W9-CTW-442

Guide to Gale Literary Criticism Series

For criticism on	Consult these Gale series
Authors now living or who died after December 31, 1959	*CONTEMPORARY LITERARY CRITICISM (CLC)*
Authors who died between 1900 and 1959	*TWENTIETH-CENTURY LITERARY CRITICISM (TCLC)*
Authors who died between 1800 and 1899	*NINETEENTH-CENTURY LITERATURE CRITICISM (NCLC)*
Authors who died between 1400 and 1799	*LITERATURE CRITICISM FROM 1400 TO 1800 (LC)* *SHAKESPEAREAN CRITICISM (SC)*
Authors who died before 1400	*CLASSICAL AND MEDIEVAL LITERATURE CRITICISM (CMLC)*
Black writers of the past two hundred years	*BLACK LITERATURE CRITICISM (BLC)*
Authors of books for children and young adults	*CHILDREN'S LITERATURE REVIEW (CLR)*
Dramatists	*DRAMA CRITICISM (DC)*
Hispanic writers of the late nineteenth and twentieth centuries	*HISPANIC LITERATURE CRITICISM (HLC)*
Native North American writers and orators of the eighteenth, nineteenth, and twentieth centuries	*NATIVE NORTH AMERICAN LITERATURE (NNAL)*
Poets	*POETRY CRITICISM (PC)*
Short story writers	*SHORT STORY CRITICISM (SSC)*
Major authors from the Renaissance to the present	*WORLD LITERATURE CRITICISM, 1500 TO THE PRESENT (WLC)*

Nineteenth-Century Literature Criticism

ISSN 0732-1864

K

Volume 74

Nineteenth-Century Literature Criticism

Excerpts from Criticism of the
Works of Novelists, Poets, Playwrights,
Short Story Writers, Philosophers, and Other
Creative Writers Who Died between 1800
and 1899, from the First Published Critical
Appraisals to Current Evaluations

Janet Witalec
Editor

Suzanne Dewsbury
Associate Editor

The Gale Group

DETROIT • SAN FRANCISCO • LONDON • BOSTON • WOODBRIDGE, CT

STAFF

Janet Witalec, *Editor*
Suzanne Dewsbury, *Associate Editor*
nna Barberi, Craig Hutchison, *Assistant Editors*
Aarti D. Stephens, *Managing Editor*

Maria Franklin, *Interim Permissions Manager*
Kimberly F. Smilay, *Permissions Specialist*
Steve Cusack, Kelly A. Quin, *Permissions Associates*
Sandra K. Gore, *Permissions Assistant*

Victoria B. Cariappa, *Research Manager*
Patricia T. Ballard, Wendy Festerling, Tracie A. Richardson,
Corrine Stocker, Cheryl Warnock, *Research Associates*

Mary Beth Trimper, *Production Director*
Cindy Range, *Production Assistant*

Gary Leach, *Graphic Artist*
Randy Bassett, *Image Database Supervisor*
Robert Duncan, Michael Logusz, *Imaging Specialists*
Pamela A. Reed, *Imaging Coordinator*

Contents

Preface vii

Acknowledgments xi

Preface

Since its inception in 1981, *Nineteenth-Century Literature Criticism* has been a valuable resource for students and librarians seeking critical commentary on writers of this transitional period in world history. Designated an "Outstanding Reference Source" by the American Library Association with the publication of its first volume, *NCLC* has since been purchased by over 6,000 school, public, and university libraries. The series has covered more than 300 authors representing 29 nationalities and over 17,000 titles. No other reference source has surveyed the critical reaction to nineteenth-century authors and literature as thoroughly as *NCLC*.

Scope of the Series

NCLC is designed to introduce students and advanced readers to the authors of the nineteenth century, and to the most significant interpretations of these authors' works. The great poets, novelists, short story writers, playwrights, and philosophers of this period are frequently studied in high school and college literature courses. By organizing and reprinting commentary written on these authors, *NCLC* helps students develop valuable insight into literary history, promotes a better understanding of the texts, and sparks ideas for papers and assignments. Each entry in *NCLC* presents a comprehensive survey of an author's career or an individual work of literature and provides the user with a multiplicity of interpretations and assessments. Such variety allows students to pursue their own interests; furthermore, it fosters an awareness that literature is dynamic and responsive to many different opinions.

Every fourth volume of *NCLC* is devoted to literary topics that cannot be covered under the author approach used in the rest of the series. Such topics include literary movements, prominent themes in nineteenth-century literature, literary reaction to political and historical events, significant eras in literary history, prominent literary anniversaries, and the literatures of cultures that are often overlooked by English-speaking readers.

NCLC continues the survey of criticism of world literature begun by Gale's *Contemporary Literary Criticism (CLC)* and *Twentieth-Century Literary Criticism (TCLC)*, both of which excerpt and reprint commentary on authors of the twentieth century. For additional information about *TCLC, CLC,* and Gale's other criticism series, users should consult the Guide to Gale Literary Criticism Series preceding the title page in this volume.

Coverage

Each volume of *NCLC* is carefully compiled to present:

- criticism of authors, or literary topics, representing a variety of genres and nationalities
- both major and lesser-known writers and literary works of the period
- 4-8 authors or 4-6 topics per volume
- individual entries that survey critical response to an author's work or a topic in literary history, including early criticism to reflect initial reactions, later criticism to represent any rise or decline in reputation, and current retrospective analyses.

Organization

An author entry consists of the following elements: author heading, biographical and critical introduction, list of principal works, excerpts of criticism (each preceded by a bibliographic citation and an annotation), and a bibliography of further reading.

- The **Author Heading** consists of the name under which the author most commonly wrote, followed by birth and death dates. If an author wrote consistently under a pseudonym, the pseudonym will be listed in the author heading and the real name given in parentheses on the first line of the biographical and critical introduction. Also located at the beginning of the introduction to the author entry are any name variations under which an author wrote, including transliterated forms for an author whose language uses a nonroman alphabet.

- The **Biographical and Critical Introduction** outlines the author's life and career, as well as the critical issues surrounding his or her work. References are provided to past volumes of *NCLC* in which further information about the author may be found.

- Most *NCLC* entries include a **Portrait** of the author. Many entries also contain reproductions of materials pertinent to an author's career, including manuscript pages, title pages, dust jackets, letters, and drawings, as well as photographs of important people, places, and events in an author's life.

- The list of **Principal Works** is chronological by date of first publication and identifies the genre of each work. In the case of foreign authors with both foreign-language publications and English translations, the English-language version is given in brackets. Unless otherwise indicated, dramas are dated by first performance, not first publication.

- **Criticism** in each author entry is arranged chronologically to provide a perspective on changes in critical evaluation over the years. All titles of works by the author featured in the entry are printed in boldface type to enable the user to easily locate discussion of particular works. Also for purposes of easier identification, the critic's name and the publication date of the essay are given at the beginning of each piece of criticism. Unsigned criticism is preceded by the title of the journal in which it appeared. Publication information (such as publisher names and book prices) and some parenthetical numerical references (such as page and line references to specific editions of works) have been deleted at the editors' discretion to provide smoother reading of the text. Footnotes that appear with previously published pieces of criticism are reprinted at the end of each essay or excerpt. In the case of excerpted criticism, only those footnotes that pertain to the excerpted text are included.

- A complete **Bibliographic Citation** provides original publication information for each piece of criticism.

- Critical excerpts are prefaced by **Annotations** providing the reader with a summary of the critical intent of the piece. Also included, when appropriate, is information about the critic's reputation, individual approach to literary criticism, and particular expertise in an author's works, as well as information about the relative importance of the critical excerpt. In some cases, the annotations cross-reference excerpts by critics who discuss each other's commentary.

- An annotated list of **Further Reading** appearing at the end of each entry suggests secondary sources on the author. In some cases it includes essays for which the editors could not obtain reprint rights.

Cumulative Indexes

- Each volume of *NCLC* contains a cumulative **Author Index** listing all authors who have appeared in Gale's Literary Criticism Series, along with cross-references to such biographical series as *Contemporary Authors* and *Dictionary of Literary Biography*. Useful for locating authors within the various series, this index is particularly valuable for those authors who are identified with a certain period but who, because of their death dates, are placed in another, or for those authors whose careers span two periods. For example, Fyodor Dostoevsky is found in *NCLC*, yet Leo Tolstoy, another major nineteenth-century Russian novelist, is found in *TCLC* because he died after 1899.

- Each *NCLC* volume includes a cumulative **Nationality Index** which lists all authors who have appeared in *NCLC*, arranged alphabetically under their respective nationalities.

- Each new volume in Gale's Literary Criticism Series includes a cumulative **Topic Index**, which lists all literary topics treated in *NCLC, TCLC, LC 1400-1800*, and the *CLC* Yearbook.

- Each new volume of *NCLC*, with the exception of the Topics volumes, contains a **Title Index** listing the titles of all literary works discussed in the volume. In response to numerous suggestions from librarians, Gale has also produced a **Special Paperbound Edition** of the *NCLC* title index. This annual cumulation lists all titles discussed in the series since its inception. Additional copies of the index are available on request. Librarians and patrons have welcomed this separate index: it saves shelf space, is easy to use, and is recyclable upon receipt of the following year's cumulation. Titles discussed in the Topics volume entries are not included in the *NCLC* cumulative index.

Citing *Nineteenth-Century Literature Criticism*

When writing papers, students who quote directly from any volume in Gale's Literary Criticism Series may use the following general forms to footnote reprinted criticism. The first example pertains to material drawn from periodicals, the second to material reprinted from books:

[1]Kim McQuaid, "William Apes, Pequot: An Indian Reformer in the Jackson Era," *The New England Quarterly*, 50 (December 1977), 605-25; excerpted and reprinted in *Nineteenth-Century Literature Criticism*, Vol. 73, ed. Janet Witalec (Farmington Hills, Mich.: The Gale Group, 1999), pp. 3-4.

[2]Richard Harter Fogle, *The Imagery of Keats and Shelley: A Comparative Study* (Archon Books, 1949); excerpted and reprinted in *Nineteenth-Century Literary Criticism*, Vol. 73, ed. Janet Witalec (Farmington Hills, Mich.: The Gale Group, 1999), pp. 157-69.

Suggestions Are Welcome

In response to suggestions, several features have been added to *NCLC* since the series began, including annotations to excerpted criticism, a cumulative index to authors in all Gale literary criticism series, entries devoted to criticism on a single work by a major author, more illustrations, and a title index listing all literary works discussed in the series.

Readers who wish to suggest authors, single works, or topics to appear in future volumes, or who have other suggestions, are cordially invited to write: The Editors, *Nineteenth-Century Literature Criticism*, The Gale Group, 27500 Drake Rd., Farmington Hills, MI 48331-3535; call toll-free at 1-800-347-GALE.

Acknowledgments

The editors wish to thank the copyright holders of the excerpted criticism included in this volume and the permissions managers of many book and magazine publishing companies for assisting us in securing reproduction rights. We are also grateful to the staffs of the Detroit Public Library, the Library of Congress, the University of Detroit Mercy Library, Wayne State University Purdy/Kresge Library Complex, and the University of Michigan Libraries for making their resources available to us. Following is a list of the copyright holders who have granted us permission to reproduce material in this volume of *NCLC*. Every effort has been made to trace copyright, but if omissions have been made, please let us know.

COPYRIGHTED EXCERPTS IN *NCLC*, VOLUME 74, WERE REPRODUCED FROM THE FOLLOWING PERIODICALS:

American Literature, v. 17, January, 1946; v. XLIV, March, 1972. Copyright 1946, 1972 by Duke University Press, Durham, NC. Both reproduced by permission.—***Books at Brown***, v. XX, 1965 for "Charles Brockden Brown as a Novelist of Ideas" by David H. Hirsch. Reproduced by permission of the author.—***Criticism***, v. XIV, Spring, 1972. Reproduced by permission.—***Early American Literature***, v. IX, Fall, 1974 for "'The Double-Tongued Deceiver': Sincerity and Duplicity in the Novels of Charles Brockden Brown" by Michael D. Bell. Copyrighted © 1974, by the University of Massachusetts. Reproduced by permission of the publisher and the Literary Estate for Michael D. Bell; v. X, Fall, 1975 for "Ambiguous Evil: A Study of Villains and Heroes in Charles Brockden Brown's Major Novels" by John Cleman. Copyrighted © 1974, by the University of Massachusetts. Reproduced by permission of the publisher and the author.—***ESQ: A Journal of The American Renaissance***, v. 18, 1st Quarter, 1972 for "Charles Brockden Brown and the Uses of Gothicism: A Reassessment" by Richard D. Hume. Reproduced by permission of the publisher and the author.—***Essays in Literature***, v. X, Spring, 1983. Reproduced by permission of Western Illinois University.—***The Personalist***, v. XLV, April, 1964. © 1964. Reproduced by permission of Blackwell Publishers.—***Religion and Literature***, v. 18, Fall, 1986. Reproduced by permission.—***Renaissance and Modern Studies***, v. 4, 1960. Reproduced by permission.—***The Serif: Kent State University Quarterly***, v. III, December, 1966. Copyright © 1966 by the Kent State University Library. Reproduced by permission.—***The Southern Review***, Louisiana State University, v. 17, July, 1981 for "Born Decadent: The American Novel and Charles Brockden Brown" by Philip Young. Copyright © 1981, by the author. Reproduced by permission of the Estate of Philip Young.—***Studies in American Fiction***, v. 24, Spring, 1996. Copyright © 1996 Northeastern University. Reproduced by permission.—***Studies in Romanticism***, v. VI, Summer, 1967. Copyright © 1967 by the Trustees of Boston University. Reproduced by permission.—***Studies in the American Renaissance***, 1993. © 1993 by Joel Myerson. All rights reserved. Reproduced by permission.—***Text and Performance Quarterly***, Vol. 2, April, 1989. Reproduced by permission of the National Communication Association.—***Theatre Research International***, v. 18, 1993 for "*It Is Never Too Late to Mend* and Prison Conditions in Nineteenth-Century England" by Daniel Barrett. Copyright © 1993 by Oxford University Press. Reproduced by permission of Oxford University Press and the author.—***Unisa English Studies***, v. IX, March, 1971. Reproduced by permission.

PHOTOGRAPHS AND ILLUSTRATIONS APPEARING IN *NCLC*, VOLUME 74, WERE RECEIVED FROM THE FOLLOWING SOURCES:

A title page for *Fashion; or, Life in New York, A Comedy in Five Acts* by Anna Cora Mowatt, London, W. Newberry, G. King Street, Holborn, 1850, photograph. The Department of Rare Books and Special Collections, The University of Michigan Library. Reproduced by permission.—A title page for *The Cloister and the Hearth: A Tale of the Middle Ages* by Charles Reade, in four volumes, Vol. I, New York, Dodd, Mead and Company, 1892, photograph. Courtesy of the Harlan Hatcher Graduate Library, The University of Michigan.—A title page for *Wieland; or, The Transformation* by Charles Brockden Brown, Philadelphia, David McKay, Publisher, 1881, photograph. Courtesy of the Harlan Hatcher Graduate Library, The University of Michigan.—Charles Reade, photograph of a painting by Charles Mercier. By courtesy of the National Portrait Gallery, London. Reproduced by permission.—Wright, Frances, engraving. The Library of Congress.

Charles Brockden Brown

1771-1810

American novelist, essayist, and short story writer.

For additional information on Brown's life and works, see *NCLC*, Volume 22.

INTRODUCTION

Brown is typically recognized as a significant figure in American literature for his attempt to earn a living as a professional writer. Hailed by many modern scholars as the first American novelist, Brown wrote fiction that, according to many critics, contained serious stylistic and structural deficiencies. Yet his works, particularly his first four published novels (*Wieland, Ormond, Arthur Mervyn,* and *Edgar Huntly*), also demonstrate Brown's intense artistic vision and his apparent struggle to reconcile his Romantic imagination with the Enlightenment ideals of reason and realism. It is this conflict that continues to draw twentieth-century scholars to Brown's work. Gothic elements in Brown's writing and the possible influences of other Gothic writers on Brown form another arena for critical debate. Brown's novels are filled with ambiguity in theme and characterization, and critics have attempted to attach a purpose to these equivocations. Finally, Brown's work reflects an interest, radical for his time, in the rights and roles of women; his apparent feminism is another attribute which entices modern critics to his writing.

Biographical Information

Brown was born to a Quaker family in Philadelphia in 1771. The religion's disdain for formal higher education resulted in the sixteen-year-old Brown's being apprenticed to a lawyer. While employed at the law office, Brown pursued his literary interests and joined the Belles Lettres Club, where he participated in philosophical and political discussions. In 1789 he published *The Rhapsodist,* a series of essays in which he analyzes the effectiveness of the government created after the American Revolution. His interest in radical social and political ideas was furthered by his reading of Mary Wollstonecraft's *A Vindication of the Rights of Women* (1792) and William Godwin's *An Enquiry concerning Political Justice* (1793). Many critics believe that these two works heavily influenced Brown's later thinking and writing. After abandoning his legal career in 1792, Brown completed his first novel, the now-lost *Sky-Walk,* in 1797. During the next several years, Brown embarked upon a period of extraordinary literary activity, publishing *Alcuin,* a fictional

dialogue on women's rights, and his first significant novel, *Wieland,* in 1798. *Ormond,* the first part of *Arthur Mervyn,* and *Edgar Huntly* all appeared during 1799. The proceeds from these works, however, were not sufficient for Brown to support himself, and as he grew increasingly interested in marrying and having a family, Brown joined his family's mercantile business in 1800. During his courtship of Elizabeth Linn in the early 1800s, Brown wrote the second part of *Arthur Mervyn* and his last two novels, *Clara Howard* and *Jane Talbot,* which were published in 1801. At this point, Brown turned to journalistic endeavors, producing political pamphlets and essays, and editing a journal. He married in 1804 and supported his wife and children on his editorial work after the family business dissolved in 1806. Brown died in 1810, of tuberculosis.

Major Works

Brown wrote essays, short stories, and political pamphlets, as well as a translation, but modern critics pay relatively little attention to these works, except as a means of elucidating aspects of Brown's major novels. The dialogue *Alcuin,* although considered a minor work, is studied attentively by modern critics in an effort to dissect Brown's feminism. In this fictional exchange between a man and a woman, arguments both for and against political and educational equality of the sexes are presented. Brown continued to explore such issues in his novels, which all contain strong female characters. Like Brown's minor works, the sentimental novels *Clara Howard* and *Jane Talbot* generate relatively little critical interest and are regarded as exhibiting Brown's shift from radical to more conservative views.

The plots of Brown's four major novels, which combine elements of the Gothic and the sentimental novel, are often considered convoluted and episodic, though highly imaginative. What unites the novels is Brown's focus on psychological aberrations and the reactions and development of his characters. In *Wieland,* the plot deals with spontaneous combustion, mass murder, seduction, and ventriloquism; *Edgar Huntly* features a case of sleepwalking. In both novels, the inability of humans to trust sense perceptions alone is explored. *Ormond* focuses on Brown's ideas regarding the necessity of educational equality for women, and also incorporates a familiar seduction plot. The plot of *Arthur Mervyn* is judged to be particularly intricate. Through it Brown examines, by way of the apparently innocent narrator's adventures, the theme of appearance versus reality. The narrator becomes incriminated in several crimes, but his declarations of benevolent intentions contradict his actions.

Critical Reception

With Brown writing at a time when eighteenth-century Enlightenment ideals were giving way to nineteenth-century Romantic principles, it is no wonder that his works contain aspects of each philosophy, and in fact, many critics have noted in Brown's work a conflict between these two distinct ideologies. Paul Witherington has maintained that the struggle between Enlightenment theories of benevolence and Romantic notions regarding character and plot "unwinds the art" of all of Brown's novels through violations in point of view, character alterations, and authorial intrusion. Further, Witherington has contended that Brown abandoned fiction not because of a "failure of imagination," but because he found the imagination to be a revolutionary force which endangered "the values of benevolence he wanted most to preserve." Similarly, Michael D. Bell has asserted that Brown's novels reveal the author's conflict between rationalism and the irrational power of the imagination, and Maurice J. Bennett has suggested that Brown's abandonment of fiction reflected his rejection of the imagination in favor of reason.

While Brown's novels incorporate aspects of Romanticism in their focus on imaginative power, they also contain some elements of the Gothic. Philip Young has observed that although Brown's novels cannot be truly classified as Gothic, Brown did write "the romance of mystery and terror." Richard D. Hume has similarly found that Brown's novels are not Gothic in more than "a superficial sense"; he has maintained that Brown is most interested in the psychology of his characters and that he employs the "trappings of Gothicism," (such as the use of suspense, apparently supernatural elements, and the isolated setting of *Wieland*) in order to provide situations to which his characters will respond. Lillie Deming Loshe and Donald A. Ringe have both examined the influences on Brown's Gothicism. Loshe argues that Brown's use of the Gothic is similar to that of William Godwin in its focus on the psychological and the revolutionary. Ringe, on the other hand, has contended that Brown created his own version of Gothicism, which was based more on German sources and English authors other than Godwin, and which eventually influenced Edgar Allan Poe and Nathaniel Hawthorne.

The ambiguity in Brown's novels is an issue of much debate among modern critics. John Cleman has noted that the haste with which Brown composed his novels and the fact that he wrote during a time when his political and moral theories were in transition are factors which could account for the ambiguity in his works. Yet many critics, including Cleman, view Brown's ambiguity as integral to his vision. Cleman has studied the major characters in Brown's novels and has asserted that the relationships among them reveal that Brown deliberately constructed the ambiguity (such as the sense of discrepancy between what seems to be virtue and what actually is vice) found in his work. Similarly, David Seed has argued that ambiguities in *Wieland* demonstrate Brown's scepticism regarding "the mind's capacity to grasp truth and order perceptions."

Twentieth-century scholars have found Brown's feminist ideas in *Alcuin* intriguing and have looked to the female characters of his novels, such as the narrators of *Wieland* and *Ormond,* to support the views outlined in the dialogue. David Lee Clark has maintained that Brown's revolutionary ideas regarding women's rights were developed prior to and were not significantly influenced by the works of Mary Wollstonecraft or William Godwin, and that Brown was particularly concerned with the economic and political rights of women. Fritz Fleischmann, however, does see parallels between Wollstonecraft's *A Vindication of the Rights of Women* and *Alcuin,* but has argued that, regardless of the view one takes on Brown's incorporation of Godwinism into his own theories, Brown's feminism is obvious and compelling.

PRINCIPAL WORKS

Alcuin: A Dialogue (fictional dialogue) 1798

Wieland; or, The Transformation (novel) 1798

Arthur Mervyn; or, Memoirs of the Year 1793. 2 vols. (novel) 1799-1800

Edgar Huntly; or, Memoirs of a Sleep-Walker (novel) 1799

Ormond; or, The Secret Witness (novel) 1799

Clara Howard (novel) 1801; also published as *Philip Stanley; or, The Enthusiasm of Love,* 1807

Jane Talbot, a Novel (novel) 1801

A View of the Soil and Climate of the United States (nonfiction) (translation of work by Constintin Francois de Volney) 1804

*Carwin, the Biloquist, and Other American Tales and Pieces. 3 vols. (unfinished novel and short stories) 1822

The Novels of Charles Brockden Brown. 7 vols. (novels) 1827

The Rhapsodist, and Other Uncollected Writings (essays and novel fragment) 1943

The Novels and Related Works of Charles Brockden Brown. 6 vols. (novels and unfinished novels) 1977-87

*Memoirs of Stephen Calvert (unfinished novel) 1978

*Carwin, the Biloquist and *Memoirs of Stephen Calvert* were published earlier in William Dunlap's *The Life of Charles Brockden Brown: Together with Selections from the Rarest of His Printed Works, from His Original Letters, and from His Manuscripts Before Unpublished,* 1815.*

CRITICISM

Richard Garnett (essay date 1902)

SOURCE: "Alms for Oblivion: The Minor Writings of Charles Brockden Brown," in *The Cornhill Magazine,* New Series, Vol. XIII, July-December, 1902, pp. 494-506.

[*In the following essay, Garnett reviews some of Brown's literary fragments, observing that these works reflect the same theme as his novels, that is, the effects of abnormal events on the development of human character.*]

Time hath, my Lord, a wallet on his back
Wherein he puts alms for oblivion.

Troilus and Cressida.

There is a celebrated dictum of Keats—not to be told in Gath, for in his day it made sport for the Philistines—to the effect that

Heard melodies are sweet, but those unheard
Are sweeter.

Such must also have been the opinion of a contemporary poet, Thomas Lovell Beddoes, for in a letter to his friend Kelsall he describes himself as the author of many celebrated unwritten productions, 'among which I particularly solicit your attention to a volume of letters to yourself.' How it is possible to melodise and not to melodise, to write and not to write, remains the secret of the poets: though De Quincey came near penetrating it when he indited a series of most affectionate epistles to his daughters, but never posted one of them. Coleridge achieved much in this line by leaving the conclusion of Christabel to the imagination; and perhaps a still further advance was effected by Nathaniel Hawthorne, whose American note-books, so incomparably superior to his European, are strewn with conceptions of unwritten stories invested with all the weird fascination of the stories which he did complete. There they are, fit for their beauty and originality to endure for ever, but for ever petrified, like those dried Indian seeds which dealers in Oriental curiosities mingle with their boxes of shells, bright and tempting to the eye as the shells themselves, but like the shells for ever incapable of germination. Nothing has more of the indefinable charm of the 'unheard melody' than the plot which none but the contriver can elaborate, and the fragment which none but the author can complete.

The silent organ loudest chants
The master's requiem.

Hawthorne is the greatest imaginative genius that America has yet produced, perhaps the only American who, when such demigods as Homer and Shakespeare have been eliminated, stands in the foremost files. Yet, like most great men, he had a precursor. Sometimes the new moon is accompanied by a spectral companion filling her imperfect orb, 'the ghost of her dead mother,' according to Shelley; 'the old moon in her arm,' according to the nameless bard

Who made
The grand old ballad of Sir Patrick Spens;

by which even the newly-created Adam or the newly-healed Bartimæus who had never seen the moon might infer that the moon he gazed upon was not the first that ever came into being. Such an antecedent luminary in relation to Hawthorne was Charles Brockden Brown (1771-1810), a man whose fragments, although unlike Hawthorne he strove to complete them, have like Hawthorne's the undefinable charm of 'melodies unheard.'

In Brown's finished writings the future Hawthorne exists like the genie in the vase, faint airy cloud, confined to narrow limits, not yet a colossal figure with one foot on the Old World and the other on the New. But if Brown, though a writer of true genius, does not possess the superb genius of Hawthorne, he is psychologically no less interesting a figure. His life is like the house of the Greek interpreter in 'Anastasius,' all homeliness without, all magnificence within. The idealist, in outward seeming gentle, patient, self-sacrificing, hardly distinguishable from a publisher's drudge, is with the pen the creator of romantic situations whose fault in art is to be, without being absolutely impossible, too persistently abnormal; and is at the same time the exponent, while too reserved to be the champion, of the most advanced speculations of the European intellect; and, like More and Campanella and the youthful Hartley Coleridge, the legislator of states existing solely in his own brain. Apart from the merits of his writings, he has two accidental but indefeasible claims to remembrance, as the first American novelist, and the first American who earned a livelihood by literature. But he is more interesting in himself, a man of great gifts repressed by feeble health, and the unfavourable conditions incidental to a country only beginning to learn to value literature, dwelling, as it were, in a penumbra, neither quite visible nor quite invisible to his contemporaries and the after-world. The fate of his completed writings is like his own, they are neither quite dead nor entirely alive. They were republished some years ago in the United States in a very handsome edition, but this was limited to five hundred copies. It is long since any of them have been reprinted in England, where perhaps they are best known from the affection entertained for them by Shelley. Peacock's account of this is worth quoting, as a brief and accurate statement of the special claims of the individual books:—

> He was especially fond of the novels of Charles Brockden Brown. The first of these novels was *Wieland.* Wieland's father passed much of his time alone in a summer-house, where he died of spontaneous combustion. This summer-house made a great impression on Shelley, and in looking for a country house he always examined if he could find such a summer-house, or a place to erect one. The second was *Ormond.* The heroine of this novel, Constantia Dudley, held one of the highest places, if not the highest place, in Shelley's idealities of female character. The third was *Edgar Huntly.* In this his imagination was strangely captivated by the picture of Clitheroe in his sleep digging a grave under a tree. The fourth was *Arthur Mervyn,* chiefly remarkable for the powerful description of the yellow fever in Philadelphia, a subject previously treated in *Ormond.* No descriptions of pestilence surpass these of Brown. The transfer of the hero's affections from a simple peasant girl to a rich Jewess displeased Shelley extremely, and he could only account for it on the ground that it was the only way in which Brown could bring his story to an uncomfortable conclusion.

> These four tales were unquestionably works of great genius, and were remarkable for the way in which

natural causes were made to produce the semblance of supernatural effects. The superstitious terror of romance could scarcely be more powerfully excited than by the perusal of *Wieland.*

This witness is true. Shelley's admiration was not misplaced. Constantia Dudley actually is one of the finest characters in modern fiction, with affinities to the Theodora of 'Lothair.' Shelley was unquestionably thinking of her when he gave the title to his lines 'To Constantia, Singing,' and the circumstance no doubt led Miss Clairmont, to whom the verses were probably inscribed, to add the name to the accumulation of names which encrusted themselves like barnacles around the original nucleus of 'Jane.' 'Nothing,' adds Peacock, 'so blended itself with the structure of Shelley's interior mind as the creations of Brown. Nothing stood so clearly before his thoughts as a perfect combination of the purely ideal and possibly real, as Constantia Dudley.' Nor did Shelley err in his admiration for the finest scenes in the other novels. The picture of the haggard somnambulist, unconsciously digging a grave for himself or another, is one of the most striking in fiction. The description of the pestilence in *Arthur Mervyn* deserves to stand beside the other world-famous descriptions of plagues by Thucydides, Lucretius, Boccaccio, Defoe, and Shelley himself in 'The Revolt of Islam.' Shelley's notion that it behoved a person of taste and feeling to have a summer-house to 'combuss' in is delicious; but Peacock's mention of it would do *Wieland* great injustice if it led to the supposition that a case of spontaneous combustion formed the leading incident of the novel. 'The superstitious terror of romance' which, as he justly says, could scarcely be more strongly excited than by the perusal of *Wieland,* is created not by the Fire King but by the Prince of the Powers of the Air. The motor is ventriloquism. When the story is finished a feeling almost of resentment arises at finding how one has been played upon by a device so ordinary with mountebanks, but the perusal is all breathless attention. It is a pregnant illustration of the Pepysian motto, 'Mens cujusque is est quisque,' that an English novel on the same theme, Cockton's 'Valentine Vox the Ventriloquist,' is farce of the broadest style, though legitimate enough in its way. Brown's other great instrument of terror was turned by Cockton to like account in 'Sylvester Sound the Somnambulist.'

It will be clear that Brockden Brown's completed novels cannot be reckoned as 'alms for oblivion,' but the same is not the case with his fragmentary writings. These sustain to the works on which his reputation rests much the same relation as the latter bear to Hawthorne's—that of a penumbral fringe, scarcely visible, but, if once caught by the eye, attractive with a strange haunting beauty. Collected and published by the pious care of his friend William Dunlap, they could not be expected to attract much attention, and have indeed drifted as far down the stream of forgetfulness as has ever been the case with works of an author of undoubted genius, not dissimilar in spirit or reputation from those to which he is indebted for his fame. The most remarkable is **Carwin the Biloquist,** a variation upon **Wieland.** Carwin is the ventriloquist whose machinations, fell in their results but innocent in intention, have brought ruin upon Wieland and his house. He appears before the survivors of his victims and relates his own story in extenuation.

Carwin, whom we have learned to know as the maleficent, though perhaps not malevolent genius of the house of Wieland, appears in his own narrative as the instrument of a still more potent personage in the background, an Irishman named Ludloe. The conception of Ludloe is characteristic of the author's age. Ever since Pythagoras, and perhaps from a much earlier period, it has been the belief of many that the regeneration of the world may proceed from a society of elect spirits, withdrawn to all appearance from active participation in its affairs, but operating all the more effectually in secret, sometimes conceived as invested with supernatural powers, sometimes as depending solely upon superiority of wisdom or the control of boundless wealth, but always as sublimely disinterested, and always, alas! eminent rather in speech than in action. Such persons exist at this day in many imaginations in the shape of the Mahatmas of Tibet; and they were something more than imaginations in the days of Brown, when Spartacus Weishaupt and the Illuminati perplexed monarchs with the fear of change, and appeared on several occasions bodily in the dock. Ludloe is such a personage. He casts his eye on Carwin as a promising disciple, and the rather as Carwin has a quarrel with society as represented by his aunt, who has disinherited him. What renders Ludloe an interesting figure, and particularly representative of his time, is that he is an incarnation of the philosophy of Godwin. While providing for all Carwin's needs with lavish generosity, he scoffs at the idea of Carwin's being under any obligation to him. What he is doing is either just or unjust. If unjust, he is highly censurable; if just he is but doing his duty. Nor will he allow Carwin to follow any occupation. 'All the liberal professions were censured as perverting the understanding by giving scope to the sordid motive of gain, or imbuing the mind with erroneous principles. The mechanical trades were equally obnoxious; they were vicious by contributing to the spurious gratifications of the rich and multiplying the objects of luxury; they were all destructive to the intellect and vigour of the artisan; they enervated his frame and brutalised his mind.'

Carwin accompanies his mysterious benefactor to Dublin, and is thence despatched to Spain to study human nature. By address and dexterity he insinuates himself into the confidence of all orders of society, and has sundry love intrigues, which he does not deem it necessary to impart to his patron, from whom he also conceals his faculty of ventriloquism. In other respects he is entirely candid, and is rewarded by the receipt of long letters, treating of the perfectibility of man. When his education in the art of reading human nature is supposed to be complete, he returns to Dublin, and Ludloe begins to open his purposes.

> A number of persons are leagued together for an enterprise of some moment. Their existence depends upon fidelity and secrecy. You are ignorant of all the members, excepting myself. Candidates have freedom of choice. Inviolable silence is necessary. To this they are not held by any promise. They must weigh consequences, and freely decide; but they must not fail to number among these consequences their own death.

> I love you. The first impulse of my love is to dissuade you from seeking to know more. Your mind will be full of ideas; your hands will be perpetually busy with a purpose into which no human creature beyond the verge of your brotherhood must pry. Believe me who have made the experiment that, compared with this task, the task of inviolable secrecy, all others are easy. To be dumb will not suffice. If the sagacity of others detect your occupations, however strenuously you labour for concealment, your doom is ratified, as well as that of the wretch whose evil destiny led him to pursue you.

> In a few years you will be permitted to withdraw to a land of sages, and the remainder of your life will glide away in the enjoyments of beneficence and wisdom.

While Carwin is endeavouring to make up his mind, an adventure befalls him. He walks by night on the road out of Dublin, and encounters a band of robbers besetting a lady in a carriage. Unseen himself, under cover of the darkness, he exerts his ventriloquistic faculty to such purpose, counterfeiting the voices of approaching rescuers, that the robbers fly; while the no less alarmed lady makes off with her equipage in the opposite direction, leaving Carwin ignorant whom he has preserved. Returning home, he is surprised and not a little discomposed to find Ludloe in his chamber. The confusion is entirely on his side, for Ludloe tranquilly explains that he has come to make a most important communication, and is awaiting Carwin's return. Would Carwin like to be rich? Will it suit him to be free and independent? Would he object to a country-house with charming grounds and the other usual appurtenances? There is one disagreeable condition annexed. He must fly in the face of philosophy, and contravene her precepts by becoming a slave-owner. He must assume absolute dominion over the person and property of another human being, now possessed of the establishment in question. 'That being must become your domestic slave, be governed in every particular by your caprice.' In plain English, Carwin must take a wife. The lady is Mrs. Bennington, widow of a merchant whom he has known in Spain; and who, as the judicious reader will have divined, speedily proves to be the identical lady whom he has rescued from the robbers. Ludloe's motives for promoting the match also peep out, and most Machiavellian they are. He desires to test to the uttermost Carwin's power of observing inviolable secrecy, and is sure that he must be equal to any trial if he can withstand the blandishments of an Irish widow.

Carwin has now two momentous problems to perpend. He derives no help from Mrs. Bennington, who is mysteriously withdrawn from observation. Ludloe himself disappears for awhile, leaving the key of his private library in Carwin's hands. Carwin makes ample use of the privilege, and comes in time upon a mysterious map. At the end of a large atlas containing maps of the usual description, appears one of an unknown country. Two islands, apparently of the size of Great Britain and Ireland, are laid down between the South Pole and the Equator, 'where the transverse parallels of the southern tropic and the one hundred and fiftieth degrees of east longitude intersect each other:' in the neighbourhood, therefore, of the Gilbert Islands. They are covered with towns with strange and unheard of names. Can this be the land of sages where Carwin is to spend a serene old age if he withstands all temptations to loquacity? He recurs to the map for more light; the atlas is gone! Ludloe has returned and carried it off; yet the key of the chamber is still in Carwin's keeping. Ludloe, then, has a duplicate key. Why not? But has he a duplicate key to every room in the house? And, if so, what may not happen to Carwin?

Carwin's mind is full of agitation. Ludloe begins to press him to make a full disclosure of his thoughts and the incidents of his life, as a prelude to his initiation. Carwin is not entirely unwilling, but shrinks from the revelation of that which distinguishes him from other men—his power as a biloquist. At the same time he cannot feel certain that Ludloe does not know this already, and that concealment may not be heavily visited upon him. In an agony of irresolution he meets Ludloe. They converse, and by-and-by Ludloe asks him:

> "Perhaps you recollect a visit which you paid on Christmas Day in the year —— to the cathedral church of Toledo. Do you remember?"

I answered in the affirmative.

> "And yet," said Ludloe with a smile, "I suspect your recollection is not as exact as mine, or, indeed, your knowledge as extensive. You met there for the first time a female, whose nominal uncle, but real

father, a dean of that ancient church, resided in a blue stone house, the third from the west angle of the square of St. Jago."

All this was exactly true.

> "The female," continued he, "fell in love with you. Her passion made her deaf to all the dictates of modesty and duty, and she gave you sufficient intimations, in subsequent interviews at the same place, of this passion, which, she being fair and enticing, you were not slow in comprehending and returning. As not only the safety of your intercourse, but even of your lives, depended upon your being shielded even from suspicion, the utmost wariness and caution were observed in all your proceedings. Tell me whether you succeeded in your efforts to this end?"

I replied that, at the time, I had no doubt that I had.

> "And yet," said he, drawing something from his pocket, and putting it in my hand, "there is the slip of paper with the preconcerted emblem inscribed upon it, which the infatuated girl dropped in your sight, one evening in the left aisle of that church. That paper you imagined you afterwards burned in your chamber lamp. In pursuance of this token, you deferred your intended visit, and next day the lady was accidentally drowned in passing a river. Here ended your connection with her, and with her was buried, as you thought, all memory of the transaction.

> "I leave you to your own inference from this disclosure. Meditate upon it when alone. Recall all the incidents of that drama, and labour to conceive the means by which my sagacity has been able to reach events that took place so far off, and under so deep a covering."

I still held the paper he had given me. So far as memory could be trusted, it was the same which, an hour after I had received it, I burnt, as I conceived with my own hands. How Ludloe came into possession of this paper, how he was apprised of incidents to which only the female mentioned and myself were privy, which she had too good reason to hide from all the world, and which I had taken infinite pains to bury in oblivion, I vainly endeavour to conjecture.

Here the story ends abruptly, leaving us no more enlightened than Carwin as to the means by which Ludloe had possessed himself of the Spanish damsel's missive. Perhaps they would have appeared disappointingly trivial. The general course of the story is easier to conjecture. Ludloe is casually mentioned in *Wieland* as an enemy whose pursuit Carwin seeks to shun. This enmity must in all probability have been occasioned by some infidelity of Carwin to his trust, and this must have been combined with the exercise of his biloquial faculty, of which hitherto he has made little use. In *Wieland* he makes too much; the first preternatural accents, as they are deemed, are intensely thrilling, but the effect wears off by repetition. Perhaps Brown himself had become tired of them; but, apart from this, his imaginative faculty was finding other means of expression. It would in most cases appear an evident proof of the decay of imaginative power if a novelist laid fiction aside and took to writing a system of geography; but topographical detail was such a passion with Brown, and he possessed such a faculty for creating foreign scenes from skeleton descriptions, that the inference would be inaccurate as regarded him. He had another taste which must have absorbed some of his creative power—that for the delineation which would often keep him for hours 'absorbed in architectural studies, measuring proportions with his compasses, and drawing plans of Grecian temples or Gothic cathedrals, monasteries or castles.'

Brown's passion for ideal geography is powerfully illustrated by two fragmentary romances, *Carsol* and *Adini*. *Carsol* was designed to have been a description of an imaginary community, in the manner of More's *Utopia*. The island is evidently intended for Sardinia, a 'hermit kingdom' whose almost total withdrawal from the current of European history during the middle ages leaves an ample field for the imagination. Brown is well acquainted with the mysterious 'nuraghe' that cover the land, and makes good use of these and other local particulars. Had his fiction like 'Utopia' been confined to the polity of the ideal state it might have been highly interesting, for Brown was a real thinker, and his thought was expressive of some of the characteristic tendencies of his time. Unfortunately he is resolved to create illusion by the minuteness and circumstantiality of alleged historical detail, and so minute and circumstantial is he as to become tedious even to himself, and hardly to arrive at the ideal community for which alone his book ought to have existed. His history, moreover, is neither fact nor fiction, but a travesty of the former which keeps the reader perpetually on the fret. He is more successful with a work more undisguisedly fictitious. Adini, a refugee Italian, takes up his quarters in an American township, and amazes the inhabitants by his opposition to their ideas of history and geography. 'If you believe De Pagès, you must believe that cunning impostor Robertson!' He seems insane on such points, but otherwise he is highly intelligent, and, if mad, there is at least a method in his madness. The story is broken off before we obtain a solution of the problem. The situation resembles one which actually at the very time existed at Bristol, where Gilbert—Southey and Coleridge's mad friend, author of 'The Hurricane'—was ranging about discoursing upon the 'Gilberti,' a nation dwelling not in the Gilbert Isles, but in the interior of Africa; of kin, as he affirmed, to the house of Gilbert, and ready to receive him with open arms as soon as he should present himself among

them. When at last Gilbert disappeared altogether, Southey, thinking that he might have gone in quest of his Ethiopian kindred, caused inquiries to be made upon every vessel bound for Africa; but, on the contrary, he had gone to America to receive a legacy, which cured him.

All Brown's novels that gained any celebrity, and all the fragments of his works that belong to the department of fiction, rest upon an identical idea, the development of a human character under the pressure of abnormal circumstances. This, if not altogether a novelty, for the definition would fit 'Hamlet,' was still in the main, so far as its application to the English novel is concerned, an invention of William Godwin's, and, if not the highest or purest form of art, did much to extend the resources of English fiction. It is a curious question whether Godwin's writings, fictitious or philosophical, will ever regain the seminal influence which they undoubtedly possessed in their own day. There are few stronger evidences of the impulse they were at one time able to communicate than the effect produced upon Brown by 'Caleb Williams,' the only romance of Godwin's which he had any opportunity of reading before he began to write his own. This was no doubt assisted by the impression he had already received from Godwin's philosophical works, as well as Mary Wollstonecraft's. *Alcuin,* his first book, a dialogue on marriage and the position of women in general, is impregnated with Mary Wollstonecraft's ideas. Yet even here the rapid transmission of thought from Britain to America is remarkable, and shows intellectual affinity overcoming political estrangement. His own idiosyncrasy considered, Brown could hardly have had a better model than Godwin, whose strong points he readily appropriated, while his invention and descriptive power veiled the dryness of Godwin's necessarianism. One defect master and disciple shared: neither had the faintest perception of humour. Brown's style, also, is exactly Godwin's, a constant succession of short, staccato sentences, more conducive to lucidity than to eloquence. This unbroken brevity of phrase becomes at length somewhat fatiguing, but has the advantage for a writer of fiction whose themes are so remote from ordinary experience as Brockden Brown's, of aiding to produce the illusion that, extraordinary as these themes may appear, they are really matters of fact. Brown has not the same power of producing this illusion as is possessed by Defoe or Borrow, but he is not very far behind them.

This pedestrian method of narrative is illustrated by a long and not very readable fragment, *The History of the Carrils and Ormes,* where the deliberate enumeration of minute pseudohistorical particulars becomes tiresome; and by Brown's only attempt at historical fiction, on a subject where the attempt to produce illusion is needless, since the tale has the warrant of history. It is the massacre of Thessalonica, perpetrated by command of the Emperor Theodosius in A.D. 390. The treatment only differs from the historical by the introduction of numerous fictitious circumstances for effect, the narration being put into the mouth of an imaginary contemporary. The slow, steady accumulation of details tries the reader's patience, but gradually produces the effect of a lowering, stifling atmosphere of terror and awe, out of which the catastrophe leaps like a thunderbolt. The conclusion well expresses the feelings of a Roman of that unhappy age, finally bereaved of all hope by the calamities of the times:

> I envy the lot of such, but it will quickly be my lot. The period of forgetfulness, or of tranquil existence in another scene, is hastening to console me. Meanwhile my task shall be to deliver to you and posterity a faithful narrative. The horrors of this scene are only portions of the evil that has overspread the Roman world, which has been inflicted by the cavalry of Scythia, and which will end only in the destruction of the Empire, and the return of the human species to their pristine barbarity.

Brown was also a writer on political questions, and an able one, but even here he characteristically adopted the methods of the romancer. His most remarkable political production is an address to the United States Government in 1803, on the advantage of acquiring Louisiana from the French. This vast trans-Mississippian territory, of which the existing State of Louisiana is but a small portion, had been ceded by Spain to France in 1801; and in 1803, Napoleon, fearful of its falling into the hands of England, was meditating the sale of it to the United States. Brown's pamphlet is to some extent, as it is described, an argumentative appeal to the United States Government, but the vital part of it is a supposititious translation of an imaginary French State paper, represented to have been drawn up by a French Counsellor of State, recommending the acquisition of Louisiana by France from Spain at the time when this acquisition, soon actually made, was being negotiated between the two countries. The counsellor, in the first place, dissuades Bonaparte from attempting the re-conquest of St. Domingo, and rather advises the colonisation of Australia. This may seem fanciful, but, in fact, Napoleon, about this very time, sent out an expedition designed to pave the way for this undertaking; and a map, reproduced in Mr. Rose's recent biography of him, adorns the southern coast of Australia with the title, 'Terre Napoléon.' Considering, nevertheless, that the project is not likely to be carried into effect, the counsellor extols the advantage to France of the possession of Louisiana, and ingeniously introduces the circumstances which ought to render the French occupation distasteful to the

United States, thus indirectly, for American readers, recommending the purchase which Brown is advocating. Can it be thought, the imaginary Frenchman asks, 'that the Americans will willingly admit into their vitals a formidable and active people, whose interests are incompatible at every point with their own; whose enterprise will inevitably interfere and jar with theirs; whose neighbourhood will cramp all their movements, circumscribe all their future progress to narrow and ignominious bounds, and make incessant inroads on their harmony and independence?' This gives occasion for drawing a picture of the American nation as, in Brown's view, it then appeared to the nations of Europe. It is thought to be weak on several accounts. From having a hostile nation of slaves in its bosom. From the clashing interests and jealousies of the States. From its division into hostile factions. From the perverse attachments and antipathies of the people to European nations. From the want of national spirit, patriotism, sense of national honour, or love of national glory. From the love of gain and the exceeding sensibility to commercial interests. From the ease with which the Indians can at all times be set on to carry fire, the tomahawk and scalping-knife into the American settlements, by any European nation having colonies on their borders.

The cradle of the young giant was indeed beset by serpents!

Louisiana was purchased from France in 1804, and the acquisition is regarded as the chief glory of the administration of President Jefferson. Brown was not a supporter of this administration. He thought Gallatin, the Financial Secretary, its ablest member. Madison, Secretary of State, and afterwards President, he considered, in Dunlap's words, 'a man of genius and industry, somewhat slow and much deficient in energy. Mr. Jefferson, as a polite scholar and accomplished gentleman, doubting received truth, and extremely credulous to whatever served to confirm his favourite theories; deficient in the science of politics, but of great address in screening himself from dangers and responsibilities.' These judgments have been substantially confirmed by posterity. Brown was a man of great sagacity, and if not an original thinker himself, was receptive of the ideas of others, as shown by his attitude towards the speculations of Godwin. Had his life been prolonged, he might have become a distinguished publicist. It must be remembered that he was not a New Englander, and was exempt from the Puritan antecedents which contributed to mould the most eminent American writers and thinkers of his day. Neither was he affected by French influences like Jefferson and his circle. He was a native of Pennsylvania, the Quaker State; his lineage was Quaker; his mental constitution exemplified that union of sobriety with mysticism which characterises the Friend.

Martin S. Vilas (essay date 1904)

SOURCE: *Charles Brockden Brown: A Study of Early American Fiction*, Free Press Association, 1904, pp. 47-66.

[*In the following essay, Vilas reviews the influence of other writers on Brown, as well as Brown's influence on Shelley and on American writers. Vilas notes that Brown did not establish a school of fiction in America and stresses the influence of William Godwin on Brown.*]

Influence of European Writers on Brown

That Brown was affected in his works of fiction by his predecessors and his contemporaries in the art has been indicated, indeed, it goes without saying. Everyone is the product of his time and his environment. Now and then an intellect stands forth that seemingly has been able so to gather impressions from the "storied urns" of the past and from the realities of the present as to "send messages into Philistia" to appear like the warning voice of a prophet, or in other words of a man in advance of his time. The effect is caused by a higher point of view or by superior comprehension, possibly by both. The question then should not be,—Was Brown affected by other writers in his field?—but,—How was he affected by them? We must take it for granted that Brown, a "literary Doge," had read De Foe, Richardson, Fielding, Smollett, and Sterne. That he was acquainted with the lesser lights that followed admits of no doubt to one who has read his works. Had he not read most of those named at least, we surely could detect the fact, though we may not be able to say we see the positive influence of a particular author. The mighty movements following the French Revolution, when the works of Rousseau, of Voltaire, Montesquieu, D'Alembert and of Diderot came to invigorate all that read the English language, bore with full weight upon Brown as is evident from his first romance, *Wieland,* and from his political essays.

It is stated [Pancoast, *Intro. to Am. Lit.,* p. 108.] that Brown was an ardent admirer of Godwin and of his almost equally famous wife, who was an extremist on the question of women's rights and from her influence seems to have arisen his *Alcuin, a Dialogue on the Rights of Women.* Dowden in his *Life of Shelley* [Vol. I, p. 472.] speaks of Brown as "Godwin's American disciple in romance." As Godwin and his wife were both ardent students of the French "Encyclopædists," we may say further that his literary friends must, in all probability, have lead him to the common fountain head. Both Godwin and Brown wrote much in the ruling spirit. Godwin was influenced by Utopian ideas and he believed, like his son-in-law, Shelley, that society should be overturned; hence his *Caleb Williams,* the underlying principle of which is a character worked out by philosophical analysis to develop certain social and political phenomena in their effects upon the mind and upon society. It was using what we would to-day call the scientific method.

It is evident that Brown adopted this mode of presentation in **Wieland, Ormond, Arthur Mervyn,** and in **Edgar Huntly.** And in all his tales there is one character that stands out before the others with a second of nearly as great consequence. In dealing with these two characters in particular, and in an especial degree with the former, Brown makes it his business to be careful in his developments of moods, to cause the changes of mind to come by gradations that we may see the effect psychologically and from it draw the lesson. Sometimes he seeks to make the demonstration from other than the principal characters, as when with much circumlocution, he endeavored to draw the irrelevant and useless moral at the end of **Wieland**. To point out the moral at the end of any tale is like telling a joke and then naming it, but in this we see some of the effects of his time which seemed to consider that we need not be expected to retain our common sense in reading or writing a novel or romance.

But in the first four of the works of fiction of Brown, and in **Wieland** in particular, there is an entirely evident attempt not merely to follow the manner of plot of Godwin, but to adopt his literary style. He endeavors by a few details, as in the description by Wieland of his crime, in the yellow fever scenes of Arthur Mervyn and in the escape from the first panther in Edgar Huntly, to impress the outlines upon the mind after the exceedingly simple but intensely sublime action of *Caleb Williams.*

If Brown read French political and social philosophy, still more likely is it that he read Locke and Hume and was, we may conclude from his political essays, familiar also with the new science of Adam Smith and with the writings of Burke.

It is common to connect the name of Jane Austen (1775-1817) with that of Brown as though she in some way influenced him, especially through her best known work, *Pride and Prejudice,* which exercised a very beneficial effect on the fiction of the time. But this novel was published in 1813, three years after the death of Brown, and all her works came forth after 1810. Accordingly, she could not have affected him and I fail to find any evidence of an influence from Brown upon her.

Influence of Brown on Shelley

I at this point consider the oft' mentioned influence of Brown upon Shelley. Dowden [*Life of Shelley,* Vol. I, p. 472.] quoted the words of Peacock, that "Brown's four novels, Schiller's Robbers and Goethe's *Faust,* were of all the works with which he was familiar those which took the deepest root in Shelley's mind and had the strongest influence in the formation of his character." But Shelley was only eighteen when Brown died and his wild, imaginative spirit was easily caught by the ruling sentiment of the fiction of the day which he attempted to represent and portray, but the "Romances of pseudo-passion and pseudo sublime" could not equal the almost blatant passion of "Zastrozzi" and "St. Irvyne the Rosicrusian." The former was written for the most part when Shelley was but seventeen. They are boyish creations and the influence of Brown can be seen only in the familiar predominence of the speculative and abnormal rather than in any one particular point of likeness. I have said Shelley attempted to portray the ruling spirit of romance but he could not do this without striving to outdo it. His nature would not admit of it. The boy gives rein to his imagination. Each character is intense. In "Zastrozzi" Matilda, Julia, the "Enchanting and congenial female," Verrezi and the towering and haughty-passioned Zastrozzi are characters that appeal to us because of an indescribable touch everywhere of an artistic fancy. Undoubtedly Brown helped to give form to this fancy, but Shelley, even as a boy, soared above Brown, for his wild images could brook nothing ever builded by another. That Brown affected permanently the tenor of Shelley's writings I am unable to verify or credit.

Influence of American Writers on Brown

Not so interesting because not so conclusive is the question of the influence of writers on this side of the Atlantic. In spite of the fact that during a part of his life speculative philosophy overshadowed Brown's religion, he was by nature deeply religious and highly moral. The intense and narrow as well as intensely narrow theological spirit of Puritan New England, the most cultivated part of America, added great stress to the conception that all writing should have a moral bearing, that nothing could be unmoral, but if not decidedly moral, everything must be immoral. Hence, the excellence of a tale was in its moral or religious strenuousness, and for that matter poetry and prose both were measured by the same cast iron standard. The horrible custom of constant self-inspection that reached its height under Hooker, the Mathers and Edwards had spent itself before the time of Brown. While the philosophy of Godwin led away from religion, Brown had the true Quaker spirit of his ancestors intensified by some lingerings of the creed of the author of the famous "Magnalia Christi Americana." Brown himself probably was unconscious of this last, yet one could not live in the culture of the north and escape it.

The great Unitarian movement had just started when Brown wrote. William Ellery Channing graduated from Harvard the same year *Wieland* appeared, but James

Freeman was re-ordained pastor of King's Chapel in Boston in 1787 with a revised Non-Trinitarian liturgy and the prenatal breathings of the work of the Wares, Andrews Norton, Theodore Parker and even of Emerson were in the air. Indeed, Brown was active in anticipating this by his adoption of the philosophic principles of Godwin, which were really the ideas of French and German thinkers modified by English minds. Moreover, the great transcendental movement meant nothing more than this; and Carlyle put into English ritual the creed of the continent which Emerson was to conform to American freedom and vigor.

Whether Mrs. Rowson and Mrs. Tenney directly affected him or not may be uncertain, as these ambitious women simply caught the temper of English minor fiction in a more gushing style than usual, but it appears to me that Brown seemed to consider that his first four works of fiction were too intensely dramatic and dealt too much with the impossible, so determined to make his others more true to life. In other words, it amounted to his dropping the philosophy of Godwin and coming down to the same basis with *Charlotte Temple* and *Female Quixotism,* a basis made more enduring in his case by his stronger hand and deeper common sense. Brown could not drop his philosophy and write good novels, but he might retain it and write good romances for the time. The latter is what he did in his first four works of fiction while his last two are merely novels a few degrees better than the milk and water productions of his two lady contemporaries.

General Critical Study of Brown

Brown's use of English is usually that of a scholar, but is what many would call over-scholarly. With him the study was not to find the simplest word or phrase to express the exact meaning but apparently to select the heaviest and most cumbersome. In *Ormond* [p. 58] he says that clothing "stood in need of ablution;" again in the same [p. 231] "all hope of happiness in this mutable and sublunary scene was fled." In *Edgar Huntly* [p. 29] is stated "my stormy passions had subsided into a calm, portentous and awful;" again in the same [p. 185] "the channel was encumbered with asperities." His characters never think or meditate, but it is their habit to "ruminate" so much that it becomes a pernicious custom. He invariably uses "somewhat" for something. One more passage will serve to illustrate fully his old-fashioned preciseness and insipid pedantry,— "Helena Cleves was endowed with every feminine and fascinating quality. Her features were modified by the most transient sentiments and were the seat of a softness at all times blushful and bewitching. All those graces of symmetry, smoothness and luster, which assembled in the imagination of the painter when he calls from the bosom of her natal deep the Paphian divinity blended their perfections in the shade, complexion and hair of this lady" [*Ormond*, p. 116].

Brown had been trained a Quaker, but that in no sense excuses him for his inaccurate uses of "thee," "thou," and "thine." They are introduced along with the newer forms with apparent indiscriminateness. One sentence uses the old, the next the new and soon the old appears again with no apparent object for the variation [*Edgar Huntly,* ps. 135-136]. The kind of diction referred to is excessively common and in the eyes of the critic to-day is far more serious than in the time of the author, serving to render neutral many of the positive excellencies of the work, as they are usually not merely faults of diction but also of style. Undoubtedly, Brown might have improved these things with better care. All the most important of his works were written within the space of ten years and his rapidity approached that of Scott for he was a very voluminous writer.

The close of our author's works is usually weak, giving the appearance that he tired as he went on or left them and became occupied in part by other things. In *Arthur Mervyn* he apparently kept increasing characters towards the close to compensate for actual dramatic action. But Brown is not lacking in invention or originality and we would never think of charging him with plagiarism or with any undue imitation of another author. He is conscientious everywhere and in everything. I agree with Prescott [*Miscellanies,* C. B. Brown, p. 53] that were his faults removed, he might not have been so good,—*"Si non errasset, fecerat ille minus."*

At any rate as he lost his Utopian ideas, his attachment for the theories of Godwin, as he came to be an ardent advocate of Christianity and endeavored to drop the extravagance of his first work, we may see in the religious experiences of Colden in *Jane Talbot,* an effort to typify himself, but in making these changes he lost his power—the ability to describe graphically and to awaken interest in us by the almost indefinable something. As says Pattee [*Amer. Lit.,* p. 105], "It is hard to lay down one of his romances unfinished; one reads on and on in a sort of ghastly dream until at length the end of the book completes the hideous nightmare."

Some men are great in themselves, others great in the eyes of the world through association with great names or because they mark epochs in events. Would Charles Brockden Brown be considered a writer of much prominence, were he not the first author of prose fiction in America? The day that would cherish writings with the style of Brown has passed. He did not possess the power, take him all in all, to entrench himself in principles of nature and of literature that are unchanging. He supplied the demands of the time with considerable credit and praise. A scholar with the instincts of a scholar, he did a scholarly work, but he had not enough individuality and keen discernment to discard the objectionable in contemporaneous literature and to write as the young prophet of the new and great America. A philosophic rather than a poetic spirit, he had not

enough of the true and exact philosophy to understand that to portray man in a form that will endure he must be portrayed as he is and that nature to be pictured so that the painting will be entitled to hang upon the galleries among the works of great artists must be tinted not in all the hues of the rainbow, unless it has the rainbow's careful blending and that reality must dominate art.

The spirit of the French renaissance united with the culture of England and with the freedom of the new nation was not sufficient to cause Brown to discard entirely the spirit of the old classical school of Pope, while the so-called "nature movement" led on by Thomson in "The Seasons" had been insufficient to turn his mind to nature in her actual form. He could not describe a cavern, a precipice or a deep ravine without letting his imagination lead him into something that is gruesome. Thus nature becomes not an emblem of the bright and beautiful, but the representation of an infinite and awful power which hangs over and around all things. This representation is expressive to us and we should study it by night time when the stars are shining, in the howl of the tempest when the sky is blackened by storm clouds, but we should study it with a nameless, indefinable dread, we should "ruminate ominously" upon it, go back to our "habitation" oppressed with melancholy and spend the night in a vague unrest with an incomprehensible and indescribable something preying upon our souls, to arise in the morning to new "ruminations." And man is, though perhaps "The proper study of mankind," yet a part of this terrible and mystic nature, is always incomprehensible and the subject of strange vagaries, whims and contrivances from on high. We study these as phenomena of nature and, particularly, as they relate to us and are "philosophical," but the more we study, the farther removed are we from ourselves, the more unfitted do we become to go on with the dull, prosaic duties that devolve upon us. But we are to "muse perpetually" upon it all, though never are we satisfied, never brightened, never go back with a glad and cheerful heart to say,—I am of nature and of God. I exist as a part of it and of Him. If he is great and wonderful, aye, awful at times in his manifestations, I rejoice in it, for it exalts me that see in it an expression of myself. The Almighty is great and powerful, so am I in a small degree as a manifestation in one form of Him. Hence, I am glad to be alive, to see these mighty movements all related to me and I to them. I breathe in the air—an extraordinary manifestation of his power—and it becomes a part of my being. I eat and thrive on the infinite resources of a miraculous Providence and I am a miracle. Therefore it is glorious to exist in such greatness and, like Walter Scott, as a boy, to lie upon the ground in a storm in the mountains and clap my hands at each thunder peal.

But these optimistic feelings were not akin to the soul of Brown. His philosophy was the philosophy of darkness and distortion. He was too sickly and shall I say too scholarly; not that he knew too much, for scholarship and knowledge are not synonymous, but his life was the morbid, introspective life of the study but little influenced by the greater life outside. He read of nature and of God from books but never fully realized that he thus was getting these subjects only from a meagre secondhand. The full, rich life of manhood, the joy of living never touched him. He realized vaguely that in the American Indian there is a creation different from the ordinary and so something that we call "original" for treatment, but the thought became a fancy before it could be fairly comprehended. It slipped from him ere he could write it down in vivid colors and he remained sombre and desolate trying to write himself into a great writer and philosophize himself into a great philosopher, though he never yet had reached the life he thought to describe save by fleeting moments and he existed ever apart from what was and is in the highest form the true, the beautiful and so the good.

But the fault lay not, I think, with himself, but that he was by Nature so incomplete a representative of man,—an illustration that he cannot be a grasper of a number of great truths that is not well or vigorous in organization. Brown had not the physical courage nor the moral force to drop his books like Thoreau and literally to "take to the woods" for long months that he might gain vigor and correct conceptions. He was bound to his desk and only broke loose when necessity drove him on brief excursions. Within the limits of his strength, he did a great work. He realized his duty to his country and to civilization to contribute as much as within him lay and he never faltered though beset constantly by weariness and disease. His patience, his conscientiousness and his unfaltering devotion to the light that came to him led him ever on with a resolute heart and, even when disease was constantly preying upon him, his smile of affection always covered the deep-seated anguish. His pure and upright life was reflected in his writings, and if he could not write brilliant facts so that they would endure, all things of him exhibited the greatest of all truths that the highest virtue consists in "the perfection of one's self and the happiness of others."

It was then a courageous thing to be an American writer and especially to attempt to be the first American novelist, but Brown constantly displayed that courage. Had he not deserved to be first, the position would not have been accorded him. If he did not set the pace, he started the movement. It is with very great respect and considerable admiration that I have studied this "brief but blazing star" that during his short and sickly life worked with such unfailing earnestness along lines that to him seemed best and highest.

Influence of Brown upon American Literature

But what has he done for us? That he was the head of an American school of fiction cannot be claimed. He lived in a transitional period in literature between the stilted, artificial style and what we are fond of denominating the "natural." Scott came soon after and prose fiction was recreated in him and never has lost his impress. Soon Brown and authors like him ceased to be read. Irving, not a romancer or a novelist, but a great prose writer, followed closely upon Brown. If Brown was the first American novelist, Irving was the first great American prose writer and his style tended to lessen further the influence of the first American novelist.

Cooper, the "American Scott," improperly so-called, ere long gave to American literature a right to look with pride upon its producers of prose fiction, and again a deep influence was exerted away from Brown. American novels that appeared soon after Brown were modeled for the most part after Scott and Cooper, as *The Buccaneers* (1827), S. B. Judah; *Rachel Dyer* (1828), John Neal; *The Betrothed of Wyoming* (1831) and *Meredith or the Mystery of the Meschanza* (1831). That Brown and others of his style will ever again be popular is exceeding improbable; we may almost say impossible.

Nevertheless, the influence of our author was considerable and valuable. Above the elements of weakness, we have shown, arose many elements of strength. The power of a great writer he had at times and we catch in ***Edgar Huntly*** shades of description and passages of strong expression that make us wonder if Cooper, though so different, may not have caught much that led him on from Brockden Brown. It is very probable. From the defects of another we see how to correct ourselves, and Cooper as he heard and read comments upon Brown could the better judge how he should act. Cooper, the painter of wild America and wild Americans is, indeed, different from Brown, the morbid mind analyst. Seemingly, then, only the touchstone of fancy could detect a derivation, but I am not one that think it necessary to be able to put the finger upon a point or principle of resemblance in one writer in order to be qualified to say with moral certainty he obtained assistance from another. It is too much to expect. We have in Brown a suggestion of Cooper. It is only a suggestion but it is enough.

For purposes of investigation and criticism, however, it amounts to but little to say that such an one, a writer, was a contemporary of another writer; therefore, the one influenced the other. We have the right to presume and assume that every man of letters reads the writings of other writers in his field and time and is affected by them, unconsciously perhaps and perhaps imperceptibly, but the influences are there and his debt to them is something; but I do not think that the spirit of the Sunday School teacher that would read a moral and religious lesson into every word of Scripture should dominate literary criticism. I am at times impatient at the manifest attempt of many commentators to force an issue where there is none and reason out an *a priori* basis until *post hoc propter hoc* seems to be the law of critical study. Generally speaking, give a commentator an analogy and he is sure to work out a derivation, but the result is frequently as far-fetched and ludicrously drawn as some of the various theories as to the origin of the English manorial system.

Irving, who came next after Brown as a prose writer, could take courage as the favorable expressions upon the "New American" came to him, and I think I detect in a few of Irving's works something in style, though so different altogether, that reminds me of Charles Brockden Brown. The debt to Brown was probably considerable of him who wrote to please and in so doing to instruct, who believed in not taking life too seriously or intensely,—a diametrical opposite of Brown.

How far Brown gave suggestions to Hawthorne, it is difficult to say. It is common to reason thus: Brown was a prose writer, morbid and sensitive, and so was Hawthorne, hence the latter probably was something of a disciple of his predecessor. But in the first place Hawthorne never to me seems morbid. He liked especially to work out a peculiar phase in the human heart, as the power of conscience in *The Scarlet Letter,* but that does not prove his morbidness. We might as well call every professor of psychology morbid because his subject is the human soul. Yet there is a very considerable likeness in conception and treatment between *The Scarlet Letter* and *Wieland* or between this and Godwin's *Caleb Williams.* Hawthorne was not a renowned painter like Cooper whose fame rested in his bold vigorous strokes, yet he was a consummate artist who delighted in delicate touches, in the subtleties of his art; but Brown was nothing of this; still even in *The Marble Faun,* I obtain a reminder of Brown. Here as usual we are unable to say one writer took his method of treatment absolutely from another. It might on as good grounds be asserted that Brown derived his manner of treating *Wieland* directly from Horace Walpole's *Castle of Otranto.* However, if Hawthorne was not affected by Brown, he certainly was affected by Brown's mode of conception and unfolding of plot.

Again, we see in Brown a suggestion of Poe, the only distinctively morbid character in American literature, but if we think he suggests Poe, because Poe was morbid, we surely cannot discern much resemblance between the morbidness of *Wieland* and *Arthur Mervyn* and that of "The Black Cat," and "The Pit and the Pendulum." But there is an actual sentiment in *Scarlet Letter* and *Marble Faun,* one that never excites our ridicule whether we agree in it or not, while in the stories of Poe we observe great genius and great art, but the genius and the art of an intensely morbid na-

ture taking the word morbid in its true sense of diseased. I cannot be sure that Brown conferred anything on Poe.

It has been said,—and rightly I think,—that to study literature correctly and determine the value of the work of each author, he should be studied with reference to himself alone first, next with reference to his place in the history of the literature. Then, Charles Brockden Brown, not what is called a great man, yet deserves the place of first American novelist and romancer because he stood forth with enough of ability above the ruling style of such writings to confer to his productions that which we denominate genius, such that he was able to please and instruct his contemporaries, to dignify America by a new title and to serve in a respectable degree as a reference and an instructor for those that followed him in the hitherto untrodden field of American fiction.

Lillie Deming Loshe (essay date 1907)

SOURCE: "The Gothic and the Revolutionary," in *The Early American Novel*, Columbia University Press, 1907, pp. 29-58.

[*In the following essay, Loshe studies the Gothic elements of Brown's novels, stressing the influence of William Godwin on Brown's writing. Loshe maintains that, like Godwin, Brown incorporated into his novels elements that were both psychological—such as characters with abnormal powers—and revolutionary—such as the "dream of an ideal commonwealth beyond the sea."*]

The period of amiable amateurishness with which American fiction began, was followed by the popularity of the first really gifted American novel-writer, the first also whose name has won the adornment of tags in the handbooks of literary history—Charles Brockden Brown, variously known as "The First American Novelist," "The Father of American Fiction," "The First American Man of Letters." Brown's novels, however, are separated from those of his predecessors less by professional handling or technical skill than by the new ideals of literature and life which they represent. In England, as in America, sentimental and didactic fiction was still produced in quantity, but the fashion of the hour at which Brown wrote was the Gothic.

Although the history of the Gothic novel goes back to 1764, when Horace Walpole had a bad dream and wrote *The Castle of Otranto,* the possibilities of the new type were not appreciated until the growing spirit of romanticism found itself in serious sympathy with the mediæval machinery and supernatural terrors which Walpole may have invented partly in a spirit of flippancy. The triumphant vogue of the Gothic novel is the peculiar glory of Mrs. Anne Radcliffe whose *Castles of Athlin and Dunbayne,* published in 1789, was followed by *A Sicilian Romance* (1790), *The Romance of the Forest* (1791), *The Mysteries of Udolpho* (1794), *The Italian* (1797). Her thrilling tales found so many imitators that after 1790 the Gothic novel may fairly be said to have reigned in English fiction. Owls hooted; trap-doors yawned; ghosts in armour walked the floor with a spectral clank; damsels swooned on secret staircases; balls of fire rolled around the best regulated houses; mysterious figures in inky cloaks waited at dark corners to pluck impetuous heroes by the sleeve and bid them "beware"; she was but a poor and old-fashioned heroine who had not been kidnapped to a mysterious castle, forced by a heartless parent to dwell in a ruined abbey, or, at the least, immured in a remote convent.

During this period, however, the Gothic romance took so many forms that the precise application of the descriptive adjective is not always apparent. The essence of the "Gothic" may be said to consist, if one may parody a well-worn phrase, in the addition of strangeness to terror. The variations of this type fall, with more or less coercion, into three groups: the supernatural Gothic of Walpole and Lewis, the mechanical or architectural Gothic of Mrs. Radcliffe, and the psychological or Revolutionary Gothic of William Godwin, which united certain characteristics of the "Gothic" and of the "Revolutionary" novels. It is from Godwin that Brown received the impulse to write the first American novels that possess any real merit.

Born in Philadelphia, in 1771, the descendant of a family of Friends who had come over with Penn, Brown was a frail child, unable to play with other boys, and consequently early addicted to books. His biographer[1] relates that even as an infant he would be found musing over the page with all the gravity of a student, and that, when he was still a child of ten, "thinking, which is to the uncultivated so laborious and irksome an occupation, became to him the most delightful of employments." As a schoolboy he tried his hand at both verse and prose, and at the early age of sixteen he had planned three epics, all on American subjects,—for the serene consciousness of national achievement which filled the country at that time was always strong in Brown.

At the end of his school days he did not allow the study of the law, upon which he then entered, to interrupt this state of "intellectual revelry"—he found time to join a debating society, to keep a journal which was a minute record of his thoughts, and feelings, and even of his letters, and to study English authors with the definite purpose of improving his style. He became one of the founders and chief ornaments of a literary society, the Belles Lettres Club, and made his first appearance in print, in a series of essays contributed to

the *Columbian Magazine,* in which, his biographer says, "he presented himself to the world in the character of a rhapsodist." On the completion of his studies Brown could not conquer his dislike to the practice of law, with what he later described as, "its endless tautologies, its impertinent conceits, its lying assertions and hateful artifices," and he displayed considerable ingenuity in the preparation of conscientious reasons for declining it.

Brown at this period seems to have been an earnest, rather over-read, young man, much given to somewhat morbid introspection, and with a slightly priggish loathing of the "common pursuits and common topics of men," acquainted with all the literary and political fads of the day, and desirous of immediately settling "the relations, dependencies, and connections of the several parts of knowledge." As a friend declined to perform the latter task he decided to undertake it himself. His devotion to literature, however, was real and enlightened. The romantic gloom and self-torture, the corroding sorrows, latent anguishes, and thoughts of suicide which leaked from his diary, where he meant to confine them, into his letters, were in part the result of youthful morbidness, and in part an expression of the self-analytical spirit of the day.

For the next few years he was without definite occupation, but seems to have considered himself in training for literature. Repeated visits to New York made him acquainted with friends of tastes thoroughly congenial with his own. At length he made his home there, and lived at first with Dunlap and afterward with Dr. Elihu Hubbard Smith. Here he seems to have done some magazine work, and to have found spiritual refreshment in the meetings of the Friendly Club, a literary society which held weekly discussions and published a review. The minds of the group were excited by the political and social speculation, and the generous enthusiasm, with which the French Revolution was filling the air. They sought "a plan to improve and secure human happiness," and, like most of the ardent young spirits of the time, evidently, looked to William Godwin as the inspired high-priest of political wisdom. Like Godwin they traced the errors of society to institutions.

It was probably as a result of these discussions that Brown wrote, and in 1797 published, his ***Alcuin,*** a dialogue on marriage. This work reflects many of Godwin's views, and discusses questions of the position and education of women which were present with Brown all his life. In other ways, also, the society in which he found himself must have been stimulating to Brown. He was surrounded by young men whose literary activity and ambitions were eager and sincere, although their actual accomplishment was not remarkable. His closest companions, Dunlap and Smith, were engaged in different kinds of literary work. Although

Smith published little not concerned with his profession, except an opera, *Edwin and Angelina,* presented in 1796, he is said by Dunlap to have written many sonnets and poems. Dunlap's services to the American stage as author, translator, manager, and later as historian, are well known. His industry as a translator and producer of sensational German dramas, especially those of Kotzebue, may have helped to bring about Brown's sympathetic attitude toward German literature.[2] However that may be, it is evident that Dunlap's friendship and example must have done much to stir Brown's literary ambitions into action.

After the publication of *Alcuin* Brown began, as he writes in his journal, "something in the form of a romance." Of this attempt he says: "When a mental comparison is made between this and the mass of novels, I am inclined to be pleased with my own production. But when the objects of comparison are changed, and I revolve the transcendent merits of *Caleb Williams,* my pleasure is diminished, and is preserved from total extinction only by the reflection that this performance is my first." This work was never finished and never received a title. According to Brown's usual system of nomenclature it should have been called *Colden, or the Mysterious Boarder.*

In 1798 the yellow fever broke out in New York. Although he had left Philadelphia in 1793 to escape the epidemic, Brown decided to rely on a systematic diet for protection, and remained in New York. The diet, possibly the hasty-pudding and water recommended in *Ormond,* did not justify his confidence; the household was stricken with the fever; Brown was very ill, and Smith died. Brown thus saw all the horrors of the disease, and gathered material for the most successful portion of his novels, realizing, as he afterwards remarked, that the events of the epidemic had been full of instruction to the moral observer.

The first of Brown's novels to be actually published was *Wieland, or the Transformation* (1798). An untoward fate had overtaken the previously completed *Sky Walk, or the Man Unknown to Himself.* It was actually in type, when the printer's death was followed by disagreements with his executor which prevented the publication of the tale.

At this time Brown, whose methods of work were somewhat erratic, had five novels in hand at once. Of these, three appeared in 1799,—*Arthur Mervyn,* which was first published as a serial in the *Weekly Magazine, Edgar Huntly, or Memoirs of a Sleep Walker,* and *Ormond, or the Secret Witness.* In April, 1799, Brown, who had fallen an early victim to the enthusiasm for magazine publishing which was over-running American literature,[3] brought out his *Monthly Magazine and American Review.* This short-lived periodical expired late in the year 1800. It shows interest in German literature, and in scientific subjects, and contains fragments of Brown's works, a specimen of *Edgar Huntly, Thessalonica,* a formless, pseudo-historical short story, and several installments of the unfinished *Memoirs of Stephen Calvert.*

In 1801 appeared his last two novels, *Jane Talbot* and *Clara Howard.* Both of these are as different from Brown's earlier tales as is *Fleetwood* from *Caleb Williams.*

In 1803 Brown returned to magazine work as editor of the *Literary Magazine and American Register,* "replete," Dunlap says, "with the effusions of erudition, taste, and genius." To this was added in 1806 the editorship of the *American Register.* During these busy years Brown, who had married and returned to Philadelphia, found time for little outside his magazine work, except for the publication of a few political pamphlets on questions of immediate interest. But he also wrote a life of his brother-in-law, John Blair Linn, made a translation of Volney, had in preparation a "system of geography" which was left unfinished at his death, and is said to have made "considerable progress in a work on Rome during the Age of the Antonines, similar to Anacharsis' Travels in Greece." Novel-writing he had apparently given up, although the success of his early tales seems to have been considerable, both in England and in America.

Brown died in 1810 after a lingering illness, bravely endured. He seems to have had the gift of attaching his friends warmly to him, and to have produced on all who were brought into contact with him an impression of intellectual ability and uprightness of character.

Brown's magazine work and his political writings, although considerable in quantity and esteemed by him the serious occupation of a life to which novel-writing was only a distraction, have done nothing to keep his name alive. To his novels he owes the distinction of being, if not still read, at least, still talked about—of being condemned as a sensation-monger on the one hand, and on the other extolled as a forerunner of Hawthorne. Of the six novels which Brown completed the first three, *Wieland, Ormond,* and *Arthur Mervyn,* show more directly the influence of *Caleb Williams.* All these tales are characterized by an exaggerated romantic individualism—they are concerned with men whose powers, whether for good or evil, are abnormal. The crimes and horrors which lend an element of external terror, making *Caleb Williams* "captivatingly frightful" to Mrs. Inchbald, are not in themselves the end of the story—they are the effect of a strong personality brought, either by force of external circumstance or by some element of its own nature, into conflict with its environment.

In Brown's novels the logic of events, however, is often destroyed by the carelessness of the composition. The author, who generally had several novels in process of construction at the same time, would send portions of a tale to the printer before he had planned the rest of the story. The result was that he apparently forgot what he had written in one installment and consequently neglected to follow it up in the next. He is never able to make a situation as clear and simple as that which Godwin achieved in *Caleb Williams.* Caleb's story, when stripped of all the didactic reflections on the administration of legal justice, on the system of land-lords, the condition of prisons,—in short, of all the passages in which William Godwin, the serene and stodgy minor prophet, pushes aside Caleb Williams, the hunted, defiant, remorseful boy,—describes the conflict of two persistent natures each driven by its ruling passion, the one by curiosity, the other by the worldly conception of honor.

The story of Caleb Williams may be summarized briefly. Caleb, a lad of unusual ability, the son of a small farmer, has become the secretary of Falkland, his landlord. In his anxiety to discover the cause of fits of melancholy and insane wandering which at times affect the be-nevolent and accomplished Falkland, Williams is led to believe that his patron is really guilty of a murder for which he has once been tried and acquitted. Hence-forth his passionate curiosity, to whose satisfaction, he says, he would have sacrificed liberty and life, leads him to attempt every means to discover the truth. Falkland comes upon Williams in the act of lifting the cover of a mysterious chest, and in a passion of impa-tience tells all the story of his guilt, and his determi-nation to hide it at any cost. Williams still loves and admires his master, whom he considers criminal only through the force of circumstances acting on his really noble qualities. But Falkland distrusts his devotion, maddens him by a petty tyranny of suspicion, and drives him to an attempted flight. Caleb is captured, and imprisoned on a charge of theft arranged by Falkland.

Williams escapes from prison, but is prevented by Falkland's emissaries from leaving the country. In London he lives the life of a hunted creature, con-stantly recognized by Falkland's spies and driven to new disguises, until he is seized and taken before a magistrate. Maddened by the long-drawn terror of his hiding, he denounces Falkland, only to be reproached with adding lying to theft. Falkland appears and tells Williams that the apparent persecution was only a test of the lad's fidelity to his oath, a test in which he has failed. Henceforth, wherever he goes, he will always be in his patron's power, and always be pursued by his revenge. To Falkland reputation is the dearest thing on earth; therefore his revenge will be to take reputation from Williams.

Thereafter Williams is followed from place to place by emissaries of Falkland, who, by spreading the story of his theft and ingratitude, make him an outcast from each community that has sheltered him. Deprived of his livelihood, his friends, his betrothed, he forgets the reverence for Falkland which has persisted through all his sufferings, returns to his native place, and brings a solemn accusation against his former master. Con-fronted with the feeble, almost dying, Falkland, Will-iams is overcome with grief for what he has done. Falkland, convinced too late of Caleb's sincerity, praises his heroic patience, acknowledges the crime, and dies. Godwin leaves his hero a prey to eternal remorse, dra-matically inquiring, "of what use are talents and sen-timents in the corrupt wilderness of human society?"

The faults of the book include the usual Godwinian preaching and pomposity, as well as the high-flown exaggeration of sentiment common in the fiction of the time and no peculiarity of Godwin or of Brown, al-though distressingly present in both. The most striking merit is the vivid representation of certain mental states, and the skill with which the narrative is built up. The book is often called the ancestor of the modern detec-tive story but the relationship is certainly remote.[4] The detection of the crime is accomplished in the first few pages. Thereafter the interest of the tale is, on the one hand, in the darkness of Falkland's mind, blackened by guilt to an insanity of remorse, yet still command-ing and still noble, and, on the other, in the slow tor-ment of Caleb's life, the sense of being watched and followed, of the imminence of an inexorable power, the final animal instinct to turn on the pursuer. In this combination of the sensational and the analytic it is the wreck of the mind, and not the shedding of blood, that gives the element of terror.

Wieland, Brown's first published novel, is like *Caleb Williams,* autobiographical in form. The narrator is Clara Wieland, a young woman of the educated and independent type then just appearing in fiction. Like Caleb Williams, and like most of Brown's other per-sonages, she begins by lamenting the singularity of her fate—"the experience of no human being can furnish a parallel; that I beyond all the rest of mankind should be reserved for a destiny without alleviation and with-out example." She then describes the Wieland family, peaceful, cultured, rathe pedantic, dwelling tranquilly on the banks of the Schuylkill. Their favorite gathering place is "what to the common eye would seem a sum-mer-house," but is in reality a temple built by the older Wieland, a religious monomaniac, who in that very temple had died a mysterious death, appar ently by spontaneous combustion. In spite of the associations of the place the family meet there daily, and pass happy hours discussing the latest German poetry, comparing texts of Cicero, "turning over the Della Crusca dictio-nary," and "bandying quotations and syllogisms."

This learned peace is soon disturbed by the arrival of a mysterious stranger, Carwin, a travelling acquain-tance of Wieland's brother-in-law, Pleyell. Carwin's strange personality and expressive voice have a fascination for Clara, which she for a time mistakes for the "first inroads of a passion incident to every female heart." Mysterious voices are heard around the temple; Wieland, on his way thither, hears his wife warning him away,—yet on returning to the house finds that she has not left her chair. A voice in the dark warns Clara of a power that would injure her, and promises protection. Strange voices are heard quarreling at night in the house in which Clara lives alone with her maid, and when she, fleeing, falls senseless on her brother's threshold, a voice of more than mortal power calls the household to her aid. Not content with establishing a supernatural reign of terror, the mysterious power convinces Clara's lover, Pleyell, of her faithlessness, by causing him to hear her voice making the most disgraceful avowals to another.

In disgust, Pleyell hastily decides to return to Germany, and Clara vainly pursues to dissuade him. On her return she finds that her brother has succumbed to the family tendency to insanity, and, at the instigation of the mysterious voices, has killed his wife and all his children as a divinely demanded sacrifice. After a long illness in another city Clara returns to her house for a farewell visit. There she is confronted with Carwin, who acknowledges that, by what he calls biloquialism or ventriloquialism, he has himself been the author of the mysterious voices. Wieland, who has escaped from prison, now appears and prepares to finish his task by the sacrifice of Clara. In order to dissuade him from the deed Carwin again assumes the mysterious voice. At its rebuke Wieland suddenly recovers from his insanity, realizes what he has done, and stabs himself. Carwin escapes. The story does not follow his adventures further, but devotes a few pages to the fate of Clara, who finally becomes the wife of Pleyell. In the last paragraph a moral is drawn, somewhat abruptly, from the events of the tale.

The story is obviously of a more sensational type than *Caleb Williams*—indeed the use of supernatural claptrap is a reminder, at least, of Mrs. Radcliffe—but the agency itself is far different from her trap-doors and mechanical devices. Instead of these Brown uses a natural, but to him mysterious and awful, power,—that control over the voice which he calls biloquialism, much as a novelist of to-day might use hypnotism. The part played by Carwin as instigator of Wieland's crimes is apparently without motive; indeed Carwin's character and history receive no adequate explanation in the novel, which is really an episode connected with the unfinished **Memoirs of Carwin, the Biloquist,** rather than an independent work.

Of these **Memoirs** only the story of the hero's early youth and education was completed. Carwin, a youth of considerable natural ability, but chiefly remarkable for his skill in ventriloquism, attracts the attention of

a distinguished and mysterious Englishman, Ludloe, who takes Carwin back to Europe with him. There Carwin is treated with affectionate indulgence, is gradually led to share Ludloe's views on the ills of society, and finally is taught the justness of dissimulation for a worthy cause. Carwin is then sent to Spain to study man and human institutions, practising "a system of deceit pursued merely from the love of truth." During his stay in Spain Carwin frequently exercises his "bilingual" power, yet still conceals its possession from Ludloe, although he has pledged himself to report every detail of his life.

On Carwin's return to England, Ludloe gradually acquaints him with the existence of a political association engaged in a great and arduous design, and leads him to desire to join it. The secret object of the association is not told, but Carwin discovers an atlas with a map of an unknown island country, and perceives that the founding of a new civilization in that place must be Ludloe's hope. Ludloe offers to make Carwin a member of the association, but insists on the dangers of undertaking the task lightly, the entire devotion required, the destruction sure to follow a breach of secrecy, and, above all, the absolute necessity of a complete confession of every detail of his past life. Carwin, although confessing everything else, and although aware that Ludloe has an unaccountable familiarity with his past actions, persists in concealing his biloquial achievements. Ludloe, evidently unsatisfied, promises him another opportunity to continue his confessions. At this point the story breaks off. From Carwin's account of himself in **Wieland** it appears that he has in some way lost Ludloe's favor, has been imprisoned on charges invented by him, and has escaped to America.

This dream of an ideal commonwealth beyond the sea was the most persistent result of Brown's early political speculations. It appears again in **Ormond,** in **Arthur Mervyn,** in the fragment of the story of Colden, and in the few pages concerning the mysterious Italian, Adini. And Dunlap explains the fragmentary *Sketches of the History of Carsol* and the *Sketches of the History of the Carrils and Ormes* as a part of a plan for extensive works combining fiction and history while imitating the air of history,—the whole to be completed by "an Utopian system of manners and government."[5]

The promoters and mouthpieces of these ideal schemes are men, like Falkland, of unusual powers and great possibilities of good, but, like Falkland, turned by the force of circumstances in part to evil. Ludloe, Carwin's patron, is only sketched in the fragment in which he appears, but he was obviously intended to have something of the sinister charm which distinguished Ormond, Brown's most finished villain, whose pursuit of the beautiful and virtuous Constantia Dudley leads him to cause the murder of her father, and finally to threaten the life of Constantia herself, who stabs him in self-defence. Ormond is the more detailed portrait of the heroic criminal sketched in Ludloe. He is said to be "of all mankind the most difficult and the most deserving to be studied." It is due to the "unexampled formation of this man's mind" that, as in the case of Falkland, his good qualities become the source of his errors—"considerations of justice and pity were made, by a fatal perverseness of reasoning, champions and bulwarks of his most atrocious mistakes." Thoroughly devoted to political schemes "likely to possess an extensive influence on the future conditions of the western world," the center of intrigues and director of all sorts of agents and fellow-workers, he still finds time to gratify his curiosity by impersonating a chimney-sweep, and thus introducing himself into his neighbor's houses. Confident in his own position, and the force of his own personality, he disregards the ordinary conventions of society and, we are told, never condescends to apply the title of Mr. or Miss to anyone. In spite of his avowed contempt for religion and for marriage, his fascination of personality and intellect is fatal to the beautiful Helena, who possesses only "attainments suited to the imbecility of her sex," and it almost proves the undoing of the grave and learned Constantia. Although in the conception of his character, in its mingling of benevolence and crime with some strange superhuman force commanding reverence, he resembles Falkland, he is as unconventional as Falkland is elegant. The contrast between their daily manners and speech is as great as that between the crude pleasure derived by the youthful Ormond from decorating his horse's mane with the heads of five Turks suspended by their gory locks, and the polished elegance with which Falkland's Italian duel is conducted.

A deeper difference between Falkland, on the one hand, and Ludloe and Ormond on the other, lies in the circumstances that have turned them to villainy. Falkland becomes a criminal in a moment of passion, and thereafter the principles which have guided his life honorably are made to lead him to infamy. But Ormond, whose crimes are set before the reader, and Ludloe, whose villainy can only be inferred from hints in the incomplete *Carwin* and in *Wieland,* have been led into evil ways while seeking a good end. One must go beyond Godwin for a model for these "systematic villains." Extricated from the fogs of indefiniteness in which Brown has purposely wrapped them, they resemble the leaders of the secret society of the *Illuminati,* or at least they resemble the popular idea of those leaders.

The order of the *Illuminati* was established in Bavaria, in 1775, by Weishaupt, a professor of Canon Law at Ingolstadt, and in 1780 was suppressed by the Elector. It is said, however, to have secretly continued its organization, to have had representatives all over Europe and to have had an active part in the French Revolu-

tion. At the time at which Brown wrote, the *Illuminati,* their wide aims, their evil methods, and their mysterious power, were a widespread cause of discussion. A good contemporary account of the order can be found in a book by John Robison, Secretary to the Royal Society of Edinburgh, with the ponderous title *Proofs of a Conspiracy against all the Religions and Governments of Europe, carried on in the secret meetings of Free Masons, Illuminati, and Reading Societies.*[6] The elders of the society were supposed to undertake the training of the novices or Minervals, just as Ludloe trained Carwin. The novices had no acquaintance with other members of the society,—each dealt with his own guardian *illuminatus,* under whose guidance he gradually imbibed new principles and forsook those in which he had been brought up; he learned, for example, that, as the object of the society was the happiness of all mankind, any narrow consideration of national patriotism must give way to this wider bond. Those higher in authority in the society were accused of absolute unscrupulousness of method and great immorality of life. A shorter account of the society was prefixed by P. Will, the translator, to a novel by the Marquis of Grosse, translated as *Horrid Mysteries*[7] (1796). Will quotes as his authority the *Uber den Umgang mit Menschen* of the Baron von Knigge, who at one time had been high in authority among the *Illuminati.*[8] The story is of the most glaringly sensational order, but the views attributed to the *Illuminati* are much like those of Ormond and Ludloe,—"let us farther suppose that the society should watch the secret process of nature, trace the means Providence employs to educate the human race and pursue the discoveries which their united exertions should stir up; let us finally suppose that these men should faithfully act as vice-regents of Providence, and strive not to improve, but to accelerate, the actions of the Supreme Ruler of the world; would these men wander from their great mark on account of the lesser troubles of this life?"[9]

More briefly, their aim is said to be the regeneration of the world by faith, dagger, and poison; but in the meantime the machinery organized for that great purpose is often employed to serve the evil ends of individuals. There was much in this mingling of idealism and infamy to appeal to the peculiar imagination of Brown, already stimulated by Godwin's high-minded criminal. In the handling of this material Brown showed a more artistic instinct than did the author of the *Horrid Mysteries* or Brown's own countrywoman, Mrs. Wood. Although in the relations of Carwin and Ludloe he followed closely the system attributed to the *Illuminati,* Brown identified his heroes with no known association, and never explained the source of their power, or the exact nature of their designs. To the mystery thus guarded, he added the idealizing element of the Utopian commonwealth, which seems to have been an addition of his own rather than a scheme popularly attributed to the *Illuminati.* Although the first impulse

to the tale of crime and of the high-minded criminal seems to have come from *Caleb Williams,* the *Illuminati* determined the form which this mixture of the magnanimous and the despicable was to take, and made Brown's tales an exposition, in a wider sense than was *Caleb Williams,* of the text *Le crime a ses héros, l'erreur a ses martyrs.*[10]

Arthur Mervyn, published in the same year as Ormond, introduces a villain of a lesser type, but still with something which sets him apart from other men, something that wakens in the youthful Arthur "emotions of veneration and awe." Welbeck's good and ill qualities, like Ormond's, come from the same source; but in his case there are no Utopian schemes for the betterment of mankind, no generous impatience of human suffering. His actions, good and ill, all proceed from the love of money and reputation; hence his crimes are sordid, and his death lingering and disgraceful.

Welbeck's worldliness is, perhaps, painted the blacker in order to enhance the simple virtues of Arthur Mervyn, the ploughboy philosopher, whom, to serve his own ends, he takes into his family. Arthur seems to have been intended for an example of the noble child of nature, instructed but not sophisticated by a few good books,—a specimen of natural excellence unspoiled by society, somewhat reminiscent of Caleb Williams.

As a story the book possesses little interest, and constitutes, indeed, practically two independent works,—for Brown apparently forgot how he was going to continue and pieced out his tale with a new set of personages. It contains, however, Brown's best known "horror," the famous description of the yellow fever plague in Philadelphia. It is the repetition of a well-worn commonplace to point out that here, for once, Brown has achieved the really horrible which he and all the race of Gothic novelists had so long and industriously sought. Yellow fever scenes are introduced in the first part of *Ormond,* and are described with a realistic detail as complete as that in *Arthur Mervyn,* but the scale of the picture is less.[11] In *Arthur Mervyn* Brown managed to give a sense of the horror of silent streets disturbed only by the rattling of the dead cart, of the terror of empty houses abandoned to the dead and the dying, of the atmosphere of disease and death hanging over the panic-stricken city in which neither food nor shelter could be bought. He describes the flight of the living, the atrocities of the hospital, and the hearse men dragging out the still breathing bodies, and illustrates the general desolation by the experiences of Arthur who, attacked by the fever, could only drag himself to a deserted house to die out of reach of the hospital cart. Brown's descriptions are of an unshrinking realism, he never trusts in suggestion or in the imagination of his reader, and yet from his loathsome catalogue of disgusting details there results an effect of simple horror.

Arthur Mervyn is the last of Brown's tales of villainy. *Edgar Huntly, or the Sleep Walker* can boast of nothing more iniquitous than a murderous madman and, for the greater confusion of the reader, two sleep-walkers. The book, like *Arthur Mervyn,* breaks in two in the middle. The early part deals with the insane Clithero, while Edgar's wilderness experiences form the second, and by far the more interesting part of the work.[12]

In 1801, two years after the publication of *Edgar Huntly,* appeared Brown's last two novels, *Clara Howard, or the Enthusiasm of Love* and *Jane Talbot.* In contrast to all his other tales these are entirely without bloodshed—not a single murder adorns the pages of either book. *Clara Howard* is entirely without a villain, and in *Jane Talbot* there is only a poor, meddling, little spinster villainess. Brown seems to be escaping from the influence of the tale of horror and indulging his natural bent toward the analytical. The form, also, differs from his early autobiographies. The story is told in letters exchanged by the hero and heroine. Although in the days when he wrote *Alcuin* Brown, with the severity of the youthful sage, had apparently scorned love stories, remarking that "the languishing and sighing lover is an object to which the errors of mankind have annexed a certain degree of importance," in these later tales he employs the conventional material of fiction; and love, which has now become in his estimation a "precious inebriation of the heart," provides the theme of the letters.

The reader of these letters is constantly reminded that they were written in the days of *The Rights of Woman.* In *Alcuin* Brown had advocated equality of education and of industrial opportunity for men and women, and in all his novels his contempt for "female metaphysics" and his enthusiasm for a more rational system of education are apparent. In Constantia Dudley, the heroine of *Ormond,* he had pre-figured the virtues of Clara Howard. Constantia's education had been conducted in Latin and English; her father had taught her mathematics, anatomy, and astronomy, and interested her in social theories, "instead of familiarizing her with the amorous effusions of Petrarch and Racine, he made her thoroughly conversant with Tacitus and Milton." As a result of this paternal forethought Constantia walked always in the light of reason, early decided that "to marry in extreme youth would be a proof of pernicious and opprobrious temerity," rejected her early suitor Balfour because of the "poverty of his discourse and ideas," and, notwithstanding the fascination which Ormond exerted over her, never fully gave him her affection because "he had embraced a multitude of opinions which appeared to her to be erroneous. Till these were satisfied and their conclusions were made to correspond, wedlock was improper." Meanwhile Constantia went on her way serene, self-poised, self-supporting, adored by a fond parent who "never reflected on his relationship to her without rapture." Her

qualities were enhanced by contrast with the women surrounding her;—the weak and yielding Helena whose early training was of the antiquated softening variety, the impulsive and sentimental Sophia, and the energetic but unbalanced Martinette de Beauvais. The latter accompanied her husband to war, "more than once rescued him from death by the seasonable destruction of his adversary," and among other Amazonian achievements, "with a fusil of two barrels," killed thirteen officers at Jemappes. Constantia, without the gentleness of Helena or the vivacity of Martinette, had a clearness of thought and a poise of character unusual in the heroines of fiction. It was probably her resolute independence, her ability to think for herself, and the unconventional nature of her conclusions, that won for her Shelley's admiration.

Clara Howard is Constantia Dudley without the hardening effects of poverty and care, and with the addition of an enthusiastic affection for a charming and guileless youth, one of Brown's gifted rustics,—a clock maker from a New Jersey village to whom Clara's stepfather plays the part of patron so indispensable in Brown's plots. In this case, however, the patron has none of the mingled nature of Ludloe or of Welbeck—he is all bland benevolence, and far too much of a philosopher to object to bestowing his daughter on a youth whose natural merits are unadorned by position, property, or anything more than a self-administered education. But Clara discovers that Stanley is already betrothed to Mary Wilmot, whom he has never loved. Mary vanishes, and Clara nobly sends the reluctant Philip in pursuit.

The letters which compose the tale are written during his absence, and are chiefly occupied by minute analysis of the writer's feelings. Clara, who is the stronger spirit, goads Philip on in his not very energetic search, and devotes many pages to the dissection of his motives and of hers. Very characteristic is the firmness with which she repulses his occasional rebellion against the programme of self-renunciation which she has laid out for him. "I am in hopes that time and reflection will instill into you better principles. Till then I shall not be displeased if your letter be confined to a mere narrative of your journey. Adieu, Clara Howard." Philip promptly retaliates by contracting an apparently mortal illness. On his recovery the correspondence proceeds, with the same alternations of enthusiastic affection and quibbling reproaches, until Mary suddenly reappears, betrothed to another. Every obstacle to happiness is thus removed, and Philip flies to the fond Clara who assures him that, with "the improvements of time," and her own judicious training, he will soon equal her in "moral discernment," and surpass her in everything else.

Their story, that of the betrothal of the poor, untrained, and unconventional, but gifted and charming country boy, to the older and more sophisticated woman of wealth and social experience, recalls the strange love affairs of Arthur Mervyn. Although Arthur has won the young affections of Eliza Hadwin, a damsel of fifteen, that "age of delicate fervour, of inartificial love," and although his heart melts with rapture when he sees her, yet he has the fortitude to weigh the matter through many pages, and finally to announce that "In consequence of these reflections I decided to suppress the tenderness which the company of Miss Hadwin produced." To her he prefers the widowed Achsa Fielding, of whom he says that "her superior age, sedateness, and prudence gave my deportment a filial freedom and affection, and I was fond of calling her 'Mamma.'" He is, as he candidly remarks, "wax in her hands," and he evidently looks forward to a life of felicity, relying on Mrs. Fielding's judgment for guidance and on her property for support. In the case of Clara Howard and Philip Stanley the difference of age and of temperament is not as great, but there is the same picture of the resolute and reasonable woman directing the gentle and irresolute boy.

The philosophical indifference to the sordid process of money-getting displayed by Arthur Mervyn, and to some extent by Philip Stanley, is even more pronounced in Henry Colden, the hero of *Jane Talbot*. "I cannot labor for bread," he frankly informs the enamoured Jane. "I cannot work to live. In that respect I have no parallel. The world does not contain my likeness. Hence it is, that if by marriage you should become wholly dependent on me it could never take place." This is the whole question in the novel; for Jane is dependent on her adopted mother, Mrs. Fielder, who disapproves of Colden because he is supposed to be a disciple of the iniquitous Godwin. Of course Mrs. Fielder believes the charge brought against him by Miss Jenny, a gossiping spinster, whose animosity is explained by the fact that she had once been in love with Jane's former husband. Both Colden and Mrs. Fielder besiege Jane with arguments and, as Jane's heart is apparently too warm to permit her judgment to be steadfast, she agrees, usually, with the one who has last written. Finally Colden is persuaded to withdraw, and starts on a voyage to China. He disappears on the way, but after the death of Mrs. Fielder returns, in time to prevent the brokenhearted Jane from marrying another man.

In this story, as in that of Clara Howard, nothing happens. The entire book is occupied with the weighing of reasons, the chopping up of motives, the analysis of emotions. Jane acknowledges her fondness for talking herself over—"It has always been so. I have always found an unaccountable pleasure in dissecting, as it were, my heart, uncovering one by one its many folds, and laying it before you, as a country is shown in a map." The portrait of Jane is evidently a careful attempt to describe an affectionate, impulsive, unconventional creature, easily bent by an appeal to her affection, yet springing back toward a reliance on her

own judgment. Unfortunately, not content with having made his Jane of a self-analytical turn like his own, Brown fell into the fatal error of trying to give her a light and playful humor. Brown himself was not a playful person, and his ideas of playfulness seem to have differed from those of the modern reader.

Jane Talbot, however, shares with Brown's other heroines the interest given by her apparent modernness in contrast with contemporary heroines, who were still blushing, and sighing, and swooning, by the rules which tales of sentiment had long and faithfully followed. Brown's women are not interesting as individuals—he never made them really live—but their unlifelikeness and the mechanical jerkings of their movements cannot conceal the author's intention to make them women of a newer type, to let them speak, and act, and love, for themselves, relying on their own judgment, and not on the conventions of society, or on the divinely inspired wisdom of a father or husband. There is an immeasurable distance between the helpless, drooping, persecuted Monima and the capable, self-reliant Constantia Dudley, yet the *Beggar Girl* was actually published four years later than **Ormond.**

It is customary to congratulate Brown on the possession of a sense of the horrible more real than that of his contemporaries. This statement, however, can perhaps be made too sweeping. Brown's mysteriously villainous heroes have an unquestionable effect of power, but his greatest success in the line of terror was in his yellow fever scenes; his murders are more gory than convincing, and the spontaneous combustion of the elder Wieland fails to thrill the modern reader. Yet to Brown and his contemporaries the center of what Miss Seward would have called "horrific greatness" in **Arthur Mervyn,** the scenes in which Brown aimed, as he said, "to wind up the reader's passions to the highest pitch,"[13] were the scenes between Mervyn and Welbeck. The yellow fever descriptions were introduced, as Brown says, to call forth benevolence to the aid of disease and poverty, and do not seem to have thrilled his contemporaries as much as did the unexplained mystery of what Mervyn really saw in Welbeck's cock-loft. Brown was a realist by nature and a terrorist by fashion. When the impulse given by *Caleb Williams* had spent itself he betook himself, in **Clara Howard** and **Jane Talbot,** to a series of analytical uneventful letters.

One effect of Brown's instinctive realism is to give his narratives an interest to-day which they can hardly have had at the time of their publication, for they give some idea of the life of America, and especially of Philadelphia, at that period. The injured maidens, the hapless orphans, and fair fugitives, of most of our early fiction might have lived in Timbuctoo as appropriately as in New York, but Brown's men and women, even if not very real themselves, are always put into a real and visible setting. One is struck by the activity and importance of Philadelphia, and particularly by the cosmopolitan character of the city, which appears in the varied nationalities of Brown's personages, the German Wieland, the English Howard, the Greek Martinette, the Italian Clemenza Lodi, the Irish Clithero, the Scottish Balfour; and the impression is deepened when one is reminded that "at that time (about 1793) there were at least ten thousand French in this city, fugitives from Marat and from St. Domingo."

Brown's most obvious debts to Godwin, apart from the political views which he adopted, and the autobiographic form of his tales, are the relation of patron and dependent, the character of the gifted self-taught country lad, and above all the hero of more than mortal force and fascination, the individuality strangely compounded of good and evil, but with a god-like ability to inspire reverence even in those cognizant of its crimes. The cult of individuality was, of course, in the air at the time, but it is clearly from Godwin that Brown derived its application to fiction. Brown has added the effect of breadth and mystery given by the secret political activities and vague schemes for the benefit of mankind in which his villains are engaged, with their hints of a regenerated human race, and of vague lands of beauty and promise beyond the pale of the civilized and the known. Godwin's noble man, criminal through circumstances, has become criminal, also, by a deliberate theory of good. If Brown has idealized the aims generally attributed to the *Illuminati,* while adopting the mystery of their far-reaching power, he has not hesitated to adopt their indifference to the employment of evil means if the end attained be good,—less intent on pointing a moral than was Godwin, he had a more vivid sense of the occasional picturesqueness of iniquity.

In the matter of style, also, Brown was early influenced by Godwin—not greatly to his advantage. There is a sad reminder of Godwin's pompously prosaic manner in the description of Wieland's conduct on seeing the flames, and hearing the shrieks which accompanied his father's mysterious death—"the incident was inexplicable, but he could not fail to perceive the propriety of hastening to the spot."

In his later years Brown's enthusiasm for Godwin seems to have cooled, perhaps like his Henry Colden he was inclined to regard it as an incident of his "dogmatic youth," but his debt to *Caleb Williams* remains. That Godwin was not unaware of the merits of his disciple appears from his own statement that he found in Brown's first novel the inspiration for one of his last.[14] "The impression which first led me to look with an eye of favor upon the subject here treated," he says in the preface to *Mandeville,* "was derived from a story-book called **Wieland,** written by a person certainly of distinguished genius, who, I believe, was born and died in the province of Pennsylvania, in the United States of North America, and who called himself C. B. Brown."

Strong and original as was Brown's work it did not establish a school in American fiction. The only one of his contemporaries who showed any disposition to follow in his footsteps was George Watterston, whose first story, *The Lawyer, or Man as he ought not to be* (1808), a dreary tale of a very small and mean-spirited villain, obviously owes its title to Bage. *Glencarn, or the Disappointments of Youth* (1810), a story on a much more elaborate plan, shows some traces of Brown's influence, particularly in the use of ventriloquism, but in general subject the tale is not unlike many contemporary romances, with a little additional salting of mystery and philosophy. It has as much in common with Bage as with Brown, and has little new machinery except the hero's experiences in a den of robbers.

Whatever fascination the schemes of the *Illuminati* may have had for Charles Brockden Brown, in the well regulated mind of the Maine authoress Mrs. Sally Sayward Barrell Keating Wood they inspired only abhorrence, and she boldly took up the pen in the cause of piety and morality. Her first novel, *Julia and the Illuminated Baron* (1800), proclaims on its title page:

> This volume to the reader's eye displays
> Th' infernal conduct of abandoned man;
> When French Philosophy infects his ways,
> And pours contempt on Heav'n's eternal plan;
> Reversing order, truth, and ev'ry good,
> And whelming worlds with ruin's awful flood.

In her preface Mrs. Wood disavows any intention to write a political novel, saying that she detests "female politicians." And it is not as political schemers that the *Illuminati* appear in her tale, but as promoters of atheism, corrupters of youthful character, and general agents of villainy.[15] Mrs. Wood had a fondness for placing the scene of her tales in Europe, a custom very unusual in our early fiction. The action of *Julia* passes chiefly in France and Spain,—there are two heirs of noble houses lost in infancy, a variety of villains, murders, abductions, and countless hair breadth escapes. Two very black miscreants, a baron who is the leading villain, and a count almost as infamous, are members of the *Illuminati;* the latter at the age of fifteen had been put into the charge of an *Illuminatus,* "one of the worst of men," who so trained his pupil that before the boy was twenty years old he had committed crimes at which even his tutor shuddered.

Mrs. Wood's next novel, *Dorval, or the Speculator,* has become practically inaccessible. Its title suggests that it may have been another anti-philosophic warning. The three books which followed, *Ferdinand and Elmira, a Russian Story* (1804), *Amelia, or the Influence of Virtue* (1802), and *Tales of the Night* (1827), are of no particular interest, either to the student or to the modern reader.

Brown's scorn of "puerile superstitions and exploded manners, Gothic castles and Chimeras" was not shared by all his countrymen. In the year after his death appeared a romance in the true Radcliffian spirit, entitled *The Asylum, or Alonzo and Melissa* by I. Mitchell, of Poughkeepsie, a man of much journalistic experience. In the same year appeared a condensed and revised version, in which the work is attributed to Daniel Jackson, Jr., then a young school teacher in Plattsburgh, where this edition was printed. The question of the true authorship of this interesting narrative has recently been clouded in controversy,[16] both Mitchell and Jackson having found partisans. The fact, however, that Mitchell's version was copyrighted December 2, 1810, and that the Jackson version did not appear until 1811, seems fairly conclusive evidence that the Jackson version, which was not copyrighted, was the later. The best known early edition is that of Brattleboro, 1824, which like all editions, except that of Poughkeepsie 1811, follows the shortened form, omitting the long episodical history of the Berger family and the "Preface comprising a Short Dissertation on Novel." In later editions this preface, which is interesting for its criticism of contemporary fiction, is reduced to a page and a half of good intentions, maintaining the original declaration of an aim to inculcate a firm reliance on Providence. The author adds that "the story contains no indecorous stimulants; nor is it filled with unmeaning and inexplicated incidents, sounding on the sense, but imperceptible to the understanding."

The opening scene[17] shows the young Alonzo, a Yale student, and the still younger Melissa, sister of his friend Edgar, sitting on a rock at New London, viewing the "drapery of nature," while "the whipperwill's sprightly song echoed along the adjacent groves." Little is said upon this occasion, but the impression is deep; and when Melissa at a later meeting says "I shall never forget the sweet pensive scenery of my native rock,"—"'Nor I, neither,' said Alonzo with a deep drawn sigh."

In these early pages much space is given to the description of nature. Although the author is found of the daylight hours, in which birds of gaudy plumage "symphoniously carolled the lay of nature," he is, perhaps, at his best in evening scenes. Alonzo's bliss as the accepted lover of Melissa is of short duration. His father suddenly loses his fortune; whereupon Melissa's heartless parent orders her to think no more of Alonzo, but to transfer her affections to his affluent rival, Beauman. When Melissa persists in her loyalty to Alonzo, she is immured in a species of Gothic castle, "situated about one hundred perches from the Sound," under the care of her spinster aunt, Miss Martha, a rough comedy character inherited from the eighteenth century novelists. Here Melissa is left alone during the night. Then Radcliffian disturbances begin. The first night she hears mysterious noises and whispers, and feels an icy hand laid on her arm. The next night the whispers become voices quarreling and menacing, and finally rise to shrieks of "Murder!" A flash of light shows in her room a tall figure "wrapped in a tattered white robe spotted with blood. The hair of its head was matted with clotted gore. A deep wound appeared to have pierced its breast, while fresh blood flowed down its garment. Its pale face was gashed and gory; its eyes fixed, glazed, and glaring; its lips open; its teeth set; and in its hand was a bloody dagger." When Melissa attempts to flee, her way is barred by a black figure, in human shape, with red flames issuing from its mouth. A large ball of fire rolls through the hall and explodes. The next day Alonzo appears, driven to seek shelter from a storm as he passes in search of Melissa. He crosses the moat on a tree-trunk which the lightning has overthrown. Later he departs to seek aid, leaving Melissa in the castle. When he returns she has vanished. After further search, interrupted by illness, Alonzo sees in a newspaper the announcement of Melissa's death at the house of her uncle in South Carolina.

The disconsolate lover decides to devote his blighted existence to his country, the Revolutionary War being then in progress, and enters the marine corps. On his first voyage he is captured and is thrown into prison, whence he escapes by a rope made of his clothing. For a time he is sheltered by a sailor of the conventional, bluff, hearty, shiver-my-timbers variety, whose aggressively nautical vocabulary is the outer accompaniment of a noble nautical heart, and by his aid is smuggled over to France. There, through Franklin's aid, he finds employment. His life of mournful solitude is interrupted when he finds in the street a miniature. The next day he sees an advertisement requesting that the picture be returned to an American hotel near the Louvre. "Determined to explicate the mystery" he goes thither; he finds Edgar, and they mourn together.

Soon after, however, Alonzo is moved by the patriotic exhortations of Franklin to return to his country and his father. At the first opportunity he visits Charleston, and there seeks the stone sacred to the memory of Miss Melissa D., "whose ethereal part became a seraph, October 26, 1776." Alonzo is overcome with grief, "he clasped the green turf which enclosed her grave, he watered it with his tears, he warmed it with his sighs." The next day a young officer tells him that his sister, who once saw in a dream the man destined to win her love, has recognized in Alonzo the man of the vision. He suggests that Alonzo might find the lady worthy of his regard, but Alonzo is firm in his loyalty to the departed Melissa. He is, however, prevailed upon to visit the lady, who appears arrayed in a sky blue silk

gown, adorned with spangled lace and jewels; a green silk veil conceals her face. She draws the veil aside, and the transported Alonzo beholds the real, the original Melissa. In their joy "their tears fell in one intermingled shower, their sighs wafted in one blended breeze." It is subsequently explained that the dead Melissa was the cousin of Alonzo's beloved, and that the Connecticut Melissa had allowed her death to be reported in order to foil her tyrannical father. The ghostly apparitions were robbers, who made the old house their headquarters, and wished to discourage interruptions. "And now, reader of sensibility," the author concludes, "indulge the pleasing sensations of thy bosom—for Alonzo and Melissa are MARRIED."

What is most striking about this tale, apart from its astonishing longevity, is the abundance and elaborateness of its descriptions of scenery. In these descriptions the Thomsonian and the Radcliffian nature vocabularies are strangely combined; while a zealous patriotism strives to give local color by the constant mention of American plants and birds, frequently garnishing the page with explanatory footnotes full of botanical and entomological information.

The whole effect is one of the greatest naïveté, and the tale, viewed as the only American product of Mrs. Radcliffe's influence, seems an inadequate representative of her school.[18] Yet it has gone through many editions, and is probably known to-day to many who have never read *The Mysteries of Udolpho*. When one considers the quantity of the Gothic output in England one wonders that the type should not have been more cultivated here. The reason, perhaps, is to be found in the somewhat aggressive patriotism of the period, which, from the first, caused American fiction to concern itself almost exclusively with American subjects, to which the mediaeval machinery of Mrs. Radcliffe was not appropriate. It was, of course, possible to erect a Gothic castle on the shores of Long Island Sound, but not even the ingenuity of a Jackson or a Mitchell could make it seem an appropriate addition to the landscape.

The question of the importance of the Gothic novel in early American fiction thus reduces itself to the importance of Charles Brockden Brown. Like all contemporary American novelists Brown sought, as was inevitable, his inspiration in British literature. It is probable that the popular German novels and dramas of horror were of some influence in strengthening the hold which the tale of heroic villainy and mysterious crime had obtained over his imagination. But *Caleb Williams* furnished the actual incentive to his criminal tales. He differed from his contemporaries, however, in that he modified the ideas thus borrowed, and added material of his own. To a certain extent he realized the general desire for novels reflecting native manners. His stories have as setting the real life of his time,—but it is only a setting. In **Edgar Huntly** he went further and devoted a large part of his book to wilderness life and Indian adventures, yet he still put forward a mysterious crime as the motive of his tale, and thus persistently identified himself with the short-lived school of terror.

Whether Brown might have done work of great and sustained excellence, if his life had fallen in a period when fiction offered more sober influences and better models, is a question which cannot be answered. As it is, he remains an interesting, but, as far as novel-writing is concerned, an isolated, figure in the American literature of his time. Although on the one hand he fulfilled in many respects the aims of contemporary American novelists, and although on the other he introduced to America the fashion then prevailing in British fiction,—yet he had no imitators in his *genre,* and he exerted no immediate influence on American fiction. In the general history of American literature he has, however, always held an important place. The influence on many greater writers which has been ascribed to him is in itself a claim to consideration. And he has always found readers to whom his emotional intensity and his command of certain effects of terror have compensated for his lack of construction and characterization.[19] In the history of early American fiction his peculiar importance comes from the fact that he is the earliest American novelist who has won reputation and influence outside his own country.

Notes

[1] The biography by his friend, William Dunlap, lacks the definiteness of modern biographical writing, but it makes accessible many fragments of Brown's works. (Philadelphia, 1815.) Dunlap's *History of the American Theatre* (New York, 1832) contains many references to Brown and his friends. See also W. H. Prescott's *Biographical and Critical Miscellanies* (1834).

[2] For Brown's interest in German literature see F. H. Wilkens, *Early Influence of German Literature in America,* p. 37-39.

[3] For Brown's magazine work see A. H. Smyth, *The Philadelphia Magazines and their Contributors.* Philadelphia, 1892.

[4] For discussion of *Caleb Williams* by Poe and Dickens see J. H. Ingram, *Edgar Allen Poe, His Life, Letters, and Opinions,* London, 1886, p. 153, and *E. A. Poe's Works,* Edinburgh, 1890, Vol. IV, p. 129.

[5] Dunlap, Vol. I, p. 258. Such a system was actually described by Henry Sherburne in his *Oriental Philanthropist* (Portsmouth, 1800), in which Oriental fairy tale machinery is used to bring about the establishment of an ideal state.

[6] The first edition of this work appeared in Edinburgh in 1797, the fourth in New York in 1798.

[7] Peacock's Scythrop Glowry, who wished to revive the work of the *Illuminati,* slept "with *Horrid Mysteries* under his pillow, and dreamed of venerable eleutherarchs, and ghastly confederates holding midnight conventions in subterranean caves." (T. L. Peacock, *Nightmare Abbey,* London, 1896, p. 143).

[8] Mr. Wilkens in his *Early Influence of German Literature in America* quotes from Dr. J. W. Francis a statement that Will lived in New York for a while before he published, in London, in 1799, his translation of von Knigge's *Practical Philosophy of Social Life.* If this is true Brown was probably personally acquainted with Will. See Wilkens, p. 26.

[9] *Horrid Mysteries,* p. 130.

[10] The *Illuminati* made a later appearance in fiction in George Sand's *Comtesse de Rudolstadt,* which gives an enthusiastically idealized account of such a society, and an elaborate description of their ceremonies. The tale is chiefly concerned, however, with a society of *Invisibles* forerunners of the historical *Illuminati,* not with the group of Weishaupt and Zwack, who appear only in a postscript. A secret society of "Brethren of the Common Weal," resembling the *Illuminati* of fiction in their combination of a noble aim with evil means, appeared in Peter Irving's *Giovanni Sbogarro* (1821), a tale said to be taken from the French with many alterations. The political secret society is lost sight of, however, in pursuing the popular German brigand-theme.

[11] The Philadelphia epidemic appears later in *Laura,* "By a Lady of Philadelphia." (New York, 1809.)

[12] For *Edgar Huntly* see Chapter III.

[13] Dunlap, Vol. II, p. 9.

[14] Margaret Fuller said that Brown and Godwin were congenial natures and that "whichever had come first might have lent an impulse to the other." Both were "Born Hegelians." *Papers on Literature and Art.* London, 1846, p. 146.

[15] In England, Sophia King's *Waldorf, or the Dangers of Philosophy* (1798) had already described, according to the *Monthly Review* (Vol. XXVI, p. 221), "a young man of talents and sensibility, deluded by a modern sceptic into a total renunciation of all restraint from religion and morality, and into a full indulgence of his favorite passions."

Tabitha Tenney, also, exclaimed: "May heaven prevent the further progress of Jacobinism, atheism, and illuminatism,—they all seem to be links of the same chain." *Female Quixotism,* p. 70.

[16] For details of this controversy, which seems to have been started in connection with a symposium on ghost stories, see *The New York Times Saturday Review of Books,* June 4, 1904, June 11, 1904, Sept. 3, 1904, Sept. 17, 1904, Jan. 21, 1905, Jan. 28, 1905, March 4, 1905. *The New York Evening Post,* Dec. 10, 1904 (with an account of Mitchell's life), Dec. 31, 1904, Feb. 3, 1905. *The Nation,* Dec. 8, 1904. *Booknotes* (Providence, R. I.), Jan. 14, 1905, Feb. 11, 1905, March 25, 1905.

[17] This brief account of the contents of the tale follows the 1824 version which has become the accepted form of the story.

[18] The reaction against the Gothic tale is represented however, by *The Hero or the Adventures of a Night,* suggested, perhaps, by *The Heroine. The Hero* is ingeniously made up by stringing together phrases and passages from the most popular Gothic novels.

[19] For varying estimates of Brown's work see *The Gentleman's Magazine,* April, 1811. *The North American Review,* 1819, Vol. IX, p. 63 and p. 26. *Blackwood's Edinburgh Magazine,* Vol. VI February, 1820. *The Retrospective Review,* 1824, Vol. IX, p. 305. S. Margaret Fuller, *Papers on Literature and Art,* London, 1846. William H. Prescott, *Biographical and Critical Miscellanies,* Philadelphia, 1882. Rufus Wilmot Griswold, *Prose Writers of America,* London, 1847. T. W. Higginson in *American Prose* (edited by G. R. Carpenter), 1898. *The Fortnightly Review,* London, 1878, New Ser., Vol. XXIV, p. 397. T. L. Peacock, *Gryll Grange,* London, 1896, p. 277.

David Lee Clark (essay date 1922)

SOURCE: "Brockden Brown and the Rights of Women," in *University of Texas Bulletin,* No. 2212, March 22, 1922, pp. 5-44.

[*In the following excerpt, Clark studies Brown's ideas regarding the rights of women, particularly in* Alcuin, *and maintains that the impact of the writings of Mary Wollstonecraft and William Godwin on Brown has been too strenuously emphasized by many critics.*]

One cannot correctly appraise the literature dealing with the social and political emancipation of women in the last third of the eighteenth century without some knowledge of the evolution of the thought of which that literature is a record. Particularly is this so in evaluating the work of Mary Wollstonecraft, William Godwin, and Brockden Brown. It is too generally assumed that the first two were the originators of the social theories

that are now so invariably associated with their names; and that their work in turn inspired Brockden Brown in America.

Although a detailed study of the struggle for the social and political freedom of women is beyond the scope of the present work, certain general tendencies in the literature of revolt in England, France, and America, will be briefly traced.

As a matter of fact neither Mary Wollstonecraft, nor William Godwin, nor yet Brockden Brown was an original thinker, for there is nothing really new in any of them. Mary Wollstonecraft in her *Rights of Women* (1792), and Godwin in his *Political Justice* (1793) and in his novels, did, however, put the arguments for the social emancipation of men and women in imperishable form, and thus established their chief claim to a place in the literature of the movement. Brockden Brown was familiar with the works of these writers, but he was also familiar with what had been done by others earlier than the time of Godwin. It can be shown that Brown was full of the revolutionary spirit before the appearance of the *Rights of Women* and *Political Justice,* and that the influence of these two works upon Brown has been overemphasized.

Theories of government and social reform are so much a part of Brown's life and writings that some account of them in relation to his predecessors seems necessary. Brown's political theories were shaped by Locke and his French and American disciples. Hobbes had asserted the absolute authority of the ruler, but Locke pointed out how the compact into which men had voluntarily entered by giving up some of their natural rights for certain advantages, was unalterably binding upon all subsequent generations, and thus were established those rights of man that no law of man or king could transgress. This theory, so generally accepted during the first half of the eighteenth century, in the hands of the radical became the basis of an argument that led straight to the American Revolution and, subsequently, to the greater revolution in France. But in the hands of the conservative it was a tool for despotism, for it gave a kind of sanction to any existing order. Permanence, not progress, became the ideal of government. According to Locke government existed solely for the good of the people. He even spoke of an ideal state, a golden age in the past, and of government as being made necessary to check the ambition and luxury that have subsequently crept in. No man, he said, should be governed except by his own consent, and no man should be punished by fallible men. Yet it is to be carefully noted that these doctrines of the natural rights of man had no marked effect upon the English people as a whole, for in England the conservative Whigs interpreted Locke as giving sanction to the position that "whatever is, is right," and it is upon this ground that Burke defended the English Constitution and condemned the French Revolution. Price, Priestley, Paine, Jefferson, Brockden Brown, and others, however, put a construction upon Locke's theory of state that embraced all the current radicalism in France, England, and America. William Godwin, indeed, was an ultraradical and would have abolished all government.

While Locke's plan of government did not specifically assign to woman a place in the body politic, by implication, at least, she was acknowledged to be an important factor in the social fabric. But women were so hopelessly low in the social scale that only the bravest men and women before 1790 ventured to suggest that women, like men, have political rights. They had first, indeed, to be emancipated socially and intellectually before any thought could be given to political and economic freedom. Woman had for centuries been considered a shallow, helpless creature, to be petted, caressed, or corrected by her superior lord, or else she was a moral being whose virtue had to be constantly guarded. The old Hebrew canon law was generally in force and was pointed to as authority for the enslavement of women. The sacred scriptures were invoked to prove that woman was created solely for the comfort of man, and as such had no liberty of active or independent judgment. Her highest virtue was obedience to the will of her lord, and her chief occupation was child-bearing. Indeed, her whole life was regulated by these considerations. She had no part in the moral, intellectual, or economic direction of her home, and no authority over her children. But, as there was no alternative course to marriage, we read much in the literature of the times of woman's use of social tricks and snares to inveigle men into marriage, and to keep them hoodwinked afterwards. This notion of woman as a mere charmer grew to such proportions that it came to the notice of the English Parliament, and as late as 1770 a law was passed that prescribed that "all women, of whatever age, rank, profession, or degree, whether virgins, maids, or widows, that shall, from and after such act, impose upon, induce, or betray into matrimony, any of his Majesty's male subjects by scents, paints, cosmetic washes, artificial teeth, false hair, Spanish wool, iron stays, hoops, high-heeled shoes, etc., shall incur the penalty of the law now enforced against witchcraft and like demeanors, and that the marriage upon conviction shall stand null and void."[1]

Oliver Cromwell in the famous civil marriage code of 1653 sought to lighten the burden for women by placing all marriages and divorces in the hands of the civil courts, in which the man and the woman were on an equality. But this law was ineffectual, for public opinion was against it. Milton's attitude toward matrimony was more nearly representative of the Puritan point of view. He pleaded vigorously for liberal divorce laws, but solely for the sake of the man. Imbued as he was with the sentiments of the scriptures Milton's position was not at all singular. There were many arguments in the literature of his time for the enslavement of women. It is not necessary in this connection to consider the social freedom of certain types of women in the *beau monde*. . . .

During the last decade of the eighteenth century, America became an asylum for the radicals and the political regugees of France and England, and as a rule these men joined in vigorously in the political disputes of the day. It is no wonder, then, that America was for a time a forum for the discussion of the rights of men and women. Nor is it surprising that Brockden Brown, then growing into manhood, was stirred by the arguments heard on every hand. Without doubt, it was during these formative years that Brown's zeal for the freedom of mankind was first awakened. And yet this is not the whole story, for there had been certain influences at work in America with which Brown must have been acquainted. Some account of these influences will now be taken.

The social condition of women in America in the eighteenth century was not markedly different from that in the mother country. There was perhaps less of social frivolity and immorality in sparsely settled America than in the crowded districts of the old world. But colonial customs and social distinctions paralleled in a remarkable way those in England. In regard to marriage the laws were strikingly similar. In America as in England the Quakers were most liberal in their views of matrimony; and owing to this liberality many false charges were brought against them. William Penn had held that marriage was a divine ordinance, and that God alone could rightly join men and women; consequently, the priest and ecclesiastical courts were ruled out. The Quakers, generally, believed that marriage was a matter to be left to the conscience of the individual man and woman. Thus it was said that they did not celebrate marriage decently.

Divorces during the eighteenth century in America on any ground were very difficult to obtain. In almost every case the laws favored the man. Connecticut, however, did insist upon the equality of men and women in matters of divorce. In New York there was not a single case of divorce during the Colonial period, and only by a special act of the legislature could a marriage be annulled. In New Jersey and Pennsylvania there is no evidence that divorces, partial or absolute, were common. In the Southern States there is not a case of absolute divorce on record before 1775.[28]

Politically, however, the women of America fared better than their sisters in England and France. The early Puritans were not enthusiasts for political freedom, but there was a tendency toward democratic principles in their management of communities, particularly in town-meetings. Yet their idea of government was theocratic rather than democratic. It was among the Quakers of Pennsylvania and New Jersey, however, that the most liberal ideas of government were to be found. As a religious sect the Quakers stood alone in maintaining the essential equality of men and women, and in all important matters women were allowed the same rights as men. The Friends believed that the form of government did not matter so much as the character of the men in whose hands the government is lodged. Good men will make good laws.

Before the American Revolution there was, however, practically no philosophical speculation on theories of government, but a steady progress toward democratization is noticeable.[29] The lofty terms of the Declaration of Independence, nevertheless, opened men's minds, as they had never before been opened, to the essential principles of government. Locke and his English and French disciples became the basis for discussions. Natural rights, laws of nature, social contract, consent of the governed, the general welfare, were terms that became familiar to all Americans. It is not surprising, then, that some of them were led into fields of speculation and dreamed of ideal commonwealths. The mildest of these held that government is a necessary evil, and that consequently the least government is the best government. This idea of the minimum of government became in time the fundamental doctrine of one of the great political parties. It was only one step from this essential fear of all government to the question of no government, or rather to the contemplation of a perfect state of society in which positive institutions are unnecessary.

In the formation of the American Constitution, however, as with the first French Constitution, the most radical became conservative to a marked degree, and the much-heralded *natural rights* and *natural equality* of the Declaration were partially, and in some instances entirely, brushed aside. The question of suffrage was an all-important one, and in the minds of the most liberal, the limitations put upon the exercise of the franchise were unjust and but one step removed from conditions in England. It was a turning back toward aristocracy. Thomas Jefferson was an advocate of universal male suffrage, but he acknowledged that those who insisted upon a property qualification were honest men, and had some solid basis of argument. Franklin held that it was an impropriety to allow the vote to those without landed property. The several state constitutions had various qualifications, and between federal and state limitations the actual voting population was but a small fraction of the male inhabitants. When all women, all slaves, all immigrants under a certain limit of residence, and all men who lacked the property qualification, were denied the franchise, it was plain to many Americans that democracy in practice was far from the ideal government that the Declaration proclaimed.

It is not strange, then, to find many who protested against this discrepancy. Although the majority of the Founding Fathers saw no inconsistency,[30] religious, property, or racial limitations were held by some, at least, to be inconsistent with the natural rights of man. There had been, nevertheless, a significant change in attitude among the leaders since 1776. This reaction is best expressed in the Constitution of 1787, and when it was submitted for ratification the great men of the time split into two camps: those that favored the limited democracy of that instrument, and those that called for a government of the people, by the people, and for the people. *The Federalist,* a series of essays by Hamilton, Madison, and Jay, took the side of the proposed constitution. Annual election, weak central government, and a more liberal franchise were advocated by the more democratic group, led by Jefferson. John Adams asserted that the people are unworthy of trust, and questioned the feasibility of any democratic government.

When the great shock of the French Revolution reached America, with a consequent swing to the Jeffersonian theories, there followed a decade of debate between Federalist and Republicans which drew to it almost every American of talent. The pamphlet war which resulted was the fiercest known in American history. John Adams was the leader of the reactionary Federalists, Jefferson of the democratic group, and around these two men the nation gathered. Jefferson was the more popular leader, with his trust in the ultimate wisdom of the mass of plain people. And his cause triumphed until the Reign of Terror in France alarmed the more conservative of his followers. This alarm over its alleged alliance with the radicals of France gave rise to a most scathing attack on the Republican party. That Jefferson's philosophy of government was largely derived from France cannot be denied, but he was far from the radical that his opponents painted him. He did highly commend the work of Condorcet, particularly *The Progress of the Human Mind,* and he may have derived some of his own ideas from this work.

In the numerous political discussions that make up so much of American history in the last quarter of the eighteenth century, a few pages at least were devoted to the rights of women. Margaret Brent of Maryland asserted her right to a seat in the legislature; Richard Henry Lee was an advocate of woman suffrage; and Abigail Adams wrote to her husband in their behalf.[31] The Quakers had always maintained, as has been already observed, the essential equality of women with men. But the general attitude toward women is best expressed in a letter by John Adams to James Sullivan, May 26, 1776, in which he said: "But why exclude women? You will say, because their delicacy renders them unfit for practice and experience in the great businesses of life, and the hardy enterprises of war, as well as the arduous cares of state. Besides, their attention is so much engaged with the necessary nurture of their children, that nature has made them fittest for domestic cares."[32]

Certain state constitutions, however, admitted women to a larger share in the life of the state than they could hope for under the federal government. This was notably the case in New Jersey, where from 1790 to 1807, women were allowed to vote, a privilege due largely it seems, to the liberality of the Quakers of that state. It should be noted, however, that they rarely exercised this right. But an occasion once arose in which the woman vote became the deciding factor, and gave rise to a most lively discussion in the press. John Condit of Newark, a Republican, and William Crane of Elizabethtown, a Federalist, were in a close race for the legislature, and in an endeavor to defeat his opponent, Crane secured many women from Elizabethtown to vote for him, but he was defeated. The newspaper war which followed, for and against woman suffrage, soon passed beyond the bounds of the state, and for some time centered attention on the rights of women.[33] This event, the exciting national election of 1796, and the criticism of the Jay Treaty, undoubtedly furnished ample incentive for Brockden Brown's *Alcuin* or *The Rights of Women*.

Such is a brief account of some of the more important phases of the emancipation of woman. We have seen that the promise which the Reformation held out was very slow in working its way into the minds of the later Puritans, but nevertheless, there were gains, however slight they may have been. It has been pointed out how in the latter part of the seventeenth century, both in France and in England, a great impetus was given to the movement by writers like Mary Astell, Defoe, Fénelon, Poulain de la Barre, and others; and how that movement increased until almost every writer of any importance was drawn to one side or the other of the question. We have also seen how, as the forces which made for the great revolutions in France and America became dominant, the rights of women were merged with the greater rights of mankind. It has likewise been observed that, although the movement had an early beginning in England, it was in France that it reached its earliest maturity. It was to France that young English and American democrats looked for inspiration. It was from France that the first principles of the works of Mary Wollstonecraft and William Godwin came. We have seen that in both France and England emphasis was first placed upon the social and intellectual emancipation of women, but that in the closing decades of the eighteenth century arguments centered around their economic and political freedom. It is of this latter side of the movement that Brockden Brown became an ardent proponent.

To say that Brown was familiar with the great body of this literature of dissent would be, of course, an unwarranted assumption; but that he was acquainted with much of it is beyond dispute. Concerning Brown's formative years, it is said "that he was a frail, studious child, reputed a prodigy, and encouraged by his parents in that frantic feeding upon books which was expected, in those days, of every American boy of parts. By the time he was sixteen he had made himself a tolerable classical scholar—and hurt his health by overwork. As he grew older he read with a hectic, desultory sweep in every direction open to him. With his temper and education, he developed into a hot young philosopher in those days of revolution. He brooded over the maps of remote regions, glowed with eager schemes for perfecting mankind."[34] This zeal for knowledge and this enthusiasm for the betterment of mankind were not at all singular in a boy reared amidst the bustle and shifting scenes of the nation's intellectual and political capital. Philadelphia thronged with French political refugees. And during these stirring days Brown is reputed to have learned the French language that he might gain a first-hand knowledge of French literature. Such names as Fénelon, La Bruyère, La Rochefoucauld, Voltaire, Rousseau, are scattered through the pages of his early essays and addresses. It must be remembered, too, that Brown had access to the best libraries in the nation, and that he frequented the home of that liberal-minded American, Benjamin Franklin. When all these facts are considered, one is not surprised that Brown showed himself familiar with all the current arguments for the social, political, and economic rights of man and woman. It appears now that he had decided opinions on such matters before the appearance of the works of Mary Wollstonecraft and William Godwin, and that those opinions were stimulated by his French reading. An analysis of *Alcuin* will show that Brown's sources were not specific, but general.

Alcuin is important as the first published volume of the first professional author in America, and it is interesting to the bibliographer as one of the rarest American books.[35] And yet the curious student will search in vain for any accurate discussion of it. According to Dunlap it was written in the "fall and winter of the year 1797,"[36] and the same year has often been referred to as the year of publication. There is reason to believe, however, that *Alcuin* was composed during the exciting fall of 1796. It was issued in book form from the press of T. & J. Swords, No. 99 Pearl Street, New York, in March, 1798, and reprinted in the *Weekly Magazine* of Philadelphia (March 17-April 7, 1798) as *The Rights of Women*. Dunlap's statement that it was written in the fall and winter of 1797 has misled every subsequent critic of Brown's work. No one, it seems, has ever suspected the existence of a sequel to *Alcuin*, and yet, by a curious circumstance, it is the sequel or second dialogue and not the original upon which discussion of the book has been based.[37] The matter is easy to explain. The original *Alcuin* as published by Swords, March, 1798, carried an "Advertisement" signed by E. H. Smith, in which he states that "the following dialogue was put into my hands, the last spring, by a friend who resides at a distance, with liberty to make it public. I have since been informed that he has continued the discussion of the subject in another dialogue." Now the Smith *Alcuin* is, as I have stated, exceedingly rare, and it appears that no critic has ever compared it with the "copious extracts" in Dunlap's *Life of Brown.* It has simply been assumed that Dunlap quoted from the original *Alcuin.* A comparison, however, shows that only three and one-half pages in Dunlap were taken from the Smith *Alcuin*— to serve, it seems, as an introduction to the second dialogue published in Dunlap's *Life* in 1815. The Smith *Alcuin* is a small volume of seventy-seven pages or approximately eleven thousand words, and is divided into two parts to correspond to Alcuin's two visits to the home of Mrs. Carter, who conducts a kind of Philadelphia salon. The dialogue as printed in the *Weekly Magazine* differs in many points from the Smith *Alcuin.* It is somewhat shorter; the title is changed to ***The Rights of Women;*** the hero is Edwin instead of Alcuin; significant references to certain famous characters and events are omitted; the slur on the professions of soldier and barber is deleted; and the last thirteen lines of *Alcuin* are lacking in the magazine edition. Why Brown made these changes is not readily seen, and why he failed to have Smith make the same alterations in the volume published by Swords, both of which appeared in print during the same month, is even more mysterious. It seems likely that Swords printed the book in the spring of 1797 or soon thereafter, but did not publish it until March, 1798. This assumption would explain the differences in the two versions.

The concluding paragraph of the Smith *Alcuin* clearly points to a sequel. "Here the conversation was interrupted by one of the company, who, after listening to us for some time, thought proper at last to approach, and contribute his mite to our mutual edification. I soon seized an opportunity of withdrawing, but not without requesting and obtaining permission to repeat by visit." The Smith "Advertisement" definitely states that the discussion was continued in another dialogue. That Dunlap's "copious extracts" are the continuation of the subject foreshadowed in *Alcuin* and clearly expressed in the "Advertisement," is beyond cavil. Then, too, the permission to repeat his visit which Alcuin sought is realized in the continuation—which begins: "A week elapsed and I repeated by visit to Mrs. Carter." The continuation, referred to hereafter as the second dialogue, was entitled *Alcuin* in the Philadelphia edition (1815) of Dunlap's *Life of Brown,* and the *Paradise of Women*[38] in the London edition of that work (1822).

It is safe to conclude, then, that it was to the second dialogue that Dunlap referred as being written in the

fall and winter of 1797. Smith and Dunlap both agree that the second dialogue was written after March, 1797. The time of the first is less certain, but more significant, as it was Brown's first publication. Reasoning from internal evidence alone, however, the date can be quite definitely established as the fall of 1796. On page eleven of *Alcuin* the priggish schoolmaster speaks of the pleasure he derives during his leisure evenings from watching a declining moon and the varying firmament with the optics of "Dr. Young." The Dr. Young here referred to was Thomas Young (1773-1829), a noted British physicist, whose paper on the structure of the eye was read before the Royal Society when he was only twenty years old, and established for him the name of founder of physiological optics. Young shortly thereafter went to Germany, and in July, 1796 received the degree of doctor of physic from the University of Göttingen. On his return to England, he was hailed as a great genius. It is not likely that Brown would refer to him as Dr. Young before July, 1796. Significant, too, is Alcuin's remark, on page fourteen, that "the theme of the discourse was political. The edicts of Carnot, and the commentary of that profound jurist, Peter Porcupine, had furnished ample materials of discussion." Lazare Nichols Marguerite Carnot (1753-1823) was a member of the French Convention, an important member of the Committee of Public Safety, and the guiding genius of the Executive Directory. He became a member of the Directory in 1795, and because of his opposition to the extreme measures of his colleague Barras, he was suspected of royalist sympathy and was sentenced to deportation in 1797. He spoke strongly against the violations of the Bill of Rights, and objected to the dictatorial and autocratic action of the Directory. But Brown's reference to the edicts of Carnot undoubtedly suggests the uncompromising measures which Carnot felt were necessary during the troublous fall of 1796. In order to put down royalist and anarchistic plots, the Directory assumed absolute power over the life and property of the citizen. It is quite certain, however, that Brown had in mind Carnot's instruction to Citizen Adet, the French minister to the United States, to address a note to the American Secretary of State reproaching the Washington Administration for the position of the President in his *Farewell Address* and for the Administration's attitude toward the Jay Treaty. Citizen Adet declared that America had violated her sacred treaty with the French Republic, and that as a solemn protest against that dereliction his government had instructed him to suspend his duties as minister. War with France or rather with the Directory seemed imminent.[39]

Peter Porcupine, mentioned in the same sentence with Carnot and referred to as a profound jurist, was William Cobbett (1762-1835). He was an English soldier, essayist, politician, editor, and farmer who came to the United States in 1792 to seek a berth with the Washington Administration. But, failing in this, he settled down in Philadelphia as a tutor in English to French political refugees. In 1794 Joseph Priestley also came to America and plunged immediately into the fight for republicanism. This action of Priestley drew Cobbett to the defense of the Federalists, and his vicious attack upon the friends of democracy stirred up the bitterest pamphlet war known in American history. He issued at Philadelphia a monthly pamphlet under the title or *The Censor* (January, 1796-to March, 1797) which he signed as Peter Porcupine. In this paper he was a vigorous and unreasonable advocate of everything British and a violent critic of everything republican. Cobbett even went so far as to place in the windows of his bookstore in Philadelphia pictures of nobles, princes, and kings—including the infamous George the Third. We first learn of him as Peter Porcupine in January, 1796, but if one may judge from newspaper allusions, he was not well known under this pseudonym until August of the same year. In September, 1796, he wrote, "What must I feel upon seeing the newspapers filled from top to bottom—with *A Blue Shop for Peter Porcupine, A Pill for Peter Porcupine, Peter Porcupine Detected,*"[40] etc. Cobbett reached the zenith of his ravings against American and French republicanism during the fall elections of 1796.

While these allusions to contemporary characters and events do not definitely fix the date of the Smith *Alcuin,* they at least point to an earlier one than has usually been assigned.

It is unfortunate that Brown is known only by the second dialogue, which is on the very face of it only an Utopian dream, not to be taken as representing Brown's real opinions. It is significant, too, that the second dialogue is one of the few pieces that remained unpublished during the lifetime of the author. It is a work of pure speculation, and as such may represent Brown's fanciful interpretation of society in Godwin's *Political Justice.* But it will be seen that the commonwealth here described has more in common with the *Utopia* of Sir Thomas More than with the speculations of William Godwin. In fact the influence of Godwin on the thought of the two dialogues diminishes in proportion as one studies them in relation to the temper of the age.

The discussions in the first dialogue, on the other hand, are thoroughly sincere and practical, and represent the most respectable democratic doctrine of the day. Indeed, it is Brown's contribution to the great debate between the Federalists and Republicans during the stormy days of 1796, and registers his protest against the conservative American Constitution. Brown, with others, had been clearly disappointed with the failure of the framers of the Constitution to embody in that document the principles of the Declaration of Independence. The Smith *Alcuin* is, furthermore, the first ex-

tended serious argument for the rights of women that had yet appeared in America, and as such it merits the praise that is the pioneer's. It is the author's plea for the natural right of women to share in the political and economic life of the nation. In this general claim for women Brown was not at all singular, as has already been pointed out, for he only gave voice to a time-honored Quaker conviction of the essential equality of women with men. Furthermore, we have seen that this conception of women's rights and capabilities was of slow growth from Mary Astell to Brockden Brown, and that it was neither fathered nor fostered exclusively by only one. So much for the general character of the work.

As *Alcuin* is almost inaccessible, a detailed account of it is advisable. In each dialogue the argument is conveyed in a conversation between the priggish schoolmaster Alcuin and the widowed Mrs. Carter, a Philadelphia blue-stocking.[41] She is familiar with the current arguments for the rights of women, and generally takes a more radical stand than Alcuin. Her argument goes beyond that of Mary Wollstonecraft, whose plea is fundamentally for the emancipation of women from low social standards through an education similar to that for men; Mrs. Carter's contention is for political and economic equality with men. Indeed, her ideas on this and other subjects are so singular that her home becomes a rendezvous for all liberal and respectable talent, so that perhaps the strongest inducement to visit her home was not the attraction of the woman, but that of the brilliant sociey that gathered there. Following the description of Mrs. Carter and her liberal coterie is a bit of philosophy on the comparative merits of reading and conversation as means of instruction. Like Swift, Alcuin sings the praises of conversation. Books are too dull and insipid, and he hates a lecturer, because his audience cannot canvass each step in the argument. Formal debate is also condemned. But conversation is free and unfettered and blends, more happily than any other method of instruction, utility and pleasure. Alcuin spends the day in repeating the alphabet or engraving on infantile minds that twice three make six, and the evening, until his acquaintance with Mrs. Carter, in amplifying the seductive suppositions, "if I were a king" or "if I were a lover." The schoolmaster longs for the liberalising influence that only the conversation of the ingenious can give, and after a careful self-analysis he decides to become a frequent visitor at the home of Mrs. Carter. We are now, after fourteen dreary pages of introduction, permitted to hear the dialogue between Mrs. Carter and Alcuin. The very dullness and narrow outlook of this prologue, the least attractive part of the book, stand in striking contrast to the liberal views that follow.

Alcuin, when the embarrassment of the introduction to the circle is over, respectfully withdraws to a corner of the room and there finds opportunity to engage the lady in conversation. He somewhat awkwardly begins: "Pray, madam, are you a federalist?" She evades the question, and replies indirectly that she has often been called upon to listen to political discussions, but never before was she asked her own opinion. Mrs. Carter declares that women, shallow and inexperienced as they all are, have nothing to do with politics; that their time is consumed in learnng the price of ribbon or tea or in plying the needle. No wonder, then, she asserts with Defoe, Swift,[42] and others, that women are narrow, and for the sake of variety they sometimes wander into the pleasant fields of scandal. Alcuin admits the force of this argument, but submits that the work of woman is not less useful and honorable than that of many proressions assigned to men, notably those of barber and soldier. He dwells on the noble character of practical, simple, everyday work.[43] He further declares that women are the equals of men in all essential respects and morally their superiors; that the distinctions based upon sex differences are of no consequence; and with the whole body of French and English advocates of the rights of women, Alcuin maintains that whatever important distinctions there are between men and women are the direct results of differences in opportunities. Women are superficial and ignorant because they are generally cooks and seamstresses.

But unlike those who believe in the infinite perfectibility of man, Alcuin takes a pessimistic view. He declares that it is doubtful whether the carecr of the species will end in knowledge, and with Locke he holds that man is born in ignorance, that habit has given permanence to error. He rejects the notion of innate ideas. Through ignorance or prejudice certain employments have been exclusively assigned to men, and the constitutional aversion of human nature to any change has confirmed this error. Mrs. Carter adds that of all forms of injustice that is most vicious which makes the circumstance of sex a reason for excluding half of mankind from the more useful and honorable professions. Alcuin falls back for a moment upon the respectable Whig doctrine of "Whatever is, is right," and replies that the real evil lies in the fact that so much human capacity is perverted.[44] Then Alcuin follows the argument of Plato, More, and Godwin in desiring to have all tasks shared in common without distinction of sex, but, unlike Godwin, Alcuin is not sure that such an arrangement would be practicable. He laments that, on account of a perverted civilization, large portions of mankind are doomed to toil, but he laments thus not because they are men or women, but because they are human bengs. This is in line with the humanitarian movement of the latter part of the eighteenth century and is not exclusively Godwinian. But Mrs. Carter insists that under any arrangement women would bear the greater burden because of the duties of motherhood. Alcuin replies that luxury and its attendant evils have greatly increased that burden. Mrs. Carter be-

lieves that woman's field of usefulness is too much limited by a consideration of her function as mother, particularly as regards the liberal professions.[45] But Alcuin insists that women are not really excluded from the higher professions, that in Europe at least women are found in such professions. He could never wish woman to stoop to the practice of law, and as for the ministry some sects (the Quakers and Methodists, of course) do not debar women from the pulpit. The Christian religion has done much to break down distinctions of rank, wealth, and sex. Mrs. Carter does not try to refute Alcuin's argument, but she points out that all professions which require most vigor of mind, the greatest contact with enlightened society and books, are filled by men only. Alcuin replies by attacking all the liberal professions, charging them with sordid motives; usefulness as such is but a secondary consideration. Benevolence, universal benevolence, should be the keynote of all the liberal callings—college degrees and examinations matter but little.

At this point Mrs. Carter broaches the question of woman's education. She takes the same line of argument as Defoe, Swift, and others that women have been educated for the profession of household slaves, that women of quality are instructed in the art of the coquette. Men believe that women should be thus educated; consequently, they are excluded from schools and colleges. Here again Alcuin takes a wholly unexpected turn in his argument by questioning the advisability of a college education, even for men, for it seems unfavorable to moral and intellectual improvement.[46] It would be indelicate to conduct mixed classes in anatomy or other such subjects. This idea of false modesty gives Mrs. Carter an opportunity to inveigh against those who urge the separation of the sexes on the score of delicacy. With Mary Wollstonecraft and Condorcet she insists that nothing has been so injurious as the separation of the sexes. They are associated in childhood, but soon they are made to take different paths, learn different languages, different maxims, different pursuits; their relations become fettered and embarrassed. With the one all is reserve and artifice, with the other adulation and affected humility: the man must affect ardor, the woman indifference—her tongue belies the sentiments of her heart and the dictates of her mind. Her early life is a preparation for marriage; her married life is a state of slavery. She loses all title to private property, and the right of private opinion; she knows nothing but the will of her husband, and she may prevail only by tears and blandishments.

Alcuin thinks this a great exaggeration, but Mrs. Carter asserts that the picture is exact, that her own life has suffered from a mistaken education. Man is physically stronger and thus in the primitive condition of society, woman was enslaved; but the tendency toward rational improvement has been to equalize conditions and to level all distinctions not based upon truth and reason. Women have benefited by this progress of reason, but they are not wholly exempt from servitude. Alcuin admits that the lot of woman is hard, but he points out that it is the preferable one, freest from the thorns of life—and then he trails off into the song of the needle, and the hand that conjures a piano. Mrs. Carter replies that this is but a panegyric on indolence and luxury, in which neither distinguished virtue nor true happiness is found. Alcuin agrees that ease and luxury are pernicious; that the rich and the poor alike are denied real happiness and peace,[47] but still their lot is better than brutal toil and ignorance. He concludes his argument by a statement that there is something wrong with society as it is now constituted, and appeals to Mrs. Carter to waive the problem of women and urge the much greater claims of enslaved human beings.

Again Alcuin inquires of Mrs. Carter whether she is a federalist; again she protests that women have nothing to do with politics, that the American government takes no heed of them, that the Constitution-makers, without the slightest consciousness of inconsistency or injustice, excluded them from all political rights, and made no distinction between women and irrational animals. In the sense that she prefers union to dissension she is a federalist; but if the term means the approval of the Constitution as a document embodying the principles of right and justice, she is not a federalist.

It is when Mrs. Carter inveighs against the Constitution of the United States as harsh and unjust that she waxes most eloquent. She scoffs at the maxims of the Constitution that proclaim that all power is derived from the people, that liberty is every one's birthright and is the immediate gift of God to all mankind, that those who are subject to the laws should enjoy a share in their enactment. These maxims are specious, and our glorious Constitution in practice is a system of tyranny. One is denied a voice in the election of his governor because he is not twenty-one; another because he has not been a resident for two years; a third because he can not show a tax receipt; a fourth because his skin is black; a fifth merely because she is a woman. So what have we to boast in the name of divinest liberty when only a small fraction of our people have a voice in our government?

Here Alcuin takes refuge in the Quaker doctrine that the spirit is of vastly more importance than the form of government; that the value of any government is measured by the character of the men who administer its laws. But this subtle distinction between power and the exercise of power does not find favor with Mrs. Carter; she wishes a voice in the choice of even the wise man. She is willing to admit that government by the wisest would be the best government, but how are the sages to be distinguished from the mediocre, and how is one to know that the wise man cannot be corrupted? That government is best, all things considered, that consults the feelings and judgments of the governed. Alcuin insists, however, that some qualifications should be required of the voter. Mrs. Carter sidetracks by saying that she is not arguing the claims of mankind in general, but the rights of women in particular; for mere sex is so purely a physical matter that to make it a basis for excluding one-half of mankind from the enjoyment of their natural rights is sheer folly.

Alcuin is most absurd in the eyes of Mrs. Carter when he suggests that women justly relinquish all claims to liberty and property when they marry; that they are contented with their present position; that they would not exercise the rights of citizens if the privilege were extended to them—this was a common argument in New Jersey where women had the privilege of voting, but very seldom took part in the elections. Alcuin admits that he is prejudiced, that he could never bring himself to sympathize with the claims of women to rights in business and politics; but he closes the argument by prudently acknowledging that since women are as thoughtful as men, and are more beautiful, they are therefore the superior sex.

Thus ends the first dialogue or the Smith *Alcuin.* Just why Dunlap elected to publish the more Utopian second is a matter that passes understanding. It is only possible that he wished thereby to re-create the speculative phase through which Brown was then (1797) passing. That Dunlap was acquainted with the first dialogue is evident from the fact he recorded in his *Diary* (April 28, 1798): "Read today Smith's publication of Brown's '*Alcuin,*' 1 & 2 parts." Then on the following day he notes that he read parts three and four. It may be suggested that Dunlap felt that the first dialogue had received sufficient publication in the Smith volume and the *Weekly Magazine.* Certainly Dunlap thought highly of the first one, for an entry in his *Diary* (August 8, 1797) states that "there is much truth, philosophical accuracy and handsome writing in the essay." Perhaps, if Dunlap had foreseen the misunderstanding growing out of his publication of the second dialogue, he would have spared his friend's reputation.

Notes

[1] *Woman: Women of England,* Vol. IX, p. 318. Cf. Pope's *Epistle to a Lady* (1735) in which woman's ruling passion is said to be "the love of pleasure and the love of sway."...

[28] *A History of Matrimonial Institutions Chiefly in England and the United States,* by George Elliott Howard, Chicago, 1904.

[29] *A History of American Political Theories,* by C. E. Merriam, New York, 1913.

[30] *A History of American Political Theories,* by C. E. Merriam.

[31] *A History of American Political Theories,* by C. E. Merriman.

[32] *Library of American Literature,* Vol. III, p. 199-200.

[33] *Smith College Studies in History,* Vol. I, pp. 165-187.

[34] Van Doren, *Cambridge History of American Literature,* Vol. I, p. 287.

[35] The only copy of which I have any knowledge is in the New York Public Library.

[36] *Life of Brown,* Vol. I, p. 70.

[37] (A) "Brown's inquisitive and speculative mind partook of the prevailing skepticism. Some of his compositions, and especially one on *The Rights of Women,* published in 1797, shows to what extent a benevolent mind may be led."—W. H. Prescott in Sparks' *"Library of American Biography,"* Vol. I, p. 129. (B) "Near the close of 1797 he published his first work, Alcuin, A Dialogue on the Rights of Women. It is not without ingenuity."—*The Prose Writers of America,* Griswold, p. 107. (C) "He wrote in the fall and winter of 1797 a work which he refers to in his journal as 'the dialogue of Alcuin, in which the topic of marriage is discussed with some degree of subtlety at least.' It was published in the same year, but its crude and hazardous theories on the subject of divorce and other social topics attracted little attention." E. A. and G. L. Duyckinck in the *Cyclopedia of American Literature,* Vol. I, p. 397. (D) "His first work, 'The Dialogues of Alcuin,' published in 1797, to which he refers in his journal as discussing the topic of marriage, attracted little attention, and many of the theories advanced on the subject of divorce were subsequently abandoned by the author."—*The National Cyclopaedia of America Biography,* Vol. II, p. 59. (E) From Mary Wollstonecraft "he derived the idea of his next work, *The Dialogue of of Alcuin,* 1797, an enthusiastic but inexperienced essay on the question of woman's rights and liberties."—*The Encyclopaedia Brittannica,* Eleventh Edition. (F) "It is not surprising, therefore, that his first publication, *Alcuin,* in 1797, dealt with the social position of woman, and advocated a very advanced theory of divorce. This brief work, in the form of a rather stilted dialogue, made little impression." Trent and Erskine in *"Great American Writers,"* p. 15. (G) "In 1797 he published a work on marriage and divorce entitled *The Dialogue of Alcuin.*"—Wendell and Greenough's *A History of Literature in America.* (H) "The spirit of Godwin stirred eagerly in Brown during the early days of his freedom. Toward the end of 1797 he bore witness by writing *Alcuin,* a

dialogue on the rights of women which took its first principles from Mary Wollstonecraft and Godwin." Van Doren, Chapter VI, *The Cambridge History of American Literature.* In an unpublished article recently put into my hands Professor Carl Van Doren, however, takes note of this confusion.

There is an entry in Dunlap's *Diary,* August 8, 1797, which lends support to the statement *Alcuin* was published in 1797. He writes: "Now S[mith] showed me 2 dialogues called Alcouin sent on by B. to be forwarded to Danies paper." It is quite likely that Dunlap—none too careful with his spelling at any time—meant to write Dennie's instead of Danies. Joseph Dennie, a friend and correspondent of Smith, was at this time editor of *The Farmer's Museum* of Walpole, New Hampshire. As I have not yet had access to the complete files of this paper, I cannot deny that *Alcuin* was published therein. But granting that it was published in 1797, its appearance did not prevent subsequent confusion with the second dialogue.

[38] In Bage's novel, *Man As He Is* (1792), France is referred to as the "paradise of women," Vol. II, p. 234.

[39] Stanwood, Edward, *A History of the Presidency,* Vol. I, 1898.

[40] *Selections from Cobbett's Political Works:* being a complete abridgement of the 100 volumes which comprise the writings of *Peter Porcupine,* London, 1835.

[41] Brown may wish to remind his readers of the famous London blue-stocking, Elizabeth Carter (1717-1806).

[42] Mary Astell, Defoe, Swift, Mary Wollstonecraft, and Godwin, whose ideas are paralleled in *Alcuin,* are not specifically mentioned; Plato, Lycurgus, Newton, and Locke are, however.

[43] Alcuin's reasoning here parallels in a remarkable way that of Fénelon in his *De l'education des filles* (1681). It is very likely that Brown was acquainted with this work, as he certainly was with *Telemaque,* for he mentions Fénelon in an address before the Belles Lettres Club.

[44] Cf. Poulain's *De l'Egalité des deux Sexes.*

[45] Cf. Poulain's *De l'Egalité des deux Sexes.*

[46] Fénelon in *L'Education des Filles* takes this same position. See also John Trumbull's *The Progress of Dulness* (1772-3). The same strictures on college education are found in the works of Hopkinson and Freneau.

[47] This point is particularly emphasized in Poulain's *De l'Egalité des deux Sexes.*

Ernest Marchand (essay date 1934)

SOURCE: "The Literary Opinions of Charles Brockden Brown," in *Studies in Philology*, Vol. XXXI, No. 4, October, 1934, pp. 541-566.

[*In the following essay, Marchand uses a variety of sources—including the prefaces to Brown's novels, literary allusions in his novels, his reviews and contributions to periodicals, and letters and passages in his journal—to examine Brown's literary and critical theories. Marchand notes in particular that Brown's literary judgments were guided by his view that the value of works of literature lies in their "moral tendency."*]

Since Charles Brockden Brown never formulated his literary or critical theories in an extended discourse comparable to Poe's "Poetic Principle" or Hugo's "Préface de Cromwell," any discussion of them must rest on the following sources: (1) the prefaces to his novels, (2) literary references and allusions found in the novels themselves, (3) his reviews of books in the several periodicals[1] which he edited, (4) his other contributions to periodicals, (5) fragmentary and passing comment made in his capacity as editor, (6) letters and passages from his Journal printed in William Dunlap's *Life of Charles Brockden Brown*. Much must necessarily remain in the uncertain region of inference. A further difficulty lies in the fact that, following the atrocious custom of the day, periodical contributions were unsigned, or, at best, signed with initials or the Latinized appellations then in vogue, such as "Adversaria," "Speratus" (which Brown himself once used), "Candidus," etc. Care, however, will be taken in this paper to ascribe no statement to Brown without citing the authority or giving the reasons therefore.[2] As for the justice of the inferences which I draw, each must judge for himself. I propose to unfold the subject under the following heads: (1) Brown's observations on the various literary *genres,* (2) his comment on individual writers, (3) his didacticism, and (4) his position as a critic.

II

The epics of Homer and Virgil, in Brown's view, loom large in our eyes chiefly because of the "reverence for what is ancient, and the influence of education." Homer belonged to a "rude" and "barbarous" age, when science was unknown and superstition was rife. In the literary productions of such an epoch "truth was deformed by tradition and credulity . . . effects were disjoined from their causes, and unattended with their circumstances . . ."; in poetry "invention supplied the defects of memory, and embellished events with causes and circumstances, grotesque, miraculous, and incredible . . .

The progress of society enlarged the views, sharpened the sagacity and refined the judgment of men. Language, bound down to a regular succession of *short* and *long,* gave place to the variety and freedom of prose; meagre, diffuse, disjointed and miraculous tales were supplanted by narratives, where invention was chastened by judgment. . . . [3]

Fantastic tales now give way to the more admirable productions of Xenophon and Thucydides, Livy and Tacitus. It is the prestige of Homer which has kept the epic in favor and stereotyped its design as to metrical form, division into books, succession of incidents, supernatural machinery, similes, battle scenes, and the rest.[4]

The old tales of the founding of Rome by the Trojan remnant led by Aeneas were but "rude and barbarous traditions current among the vulgar." For Virgil, therefore, to incorporate these "monstrous fables, absurdities and contradictions," about "brutal men and sanguinary deities," into his poem in an effort to supply Augustus, the destroyer of Roman liberty, with a distinguished ancestry was "a remarkable instance of servile adulation to tyrants, and superstitious reverence for antiquity." We may admire the poet's description of burning Troy and the despair of Dido, and yield to the music of his verse, but we must censure his choice of such a defective model as Homer, and the devotion of his talents "to the embellishment of childish chimeras . . . and the propagation of slavish maxims and national delusions."[5] Pope nearly fell into the same folly when he proposed an epic on the Brutus legend.

The selection of a great theme, after the author had pieced out the gaps left by history, being careful, however, to conform the efforts of imagination to "the most rigid standard of probability," all for the purpose of conveying "beneficent truths" to the reader, Brown believed to be one of the loftiest tasks which the mind may undertake. If he has not already sufficiently done so, Brown reveals his kinship with the age of prose and reason and prefers prose to poetry in stating that "all that constitutes the genuine and lasting excellence of narratives; all the subtilties of ratiocination, the energies and ornaments of rhetoric, and the colors of description, are compatible with prose. Numbers are an equivocal, or, at least, not an essential attribute of a moral and useful tale."[6]

Further general remarks on the subject of poetry are but scanty in Brown's writings, but a few may be noticed. The importance attached in the foregoing observations on the epic to credibility, "truth," probability, is seen again in his review of Samuel Low's *Poems,* where he takes that worthy to task for exercising the poet's authority over nature (i. e., in employing what we know as the pathetic fallacy) "with a pretty high hand." When death robs the poet of his friend, "he prescribes a general mourning through all the realms of nature: the face of heaven is overspread with gloom, and all the flowers of the field droop with despondence. . . ."[7] Likewise he stickles for precision in imagery, criticising Low for allowing the storm to break the "formidable surges," which, says Brown, are not so powerful as to require a storm to break them.[8]

Desirable qualities of verse are "strength," "originality of idea," "beauty of simile," "ingenuity of description," "harmony,"[9] "energy of thought," "gracefulness of diction," "ardour of fancy,"[10] "gay images," "lively numbers."[11] I submit a specimen which, Brown declares, possesses the last two of these poetic virtues:

> Dear Spirit of our happy clime,
> With star-deck'd Tiar', and port sublime,
> Who hear'st the savage yell of *war*,
> And giv'st to pity many a *tear;*
> Can'st thou believe, oh! Goddess blest!
> Such Stygian fiends thy realm infest?[12]

A "poet of superior genius," he asserts of this forgotten poetaster, "has not yet risen among us."[13]

A further principle of poetic composition—congruity and fitness—is violated in the attempt of John Blair Linn to fasten the machinery of Ossian on American scenes and characters. Such an exercise may "amuse" and "surprise" but "the scrupulous might deem such combinations uncouth, grotesque, and, perhaps, debasing."

> . . . he has transported us to the age of Fingall and Ossian. He has given us their mists, halls, and harps, but he has improperly introduced, into such company, Vernon, Potowmack, . . . Boston, . . . and Braddock; . . . In carrying us to the Hebrides, these and all images foreign to our new abode, should have been left behind.[14]

That the ancient question, What is poetry? was a live issue among Brown's contemporaries, as with us, who have heard the angry cries of the contestants around the free verse writers and other innovators, is seen in a passage from **"A Student's Diary,"** contributed by Brown to the *Literary Magazine:*

> This evening the conversation of the company turned upon the ingredients of poetry. Some maintained that verse and even rhyme were indispensable. Others were satisfied with verse alone, but differed . . . as to the criterion . . . some restricting it by very rigorous laws, and others extending its bounds so as to comprehend much of what is vulgarly called prose.

> Some . . . confined their views entirely to thought and imagery, and maintained that strength and beauty in these respects, constituted poetical excellence. . . .

> Another set extended the limits of poetry still further, and made it comprehend every effort of the imagination, whether conveyed by means of sounds, or colours, or figures.[15]

He laments the imperfections of language which make such disagreements possible: "There is not one word in ten in the English language, the meaning of which is settled with absolute precision."[16]

Brown's scattered, meagre remarks on some of the other literary categories may be gathered up in a paragraph. Satire suffers if it refers to "local circumstance" and "obscure individuals."[17] Despite his friendship with the chief American playwright of the period, he has practically nothing to say on the drama or the stage. He once, however, wrote to Dunlap (November 28, 1794), "My imagination is too undisciplined by experience to make me relish theatrical representations." He could not, as could others, "separate with ease the dramatic and theatrical."[18] Controversial writing he distrusted, believing that preoccupation with one side of an abstract subject breeds intolerance, and suspicion of the knowledge and intentions of our opponents. "Instead of concentering all our energies in argument . . . we are likely to deal too much in sarcasm and invective."[19] In the writing of history it is the "deduction of general causes" and "the statement of wide-spread, yet latent; of slow, yet incessant, revolutions in opinion and practice" which are important and in comparison with which "luxuriance of style and eloquence of narration are common and trivial."[20] In biography it is less important to explain the opinions of the subject, where these are generally known, than "to show the progress of his mind in forming them." To this end his "choice of books and companions, his methods of study, meditation, and converse . . ." are things worthy to be known if the biographer wishes to reveal the social, moral, and intellectual quality of a life.[21] Explicit statement of general principles of literary criticism is hardly to be found, but Brown delivered himself of the following observation on Shakespeare criticism. The critics, he thought, might be divided into two schools. The first, best represented by Johnson and Richardson, study the poet's plots and characters, and "banquet on his beauties." The second, "of which Malone is the Magnus Apollo, fasten on his words, and feast upon his crudities, his pedantry, his absurd and unintelligible parts. They labour to explain, what, in relation to the poet, is not worth knowing,"[22] and which can be of interest only to philologers and antiquarians.

When we come, however, to Brown's own field, the novel, we find more copious pronouncements. We have already seen in his remarks on the epic, how he held prose to be as suitable a medium as verse for fictitious narrative, if not superior. In general the novelist must have regard to the credibility and probability of the events which he recounts. Hence, in the prefatory "To the Public" of *Edgar Huntly* Brown associates "Gothic castles and chimeras" with "puerile superstition and exploded manners." *Robinson Crusoe* is commended for "the exquisite judgment displayed in giving conduct and feelings to the hero of the tale, suitable to his education, character, and situation. . . ."[23] This concern for verisimilitude is everywhere manifest. Writing to his brother James (February 15, 1799) of the newly published *Arthur Mervyn,* he declares that "to excite and baffle curiosity, without shocking belief, is the end to be contemplated."[24] In the Preface he offers the book as "a faithful sketch of the condition" of Philadelphia during the plague. In the letter just referred to he asks James to delete, if the progress of the printing will allow it, a passage in which Mervyn says a fifteenth of the population dies daily. "One in five hundred is nearer the truth. . . ."[25] *Edgar Huntly* is recommended to the public because "Similar events have frequently happened on the Indian borders; but, perhaps, they never were before described with equal minuteness."

> As to the truth of these incidents, men acquainted with the perils of an Indian war must be allowed to judge. Those who have ranged along the foot of the *Blue-ridge,* from the *Wind-gap* to the *Water-gap,* will see the exactness of the *local* descriptions. It may also be mentioned that *Old Deb* is a portrait faithfully drawn from nature.[26]

In *Wieland* the author hopes "the solution will be found to correspond with the known principles of human nature."[27] *Ormond* is not a tale "flowing merely from invention," but is an authentic picture of "society and manners."[28]

In connection with this desire for realistic and credible narrative Brown's interest in science, which he early displayed, is of some significance. In his journals for about 1789, when he was eighteen years old, he attempted a detailed classification of the sciences.[29] His intimates in the New York Friendly Club included Elihu Hubbard Smith, a physician; Edward Miller, a surgeon and one of the editors of the *Medical Repository;* Samuel Latham Mitchill, icthyologist and professor of chemistry at Columbia College.[30] The American edition of the great French *Encyclopedia* was published at Philadelphia in 1798. Brown reviewed it[31] in his *Monthly Magazine,* and, in all probability, drew on it for his knowledge of ventriloquism. In *Wieland*[32] he cites Erasmus Darwin's *Zoonomia* in a footnote as authority for the occurrence of cases of delusion similar to Wieland's. In two other learned footnotes he refers to a Florentine journal and to Merrille and Muraire in the *Journal de Medicine* for instances of spontaneous combustion, and to the Abbé de la Chapelle and Dr. Burney's *Musical Travels* for an account of ventriloquism.[33] For the immediate plot of *Wieland* he seems to have made use, like Poe for the *Mystery of Marie Roget,* of a contemporary newspaper account.[34]

The business of the novelist is to exhibit "depth of views into human nature" and "the subtilties of reasoning";[35] to illustrate important branches of the moral constitution of man."[36] Popular tales designed to amuse the idle and thoughtless by mere incident cannot do this. It is only by the presentation of "audacious" characters governed by "powerful motives" that the intelligent reader can be appealed to. "The world is governed, not by the simpleton, but by the man of soaring passions and intellectual energy. By the display of such only can we hope to enchain the attention and ravish the souls of those who study and reflect."[37] Bedloe in *The Man at Home* in advising Miss De Moivre to write her story, employs the same strain:

> In the selection of subjects for a useful history, the chief point is not the virtue of a character. The prime regard is to be paid to the genius and force of mind that is displayed. Great energy employed in the promotion of vicious purposes, constitutes a very useful spectacle. Give me a tale of lofty crimes, rather than of honest folly.[38]

It must not be thought, however, that his argument here indicates any strain of diabolism in him. He shows always the most tender regard for Christian morality. Indeed, the ultimate purpose of the novelist is the inculcation of virtue. But I shall leave this for my discussion of Brown's didacticism.

The loosely constructed tale in which incident follows incident without any attempt to excite curiosity, to build up suspense, to thrill and astound the reader, would not meet Brown's approval, if we may judge by several scattered remarks. The novel should be a "contexture of facts capable of suspending the faculties of every soul in curiosity."[39] The defect of Southey's *Joan of Arc* as a narrative is that in plan it is "simple and artless; attention is never roused by expectation, or held in suspense. . . . Incidents are touched lightly and connected loosely . . . the narrative awakens neither curiosity nor suspense."[40] Brown's letter to his brother James, often quoted as evidence of his return to literary respectability, in which he promised to abandon the "gloominess" with which he was charged, and to substitute "moral causes and daily incidents in place of the prodigious or the singular," by which he had previously sought the interest of his readers, must be received with a certain reserve. He was not convinced, but at best only yielded to expediency and average opinion. The objections "if they be not just in their full extent, are, doubtless, such as most readers will make, which alone, is a sufficient reason for dropping the doleful tone and assuming a cheerful one."[41] What there is "doleful" in novels dealing with borderline or abnormal states of consciousness is hard to make out. There are just two things to note in Brown's letter: the sad spectacle of an artist bowing to popular prejudice; and the operation (thus early) of the American passion for the happy ending and for "optimistic" views of life, with its converse morbid fear of the "morbid."

The novel in Brown's day was pretty generally under fire from the lingering religious prejudices of an earlier century. In order to make its way at all it had to surround itself with a thick coating of moral sugar, not always with success, for the alert godly frequently detected the bitter pill of sin underneath.[42] The magazines of the period contain numerous discussions pro and con of the religious, moral, and social effects of the craze for novel reading. "Novels," says a writer in the *Weekly Magazine,* March 10, 1798, "not only pollute the imaginations of young women, but likewise give them false ideas of life. . . ."[43] A contributor to Brown's *Literary Magazine* for July, 1805, grants that Richardson, Fielding, Mrs. Radcliffe, and Fanny Burney are harmless, but believes the bulk of novels "which usually crowd the shelves of a circulating library, or are seen tumbling on the sophas of a fashionable drawing room" corrupt morals, language, and religion, and tend to subvert government.[44] Another in the same periodical declares the *Sorrows of Werther* unfit for the young to read or booksellers to dispense.[45] Brown's contribution to the subject is contained in an imaginary dialogue between "a gentleman" and "a lady." The lady confronts the opponents of novel reading with two arguments: first, "a just and powerful picture of human life in which the connection between vice and misery, and between felicity and virtue is vividly pourtrayed, is the most solid and useful reading that a moral and social being . . . can read"; second, many who read trashy novels will read nothing else, and may as well be permitted a pastime which will keep them out of worse mischief. The gentleman agrees to the lady's argument, adding that the fear of corruption from novels rests on a profound ignorance of human nature, "the brightest of whose properties is to be influenced more by example than by precept."[46]

This section may be concluded with noticing a few remarks on style, gleaned from Brown's reviews. "Conceit, glitter, and bombast" should not be mistaken for "eloquence and sublimity." "Laboured antithesis, and sentences balanced with nice adjustment . . . mark the efforts of art and contrivance, but not taste, good sense, or feeling."[47] Brown likewise ridiculed the inflated, windy style then current among newspaper writers who were especially fond of letting themselves out in the description of fires, bursting into such blooms of eloquence as "'the peaceful slumbers of the inhabitants were broken by *vociferated fire!*' . . . In spite of the exertions of the citizens, such and such buildings were 'swallowed up by the conflagration;' or . . . 'became victims to the devouring element;' or, 'fell a prey to the remorseless fury of the flames.'"[48] Like Poe he frequently descended to minute particulars in commenting on books. Thus he takes Noah Webster to task for using *originate* as a transitive verb, and for referring to

the plague as "that all-devouring scourage, which has swept away a large portion of the human race." A scourge, says Brown, "neither devours nor sweeps."[49] His sole essay in iconoclasm occurs in a **"Critical Notice"** in the *Literary Magazine* for June, 1804, where he tosses a pebble at the mighty Milton. "How few there are," he writes, "who stop to enquire into the propriety or reasonableness of what they read! They are told beforehand that this or that is a sublime production . . . take the work as a criterion of taste and excellence, and seldom venture . . . to derive the reasons for their approbation from the unbiassed and original suggestions of their own minds."[50] Out of this bold thunder issues a feeble remonstrance against Milton's lines " . . . Black as night; Fierce as ten furies; terrible as hell." In the first place, he argues, the blackness of night is not absolute—black as ebony would have been a better comparison; in the second place, ten furies are no fiercer than one; and in the third place, death is terrible as hell to sinners, not necessarily to others.[51]

Brown's own style is rapid and nervous, his sentences are short for the most part, without excessive balance and antithesis, and with little initial periodicity. But his diction is extremely stilted and he is very fond of periphrasis. Huntly, having resolved to do some digging by night beneath an elm, "repairs thither" ("hither," Brown has it), not with a shovel or spade, but "with a proper implement."[52] On his rambles through the woods he carries no musket or hunting knife, but "the means of defence."[53] Awaking at night he produces a light by means of "a common apparatus," rather than by flint and steel.[54] A bad piece of observation still in use occurs in **Wieland,** where Wieland clasps his hands "with a force that left the print of his nails in his flesh."[55] Another old friend is too good to omit: Pleyel's wife dying in childbirth is "snatched from him . . . in the hour in which she gave him the first pledge of their mutual affection."[56] The language of the characters is likewise preposterous: try to imagine a man who has just killed another saying to an unexpected arrival, "aid me in hiding these remains from human scrutiny."[57]

Little of the Keatsian delight in the sensuous apprehension of the world is to be found in Brown. His characters walk through streets, live in houses, have more or less intimate acquaintance with chairs, tables, fireplaces, windows, walls, pictures, bric-a-brac, and the other appurtenances of daily living; presumably eat and drink, wear clothes, smell odors good and bad, hear sounds sweet and harsh, and are played upon by all the infinite appeals to sense, but we feel it only imperfectly in these pages. I cannot recall a color image, unless it be the pale or livid hue of a countenance.

III

When we turn to Brown's observations on individual writers, we find them disappointingly few, brief, and general, as regards writers of front rank. The bulk of his reviews is devoted to obscure nobodies who have been totally forgotten. His interests, moreover, were as much political and scientific as literary.[58] The three volumes of the magazine he first edited, the *Monthly Magazine and American Review,* extending from April, 1799, to December, 1800, contain, if my count is correct, 150 reviews, which may be classified as follows: history, seven; biography and memoirs, four; natural history, one; philosophy, one; theology and religion, six; ecclesiastical history, one; law, one; politics and economics, sixteen; science, three; anthropology, one; geography, one, agriculture, one; medicine, three; crime, two; reference works, five; fiction, two; drama, four; poetry, ten (of which three are effusions on Washington); sermons, twenty-two; and addresses and orations, fifty-three (of which forty-two were evoked by the death of Washington). The reviews in the two latter categories are, it is true, often short—a few lines or a paragraph—but many are full length and the total bulk is far out of proportion to their significance. Notices of addresses and orations on Washington alone, for example, occupy forty-three pages, as against twenty-seven pages for reviews of poetry.

Brown's opinions of his contemporaries and predecessors must be sought, outside his reviews, in brief references and allusions scattered through his novels, periodical contributions, and editorial comment. The names which recur, and the tenor of the remarks, lead to the conclusion that the established writers of the eighteenth century were most in his eye. If he wrote the "European Literary Intelligence"[59] for the *Literary Magazine* for October, 1804, he ascribes to Richardson high "moral and literary excellence," speaks of his "genius," and declares he could have no better historian than Mrs. Barbauld, whose life of the novelist had just appeared.[60] Goldsmith's *Citizen of the World* "does not please me," he wrote in his journal (July 10, 1801). "The fiction is ill supported, the style smooth and elegant, but the sentiments and observations far from judicious or profound."[61] The coolness shown here should not, however, be taken to signify a general disapproval of Goldsmith, for elsewhere he puts him, by implication, in an assured place with Gray and Campbell, into whose company such a poet as his countryman Samuel Low can hardly enter.[62] A contribution to the *Literary Magazine* for June, 1805 (signed "B" and probably Brown's) contains the opinion that "No themes of poetry are nobler than those of Goldsmith, and no genius ever poured out on such themes, richer and more polished strains."[63] The writer continues:

[Johnson's] eastern tales have all the merit compatible with plans so wild, grotesque and unnatural; but no man of just taste, in morals or in composition, can hesitate a moment in preferring . . . Goldsmith's simple and natural tales, to . . . the pompous and gloomy fictions of Johnson.[64]

Cowper is "a glory and blessing to humanity."[65] In a series of ten "Critical Notices"[66] running in the *Literary Magazine* from October, 1803, to December, 1804, the names which occur are Milton, Young, Thomson, Cowper, Dryden, Gray, Pope, Goldsmith, Virgil, Tasso, Voltaire, Wordsworth. The *Aeneid* is disparaged. In a comparison of Dryden and Pope as translators, Dryden's *Iliad* (Book I) is said to be "more forcible and natural" than Pope's; but Pope has "more harmony and . . . uniform magnificence" than Dryden.[67] Voltaire's *Henriade* is praised with some reservation.[68]

After he had finished his first romance,[69] Brown wrote in his journal, "when . . . I revolve the transcendant merits of Caleb Williams, my pleasure is diminished, and is preserved from a total extinction only by the reflection that this performance is the first."[70] Opinions vary as to the extent of Godwin's influence on Brown. Professor Clark holds that his letters and Journal furnish "conclusive evidence that his mind was set before Godwin had published a word."[71] Professor Pattee also believes that the influence has been overstressed.[72]

The position which Scott had achieved in America by 1808 is indicated by a brief reference in the *American Register* for the last half of that year. In a **"Review of Literature"**[73] Brown writes, "We receive with delight and avidity, new presents from Walter Scott and Mrs. Opie,[74] with whom every man of taste has made himself long ago acquainted."[75] This is the sole reference to Scott which I have discovered. Burns receives a bare mention in the same notice in connection with some of his literary remains, recently discovered, but there is no expression of opinion on him. "We look in vain," Brown laments, "for some precious bequest from the hand of Miss Edgeworth or Mrs. Opie,"[76] that is, in the field of the novel for 1808. "Anne Radcliffe," declares the "gentleman" in one of Brown's characteristic dialogues, "is, without doubt, the most illustrious of the picturesque writers. Her 'Travels on the Rhine and in Cumberland' is, in this view, an inestimable performance. . . ."[77] *The Mysteries of Udolpho* and *The Italian* are word pictures in which the narrative and characters bear subordinate parts; " . . . to limit the attention, as is usually done, to her human figures, is no less absurd than to look at nothing in a seaview but the features of the pilot."[78]

The immediate heirs of the romantic period attach great interest to what the men of that time had to say about the new literature, and especially about the authors of the *Lyrical Ballads,* and they tend to measure all others by their attitudes toward these two men and toward the romantic poetry in general. In the whole mass of Brown's work I find but one meagre reference to Wordsworth, that one damning the poet by implication. In a plea for intellectual tolerance, he argues that an "enlightened mind" will not hold another man's hobby or taste in contempt. "Such a one will perceive the ties which connect all the objects of human knowledge. . . . He will extract useful and delightful knowledge from a treatise upon heraldry: or a catalogue of Scottish kings, who reigned before the flood: or a volume of year books: or one of Wordsworth's pastorals. . . ."[79] To the same issue of the magazine in which these words appear, Brown admitted a notice of the *Lyrical Ballads* signed by one "I. O.," who abuses that work in the conventional terms. "I know few performances," writes this critic, "which have assumed the name of poetry and which have obtained a considerable share of celebrity, so truly worthless. . . ."[80] The objection is, that though Wordsworth aimed at simplicity, he did not know what simplicity was, nor how to distinguish it from affectation. "The Thorn" and "The Idiot Boy" are singled out as specimens of that affectation. Two months later the same reviewer in a notice of one Peter Bayley's "The months later the same reviewer in a notice of one Peter Bayley's "The Fisherman's Wife, dedicated to all admirers of the familiar style of writing, so popular in 1800," and designed to burlesque the *Lyrical Ballads,* "which we have already in this work justly condemned," praises it as "vastly superior" to "The Thorn" or "The Idiot Boy."[81]

Of the ten reviews of works of poetry in the *Monthly Magazine,* the only ones which deal with a writer of even second rank are a notice of Southey's *Joan of Arc,* which Brown reviews at some length, and a shorter notice of the first American edition of *Poems,* containing Southey's youthful verse. The author of *Joan of Arc,* he grants, has true genius, as appears in his "happy epithets, vivid descriptions, copious imagery, and tender sentiments."[82] He would give him, perhaps, the highest place among the "serious and pathetic poets" of the time.[83] Only Cowper excels him in "vigor and sprightliness of fancy" and in "equable, melodious, moral, and pathetic" strain.[84] His faults as revealed in *Joan of Arc,* are (1) a genius "not chastened by discipline and knowledge," (2) "feeble and rugged numbers," (3) "harsh and new coined terms," (4) "affectations," (5) "obscurities," (6) a "simple and artless" plan, loose in construction and failing to make use of suspense, (7) weak portrayal of characters, giving "no distinct images of the habits and motives connected with them," (8) conspicuous failure to draw from his theme the great lessons which it is calculated to teach, although he deserves credit as first to exploit it. The lessons are four: "a powerful lesson on the principles of human nature," the "tendency of the feudal system," the "evils of ambition and war," and the "operations of religious enthusiasm and popular passions."[85] One or two of these faults deserve more particular notice. He has particularly failed to give the real character of Joan, retaining the miraculous elements of her history in the face of the example which he might have followed from Hume, who had happily exploded these supersti-

tions. Such fantastic errors, although Southey no doubt thought them more suitable for poetry than sober truth, "in reality degrade it and destroy its usefulness."

> . . . some disgust and disappointment were awakened in our minds, on finding the bold, natural and instructive features of her history displaced by the tasteless and trite fictions of an hermit's cell, miraculous skill in the cure of diseases, Orlando's sword, the innocent amusements of a shepherdess, the sorrows of fantastic love, and lastly the serious assertions of preternatural impulse. . . .[86]

The struggle of Joan, a woman of humble birth and "servile education," against "aristocratical pride" and "lordly and martial presumption," and her triumph, are displayed only in a "frigid, indirect, and feeble manner."[87] In these several pronouncements the voice of the rationalist and the republican, even of the democrat and social radical, is plainly heard.

Two of the pieces in Southey's early volume—"Inscriptions" and "Hymn to the Penates"—are reminiscent, Brown thinks, of Akenside, the second poem reminding him of the latter's "Hymn to the Naiads," which, however, is "superior in imagery and numbers." Southey's "Inscriptions," although it has "beauty of sentiment, vivid description, and pure morality," has "less elegance and classic purity of ornament and expression" than the verse of the earlier poet.[88]

I find nowhere any mention of Coleridge, and if Byron's early volume of 1807 and the hostile review of it the next year in the *Edinburgh* stirred up a ripple on this side of the Atlantic, there is no sign of it in Brown's periodicals. Altogether, notices of the romantic writers, small or great, are scanty; and if the editor's taste may be inferred from the authorship of the poems which he admitted to his magazines, it is still in the neo-classic tradition. According to Professor Clark, of the seventy-four poems in the *Monthly Magazine,* "thirty-three were by John Davis, seven by Richard Alsop,—largely translations from the Latin and Italian—and the rest were by numerous *Mathildas, Della Cruscans,* and *Peter Pindars.*"[89] There were also five by Cowper, one by Dr. Burney, one by Colman, and one by Southey.[90] The eight volumes of Brown's second journalistic enterprise, the *Literary Magazine and American Register,* contain a total of forty-one poems, of which three are by Cowper, one by Darwin, two by Burns, two by Campbell, and two by Moore.[91] The *American Register,* last of our editor's ventures, contains in its seven volumes only fourteen poems, including one by Scott, the "Epistle to J. M." Thus of British poets Brown prints more poems by Cowper than by any other, eight altogether. We turn now to his comment on American writers.

Professor Clark says that "though a friend of the Hartford wits, Brown lightly esteemed the artificial lyrics and satires from that 'tuneful nest' . . ."[92] He does not state, nor am I able to discover, on what he bases his assertion. On the contrary, Brown seems to assume the preëminence of this group in American poetry. Deploring in 1800 the poetic sterility of America, he added: "A Trumbull, a Dwight, a Barlow, will ever be excepted in the general observation."[93] Some years later, in announcing the appearance of the *Columbiad,* he remarks, "In the department of the fine arts, we meet with a work which, in extent and value, cannot be expected to present itself very often."[94] Whether this "value" applies to the work as poetry, or to its "typographical splendour" is not altogether certain. Speaking of Dwight, he believes the great reputation of that "distinguished divine, orator, and scholar" is deserved, but does not specifically mention his rôle of poet.[95] A notice of Trumbull's *M'Fingal* which appeared in the *Literary Magazine* for July, 1806, I believe to be Brown's because of its use of the editorial "we" and general assumption of the editorial manner. In it the writer remarks on the once great popularity of *M'Fingal,* but fears it is now unknown to readers "to whom the revolution is an obscure and antiquated story. . . ." He believes a work "which has been universally acknowledged to be in no respect inferior, and in several respects much superior to the far-famed Hudibras," is worth reintroducing to the public. The points of superiority to *Hudibras* are two: first, "the adventures . . . are more coherent, intelligible, and consistent"; second, "the language is not usually so careless as Butler's." Probably misled, however, by his model, Trumbull too uses "slovenly rhymes."[96] Joseph Dennie sometimes admits to the pages of the *Port Folio* "poetical effusions" at which Brown is disposed to cavil, but he "warmly" approves his zealous labors for literature.[97] Elsewhere he dissents from Dennie's too severe censures of American materialism.[98] The Pennsylvania writers, Hopkinson and Brackenridge, are nowhere mentioned. An announcement in the "Literary Intelligence" department of the *Literary Magazine* for June, 1805, of Dunlap's proposed collection of his dramatic works commends his "extensive experience and mature taste" and advances his claim to patronage on the score that he is almost the only native American dramatist.[99]

Brown showed a considerable interest in German literature and things German. His *Monthly Magazine,* says Professor Clark, "was one of the leading forces in making known German literature to America."[100] In one of Brown's **"Dialogues of the Living,"** Harry, who is studying German, replies to the questions of Tom that he does not expect to go to Germany, marry into a German family, associate with Germans, teach German, translate from the German to "profit by the popular age for translations," nor does he believe the Germans have more eloquent historians, more "valuable" poets, epic and dramatic, than "our own Spencer

[*sic*], Milton, and Shakespeare; Pope, Dryden, and Thompson" [*sic*], nor better "dealers in fictitious narration" than Fielding, Smollett, Richardson, and their followers, "whose works, whether resorted to for entertainment or instruction, will afford plentiful employment even to him who reads nothing else. . . ." His object is "merely to read and understand their authors . . . I meditate nothing but intellectual pleasure and improvement." He hopes to read all classes of German writers worth the study—"This Kotzebue, they talk so much of," Gesner [*sic*], Ifland, Weiland [*sic*], Haller, Schiller, Goethe.[101] Brown's friend Dunlap was busying himself with translating the plays of Kotzebue, then popular on the American stage. Three or four reviews of these plays may be found in the *Monthly Magazine,* comparing the work of several translators with that of Dunlap, to the latter's advantage. Only one of these, however, am I able to identify as Brown's.[102] Kotzebue, if tried by the rules of Aristotle, will be found wanting, but if we allow him the freedom which liberal critics grant to Shakespeare, he will appear in a better light.[103] It is apparent that in the midst of the Kotzebue craze Brown maintained a certain reserve. He doubts whether the German playwright's fame will last; " . . . the present *teutonick* fashion of writing may be as transient as any other kind."[104]

But Brown's German interest, however tempered, is reflected in the novels. The grandfather of Clara Wieland was of a noble Saxon family, and is said by her to be the ancestor of the poet Wieland.[105] Clara, violently agitated by her first glimpse of the mysterious Carwin, after a night of wakefulness and a day spent in gloomy foreboding, attempts to distract her thoughts with "a ballad which commemorated the fate of a German Cavalier, who fell at the siege of Nice under Godfrey of Bouillon."[106] Wieland himself receives from Germany a new book, a tragedy by a Saxon poet. The hero is Zisca, a Bohemian.

> According to German custom, it was minute and diffuse, and dictated by an adventurous and lawless fancy. It was a chain of audacious acts, and unheard-of disasters. The moated fortress, and the thicket; the ambush and the battle; and the conflict of headlong passions, were pourtrayed in wild numbers, and with terrific energy.[107]

Pleyel, Wieland's brother-in-law, has recently returned from Germany, where he has left his fiancée, Theresa de Stolberg.

IV

The most conspicuous and the most consistent element in Brown's literary judgments, as in his own practice, is his thorough-going didacticism. We have already seen how he applied didactic standards to Homer and Virgil and to Southey's *Joan of Arc,* and how he defended the novel on the ground of its capacity to present powerfully the connection between "vice and misery, felicity and virtue." It is characteristic of his period, which saw the rise of a middle class morality, that the classics, hitherto accepted in their entirety by an aristocratic society, without any cavil at their frank animality, should be reweighed in moral scales. Brown now launches an indignant assault on Anacreon. "How much," he exclaims, "are mankind misled by names . . . the mirth and love of Anacreon and Horace shall be listened to with reverence . . . and yet reduced into plain English . . . they are nothing but drunkenness and lewdness. Anacreon is neither more nor less than a hoary debauchee. . . ."[108]

> I see nothing here . . . but those fires which are raised and quenched in a brothel, which are excited by mere sex . . . I see nothing but a gross appetite, distinguished by no humanity, no delicacy, from that which stimulates the goat and the bull.[109]

A correspondent of the *Monthly Magazine* who signs himself "A. Z." wishes that the editor would devote "a much larger portion of your magazine to the labours of the moralist." He doubts that scientific articles will "benefit" the majority of readers. Brown defends himself for allowing his attention to stray for a moment from the all-important labors of the moralist as follows:

> Literature and science have a strong connection with morality: and, although the editor is not less sensible than A. Z. of the superior importance of those performances which have immediate relation with the latter, he cannot but think that a plan which comprehends other branches of knowledge, will be approved by the majority of readers.[110]

In urging American novelists to turn their eyes from foreign models and from books and to "paint from nature," he declares that the value of such works will lie "without doubt in their moral tendency."[111] He offers **Wieland** as a work whose "usefulness," he hopes, will secure it a lasting reputation, his aim being to illustrate, "some important branches of the moral constitution of man,"[112] and he makes Clara Wieland say that she writes her history "for the benefit of mankind" and to "inculcate the duty of avoiding deceit." In the foreword to **Edgar Huntly** Brown announces his purpose to employ some of the numerous "sources of amusement to the fancy and instruction to the heart" peculiar to American life. The old Horatian pair—amusement and instruction—are never divorced in his thought. The emphasis, however, is always felt on the instruction, for without it the amusement would fall under suspicion of sin. The Preface to **Arthur Mervyn** assures the reader that "he who portrays examples of disinterestedness and intrepidity confers on virtue the notoriety and homage that are due to it, and rouses in

the spectators the spirit of salutary emulation." The "Editor's Address to the Public" in volume one of the *Literary Magazine* promises that "in the conduct of this work a supreme regard will be paid to the interests of religion and morality . . .

> Everything that savours of indelicacy or licentiousness will be rigorously proscribed. His poetical pieces may be dull, but they shall at least be free from voluptuousness or sensuality; and his prose, whether seconded or not by genius and knowledge, shall scrupulously aim at the promotion of public and private virtue.[113]

V

As a reviewer Brown was, on the whole, cautious, and tender toward literary sensibilities. A typical statement about a work under notice is "We cannot sincerely applaud, neither shall we very earnestly condemn the design."[114] Commenting on one of the perfervid eulogies of the period, he says of its rhetoric, "What one shall esteem luxuriant and magnificent, another may despise as puerile, jejune, and flat,"[115] but refuses to commit himself directly. In his last magazine, the *American Register,* he gave up reviewing altogether, and contented himself with a bare catalogue of new books, giving as his reason "the number of those whom censure would mortify or irritate."[116] Despite his earnest efforts to please the public, he frequently, as all editors must, aroused the ire of subscribers, but credit is due him for admitting their grievances freely to his columns.[116a] There is, I feel, a good deal of justice in the complaint of one reader about the reviews: "Sir, they are anything but reviews. They are feeble, indecisive worthless things. No man can tell what to think of an author, after their account of him. . . ."[117]

Brown's critical vocabulary was feeble and trite, full of such terms as "lively numbers," "strength," and "gracefulness of diction," which mean nothing without analysis of the objects to which they are applied, or at least specific reference to those objects—an analysis and a reference which he hardly attempts. That he occasionally made a common sense observation on literature or style is not to be denied. What he says on biographical and historical writing is what has been said before and since, and what few will deny, more than they will deny that "conceit, glitter, and bombast" are bad qualities of style. But this is hardly sufficient to establish the reputation of a critic. He was slow, says Professor Clark, to recognize genius, "but when his mind was once clearly made up his judgments were nearly always to be relied upon."[118] Considering that the American literary horizon was as empty of genius at the time as it could well be, that he was concerned almost entirely with obscure and forgotten men, that of the half dozen poets he reviewed only Southey is remembered, the judgment rather lacks point. Hence to say, as does Professor Clark, that he was the greatest critic in America before Poe,[119] though one may assent to it, is to say little—is a good deal like saying that the greatest naturalist in Europe before Linnaeus was Pliny; and to say that "his natural bent was toward literary criticism of a high order,"[120] is to say too much. Brown's standards were those of the fag end of neo-classicism, with its talk of "correctness," "elegance," and "propriety," the whole overlaid with an enervating moral didacticism. He is chiefly interesting as one of the earliest American writers to issue the call for literary independence, and as a man who wrote some very readable tales employing native materials and original themes, and avoiding, in the main, the absurdities which filled the novels of the day.

Notes

[1] These were the *Monthly Magazine and American Review,* 3 vols., New York, April, 1799-Dec., 1800; the *Literary Magazine and American Register,* 8 vols., Philadelphia, Oct., 1803-Dec., 1807; the *American Register or General Repository of History, Politics and Science,* 7 vols., Philadelphia, 1807-10. They will be referred to hereafter by their shorter titles. Of the *American Review and Literary Journal* (2 vols., New York, 1801-1802), a quarterly, successor to the *Monthly Magazine,* I find three statements: (1) Brown had no connection with it (David Lee Clark, "Brockden Brown's First Attempt at Journalism," *Univ. of Texas Bulletin,* No. 2743 [Nov. 15, 1927], p. 174); (2) Brown was the editor (Frank Luther Mott, *A History of American Magazines 1741-1850,* p. 219); (3) Brown edited it in part (Annie Russell Marble, *Heralds of American Literature,* Chicago and London, 1907, p. 296).

[2] Reviews are signed in the *Monthly Magazine* only in Vol. I. Five bear Brown's initial, as follows: (1) Eulogium on the late Dr. Samuel Cooper. By Charles Caldwell (April, 1799). Signed "B." (2) New Views of the Origin of the Tribes and Nations of America. By Benjamin Smith Barton (May, 1799). Signed "C. B." (3) The History of America. Books IX and X. By William Robertson (May, 1799). Signed "B." (4) The History of Pennsylvania. By Robert Proud (June, 1799). Signed "B." (5) Joan of Arc. By Robert Southey (June, 1799). Signed "B." Other reviews in this magazine I ascribe to Brown on the authority of Professor David Lee Clark, who has had access to rare manuscripts in the possession of Brown's grandson, Mr. William Linn Brown, of Philadelphia. See the preface (dated Austin, Texas, April, 1923), to the forty-nine page abstract of his Columbia dissertation, which is there said to be "in process of revision for publication." All interested in Brown will look forward to Professor Clark's book. The statements on which I depend for identification of reviews will be found in

his article in the *University of Texas Bulletin,* referred to in the preceding note. In several instances it is not clear from his wording whether the piece under discussion is by Brown or another, but such pieces I have not used. The pages in the *University of Texas Bulletin* on which the statements will be found, and the reviews by Brown which they identify, are as follows: p. 167, A Brief History of Epidemic and Pestilential Diseases. By Noah Webster; p. 167, Poems. By Robert Southey; p. 169, Poems, chiefly occasional, by the late Mr. Cliffton; p. 169, Mount-Vernon, a Poem. By John Searson; p. 170, Poems. By Samuel Low; p. 170, Eulogy on the Life of General George Washington. By Thomas [i.e., Robert Treat] Paine; p. 170, A Discourse delivered April 1st, 1800 . . . before the New York Missionary Society. By William Linn, D. D.; p. 172, Pizarro in Peru . . . a play . . . From the German of Kotzebue, by William Dunlap; p. 172, Dialogues of the Living. Dialogue III (not a review, but an original contribution by Brown). Professor Clark also ascribes (p. 42 of abstract of thesis before mentioned) to Brown a review of The Death of Washington, a poem, in imitation of the manner of Ossian. By Rev. John Blair Linn.

An early composition of Brown's, "The Rhapsodist," contributed to Volume III of *The Columbian Magazine,* 1789, appeared in four parts (August, September, October, and November) signed successively "B," "R," "O," "W"; one more would have completed his name. I suspect that here is a clue to the identification of his periodical contributions, and that any piece signed with one of these letters will be found to be his. Professor Clark, for example, who has had access to hitherto unexamined documents, credits him with the review, signed "W," of Southey's *Poems, Monthly Magazine,* May, 1799.

[3] Review of Southey's "Joan of Arc," *Monthly Mag.,* I (June, 1799), 226.

[4] *Ibid.,* p. 225.

[5] *Ibid.,* p. 226.

[6] *Ibid.,* p. 227.

[7] *Monthly Mag.,* III (July, 1800), 57.

[8] *Ibid.* (Oct., 1800), 268.

[9] *Ibid.* (July, 1800), p. 58.

[10] *Ibid.* (Dec., 1800), p. 430.

[11] *Ibid.* (Dec., 1800), p. 431.

[12] *Monthly Mag.,* III (Dec., 1800), 431. "Rhapsody on the Times," in *Poems* . . . by the late Mr. Cliffton.

[13] *Ibid.,* p. 433; also p. 234.

[14] *Monthly Mag.,* II (Apr., 1800), 308.

[15] I (Dec., 1803), 165. Attributed to Brown by Clark, *Abstract of Thesis,* p. 48.

[16] *Literary Mag.,* I (Dec., 1803), 166.

[17] Review of Cliffton's *Poems, Monthly Mag.,* III (Dec., 1800), 430.

[18] William Dunlap, *Life of Charles Brockden Brown* (Philadelphia, 1815), II, 91.

[19] Review of Noah Webster's *Brief History of Epidemic and Pestilential Diseases, Monthly Mag.,* II (Feb., 1800), 115.

[20] Review of Robertson's *Hist. of America, Monthly Mag.,* I (May, 1799), 131.

[21] Review of Charles Caldwell's "Eulogium on . . . Dr. Samuel Cooper," *Monthly Mag.,* I (April, 1799), 51. It is to be regretted that Brown himself could not have had such a biographer, for a feebler production than Dunlap's *Life* has seldom passed under the name of biography.

[22] "Review of Literature," *American Register,* IV (1809), 117.

[23] "A Student's Diary," *Lit. Mag.,* I (Feb., 1804), 324.

[24] Dunlap, *Life,* II, 97. Brown, of course, was not unique in his desire for realism. It was a fashion of the day to claim truth for fiction. See the bibliographhy in Lillie Deming Loshe's *The Early American Novel* (New York, 1907).

[25] Dunlap, *Life,* II, 98.

[26] Note addressed "Mr. Editor" (Brown himself), and signed "E. H.," prefaced to "Edgar Huntly: A Fragment," *Monthly Mag.,* I (April, 1799), 21.

[27] Prefatory "Advertisement."

[28] Prefatory note.

[29] Dunlap, *Life,* I, 18-20.

[30] D. L. Clark, *Univ. of Texas Bul.,* No. 2743, p. 162.

[31] Statement of Fred Lewis Pattee in Introduction to *Wieland* (New York, 1926), p. xxi. The review, which appeared in the *Monthly Magazine,* I (May, 1799), 134-35 is unsigned.

[32] Edition cited, p. 202.

[33] *Ibid.,* pp. 21, 223.

[34] The story may be found in the *New York Weekly Magazine,* July 20 and 28, 1796. See Carl Van Doren, "Early American Realism," *Nation,* XCIX (Nov. 12, 1914), 577-78.

[35] Letter "To the Editor of the Weekly Magazine" announcing the forthcoming appearance of Brown's novel *Skywalk, Weekly Mag.,* I (March 17, 1798), 202.

[36] *Wieland,* prefatory "Advertisement."

[37] Letter (note 35 above), *loc. cit.*

[38] *Weekly Magazine,* I (March 31, 1798), 257.

[39] "To the Editor of the Weekly Magazine," *Weekly Mag.,* I (March 17, 1798), 202.

[40] Review in *Monthly Mag.,* I (June, 1799), 228.

[41] Dunlap, *Life,* II, 100. Letter dated New York, April, 1800.

[42] On this whole subject see the discussion of V. F. Calverton, *The Liberation of American Literature* (New York, 1932), pp. 216 ff.

[43] I, 185.

[44] IV, 7-8.

[45] VI (Dec., 1806), 451.

[46] "A Student's Diary," *Literary Mag.,* I (March, 1804), 404-05.

[47] Review of Thomas [i. e., Robert Treat] Paine's "Eulogy on the Life of General George Washington," *Monthly Mag.,* II (May, 1800), 354.

[48] "Extracts from a Student's Diary," *Literary Mag.,* I (Oct., 1803), 7.

[49] Review of Webster's "Brief History of Epidemic and Pestilential Diseases," *Monthly Mag.,* II (Jan., 1800), 31, 33.

[50] This passage, though pruned down, is a fair specimen of Brown's prolixity.

[51] II, 176-79. I attribute this piece to Brown on the evidence of a letter to his brother-in-law, the Reverend Dr. John Blair Linn, in which he says he was obliged to write the whole original department of the June and July numbers, with one exception, which he names. See Dunlap, *Life,* II, 111.

[52] *Edgar Huntly* (New York, 1928), p. 118.

[53] *Ibid.,* p. 129. Carwin, walking about Dublin at night, had about him "the usual instruments of defence." *Wieland, ed. cit.,* p. 323.

[54] *Ibid.,* p. 139. Cf. *Wieland,* p. 95, "a lamp and the means of lighting it."

[55] Edition cited, p. 153.

[56] *Ibid.,* p. 267.

[57] *Arthur Mervyn* (Philadelphia: McKay, n. d.), I, 109.

[58] The review of Webster's *Brief History of Epidemic and Pestilential Diseases* occupies twenty-seven pages, and that of Count Rumford's *Essays: Political, Economic, and Philosophical,* twenty-six.

[59] In the preceding July he announced that he would devote two or three pages in each number to a list of new publications, "as a general reference in the selection of books to purchase, and as exhibiting a tolerably correct view of the prevailing taste for reading and the progress of literature in the United States." Vol. II, p. 318.

[60] II, 532-33.

[61] Brown picked up the book aboard the boat on which he was travelling up the Hudson. Together with a volume on navigation and Dillworth's *Arithmetic* it formed the captain's whole library. He mentions, also, another passenger as absorbed in Mrs. Bennet's *Beggar Girl.* See Dunlap, *Life,* II, 53.

[62] Review of Samuel Low's *Poems, Monthly Magazine,* III (July, 1800), 58.

[63] III, 403.

[64] III, 404.

[65] "Extracts from a Student's Diary," *Literary Mag.,* I (Oct., 1803), 10. Remarks on the niggardliness of kings and nobles toward genius, inspired by "reading Burke's speeches on Economical Reform." Bare allusion to *The Task* in "The Man at Home," *Weekly Mag.,* I (March 10, 1798), 168.

[66] Four are signed "I. O." Only one is certainly Brown's, that criticising Milton's simile. See *ante,* note 51.

[67] Vol. I, Nov., 1803.

[68] Vol. II, April, 1804.

[69] This was never published. The series of letters between "Sophia" and "Jessica" printed by Dunlap (*Life,* I, 108-69) is, according to him, part of it.

[70] Dunlap, *Life,* I, 107.

[71] *Edgar Huntly, ed. cit.,* p. viii (Introduction).

[72] Introduction to *Wieland,* p. xxxv.

[73] This department of the magazine bears every mark of the editorial hand.

[74] Amelia (Alderson) Opie, novelist and poetess, intimate of Godwin and Mary Wollstonecraft, and an admirer of Horne Tooke.

[75] IV, 117.

[76] *Ibid.,* p. 116.

[77] "On a Taste for the Picturesque," *Lit. Mag.,* II (June, 1804), 165.

[78] *Loc. cit.*

[79] "A Student's Diary," *Literary Mag.,* I (Feb., 1804), 328.

[80] *Ibid.,* p. 336.

[81] *Literary Mag.,* II (April, 1804), 17.

[82] *Monthly Magazine,* I (June, 1799), 228.

[83] It is difficult to know in precisely what sense Brown uses the word "pathetic," whether in the older meaning of "stirring," or "exciting," or in the later one of moving to "pity" or "compassion," or in the general one of producing sympathy by the display of any kind of feeling or passion. Since he finds *Joan of Arc* devoid of suspense or dramatic excitement, perhaps he intends the latter. See J. W. Bray, *A History of English Critical Terms* (Boston, 1898), pp. 221-23, for a discussion of the term, with examples of its use in different periods.

[84] *Monthly Magazine,* I, 229.

[85] *Ibid.,* I, 227.

[86] *Ibid.,* I, 228.

[87] *Ibid.,* I, 229.

[88] *Ibid.,* I (May, 1799), 136.

[89] My count shows eighty-one. Professor Clark has depended on the indexes, which in several instances

place more than one poem under a single title. Doubt-less he intends the names Mathilda, Della Cruscan, etc., to be typical, as no such names appear. Only two poems are signed with this type of name—one, Calista, the other, Juvenia (September, 1800).

[90] This was the piece entitled "On my own Miniature Picture, Taken at two Years of Age"; it appeared in Vol. I (June, 1799), 240.

[91] Moore's "Lines Written on Leaving Philadelphia" (issue for January, 1805; no author given) have some interest as reflecting his American visit.

[92] Abstract of thesis, p. 41.

[93] Review of Low's *Poems, Monthly Mag.,* II (Oct., 1800), 266.

[94] "Sketch of American Literature for 1807," *American Register,* II, 159.

[95] "Notices of American Writers and Publications," *Literary Magazine,* II (August, 1804), 345.

[96] VI, 57.

[97] "Notices of American Writers and Publications," *Lit. Mag.,* II (August, 1804), 344.

[98] "Literary . . . Intelligence," *Monthly Mag.,* III (Sept., 1800), 234.

[99] III, 480.

[100] *Univ. of Texas Bul.,* No. 2743, p. 172. Professor Goodnight finds that in eighteenth century America German literature was almost wholly ignored. "Only occasional works, as Gessner's *Death of Abel,* and Goethe's *Werter,* find temporary favor. The writers most generally known, Gessner, Lavater and Goethe (*Werter*), illustrate well the literary tastes of the age, of which the chief characteristics were pietism and sentimental-ism.

"The most striking phenomenon of the first quarter of the new century is the vogue of Kotzebue's plays and Schiller's *Robbers.* These antagonized the Puritanic element and were vigorously attacked, but held their place in the regard of the theatre-going public re-markably well, especially the Kotzebue dramas in Dunlap's skillful rendering. But, with a few striking exceptions . . . the first two decades show little sym-pathy for German literature in general, the general attitude being well shown by the article of 1816 ["On the State of Polite Literature in Germany," *The Portico* (Baltimore), II, 17-25], which declares all Ger-man writers, with the single exception of Gessner, to be utterly deficient in taste." Scott H. Goodnight,

German Literature in American Magazines Prior to 1846 (Madison, Wisconsin, 1907), p. 105.

[101] *Monthly Magazine,* II (April, 1800), 284-87.

[102] With the aid of Professor Clark; he quotes (*Univ. of Texas Bul.,* No. 2743, pp. 172-73) another passage as, presumably, from one of these reviews, which, how-ever, I am unable to locate.

[103] Review of "Pizarro in Peru . . . a Play . . . From the German of Kotzebue, by William Dunlap," *Monthly Mag.,* III (Dec., 1800), 454-55.

[104] *Ibid.,* p. 454.

[105] *Wieland,* p. 7.

[106] *Ibid.,* p. 63.

[107] *Ibid.,* p. 88.

[108] "A Student's Diary," *Literary Mag.,* I (Dec., 1803), 165.

[109] *Ibid.,* p. 164.

[110] III (Oct., 1800), 265.

[111] Letter to the editor announcing *Skywalk, Weekly Magazine,* I (March, 17, 1798), 202.

[112] Prefatory "Advertisement."

[113] Dated Sept. 1, 1803. Quoted with pious approval by Prescott, *Biographical and Critical Miscellanies,* new ed. (Boston, 1857), p. 42.

[114] Review of Linn's "The Death of Washington, a poem in imitation of the manner of Ossian," *Monthly Mag.,* II (April, 1800), 307. See above, p. 561, on Kotzebue; shall we judge him by the rules of Aristotle, or not?

[115] Review of Caldwell's "Eulogium on . . . Cooper," *Monthly Magazine,* I (April, 1799), 51.

[116] Preface (dated May 20, 1809) to Vol. IV. Professor Clark says (Abstract of Thesis, p. 42) that Brown could be severe, basing his opinion on a review of John Searson's poem *Mount Vernon* and on the review of Linn's *Washington.* The first is a notice of ten or a dozen lines in which Brown calls the poem "the intel-lectual drivellings of a harmless simpleton" (*Monthly Mag.,* III, 144). These, so far as I have discovered, are the harshest words Brown ever wrote. Linn's piece he would "not very earnestly condemn."

[116a] Webster replied in nine pages (*Monthly Mag.,* III [Nov., 1800], 332-40) to Brown's strictures on the bad

organization of his *History of Epidemic . . . Diseases,* and on his lack of technical knowledge.

[117] "Dialogues of the Living, No. II," *Monthly Mag.,* II (Feb., 1800), 97.

[118] Abstract of Thesis, p. 41. In his later paper in the *University of Texas Bulletin* (pp. 166-67) the phrase is not "nearly always," but "always to be relied upon."

[119] *University of Texas Bulletin,* No. 2743, p. 166.

[120] Abstract of Thesis, p. 42.

Arthur Hobson Quinn (essay date 1936)

SOURCE: "Charles Brockden Brown and the Establishment of Romance," in *American Fiction: An Historical and Critical Survey,* D. Appleton-Century Company, 1936, pp. 25-39.

[*In the following essay, Quinn argues that Brown's novels reflect his interest in both the romance genre and in American material. Quinn goes on to study the romantic elements of* Wieland, Arthur Mervyn, Edgar Huntly, *and* Ormond.]

The foundations of American fiction were laid by writers who, with few exceptions, were the creators of one novel, or were sporadic in their efforts. In the work of Charles Brockden Brown, however, we have the professional man of letters, with an achievement which may be estimated in terms both of quality and quantity.

That he wrote romances was of course inevitable. But in speaking of his work as romantic, it is important to employ this misused term correctly. Much confusion would be avoided if the name "romantic" were kept to describe the material of a novelist who rejects the familiar in order to secure the interest which is given to the strange or the new. Its antithesis is not "realistic" but "classic," if again we use that term, in its proper sense, to signify that material which attracts a reader through his familiarity with it and allows him to exercise the faculty of recognition, just as the romantic material kindles the faculties of wonder and surprise. "Realistic" and "idealistic" should be preserved for the methods of treatment, for they adequately describe, on the one hand, a faithful depiction of life, and, on the other, a heightened portraiture which emphasizes one trait, often to the exclusion of others. Fiction may be romantic in its selection of material, and either realistic or idealistic in its treatment. Usually romantic material and idealistic treatment are united, as in *Ivanhoe* or *The Last of the Mohicans,* and classic material and realistic treatment, as in *Silas Marner* or *The Rise of Silas Lapham;* but when the unexpected combinations

occur, as in *The Scarlet Letter*—where selection of romantic material is developed through the realistic portrayal of character, or in *Bleak House*—where familiar life is depicted through types as well as individuals, we often have the greatest productions of fiction.

True romance, while it deals with the unusual, is not an inartistic departure from truth, but is based upon truth, for when it is a deliberate departure from exact fact, the result is often the discovery or the suggestion of a truth more profound than fact. By the time Brown began to write **Wieland,** romance in English fiction had passed from the absurd impossibilities of *The Castle of Otranto* into the prosaic explanations of *The Mysteries of Udolpho,* and the tentative approach in the work of American novelists to new fields, such as Indian warfare, the frontier, and the history of the Revolution, has been already noted.

Charles Brockden Brown was born in Philadelphia, January 17, 1771. He was a great reader, and matured rapidly from an intellectual point of view. Those who are disconcerted at the precocity of his heroes forget that Brown saw nothing improbable in the language of Arthur Mervyn, for at the age of ten he apparently talked in the same way. The extraordinary activity of his mind was fostered by his custom of taking long walks in the neighborhood of Philadelphia, where the habit of brooding over ideas drawn from his reading resulted in abstractions often powerful and often absurd.[1] This quality again was transferred to his heroes, as well as the tendency toward tuberculosis which led to the solitary rambles in the open air. Brown was educated by reading; he speaks scornfully of the routine of college training, which he never had; what he needed most was advice which would have taught him some principles of construction. He was greatest at planning and, while his projected epics on the discovery of America, on the conquest of Peru and on the conquest of Mexico, which he had outlined at the age of sixteen, did not materialize, they show his preference for American scenes.

It is not surprising that the first native professional novelist in the United States should have hesitated before he devoted himself to the sphere in which his real strength lay. Novels, like plays, were still frowned upon by a large part of the respectables of the time. Seventeen years later Scott was to publish *Waverley* anonymously. The profession of the novelist in America simply did not exist, and Brown's first claim to our consideration rests upon his foundation of that profession.

To understand him thoroughly one must read his journals, his beginnings in essay and essay-like fiction, recorded in the magazines or in the sympathetic biography by his friend William Dunlap, who was endeavoring to lay the foundations of our drama. Brown's extended visits to New York brought him into contact with the group of writers who formed the Friendly Club, and gave him inspiration for the large amount of work which he accomplished from 1797 to 1800. His letters then and later, to Dunlap, to John Howard Payne, as well as his deep friendship for Elihu Hubbard Smith, reflect that mutual encouragement which was building up, under such discouraging circumstances, the beginnings of national literature.

In *The Man at Home,* published anonymously in *The Weekly Magazine* from February 3 to April 28, 1798, Brown introduces the pestilence of 1793 and, in the relation of the death of M. de Moivre and the miseries of his daughter, points forward to incidents later developed in *Arthur Mervyn* and *Ormond.* The teller of the story finds a manuscript account of the Revolution, but Brown, after exciting our interest, stops the narrative. The fragment shows his methods, just as his *Alcuin, a Dialogue on the Rights of Women* (1798), reprinted in part in the *Weekly,* with additions, reveals his Federalist leanings and shows his interest in reforming the institution of marriage, although, as is usual in such discussions, he provides no remedy or substitute. That he never completed a projected romance, of which Dunlap gives sample passages, is not to be regretted. While the letters passing from "Jessy" to "Sophia" or "Julia" reveal some knowledge of feminine psychology, they are not really interesting.

That Brown was prompted by native inspiration is shown in a letter by "Speratus," which is probably his. He speaks of a new work to be projected by him and continues:

> To the story telling moralist the United States is a new and untrodden field. He who shall examine objects with his own eyes, who shall employ the European models merely for the improvement of his taste, and adapt his fiction to all that is genuine and peculiar in the scene before him, will be entitled at least to the praise of originality.[2]

Of the many forms which romance may assume, Brown used chiefly the deliberate selection of remarkable incidents of contemporary life. His first completed story, *Wieland* (1798), was based in part upon an actual occurrence. A farmer in Tomhannock, New York, suddenly went crazy under the influence of two angels whom he saw in a bright light and who urged him to "destroy his idols." He killed his horses, then his children and his wife, and, visiting his sister with apparent intent to destroy her, was captured and confined as a lunatic. What makes the novel important, however, is not one incident, but the portrayal of the soul of Wieland. When he was quite young his father was killed, apparently by a supernatural agency, because he had failed to obey a mysterious command

which produced in his soul a dreadful conflict. Wieland's life, however, passed peacefully on the outskirts of Philadelphia, with his wife Catherine, his children, and his sister Clara, who is the narrator of the story. Clara describes the effects of a mysterious voice which is heard by herself, her brother Wieland, and Henry Pleyel, his brother-in-law, with whom she is in love. It resounds especially in her own room, upon a terrace, and in the "Temple," which Wieland's father had built. It warns Wieland not to go to Lusatia to claim a great inheritance; it convinces Henry Pleyel of Clara's illicit relationship to a certain Carwin, who has taken up his abode in the neighborhood. It appears to save her from evil, and yet it plunges her into misery. Brown shows his ability in working up to a climax. Wieland, brooding over the messages he has received and animated by the memory of his father's death, is ripe for the reception of abnormal suggestions. They come from the same voice, which tells him, "Thy prayers are heard. In proof of thy faith, render me thy wife. This is the victim, I chuse. Call her hither, and here let her fall." He kills his wife and his children, and goes to Clara's house to kill her. She is warned, as she enters the house, in a scene which shows Brown's ability to write effective narrative:

> I have said that I cast a look behind. Some object was expected to be seen, or why should I have gazed in that direction? Two senses were at once assailed. The same piercing exclamation of *hold! hold!* was uttered within the same distance of my ear. This it was that I heard. The airy undulation, and the shock given to my nerves, were real. Whether the spectacle which I beheld existed in my fancy or without, might be doubted.

> I had not closed the door of the apartment I had just left. The stair-case, at the foot of which I stood, was eight or ten feet from the door, and attached to the wall through which the door led. My view, therefore, was sidelong, and took in no part of the room.

> Through this aperture was an head thrust and drawn back with so much swiftness, that the immediate conviction was, that thus much of a form, ordinarily invisible, had been unshrouded. The face was turned towards me. Every muscle was tense; the forehead and brows were drawn into vehement expression; the lips were stretched as in the act of shrieking, and the eyes emitted sparks, which, no doubt, if I had been unattended by a light, would have illuminated like the coruscations of a meteor. The sound and the vision were present, and departed together at the same instant; but the cry was blown into my ear, while the face was many paces distant.

Wieland is confined but escapes, and Clara is saved once more from him by Carwin's powers as a ventriloquist.[3] To some critics, this natural explanation of the mysterious voice is irritating. But when Brown used the device, it had not been so definitely associated with trickery, and the scene in which Carwin through its use strips Wieland of the illusion that had lifted him into a state of moral ecstasy and brings him to suicide is masterly. Clara marries Pleyel ultimately, and Carwin sinks out of sight.

The theme of ventriloquism was treated again in the fragment *Carwin the Biloquist,* published in Brown's magazine (1803-1805) but according to Dunlap's Diary, being in manuscript in 1798. This is an account of the early life of Carwin, who is led to the exercise of his power by an echo heard in his youth. The main interest of the fragment lies, however, in the relations of Carwin to his benefactor, Ludloe, who takes him to Dublin and who is about to initiate him into the secrets of a mysterious society, when the account ceases. The terror which Carwin feels for the possible results of his determination to conceal his exercise of "biloquial" power, knowing that this concealment will render him liable to death if discovered, is not badly done.

Brown's concern with native material is illustrated most definitely, perhaps, by his picture of the yellow fever, in *Arthur Mervyn, or, Memoirs of the Year 1793,* which began to appear in the *Weekly Magazine* in June, 1798, but remained a fragment, owing to the suspension of the journal in August, and was published in two parts in 1799 and 1800. The fever is not merely a background; it makes probable the sudden disappearance and reappearance of the characters, and creates that atmosphere of confusion, in which anything may happen, which suited admirably the peculiar gifts of Brown. Moreover, the brooding sense of terror which hangs over the city is an accessory to romance. The romantic material and the highly idealized characters are held in check by the realistic description of the plague, not to be surpassed until Weir Mitchell wrote *The Red City.* The description of the fugitives as Mervyn enters the city, the loathsome details of the hospital, tie the novel to earth. Brown had escaped the plague in Philadelphia in 1793, but he had suffered from it in 1798 in New York, and he simply transferred his experience to his native city. He was exposed to the infection through the generous action of his friend Elihu H. Smith, the physician and playwright, who took an Italian, Dr. Scandella, into the house where both the friends were living. Brown used the incidents of Scandella's death in *Arthur Mervyn.*

The plot of *Arthur Mervyn* is the most complicated of all Brown's novels. It is told partly by Dr. Steevens and partly by Arthur Mervyn, a boy of nineteen whom Steevens finds near his door, stricken with the fever. Suspicion being cast upon Mervyn, he is practically required to give an account of himself. He has had startling adventures, mainly in connection with a cer-

tain Welbeck, who has betrayed, robbed or murdered nearly every one of his associates. Arthur Mervyn is one of those imperturbable heroes who acts with courage and resourcefulness in all emergencies, but, unlike the striplings of Gothic romance, he fights with his brain rather than his sword. When he faces the brutal uncle of Eliza Hadwin, the girl of fifteen who worships him and whose farm he is trying to save, his clever handling of a man who could have crushed him is a relief from the methods of earlier and later romancers who would have made him, in defiance of all probability, knock his enemy down with one blow.

The influence of *Caleb Williams,* by William Godwin, is more evident in *Arthur Mervyn* than in *Ormond.* Arthur is propelled by an insatiable curiosity disguised, even to himself, as benevolence, and he preserves an almost painfully virtuous attitude toward life, as Caleb does. But he has a loyalty even to Welbeck, to which Caleb is a stranger, and Brown endows him with a reticence in the telling of his relations with women which is refreshing. His solemn announcement to Eliza Hadwin that he is destined to grow in intellectual stature to a height to which she cannot follow him is, of course, absurd, but his ignorance of his attraction for all the other women, except Mrs. Wentworth, who thinks he is a lunatic, is not the least of his merits. In her eyes, which were those of the eighteenth century, anyone who tried to benefit others without reward was a lunatic. But here, as in Eliza Hadwin's vigorous putting of the woman's position, Brown was in advance of the social and humanitarian progress of the time. With all its inconsistencies and lack of unity, *Arthur Mervyn* holds our interest through two volumes, and the central character remains of all his creations longest in our memory.[4] And it must always be remembered that when Hawthorne placed the bust of its creator in his Hall of Fantasy, with Homer, Shakespeare, Fielding and Scott, it was as "the author of *Arthur Mervyn.*"

According to Dunlap, *Ormond* (1799) was completed in December, 1798, while *Arthur Mervyn* was still in the making. The yellow fever is once more used as a background, but while the details are told with Brown's usual realistic portraiture, the pestilence is used only as a means of heightening the difficulties of Constantia Dudley and her father. Constantia, who excited such warm praise from Shelley, combines the qualities of a real woman with those of an ideal heroine. She meets calamity with energy, and, while her calm disregard of Ormond's desertion of his mistress, Helena, and the latter's suicide, seems at first incredible, it accords with her usual acceptance of the accomplished fact. Constantia's growing interest in Ormond, who loads her with benefits, is no more out of keeping than is her final defence of her honor in the lonely dwelling where he meets death at her hands. Ormond, on the contrary, is so much a bundle of oddities that he hardly comes alive. Brown tried to draw in Ormond a superman, strong and completely selfish, but his hero remains an abstraction, whose conversation is usually absurd. The supposed resemblance to Godwin's Falkland in *Caleb Williams* is slight. Falkland is much more human, and the fundamental differences between the characters are greater than any superficial resemblances.

In *Edgar Huntly* (1799) Brown once more based his novel upon a human aberration from the normal, that of sleep-walking. At the very beginning he drew with uncommon power the picture of the sleep-walker, Clithero, through the eyes of Edgar Huntly. At the same time, he secures sympathy with Clithero and establishes the sense of the wonderful. Notice the directness of language:

> He stopt, the spade fell from his hand, he looked up and bent forward his face towards the spot where I stood. An interview and explanation were now, me thought, unavoidable. I mustered up my courage to confront and interrogate this being.

> He continued for a minute in his gazing and listening attitude. Where I stood I could not fail of being seen, and yet he acted as if he saw nothing. Again he betook himself to his spade, and proceeded with new diligence to fill up the pit. This demeanor confounded and bewildered me. I had no power but to stand and silently gaze upon his motions.

> The pit being filled, he once more sat upon the ground, and resigned himself to weeping and sighs with more vehemence than before. In a short time the fit seemed to have passed. He rose, seized the spade, and advanced to the spot where I stood.

> Again I made preparation as for an interview which could not but take place. He passed me, however, without appearing to notice my existence. He came so near as almost to brush my arm, yet turned not his head to either side. My nearer view of him made his brawny arms and lofty stature more conspicuous; but his imperfect dress, the dimness of the light, and the confusion of my own thoughts, hindered me from discerning his features. He proceeded with a few quick steps along the road, but presently darted to one side and disappeared among the rocks and bushes.

The story of Clithero, which he is required to tell, because he is under suspicion of the murder of Waldegrave, the brother of Huntly's fiancée, is a novel in itself, and is woven into the main narrative with more skill than is usual with Brown. The search which Huntly institutes for this strange being, who is haunted with the sense of guilt for the murder of the mistress whom he had loved, leads to one of the best passages in Brown's novels, that in which Huntly finds himself at the bottom of a pit,

without any memory of recent events. The reader suspects that Huntly has become a sleep-walker, but Brown's art is such that, although the motive has been introduced earlier, there is no prosaic explanation as there was in *Wieland.* Huntly's description of the pit proceeds by that effective method of denying the natural order which Poe was to use so often. The following events, including his escape from the Indians who are at the mouth of the cave, his rescue of the captive, his killing of the Indians, his flight down and across the Delaware, finally come to a point where credulity begins to cease. The last part of the novel is not up to the level of the beginning. But the Indians, including "Old Deb," are painted in real colors, and the motive of revenge for Huntly's parents who have been their victims is introduced sufficiently well. This element in the story was its germ, as the fragment published in his *Monthly Magazine*[5] indicates.

Clara Howard (1801) and *Jane Talbot* (1801) are not to be ranked with the four other completed romances. The first is the expansion of a minor incident in *Edgar Huntly,* and both are love stories, for which Brown had no especial talent. In fact, the characters seem absurd, especially in their letters and conversations. The establishment of the wonderful in terms of the natural is absent from both of them, and while one cannot help sympathizing with Philip Stanley, bewildered between two women, each apparently trying to renounce him in favor of the other, while they are really holding on to him at the same time, one soon loses patience even with him.

Of more interest are the fragments, in some cases of considerable length, which reveal Brown's power in other directions. **"Thessalonica"**[6] is a vivid description of the massacre of the people of this Roman city about 400 A.D. and shows not only Brown's ability to sketch the development of a great tragedy from a trivial occurrence, but also proved his power to visualize an historic period. The power was evidenced even more clearly in the **"Sketches of a History of Carsol,"** which Dunlap states was written later than 1800. It is an account of an imaginary kingdom, laid in an island in the Mediterranean, which goes back to pre-Roman days and has been governed successively by Romans, Vandals, Saracens and the descendants of Charles Martel. The interest which Brown excites in the purely imaginary history is due to the singular air of reality which he succeeds in creating, and to the direct style, free from his usual eccentricities. So plausible is his narrative method that it seems as though there should have been such a country. By constantly referring to actual sovereigns of other countries as contemporary, he gives an additional sense of historic accuracy. His social ideas have here an outlet, also. His ideal seems to be that of a despotism ruled by a virtuous and enlightened prince, who subdues the barons and secures uniformity and harmony in religious and economic life. Belonging to the same category, but not quite so successful, are the **"Sketches of a History of the Carrils and Ormes,"** an account of an imaginary earldom in England. Evidently not revised, for there are many inconsistencies, it afforded Brown another opportunity to express his ideals of society, and it reveals a knowledge of architecture of respectable proportions.

The most striking characteristics of Brown are his remarkable inventive power, his ability at description and narration, his sympathy and understanding of human beings laboring under powerful emotions, and the art with which he made even the impossible seem probable. No one save a superman could have survived the exploits of Edgar Huntly and Arthur Mervyn, but we forget these facts as we read. His achievement can be realized only by those who study not only his completed novels, all composed in three years, but also the shorter tales, essays and criticism with which, usually anonymously, he filled the pages of *The Weekly Magazine* and *The Monthly Magazine.* His wide interest, in topics native and foreign, is revealed also in his later editorship of *The Literary Magazine and American Register* (1803-1807), although by this time his period of fiction was largely over.

He was, to use his own expression in *Edgar Huntly,* a "moral painter." His fine spirit, shot through with aspirations for the best in thought and life, poured itself out not only in the pleas for right living which too often impede the progress of his narrative, but, more effectively, in the creation of his characters. They are the incarnations of his love of duty which seeks no reward but the securing of an invincible self-respect. Brown knew, however, that rectitude was not enough to secure for his characters interest and sympathy. He endowed them, therefore, with courage, a love of adventure and, above all, curiosity. The importance of this quality in fiction lies in its being an active, even a driving force. It is not an endearing trait—as he remarks in *Edgar Huntly,* "Curiosity, like virtue, is its own reward." But without it, Clara Wieland, Arthur Mervyn, Constantia Dudley, Edgar Huntly, would be impossible. It keeps the novels moving rapidly, for notwithstanding all dangers and rebuffs, his characters dare fever and famine, savages and supermen, lofty mountains and dim vaults, to find out what they wish to know. Brown imbued his characters with curiosity deliberately. He remarks in his first book, *Alcuin,* "But though we may strive, we can never wholly extinguish, in women, the best principle of human nature, curiosity."

Brown's novels are a protest against the tyranny of narrow minds. In the same magazine in which vehement protests were printed against Thomas Jefferson's candidacy for the Presidency because of his attitude toward orthodox religion, Brown was contending in *Arthur Mervyn* for the intellectual rights of the individual. Arthur Mervyn "could not part with the privilege of observing and thinking for himself," and the same character remarks, apropos of certain slanders circulated in his town, "It was sufficient that the censure of my neighbors was unmerited, to make me regard it with indifference." Wieland and his sister, Constantia and her father, Ormond, Achsa Fielding, Edgar Huntly all arrange their lives without reference to public or private criticism. They suffer in consequence, but it is to be noticed that Eliza Hadwin, who is perhaps closest to the average woman in her nature, is left at the end of *Arthur Mervyn* unrewarded for her obedience and a prey to her emotions. It is easy to attribute this tendency to revolt to his reading of Godwin and his school, but to attribute to foreign inspiration such an impulse on the part of an American novelist who was born three years before Lexington was fought and who grew up in the atmosphere of the last two decades of the eighteenth century in Philadelphia and New York is really unnecessary. That the influence in the case of Godwin and Brown was mutual has often been shown.[7]

That Brown was conscious of his native inspiration is evident. In the preface to *Edgar Huntly* he says:

> America has opened new views to the naturalist and politician, but has seldom furnished themes to the moral painter. That new springs of action, and new motives to curiosity should operate; that the field of investigation, opened to us by our own country, should differ essentially from those which exist in Europe, may be readily conceived. The sources of amusement to the fancy and instruction to the heart, that are peculiar to ourselves, are equally numerous and inexhaustible. It is the purpose of this work to profit by some of these sources; to exhibit a series of adventures, growing out of the condition of our country, and connected with one of the most common and wonderful diseases or affections of the human frame.

> One merit the writer may at least claim; that of calling forth the passions and engaging the sympathy of the reader, by means hitherto unemployed by preceding authors. Puerile superstition and exploded manners; Gothic castles and chimeras, are the materials usually employed for this end. The incidents of Indian hostility, and the perils of the western wilderness, are far more suitable; and, for a native of America to overlook these, would admit of no apology. These, therefore, are, in part, the ingredients of this tale, and these he has been ambitious of depicting in vivid and faithful colors. The success of his efforts must be estimated by the liberal and candid reader.

Too much stress entirely has been laid upon the foreign influences upon Brockden Brown. The supposed resemblance of *Wieland* to Schiller's *Der Geisterseher* vanishes upon a reading of them both. He knew German literature, but to call his novels "Gothic" is a

facile but not significant classification. His mention of the novels of "Mademoiselle Scuderi" as powerfully affecting the nature of Stephen Calvert might be misleading if he did not also give us the names of the leading characters, "Statira, Lysimachus and Perdiccas,"[8] which are found in the novels not of Scuderi but of La Calprenède.

The most serious criticisms that must occur to readers of Brown's novels are, first, the lack of unity in construction and, second, the stilted language often used by the characters. The first defect arose partly through the very wealth of his imagination, which presented enough material for three novels in one. But it came also from his association with periodical literature. If those portions of **Arthur Mervyn** which appeared in *The Weekly Magazine* are read, it will be noticed that, so far as possible, the installments end in such a manner as to pique the curiosity of the reader. That Brown began to publish his fiction before it was completed is shown not only here, but in his **Memoirs of Stephen Calvert,** whose progress through *The Monthly Magazine* was interrupted in May, 1800, and a note inserted which is little better than an advertisement.

The effect upon his work was on the whole unfortunate. The stopping of the dramatic scene in **Ormond,** when Constantia kills Ormond in defence of her honor, and the return to Sophia's narrative with the words, "It will be requisite to withdraw your attention from this scene for a moment and fix it on myself," is artificial to say the least. In any criticism of his novels for their lack of unity, the fact that they were written with the possibility of periodical publication in mind, must not be overlooked.

His style, while no one would care to defend it in its pompous moments, is to be judged again in the light of the delusion current at the time that the expression of moral truth endowed the fictional character who possessed it with a dilated vocabulary. Indeed, a supreme artist like Jane Austen was not entirely free from this opinion. Brown could write direct and stirring narrative, or vivid descriptions of scenery, but he seemed to lose his skill as soon as his characters open their mouths. Here again the fact that practically all his work is communicated by one character to another in letters had a tendency to add to its formality.

Brown's later activities as editor and his writings on public questions fall outside our province. They show his ability as a close reasoner, and his prophecy of our future continental expansion reveals his imaginative power. He died on February 22, 1809, a victim to tuberculosis.

Brown's influence upon later writers was noteworthy. Thomas Love Peacock has made clear the deep impression his fiction made upon Percy Shelley:

Brown's four novels, Schiller's *Robbers* and Goethe's *Faust* were, of all the works with which he was familiar, those which took the deepest root in his mind and had the strongest influence in the foundation of his character. . . .

Nothing so blended itself with the structure of his interior mind as the creations of Brown. Nothing stood so clearly before his thoughts as a perfect combination of the purely ideal and possibly real as Constantia Dudley.[9]

Brown's general influences upon Shelley's immature prose romances, *Zastrozzi* (1810) and *St. Irvyne,* are purely conjectural, since we do not know exactly when he read Brown's works. The habits of the characters like Verezzi, who takes long walks in the woods, runs several miles after escaping from a cave, and is prompted by an unusual curiosity, and the escape of Wolfstein and Megalena from the robbers' cave might have been prompted by Brown's novels. But they also might be due to other influences. Since we know from Peacock's testimony that "the summer house in **Wieland** made a great impression on Shelley," "the altar and the temple bright" in *Rosalind and Helen* seems more definite an inspiration. The vivid description of the pestilence in *The Revolt of Islam,* Canto X, especially those stanzas which describe the immolation by the sufferers of their own "infidel kindred" to appease the god, and the influence of terror which produced death even without infection, may owe its inspiration to Shelley's memories of **Wieland, Ormond,** and **Arthur Mervyn.**

In the list of books read by Mary Wollstonecraft Shelley in 1815, **Wieland** and **Ormond** appear,[10] and in her romance of *The Last Man* the description of the pestilence shows the influence of **Ormond** and **Arthur Mervyn.** Her own testimony is direct, for the imaginary narrator who describes the plague which at the end of the twenty-first century destroys the human race tells us:

While every mind was full of dismay at its effects, a craving for excitement had led us to peruse DeFoe's account, and the masterly delineations of the author of **Arthur Mervyn.**[11]

The approach of Lionel Verney to London, and the description of the hospital, are in the manner of Brown.

Brown's immediate influence upon American fiction was not marked. It is possible that his insistence upon American themes may have animated such visitors as John Davis, an Englishman who insisted upon the fact that "The United States is the country of my literary birth." Davis came to New York in 1798,[12] and proceeded to turn his wanderings in America, which appear to have been extensive, into narrative which can

be called fiction only through courtesy. In *The Farmer of New Jersey* (1800), a domestic tale laid in New Jersey and Georgia, written with such haste that he forgets the names of his characters and has to publish a list of corrections, he introduces the Pocahontas story through one of the characters. In 1805 he developed this theme in *Captain Smith and the Princess Pocahontas*, expanded with revisions into *The First Settlers of Virginia* (1805). These are little more than rearrangements of Captain John Smith's *General History of Virginia*, with a desperate attempt to create a love story between Smith and Pocahontas. Davis was intensely interested in the Indians, and in his *Walter Kennedy* (1805) he takes his hero through the southwestern tribes, even marrying him to Oosnoqua of the Kaskaskias tribe, at the end. The various editions of Davis's books attest their popularity, but their realism rather than any constructive ability must account for it.

Certainly an absurd production like *The Asylum; or, Alonzo and Melissa* (1811)[13] by Isaac Mitchell (c. 1759-1812) stems from Mrs. Radcliffe and not from Brown. This love story of a young Yale student with the daughter of a cruel father is laid partly in a Gothic castle mysteriously located near Long Island Sound. The shrouded figures in Melissa's bedroom, her seeming death, Alonzo's foreign trip where he meets Franklin, and their final marriage are told in an older manner. Equally as unaffected by Brown's firm grasp of his material was Samuel Woodworth's *The Champions of Freedom, or, The Mysterious Chief* (1816), a romance purporting to deal with the events of the War of 1812, with a backward glance at the Revolution. George Washington Willoughby, "a child of nature," is subjected to as many dangers from the opposite sex as the heroine of the seduction romance, but his escapes from a brothel and the battlefield do not make him quite immune. When a married flirt pursued him to the army, Woodworth remarks:

> I have never asserted that my hero was more than a man. Sophia conquered. Let fastidious virtue close the volume. I write nothing but the truth.

Somewhat better is *Laura* by "a Lady of Philadelphia" (1809), and here the description of the yellow fever in Philadelphia is reminiscent of Brown and has some reality. *Kelroy* (1812), by "a Lady of Pennsylvania," stands out even more definitely from its contemporaries. It has no seduction to its discredit, and the character of Mrs. Hammond, the mother who deliberately spends her capital in two years in order to marry her daughters advantageously, then wrecks Emily's happiness because of her hatred for her intended son-in-law, Kelroy, is a real person. The book has been attributed to Rebecca Rush, daughter of the famous physician of that day.

Brown's influence upon Poe was definite, as a comparison of the fifteenth chapter of **Edgar Huntly** with "The Pit and the Pendulum" will indicate. Hawthorne's tribute in "The Hall of Fantasy" is sufficient evidence of his study of his predecessor in the novel of human conscience. Through the nature of Poe and Hawthorne, the influence of Brown was principally of a general character. But his very existence was an inspiration to the American novelist. Without any strong love interest in his fiction, with a scorn for the sentimental excursions into the sensual with which he was surrounded, he proved that an artist could depict with insight and sympathy a human soul under temptation to commit crime or bending under the load of crime already committed. Under his touch the abnormal took on dignity. Wieland's defence at the trial while he is still insane, Clara Pleyel's fear that she herself is going insane, are not unworthy of the two greater artists who succeeded him in the treatment of such themes.

Notes

[1] "Overpowered with fatigue, I am prompted to seek relief in walking, and my mind untuned and destitute of energy, is lost in a dreary confusion of images." Letter V, *Weekly Magazine,* II (May 5, 1798), II.

[2] *Weekly Magazine,* I (March 17, 1798), 202.

[3] Brown does not use this term. He speaks of Biloquism or ventrilocution, the idea of which he seems to have obtained by reading the work of the Abbé de la Chappelle.

[4] See Brown's defence of the probability of certain incidents in his letter to his brother, February 15, 1799, printed in Dunlap's *Life,* Vol. II, pp. 98-100.

[5] I (April, 1799), 21-44.

[6] *Monthly Magazine,* I (May, 1799), 99-117.

[7] See Godwin's Introduction to his own novel, *Mandeville.*

[8] William Dunlap, *Life of Charles Brockden Brown,* Vol. II, p. 389.

[9] Peacock, T. L., *Memoir of Percy Bysshe Shelley, Works,* ed. by H. Cole (1875), Vol. III, pp. 409-410.

[10] *Letters of Mary W. Shelley,* Int. by Henry H. Harper (The Bibliophile Society, Boston, MDCDXVIII), pp. 11-12.

[11] *The Last Man,* by the author of *Frankenstein,* Vol. II, p. 208.

[12] See his "A Voyage from Bristol to New York," *Monthly Magazine,* III (1800), 167-172.

¹³ Published first over his own signature as "Alonzo and Melissa," in *The Political Barometer,* a weekly paper of Poughkeepsie, New York, in 1804. A pirated version was published in 1811 by Daniel Jackson, Jr. and was reprinted at late as 1876. See article by D. S. Rankin in *Dictionary of American Biography,* Vol. XIV.

Lulu Rumsey Wiley (essay date 1950)

SOURCE: "Methods of Composition," in *The Sources and Influence of the Novels of Charles Brockden Brown,* Vantage Press, 1950, pp. 189-206.

[*In the following essay, Wiley appraises the plots, characters, and style of Brown's novels, contending that his plots are "original, exceptional, and forceful," although they lack coherence. Wiley also notes that Brown's style may seem inflated, but that it reflects the "prevalent pedantry of the times."*]

The plots of Brown's novels are original, exceptional and forceful, though defective in unity of design. Each main narrative consists of a series of episodes slightly connected with each other, but all connected to the purpose and developing it. They are like clothes hanging on a line, grouped, however, as a good housewife would hang them. A contemporary of Brown, Royall Tyler, said of him:

He never mastered the art of fiction well enough to produce a book that deserved anything more than the name of narrative.

Brown may have been negligent of his plots, but he certainly was never at a loss for a breath-taking adventure or for creating suspense,—not inferior to Cooper in this respect. The incidents of his novels are many of them dramatic, yet he made little attempt to dramatize his plots. He makes a conscious effort in *Edgar Huntly.* Dramatic terms are used in the story; for example,—

To comprehend it (the "drama in which his mind was busy") demands penetration into the recesses of his soul. . . . Was the narrative of Clithero the web of imposture or the raving of insanity? . . . He had appeared. The strange being is again upon the stage."   "I was left to mark the progress of the drama. . . . At length the drama is brought to an imperfect close, and the series of events that absorbed my faculties ("my mind had been the theatre") . . . has terminated in repose.

A few other times the words—drama, stage and scene—are found here and in his other novels, as in *Wieland:* "this the stage on which that enemy of man (Carwin) showed himself for a moment unmasked."

These words of the author are relevant in this connection, when the press was publishing each part as fast as he could supply it:

I commenced something in the form of a Romance. I had at first no definitive conceptions of my design. As my pen proceeded forward, my invention was tasked, and the materials that it afforded were arranged and digested. Fortunately I continued to view this scheme in the same light in which it had at first presented itself. Time therefore did not diminish its attractions. The facility I experienced in composition, and the perception of daily progress, encouraged me, and my task was finished on the last day of December. . . . It was at first written in a hasty and inaccurate way. Before I can submit it to a printer, or even satisfactorily rehearse it to a friend, it must be wholly transcribed. I am at present engaged in this employment. I am afraid as much time will be required by it, as was necessary to the original composition.¹

One might think he had in mind the words of Sterne when he began *Tristram Shandy,* "with no real idea of how it was to turn out." He also said in that novel (Chapter 19, p. 2): "Writers had need look before them, to keep up the spirit and connection of what they have in hand."

In strong contrast to this obvious irregularity of plot is Brown's ever-present, ever-evolving moral or psychological purpose, as illustrated in the treatment of Clithero mentioned above. The author always had a purpose, if not always a plan. Griswold wrote: "the metaphysical unity and consistency of his novels are apparent to all readers familiar with psychological phenomena."² This predetermined purpose or aim has the advantage of giving such an air of truth that his readers almost forget that they are not reading statements of some serious matter of fact and are unconscious of the abnormal phases of the subject. Brown "is inferior to all great story tellers in his sacrifice of universal truth to the situation, the moment,"³ remarked Blake. It would seem that Brown had not sacrificed the truth, but rather had not sufficiently elaborated it or had too many truths.

"In sheer power of gripping plots and masterful climaxes Brown has few superiors. His weakness, on the other hand, lies in his inability to resolve his plots and scenes into their realizable effects," said David Lee Clark in his Introduction to *Edgar Huntly.*

One reason for Brown's lack of plot unity was his not having in mind the completed story in the beginning, which led to necessary changes of plan in the prosecution of the work. Brown completed *Wieland* and three years after the romance itself wrote an additional chapter to clear up the unfinished incidents as promised at the close of the story and put the finishing touches on several characters—Clara and Pleyel, Carwin, Stuart and Maxwell. Another continuation of *Wieland* was made—*Memoirs of Carwin, the Biloquist, a fragment,* of which Brown says in the Advertisement of *Wieland:*

> The memoirs of Carwin, alluded to at the conclusion of the work, will be published or suppressed according to the reception which is given to the present attempt.

In similar fashion, Brown finished *Arthur Mervyn* with its theme of yellow fever and later wrote another volume to conclude the incidents of the first and to give Arthur time and opportunity to perform his benevolences. When Arthur has completed his projects and knows not that Achsa loves him and that he loves her, Dr. Stevens apprises him of the fact in dramatic terms: "This scene is quite new. . . . This is a necessary part of the drama," showing Brown's intention to unwind the story with the expected love-marriage ending. The episodical style in this book was due to the fact that Brown had published the early chapters as a series, as he had done with earlier writings, like *The Rhapsodist, The Rights of Women* and *Sky-Walk.* So this style became a habit. Besides, it was found effective in sustaining the interest of his readers. Parts of several of his novels were published in magazines serially, which accounts for the large number of striking incidents or crises at intervals,—also for the lack of well-developed plot construction and likewise for the author's lack of time for sufficient revision and transcription.

Dunlap, with whom Brown lived for a time and who knew him better than anyone else did, testified to his methods:

> He began to write a novel after having only determined upon one leading circumstance, character or idea, and trusted to the growth of one incident from another, and the appropriate sentiments from the incidents. One volume would be finished and printed before he had formed any plan for the beginning of the second, or any plan for the continuation, developement or denouement of the story. . . . It is very evident that this unsystematic mode of composition must give a motley appearance. . . . The parts must occasionally be disproportioned to each other, and incidents imagined which excite great expectations in the reader, and involve the story in mystery, which the author trusting to after thought for the explanation or the sequel, and not finding . . . any adequate solution of difficulty or termination of adventure, the event either does not answer the expectation raised, or the reader is put off with the intimation of a continuation at a future time.[4]

There are episodes which seem irrevelant, as it were, to the plot because they are based on the author's experiences and opinions. Brown was inexpert in portraying familiar characters against his real backgrounds.

The portrayal of unusual characters with reality of settings produces an effect of confusion at times, seen not only in his construction of incidents, but in his designs.

Confusion is also occasioned by the use of the epistolary method, which requires a change of viewpoint with each different letter writer. Clara Wieland tells the Wieland story, but there are introduced confessions of Wieland and Carwin in their own persons. In *Arthur Mervyn,* Arthur relates the history of his own life and of the yellow fever; Dr. Stevens opens both parts of the story and enters at other times; Welbeck's two or three confessions are within Arthur's story; the early life of Arthur is told by a country neighbor woman and then he gives his version of it; in his attempts to alleviate the final distresses of all characters, there is conversation, presenting opposing viewpoints. Despite these "venial faults (dramatic bounds of time and action) the beauties of Arthur Mervyn are splendid,"[5] said Dunlap.

An additional cause of Brown's unskilfully wrought plots, involving cumulative incidents, unfinished incidents and narrative within narrative, was the celerity with which he wrote. Dunlap said that, in the year 1799, Brown had begun five novels, all of which were in a state of progression. Critics agreed that he had no time to perfect either plots or style, due to haste of composition.

The spur that set Brown on his extraordinary spree of writing five novels at once, after *Wieland* was begun, was the immediate popularity at home and abroad of its first chapters. Doubtless, these novels contain much material from his earlier writings or from his pre-contemplated plans and even outlines, as from social and political treatises, evident in *Wieland* and *Ormand,* from *Sky-Walk* in *Edgar Huntly,* from the *Romance* of Sophia and Jessy the Zisca incident in *Wieland* and so on. Brown's writing of all but one of his novels simultaneously speaks in a more forceful way than can any encomium upon the varied talents of the author. It was the exhilirating realization that he had now found a proper medium of expression for the teeming thoughts that circled in his brain and his exuberant youthfulness displaying itself with the thrill of accomplishment.

In a letter to his brother Armit, Brown wrote:

> Some time since I bargained with the publisher of Wieland for a new performance, part of which only was written, and the publication commencing immediately, I was obliged to apply with the utmost diligence to the pen, in order to keep pace with the press. . . . I call my book Ormond, or the Secret Witness. I hope to finish the writing and the publication together before new year's day, when I shall have a breathing spell.[6]

As a commentary justifying Brown's rapidity of writing are words from *Edgar Huntly:*

> In proportion as I gain power over words, shall I lose dominion over sentiments. In proportion as my tale is deliberate and slow, the incidents and motives which it is designed to exhibit will be imperfectly revived and obscurely portrayed.[7]

Although Brown usually contrived thrilling incidents, his object was not the relation of the incidents but the recording of impressions. He uses the word "sentiments."

Scott's method a few years later reflects that of Brown. He said after completing the second volume of *Woodstock:*

> Now I haven't the slightest idea how the story is to be wound up to a catastrophe. . . . I never could lay down a plan. . . . I only tried to make that which I was actually writing diverting and interesting, leaving the rest to fate. . . . When I chain my mind to ideas which are purely imaginary, . . . I think away the whole vivacity and spirit of my original conception, and the results are cold, tame, and spiritless. . . . Wrote to the end of a chapter, and know . . . no more than a man in the moon what comes next. . . . I love to have the press thumping, clattering, and banging in my rear; it creates the necessity which almost always makes me work best.[8]

Writing with the publishers always calling for copy forbade Brown's rounding out events, mysteries, incidents and characters, no doubt to his discomfiture. The words of Clara with regard to her relation by letter of the account of the Wieland family well applies to Brown himself:

> Yet I will persist to the end. My narrative may be invaded by inaccuracy and confusion; but, if I live no longer, I will, at least, live to complete it. What but ambiguities, abruptnesses, and dark transitions, can be expected from the historian who is, at the same time, the sufferer of these disasters?[9]

One may readily speak of Brown as a sufferer, because of his lifelong uncertainty of health and his foreknowledge of consumption ever in the offing. However much the versatility and industry of the author may be admired, the loss of excellence and reputation that it occasions him and the loss of amusement and instruction to his readers must be forever deplored (Dunlap).

Many of Brown's characters are living, assertive beings. A few act as if they were the puppets of superior powers or the victims of a vague and dreadful fatality, almost subservient to the circumstances that surround them, which accords with the author's purpose to study character in unusual situations. He identifies himself with the working of their minds and develops each as a specific, psychological personality troubling himself little to individualize them in the details of their outward lives. He uses them as material in his hands to work out his purposes. In accordance with the characteristics of solitariness, mystery and gloom of his own temperament, he loves to present the heart as desolate, foreboding, self-dependent and at times plotting evil or good. When he would exhibit strength of mind or purpose to most advantage, he takes away all external succour and encircles the person with circumstances that rouse vague apprehensions of danger or uncertainty. The individual must then estimate the approaching evil, comprehend its worst consequences and act accordingly, thus revealing the latent, potential virtue within him. Clara Wieland and Constantia Dudley, for example, have loving, gentle natures, but have also thinking minds, full of resourcefulness, constancy and courage. Arthur Mervyn with no money does many helpful services. Edgar Huntly reasons on the behavior of the panther and on his chances and on the necessity of killing the Indians, with no human aid at hand. Brown's women are equal to his men. Nearly all of them show minds of their own and somewhat of womanly devotion, helpfulness and self-sacrifice. Clara is almost as much the heroine of *Wieland* as her brother is the hero, in her education, independence, ability to meet situations, love-life and authorship. In comparison with Brown's female characters, a generation later Cooper's women are so limited by narrow conventions as to be insipid, helpless and ill-defined; to use his own phrase, they belong to the type "of religion and female decorum." They think, act and talk with fastidious propriety.

The principal characters of Brown's earlier novels are simple, impelled or motivated by some one ruling passion, which sets them apart, as it were, from their fellow men and drives them irresistibly to their doom, as Wieland, Carwin, Ormond, Welbeck and Clithero. Character grouping, whether in the social life of the city or country or in happy home relations, is a requisite for the true novel. Brown held himself aloof and probably did not perceive the value of it. He says, "my powers do not enable me to place the common place characters around me in an interesting or amusing point of view."[10] By nature and training, Brown was unacquainted with the complex relations of life, which are a necessary preparation to a novelist who would attain effective character grouping. His characters are more disposed to soliloquize than to talk. They deliberate. They bring before the mind all the pros and cons regarding a subject, which reveals their author's legal training, before they finally decide to act.

This process of reasoning, making mention of a thousand minute particulars, at times becomes tedious and seems affected; yet this being the way in which the larger part of the world reasons, Brown has convinced his readers of the truth of his facts and produces an atmosphere of circumstantiality. A modern novelist, like the dramatist, develops his characters more by action; but Brown more often has his characters make themselves known by their self-analyses and explanations, interspersed by his own comments. He uses dialogue sparingly, which correlates with the private musings of his characters. However, his chief characters speak in dialogue as befits them under proper conditions. Many of their conversations employ the thou-and-thee, old-style Quaker forms. One of the most natural conversations is that between Arthur Mervyn and the unlearned, indigent person from whom he tries to learn who owned the house where he was locked in. Arthur inquires of the name, profession, whether married. The man replies:

> It would be an odd thing if he was married. An old fellow, with one foot in the grave—comical enough for him to *git a vife!*" Concerning the death of the baby, he says: "She (the mother) is not quite out of *the dumps* yet. . . . I'll war'n' they'll have enough of them before they die.[11]

In his later works, Brown attempted a somewhat wider range of characters and personalities of mixed and complicated natures, rather than agents of a single, dominant control. Constantia Dudley, Queen Mab, Arthur Mervyn and Edgar Huntly are quite original in conception and evolution. Though at times the women are sentimental and weakly portrayed, they are on the whole superior in strength and in reality to most of the women characters in the novels of the time; for example, Achsa Fielding in *Arthur Mervyn*. Mrs. Fielding is one of the author's choice characters, she who is the modern, refined, sensitive, well-educated woman, sharing as heroine with Eliza, the simple, unspoiled country girl. This is a case where an American, Arthur, marries an immigrant English lady, who is also a Jewess. The English seem to have become congenial and reconciled to the Americans soon after the Revolution; or, perhaps, Brown is trying to help bring about better relations between them. Evidently, he chose the Hebrew name Achsa from the Biblical character, which indicates his familiarity with the Bible,—a fact that comes out in several instances.

Sometimes Brown introduces too many and too unimportant characters for a single performance, as Harwick, Waring, the Walpoles, Keyser, Austin, Capper, in *Arthur Mervyn;* and important personages disappear altogether, as Mrs. Wentworth, Wallace and Eliza, abandoned both by the author and the hero, in the same novel. Again characters causing new complications are introduced unnecessarily, as Stuart, Maxwell and Dashwood, in *Wieland.* From a general study of Brown's novels, one can see that he is limited in the creation of characters and accepts some standardized models.

"Like some other dealers in fiction," Brown says, "I find it easier to give new names to my visionary friends, and vary their condition, than to introduce a genuine diversity into their characters."[12] He brings in a large number of characters, but fashions fully only the opposing principals. Even in the case of those most fully treated, the treatment is chiefly mental to accord with his purposes and themes.

Supposing inheritances in names may be made a game, whether true or false. Fannie Burney's *Evelina* may have given Brown ideas besides the father-daughter incident,—as Arthur and the Villars family from the benevolent Arthur Villars, Louisa Conway from Lady Louisa, followed by the authoress of "Sabina" of her book *Louisa,* Lovel, mentioned but once by Brown, from her Lovel, and Clemenza from Clement. The same names are used in different novels: *Arthur Mervyn* and Arthur Wiatte in *Edgar Huntly,* in which Mary Waldegrave occurs; in *Ormond* are two Marys—Mary Mansfield and Mary Ridgefield; Talbot in *Ormond* and *Jane Talbot;* Watson, Wentworth, Lucy and Betsy in *Ormond* and *Arthur Mervyn;* Sarsefield in *Ormond* and in *Edgar Huntly;* Clara Wieland and Clara Howard. Following this author the name Wentworth is used by Dana in *Tom Thornton.* A few names have been noted heretofore.

In 1751, Mrs. Eliza Haywood published a novel, *Miss Betsy Thoughtless.* Betsy was of a scatter-brain nature, falling into trouble, flattered by lovers, meeting Mr. Trueworth, but losing him for a time by associating with a virtueless friend. She enters into a sham marriage with the worthless rascal and is finally rescued by Mr. Trueworth. There may be a connection between her and Betty Lawrence in *Arthur Mervyn;* she was a loud, lover-possessed, ignorant person, whom Arthur's father was enticed into marrying, causing Arthur to leave home. The two Elizas in the same novel may take their name from Mrs. Haywood's given name, if Brown knew her novel.

Characters must be representative men and women to make them lasting fictional personalities. To invest them with the illusion of reality, whether factual or fictitious, they must be individualized by certain personal traits that distinguish them from all other representatives or members of their class. To make them interesting, they must act their parts,—be dynamic, not static. A few of Brown's best characters seem to measure up: Wieland, Ormond, Constantia, Dudley, Huntly, Queen Mab, Arthur Mervyn, Stanley, Carwin. These and, perhaps, others have been copied and handed down by later writers,—by Godwin, Shelley, Mrs. Shelley, Scott, Irving, Cooper, Poe, Maria Edgeworth, Wallace, Ainsworth, Meredith, of lasting fame.

Repetitions, confusions and inconclusions are not hard to find. Brown commits the fault of having two somnambulists in *Edgar Huntly.* Arthur Mervyn resembles both young Lodi and Clavering, with little reason for the fact in the story; and the purpose of the cockloft in Welbeck's home is unexplained. The author commenced a new novel before having completed a former one, thus repeating the same ideas without knowing it. Duplicate stories are found in the circumstances of Edgar Huntly and his two sisters and in those of Philip Stanley and his sisters. All are left orphans and provided for in each case by an uncle; but the young men are early compelled to shift for themselves. Each finds a friend and instructor in an English immigrant, who finally returns home to England, marries a former lady friend, a second marriage for her, and returns again to America.

The brother of Jane Talbot is like the brother of Mrs. Lorimer, in *Edgar Huntly.* Each recklessly squanders the patrimony of his father and tries to rob his sister. Jane says of her brother:

> My brother's temper grew more unmanageable as he increased in years. . . . I do not remember a single direct kindness that I ever received from him; but I remember innumerable ill offices and contempts. Still, there was some inexplicable charm in the mere tie of kindred, which made me more deplore his errors, exult in his talents, rejoice in his success, and take a deeper interest in his concerns than in those of any other person.[13]

> Mrs. Lorimer had a twin-brother, . . . but the powers that in one case were exerted in the cause of virtue were, in the other, misapplied to sordid and flagitious purposes. Arthur Wiatte . . . had ever been the object of his sister's affection. . . . All her kindness was repaid by a stern and inexorable hatred. . . . He exceeded in depravity all that has been imputed to the arch-foe of mankind. . . . He seemed to relish no food but pure unadulterated evil. He rejoiced in proportion to the depth of that distress of which he was the author. . . . At their (parents') death the bulk of their patrimony devolved upon him. This he speedily consumed in gaming and riot.[14]

Parallel incidents are found in the brother of Mary Wilmot, in *Clara Howard,* and in Waldegrave, the friend of Huntly. Each receives and deposits money, dies, leaves an inheritance to his sister, and each deposit is sought by a claimant. Waldegrave left certain property in the care of Huntly. "It was money, and consisted of deposits at the Bank of North America. The amount was little short of eight thousand dollars. . . . His sister was his only kindred, and she is now in possession of it." Weymouth, a stranger to Huntly, on inquiring about the property, says:

> I invested the greatest part of my property in a cargo of wine from Madeira. The remainder I turned into a bill of exchange for seven thousand five hundred dollars. . . . To him (Waldegrave) therefore I determined to transmit this bill. . . . I remember when we parted, he was poor. He used to lament that his scrupulous integrity precluded him from all the common roads to wealth. . . . His religious duty compelled him to seek his livelihood by teaching a school of blacks. . . . It scarcely supplied the necessities of nature, and was reduced sometimes even below that standard by his frequent indisposition." (Huntly replies:) "I was not only unapprised of any other employment of his time, but had not the slightest suspicion of his possessing any property besides his clothes and books.[15]

No conclusion is given of the return of the money to Weymouth; and the difficulty of accounting for Morton's false claim in *Clara Howard* is unsolved. The brother of Mary Wilmot was drowned and he "was found to be credited in the Bank of P——— for so large a sum as five thousand dollars." This credit had been given two years before his death. "This money was the gift of Mr. Sedley to my brother." His intimate associates had never heard the slightest intimation of his possessing anything beyond the scanty income of his school. His expenses were kept within his meager salary. Sometime afterward, Morton, a former acquaintance of Stanley, appeared and sought Wilmot, saying,

> His property he partly invested in a ship and her cargo, and partly in a bill of exchange for five thousand dollars. This bill he transmitted to his friend Wilmot.[16]

There is practically no true humor in Brown's novels to relieve the prevailing seriousness. The few attempts, particularly in *Arthur Mervyn,* are failures. One passage in the report of Brown's visit to Rockaway serves as an unconscious criticism in this respect, of his novels written later:

> As to our talk at dinner, there was perfect good humour, and a good deal of inclination to be witty, but I do not recollect a single *good thing* that deserves to be recorded.[17]

Dunlap said of Brown's humor: "He had no portion in himself, nor any adequate conception of it in others."

Clara Wieland contrasts herself, Catharine and Pleyel with her brother, in relation to humor:

> The images that visited us were blithesome and gay. . . . I scarcely ever knew him to laugh. He never accompanied the lawless mirth of his companions with more than a smile.

Quite a number of expressions refer to the mirth of Pleyel: "His gayety had flown. . . . His vivacity had indeed been damped; . . . His conversation abounded with novelty. His gayety was almost boisterous; . . . His conceptions were ardent but ludicrous, and his memory . . . was an inexhaustible fund of entertainment." . . . (He said) "They may doze away their days on the banks of the Schuykill; but, as for me, I go in the next vessel."[18]

Pleyel notices Carwin's effect upon Clara, who resents his banter:

> It was a hint to rally me upon my prepossessions, and to amuse us with a thousand ludicrous anecdotes. . . . His conversation was occasionally visited by gleams of his ancient vivacity. . . . This would . . . call forth new railleries. His mirth, when exerted upon this topic, was the source of the bitterest vexation. . . . He was as whimsical and jestful as ever, but he was not happy. . . . The levity which had formerly characterized the behaviour of this man tended to obscure the greatness of his sentiments. . . . Pleyel was a devoted lover, but . . . a man of cold resolves and exquisite sagacity. To deceive him would be the sweetest triumph I had ever enjoyed (because of his distrust of her honor and his fierce upbraiding)." (He said), "The spirit of mischievous gayety possessed me. I proceeded on tip-top . . . till I was able to overlook your shoulder.[19]

Dr. Stevens investigated Arthur's boyhood and heard tales from a countrywoman:

> Here, in the chimney-corner, seated on a block, I found Arthur busily engaged in *knitting stockings!* I thought this a whimsical employment for a young active man. I told him so, . . . but he smiled in my face, and answered, without the least discomposure, 'Just as whimsical a business for a young active woman. Pray, did you never knit a stocking? . . . You see, though a man, I use your privilege, and prefer knitting yarn to threshing my brain with a book or the barn-floor with a flail.' . . . 'I wonder,' said I, contemptuously, 'you do not put on the petticoat as well as handle the needle.' . . . 'Do not wonder,' he replied, 'it is because I hate a petticoat encumbrance as much as I love warm feet'.[20]

The foolish colloquy of the ignorant continues in her report. Arthur, in speaking of his having left home and making up his bundle, says:

> My whole stock of linen consisted of three check shirts. Part of my winter evenings' employment, since the death of my mother, consisted in knitting my own stockings. Of these I had three pair.[21]

Brown uses a sort of humor when he has Dr. Stevens employ a bit of ridicule or sarcasm to open Arthur's eyes to his standing with Achsa:

> She can find nothing in you to esteem! . . . Incredible, indeed! You, who are loathsome in your person, an idiot in your understanding, a villain in your morals! deformed! withered! vain, stupid, and malignant. That such a one should choose *you* for an idol!

to which Arthur replies, "Pray, my friend, jest not.[22]

This statement may smack of humor or irony: "He was too old a bird to be decoyed into the net by *such* chaff,"[23] speaking of Jamieson's financial dealings with Welbeck.

It has been said that the greatest novelist must be essentially a humorist, just as the greatest romancer must be essentially a poet. Certainly Brown was lacking in humor. He had tried his hand at poetry and one can see poetical phraseology on many pages of his novels, noticeably in his descriptions of nature.

The style of Brown's novels partakes of the style of those of his contemporaries. He put great pains on his choice of words and on the formation of his sentences, which emphasize the prevalent pedantry of the times in letters exchanged between friends and in the books that were written. His style contrasts singularly with his natural simplicity of taste; and his care-free composition contrasts ofttimes with the preparation which he made in the study of words and sentences. For Dunlap tells how Brown used to copy in his Journal letters sent and received, besides other material, to improve his composition. This policy of letter-copying is mentioned by Brown when he has Huntly write to Mary Waldegrave of her brother's letters:

> The scheme of transcribing, for thy use, all the letters which, during his short but busy life, I received from him . . . occurred to my thoughts.[24]

On the whole Brown's words accord with the subject matter,—solemn diction for morbid incidents, sentimental words for expression of feelings, heady words for psychological introspection. Latin derivatives are used where Anglo-Saxon words would have been just as forceful. Many unusual words and peculiar combinations of words are to be found. The impression that the words make remains with the reader rather than the words themselves, unless he rereads for the words' sake.

> His language was downright prose—the natural diction of the man himself—earnest—full of substantial good sense, clearness, and simplicity;—very sober and very plain, so as to leave only the *meaning* upon the mind. Nobody ever remembered the words of Charles Brockden Brown; nobody ever thought of the arrangement; yet nobody ever forgot what they conveyed.[25]

Some sentences are lengthy, run-on and awkward in grammatical construction. As if to offset the heaviness of such sentences, the author has fallen into the opposite extreme, using short, condensed statements, questions, exclamations and elliptical expressions, sometimes following one another in a series for a whole page, until they become monotonous.

The word *bombastic* was applied in a former chapter to Revolutionary-period writers' language. Like a goodly number of their predecessors, Brown does use inflated speech and magniloquent words when he wishes to make his characters seem impressive and learned. Their conversations often sound like set speeches. The language is then verbose, melodramatic or absurdly sentimental. At times one feels the incongruity between the strong, passionate, terrific enterprises of the characters and the pedantic language in which they are presented. He suddenly realizes that the author is doing the speaking.

"Simple, heart-felt expressions generally serve realism best," some one has said. Brown claimed to aim at realism; yet his fondness for long words and his avalanches of sentimental words are conspicuous on many a page. A few of his favorites are listed. *Ruminate* is used scores of times in place of think, which by inference has that meaning; but its frequent occurrence gives the impression that the speaker is putting on. Among words to watch, in alphabetical order, are adscititious, ambiguities, ambiguous, ambiguousness, animadvert, asperities, aspersions, assiduities, assiduous, attemper, austerities, bemazed, caprice, capricious, circuities, contumacious, conversible, deliquium, ductile (to her will), ebullitions, flagitious, immutable, incongruousness, indefatigable, inexhaustible, inexplicable, insuperability, interrogatories, lucubrations, mellifluent, metamorphosed, mutable, mutate, mutations, nugatory, obsequiously, obsequiousness, opprobrious, paniful, pregnant (of meaning), presages, prognostics, prothonotary, punctilio, punctiliousness, pusillanimity, ratiocination, remediless, repugnant, sedulously, specious, spirituous, umbrage, undulation, unplausible.

Besides these there are hundreds of other words of four and five syllables and some of six and seven syllables. It is significant to recall how authors whom Brown influenced almost invariably used a score or more of his most unusual words. Nearly half of these listed words are found in *Caleb Williams,* showing either Godwin's influence or a common inheritance among writers.

Critics of Brown's language denounced it as melodramatic, involved, ornate, stiff and stilted. One would not want it otherwise, except that he did not take time to do as well as he knew—to substitute different words for those he uses so often. The so-called simple language of today would have made his writings out of place in his generation. A person need only read the fiction and the poetry of the years immediately suc-ceeding Brown's short span of life to know that their language was far more ornate in expression, involved in construction grammatically and more impassioned in conversation than that of the present.

William H. Prescott, who wrote a memoir of Charles Brockden Brown for Jared Sparks' *American Biography* (1834), only twenty-four years after his death, in discussing his language, said:

> It must be remembered, too, that his novels were his first productions, thrown off with careless profusion, and exhibiting many of the defects of an immature mind, which longer experience and practice might have corrected.

He quoted a few of Brown's phrases—"fraught with the persuasion," "appended to it," "hoarser aspirations," "on recovering from deliquium," "fraught with the apprehension that my life was endangered," "his brain seemed to swell beyond its continent," "by a common apparatus, that lay beside my bed, I could instantly produce a light." "By this last circumlocution he meant to say that he had a tinderbox." Elsewhere Brown says, "a taper, a flint, tinder, and steel."

The spot-light might be turned on Prescott. By this circumlocutory remark, he said that Brown was born a Quaker:

> He was descended from a highly respectable family, whose ancestors were of that estimable sect, who came over with William Penn to seek an asylum, where they might worship their Creator unmolested in the meek and humble spirit of their own faith.[26]

Here are additional typical Brownesque expressions. Arthur Mervyn struck his head and made a gash: "My ensanguined visage . . . my clothes were moistened with the unwelcome effusion." "My horse stood near, docile and obsequious." "This action was sufficiently conformable to my prognostics." "Washing was her trade"—the trade of kind Sarah Baxter—she "punctually visited the Dudleys once a week, and carried home with her whatever stood in need of ablution." "The voice was that of Constantia (after killing Ormond). It penetrated to my heart like an ice-bolt."

Corrode in literature is a pedigreed word. "The vexations and tumults of public affairs, which too frequently corrode the heart and vitiate the taste," are words of Mrs. Radcliffe. Godwin used "corrosive bitterness" in *Caleb Williams.* Clara Wieland says, when considering Carwin's words and Pleyel's suspicions, "But now my bosom was corroded by anxiety. I was visited by dread of unknown dangers." "Mr. Dudley's . . . features (were) corroded by his ceaseless melancholy." Brown said of himself, "Forget that any latent anguish or corroding sorrow" disquiet me, quoted more fully in Chapter I.

After Brown, Godwin says, "corrode his vitals" and "corroding cancer" in *Mandeville,* and Maturin in *Fatal Revenge* says, "corroded mind" and "erosions of conscience."

Adders, vipers and scorpions slide through the pages of novels. "Viper in my bosom" of *Caleb Williams* becomes "adders lodged in my bosom" in **Wieland,** repeated by "viper in my bosom" in *Mandeville.* In *Tom Jones* (Fielding) many years earlier are the expressions: "a scorpion in her bosom" and "that wicked viper which I have so long nourished in my bosom." Lady Shelley in *The Last Man* carries on the tradition: "His praises were so many adder's stings infixed in my vulnerable breast," "and ideas, horrid as furies, cruel as vipers."

In relation to Brown's style, the words of Blake are appropriate:

> His books, if they seem to us the crude expression of youth, are the expression of a literature's youth no less than the author's. . . . His language seems to us prolix and pretentious only if we go to it direct, instead of from the reading of his British predecessors. . . . Moreover, Brockden Brown was found remarkable—even in his day and generation,—for writing in a style that is nervously instinct with repressed energy. His sentences are short, like the modern writer's, monotonously so; but experiment, even literary experiment, is better than stagnation.[27]

Notes

1 Brown, His Journal, in Dunlap, *op. cit.,* I, 107.

2 Griswold, *The Prose Writers of America,* 29.

3 Blake, "Brockden Brown and the Novel," in *The Sewanee Review,* XVIII, 436.

4 Dunlap, *op. cit.,* I, 258, 259.

5 *Ibid.,* II, 29.

6 Brown, Letter to his brother Armit, New York, Dec. 20th, 1798, in Dunlap, *op. cit.,* II, 93.

7 *Edgar Huntly,* 1-2.

8 Scott, *Journal,* 1825-1832, 117, 122, 151.

9 *Wieland,* 166.

10 Brown, Record of a Trip to Rockaway, in Dunlap, *op. cit.,* I, 66.

11 *Arthur Mervyn,* I, 60-1.

12 Brown, "Alcuin," in Dunlap, *op. cit.,* I, 74.

13 *Jane Talbot,* 9.

14 *Edgar Huntly,* 43, 44, 46.

15 *Ibid.,* 147, 150, 148, 149.

16 *Clara Howard,* 320, 389, 322.

17 Brown, Report of a Visit to Rockaway, in Dunlap, *op. cit.,* I, 66.

18 *Wieland,* 42, 43, 67, 68, 44-5, 64.

19 *Wieland,* 81, 89, 96, 202, 229, 143.

20 *Arthur Mervyn,* II, 18.

21 *Ibid.,* I, 24.

22 *Arthur Mervyn,* II, 217.

23 *Ibid.,* II, 29.

24 *Edgar Huntly,* 135.

25 Neal, in *Blackwood's Magazine,* XVI, 421, October, 1824.

26 Prescott, "Memoir of Charles Brockden Brown," in Sparks, *Library of American Biography,* I, 119-80.

27 Blake, "Brockden Brown and the Novel," in *The Sewanee Review* XVIII, 435.

Kenneth Bernard (essay date 1964)

SOURCE: "Charles Brockden Brown and the Sublime," in *The Personalist,* Vol. XLV, No. 2, April, 1964, pp. 235-49.

[*In the essay that follows, Bernard argues that the praise Brown has received for his descriptions of the "American scene" is undeserved: the few occasions when Brown does discuss the American scene, he does so within the constraints of eighteenth-century aesthetics of the sublime and the picturesque.*]

Charles Brockden Brown (1771-1810) has often been praised for his description of the American scene in his novels.[1] But, although Brown deserves much praise, it is by no means certain that he deserves it for his description of the American scene. It is surprising, first, how infrequently Brown describes the American scene at all. Second, when he does describe it, he does so almost invariably in terms of the eighteenth-century esthetics of the sublime and of the picturesque. Twentieth-century critics, perhaps eager to extend the limits of American literary independence from Europe, have claimed too much for Brown. Earlier critics correctly found Brown's descriptions artificial, closer, for example, to a painting of Salvator Rosa than to any real scene.[2]

Brown himself refutes the notion that he is a close observer of nature. William Dunlap has reproduced in his biography of Brown letters Brown wrote on a trip to Rockaway, New York, and on a trip up the Hudson. Brown's most specific description is of the Hudson: "The scenery around is sweetly picturesque, swelling fertility and the wild music of birds."[3] Even more revealing, Brown says, "How shall I describe them [the scenes]. I cannot particularize the substance of the rock, or the kind of tree, save oaks and cedars."[4] The Rockaway trip was equally barren in observation:

> You will of course ask me, how the fields are enclosed? How they are planted? What portion is tilled? What is wood, and what is waste? Of what number, materials, dimensions, and form, are the dwellings, the granaries, the churches, the bridges, the carriages? What is the countenance, the dress, the deportment of the passengers, and so forth? through an endless catalog of interrogatories.

> Now I cannot answer a word to all these questions . . . I, alas! am one of those whom fifty years of observation would leave in the same ignorance in which they found me.[5]

A little later he writes,

> I confess to you then that my mind was much more busily engaged in reflecting on the possible consequences of coming off without several changes of clothes in my handkerchief, and without an umbrella to shelter me from sunshine and rain, than with the fields and woods which I passed through.[6]

He shows the same indifference to scene at the end of the trip:

> On my return, I was just as unobservant of the passing scene as before, and took as little note of the geography of the isle. Set me on the same journey again, and I should scarcely recognize a foot of the way. I saw trees and shrubs and grasses, but I could not *name them, being as how* I am no botanist [sic].[7]

It is unlikely, in view of Brown's poor powers of observation, that he could celebrate the American or any other scene very much.[8] What, then, does Brown describe in his novels?

In all his novels but one, Brown gives almost no description of the American scene. *Ormond* and *Arthur Mervyn* are set primarily in the city.[9] *Arthur Mervyn* has a country interlude, idyllic in nature; however, Brown gets no more specific than to say that the Hadwin farm is surrounded by "pure airs" and "romantic walks." In *Wieland* he has one long scenic description, and that clearly showing his relationship with the eighteenth-century esthetic. Contrasting a river scene with one of higher elevation, he writes:

> No scene can be imagined less enticing to a lover of the picturesque than this. The shore is deformed with mud and encumbered with a forest of reeds. The fields, in most seasons, are mire, but when they afford a firm footing, the ditches by which they are bounded and intersected, are mantled with stagnating green, and emit the most noxious exhalations. . . . The scenes which environed our dwellings at Mettingen constituted the reverse of this. Schuylkill was here a pure and translucid current, broken into wild and ceaseless music by rocky points; murmuring on a sandy margin, and reflecting on its surface, banks of all varieties of height and degrees of declivity. These banks were chequered by patches of dark verdure and shapeless masses of white marble, and crowned by copses of cedar, or by the regular magnificence of orchards, which at this season, were in blossom, and were prodigal of odours. The ground which receded from the river was scooped into valleys and dales. Its beauties were enhanced by the horticultural skill of my brother, who bedecked this exquisite assemblage of slopes and risings with every species of vegetable ornament, from the giant arms of the oak to the clustering tendrils of the honeysuckle. (V)[10]

Phrases like "lover of the picturesque" and "broken into wild and ceaseless music by rocky points" help to place this passage in proper context. It is interesting to observe that the first part of the description, the "unpicturesque" part, is rendered straight-forwardly and realistically; the second or "picturesque" part is rendered artificially (note the rhetoric of phrases like "prodigal of odours") and unspecifically ("banks of all varieties of height and degrees of declivity," "exquisite assemblage of slopes and risings"), as if it were a balanced composition by a painter rather than a real scene.[11]

The book on which Brown's reputation as a writer of the American scene rests is *Edgar Huntly.* In the introduction to the book he announces that he wants to break away from European themes and materials. Yet, Brown's detailed descriptions are few and conventional, his Indians a mixture of real and romantic, and his intentions laudable but fulfilled in ways he did not suspect. Brown has only one extended description of the Norwalk wilderness in *Edgar Huntly.* After giving its dimensions, he says:

> The hollows are single, and walled around by cliffs, ever varying in shape and height, and have seldom any perceptible communication with each other.

These hollows are of all dimensions, from the narrowness and depth of a well, to the amplitude of one hundred yards. Winter's snow is frequently found in these cavities at midsummer. The streams that burst forth from every crevice are thrown, by the irregularities of the surface, into numberless cascades, often disappear in mists or in chasms, and emerge from subterranean channels, and, finally, either subside into lake, or quietly meander through lower and more level grounds.

Wherever nature left a flat it is made rugged and scarcely passable by enormous and fallen trunks, accumulated by the storms of ages, and forming, by their slow decay, a moss-covered soil, the haunt of rabbits and lizards. These spots are obscured by the melancholy umbrage of the pines, whose eternal murmurs are in unison with vacancy and solitude, with the reverberations of torrents and the whistling of the blasts. Hickory and poplar, which abound in the lowlands, find here no fostering elements.

A sort of continued vale, winding and abrupt, leads into the midst of this region and through it. This vale serves the purpose of a road. It is a tedious maze and perpetual declivity, and requires, from the passenger, a cautious and sure foot. Openings and ascents occasionally present themselves on each side, but always terminate, sooner or later, in insuperable difficulties, at the verge or the bottom of a steep. (IX)

He gives a shorter description of one part of the area when Edgar Huntly is fleeing the Indians:

No fancy can conceive a scene more wild and desolate than that which now presented itself. The soil was nearly covered with sharp fragments of stone. Between these, sprung brambles and creeping vines, whose twigs, crossing and intertwining with each other, added to the roughness below, made the passage infinitely toilsome. Scattered through this space were single cedars with their rugged spines and wreaths of moss, and copses of dwarf oaks, which were only new emblems of sterility. (XVIII)

Aside from these descriptions, Brown writes only comments like "It was in the highest degree rugged, picturesque, and wild" (II). The last quotation, in a few words, gives the essence of Brown's descriptions. He is not describing any real landscape. The fantastic cliffs, gloomy hollows, irushing streams, dangerous chasms, mists, dead trees, moss, storms, mazes, and so on were all commonplaces of eighteenth-century prose and poetry. He is describing sublime or picturesque landscapes according to principles laid down by such writers as Edmund Burke and William Gilpin, depicted by certain painters like Salvator Rosa and Claude Lorrain, and used by such writers as Ann Radcliffe.

The sublime, the beautiful, and the picturesque have a complex history in eighteenth-century England.[12] The sublime in this paper refers to that esthetic of which Edmund Burke may be called the high priest. With Burke the connection of the sublime with the pathetic (feeling) was firmly established in England. He considered terror the feeling most closely connected with sublimity; a person felt sublime as his thoughts turned on the idea of pain. "Indeed," writes Burke, "terror is in all cases whatsoever, either more openly or latently, the ruling principle of the sublime."[13] For example, when Edgar Huntly has braved the dangers of the cave to seek Clithero, he experiences a sublime feeling:

A stream, rushing from below, fell into a cavity, which its own force seemed gradually to have made. The voice and the motion equally attracted my attention. There was a desolate and solitary grandeur in the scene, enhanced by the circumstances in which it was beheld, and by the perils through which I had recently passed, that had never been witnessed by me. (X)

The recent danger and present grandeur make the moment and the scene thrilling. At another point in the book, Huntly, amid the dangers of the cave, says, "At that moment, torrents of rain poured from above, and stronger blasts thundered amidst these desolate recesses and profound chasms. Instead of lamenting the prevalence of this tempest, I now began to regard it with pleasure. I conferred new forms of sublimity on this scene" (XIII). In **Arthur Mervyn,** the hero says, "A certain sublimity is connected with enormous dangers that imparts to our consternation or our pity a tincture of the pleasing" (XIV).

If Burke was the high priest of the sublime, William Gilpin was the high priest of the picturesque.[14] Gilpin, in a series of travel books, essays, and poems which began appearing in 1782, enunciated an elaborate set of principles by which a viewer could judge beauty in nature. Gilpin deferred to Burke on the sublime,[15] but he felt there were aspects of beauty that did not come under Burke's esthetic. The term he used to describe these aspects was picturesque, "that kind of beauty which would look well in a picture."[16] Thus toward the end of the century there developed an esthetic of nature that had nothing to do with nature:

Nature, one sometimes believes, was sought not so much for what she was, as for what she was not. The picturesque traveler approached her with his head full of vistas and lights and foregrounds and points of view and side-screens; and he stayed to commend when she could offer to "Taste" a scene which in some way resembled the compositions of those Gemini among landscape artists, Claude and Salvator.[17]

Brown's two most direct sources of influence for scenery were Radcliffe and Gilpin. In a short essay, Brown wrote:

> Much may be done . . . by solitary efforts to analyze the scene before us, and nothing can be done [to appreciate scenery] without such efforts. It is likewise of great use to examine the works in this kind of celebrated painters; but that is an advantage scarcely to be hoped for by us who stay on this side of the ocean. Books are of the most use, but I know of but one writer anyways eminent for displaying the principles of landscape; I mean Mr. Gilpin, whose works ought to be familiar to every mind endowed with virtuous propensities and true taste.
>
> There is another set of writers who are in some sense to be regarded as commentators upon Gilpin; who have traveled and written books for little other purpose than to deduce the application of the principles of this kind of beauty, and to furnish in a set of pictures, *in words,* as Verney, Claude, and Salvator, exhibited on canvas.
>
> Ann Radcliffe is, without doubt, the most illustrious of the picturesque writers. Her "Travels on the Rhine and in Cumberland" is, in this view, an inestimable performance. . . . Her last two romances, "Udolpho," and "The Italian," are little else than a series of affecting pictures, connected by a pleasing narrative, and in which human characters and figures are introduced on the same principles that place them on canvas, to give moral energy and purpose to the scene. This is the great and lasting excellence of her works.[18]

Brown is not interested in nature as nature. One must approach nature with a set of principles, such as those of Mr. Gilpin; it is also useful in the analysis of nature to study certain painters, like Salvator, and certain writers, like Mrs. Radcliffe. But Gilpin saw nature through picture frames. A scene is sublime or picturesque as it approaches what one or another painter might have put on canvas. His favorite painters, Salvator and Claude,[19] had never aimed at realistic depiction. Mrs. Radcliffe herself is completely painter-oriented in her novels. She never saw the Italian scenes depicted in *Udolpho* and *The Italian.* It was only after they were written that she travelled abroad. "Her pictures are manifestly taken from the painters' landscapes, not from nature. She had not indeed travelled farther south than part way down the Rhine; but what was the need? The pictures of Claude and Salvator gave her precisely what she required."[20] Thus, two people whom Brown admired very much and whose scenic descriptions made deep impressions on him did not at all take their cue for description from nature itself, but from painters. As much as Brown may have wanted to display the American scene, he was incapable of doing so realistically because of his esthetic affinities.

An aspect of the sublime esthetic in Brown not yet mentioned is the tableau or picture effect he achieves with figures on occasion. Brown says that Radcliffe's novels are no more than a series of "affecting pictures." He too has such pictures, though not perhaps in series. The description of Clithero in *Edgar Huntly,* abstracted high on his sheer cliff, a chasm all around, a raging torrent at the bottom of it, is such a picture:

> The wilderness, and the cave to which you followed me, were familiar to my Sunday rambles. Often have I indulged in audible griefs on the cliffs of that valley. Often have I brooded over my sorrows in the recesses of that cavern. This scene is adapted to my temper. Its mountainous asperities supply me with the images of desolation and seclusion, and its headlong streams lull me into temporary forgetfulness of mankind. (VIII)

The conventional romantic pose here is obvious. The most dramatic picture is one of Huntly himself. It also seems the most obviously staged for pictorial effects. Huntly has just saved a girl held captive by the Indians. He has killed several of them and been wounded himself in the process. Here is the picture Brown paints:

> I sat upon the ground, supporting my head with my left hand, and resting on my knee the stock of a heavy musket. My countenance was wan and haggard, my neck and bosom were dyed in blood, and my limbs, almost stripped by the brambles of their slender covering, were lacerated by a thousand wounds. Three savages, two of whom were steeped in gore, lay at a small distance, with the traces of recent life on their visages. Hard by was the girl, venting her anguish in the deepest groans, and entreating relief from the newcomers. (XIX)

Such "affecting pictures" amidst sublime settings were, of course, congenial to the romantic writers.

Huntly's prodigiousness may itself be considered an aspect of sublimity in that it hints of great power. Typically he says, after he has killed the Indians, "The destruction I witnessed was vast. Three beings, full of energy and heroism, endowed with minds strenuous and lofty, poured out their lives before me. I was the instrument of their destruction. This scene of carnage and destruction was laid by me" (XIX). Huntly acts on the grand scale. When he destroys, his destruction is cataclysmic. It is worth noting that here, with Huntly in a characteristically heroic pose, Brown has him reflect a more Rousseauistic view of the Indian, the traditionally romantic one ("full of energy and heroism," "minds strenuous and lofty"), whereas elsewhere in the book he credits them with savagery and low qualities, a realistic fact for which Brown has been praised. A short while later, Huntly modestly speaks of himself thus:

I had delighted, from my childhood, in feats of agility and perserverance. In roving through the maze of thickets and precipices, I had put my energies, both moral and physical, frequently to the test. Greater achievements than this had been performed, and I disdained to be outdone in perspicacity by the lynx, in his surefooted instinct by the roe, or in patience under hardship, and contention with fatigue, by the Mohawk. I have ever aspired to transcend the rest of animals in all that is common to the rational and brute, as well as in all by which they are distinguished from each other. (XX)

Huntly's powers of endurance are phenomenal. He spends two and a half days in a cave without food and water (except for raw panther meat and blood, which give him violent cramps). He then rescues the girl and kills the Indians. Then, after being wounded and having had water and only a little food, he travels over mountainous terrain for thirty hours without sleep, part of that time wet to the skin from a plunge into a mountain stream from a high cliff. This was "enough to annihilate the strength and courage of ordinary men" (XXIII). He then travels fifteen miles more to the house where he meets his old tutor, Sarsefield, who, almost incredulously, relates Huntly's adventures with the Indians, the amazing distances he has covered, and his now legendary appearances and disappearances, deaths and reincarnations. "Surely my fate has never been paralleled!" (XXII) Huntly ejaculates at one point.

Brown's heroic villains may be considered still another aspect of the sublime, for they have characteristics analogous to sublime scenery. For example, all the dramatic contrast of Carwin's frame, visage, and character in **Wieland** contribute much to Clara Wieland's "sublime" prostration. When she first sees him he appears as

> ungainly and disproportioned. Shoulders broad and square, breast sunken, his head drooping, his body of uniform breadth, supported by long and lank legs. (VI)

Just after, when she has heard his voice, she says of it:

> I cannot pretend to communicate the impression that was made upon me by these accents, or to depict the degree in which force and sweetness were blended in them. They were articulated with a distinctness that was unexampled in my experience. . . . The voice . . . imparted to me an emotion altogether involuntary and uncontroulable [sic]. . . . I dropped the cloth that I held in my hand, my heart overflowed with sympathy and my eyes with unbidden tears. (VI)

There are several other contrasts. His teeth are "large and irregular" but "brilliantly white." His eyes are "sunken" but "lustrously black." His forehead is "overshadowed by course straggling hairs" (VI), but some-how impressive. His total effect on her is overwhelming. As William Dunlap wrote of Carwin, he is "a character approaching to the sublime, from the mystery thrown about him."[21] No small part of that effect is the result of certain sharp contrasts, irregularities, and purities, which can also be observed in landscape.

Although Brown is without doubt describing scenery out of the same tradition as a writer like Ann Radcliffe, his use of it is noticeably different. Radcliffe uses scenery as a decorous backdrop to heighten her drama. In fact, there is nothing so important that it cannot stop for a moment while the characters and readers enjoy a litany of praise for the wild, the grand, the sublime. To the modern reader, this appreciation is out of keeping with the dramatic narration. Setting can give significance to a character, but the mutual interplay of setting and character is different from a mechanical conjunction of them. When Ellena in *The Italian* has been kidnapped and is being rushed to a remote region by ruffians, Radcliffe writes:

> The road, therefore, was carried high among the cliffs that impended over the river, and seemed as if suspended in air; while the gloom and vastness of the precipices which towered above and sunk below it, together with the amazing force and uproar of the falling waters, combined to render the pass more terrific than the pencil could describe, or language express. Ellena ascended it not with indifference, but with calmness; she experienced somewhat a dreadful pleasure in looking down upon the irresistible flood; but this emotion was heightened into awe, when she perceived that the road led to a slight bridge, which thrown across the chasm at an immense height, united two opposite cliffs, between which the whole cataract of the river ascended.[22]

Later, when she is imprisoned, she looks at a scene: "The consciousness of her prison was lost, while her eyes ranged over the wide and truly sublime scene without."[23] She is never in so much danger that she cannot become an epicure of the sublime. Brown's characters rarely do this. Although they have some words for the scenery, in only one instance do they approach the suspension of dramatic moment in Radcliffe. When Huntley has escaped from the cave and is exhausted, wounded, hunted, and hungry, he comes to a cliff: "I pondered for a while on these stupendous scenes. They ravished my attention from considerations that related to myself, but this interval was short" (XXI).

Brown does, however, *use* his scenery, and it is this use that represents a change. In Radcliffe, even though the mountain scenery is intended to increase the thrill of the narrative, it is still essentially decorative. In Brown it becomes functional in several ways. For example, night scenes appeal to Radcliffe for much the same reason they appealed to Burke: "But darkness is more productive of sublime ideas than light."[24] To

Brown they appeal for another reason besides: "Intense dark is always the parent of fears." (*Edgar Huntly,* X) Brown, perhaps intuitively, realized that the tale he had to tell would achieve greater effect in scenes of darkness than light. The dark is much more suitable in telling a tale of the mind, especially the less known parts of the mind. Again, Brown uses mountain scenery, and was certainly aware of its sublime effects, but the opportunity it gave him for frequent depth images makes it functional rather than decorative, as the depth images reinforce significantly the main idea, Huntly's near loss of mind, his plunge into the unknown portion of his mind, the dark portion. Finally, the rough, shifting terrain, the mazes, and lastly the cave, which contains a summary of all the previous images (darkness, dangerous heights, confusion), are hardly pictorial only; nor do they simply reinforce the main idea: they function on the level of symbol, representing in a large way the same human drama that the reader is following most obviously. If Brown's use of landscape is to be considered "native" or American, it is so not because his scenes are accurate descriptions but because they are charged with symbolic significance. Lewis Mumford recognized this use of landscape in American literature when he wrote, "At heart, the American novelists were all transcendental. The scene was symbol; they hardly had the patience to describe it; they were interested in it only because it pointed to something more important."[25] Consider, for example, the Norwalk wilderness in *Edgar Huntly.* No one knows it better than Huntly, yet Clithero, who has been there only a few years, leads him to places Huntly has never been. When Clithero disappears, Huntly fears that "his concealment was not to be traced." And when Huntly ponders over the valley into which Clithero has led him, he says,

> I had a faint remembrance of the valley into which I had descended after him; but till then I had viewed it at a distance, and supposed it impossible to reach the bottom but by leaping from a precipice some hundred feet in height. The opposite steep seemed no less accessible, and the cavern at the bottom was impervious to any views which my former positions had enabled me to take of it. (IX)

Yet Clithero does lead Huntly into this inaccessible valley and into the hidden cave, where Huntly nearly dies. What else is all this landscape but a symbolic representation of the book's conflict, a landscape of mind, a geography of Huntly's mental breakdown, a topographical interplay between Huntly's ego and alter-ego, conscious and subconscious? Such functional uses of scene were not the province of Radcliffe. Brown, in putting a conventional landscape to new uses, has gone a step further, and in so doing advanced a method that, while not exclusively American, became for later writers significantly American.

Notes

[1] For example, Richard Chase, *The American Novel and Its Tradition* (New York, 1957), p. 36: "And certainly *Edgar Huntly,* with its setting of remote farms, of rugged hills, forested valleys, swift streams, bogs, fens, caves, precipices, sudden storms and night winds, hidden trails, and Indian retreats, successfully claims the American wilderness for fiction." See also Warren Barton Blake, "Brockden Brown and the Novel," *Sewanee Review,* October, 1910, p. 433; Albert Keiser, *The Indian in American Literature* (New York, 1933), p. 34; and Lulu Rumsey Wiley, *The Sources and Influences of the Novels of Charles Brockden Brown* (New York, 1950), pp. 30, 170.

[2] For example, Richard Henry Dana, "The Novels of Charles Brockden Brown," *Poems and Prose Writings* (New York, 1850), II, 328: " . . . we know of none who appear from their writings to have looked less at nature, or to have been less open to its influences. With the exception of Mervyn's return to Hadwin's, and his last journey thence, and the opening of Carwin, with one or two more slight instances, Brown seldom attempts a description of real scenery; or where he does, and labors it most, it is confused and indistinct, as, for instance, in Edgar Huntly." See also Evert A. and George L. Duyckinck, *Cyclopaedia of American Literature* (New York, 1856), I, 590-591; and William H. Prescott, "The Life of Charles Brockden Brown," *American Biography,* ed. Jared Sparks (New York, 1839), p. 152.

[3] *The Life of Charles Brockden Brown* (Philadelphia, 1815), II, 54.

[4] *Ibid.,* II, 52. Wherever in Brown's novels he does describe scenery, oaks and or cedars are nearly always present. See quotations below.

[5] *Ibid.,* II, 58-9.

[6] *Ibid.,* II, 60.

[7] *Ibid.,* II, 66. He implies, p. 67, that he is not a mineralogist or naturalist either.

[8] Miss Wiley, pp. 326-7, finds in Brown's novels careful descriptions which had their origin in youthful rambles taken for health. However, Harry Warfel, *Charles Brockden Brown: American Gothic Novelist* (Gainesville, Florida, 1949), p. 38, indicates just the opposite: "Although he [Brown] wandered through the fields, he never brought home a flower, a leaf, a feather, or a stone as a specimen. Unlike most lads, he never made a collection of natural objects. He simply had no capacity for close observation." Further, Miss Wiley supports Brown's realistic descrip-

tions elsewhere, p. 165, by comparing them favorably with those of Mrs. Radcliffe—a writer whose scenes are totally derivative (See n. 20): "He surpasses in wildness, but not in grandeur, perhaps, the scenic effects produced by Mrs. Radcliffe." Miss Wiley herself, as indicated by the terms "wildness" and "grandeur," seems to be functioning out of the eighteenth-century esthetic tradition.

9 Even Brown's city scenes are rarely distinctive. For example, in *Arthur Mervyn* there is almost no mention of particular streets or particular places in Philadelphia.

10 All quotations from Brown's novels are cited only by chapter, in parentheses, after the quotation.

11 Ernest Marchand, ed., Introduction to *Ormond* (New York, 1937), p. xxii, seems to recognize Brown's derivative scenic description when he writes, "Even so, he shows several of the traits of literary romanticism, of which the love of picturesque nature is well seen in *Wieland* and *Edgar Huntly.*

12 No one has examined that history better than Samuel H. Monk, *The Sublime: A Study of Critical Theories in XVIII-Century England* (New York, 1935).

13 Edmund Burke, "On the Sublime and the Beautiful . . . ," *The Writings and Speeches of Edmund Burke* (Boston, 1901), I, 147. See also p. 110: "Whatever is fitted in any sort to excite the ideas of pain and danger, that is to say, whatever is in any sort terrible, or is conversant about terrible objects, or operates in a manner analogous to terror, is a source of the sublime; that is, it is productive of the strongest emotion which the mind is capable of feeling." And p. 125: "To draw the whole of what has been said into a few distinct points: The passion which belong to self-preservation turn on pain and danger; they are simply painful when their causes immediately affect us; they are delightful when we have an idea of pain and danger, without being actually in such circumstances: this delight I have not called pleasure, because it turns on pain, and because it is different enough from any idea of positive pleasure. Whatever excites this delight, I call *sublime."*

14 One critic, in fact, Christopher Hussey, *The Picturesque: Studies in a Point of View* (London, 1927), p. 111, so designates him.

15 *Remarks of Forest Scenery and Other Woodland Views* (London, 1808), I, 262.

16 *Observations on the Western Parts of England* (London, 1808), p. 328. For a discussion of Gilpin's influence, which was considerable, and his rivals, see E. W. Manwaring, *Italian Landscape in Eigh-*

teenth Century England (New York, 1925), as well as Hussey and Monk.

17 Monk, p. 204. Salvator's paintings became perfect illustrations of sublime scenery: mountain scenes full of danger, banditti on craggy coasts, tumultuous, storm-lashed waves. Claude's served more to illustrate the beautiful: hazy dawns and misty twilights, pleasant, balanced pastoral vistas.

18 "On a Taste for the Picturesque," *Literary Magazine and American Register,* I (June, 1804), 165. It is likely that by Verney, Brown means the painter Joseph Vernet (1714-89), often mentioned with Claude and Salvator.

19 *Forest Scenery,* I, 9, 225; *Observations on the Western Parts of England,* pp. 75-76. See also Myra Reynolds, *The Treatment of Naturein English Poetry* (Chicago, 1909), p. 189. A typical Gilpin remark on a scene in nature is, for example, *Forest Scenery,* I, 8: "What is more beautiful, for instance, on a rugged foreground, than an old tree with a *hollow trunk,* or with a *dead arm,* or a *drooping bough* or a *dying branch?"*

20 Manwaring, p. 213. See also Eino Railo, *The Haunted Castle* (London and New York, 1927), p. 26.

21 II, 15.

22 *The Confessional of the Black Penitents; or, The Italian* (Cincinnati, 1853), p. 33.

23 *Ibid.,* p. 45. Cf. p. 33, when Ellena is awaiting the return of the "ruffian," and p. 78, when she is escaping with Vivaldi. The occurrence is common.

24 p. 156.

25 Lewis Mumford, *The Golden Day* (New York, 1926), p. 140.

David H. Hirsch (essay date 1965)

SOURCE: "Charles Brockden Brown as a Novelist of Ideas," in *Books at Brown,* Vol. XX, 1965, pp. 165-84.

[*In the following essay, Hirsch maintains that Brown utilized a combination of genres—the sentimental novel of seduction and the gothic romance—in order to advance his French-influenced philosophic ideas.*]

The historian Bernard Faÿ observes "a curious phenomenon" in serious American literature of the late eighteenth century: "French writers roused American minds and created original reactions in them at a time when English writers were less interesting and stimulating, but afforded examples that could easily be utilized and imitated. French culture in America was a means of liberation, not a model to be copied. Indeed its great role seems to have been to aid hardy and simple minds, who might have lacked enterprise or imagination, to find themselves and adopt a new spirit that should lead them to create a new form for themselves."[1] This "curious phenomenon" of turning to France for ideas and to England for form may throw some light on the critical problem of Charles Brockden Brown's achievements and shortcomings as a novelist.

Reared in Philadelphia, "the cultural capital of, . . . and least provincial spot in America, . . ."[2] during the 1770s and 1780s, Brown " . . . was exposed to all currents of thought, European and American, that were molding a new country and a new people."[3] Brown, however, was not merely exposed to contemporary currents of thought, he plunged into them with reckless enthusiasm. And in spite of the occasional absurdity of his intellectual commitments, he was primarily a man of ideas, or at least conceived of himself as one. David Lee Clark describes the variety of his intellectual interests (literature, geography, history, architecture, utopian thought), and adds that he was sufficiently committed to ideas that " . . . even his novels bear witness to Brown's deep concern about the issues facing the new nation."[4]

Like the early English Romantics (Brown was born a year after Wordsworth), Brown was soon caught in the tide of French ideas. Clark states that " . . . young Brown was an eager reader" of French philosophy, especially Montesquieu, Helvetius, and Holbach.[5] This intellectual influence was further intensified by Brown's association with French emigres who apparently became quite numerous in Philadelphia in the 1790s. Brown actually became the tutor of the daughter of one of them, and in a letter written while he was thus employed, he defended French ideas vigorously.

The situation confronting Brown, as an incipient novelist, was not unusual. Possessed of ideas, Brown was anxious to find some way to promulgate them and get them on the market-place. He tried a series of philosophical essays significantly called *The Rhapsodist,* but these evidently were little read. As a result, it must have become quite obvious to Brown that as a writer of philosophical essays he had little hope either of bringing his ideas to a large audience or of becoming a professional man of letters. Nevertheless, there was a possibility of achieving both these goals at one stroke, and that was by writing novels. Acutely sensitive to public taste, Brown chose to spread his ideas through the two forms which had proved their ability to capitivate the American and English reading publics—the sentimental novel of seduction and the gothic romance.

The inspiration to write a novel was in Brown's mind by at least 1793. Clark states that Brown " . . . had no notion before 1793 of undertaking a work of fiction. That he entertained such a notion in the summer of 1793 while in Hartford and New York may be seen in an unpublished letter to his brother James, dated October 25, 1796, from New York."[6] The pertinent passage of the letter reads:

> . . . I was talking of the yellow fever, or rather of the plague . . . When I mentioned to you my treatment [of it] at Hartford in ninety-three, I was half disposed to instruct myself, and possibly amuse you, by recalling and putting [it] on the paper before me, during a residence of two or three days there.

"The important fact which this letter affirms," says Clark, "is that as early as 1793 Brown's mind was busied with plans for works of fiction, and that the subject then uppermost in his mind was the yellow fever. . . ."[7]

Actually, Brown may have started experimenting with the novel even before 1793. In his Journal there is a series of letters addressed to a "Henrietta G." Clark insists that the letters are autobiographical, but there remains, nonetheless, a good possibility that they represent an early attempt to write an epistolary novel.[8]

Whatever the answer to the Henrietta riddle, it is certain that by 1797, Brown's notion of embodying ideas in the form of romance had jelled. He states in a journal entry of that year: " . . . I commenced something in the form of a Romance. I had at first no definite conceptions of my design"[9] The advertisement to Brown's projected romance, *Skywalk,* is highly illuminating:

> To the story-telling moralist the United States is a new and untrodden field. He who shall examine objects with his own eyes, who shall employ the European models merely for the improvement of his taste, and adapt his fiction to all that is genuine and peculiar in the scenes before him, will be entitled at least to the praise of originality. . . .

> The value of such works lies without doubt in their moral tendency. The popular tales have merit, but there is one thing in which they are deficient. They are generally adapted to one class of readers only. By a string of well-connected incidents, they amuse the idle and thoughtless; but are spurned at by those who are satisfied with nothing but strains of lofty eloquence, by the exhibition of powerful motives, and a sort of audaciousness of character. The world is governed, not by the simpleton, but by the man of soaring passions and intellectual energy. By the display of such only can we hope to enchain the attention and ravish the souls of those who study and reflect. To gain their homage it is not needful to forego the approbation of those

whose circumstances have hindered them making the same progress. A contexture of facts capable of suspending the faculties of every soul in curiosity, may be joined with depth of views into human nature and all the subleties of reasoning.[10]

Brown, in this preface, already perceives that while the novelist may work from European models, he must eventually shape these models to the exigencies of native materials. More striking, however, is the fact that, like Hawthorne and Melville after him, Brown deliberately plans to "hoodwink" the common reader by writing a fiction that will excite the passions of all men, but that will have an especial appeal to the mind of the intellectual. He will somehow revitalize moribund forms by transfusing them with the blood of new ideas. The sop to the common reader is "a string of well-connected incidents . . . ," in a word, narrative. The main dish is the display of the hero with "soaring passions and intellectual energy." He will present ideas and speculation by presenting characters who are obsessed by ideas; characters who themselves are interested in speculation.

By 1798, when, in a fantastic burst of creative energy, he apparently wrote a good portion of his major novels, Brown had essentially abandoned the notion of an epistolary romance. Both *Wieland* and *Ormond,* it is true come to the reader in the form of an epistle. But both narratives are told in one long letter, rather than in a series of letters written by different people. Brown, by this time, had also abandoned the notion of the typical sentimental novel of seduction. He had, instead, settled on a combination of this and the gothic romance.

Leslie Fiedler and Richard Chase have made a great deal of this decision. Chase, of course, sees in it unmistakable symptoms of the American author's irresistible attraction to "romance," his desire to flee from social reality, and so on. And Fiedler, after tormenting himself with the question ("But why, one is driven to ask, *why* has the tale of terror so special an appeal to Americans?")[11] concludes that the success of the tale of terror

> must be derived in part from the failure of love in our fiction; the death of love left a vacuum at the affective heart of the American novel into which there rushed the love of death. The triumph of the genteel sentimental incapacitated even our most talented writers, left them incapable of dealing with the relations of men and women as subtly and convincingly as the prose writers in the great novelistic tradition of France. Our novelists, deprived of the subject that sustained Stendahl or Constant, Flaubert or Proust, that seemed indeed to them *the* subject of the novel, turned to fables of loneliness and terror.[12]

A more reasonable conclusion, however, is that Brown grasped at a ready-to-hand form that would insure a certain amount of popular acceptance and at the same time provide a vehicle for his ideas, thereby establishing him as both a literary man and a philosopher. As the newest and most daring form, one which Godwin had used so successfully for didactic, if not speculative ends, the gothic novel would seem to have been the most natural choice. Fiedler himself, when not lost in the deepest recesses of the psyche perceives this:

> To promulgate notions of social justice and to write novels, to revolutionize American life and to achieve literary fame: this double ambition he came to feel as a single impulse, not unlike certain young radical writers in the United States of the 1930's. The literary form which eminently suited both such political allegiances, and such literary aspirations was at the moment he began to write (the 1790's were almost gone) the "new novel," which is to say, the gothic romance in its doctrinaire Godwinian form. "To equal Caleb Williams" was the best Brown could hope for himself.[13]

Brown apparently felt that some combination of the novel of seduction and the gothic romance would provide the best salable vehicle for both his ideas and the hero of "soaring passions and intellectual energy." But once committed to this mixture, Brown found himself unable to fuse the individual elements into a new, whole, and significant substance. And it is this that partly explains the chaos of his novels. Having adopted the structure of the gothic, and devices of the sentimental novel, Brown found himself stuck with their rhetoric as well, and he never did figure out quite what to do with it.

Brown's confusion is apparent in *Wieland,* his first important published work of fiction. Clark says of the preface to the novel that "Here Brown clearly goes beyond his formula as stated in the preface to *Skywalk;* he denounces the puerile gothic novels, and the sentimental stories of love and seduction fathered by Richardson, and adopts the principles of the Novel of Purpose, made prominent by Holcroft, Bage, and Godwin. Henceforth he will lay bare the hidden motives of men of soaring passions and raging wills; he will choose for his characters men and women who are under some horrid mental or moral delusions, some obsession or perversion of mind."[14] But far as Brown may go, he never manages to go far enough to break the shackles of the sentimental novel and its language. So, although Wieland is intended as the man of "soaring passions, etc.," he is instead cast inevitably into the mold reserved for characters in sentimental fiction, as is evident in the narrator's description of him:

His deportment was grave, considerate, and thoughtful. I will not say whether he was indebted to sublimer views for this disposition. Human life, in his opinion, was made up of changeable elements, and the principles of duty were not easily unfolded. The future, either anterior or subsequent to death, was a scene that required some preparation and provision to be made for it. These positions we could not deny; but what distinguished him was a propensity to ruminate on these truths. The images that visited us were blithesome and gay, but those with which he was most familiar were of an opposite hue. They did not generate affliction and fear, but they diffused over his behaviour a certain air of forethought and sobriety. The principal effect of this temper was visible in his features and tones. These, in general, bespoke a sort of thrilling melancholy. I scarcely ever knew him to laugh. He never accompanied the lawless mirth of his companions with more than a smile, but his conduct was the same as ours.[15]

In his gravity, pensiveness, and melancholy Wieland is a bonafide hero of the gothic romance. But there is a significant difference between him and his forebears. Wieland's melancholy is not motivated, as in most seduction novels, by thwarted love or lust, but by an excessive preoccupation with the general problem of human mortality. Wieland, like Brown himself, *would* ruminate on the great truths of death and mortality, but the verbal structure of which he is composed will not permit him to.

It is interesting to note what Richard Chase has to say on this point:

> In **Wieland** emotions are conventionalized . . . The language too is highly formalized and often stilted. But whereas there is some sense in the complaint that Brown writes "he had not escaped the amorous contagion" instead of "he fell in love," this is really to miss the point. A stately and elevated language, like the measures of a classic ballet, is as useful in the aesthetic economy of the book as is the tireless rationalism of the conversation. The related complaint that Brown's characters are not realistic may also becloud the fact that the melodramatic method demands characters of a somewhat abstract and conventionalized sort, so that in the extremities of the action they become less human beings than *loci* of the clash of ideas and forces.[16]

That Chase begs the question is quite obvious. To be sure, no one will deny that "stately and elevated language" *can* be of use in the "aesthetic economy" of a novel. The question is whether it is so in **Wieland** and Brown's other novels. The answer is by no means simple, but there is sufficient reason to believe that the diction of eighteenth century novels became a straitjacket which strangled Brown almost completely.

But if Brown was never able to break out of the language and stereotypes of sentimental and gothic fiction, he nevertheless tried manfully, and it is the effort, albeit only partly successful, that is significant.

Brown's debt to Godwin for the "philosophial novel" was recognized as early as 1830 in an article in the *American Quarterly Review*. But Godwin, for all the radicalism of his social and political theories, was fairly conventional as a novelist. He wrote *Caleb Williams* (1794) in order to dramatize some of the views he had promulgated a year earlier in *Political Justice*. But he did not project his utopian speculations into his fiction. Instead, he exposed existing evils of society through characters who were not novel or extraordinary. Certainly, the oppressed servant was not new to the English novel (after all, Pamela was one, and so was Joseph Andrews). But Godwin was able to use the situation to emphasize the fact that oppression comes not only from an occasional mean master but from a society which sets a higher value on a man with property than on one without it.

No more unusual than the oppressed servant in the English novel is the cruel squire. But here again Godwin very skillfully and beautifully played a slight variation on an old theme. Falkland, Caleb's oppressor, turns out to be as much a victim of the social order as is his servant, since society has imbued him with the false sense of honor that, ironically, leads to his most dishonorable acts and eventually to his destruction. Godwin criticized the institutions that made a Squire Western, a Squire Allworthy, and a Tom Jones by showing that the same institutions could also make a Barnabas Tyrell, a Falkland, and a Caleb Williams. There was no need for Godwin to experiment in character. All that was necessary was to show the old stock characters in a new light.

Charles Brockden Brown's road was a little rougher. To begin with, many of the evils that Godwin had set out to criticize in the light of new equalitarian ideas had already been abolished, at least theoretically, in this country. There was no monarchy and no legally recognized hereditary aristocracy. In theory, all men were recognized as equal. But since in actuality, men had not progressed sufficiently to live by the rule of Reason, revolutionary ideas still seemed to be valid, and Brown found them still stimulating. He picked up where Godwin had left off, proceeding in some respects to push beyond the master, and in others merely to confuse his teachings. Whereas Godwin had saved most of his speculation for *Political Justice,* contenting himself in *Caleb Williams* with exposing present evils, Brown, in his fiction, was at least as interested in the problematic nature of good and evil as in the evils that flourished before his eyes. The revolutionary ideas promulgated by Godwin grew out of, and were intended to remedy, an immediate situation; but for Brown they always remained largely abstract and speculative. The acute *American Quarterly Review* critic of 1830 had recognized the vagueness of Brown's ideas. Explaining the public hostility to Brown, he asked, " . . . To what end did philosophizing ever come? Who can set bounds to speculation; or limit the wandering of his thoughts when he has fairly embarked amidst the perplexing wilds and interminable labyrinths of metaphysics? It is this unfortunate propensity to prolixity in the philosophical novelist, together with his frequent and inevitable lapses into mysticism and obscurity, which renders his productions . . . less readable, and . . . less popular than those of the describer in fiction. . . ."[17]

It is not merely that Brown philosophizes while Godwin does not, but that Brown adds to Godwin's eighteenth-century rationalism an interest in the problematic and transcendental that involves him in the "interminable labyrinths of metaphysics," in "lapses into . . . obscurity." It is in just such labyrinths that Brown becomes involved in *Wieland.* In it, he tries to test the possibilities of a kind of intellectual aristocracy whose members live a life of reason. So, Wieland, whose grandfather spent his life " . . . in the composition of sonatas and dramatic pieces," which were " . . . not unpopular, but merely afforded him scanty subsistence," and whose father was a fanatic who built his own temple on the Schuylkill, sets up his own little intellectual community, consisting of himself, his sister, his wife, and his brother-in-law, Henry Pleyel. The entire arrangement resembles a Godwinian Utopia in which the life of reason is finally realized. But the first thing that becomes evident is that the life of at least one member of the community is not founded on reason. This member is Wieland himself, who inherits not only his grandfather's interest in literature and his father's fanaticism, but also his father's sense of some sort of ineffable and undefinable guilt. Wieland père believed that "a command had been laid upon him, which he had delayed to perform. He felt as if a certain period of hesitation and reluctance had been allowed him, but that this period was passed. He was no longer permitted to obey. The duty assigned to him was transferred, in consequence of his disobedience, to another, and all that remained was to endure the penalty" (p. 32). A similar sense of guilt became a crucial factor in his son's later behavior.

Wieland's inordinate gravity and concern with man's mortality has already been described. His sister (the narrator) elaborates further, stressing the relationship between this gravity and his father's fanaticism:

> In his studies, he pursued an austere . . . and . . . arduous path. He was much conversant with the history of religious opinions, and took pains to ascertain their validity. He deemed it indispensable to examine the ground of his belief, to settle the relation between motives and actions, the criterion of merit, and the kinds and properties of evidence.

> There was an obvious resemblance between him and my father in their conceptions of the importance of certain topics, and in the light in which vicissitudes of human life were accustomed to be viewed. Their

characters were similar; but the mind of the son was enriched by science and embellished with literature. (p. 43)

The melancholy and fanaticism are further combined with an obsessive desire to plumb the depths of the human mind. "I said, This man is of an ardent and melancholy character. Those ideas which, in others, are casual or obscure, which are entertained in moments of abstraction and solitude and easily escape when the scene is changed have obtained an immovable hold upon his mind. . . . All his actions and practical sentiments are linked with long and abstruse deductions from the system of divine government and the laws of our intellectual constitution. He is in some respects an enthusiast, but is fortified in his belief by innumerable arguments and subtleties" (p. 55).

But strangely enough, in spite of his "enthusiasm," Wieland is strongly influenced by the Ciceronian image of the gentleman.[18] To adorn his father's temple he purchases a bust of Cicero, and though he is "an indefatigable student" who is well versed in many authors, "the chief object of his veneration was Cicero. He was never tired of conning and rehearsing his productions. . . . Not contented with this, he was diligent in settling and restoring the purity of the text. For this end, he collected all the editions and commentaries that could be procured, and employed months of severe study in exploring and comparing them. He never betrayed more satisfaction than when he made a discovery of this kind" (p. 44). All in all, Wieland is a baffling mixture of types: the religious fanatic, the man of science, the Ciceronian gentleman, the litterateur and diletante.

The foil set against him is Henry Pleyel. They are alike in their admiration for Latin authors: "It was not till the addition of Henry Pleyel . . . to our society that his [Wieland's] passion for Roman eloquence was countenanced and fostered by a sympathy of tastes" (p. 44). And, too, Pleyel " . . . was not behind his friend in his knowledge of the history and metaphysics of religion" (p. 45). But here the resemblance ends, for Pleyel does not usually (though he can when necessary) match the lugubriousness of Wieland. Pleyel's " . . . conversation abounded with novelty. His gayety was almost boisterous, but was capable of yielding to a grave deportment when the occasion required it. His discernment was acute; but he was prone to view every object merely as supplying materials for mirth. His conceptions were ardent but ludicrous, and his memory, aided . . . by his invention, was an inexhaustible fund of entertainment" (pp. 44-45).

The difference in temperaments results in a difference in belief:

> Their creeds . . . were in many respects opposite. Where one discovered only confirmations of his faith, the other could find nothing but reasons for

doubt. Moral necessity and Calvinistic inspiration were the props on which my brother thought proper to repose. Pleyel was the champion of intellectual liberty, and rejected all guidance but that of his reason. Their discussions were frequent, but, being managed with candour as well as with skill, they were always listened to by us with avidity and benefit. (p 45)

Pleyel, then, is more the Godwinian, although precisely how much of a Godwinian is never made quite clear, since his discussions with Wieland are never dramatized. And as things turn out, Pleyel eventually finds happiness, while Wieland, spurred on by his fanaticism, plunges with great gusto to his destruction. Eventually another member is added to this intellectual group. Carwin pops up from out of nowhere and for no particular reason. In appearance he is totally outlandish:

> His pace was a careless and lingering one, and had none of that gracefulness and ease which distinguish a person with certain advantages of education from a clown. His gait was rustic and awkward. His form was ungainly and disproportioned. Shoulders broad and square, breast sunken, his head drooping, his body of uniform breadth, supported by long and lank legs, were the ingredients of his frame. His garb was not ill adapted to such a figure. A slouched hat, tarnished by the weather, a coat of thick gray cloth cut and wrought, as it seemed, by a country tailor, blue worsted stockings, and shoes fastened by thongs and deeply discoloured by dust, which brush had never disturbed, constituted his dress. (p. 70)

But this initial impression is misleading for " . . . his forehead, . . . his eyes lustrously black, and possessing, in the midst of haggardness, a radiance inexpressibly serene and potent, and something in the rest of his features which it would be in vain to describe, but which served to betoken a mind of the highest order, were essential ingredients in the portrait" (p. 73).

Carwin turns out to be " . . . sparing in discourse . . ." But " . . . not withstanding the uncouthness of his garb, his manners were not unpolished. All topics were handled by him with skill, and without pedantry or affectation. . . . His observations denoted a mind alive to every generous and heroic feeling. They were . . . accompanied with that degree of earnestness which indicates sincerity" (p. 90).

Because of his "indisputably great . . . intellectual endowments," Carwin is soon completely accepted by the group, though his past remains cloudy. Pleyel provides some enlightenment on this score. Some years before the action of the novel takes place, Pleyel had met Carwin in Spain, where the latter " . . . had embraced the Catholic religion, and adopted a Spanish

name instead of his own, which was CARWIN, and devoted himself to the literature and religion of his new country. He pursued no profession, but subsisted on remittances from England" (p. 87).

Carwin's function in the book is somewhat puzzling. On the one hand, it seems as if Brown intended him as a diabolic character, as is indicated by his grotesque appearance, by the horror with which the narrator recalls his name, and finally by the fact that his sinister (and yet scientifically explainable) ability to project his voice, working on Wieland's fanaticism, initiates the series of actions that culminates in Wieland's total ruin. On the other hand, Carwin's diabolism is unwitting. Moreover, he is not totally evil. The narrator, as has been pointed out, admires his generous and heroic mind, and her attraction to him seems to imply that high minds are attracted to each other in spite of physical impediments. This inference is further encouraged when Pleyel, who is soft on Clara, becomes jealous of Carwin.

It is perhaps fitting that both the romantic contenders for Clara's affection should have European backgrounds. The fact that Pleyel has vague, mysterious ties in Germany, and Carwin in Spain, seems, in a sense, to anticipate the two veins of romanticism (the nostalgic and the supernatural) that Washington Irving was to exploit some twenty years later.

At any rate, these male characters (Pleyel, Carwin, and Wieland) form an interesting triumvirate. Pleyel is a man of reason and learning who is on the whole ineffectual. He thinks of himself as a moralist, and is indeed pompously self-righteous, but he seldom does anything which even remotely resembles a contribution to the good of manking. He is, in the last analysis, a weak character who is dominated by women, but who eventually marries the right one, the heroine, and in so doing supplies the one pleasant note in an otherwise sordid situation.

Carwin is essentially amoral, but his amorality ends in unintended diabolism. He uses his talent of ventriloquism to benefit himself, but his unthinking egocentricity initiates a series of bloody events. As he rather lamentably confesses to Clara (the narrator), he never meant to harm anybody. He just did not foresee the consequences of his actions. It is not difficult to see operating in him the machinations of the modern technological mind.

Wieland in his ardor, though not in his faith, resembles the new intellectual emerging out of the French Revolution. He is, in the fullest eighteenth-century meaning of the word, "an enthusiast." So possessed does he become by his ideas that he kills his wife and children, and later tries to murder his sister. Wieland's confession is excessively verbose and lengthy, but it is also very revealing. He admits that he has done the killing, and then goes on:

"It is needless to say that God is the object of my supreme passion. I have cherished in his presence a single and upright heart. I have thirsted for the knowledge of his will. I have burnt with ardour to approve my faith and my obedience.

"My days have been spent in searching for the revelation of that will; but my days have been mournful, because my search failed. I solicited direction; I turned on every side where glimmerings of light could be discovered. I have not been wholly uninformed; but my knowledge has always stopped short of certainty. Dissatisfaction has insinuated itself into all my thoughts. My purposes have been pure, my wishes indefatigable; but not till lately were these purposes thoroughly accomplished and these wishes fully gratified.

"I thank thee, my Father, for thy bounty; that thou didst not ask a less sacrifice than this; that thou placedst me in a condition to testify my submission to thy will! What have I withheld which it was thy pleasure to exact? Now may I, with dauntless and erect eye, claim my reward, since I have given thee the treasure of my soul." (p. 184)

Wieland's is the absolutist mind. He demands certainty, and he demands it passionately. He demands it even at the cost of his own destruction. In this he is like Melville's Ahab, who must run down the white whale, no matter what the consequences. But ironically, when Wieland does find certainty he has only found a delusion, after all.

Wieland describes his state of mind immediately preceding the murders by saying that it " . . . was contemplative and calm. . . ." His contemplations, he says, ". . . soared above earth and its inhabitants. . . ." He wanted " . . . the supreme delight of knowing [God's] will, and of performing it." His ardor is finally rewarded with a vision of "heaven," all "luminous and glowing." And then he hears " . . . a shrill voice behind. . . . As it spoke, the accents thrilled my heart:—'Thy prayers are heard. In proof of thy faith, render me thy wife! . . .'" The request is not an easy one, even for a fanatic. "'Substitute some other victim,'" he begs. "'My own blood is cheap. This will I pour out before thee with a willing heart . . .'" This is the Abrahamic dilemma descended from the sublime to the melodramatic. And yet, it is typical of Brown that he should have stumbled onto one of the crucial intellectual dilemmas of the nineteenth century—one handled with magnificent sophistication by Kierkegaard in *Fear and Trembling* and by Melville in *Billy Budd*—while at the same time reducing the problem itself to ludicrosity because of his inability to shake off the weakest aspects of Gothic diction and claptrap.

Then, recounting his emotions following the murder of his wife and children, he asserts,

This was a moment of triumph. Thus had I successfully subdued the stubbornness of human passions: the victim which had been demanded was given; the deed was done past recall . . . I imagined I had set myself forever beyond the reach of selfishness.

You [the jury] say I am guilty. Impious and rash! thus to usurp the prerogatives of your Maker! to set up your bounded views and halting reason as the measure of truth! (pp. 191, 195)

There are many ironies here, and many questions raised, but one is never sure whether Brown was aware of them. To begin with, Wieland seems to think that he has acted very reasonably. He has subdued his human passions to perform a difficult task that was required of him. He somehow imagines that he has made a sacrifice to benefit the human race. And except for its violence, his act would appear to be in accord with Godwin's philosophy. Godwin had concluded that a reasonable man who had the choice between saving Archbishop Fenelon or Fenelon's butler should choose to save the Archbishop because of his greater value to mankind. Then Godwin added that it would be immaterial if the butler happened to be the brother or father of the individual who had to make the choice. Thus, for Wieland, an act of madness becomes an act of reason.

The questions raised by the situation could be disturbing. How is it possible to choose between natural affection and the demands of faith? Moreover, when does an act of faith become an act of madness, and who is capable of judging between the two? Where does one draw the line between faith and fanaticism? More disturbing yet, where does one draw the line between fanaticism and reason?

Brown does not push the questions or the ironies. Indeed, one tends to doubt that he saw them. But their presence, even by implication, tends to cast an air of uncertainty over all human actions, an uncertainty that Brown could not have gotten directly from his preceptor. Godwin had great confidence in man's ability to act constructively, and he believed "Human inventions susceptible of perpetual improvement."[19] Godwin was firmly convinced that through Reason, which in itself was not problematic, man could define benevolence, and then proceed to act benevolently.

But Wieland's situation casts doubt on both the capacity of human Reason and the efficacy of human benevolence. Wieland is convinced that his violent act was the very epitome of unselfishness, the very summit of benevolence. His own Reason, he feels, transcends the "halting" reason of ordinary men. And yet, in the eyes of other men, his behavior has been monstrous.

The full ambiguity of human action, however, occurs after Wieland, through the agency of Carwin's ventriloquism, is awakened out of his state of delusion. Clara describes the scene:

> Fallen from his lofty and heroic station; now finally restored to the perception of truth; weighed to earth by the recollection of his own deeds; consoled no longer by a consciousness of rectitude for the loss of offspring and wife,—a loss for which he was indebted to his own misguided hand,—Wieland was transformed at once into the *man of sorrows!*

> He reflected not that credit should be as reasonably denied to the last [the voice he has just heard] as to any former intimation [the visionary voices]; that one might as justly be ascribed to erring or diseased senses as the other. He saw not that this discovery in no degree affected the integrity of his conduct; that his motives had lost none of their claims to the homage of mankind; that the preference of supreme good, and the boundless energy of duty, were undiminished in his bosom. (p. 249)

Clara's attitude is somewhat peculiar. She shrewdly points out that there is no reason why Wieland should not consider the ventriloquized voice as illusory and continue to believe the hallucinated voice which had originally told him to make the sacrifice. But then she comes to the surprising conclusion that even if he has been deluded and has committed horrible crimes as a result of his delusion, his conduct is still noble, for in any case he has acted with the intention of benefiting mankind.

In his next hero "of soaring passions and intellectual energy," Brown turns from his concentration on the dilemmas of religious fanaticism to a consideration of the problem of political commitent, especially the kind of zealous ideological commitment which characterized the eighteenth-century European revolutionaries.

Like Wieland, Ormond occupies himself with "ultimate" questions, and, also like Wieland, he is an "enthusiast." But while Wieland's meditations confirm him as a religious enthusiast, Ormond's meditations intensify his religious skepticism.

> His disbelief was at once unchangeable and strenuous. The universe was to him a series of events connected by an undesigning and inscrutable necessity, and an assemblage of forms to which no beginning or end can be conceived. Instead of transient views and vague ideas, his meditations, on religious points, had been intense. Enthusiasm was added to disbelief, and he not only dissented but abhorred.[20]

As is typical of the revolutionary intellectual, Ormond fills the emotional hiatus left by the absence of religious belief with his fervid political involvement. "His political projects," the reader is informed, "are likely to possess an extensive influence on the future condition of this Western World" (p. 92). The political projects seem to be rooted principally in revolutionary activity, in which Ormond has become engaged at a young age.

> . . . He had embraced, when almost a child, the trade of arms; . . . had found service and promotion in the armies of Potemkin and Romanzow; . . . had executed secret and diplomatic functions at Constantinople and Berlin; . . . in the latter city . . . had met with schemers and reasoners who aimed at the new-modeling of the world, and the subversion of all that has hitherto been conceived elementary and fundamental in the constitution of man and of government. . . . Some of these reformers had secretly united to break down the military and monarchical fabric of German policy. . . . Others, more wisely, had devoted their secret efforts, not to overturn, but to build, . . . [and] for this end . . . embraced an exploring and colonizing project. [Ormond] . . . had allied himself to these, and for the promotion of their projects had spent six years of his life in journeys by sea and land, in tracts unfrequented till then by any European.

> What were the moral or political maxims which this adventurous and visionary sect had adopted, and what was the seat of their newborn empire—whether on the shore of an *austral* continent, or in the heart of desert America—he carefully concealed. (pp 208-209)

The secret society to which Ormond allied himself was apparently the Illuminati, a sect founded in Bavaria by Theodore Hauptmann, a renegade Jesuit, in 1776. At the time ***Ormond*** was published the sect was under heavy attack from conservative clergy as a fountainhead of world conspiracy. Though Ormond has managed to conceal from the narrator (Sophia Westwyn) the maxims of the society, nevertheless she is able to " . . . explain the maxims by which he was accustomed to regulate his private deportment" (p. 92), and these give us at least some insight into Ormond's political beliefs and their influence on his actions.

> No one could entertain loftier conceptions of human capacity than Ormond. But he carefully distinguished between men in the abstract, and men as they are. The former were beings to be impelled, by the breath of accident, in a right or a wrong road; but whatever direction they should receive, it was the property of their nature to persist in it. Now, this impulse had been given. No single being could rectify the error. It was the business of the wise man to form a just estimate of things, but not to attempt, by individual efforts, so chimerical an enterprise as that of promoting the happiness of mankind. Their condition was out of the reach of a member of a corrupt society

to control. A mortal poison pervaded the whole system, by means of which everything received was converted into bane and purulence. Efforts designed to ameliorate the condition of an individual were sure of answering a contrary purpose. The principles of the social machine must be rectified, before men, can be beneficially active. Our motives may be neutral or beneficent, but our actions tend merely to the production of evil. (pp. 92-93)

This initial set of tenets, apparently the result of a misunderstanding of Godwin's then revolutionary theory of ethics, puts man in an impossible position. Man (as he is) cannot improve his lot without first rectifying "the principles of the social machine." But as a product of the machine and a part of it, there is little he can do to rectify it. Wieland had experienced, to his sorrow, the knowledge that actions performed out of the noblest motivation could have not only disastrous but meaningless results. Ormond has already perceived this intellectually, and so he has reached the conclusion that man is faced with a horrible paradox: all human action, motives notwithstanding, ultimately produces evil.

But this is not the worst of the paradox, for many can not rely on inaction either. As far as Ormond is concerned,

> The idea of total forbearance was not less delusive. Man could not be otherwise than a cause of perpetual operation and efficacy. He was part of a machine, and as such had not power to withhold his agency. Contiguousness to other parts—that is, to other men—was all that was necessary to render him a powerful concurrent. (p. 93)

Still, Ormond unaccountably continues to believe that "a man may reasonably hope to accomplish his end, when he proposes nothing but his own good. Any other point is inaccessible." Oddly enough, Ormond also believes that a man " . . . must not part with benevolent desire: this is a constituent of happiness. . . . A wise man will relinquish the pursuit of general benefit, but not the desire of that benefit, or the perception of that in which this benefit consists, because these are among the ingredients of virtue and the sources of his happiness" (p. 93).

Ormond's ethics seem to resolve as follows: All human action eventually produces evil, and yet all men must act. Since a man can achieve happiness only for himself, he must live selfishly. But in pursuing happiness for himself, he must also retain a sense of universal benevolence. This universal benevolence a man must continue to desire as a goal even though he must refrain from trying to achieve it, and even though it is not quite clear what maintaining the desire is intended to accomplish.[21]

In the face of this belief in the futility of all individual action, it is not surprising that Ormond uses his wealth principally to gratify his own pleasures rather than to promote the betterment of man.

> He thought himself entitled to all the splendor and ease which it [his wealth] would purchase, but his taste was elaborate and correct. He gratified his love of the beautiful, because the sensations it afforded were pleasing, but made no sacrifices to the love of distinction. (p. 94)

To spend his money for philanthropic ends would, of course, have been ridiculous, since "The use of money was a science, like every other branch of benevolence, not reducible to any fixed principles. No man, in the disbursement of money, could say whether he was conferring a benefit or injury. The visible and immediate effects might be good, but evil was its ultimate and general tendency" (p. 110).

Neither, however, does Ormond squander his money on the trappings of aristocracy. Though a man of "elaborate and correct" taste, in dress, manners, equipage, and human relationships, he is a democrat:

> Pompous equipage and retinue were modes of appropriating the esteem of mankind which he held in profound contempt. The garb of his attendants was fashioned after the model suggested by his imagination, and not in compliance with the dictates of custom.

> He treated with systematic negligence the etiquette that regulates the intercourse of persons of a certain class. He everywhere acted, in this respect, as if he were alone, or among familiar associates. The very appellations of Sir, and Madam, and Mister, were, in his apprehension, servile and ridiculous; and as custom or law had annexed no penalty to the neglect of these, he conformed to his own opinions. It was easier for him to reduce his notions of equality to practice than for most others. (p. 94)

But in spite of his democratic manners and in spite of his belief in the futility of individual human action, Ormond never overcomes the drive to violence which characterized his early revolutionary career. In order to expedite his seduction of the heroine of the novel, Constantia Dudley, he kills her father. For the same reason he kills a character named Craig. And finally, when the fortress of Constantia's virtue turns out to be invulnerable to deception, he tries to rape her. By this time, however, he has degenerated into a madman. It has been part of his creed that "Love, in itself, was . . . of little worth, and only of importance as the source of the most terrible of intellectual maladies. Sexual sensations associating themselves, in a certain way, with our ideas, beget a disease which has, indeed, found no place in the catalogue, but is a case of more entire subversion and confusion of mind than any other" (p. 132). He himself contracts the malady, and it does indeed prove fatal.

Ormond is not the only intellectual on the scene. In this novel as in **Wieland**, Brown tries to experiment with the possibilities of a group of intellectuals. Constantia herself is the most intellectual of women. She is " . . . thoroughly conversant with Tacitus and Milton," and familiar with Newton and Hartley. Her father has " . . . unveiled to her the mathematical properties of light and sound, taught her, as a meta-physician and anatomist, the structure and power of the senses, and discussed with her the principles and progress of human society" (p. 28). She has " . . . always been solicitous for mental improvement" (p. 146), and her beauty is "animated by . . . intelligence" (p. 131). It is largely her mind that attracts Ormond: "Her discourse tended to rouse him from his lethargy, to furnish him with powerful excitements, and the time spent in her company seemed like a doubling of existence" (p. 131). Likewise, it is to Ormond's mind that Constantia is attracted. "The conversation of Ormond was an inexhaustible fund. By the variety of topics and the excitements to reflection it supplied, a more plenteous influx of knowledge was produced than could have flowed from any other source. There was no end to the detailing of facts, and the canvassing of theories" (p. 146). Furthermore, "The novelty and grandeur of his schemes could not fail to transport a mind ardent and capacious as that of Constantia" (p. 147).

This introduction to revolutionary ideas is supplemented by an introduction to revolutionary actualities when Constantia meets Martinette de Beauvais. Martinette is also an intellectual woman, and though her education has been similar to Constantia's, her life has been richer and more varied. Born in the middle eastern city of Aleppo, she has been exposed to a broad slice of life.

My father [she informs a wide-eyed Constantia] talked to me in Sclavonic. My mother and her maids talked to me in Greek. My neighbors talked to me in a medley of Arabic, Syriac, and Turkish. My father's secretary was a scholar. He was as well versed in Lysias and Xenophon as any of their contemporaries. He labored for ten years to enable me to read a language essentially the same with that I used daily to my nurse and mother. . . . To have refrained from learning was impossible. Suppose a girl, prompt, diligent, inquisitive, to spend ten years of her life partly in Spain, partly in Tuscany, partly in France, and partly in England. . . . Would it be possible for her to remain ignorant of each of these languages? (p. 159)

Martinette's chief attraction is not the quality and breadth of her formal education, but

. . . a knowledge of political and military transactions in Europe during the present age, which implied the possession of better means of information than books. She depicted scenes and characters with the accuracy of one who had partaken and witnessed them herself.

Constantia's attention had been chiefly occupied by personal concerns. Her youth had passed in contention with misfortune, or in the quietudes of study. She could not be unapprised of contemporary revolutions and wars, but her ideas respecting them were indefinite and vague. Her views and her inferences on this head were general and speculative. Her acquaintance with history was exact and circumstantial in proportion as she retired backward from her own age. She knew more of the siege of Mutina than of that of Lille; more of the machinations of Catiline and the tumults of Clodius, than of the prostration of the Bastille and the proscriptions of Marat.

She listened, therefore, with unspeakable eagerness to this reciter, who detailed to her, as the occasion suggested, the progress of action and opinion on the theater of France and Poland. . . .

But, while this historian described the features, personal deportment, and domestic character of Antoinette, Mirabeau, and Robespierre, an impenetrable veil was drawn over her own condition. (pp. 157-158)

Indeed, as it turns out, Marinette has been an intimate participant in the events of the French Revolution, and has been motivated by true revolutionary zeal. When Constantia, at one point, naively asks, "Does not your heart shrink from the view of a scene of massacre and tumult, such as Paris has lately exhibited and will probably continue to exhibit?" Martinette coolly answers:

"Thou talkest, Constantia, in a way scarcely worthy of thy good sense. Have I not been three years in a camp? What are bleeding wounds and mangled corpses, when accustomed to the daily sight of them for years? Am I not a lover of liberty? and must I not exult in the fall of tyrants, and regret only that my hand had no share in their destruction?" (p. 171)

And exult in the sight of blood she does. When " . . . she communicated the tidings of the fall of the sanguinary tyranny of Robespierre, her eyes sparkled, and every feature was pregnant with delight, while she unfolded, with her accustomed energy, the particulars of this tremendous revolution. The blood which it occasioned to flow was mentioned without any symptoms of disgust or horror" (p. 170).

It is only natural that in her wide experience Martinette should have encountered other intellectuals and revolutionaries. One is a priest whose " . . . passion for science," Martinette tells Constantia, "was at least equal to that which he entertained for me, and both these passions combined to make him a sedulous instructor. He was a disciple of the newest doctrines respecting matter and mind. He denied the impenetrability of the first, and the immateriality of the second. These he endeavored to inculcate upon me, as well as to subvert my religious tenets . . ." (p. 162). It is on these startling ideas that Martinette has been nurtured.

But she is initiated into first-hand revolutionary activity through love of a young, idealistic Englishman named Wentworth, who is remarkably anticipatory of the Byronic hero, and actually of Byron himself. He changes the entire orientation of Martinette's previous education: "From the computation of eclipses I now betook myself to the study of man. . . . Instead of adulation and gallantry, I was engaged in watching the conduct of states and revolving the theories of politicians" (p. 166). Wentworth himself, in his youth, " . . . proposed no other end of his existence than the acquisition of virtue and knowledge" (p. 164). He is a member of the nobility, and his character is one " . . . not frequently met with in the world. He was a political enthusiast, who esteemed nothing more graceful or glorious than to die for the liberties of mankind. He had traversed Greece with an imagination full of the exploits of ancient times, and deprived, from contemplating Thermopylae and Marathon, and enthusiasm that bordered upon frenzy" (pp. 166-167).

In search of a cause, he joins the Colonists in the American Revolutionary War. He is wounded in the fighting, and eventually his wounds prove fatal.

These vignettes of subordinate characters are typical of Brown's method. But at least in *Ormond* they are understandable. Brown seems to be trying to encompass the character of the new intellectual, but he is never in sufficient command of his material to achieve his end within the dramatic framework of the novel.

This weakness in development of character extends into his attempts to deal with ideas. Never does he appear able to control ideas within the context of the materials and language of fiction. He sets out to portray men and women of ideas, who are apparently supposed to be eloquent, but they wind up mute. When they do speak, it is in the conventions of the heroes and heroines of sentimental and gothic fiction. Brown plunges courageously into Godwinian and French ideas only to become hopelessly entangled in them. Without reason or motivation characters contradict themselves, and frequently their actions seem to contradict their ideas. In many cases, moreover, the very ability to articulate ideas, which was ostensibly intended to make them heroes, turns them into incorrigible villains.

And yet Brown's very confusion is revealing. Like many an American author after him, he wanted the approval of both the public and the intelligentsia. He

had said as much in the "Advertisement" to *Skywalk.* Nor was it an accident that he sent a copy of *Wieland* to one of the outstanding intellectuals of the day, Thomas Jefferson, in the hope that " . . . an artful display of incidents, the powerful delineation of characters and the train of eloquent and judicious reasoning which may be combined in a fictitious work, will be regarded by Thomas Jefferson with as much respect as they are regarded by me."[22]

But there is no evidence that Jefferson was impressed. To satisfy the public, Brown had to provide entertainment in accepted fashion and at the same time avoid the open expression of unpopular ideas; to satisfy "those who study and reflect" he had to provide intellectual substance. He succeeded in satisfying neither.

Perhaps Jefferson's silence is as meaningful as anything he could have said. Most likely, he was baffled. For though many of Brown's insights were sound, he never seemed fully able to comprehend them intellectually, nor to articulate them meaningfully. He sensed the situation of the new intellectual—his derivation from the reasonable Ciceronian gentleman, his unreasoning impassioned elevation of reason into a goddess, his fatal political zeal—but he lacked the intellect or imagination that would have fused these elements into a consciously significant work of art. Probably Brown's most brilliant insight into his intellectual characters is his having conceived their violence against a European background, even though the main setting of the action is always American. Wieland, for example, is deeply involved in his Saxon ancestry. Ormond's past is mysterious, but he has been engaged in European revolutionary intrigue since boyhood. Martinette was born in Aleppo, has lived all over the continent, and has been involved in all the major revolutions of the late eighteenth century. Pleyel, when he arrives on the scene, has just returned from Europe. Achsa Fielding (in *Arthur Mervyn*) is a Jewess born in England. Carwin was born in England and has lived a great deal on the Continent. Two lesser Falkland-like intellectual villains, Welbeck (in *Arthur Mervyn*) and Ludlow (in *Carwin the Biloquist*), are both of European origin. But Brown himself never seemed to know quite what to make of his own insight. If he had, he might have been our first great novelist and not just a historical curiosity.

Notes

[1] *The Revolutionary Spirit in France and America* (N.Y., 1927), p. 465.

[2] Vernon L. Parrington, *Main Currents in American Thought* (Harvest Books, N. Y., 1954), II, 177.

[3] David Lee Clark, *Charles Brockden Brown, Pioneer Voice of America* (Durham, 1952), p. II.

[4] Ibid., p. 6

[5] Ibid., p. 5.

[6] Ibid., p. 155.

[7] Ibid., p. 157.

[8] Ibid., pp. 54 ff.

[9] Ibid., p. 158.

[10] Charles Brockden Brown, *The Rhapsodist and Other Uncollected Writings,* ed. Harry Warfel (N.Y., 1943), pp. 135-136.

[11] Leslie Fiedler, *Love and Death in the American Novel* (N.Y., 1960), p. 126.

[12] Ibid., pp. 126-127.

[13] Ibid., p. 132.

[14] Clark, pp. 164-165.

[15] Charles Brockden Brown, *Wieland, or the Transformation* (Phila., 1887), pp. 42-43. Page references in the text are to this edition.

[16] *The American Novel and its Tradition* (Anchor Books, N. Y., 1957), pp. 38-39.

[17] "Brown's Novels," *American Quarterly Review,* VIII (1830), 318.

[18] For a discussion of the Ciceronian gentleman in America, see Edwin H. Cady, *The Gentleman in America* (Syracuse, 1949).

[19] William Godwin, *Political Justice* (Toronto, 1946), Bk. II, Chapter I, 109.

[20] *Ormond, or the Secret Witness,* ed. Ernest Marchand (N. Y., 1937), p. 149. Page references in my text are to this edition.

[21] To say that there is an "ethic" here is probably an overstatement. Rather, the entire passage seems to be a botching of Godwin's implicit utilitarianism.

[22] Clark, p. 163.

Warner Berthoff (essay date 1966)

SOURCE: "Brockden Brown: The Politics of the Man of Letters," in *The Serif: Kent State University Library Quarterly*, Vol. III, No. 4, December, 1966, pp. 3-11.

[In the following essay, Berthoff surveys Brown's political philosophy as exhibited in his novels and maintains that it remained consistent throughout his literary career. Berthoff explains that Brown's political theory centered on human personality and self-fulfillment as ways of evaluating the problems of the state; in Brown's earlier novels he focuses on the potential destructiveness of self-interest, while in his later novels, Brown emphasizes the success of self-interest.]

Charles Brockden Brown's last two novels, ***Clara Howard*** and ***Jane Talbot,*** were published in 1801. Their general feebleness seems to anticipate directly his abandonment of the novel as a literary instrument. Actually these books, epistolary in form, are in some ways more competently executed than the four better-known novels Brown had rushed into print in the brief and turbulent period, 1798-99, when his most important writing was done. But the force of mind, the psychological intensity and energy of analysis that characterized this earlier work have gone out of Brown's story-telling. He is still committed as a novelist to the serious exploration of moral ideas and their practical human consequences and to the projection of a sharply monitory image of the troubling anomalies of the moral life. His leading characters, their presumptions to an understanding of moral right and wrong thoroughly chastened, still must learn that "the wisdom of men, when employed upon the future, is incessantly taught its own weakness."[1] The temper of the exposition, however, is distinctly cooler and more complacent, the narrative resolutions much more nearly in accord with common wisdom. Marriage and civil happiness now reward those who overcome excesses of sensibility or of ideological passion and move toward a prudent acquiescence in the imperfect custom of human existence.

It would seem that as Brown's own ideas about right conduct and worldly probabilities settled down, his novels lost their melodramatic urgency. In any event these last two speak not for the confused philosophic quest of his early manhood but for the sensible compromises of his later career as a magazine editor, chronicler of contemporary history, and family man. He wrote no longer to the end of a purgative moral excitement but in the service of a tolerable civil settlement. From the metaphysics of spiritual "transformation" (the subtitle of ***Wieland***) he turned to the mechanics of practicable social compromise. It is this latter interest that finds expression in Brown's political writings, the great bulk of which was produced after 1801. His preoccupations as a writer cease now to resemble those of a Poe or Hawthorne and approach those of a Fenimore Cooper. For Cooper's studied methods of advancing political opinions and social judgments in fiction, however, Brown had neither talent nor interest. He simply changed his métier. He had used the novel as a means of intellectual growth, and he had now outgrown the point of view, the special concerns, that brought dramatic life into his management of it. Yet in turning to journalism and pamphleteering, to history and politics, his serious critical interest in ideas and their practical consequences in no way diminished; the work of his last decade continued to register the intellectual dedication that despite every crudeness of form had made his novels so curiously memorable.

Before the nineteenth century, to be "liberal" (the word did not come into use as a noun until about 1820) meant to be cultivated, to show a generous and informed interest, free from the necessity of any immediate serviceability, in learning, science, the arts, politics, all the activities of civilized culture. In this sense of the word it would be accurate to speak of Brockden Brown's politics as "liberal." The "liberal" attitude in politics was above partisanship; the "liberal" concern was not primarily with the organization and administration of government but with its spirit and ends. The ends in view were the cultural and moral improvement of individual human beings in their natural relationships, the amelioration of their fortunes, the progress of the species. The "liberal" attitude, in fact, tended to postulate a deep division, even antipathy, between government and society. The forms of government were artificial, arbitrary, inevitably unjust, inimical to true morality. But the forms of human society were natural, organic, capable of indefinite betterment—and therefore more expressive of the innate capacities of individual men, the proper development of which lay at the heart of the whole disagreeably necessary matter of politics.

The critical question was: were these capacities free to develop? On issues of policy, liberalism was eventually to evolve an embarrassing instinct for self-contradiction, as in its conflicting impulses to leave society and individuals alone and to hurry along, by force and repression if necessary, their "inevitable" progress. But beneath all conflict over policies there was agreement on first principles: that no theoretical or statutory design and no fixed institutions could fairly represent the multiform actuality of natural social enterprise or do justice to the irreducible singularity of individual temperament.

A classic, and extreme, expression of this outlook in the English-speaking world at the end of the eighteenth century was William Godwin's influential *Enquiry Concerning Political Justice* of 1793. In the anti-Jacobin reaction of the 1790's Godwin was known in England as a dangerous radical, though his book escaped prosecution by reason of its price; no publication costing three guineas, it was sensibly decided, was likely to inflame the popular mind. But *Political Justice* in any case is a very different book from Paine's *Rights of Man,* which appeared a year later. Godwin so idealized his concept of justice as to put it altogether above

practical politics. His thesis was that human reason and moral will, if they would act *sincerely,* could by themselves establish absolute justice and institute moral perfection in society. The revolution *Political Justice* projects is a moral and psychological revolution. Though it prophesies an age without government and without policy, sharing with Rousseau and Marx the ultimate myth of "the dissolution of political government," it specifies no particular outward convulsion by which the chains of tyranny and injustice are to be cast off. The reformer's task is not revolt but education and enlightenment (though on this ground there is a strain of the cultural commissar in Godwin's thinking, on the subject of purifying common human relationships and reforming ordinary behavior). "A certain quantity of truth will be sufficient for the subversion of tyranny and usurpation," Godwin confidently asserted, for "it is the property of truth to spread." "The chains of tyranny fall off of themselves, when the magic of opinion is dissolved." The *Enquiry* reads now, and must have read even then, as a visionary idyll of reason and triumphant human virtue; by contrast both Tom Paine and Edmund Burke may seem rather sordidly Machiavellian. "A metaphysical and logical commentary on some of the most beautiful and striking texts of Scripture": so Hazlitt was to describe the book thirty years later,[2] when its influence had long since departed from public debate to be diffused into the more abstruse prophecies of Shelley's poetry.

When Brockden Brown, erstwhile Godwinian, abandoned the novel and turned to political journalism, this, broadly speaking, was the point of view he instinctively adopted. He wrote as a "speculatist,"[3] a public moralist of broadly liberal persuasion. His first concern was not the analytical critique of institutions nor the science of legislation nor the Idea of the State nor the laws of history (though all of these preoccupations were taking shape in western thought during his lifetime) but, more traditionally, the moral temper and cultural accomplishment of society. It was Godwin's attitude without Godwin's inflationary evangelism. Like the hero of his own *Jane Talbot,* who had to outgrow an excessive devotion to the book, *Political Justice,* before being allowed to win the girl, Brown foreswore the letter of Godwinism as a "vanity of disputation" but clung to the generosity of its vision.

This suprapolitical attitude did not inhibit active partisanship. When the party divisions of the early republic became fixed in the administrations of Adams and Jefferson, Brown took his stand with the "liberal" Federalism of the seaboard commercial centers. He published three pamphlets criticizing Jefferson's foreign policy. His *American Register,* the semi-annual review of current history which he conducted from 1806 until his death, clearly reflects his merchant bias, and gains understanding and imaginative strength from it. And though he kept his *Literary Magazine and Ameri-*

can Register (1802-1807) studiously neutral, its editorial sympathies are unmistakably with an enlightened conservatism. But in contrast to the vitriolic party press of the period, the journalism of Bache, Duane, Freneau, Cobbett, Brown remained aloof and dispassionate.

So when he ventured to attack the Jefferson administration, he attacked nothing short of what he took to be its essential and defining temper. The point of his criticism was not that the administration was pursuing dangerous or unwise policies but that it lacked policy altogether, that it did too little, took too short a view of the national welfare, that its exercise of government was small-minded and materialistic. In short it lacked a "liberal" understanding of the ends of government. "The whole purpose of government," Brown wrote in 1804, "is vulgarly supposed to consist in repelling external enemies, and restraining the fraud or violence of individuals when immediately directed against the person or property of each other." But there is more to good government, he contended, than the operation of an efficient constabulary. What the mere "politician" fails to look to is "the health or morals of the people, so far," Brown added rather obscurely, "as these arise from the regulation of the passions and discipline of the manners."[4]

What he meant by this seems as vague as his disapproval was sharp. How far was he willing to admit social "regulation" and in what form? He never gave a clear answer. Certainly he would countenance no statutory supervision of private life; the rationalist version of tyranny was no more to be endured than the feudal or imperial. That man's life was the subject of intricate relations, and encompassed by a bewildering variety of claims, as Brown had written in "Walstein's School of History" and as he had shown systematically in his novels, was as true for the political theorist as for the story-telling moralist. Brown's mature attitude merely reinforced what he had long before concluded from his brief study of the law, that there was no greater source of injustice than the subordination of particular human actions to abstract legislative principle.

In retreating from the prescriptive element in Godwinism, Brown, let it be said, had not given up the ideal of an ultimate political justice. Rather he had come to understand what positive harm a rationalism that was inflexible, a benevolence that would not compromise, could do to the worthiest ends. (His novels had said as much, though more ambiguously.) Men do not yield up their vices, or their sympathies, to righteous bullying. The reformer's first task must be to get himself privately trusted and respected: "so long as men are led by their affections, I destroy in myself the power of doing good, if I declare open hostilities with their follies and weaknesses, and thus forfeit that esteem by which alone I can hope to influence their judgments to choose the good and refuse the evil."[5] We can see him here not outlining a program but establishing a position, a broad social "liberalism" that was, with respect to political action, conservative and gradualist. So long as men *are* led by their affections, Brown now believed, such advance in general welfare as is possible in any era may be entrusted to the stabilizing power of society's received institutions; Brown ridiculed those "politicians" who "have of late imagined that no government could safely rest upon custom and tradition, that no nation can be supposed to have any constitution which is not reduced to writing. . . ."[6] From the Utopian goal of an immediately perfected political justice (to which, Dunlap's biography tells us, he had devoted himself in his first youth) Brown had come around to the goal of a mediate stability; from righteous severity to a benign watchfulness. "Treat the world at large," his "Speculatist" argues, "somewhat as the skillful nurse treats a wayward child; that is, make some sacrifices to its caprices in matters of less importance, in order to obtain the power of controverting it in those of greater."[7]

These positions are of interest not as new departures in political theory but as American responses to the convulsions of 1789 and after, not less ominous because they were taking place an ocean away. Brown's tentativeness and vagueness are themselves a measure of the rapid unsettling, around 1800, of Enlightenment categories of political understanding. The language of discussion had been conditioned for nearly a decade by the French Revolution: by the volumes of controversy in the wake of the Burke-Paine debate, and by that ultimately more decisive event, the experience of aggressive revolutionary warfare by a truly national army whose power was essentially ideological. A French Revolution in some form had been predictable from the logic of eighteenth-century social criticism and from the philosophically satisfactory example of the American Revolution. But long before it was over, it was clearly not the Revolution that had been foreseen, not a beneficent climax to the century of enlightened progress now past, but an ominous index to an obscure and alarming future. So it appeared in the speculative and literary precincts of European culture, where the ends of political association, as of man's life and of creation itself, were rapidly passing out of the realm of self-evident truth. Received truths were everywhere being challenged; the very scope of political thought was decisively broadened. The romantic obsession with personality, with the flowering of genius and the release of energy and imagination, gave new force to the view that *no* known form of political association could ever finally be *good* for its members. Political thought was reaching out to two characteristic nineteenth-century extremes, both alien to the common-sense formulations of the Enlightenment: one was the concept of an absolute anarchism of personal independence, the other the concept of an absolute State which would perfectly realize the entire potential of society and all its members.

Brown's own political thinking reached neither of these extremes, but he could not help sharing in the movement of thought that produced them (to the point of projecting, in the curious imaginary histories he was piecing together after 1800, an ideological police state to enforce cultural homogeneity).[8] His brand of conservatism suggests a sympathy with the ideas of Edmund Burke, whose defense of traditional order—not always tenable, with regard to the actual circumstances of the French Revolution, in the face of Paine's cross-examination—was nevertheless to become authoritative for anti-radical thought. Burke's powerful imagination had visualized the destructive effect of revolutionary change on manners and institutions, on social custom, on civilization itself. To a reader who shared with Burke the point of view of the moralist and man of liberal culture, the *Reflections* could provide a philosophic platform to stand on whether or not he accepted every detail of the anti-revolutionary case. Brown, however, was no disciple of Burke.[9] He was instinctively more sympathetic to the democratic sentiments of Paine; he shared with Paine a common Quaker heritage, a respect for the sanctity of individual experience, a preference for a truly communal democracy. But for Brown the starting point of political speculation was no longer the natural rights of men, as it was for Paine, but their natural capacities. And his understanding of "natural" was infected by that subjectivist contagion which was transforming every aspect of Enlightenment thought and of which his own novels, with their melodramatic analysis of minds under extreme stress, were a conspicuous symptom. He measured the problems of the state by standards of human personality and individual self-fulfillment, which is to say by precisely those considerations which had occupied him in fiction.

The consistency of Brown's political thinking will be apparent if we bear in mind the preoccupations, and the lessons, of his fiction. A "speculatist" in public affairs as well as in the novel, his unspoken first principle was (to adapt Professor Crane Brinton's sentence about Wordsworth) "to make 'the sentient, the animal, the vital' in human life the guide to a social and political state where these most natural elements can find the satisfaction they demand."[10] The lesson of **Wieland, Ormond,** and **Edgar Huntly,** however, had been that the 'sentient' and 'vital,' the qualities of energy and feeling, were as ambiguous and potentially destructive as they were fulfilling. Only by firm management of the outward circumstances, the social milieu, could it be guaranteed that human energy would always be guided by reliable motives. Even then, experience seemed to demonstrate that there was always some self-generating demonism in the man of energy, some fatality at the root of his experience, which would resist public disciplining and subvert any compromise or armistice imposed by social decorum. In **Arthur Mervyn** and the two last novels Brown had shifted his ground; there the lesson had been of the successes of self-interest, and the outcome a more or less politic compromise with things-as-they-are.[11] A characteristic American practicality and ideological reserve (such as, not without traces of provincial smugness, had conditioned the middle-of-the-road American attitude toward the doctrinaire politics on both sides of the French Revolution) kept Brown from moving directly into any of the doctrinaire positions of Romantic liberalism. He recognized, as the Godwin of *Political Justice* had not, the specifically political consequence of the liberal premises; that is, he understood that the unconditional medicines of disinterested sincerity and rational justice could not be administered to the whole body of society except through political compulsion. And the politics of compulsion would require a willingness to compromise, to be tolerant of half-way measures, if it were not to be worse than the original sickness.

To wind up so respectably in the middle way is no proof of great political wisdom. But Brown's political imagination was at least as alert and responsive as the psychological understanding displayed in his novels. It was given positive direction by the special roles he played in the liberal, professional society of the early republic: the role of merchant that he had inherited and the role of author and editor that he had chosen. As a Philadelphia merchant he made a good deal more of his serious political journalism than special pleading for the mercantile interest; so he grounded his case against the non-intercourse policy in a broad, a truly "liberal" conception of the sociological and cultural function of international commerce. As a professional man of letters he worked in the magazines he edited to foster the essentially political notion of a national culture. His task was not to defend a standing order from revolutionary assault but to look for means of securing and cohering America's already revolutionary institutions.[12] His avoidance of partisanship in advancing these large conceptions was backed increasingly by his concern for the perspective of history, for exposing the immediate event to the long view. In his political writing Brown had begun with Utopian romance; he ended with history, even (one may wish to say, after studying the "Annals of Europe and America" he was writing in the last years of his life) with an incipient historicism. Through all the stations of his activity as a political and historical journalist he maintained a consistent objective: that cultural progress of the whole people which alone would safeguard the young republic.

Notes

[1] *Clara Howard, or, The Enthusiasm of Love, Charles Brockden Brown's Novels, Volume VI* (Philadelphia, 1887), p. 350.

[2] "William Godwin," *The Spirit of the Age* (1825).

[3] A short-lived department in Brown's *Monthly Magazine and American Review* was called "The Speculatist"; it appeared in April (II, 4) and in September and October (III, 3, 4) of 1800.

[4] This passage is to be found in a translator's footnote in C. F. Volney, *A View of the Soil and Climate of the United States of America,* translated, with occasional remarks, by C. B. Brown (Philadelphia, 1804), p. 259n.

[5] "The Speculatist: No. III," *The Monthly Magazine and American Review,* III, 4 (October, 1800), pp. 241-243.

[6] "The Polemical Passion," *The Literary Magazine and American Register,* IV, 23 (August, 1805) pp. 128-129. The essay is signed "B."

[7] "The Speculatist: No. III," *The Monthly Magazine and American Review,* III, 4 (October, 1800), pp. 241-243.

[8] These are printed in William Dunlap, *The Life of Charles Brockden Brown,* 2v. (Philadelphia, 1815), I, pp. 170-258, 262-396, as "Sketches for a History of Carsol" and "Sketches for a History of the Carrils and Ormes." For an interpretation of this work see W. B. Berthoff, "Charles Brockden Brown's Historical 'Sketches': A Consideration," *American Literature,* XXVIII (May, 1956), pp. 147-154.

[9] It is difficult, on the basis of only a few direct references, to determine what Brown's judgment of these controversial figures was, or whether he had formed one. One finds in Brown's magazines a number of more or less Burkean reflections on political affairs but very few bearing any resemblance to Paine's thought. See, for example, "On 'The Enlightened Public' and 'The Age of Reason,'" *The Literary Magazine and American Register,* IV, 23 (August, 1805), pp. 110-114: "He who thinks, will perceive in every enlightened nation, three kinds of people; an inconsiderable number instructed by reason, and glowing with humanity; a countless multitude, barbarous and ignorant, intolerant and inhospitable; and a vacillating people with some reason and humanity, but with great prejudices, at once the half-echoes of philosophy, and the adherents of popular opinion." But in 1809 we find Brown referring, in a pamphlet written to oppose the Embargo, to "the imagination of Burke, teeming with so many monsters. . . ." (*An Address to the Congress of the United States. . . . ,* Philadelphia, 1809, p.4n.)

[10] *The Political Ideas of the English Romanticists* (London, 1926), p. 63.

[11] On *Arthur Mervyn,* see W. B. Berthoff, "Adventures of the Young Man: An Approach to Charles Brockden Brown," *American Quarterly,* IX (Winter, 1957), pp. 421-434.

[12] Brown's thought, it appears, was moving towards the positions occupied in succeeding decades by those lawyers and legal theorists whom the late Perry Miller brought freshly to our attention in Book Two, "The Legal Mentality," of his posthumous *The Life of the Mind in America* (New York, 1965).

For a detailed review of Brown's political and historical journalism, see my unpublished dissertation, *The Literary Career of Charles Brockden Brown* (Harvard, 1954), Part Three, "Political Writings."

Arthur G. Kimball (essay date 1967)

SOURCE: "Savages and Savagism: Brockden Brown's Dramatic Irony," in *Studies in Romanticism,* Vol. VI, No. 4, Summer, 1967, pp. 214-25.

[*In the following essay, Kimball examines Brown's use of the term "savage," arguing that Brown uses the term ironically, not as a reflection of "New World experiences" with Indians, as many critics have contended, but as a way of commenting on the human capacity for violence.*]

Critics of Charles Brockden Brown's *Edgar Huntly* (1799) have taken the titular hero at his word. "My parents and an infant child were murdered in their beds," he says. Thus "I never looked upon or called up the image of a savage without shuddering."[1] Accordingly, critics say that Huntly's attitude reflects New World experience with the red man, and that Brown considers the Indian a murderous savage "whose every action if not closely circumscribed leads to tragedy."[2]

This approach overlooks Brown's ironic use of the term "savage" and the idea of savage violence as commentary, not on the red man, but on the white. The Indians in *Edgar Huntly* are really foils for the savage potential of Brown's hero. "What light has burst upon my ignorance of myself and of mankind!" says Huntly as he reflects upon his adventure. "How sudden and enormous the transition from uncertainty to knowledge!" (p. 6). The new knowledge results from a nightmare series of wilderness encounters in which Huntly, stripped of all outward signs of civilization (except an army musket), drinks the warm, reeking blood of a panther, slaughters five Indians, and emerges, marked by the "ruthless passions" he has experienced.

Huntly's discovery of his savage potential provides a key to Brown's major fiction. Through his art, Brown protests Enlightenment optimism with its assumption of man's innate virtue and its overly optimistic hopes for the New World. He indicates that from the hidden corners of man's mind there is likely to issue as much darkness as light. That darkness, in the form of savage violence, is a central theme in **Wieland, Ormond,** and a short story, **"Thessalonica,"** as well as in **Edgar Huntly.** Through ironic variations on the theme of "savagism," Brown suggests that a recognition of man's capacity for violence qualifies unrealistic visions of progress.

I

Antoine-Nicolas De Condorcet provides a good example of the optimism that prevailed with many at the time Brown was writing novels. In his *Sketch for a Historical Picture of the Progress of the Human Mind* (1795), Condorcet said that he would "show by appeal to reason and fact that nature has set no term to the perfection of human faculties; that the perfectibility of man is truly indefinite; and that the progress of this perfectibility, from now onwards independent of any power that might wish to halt it, has no other limit than the duration of the globe upon which nature has cast us."[3] Condorcet said that John Locke had provided the key to knowledge and progress. Brown, like many others at the end of the eighteenth century, was affected by Lockean ideas. But Brown suspected that there were shadowy corners in man's psyche for which Locke's *tabula rasa* had not provided. He incorporated his insights into his novels.

In **Wieland; or, the Transformation** (1798), his first major novel, Brown showed how the Lockean association of ideas could be disrupted by, of all things, a ventriloquist. In the course of the novel, nearly every character finds his senses deluding him. Thanks to the ventriloquist, people hear voices—and draw conclusions from the sense data—which turn out to be false. Chaos results. But Wieland, not the ventriloquist, provides the real irony in the novel. He too hears voices, but he is mentally sick and thinks God commands him to kill his wife and children. He slaughters them with an axe and nearly kills his sister, Clara, the narrator of the book. Clara Wieland, terrified by the nightmare change in her life, exclaims, "I live not in a community of savages; yet . . . I am in perpetual danger of perishing; of perishing under the grasp of a brother!" Later she addresses her killer-brother as, "Thou whom thy fate has changed into parricide and savage!" (pp. 208, 250). Wieland, like Edgar Huntly, becomes a symbol for civilized man's savage potential.

Central to an understanding of **Wieland** is Clara's symbolic private closet. For Brown, an inheritor of Lockean sensationist psychology, it is a striking metaphor for Locke's "dark room of the mind." Like Edgar Huntly's wilderness cave, it harbors the shadowy night-side of the id; it is Clara's version of what Leslie Fiedler calls the gothic "world of dreams and of the repressed guilts and fears that motivate them," and part of Brown's "vocabulary of symbol and myth capable of bootlegging past the guardians of Reason perceptions of the irrationality of experience and life itself."[4]

Appropriately, the climax of **Wieland** takes place in Clara's room, near the closet which houses the manuscript which in turn contains, in Clara's words, "the most secret transactions of my life." Equally appropriate is the heroine's description of the scene: "I have said that the window-shutters were closed. A feeble light, however, found entrance through the crevices. A small window illuminated the closet, and, the door being closed, a dim ray streamed through the keyhole. A kind of twilight was thus created, sufficient for the purposes of vision, but, at the same time, involving all minuter objects in obscurity" (p. 212). Clara's words describe **Wieland** itself. The heroine's emotional nightmare finally ends with her brother's suicide (does the knife in the neck imply an insane attempt to "kill" the voice?) and her own ambiguous comment, which suggests that some symbolic taint has passed from her brother to herself (and perhaps from Clara to the reader): "He was stretched at my feet; and my hands were sprinkled with his blood as he fell" (p. 250).

What has emerged from Clara Wieland's dark room? What strange chimeras of the fancy are recognizable in the twilight atmosphere of her narrative? Some we can name. The closet contains at different times the "memoirs" of her father, the incarnate irrationality which is Carwin, a "lancet and other small instruments" with which Clara contemplates suicide, a manuscript of her innermost secrets, countless fears associated with her brother's madness, and a host of other vague terrors of physical violence, death, seduction, and incest, which, like the "minuter objects" in the final scene, remain in obscurity. Brown's portrait of the irrational is a triptych whose outer panels—Wieland's insanity and Carwin's manipulations—frame and give dimension to the central picture, Clara's dimly lit closet. For Clara Wieland, a peaceful vision in America ends in gloomy memories thousands of miles from her native land. Clara's riverbank retreat emerges as another important symbol, a microcosm of the novel's major action. Its change from a place of happy meditation to a place of terror, one of the book's many "transformations" (cf. the full title), reflects the change in Clara's knowledge resulting from her traumatic confrontation with her own psyche and the irrational, savage violence of her brother. The words in Brown's "Advertisement" prove hauntingly ironic: "It is hoped . . . that the solution will be found to correspond with the known principles of human nature."

Brown analyzed savagism in a more covert form with a short story in his own *Monthly Magazine* early in

1799. "**Thessalonica, A Roman Story**" is a study in violence. The action starts when a citizen, Macro, attempts to enter a gate by which the senators pass to their seats at the stadium. Repulsed by guards, Macro resists, is slightly wounded, the citizens explode in fury, and the guards run in terror. "At length the soldiers sought their safety in flight. The mob poured into the passages. One of the fugitives was overtaken in a moment. The pursuers were unarmed, but the victim was dashed against the pavement, and his limbs were torn from each other by the furious hands that were fastened upon him. . . . All around them was anarchy and uproar, and passion was triumphant in all hearts." The "savage ferocity" of the Thessalonians brings about their own slaughter and the story ends with a statement threatening "the return of the human species to their original barbarity."[5]

That Brown's Roman story has universal application is underscored by a review he wrote for his paper. "**Thessalonica**" appeared in the May issue; in June Brown reviewed a Fourth of July, 1798, oration by Josiah Quincy of Boston. Quincy described how Rome subjugated the nations of the world, and added that in Roman history "may be seen the reflected image of the rulers of France, who, with the professions of Roman virtues, have practiced all the arts of Roman ambition, and all the schemes of Roman conquest and injustice." In his review Brown commented that "in these times of discord and contention, to look for the empire of benevolence and justice in the minds and hearts of men may be delightful as a vision of the fancy, but experience teaches us it is almost a chimerical hope."[6]

In **Ormond,** written only four years after Robespierre's death, Brown overtly states his concern with savagism, and reveals with considerable irony a new world man's shocked reaction to the savage violence that could perpetrate a Reign of Terror. Constantia Dudley learns much about men and savagery from the wild adventures of Martinette Beauvais, a participant in both the American and French revolutions:

> Each incident fastened on the memory of Constantia, and gave birth to numberless reflections. Her prospects of mankind seemed to be enlarged, on a sudden, to double its ancient dimensions. Ormond's narratives had carried her beyond the Mississippi, and into the deserts of Siberia. He had recounted the perils of a Russian War, and painted the manners of Mongols and Naudowessies. Her new friend had led her back to the civilized world and portrayed the other half of the species. Men, in their two forms, of savage and refined, had been scrutinized by these observers; and what was wanting in the delineations of the one was liberally supplied by the other.

Constantia discovers Martinette's delight in violence. "Her eyes sparkled, and every feature was pregnant with delight, while she unfolded, with her accustomed energy, the particulars of this tremendous revolution. The blood which it occasioned to flow was mentioned without any symptoms of disgust or horror" (pp. 200-201). Ormond's experience is bloodier still. He has spent eight years of a military career "in a warfare the most savage and implacable . . . which history records" (p. 256). Appropriately, these two savages turn out to be brother and sister.

Brown's sources of the irrational in **Ormond** include also the yellow-fever setting (Rush and other physicians debated fiercely over its origin) and sexual desire. The plague causes moral anarchy in the city; the villain Ormond's passion drives him insane. Constantia survives the terrors of the diseased city only to confront the crazed villain. Ormond is a man of colossal ego, an incarnate parody of Reason. He desires unlimited power, and seeks to control and manipulate others. Ironically, for lack of self-understanding, he cannot control himself. The motivational joker in the deck proves to be the oldest passion in the world. The narrator, Sophia (Wisdom?), has said, "sexual sensations associating themselves, in a certain way, with our ideas, beget a disease which has, indeed, found no place in the catalog, but is a case of more entire subversion and confusion of mind than any other" (p. 156).

She is right. Near the end of the novel Ormond traps Constantia in the house on her Jersey estate. Like the riverbank recess of Clara Wieland, this retreat is a symbol of past happiness, and like Clara's sanctuary it is transformed into a place of terror. And like **Wieland, Ormond** has many transformations, for the villain's experience of the dark possibilities of human nature has at some point turned to insanity. Ormond has murdered Constantia's father; now he seeks to rape her. She defends her honor—that airy notion, as Ormond regarded it—with what has been happily described as her "very substantial little pen knife,"[7] but her experience transforms her world. Constantia's confrontation of the irrational in terms of murder, seduction (she had found Ormond strangely attractive), and savage violence leave her sad and troubled. At the end of the novel she embarks for Europe.

II

When Brown wrote, much irony surrounded the term "savage." There were "noble" savages, and, as captivity narratives demonstrated, ignoble savages. Savagism could refer to man in a primitive, unspoiled state, or to man at his wildest and most barbarous. Some writers questioned whether society was progressing from, or relapsing into a state of savagism. Noah Webster captured some of the ironic ambivalence in his definition:

Savage, *n.* A human being in his native state of rudeness; one who is untaught, uncivilized or without cultivation of mind or manners. The *savages* of America, when uncorrupted by the vices of civilized men, are remarkable for their hospitality to strangers, and for their truth, fidelity and gratitude to their friends, but implacably cruel and revengeful toward their enemies. . . .[8]

Political writers, especially, exploited the term "savage." For example, after the Reign of Terror American Federalists associated their political opponents, the Republicans, with French Jacobins and quickly labelled their rivals "savages." The Terror, the American Revolution, and frontier experience with the red man combined to invest the idea of "savagism" with ironic ambiguity. The heart of the matter was pin-pointed in the *Newhampshire and Vermont Journal* of February 21, 1797, where the editor, in an article entitled "Savages," said, "There were savages then, there are savages now, of fair face, and who never shot arrows from a bow."[9]

As his novels indicate, Brown knew what the term could imply. In 1804 he published his translation of C. F. Volney's *A View of the Soil and Climate of the United States of America,* a work which was to be part of an extensive study of the new American nation. Volney stated candid opinions and Brown made numerous corrections and comments throughout in the form of translator's notes. In the section "On the Indians or Savages of North America," Volney said, "As to the practice of burning and devouring captives, every narration of an Indian war informs us that captives are fastened to a stake, near a pile of burning wood, there to be tormented in all the ways which savage vengeance can devise." After some illustrations, including a description of a scalping, Volney concluded that these tales "would not be credited by civilized nations, were they not well authenticated, and posterity, who will know no savages will treat such tales as fabulous." "Alas!" lamented Brown in a footnote, "what a mistaken notion that cruelty prevails only among hunting tribes, and that posterity will cease to be governed by the same ferocious passions, or prompted by them to the same excesses."[10]

Brown had incorporated these sentiments into his fictions, of which *Edgar Huntly; or, The Memoirs of a Sleepwalker* climaxes his commentary on savages and savagism. Here he again probes the dark depths of the soul, adding to the themes of his earlier works—madness and savage violence—his peculiarly American source, the red man, and the ideas of self-preservation and revenge. The result is a complex and ironic delineation of man's capacity for irrational and savage behavior reflecting the problems of "civilized" society in general, and in particular, those of the new American nation.

In words addressed "to the public," Brown says his purpose is "to exhibit a series of adventures, growing out of the condition of our country, and connected with one of the most common and most wonderful diseases or affections of the human frame." On the surface Brown alludes to sleepwalking, but the "affection" which emerges from the narrative is the death-dealing potential couched in the hidden depths of man's being. To link this insight with a display of somnambulism was, however, a brilliant thrust, for sleepwalking in Brown's day was thought to be a kind of madness, a temporary lapse into irrationality. "Dreaming," said Benjamin Rush, "is a transient paroxysm of delirium. Somnambulism is nothing but a higher grade of the same disease. It is a transient paroxysm of madness."[11] When Edgar Huntly first encounters Clithero Edny and realizes the latter is asleep, he reflects: "The incapacity of sound sleep denotes a mind sorely wounded. It is thus that atrocious criminals denote the possession of some dreadful secret. The thoughts, which considerations of safety enabled them to suppress or disguise during wakefulness, operate without impediment, and exhibit their genuine effects, when the notices of sense are partly excluded, and they are shut out from a knowledge of their entire condition" (p. 13).

Brown has been underrated as an ironist. Huntly's own primitive instincts soon "operate without impediment" as he undergoes a nightmare series of adventures in search of Clithero, and his words form the matrix from which the novel germinates when he reflects that Clithero's action "was part of some fantastic drama in which his mind was busy," and that "to comprehend it, demands penetration into the recesses of his soul" (p. 13). The penetration is a pursuit through a symbolic mental wilderness to the blackness of a cave hidden in its depths. Here Huntly finds Clithero in a primitive state. "His scanty and coarse garb had been nearly rent away by brambles and thorns; his arms, bosom, and cheeks were overgrown and half concealed by hair. There was somewhat in his attitude and looks denoting more than anarchy of thought and passions. . . . My surprise and my horror were still strong enough to give a shrill and piercing tone to my voice. The chasm and the rocks loudened and reverberated my accents while I exclaimed: *'Man! Clithero!'* " (p. 100).

When Huntly finds "man" at the dark center of the cave, he finds himself as well. Later, in a sleepwalking trance, he again seeks Clithero in the Indian-infested wilderness. He finds his way to the cave, only to fall into a pit. When he regains consciousness, "immersed in palpable obscurity," he gropes about; the first object he encounters is an Indian tomahawk (he is an expert in its use!). "This incident afforded me no hint from which I might conjecture my state," says Huntly. The reader need not remain in such darkness. Hunger and fear reduce Edgar to an instinctual, savage state; he contemplates suicide with the tomahawk, then uses it to kill a panther (which he calls a "savage"), gorges himself on the warm flesh, and eventually fights his way back to civilization, slaughtering five red men along the way.

In the first part of the novel, Clithero tells Edgar how his troubles all started. One night, while carrying a large sum of money for Mrs. Lorimer, his European benefactress and employer, Clithero was attacked. A bullet grazed his forehead and in the darkness he glimpsed the flash of a knife. He reacted instinctively, in self-defense, and killed the attacker—who turned out to be Mrs. Lorimer's villainous brother. Unhinged by this unforeseeable event, Clithero nearly killed Mrs. Lorimer and, thinking he had caused her death, escaped to America where he met Huntly. After hearing Clithero's story, Huntly concludes that he is innocent, and that "it was the instinct of self-preservation that swayed him" (p. 87).

Critics, failing to note the significance of the self-preservation motif, have charged Brown with structural inadequacy. "The book, like *Arthur Mervyn,* breaks in two at the middle," says Lillie Deming Loshe.[12] But during his wilderness sojourn, Huntly is threatened too, first by a panther and then by five Indians. He kills the animal "from the self-preserving and involuntary impulse," he explains (p. 161), and later buries a tomahawk in the breast of one of the red men with a stroke "quick as lightning." "How otherwise could I act?" he asks. "The danger that impended aimed at nothing less than my life. . . . In an extremity like this, my muscles would have acted almost in defiance of my will" (p. 171).

Eighteenth-century philosophers like Edmund Burke, Henry Home (Lord Kames), and Adam Ferguson saw "self-preservation" as a particularly significant motive. Fear and anger operate instinctively, says Kames, and therefore the passion of self-preservation often is exerted "even in contradiction to reason."[13] But Ferguson, especially, by linking this irrational passion to the idea of "property," provides a fertile source of irony for the novelist. Ferguson explains that "the dispositions which refer to the preservation of the individual, while they continue to operate in the manner of instinctive desires, are nearly the same in man that they are in the other animals: but in him they are sooner or later combined with reflection and foresight; they give rise to his apprehensions on the subject of property, and make him acquainted with that object of care which he calls his interest. . . . He apprehends a relation between his person and his property." Under these apprehensions, Ferguson warns, man may enter, "if not restrained by the laws of civil society, on a scene of violence or meanness, which would exhibit our species, by turns, under an aspect more terrible and odious, or more vile and contemptible, than that of any animal which inherits the earth."[14] Huntly's adventures take place on what

was once Indian "property," and during his escape from the wilderness, he arrives at the primitive log hut of Old Deb, a woman of the tribe of Delawares or Lenni-Lennapee who has remained stubbornly to occupy the land her countrymen have been forced to abandon, for, Huntly says, "all these districts were once comprised within the dominions of that nation. About thirty years ago, in consequence of perpetual encroachments of the English colonists, they abandoned their ancient seats" (p. 197). Here Huntly kills three Indians.

The irony is compounded many times during Huntly's return to civilization, in part through Sarsefield, Huntly's friend and former tutor. Like the self-preservation theme, the figure of Sarsefield helps link Clithero's European troubles with Huntly's wilderness experience. Sarsefield has been a suitor of Mrs. Lorimer, and a former friend of Clithero. Again, when Huntly kills one of the Indians, he takes a gun which he later recognizes to be the ingeniously designed weapon Sarsfield had given to him. Designed for war not sport, Huntly explains, the gun had been given to Sarsefield by an English officer who died in Bengal. With it Huntly dispatches two Indians and wounds a third, ending the latter's dying agonies with the gun's bayonet. After killing the red man, Huntly moralizes: "Such are the deeds which perverse nature compels thousands of rational beings to perform and witness! Such is the spectacle . . . of which habit and example, the temptations of gain, and the illusions of honor, will make us, not reluctant or indifferent, but zealous and delighted actors and beholders!" He adds, ironically, "I left the savage where he lay, but made prize of his tomahawk. I had left my own in the cavern" (pp. 193-194).

The successive dwellings Huntly encounters on his way out of the wilderness furnish more irony. After killing three Indians at Deb's hut, Huntly staggers to a frame dwelling painted white, with windows and a door "embellished with mouldings and a pediment." He expects to find marks of progress here, and an end to violence, and concludes that it is "the abode of rural competence and innocence"; he finds instead a drunken ruffian who has driven his wife and infant from their home. The sleepwalker's weird experience finally ends at a tree-lined estate where he meets Sarsefield. A happy reunion and explanations follow; ironically, Huntly's story reveals that he and Sarsefield have almost killed each other, each mistaking the other for a "savage" (pp. 230, 271). The joy ends abruptly, for Clithero's body is discovered, mangled by a tomahawk, and Huntly asks Sarsefield for help. A doctor and teacher, Sarsefield embodies the humane skill and learning which mark a civilized nation. He refuses to aid Clithero because of an old grudge. In this last dwelling, which should have epitomized the farthest reaches of culture, Huntly finds only hatred determined on revenge. Brown has reduced a popular account of the stages of society's progress, related by Crèvecoeur, Thomas Jefferson, and others, to a tale of ironic equality in terms of instincts and dark motives. Huntly's nightmare flight, hunted, it turns out, by both red man and white, dramatizes the message. Huntly's penetration into the recesses of the soul is almost complete.

The ambiguous possibilities of "savagism" are further underscored by Brown's use of the Indians and by the ending of his novel. Brown is ambivalent toward the red men, for they are a threat; they haunt the wilderness, mangle Clithero, and prove to be murderers after all. But the terror which "broods over the perils of Brown's fictional world" is not the Indian, as Fiedler claims, but the terror of Huntly's self-discovery.[15] Despite Sarsefield, Clithero Edny recovers—with the aid of some old Indian remedies!—and for a time secludes himself in the wilderness in Deb's hut (a symbolic rejection of the "civilized" world?). Clithero had come to America eager to embrace a "new world"; he ends a lunatic who drowns himself trying to escape from his guards. "May this be the last arrow in the quiver of adversity!" says Sarsefield in the last sentence of the book. But Huntly's statements linger on. "Disastrous and humiliating is the state of man!" says Edgar. "By his own hands is constructed the mass of misery and error in which his steps are forever involved. . . . How little cognizance have men over the actions and motives of each other!" (p.267). In words which sum up much of the book's irony, Huntly concludes that "no one knows the powers that are latent in his constitution. Called forth by imminent dangers, our efforts frequently exceed our most sanguine belief" (p. 159). Thus, in **Edgar Huntly,** the underlying irony is Brown's exposé of the savage potential, not of the red man, but of the white.

Apparently Brown's ironic suggestions about man's potential for violence and irrational behavior were lost on his contemporaries. His insights did not appeal to those, like Condorcet, who envisioned great strides of progress. New Bedford's Abraham Holmes said that at last America had "provided the proper environment for realizing man's potentialities."[16] Some, however, sensed a potential source of tyranny in man's nature for which no philosophical system, including Enlightenment optimism, could adequately account. Brown was one, and Margaret Fuller was right in saying that he spoke to "the soul of things" and at least partly right in that it was the "dark deep gloom" of his novels that prevented their being more popular.[17] James Fenimore Cooper was less perceptive. In the preface to *The Spy* he doubted that readers would relish the cave scene in **Edgar Huntly,** because it contained "an American, a savage, a wild cat, and a tomahawk, in a conjunction that never did, nor ever will occur."[18]

But Brown's symbolic conjunction did occur. Brown died in 1810, and two years later America was at war with England. And by the 1860s Edgar Huntly's tomahawk had become a Civil War musket and the wildcat

a guerilla marauder. Americans demonstrated again their potential for savage violence and parricide. Brown did have something to say as to the soul of things. His premonitions continue to be relevant for an age of progress.

Notes

[1] *Charles Brockden Brown's Novels* (Port Washington, N.Y., 1963), pp. 165-166. All references to Brown's novels are to this reprint of the 1887 David McKay edition.

[2] Albert Keiser, *The Indian in American Literature* (New York, 1933), p. 36. Cf. David Lee Clark, *Charles Brockden Brown; Pioneer Voice of America* (Durham, N.C., 1952), p. 176; and Roy Harvey Pearce, *The Savages of America* (Baltimore, 1953), pp. 198-199. Mabel Morris, "Charles Brockden Brown and the American Indian," *AL,* XVIII (1946), 244, disagrees, but fails to apply her insight toward an understanding of Brown's fiction.

[3] Tr. June Barraclough (New York, 1955), pp. 4, 132.

[4] *Love and Death in the American Novel,* rev. ed. (New York, 1966), p. 140.

[5] *Monthly Magazine and American Review* (New York, 1799-1800), I, 103.

[6] *Monthly Magazine and American Review,* I, 220.

[7] Alexander Cowie, *The Rise of the American Novel* (New York, 1948), p. 78.

[8] *An American Dictionary of the English Language* (New York, 1828).

[9] *The Newhampshire and Vermont Journal; or, The Farmer's Weekly Museum* (Walpole, N.H.). See also the issue of Aug. 9, 1796, and for an example of a satiric political exchange see *The Echo, With Other Poems,* ed. Richard Alsop and Theodore Dwight (New York, 1807), pp. 31-32, 35.

[10] (Philadelphia, 1804), pp. 402, 402 n.

[11] *Medical Inquiries and Observations upon the Diseases of the Mind* (Philadelphia, 1812), p. 304.

[12] *The Early American Novel* (New York, 1907), p. 45.

[13] Henry Home (Lord Kames), *Elements of Criticism* (Edinburgh, 1762), I, 95-96.

[14] *An Essay on the History of Civil Society* (Edinburgh, 1767), pp. 17-18. The section deals with the "universal qualities" of man's nature.

[15] *Love and Death in the American Novel,* p. 160.

[16] See Merle Curti, "The Great Mr. Locke, America's Philosopher 1765-1865," *Huntington Library Bulletin,* XI (April 1937), 120.

[17] *The Writings of Margaret Fuller,* ed. Mason Wade (New York, 1941), p. 374.

[18] *The Spy; A Tale of the Neutral Ground* (New York, 1821), pp. vi-vii.

Cecelia Tichi (essay date 1972)

SOURCE: "Charles Brockden Brown, Translator," *American Literature*, Vol. XLIV, No. 1, March, 1972, pp. 1-12.

[*In the following essay, Tichi contends that Brown's 1804 translation of C. F. de Volney's* A View of the Soil and Climate of the United States *reveals Brown's nationalistic bias.*]

In his lifetime Charles Brockden Brown translated one work only: C. F. de Volney's *A View of the Soil and Climate of the United States.* For the novelist-editor-critic and, as of 1803, political pamphleteer, the translation of Volney in 1804 seems an odd choice, Although he was America's formost litterateur, Brown rendered into English no romantic tale in the tradition of Chateaubriand's *Atala,* but "the first book to give an organized synthesis of the physiographic and geologic regions of the United States and of the climatology of the continent."[1] The choice for translation seems doubly puzzling when we consider that a London English language edition was already available in America even as Brown labored at its American counterpart. And without engaging in the perpetual debate over the noblesse oblige of literary translators, one must upon examination of Brown's work concur with a reviewer for the *Monthly Anthology and Boston Review* that Brown "omitted notes that did not accord with his own ideas" and "wholly altered the form of one of the appendices."[2] But while his biographers have viewed Brown's effort as an anomalous, quasi-literary interlude between his novels and his political-historical activities, such easy dismissal of the translation may leave neglected a significant aspect of Brown's thought. The *Monthly Anthology* reviewer had denounced Brown's alterations of Volney as "wholly unpardonable," both dishonorable and unjust. Yet a close look at the eccentricities of Brown's translation suggests that Volney stimulated the Philadelphian both to define the American in relation to his nation and continent, and to attempt actuation of the territorial expansion which, as of his first political pamphlet, Brown evidently believed would insure national progress. Indeed, the special biases Brown reveals in his translation make it quite clear that the effort was no perfunc-tory exercise in a language self-taught, nor a task undertaken only at the urging of Brown's fellows in the Friendly Club. Rather, Brown's translation of Volney appears to be the work of a mind bent upon using the pen for specific nationalistic purposes.

Brown's interest in, and encouragement of, American national self-consciousness in varied areas of life has been well documented.[3] For example, his brief editorial tenure at the *Monthly Magazine and American Review* (1799-1800) had found him reviewing "more or less critically" some "one hundred and fifty American publications."[4] And his later journalistic ventures in editing the *Literary Magazine and American Register* (1803-1806) and then the *American Register, or General Repository of History, Politics, and Science* (1807-1809) reveal by their contents—and even by their titles—the value Brown placed upon preserving the current record of the growing nation. Moreover, as a novelist Brown had used fiction to define the American experience. His portrait of the American wilds in **Edgar Huntly** was no happenstance of setting, for "the work unites Old World intrigues with the hazards of a New World civilization."[5] Further, **Arthur Mervyn** has recently been called a novel in which "self realization occurs on American soil and in American terms . . . in more complex ways than most readers have imagined."[6] But Brown published no fiction after 1801, and Warner Berthoff finds in the "feebleness" of his last two novels an anticipation of Brown's "abandonment of the novel as a literary instrument." It was in "journalism and pamphleteering, history and politics" that Brown was thereafter to focus "his serious critical interest in ideas and their practical consequences."[7] Certainly one of Brown's major ideas concerned American nationalism, a term whose political ramifications are perhaps best revealed in the kinds of liberties Brown took with Volney's text and in the cast his marginal notes gave that work.

It is important to recognize the tradition of which Volney's *View of the Soil and Climate* is part. Misleadingly, Joseph Dennie had called it "these travels."[8] But Volney did not write the kind of impressionistic, anecdotal travel narrative that was fast becoming a literary genre all its own, especially for disgruntled European visitors eager to excoriate America for its crudities. On the contrary, Volney, an "accomplished French linguist, philosopher, politician, scientist, author, and extensive traveler in Africa and Asia Minor," followed his scientific predecessors Buffon and de Pauw, both of whom had concluded by deduction that natural conditions in America could not promote population growth nor support a healthy populace.[9] In sum, Volney, a friend of Jefferson and Fellow of the American Philosophical Society, did not present himself as one French traveller piqued by drafty coaches and greasy dinners, but as a savant prepared to assert in the authoritative language of disinterested science that

America was thoroughly pestilential and rife with threatening savages, that of its vast area the only sites fit for civilized life were "the southern point of Rhode Island, or the south-west chain in Virginia between the Roanoke and Rappahannock," or the "high-lands of Florida and Georgia," or the shores of Lake Erie "a hundred years hence" when "it will not as now be infested with fevers" (p. 264).

Volney's caveats appeared in the same year as Brown's first political pamphlet, which urged the expropriation of the Louisiana Territory Spain had recently ceded to France. Brown's main intent in *An Address to the Government of the United States on the Cession of Louisiana* was to alert Americans to imminent colonial danger, but the boldness of his proposal contrasts sharply with Brown's recognition of the awesome vastness of the United States as currently bounded, and of the nation's self-induced vulnerability through interregional strife. In 1800, three years earlier, Brown had described the enormous area and maze of divisions in his country:

> Only reflect upon the motleyness, the endless variety of habits, ranks, and conditions in our country. The theatre itself is too wide for you to traverse: a thousand miles one way and fifteen hundred the other: various in climate from the ceaseless ardors of the tropics to the horrors of the arctic winter; divided into near a score of separate states, in each of which there are very great peculiarities of constitution and laws; each of which has climate, soil, productions, distributions of property and rank somewhat different from those of its neighbors.[10]

Brown's reflections on the multiplicity of the country are not singular for himself or his time, for American periodicals were reiterating the difficulties of defining the interrelation of citizen to nation to continent, and of deriving a national identity from disparate peoples in disparate geopolitical regions. Brown's own *Monthly Magazine* tried to distill the "American spirit," and his *Literary Magazine* contained warnings of regional disputes and perspectives on the American character.[11] Similar writings appeared in the *American Museum,* the *Monthly Anthology,* and the *Port-Folio.*[12] Nor did Brown neglect such matters in his *Address to the Government.* Seemingly his horror of Americans' myopic parochialism (and concurrent indifference to their fellow citizens in other regions) led him to cry in his political pamphlet, "Do the people of the coast regard as aliens and enemies those beyond the mountains? Those of the northern states, however distant in place and dissimilar in manners, do they regard with no paternal emotions the happiness or misery of their Southern countrymen?"[13]

Yet boldly in his *Address to the Government* Brown asserted the importance of United States territorial imperatives over the "lesser" matters of cultural and regional variance among Americans. Righteously he called for seizure of the Louisiana Territory. "We have looked on with apathy," he wrote, "while European powers toss among themselves the property which God and Nature have made ours. . . . America is OURS . . . and therefore Louisiana is ours." He urges that the Territory be secured "for removing all obstacles to the future progress of our settlements." Minimizing current difficulties, Brown's tone becomes visionary as he legitimizes the expropriation of land as ordained by higher powers, "God and Nature." David Lee Clark has observed that "Brown was moved primarily by wholesome patriotism—the desire to see his country expand from ocean to ocean."[14] But indications are that Brown's position required a striking imaginative leap both geographically and temporally, as well as politically.

Thus committed to the view that America's destiny lay in future continental expansion, Brown used his translation of Volney both to reaffirm his view and to actuate that expansion by nullifying Volney's charges about savage Indians and unhealthy natural conditions. At the very outset Brown takes his visionary stance, his imagination fueled by the Louisiana Purchase:

> The recent addition of Louisiana has carried the western limit far beyond the Mississippi, and embroiled it in a world of unexplored deserts and thickets. The circumstance has aided the imagination in its excursions into futurity; and instead of anticipating the extension of this empire merely to the sea on the south, and to the *great river* on the north, we may be sure that, in no long time, it will stretch east and west from sea to sea, and from the north pole to the Isthmus of Panama. (p. 2n.)

Just as his *Address to the Government* has emphasized the importance of United States geographical extension, so in the translation Brown characterizes Americans by their reach upon the continent, seeming to settle for himself the question of who is properly an American citizen:

> The want of a peculiar geographical appellation, and their superiority in numbers and importance to every other nation, exotic or indigenous, of America, has given to the people of the United States the name of "Americans," among their neighbors and among Europeans. . . . Instead of regretting this circumstance . . . I think it rather a cause of pride and exultation. We should . . . ardently anticipate the period, when the extension of our empire will make the national appellation of *Americans* a strictly geographical and precise one. (p. 338n.)

Yet the plausibility of "extension of our empire" from "sea to sea" over the entire North American continent obliged Brown to counter Volney's indictments of America as unhealthy territory riddled with incorrigible savages.

Throughout the *View of the Soil and Climate* Volney had revealed his distaste for Rousseau, "who, having created for himself an airy and fantastic world, knew as little of the society of which he was born a sequestered member, as of Indians, of whom all his notions were gathered from the woods of Montmorenci" (p. 386). With satisfaction Volney portrays the indigenous American as the ignoble savage, at best a herd animal, at worst a cannibal devouring enemies alive. He is delighted that Floridian traveller Bernard Romans agrees that the Indian race is "sottish, filthy, idle, pilfering, and haughty," not to mention "vain, irritable, vindictive, and ferocious" (p. 272). In large part Charles Brockden Brown might be expected to concur with these views, for in *Edgar Huntly* (1799) he had by no means portrayed the Indian sympathetically. Of necessity Edgar slays five savages in the course of the action, and in the narrative recounts how "notwithstanding the progress of population, and the multiplied perils of such an expedition, a band of them had once penetrated into Norwalk, and lingered long enough to pillage and murder some of the neighboring inhabitants."[15]

But while Brown perceived the Indian as a rich resource for fiction, using him in Roy Harvey Pearce's term, for "the luxury of horror," still his translator's notes do not accede to Volney's view of the Indian as a violent threat to civilization.[16] The Indian refusing accommodation to a reasonable mode of civilized life is, Brown says, simply a despicable creature of habit, much like his white counterparts (p. 376n.). "The true problem is not why the Indian cannot be changed into a shopkeeper or mechanic," but why he stubbornly resists an agrarian life which "is all that the welfare of the United States" and his own "happiness and dignity" require of him (p. 377n.). Yet the example of Chief Little Turtle heartens Brown that "an Indian can abjure his habits, and adopt all the modes of the whites which are worthy of adoption." Brown neither patronizes nor condescends, but firmly resists agreement with Volney. In fact, Brown suggests Indian *extinction* is likely in the offing, for while the native peoples "have already probably taken several steps toward a total assimilation to the customs of the whites, they are hastening to extinction with a much quicker pace than to civilization" (p. 381n.). So much for that threat to national expansion.

On the subject of health Volney had charged that even the most populous and civilized portions of the United States were debilitating. Philadelphia in midsummer is so intensely hot, he complains, "that the streets are deserted from noon till five o'clock, and most of the inhabitants retire to repose after dinner" (pp. 107-108). Yet the northeast wind "fills the air with the chilliest

and most benumbing fog" which "oppresses the brain, and produces torpor and headache" (p. 137). Volney extends the pathology to the national character, implying that America is distinguished by "torpor and feebleness of mind" (p. 138). He complains of drenching rainfall and, as if water, wind, and heat were not abusive enough, warns that when he "first saw thunder storms at Philadelphia, the electric fluid appeared so copious, that all the air was on fire." Lightning bolts, he adds, "often occasion the most disastrous accidents" (pp. 198-199).

Brown discredits Volney with light irony, declaring risible the Frenchman's avowals of prostrating heat and citing himself as a Philadelphian active in all weathers. "The writer of this note," he says, "has been sitting at his ease, in a spacious room in an airy situation, surrounded by trees" and "at six o'clock P. M., observing the noon-day heats remitting, he has looked at the glass and found it 89 degrees." No sedentary creature, Brown "has himself walked five miles in a dusty, shadeless road at noon day, with a black beaver hat on his head, when the heat was 91 in the shade of an adjacent wood" (p. 108n.). As for the wind-induced headache and torpor, Brown writes that most Philadelphians and visitors experience nothing but the consequences of dreary weather "rather uncheering to the fancy than directly hurtful to the health" (p. 137n.). And those lightning accidents are "rare," though with irony Brown adds that the "terror of lightening," especially among the ladies, "is a genuine and formidable evil in America" (p. 199n.). But Brown takes umbrage at Volney impugning the national character. "It is somewhat surprising," he says caustically, "that notions so crude and generally exploded, should be countenanced by our author" (p. 138n.). But he cannot resist exploding the notions anew.

Far more serious are Volney's imprecations about diseases in America, for at length he describes those "whose prevalence entitle them to be considered as the direct offspring of the soil of this country" (p. 223). Volney charges that fatal consumption is caused by widely fluctuating American temperatures. Further, fevers are rife and while "not immediately fatal," they "sensibly enfeeble the constitution and shorten life" by fifteen to twenty years (p. 229). Volney's gravest accusation, however, is that "the yellow fever prevails more and more in the United States" (p. 237), and that, contrary to the accepted medical hypothesis, it is not a disease imported from the Caribbean via infected sailors, but an indigenous malady engendered by the soil and climate of the United States. He lists each symptom until "death hastens to close the scene"; and then Volney offers a chilling geographical profile of the disease reaching inexorably northward in America throughout the eighteenth century. "Louisiana and the southern coasts of the United States, where heat and moisture combine their pestilential influence, were never strangers to it," nor were "New Orleans, Pensacola, Savannah, Charleston, and Norfolk" usually "free from it for five years together." The Potomac River had long been its boundary, but the disease had got such a stronghold beyond it that "it may be now considered as congenial to the northern as well as to the southern states." It had "appeared at Philadelphia as a pestilence," had "raged at New York," and "ravaged Baltimore, Norfolk, Charleston, and Newburyport." It had also been diagnosed at Boston, Harrisburg, Oneida, and "the Miami of Lake Erie" (pp. 240-241). Yet even as the disease gained ground, Volney charges, the American medical profession had through a sense of national pride conspired to deceive the public into belief that the yellow fever was imported. On the contrary, Volney suggests that it "is capable of being generated within the country, by a concurrence of certain incidents of time and place" (p. 246).

Brown likely prepared his refutation in counsel with his medical colleagues in the Friendly Club. Of course he could not dispute the Frenchman's statistics, so instead he emphasizes the efficacy of preventive measures. Evidently Brown was convinced that a well-regulated life made the body a healthy garrison for warding off disease. This was his position in *Arthur Mervyn*, in which the narrator, Dr. Stevens, says that in the midst of the epidemic his family "enjoyed good health" and were "hopeful" of escaping infection because they followed a regimen of "cleanliness, reasonable exercise, and wholesome diet," rather than of fumigation or flight from the zones of disease.[17] Mervyn himself becomes ill only when he abuses his body by ignoring advice to eat and rest, and he hears a companion impute the disease, "not to infectious substances imported from east or west, but to a morbid constitution of the atmosphere, owing wholly or in part to filthy streets, airless habitations and squalid persons."[18] Noteworthy here is the attribution of the fever, not to an indigenously pestilential soil and clime, but to an hygienically insulting condition created by men, and presumably correctable. In his translation Brown indicates that corrective measures are indeed underway, observable in Philadelphia's new public water system, which had been installed after Volney departed the country secure in his conviction that the quays of New York and Philadelphia "surpass, in public and private nastiness, any thing [he] ever saw in Turkey" (p. 255).

In defending the healthful virtues of a well-ordered life, Brown attacks European customs and chides his countrymen for aping them. Diseases, he believes, "are owing to absurd modes and vicious habits," and he regrets that "the dress and diet of Europe are assiduously copied in America, where it is far more injurious from the nature of the climate" (p. 225n.). He castigates Americans frequently for alcoholic abuses and complains that "men are every where reckless of health." Regrettably, "habit reconciles us to every

thing, and a stupid confidence in our own good fortune possesses us" (p. 231n.). Nonetheless, Brown vehemently denies that America is unhealthy. He credits the "middle and eastern states" with having "the strongest physical claim to salubrity," and to these adds "New England, the inland of New Jersey, and the eastern part of Pennsylvania" as being "entitled equally, and in a high degree, to this praise, and as long life, with as few diseases [as] are to be found in . . . France, Spain, or Italy." Likely projecting American national expansion into Canadian territory, Brown adds that "a northern climate, and a social and agricultural state similar to that of Norway and Scotland, is doubtless still more favorable to health and longevity" (p. 264n.).

Significantly, Brown's translation includes prescriptive treatment for the fevers Volney only warns against. Brown reprints these cures from Bernard Romans's *Concise Natural and Moral History of East and West Florida* (New York, 1775). Volney himself had excerpted from Romans brief passages which comprised an "Appendix." But the Frenchman used the excerpts to document Indian brutality in the Southeast, and to reveal which horrible diseases awaited the unsuspecting there. Dutifully Brown translated those passages without comment. But then he expanded that portion of the "Appendix" to four times its original length—an alteration which incensed the *Monthly Anthology* reviewer. But Brown had special reason to quote extensively from Romans, for not only did the Floridian traveller concur with Brown about the enervations of alcohol and the virtues of life free of all debauchery (including carousing and gormandizing), but he further prescribed specific cures for tetanus, sunstroke, fluxes, and even the yellow fever. Thus Brown's version of the "Appendix" becomes in part a layman's practical pharmacopoeia. The inclusion of these cures markedly alters the tone of Volney's work. For by implication, disease, once contracted, can be dealt with successfully. It need not be a deterrent to salubrious life in the United States, nor to national expansion into southeastern American territory.

Brown's generous quotation from Romans evinces in other ways his motives for actuating national territorial expansion. He inserts a lengthy passage extolling the natural resources of the region. There is pine that makes "both excellent and good timber," on land which maintains "immense stocks of cattle." "Barren and unfavorable soil" nonetheless sustains "peach and mulberry orchards," and rice production yields an abundant crop "very willingly" and, "if sufficiently made dry, always proves the best for corn, indigo, and hemp." Romans has seen "very good corn and rice together, with two kinds of melons, and cucumbers in great perfection on this species of soil" (pp. 273-282).[19] Brown's permutation of Volney's "Appendix" reads, in short, like an invitation to colonization of the southeastern regions. Agricultural industry is promised bountiful rewards there. Brown says that he "has extended a little the quotations of Volney" because "B. Romans' information on the soil and diseases of those provinces is very curious and authentic" and because "his book is out of print, and extremely rare" (p. 273n.). But surely Brown affects the guise of a bibliophile, a posture he really belies at the conclusion of his altered "Appendix," where he regrets that Romans's work has not been reissued, since "the vicinity of Florida to the United States, and the probability of its being incorporated with our territory in a little time, would render its contents uncommonly interesting to the present, and still more to the next generation" (p. 316n.). Once again looking to the future, Brown spurs the appropriation of lands "God and Nature" intend to be a part of the United States.

All along, with the imperative of American national expansion fixed in mind, Brown refuses the self-effacing role his London counterpart followed in translating Volney. Brown, in fact, insists upon being a dialectic voice throughout the work. And he manages, at least in part, to make translation the metamorphic means for turning an unfavorable view of the soil and climate of the United States into one inviting Americans to fulfill their destiny by taking dominion of a potentially rewarding land. Expectedly, the "Americanization" of Volney's work met with the plaudits of Brown's associates. S. L. Mitchill observed that "the Philadelphia translation contains many critical and explanatory notes by the ingenious Mr. Brown."[20] And William Dunlap, mindful of the London translation, archly remarks that "to give an English dress to the crude and often unfounded opinions of Volney respecting this country, was neither congenial with the talents nor feelings of Charles Brockden Brown."[21] Nor, one might add, with the expansionist motivations of the Philadelphian.

Brown's politically visionary translation of Volney was no intellectual cul-de-sac, for the subsequent prospectus of his General Geography indicates that he hoped to make that work an instrument of the nation's comprehension of its possibilities. Promising a special emphasis on America, Brown writes that "with respect to North America, the daily and rapid extension of our geographical knowledge is notorious, while the rapid progress of this portion of the world, in population and riches, continually calls for new pictures."[22] He adds that "every geographical writer justly regards the description of his own country as of chief importance," a topical focus which Brown vows to imitate, promising "one volume, or the greater part of it, to America in general, and particularly to the United States." Of course Brown's death prior to completion of the project makes discussion of it conjectural. But it seems probable that in it Brown planned to convey his beliefs about the nation's territorial growth and progress. Certainly a geography was the ideal genre in which to be informative and visionary, yet also to

help realize that vision by enticing readers to emigrate over the landscape. If truly the Lewis and Clark Expedition was Jefferson's instrument of vision, "the enactment of a myth that embodied the future," then plausibly Charles Brockden Brown's very similar vision was to be conveyed in a geography.[23] Here would be a work more efficacious for his purpose than fiction, and one whose practical nature would link it with the American-produced volumes Brown continued to review as a journalist. Doubtless Brown planned to supersede Jedidiah Morse, whom he praised for having given Americans "that knowledge of their country which they would seek in vain in any foreign publication."[24] That Volney was uppermost in his mind seems indisputable, and perhaps in retrospect Brown's own translation seemed to him a stop-gap measure. Yet on the continuum of his career it must be viewed as a logical connection between his *Address to the Government* and his proposed Geography, and as an expression of Brown's nationalism for pragmatic and idealistic ends.

Notes

[1] George W. White, "Introduction," Charles Brockden Brown, trans. *A View of the Soil and Climate of the United States,* by Constintin Francois de Volney (New York, 1968), p. v. All references are to this edition; page references will hereafter be cited in my text.

[2] *The Monthly Anthology and Boston Review,* V (July, 1808), 442.

[3] See David Lee Clark, *Charles Brockden Brown: Pioneer Voice of America* (Durham, 1952), pp. 137-154.

[4] Frank Luther Mott, *A History of American Magazines, 1741-1850,* I (Cambridge, 1958), 219-220.

[5] Clark, *Charles Brockden Brown,* p. 175. See also Donald A. Ringe, *Charles Brockden Brown* (New York, 1966), pp. 86-107.

[6] James H. Justus, "Arthur Mervyn, American," *American Literature,* XLII (Nov., 1970), 305.

[7] Warner Berthoff, "Brockden Brown: The Politics of the Man of Letters," *Serif,* III (Dec., 1966), 3-4.

[8] *The Port-Folio,* IV (1804), 269. Dennie advertised Brown's forthcoming translation as "fully equal, if not superior, to the foreign," and he urged that "these travels may be purchased with avidity, and criticized with candour," though it is doubtful that he anticipated the acerbic forthrightness of the *Monthly Anthology* reviewer.

[9] White, "Introduction," *View of the Soil and Climate,* p. v.

[10] "On a Scheme for Describing American Manners," *Monthly Magazine and American Review,* III (July, 1800), 8-10.

[11] *Literary Magazine and American Register,* II (1804), 215-220, 252-257.

[12] See *American Museum,* VII (1790), 237-241; *Monthly Anthology and Boston Review,* I (1804), 293-297; *Port-Folio,* II (1809), 302-303; V (1811), 388-389.

[13] Quoted from Clark, *Charles Brockden Brown,* pp. 265-268. Clark reprints large sections of Brown's pamphlets because of their general unavailability.

[14] Clark, *Charles Brockden Brown,* p. 269.

[15] *Edgar Huntly,* ed. David Lee Clark (New York, 1928), p. 181.

[16] *The Savages of America* (Baltimore, 1965), p. 198.

[17] *Arthur Mervyn,* ed. Warner Berthoff (New York, 1962), p. 4.

[18] Ibid., p. 153.

[19] Published on the eve of the American Revolution, Roman's work can readily be interpreted as a colonization tract. He encourages England to permit her colonists to settle at will throughout the Floridas, which Romans foresees as "the seat of trade and its attendant riches in North America" (p. 91). "This noble country" will "afford not only all the necessities, but even the superfluities of life" if only agriculture is the principal object of "our most arduous pursuits" in a land in which "all the products of the torrid zone as well as of the temperate are capable of being produced" (p. 117). Then Romans lists a dazzling array of cultivatable food and fiber.

[20] *Medical Repository,* IX (1806), 286.

[21] William Dunlap, *The Life of Charles Brockden Brown* (Philadelphia, 1815), II, 85.

[22] "A System of General Geography" (Philadelphia, 1809), pp. 6-7.

[23] Henry Nash Smith, *Virgin Land* (New York, 1950), p. 18.

[24] "System of General Geography," p. 3. It is likely that Volney's work first came to Brown's attention as a useful research source for the Geography. Dunlap— *Life of Charles Brockden Brown,* II, 68, 85—says that geography was Brown's "favorite science" and that his "early and constant passion for that science" led him to become intimately acquainted with it.

Paul Witherington (essay date 1972)

SOURCE: "Benevolence and the 'Utmost Stretch': Charles Brockden Brown's Narrative Dilemma," in *Criticism,* Vol. XIV, No. 2, Spring, 1972, pp. 175-91.

[*In the following essay, Witherington analyzes Brown's abandonment of fiction as a result of his failure to reconcile the two strains of his thought: the principles of objectivity and reason associated with the Enlightenment and the revolutionary and imaginative impulses of Romanticism.*]

The titles of Charles Brockden Brown's novels suggest the steps backward his fiction took from 1798 to 1801, and the failure of his plans for an American literature. The mythic sounding **Sky-Walk** is lost to us today, but an advertisement remains, claiming "strains of lofty eloquence, the exhibition of powerful motives, and a sort of audaciousness of character."[1] **Wieland** and **Ormond,** the next novels, offer romance and exotic singularity. **Arthur Meruyn** and **Edgar Huntly** take up everyday names, which **Clara Howard** and **Jane Talbot** turn toward the woman's market, Brown's last effort to come to terms with fiction. There was no failure of imagination. Brown simply found that imagination was revolutionary, that it threatened the values of benevolence he wanted most to preserve.

Although Brown is respected today for his fathership of nineteenth-century American fiction, he often behaves more like a child of the eighteenth century. Writers of the Enlightenment assumed that knowledge led to benevolence. Sometimes a short circuit seems to have occurred, though, and the formula read "knowledge *is* benevolence." This led to excesses of sensibility and endless exchanges of woeful tales, all in the name of benevolence. Thus the moral belief that secrecy marks a villain, and an aesthetic belief that mystery in fiction, and even the mystery *of* fiction, is a necessary evil, valuable only in proportion to its service of Truth.

Deriving from that tradition, Brown's concern for benevolence unwinds the art of all his novels, leaving behind traces of his inner struggle. Benevolence typically works by an exchange of confidences, often spoken of as a flow—tears or words or letters travelling from one supercharged creature to another. In **Ormond,** Constantia and Sophia meet after long years apart and reveal every detail of their history, relieving the fullness of their "precious inebriation of the heart."[2] Edgar Huntly greets his old friend Sarsefield with tears: "I wept upon his bosom; I sobbed with emotion which, had it not found passage at my eyes, would have burst my heart strings." (**E.H.,** [**Edgar Huntly**] p. 231) These sentimental effusions are not merely appendages to the real action. They are the real action. They signify a moral center, a strength of benevolence present in the most Gothic circumstances that will eventually defeat all unsocial forces, and the ego and indirection of art itself. For Brown, the Gothic "audaciousness of character" becomes an aberration that is purged from even the early novels until the "unbosoming of souls" (**J.T.,** [**Jane Talbot**] p. 140) is virtually unopposed.

Constantia is supposedly narrating **Ormond** in a letter to her friend Sophia, who is in Europe. After a time of poverty, Constantia is rescued by the apparently endless generosity of Ormond, a man of secrecy whose ability to find out and exploit the secrets of others is supernatural. Ormond's methods of social control include a lofty imagination, imitation, and disguise, which earn him a kind of omniscience. Constantia says, "He blended in his own person the functions of poet and actor, and his dramas were not ficticious but real." (**O.,** [**Ormond**] p. 114) In short, he is an artist, manipulating people as other artists manipulate their creations.

Although Constantia is as well-educated and emotionally secure as most men, she lacks the wisdom to see beyond Ormond's surface benevolence and pretentions to honesty. That is where Sophia comes in—literally—violating the point of view by materializing in time to lend Constantia her worldly experience. Sophia instantly recognizes that Ormond's secrecy is the heart of his evil: "Not to reveal too much, and not to tire curiosity or overtask belief, was his daily labour. . . . I had seen too much of innovation and imposture, in France and Italy, not to regard a man like this with aversion and fear." (**O.,** p. 245) Real benevolence, she teaches Constantia, is an open exchange.

Ormond has a henchman, Craig, who is something of an alter-ego, a Fedallah to Ormond's Ahab. But the day belongs to sisterhood, and when Ormond is dispatched, Constantia and Sophia leave for Europe, abandoning the uncertainties of America. Ormond is set up for the kill by a last minute change in character. The rational Gothic benefactor, for whom evil is an accidental quality inherent in his superhumanity, is exchanged for an irrational Gothic madman whose essence is depravity. When he threatens Constantia with rape at her father's mansion, he is a little too brutish to jibe with his earlier image as an intellectual, and when he falls to her penknife, a little too fallible to correspond with hints of the supernatural.

The art that is slain here goes beyond violated point of view and character alterations. As Ormond collapses—in effect Brown kills him before Constantia does—the mystery of fiction collapses before a notion that the novel itself exists because of benevolence, that art is a flowing gift, the more perfect as it is more easily and fully understood. The author's intrusions with asides, coincidence, and unprepared-for endings, all eighteenth-century hangovers, function to offset the intrusions of Gothic villains. That

is, a direct, benevolent ego counters an indirect, malicious ego. In Brown's prose the egos eventually cancel themselves out to produce the disciplined but flat form of the last two novels.

One short passage in **Wieland** illustrates a number of Brown's narrative assumptions. When Clara tells of returning to her house one night and finding Carwin inside, words fail her for a moment. Then she continues: "Yet I will persist to the end. My narrative may be invaded by inaccuracy and confusion; but, if I live no longer, I will, at least, live to complete it. What but ambiguities, abruptnesses, and dark transitions, can be expected from the historian who is, at the same time, the sufferer of these disasters?" (**W.,** [**Wieland**] p. 166)

First, the choice of "invaded" suggests a comparison between Carwin's entry into Clara's house—an analogue throughout the novel of the sexual invasion she fears—and what is happening to her language. In both cases, the intruder represents the irrational, the unknown, and by extension, the contents of Clara's unconscious mind which emerge throughout the story in half-explained dreams that are eventually repelled. Invasion, like rape, is largely a Gothic motif whereby response is stolen rather than exchanged.

Second, the indiscriminate linking of inaccuracy, confusion, ambiguity, abruptness, and transition suggests that Brown may have been unaware of the good effects he occasionally creates in moments of high tension, that he may have made no distinction between a confused narrative and a narrative about confusion. Brown's fourth novel has a parallel scene. When Edgar Huntly begins to relate his own sleep-walking experiences, paralleling Clithero's earlier, he hesitates: "One image runs into another; sensations succeed in so rapid a train, that I fear I shall be unable to distribute and express them with sufficient perspicuity." (**E.H.,** p. 151)

It may be argued that Clara and Edgar are personae, not mouthpieces for Brown himself, and perhaps this is true at the outset of each novel. But as the "invasions" of complexity are repelled, so the distance shrinks between author and character, indicating that Brown began to regard the mask of fiction itself as an invasion. He seemed to believe it inconsistent with benevolence that a character's darkest agony might be aesthetically delightful to a reader.

Third, Clara's remark that she must live to complete her tale, but perhaps no longer, is a conventional pose of narrators in Brown's time, expressing the notion that art has an obligation to the reader. That it cannot be relinquished until all the vital moral juices are squeezed from each incident is guaranteed by a first-person narrator who speaks as long as the novel speaks, "the historian who is, at the same time, the sufferer."

Clara's hesitation before an experience that seems to transcend language is a typical pre-romantic and romantic pose that led, for some writers, to a kind of heroic language of paradox, Thoreau's puns that bring cliché alive, Melville's rhetoric of "madness maddened," and Poe's poetical incantations ("But we loved with a love that was more than love"). But for Brown language is not liberating in a romantic sense. Rather, language serves experience as it serves art, retreating always from paradox. Pose is continually collapsing into position.

The sentimental exchanges of *Clara Howard* and *Jane Talbot* are expressed through letters, the writers say, because more direct methods of conversation are impossible. Art is collapsed into artificiality. Letters occur because of a sick friend or a stagecoach accident or inclement weather—any accidental, temporary reason for separation. As Philip writes to Clara Howard, "This is a mode of conversing I would willingly exchange for the more lively and congenial intercourse of eyes and lips; but 'tis better than total silence." (*C.H.,* [*Clara Howard*] p. 359) Again, a pose, but one that Brown eventually believed, like the insipid verses on a modern greeting card which begin, prophetically, "Words cannot tell. . . ."

Brown is also seduced to the epistolary novel because it more nearly resembles the writing of "real" letters.[3] Early authors used the letter form to claim verisimilitude, and all Brown's novels are technically epistolary, although the long letters that form *Wieland, Ormond,* and *Edgar Huntly* disappear for most readers. Years before the novels Brown's tone was set. In a 1789 piece written for the *Columbia Magazine,* he defines himself as a "rhapsodist" who "delivers the sentiments suggested by the moment in artless and unpremeditated language. . . . In short he will write as he speaks, and converse with his reader not as an author, but as a man."[4] In those days letter-writing was as comfortable an entry into fiction as today's "autobiographical" first novel. That this form constitutes Brown's exit from fiction illuminates again his problem. Technique had not failed him, but it had blocked his moral ends.

Ormond seems indivisible, the witness unwitnessed. But in *Wieland* and *Edgar Huntly* the ambiguities of innocence and experience are more pronounced, and we follow Clara and Edgar to the uncertain border between benevolence and the ego that Brown believed must eventually destroy itself. Carwin's ventriloquism—a phenomenon still mysterious in Brown's time—illustrates the separation of sight and sound, as Clara indicates when she identifies Carwin to Wieland: "He is able to speak where he is not." (*W.,* p. 237) Brown uses this discrepancy between the two primary senses to argue that, in a world where perception is often illusory, defense against the seductions of subjectivity depends on proper training and habits of benevolent interaction.

But Carwin's talents also echo the seductiveness of art. Ventriloquism represents the pose of fiction itself, the split between author and actor, doubleness in point of view and tone. Mimicry, Carwin's other talent, represents the artist's ability to copy reality. Together—Carwin never separates them—they form the artist's paradox of distance (the "thrown" voice) and involvement (mimesis).

Clara says Carwin's art is that of a rhetorician. His "tones" have a "magical and thrilling power" as he tells the Wielands elaborate tales "constructed with so much skill, and rehearsed with so much energy, that all the effects of a dramatic exhibition were frequently produced by them." (*W.,* pp. 88, 93) Like Ormond, he is the irresponsible artist who toys with great talent to manipulate other people. His "engine," as he calls it, is an extension of his ego in which he is subsequently trapped.

To a modern reader Carwin's trap seems preferable to that of the Wieland family: the remoteness of their house, their separation from all outside company, their obsession with the past insanity of their father and grandfather, their almost puritanical self-denial without the benefit of Puritan faith, and even the novelty-denying syllogisms they play at in their leisure. They are thoroughly prepared to fall into the final trap of logic itself, voiced first by Wieland when he has just heard Carwin's imitation outside: "Either I heard my wife's voice at the bottom of the hill, or I do not hear your voice at present." (*W.,* p. 52)

Carwin tests the Wielands, but offers them in so doing an alternative, escape from their confining situation to the resonances of art, which can liberate or destroy. Refusing the risk, they retreat to their old world—Wieland to the sins of his fathers, Pleyel (a close friend) to the safety of reason, and Clara to her self-sufficiency. Midway in the action, Clara begins to sense a split in herself as outer complexity works its way in: "The poet's chaos was no unapt emblem of the state of my mind." (*W.,* p. 160) But later, she remarks, "I was desirous of freeing my imagination from this chaos." (*W.,* p. 194) Thus she simplifies continually, until the split she feels—psychological and aesthetic—has been healed and Carwin, the artist, is dismissed as a "double-tongued deceiver." (*W.,* p. 263)

So Clara's escape from her brother at the end, with Carwin's help, is anticlimactic and thematically false. Symbolically she has already repelled the ultimate seduction of art. Moreover, by saving her from Wieland, Carwin damns himself along with her to Wieland's limited view. By playing God and commanding Wieland to "hold," he becomes in effect the certainty, the deterministic religion the Wielands have practiced throughout. His imaginative art is destroyed in the service of a rigid fate.

The real seducer may be Wieland after all, for his mad rationalization triumphs over the novel.[5] Critics who say that multiple-focus point of view in *Wieland* indicates an ethical relativism are ambitious for Brown, but basically in error.[6] If anything, the relativism Brown senses through his experimental point of view frightens him back to more conventional modes. The novels that follow do not sustain ambiguity through point of view.

The final chapter of *Wieland,* a letter written three years after the long first letter, betrays ambiguity and art. Carwin is returned to a farm, apparently giving up his powers, or using them only on livestock. He appeared on the scene as a stranger rich in European mythology and dressed in rustic clothes, almost an emblem of the American artist exhibiting old ideas in new forms. Now as a farmer, only the shell remains. In the final chapter Clara dreams of a fire and wakes to find it real. Her house burns and she narrowly escapes. The surreal becomes real, art reduces to life.

The subtitle of *Wieland,* "The Transformation," refers to Wieland's alterations which are avoided, supposedly, by Clara. But it suggests also the transformation that is the essence of art, experience rendered mysterious. Transformation in sophisticated Gothic literature, as in art, may be liberating or damning, as Mary Shelley's *Frankenstein* shows. The creator may be destroyed by his creation, or the artist by the hellfire of his work, Melville in the grasp of *Moby-Dick.*

Like Clara, Edgar Huntly resists transformation. Late in the novel, he says, "The miracles of poetry, the transitions of enchantment, are beggarly and mean compared with those which I had experienced. Passage into new forms, overleaping the bars of time and space, reversal of the laws of inanimate and intelligent existence, had been mine to perform and to witness." (*E.H.,* p. 228) Brown seems to believe that Edgar's Poe-like experiences, like Clara's chaos, are stimuli unuseful to art. Henry Colden's voyage, crucial to his conversion to Christianity, remains in the background of *Jane Talbot.* Colden says it will be told in full only in "future conversations." (*J.T.,* p. 231)

The sections of *Edgar Huntly* after Edgar wakes in a cave and begins his "ramble" through the woods indicate that he has unconsciously been led into his personal and racial past. Sleepwalking, like ventriloquism, represents a divided state, but one where man is out of touch with his primitive consciousness. By a number of parallels, Edgar, Clithero who is Edgar's double, and the shadowy, deadly Indians are brought together in a wilderness that represents both particu-

lar and universal guilt.[7] Sleepwalking also suggests the process of art, the interaction of conscious and unconscious minds to dramatize an inner design. Edgar, like Clara, faces doubleness, the frontier of art that lies between the real and the unreal.

In the cave, Edgar hears an echo of his voice, walks in a circle, and meditates suicide. He feels a strong urge to bite his own arm, to tomahawk himself and drink his own blood while he dies. He does drink his own sweat and his own urine.

The alternative to this trap of self is not entirely clear. Benevolence itself fails at the end, perhaps because it borders on egotism. Edgar speaks of "phantoms in the mask of virtue and duty." (*E.H.,* p. 277) At one point, he finds in Clithero's room a strange box, six-sided and perfect in construction. Despite Edgar's own skill as a cabinet-maker, he cannot find the principle of its junctures or lid. He finally opens it by accident, intending to find something that will help Clithero, but he sees nothing in the numerous compartments except some tools of "curious constructions." (*E.H.,* p. 112) Finally, he realizes that it has been rigged to stay open. The box becomes a trap to Edgar's rash invasion of privacy, and an analogue to the "infection" he received from Clithero's confession earlier.

One thinks also of Pandora's box, a womb of the imagination the cost of opening which is the blasting of complacency and peace. The box is art, misunderstood and abandoned. Edgar cannot understand it just as he cannot understand Clithero's story until he has literally followed in his footsteps through the wilderness. Edgar ruins the box as he ruins Clithero later by his intended benevolence. For Clithero is the real artist, self-exiled from a civilization that has gone sour. He has buried his "art," a manuscript, in the ground. Edgar, his social counterpart, unearths it.

These destructions of art foreshadow Edgar's final destruction of the artist. By interfering in Clithero's secrets once again, Edgar forces him from his wilderness home to a wild escapade ending in suicide at sea. Edgar's inartistic survival—Ishmael without Queequeg's coffin, so to speak—reflects Brown's abandonment of Gothic forms and then of the novel itself. Brown's response to his brother's hostile criticism of *Edgar Huntly* simply makes conscious the unconscious resolution of the novel. "Your remarks upon the gloominess and out-of-nature incidents of Huntley [sic], if they be not just in their full extent, are, doubtless, such as most readers will make, which alone, is a sufficient reason for dropping the doleful tone and assuming a cheerful one, or at least substituting moral causes and daily incidents in place of the prodigious or the singular. I shall not fall hereafter into that strain."[8]

One effect of Brown's new strain in *Jane Talbot* is the removal of all ambiguity from the drama of self and benevolence. Colden is described by Mrs. Fielder (Jane's benefactress) as a dangerous egotist, "a poet, not in theory only, but in practice." (*J.T.,* p. 69) Actually, he seems to us more a caricature of the romantic poet who is fitted for no activity but writing and torn apart by that. "Writing always plants a thorn in my breast," he says. (*J.T.,* p. 103) Colden's confession is inward. "Let me unfold myself *to* myself," he says on one occasion. (*J.T.,* p. 199) After describing his inactivity as an aimless moving around a post to examine all sides, he adds: "The only post, indeed, which I closely examine, is myself." (*J.T.,* p. 137) Unlike Thoreau's "I" which expands to a universal eye, Brown's final egotist seems myopic, and his conversion late in the novel (more to benevolence than to Christianity) is hardly a loss to art.

Brown brought the Gothic novel to America and abandoned it. The intense introspection demanded by Gothic gave the novel a new depth. The doubleness of Gothic—paradox, psychological projection, and symbolism—helped establish the novel as an art form.[9] But Brown rejected the egotism of the one, and the indirection of the other. He discovered that Gothic form itself was too often a disguise for irrationality and revolution.[10]

Because of its significance in the conflict and contact between innocence and experience, curiosity is an effective barometer of Gothic tendencies, but it is also a measure of the art of fiction. In an early piece, Brown says that a good novel is "a contexture of facts capable of suspending the facilities of every soul in curiosity."[11] Through the novels, however, he begins to distrust curiosity that is not firmly lodged in benevolence. In early works, curiosity is used with adjectives like "excited," "awakened," "roused," "turbulent," and "alive." In *Arthur Mervyn* it appears with imagery of fire. (*A.M.,* [*Arthur Mervyn*] I, pp. 44, 74, 95) But in *Edgar Huntly* curiosity is "vicious," "ungovernable," and "lawless." (*E. H.,* pp. 16, 28-9, 228) Interesting that the language used to describe it has become not only unambiguous but less metaphoric, a double denial of art. Looking back on his days of creative writing, Brown says, almost condescendingly, "The days of youth are certainly days of curiosity," and he goes on to argue the use of curiosity in everyday life rather than in "wild narratives of the imagination."[12]

Early American novelists had to fight two prejudices, that against fiction itself and that against American writing of any kind. Thomas Jefferson's censure of novels is typical: "A great obstacle to good education is the inordinate passion prevalent for novels, and the time lost in that reading which should be instructively employed. . . . The result is a bloated imagination, sickly judgment, and disgust towards all the real busi-

nesses of life."[13] Commenting on the unevenness of Brown's work, William Hazlitt says, "This is to be expected, we apprehend, in attempts of this kind in a country like America, where there is, generally speaking, no natural imagination."[14] In the early nineteenth century, the fight for survival was literary as well as political.

Add to the young artist's feelings of inferiority the acute self-awareness encouraged by the new romanticism. And Brown's personal conflicts: his attempts to reconcile Enlightenment theories of benevolence with romantic impulses in character and plot; his antipathy to poses and falsehoods, even as narrative techniques; and his attempts to earn a living from a profession that had not yet yielded any American a living. Since American literature began self-consciously, early writing often borders on allegories of the artist and art in America.

Three types of artist-hero occur in Brown, in contexts that resemble allegories. One, a mythic hero, has already been discussed. He is a superman of duplicity, like Carwin and Ormond, whose life itself is an art. Another is a self-conscious folk hero, a rustic, naive character, like Arthur Mervyn and Edgar Huntly, who confronts urban sophistication with rural virtue. This type has been well described by Constance Rourke, Daniel Hoffman, and R. W. B. Lewis.[15] In Brown's allegory he might be described as raw material in the process of becoming art. Both types have omnivorous egos, prototypes of Melville's Ahab and the "I" of Whitman's "Song of Myself." The mythic hero represents the condition of art itself which, Brown feels, may be self-destructive. The rustic hero represents the attempt to found a truly American literature, an attempt that collapses on its own self-consciousness. Finally another type emerges to counter these egos, the anonymous artist like Dudley (in *Ormond*) and Colden who submit to the financial realities of America and to moral imperatives for a fading personality.

Arthur Mervyn is usually regarded as an initiation story,[16] but it is more of a parable. Instead of being ravished by the city, or compromising with it, Arthur transforms it to his terms—actually Brown's terms—which include the abandoning of artistic motifs developed throughout the novel.[17] From the beginning Arthur mentions his dependence on the pen for making a living in the city as a copyist, and this phase leads him to the translation of a manuscript. Finally it emerges that he is actually writing the novel we are reading, a strange switch in point of view that will be discussed later.

Arthur's name, punning on "author" and suggesting kingship and romance, may be an intentional clue to his role. A mysterious hereditary illness mentioned in the early parts of the novel, something of an artist's ailment, is later disregarded. This may be significant in view of Brown's own illness, tuberculosis. Perhaps his rejection of fiction—like Arthur's—expressed a futile hope that giving up art could cure the illness, biological or moral, that is customarily associated with the artist.[18]

When he believes Welbeck is dead and the career with his city benefactor finished, Arthur searches out a manuscript that was given to Welbeck by a dying man. In the solitude of the country, he begins to translate it (from the Tuscan), a process, he says, that "afforded me unspeakable pleasure." (*A.M.,* I, p. 127) The story he translates regards a hidden treasure. Ironically at this point Arthur finds pages glued together, holding $20,000. Translation stops permanently, and the money that came from the art—accidentally of course—becomes more important to Arthur than the art itself. This development is paralleled and foreshadowed by Welbeck's early intentions (he tells Arthur) of pirating the manuscript. Welbeck's perversion of art becomes Arthur's, just as Welbeck's city immorality "infects" Arthur's rural innocence.

Arthur plans to use the money to fight the yellow fever plague then in progress, but at the climax to Part One he burns the bill when Welbeck, who is alive after all, tells him—lying of course—that they are forged. This scene vexes critics who think Arthur's folly is emphasized too strongly for the good intentions Brown ascribes to him. But Brown seems quite serious in praising Arthur's intentions.[19] The money, after all, is relatively unimportant to the plot since further money is found in Part Two. But the manuscript is simply discarded.

The plagiarism of art motif becomes the forgery of money motif, which then changes to humorous character duplications, a comedy of errors. At the end of Part Two Arthur asks repeatedly for a "copy" or "counterpart" to Achsa, failing to realize that the flesh and blood Achsa is willing to marry him. These shifts stress Brown's point, that the artist in America needs a patron. Most of Brown's characters are either orphans by fate or by preference, seeking wealthy benefactors who will endow them with leisure. But money diverts the artistic impulse to an impulse to perform benevolence more directly, through social intercourse. The scene ending Part One, the burning of the money, is therefore a fulcrum to the novel, dividing concern with art from concern with society, and linking the two with the money which makes the difference between what art might have been and what it actually becomes.

Arthur's relationship with the dark, ugly, anti-sentimental heroine, Achsa, as many critics note, is an election of experience over innocence, and as some have suggested, a surrender of masculinity to the devouring "mamma," Arthur's name for her. This seems reasonable, as does the argument that the "pen" that is given up represents the phallus.[20] But the castration of the artist is more important here than the castraion of the man.[21] The early Arthur, in his words, "loved to leap, to run, to swim, to climb trees and to clamber up rocks, to shroud myself in thickets and stroll among woods, to obey the impulse of the moment." (*A.M.,* II, p. 125) Rumors of Arthur's femininity—one neighbor says he liked knitting—and his wild, ungovernable imagination can be regarded as characteristics a sensitive artist might have. (*A.M.,* II, pp. 18 ff.) But when he yields to the "gratification of social intercourse" (*A.M.,* II, p. 179), he loses not only the phallus but feminine imagination and spontaneity. The anima of the playful girl is exchanged for the anima of the dark mother.

Achsa's magic of love, her "power to bewitch" (*A.M.,* II, p. 218), replaces the magic of art. Arthur chooses Achsa freely, though abandoning art because he cannot imagine its ends serving the ends of life. "What is given to the pen would be taken from her." (*A.M.,* II, p. 229) His final words are an apostrophe to his pen: "Take thyself away, quill. Lie there, smug in thy leathern case, till I call for thee, and that will not be very soon." (*A.M.,* II, p. 230) Thus the symbolic "death of Arthur." The pen will be reborn, he says, but not in the same form.

The dilemma of the artist's loss of identity affects the structure of this novel, as it affects *Ormond*. Midway through the second volume, Arthur's point of view breaks loose from the outer "frame," Dr. Stevens' point of view which has previously bracketed the novel. Arthur justifies this switch by explaining that Mrs. Wentworth (one of the minor characters), for some reason she will disclose later (she never does), has asked him for a narrative of his adventures, presumably for publication. Luckily, Stevens has saved more than half the trouble by keeping Arthur's history up to this point. Brown's lapse could be explained partially by Arthur's new maturity, and by the increasing simplicity of the story. Irony of contrasting situations has been the frame's primary benefit, and with Gothic conflicts removed, irony is altered to more social specifications.

Primarily, though, the removal of the frame constitutes a denial of indirection, and of art. Arthur always insists on absolute honesty. He says, "There was no tribunal before which I should falter in asserting the truth, and no species of matyrdom which I would not cheerfully embrace in its cause." (*A.M.,* I, p. 201) But the martyr becomes art itself, as he indicates unconsciously in a later remark: "I will not describe my dreams. My proper task is to relate the truth." (*A.M.,* II, p. 154) Arthur's objection to indirect fiction is stated explicitly: "Books are cold, jejune, vexacious. . . . They talk to us behind a screen." (*A.M.,* II, p. 211)

One final hero must be mentioned—the anonymous hero. Constantia Dudley's father is a genteel artist, a painter. A decline in fortune forces him into a business which he quickly loses, and since he cannot market his art, he depends on Constantia for his livelihood. He becomes blind, and evidently gives up painting, although this is only suggested through the pawning of his lute, symbol of his artistic powers. He regains sight by a miraculous operation, but his art is not mentioned again. Finally he is murdered by Craig, acting for Ormond.

Dudley is the artist rendered anonymous by social pressures. He appears later as Colden who is robbed of his ego by Jane Talbot. Significantly, Colden is the hero of that later novel, not a background character like Dudley. The background character in *Jane Talbot* is Frank, a kind of Ormond who is dispatched to Europe and reformed before the main action of the novel begins. So anonymity becomes the moral center for Brown's novels. In *Clara Howard* it takes the form of social paralysis. Clara won't marry Philip until he has fulfilled his vows to Mary, who won't take him because she knows he loves Clara. Benevolence carried to this extreme, without benefit of satire, paralyzes art itself.[22] But the condition of *Clara Howard* is the anonymity toward which all Brown's characters move. The great egos of the earlier novels are destroyed, like Ormond, Wieland, and Welback, or converted like Carwin, Arthur, and Colden to self-debasing advocates of benevolence.

As an editor, Brown could exercise the personal anonymity he desired, since editors of that day, and journalists in general, were not accustomed to seeing their names in print. In his preface to *The Literary Magazine and American Register* (1803), Brown is very coy about his namelessness. He won't give his name, he says, but "any body may know it who chuses to ask me or my publisher." He follows these remarks with deprecatory comments on his past writing, presumably the novels: "I should enjoy a larger share of my own respect, at the present moment, if nothing had ever flowed from my pen, the production of which could be traced to me."[23]

Brown rejects the frontier even as he establishes it, for the first time, in our fiction. The setting of *Edgar Huntly* dramatizes a rejection of art that is actually three rejections: of the American experience itself, of the excesses of romanticism, and of the process of fiction. The setting, Norwalk, is a place of fluctuations, "continual succession of hollows and prominences." (*E.H.,* p. 175) Things are not as they seem. Limestone caves underlie the entire area, and deceptions of height and depth function like light and sound in *Wieland.* Routes are circular, leading to dead ends and barriers. It is described as a "tedious maze." (*E.H.,* p. 58)

Norwalk is the irrationality of the American experience, the savage that lives at the heart of the American dream. Just as Clara Wieland and Constantia find their rational paradises shattered by Gothic egomaniacs, Arthur and Edgar find the real America full of fierce contradictions. Clara Howard says, "This is a land of evils—the transitions of the seasons are quick, and into such extremes. How different from the pictures which our fancy drew in our native land!" (*C.H.,* p. 408)

Norwalk is also a fruitless, barren land. The whole region is "the termination of a sterile and narrow tract." (*E.H.,* p. 165) As an editor, Brown remarks that the soil of American letters is "comparatively sterile," and that periodical publications might do more to cultivate it than other forms of literature.[24] This was in January, 1801, the year that Brown gave up writing novels, and nine months after the letter to his brother promising not to repeat the "gloominess and out-of-nature incidents of Huntley." He adds in that letter: "Book-making, as you observe, is the dullest of all trades, and the utmost that any American can look for, in his native country, is to be reimbursed his unavoidable expenses."[25]

The frontier represents romanticism, a movement Brown sensed in American literature and drew back from. As Richard Chase puts it, American romance is "a kind of 'border' fiction,"[26] a place or a state of mind where paradise meets paradise lost. "Many of romantic structures were found within the precincts of Norwalk," Edgar says. (*E.H.,* p. 22) At first he admires the frontier, but when he sees himself in the wildness of Clithero, "denoting more than anarchy of thoughts and passions" (*E.H.,* p. 100), he retreats to the objectivity and reason of society. In late essays Brown attacks all novels not grounded in truth or strong probability. He says, "The pages of history . . . will contain more variety and entertainment, than the utmost stretch of fiction could have produced."[27]

Finally, the frontier represents fiction itself—metaphor that expresses fundamental human conflicts. Brown's major works have controlling metaphors: ventriloquism, sleepwalking, plague, city, and frontier. When the conflicts generated function as simple alternatives, the result is a dialectic, an "agitation and concussion" (*W.,* p. 43) which Brown believes will lead to truth and to benevolence.[28] A kind of debate enters all the novels, especially through soliloquies in which characters take time out from immediate dangers for a silted analysis of their situation. At best it builds suspense, dramatizing the horror and sometimes the pleasure of alternatives. At worst, it becomes absurdly like a syllogism stated in full. Arthur, for example, hears a pistol shot and remarks that a human hand must have pulled the trigger. (*A.M.,* II, p. 84)

In the early novels argument seems almost a good in itself, a savouring of intellectual possibilities (one of Brown's favorite words is "ruminate") through lofty situations. But when the frontier gets out of hand, when the controlling metaphors begin to radiate in a number of directions, Brown drops them for quiet and more direct argument. In a late essay Brown explains the theory behind his separation of metaphor from reason. Distinguishing between poetry and prose, Brown argues that a more meaningful division would be into poetry (the language of fancy, sentiment, and passion) and philosophy (the language of reason). "Metaphorical language, being more powerful than general terms, is best suited to poetry."[29] Indirectly, this explains Brown's abandonment of all fiction, for he must have realized through **Clara Howard** and **Jane Talbot** the poverty of literature without metaphor.

Lacking a literary heritage and social context, early American writers often grounded their ideas in their own inner conflicts, producing, ironically, a sophisticated literature of symbolism, allegory and myth.[30] In many ways, American literature survived and prospered by this internalization, by going underground in a cultural sense. Melville's Pierre describes the process in a metaphor that dominated American romanticism: "I shall follow the endless, winding way,— the flowing river in the cave of Man."[31] Brown does not sustain the inner way in his fiction because he does not trust the "utmost stretch" of imagination. The cave in **Edgar Huntly** led on to Poe's vaults and Hawthorne's forests, but for Brown it was a dead end. And so his ideas remain a little too abstract, and the brief sorties inside his characters are often psychological and aesthetic disasters, inviting us to believe that he was purging himself rather than his heroes.

Notes

[1] "Advertisement to *Sky-Walk: The Man Unknown to Himself*," *The Weekly Magazine*, I (March 17, 1798), 202.

[2] *Ormond*, p. 243. The text of the novels discussed will be that of the 1887 edition, *The Novels of Charles Brockden Brown*, 6 vols., Philadelphia: David McKay. Subsequent references will appear in parentheses in my text.

[3] In her introduction to an anthology of epistolary novels, Natascha Würzbach discusses the fact that first-person epistolary narrations are extremely difficult to distinguish from genuine correspondence. (*The Novel in Letters: Epistolary Fiction in the Early English Novel 1678-1740*, Coral Gables, Florida, 1969, p. x.) Examination of Brown's letters shows little difference in style and tone between the real and the fictional.

[4] *The Rhapsodist, and Other Uncollected Writings by Charles Brockden Brown*, ed. Harry R. Warfel (New York, 1943), p. 5.

[5] Clara has an early dream that her brother is luring her into an abyss (p. 82), and a later comment indicates that she unconsciously recognizes him as her seducer: "Ideas exist in our minds that can be accounted for by no established laws. Why did I dream that my brother was my foe?" (p. 106)

[6] See William M. Manly, "The Importance of Point of View in Brockden Brown's *Wieland*," *American Literature*, XXXV (Nov., 1963), 311-21, and Donald A. Ringe, *Charles Brockden Brown* (New York, 1966), pp. 46-48.

[7] Recent interpretations of *Edgar Huntly* have stressed Clithero as Edgar's double. See Kenneth Bernard, "*Edgar Huntly*: Charles Brockden Brown's Unsolved Murder," *Library Chronicle*, XXXIII (1967), 30-53, and my article, "Image and Idea in *Wieland* and *Edgar Huntly*," *The Serif*, III (Dec., 1966), 19-26.

[8] Letter of April, 1800, to James Brown, quoted in William Dunlap, *The Life of Charles Brockden Brown*, II (Philadelphia: James P. Parke, 1815), p. 100. Dunlap's biography (begun by Paul Allen and taken over by Dunlap) is indispensable to Brown criticism because it includes much primary material as well as a number of first-hand impressions.

[9] Devendra P. Varma's excellent comments in *The Gothic Flame* (London, 1957, pp. 213 ff.) credit Gothic literature with initiating many techniques of the modern novel.

[10] See Leslie Fiedler, *Love and Death in the American Novel* (New York, 1966) Rev. ed., p. 140.

[11] "Advertisement to *Sky-Walk: The Man Unknown to Himself*," *op. cit.*, p. 202.

[12] "On the Cause of the Popularity of Novels," *The Literary Magazine and American Register*, VII (June, 1807), 412.

[13] Thomas Jefferson, letter to Nathaniel Burwell (Monticello: March 14, 1818), *The Writings of Thomas Jefferson*, ed. Paul Leicester Ford, X (New York, 1899), pp. 104-05.

[14] "William Ellery Channing's Sermons and Tracts," *Edinburgh Review*, L (October, 1829), 127.

[15] Rourke, *American Humor, a Study of the National Character* (New York, 1931); Hoffman, *Form and Fable in American Fiction* (New York, 1961); Lewis, *The American Adam* (Chicago, 1955).

[16] See Lewis, *op. cit.,* pp. 92-98; Kenneth Bernard, "*Arthur Mervyn:* The Ordeal of Innocence," *Texas Studies in Literature and Language,* VI (Winter, 1965), 441-59; and James H. Justus, "Arthur Mervyn, American," *American Literature,* XVII (Nov., 1970), 304-24.

[17] Although *Arthur Mervyn* was published in two separate volumes, over a year apart, I will treat the work as a whole. All Brown's novels show some signs of a split, for he almost never revised his work.

[18] Comments by Lewis (*op. cit.,* p. 96) are pertinent: "Brown was an early American illustration of the alliance between art and illness—between art, moreover, and the knowledge, which may derive from the experience, of evil. But he illustrates at the same time the special intensity—indeed, the sense of outrage—with which the American has characteristically acknowledged that alliance."

[19] For an opposing view, see Patrick Brancaccio's recent article, "Studied Ambiguities: *Arthur Mervyn* and the Problem of the Unreliable Narrator," *American Literature,* XLII (March, 1970), 18-27.

[20] Fiedler, *op. cit.,* pp. 151-52; Brancaccio, *op. cit.,* pp. 25-26.

[21] Fiedler notes that Arthur's abandonment of Eliza, his country sweetheart, represents "his turning away from a Romantic commitment of art to an acceptance of the responsibilities of bourgeois life." (*Op. cit.,* p. 152)

[22] Fiedler says, "Thanks to the sentimental novel, the artist came quite soon to be thought of not as one who makes things, a man with a talent or a skill, but as one who feels them, a quivering sensibility." (*op. cit.,* p. 116)

[23] "The Editor's Address to the Public," *The Literary Magazine and American Register,* I (Oct. 1, 1803), 4.

[24] *The American Review and Literary Journal,* I (Jan. 1, 1801), 3.

[25] Letter of April, 1800, to James Brown, *op. cit.,* p. 100.

[26] *The American Novel and Its Tradition* (New York, 1957), p. 19.

[27] "On the Cause of the Popularity of Novels," *op. cit.,* pp. 411-12.

[28] Warner B. Berthoff suggests that Brown's dialectic was "an instrument for *discovering* ideas, for exploring and testing them out." "'A Lesson on Conceal-ment': Brockden Brown's Method in Fiction," *Philological Quarterly,* XXXVII (January, 1958), 46.

[29] "The Distinction Between Poetry and Prose," *The Literary Magazine and American Register,* I (Oct. 1, 1803), 585-86.

[30] See F. O. Matthiessen, *American Renaissance,* New York, 1941, p. 233, and Marius Bewley, *The Eccentric Design,* London, 1959, p. 16.

[31] *Pierre* (New York, 1930), p. 121.

Robert D. Hume (essay date 1972)

SOURCE: "Charles Brockden Brown and the Uses of Gothicism: A Reassessment," in *ESQ: A Journal of The American Renaissance*, Vol. 18, No. 1, 1st Quarter, 1972, pp. 10-18.

[In the essay that follows, Hume differentiates between the Gothic novel and the presence of Gothic elements in a novel, measuring Brown's work against these standards. Hume concludes that Brown is concerned in all his novels with the psychology of his characters and that he utilizes the "trappings of Gothicism" in order to create situations to which his characters react, but that his novels are not truly Gothic.]

Although Charles Brockden Brown has long been thought of as the first American Gothic novelist—essentially a forerunner of Poe—recent critics have been turning away from this view of him, and we may well wonder just how much substance there is in the Gothic ascription.[1] Certainly to date no one has shown that in sources or mode Brown was drawing significantly on contemporary English Gothic novelists; and indeed, I shall try to prove the opposite. In truth the form of his novels seems more influenced by Godwin, Bage, and Holcroft than by the Gothicists. This has led several critics, notably Clark, to view them as "novels of purpose"—the purpose being "dissemination of . . . radicalism."[2] But this description represents Brown's work no better than earlier labels.

Brown can actually be usefully viewed in a number of contexts. He is a writer of novels of feminine distress in the tradition of Richardson, a point rightly emphasized by Leslie Fielder. At the same time he is often much concerned with "manners" in the fashion of Fanny Burney and others. As a journalist and social thinker he invites explication with reference to his nonfictional work. His obvious use of Godwin further encourages the notion that he was a novelist of ideas. As the forbear of Cooper and Poe and as the object of Shelley's admiration, Brown becomes the subject of a hunt for other men's sources and hence an object of "historical" curiosity. Finally, of course, Brown can be viewed as a writer of Gothic novels.

Critical accounts of Brown agree on some points—especially his slovenly construction—but diverge wildly on others: all four of the major novels have been firmly upheld as the "best." I suspect that this heterogeneity of opinion results from critics coming to Brown with different purposes and concerns in mind, and the resulting chaos makes me the more anxious to state my aims and biases at the outset. I take it as beyond question that Brown does extensively employ the trappings of Gothicism; whether any of his novels is "Gothic" in more than a superficial sense is another matter. I think it useful, therefore, (1) to consider how central the conception of the Gothic is to Brown's novels; (2) to inquire precisely what part it plays in them; and (3) to contrast Brown's work with the Gothic types produced by his contemporaries and predecessors.

I

Although critics speak glibly of "the Gothic novel" and "the Gothic imagination," these entities are in fact exceedingly ill-defined. Even in the 1764-1820 period in England, the Gothic novel does not exist as a clear and independent form, and it would be hard to claim even that a special Gothic tradition was developing. A distinction between Gothicism and the Gothic novel is crucial. Gothic devices—midnight scenes, haunted castles, and the like—appear almost ubiquitously in late eighteenth-century fiction.[3] Writers like Clara Reeve and Sophia Lee use Gothicism to enliven otherwise ordinary sentimental or historical tales, just as Godwin is not above doing so in his mechanistically didactic *Caleb Williams* (1794). In the brief period when Brown was writing novels (1798-1801) no real Gothic "school" was apparent. Mrs. Radcliffe's sentimental-distress tales were all the rage, and Lewis' *The Monk* (1796) was a *succès de scandale,* but no distinct form had jelled. With the benefit of hindsight, modern critics can see in the works of Walpole, Radcliffe, and Lewis potentialities and devices which were later to be exploited by such writers as Mary Shelley, Maturin, and Emily Brontë; nonetheless, in studying Brown we have to recollect that he would not have conceived the Gothic novel as a special and distinct form or regarded it as possessing special psychological and affective characteristics.[4]

The sub-categories employed by Montague Summers (sentimental-Gothic; terror-Gothic; historical-Gothic) are unhelpful, for they lump together very dissimilar works and lead to the supposition that the generic conception of the Gothic is more important than usually it really is: thus *The Old English Baron,* for example, is in reality a rather soupy romance, and its ghosts are strictly additives. On the other hand, in a few cases a novel's defining characteristics and central thrust seem to rely on its use of Gothic materials. And since several such works exhibit common features, it is natural to view them loosely as a group. But the radical dissimilarity of Brown's works to this group is revealing. First, none of his novels has the characteristic "distinct setting" removed from ordinary standards of probability. His settings are largely urban and realistic: Brown frequently names real streets. English writers were setting their stories in Southern France, Spain, Italy, or the near East, and generally in the past as well. Brown's time is strictly contemporary. Second, Brown's stories lack truly impressive villain-heroes. As I will suggest in more detail later, Wieland, Carwin, Craig, Ormond, Clithero, and Welbeck all lack tragic stature; worse, they all turn out to be rather mean figures; whining, tricky, or demented, but not terrifying or possessed of a moral complexity which also rouses sympathy. Third, the English Gothic writers generally place the innocent in a position where virtue and reason apparently cannot prevail against the villain's Machiavellian evil; a by-product is a prevailing skepticism about reason and religion which produces a marked anti-clericalism, even in so bourgeois a writer as Ann Radcliffe. Brown, though he does place his characters in jeopardy, makes a point of allowing their virtue and strength of mind to protect them; he displays no anti-clericalism; and his ethical system is strictly ordinary. None of his villains is fearsomely attractive, and none is granted the suspension of moral judgment common in the English novels.

Certainly Brown does not write in any of the modes established by his English predecessors. He has only contempt for the supernatural marvels favored by Horace Walpole; indeed, he not only explains all apparently supernatural events but also takes the trouble to annotate his explanations with references to recent scientific discoveries. Brown does sometimes, like Mrs. Radcliffe, hold the reader in long drawn-out suspense, but unlike her he is entirely willing to cross the boundary into out and out horrors—Wieland's mass-murders, the plague scenes and deaths in **Ormond** and **Arthur Mervyn,** the butchery in **Edgar Huntly.** With his realism (a far cry from *The Monk*), his outright horrors, and his ethical simplicity, Brown is considerably removed from the modes favored by his most Gothic predecessors. In fact, his extensive concentration on feminine distress places him closer to Richardson than to the Gothicists, and this relationship deserves a closer look.

For our purposes, several points about Richardson are important. In his novels distressed females figure prominently; suspense is well drawn out but actual horrors (for example, Clarissa's rape) can occur. Lovelace is the sort of half-attractive villain we see in Ormond, though he too lacks Gothic stature. Perhaps most important is Richardson's emphasis on elaborate psychological analysis. This becomes prominent in later Gothic fiction, but is much less developed in the pre-1800 examples. Compared with his Gothic successors, Richardson places a great deal of emphasis on virtue and moral propriety. Of course, Mrs. Radcliffe is proper enough, but for her the virtuous heroine is a *donné*, not a subject to be explored in great detail. Here Brown's interest closely parallels Richardson: we can easily see why Shelley rhapsodizes over Constantia Dudley, but could well be indifferent to the commonplace rectitude of Emily St. Aubert. Here indeed is a point on which Brown markedly differs from the Gothicists: they tend to concentrate on the psychology of the villain and leave their technical lead characters rather bland, while Brown concentrates on his virtuous hero or heroine and leaves the villains somewhat undernourished.[5]

No doubt any schematic description of the types of fiction prevalent in a given period is an oversimplification, but such a device can be useful, and some account of the English novel before Brown seems necessary. Perhaps the most salient point in any survey is the multiplicity of aims, concerns, and methods which appears in late eighteenth-century fiction. The novel's antecedents in romance, personal history, and intellectual or moral fable continue to exercise a strong influence on form. (I have in mind seventeenth-century French romances, Defoe, and *Gulliver's Travels* as representative of such modes.) Distinctions are sometimes made between the epistolary-psychological technique of Richardson and the third-person, "History of" approach of Fielding; to some degree they have distinguishable followings. Sterne's highly individual psychologizing is sometimes cited as a third possibility, though he attracted less imitation. But perhaps a more meaningful set of categories would be the following. (1) Personal history with adventures; for example, Fielding, Smollett, and later imitators. (2) Domestic or "manners" novels, which appear in a number of guises: historical (Sophia Lee), education and morals (Fanny Burney), straight sentimental (Mackenzie's *Man of Feeling*). (3) Serious, didactic novels (Godwin, Bage, Holcroft). (4) "Gothic" novels (Walpole, Mrs. Radcliffe, Lewis). What, we must ask, is the special nature and thrust of the Gothic form, at least as distinguishable in retrospect?

In the Preface to the second edition (1765) of *The Castle of Otranto*, Horace Walpole gives a good account of his enterprise, saying in essence that he tried to combine the imaginative freedom of older romances with the psychological realism of recent novels.[6] We see the same kind of aim in Coleridge's part of the *Lyrical Ballads*. But although the Gothic novels do exhibit concern for this kind of psychological realism, the reader is principally enthralled not by character but by events or suspense. True, we can be intrigued by the villain-hero, but in the early novels we tend to see rather little of him except from some distance. Seldom are we close enough to hero or heroine to take their perils with more than a conventional seriousness. Even in *The Italian* I think we are less genuinely concerned

for the protagonists than we are bothered by the excruciating social embarrassments in Fanny Burney or Jane Austen. My point is simply that in reading the early Gothic novels we respond less to the characters (even the villains) than to the suspense or horror devices to which we are subjected. These works are designedly *affective;* their object is to rouse the imagination and feelings of the reader, but unlike *Clarissa* they do not go about it by bringing the reader as close as possible to the main character, and unlike sentimental tales of the time, the feelings they try to rouse are not principally pity for distress.

Oversimplifying only a little, we can say that the principal aims of the various sorts of novels I have distinguished are significantly different. The realistic historian entertains and instructs in the straightforward fashion of Defoe or Fielding. Domestic novelists pursue much the same aims in a different theater, and they are likely to emphasize feelings, psychology, or sentiment at the expense of action, though in only a few cases is the reader inclined to hang himself for want of plot. The didactic novelists aim to embody social or political ideas in a fictional framework; here the story exists principally as vehicle for an extrinsic concept, and our response is more intellectual than emotional. No doubt the Gothic writer is glad enough to instruct and entertain, but his efforts are really bent to giving the reader an emotional workout, and the vein he chooses to exploit is the imaginative rather than the sentimental; the Gothicist gives us the sublime and the terrible, not tear-jerking pathos or touching benevolence.

The devices which seem so hoary to us—haunted castles, extinguished candles, and so forth—were originally introduced in an effort to sensitize and liberate the reader's imagination, to free the resources of fancy, as Walpole says. Naturally enough they were seized upon and exploited for pure thrill value and quickly became hackneyed—hence *Northanger Abbey* and hence Brown's sneers at the Gothic in the Preface to *Edgar Huntly.* But the mere presence of Gothic flummery in a novel does not define its type. If we look beyond such trappings, Brown's novels quite obviously are of a different sort than those of contemporary Gothicists; we are left to ask whether Brown's use of their devices is simply so much frosting to a sentimental-domestic cake. I think not. If we turn from arguments about what generically "constitutes" a Gothic novel and look instead at what Brown does with the "devices," we can see that, though Gothicism is not central to his endeavor, he makes effective use of it as a means toward his own ends.

II

Of Brockden Brown's major novels, two, *Clara Howard* and *Jane Talbot,* cannot by any stretch of a definition be termed Gothic; and a responsible critic is more or less obliged to explain their relationship—or lack of it—to the rest of the corpus. The critic's difficulties are compounded by the lack of any tidy pattern of development in Brown's novels: since he wrote the first four more or less simultaneously (and incorporated older work in some places) we can hardly argue that the lessons learned in writing one appear in the management of the next. *Clara Howard* can fairly be called a dry run for *Jane Talbot,* but each of the first four is distinct in type and concerns.

Wieland, the first completed, is the most overtly Gothic and by far the closest to English Gothic models. Clara Wieland's virtue and life are threatened; in Radcliffean fashion we are held in suspense for long periods, and the apparently supernatural is ultimately given natural (if here scientific) explanation—spontaneous combustion, ventriloquism, and so forth. But unlike Radcliffe, Brown is perfectly willing to butcher the innocent, and so his stage is liberally strewn with the bodies of women and children—a direct assault on our sensibilities of the sort favored by M. G. Lewis. But unlike Lewis or Beckford, Brown does not exaggerate his horrors to the verge of burlesque or beyond. *Wieland* is unique among Brown's novels in having the sort of isolated, largely self-contained setting common in Gothic novels; lack of social realism is almost a *sine qua non* for this sort of terror story. Two major points, however, differentiate *Wieland* from what are usually thought of as Gothic novels. First is the lack of a true villain-hero. Carwin is responsible for some of the terrors and misunderstandings, but we finally see him as a snivelling apologist for his doings rather than as a self-willed *Übermensch* who glories in his own damnation. The novel's actual horrors are enacted by Wieland himself, but he is not consciously doing evil, and when his religious dementia is punctured his horror and remorse lead him immediately to suicide. Again, this is not the stuff of which a Gothic villain is made: we regard Wieland not with awe but with horror and pity. The lack of a fearsomely attractive villain leads to a second point of differentiation: the suspense and horrors of the novel do not work directly on the reader's imagination, for our interest is really directed elsewhere. As a recent critic puts it, "The dramatic heart of the novel is not in the events themselves but in the reaction of Clara and Wieland to them."[7] This seems to me a crucial point. Even in *Wieland,* the most ostentatiously Gothic of Brown's novels, the trappings of terror and horror are employed not to work upon the reader but to produce reactions in the characters, and the reactions then become the subject of close analysis. We will see this pattern repeated in other novels.

Ormond can be characterized as domestic, realistic, and didactic. The struggle of Constantia Dudley to support her blind and broken father amid the ravages of plague (etc., etc.) is a straightforward sentimental-domestic story whose realism and financial detail make it an exceptionally effective specimen of its type. Constantia is an idealized character, but Brown scrupulously avoids emotional excess, even in bathetic situations. Against the background of this realistic tale of poverty is set Ormond. Among Brown's villains he comes closest to the usual Gothic recipe: great spirit and ability perverted to evil ends. Ormond's pseudo-rationalistic principles and hunger for absolute power over others are reminiscent of the villains of Lewis and Radcliffe. His relative indifference to Helena's suicide suggests a moral callousness appropriate to such a figure. Nonetheless, a number of factors combine to undercut his stature. Constantia is so virtuous by nature that we cannot imagine her succumbing to his blandishments, however plausible.[8] Ormond is a serious threat only in a physical sense, which turns out to be awkward, for when he engineers Dudley's murder and tries to rape Constantia he has come such a way from his previous character that the whole story alters its character too and becomes a melodrama. Brown's clumsy attempt to prepare for the rape scene by abruptly introducing a gory anecdote about Ormond's past (Chap. 27) is indicative of his difficulties.

Indeed, our whole view of Ormond is made awkward by the narrative standpoint of the novel, which is supposedly told by Constantia's friend Sophia Courtland, who is an observer only in the last chapters. This device permits Brown to dwell lovingly on Constantia's virtues, but it means that our view of Ormond is second and third hand: except for some *ex post facto* hint dropping, Ormond appears during most of the story filtered through Constantia's rather good opinion of him, which considerably reduces his impressiveness as a villain. Such imaginative excursions as Miss Courtland makes into his mind take place in his free-thinking phase, so we are the more surprised when he turns out to be a villain of the deepest dye. In patches *Ormond* is a striking piece of work, but overall it seems to me the least cohesive of Brown's novels. From a sentimental novel of manners and morals it abruptly turns into a suspense thriller, and the gap is not comfortably bridged. Our extrinsic view of the title villain gives him neither tragic stature nor even real impressiveness. In this respect Brown's villains are constantly disappointing. None of them is really morally complex (as is Mrs. Radcliffe's Schedoni), or psychologically maimed (as is Brontë's Heathcliff), or doomed to destruction by perverse self-will (Melville's Ahab). Brown's creations turn out to be insane (Wieland, Clithero), or essentially bestial (Ormond), or not evilly intentioned (Carwin), or simply to be tricky rogues (Thomas Craig, Welbeck). We never get inside these men as we do even Schedoni or Lewis' Ambrosio; we see no great potentiality for good in them (definitely a characteristic of most Gothic villains); and the audience finds them more to be pitied or hated than feared.

Perhaps one of the strongest objections to calling Brown's novels Gothic is the limited stature of his villains. They simply do not loom large enough. In the novels of Walpole, Radcliffe, and Lewis we do technically follow the hero or heroine, but the whole nature of the story is conditioned by the character and machinations of the villain. Brown's villains seem less central, and none of them possesses a conscious mixture of good and evil; those with good in them do not consciously do great evil, while the rogues care nothing for good.

Wieland and *Ormond,* despite their titles, concentrate on the character and psychology of the heroine. Constantia is the more interesting, but the first person narrative scheme of the former novel makes it more internally cohesive. *Edgar Huntly* and *Arthur Mervyn* are quite different in kind. Both follow young men; both are quite overtly adventure stories. The brief Preface to the former novel helps clarify Brown's aims. He will give us a history of adventures but with two new twists. The scene will be American, and hence fresh. More important, he will seek to excite the reader's imagination not by employing "puerile superstition and exploded manners, Gothic castles and chimeras," but by turning to a medical phenomenon (sleepwalking) and "the incidents of Indian hostility, and the perils of the Western wilderness." This explicit rejection of Gothic trappings need not mean, of course, that Brown is rejecting Gothic aims; indeed, when he speaks of "calling forth the passions and engaging the sympathies of the reader by means hitherto unemployed by preceding authors," he sounds very like contemporary Gothicists.

Nonetheless, though *Edgar Huntly* is a rousing adventure story, its basis is not the terrors—Indians, panthers, and so forth—with which it is liberally supplied. Rather, the novel is really a bungled *Bildungsroman.* We follow the narration of Edgar very closely, and our interest is almost entirely concentrated on his struggles against elemental forces. In retrospect, two points stand out in the reader's mind: the sheer excitement of Edgar's puzzles and predicaments, and annoyance at an infelicitous narrative scheme. Brown holds us rigidly to what Edgar knows, which is fine up to a point. He does not know about his sleep-walking, and though a reader might suspect from the secret-compartment episode, we share his assumption that Indians must have cast him into the pit in the cave, while presumably carrying off his sister. This supposition is ingeniously supported by the appearance of Edgar's gun in Indian hands. This is gimmicky, but perfectly good adventure story technique. The first person narration necessary to this device, however, becomes a major problem at the end of the story. Brown attempts to avoid a predictable, bland conclusion by making Edgar's view of Clithero completely wrong. Against all previous evidence Clithero turns out to be a homicidal maniac, and Mrs. Sarsefield's miscarriage (the result of fright) pre-

sumably teaches Edgar to "be more circumspect and more obsequious for the future," but since we had every reason to think Edgar's judgment correct, this ending is distinctly disconcerting. If we take the conclusion as proof of ironic undercutting of the hero, what are we left with? Edgar's education comes in a single lump, and the rest of the tale seems irrelevant to it.[9]

Arthur Mervyn is likewise a *Bildungsroman,* but of a very different order. Instead of adventures in the woods, it gives us an account of a young man's mishaps in a plague-stricken city. Though specific Philadelphian detail is sparse, the descriptions are strikingly plain and realistic. But unlike Defoe's *Journal of the Plague Year,* the novel is not simply a descriptive account. Here young Mervyn's experiences are central, and the plague is merely background for his struggles to make his way and his unlucky involvement with the villain Welbeck. The narrative perspective is distinctly complicated: it consists essentially of a Chinese box of story within story.[10] Early in Part II Brown succeeds in casting serious doubt on the reliability of Mervyn's earlier narration: this fact, added to the multiplicity of narrators, makes the reader's response to *Arthur Mervyn* less straightforward and trusting than in the other novels. The result is an increase in complexity and a more active speculation about the truths of the case. Despite innumerable loose ends and some ill-motivated actions (for example, Wallace abandoning Mervyn in a friend's bedroom) the story is gripping and the truth stimulatingly uncertain. Several plot lines are continually left hanging fire, which builds suspense and anticipation, while the plague provides plenty of horrors. Nonetheless, I could not call *Arthur Mervyn* a Gothic novel. For one thing, Mervyn is menaced not by a titanic villain or by vague but terrifying powers; rather, he is endangered by poverty, disease, and his peripheral involvement in Welbeck's criminal activities. For another thing, the type of narrative employed keeps our attention more on the reactions of the teller than on the events he is relating. This last point is worth expanding, for I think it is one of the key differentiations of Brown's novels from contemporary Gothic work.

III

First-person narration by the protagonist is not well suited to eliciting the sort of effect Gothic writers try to produce in the reader. The imaginative involvement of the reader in a dark and irrational world—usually a world removed from the ordinary—which the Gothicists seek is missing in Brown. His realistic settings and emphasis on science and reason place his fiction on a more ordinary plane of existence. Nowhere do we find any of his villains really impressive or attractive. Where one of them temporarily appears so—as Ormond does to Constantia—we are quickly assured that it is so only because she has not the experience and insight which would let her judge correctly. The presence of a large-scale villain is a prime characteristic of eighteenth-century Gothic novels; however not only do Brown's villains lack stature, but we see them wholly from the outside. Brown's concentration on the viewpoint of hero or heroine brings us very close to these characters: the result is that we are more interested in their reactions than in the events which occasion them.

Critics who overemphasize the presence of pseudo-Gothic elements in the first four novels are generally less than pleased with *Clara Howard* and *Jane Talbot*. These two works are epistolary, and the letters are not, as in the earlier novels, lengthy recollected accounts. The subject in each instance is social, moral, and family barriers to a marriage. Action is almost entirely of the drawing room variety, or off stage. The substance of these novels, especially the long drawn-out *Jane Talbot*, consists of minute analysis of the feelings of heroine and hero as they respond to a seemingly endless series of ethical dilemmas and social contretemps. What we see in these novels, I believe, is not a radical shift in Brown's subject and interests, but simply an increasingly exclusive concentration on psychological analysis at the expense of action. Even in *Wieland* the psychological bias is very strong. Nowhere in Brown's novels are we really gripped principally by suspense about intrinsic events (*Edgar Huntly* comes closest to doing this); rather, we live inside the lead characters and are preoccupied with them. In this respect the novels are far more Richardsonian than Gothic. Even in his most action-oriented stories Brown includes a substantial admixture of "manners." In his ethical concerns, education themes, and sentiment, Brown can justly be compared with late eighteenth-century domestic novelists like Burney. The comparison is most apt in the last two novels, but these elements are present earlier, though they are less prominent.

Yet the intriguing suggestion that Brown writes "novels of purpose" does not seem to me fully tenable, though some support for it can be found in Brown's prefaces, essays, and letters. This is not the place for a thorough consideration of the matter: I raise it merely for purposes of clarification. In correctly rejecting Gothicism as Brown's principal concern, several critics have maintained that he is "a novelist of ideas" in the fashion of Godwin and Holcroft. But unlike those writers Brown does not seem to construct his novels to convey a clearly defined idea or argument—at least, no one has yet explained what they might be in each instance. Warner Berthoff wisely qualifies this view by saying that "narrative for Brown was not merely a means of illustrating and embellishing pre-established ideas; it was capable of a more positive and creative kind of statement; it was an instrument for *discovering* ideas, for exploring and testing them out; it was, we may say, an alternative to formal, systematic speculative thought."[11] Fair enough: all of the novels are laden

with bits and pieces of moral and social speculation. I would say, however, that this is merely the natural result of Brown's preoccupation with such matters in his other writings. At least for me, what stands out in Brown's fiction is not ideas but people. I do not mean that many of his characters are particularly memorable as individuals, but that his concentration on his protagonists' responses seems to be the defining characteristic of his method.

If this is a reasonably accurate account of Brown's fiction, the relation of his work to the English Gothic novel should not be hard to define. Unlike Walpole, Radcliffe, and Lewis, Brown is not principally an *affective* writer. In mode he is *sui generis:* his combination of personal history with domestic manners, morals, education, didacticism, and psychological analysis is based on no one model. What gives rise to the persistence of the Gothic label is Brown's undeniable employment of quasi-Gothic devices and situations. The midnight scene, the extinguished candle, the threat to female virtue, and so forth, though not exclusively the property of the Gothicists, are all too often considered the defining features of the Gothic novel, and the label too hastily applied. Actually, Brown's narrative perspective, his villains, his realistic settings, and particularly his rigorous morals are all quite inappropriate to the sort of novel in which the Gothic element is central to the nature and impact of the work. But Brown's Gothicism is not mere windowdressing. Unlike such popular writers as Clara Reeve and Sophia Lee, Brown does not produce sentimental romances in which scary episodes and mock-supernaturalism add a *frisson* for the customer's greater entertainment. When he employs such devices, his object is to produce a reaction in the *character,* not the reader. Considered as suspense stories, or proto-Poe, Brown's novels seem pretty poor stuff. But to view them this way is unjust, for what Brown really seems to be after in each of his six major novels is close attention to the psychology of his characters—and it is this concentration which makes any reader but the most captious critic relatively unworried by Brown's botched structures and loose ends. Brown's perpetual emphasis on the reactions of his characters to events rather than on the events themselves accounts for the curious role of the Gothic in his novels. For though the Gothic does not serve a merely decorative function, it is employed not for the affective purposes we expect, but to provide situations, problems, and trials for the characters to respond to.

Notes

[1] For example, Warner Berthoff says at the outset of one of the best studies of Brown's fictional mode and method: "The assumption underlying this article is that Gothic sensation and even the touches of realism and psychological penetration are but the secondary and incidental properties of Brown's fiction; that it is es-

sentially a fiction of ideas." See "'A Lesson on Concealment': Brockden Brown's Method in Fiction," *Philological Quarterly,* 37 (1958), 45-57.

[2] David Lee Clark, *Charles Brockden Brown* (Durham, N.C., 1952), p. 192. No remotely adequate study of Brown's "sources" exists; probably none could be written. Brown himself acknowledges Godwin's influence; Dunlap's *Diary* attests his knowledge of Holcroft.

[3] For an account of the use of Gothic trappings in several types of novels, see J. M. S. Tompkins, *The Popular Novel in England 1770-1800* (1932; rpt. Lincoln, 1961), Chap. 7.

[4] For an attempt at this kind of *ex post facto* definition (relevant mainly to later writers) see my "Gothic versus Romantic: A Revaluation of the Gothic Novel," *PMLA,* 84 (1969), 282-290.

[5] The one major instance in which he does follow such a character—*Carwin the Biloquist*—breaks off before the man has actually become a villain.

[6] "It was an attempt to blend the two kinds of romance, the ancient and the modern. In the former all was imagination and improbability: in the latter, nature is always intended to be, and sometimes has been, copied with success. Invention has not been wanting; but the great resources of fancy have been dammed up, by a strict adherence to common life. But if in the latter species Nature has cramped imagination, she did but take her revenge, having been totally excluded from old romances. . . . The author of the following pages thought it possible to reconcile the two kinds. Desirous of leaving the powers of fancy at liberty to expatiate through the boundless realms of invention, and thence of creating more interesting situations, he wished to conduct the mortal agents in his drama according to the rules of probability; in short, to make them think, speak and act, as it might be supposed mere men and women would do in extraordinary positions. He had observed, that in all inspired writings, the personages under the dispensation of miracles, and witnesses to the most stupendous phenomena, never lose sight of their human character: whereas in the productions of romantic story, an improbable event never fails to be attended by an absurd dialogue." *The Castle of Otranto,* ed. W. S. Lewis (Oxford, 1964), pp. 7-8.

[7] William M. Manly, "The Importance of Point of View in Brockden Brown's *Wieland,*" *American Literature,* 35 (1963), 311-321; quotation from p. 320.

[8] Brown does attempt (Chap. 18) to suggest that her lack of religious principles endangers her virtue, since "all opinions in her mind were mutable." But I doubt that many readers are convinced, especially as we never see Constantia waver in her principles.

[9] Arthur G. Kimball, in "Savages and Savagism: Brockden Brown's Dramatic Irony," *Studies in Romanticism,* 6 (1967), 214-225, ingeniously explains the conclusion as part of a systematic irony. But if Brown was aiming at this, I don't think he brought it off.

[10] For a disentanglement, see Kenneth Bernard, "*Arthur Mervyn:* The Ordeal of Innocence," *Texas Studies in Literature and Language,* 6 (1965), 441-459.

[11] Berthoff, "A Lesson on Concealment," p. 46.

Michael Davitt Bell (essay date 1974)

SOURCE: "'The Double-Tongued Deceiver': Sincerity and Duplicity in the Novels of Charles Brockden Brown," in *Early American Literature*, Vol. IX, No. 2, Fall, 1974, pp. 143-63.

[*In the following essay, Bell addresses the "dialectic between innocence and experience" in Brown's novels, maintaining that in novels such as* Wieland, *Brown explores the conflict between Lockean-style rationalism and the irrational forces of the imagination. Bell further claims that this struggle has philosophical, political, psychological, and literary dimensions.*]

The four best-known novels of Charles Brockden Brown turn on a contest between two recurring figures: a virtuous but inexperienced protagonist (Clara Wieland, Constantia Dudley, Edgar Huntly, Arthur Mervyn) and an antagonist (Carwin, Ormond, Clithero Edny, Welbeck) whose attitudes and experience threaten the protagonist's conception of virtue and order. At the center of these novels is a dialectic between innocence and experience or, to use the terms Brown himself preferred, between "sincerity" and "duplicity." Brown's plots reveal the difficulty of living by honesty and idealism, a difficulty he had already noted in the early 1790's:

> I think it may safely be asserted that of all the virtues mankind is most universally deficient in sincerity. . . . How many motives are there for concealing our real sentiment, for counterfeiting approbation and conviction? And how many occasions are there, on which, if its immediate and temporary effects only be considered, sincerity is criminal, and when a strict adherence to it would be, not only an infraction of politeness but a deviation from rectitude?[1]

Here we see the curiously hypothetical reasoning from principle to complication that characterizes the novels. They present, in the figure of the antagonist, the logical and duplicitous extreme of that sincerity by which the protagonist attempts to live. It is in such terms that the central struggle of the novels must be understood.

The meaning of this struggle, however, may be approached in various ways. Brown's enthusiasm for such terms as "sincerity"—of great importance in the writings of Enlightenment political philosophers—has led some readers to emphasize the political side of his thought. To be sure, political ideas are important to Brown. In the late 1790's, during the very years in which his novels appeared, he was undergoing an intellectual transformation from radical idealism to pragmatic conservatism—from a belief in absolute sincerity to a recognition of the supremacy or inevitability of circumstance. And some of the antagonists in his novels, notably Carwin and Ormond, are linked with the excesses of the revolution in France. But such figures as Carwin and Ormond have little real political substance. Their schemes and ideals are vague and often quite preposterous. In his portrayal of them Brown substitutes melodramatic stereotype for serious political analysis.[2]

The real threat to the equanimity of Brown's protagonists seems to be psychological rather than political. As many readers have noted, Brown is centrally concerned with those forces that threaten eighteenth-century ideas of psychological order, ideas derived from Locke's *Essay Concerning Human Understanding*. For instance in *Wieland* (1798), Clara Wieland tells the story of her brother Theodore's growing insanity. At the behest of what he takes to be supernatural voices Theodore murders his wife and children and attempts to kill Clara. Clara attributes these voices to the ventriloquism of the mysterious intruder, Carwin. Her sense of psychological order is based on the Lockean model, in which all ideas and resulting motives derive from sense impressions, and in the course of the novel this model is undermined in two ways. Carwin's ventriloquism reveals the complexity and unreliability of the sensory apparatus, on which all else depends. And Wieland's insanity, which turns out to have arisen from his own mind and not from Carwin's deceptions, suggests a process of idea-formation quite outside Locke's theory of the mind. In psychological terms, then, *Wieland* portrays the contest between Lockean rationalism and the power of the irrational.[3]

Irrational psychology is important in *Wieland*. But tied to it is a more specific sense of what threatens Clara and her view of the world. What destroys the Wielands' idyllic American community is the force of imagination, of voices heard and visions seen in dreams. These dreams may represent the power of the repressed subconscious, but it should also be recalled that the Wieland family is related to "the modern poet of the same name." Their grandfather devoted his youth "to literature and music" and might be regarded, as Clara informs us, "as the founder of the German Theatre." (7)[4] These aspects of the Wieland family background suggest that among those

irrational forces threatening Clara's sense of order is the force of literary art and literary imagination.

Well into the nineteenth century it was the consensus of American critics, ministers and moralists that novels were at best frivolous and usually dangerous. Such hostility toward fiction was hardly unique to America, but it was particularly virulent in a new nation whose beginnings were in Puritanism and whose accepted official philosophy derived from the ethical realism of the Scottish Common Sense School.[5] Thus the Rev. Samuel Miller, whom Brown knew as a member of the New York Friendly Club, complained in 1803 that novel-reading had "a tendency too much to engross the mind, to fill it with artificial views, and to diminish the taste for more solid reading." "To fill the mind with unreal and delusive pictures of life," he claimed, "is, in the end, to beguile it from sober duty, and to cheat it of substantial enjoyment."[6] Miller's attack is thoroughly representative. And behind such attacks there lay, as Terence Martin has observed, "a predisposition of the American mind to be suspicious of imaginative experience." The attacks on the novel, Martin writes, were "based ultimately . . . on the primary metaphysical principle that the order of possibility is delusive, distorted and dangerous."[7]

Confirmation of this principle was not hard to find; one had to look no farther than Hugh Blair's *Lectures on Rhetoric and Belles Lettres* (1783), whose influence on official American thought was omnipresent and for which Brown expressed admiration as early as 1787.[8] Imaginative literature, according to Blair's *Rhetoric,* is more characteristic of primitive than of modern societies: "The imagination is most vigorous and predominant in youth; with advancing years, the imagination cools, and the understanding ripens." Imagination partakes, therefore, of the other salient quality of youth and barbarism: "In the infancy of all societies, men are much under the dominion of imagination and passion." *Imagination and passion:* this equation, which Blair could simply assume in 1783, explains the alarm of Samuel Miller and his fellow moralists. "Poetry," in Blair's definition, is "the language of passion, or of enlivened imagination."[9] "Understanding" is the cement of a settled society. Since "passion" is foe to both so, too, is "imagination." It is no coincidence that Blair associated imagination with that very state of society to which Rousseau and his followers appealed for the sanction of their revolutionary doctrines. As Martin puts it: "The world of the imagination thus became in a special way a region of terror. . . . In the United States, with the imagination regarded as a threat to society, the terror took on a new and local dimension."[10]

Most contemporary novelists, oddly enough, shared this fear of fiction and imagination. Following the logic of Blair's equation such writers as William Hill Brown

WIELAND;

OR,

THE TRANSFORMATION.

BY

CHARLES BROCKDEN BROWN.

PHILADELPHIA

DAVID McKAY, PUBLISHER

604–8 SOUTH WASHINGTON SQUARE

and starvation of his beloved), and Archibald is converted into a raving maniac. "He has remained for some years," the narrator moralizes, "an example of the fatal effects of addicting the undisciplined mind to books, in which Nature is so fantastically and egregiously belied."[12] The point is made even more clearly in the revised version of the story published in 1809 in Joseph Dennie's *Port Folio* as **"Insanity: A Fragment."** In this version the narrator's husband intrudes at the close to reveal that the experience to which Archibald attributes his insanity never happened, but derived solely from the effect of books on his sensibility, "that the whole existed only in his own imagination: . . . that the whole is a dream, regarded by him indeed as unquestionable reality, but having not the slightest foundation in truth."[13] Such, for Brown, were the dangers of exposing the mind to unreal and delusive pictures of life.

The same dangers lie behind the disastrous events of **Wieland** which also culminates in insanity. At the close of her story, still believing that Carwin's ventriloquism produced Theodore's supernatural voices, Clara moralizes: "If Wieland had framed juster notions of moral duty, and of the divine attributes; or if I had been gifted with ordinary equanimity and foresight, the double-tongued deceiver would have been baffled and repulsed." (273) Carwin is only indirectly responsible for Wieland's madness. His vocal deceptions only unsettle Theodore's ability to distinguish between fact and fiction, leading him to accept the reality of voices produced by his own imagination. But this is precisely the sense in which moralists, including Brown, feared that fiction would unsettle the mental balance of novel-readers.

And there is much else in Brown's novel to link Carwin's ventriloquism with the art of the novelist. Early in 1798 Brown wrote that the purpose of the novelist's "lofty eloquence" is to "enchain the attention and ravish the souls of those who study and reflect."[14] On first meeting Carwin, Clara has an almost sexual reaction to the power of his voice:

> The voice was not only mellifluent and clear,
> but the emphasis was so just, and the modulation
> so impassioned, that it seemed as if an heart of
> stone could not fail of being moved by it. It
> imparted to me an emotion altogether involuntary
> and uncontrollable. When he uttered the words,
> "for charity's sweet sake," I dropped the cloth
> that I held in my hand, my heart overflowed with
> sympathy and my eyes with unbidden tears. (59)

Here is the writer's passionate eloquence, uncontrollable in its appeal, irrational in its effects. Clara is "ravished" by its power. And Carwin is also a teller of tales, a literary artist. "His narratives," Clara writes, "were constructed with so much skill, and rehearsed

turned the seduction novel's warning against the triumph of passion into the critic's warning against the dangers of novel-reading. In a long footnote to *The Power of Sympathy* (1789) Brown draws a clear moral from the seduction of Elizabeth Whitman, a woman possessed of "a poetical imagination." "She was a great reader of novels and romances," he writes, "and having imbibed her ideas of the *characters of men,* from these fallacious sources, became vain and coquettish, and rejected several offers of marriage, in expectation of receiving one more agreeable to her fanciful idea."[11] Miss Whitman, illustrating Brown's logic, is seduced by novel-reading.

The same logic dominates the writings of Charles Brockden Brown. In 1798 he published a story, **"A Lesson on Sensibility,"** which tells of one Archibald, "a youth of lively parts," but one whose "sensibility had become diseased by an assiduous study of those Romancers and Poets, who make love the basis of their fictions." Through a process too involved to relate here, his diseased sensibility leads to a rather gruesome disappointment in love (involving the premature burial with so much energy, that all the effects of a dramatic exhibition were frequently produced by them." (84)

Carwin is a special sort of artist. Clara assures us repeatedly that her own tale is true, that she is disguising nothing. Not so with Carwin: "His tale is a lie, and his nature devilish." (243) "It would be vain," Clara writes, "to call upon Carwin for an avowal of his deeds. It was better to know nothing, than to be deceived by an artful tale." (145) In Clara's contest with Carwin, then, the conflict between sincerity and duplicity acquires a specifically literary dimension. In *The Rhapsodist* (1789), his first important literary production, Brown had his persona insist on the ideal of absolute literary truthfulness: "I intend that the sincerity of my character shall be the principal characteristic of these papers. . . . I speak seriously, when I affirm that no situation whatsoever will justify a man in uttering a falsehood." And yet even the Rhapsodist feared that his literary performance might be considered "as an artful contrivance, designed to show the skill and ingenuity, rather than the fidelity, of the author's pencil."[15] If Clara represents the Rhapsodist's ideal of absolute literary sincerity, then Carwin represents his fear that all literary expression, being "artful," leads inevitably to artificiality and deception.

Such fears were elaborated in 1800 in a series of essays, entitled *The Speculatist,* probably written by Brown. In one of these essays a friend of the Speculatist wonders whether even the man of benevolent sincerity may be but "performing a part in order to obtain [the world's] good opinion." If so, the friend concludes, "life appears like one great masquerade, at which every object is decked in false colours, and the attention of observers diverted from an useful analysis of the genuine character, by the vagaries of one which is assumed."[16] It is fitting that Carwin's eloquence should find its ultimate expression in ventriloquism, vocal masquerade.

An essayist in Brown's *Literary Magazine* wrote in 1803 that the artist gains his ends, "not by imitating the works of nature, but by assuming her power."[17] Such ideas particularly alarmed contemporary critics of fiction, who ultimately rested their case against imagination on the contention that the artist in his manipulations of reality usurps the power of God.[18] Clara declares to the "doubletongued deceiver": "Thou art the author of these horrors! . . . I adjure thee, by that God whose voice thou hast dared to counterfeit, to save my life!" (255) Carwin, "*author* of these horrors," masquerades as God. In so doing he sets forward a chain of circumstances leading to Wieland's illusory visions of divinity.

At the close Clara assures us that Carwin "saw, when too late, the danger of imposture." (267) She claims herself to have avoided this danger by adhering to an art based on sincerity. Yet when Theodore's imaginary voices turn him against her, Clara appeals to the imposter Carwin to save her. He does so by counterfeiting the divine voice which has urged Wieland on, and by having that voice attest to the "truth" of its own non-existence. This conclusion is doubly ironic. To communicate the *truth* Carwin must resort to *imposture.* And his "truth" destroys Wieland just as surely as illusion destroyed Wieland's wife and children. "Now finally restored to the perception of truth," writes Clara, "Wieland was transformed into the *man of sorrows!*" (258) Sincerity is once again corrupted by "artful" duplicity. Clara's true story has been opposed all along to Carwin's imposture. At the end, however, she can only declare to her remembered brother, who has committed suicide in his despair: "O that thy phrenzy had never been cured! that thy madness, with its blissful vision, would return!" (259) Even Clara turns at last from "truth" to the "blissful vision" of imagination and insanity. Her anti-fictional sincerity finally collapses under the weight of moral and artistic confusion.

The same confusion permeates the world of *Ormond* (1799). Constantia Dudley, another figure of sincerity and virtue, confronts the trials of poverty, of pestilence and ultimately of the villainous advances of Ormond, who announces at their first interview: "I will put your sincerity to the test." (17)[19] Ormond is Brown's fullest representation of the descent from idealism to villainy. He rigidly separates his high ideals from his practical actions. He is also, of all Brown's characters, the most sexually aggressive and the most clearly linked to the ideals and excesses of the French Revolution. All of these forces—depraved idealism, sexual passion and political radicalism—are brought to bear against Constantia's virtue, against both her virginity and the ideals by which she tries to live. But Ormond has another attribute which seems inexplicable in terms of his function in the novel. "In early youth," writes the narrator, Sophia Courtland, "he discovered in himself a remarkable facility in imitating the voice and gestures of others." (95) We are told at some length the steps by which this facility became habitual. And yet after his first visit to Constantia disguised as a chimney-sweep, Ormond's love of disguise, so elaborately introduced, has no function in the plot.

On a symbolic level, however, his "remarkable facility" is quite appropriate. His abilities, we are told, "would have rendered his career, in the theatrical profession, illustrious." (95) Sophia writes that he "blended in his own person the functions of poet and actor, and his dramas were not fictitious but real." For Ormond the goal of such "real" drama is power: "Ormond aspired to nothing more ardently than to hold the reins of opinion—to exercise absolute power over the conduct of others, not by constraining their limbs or by exacting obedience to his authority, but in a way of which his subjects should be scarcely conscious." (96) It is in this sense that his "remarkable facility" is turned on Constantia: "By explaining his plans, opportunity was furnished to lead and to confine her meditations to the desirable track. By adding fictitious embellishments, he adapted it with more exactness to this purpose. By piecemeal and imperfect disclosures her curiosity was kept alive." (148) In 1798 Brown had characterized the novel as "a contexture of facts capable of suspending the faculties of every soul in curiosity."[20] Like Carwin, then, Ormond acts in a sense as a figure of the artist as master of duplicity.

Half way through *Ormond* Sophia introduces her title character, and begins by confessing her difficulties:

> I know no task more arduous than a just delineation of the character of Ormond. To scrutinize and ascertain our own principles are abundantly difficult. To exhibit those principles to the world with absolute sincerity can scarcely be expected. We are prompted to conceal and feign by a thousand motives; but truly to portray the motives and relate the actions of another appears utterly impossible. (92)

Sophia's confession indicates that for Brown the problem of fictional portrayal of character was analogous to the more general problem of literary sincerity. Both presented the writer with the difficulties of knowing and expressing the truth. In presenting himself, or in presenting the motives of another character, the writer was tempted into artfulness. And since he could only establish patterns of motivation through conjecture, he was forced to rely on imagination. In an 1800 essay, **"The Difference between History and Romance,"** Brown identified the novelist's analysis of motive with "romance," with fiction.[21] And a few months after publishing *Ormond* he admitted the difficulty of such reliance on conjecture: "No situation can be imagined perfectly similar to that of an actual being."[22] Thus in spite of her prefatory claim that Ormond "is not a creature of fancy" (3), Sophia is finally forced to admit that her portrayal of him is nonetheless a work of imagination.

What happens in Sophia's story is that the imaginary quality of her *delineation* of Ormond becomes embodied in the character of Ormond as he acts in the novel. In 1798 Brown wrote that the writer's "eloquence" finds its fit object in "the man of soaring passions and intellectual energy."[23] In Brown's novels this man emerges, again and again, as not only the object but the objective correlative of this eloquent "energy" and of its terrors. In *The Rhapsodist* and in his portrayal of Carwin, Brown reveals his fear that such energy will be falsified by the effort to communicate it. The outcome of *Ormond* suggests that he feared equally what would happen if such communication were successful. Toward the close Ormond begins to abandon his habit of imposture. "The veil

that shrouded this formidable being," writes Sophia, "was lifted high enough to make him be regarded with inexplicable horror." (227) She writes of Ormond, already associated with revolutionary violence, that "that in which he chiefly placed his boast was his sincerity." (94) Hugh Blair equated imagination with passion, and implied that both threatened society. In his final interview with Constantia, Ormond, figure of revolutionary sincerity and of the novelist's power, is transformed into the conventional villain of the seduction novel. All else failing, he determines to rape his fair antagonist. He thus reveals the purpose, the energy, at the heart of his elaborate masquerade: "My avowals of love were sincere; my passion was vehement and undisguised." (233) Confronted with this figure of vehement sincerity Constantia has no choice; she kills him.

Carwin and Ormond, men "of soaring passions and intellectual energy," become at last figures of the artist, trapped between sincerity and imposture, between literary energy and the artfulness of literary order. To say this is not to reduce Brown's first two novels to the status of allegorical portraits of the artist. Rather in these novels the artistic conflict between sincerity and duplicity emerges as only one aspect of a more general opposition—literary, psychological and political—between energy and order. Brown's villains are *at the same time* seducers, revolutionaries and artists. As such they embody a whole complex of related forces allied against eighteenth-century ideas of stability. Brown was hardly original in perceiving the similarity between that passion which overthrows the understanding and those revolutionary doctrines which threaten to overthrow settled governments. Nor was he unique in perceiving the relationship of such revolutionary passion to the artistic imagination. In fact in portraying these forces acting in concert Brown was only expressing, in fictional form, the conventional wisdom of his age. Blair assumed the equation of imagination with passion. And there was clearly a close intellectual relationship between the conservative American fear of fiction and the contemporary fear of the spread of the French Revolution.

What makes Brown fascinating is the self-consciousness with which he made the conventional fear of fiction a central preoccupation of *works of fiction.* In this self-consciousness he seems quite modern. Carwin and Ormond threaten the order not only of the mind and the community but of the work of art as well. If they represent the disastrous practical consequences of the doctrines of sincerity by which Clara and Constantia attempt to live, they also represent the hazards of that literary sincerity by which Brown was attempting to write. In the horrible consequences of their impostures, and in their own precipitate descents from sincerity to masquerade, they express Brown's fears about the truth and the effects of fiction. In *Wieland* and *Ormond* such fears are embodied mainly in the figures of the villains. In *Edgar Huntly* and *Arthur Mervyn* they are embodied, as well, in the narrative structures of the novels.

In *Edgar Huntly* (1799) Brown is concerned neither with revolution nor with the inevitable descent from sincerity to deliberate imposture. As the narrator of his own tale, however, Edgar *is* concerned with the conflict between literary energy and literary order. He believes in the need for "order and coherence" in narrative and yet fears that such coherence may be irreconcilable with the emotional "truth" of his adventures: "Time may take away these headlong energies, and give me back my ancient sobriety; but this change will only be effected by weakening my remembrance of these events. In proportion as I gain power over words, shall I lose dominion over sentiments." (5)[24] This problem is central to Edgar's narrative. His story turns on the implications of telling and hearing tales, and on the ways in which rational forms of order ("words") obscure or repress the irrational sources of artistic energy ("sentiments"). In the narrative structure of *Edgar Huntly* Brown explores the means by which certain kinds of literary response attempt to reverse or overcome the revolutionary impulses revealed in *Wieland* and *Ormond.*

At the beginning of his story Edgar is seeking the murderer of his friend Waldegrave. He comes to suspect a mysterious somnambulist. Clithero Edny, and follows him into the wilderness to extort a confession. When Clithcro does confess, however, it is to a quite different crime. *His* story, nested within Edgar's, tells of his having been raised by a Mrs. Lorimer, a benevolent woman persecuted by her villainous brother, Arthur Wiatte. In spite of Wiatte's treachery Mrs. Lorimer was convinced that her own survival depended on his continued existence. One night Clithero killed a thief in self defense, and then discovered to his horror that the assailant was Wiatte. Overwhelmed by guilt, in spite of his blameless motives, Clithero succumbed to an irrational compulsion to "save" Mrs. Lorimer from knowledge of her brother's death by killing her, too. His attempt failed, but she collapsed from shock, and Clithero fled convinced that his actions led to her death. Tormented by his "inexpiable guilt" he has come to the American wilderness.

As soon as he finishes his tale, which occupies six chapters of Brown's novel, Clithero vanishes into the forest. Edgar is deeply impressed by what he has heard. "I had communed," he writes, "with romancers and historians, but the impression made upon me by this incident was unexampled in my experience." (86-87) From here on the novel's action turns on Edgar's response to Clithero's narrative. Consciously, he is filled with compassion, with a sympathy that overwhelms moral judgment—which is to say that on the conscious level he reacts to Clithero's story like a good reader of

sentimental fiction, substituting charity for censure. He sets out to exonerate Clithero and thus to "save" him. "It must at least be said," he argues, "that his will was not concerned in the transaction. He acted in obedience to an impulse he could not control or resist. Shall we impute guilt where there is no design?" (87) The rational judgment of irrational behavior is that only a deliberate, rational act of the will can lead to the imputation of guilt.

Unconsciously, however, Edgar reacts to Clithero's story with a very different sort of sympathy. "My judgment," he writes, "was, for a time, sunk into imbecility and confusion. My mind was full of images unavoidably suggested by this tale, but they existed in a kind of chaos." (87) Just as Clithero acted against Mrs. Lorimer "in obedience to an impulse which he could not control or resist," and just as Clara Wieland's reaction to Carwin's voice was "altogether involuntary and uncontrollable" (59), so Edgar is propelled "unavoidably" into "a kind of chaos." Even as he consciously dismisses the importance of Clithero's irrational behavior, he unconsciously begins to imitate it. He is himself transformed into a somnambulist, thereby manifesting a guilt in some obscure way comparable to Clithero's. He follows Clithero into a wilderness clearly symbolic of the unconscious mind.[25] And his new life, described as a "hideous dream," becomes at last quite literally dreamlike. After retiring to sleep in his uncle's house he awakens in a cave, from which he emerges to battle Indians and panthers and to make hundred-foot leaps into the Delaware River. As he notes himself, these fantastic adventures must seem to the reader "the vision of fancy, rather than the lesson of truth." (185)

Edgar's response to Clithero's story hints at a profound unconscious sympathy between artist and audience. Many details both of the story and of Edgar's response to it hint further at the mechanism by which such irrational sympathy operates. For instance Clithero notes, almost casually, of his murder of Wiatte: "I was impelled by an unconscious necessity. Had the assailant been my father, the consequence would have been the same." (70) Edgar pursues, and yet becomes curiously identified with, Indians who years before killed *his* father. He uses a rifle given to him by his paternal teacher, Saresfield. At the beginning of his dream-adventure he finds this rifle in the possession of one of his Indian victims; he learns later that it had just been used to kill his uncle, who adopted him after his father's death. And near the close he "unwittingly" turns this rifle on his last remaining father-figure, Saresfield, who had given him the weapon in the first place. Both Edgar and Clithero, it would seem, are plagued by unconscious urges to slay figures of paternal authority, and by the "irrational" guilt consequent to these urges. They even have a "father" in common: Saresfield turns out to be Mrs. Lorimer's long-lost fiancé. Thus it is small wonder that Edgar reacts so powerfully to Clithero's strange tale. It reveals, symbolically, his own repressed dreams and impulses.

The oedipal patterns in Clithero's and Edgar's stories, only sketched here, are quite blatant to the modern reader. One can only speculate about Brown's awareness and intention in portraying such patterns. What *is* clear, though, is that in the course of the novel irrational motivation and identification, whatever their source, trimph over the rational sympathy with which Edgar attempts to control his response to Clithero's story. This is the essential action of *Edgar Huntly,* Rational sympathy (the "charity" of sentimental fiction) is undercut by unconscious sympathy. At the end of the novel, having fortunately missed his shot at Saresfield, and having emerged from his own wilderness of guilt, Edgar tries to work out a similar deliverance for Clithero. He rushes into the wilderness to tell him that Mrs. Lorimer is not dead after all, but married to Saresfield and living in New York. "I come," he announces, "to outroot a fatal but powerful delusion." (275) His information has, however, precisely the contrary effect from what he intends. He simply reawakens Clithero's compulsion to murder his benefactress, driving him to New York where he is arrested and where he commits suicide on the way to an asylum.

Edgar has maintained throughout that "the magic of sympathy, the perseverance of benevolence, though silent, might work a gradual and secret revolution, and better thoughts might insensibly displace those desperate suggestions which now governed [Clithero]." (107) At the close he finally agrees with Saresfield that Clithero's "understanding" has been "utterly subverted" (277), making him immune to the workings of benevolence. But Edgar never makes the final step; he never consciously understands the implications of Clithero's insanity for his own and Clithero's narratives, and for narrative in general. He is never willing or able to admit, even to himself, that the appeal of Clithero's tale, the "magic" of its "sympathy," derived not from "better thoughts" but from the "desperate suggestions" at its heart. Edgar thus pulls back from the fullest implications of his own story. If Brown's novel records the undercutting of charity by compulsion, of "better thoughts" by "desperate suggestions," it does so only through narrative irony. Overtly, in Edgar's account, "words" do finally triumph over "sentiments."

The protagonist of Brown's fourth novel even more persistently submerges "desperate suggestions" beneath "better thoughts." *Arthur Mervyn* was published in two parts. The first appeared early in 1799, before *Edgar Huntly.* Part two was given to the printer early in 1800. The first part is very much in the manner of *Wieland* and *Ormond.* A sincere protagonist, this time a young man from the country, enters an alien city-world dominated by "perils and deceptions." (43)[26] Like Constantia

Dudley he confronts the smallpox epidemic of 1793. And he encounters an older man whose character is strongly reminiscent of Carwin and Ormond. Welbeck's villainy has mainly to do with sexual licentiousness and financial fraud, but it is also associated with literature. "My ambition," he declares, "has panted, with equal avidity, after the reputation of literature and opulence." (95) He thus assumes familiar poses of the artist-figure in Brown's fiction: as forger, and as vocal imposter counterfeiting the voices of others. In the relationship of Arthur with Welbeck, then, we have the familiar contest between sincerity and duplicity. As Arthur is physically wasted by fever, so his reputation is blasted by his association with Welbeck. He is saved at the end only through the charity of a Dr. Stevens, to whom he tells his story, and whose own voice frames the narrative of the first part.

In part two Arthur's adventures take a different direction. Sincerity and virtue triumph. Welbeck dies repentant. Through an almost obsessive course of benevolence Arthur rescues his reputation, rising into circles of affluence and finally marrying a rich widow. He does all this by insisting on absolute sincerity of conduct. Even his view of the city changes. Wider experience of Philadelphia convinces him "that if cities are the chosen seats of misery and vice, they are likewise the soil of all the laudable and strenuous productions of mind." (95) Part one's vision of evil is transformed, in part two, into a vision of opportunity.

Part two also transforms the earlier treatment of literary truth and deception. In part one Welbeck's inveterate imposture is contrasted with Arthur's insistent honesty—just as, in *Wieland,* Carwin's duplicity is contrasted with Clara's sincerity. In part two Welbeck's importance subsides, and it is Arthur himself who comes under suspicion of fraud. In fact part two functions as a sort of commentary on the narrative Arthur presents in part one. It begins with the efforts of Dr. Stevens' friends to convince him of the falsehood of Arthur's tale. One merchant argues, as Stevens writes:

> that Mervyn was a wily imposter; that he had been trained in the arts of fraud, under an accomplished teacher; that the tale which he had told to me, was a tissue of ingenious and plausible lies; that the mere assertions, however plausible and solemn, of one like him, whose conduct had incurred such strong suspicions, were unworthy of the least credit. (215)

The action of part two turns mainly on the question of whether or not Arthur will be able to prove his sincerity against such aspersions.

Arthur's problem recalls that of Godwin's Caleb Williams.[27] Like Caleb he has nothing to support his tale but the air of sincerity with which he tells it. But there is an important difference of emphasis in *Arthur Mervyn.* Godwin's concern with Caleb's predicament—with his inability to disprove the false accusations of Falkland—is almost entirely social and psychological. He is concerned with the possibility of justice in a legal system based on corroborative evidence, and with the psychological consequences of Caleb's exposure of Falkland. For Brown what is at stake is not justice in society but belief in truth as an abstract ideal. "If Mervyn has deceived me," Stevens confesses to one of his suspicious friends, "there is an end to my confidence in human nature. All limits to dissimulation, and all distinctions between vice and virtue will be effaced. No man's word, no force of collateral evidence shall weigh with me an hair." (236-37)

And such confidence has a specifically literary dimension. By shifting the narrative point of view from Arthur to Stevens, Brown calls attention to the fact that Arthur's narrative *is* a narrative, possibly a work of fiction. "Nothing but his own narrative," writes the doctor, "repeated with that simple but nervous eloquence, which we had witnessed, could rescue him from the most heinous charges. . . . His tale could not be the fruit of invention; and yet, what are the bounds of fraud? Nature has set no limits to the combinations of fancy." (218) As Melville would do half a century later in *The Confidence-Man,* Brown in *Arthur Mervyn* links confidence in human nature with confidence in literary truth, and subjects both to powerful scrutiny. To believe in Arthur (or "author"?) one must trust the art, the "nervous eloquence," of his story.

The novel's comic conclusion seems to vindicate both Arthur and the possibility of sincerity in literature. Throughout the second part Arthur insists on the efficacy of telling the truth, "without artifice or disguise." (294) His sincerity is rewarded with the restored confidence of Stevens' skeptical friends. And yet the reader's skepticism, once aroused, is not so easily quieted. The very complexity of the novel's narrative structure raises doubts about the reliability of all narrative. And while one hardly suspects Arthur of the deliberate sort of fraud practiced by Welbeck, one cannot avoid the suspicion that he is at least deceiving himself.[28]

For one thing, his benevolent honesty often has quite disastrous consequences for others, as he himself acknowledges. "Good intentions," he admits, "unaided by knowledge, will, perhaps, produce more injury than benefit." Yet he insists that only conscious intention matters, whatever the result. "We must not be inactive because we are ignorant. Our good purposes must hurry to performance, whether our knowledge be greater or less." (309) This obliviousness is not, however, completely ingenuous. If Arthur ignores the hazardous consequences of his sincerity for others, he seldom

forgets the possible beneficial consequences of that sincerity for himself. He always seems to have a *reason* for telling the truth. And the prosperity of the novel's conclusion suggests that virtue is to be regarded not as its own reward but as a particularly efficacious way to wealth. One recalls the friend's musings in the *Speculatist* essays, published four months after part two of *Arthur Mervyn* went to the printer—his suspicion that even the benevolent man is but "performing a part in order to obtain [the world's] good opinion." Dr. Stevens, at the outset, provides Arthur's adventures with a fitting motto. "Sincerity," he observes, "is always safest." (11)

If the reader has cause to suspect the motive behind Arthur's sincerity of behavior he has even more cause to suspect the motive behind his narrative. Arthur's story is offered as a didactic illustration of the triumph of virtue over vice, of benevolence over corruption. Each confrontation with evil simply provides another opportunity to display the corrective power of sincerity. Like Edgar Huntly, with whom he also shares a belief in the supremacy of the rational will, Arthur believes in the ability of "better thoughts" to overcome "desperate suggestions," and this belief functions as the moral of his tale. And yet such desperate suggestions emerge in spite of Arthur's conscious narrative purpose. The sense of pestilential depravity pervading Philadelphia is never quite washed away by the second part's comic momentum. And Arthur's benevolent moral is undercut by his own story—the story of a young man who idolizes his dead mother, loathes his father (for having "victimized" her), and leaves home when his father takes a second wife, a woman whose "superabundant health" (16) disturbs Arthur. The suspicions of Dr. Stevens' friends focus mainly on Arthur's account of his childhood and youth. In their view Arthur simply rebelled against his father's just authority. They have also heard, from other sources, that Arthur has had sexual relations with his stepmother.

At the end of his story Arthur spurns the love of a beautiful young woman in order to marry his heiress, Achsa Fielding, an older widow to whom he repeatedly refers as "Mamma." Just before their marriage he confesses to feeling a "nameless sort of terror" (419) and has a dream in which Mrs. Fielding's first husband (presumably his "Papa") returns to kill him. This dream suggests that Arthur's motives, for all his overt benevolence, are not very different from those of Clithero Edny or Edgar Huntly. The dream even induces in Arthur a brief bout of somnambulism. What matters, though, is his utter rejection of the dream's implications, both psychological and literary—paralleling his earlier rejection of the pestilential evil of Philadelphia. "I hate your dream," says Achsa. "It is a horrid thought." "Why," replies Arthur, "you surely place no confidence in dreams." (429) If Arthur feels unconscious guilt for leaving his father and marrying his "Mamma," he refuses to admit it to the reader or to himself. On learning of his father's death he writes: "I was greatly shocked at this intelligence." But then "better thoughts" come to the fore. After some time, he writes, "my reason came to my aid, and shewed me that this was an event, on the whole, and on a disinterested and dispassionate view, not unfortunate." (376-77)

Many readers have noticed the irony of *Arthur Mervyn,* but they have generally been hesitant to give Brown full credit for it.[29] It would seem, however, that the book's irony is full, deliberate and devastating. Against Arthur's profession of virtuous intention stands his unacknowledged but persistent self-interestedness. Against the novel's apparent vindication of narrative sincerity stands the welter of suppressed motives revealed briefly in the final dream. In 1789 Brown's Rhapsodist wrote: "It is a very whimsical situation when a person is about to enter into company, and is at a loss what character or name to assume in it."[30] Arthur is the first of Brown's protagonists to "enter into company" with complete success, without agonizing over the question of what "name or character" to "assume." But he does not resolve the Rhapsodist's doubts; he simply suppresses them. He maintains his faith in social and literary order by averting his eyes from the dangerous psychological sources of literary energy and from the Rhapsodist's fear that all literary character is "assumed." Arthur turns sincerity on its head. He is a *pragmatic* idealist, wilfully ignoring all those aspects of his idealism and its consequences which terrified Brown's earlier protagonists. His trick, as a good American, is to act and write artificially without knowing it. He completes the process begun by Edgar Huntly, who at least admitted that Clithero was immune to benevolent salvation. Arthur's earnestness is never daunted. But it is the earnestness, as Brown's irony makes clear, of the confidence-man.

Brown's first four novels, then, portray the complex collision of sincerity with duplicity on many levels—philosophical, political, psychological, literary. It is on this last level that they are most interesting to the student of later American fiction. Their importance is not mainly a matter of influence, although such writers as Cooper, Poe and Hawthorne knew Brown's work.[31] Rather they are interesting because they show how the intellectual and literary climate of America led an early novelist toward preoccupations which would characterize the best American fiction of the next sixty years and beyond. Such critics as Charles Feidelson, Richard Chase and Leslie Fiedler have found in the American novel such distinctive qualities as pervasive psychological symbolism, intense self-consciousness about literary form and formal reliance on extreme and abstract conflicts and oppositions. They have also explored, in various ways, the relationship of such literary qualities to more general social and intellectual patterns in American culture.[32] What Brown's example demonstrates is the relationship of such literary qualities to the specific predicament of an author trying to write fiction in America.

The divergence of American fiction from British has long been recognized. The tradition of Fielding, Austen, Scott and Eliot, whatever the great differences between these writers, presents a world of social reality, controlled by an author whose wisdom and fairness qualify him for the trust of his audience. It is generally supposed that the failure of American fiction to take such a course results from such things as the lack of intelligible social reality in America, the abstract nature of American intellectual culture, the enduring Puritan habit of introversion or the prevailing symbolic bias of the American imagination. All of these factors, surely, played their part in forming our literature. But Brown's novels suggest that what was ultimately in question was not the sort of reality to be portrayed but the very act of portrayal. One reason social reality is generally absent in our fiction is that both readers and writers, whatever their views about the intelligibility of *society,* were predisposed to distrust fictional *reality.* Thus the novelist's attention was continually deflected from his world to his art. In Brown's novels political and social conflict are absorbed in the prior problem of artistic conflict. Social initiation, finally, becomes a kind of metaphor for the literary process. Behind the political and philosophical debates that inform the plots of Brown's novels one finds the Rhapsodist's question of what "character or name" an author could or should "assume" when "about to enter into company."

And thus, too, the sane controlling intelligence of the novelist is replaced by the figure of the artist as imposter, the "double-tongued deceiver." Brown turns from those forms in which a reliable narrator mediates between the audience and the world of the novel. He turns instead to the forms which pretend to authenticity and immediacy—letters, memoirs, confessions. And yet the paradoxical effect of this immediacy is to *subvert* authenticity, to bring narration into the action and thereby to raise questions about the novel's overt sincerity. All four novels reveal a basic fear, essentially similar to the fears of contemporary moralists, of both the illusoriness and the consequences of imaginative fiction. The novel's unreal and delusive picture of life unsettles the balance of the mind; and in so doing it releases that repressed psychological energy which threatens not only the order of society but also the order of fiction—of the narrative communication between author and audience. Deliberately writing just the sort of fiction men like Samuel Miller feared, and fearing it himself, Brown inevitably entangled himself in the strange relationship between narrative unreliability and irrational psychology. Whatever its overt adherence to moral order ("understanding," "charity," "better thoughts"), the novel ultimately probed and liberated the imagination ("passion," "unconscious necessity," "desperate suggestions").

This same configuration—fear or distrust of art, concern with irrational psychology, use of deceptive narrators—appears again and again in the fiction of Irving, Poe, Hawthorne and Melville. It is no coincidence that Brown, while he lacked the skill of these later writers, stumbled upon their central preoccupations and themes. In 1789 the Rhapsodist identified the new American literature with the cult of sincerity over calculation, truth over style, justice over social custom and habit. Sixty-one years later, in his famous review of Hawthorne's *Mosses from an Old Manse,* Melville still linked the literary genius of America with the doctrine of literary sincerity, "the great Art of Telling the Truth." "No American writer," he declared, "should write like an Englishman, or a Frenchman; let him write like a man, for then he will be sure to write like an American."[33] The Rhapsodist, Brown had written, "will write as he speaks, and converse with his reader not as an author, but as a man."[34]

Within two years of the Hawthorne review Melville recorded in *Pierre* his agonizing recognition that novels are unreliable, that "truth-tellers" are in fact confidence-men, that "like knavish cards, the leaves of all great books [are] covertly packed."[35] And even in the review of Hawthorne's *Mosses* he acknowledged the need to "insinuate" truth "craftily."[36] In the third and fourth **Rhapsodist** essays Brown introduced a "correspondent" whose sole function is to undermine the Rhapsodist's pose of sincerity by revealing its artificiality. "First appearances deceive me," he writes, "more specially in *an author* [Brown's italics], who speaks, as it were from behind a curtain." The Rhapsodist promised to address the reader "not as an author, but as a man." "Permit me," writes the correspondent, "to address you as an author."[37] Already in 1789, then, we have the vision of Brown's major novels, and of so much later American fiction. It is the vision the Speculatist would articulate eleven years later: "Life appears like one great masquerade, at which every object is decked in false colours."[38] This is also the vision Hawthorne would embody in 1852 in *The Blithedale Romance,* and Melville in 1857 in *The Confidence-Man.*

Notes

[1] "Journal Letters to Henrietta G.," in David Lee Clark, *Charles Brockden Brown: Pioneer Voice of America* (Durham, N. C., 1952), p. 102. Clark dates these letters, which may in fact be a fragmentary draft of an epistolary novel, around 1790-93.

[2] It should be recognized that contemporary political discourse was at times as conventionally melodramatic as Brown's political villains. Thus Timothy Dwight could declare of the secret Order of the Illuminati, founded in Bavaria and popularly supposed to have caused the French Revolution and to be plotting similar disasters for America: "Adultery, assassination, poisoning, and other crimes of the like infernal nature, were taught as lawful, and even as virtuous actions." (*The Duty of Americans, at the Present Crisis . . .* [New Haven, 1798], p. 12.) On Brown's exploitation of popular alarm about the Illuminati see Lillie Deming Loshe, *The Early American Novel* (New York, 1907), pp. 41-43; and Clark, *Charles Brockden Brown,* pp. 188-92. On general American reaction to the Illuminati see Vernon Stauffer, *New England and the Bavarian Illuminati* (New York, 1918); and, for a briefer account, Howard Mumford Jones, *America and French Culture* (Chapel Hill, 1927), pp. 397-400.

[3] See, for instance, Larzer Ziff, "A Reading of *Wieland,*" *PMLA,* 77 (1962), 51-57. An earlier and fuller reading of *Wieland* along these lines is Chapter 5, "*Wieland:* Reason and Justice," in Warner Berthoff's "The Literary Career of Charles Brockden Brown," Diss. Harvard 1954. The fullest study of the breakdown of Lockean assumptions in all of Brown's fiction is Arthur Kimball's invaluable *Rational Fictions: A Study of Charles Brockden Brown* (McMinnville, Ore., 1968). Kimball develops his argument much more briefly in his article, "Savages and Savagism: Brockden Brown's Dramatic Irony," *Studies in Romanticism,* 6 (1967), 214-15.

[4] All parenthetical page references to *Wieland* are to the edition of Fred Lewis Pattee, *Wieland, or The Transformation, together with Memoirs of Carwin, the Biloquist, A Fragment* (New York, 1926).

[5] Attitudes toward fiction in early America are discussed in G. Harrison Orians, "Censure of Fiction in American Romances and Magazines, 1789-1810," *PMLA,* 52 (1937), 195-214; in William Charvat's chapter on "Criticism and Fiction" in *The Origins of American Critical Thought 1810-1835* (Philadelphia, 1936), pp. 134-63; and especially in Terence Martin's *The Instructed Vision: Scottish Common Sense Philosophy and the Origins of American Fiction* (Bloomington, Ind., 1961).

[6] *A Brief Retrospect of the Eighteenth Century* (New York, 1803), II, 179, 176.

[7] *The Instructed Vision,* pp. 54, 76.

[8] Brown's mention of Blair occurs in an address given at the opening meeting of the Belles Lettres Society, a group of young Philadelphia law students devoted to the discussion of philosophy and literature. (Reprinted in William Dunlap, *The Life of Charles Brockden Brown* [Philadelphia, 1815], II, 27.) On the influence of Blair's *Rhetoric* in

America see Martin's *The Instructed Vision* and Charvat's *Origins of American Critical Thought.*

[9] *Lectures on Rhetoric and Belles Lettres* (Philadelphia, 1844), pp. 77, 66, 421.

[10] *The Instructed Vision,* p. 107.

[11] *The Power of Sympathy,* William S. Kable, ed. (Columbus, 1969), pp. 33, 32n-33n.

[12] Philadelphia *Weekly Magazine,* 2 (1798), 71, 72.

[13] *Port Folio,* 3rd Series, 1 (1809), 168. For the relationship between these two stories, and for the evidence that they were written by Brown, see Robert Hemenway, "Brockden Brown's Twice-Told Insanity Tale," *American Literature,* 40 (1968), 211-15.

[14] "Advertisement for *Sky Walk*" (a novel completed but never published) in Harry R. Warfel, ed., *The Rhapsodist and Other Uncollected Writings by Charles Brockden Brown* (New York, 1943), p. 136.

[15] Warfel, ed., *The Rhapsodist,* pp. 1, 9. *The Rhapsodist* reveals that for Brown, even at the very beginning of his career, sincerity was problematic on the various levels described by Henri Peyre: "aesthetic (Does language necessarily betray? Does technique imply artifice and distortion?); psychological (Does sincerity to oneself ever penetrate into all that, in ourselves, lies hidden from us, impervious to analytical probing?); social (Is our social self to be slighted? Or do truth to others and the commitment of the author to wider groups constitute higher duties than those to ourselves? . . .)" (*Literature and Sincerity* [New Haven, 1963], pp. 306-07). Behind all these problems, according to Peyre, lies the central question: "Can literature be sincere?" (*Ibid.,* p. 306). In addition to this question, however, Brown was troubled by a prior one: *should* literature be sincere?

[16] *The Monthly Magazine and American Review,* 3 (1800), 161-62. Brown edited the *Monthly Magazine* from 1799 to 1800, and apparently wrote much of the material (generally unattributed) that appeared in it. Professor Clark concludes that although "Brown's authorship of the *Speculatist* is uncertain . . . it is reasonably safe to assign these essays to his pen" (*Charles Brockden Brown,* p. 142n).

[17] *The Literary Magazine and American Register* (which Brown edited from 1803 to 1807), 1 (1803), 150.

[18] On this point see Martin, *The Instructed Vision,* pp. 61-63.

[19] All parenthetical page references to *Ormond* are to the edition of Ernest Marchand, *Ormond* (New York, 1962).

[20] "Advertisement for *Sky Walk,*" Warfel, ed., *The Rhapsodist,* p. 136.

[21] *Monthly Magazine,* 2 (1800), 251-53.

[22] "Walstein's School of History," in Warfel, ed., *The Rhapsodist,* p. 154.

[23] "Advertisement for *Sky Walk,*" Warfel, ed., *The Rhapsodist,* p. 136.

[24] All parenthetical page references to *Edgar Huntly* are to *Edgar Huntly, or Memoirs of a Sleep-Walker* (Philadelphia, 1887).

[25] On Brown's use of landscape in *Edgar Huntly* for the purpose of psychological symbolism see Kenneth Bernard, "Charles Brockden Brown and the Sublime," *The Personalist,* 45 (1964), 235-49; and Paul Witherington, "Image and Idea in *Wieland* and *Edgar Huntly,*" *The Serif,* 3, No. 4 (Dec. 1966), 19-26. For a more general discussion of the psychological dimensions of *Edgar Huntly,* and of Brown's fiction as a whole, see Chapter 5, "Charles Brockden Brown and the Invention of the American Gothic," in Leslie Fiedler's *Love and Death in the American Novel* (Cleveland, 1962).

[26] All parenthetical page references to *Arthur Mervyn* are to the edition of Warner Berthoff, *Arthur Mervyn: or Memoirs of the Year 1793* (New York, 1962).

[27] The influence of *Caleb Williams* (1794) on Brown's fiction, and particularly on *Arthur Mervyn,* is quite evident and has received much comment. Dunlap assures us that in the 1790's Brown "was an avowed admirer of Godwin's style, and the effects of that admiration, may be discerned in many of his early compositions" *(Life, II, 15).* Describing a work in progress—"something in the form of a romance"—in his journal in 1797 Brown referred to *Caleb Williams* as the standard by which such a work should be judged (*Ibid.,* I, 107).

[28] On the question of the truthfulness of Arthur's narrative see especially Patrick Brancaccio, "Studied Ambiguities: *Arthur Mervyn* and the Problem of the Unreliable Narrator," *American Literature,* 42 (1970), 18-27. The novel's elaborate narrative structure is described in detail in Kenneth Bernard, "*Arthur Mervyn:* The Ordeal of Innocence," *Texas Studies in Literature and Language,* 6 (1965), 441-44.

[29] Warner Berthoff, for instance, writes that "the moral irony in the contrasts between the hero's priggish reflections on events and the melodrama of his actual career is remarkably consistent," but feels compelled to insist that "one does not wish to claim too much for Brown as a comic artist manqué, nor as an ironist"

(Introduction to Berthoff, ed., *Arthur Mervyn*, p. xviii). James H. Justus gives Brown more credit in his excellent recent article, "Arthur Mervyn, American," *American Literature*, 42 (1970), 304-24.

[30] Warfel, ed., *The Rhapsodist*, p. 3.

[31] In his original preface to *The Spy* (1821) Cooper referred disparagingly to the cave scene in *Edgar Huntly*, containing "an American, a savage, a wild cat, and a tomahawk, in a conjunction that never did, nor ever will occur" (Reprinted in *The Spy*, J. E. Morpurgo, ed. [London, 1968], p. 1). Poe and Hawthorne were kinder. The former, in a review of Cooper's *Wyandotté*, distinguished between "popular" writers, such as Cooper, and writers of "more worthy and more artistical fictions." In the latter category he included Brown along with John Neal, William Gilmore Simms and Nathaniel Hawthorne (*The Works of Edgar Allan Poe*, Edmund Clarence Stedman and George Edward Woodberry, eds., 10 vols. [New York, 1914], VII, 4-5). In "The Hall of Fantasy," after discovering Fielding, Richardson and Scott on "conspicuous pedestals," Hawthorne writes: "In an obscure and shadowy niche was deposited the bust of our countryman, the author of Arthur Mervyn" (*Mosses from an Old Manse* [Boston, 1882], p. 198).

[32] See Charles Feidelson, Jr., *Symbolism and American Literature* (Chicago, 1953); Richard Chase, *The American Novel and Its Tradition* (Garden City, N. Y., 1957); and Leslie Fiedler, *Love and Death in the American Novel*.

[33] "Hawthorne and His *Mosses*" (1850), in Edmund Wilson, ed., *The Shock of Recognition* (New York, 1955), pp. 195, 194.

[34] Warfel, ed., *The Rhapsodist*, p. 5.

[35] *Pierre: or, The Ambiguities*, Henry A. Murray, ed. (New York, 1949), p. 399. Already in 1849, of course, Melville had registered a milder disillusionment with the reliability of books in the guidebook episode of *Redburn*.

[36] Wilson, ed., *The Shock of Recognition*, p. 193.

[37] Warfel, ed., *The Rhapsodist*, p. 18.

[38] *Monthly Magazine*, 3 (1800), 162.

John Cleman (essay date 1975)

SOURCE: "Ambiguous Evil: A Study of Villains and Heroes in Charles Brockden Brown's Major Novels," in *Early American Literature*, Vol. X, No. 2, Fall, 1975, pp. 190-219.

[*In the following essay, Cleman studies the main characters in Brown's major novels and argues that their interrelationships demonstrate that the ambiguity in Brown's work was purposeful and carefully constructed.*]

In the first issue of his *Weekly Magazine* Charles Brockden Brown wrote, "Great energy employed in the promotion of vicious purposes, constitutes a very useful spectacle. Give me a tale of lofty crimes, rather than of honest folly."[1] Such morbid intentions were certainly carried out, for in his major works—*Wieland* (1798), *Ormond* (1799), *Arthur Mervyn* (1799, 1800), and *Edgar Huntly* (1799)—Brown created a remarkable array of villains and "lofty crimes."[2] For some time, the usual treatment of these characters was to see them as simply conventional figures embodying certain ideas to be tested in the course of the novel. David Lee Clark, for example, feels that most of Brown's villains are in some sense connected with or actually represent members of the *Illuminati*, socio-religious fanatics who set about indoctrinating youths,[3] and Lulu Rumsey Wiley observes that Brown "based all the actions of the hero on his right intentions and habitual benevolence of heart, after the manner of Fielding."[4] One basis for this way of looking at Brown, of course, is his interest in the political issues of the 1790s and his debt to such writers as Richardson, Fielding, and especially Godwin. One student of the Godwin-Brown link sees Brown's greatest work to be "the product of an intellectual debate for which the ideas of Godwin provided a powerful and germinal source of inspiration."[5] From this point of view, shared by most of those who have emphasized the relation between Brown and Godwin, has come the most frequently noted distinction between Brown's heroes and villains: villains exemplify subverted reasoning and heroes good intentions, even if the benevolence is not tempered by knowledge.

Another basis for this tendency to describe Brown's villains in rather static moral and ideological terms is that Brown was clearly, at least in intent, a didactic novelist. Ernest Marchand, in a study of Brown's critical theory, concludes: "The most conspicuous and the most consistent element in Brown's literary judgment, as in his own practice, is his thoroughgoing didacticism."[6] As Brown says in the "Advertisement" to *Wieland*, "it is the business of moral painters to exhibit their subject in its most instructive and memorable forms" (*W*, [*Wieland*] p. 24), and he expresses a similar sentiment in the preface to *Edgar Huntly:* his objectives are "amusement to the fancy and instruction to the heart" (*EH*, [*Edgar Huntly*] p. 3). However, it seems reasonable that if instruction is to occur the moral types represented by the central characters must be reasonably clear, but this is not the case. We may feel Brown is trying to tell us something, but after reading one or a number of his novels carefully we are not sure exactly what the message is.

One explanation for this is that Brown was not the most accomplished of artists. In addition to glaring weaknesses in style,[7] the major novels were written in great haste, with little revision, and at a time when his political and moral ideas were changing, and these factors, among others, contribute to a considerable amount of ambiguity. Yet, however much this ambiguity is a failure of art, it holds a continuing fascination for Brown's readers. In recent years this ambiguity has become a major focus of critical investigation of his work and is seen as a result of artistic strength, not weakness, as a source of his power and as the basis of his particular role in the mainstream of American fiction. As summed up by Williams Hedges in a recent treatment of Brown's novels: " . . . the darkness and ambiguity of Brown's fiction are taken to be more or less the same darkness and ambiguity that supposedly begin to haunt American literature more persistently after 1830. Current criticism of Brown feeds unstintingly on the overlapping assumptions of Lewis, Fiedler and Chase which make the theme of innocence, the motive of suppressed sexuality and the form of the romance central to American fiction."[8] Thus, whereas earlier observers were often either superficial or simplistic in their views of Brown's moral messages and the ways he attached them to individual characters, the modern view is to accept Brown's ambiguities as part of his vision and to describe them in terms of a dialectic, whether it be innocence and experience,[9] savagery and civilization,[10] sincerity and duplicity,[11] or the search for identity without the capacity to discover it.[12]

As a result of this acceptance of Brown's ambiguity, the more recent critics have had little trouble recognizing that his characterizations are not as single faceted, not as clearly limned, as they once seemed. The villainous and virtuous are not as easily separable as we might suspect from a writer who proclaimed himself a "moral painter." Much of the focus of this kind of realization has been on *Arthur Mervyn* and to a somewhat lesser extent on *Edgar Huntly.* These two novels, perhaps because of the moral ambiguities in their protagonists, have become the favorites of the modern critic, and debunking Arthur Mervyn's moral character has become fairly common practice.[13] But this kind of approach has been taken much less frequently, much less thoroughly, and much less successfully with other characters in Brown's novels. The nature of Brown's villains and heroes, the particular relationship they bear to each other, remains an aspect of his fiction deserving critical attention. That Brown was interested in moral issues is obvious, and that he was interested in character types seems equally apparent, partly because of the ways he would parallel his fictional models but also because of the protagonist-antagonist structuring of his fiction. There are characters in Brown's novels who at first glance seem easily to fit the general notion

of villains and others who seem to qualify as virtuous heroes or heroines, and the natural inference is that their behavior would reflect the moral dimensions or moral purpose of his work. In the present study I examine a number of these characters in his four major novels not only to suggest further the extent of ambiguity in them, but also to explore the particular relationships these characters have to each other both within individual works and among them. It is in these relationships that I find Brown's ambiguities most significantly and purposefully worked out.

By focusing on character delineation I do not mean to suggest that non-human harm or evil is absent from Brown's novels, but too much has been made of this as part of Brown's dark vision. To be sure, in each of these four works some element of natural or supernatural villainy is potentially and visibly present, in each case cloaked with mystery that enhances the terror. The elder Wieland's spontaneous combustion, for example, and the voice that directs Theodore Wieland to kill might be seen as non-human agents producing harm. But, these have close ties to the psychology of the two Wielands, and the plague in *Ormond* and in *Arthur Mervyn* may represent such non-human evil more obviously, particularly since the sources of the disease were then unknown and its ways not connected with anything in man's moral life visiting the good and bad, the cautious and incautious, indiscriminately. But Brown's interest in the plague seems more in the kinds of human horrors it occasions. In *Arthur Mervyn,* for example, the debauched hospital attendants, the callousness, even toward burying the living, of the hearsemen, and the instances of abandoning sick friends and relatives arouse more disgust than do the few scenes of actual suffering from the fever. The lions in *Edgar Huntly* more purely represent a natural, non-human evil, but they are still mostly a potential for harm and generally require that human volition bring a man into the area of danger. Similarly, the Indians in *Edgar Huntly,* insofar as they are seen as a simple, natural, savage force in the novel, have become dangerous mainly because of the settlers' encroachments into their territories. Their motivation, at least in the killing of Waldegreve, stems from feelings of resentment at that encroachment and borders on both simple savagery and the very human desire for vengeance. Moreover, when Edgar Huntly describes the Indians he has just killed as "Three beings, full of energy and heroism, endowed with minds strenuous and lofty" (*EH,* p. 185), he is hardly relegating them to pure savagery.[14] That Edgar or Brown can entertain this view of them and also the view that they are vicious and brutal begins to suggest the kind of ambivalence that appears in Brown's characters.

In short, the instances of non-human evil, or harm not the result of human action, are rare in Brown's major novels, and the examples that do appear are never left without a sense of the human connection. The focus of attention on non-human evil or harm inevitably shifts to the link of that evil with human motive or activity. Even the mysterious evil force, the rather strange compulsion for doing wrong in such figures as Carwin, Clithero, Ormond, and Welbeck, which at times seems pervasive rather than character-linked in the novels, must ultimately be described in terms of particular psychological states. Brown's Gothicism, in fact, is characterized by giving natural explanations to what seem to be supernatural phenomena, by replacing the "puerile superstitions and exploded manners, Gothic castles and chimeras" (**EH**, p. 4) of the popular English tale of terror with truly American materials—mountain lions, Indians, dark frontier forests, and foreboding mountain cliffs and caves. But even more, the startling and terrifying effects in his novels stem from abnormal and morbid states of mind, from the deeds of villains and misguided heroes attempting to carry out pernicious, or simply unfortunate, ideas.

If looking for evil in Brown's novels means looking for it in men, then it would be useful to discover some unmitigated villain to examine as a pure type. And, although Alexander Cowie's observation seems true, that "Indeed there is no call to hiss the villain heartily in any of Brown's novels,"[15] several of Brown's villains, at least in the final analysis, seem almost totally depraved. Perhaps the most extreme of these is Mrs. Lorimer's brother Wiatte in **Edgar Huntly**, who is described by Clithero Edny as " . . . sordidly wicked,— a hoary ruffian, to whom the language of pity was as unintelligible as the gabble of monkeys. His heart was fortified against compunction, by the atrocious habits of forty years; he lived only to interrupt her [Mrs. Lorimer's] peace, to confute the promises of virtue, and convert to rancour and reproach the fair fame of fidelity" (**EH**, pp. 70-71). His specific crimes are seducing and abandoning the mother of Clarice, gambling, attempting to turn his parents against his sister, bringing about his sister's separation from her lover, and generally tormenting Mrs. Lorimer to the point of posing a possible threat to her life. In short, "he seemed to relish no food but pure unadulterated evil" (**EH**, pp. 43-44), and he is seen in this light from the start. Despite the hopes Mrs. Lorimer holds out for him, there seems to be no chance for his redemption, and in this respect, he is described by Clithero as "an exception to all the rules which govern us in our judgments of human nature" (**EH**, p. 43). Indeed, while sibling rivalry—jealously toward a parentally favored sister—might seem a reasonable explanation for his behavior, the way he is presented suggests something closer to Poe's concept of the perverse. Wiatte is a kind of horrible freak, who on the one hand, because he is Mrs. Lorimer's twin, represents the insignificance of heredity in determining moral character,[16] on the other provides the first unmistakable clue to the ineffectiveness of simple benevolence in redeeming lost

souls. Perhaps he belongs in the category of non-human evil, an example of natural depravity—a Claggart to Mrs. Lorimer's Billy Budd—but we simply do not know enough about him, and what we know is a reflection of Clithero's obviously biased point of view. Whatever we might wish to make of him, the extremity of Wiatte's villainy remains largely an exception in Brown's work.

The closest approximations to Wiatte are Craig in **Ormond**, and Thetford, Betty Lawrence and possibly Colvill in **Arthur Mervyn**, all of whom share the capacity to do harm, to commit clear moral wrongs when in complete control of their wills and without qualms of conscience. Like Wiatte they are not ideological villains; they are neither dangerous utopianists nor well-meaning fanatics of any sort, but are primarily bent on satisfying their own desires. Of these Craig is the most criminal—chronically lying, refusing to support his mother, embezzling, and eventually murdering. Harry Warfel describes Craig as having "the criminal type of mind. This typical villain, . . . represents undisguised, crude, unintellectual, and ungifted dishonesty."[17] However, as with Wiatte our knowledge of Craig is limited, and, unlike Wiatte's, Craig's villainy does not seem largely gratuitous. Thetford is similarly cruel, deceitful, licentious, and grasping, but again not gratuitously so. His worst crimes are committed out of terror over the plague, and our first glimpses of him are pleasantly domestic. Betty Lawrence, who rises from lusty milk-maid to lusty paramour by eventually ruining Arthur's father, is not so much bent on harm as she is lascivious and unscrupulous.

Colvill is the least villainous of the group, for, although, he is shown as a multiple seducer (including among his conquests Arthur Mervyn's sister, which certainly would not enhance the description of him in Arthur's narrative), he is also capable of acts of generosity and kindness in sheltering Welbeck and nursing him back to health. These acts may represent only some kind of natural camaraderie among villains, an ironic, temporary merging of two parallel destinies, or simply a contrived plot manipulation, but they tend to suggest a greater complexity in his character than is apparent in Arthur calling him an "arch-villain" (**AM,** [**Arthur Mervyn**] I, p. 188). When he first appears in the Mervyns' district he demonstrates "learning and genius" (**AM**, I, p. 189), acquires the position of schoolmaster, and lives a quiet, modest, secluded contemplative, "abstemious and regular" (**AM**, I, p. 189) life. The terms of his guilt, seen from Arthur's point of view, remain sketchy, but even with that limitation the greatest suffering, harm, and furor (including Colvill's desertion) comes after the scouring for victims begins and after the Mervyn girl is upbraided and censured for her failings. Moreover, according to Wiley the description of Colvill as he first appears to the village—modest, meditative, reclusive—fits Brown closely. Since Mervyn is also generally regarded as being a partially autobiographical figure, and since Mervyn hates Colvill more than any other figure, something like a conflict of self-love and self-hate seems to center in the development of these two characters. More important, whether Colvill is to be considered a man of great promise, unfortunately prey to his passions, or some kind of willfully depraved intellectual, the main problem in determining his character, both for the reader and for other characters in the novel, is the disparity between appearance and reality, between what a man seems to be and what he is.

This concern with the deceptiveness of appearances is one of Brown's most pervasive literary interests. It is at the center of action in *Wieland* and part of the central mystery in *Edgar Huntly.* Ormond's powers of knowledge are played off this theme, and on the most obvious level the structure of *Arthur Mervyn* grows out of the need for Mervyn to explain that the appearances of guilty behavior charged to him are not real. In fact, in each of these four novels characters regularly appear who turn out to be something other than what their first impression would suggest. This applies not only to Craig, who deceives the Dudleys, and to Thetford, who deceives many, but to Wallace, Colvill, Betty Lawrence, Carwin, Ormond, Clithero, and Welbeck. The worst of Brown's villains, then, with the exception of Wiatte, suggest this common denominator of deceptive appearances, which Michael Bell has characterized even more strongly as duplicity, a conscious deceitfulness on the part of Brown's villains, which separates them from the virtuously sincere. In addition, Wiatte's twinship with Mrs. Lorimer, Craig's ties with Ormond, and Colvill's link with Arthur suggest the kind of pairing of characters which is obvious in the Clithero-Huntly, Mervyn-Welbeck relationships and which will be shown to exist on a much broader and more complex basis. Still these characters are relatively minor in the works, serving a purpose parallel to Carwin's catalytic role in *Wieland* in which a chain of disasters is initiated out of proportion to the evil of the original act.

The villainy of such characters as Ormond, Clithero, Welbeck, Carwin, and Theodore Wieland, however, is much more complex. Ormond and Welbeck seem the blackest of these, and Ormond's is certainly the most commanding presence. Like Craig and Colvill, Ormond's first appearances in the novel present him in a favorable light. He seems to be a fairly pleasant, well-to-do man with an inclination toward inconspicuous philanthropy, but gradually we discover he holds extremely radical ideas about the nature of society and particularly about the institution of marriage, and finally he is seen to be capable of such extreme crimes as rape and murder. But whereas the villains like Wiatte, Craig, Thetford, Colvill, and Betty Lawrence are motivated by a simple, unintellectual, almost compulsive

desire to gratify their personal wants, Ormond's villainy has the appearance of being more calculated, cerebral, the result of a certain ideological bent. If like the others he often indulges his passions, he usually does so in relation to a specific philosophical framework. "Yet," as the narrator in *Ormond* points out, since "there was more of grossness and licentiousness in the expression of his tenets, than in the tenets themselves" (*O,* [*Ormond*] p. 115), the appearances of Ormond's villainy may prove deceptive.

The attitudes and ideas espoused by Ormond are extensively described in chapter twelve of the novel. Basically his philosophy is characterized by the Godwinian belief that evil results from a corrupt social system and therefore that "efforts designed to ameliorate the condition of an individual were sure of answering a contrary purpose. The principles of the social machine must be rectified, before men can be beneficially active" (*O,* p. 110). No matter what an individual does, " . . . whether he went forward or stood still, whether his motives were malignant, or kind, or indifferent, the mass of evil was equally and necessarily augmented. It did not follow from these preliminaries that virtue and duty were terms without a meaning, but they require us to promote our own happiness and not the happiness of others" (*O,* p. 110). Ormond's scheme, then, is benevolent in outlook; if a man hopes to achieve good, he must realize that it can only be hoped for and not attained, and therefore the only practical means of producing any measure of good is for the benevolent man to pursue exclusively his own benefit.

Through all its turnings this philosophy of benevolent self-interest effectively equips Ormond with an easy escape from any guilt feelings which might ordinarily result from committing numerous moral and legal crimes. It raises him above the affairs and limitations of ordinary men and thereby gives him the quality which Helena Cleves and Constantia Dudley find particularly fascinating. Constantia is even more awed by the force of his mind, which she thinks borders on the supernatural because of his knowledge of her private conversations, but is actually the result of his abilities to act and disguise himself in her presence. His self-elevation is also manifested in a frankness which disregards the feelings of others in order to serve his delight in his own sincerity; in an enjoyment of wealth, not to impress anyone else, but to give the fullest indulgence to his own pleasures; and curiously, in a total disregard for the formalities of class distinction, which could only come from an absolute assurance of his own superiority.

All of these aspects of Ormond, however, are not inherently wicked; his philosophy does not, of itself, automatically lead to the crimes he commits. As a matter of fact his first and most heinous crimes—rape and murder of a captured Tartar girl, killing of his best friend, and slaughter of five Turkish foragers, all as an eighteen-year-old volunteer in the Russian army (*O,* p. 255)—are clearly acts more of passion than of philosophy in which the murder of the Turks and girl are to expiate a sense of guilt over the death of his friend. Whatever the state of his philosophy at that time, Sophia Westwyn's sententious observation, which precedes this episode and which suggests its connection with Ormond's involvement in Mr. Dudley's death, can perhaps help illuminate the more general moral feelings in Ormond's character. She says, "Human life is momentous or trivial in our eyes, according to the course which our habits and opinions have taken. Passion greedily accepts, and habit readily offers, the sacrifice of another's life, and *reason obeys the impulse of education and desire*" (*O,* p. 255 [emphasis mine]). Earlier she had made the point that "Ormond was, for the most part, governed, like others, by the influences of education and present circumstances" (*O,* p. 110), that his thinking was as much guided by his experience as his actions were directed by his thinking. For example, "his aversion to duplicity had flowed from experience of its evils. He had frequently been made its victim; in consequence of this his temper had become suspicious . . ." (*O,* p. 113). Furthermore, his attitudes toward love and marriage are ascribed to his never having met the right woman.

The primary significance of this is not that it shows Brown employing Godwinian notions of the importance of environment and events on moral growth, but that it indicates the flexibility, to the point of vapid formlessness, of Ormond's philosophy. The intellectual construct, at least potentially, is as much the servant of his physical passions as it is the director of them. If that philosophy presented in chapter twelve smacks of sophistry, note that immediately in chapter thirteen Ormond, in persuading Helena Cleves to become his mistress, purports to rely on nothing but reason and absolute sincerity, simply to lay the whole truth before her and allow her free choice; while as a matter of fact, says Miss Westwyn,

> It cannot be supposed that Ormond, in stating this proposal, acted with all the impartiality that he pretended; that he did not employ fallacious exaggerations and ambiguous expedients; that he did not seize every opportunity of triumphing over her weakness, and building his success rather on the illusions of her heart than the convictions of her understanding. His conclusions were specious but delusive, and were not uninfluenced by improper biases; but of this he himself was scarcely conscious, and it must be at least admitted that he acted with scrupulous sincerity. (*O,* p. 120)

In pursuit of sexual pleasure, then, Ormond's scruples and high intellectual principles offer no guides or controls at all; he simply takes the course which seems most likely to succeed. The farthest reach of this, of course, is that with the same facade of reasonable action and argument, he not only kills Constantia's father and directly threatens her with rape, but even suggests necrophilia if necessary, saying: "Living or dead, the prize that I have in view shall be mine" (*O,* p. 276). Ormond has, in short, philosophically created moral loopholes in his conscience to the extent that effectively it no longer exists. His reasoning has rendered him basically amoral and ironically and tragically self-deceived about his own motives.

Considered in this light, Ormond's villainy derives from the same sources as the villainy of Wiatte, Thetford, Craig, Colvill, and Betty Lawrence. Gratification of personal desires or passions, especially the sex urge, is the main wellspring of evil in Brown's arch-villains, and Ormond's distinction in this group is not, as Warfel would have it, that "in him [Ormond] evil flourishes as a result of an intellectually conceived principle."[18] The main distinction is that Ormond *claims* benevolence and a philosophical framework as the basis of his actions, whereas the others do not. The disparity between good or benevolent intentions and their realizations is a recurring theme in Brown, and Ormond must be seen as not so much an example of specific, mistaken ideas as an instance of human frailty much like the worst of Brown's villains and, we will discover, similar to the failings of his heroes.

It might seem that Welbeck in ***Arthur Mervyn*** ought to be included among these arch-villains. The fact of his guilt and the enormity of his crimes are inarguable, and the sources of his wrongdoing are clearly sexual desire and the pursuit of luxury and fame. Like Ormond, Colvill, and Craig he is initially an attractive figure, and although in his final appearances in the novel, he, like Colvill, performs some kind of redemptive act, the sum of the villainous deeds of his whole career seems ultimately a few shades darker than that sum known of Betty Lawrence or Colvill. But, Welbeck is different from these others in one major respect: through the course of his infamy, he periodically displays considerable remorse and what seem to be honest guilt feelings over what he has done. Remorse and repentence, of course, do not keep Welbeck from continuing in his villainy, do not lessen the consequences of his actions, but they are, like good intentions, frequent ways Brown postulates redemption for the fallen.

The sincerity of Welbeck's remorse, however, is not easy to be sure of. Like Ormond he embodies many principles of Godwinian radicalism and has several parallels with Falkland in Godwin's *Caleb Williams,* but his compulsions are not of an ideological caste. As one critic accurately observed, all his problems seem explicable by the then contemporary notion that vice proceeds from a life of leisure.[19] He was too used to living off others, which weakened his moral fiber to the point where he could become involved with a woman "who was unchaste, perverse and malignant" (*AM,* I. p. 87), and from there his moral life was all down hill. At least from his own description of himself, he has not, as Flanders assumed, "sprung into being black with malice, destined for villainy,"[20] but seems to have grown increasingly susceptible to selfish ambitions and sexual desire—one crime making the next one easier and more likely to occur. For this reason he appears more malignant at the end of the first part of *Arthur Mervyn,* not only because we know more about him, but also because he has actually grown worse.

Welbeck's plight, then, is that he feels compelled to seek fame, fortune, and physical pleasure by any means but cannot wholly free himself from a sense of guilt. After discovering he has made pregnant the married sister of the man who has sheltered him, Welbeck reflects, "Then I began to resolve the consequences, which the mist of passion had hitherto concealed. I was tormented by the pangs of remorse, pursued by the phantom of ingratitude" (*AM,* I, p. 89). At a later stage of his degradation he claims to discover a solution: "To free myself from self-upbraiding and to shun the persecutions of my fortune was possible only by shaking off life itself" (*AM,* I, p. 91). The problem is that Welbeck never carries through with this intention, and his primary motivation for suicide has more to do with his sense of ignominy from being poor. The prospects of renewed fortunes easily draw him away from the river bank on the first occasion and are ultimately linked with his inability to stay down on the last. To his favor, he comes away from the river on the second attempt out of concern for the fate of Clemenza Lodi, whom he would be deserting; he recognizes his own sins as sins in the account he gives of his life; and on his deathbed he not only again shows genuine interest in Clemenza, but returns Watson's gold belt to Arthur's honest hands, which he knows will carry it back to the owners.

If a list were drawn up of Welbeck's moral debits and credits, it would certainly not conclude in his favor, but it would show that feelings of remorse, concern for others, and final attempts to set matters right, to end a chain of sins, all have their redemptive value. Moreover, in his final deathbed scenes Welbeck is almost pitiable as a victim of his own weaknesses, the deceptions of others, and the remorseless plaguing of Arthur, who serves the role of his conscience in many respects. Even considered in isolation, Welbeck's character has its ambiguities that are not entirely the result of conscious or unconscious duplicity on his part. His guilt is measured somewhere between his acts and the confessions which seem to temper the acts but whose meaning may be blurred by the motives of the confessor and the perception of the listener. Brown seems to toy with these ideas when immediately after Welbeck has made

his confession to Arthur and they have gone to the cellar to bury Watson's body, Welbeck disappears, and Arthur suspects him of desertion, a treachery greater than his declared motives had promised, and greater also than what has actually happened. Acting on this suspicion Arthur wanders literally, and perhaps figuratively, through the wrong passageway until he arrives at a locked door which seems to confirm his beliefs. The juxtaposition of the confession and wrong-passageway scenes suggests at least to the reader the difficulty in determining a character such as Welbeck's. There is the possibility both of deceit and of misapprehension, which are once again disparities between appearances and reality.

In *Wieland* the character of Carwin presents many of the same ambiguities as Welbeck's, but he is much less of a villain and not at all as well developed.[21] Like Ormond he is strongly influenced by eighteenth-century radicalism, again with particular regard to the conventions of marriage and chastity. His primary crimes are in misusing his gift of ventriloquism, in whoring with Clara's maid, and in attempting Clara's seduction, but like all Brown's other villains except Wiatte, Carwin first appears to us in a favorable light. Clara finds him initially an innocent rustic and then strangely, compellingly attractive. When at last Carwin confesses his involvements in the strange events surrounding the Wieland household, his motives are anything but singular, certainly not depraved. At first he uses his ventriloquism out of a kind of Faustian delight in his unusual powers, hoping to gain wealth and pleasure. Then, when he deceives Wieland for the first time and on several occasions after that, he acts out of "habit and the influence of present convenience" (*W,* p. 219) to avoid some embarrassing confrontation. At other times he is moved by the irresistible "temptation to interfere" (*W,* p. 219), by a perverse mischief, and by the urge to experiment with Clara's fortitude. He is convinced that his intentions have not been evil and is continually contrite over the mischief he causes.

The issues of absolution raised by Carwin's avowals of his own motives are strikingly close to those we have observed in Welbeck's confessions and similarly parallel to key aspects in the development of Ormond's and Clithero's characters. In fact, the self-exculpating confessional mode is, along with the contrast of appearance and reality and close pairing of character roles, among Brown's favorite fictional patterns. He uses it for Carwin, Theodore Wieland, and much more subtly for Clara in *Wieland,* for Clithero and Edgar in *Edgar Huntly,* for Arthur and Welbeck in *Arthur Mervyn,* and perhaps in an inverted way for Ormond in the final scenes of that novel. What Carwin says about himself is made suspect not only by the nature of his actions, particularly by his admitted capacity for deception, but also by our realization that what he says may be colored by the needs of the moment. Thus, when he confesses to Wieland that he "did appear—in the entry— did speak" (*W,* p. 239), he is responding to Clara's charge that he has deceived Wieland. His confession is demanded as a way of saving Clara, which Clara eventually realizes may place his life in jeapordy, and the admission is therefore hard in coming. When the immediate danger is no longer present, Carwin once again reaffirms his innocence.

However much Carwin may convince the reader, Clara believes him guilty, for when she stops to reflect on all that has happened, she says, "Let me tear myself from contemplation of the evils of which it is but too certain that thou wast the author, and limit my view to those harmless appearances which attended thy entrance on the stage" (*W,* p. 57). While this statement comes with Carwin's confession fully in Clara's mind, although not the reader's, it leaves Carwin's motives and the extent of his guilt unaccounted for. Carwin's actions, his voice throwing as well as his willingness to confess, have rendered, as Clara admits, "the secrecy of . . . [his] purposes unfathomable" (*W,* p. 56), but what is important here is not so much the fact of the ambiguity itself as the way Brown systematically establishes it. Like Welbeck in his confessions, Carwin's guilt is a function of both his potential deceptiveness and an observer's capacity to perceive. In writing the first twenty-six chapters Clara is recording experiences recently past, with impressions fresh on her mind that she is trying faithfully to recall, as she is gradually slipping into madness. The reader's sense of Carwin, therefore, is explicitly a function of the way the none-too-reliable Clara tries to remember him at each stage of his role in the events. Carwin's statements, like Wieland's and like hers, only have a meaning or validity with respect to each other, but for Clara the question of Carwin's precise role in the disasters is not only indeterminate but irrelevant. In the last horrifying scenes Clara loses all interest in Carwin's guilt. "I care not," she says, "from what sources these disasters have flowed; it suffices that they have swallowed up our hopes and our existence" (*W,* p. 252). Whatever his intentions were and however far he actually went with his manipulations, once Carwin has begun them he has, as he realizes, "set in motion a machine, over whose progress . . . [he] had no control . . ." (*W,* p. 234). Like Marlowe's Faustus and also like Welbeck, Carwin's first sins prescribe the course of sins to follow, and the importance of individual agency gradually disappears. But, we are not made to feel that the disasters at Mettingen are the result of perverse fate, a dark, blighted order of existence, mere chance, or even some pervasive blot on human character. If the importance of individual human agency disappears, the importance of human responsibility does not. Carwin's role in the evil remains necessarily ambiguous, and we end up focusing our attention not on the question of Carwin's personal guilt, nor on Wieland's guilt either, but on the wrong of the thing that was done by the two together.

We can see this point even more clearly when we examine Wieland's responsbility for what happens. Wieland may be classed with Clithero Edny as among villains who actually commit or attempt unmistakably serious crimes, but are partially exonerated because they are insane at the time. They both have the most benevolent intentions behind their misdeeds, but therein lies a problem. While neither is ostensibly driven by passions for sex, fortune, or reputation, their selflessness is nevertheless problematical. Wieland's passion, for example, is religious fanaticism, an apparent heritage from his father. Unlike his sister, whose religion is an informal attitude toward nature and a reserve solace for bad time, Wieland takes his religion seriously, broods about it, studies its history, arrives at conclusions similar to the Calvinistic views of his father. The religious background allows him to accept supernatural explanations for the voices he hears and ultimately to obey what he thinks is a command from God to destroy his wife and children. But full realization that he is insane does not come until, confronted by Carwin's admission of having produced many of the voices, Wieland attempts to kill his sister anyway. He is shaken by Carwin's confession, but he chooses to obey an inner voice which convinces him that Carwin is a demon sent to lead him astray and that he must carry through with his original plans.

To the extent that Wieland's fanaticism partakes of religious selflessness—the giving of oneself to something other than oneself—his actions cannot be considered selfish. But in his plea which precedes the vision and command to kill, "O! That I might be admitted to thy presence that mine were the supreme delight of knowing Thy will, and of performing it!—the blissful privilege of direct communication with thee, and of listening to the audible enunciation of the pleasure!" (*W,* p. 185), there is the sense of his wishing a very private experience. This is not the voice of a skeptic painfully begging to have his doubts blasted; he wants, in a literal sense, to be made a saint. Private, individual worship was the nature of his father's religion, and it is in keeping with what are, in the final analysis, selfish acts. Wieland is willing to place his own contact with God above the happiness and safety of his sister, wife, and children. His laughter over the corpse of his wife signals joy at what he has accomplished for himself; there is, at first, not a trace of sorrow over what the killing has cost her.

Wieland, however, does not see matters in this light. His concept of selfishness, characteristically puritanical, is his thinking of sparing his wife. To his mind the selfish response is the human response, for when, as he says, he "sunk into *mere man*" (*W,* p. 192) after the religious transport leaves him, he then grieves deeply over his wife's death. And when he begins to consider how his children will provide him comfort for the loss of their mother, he rejects those feelings as "the growth of selfishness" (*W,* p. 192) and, in retrospect, recognizes the need for a second command which completely purges him of the self-indulgence of a family.

Such perverted notions of self-interest and selflessness make it difficult to see Wieland sympathetically as victim or sufferer. Yet, this seems to be Clara's intent when she moralizes at the very end: " . . . it will not escape your notice, that the evils of which Carwin and Maxwell were the authors, owed their existence to the errors of the sufferers" (*W,* p. 263). Wieland assumes the role of sufferer, according to Clara, when he finally realizes, by virtue of a final *divine* message, that he has acted insanely; the realization transforms him "at once into the *man of sorrows!*" (*W,* p. 249). Furthermore, Clara sees this transformation as a change for the worse. She seems to feel that Wieland's recognition of the state of mind under which he acted should not make him feel any more sorry. She explains, "He saw not that his discovery in no degree affected the integrity of his conduct; that his motives had lost none of their claims to the homage of mankind . . ." (*W,* p. 249). For Clara, then, Wieland's suicide is an especially shattering blow and one for which Carwin is again made to seem guilty; "What his agency began, his agency conducted to a close" (*W,* p. 252). Thus, in his most sincere attempt at genuine good, using the only means that would have halted Wieland, Carwin plays a direct part in Wieland's final destruction, thereby insures Clara's final unforgiveness, and almost brings about her death as well.

The events have, in short, degenerated into a moral morass in which good and evil both lead to the same unfortunate result. We might agree with Clara's final judgment, that "If Wieland had framed juster notions of moral duty, and of the divine attributes; or if . . . [she] had been gifted with ordinary equanimity or foresight, the double-tongued deceiver [Carwin] would have been baffled and repelled" (*W,* p. 263). But we might wish to qualify the moral dichotomy that it implies. The same ambiguity that surrounds Carwin's motives envelops Wieland's as well, and it may not be enough to ascribe his errors only to misguided theology. He is insane, but it is the terms of his insanity that we are interested in. At what point and in what ways does Wieland become insane? When does it become too late for him to frame "juster notions of moral duty"? The answers to such questions are made even more difficult by the fact that Clara's moral standards, when she describes Wieland's motives as worthy of "the homage of mankind," are almost exactly those of her brother at the time when he is clearly mad. We are left, as Clara realizes, with a situation in which guilt is shared at least three ways, but even more in which, as she seems not to realize, the terms good and evil have no definite place, no specific area to describe.

This notion of complicity that Clara points to in the last paragraph of *Wieland* deserves special attention. *Wieland, Edgar Huntly* and *Arthur Mervyn* all share elements with the detective story, but rather than simple whodunits, they are moral whodunits—they ask, "Who is responsible?" rather than, "Who pulled the trigger?" Even *Ormond,* which at first does not seem to have the same resolution-of-mystery structure as the others, presents the same issues in the way Clara's father is killed (is Craig guilty by actually committing the act, or Ormond by directing it?), in Helena's suicide (was she weak and foolishly sentimental or Ormond cruel and overmastering?), and in the death of Ormond himself (is Constantia as guilty as she feels, or is she exonerated by having been driven to it?). This complicity seems inevitably to imply that motive or intention, even sincerity, is not the key factor in judging moral responsibility or in avoiding harmful acts.

Clithero Edny illustrates this implication clearly and is instructive in our understanding of Wieland, Ormond, and Arthur Mervyn, as well as Edgar Huntly. Like these others Clithero is ostensibly motivated out of some form of benevolence, some sense of good. As a matter of fact, Clithero's entire history serves to illustrate that unenlightened benevolence leads to misfortune. When he tattles on Mrs. Lorimer's son, Clithero does it to benefit him; when he attempts Mrs. Lorimer's life, Clithero does it to benefit her; when Edgar Huntly presses to hear Clithero's tale, which results in Clithero's self-imposed exile and attempt at starvation, it is to help Clithero; when Edgar reveals to Clithero that Mrs. Lorimer is not dead, an act which sets the madman off to finish his duty,[22] it is again with the idea of aid; and the principles Mrs. Lorimer holds which allow Wiatte to get away with what he does, which lead Clithero to think he has wronged her by accidentally killing her brother, and which finally suggest to Clithero that her fortune and her brother's are one, are characterized by excessive benevolence. Clithero's villainy, which is largely the harm he attempts but does not carry out, is in this way intertwined with the acts and the beliefs of others. Wiatte's depravity necessitates Clithero's killing him in self-defense, and Mrs. Lorimer, who is not herself evil for taking Clithero out of his lower station in life, may be accused of engaging in a foolishly short-sighted act by helping him. Even more, Edgar's and Clithero's involvement in Mrs. Lorimer's miscarriage may be compounded by Sarsefield's precipitate assumptions of Clithero's intent and by his lack of compassion in dealing with him.

Clithero's case, like Wieland's, is complicated even further by his apparent madness. When Sarsefield and, shortly after, Wiatte reappear, Clithero begins to brood over the future and finally loses hold of his reason as he ponders the implications of his shooting Wiatte in self-defense. Realizing Mrs. Lorimer's devotion to her wicked brother, Clithero feels he has failed her trust and his obligations to her. He decides to kill her because he believes her contentions that her fortune was linked to her brother's, that Wiatte's death would automatically signal hers, and that by stabbing her in her sleep he can save her the anguish of waking to hear of and wait out her fate. Clithero's own conception of these thoughts and actions is that "it was the demon that possessed" him (*EH,* p. 79), and, in fact, much of his reasoning takes place while he is sleepwalking, which is the main clue to insanity in the novel. Thus, he may be an example of one with "a diseased condition of his frame" (*W,* p. 55), as Clara Wieland suspects of her brother, but we must also recall that Clithero's madness is, in part, his taking too far beliefs originating with Mrs. Lorimer.

Thus, just as it is not precisely Ormond's social philosophy or Wieland's religion that is to blame for their respective crimes, Clithero's benevolence is not itself the sole culprit. Not only is he mad, but the benevolence is mixed up with other aspects of his character. He appears to share Wieland's rather stiff sense of proper moral conduct, for his falling out of favor with Mrs. Lorimer's son results from his priggishly reporting the son's activities. He deems it his "privilege, as well as duty, to sit in judgment on his [Mrs. Lorimer's son's] action" (*EH,* p. 38), but again this does not come from religious fanaticism or from enlightened, radical philosophy. Clithero, it appears, has an inordinate, almost exquisite, sense of his place, his duties and obligations to those above him, and his advantages over those below. His rise from tenant farmer's son to Mrs. Lorimer's steward, or as Clithero likes to think, to "a member of her own family" (*EH,* p. 39), puts him in a special position: " . . . She treated me in a manner in some degree adapted to the difference of rank and the inferiority of my station, and yet widely dissimilar from that which a different person would have adopted in the same circumstances. The treatment was not that of an equal and a friend, but still more remote was it from that of a mistress. It was merely characterized by affability and condescension, but as such it had no limits" (*EH,* p. 41). Such strong class feelings produce a conflict for him when he falls in love with Clarice, his protectoress' niece, and these feelings are also, insofar as they imply an unusual sense of duty, involved in his attempt to kill Mrs. Lorimer. Even more, once he becomes aware of larger possibilities in life than he knew as a peasant's son, he becomes somewhat ambitious: "In proportion as my views were refined and enlarged by history and science, I was likely to contract a thirst of independence, and an impatience of subjection and poverty" (*EH,* p. 37). Thus, if we can accuse Wieland of being suspiciously self-serving in his selflessness, we must recognize that Clithero's class consciousness and sense of duty are in fact self-serving insofar as they help ingratiate him with Mrs. Lorimer and thereby further his advance in life.

From the discussion so far we can see that there is a rather wide range of villainy found in Brown's major novels from the unusually unmitigated depravity of Wiatte, to figures such as Wieland and Clithero, who might not qualify as villains at all, despite the considerable evil they either participate in or bring about. The ambiguity of these figures and of the moral world Brown creates becomes even more problematical when we consider those characters who seem to be heroes or heroines in his works—Clara, Constantia, Edgar, and Arthur. In fact, the idea of complicity we have seen to apply to the Wieland-Carwin, Clithero-Edgar relationships extends even further to include these so-called heroes and heroines, and their characters are frequently developed along lines similar to those of their darker parallels.

One distinction between hero and villain might seem to be whether or not the character seeks to do or actually does physical or moral harm to an innocent person, and yet Arthur Mervyn is the only one of Brown's major characters who would seem to qualify as hero. For example, Clara Wieland not only thirsts for Carwin's blood, at one point (*W,* p. 240), but also is on the brink of using a knife on either her brother or herself; Constantia Dudley ends up stabbing Ormond; and Edgar Huntly is prolific in his destruction of Indians. The key concept then would appear to be the innocence of the victim.

Ormond, Wieland and the Indians are hardly innocent in what they have actually done, but Wieland, at least, is not entirely responsible for his actions and especially not in Clara's eyes. Therefore, when she recalls how she considered stabbing her brother she is horrified: "O, insupportable remembrance! hide thee from my view for a time; hide it from me that my heart was black enough to meditate the stabbing of a brother! a brother thus supreme in misery; thus towering in virtue!" (*W,* p. 242). In some sense, then, Clara Wieland contemplates physical harm to someone who is in her mind undeserving of injury, if not morally innocent, and for it she sees herself as having failed a test of her character under stress. In this situation, at least, the question of innocence is not clearcut, since Clara, who hardly seems evil, would have to classify herself as being villainous for a while. The point, however, is that Brown again neatly underscores and undercuts the actions and motives of one of his characters with those of another. Theodore's "selfless" justifications for murder mock Clara's selfish motives of self-defense; whereas in his mind the selfish act would have been saving his loved ones, in hers it would be destroying one of them, so that for a moment they merge their wills and consciences, acquiescing to what amounts to suicide for her, and one more murder for him.

In Constantia's case there is little doubt about the victim's guilt, but there are other ironies implicit in the final confrontation with Ormond. Prior to that confrontation Constantia has been developed as a courageous, forthright, practical, reasonable, independent woman who is well able to make her own way in the world and to resist evil despite the one flaw in her moral make-up—she is "Unacquainted with religion" (*O,* p. 175). More to the point, "matrimonial as well as every other human duty . . . [is] disconnected in her mind with any awful or divine sanction. She . . . [forms] her estimate of good and evil on nothing but terrestrial and visible consequences" (*O,* p. 175), and therefore she is susceptible to Ormond's insidious logic. Against Ormond's egocentric, rapacious desire to have her at any cost, all she has for a defense is a pragmatic rational sense of what serves her own good. She is able to avoid impractical offers of marriage, but when in the final scene she faces Ormond's seductive arguments, then his declaration to rape her if she doesn't willingly submit, and finally his avowal to have his way whether she is alive or dead, Constantia is left in an impossible dilemma. Her sense of societal honor and virtue will not ler her submit. Her reliance on reason and on "appeals to his compassion and benevolence would counteract her purpose, since, in the unexampled conformation of this man's [Ormond's] mind, these principles were made subservient to his most flagitious designs" (*O,* p. 275). Such principles have been the mainstays of her rational outlook, and they are the basis of a prior appeal for help when she relies on a simple presentation of truth and reason attempting to stir Craig's benevolence, conscience, and reason in restoring some of what he had cheated from her father. Therefore, to kill either Ormond or herself would be an admission of failure for those principles and of his ultimate power over her. The possibility of killing Ormond is even more antithetical to her notions because she senses that attempting it would be impractical and that matters would probably be worse if she failed. Ormond's social and moral philosophy not only obliterates *his* conscience, but effectively neutralizes Constantia's rational moral system as well. It is ironic, finally, that the man whose reasoning obeys his natural impulses is brought down by an impulse which is similar to many of his and which disobeys her sense of reason, because that sense has been so effectively stymied by his.

Thus, for both Clara and Constantia the question of taking life, either suicide or homicide, is difficult and closely tied to the beliefs and values of their intended victims. Both women are driven to a decision about killing by necessity, by a lack of other alternatives to save their own lives, but necessity does not seem to make the killing morally excusable. Looking back on her thoughts of killing, Clara exclaims, "Alas! nothing but subjection to danger, and exposure to temptation, can show us what we are. By this test was I now tried, and found to be cowardly and rash" (*W,* p. 241). Similarly, "a momentary frenzy" (*O,* p. 282) is what leads

Constantia to stab Ormond, and Clara's feelings about what she considers doing match Constantia's feelings for what actually happens. Sophia attempts to assure her that the act was justified by Ormond's complete wickedness, but she is not immediately successful, since Constantia's position has been, as she evidenced in her feelings toward Martinette's adventures: " . . . how can the heart of women be inured to the shedding of blood?" (*O,* p. 201). Moreover, she shows additional outrage that Martinette should consider suicide even out of necessity and the love of liberty. The extent of Brown's Quakerism and how much of an aversion to bloodshed it may have produced are not clearly known, but in his novels killing seems to be the avenue by which ordinarily virtuous heroes and heroines are drawn into a kind of involvement in evil.[23] The distinction of innocent victims is only partially a saving grace.

Perhaps the best representation of this involvement is found in the exploits of Edgar Huntly. From the moment he finds himself in the cave faced by a ferocious mountain lion, which he kills and eats raw, there is a foreshadowing of an unusual kind of adventure about to begin. There can be little doubt that killing the lion is necessary and justifiable, but the savagery of it suggests his entrance into a world where one savage act inescapably leads to others.[24] Yet his commitment to this world is not immediately complete, for when he faces the first of the five Indians he struggles with his conscience for a long time before finally burying a hatchet in the Indian's chest. The question for Edgar is whether the consequences of not killing the Indian are sufficient to warrant taking another man's life; or as he puts it, "My aversion to bloodshed was not to be subdued but by the direst necessity" (*EH,* p. 171). The situation would seem dire enough for most men, for not only is the Indian blocking his only escape route but Edgar's parents were massacred by Indians, perhaps, as he suggests, by the same ones he now faces. Despite these reasons of necessity, made still worse by his desperate thirst, hunger, and weakness, Edgar is willing to crawl back through the cave where the four other Indians are sleeping, back to the darkness where he has previously been, in order to avoid using his gun or hatchet. He says, "The hazards attending my reentrance were to be boldly encountered, and the torments of unsatisfied thirst were to be patiently endured, rather than imbue my hands in the blood of my fellow men" (*EH,* p. 171).

The final blow comes only when Edgar has clearly no choice but to strike or be detected; the act is almost involuntary but still Edgar cannot help feeling remorse. After this, however, and after he quenches his thirst, Edgar begins to show signs of responding to danger for reasons other than necessity. Whereas before killing the one brave he was willing to leave the girl with the others while he went for aid, Edgar now decides to rescue the girl himself, and in some sense this act of bravery necessitates his killing the three Indians who follow him and the girl to Queen Mab's cabin. Although there is still a kind of necessity in these killings it is not as great as in the first; flight is a more practical possibility at any stage in the second series of deaths, and Edgar begins to sense that he is being drawn into something undesirable. As he says, looking at the dead Indians, "This scene of courage and blood was laid by me. To this havoc and horror was I led by such rapid footsteps" (***EH,*** p. 185).

When he escapes the cabin and resumes his journey home he declares himself even more loath to shed blood, but this encounter with the last Indian reveals that his attitudes have actually changed in the opposite direction. From a position which he describes as "shaded from the observation of others" (***EH,*** p. 190), Edgar watches the last Indian crawling in the grass across a clearing and once again ponders what to do. But this time his thoughts lead him almost directly to killing rather than to flight. As he sees it,

> The mark was near; nothing obstructed or delayed; I incurred no danger, and the event was certain.

> Why should he be suffered to live? He came hither to murder and despoil my friends; this work he has, no doubt, performed. Nay, has he not borne his part in the destruction of my uncle and my sisters? He will live only to pursue the same sanguinary trade; to drink the blood and exult in the laments of his unhappy foes and of my own brethren. Fate has reserved him for a bloody and violent death. For how long a time soever it may be deferred, it is thus that his career will inevitably terminate. (***E.H,*** p. 191).

From these arguments of fate and vengeance, which are quite different from his previous positions and which are wrong as to the Indians' motives and the extent of their guilt, he proceeds to argue for the necessity of killing the Indian, and finally, whether he intends it or not, actually precipitates that necessity by cocking his gun. Because of last minute doubts his aim is bad, he has to shoot the brave again, and finally he stabs him to put him out of his misery. But if this gory savagery were not enough, a final shot is mistakenly aimed at the head of a friend, and thus his involvement in the brutal, elemental life very nearly leads him to kill an innocent man.

Most significant, his reasoning is ironically parallel to Clithero's justification for speeding up Mrs. Lorimer's fate. The point seems to be that like Ormond, like Clithero, and, perhaps, like Wieland as well, once a man kills for the first time, however excusable an act it may be, it becomes much easier for him to kill again, not only in terms of acquired prowess, but especially in terms of accommodating his mind and conscience to the act. From the hero's point of view such a killing,

even when a matter of self defense, is always seen as a kind of evil, an evil that involves hero and villain alike.

The links and parallels between Edgar Huntly's and Clithero's careers are quite obviously extensive. As critics have regularly pointed out, they are in many ways mirror images of each other: both are forced to take one man's life, which act leads them at least to consider (in Clithero's case) taking others; both entertain benevolent ideas which lead to disasters; both are motivated also by curiosity; both have manuscripts which they are secluding; and both are afflicted by sleepwalking, which comes to represent a similar insanity. Moreover, however much Edgar's killings may be considered crimes, Clithero, by the curiosity and concern he arouses in Edgar, plays a major role in getting him into the cave and therefore into contact with the Indians. In the latter stages of the novel, Clithero and Edgar even more directly interact to terrorize Mrs. Lorimer. The temptation is to describe these characters as among the "various pairs of devil-and-innocent" which R.W.B. Lewis thought were Brown's tools for mastering the conditions of a similarly divided world.[25] But such a division is not easily made; borrowing from Brown's own approach to such matters we might say that what first *appears* to be the case, upon examination turns out to be, in reality, something other. Thus, if Clara Wieland can see herself as partially guilty for all the evil that happens in that novel, if Constantia Dudley can be blamed for not having the proper moral make-up to withstand Ormond and thereby avert the final disaster, then certainly Edgar Huntly, despite all his claims to good intentions, must share some moral guilt for the suffering he finally brings to Mrs. Lorimer and Sarsefield. His similarities to Clithero suggest that, seen from a point of view other than Edgar's, the action of the novel would less clearly distinguish the guilt of the two men's actions. Edgar is not malicious, but then Clithero is not clearly so either, and both are interested in improving their lots by attaching themselves to wealthy, wordly mentors. As we have seen before, avowed motives seem not to matter so much (if Sarsefield had killed Edgar in the mountains that act would have been damned as precipitate), and by the analogies with Clithero, by sneaking into locked caskets and other furtive actions, and by his period of semi-insanity, Edgar comes off less than lily-white.

While it no longer seems necessary simply to debunk the purity of Arthur Mervyn's behavior, the ways in which his character is drawn along the lines we have been considering are significant. Arthur is obviously similar to Edgar Huntly and Clithero Edny, but less obviously parallel to Carwin and Ormond, and perhaps even to some of Brown's blacker villains. What Arthur *seems* to be is relatively clear—a semi-educated rustic, innocent of the ways of the world, who aspires to wealth and education, and who holds as his highest virtues unmitigated honesty and benevolence of purpose. On the surface he seems the supreme do-gooder. Of course, since Arthur reveals most of the circumstances of his life in a narrative designed to allay doubt about his character resulting from the charges of some other, perfectly respectable viewer, he is generally on the defensive. He is trying to provide a more favorable account of appearances and relying, in the final analysis, on his own appearance or manner of forthrightness and sincerity to convince his listeners. However, as several critics have recognized, either beneath the surface of benevolent virtue or part of that surface character itself are a number of opposite traits. Warner Berthoff, arguing from the fact that Arthur has been doomed by his heritage both morally and physically (he believes all of his line must die at an early age), says, "If the alternative is death, he must take hold of life at any cost. This is the crux of his education out of moral inertia. The 'selfishness' of this necessity requires for compensation just that energy of comparison which he displays in the novel, for the cost of his educaiton, in Brown's narrative, is an underlying strain of cruelty and inhumanity."[26] Others, in noting Arthur's similarity to Benjamin Franklin or other models of the American, acquisitive prototype, see a conflict in Arthur's character between the impulses for freedom and independence on the one hand and the democratic spirit on the other.[27]

The recent concensus is that Arthur is to some degree selfish or self-serving, and this suggests several comparisons with other Brown characters. Most obviously he shares Edgar's and Clithero's aspirations as common-born individuals seeking a higher place in the world by ingratiating themselves with some wealthy patron or patroness for whom they have almost incestuous feelings. If Arthur is a Franklinian type, he is going to succeed less on industry and frugality than on charm and the appearance of virtue alone. Whether or not due to his defensive posture, there is also in Arthur a priggish, smug, and inordinately self-righteous tone in all his claims of benevolence, which suggests that he attempts to do good and be brave mainly to please himself. This may again suggest something of Franklin, but it also recalls Clithero and Wieland. Similarly, like so many of Brown's villains, particularly the worst, Arthur has a more than healthy sex drive; he seems to be quite literally "on the make," for after seeing Clemenza Lodi only once, his thoughts run ahead to envision marriage with the girl, who is in his mind wealthy; this fancy is replaced by affections for the also wealthy Eliza Hadwin, a fleeting admiration for Fanny Maurice, and finally a preference for the wealthier and more worldly Ascha Fielding. Of course, he denies any entanglement with the lascivious Betty Lawrence, and he may be right as to acts committed, but his descriptions of her advances, which he says he watched

as he "regarded a similar deportment in the *animal salax ignavumque* who inhabit the sty" (*AM,* II, p. 129), include a rather oddly appreciative assessment of her charms: "Betty had many enticements in person and air. She was ruddy, smooth, and plump. To these she added—I must not say what, for it is strange to what lengths a woman destitute of modesty will sometimes go" (*AM,* II, p. 130). Arthur's momentarily losing himself in what would appear to be rapt recollection of what Betty's destitute modesty revealed to him is amusing and revealing. If he is as libidinous as he sometimes seems, it gives him something in common with all the seducer villains in Brown's novels, and particularly with Welbeck and Colvill, whose several links with Arthur center around sexual crimes.

Arthur's shift of affection from Eliza Hadwin to Ascha Fielding is perhaps the clearest example of Arthur's selfishness. In apperance the pretty Eliza Hadwin is hardly rivalled by Mrs. Fielding, whom Arthur describes as lovely, yet " . . . in stature she is too low; in complection [sic], dark and almost sallow; and her eyes, though black and of piercing lustre, have a cast, which . . . lessens without destroying their lustre and their force to charm" (*AM,* II, p. 197). Yet his consistently expressed desire to learn about the world makes Mrs. Fielding, who is several years older than Arthur, has travelled, been married, given birth, and been deserted, who is above all educated both traditionally and in the ways of the world, a likely choice over the younger and more innocent Eliza. The switch is, as a matter of fact, well prepared for in the second part of the novel when shortly before he visits Phillip Hadwin he explains to Eliza the reasons why he feels he cannot marry her at that point. He tells her of his ambitions for greater things in the way of world knowledge than she can offer him, or, in essence, that he feels through his experiences in the city he has outgrown her. There is a considerable lack of tact in his approach and a high degree of male ego, and to his surprise she upbraids him for his views, providing a clear appraisal of what they really amount to: "What angers and distresses me," she says,

> is, that you think me unworthy to partake of your cares and labors; that you regard my company as an obstacle and incumbrance; that assistance and counsel must all proceed from you; and that no scene is fit for me, but what you regard as slothful and inglorious.

> . . . You desire to obtain knowledge, by travelling and conversing with many persons, and studying many sciences; but you desire it for yourself alone. (*AM,* II, p. 80).

Certainly he provides better for her education in the end, but his self-interest seems to undergo no change.

In his dealings with Eliza what may be even more suggestive is his capacity to provide sometimes elaborate, but always rational sounding, moral justifications for what he does. Although Arthur is certainly no ideologue like Ormond, there is something of that man's pliable ethics in the way Arthur explains a good deal of his behavior. Thus, for all his moral uprightness, which he extols in its consistency, Arthur has no compunctions about not paying to cross the toll-bridge in and out of town, because, as he explains, "All that honour enjoins is to pay when I am able" (*AM*, I, p. 27), and "so slight an incident would have precluded that wonderful destiny to which I was reserved" (*AM*, I, p. 27). Such "situation ethics" also keep him honor bound by his pledge to Welbeck not to reveal the secret of his past to anyone. The first test of this pledge comes when he realizes he has foolishly begun to reveal part of his history to Mrs. Wentworth and must simply remain silent to avoid telling her more. Although he clearly causes Mrs. Wentworth considerable anguish by not revealing the full of his knowledge of Clavering, he reasons: " . . . to forget the compact which I had so lately made, and an adherence to which might possibly be, in the highest degree, beneficial *to me* and to Welbeck—I was willing to adhere to it . . ." (*AM*, I, p.68 [emphasis mine]). This is, however, the last point at which he is so scrupulous about keeping the pledge, for he relates his past to Mr. Hadwin without any qualms in order to secure a job. In addition he breaks a second pledge to Welbeck not to reveal the history of their connections when he tells his story to Dr. Stevens in order to clear his reputation. This second pledge, which he goes along with for awhile, includes secretly burying Watson and the knowledge of several other crimes by Welbeck, and the breaking of it brings Welbeck's charge of betrayal down on Arthur's head. In all these matters, while Arthur might not be accused of outright falsity, his honor seems to depend considerably on his own interest in particular situations.

A similar standard of ethics is revealed in connection with his curiosity. This trait marks another of Arthur's similarities to other of Brown's characters, such as Carwin, Clithero, and Edgar Huntly, and is again, as Arthur Hobson Quinn points out, "disguised, even to himself, as benevolence. . . ."[28] It is what drives Arthur out into the world, into other persons' houses and private chambers, but always with the strongest avowals of honesty.[29] At one point his insatiable curiosity leads him to take the Lodi manuscript from Welbeck's house. even though he recognizes Mrs. Wentworth's claim to everything there. His explanation is simple: " . . . I felt an irresistible desire, and no scruples which should forbid me . . ." (*AM*, I, p. 120).

Even more striking are Arthur's similarities to Welbeck. As one commentator has observed, if Arthur had remained at the level of "moral benevolence" where we find him when he first leaves the city, "he might even-

tually only have repeated the life of Welbeck."[30] Both have been deprived of family inheritances and both have been used to lives of ease and relative independence in all matters except finances. When Arthur comes to Philadelphia and becomes Welbeck's protégé, it somewhat matches Welbeck's living off his relatives. Both are tempted by licentious women, and while we can be sure of Welbeck's succumbing and its significance on his later history, we are faced with conflicting claims about Arthur's involvement—he denies what his neighbors and Betty Lawrence assert. Nevertheless the pattern of Arthur's love interests demonstrates an inclination, if not a series of achievements, parallel to Welbeck's. Finally, even in the second part of the novel, it becomes clear that Arthur's ambitions in life are almost exactly Welbeck's, aspiring to wealth, knowledge, and social recognition based on something other than manual labor, or really any other kind of work of any specific sort.

This connection with Welbeck goes beyond what Kenneth Bernard describes as a symbiotic relationship in which Welbeck provides education for Arthur, while the young innocent is Welbeck's conscience. The first part of the novel, in fact, closely follows the structuring of *Edgar Huntly, Wieland,* and *Ormond* in that the destruction of the Lodi fortune, which in turn ruins Welbeck, and the death of Eliza's father, which brings ruin to her family, are the results of complex agency. Somewhat like Craig with Ormond or Wieland with Carwin, Arthur actually destroys the fortune, but it is the result of Welbeck's deception. Similarly, Eliza's father comes to the city because of the tardiness of Wallace and the failure of Arthur to tell anyone of his plans when he goes himself to the city. But, in *Arthur Mervyn* this is really more a feature of the first part of the novel than of the second. Considered as a sequel or separate novel, the second part is different in structure and different in tone from any other of Brown's major works. Not only does it not end in quasi-disaster, it lacks the contesting force of an antagonist that marks the rest of his work. Mainly, Arthur engages himself in tying up the loose ends, in righting the wrongs of the first part and, of course, in cementing himself into the higher reaches of society. However, at the same time that the antagonist is done away with, Arthur's character is felt to be increasingly suspect, or at least the conflicts in his character that are set down in the first part of the novel become more visible, the tensions more irreconcilable. This is not to say that *Arthur Mervyn* should be read as two separate novels; both parts are too closely linked with each other and each is too incomplete for such a reading. Nor is this to say that there is in *Arthur Mervyn,* or in any of Brown's major works, a clear contest of dark and light forces that become internalized in Arthur in the second part. The pairing of traits between the characters in Arthur's case as in others is too close to allow such a dichotomy. My point is rather that in the absence of a contending figure to add the kind of complication he regularly employed, Brown seems to have heightened the complexity of the single character, and this is one of the reasons Arthur is so interesting to modern readers.

What I hope to have shown in this study of Brown's heroes and villains is not only that these characters are more ambiguous than is always recognized, even among modern critics, but, more important, that the ambiguities seem to be worked out along purposeful lines. The complicity of agents within individual works, the way characters frequently are seen as doubling some other character or characters, and the echoing of character traits from novel to novel belie the notion that the confusion or ambiguity of Brown's work is entirely accidental. Rather, the development of this complicity and character pairing and the constant sense of disparity between the appearance of virtue and the reality of vice, or the opposite, seem designed to make the point at the end of *Wieland, Ormond, Edgar Huntly,* and at least the first part of *Arthur Mervyn* that intentions, however virtuous, are not the key factors in preventing evil or harmful acts. To make this point satisfies, I think, some of Brown's didactic inclinations, but I would also suggest that the point goes beyond the assertion that programs to rectify society through benevolent action are doomed to failure. The theme of self-promotion versus other-promotion, egotism versus altruism, is clearly a part of *Ormond* and *Arthur Mervyn,* less obviously of *Edgar Huntly* and *Wieland,* and the irreconcilability of these impulses has been recognized as one of the central tensions of Brown's fiction and of his social and political thought. The development of Brown's characters suggests that those tensions are really part of a rather intricate combination of external circumstances, unrecognized motivations, and the involvement of others, all of which seem to stifle purpose, to short-circuit virtue and vice alike. Rather than drawing the lines too narrowly between self and other, Brown's purpose seems to be thoroughly and purposefully reductionist, to create final situations of moral blankness or paralysis. Even *Arthur Mervyn* may qualify for this judgment insofar as we may feel that his final success is paid for by something in his humanity, but it is more clearly the case in the sad endings of the other works.

The complicity of agents that appears in all these novels recalls the ending of Stephen Crane's "The Blue Hotel," in which the Easterner reappears to give an account of how each character in the story has played a role in the death of the Swede. Once the enumeration begins, of course, we may feel able to extend it to include something like man's fate in an overwhelming universe, but Brown does not develop his theme on such a broad cosmic scale. His major novels are, indeed, characterized by a dark vision, by a world of terror, of "confusion, complication, misfortune and calamity,"[31] but whereas this darkness may at first seem to stem from some malign external power, intelligence, or order, the ultimate locus of malignity is placed squarely in man and his society. In this Brown seems less like Edwards, Hawthorne, Melville, and Poe, with whom he is usually associated, than the darkness itself would suggest. Despite the emphasis on various kinds of compulsive behavior and despite the obviously catastrophic events surrounding them, Brown's characters seem less driven, less victims of fate than do so many of the figures in the works of America's other dark fictionists. In the plagues, the mountain lions, the shipwrecks, the bizarre coincidences, the dementia of Wieland, Clithero, and Edgar there is little of the human compelling force felt in Edwards' God, Hawthorne's Satan, Melville's whale, Poe's maelstrom, or even Dreiser's Spencerian laws of nature.

A more natural comparison may be with William Dean Howells in *The Rise of Silas Lapham,* in which Silas' economic fall is felt to be the result of a melange of events, motives, and characters, to be a product of his own doing and of others, and in which at the end the moral meaning of all that has happened (except that Silas is a better man) remains a mystery. Thus, such a comparison, which might also be made with other late nineteenth-century writers—even James—who are concerned with society *and* morals, suggests precisely where the emphasis lies in Brown's work. He is certainly interested in psychology, including mysterious, subconscious forces, and there are many inexplicable vicissitudes in external events. But, what produces the moral blank is a rather close set of interpersonal involvements—for example, Carwin with the group at Mettingen, Craig and Ormond with Constantia, Clithero, Wiatte, Mrs. Lorimer, and Sarsefield with Edgar, Welbeck and the Hadwin group with Arthur—that come to represent the interactions of society in general. Society as it is embodied in institutions and mores is an important part of these novels, but it is society as it is embodied in interactions of central characters that I think is key.

Notes

[1] Quoted by Ernest Marchand, "The Literary Opinions of Charles Brockden Brown," *Studies in Philology,* 31 (October 1934), 549.

[2] All future references to these four works will be included within the text and will refer to *Charles Brockden Brown's Novels,* 6 vols. (Philadelphia, 1887). For clarity, this internal notation will include the following symbols in referring to individual works: *W* for *Wieland; O* for *Ormond: EH* for *Edgar Huntly;* and *AM, I,* or *AM, II,* for the two volumes of *Arthur Mervyn.*

[3] *Charles Brockden Brown: Pioneer Voice in America* (Durham, N.C., 1952).

[4] *The Sources and Influences of the Novels of Charles Brockden Brown* (New York, 1950), p. 62.

[5] Jane Townend Flanders, "Charles Brockden Brown and William Godwin: Parallels and Divergences" (diss. University of Wisconsin, Madison, 1965), pp. 21-22.

[6] Marchand, p. 561.

[7] William Hedges in "Charles Brockden Brown and the Culture of Contradictions," *Early American Literature*, 9 (Fall 1974), 129, credits Brown with a "crude strength," but Brown's style is more frequently and more obviously an embarrassment—strained, latinate, circumlocuted, bad.

[8] *Hedges*, p. 108.

[9] R. W. B. Lewis, *The American Adam: Innocence, Tragedy, and Tradition in the Nineteenth Century* (Chicago, 1955), pp. 92-98.

[10] Arthur G. Kimball, "Savages and Savagism: Brockden Brown's Dramatic Irony," *Studies in Romanticism*, 6 (Summer 1967), 214-25.

[11] Michael Davitt Bell, "The Double-Tongued Deceiver': Sincerity and Duplicity in the Novels of Charles Brockden Brown," *Early American Literature*, 9 (Fall 1964), 143-63.

[12] Hedges, pp. 107-42.

[13] See especially Patrick Brancaccio, "*Arthur Mervyn* and the Problem of the Unreliable Narrator," *American Literature*, 42 (March 1970), 18-27.

[14] They may even recall the characters of "soaring passions and intellectual energy" Brown believed to govern the world and to be the most desirable subjects for literature. See "'Advertisement' for 'Sky Walk,'" in *The Rhapsodist and Other Collected Writings by Charles Brockden Brown*, ed. Harry Warfel (New York, 1943), p. 136.

[15] *The Rise of the American Novel* (New York, 1948), p. 80.

[16] In this Brown seems to be demonstrating the Godwinian notion that the characters of men are determined by environment and events. (See Flanders, p. 354.) But exactly how environment or circumstances have affected Wiatte is not clearly worked out in the novel. He seems to have simply gone bad as a natural reaction to his sister's goodness.

[17] *Charles Brockden Brown: Gothic Novelist* (Gainesville, Fla., 1949), p. 134.

[18] *Ibid.*, p. 132.

[19] David Brion Davis, *Homocide in American Fiction* (Ithaca, N.Y., 1957), pp. 131-32.

[20] Flanders, p. 117.

[21] Some of the range of the critical estimates of Carwin's character can be seen in David Lee Clark's view that Carwin is "impelled to wickedness, not because of innate maliciousness, but because of the fascination of evil itself" (p. 169) and in William Manly's that Carwin is "more of a pathetic bumbler than a figure of soaring sexual passion" ("The Importance of Point of View in Brockden Brown's *Wieland*," *American Literature*, 35 [November 1963], 319). Larzer Ziff in his "A Reading of *Wieland*," *PMLA*, 77 (March 1962), 52, provides an explanation for this variance in arguing that Carwin's role changes from seducer (of the type found in a Richardsonian sentimental novel) to something else, perhaps a manipulator villain more like Ormond or Welbeck. Up to the point where he confesses his intentions to seduce Clara, Ziff argues that we have assumed him to be a standard villain, but at that point by his revealing only the terms of that standard villainy and not his ventriloquial powers, our understanding of his role changes.

[22] As Hedges points out, Clithero's purpose, whether murder or suicide, is not certain, but it is sufficient for my point here that the result is clearly disastrous.

[23] Wiley tells us that from the Friends " . . . he received a hatred of war and of slavery, repugnance toward military service, capital punishment and suicide . . ." (p. 2). Also, Howard Hintz in *The Quaker Influence in American Literature* (Port Washington, N.Y., 1965) concurs that "there is evidence . . . to show that he already held pacifist views in his early youth" (p. 38). The amount of space Brown devoted to characters agonizing over whether or not to resort to violence, especially in situations where there seems to be little real choice, suggests how important pacifist views were to Brown.

[24] Kimball argues this effectively at some length, pointing out how Brown's treatment of this theme was an ironic undermining of optimistic Lockean psychology.

[25] Lewis, p. 96.

[26] "Adventures of the Young Man: An Approach to Charles Brockden Brown," *American Quarterly*, 9 (Winter 1957), 430.

[27] For a more thorough examination of the Franklin parallel see James H. Justus, "Arthur Mervyn, American," *American Literature*, 42 (November 1970), 304-24.

[28] *American Fiction* (New York, 1936), p. 30.

[29] Note the similarities between his descriptions of motives and the later rationalizations of the antiquarian after the Jeffrey Aspern letters in James's *The Aspern Papers.*

[30] John Stephen Martin, "Social and Intellectual Patterns in the Thought of . . . and Charles Brockden Brown" (diss. University of Wisconsin, Madison, 1965).

[31] Hedges, p. 107.

Philip Young (essay date 1981)

SOURCE: "Born Decadent: The American Novel and Charles Brockden Brown," in *The Southern Review*, Vol. 17, No. 3, July, 1981, pp. 501-19.

[*In the following essay, Young asserts that although Brown's novels cannot properly be characterized as Gothic, Brown did write "the romance of mystery and terror." Young further argues that the "dark secret" of Romanticism—love between members of the same family or same sex—is also reflected in Brown's works.*]

> " . . . the Writer must appeal to Physicians and to men conversant with the latent springs and occasional perversions of the human mind."
>
> —Brown, Advertisement to Wieland, *1798*

Great ages of practically everything decline and fall, but it takes time. *Fin de siècle* cannot close in without a *siècle* behind it, and when Charles Brockden Brown came along the history of American fiction was not quite a decade old. Such an infant, indeed, was the American Novel that he is still called the Father of it. Yet he might as reasonably be considered the descendant of others. Late eighteenth-century America remained culturally colonial; our fiction grew out of England's. England had known the great age of Fielding, Richardson, Smollett, and Sterne, and then well before the turn of the century its novel was on the wane. Thus if Brown shows signs, and he certainly does, of the deterioration said to characterize the close of a major period—self-consciousness, restless curiosity, sensationalism, and moral perversity are symptoms commonly noted—he is the foremost native representative of the decline of fiction in the motherland.

There is only one point of view from which our novel can be looked on as born of him. He could be cast as heir to provincial forces and failings fathered or—so many of those early American writers were female—mothered in the years just before him. Or if it's argued that things didn't really get going until Cooper, a full generation after him, he is essentially a forerunner of

others: Poe, Hawthorne, even Faulkner. The matter is untidy, and only one claim is clean. For as long as he could hope to make a living at it, Brown was our First Professional Novelist. He was, to boot, the first American novelist who can be taken seriously.

It would be all right with a lot of people if our fiction, having thrived off and on for something like 150 years, had been born healthy. Or at least if, of all the tags pinned on Brown, a respectable and roughly accurate one would stay put. But the labels regularly assigned won't stick—partly because of the odd way the author was put together. He was for a time, as alleged, a "Godwinian liberal and humanitarian," but a destructive drive to his tales was always undercutting the position, and anyway he turned conservative. If he was an Enlightenment Rationalist, the ideas that made him one usually got carried away by an essentially narrative and dramatic imagination. He called himself a "Quaker outcast," but admitted when he said it that he had not cast out that training—and besides the Inner Light had always a bloody tinge to it. He could be a strident moralist, but was as powerfully drawn to what he regarded as Flagitious Immoralities, confessed to secret hopes he called "criminal," and heartily favored stories of "lofty crimes"—of "great energies employed in the promotion of vicious purposes" (his terms). Perhaps, as he thought, literature should instruct, but he was more eager to "ravish the souls" of his readers with "soaring passions."

The usual name for Brown is "Gothic," a category said to have three principal hallmarks: the ruined castle for a setting, the supernatural freely invoked and rarely rejected, the villainous hero dominating. On such a count he comes near striking out. Brown's dank dungeons and medieval castles (whence the very name of the game) are for the most part Pennsylvania caves, forests, and hospital wards. (There are a couple of dark closets, and one garden temple with a lurid sheen.) The weird occurrences for which his books are occasionally remembered could be explained to his own satisfaction in such natural terms as somnambulism, spontaneous combustion, and ventriloquism. His heart was never in his villains, who were not nearly so potent as the genre called for. But he did write "the romance of mystery and terror," did have a real feeling for the obsessed, the macabre, the demonic. The adventures are indisputably wild, the conceptions outré, the language extravagant. And the term "Gothic horrors" will cover such moral perversity as decadence is said to display.

Right along this line Brown may find a firmer hold on what is called Gothic. A distinction of the movement, as almost any textbook has it, is that it produced seeds which flowered in the great age that followed; hence the associated term "pre-Romantic." And if it is true, to move briskly, that Romanticism, at least in England, had an "ultimate and darkest secret"—when the business was not in the open—and that the secret was Incest, then this is surely one of those germs. It will do to recall Horace Walpole, who wrote *The Castle of Otranto, a Gothic Story* (1764), turned his establishment at Strawberry Hill into "a little Gothic castle," and told what might be the most horrendous of all incestuous tales in *The Mysterious Mother* (1768). In fact the subject of incest surfaced in all kinds and conditions of the novel in England in the 1770s and 1780s. Romantic poets soon to mature absorbed it in books as boys, to exploit it later on in such ways as Americans in general would not put up with.

This is presumably where our fiction got the topic at its start. In 1789, the year of the founding of the Republic, the First American Novel appeared: William Hill Brown's *The Power of Sympathy* focused on a love affair, ending in tragedy, between a sister and her brother. Within three decades such soiled material in the hands of native writers would no longer wash. What readers could handle instead, among many things, was repeated exposure to a figure conspicuous in American Romantic literature, who would be known as the Dark Lady. Her attributes settled into a familiar mold. She was a magnetic, even fatal beauty, erotic, exotic, sensual, seductive. Dark, often black, of hair, dark of eye and complexion, she was sexually experienced—also intelligent. Her fate was the rest of the formula. She frightened the young men she attracted, so that they ended rejecting remarkable opportunities, and settled for her equally traditional opposite. Not usually so striking as to be actually blond, the Fair Lady is often blue-eyed and always fair of face. Virginal if not virtually sexless, domestic, compliant or downright submissive, she is neither a physical nor an intellectual threat.

That this pattern was potentially dangerous became clear eventually, but it insinuated itself into American fiction without any opposition at all. Gently introduced in the unexceptionable romances of Sir Walter Scott, it passed into respectable versions by James Fenimore Cooper. Poe and Hawthorne explored more deeply. And then in 1852 Melville's *Pierre, or the Ambiguities* made it plain that the Dark Lady could be the incarnation of the preoccupation with incest that had gone underground.

Nothing here that has not been said one way or other several times before. What has been left out is that it really fell to Charles Brockden Brown of Philadelphia—well before Scott or Cooper, and almost by accident, as it will seem—to introduce the Dark Lady to American letters. And to stumble as well on Romanticism's dark secret, which was her own.[1]

The heedless speed at which Brown improvised permitted inspired accidents as well as other kinds. We remember him, when at all, for four novels—***Wieland, Ormond, Arthur Mervyn, Edgar Huntly***—and except for a sequel, ***Arthur Mervyn,*** volume II, he published them all in the months between September of 1798 and the summer of 1799. "More or less simultaneously" he wrote them all; according to William Dunlap, his close friend and first published biographer, he once had five books under way at the same time, mostly during a sojourn in New York. On finishing ***Wieland*** in less than a month, so we are told, he cultivated an offshoot called ***Memoirs of Carwin, the Biloquist,*** filed it, turned to the ***Memoirs of Stephen Calvert,*** completed a volume of them, and quickly composed three other books. At or about the same time he wrote the lost novel ***Sky-Walk,*** a substantial and recently anthologized piece described as "A Lesson on Concealment," a number of other fictions issued in magazines, and some hefty fragments—notably, **"Jessica"**—started a magazine of his own, and contracted but survived yellow fever, all before bringing out his last two, widely-unread novels in 1801. His effective career lasted about two years.

The cost of such haste is demonstrable. A search for what few of his papers exist in Philadelphia turns up, to be sure, spotless sheets of calligraphy that resembles engraving. A difficult scrawl would better have reflected the product. Brown's novels end spasmodically, leaving bits of plot to twitch involuntarily. The narratives are controlled, in a manner of speaking, as much by coincidence as by any other design. (The author's best friend, Elihu Hubbard Smith, had the first and last word on the structure: Brown "starts an idea," he observed, "pursues it a little way; new ones spring up; he runs a short distance after each; meantime the original one is likely to escape entirely.") We are accustomed to prolific nineteenth-century novelists who habitually wrote themselves half-way into a story without knowing how it would turn out; Brown never seems to know for sure where he is headed until he gets there—whereupon he glances about and either rushes on or quits. The modes of narration, further, can be radically dislocated. At one point in ***Arthur Mervyn*** we are reading a story within a story within a story that is within the original story. In another novel the author forgets the name of one of two principal characters; we frequently learn the names, origins, and purposes of significant figures when we are perilously close to no longer caring. As for rewriting, it was out of the question. (The allegation is that he never read the stuff over.) In some belatedly published fictional letters to a hypothetical girl, Brown explains how he regularly seems to have composed: "I cannot hesitate in the choice of words"; the first to offer themselves are "instantly adopted . . . unsolicitous of elegance or accuracy," regardless of selection or arrangement. And "why should I revise and correct what I have written?" The answer is so obvious one is shamed at not having thought of it himself: "I might with the same propriety repeat what I say."

Yet the results cannot always be dismissed out of hand. Peacock remarked of Shelley that "nothing so blended itself with the structure of his interior mind as the creations of Brown." The heroine of **Ormond,** Constantia, "held one of the highest places, if not the very highest place, in Shelley's idealities of female character." He is believed to have named a poem after her. Keats and Hazlitt were of roughly like opinion. Poe and Hawthorne paid more temperate tribute in America; Brown had been dead quite a while when Margaret Fuller argued that he "ought to be the pride of the country."

What is clear today is that to read the man extensively—from the present lonely viewpoint at any rate—is very different from reading about him, especially when the critic or plot-summarizer (which is frequently all that criticism of Brown comes to) appears not to have read, or anyway not to have finished, the work in question. For one thing, and despite Shelley, the author is best known for his male characters. All of his foremost titles name men. Males in Brown become religious maniacs, spontaneously combust, speak out of unlikely places, tramp off in their sleep, murder (with one exception), or, what is worse, despoil. Men advance most of the ideas the author is supposed to be making into novels. But to speak truly these ideas are not engrossing, unless conceivably when a female entertains them; the villains are half-hearted; the ravishers generally fail the assignment. The central characters in Brown's first two novels are in fact women, and the male protagonists of the second two are essentially in search of the substitute mothers they ultimately find. The last two novels are named for the heroines—**Clara Howard** and **Jane Talbot.**

Likewise with the very earliest works. *Alcuin,* also 1798, is a feminist tract which argues for equality of education, hence of career rights, for women, and for the right of divorce. **"Letters to Henrietta G.",** the long start of an epistolary novel, was published in 1952 by a biographer who took them as the record of Brown's real-life love affair, running from 1790 to 1793, with a girl he met "in the spring of 1792." The orientation of the correspondence is feminine, featuring a mammary fixation unprecedented for frenzy in our literature to that time and perhaps not matched for half a century—not until 1844, when another Philadelphian, George Lippard, composed his notorious *Monks of Monk Hall* (which, though Lippard could not have seen these letters, is Inscribed to the Memory of Brown).

There is nothing of the sort in the author's four-year correspondence with the young woman he married. Indeed she seldom wrote him, and she returned his letters after a single reading. It was during these years, 1800-1804, that he ran out of gas as a novelist, married, and fathered the twins that his fiction may have seemed to have called up. Before long he was announc-ing that a magazine he would edit "rigorously proscribes" everything that "savors of indelicacy or licentiousness." The "child of passion and inconstancy," as he once described himself to Smith, "the slave of desires that cannot be justified," was no more. The man lived until 1810.

That slave or child dreamed up Brown's women, who are more lively than the aspects of his work commonly labored over. This is partly because, as is vital to note but goes everywhere unnoticed, Brown wrote at a time when a radical discovery, which would inform our fiction for a considerable period, had yet to be made: namely, that women do not possess sexual appetites. Thus his females have an ingratiating dimension that would soon be largely missing from contemporary portraits. Traditional accounts of his books keep so busy expressing gratitude for his employment of American ingredients—scenery, Indians, and historical events (chiefly yellow fever epidemics), stressing the influence of foreign thinkers like Godwin and his eventual wife Mary Wollstonecraft, and unraveling the plots, that only recently have they found space for much else. Women are crucial to the stories, but **Ormond** has been recounted at length without reference to the female who narrates it and in the end dominates the action; the bride who climaxes both volumes of **Arthur Mervyn** in astonishing fashion is skipped over as just one character among too many; the woman at the heart of the mystery in **Stephen Calvert** is never mentioned in one account of that work; and in a summary of the long fragment **"Jessica"** the co-star Sophia is simply ignored, as she was in **Ormond.**[2] Either there has been a widespread failure to read what Brown wrote or an inability to comprehend it or a lobotomizing aversion to what it says.

Wieland; or, The Transformation, Brown's first and best-known novel, is narrated by an ideal beauty, Clara Wieland, and is often taken to focus on her brother Theodore, for whom the book is named. (It was their father who combusted spontaneously; the author had apparently read in a magazine of such an occurrence.) Theodore marries Catharine Pleyel, who is rich, and sister Clara lives nearby. An extremely close trio, they are joined by Henry, Catharine's brother, whose touch throws Clara into tumults. Children are born to the wedded Wielands. Then after six years the group is further joined by a Gothic or pre-Byronic type named Carwin, who alone of the characters is described: "sunken eyes . . . lustrously black" and "potent"; cheeks "sallow . . . pallid and lank"; "coarse, straggling hairs." Clara, following a bad dream involving not him but her brother, begins to fear for her life. She also thrills to the suspicion that the charming Pleyel loves her honorably. Carwin's intentions are of course different. He confronts her frankly, all muscle, to bring about her ruin. "What injury," he asks, "is done?" "Unspeakably more dreadful" than death, she replies.

It never happens, but because of Carwin's powers of ventriloquy Pleyel is convinced that Clara's charms, "so awful and so pure," are lost to the villain—"polluted by grovelling vices," devoted to "brutal gratifications." Brother Theodore also believes the worst of her, and when Clara finds his wife dead and disordered in bed she thinks her friend has been violated and killed in her place. The murderer, however, is Theodore, who in a fit of religious madness has done away with all his children too. He comes close to killing Clara as well but commits suicide instead, and Clara, exonerated, lives to tell the tale, her passion for Pleyel reborn in their union.

Ormond; or, The Secret Witness is really concerned with the fortunes of Constantia Dudley, as related by her "distant friend." At the start she is sixteen, and "no stranger to the pleadings of love . . . but its tumults were brief. . . ." Ormond, something of a freethinker and clairvoyant, has a voluptuous mistress whom he finds lacking in intellect. ("Marriage is absurd," he says. "To make her wise it would be requisite to change her sex.") He is aware that carnal impulses beget a disease "of more entire subversion and confusion of mind than any other"; its victim is "callous to the sentiments of honor and shame." That he is, and he underestimates Constantia. Confident of her when her father dies, he abandons the mistress.

Four years parted from her beloved Sophia Westwyn, Constantia has become "daily more enamoured" of Ormond's sister Martinette, a woman of great vigor and strong military propensities. On learning of her savagery at arms, Constantia cools, and it is here that Sophia, after 184 pages in the modern edition, identifies herself as the narrator and enters the action. Deserted at birth by her disreputable mother, Sophia had lived until maturity with Constantia and Constantia's father. She is now in Rome, where for some reason she has just married. Immediately departing solo for America, she searches for her sisterly friend and implausibly finds her. Meanwhile Ormond (who murdered Constantia's father) tells the girl that a disaster awaits her—a mighty evil with no witnesses. He has come to take what she has refused him. His intention dawns on the heroine like an "electrical flash"; she naturally prefers death by her own penknife. It makes no difference to him: "Living or dead," he announces icily, "the prize I have in view shall be mine." In something of a rerun of Clara Wieland, Sophia finds her friend on her back in disarray, but alive and unharmed. Ormond is finished, stabbed in the heart by Constantia—who, having rejected all suitors, leaves for England with Sophia.

Though Brown proclaimed that "the most momentous topic" for human beings is Property, as he never forgot, he liked to display "a virtuous man in those situations that arise from sex." Hence, conceivably, ***Arthur***

Mervyn; or, Memoirs of the Year 1793 (a reference to plague in Philadelphia). At any rate these declarations tend to unify the many strands of a staggering plot. Arthur is a curious chap—the "chameleon of convenient virtue" he has been called. A farm boy whose beloved sister, unwed and pregnant, was cast out to her death, and whose father has replaced his deceased mother with a girl whom Arthur has witnessed in the exercise of her "morals defective," he escapes to the city at eighteen. Much like Ben Franklin, he arrives in Philadelphia to build "a name and a fortune" with a few coins and fewer spare clothes, soon to be deprived of both. He has only his author's "elegant penmanship" to trade on (and consumption to fear, which Brown would die of). Falling in with a criminal named Welbeck, he is set up handsomely as a copyist. The events of a chaotic saga are initiated by his zealous curiosity about Welbeck's affairs. That and his fiendish virtue. "Life," Arthur observes, "is a trivial sacrifice in the cause of duty."

Living with Welbeck is his specious daughter Clemenza, an attractive girl who is struck with Arthur's resemblance to her brother; it takes no time at all for the boy to conceive that his employer will adopt and the daughter marry him. A "stranger to what is called love," he is shaken to discover that Clemenza is pregnant, and in his excitement it is hard to say whether he is more shocked that Welbeck has betrayed the girl or, if she be really his daughter, has committed "the blackest and most stupendous of crimes." Now entangled in his master's other misdeeds, Arthur helps him bury a corpse, then has reason to think that Welbeck has expired too. Moving in with a rural Quaker family, he is quickly taken with a genuine daughter, Eliza. Yellow fever hits the city—as famously described in passages that have still the power to shock. A hideous hospital is staffed with male and female drunks; Arthur naturally thinks he should be in charge of it. Welbeck turns up alive and begs him to save Clemenza from "the blackest imputations . . . dungeons . . . the gallows!" Arthur will certainly try, and the volume ends with the amazing announcement that "a particular series of adventures is brought to a close," perhaps to be followed by more. Brown wrote his brother that Arthur was going to marry the farm girl Eliza.

But first he composed and published ***Edgar Huntly; or, Memoirs of a Sleep-Walker,*** also a digressive, moralizing tale—narrated by a half-mad altruist for the edification of his fiancée, Mary. Hallucinated, violent, and grotesque as well, the book begins with Huntly (identified for us when the novel is half done) searching for the murderer of Mary's brother. Discovering one Clithero digging near the scene of the crime—in his sleep, as it happens—he sets out in compulsive pursuit of the suspect (whom he wishes to help). Somnambulism proves contagious; Edgar wakes to find himself in a deep and awful pit. He kills a panther and eats it raw. He also kills several Indians, among them the murderer he was seeking (though the book is sufficiently hallucinated that one ingenious interpreter has identified the guilty party as Huntly himself). This Clithero, we learn, is devoted to a benefactress, Mrs. Lorimer, who is the aunt of *his* fiancée, Clarice. Clarice is the daughter of Mrs. Lorimer's twin brother, an irredeemable villain named Wiatte. Otherwise a flawless woman, Mrs. Lorimer holds such "absurd opinions of the sacredness of consanguinity" as to be convinced that when her twin dies she will too. Clithero, in self-defense, kills a man; when he learns that the victim is Wiatte, he feels bound to kill the sister too, sparing her knowledge of her imminent doom. (Huntly considers this thoughtful of him.) Believing he has accomplished his purpose (actually he nearly murdered his sweetheart, Clarice), Clithero eventually drowns. Huntly in the end has fulfilled "the duty of preserving my life for the benefit of mankind." And, having forgotten the fiancée for whom the whole tale was told, he is left to rejoice in a new set of parents—a "mother," as she is called, in Mrs. Lorimer and an almost-father in Edgar's old teacher whom she has married.

There was a lot left over, as it turns out, from the opening volume of **Arthur Mervyn**. More, for instance, about the criminal Welbeck and his ex-mistress Clemenza, now installed in the opulent residence of a woman whose daughters support the place on the Wages of Pollution. Arthur now has three females on his incompetent hands. His father's slut is in town with the rumor that he is among the many men in her past; to save Clemenza he will search her out in the whorehouse; at fifteen Eliza the farm girl is alone in the world. "Not exempt from passion," she begs to join the lad: "and did I not pant after the . . . boundless privileges of wedlock?" Besides, she now owns the family farm. But Arthur dutifully crashes the brothel instead, and finds there with the merchandise Clemenza, whose infant perishes in front of them. Here he meets a fourth woman, Mrs. Achsa Fielding, who is unaware of the purpose of the place.

Mrs. Fielding is rich, and Arthur immediately decides that she should accomplish the salvation of Clemenza by taking her in. The plan fails, but he and the older woman exchange histories, Arthur confessing his love of the beautiful Eliza. Why doesn't he marry her, Mrs. Fielding wants to know. What does she lack? Everything, he explains: "Age, capacity, acquirements, person, features, hair [?], all. . . ." His wife must be the counterpart of Achsa herself, with her "hues." What Achsa has in the way of coloring that Eliza hasn't then becomes clear, as Brown offers the first description of a character he has introduced since Carwin—whom Mrs. Fielding oddly resembles. She is "in complexion dark and almost sallow," her eyes "black and of piercing luster." (His friends tell him she is "tawny as a Moor" with the "eye of a Gipsy" and "unsightly as a

night-hag." He admits she is short.)[3] But for Arthur she is truly *"lovely,"* has the "power to bewitch" and the "wisdom of men and books." In addition, moreover, to being much older than he, wealthy, once married and a mother, she is, as he guesses with a great thrill, *"a Jew."* (She is thought to be the first fictional Jew, in America, in American literature, perhaps the first unstereotyped Jew in all literature in English.) The daughter of a Portuguese, she was at sixteen carried away by her passions and married to an English nobleman, now dead, who ran off with a friend of hers, leaving her with one surviving child, now at a distant school. She agrees to take Eliza into her household as a sort of daughter, and the grateful Arthur, who has been deporting himself as a sort of son—with a "filial freedom and affection"—now means to kneel to her as to a mother or deity. But in a moment of "insanity" he "clasped her in my arms, and kissed her lips fervently." "Mamma" he calls her, and never anything else. When Eliza arrives she calls her mamma too.[4]

At the thought of being wholly Arthur's, Achsa is agreeably shaken. So is he. And why not? "Was she not the substitute of my lost mamma? Would I not have clasped that beloved shade?" Thus at the very end of his effective career as a novelist, Brown comes up with the first full-blown Dark Lady of our literature, a sexually ripe, exotic opposite to the undescribed but transparently fair Eliza—the domestic, selfless virgin Arthur in his unspeakable chastity should have chosen. At once creating and embracing our Dark Lady, Brown plunges into her ultimate secret: sacred consanguinity, mamma. At this point, a psychoanalytic shade out of Vienna descends anachronistically on the ending of the book. As Arthur, delirious with excitement, approaches the consummation of his marriage to Mrs. Fielding, anxiety mounts; a "nameless terror" fills him. In a nightmare, the dead Fielding—a father-figure if he ever had one—comes for his wife and stabs the boy in the heart. But as the hour nears, Arthur "abjures," as he says in the novel's last sentence, his pen—which he will not need, so he believes, any more.

Rich woman triumphs over peasant girl: the reason this climax upset Shelley is that his politics triumphed over his attraction to incest—that "very poetical" subject, as he called it. Dunlap simply pronounced the whole business "as unexpected as disgusting." What is likely is that no one expected it less than the author. Yet in some odd way, as if Brown had come to it sleepwalking, the climax was prepared for. Having protected his real mother from his father while she lived, Arthur was commanded to treat like a mother the easy woman his father then married. Treating him not precisely like a son, she tried to seduce him, and when this failed became "shameless and direct." (It is strange, Arthur observes, "to what lengths a woman destitute of modesty will sometimes go.") Then there was the general notion that the boy might marry Clemenza for the reason that they looked enough alike to be brother and sister, not to mention the perished thought that she might be pregnant by her father. Given the drift of the novel, it is no surprise that Eliza also finds a new parent in Mrs. Fielding, so that Arthur at the close has replaced both his lost mother and the sister he grieved for.

Quite different considerations have led a few to call Mervyn "our first representative hero." If he is a peculiar one, it is true that his book is our first thematically mature fiction: an "initiation novel" in which the protagonist moves from country to city, from rags to riches, from total innocence to the threshold of adulthood and the promise of very broad experience. In joining Achsa he means to take to himself not only her and her money, but her experience, her knowledge, and the power that comes with them.

Hindsight if nothing else will show that the ending of this novel was prepared for by previous ones as well. It is perfectly clear, to return to *Edgar Huntly,* that its hero had virtually no interest in his fiancée. His ultimate joy is in being told that Mrs. Lorimer "longs to embrace you as a son"—"truly." Family ties in this book are tight and tangled. The profundity of Mrs. Lorimer's relationship with her twin brother is intentionally mysterious; they are, we are told, exceptionally intimate; their resemblance to each other is "almost incredible." Nothing Wiatte can do to hurt her diminishes her love, and the power of consanguinity spins off in curious ways. Wiatte has seduced a woman who bore a daughter, Clarice, and died; his sister takes in the child as her own. She clings to the girl with more ardor than to the son she bore herself; the resemblance of brother to sister is "completely realized in his offspring." In this house of mirrors it is much as if Mrs. Lorimer thought of the girl as hers by Wiatte, and as if to confirm a wishful union with him she hopes (in vain) that Clarice will marry her look-alike half brother as her foster mother could not marry her twin. Clithero had found a mother in Mrs. Lorimer before Edgar did— "I her son," he declares himself—and then had fallen in love with her "darling daughter" Clarice, whose father he murdered. In this book Brown, the once hopeful rationalist, makes his single reference to "universal depravity."

Lust and murder had exploded out of a steamy situation in *Wieland.* From one clear angle the issue of the novel is Chastity's Destiny; or, The Fate of Clara Wieland. She is powerfully drawn to both her brother and his wife, whose rich beauty "added force to the love I bore her, which was amply returned." She lives near—not with—the married ones because self-denial was "one means of enhancing our gratifications," of satisfying "every craving." Then when she suspects that Pleyel loves her, a "nameless ecstasy thrilled

through my frame." She cannot wait for the "burning blushes and the mounting raptures of that moment" when he will tell her, though she calls these "hateful and degrading impulses." Such shame would better suit her response to the pallid, sunken-eyed Carwin—in whose presence her bosom heaves. "Perhaps," she concedes, "the first inroads of a passion" might be detected here; both repelled and attracted, she wonders if he is to be "dreaded or adored." But in the nightmare when she is beckoned into a pit that would be her real ruin, "he that tempted me to destruction, was my brother," and what she fears is his "suffocating grasp." She knows that ideas exist in our minds that can be accounted for by "no established laws." But "what monstrous conception is this? my brother!"

Pity poor Clara. (Like Clarice's, one suspects, her name derives from Clarissa, a great favorite of Brown's.) She has a conscious passion for the brother of her beloved sister-in-law, a half-conscious passion for an apparently unattractive villain, and an unconscious passion for—or what may mask a passion, a sexual fear of—her brother. Yet this plot has a happy ending.

The situation in **Ormond,** on the last side of this warped quadrangle, is entirely different. This is an "old-fashioned tale," we are assured by a modern editor of it, of an Ideal Heroine of the Enlightenment—Constantia Dudley, who "yielded nothing to caprice or passion"—and of her devilish though failed seducer. So it might seem if one doesn't read to the end of the book, by which point the narrator Sophia has come to dominate both the action and the heroine. By then Constantia's "love" for the militant transvestite Martinette has changed to "antipathy." But Sophia, who confesses her love of Miss Dudley, is not much more ordinary. Living in Rome, she hopes to bring Constantia to Europe or, failing that, to live and die with her elsewhere. Marrying one day, she embarks the next for New York in search of the heroine, leaving behind her one night's husband. She "has never been wise," she tells us; she disdains discretion. So she does. When she eventually finds Constantia, she explodes in rapture: "O precious inebriation of the heart! O pre-eminent love!"

> The succeeding three days were spent in a state of dizziness and intoxication. The ordinary functions of nature were disturbed . . . lost amidst the impetuosities of a master passion. . . . I would not part from her side, but eat and slept, walked and mused and read, with my arm locked in hers, and with her breath fanning my cheek.

These tumults "did not speedily subside." Nor when Ormond shows up does Sophia want him as a "competitor." Her "disclosures were of too intimate and delicate a nature for any but a female audience"—not to mention a man with his own designs on Constantia. Once the ideal heroine has killed the villain, she and Sophia—indeed yielding nothing to passion—depart for abroad. Sophia's husband, a born loser, is mentioned again only once—as having been in Paris with Martinette. Concerning the life of the young women in England, Sophia says only of Constantia that we have been witness to "her personal deportment and domestic habits. . . . Farewell." Margaret Fuller was a great admirer of this book; she did not specify what "precious revelations" she found in it.

The two novels on which Brown's reputation does not rest were epistolary and relatively genteel. *Clara Howard; or, The Enthusiasm of Love,* as it was once subtitled, presents yet another green youth taken in by a rich man—who has a beautiful stepdaughter. Inevitably the pseudo-siblings fall in love, but the boy has reluctantly promised himself to another woman. *Love,* the author once speculated, might be regarded as a form of disease; the thought that he intended *Enthusiasm* in the eighteenth-century sense of fervid, misdirected emotion is also useful. Nothing less, at any rate, will explain what happens. The girl insists that the young man honor his previous commitment and gives him half her fortune to make possible his marriage to the other woman. Thus he seeks to find and wed the female he does not love in order to please the one he does. Toward all this the author's attitude is not clear, but he seems gratified when the tale ends happily for all, including the reader.

Jane Talbot, A Novel is much longer and not much more important. Jane, a young widow, loves Colden, a "Godwinian radical" strongly opposed by her foster mother, Mrs. Fielder, who for some reason still controls her. Jane and Colden were adulterous while Jane's husband lived; so, anyway, believes Mrs. Fielder, and in truth the young man was after her. But Jane complains that he is too tame—"not quite passionate enough"—and to be sure he is a remarkably chaste radical, in awe of the older ex-wife. He has not "banished discretion," Jane objects, but Mrs. Fielder hardly agrees: he is "an opponent of marriage, and . . . denied . . . that any thing but mere habit and positive law, stood in the way of marriage; nay, of intercourse without marriage, between brother and sister, parent and child!" However this might have been worked into other novels, it has no bearing here; anyway Colden mellows, the foster mother is placated, and the resigned widow marries the virginal villain.

Better that Brown had returned to a couple of his abandoned projects—"Stephen Calvert," for one, a complex but viable tale involving the hero and his identical twin whom the heroine, if that's what she is, confuses (as may the reader confuse them). Stephen has an unseen cousin, Louisa, and since he shrewdly infers

that she has sexual impulses he is confident of seducing her. In the flesh she turns out to look a bit like Achsa Fielding: small, dull brown in complexion, but also pock-marked. The crusher is that she decides he is too young and inexperienced for her. But scarcely for Clelia, whose life he saves in a scene out of Godwin's *Caleb Williams* (1794). Clelia levels with him: "I will withhold nothing." But as for marriage, "I am—*a wife already!*" Regarding her husband, however, she harbors "horrid images of voluptuousness": his "heroic ardours" have not "a name I can utter." All his associates were men, and "so shameless was his conduct . . . my own eyes were allowed to witness—. I cannot utter it: I was frozen with horror."

Cousin Louisa tells Stephen that Clelia doesn't deserve him. She is "dazzling, but sensual and fickle"; marriage to her is "no requisite." Having before her wedding seduced her father's clerk, she is apparently still at it even as Stephen attends her. But the clerk seems to be Stephen's lost twin, whom Clelia cannot tell from Stephen. The booklength first act of a "five-act drama" ends in some confusion, leaving in doubt the moral nature of Clelia and the fate of the dark Louisa.

Another fragment is **"Jessica,"** of which Brown observed in his notebook, "these memoirs should be interesting. The character no common one." That she is not—nor yet unique. Brown began her book before he wrote *Ormond,* but here is the known Sophia—repeatedly in the general excitement called Julia—this time in correspondence with Jessica. Jessica, Sophia complains, doesn't know "how passionate I can be. . . . Your lips distill nothing but sweetness." There is no one like her—"at least in the form of a *man.* Single, then, Jessica, shall I ever be." (But "my passion is again at work. I must lay down my pen.")

Jessica does not love men either; she cannot describe her feelings, she writes, when Sophia "first made advances to me. . . . *Come back again.*" Such qualities as hers "I would doat on in a man. . . . Where then is the difference?" Perhaps in Colden, who now anticipates himself in *Jane Talbot.* But Jessica cannot forget the night she spent in Sophia's "humble cot"— "locked in your arms": it "gave new . . . existence to the love which before united us; often we shall pass such nights. . . ." Alas, Sophia has heard that she is falling for Colden; Jessica plaintively writes "send for me, Sophia. . . ." And over this cliff the text is left hanging.

Left hanging as well—permanently, it would appear—are Jessica and Sophia. It is not easy to explain how two young women made fast in print over 150 years ago could remain in a position so awkward for their time and place and attract no attention whatever. Regarding Sophia and Constantia, Leslie Fiedler puts a question: what in the world were Brown's readers to make of the way they bring *Ormond* to its happy ending? The audience, he submits, could only have been baffled. Possibly so, though it could be shown how women of the age enjoyed a latitude in relation to other women that would have raised eyebrows later on. It does not appear, as might be argued, that hyperbolic rhetoric in the portrayal of heated female friendships has falsified them. What has not been considered at all is how such affairs got into Brown's fiction in the first place.

One lead begs to be pursued. Elihu Hubbard Smith, the author's bosom friend, was an enthusiastic student of Dr. Benjamin Rush of Philadelphia, the Father of American Psychiatry, who lectured on psycho-sexual subjects as early as 1786 and in 1812 published the first "psychiatric" American book, *Medical Inquiries and Observations Upon the Diseases of the Mind.* This volume deals with somnambulism, love as a disease, and "the Morbid State of the Sexual Appetite," among other maladies. But the path goes nowhere. Of somnambulism we learn nothing useful to *Edgar Huntly;* only when severely disappointed—not the case in *Clara Howard*—is love a disease. Sexually "morbid" means nothing but "excessive" (though here worth remembering is a young man whose "system is so very irritable, that . . . even combing his hair, *seminis emissionem inducunt*").

Nor can we explain a mother-complex in Brown as we might, say, in Rousseau—who was made awfully conscious that his own mother died in giving him life. Mrs. Brown lived to write in her tiniest of notebooks (ellipses hers):

> Departed this Life my
> Dear Sun Charles Brockden Brown . . .
> in the Fourt^{e}h year of his age . . .
> 39 yrs, 1 mo & 4 Day.

All we can be sure of is that we know so little about what may have shaped the author's psyche that we cannot begin to account in personal terms for the unexpected twists he would give some early American novels.

Fortunate, then, that his two most irregular subjects, women without men and the bride as mother, can be approached in a different way. What is peculiar about Achsa Fielding as a Dark Lady is not at all that she is Jewish. So would be the most popular specimen of the coming age, Rebecca of Scott's *Ivanhoe* (whose original is thought to have been the lovely Rebecca Gratz of Philadelphia). That's simply the "exotic" element. What's odd is that just as Rebecca is not "experienced" so Achsa is not beautiful—to anyone but Arthur Mervyn. She is too short, too dark, and almost sallow; even her black eyes are frowned on. Given the influence of Godwin, it is no surprise to

find that the heroine of *Caleb Williams* is likewise "far from being entitled to the appellation of a beauty. Her person was *petite* and trivial; her complexion savoured of the *brunette:* and her face was marked with the small pox." She had long dark eyebrows. Mrs. Fielding is not scarred, but Brown's other Dark Lady, Stephen Calvert's Louisa, is also little, "dun" in complexion, and pockmarked.

If we hesitate to risk inferences about the author's secret immoralities—dangerous, even from the books—all the more useful the guess that each of these look-alike ladies evolves from a real-life woman of some literary consequence. This time Smith offers a better lead—in writing to his friend in May of 1796 that the "charms" of Jean-Jacques Rousseau "incite you to imitate him." Imitate what, Smith does not say. But Rousseau's marvelously influential *Julie; ou La Nouvelle Héloïse* had just been published in this country in translation, and Smith was shortly to write his sister at length about the novel. Rousseau's *Confessions,* which already had an audience here as in England, he had not yet read. Brown evidently had. It is in the *Confessions* that the autobiographer explains that after he had written (in "erotic transports") the first two parts of the novel *Julie,* inventing the heroine and casting himself as her lover, he met the "only love" of his life. This was Sophie, the Countess d'Houdetot, who then *became* Julie in the last three parts. He describes Sophie thus: she "was approaching her thirtieth year, and was by no means handsome. Her face was pitted with small-pox, her complexion was coarse. . . . Her eyes were rather too round, but . . . her features were attractive. She had an abundance of luxuriant black hair."

Irresistible the hunch that in conceiving his memorable female friends Brown was inspired by the same Sophie or Julie—precisely the names he confuses in Sophia-Julia's affair with Jessica. The whole concept of the innocent youth in love with the older, experienced woman has been attributed to Rousseau, where for whatever reason Brown may have found it appealing. Among other "charms," he could not possibly have failed to notice the ardent passion that Julie, however devoted to her lover, maintains for her cousin Claire. After watching her in Claire's arms, the hero writes Julie of "new sentiments which I had not even imagined . . . unknown delights . . . pure bliss which has nothing to equal it. . . . Gods!"

> What a ravishing sight . . . what ecstasy to see two such touching beauties tenderly embracing, your head reclining on Claire's bosom, your sweet tears mingling with hers and bathing that charming bosom just as the dew from Heaven moistens a freshly opened lily! I was jealous of so tender a friendship. I found in it something indefinably more interesting than in love itself. . . . Nothing on earth is capable of exciting so voluptuous a tenderness as your mutual caresses.

Miss Howe wrote Clarissa Harlowe, "I love you, as never woman loved another." But not theirs the love of Rousseau's cousins (and Rousseau afflicted with the same rhetorical extravagance as Brown). Not theirs, as Claire writes Julie, like one of those "friendships between women so lukewarm and so short-lived." Inseparable since childhood, "we must be so until death." And so they are. Claire comes to Julie for the last time "crying in an ecstasy impossible to describe, 'Cousin, forever, forever, until death!'" Both pass out cold, falling entwined. The men in attendance behave predictably. At the sight of the girls, Julie's lover goes into convulsions. Her husband is smarter, throwing himself into a chair "in order to contemplate this ravishing sight eagerly. 'Do not fear anything,' he said. . . . 'These scenes of joy and pleasure exhaust our nature only to rekindle it with a new vigor.'" Once the ladies regain consciousness they can do nothing all day but "look at and embrace each other with fresh ecstasies." Julie soon perishes; Claire rolls on the floor in grief and bites the legs of chairs.[5]

The Dark Lady's secret, *enfin*—broadcast by the filial Arthur Mervyn—has plain precedent in the *Confessions*. In detail Rousseau recounts how at sixteen, "thirsting after women" though "I had never touched one," he met Madame de Warens, twenty-eight, to whom he was submissive and from whom he delighted to get "kisses and the tenderest caresses of a mother." Soon he began calling her *Maman,* and having "so long called her mamma, having enjoyed the intimacy of a son, I had become accustomed to look upon myself as one." Then at long last, to protect him from others, she told him it was time he learned as a man about women and she taught him.

"Was I happy? No; I tasted pleasure." But a "certain unconquerable feeling of melancholy poisoned its charm": *"J'étais comme si j'avais commis un inceste."* The affair lasted for years, and *Maman* it remained. So Rousseau remained—"perpetually guilty," always afflicted by "a secret oppression of the heart."

Very belated insight reveals that Brown was "rapturous" over Rousseau, and over the possibilities of love between members of the same family or sex, while still boyish and before his career had fairly begun. In **"The Story of Julius"** (1792)—a manuscript not known to exist until 1973—he named himself after *Julie* and explicitly proposed to do for a "refined and exquisite relation" between a brother, Julius Brownlow, and his twin, Julietta, what the Frenchman's "seductive" and "forbidden" *Julie* had done for friendship between women.

It looks as if Romanticism was born decadent. Whatever. We need only remark that a professional pornographer, writing in late 1976 on his trade in the New York *Times,* revealed that the most popular current subject for his kind of novel was incest, which had recently supplanted the second most popular subject, lesbianism. This, whatever Charles Brockden Brown might make of it, in whichever frame of mind, is approximately where we came in.

Notes

[1] The "brotherly love" that the author's hometown was named after harks back three centuries before Christ to the Egyptian princess Arsinoë, who, after she married her brother Ptolemy II, was known as Philadelphia.

[2] The easy winner of this competition for misrepresentation is David Lee Clark in his self-censored *Charles Brockden Brown: Pioneer Voice of America* (1952), but there are many contestants—among them Harry Warfel, who collapsed over *Arthur Mervyn* in the midst of his *Charles Brockden Brown, American Gothic Novelist* (1949).

[3] Her namesake, Achsah, makes a single appearance in the Bible as the daughter of Caleb (see Joshua 15:16-19 and Judges 1:12-15, which are the same). In the translation of the New English Bible it is a memorable little scene: "As she sat on the ass, she broke wind, and Caleb asked her, 'What did you mean by that?'"

[4] Via a different route which reaches different conclusions, Patricia Jewell McAlexander touches on Mrs. Fielding in a way to be pursued here. See "*Arthur Mervyn* and the Sentimental Love Tradition," *Studies in the Literary Imagination,* 9 (Fall, 1976), p. 33, nn. 12 & 13.

[5] In creating his enamored females, Brown was almost certainly mindful as well—particularly in "Jessica"—of the story of Mary Wollstonecraft and Fanny Blood. William Godwin had just published it in *Memoirs of the Author of A Vindication of the Rights of Woman* (1798), his biography of his late wife Mary. Brown could previously have seen her own vaguer version of the affair in *Mary; a Fiction* (1788). And he may also have read Diderot's *The Nun,* which appeared in English in 1797. (We know from Smith's diary that his friend did.)

Donald A. Ringe (essay date 1982)

SOURCE: "Charles Brockden Brown," in *American Gothic: Imagination and Reason in Nineteenth-Century Fiction,* The University Press of Kentucky, 1982, pp. 36-57.

[*In the following essay, Ringe states that while the liberal ideas of William Godwin and Mary Wollstonecraft may have been important to Brown, it was British and German Gothic writers such as Matthew Gregory Lewis,*

*Eliza Parson, and Cajetan Tschink who influenced the
style and substance of Brown's fiction. Ringe further
argues that in* Wieland *and* Edgar Huntly *Brown attempts to establish his own interpretation of the Gothic
mode, adapted to the conditions of American life.*]

To discuss the novels of Charles Brockden Brown
only in terms of contemporary Gothic fiction is to
view them from an admittedly limited point of view.
A man of strong intellectual curiosity, Brown read
widely in both traditional and contemporary literature. Echoes of Shakespeare and Milton are heard
throughout his works, and the influence on his books
of both the fiction and nonfiction of his own age was
great. Biographers have stressed the importance of
William Godwin, Mary Wollstonecraft, and Robert
Bage in the development of Brown's ideas, and no
single book was perhaps more important than Godwin's
Caleb Williams (1794) in teaching the young man about
the form and purpose of fiction. To emphasize these
influences, however, is to create a bias in favor of the
liberal ideas that are introduced, discussed, and tested
throughout his works—a bias that warps our view of
Brown away from his real importance as the father of
American fiction.[1] For however important those liberal
books and ideas may have been to the aspiring young
writer of the 1790s, it was the side of his fiction derived from the British and German Gothic writers that
gave him his characteristic mode of expression and
established a kind of fiction that was to become peculiarly American.

In developing the Gothic strain, however, Brown
confronted a problem that would trouble many of
his successors in nineteenth-century America: how
to adapt a European mode of fiction to the very
different conditions of American life. The Gothic
novel had begun in England as a tale of Gothic
times, set in the distant past and pretending to
imitate the manners of the medieval age. Even those
novels detailing more recent events were either set,
like *The Italian,* on the continent of Europe, or, if
laid in Great Britain, like *The Old Manor House* or
The Children of the Abbey, used an old and usually
decaying castle or similar ancient building as a
source of Gothic terror. Neither of these alternatives was suitable for an American writer of the
late eighteenth century who wished to develop a
distinctively American literature, and in his preface
to **Edgar Huntly** (1799), Brown announced to his
public that he had eschewed the "puerile superstition and exploded manners, Gothic castles and chimeras" (4: 4) usually employed to engage the interest of the reader. But although Brown turns in that
book to scenes of the wilderness and the incidents
of border warfare to embody his theme, the fact
that he makes the statement at all indicates that he
was without question thinking of his book in terms
of the contemporary Gothic mode.

How much Brown learned from contemporary Gothic
fiction remains an open question, for his sources in
this genre have never been properly explored. Some
critics have mentioned both Schiller's *The Ghost-Seer*
and Tschink's *The Victim of Magical Delusion* as possible sources for **Wieland** (1798), while others have
suggested the romances of Ann Radcliffe as a possible influence on him.[2] The problem, of course, is
that Gothic devices soon became the property of all
the practitioners of the mode, and one can never be
sure whether a specific device is a source or an analogue for another's use of it. Thus, although Carwin
in **Wieland** may resemble in some respects both the
Armenian and Hiermansor in Schiller's and Tschink's
romances, he is also much like Volkert, the pretended
sorcerer in Kahlert's *The Necromancer.* And if both
Clara Wieland and Constantia Dudley face terrifying
situations alone in their rooms at night, so too do the
heroines of not only Ann Radcliffe's romances but also
those of practically every other book by her numerous
imitators. To seek a specific source from among so
many possible contenders is difficult at best and may
in the final analysis be simply futile.

One can point out, nonetheless, some interesting parallels. Eliza Parsons's *The Mysterious Warning* (1796),
for example, stands in a close relationship to Brown's
Wieland in the important use they both make of apparently supernatural voices. Ferdinand, in the former book,
believing himself to be disinherited, hears a voice in
the chamber of his dead father promise him pardon
and peace. Though he has always discredited "supernatural interpositions," he is convinced that the voice
is "not the illusion of his senses" (p. 12), and his certainty is reinforced when it warns him against his corrupt brother and later tells him to avoid his unfaithful
wife. Since both he and his wife hear the third message, he believes he must accept it as a warning from
the dead. Though all three messages are the work of
Ernest, an old steward who is loyal to Ferdinand, his
corrupt brother, Rhodophil, begins to hear voices too.
Since those that Rhodophil hears have no objective
source in the real world, they must be the product of
his guilt or of a diseased fancy. The parallel with
Wieland, where Carwin's biloquial tricks are interpreted
by Clara and Theodore Wieland as supernatural messages, and where Wieland himself begins to hear other
voices not made by Carwin, is perfectly obvious.

An equally interesting analogue to **Wieland** may be
found in Kahlert's *The Necromancer* (1794), a story
told through the use of a multiple point of view. Each
of three characters recounts the striking experiences he
has had independent of the others, and it is not until
the end of the book, when the culprit confesses, that
each experience in turn is revealed to have been the
deception of a man named Volkert. He early learned
how easy it is to play on the credulity of others for his
own purposes and soon acquired the reputation of being

a sorcerer. Besides the fact that Volkert bears some resemblance to Carwin, in form *The Necromancer* may have provided Brown with a model for *Wieland,* where a series of strange events also occurs, only to be explained finally in the confession of Carwin. One can, of course, make too much of such parallels. The voices of *The Mysterious Warning* and the technique of *The Necromancer* may—or may not—have influenced Brown when he was composing *Wieland.* But the question of sources is not really the point. What the parallels certainly indicate is the close relation of Brown's fiction to the kind of thing being done by his British and German contemporaries.

We should seek the sources of Brown's inspiration, therefore, not so much in specific works as in general types of fiction. Though a writer may sometimes borrow a particular episode or event from another, he is usually more profoundly affected by the broader aspects of the fiction he has read. Brown's probable use of the German romance is a case in point. What he got from the fiction of Schiller and Tschink, and perhaps also of Grosse, was the use of a mysterious band of political adventurers who seek to manipulate others for their own advantage. Since each of their books deals with a different kind of political intrigue, Brown could only have derived from them the general idea. He had to select for himself the kind of society he wished to use. He found what he wanted in the Society of the Illuminati, a real group that was much discussed in those days. Both the end-note to the English edition of *The Ghost-Seer* and the long introduction by Peter Will to his translation of *Horrid Mysteries* contain information about it, and John Robison's *Proofs of a Conspiracy* includes a long discussion of it.[3]

When William Dunlap read the manuscript of *Memoirs of Carwin, the Biloquist* in 1798, he immediately saw what Brown was about, for he wrote in his diary on September 14: "read C B Browns beginning for the life of Carwin—as far as he has gone he has done well: he has taken up the schemes of the Illuminati."[4] Though Brown does not mention the society by name in any of his fiction, it figures prominently in at least two of his important works, and suggestions of it appear as well in *Wieland.* In both *Memoirs of Carwin* and *Ormond* (1799), he includes a mysterious character who belongs to a utopian society and who, like the secret leader in *Horrid Mysteries,* recruits promising young men to the cause. Ludloe, in the former work, seeks to enlist Carwin when he learns of his talent as a ventriloquist, but the fragment ends before we discover the use that is to be made of him. Ormond, in the latter book, has at his command "numerous agents and dependants" (6: 170-71), such as the surgeon who cures Stephen Dudley's blindness, all of whom are used for the furtherance of his political goals.

This political purpose is so veiled in secrecy that only the vaguest hints and most oblique allusions suggest to the other characters what is really afoot. Even Sophia Westwyn Courtland, the narrator of *Ormond,* tells us twice that she does not have complete knowledge of Ormond's actions and that it would not be prudent for her to reveal the means by which she acquired the information which she does have. Carwin's fragment breaks off long before he learns much of Ludloe's plans, but both he and Sophia reveal enough to suggest that the secret societies aim, in her words, at nothing less than "the new-modelling of the world, and the subversion of all that has hitherto been conceived elementary and fundamental in the constitution of man and of government" (6: 245). Though subversion seems to be part of their schemes, both Ludloe and Ormond are also concerned with constructing new societies in unexplored parts of the world. Carwin discovers a map among Ludloe's things which places his colony on some islands in the South Pacific,[5] and though Ormond conceals the location of his society, Sophia believes that it must be in some out-of-the-way place: "on the shore of an *austral* continent, or in the heart of desert America" (6: 245).

For the furtherance of their schemes, these utopian projectors use powers that are so mysterious as to border on the incredible. Like Hiermansor in *The Victim of Magical Delusion* or Don Carlos's servant, Alfonso, in *Horrid Mysteries,* Ormond is the master of disguise. Having once been the dupe of misleading appearances, he has used his talent to penetrate the duplicity of others and has been so successful in each attempt that he uses this means repeatedly to attain his ends. Both he and Ludloe, moreover, are extremely adept at penetrating the secrets of others. Carwin is amazed to learn that Ludloe knows all about an event in his life which he has taken great pains to conceal, and he even produces a paper that Carwin thought he had burned. In a similar fashion, Ormond reveals to the astonished Constantia Dudley his total knowledge of conversations she had had with Sophia Courtland—conversations that had taken place under such conditions that it would appear impossible for anyone to have overheard them. Thus, like their German counterparts, both Ludloe and Ormond seem to possess a number of powers that border upon the miraculous.

But Brown does not exploit the marvelous aspects of this material. Unlike the German romancers, whose pretended sorcerers use spectacular displays to play upon the credulity of their victims, Brown avoids any suggestion of deliberate magical delusion. Even Carwin employs his voices in *Wieland* not to dupe the superstitious but first to extricate himself from tight situations and later to test the fortitude and rationality of Clara Wieland and Henry Pleyel. In no instance does he attempt to delude them for a political or social end. In a similar fashion, the powers of Ludloe and Ormond are not manifested through the magical tricks of their German counterparts, nor do they attempt to create a feeling of superstitious fear in their victims. They never pretend that their powers are anything but natural, and Ormond even admits to Constantia toward the end of the book that he has merely used secret passages and canvas walls in acquiring his knowledge of her private affairs. A sense of mystery is, of course, present in all these incidents, and *Wieland,* in particular, has about it an aura of the supernatural, but Brown has avoided even the suggestion that his projectors employ either real or supposed supernatural means to attain their ends.

In other matters, too, Brown's use of this material differs sharply from that of the German romancers. For Schiller, Tschink, and Grosse, the political theme is the center of focus, and for the former two, the story exists merely to show how clever men may play upon the superstition of others for their own ends. In Brown's completed works, however, the mysterious projectors play only a subordinate role. Although Carwin's use of ventriloquism in *Wieland* may remind one of the magical deceptions of the Germans, the main emphasis of the book is on Clara and Theodore Wieland and the intellectual problems posed to them by the seemingly inexplicable phenomena they perceive. In *Ormond,* the main point of the book is not the secret machinations of the projector but the strength and fortitude of Constantia Dudley, who, because of her rational education, is able to act with intelligence and resolution when confronted with all kinds of challenging situations.[6] Only in *Memoirs of Carwin* did Brown attempt an entire book focused upon the material he found in the German romances, but he did not bring the work to completion. His primary interest apparently lay in other directions.

Brown was concerned, not with political themes or attacks upon supersision, but with the serious moral and intellectual issues raised by the principles and actions of his utopian projectors, questions like the relation of means to ends and the value of unrestrained intellectualism as a guide to life. He gives his projectors a fair hearing for their ideas, but the actions of his books make clear the appalling consequences that can result from the application of those principles. Though "Memoirs of Carwin" is only a fragment, the fate of Carwin in *Wieland,* accused of robbery and murder by his erstwhile benefactor and pursued as a common criminal, clearly indicates the fate of one who, for whatever reason, incurs the wrath of the secret society. The arrogant intellectualism of Ormond leads him into hideous excesses: the murder of Constantia's father and the attempted rape of the girl herself. And the biloquial tricks of Carwin in *Wieland* illustrate clearly the danger of setting in motion, even in an innocent manner, a chain of events the end of which no one can predict. In developing his books in this way, Brown

greatly improved on his sources. He turned a limited kind of fiction—at once both sensational and aridly rationalistic—into an interesting vehicle for testing significant ideas.

Brown's handling of other Gothic materials—the Gothic horror, for example, that was just coming into prominence at that time—illustrates further his ability to adapt a convention to his own artistic ends. In *A Sicilian Romance,* Ann Radcliffe had included a brief episode in which two characters are trapped in a vault with the decaying bodies of some bandits' victims, and Karl Grosse, in *Horrid Mysteries,* includes a series of episodes in which a character named Elmira seems to die and reappear, undergoes premature burial, and even reappears once after her husband has retained her dead body until there can be no doubt that it must be buried. In Matthew Gregory Lewis's *The Monk,* moreover, such materials are given an unusually prominent place for British Gothic fiction. The story of the Bleeding Nun and the description of putrescence and physical decay in the charnal house of the convent are among the most striking and sensational elements in the book. One would expect, perhaps, that a young intellectual like Brown, so deeply concerned with moral and philosophical questions, would have had little interest in such material. Yet in *Ormond* and *Arthur Mervyn* (1799-1800),[7] Brown includes a number of elements that are closely related to it.

The yellow fever epidemic in Philadelphia in 1793 provided Brown with the means for creating a sense of Gothic horror without resorting to the kind of device he dismisses in the preface to *Edgar Huntly.* In *Ormond,* for example, a character named Whiston flees in terror when he learns that his sister is infected, only to die alone in a barn, his body left to decay because everyone fears to approach it. Another, named Baxter, is watching the house of a Frenchman one night when he sees the man's daughter drag a body from the house to bury it in a shallow grave. When she pauses a moment in her work, she looks up, catches sight of Baxter's face, and shrieks. He, in turn, flees in such panic that the disease, which he otherwise might have resisted, takes hold of him and kills him. A feeling of intense fear pervades these scenes in *Ormond.* The characters face the horror of the plague with enervating terror and perceive the gruesome effects of sickness and death. The stench of the disease fills the atmosphere, and the horror of physical dissolution is constantly held before the eyes of the onlooker.

Brown develops an even greater sense of horror in the first part of *Arthur Mervyn.* Though he certainly had no use for tales like that of the Bleeding Nun, he does allow Arthur Mervyn to experience the psychological equivalent of perceiving such an apparition. In plague-ridden Philadelphia, Mervyn has learned that a man he has been searching for is dead, and looking through his house to recover what property he has left, he hears footsteps approach him.

> The door opened, and a figure glided in. The portmanteau dropped from my arms, and my heart's-blood was chilled. If an apparition of the dead were possible, and that possibility I could not deny, this was such an apparition. A hue, yellowish and livid; bones, uncovered with flesh; eyes, ghastly, hollow, woe-begone, and fixed in an agony of wonder upon me; and locks, matted and negligent, constituted the image which I now beheld. My belief of somewhat preternatural in this appearance, was confirmed by recollection of resemblances between these features and those of one who was dead. In this shape and visage, shadowy and death-like as they were, the lineaments of Wallace, . . . whose death I had conceived to be incontestably ascertained, were forcibly recognized. [3: 166-67]

Though Wallace turns out to be alive, Mervyn has for the moment perceived him as a specter.

Nor is this all. The men who collect the dead sometimes thrust living persons into the coffins, and Mervyn himself almost undergoes premature burial. While searching a house in the hope of finding Wallace, Mervyn looks into a mirror and thinks he sees an apparition approaching him. When he turns to confront it, a blow to his forehead renders him senseless. He dreams that two gigantic figures are trying to cast him into a pit, and he awakes to find two men who, thinking him dead, are about to place him in a coffin and nail down the lid. Other men in the city collect the sick and carry them to the hospital, the equivalent, in Brown's universe, of the charnal house of the conventional Gothic romance. Here Wallace had been sent when he contracted the fever, and he was placed on a mattress "whose condition proved that an half-decayed corpse had recently been dragged from it" (3: 173). The horrors of the sick and the dying are made worse by the carousals of those who are supposed to care for them, and a dying victim is sometimes forced by his position to look at "the ghastly writhings or deathful *smile* of his neighbour" (3: 173).

Passages like these are closely allied to the kind of Gothic horror that Lewis includes in *The Monk* and that was to become a staple of one type of Gothic fiction down to the works of Edgar Allan Poe, Ambrose Bierce, and even William Faulkner. What makes Brown's use of the material so interesting is his ability to create the effect of Gothic horror without resorting to the more conventional literary devices. His use of the yellow fever may, in fact, have intensified that effect. The threat of death and the horror of dissolution are especially frightening during an epidemic, the fear of premature burial becomes a very

real as well as a deeply psychological terror, and the sights and smells of the hospital create a sense of horror not to be matched by those of a charnal house in the vaults of an ancient convent. By describing a real situation, moreover, Brown was able to use these Gothic materials for a serious social purpose. The hospital scenes, in particular, serve an important function in revealing what were, after all, the true conditions of the time, and some of the incidents clearly show the strength and weakness of human nature in the face of such actual terrors.

Brown was equally adept at turning the Gothic strain of Ann Radcliffe and her successors to his own artistic ends. The influence of this school is especially strong in *Wieland,* where many of the devices of British Gothic fiction appear. Clara Wieland, who narrates the book, resembles in some ways the Gothic heroines of the Radcliffe school. She flees in terror once from apparently inexplicable phenomena, she is threatened with rape, and she is separated from her lover for a time before their ultimate reunion and marriage. The setting, too, sometimes takes on a Radcliffean atmosphere, and it affects the mind of the heroine in the expected way. Alone in her room at night and frightened by a mysterious voice, Clara observes: "Solitude imposes least restraint upon the fancy. Dark is less fertile of images than the feeble lustre of the moon. I was alone, and the walls were chequered by shadowy froms. As the moon passed behind a cloud and emerged, these shadows seemed to be endowed with life, and to move. The apartment was open to the breeze, and the curtain was occasionally blown from its ordinary position. This motion was not unaccompanied with sound. I failed not to snatch a look, and to listen when this motion and this sound occurred" (1: 86). Though the style is his own, Brown is attempting to create the kind of effect made popular by the British romancers.

Yet numerous though such Gothic devices may be, they receive in *Wieland* a markedly different emphasis, derived in part from the serious treatment given the whole question of supernaturalism. Instead of the somewhat trivial purposes it sometimes serves in even Radcliffe's romances, it provides the intellectual center for the entire book. The tenor is firmly established in the opening chapters when the elder Wieland dies under extraordinary circumstances, his arm hurt, his body burned, and a strange light pervading the atmosphere. Though his death may be explained as the result of spontaneous combustion, his own report, before he expires, of what had happened to him in his temple of worship—a report which suggests that he has not told all that occurred—leaves open the question of whether or not some nonmaterial influence may have been present.[8] A degree of uncertainty is thus introduced in the minds of his children, which leaves them prone to believe that direct supernatural intervention may have been instrumental in bringing about their father's death. When Carwin later projects his voice, therefore, both Theodore and Clara Wieland are prepared to believe that messages may be received from supernatural powers.

Wieland is thus inclined from the beginning to accept the voices produced by Carwin as supernatural phenomena, and his view of the world is such that he sees his decision as a perfectly rational one. In the course of the novel, however, Wieland goes insane and believes he hears a voice that has no basis in reality. When it tells him to murder his family, he assumes he has received a divine command and proceeds at once to obey it. Clara, on her part, is much more likely to weigh the evidence and balance one interpretation of strange phenomena against another. But she is soon subjected to a series of frightening experiences, all directly caused by Carwin, in which a voice seems to preserve her from harm and warn her away from danger. Clara is not superstitious. She scorns the tales of ghosts and apparitions that so often unnerve the unwary, and she considers herself "a stranger even to that terror which is pleasing" (1: 45). So real and so inexplicable are the events that happen to her, however, that she begins to believe an invisible protector is shielding her from evil.

Because it lays such stress on the question of supernatural intervention, **Wieland** stands somewhat apart from the novels it most resembles. Though the use of Carwin's ventriloquism to suggest supernatural events may remind one of the romances of Schiller, Tschink, and Kahlert, Brown does not dismiss the phenomena as merely political trickery or magical delusion, and in the mania of Wieland he adds a dimension to the problem of interpreting strange phenomena untouched by the German romancers. In a similar fashion, though Clara Wieland bears an obvious resemblance to the heroines of Ann Radcliffe and her imitators, her encounters with mysterious occurrences are more extended and more terrifying than those of her British counterparts, and her ultimate descent into madness, after Wieland murders his family, sets her further apart from them. Clara is depicted, too, as more intelligent and better educated than the usual Gothic heroines, she ponders more deeply on the strange events she experiences, and in the course of her adventures she exhibits psychological depths not to be found in them. To reveal her psychic state Brown employs two stock Gothic devices that he had undoubtedly picked up in his reading, but which, characteristically, he turns to his own purposes: the presentiment and the prophetic dream.

Early in the book, Clara experiences a strange but accurate presentiment of what is to come. When she first sees Carwin, she is much disturbed by the strange inconsistency she perceives between his melodious voice and his unattractive countenance. She quickly sketches his visage, and during the stormy day that follows, she spends her time in deep contemplation of both the image and the tempest. When night returns, her mind is "absorbed in thoughts ominous and dreary" (1: 54). She sees in the tempest a possible sign of impending ruin, the portraits of her brother and his children increase her mournfulness, and although their images are as serene as ever, she thinks of them "with anguish. Something whispered that the happiness we at present enjoyed was set on mutable foundations" (1: 54). As yet she is unaware of any connection between Carwin and her family, and though the stormy day may have had a depressing effect on her, there is no reason for Clara to expect an early end to their happiness. Yet her foreboding is accurate: Wieland in his madness will soon destroy his wife and children, and Clara herself will eventually be driven to insanity.

A presentiment of this kind is a far cry from those to be found in *The Mysteries of Udolpho* or *The Italian*, for it seems to rise from a source deeply imbedded in the character's psyche. So too does an odd series of experiences that Clara undergoes in which a prophetic dream and presentiments of the future are strangely intermixed. Having fallen asleep in the summerhouse one evening, Clara dreams that she is near her brother's house and walking toward a pit of which she is unaware. Her brother stands on the other side, beckoning to her and bidding her make haste. But just as she is about to plunge into the abyss, a voice cries out "Hold! hold!" and she starts awake (1: 62). In the waking world the voice is Carwin's, but as so often happens in sleep, it also functions in her dream. Clara is of course disturbed by this occurrence, but she is more deeply affected by the voice she subsequently hears than by the dream itself. Indeed, it does not recur to her memory until one night when she is alone in her room and she has another presentiment of evil.

On this occasion Clara is about to go to her closet to get her father's manuscript, which she intends to read. Because she has previously heard voices there threatening her life, she is understandably nervous, but as she approaches the door, she feels "unconquerable apprehensions. A sort of belief darted into my mind," she writes, "that some being was concealed within, whose purposes were evil" (1: 84). Though Clara does not know it, Carwin is concealed in the closet, and when she puts her hand on the lock, she hears the same command she heard in the dream. This cry makes her remember who it was in the dream that beckoned her to destruction, and she leaps at once to the conclusion that Wieland lurks within and is waiting to kill her. From one point of view, of course, her presentiment is wrong. There is no one there with any intent to harm her, for Carwin has simply been led to her room by a desire to see her father's manuscript. From another, however, the presentiment is deadly accurate. It is Wieland she must fear, and before the book is finished, he will come to kill her in that very room.

In the ensuing action Clara undergoes a series of experiences that confirm at last the prophecy of her dream. The death of Wieland's wife and children drives her temporarily insane before she can learn who the murderer is, and when she recovers her sanity, she assumes it is Carwin. It is only then that her uncle reveals to her that Wieland has confessed his crimes, and he places in her hands her brother's testimony before the court. Shocked though she is, she requests to see him, only to be told that Wieland considers his task as yet incomplete, and should she enter his dungeon, he would try to kill her. Indeed, he had already twice escaped in an attempt to complete the murders that he thinks are commanded by God. At this point Clara recalls her dream in the summerhouse. "I recollected the omens of this destiny; I remembered the gulf to which my brother's invitation had conducted me; I remembered that, when on the brink of danger, the author of my peril was depicted by my fears in his form: Thus realized, were the creatures of prophetic sleep, and of wakeful terror!" (1: 189-90). From a deep recess in Clara's mind there has arisen a finciful image of her true danger.

Other aspects of Gothic fiction also receive an emphasis in *Wieland* not usually found in the genre. Like most of its British and German predecessors, the book is concerned with the problem of perception: the characters are mystified by the phenomena they perceive and, in some cases, interpret them as supernatural. In most of the British romances, however, the uncertain vision is only a subordinate element usually employed to project the fears of the isolated heroine, and in the German books it is always presented as a deliberately induced delusion. In *Wieland,* however, the problem of perceiving reality is of the utmost importance in the book, the interest in it is sustained throughout, and the source of the delusion is as much internal as it is externally induced. In addition, Brown lays heavy stress on the sense of hearing rather than that of sight. This in itself was an important shift in emphasis from the typical Gothic romance, where most apparitions are visual. An aural delusion cannot be dismissed by a simple change of light or shift from night to day, and since sight is the primary sense on which the characters must rely for knowledge, they are likely to believe that the voices they hear have no physical source when none is visible.

In their reactions to the problem, moreover, the characters in *Wieland* differ from those most often found in Gothic fiction. Both Clara and Theodore Wieland are intelligent and educated persons whose qualities of mind should prevent their succumbing to the kind of belief in supernatural agencies usually reserved for the ignorant lower classes, but their strange family history and personal psychology render them incapable of penetrating the appearances they perceive to the truth that lies behind them. Even their rationalist friend,

Henry Pleyel, whom Clara loves, is markedly different in his behavior from the character he most resembles in the British Gothic. Both he and Lord Mortimer in Roche's *The Children of the Abbey* fall prey to mistaken perceptions deliberately caused by others. They believe the evidence of their senses that the heroines of the books, Clara Wieland and Amanda Fitzalan, have become the mistresses of unsavory characters, Carwin and Colonel Belgrave. Each confronts the girl with his accusations, but whereas Lord Mortimer, in true sentimental fashion, is immediately convinced of Amanda's innocence when she explains what has happened, Pleyel insists in his passion that his senses have reported the truth, and he leaves Clara protesting, but unable to prove, her innocence.

Because the delusions of the characters in *Wieland* are so strong and deepseated, the cure is by no means as easy to effect as it usually is in the romances of the Radcliffe school. There the sources of error are always clearly presented as superstition, emotion, or an ardent imagination, and the cure is brought about by a return to the rule of reason, which enables one to distinguish fact from fancy. In Brown no such unqualified solution appears. Though he, like his predecessors, clearly recognizes the deceptive power of the imagination and the influence of the emotions in leading men astray, he makes it abundantly clear that the cause of error is not simple nor the cure easy. Wieland, after all, insists that he put the passion of love aside and acted reasonably in following the evidence of his senses—the divine command he imagines he heard—in destroying his family, and both Clara and Pleyel are equally sure that they have acted on sensory evidence and arrived at rational conclusions, even when the one believes that she is under supernatural protection and the other is certain that he has perceived her dishonor.

Reason, of course, does enter the book in the character of Clara's uncle, a rationalist physician who nurses her back to sanity after her ordeal and who arranges for Carwin to disabuse Pleyel of his mistaken opinion of her. But so thoroughgoing is Brown's treatment of the unconscious sources of human error that reason cannot be seen as ever in full control, not even at the end of the book. Throughout, the characters are lost in the maze of their own perceptions, and even after her uncle's explanation, Clara's final analysis of the characters' "errors" does not really establish a basis on which sound knowledge could have been derived from their perceptions. Despite all the evidence to the contrary, she still perceives Carwin as a "double-tongued deceiver" and the author of the evils they have experienced (1:244), whereas the action of the book clearly reveals to the reader that the sources of error lie within and cannot be so glibly assigned an external cause. Brown permits no easy solution to the problems he raises, and unlike the Gothic novelists from whom he derived so much, he retains an aura of ambiguity and uncertainty right to the end.

What Brown did in *Wieland,* therefore, was to take the problem of perception that he found in the British and German Gothic romances and examine it in terms of its deepest philosophic meanings. In his hands, the device of mistaken perception is used not merely to suggest that people frighten themselves with chimeras, but to examine the very basis of human knowledge and to probe, as he writes in the preface to *Wieland,* "the moral constitution of man" (1:3). He looks deeply into the springs of human motivation, touches the unconscious sources of terror, and suggests that the causes of madness—the ultimate misapprehension of reality—may lie in one's childhood experience or in the traits inherited from one's forebears. Though the book must surely be seen as derived primarily from one branch of the late eighteenth-century Gothic mode, it goes far beyond its predecessors in adapting that form to a serious psychological purpose. *Wieland* marks a real advance over the Gothic tales of Ann Radcliffe and her successors, and it establishes once and for all in America a type of Gothic fiction that was to undergo a great deal of additional development.

The most original use that Brown made of this material was undoubtedly in *Edgar Huntly,* a book which, true to its preface, employs no major Gothic devices, but which represents nonetheless the culmination of Brown's Gothicism. Many of its most striking effects derive, of course, as do those of the usual Gothic romance, from the characters' misapprehension of the reality that impinges upon them and their inclination to interpret the strange phenomena they experience as supernatural. But there are significant differences, too. The characters in *Edgar Huntly* do not confront bizarre external phenomena. There are no spectacular deaths like that of the elder Wieland to suggest supernatural interference in the affairs of men, no voices like those projected by Carwin to baffle interpretation, indeed, no accurate presentiments of evil, no truly prophetic dreams. The world that the characters face is by and large the natural one, and the sense of mystery and terror derive not so much from the external world itself as from the inner workings of their individual minds. What they perceive, therefore, is an index to the world that lies within, and the book, perhaps even more than *Wieland,* is deeply psychological.

Consider the reactions of three of the characters to the strange experiences they have in the actual world. All three suggest supernatural explanations for what has occurred, and each interpretation reveals the mental state of the character. The skeptical Sarsefield, for example, is undismayed by a series of seemingly miraculous events he has observed. While searching for Huntly during the Indian incursion, he twice witnesses his apparent death and return to life, he becomes aware of the incredible distance Huntly has covered in a short period of time, and he sees the Indians Huntly had killed while presumably unarmed. Thus, when he finally meets Huntly in a farmhouse where he least expects to find him, he declares himself ready to abandon his lifelong spirit of skepticism. Though he has never placed "credit or trust in miraculous agency" (4:232), were he called upon to testify, he would have to swear that Huntly has been dead and restored to life, and has exhibited preternatural powers. Sarsefield, of course, is not really serious in this statement. To rely on his senses alone would indeed enforce this conclusion, but as a rational man he believes there must be a natural explanation, and he actively seeks it.

Edgar Huntly, on the other hand, draws a quite different conclusion when he discovers that some papers he had hidden in a secret cabinet are missing. Utterly unable to account for the phenomenon, he experiences a feeling of ominous terror—"a whispering intimation that a relic which [he] valued more than life was torn forever away by some malignant and inscrutable destiny" (4:128). This sense of helplessness before a mysterious force stays with him. After he awakes in the cave totally at a loss to explain how he got there, he fancies, in a kind of wakeful dream, that he has been imposed upon by "some tyrant who had thrust [him] into a dungeon of his fortress" (4:154), and even when he escapes from the cave, he wonders if "some mysterious power [had] snatched [him] from the earth, and cast [him], in a moment, into the heart of the wilderness" (4:164). Finally, when he rediscovers his papers in the farmhouse where he meets his mentor, Sarsefield, he can only conclude that the power who has afflicted him is beyond conjecture. Though Huntly's experience has, of course, been much more disturbing than Sarsefield's, his mind is more apt to leap to a belief in a supernatural agency.

A related but much more ominous conclusion is drawn by Clithero Edny, who undergoes an even stranger experience. While he has still in Europe serving a Mrs. Lorimer, he became involved in a series of events that led him to kill Arthur Wiatte, her evil twin brother. Clithero is innocent of any intent to murder. He fired in self-defense at an assailant whom he did not recognize. His mind, however, goes through a strange and irrational series of thoughts which eventually leads him to conclude that because of this deed he must kill Mrs. Lorimer as an act of benevolence, and he immediately sets out to do so. When he fails in his attempt to murder her, Mrs. Lorimer faints, and Clithero leaves the scene convinced that she has died because of her strange belief that her life must end with that of her twin. In telling his story to Edgar Huntly in America, however, Clithero insists that some evil power had ordained this fate for him. He believes that his mind had "been perverted by diabolical instigations" (4:65) and that the act of attempted murder was not actually his but that of the daemon who possessed him.

Though Clithero draws by far the darkest interpretation of events, both he and Huntly are alike in seeing themselves as pawns in the hands of some inscrutable power. The influences they feel are, to be sure, entirely subjective and derive from aberrations of mind, but they seem to them as real as any demonstrable influence in the physical world. Of the two, Clithero is, as his interpretation suggests, the more seriously disturbed. His behavior is obviously bizarre. When Huntly first sees him, he is burying a box beneath an elm tree while asleep; on the second occasion he wanders through the wilderness of Norwalk at night and darts into a cave; and after telling his story to Huntly, he flees to an isolated peak in the wilderness where he intends to starve himself to death. From their first encounter Huntly realizes that Clithero is a sleepwalker, and he knows that the inability to sleep soundly is the sign of a "sorely wounded" mind (4: 13), but he also believes that a sympathetic and understanding friend may restore him to sanity. For this reason Huntly makes several trips to the wilderness retreat to seek him out, fells a tree across a chasm in order to reach him, and brings him food so that he will not perish.

What Huntly fails to perceive is that he himself is so mentally disturbed that his judgments are not to be trusted. He is aware, of course, of some of his own aberrations. He knows that his friend Inglefield has had to correct "the wanderings of [his] reason and [his] freaks of passion" (4: 24), and he recognizes the folly of repeatedly searching the spot where another friend, Waldegrave, was killed in the hope of finding some clues to his murder. When he decides to help Clithero, however, he thinks he is acting rationally, even though his pursuit of him becomes increasingly strange. He begins, indeed, to resemble the man he is trying to help, for, completely unknown to himself, he has become a sleepwalker. While in the somnambulent state, he, like Clithero, hides papers from himself, goes wandering into the wilderness, and enters a cave. Unlike his double, he falls into a pit in the cave and later awakes with no recollection of how he has come there, but on his return to the settlements he discovers a bloodthirsty side of himself that he did not know he possessed, and he feels, in killing some Indians, as if "a spirit vengeful, unrelenting, and ferocious" has taken possession of him (4: 184).

The aberrations of mind from which Huntly suffers create a world that is intensely Gothic in its effects. Because of his compulsive search for clues to Waldegrave's murder and his obsessive pursuit of Clithero through the wilderness, Huntly both perceives and describes for the reader a number of strange and mysterious scenes: Clithero digging under the elm tree late at night, and the tangled labyrinth of Norwalk through which they move in darkness. Huntly's gradual return to consciousness when he awakes in the cave, moreover, provides a series of adventures filled with mystery, and his journey back to Solesbury during the Indian incursion, his encounter with the warriors, his flight from apparent pursuers by diving into the river at night, and his strange adventures in the houses he enters provide the kind of suspense and terror that other Gothic novelists had created through the use of more conventional devices. What is especially significant in *Edgar Huntly,* however, is that the universe of the book is a reflection of Huntly's mind. It must be dark and mysterious so long as Huntly remains a man unknown to himself.[9] Should he acquire self-knowledge, he would presumably see a world approximating that of Sarsefield.

Such enlightenment seems to come when Huntly meets Sarsefield in the farmhouse and, in the course of their long conversation, the mystery of what has happened to him is at last unraveled. Once he learns from his mentor that he, like Clithero, has been a sleepwalker, the disappearance of his papers and his presence in the cave are easily explained, and as he and Sarsefield recount their adventures to each other, what had seemed strange and inexplicable becomes perfectly clear. Huntly's return to rationality, therefore, would seem to have been easily effected by the interposition of Sarsefield's mind, which, viewing the phenomena dispassionately and observing their true meaning and significance, can help him to reestablish in his mind the rational order of things. Huntly believes that something like this has indeed happened, for after the experience is over and he begins to write the narrative of his adventures, he exclaims: "What light has burst upon my ignorance of myself and of mankind! How sudden and enormous the transition from uncertainty to knowledge!" (4: 6). Huntly retains this view throughout the book, concluding his account of what has happened in the assurance that all mysteries have been solved and his return to rationality is complete.

The book does not end with Huntly's narrative, however, but goes on to a final episode that brings this conclusion into serious doubt. Huntly's career has so closely paralleled Clithero's that a question remains of whether Clithero too can be saved. Sarsefield does not think so. He believes that Clithero is probably an incurable maniac, and he tries to persuade Huntly to this opinion. Huntly, on his part, should have learned by now that he ought to distrust his own judgment, but he still believes that Clithero can be cured. Three letters appended at the conclusion of Huntly's narrative show the results of his acting upon that assumption. As he did in the early part of the narrative, Huntly seeks out Clithero in the wilderness in an attempt to cure him of his madness by revealing that Mrs. Lorimer is alive and in America. But much to Huntly's dismay, the insane Clithero sets out at once to murder her. Despite his vaunted self-knowledge and enlightenment, Huntly has acted rashly, and only a hasty letter to Sarsefield prevents a total disaster. Mrs. Lorimer is not killed, but she loses the child she is carrying, and Clithero ends a suicide.

As he did in *Wieland,* therefore, Brown ends his book not with the triumph of reason but with the major character still deeply disturbed and inclined to fall into the same error he has succumbed to through the book. Though the voices of Clara's uncle and of Sarsefield reaffirm an ideal of reason, the action of both books seems to indicate the fallibility of the human mind, the powerful influence of its unconscious forces, and the inability of men to predict the outcome of their actions. The dark world of Gothic terror would seem therefore to be more real than the bright and ordered world of the rationalists, even though that Gothic world derives from the consciousness of the characters who perceive it. If this interpretation is correct, the Gothic novels of Charles Brockden Brown are significantly different from their English and German counterparts. The external world of Gothic terror in *Wieland* and *Edgar Huntly* is no chimera that can be easily dismissed by the influx of light, either physical or mental. It is, rather, an accurate indication of the reality that lies within the tortured minds of the protagonists—a reality that is not to be changed by any simple means.

The Gothic devices that Brown uses are for this reason more highly charged with symbolic significance than are those of his predecessors. The best of the British Gothic romancers had, of course, always sought to make their settings more than mere sources of terror. The castles and abbeys, darkened rooms, moonlit galleries, and subterranean labyrinths that abound in their books not only provide an appropriate atmosphere but sometimes suggest as well the physical and mental condition of the characters who move through them. An abbey set deep in the woods in Ann Radcliffe's *The Romance of the Forest* appropriately suggests not only the physical isolation of the central characters but also to some extent their psychological insecurity, while the intricate paths through which Ferdinand wanders when his mind is distraught in Eliza Parsons's *The Mysterious Warning* are an effective physical representation of his psychological state. But few, if any, of the British Gothic writers develop the material so fully as Brown does in *Wieland* and *Edgar Huntly.* In his hands some of the objects of the external world take on a symbolic meaning, which, closely related to the mental condition of his characters, is consistently maintained throughout the book.

Like all Gothic romances, Brown's two books are full of enclosures—the temple, the summerhouse, and Clara's bedroom and closet in *Wieland,* and the cave in *Edgar Huntly*—all of which reflect the various characters' minds.[10] The temple in *Wieland,* for example, isolated on the top of a steep hill and used for different purposes by its successive owners, is clearly the counterpart of the minds of those who possess it. As the bare and forbidding site of the elder Wieland's solitary worship, it appropriately reflects the mental state of a man whose religious obsessions separate him from his family and eventually consume him. As a place of social and intellectual pleasure for his children and their friends, on the other hand, it comes to represent, with its harpsichord and bust of Cicero, the supposed enlightenment of minds that have been educated according to just principles. But because the temple, however changed, remains the one in which their father perished, it serves as the constant reminder of a mysterious past from which their minds can never be entirely free. The temple is thus much more than merely a physical object. It embodies as well a large amount of thematic meaning of the utmost importance to the development of the story.

In a similar fashion the many isolated enclosures in which Clara finds herself become symbolic of her mind. Both the summerhouse, where she has her prophetic dream, and the bedroom of her residence, where it is almost fulfilled, are isolated places. The summerhouse can be reached only by a difficult path, her house is far removed from that of her brother, and her upstairs bedroom with its adjoining closet is her most intimate retreat. All of these places are violated by the voice of Carwin, which, operating by chance with the material of her dream, sets her mind working in a way that reveals her unconscious fears of her brother. What happens in these enclosures is happening in Clara's mind, so that in a sense the two become one. It is therefore highly significant that, once she faces the murderous Wieland and survives, she retires to her house and refuses to leave—an obvious retreat into her own inner consciousness—and it is not until her house is destroyed by purging flames and her uncle takes her away to Europe that Clara is able to recover the degree of sanity that she reaches at the end of the book.

A related enclosure, the cave, appears in *Edgar Huntly,* though here it achieves its fullest significance only if seen in relation to another device of equal import, the journey through an intricate maze or labyrinth. Both Clithero and Huntly thread their way through the tangled wilderness of Norwalk, only to plunge into a cave or penetrate to another wilderness retreat. Because the most important of these journeys take place while they are asleep, the maze through which they go may be seen as a mental one, and the place where they arrive as the inner self to which they withdraw when reality is more than they can face. Though Clithero leaves his innermost retreat, he never really emerges from the labyrinth of his mind. He takes up his permanent abode in Norwalk, and there he would have remained had Huntly not provoked him to seek out Mrs. Lorimer. Huntly, on his part, emerges from the labyrinth only with the greatest difficulty. After awaking in the cave and gradually reorienting himself to reality, he manages to work his way back to the external order of the settlements. But his recovery is not complete. Huntly still faces the danger of repeated relapse, as his final trip to the wilderness and its disastrous results so clearly show.

Because he lays such stress on the psychological state of his characters, the major Gothic romances of Charles Brockden Brown make a new and significant contribution to the developing Gothic mode. The works that he found on the shelves of the bookstores and lending libraries of New York or Philadelphia had no doubt taught him much about the craft and purposes of fiction, and one can certainly trace the influence of some of these books on his own romances. But Brown was not the slavish imitator of any school of fiction, and although he might derive what he could from a Schiller or Tschink or Radcliffe or Parsons, he developed the material in a highly individual way. He apparently saw at once the possibilities of the Gothic mode as a vehicle for psychological themes, and he quickly found a way to relate the mental states of his characters to the objects of external reality. In both **Wieland** and **Edgar Huntly** he established at once his own version of Gothic, creating thereby an American branch of the mode that was to reach its fullest development a generation later in the works of Edgar Allan Poe and Nathaniel Hawthorne.

Notes

Throughout this chapter, text citations of *Wieland* and *Arthur Mervyn* are to volumes 1 and 3 respectively of the Bicentennial Edition of *The Novels and Related Works of Charles Brockden Brown* (Kent, Ohio, 1977, 1980). Citations of *Ormond* and *Edgar Huntly* are to volumes 6 and 4 respectively of *Charles Brockden Brown's Novels* (Port Washington, N.Y., 1963), a reprint of the edition of 1887.

[1] See David Lee Clark, *Charles Brockden Brown: Pioneer Voice of America* (Durham, N.C., 1952), where this aspect of Brown's work is emphasized.

[2] A study of Brown's novels in relation to British Gothic fiction is Robert D. Hume, "Charles Brockden Brown and the Uses of Gothicism: A Reassessment," *ESQ,* 18 (1st Quart. 1972): 10-18. Hume minimizes the influence of the Gothic novel, however, and does not really analyze the sources of Brown's Gothicism. The influence of Schiller's romance on *Wieland* was noticed by John Keats as early as 1819. See Hyder E. Rollins, ed., *The Letters of John Keats, 1814-1821* (Cambridge, Mass., 1958), 2: 173. Recent scholars have stressed the influence of Tschink; see Harry R.

Warfel, "Charles Brockden Brown's German Sources," *Modern Language Quarterly,* 1 (Sept. 1940): 357-65; and Henry A. Pochmann, *German Culture in America: Philosophical and Literary Influences, 1600-1900* (Madison, Wis., 1957), pp. 361-62. On Radcliffe's influence see especially Fred Lewis Pattee, introduction to *Wieland: or, The Transformation, together with Memoirs of Carwin, the Biloquist, a Fragment* (New York, 1926), pp. xxxviii-xl; and Harry R. Warfel, *Charles Brockden Brown: American Gothic Novelist* (Gainesville, Fla., 1949), pp. 109, 129, 138-39, 156.

[3] See Chapter 2, notes 31 and 32, above.

[4] *Dairy of William Dunlap (1766-1839)* (New York, 1930), pp. 338-39. The *Diary* is paged continuously throughout its three volumes.

[5] The latitude and longitude he gives would, however, place it just inside the east coast of Australia.

[6] These aspects of Constantia's character are stressed throughout, her only weakness being her lack of training in religion, which places her in danger of succumbing to Ormond's radical arguments (6: 175).

[7] *Arthur Mervyn* was published in two parts, the first in Philadelphia in 1799, the second in New York in 1800.

[8] Because he copied the details of the elder Wieland's death from the account of a supposedly real occurrence reported in *Literary Magazine, and British Review,* 4 (May 1790): 336-39, Brown clearly intended the event to be a completely natural one, and he signaled his intention to the reader by providing a footnote to additional sources (1: 19). But for the elder Wieland's children, Theodore and Clara, he deliberately leaves unresolved the question of supernatural influence, and they are left to interpret the nature of the event for themselves.

[9] "The Man Unknown to Himself" had been the subtitle of Brown's now-lost first novel, *Sky-Walk,* parts of which, William Dunlap believed, were later incorporated into *Edgar Huntly* and other works. See William Dunlap, *The Life of Charles Brockden Brown: together with Selections from the Rarest of His Printed Works, from His Original Letters, and from His Manuscripts Before Unpublished* (Philadelphia, 1815), 1:259.

[10] The material in this and the two following paragraphs I have discussed in greater detail in "Charles Brockden Brown," in *Major Writers of Early American Literature,* ed. Everett Emerson (Madison, Wis., 1972), pp. 280-88. See also Arthur Kimball, *Rational Fictions: A Study of Charles Brockden Brown* (McMinnville, Ore., 1968), pp. 49-74.

Fritz Fleischmann (essay date 1982)

SOURCE: "Charles Brockden Brown: Feminism in Fiction," in *American Novelists Revisited: Essays in Feminist Criticism*, edited by Fritz Fleishmann, G. K. Hall & Company, 1982, pp. 6-41.

[*In the essay that follows, Fleischmann explores Brown's "systematic treatment" of women, their rights, and their roles in his novels. Fleischmann argues strongly in favor of the view that Brown was a feminist and also advocates Brown's "competence as a writer," but notes that there is no consensus (feminist or otherwise) in Brown scholarship.*]

I

Charles Brockden Brown (1771-1810) is the first novelist to be considered here, because he was the first born. But it would also be appropriate, for other than chronological reasons, to place him at the beginning since he already has a long history of feminist criticism, a history that many would consider disheartening, for it has neither produced a consensus on Brown's feminism nor left much impact on his status in the canon of American writers.

At least three generations of feminist critics have remarked on Brown's women characters; a feminist reading of his novels goes back at least as far as Margaret Fuller's comment that "it increases our own interest in Brown that, a prophet in this respect of a better era, he has usually placed his thinking royal mind in the body of a woman . . . a conclusive proof that the term *feminine* is not a synonym for *weak*."[1] Thomas Wentworth Higginson, a supporter of women's rights and sympathetic biographer of Fuller, noted Brown's "advanced views as to the rights and education of women."[2] The subject, although never ignored by Brown scholars,[3] was picked up again by the generation of feminists who wrote after the passage of the Nineteenth Amendment. In 1925, Augusta Genevieve Violette included Brown in her discussion of "economic feminism," claiming that the radical sentiments in *Alcuin* "express Brown's own feelings on social usages of his time."[4] Mary Sumner Benson, in her pioneering work on women's history published in 1935, wrote of Brown's fictional women that they "could . . . think for themselves" and that "they marked an altered attitude toward women."[5] Dorothy Yost Deegan, in 1951, thought that Clara Wieland and Constantia Dudley "were unusually independent women of their day," and that before Hawthorne, Brown was the only novelist who "dared to present the unmarried woman as somewhat admirable."[6]

If this sounds like a consensus, the impression vanishes with a look at the contemporary critical scene. Brown's place in the American literary canon as "the first writer of prose fiction of which America could boast"[7] appears secure, if the quantity and general quality of recent criticism is any indication.[8] His niche in the American feminist pantheon should also be well established. Not only did he create striking, memorable women characters in his fiction, but he was also the first major writer of the Republic to examine women's rights and roles systematically and sympathetically. On both counts one would expect far-reaching agreement as to the quality of his achievement as well as to the reasons for his continuing critical appreciation.

But there is no such consensus in Brown scholarship, be it feminist or not Brown's status as a novelist of rank is still being contested;[9] and although the appreciative majority of his critics agree that his fiction is important because it "examined issues that have remained germane,"[10] there is much disagreement on what those issues are and how they have been presented. Critical opinion on Brown's women is in similar disarray. Its feminist tone re-emerges with the women's movement of the late 1960s and early 1970s and the growth of women's studies as an academic discipline.[11] By the mid-seventies, women as a topic had become academically respectable; the political lines are often no longer clearly discernible.[12] Brown criticism in this period shows how problematic the label "feminist" can be in characterizing critical positions. But the fact remains that an interest or disinterest in the "women's issue" makes a difference in scholarship. Currently, the best arguments for the consistent quality, coherence, and thematic unity of Brown's work come from two critics who pay close and sympathetic attention to Brown's feminist views as well as his women characters, although their tone does not categorize them as political feminists.[13] Brown's own systematic treatment of the issue deserves our attention first.

II

Anyone who doubts Brown's feminism or his competence as a writer should go back to *Alcuin.* Far from being "an extremely clumsy work"[14] or the product of "an apprentice writer still working out his basic techniques,"[15] it is a small masterpiece, sophisticated and occasionally witty. (Brown had worked on the problem of combining dialogue and narrative as early as 1792, when he wrote the "Henrietta" letters.)[16] Alcuin's preposterous question to Mrs. Carter ("after much deliberation and forethought"!), "Pray, Madam, are you a federalist?" (p. 9)[17] sets the ironic tone that controls the subsequent exchanges.

Alcuin, a city schoolmaster with an active fantasy life, as little money as worldly experience, and but a slender stock of the social graces, descends upon the home of Mrs. Carter, a widow who hosts an intellectual salon for her brother, a physician and "man of letters";

he invites the guests whereas his sister is "always at home" (p. 4). Alcuin's opening gambit is preceded by a careful buildup which establishes the character of the disputants and their social background, creating enough *vraisemblance* to make the discussion realistic. Alcuin is the namesake of Charlemagne's friend and philosopher-teacher, perhaps "to hint that many of [his] opinions . . . should be considered medieval." Mrs. Carter is probably a reference to the famous English bluestocking Elizabeth Carter, "whose views would necessarily be both more modern and more radical."[18]

Mrs. Carter reacts to Alcuin's question about her politics with a smile—and ironic incredulity. Why ask *her?* "We are surrounded by men and politicians. You must observe that they consider themselves in an element congenial to their sex and station" (p. 10). Alcuin jumps to defend the status quo by explaining that, under the existing arrangements, men and women "may all equally be said to stick to their lasts" (p. 10). In so doing, he must also defend women as they now are, ascribing their defects ("perfectly natural and reasonable") to the "limited sphere" in which they properly belong (p. 12). His hostess is far more critical of women and therefore of the circumstances that have made them what they are. This pattern of argument—chivalry/apology versus criticism—follows the distinction Mary Wollstonecraft made in *A Vindication of the Rights of Woman* (1792).[19] As we shall see, such parallels abound. Even the basic analogy is the same: Mrs. Carter derives her demands for women's political rights from the American Revolution and its concomitant documents, just as Wollstonecraft had insisted on equal treatment of women by the French revolutionaries.

Her steadily developing argument is counterpointed by Alcuin's much jumpier tactic of defense and assault that usually gets him to concede a point of principle even while he gains one of circumstance. Alcuin, though mostly the target of irony, is not devoid of wit himself. "You might as well expect a Laplander to write Greek spontaneously, and without instruction," he jokes, as a woman to be learned without an opportunity to learn. But his wit is labored, a warning that he will have to eat his own words.

> I humbly presume one has a better chance of becoming an astronomer by gazing at the stars through a telescope, than in eternally plying the needle, or snapping the scissars [*sic*]. To settle a bill of fare, to lard a pig, to compose a pudding, to carve a goose, are tasks that do not, in any remarkable degrees, tend to instil the love, or facilitate the acquisition of literature and science. Nay, I do not form prodigious expectations even of one who reads a novel or comedy once a month, or chants once a day to her harpsichord the hunter's foolish invocation to Phoebus or

Cynthia. Women are generally superficial and ignorant, because they are generally cooks and sempstresses. [Pp. 13-14]

All this he advances to prove that "human beings are moulded by the circumstances in which they are placed. In this they are all alike. The differences that flow from the sexual distinction, are as nothing in the balance" (p. 13). An inch gained, a mile lost; Alcuin's struggle is doomed. He must admit so many single points in order to defend the overall status quo that he becomes hopelessly entangled in his own web. Lee R. Edwards calls Alcuin "the fossil prototype of the much denounced contemporary liberal" (*Alcuin,* p. 98) whose arguments, dismaying to watch, reappear throughout the nineteenth and well into the twentieth century. Some examples:

> 1. Human nature itself impedes progress. ("It is doubtful whether the career of the species will ever terminate in knowlege" [p. 14].)

> 2. Unpleasant social tasks are unavoidable. Those who have to carry them out have a right to feel "abundance of injustice," but "it matters not of what sex they may be" (p. 14). "The evil lies in so much human capacity being thus fettered and perverted" (pp. 14-15).

> 3. Women are excluded from the professions because they don't really care for them. Besides, the professions are in reality demeaning and full of abuse, and hence not terribly desirable in the first place (pp. 16-21). ("It is evident," Mrs. Carter retorts, "that, for some reason or other, the liberal professions . . . are occupied only by men" [p. 20]. The assumption that women's lot is more desirable ignores the life of the vast majority.)

> 4. Should women feel bitter about their exclusion from schools and colleges? Alcuin (a schoolmaster!) wonders "whether a public education be not unfavourable to moral and intellectual improvement" (p. 22).

> 5. Society and its laws—"which have commonly been male births" (p. 26)—may be defective, but men suffer more than women: "Let us inquire, whether the wives, and daughters, and single women, of each class, be not placed in a more favourable situation than the husbands, sons, and single men, of the same class. Our answer will surely be in the affirmative." The only hope lies in historical progress. "Human beings, it is hoped, are destined to a better condition on this stage, or some other, than is now allotted to them" (p. 28).

With this outlook, Alcuin has the last word of Part I. Like Part II and sections of Part III, it is strongly imbued with Wollstonecraftian rhetoric, even on Alcuin's side, and goes over all the major points from the Vindication. The faultiness of women's education, the false delicacy which causes the separation of the sexes in childhood, the socialization of children into sexual roles with different "systems of morality" (p. 24), the inevitable hypocrisy in marriage ("she must hope to prevail by blandishments and tears; not by appeals to justice and addresses to reason" [p.24]—these points are directly, often almost literally, derived from Wollstonecraft, down to Mrs. Carter's caution that she herself is an exception to the picture she has described.

Alcuin II moves on to the political and legal rights of women, with Mrs. Carter lecturing more and more, reducing poor Alcuin to inanity. Her cool and systematic destruction of his positions should overcome any remaining suspicions that Brown did not know what he was about. The movement of the text is as follows. Alcuin's repeated question, "Are you a federalist?" is rejected as irrelevant, since the constitution has excluded women from the body politic, together with minors, recent immigrants, paupers, and black people. Here is Mrs. Carter on the poor: they "vary in number, but are sure to increase with the increase of luxury and opulence, and to promote these is well known to be the aim of all wise governors" (p. 33). She gives a spirited defense of democratic government, but Alcuin's attempts to muddle the issue by general reflections are repelled. "I plead only for my own sex"—let other groups fend for themselves; for women "the injury is far greater, since it annihilates the political existence of at least half of the community" (p. 38). Alcuin's faint objection that the marriage laws, by taking away "both the liberty and property of women," deprive them of "independent judgment" in politics, gets Mrs. Carter started on those laws, not without another shot at the "independent judgment" of male officeholders ("Most of them seem not to have attained heights inaccessible to ordinary understandings" [p. 39]). Alcuin sounds a note of humility, admitting his prejudices (men's "teachers have been men"), and proposing women's intellectual equality, even their overall superiority, a kind of higher nature. (His tail is between his legs here, because this is the "specious homage" that Wollstonecraft had criticized.) Nevertheless, he tries hard and ends Part II with the *Vindication*'s analogy between the battle of the sexes and class war. Men's assumption of superiority "is a branch of that prejudice which has so long darkened the world, and taught men that nobles and kings were creatures of an order superior to themselves" (p. 43). At this point, the conversation is interrupted by an intruder "who, after listening to us for some time, thought proper at last to approach, and contribute his mite to our mutal edification" (p. 43).

Parts III and IV, not clearly separated, cover Alcuin's imaginary visit to the "paradise of women," his report of the "voyage" to Mrs. Carter, and a lengthy discussion of marriage. The "paradise of women" is a utopian island of complete gender equality. Alcuin's remarks about sexual distinctions are constantly rebuffed by his guide, who misunderstands them as questions about *anatomical* differences of which Alcuin must be "doubtless apprised" (p. 50). The views and customs that the visitor reports from his own country are denounced, in good utopian fashion: "Common madness is unequal to so monstrous a doctrine" as gender inequality (p. 62). While the education of children is discussed in Wollstonecraftian terms, Brown prepares the way for Part IV, a Godwinian critique of marriage, by introducing elements from *Political Justice* along the way. "Man" (the term is used generically throughout) "is a progressive being, he is wise in proportion to the number of his ideas" (p. 58), which are products of his environment, creating differences between individuals far greater than those of sex. The utopian island has egalitarian traits ("A certain portion of labor will supply the needs of all. This portion then must be divided among all" [p. 61]). The truth (correct opinions) will automatically change human behavior ("My actions will conform to my opinions" [p. 63]). Alcuin's idea that the oppression of women in his homeland may be a male conspiracy cannot be imagined by the guide, as the introduction of such a system ("by force or persuasion" [p. 64]). is impossible where women are mentally and physically as capable as men.

When Alcuin introduces marriage ("that relation which subsists between human beings in consequence of sex" [p. 64]), he interrupts his narrative for fear of offending Mrs. Carter's sense of propriety. This interruption of almost four pages may seem beside the argument, but it is not. Decorum (what is fit for female eyes or ears) had been recognized by Mary Wollstonecraft as a feminist issue, and it was to remain one throughout the nineteenth century.[20] Here is Brown speaking through Mrs. Carter: "The impropriety methinks must adhere to the sentiments themselves, and not result from the condition of the author or his audience" (p. 65). She insists on her willingness and qualification to discuss marriage, because "the lowest stupidity only can seek its safety in shutting its ears," and "to sophistry . . . the proper antidote is argument" (pp. 67, 68).

Sydney J. Krause has discussed Godwinian attitudes toward marriage extensively in his notes to the KSU *Ormond*.[21] "Fascinatingly," he writes, "whereas in *Ormond* Brown made Godwin a straw man for the criticism of views that disadvantaged women, in *Alcuin* III and IV, he had gone the other way, using Godwinian liberalism *to uphold* women's rights." Mrs. Carter "point by point takes up all of Godwin's revolutionary initiatives, beginning, as Godwin did, with the evils of cohabitation: harmony can be achieved only at the cost of one's individuality; cooperation really means accommodation, which thwarts personal preferences, stultifies reason and inhibits individual judgment; and all of this finally leads to bickering, frustration and unhappiness"; "other objections exactly mirror the Godwinian argument, as with: the inflexible restraints of the contractual relationship, the supreme importance of choice, the need to allow for change and remedy, and, on the positive side, for the supports of free consent, friendship and spontaneity. Seen by themselves, the words might be easily mistaken for Godwin's." Mrs. Carter defends the idea of marriage as "sacred," but its reality has been made unbearable by unjust laws, which can only be remedied by "unlimited power of divorces" (p. 75). The *Vindication* had suggested that unhappy wives often make good mothers;[22] Mrs. Carter argues that the children suffer more in unhappy marriages than from divorces (p. 85). This goes beyond Wollstonecraft, although it remains true to her method of employing a critique of women's condition and the false ideals of femininity as a critique of society. Where the *Vindication* falls short of supplying a model for a just society, *Alcuin* can draw on the most widely known program for one, Godwin's *Political Justice* (1793; second and third editions in 1796 and 1798). As Professor Krause puts it, "On the requirements of free choice, removal of unnatural constraints and allowance for change," Mrs. Carter's Godwinism "is adamant, and reasserted."

Unfortunately, Mrs. Carter has introduced her whole lecture by warning Alcuin that "[a] class of reasoners has lately arisen, who aim at the deepest foundation of civil society," and that his utopian journey is to be regarded "as an excursion into their visionary world" (p. 68). A little later, she refers to Godwin himself by denouncing "that detestable philosophy which scoffs at the matrimonial institution itself, which denies all its pretensions to sanctity, which consigns us to the guidance of a sensual impulse, and treats as phantastic or chimerical, the sacred charities of husband, son, and brother" (p. 70). In ascribing such views to her, she informs Alcuin, "you would hardly be justified by the most disinterested intentions" (p. 70).

Where does this leave us? How could this be followed by the "boiler plate Godwinism" (S.J. Krause) we have heard? The answer lies, I think, in a game Brown plays with his readers. His frequent disavowals of his radical affiliations have been a persistent problem for scholars. In *Alcuin,* they occur twice, once in the unexpected attack on Godwin and company just mentioned, the other time much earlier, toward the end of Part I. Both times Mrs. Carter has the word, and both times, it appears, she (or Brown) is pulling somebody's leg. *If* Brown is hedging on his radicalism here, as has been alleged, he does so tongue in cheek, relying on his readers' wits and sense of irony. His later works show that he never abandoned his feminism and that he continued to hope for social reform, if not necessar-

ily along Godwinian lines. Why then these disavowals? And why did Brown only publish Parts I and II?

S.J. Krause has followed the writing and publishing history of *Alcuin,*[23] and found that there was much debate on Godwin and the drafts of *Alcuin* among Brown and his closest friends, considerable support at least from Elihu Hubbard Smith (who read Parts III and IV three times in all), and plenty of opportunity for Brown to find publishing space. Yet III and IV did not go into print during Brown's lifetime. We are reminded that "divorce remained so touchy a subject that *Alcuin* III and IV could not even be published posthumously in 1815 without benefit of an extended apology."[24] Brown may have noticed the pattern of critics' reception of Wollstonecraft and Godwin during the 1790s.[25] Those who had read the texts tended to be fairly objective, even in disagreement. The hearsay reaction, on the other hand, which picked up on the vague dangers and alleged moral "looseness" of the "new philosophy," was mostly slanderous and abusive. (The news of Godwin's marriage to Mary Wollstonecraft in 1797 did not help the sincerity of his professed antimatrimonialism; and his publication of the posthumous *Memoirs of the Author of "A Vindication of the Rights of Woman"* the following year, with its exposure of Wollstonecraft's private life, destroyed the moral reputation of both writers.) The obstreperous Mrs. Fielder in *Jane Talbot* is a caricature of such ignorant anti-Godwinism.[26] Brown seems to expect the informed reader to recognize the truth, even as he tweaks the noses of the uninformed by presenting the argument while obscuring its source. That he decided not to publish *Alcuin* III and IV would indicate that he was not entirely sure of his audience, fearing "how grossly his own views might be misunderstood."[27]

To return to *Alcuin* I, and the first instance of this game of hide-and-seek: At the end of a long harangue, Wollstonecraftian in substance as well as imagery (the wife as a fawning dog; Wollstonecraft had specified a spaniel), Alcuin gets suspicious of the picture Mrs. Carter has drawn. "You derive it from some other source than your own experience, or even your own observation." She sweeps the charge aside—"No; I believe the picture to be generally exact"—and embarks on another lecture from the *Vindication,* ending with the purest Wollstonecraft: "Men and women are partakers of the same nature. They are rational beings; and, as such, the same principles of truth and equity must be applicable to both" (pp. 25, 26). Brown gives an ironical turn to the screw each time he puts Wollstonecraft's diction in Alcuin's mouth (as he later makes Mrs. Fielder pick up pseudo-Godwinian vocabulary). This occurs a number of times in *Alcuin,* but nowhere more blatantly than just after Alcuin has smelled the rat. Wollstonecraft had drawn an insistent parallel between the parasitical privileges of aristocrats and women, resulting in warped minds and morals. Alcuin now draws a charming picture of woman's existence ("Yours are the peacefullest recesses of the mansion: your hours glide along in sportive chat, in harmless recreation, or voluptuous indolence . . ." [p. 26], which Mrs. Carter promptly condemns both as unrepresentative of reality and as "a panegyric on indolence and luxury" (p. 27). Alcuin caves in and reverts to Wollstonecraft: "I have only attempted to justify the male sex from the charge of cruelty. Ease and luxury are pernicious. Kings and nobles, the rich and the idle, enjoy no genuine content." In Chapter 9 of the *Vindication,* the most widely quoted section of her book, the author had idolized the middle class. *Vide* Alcuin: "There must be one condition of society that approaches nearer than any other to the standard of rectitude and happiness. For this it is our duty to search; and, having found it, endeavour to reduce any other condition to this desirable mean" (p. 27).

In Part IV, Mrs. Carter adopts Godwin's position on divorce and cohabitation but rejects his outright condemnation of marriage. (This again may be Wollstonecraft turned against Godwin, who himself described his wife as "a worshipper of domestic life.")[28] She ends the discussion with a refusal to discuss what one should do if the commonly accepted form of marriage conflicted with one's "notions of duty" (p. 87): "That indeed, returned she, is going further than I am willing to accompany you." But she reasserts her own, radical redefinition of marriage.

> Marriage is an union founded on free and mutual consent. It cannot exist without friendship. It cannot exist without personal fidelity. As soon as the union ceases to be spontaneous it ceases to be just. If I were to talk for months, I could add nothing to the completeness of this definition. [P. 88]

However one looks at Brown's treatment of Godwinism, his own feminist loyalties emerge clearly: "His oscillations themselves become ancillary to this cause. The case for it is that compelling, that simple."[29] The cause Brown makes for women's rights extends to all his novels. It survives even the end of his career as a novelist to turn up again in later writings. Critics have also begun to recognize that "*Alcuin* anticipates Brown's later novels and is consequently at least as noteworthy for its manner as for its matter," thus providing "an early illustration" of, among other techniques, "how Brown could shape his narrative to serve the two separate ends of moral didacticism and psychological realism."[30]

III

Brown's scattered programmatic statements on writing share a didactic bent. The writer is described as a "moral painter,"[31] a "story-telling moralist,"[32] whose task it is to "exhibit, in an eloquent narration, a model of right conduct."[33] Even if this formula sounds like a recipe for socialist realism, Brown knew how difficult his project was. The depiction of "virtuous activities"[34] could not ignore the limitations imposed upon the actors by their relations with others and by their fragmentary understanding of reality.

Human relations are determined by two main factors, property and sex. "Opinions, relative to property, are the immediate source of nearly all the happiness and misery that exist among mankind." "Next to property, the most extensive source of our relations is sex. On the circumstances which produce, and the principles which regulate the union between the sexes, happiness greatly depends."[35] The social unit that is based on both property and sex is the family. Brown's fictional practice conforms to his theory because the family is a main source of conflict in his novels. Justifying his preoccupation with sexual politics, Brown also establishes his place vis-à-vis the sentimental tradition.

> Fictitious history has, hitherto, chiefly related to the topics of love and marriage. A monotony and sentimental softness have hence arisen that have frequently excited contempt and ridicule. The ridicule, in general, is merited; not because these topics are intrinsically worthless or vulgar, but because the historian was deficient in knowledge and skill.[36]

These are the methods of the "fictitious historian":

> The observer or experimentalist . . . who carefully watches, and faithfully enumerates the *appearances* which occur, may claim the appelation of historian. He who adorns these appearances with cause and effect, and traces resemblances between the past, distant, and future, with the present, performs a different part. He is a dealer, not in *certainties,* but in *probabilities,* and is therefore a romancer. [emphases mine].[37]

The much-discussed question of Brown's "unreliable" narrators is brought into perspective by this stated intention. Whether deceptive or themselves deceived, these narrators hand out probabilities at best; we should never expect certainties from them. (The "narrator"-correspondents of *Clara Howard* and *Jane Talbot* are not excluded since letter writers, by implication, know only part of the truth.) And, of course, this caution automatically qualifies the sentimental formula of virtue in distress, as virtue itself is reduced to a "probability."

"The Man Unknown to Himself" is the subtitle of Brown's first novel, the lost *Sky-Walk. Wieland* is subtitled "The Transformation." What is being transformed is human identity, most commonly derived from the family. Wieland is the name of a family.

William J. Scheick has recently commented on "the orphan condition of so many of the characters" in *Ormond,* noting that "the image of the orphan serves as a metaphor for the psychological condition of Americans." Concerned with the origins of knowledge and identity as a theme in *Ormond,* Scheick states that "so long as a person . . . defines himself primarily in relation to the family . . . into which he is born, he can displace questions pertaining to the source of his knowledge and behavior by focusing on the comforting extrinsic biological reference provided by his parents."[38] In *Wieland,* the origination of self in the family is precisely the problem.

Two young orphans, Theodore and Clara Wieland, grow up under the liberal regime of an aunt. Their closest friend is Catharine Pleyel, who later becomes Theodore's wife. Catharine's brother, returned from travel in Europe, also joins them. After the marriage of Catharine and Theodore, the four live on pastoral estates near Philadelphia in close contact, spending their time in musical activities and enlightened discussion. Mettingen, the Wieland estate, is described as a virtual utopian *locus amoenus.* Clara remembers growing up there with Theodore and Catharine: "The felicity of that period was marred by no gloomy anticipations. The future, like the present, was serene" (p. 21).[39] Not so the past. The happy present is centered on a symbol of the past—the summerhouse on a rock above the river, where the elder Wieland worshiped in somber loneliness and where he found his death, has become a place of joyous community.

In the first three chapters of the novel, Brown constructs a gloomy family history that overshadows the present. Its origins reach far back into the past and the Old World. Clara and Theodore's paternal grandfather was a fallen aristocrat and unsuccessful provider. His son had to be apprenticed to a merchant and engaged in such mind-narrowing labor that "his heart gradually contracted a habit of morose and gloomy reflection" (p. 7). Having accidentally adopted a "bizarre theology,"[40] he spent his life in a "sentiment of fear" and a sense of unfulfilled obligation. After emigrating to America, he married "a woman of a meak and quiet disposition, and of slender acquirements like himself" who could be easily "intimidated into silence" (pp. 9, 10, 15). He died under mysterious and violent circumstances, soon followed by his wife.

This unresolved past, never far from the younger Wielands' consciousness, breaks loose with a vengeance when mysterious voices begin to be heard. We later learn that they are ventriloquist tricks played by Carwin, the serpent in the garden, but their immediate effect is to activate the past. Theodore's extreme identification with his father predisposes him for the madness he develops, during which he believes himself under divine command to kill his family. His madness follows an inherited desire to appease a patriarchal god, transforming the victim from "the glory of his species" (p. 197) into a demented murderer. The transformation is undone by a final flash of recognition followed by suicide, and Theodore dies at his sister's feet.

As critics have noted, this is a flawed transformation, and Theodore is an unsatisfactory hero. He disappears from the narrative for long stretches of time, only to re-emerge as a madman. Far more interesting is the transformation of Clara, the narrator of the story. She, of course, is as little "clear" about the events as Theodore is a "gift of God." But she makes it clear that *"she too* is a Wieland,"[41] and that hers is a family tragedy.

Clara resists the family madness more successfully than her brother, although she is not untouched by it. Portrayed as a woman of extraordinary intellect and firmness of character, she enters the scene as Brown's "new woman." But although she is clearly the strongest of Carwin's victims, the fact of her gender creates specific complications for her. The character also makes sense as the instrument of a larger philosophical design, as a "representative of humanity," as Alexander Cowie has noted, a humanity shown as "cowering in a frightening, lonely, ambiguous universe,"[42] but it is significant that the author of *Alcuin* chose a woman to guide us though this universe. She is an admittedly confused guide. "What but ambiguities, abruptnesses, and dark transitions, can be expected from the historian who is, at the same time, the sufferer of these disasters?" (p. 147). Her confusion arises from a double burden: she is a Wieland and a woman.

Thrown into a universe of male-created madness (the Wieland heritage activated by Carwin's voices), her rational defenses are further weakened by her awakening sexuality. This is a significant aspect for a feminist interpretation, as a closer look at the sexual politics involved will show us. Although Clara herself is an agent in this process, she is primarily an object of manipulation. Her situation is circumscribed, her agency limited by gender. She recognizes the limitations which convention imposes on her and the conflicts which result; her experience and interpretation of her own sexuality are informed by this consciousness.

Clara has relationships with three male protagonists (discounting her uncle, who is not part of her crises): Theodore, Pleyel, and Carwin. Theodore, although a threat, is not involved in the sexual politics; until the final confrontation, he even supports Clara.

She is in love with Pleyel, engaged to another woman who is said to be dead during a crucial stretch of the plot. Clara, like so many of Brown's women, does all the wooing, trying to create situations wherein Pleyel may declare himself. She is restricted by social custom which requires the male to play the active part—a restriction under which Clara chafes but which she finds herself unable to overcome.

> I must not speak. Neither eyes, nor lips, must impart the information. He must not be assured that my heart is his, previous to the tender of his own; but he must be convinced that it has not been given to another; he must be supplied with space whereon to build a doubt as to the true state of my affections; he must be prompted to avow himself. The line of delicate propriety; how hard it is, not to fall short, and not to overleap it! [P. 79]

Later, while writing down the story, she reflects:

> My scruples were preposterous and criminal. They are bred in all hearts, by a perverse and vicious education, and they would still have maintained their place in my heart, had not my portion been set in misery. My errors have taught me thus much wisdom; that those sentiments which we ought not to disclose, it is criminal to harbour. [P. 80]

Right out of Wollstonecraft and *Alcuin*. Clara's problem is that she is dealing with a patriarch of the first order, the cheerful Pleyel. Most critics have treated him as the "nice guy" of the story, the voice of reason and "champion of intellectual liberty" (p. 25) who, alas, becomes another victim of deception. But he is neither nice nor reasonable. His character corresponds to his structural function in the plot, as counterpart to Carwin. They both see women as the Other and indulge in relentless reification of Clara, according to their own needs. (I refer to "the Other" in Simone de Beauvoir's formulation in *The Second Sex* that "humanity is male and man defines woman not in herself but as relative to him; she is not regarded as an autonomous being."[43]) Their needs are diametrically opposite, but their methods are the same. Pleyel, pursued by Clara, puts her on a pedestal as an ideal of womanhood to be admired but not touched (by him *or* anyone else). He prescribes her as a role model to his future wife (p. 123); like Clara, she is to be an exemplum of "that union between intellect and form, which has hitherto existed only in the conceptions of the poet" (p. 121). His own role is that of chivalric adoration. "In the midst of danger and pain, my contemplations have ever been cheered by your image" (p. 123). Carwin's interest, on the other hand, lies in the destruction of Clara's image as this "prodigy" by subjecting her to cruel tests. "I was desirous of ascertaining whether you were such an one" (p. 202). Both commit the "unpardonable sin" of manipulation, doing violence to her personality.

Early in the novel, Clara thinks that "there was nothing to dread from [Pleyel's] malice. I had no fear that my character or dignity would suffer in his hands" (p. 61).

But despite his confessed adoration of Clara, Pleyel is quick to jump to horrible conclusions; another twist in his evasion of her pursuit. A "precipitate and inexorable judge" (p. 114), he rejects Clara without a hearing when he thinks she is Carwin's mistress, and he prepares to run away from her, quite literally. Clara is aware of the Kafkaesque "transformation" which women undergo who offend against the moral standard. "The gulf that separates man from insects is not wider than that which severs the polluted from the chaste among women" (p. 113). Now she, despairingly, finds herself subjected to such a transformation by Pleyel; she senses betrayal. "There is a degree of depravity to which it is impossible for me to sink; yet, in the apprehension of another, my ancient and intimate associate, the perpetual witness of my actions, and partaker of my thoughts, I had ceased to be the same" (p. 113).

Pleyel's betrayal, however, is simply the way he treats women. Earlier on, he tries to conspire with Theodore against Clara and Catharine, hoping to persuade him to move his family to Europe. When Clara catches on, Pleyel wants to draw her into the conspiracy in order to keep the secret from Catharine. With arguments almost verbatim from Alcuin's "paradise" guide, Theodore refuses to manipulate the women: they "'are adversaries whom all your force and strength will never subdue.'" Pleyel operates on the assumption "that they would model themselves by [Theodore's] will: that Catharine would think obedience her duty. He answered, with some quickness, 'You mistake. Their concurrence is indispensable. It is not my custom to exact sacrifices of this kind. I live to be their protector and friend, and not their tyrant and foe'" (p. 43). Theodore refuses the patriarchal role which Pleyel wants to exploit. Pleyel's attitudes toward women accord with his monarchist and feudal inclinations (pp. 37-39). Wieland, on the contrary, refuses an inheritance fallen to him by "the law of male-primogeniture" and decides to stay in America, content in "the happiness of mediocrity" (pp. 37, 43).

Like Carwin, Pleyel pries into Clara's papers, using the same excuse that he was "prompted by no mean or selfish views" (p. 128). Like Carwin, he "lie[s] in wait" (p. 133) to satisfy his curiosity. He teases and torments Clara mercilessly about her alleged love for Carwin (pp. 61, 69-70). Although he is engaged to another woman, his jealousy is so strong that Carwin can use it against him: "To deceive him would be the sweetest triumph I had enjoyed" (p. 210). Clara derives "gratification" (p. 235) from her trials, but when she finally gets her Pleyel, all she has to say is that she is "not destitute of happiness" (p. 234). Small wonder.

Carwin is the catalyst for the maddening resurgence of the past and for Clara's sexual awakening. From Clara's perspective, the two go hand in hand, hence her experience of passion is closely allied to madness.[44] Carwin's manipulation of Clara begins with the first mysterious voice heard at Mettingen. Susceptible to supernatural notions as much as her brother, Clara experiences "a thrilling, and not unpleasing solemnity" when she learns about it (p. 35). The second voice, which tells Pleyel that his German fiancée is dead, results in "a sentiment not unallied to pleasure" in Clara, as she increasingly realizes her love for Pleyel: "For though this object of his love be snatched away, is there not another who is able and willing to console him for her loss?" (pp. 48, 46). When Clara finally gets to hear a voice herself, it is Carwin's own natural voice. She is completely overwhelmed by it and loses all self-control: "It seemed as if an heart of stone could not fail of being moved by it. It imparted to me an emotion altogether involuntary and incontroulable . . . I dropped the cloth I held in my hand, my heart overflowed with sympathy, and my eyes with unbidden tears" (p. 52). At first sight, Clara has mistaken Carwin for a "clown," "rustic and aukward" (p. 50). His voice changes her visual perception; now his face has "a radiance inexpressibly serene and potent" (p. 53). Almost paralyzed, she finally rallies to make a sketch of "this memorable visage" (p. 53) and spends half the night staring at it. The next day (which "arose in darkness and storm") is still spent in looking at the sketch. Night brings melancholy premonitions ("Was the tempest that had just past a signal of the ruin which impended over me?") and anquished thoughts about Theodore's family (p. 54). The sound of her father's clock reminds her of death. Just after midnight, she hears threatening voices in her closet and flees to her brother's house, where she faints, "exhausted by the violence of my emotions, and by my speed" (p. 58).

This sequence shows the skill with which Brown has linked sexuality, madness, and death in Clara's mind. The climax of Clara's first brush with Carwin and her flight to her brother's house is a key scene. Is she succumbing to the family madness? If so, why at this point? It may be that she seeks refuge in the family (her parents'/brother's house), away from her self-sought place in the world (her own house, where she wants to live independently and in control of her own life), since it turns out to be the locus of sexuality and death. But her "ancient security" (p. 60) is gone; there is no way back. This is the meaning of Clara's subsequent dream in which her brother beckons to her across an abyss. Her wish to return to the past is dangerous, for surely she would turn mad.

Clara's dreams and visions show her double fear of sexuality and madness. Even a brief dip into Freudian dream analysis will show the pieces falling into place. (Although Freud has been in bad repute among feminists for confusing culturally conditioned phenomena with anthropological constants, he created important tools for our understanding of human behavior. A feminist analysis must apply the tools properly, not reject them out of hand.) The text itself suggests this approach; an early twentieth-century critic hailed Brown as "the veritable forerunner of the new psychic school of fiction as practiced by the adherents and disciples of the psycho-analytic school."[45] Freud himself defended it: "It sometimes happens that the sharp eye of the creative writer has an analytic realization of the process of transformation of which he is habitually no more than the tool."[46] "Transformation"—indeed! What makes the case so compelling is Clara's own conscious realization of her sexuality as a handicap. She interprets it in Wollstonecraftian fashion; under the existing circumstances, love makes a woman a prisoner, "a passion that will never rank me in the number of its eulogists; it was alone sufficient to the extermination of my peace" (p. 83). (This is only what it does to her psyche; with Mrs. Carter, she might have added that love's consequence, marriage, also makes a woman a physical prisoner.) In a lucid moment, Clara decides to "henceforth intrust my felicity to no one's keeping but my own" (p. 81).

The symbolization process on both levels of creation (Brown's and Clara's) firmly links madness with sexuality. The Wielands' family life centers around a phallic rock overlooking a river (water, a symbol of female sexuality and frequently of birth).[47] Brown places the lovers, Clara and Pleyel, in symbolic landscapes that express their difference. Clara walks in picturesque, gardenlike scenes along the Schuylkill; Pleyel, brooding over the alleged death of his fiancée (who has no function in the plot other than to shield him from Clara's desire), seeks out "deformed," "stagnating," "noxious" areas along the Delaware (p. 47). But the symbols that Clara herself creates are more interesting, and central to this discussion.

Whereas Clara's distraction by Carwin's sensual impact comes as an unwelcome and sudden surprise to her, her attraction to Pleyel develops gradually; her awareness of it gains in intensity as she encourages Pleyel to respond to her feelings. After the dramatic sequence ending in her flight from her house, Pleyel moves in with her for protection, "in order to quiet my alarms" (p. 60). Proximity does not create closeness, however, "as it was wholly indifferent to him whether his nights were passed at my house or at my brother's" (p. 60). Clara's famous dream in the summer house by the river takes place some weeks later (p. 61). while Pleyel is still living with her. She falls asleep in an intensely sensual, erotic place characterized by female and male genital symbols; the building is in a "recess" or cave in the riverbank above the river and next to a waterfall. But her dreams are "of no cheerful hue." After a while,

> I . . . imagined myself walking, in the evening twilight,
> to my brother's habitation. A pit, methought, had

been dug in the path I had taken, of which I was not aware. As I carelessly pursued my walk, I thought I saw my brother, standing at some distance before me, beckoning and calling me to make haste. He stood on the opposite edge of the gulph. I mended my pace, and one step more would have plunged me into this abyss, had not some one from behind caught suddenly my arm, and exclaimed, in a voice of eagerness and terror, "Hold! hold!" [P. 62].

It is important to realize that Clara is walking toward her brother in the dream while Pleyel, at this time, is living at her house. She walks away from Pleyel, now one with her house (seat of her sexual longing) but unresponsive to her wooing. Clara repeats in her dream the flight back to her family which she performed in the previous chapter. Her brother is seen as encouraging her, and Clara is ready to fall into the abyss when she is stopped. Although she cannot resist the pull, Clara realizes that Wieland's transformation into a madman has already created a barrier between them. Here is one instance where Theodore's progress toward insanity is noticed, albeit subconsciously, by another protagonist. A dream, says Freud, is always "the hallucinated fulfillment of a wish."[48] Clara wishes to reunite with her brother (her family, her past) in order to regain her "ancient security." In Freudian terms, the gulf represents the censorship that distorts her dream into an anxiety dream. "Anxiety dreams," Freud notes, "are as a rule also arousal dreams; we usually interrupt our sleep before the repressed wish in the dream has put its fulfilment through completely in spite of the censorship."[49]

Even a sexual interpretation of this dream content, which explains the dream as the attempted fulfillment of an incest wish, does not change the fact that Clara sees a danger in her brother. The point is that sexuality (the erotic setting for the dream) triggers the madness latent in the family (the family, to Clara, being identical with Theodore). Clara must resist this double temptation. The "gulf" as Clara's central image is appropriate; to yield is to fall (a falling sensation signifies sexual intercourse), is to succumb to sexuality and madness at the same time. It can only end in death. Clara's *last* use of the image shows its meaning fully developed— the grave. "I will die. The gulph before me is inevitable and near" (p. 228).

After Clara's stunned awakening from the dream, Carwin's threats associate the summer house in the "recess" with the one on the rock, place of her father's mysterious end. The seat of eros becomes the scene of death. Clara is fantasizing her father's death scene while she is being "rescued" by Pleyel (pp. 63-64).

Her increasingly intense association of sexuality with madness and death is shown in her physical surroundings as well as in her fantasies. Her closet, a sexual symbol transformed into the object of her death fantasies, is the place where Carwin hides, where her father's autobiographical manuscript is kept, and where she expects to find her brother. Her fantasies incorporate elements as well as symbolizations of her experience. Her last dream is a mixture of sexual dream symbols: rising and falling, water and fire, mountain and abyss; the only constant is Clara's self-perception as a victim (p. 236).

Once more back to Pleyel and Carwin: both are associated with water, of which Clara has a "hereditary dread" (p. 83). She experiences "floods of passion," her heart "overflowed with sympathy," she is "set afloat upon a stormy sea" or a "sea of troubles" (pp. 50, 52, 151, 68). Carwin is first introduced asking for a drink and receives a cup with which to get water; she sees him from her window standing on a riverbank and, of course, he takes over her summer house by the waterfall. Carwin fits well into this symbolic landscape, but Pleyel is fearful of sexuality. In Clara's fantasy, she sees him in danger of drowning (p. 83), whereas he reacts to her alleged immorality with a "flame of resentment" (p. 134).

Clara has to survive a fire and cross the Atlantic before she can marry Pleyel. After her nervous breakdown, she finds herself the last surviving Wieland. In a similar catharsis, she has to go through a process of complete identification with her brother at his worst moment. "Was I not likewise transformed from rational and human into a creature of nameless and fearful attributes? Was I not transported to the brink of the same abyss?" (pp. 179-80).

In Alcuin's world of male politicians, women has no place; a "paradise" had to be invented for them. The Wieland world is one of male eccentricity where women are both victims and carriers of madness. In *Ormond*, paternal failure starts a young woman's initiation into a world of men where women are objects, where utopian "alternatives" are constructed by misogynists, and where the only happiness comes from the company of other women. Themes from *Wieland* are continued: masculine failure and hubris; a young woman's survival of the "complicated havoc" (*Ormond,* p. 239)[50] created by men; the possibilities of an independent subsistence for women; the support from women's friendships.

Constantia Dudley has had a superior education for a woman; she is intelligent, but not otherwise a "prodigy." Her strength of mind is the result of her unusual upbringing. This proves helpful when her father turns bankrupt, defrauded by a younger man. Canstantia's mother (another weak wife) dies of grief; her father moves from drink to blindness and childlike dependence on his daughter, and by the time she meets Ormond, Constantia has reached the bottom of her social decline. She has survived pestilence and poverty, been rescued from a rape attempt, and rejected an offer of marriage which would have ended her economic problems. Since **Ormond** is a novel *about* sexual politics, it is important to consider Constantia's reasons for rejecting her suitor, Balfour.

Her obvious reason is that she has "no sympathy, nor sentiments in common" with Balfour (p. 69); the prospect of economic security is not enough to tip the scales. Constantia's deliberations, according to the narrator, her friend Sophia, are spontaneous and not indebted to any source. "What are the genuine principles of that relation, and what conduct with respect to it is prescribed to rational beings by their duty, she had not hitherto investigated" (p. 68). But her explanations of her decision would be recognized by informed readers as Wollstonecraftian and potentially anti-Godwinian.

> Now she was at least mistress of the product of her own labor. Her tasks were toilsome, but the profits, though slender, were sure, and she administered her little property in what manner she pleased. Marriage would annihilate this power. Henceforth she would be bereft even of personal freedom. So far from possessing property, she herself would become the property of another.

She disdains to manipulate a man by the "soft artillery of blandishments and tears" that Rousseau had recommended and Wollstonecraft criticized. "She would not stoop to gain her end by the hateful arts of the sycophant and"—her potshot at Godwin—"was too wise to place an unbounded reliance on the influence of truth." Her conclusion: "Homely liberty was better than splendid servitude"—another Brownian reminder of the American Revolution (p. 69).

Ormond is introduced as a utopian reformer whose political philosophy is "to be intimately identified with the Godwinian model" (S.J. Krause),[51] nowhere more so than in his views on marriage. A whole chapter is devoted to his political and moral principles, already contrasting "discourse" and "actions" (p. 95), and pinpointing Ormond's "delight" with personal power (p. 96). It concludes with his "belief that the intellectual constitution of females was essentially defective" and that love based on equality does not exist (p. 97). The following chapter proceeds from theory to practice by describing his relationship with the beautiful Helena, who loves him but has to subsist as his kept woman. She is the perfect result of the feminine upbringing that outraged Wollstonecraft; a textbook case for Drs. Fordyce and Gregory (next to Rousseau, the primary targets of the *Vindication*), she is "calculated to excite emotions more voluptuous than dignified" (p. 98). Yet she is not "silly or ignorant" (p. 98). She has wonderful "accomplishments," is a talented, even original, artist, and proves Ormond's equal at chess. But she

has not been taught to reason, and Ormond does not encourage it ("he was accustomed to regard her merely as an object charming to the senses"). Her education, likewise, has not prepared her to be self-supporting when her father dies penniless; she must submit to "a life of dependence" (pp. 98-99).

Sophia, always reasonable, does justice to Helena. "Her understanding bore no disadvantageous comparison with that of the majority of her sex, but when placed in competition with that of some eminent females or of Ormond, it was exposed to the risk of contempt" (p. 98). No match for Ormond—yet he expects her to function as an equal in their "voluntary union" and to overcome social "prejudice" by force of reason. To "annihilate" those "inconveniences" of social ostracism, "it was only necessary to reason justly" (p. 101). Ormond uses the fiction of equality (basis of every contract) while dictating his own terms—and at the same time insisting that women, by virtue of gender, can never be the equals of men. His whole critique of marriage is based on "the general and incurable imperfection of the female character" (p. 100). To appease Helena's chronic unhappiness, he reasons with her, fully expecting "the influence of truth" to work, with the predictable result that his "maxims were confuted in the present case." In despair, he concludes that "[to] make her wise it would be requisite to change her sex" (pp. 103, 106).

Helena's flaws are those of the society that made her. Only women do her justice; even the critical Constantia grants her "greatness of mind" (p. 139). To Ormond, she is a plaything for his "amusement." "He must occasionally unbend, if he desires that the springs of his mind should retain their due vigor" (p. 108). From the beginning, Ormond is characterized as a pseudo-Godwinian, a coldhearted liar and power-hungry manipulator of men and women. Although his utopian plans remain behind the scenes, it is clear that they follow the same principles and motives as his visible actions. The greatest of Brown's "liberal" scoundrels, he constantly exposes his political designs for what they really are—dishonest power schemes—by his violations of human dignity, particularly that of women.

Enter Constantia, attempting to persuade Ormond that he must marry Helena. She scores in an unexpected quarter. "He was suddenly changed, from being one of the calumniators of the female sex, to one of its warmest eulogists" (p. 131), and he decides to drop Helena for Constantia. After Helena's suicide (her parting letter a model of dignity and logic), Ormond courts (and spies on) Constantia by all the means in his power. It is a *power* struggle. "Ormond aspired to nothing more ardently than to hold the reins of opinion—to exercise absolute power over the conduct of others" (p. 147). His pursuit of Constantia, ending in his rape attempt and death, begins with a recognition of her intellectual equality; but this equality only spurs his need to dominate. It raises the stakes, but does not change his game. His disdain of marriage was based on woman's flawed nature—this basis is gone. Yet, "Constantia was to be obtained by any means" (p. 148), marriage being only a last resort. ("Any means" includes the murder of her father when he appears to be in the way.) Failing to persuade Constantia, he resorts to rape, preceded by ceremonious warnings (pp. 214-15). It is now revealed that Ormond has been a rapist since his youth. Sophia's narration of this background story shows that Brown had an uncanny insight into the mechanics of rape: an act of power, not of sex, woman as pawn in a male struggle for dominance.

> A youth of eighteen, a volunteer in a Russian army encamped in Bessarabia, made prey of a Tartar girl, found in the field of a recent battle. Conducting her to his quarters, he met a friend, who, on some pretence, claimed the victim. From angry words they betook themselves to swords. A combat ensued, in which the first claimant ran his antagonist through the body. He then bore his prize unmolested away, and having exercised brutality of one kind upon the hapless victim, stabbed her to the heart, as an offering to the *manes* of Sarsefield, the friend whom he had slain. Next morning, willing more signally to expiate his guilt, he rushed alone upon a troop of Turkish foragers, and brought away five heads, suspended, by their gory locks, to his horse's mane. These he cast upon the grave of Sarsefield, and conceived himself fully to have expiated yesterday's offence. In reward for his prowess, the general gave him a commission in the Cossack troops. [P. 218]

In his final confrontation with Constantia (following another murder), Ormond sardonically reveals that this logic of power originates in hubris, a form of madness. Ormond, the "secret witness" (the novel's subtitle) of human deeds, assumes the role of God. His motives are impersonal, his actions irresistible. "I am not tired of well-doing," he asserts, despite the ingratitude he has encountered. Being raped, he tells Constantia, will "afford you an illustrious opportunity to signalize your wisdom and your fortitude" (p. 232). Rejection is something he cannot brook. "What thou refusedst to bestow it is in my power to extort. I came for that end" (p. 233). He is struck by Constantia's penknife and expires at her feet, a fitting climax, as S.J. Krause has observed, "not so much of the traditional battle of the sexes, as a battle over sexism."[52]

The villain slain, Constantia and Sophia sail for Europe. In this novel, as in *Wieland,* "communities of women" (Nina Auerbach) offer the only escape from the mad world of men. Clara Wieland has several women friends: Mrs. Boynton whom she frequently visits; her sister-in-law Catharine, "endowed with an uncommon portion of good sense" (p. 34); and Louisa Conway, murdered by Theodore so cruelly that *"not a lineament remained!"* (p. 157). Clara remembers sadly that Louisa "never met my eye, or occurred to my reflection, without exciting a kind of enthusiasm. Her softness, her intelligence, her equanimity, never shall I see surpassed. I have often shed tears of pleasure at her approach, and pressed her to my bosom in an agony of fondness" (p. 27).

Constantia Dudley develops a great fondness for the aptly named Martinette, growing "daily more enamored of her new acquaintance" (p. 157), although shocked by her friend's sanguinary exploits (as it turns out, she is Ormond's sister) from whose perspective Constantia appears as "a frail mimosa" (p. 160)! But her great love belongs to Sophia. Their reunion throws them into a three-day "state of dizziness and intoxication." Sophia reports, "The ordinary functions of nature were disturbed. The appetite for sleep and for food were [*sic*] confounded and lost amidst the impetuosities of a master passion. To look and to talk to each other afforded enchanting occupation for every moment. I would not part from her side, but eat [*sic*] and slept, walked and mused and read, with my arm locked in hers, and with her breath fanning my cheek" (p. 207). Ormond jealously mocks their "romantic passion for each other" (p. 212), but to them, it is a great celebration: "O precious inebriation of the heart! O pre-eminent love! what pleasure of reason or sense can stand in competition with those attendant upon thee? . . . surely thy sanction is divine, thy boon is happiness!" (p. 207).

IV

Whereas *Wieland* and *Ormond* assume a woman's perspective, *Stephen Calvert,* **[SC]** *Edgar Huntly [EH]* and *Arthur Mervyn* **[AM]** have male narrators and deal with problems of young men seeking to establish a place for themselves in the world. This was a theme already developed in the *Carwin* sequel to *Wieland.* The common starting point of these stories is the death or failure of a father (death in *SC* and *EH,* cruelty in *Carwin* and *AM*); in each, the young man's path to success lies through a woman's fortune. The *Carwin* fragment breaks off before the hero's marriage to a rich widow. Stephen Calvert gains a fortune which rightfully belongs to a young woman disinherited by a tyrannical father.[53] Edgar Huntly is willing to marry a young woman when she comes into money; when she loses it, she also loses him. Edgar's sleepwalking *Doppelgänger* Clithero has made a career through a woman's affection—and spoiled it through hubris. Arthur Mervyn even has a choice of two women— and chooses the unattractive, rich widow over the pretty but poor young girl. These plots are complicated, because they also involve issues of cultural and personal identity. Critics of *AM* have tended to see in Arthur's final decision a capitulation, a regression to the security of the womb, a sacrifice of his own potential identity to the maternal embrace, even a "self-abasement."[54] It could be argued in Arthur's defense that his final leap into "matronage" follows the previous failures of "patronage"; as Ludloe in *Carwin*, so Welbeck in *AM,* proves treacherous. And yet the matter is more complex than this; for why can't these young men stand on their own feet? A recent critic has recognized the "balance between sex and property" as "basic to *Arthur Mervyn.*"[55] Since *AM* is the central and most finished text of this phase, I will use it to demonstrate the problem.[56]

Mervyn is a country boy thrown into the turmoil of the city. He upholds the ideals of country life and experiences the city as a place of fraud, deception, and pestilence. But this simple contrast does not hold. Neither Mervyn's world nor his own character can be drawn in black and white; both are mixtures of good and evil. Arthur's world, like that of Clara and Constantia, "is a world of failed fathers and ruined families,"[57] a world that transcends city and country. Arthur flees from the country where he has become an "alien" (*AM,* p. 21) because of a hostile and jealous father. The elder Mervyn, after the death of his wife, falls for the wiles of a milkmaid (who has also made advances to Arthur) and kicks his son out of the nest. Arthur's fate has a number of parallels in the novel. As Emory Elliott points out, "The fathers of Mervyn, Welbeck, and Achsa desert or abandon their children while those like Mr. Hadwin, Watson, and the elder Lodi die prematurely from disease, crime, and political havoc."[58] The orphaned condition of so many characters is a microcosmic version of the human condition created by the yellow fever, which destroys not only real families but also the human family, the sense of community. Under these conditions, the ethical ideals that Arthur carries so self-consciously on his standard are bound to be subverted by the promptings of self-interest necessary to survival and advancement. Arthur is a mixed character because he must adapt himself to a "culture of contradictions,"[59] like himself the product of the historical moment. "Neither picaresque saint nor complete confidence man, Mervyn, a name suggestive of Everyman, is a symbol of the amoral, unschooled but intelligent individual struggling to survive in the social turmoil of the post-revolutionary age."[60] True, but what about the fact of gender? Is it correct to speak of "Arthur Mervyn, American"[61] as a representative figure? Women in the early Republic faced special problems not encountered by men, and they face some of them in this novel. We are shown how Arthur slips in and out of the roles of child, lover, and man-of-the-world with little difficulty, whereas a comparably situated young woman, Eliza Hadwin, is confined to the role of dependent. And she is not even much of a victim (despite Arthur's betrayal of her love), if her fate is compared to that of some other young women: Clemenza Lodi, seduced, defrauded, and abandoned in a brothel; Arthur's own sister, seduced, abandoned, and driven to suicide by her father; Eliza's sister Susan, dying from imagined abandonment, and buried by Arthur like a dog.

This hero's interest in women is inevitably property-related, whether his approach to that property follows the route of patronage or matronage. In the patronage model, the property belongs to the real or apparent father (Hadwin/Welbeck), and the young woman represents either access to the property via inheritance (Eliza) or simply an added benefit (Clemenza). In the matronage situation, the woman herself owns the property. These schemes recur with variations in the other major fiction of the same phase. In *Carwin*, the adoptive father procures the rich widow for the young man.[62] Edgar's Mary has her own modest fortune (at least for a while); Clithero's adoptive mother prepares a match between her adopted daughter and Clithero. Stephen Calvert's mother has taken up the young woman whose property he inherits from her father; Stephen loses interest in her when he meets a more attractive and wealthy woman. (This woman in turn was adopted by an aunt after escaping from a miserable, arranged marriage.)

In *AM,* the acquisition of property through patronage fails. This does not mean that Arthur does not find a substitute father and mother. But Dr. Stevens (narrator of large portions of the story) and his wife represent an option that Mervyn ultimately rejects—independence and identity through "useful exertion"—and they bear little relation to the property/sex complex. Instead, Arthur's "apprenticeship" takes place under the roof of a man who has a long history of sexually and financially exploiting women. The apprentice, it is true, renounces his master and eventually has a chance to restore some of the damage Welbeck has done. But Welbeck's patronage brings out that aspect of Arthur's character that predisposes him to accept the world's gifts as his due and causes him to spend so much time on his self-stylization as a worthy and "undepraved" recipient. On his first errand for Welbeck, Arthur reflects:

> But what was the fate reserved for me? Perhaps Welbeck would adopt me for his own son. Wealth has ever been capriciously distributed. The mere physical relation of birth is all that intitles us to manors and thrones. Identity itself frequently depends upon a casual likeness or an old nurse's imposture. Nations have risen in arms, as in the case of the Stewarts, in the cause of one, the genuineness of whose birth has been denied and can never be proved. But if the cause be trivial and fallacious, the effects are momentous and solid. It ascertains our portions of felicity and usefulness, and fixes our lot among peasants or princes. [Pp. 57-58]

This readiness to passively accept a "fate" is in stark contrast to Arthur's pronounced curiosity and his tendency to play Fate himself by interfering in the affairs of other people. (A fine testing ground for his chameleon ethics "Honest purposes," he reasons, "though they may not bestow happiness on others, will, at least, secure it to him who fosters them" [p. 270]. Arthur's quest for a place in the world is marked by this contradiction, which is also expressed in his changing resolves, his frequent changes of place, his vacillation between the roles of observer and actor, between naiveté and wisdom. There are important clues that he even vacillates between gender roles. This is not your hairy-chested, powerful seducer type. We learn that, back on the farm, he used to knit stockings and stay away from young men's activities, reason enough for a neighbor to doubt if all is right with Arthur. He

> moped away his time in solitude, never associated with other young people, never mounted an horse but when he could not help it, and never fired a gun or angled for a fish in his life. Some people supposed him to be half an idiot, or, at least, not to be in his right mind; and, indeed, his conduct was so very perverse and singular, that I do not wonder at those who accounted for it in this way. [P. 233]

This repudiation of prescribed gender roles is more important than it at first appears. I have referred to the special problems that women at the end of the eighteenth century were facing. Not the least of them was an increasing pressure to marry (as women's independent subsistence was more and more endangered) while, at the same time, their opportunities to marry dwindled.[63] To advance in the world or simply to obtain a respectable place in it, women *had* to marry. Whether or not Brown was aware of the historical trends, whether he picked up the pattern from the sentimental tradition or any other context, is irrelevant here, because this is so clearly identified as a feminine pattern of behavior. It is the pattern that Mervyn follows. Amidst all his waverings, he constantly exhibits androgynous traits (which do not prevent him from sexist behavior, as we shall see). In the end, he settles for a typical woman's "career"; he marries a wealthy older person, better educated and more sophisticated than he. Arthur is "wax in her hand" (p. 428) and calls her his "mamma," just as a young bride might call an older husband "daddy." Arthur, it turns out, is Everyman *and* Everywoman, after all; but is he really the representative American? No, because he is still a man. The irony of his rise from rags to riches is a double one. He not only chooses a woman's career (the critic's charge of "self-abasement" suddenly gains new dimensions!), but he does so out of a man's arsenal of possible choices. This gives new depth to his much-discussed opportunism—if *he* needs it, how much more a woman? What choices among "honest purposes" does *she* have?

Two more touches from the broad palette of what is perhaps Brown's best novel, one tragic, the other tragicomic. Eliza's rejection by Arthur as a companion and future wife is tragic for her. The decision, typically, is not final until after she has lost her inheritance to a greedy uncle; Arthur's rationalizations of what is to become of her are pitiful (p. 311). But he distances himself from her even earlier, as she appears to be in the way of his plans for a future (p. 293). As Elliott has recognized, "Eliza makes a powerful argument from the position of women's rights for sharing in his years of learning and experience":[64]

> You think me unworthy to partake of your cares and labors; . . . you regard my company as an obstacle and incumbrance; . . . assistance and counsel must all proceed from you; and . . . no scene is fit for me, but what you regard as slothful and inglorious.

> Have I not the same claims to be wise, and active, and courageous as you? If I am ignorant and weak, do I not owe it to the same cause that has made you so; and will not the same means which promote your improvement be likewise useful to me? You desire to obtain knowledge, by travelling and conversing with many persons, and studying many scenes; but you desire it for yourself alone. Me, you think poor, weak, and contemptible; fit for nothing but to spin and churn. Provided I exist, am screened from the weather, have enough to eat and drink, you are satisfied. As to strengthening my mind and enlarging my knowledge, these things are valuable to you, but on me they are thrown away. I deserve not the gift. [P. 296]

Arthur is "shaken" but not convinced. Eliza ultimately arrives to live as a dependent in Achsa's household, also calling her "mamma," thus becoming a sister/daughter to Arthur. There she appears (small poetic justice) in Arthur's Oedipal dream just before his marriage to Achsa Fielding.

Although tragic to Arthur (and Achsa, who nearly breaks off the engagement), this dream must give a sense of satisfaction, even amusement, to readers who feel qualms about Arthur's success. It hints at the price he may have to pay. The dream is caused by Arthur's sudden panic at the prospect of marriage. Its two parts show the reasons for his panic—fear of sexuality and fear of his "mamma's" past in the shape of her first husband, now to become his "father." (A Freudian interpretation might argue that the dream's "wish" is the appearance of the first husband as an obstacle to the marriage.) Part one, not a proper dream but "a nameless sort of terror," is a replay of Pleyel's drowning in *Wieland,* this time from the perspective of the victim. "Methinks, that one falling from a tree, overhanging a torrent, plunged into the whirling eddy, and gasping and struggling while he sinks to rise no more, would feel just as I did then" (p. 436). Part two is a visit to Achsa's house, complete with Eliza as parlormaid, only to find Achsa's first husband there.

> What, said he, mildly, is your business with my wife? She cannot see you instantly, and has sent me to receive your commands.
>
> Your *wife!* I want Mrs. Fielding.
>
> True; and Mrs. Fielding is my wife. Thank Heaven I have come in time to discover her, and claim her as such.
>
> I started back. I shuddered. My joints slackened, and I stretched my hand to catch something by which I might be saved from sinking on the floor. Meanwhile, Fielding changed his countenance into rage and fury. He called me villain! bad me avaunt! and drew a shining steel from his bosom, with which he stabbed me to the heart. [P. 437]

This classic Oedipal triangle ends a story which had started with one, Mervyn's banishment by his natural father. Ironically, *AM* ends with the young man fantasizing about future fatherhood (p. 446).

V

In the view of a 1970s feminist critic, "The final resolution of Arthur and Achsa's difficulties offers the maternal role as one possibility in coming to terms with the feminine."[65] This would imply that Brown intended woman as the Other, the nonhuman, the "object" one must come to terms with. It would also mean that the novelist is to be identified with Arthur and the other young men of this phase. That this is patently wrong and that Brown was aware of the punishment such treatment would bring on the heads of the perpetrators is already hinted at in the fate that awaits Arthur in his marriage. Still, Achsa might let him get away with it. The young man in Brown's next novel, *Clara Howard,* is not so lucky.

Brown's last two novels continue to evolve themes that the earlier ones had developed. They represent a high point in awareness, as well as in craftsmanship, technical finesse. They have even been claimed as Brown's "most mature novels."[66] Thematic evolution, as I see it, also accounts for the apparently "regressive" epistolary form that has raised critical eyebrows.[67] Brown's novels began with female narrators (*Wieland/ Ormond*), moved on to male narrators (*Carwin /SC/ EH/AM*), and end now with letters written by both men and women. The form itself is a statement.

The strongest case for *Clara Howard* [CH] and *Jane Talbot* [JT] as a continuation of earlier efforts was made in a recent essay by S. J. Krause, who finds in them "an extension of the same basic investigation of the 'moral constitution of man' that concerned him" before.[68] His essay places them in the context of Brown's running argument with Godwin and Godwinism. Thus, it finds Clara "a pillar of Godwinian moral theory," "the original Iron Maiden of American literature" who exhibits the absurdities of extreme adherence to "disinterest" (Krause, p. 187). *JT* continues the argument with the result that "Godwin is not just tested, he is corrected; Jane and Colden dispense with theoretical obligations, as it becomes plain that one partner can in no way receive a happiness conferred at the expense of the other's happiness" (Krause, p. 187). To achieve this resolution, Rousseau's radical reliance on feeling is employed as the novelist's "counter-theory" supporting the notion that "acute feelings are heuristic; through the acutest of them we learn virtue" (Krause, p. 191).

This battle of ideas, Godwin versus Rousseau, must be seen in connection with the ongoing battle of the sexes. With respect to both, S. J. Krause's contention can be upheld "that the last two novels are indeed counterparts which have to be read together, in sequence, as they were written, *Jane* in the context of *Clara.* Not only was *Jane* begun almost immediately after *Clara* was finished, but it is its intellectual complement suggesting a progression of where we go from *Clara,* and where we do not. From the negative analysis on which *Clara* ended, we move on to a consideration of alternatives." (p. 202).

In *CH,* the young man continues the game of sex and property, garnished with the usual claims of high-minded disinterest and the most rigorous ethical standards. For the first time, the patronage model seems to work. Edward/Philip, another talented country lad,[69] becomes the protégé of his teacher, Mr. Howard. "He had reason to regard me, indeed, somewhat like his own son. I had no father; I had no property" (XIII, p. 31). Howard leaves the country and returns, years later, with a rich wife and a beautiful, accomplished stepdaughter, Clara, whom he has destined to marry Philip. In the meantime, however, Philip has become engaged to Mary Wilmot, whom he does not love but who loves him and has suddenly come into some money through her brother (this part of the plot is lifted from *EH*). Mary in turn is loved by Mr. Sedley whom she does not love. Almost simultaneously, she finds out that she lost the money (as Mary in *EH*) and that Philip has met Clara, has in fact moved in with the Howards. Mary breaks the engagement to set Philip free for the inevitable and vanishes from the scene. Patronage has superseded matronage; the prize is beautiful, rich, and also in love with Philip. Open season, at last?

Unfortunately, Philip meets what he deserves, a woman who takes him at his word. When he was urging Mary to become his wife, he used the vocabulary of benevolence, as she recalls:

> I was not so base as to accept your hand, without your heart. You talked of gratitude, and duty, and perfect esteem. . . . Your reason discerned and adored my merits, and the concurrence of the heart could not but follow. . . . I doubted not your fidelity, and that the consciousness of *conferring happiness* would secure your contentment. [II, pp. 12-13; emphasis mine]

When Clara learns about Mary, she tells Philip that these were, indeed, valid reasons; that he has to go find Mary and marry her. His earlier claims of disinterestedness are taken seriously and promptly turn against him. And in keeping with the "higher nature" that Mervyn and company have routinely ascribed to the objects of their love, Clara remains adamantly disinterested herself, yielding no ground to the impulses of self-interest (although she loves Philip).

Although the basic plot is an elaboration of a catch-22 that Brown had discussed with his friend William Wood Wilkins around 1792 (boy loves girl but is loved by another girl),[70] it is significantly transformed by the property aspect at the time it becomes **CH**. The gentleman doth protest too much—and has to eat his own words. He tells Clara:

> Your decision has made me unhappy. I believe your decision absurd, yet I know your motives are disinterested and heroic. I know the misery which adherence to your schemes costs you. It is only less than my own. Why then should I aggravate my own? It is the system of nature that deserves my hatred and my curses—that system which makes our very virtues instrumental to our misery. [III, p. 16]

Whether or not the "system of nature" is Goodwin's moral system or Rousseau's "nature of things" (*Contrat Sociale*), it is reason that Philip is told he lacks; "Thy spirit is not curbed by reason" (VII, p. 22). Or as the *Vindication* has it, "to submit to reason is to submit to the nature of things."[71] This does not mean that Philip is not able or does not try to reason with Clara. "That conduct which in me is culpable, is no less culpable in others. Am I cruel and unjust in refusing my love to one that claims it? So are you, whose refusal is no less obstinate as to me, as mine with respect to another; and who hearkens not to claims upon your sympathy, as reasonable as those of Mary on mine" (XXIV, p. 94). But the twisting of words does not help. The moral tenets that Philip claimed as the basis for his actions are rubbed in his face until he nearly chokes. Moreover, the re-emerged Mary refuses to take him back, urging the same reasons. "She was too blind an admirer, and assiduous a follower of Clara Howard"

(XXVI, p. 98). Knight that he is, Philip is sent on this impossible crusade by his fair lady until he goes insane. She gives in briefly once, when he nearly dies (from jumping into water!), but she recovers and sends him out again. This time, he goes mad. "Alas, my friend! you are not in your right mind," Mary informs him. "Disappointment has injured your reason" (XXVIII, p. 112). The dilemma gets resolved only when Mary agrees to marry Sedley. Philip recovers slowly: "In truth, I have been sick; . . . I have been half crazy, shivering and glowing by turns; bereft of appetite and restless—every object was tinged with melancholy hues" (XXXI, p. 120).

Selfishness masked by high purposes is unmasked by high purposes; by accepting Philip's premises, Clara becomes the Other with a vengeance-she turns nonhuman by living the proposition to its bitter end. Philip feels the nightmare reality of what, normally, would be conventional verbiage; he must "submit to one whom I deem unerring and divine"; "an angel in the heavens like thee, is not a fit companion for a mere earthworm like Philip Stanley" (XVIII, p. 75). Clara, the "heavenly monitor" (XXXI, p. 119), is firmly established as his preceptress who will teach the young man "moral discernment." In her words, "Our modes of judging and our maxims shall be the same; and this resemblance shall be purchased at the cost of all my patience, my skill, and my love" (XXXII, p. 122). A double wedding in sight, Clara writes to Mary, "At present, I must devote myself to console this good lad for his sufferings, incurred, *as he presumes to say,* entirely on my account" (XXXIII, p. 122; emphasis mine).

With respect to our theme, *Jane Talbot* is both summary and resolution of Brown's incredible three-year spell of creativity (1798-1801) that produced all his novels. This comedy has familiar scenes and characters, but the romantic leads have changed. Its greatest innovation is the young man, Colden. He is Brown's epitaph written by himself (with a great deal of wishful thinking), the closest he ever came to a fictional self-portrait. A penniless writer with a suspiciously radical background, he is won to love, marriage, and rational Christianity by Jane who, in turn, changes from a Betsy Thoughtless to a young woman of rational persuasions.

The plot, too, is a synopsis of the familiar. Jane, bereft of her mother as a child, is exposed to masculine failure and tyranny in the persons of her weak father and rakish brother, the latter a cartoon-character misogynist. Jane, an "April girl" who cannot resist an appeal to her emotions, loses half her money to him despite the fact that she knows better—a prefiguration of things to come, for she is a sitting duck for manipulators. Adopted by her aunt, Mrs. Fielder, she follows the advice to marry an older man whom she does not love (Talbot). During his absence, she meets Colden whom she falls to loving and wooing. Although she does not break her marriage vows, a forged letter convinces both her husband and her aunt that she has; Colden is marked as a seducer, and his alleged radicalism is the motive presented by the prosecution. This is the state of affairs when the curtain rises. Talbot is dead, and Jane wishes to marry Colden. Enter the obstacle: Mrs. Fielder, who abhors the young man and his suspected views; she will disinherit Jane if she marries Colden, whereupon the elder Colden (another tyrant) disinherits his son for wanting to marry a poor girl. A conspiracy of the elders, patriarchy and matriarchy coming together in perfect cacophony.

Although Jane's conflict is one between love and duty, the traditional parameters have been discredited. On the one hand, Mrs. Fielder (her "mother") is shown to be as power-hungry and manipulative as she suspects Colden to be; she interprets relationships in terms of power—a form of thinking Jane herself has adopted and must unlearn. Mrs. Fielder raves at Colden that Jane is "an unhappy girl who has put herself into your power" (p. 75);[72] Jane speaks of "my mother's government" (p. 206); at times she promises to "reign" over Colden (p. 93), at other times she slips into a traditional woman's role and craves governance from him. "Let me lose all separate feelings, all separate existence, and let me know no principle of action, but the decision of your judgment; no motive or desire but to please; to gratify you" (p. 91).

On the other hand, Colden is a male feminist who refuses to play any of these games. He wants Jane, not her money. (When interrogated by Jane's brother about "the basis of this engagement," his response is totally deadpan: "Mutual affection, I believe, is the only basis" [p. 123].) He wants Jane to make her own decisions, not follow his; he is firm but unassuming, loving but rational. His lesson is Wollstonecraftian: "It is a farce to call any being virtuous, whose virtues do not result from the exercise of its own reason."[73] Where Jane's worst crimes, in Mrs. Fielder's eyes, are crimes against the family ("the faithless wife and the ungrateful child" [p. 76]), Colden insists that Jane be herself, not a wife or a daughter. In the tug-of-war between Mrs. Fielder and himself, he turns down his final chance to win Jane over to his side; "she has made her election" (p. 212). Jane is a responsible person; this is her choice, which he respects.

Mrs. Fielder's comic ravings about Colden's "radical" views supposedly derived from Godwin are "pure fantasy," as S. J. Krause has shown,[74] and only serve to discredit her, just as her attempts to bribe Colden do. According to her, Colden is

> the advocate of suicide; a scoffer at promises; the despiser of revelation, of providence and a future state; an opponent of marriage, and . . . one who

> denied (shocking!) that any thing but mere habit and positive law, stood in the way of marriage; nay, of intercourse without marriage, between brother and sister, parent and child! [P. 68]

Colden does, in the end, return as a rational Christian to marry Jane, but she has already met him halfway. The "reformation" is mutual, the happy end believable.

Received opinion has it that **Clara** and **Jane** were Brown's last attempts at fiction. Charles E. Bennett has recently pointed out that this is not the case and that Brown developed an interest in historical fiction which lasted well into his last decade.[75] We have already seen that the last two finished novels are no evidence of a "growing conservatism" with respect to Brown's views on women. The surviving fragments of his large-scale project in fictional history show that he placed special emphasis on strong, independent women even then. His magazine articles of the last decade, laboriously nonpartisan as they are, also indicate that he never lost interest in women's issues.

If Brown neither abandoned the pursuit of fiction nor lost his feminist impulse, why did he not finish another novel for the ever-growing audience of women readers in America? The answer must be that he had realized the impossibility of making a living as a writer of fiction—*his* fiction, anyway. **Clara** and **Jane** "were his last-gasp efforts to cultivate a following."[76] In 1801, the year these two appeared, Brown met his future wife whom he married in 1804. Henceforth, unprofitable fiction had to give way to more solid sources of income; an unremunerative career as a novelist was no way to satisfy the demands of a family.

Notes

[1] Margaret Fuller, "Papers on Literature and Art" [1846], in *Critical Essays on Charles Brockden Brown,* ed. Bernard Rosenthal (Boston: G. K. Hall, 1981), p. 63.

[2] *Carlyle's Laugh and Other Surprises* (Boston and New York: Houghton Mifflin, 1909), p. 58.

[3] See, for instance, Lillie Deming Loshe, *The Early American Novel 1789-1830* (1907; reprint ed., New York: Fredrick Ungar, 1958), Ch. 3; and David Lee Clark, *Brockden Brown and the Rights of Women* (Austin: University of Texas Bulletin No. 2212, 1922).

[4] Augusta Genevieve Violette, *Economic Feminism in American Literature Prior to 1848* (Orono: University of Maine Studies, 1925), p. 47.

[5] Mary Sumner Benson, *Women in Eighteenth-Century America: A Study of Opinion and Social Usage* (New York: Columbia University Press, 1935), pp. 200-201.

6 Dorothy Yost Deegan, *The Stereotype of the Single Woman in American Novels* (New York: Columbia University Press, 1951), pp. 130-31.

7 *Retrospective Review* 9 (1824), p. 317. Quoted in Rosenthal, Introduction, *Critical Essays,* p. 5.

8 The most useful bibliographies of Brown criticism are Robert E. Hemenway and Dean H. Keller, "Charles Brockden Brown, America's First Important Novelist: A Checklist of Biography and Criticism," *Papers of the Bibliographical Society of America* 60 (1966):349-62; Paul Witherington, "Charles Brockden Brown: A Bibliographical Essay," *Early American Literature* 9 (1974):164-87; Patricia Parker, *Charles Brockden Brown: A Reference Guide* (Boston: G. K. Hall, 1980); Charles A. Carpenter, "Selective Bibliography of Writings about Charles Brockden Brown," in Rosenthal, *Critical Essays,* pp. 224-39.

9 A prominent recent example is Nina Baym, "A Minority Reading of *Wieland,*" in Rosenthal, *Critical Essays,* pp. 87-103. In Baym's opinion, "there is no real evidence that [Brown's] novelistic aims were very high" (p. 87); critical emphasis on Brown's ideas ("a list of truisms"), although no valid reason for the high appreciation of his fiction, is caused by "the intense didactic bias" in academic criticism (p. 88).

10 Rosenthal, Introduction, *Critical Essays,* p. 2.

11 See, for instance, Judith Ann Cunningham, "Charles Brockden Brown's Pursuit of a Realistic Feminism: A Study of his Writings as a Contribution to the Growth of Women's Rights in America" (Ph.D. diss., Ball State University, 1971); Mary A. McCay, "Women in the Novels of Charles Brockden Brown: A Study" (Ph.D. diss., Tufts University, 1973); Ann Stanford, "Images of Women in Early American Literature," in *What Manner of Woman: Essays on English and American Life and Literature,* ed. Marlene Springer (New York: New York University Press, 1977), pp. 184-210; Nina Baym, "Portrayal of Women in American Literature, 1790-1870," ibid., pp. 211-34.

12 Examples are Ernest Earnest, *The American Eve in Fact and Fiction, 1775-1914* (Urbana: University of Illinois Press, 1974); Patricia Jewell McAlexander, "The Cultural Dialogue on the Nature and Role of Women in Late Eighteenth-Century America," *Early American Literature* 9 (1975):252-66.

13 Cathy N. Davidson, "The Matter and Manner of Charles Brockden Brown's *Alcuin,*" in Rosenthal, *Critical Studies,* pp. 71-86; and Sydney J. Krause, "*Clara Howard* and *Jane Talbot:* God win on Trial," ibid., pp. 184-211.

14 William Hedges, "Charles Brockden Brown and the Culture of Contradictions," *Early American Literature* 9 (1974):115.

15 Davidson, "Brown's *Alcuin,*" p. 75.

16 This body of work includes the letters between "Henrietta" and "C. B. B." in David Lee Clark, *Charles Brockden Brown: Pioneer Voice of America* (Durham, N.C.: Duke University Press, 1952), pp. 55-107, as well as Brown's correspondence with friends in which "Henrietta" is mentioned. My reference is specifically to Brown's letter "To J. D———n" (MS at the Humanities Research Center, University of Texas at Austin) listed as no. 2 in Charles E. Bennett, "The Letters of Charles Brockden Brown: An Annotated Census," *Resources for American Literary Study* 4, no. 2 (1976):167.

17 All citations in text are from Lee R. Edwards, ed., *Alcuin: A Dialogue* (New York: Grossman, 1971).

18 Edwards, Afterword, *Alcuin,* p. 94.

19 All references are to the second edition of 1792 in the facsimile reproduction of Gregg International Publishers (Farnborough, England, 1970). Its appendix contains Godwin's biography of Wollstonecraft first published in his *Memoirs of the Author of "A Vindication of the Rights of Woman"* (1798), which will be cited hereafter as *Memoirs.*

20 It was also a big headache for a writer addressing a predominantly female audience. Hawthorne's much-maligned diatribe against the "scribbling women" was directed at the sentimental bowdlerization of issues that, in his opinion, called for franker treatment.

21 I wish to thank Professor Sydney J. Krause, general editor of the CEAA/CSE Bicentennial Edition of Brown, for making available to me the resources of the Kent State University Bibliographical and Textual Center and, especially, for permitting me to use his manuscript notes to *Ormond,* which will appear as vol. 2 of the edition. All quotations here are from his lengthy commentary on marriage (passages 140.35-141.2; 141.22-26; 147.24-28 in the KSU *Ormond*), henceforth cited as KSU *Ormond.* I also wish to thank Ms. Bobbie Trowbridge at the center for clerical support during my stay.

22 Wollstonecraft, *Vindication,* p. 59.

23 Krause, KSU *Ormond.*

24 Ibid.

25 See Ralph Wardle, *Mary Wollstonecraft: A Critical Biography* (Lawrence: Kansas University Press, 1951),

p. 158 ff.; R. M. Janes, "On the Reception of Mary Wollstonecraft's *A Vindication of the Rights of Woman*," *Journal of the History of Ideas* 39 (1978):293-302; Marcelle Thiébaux, "Mary Wollstonecraft in Federalist America: 1791-1802," in *The Evidence of the Imagination: Studies of Interactions between Life and Art in English Romantic Literature,* ed. Donald H. Reiman et al. (New York: New York University Press, 1978), pp. 195-245. For Philadelphia, see Bertha Monica Stearns, "Early Philadelphia Magazines for Ladies," *Pennsylvania Magazine of History and Biography* 64 (1940): 479-91.

[26] Krause, KSU *Ormond;* and Krause, "*Clara Howard* and *Jane Talbot,*" pp. 196-97.

[27] Krause, KSU *Ormond.*

[28] Godwin, *Memoirs,* p. 166.

[29] Krause, KSU *Ormond.*

[30] Davidson, "Brown's *Alcuin,*" p. 75.

[31] Most often quoted from Brown's preface to *Edgar Huntly* (1799). See David Lee Clark, ed., *Edgar Huntly, or Memoirs of a Sleep-Walker* (New York: Macmillan, 1928), p. xxiii.

[32] Advertisement for *Sky-Walk, The Weekly Magazine* (Philadelphia), 17 March 1798, p. 202, reprinted in *The Rhapsodist and Other Uncollected Writings by Charles Brockden Brown,* ed. Harry R. Warfel (New York: Scholars' Facsimiles & Reprints, 1943), pp. 135-36.

[33] "Walstein's School of History. From the German of Krants of Gotha," *The Monthly Magazine and American Review* (New York), August-September 1799, p. 408, reprinted in *The Rhapsodist,* p. 151.

[34] "Walstein's School," *Rhapsodist,* p. 152.

[35] Ibid.

[36] Ibid.

[37] "The Difference between History and Romance," *Monthly Magazine and American Review,* April 1800, p. 251, reprinted in Alfred Weber, "Essays und Rezensionen von Charles Brockden Brown," *Jahrbuch für Amerikastudien* 6 (1961):185.

[38] William J. Scheick, "The Problem of Origination in Brown's *Ormond,*" in Rosenthal, *Critical Essays,* pp. 127-28.

[39] *Wieland or The Transformation. An American Tale/ Memoirs of Carwin the Biloquist (1798),* Bicentennial Ed. vol. 1, ed. Sydney J. Krause and S.W. Reid (Kent, Ohio. Kent State University Press, 1977). All citations are from this edition.

[40] Rosenthal, "The Voices of *Wieland,*" in *Critical Essays,* p. 109.

[41] Sydney J. Krause, "Romanticism in *Wieland:* Brown and the Reconciliation of Opposites," in *Artful Thunder: Versions of the Romantic Tradition in American Literature* in Honor of Howard P. Vincent, ed. Robert J. DeMott and Sanford E. Marovitz (Kent, Ohio: Kent State University Press, 1975), p. 19.

[42] Alexander Cowie, "Historical Essay," KSU *Wieland/ Carwin,* p. 348.

[43] Repr. in Alice S. Rossi, ed., *The Feminist Papers* (New York: Bantam, 1973), p. 675.

[44] James R. Russo has pointed out that Carwin is a notorious seducer in the "Carwin" fragment, where he uses his magnificent vocal gifts to gain control over women ("'The Chimeras of the Brain': Clara's Narrative in *Wieland,*" *Early American Literature* 16 (1981):87-88, n. 18). In *Wieland,* the ventriloquist confesses to a "voluptuous temper" (p. 201), but is not physically interested in Clara. He goes to bed with the maid while engaging in a power play with the mistress.

[45] Dorothy Scarborough, *The Supernatural in Modern English Fiction* (New York: G. P. Putnam's Sons, 1917), p. 39. Quoted in Cowie, "Historical Essay," p. 347.

[46] Sigmund Freud, *The Interpretation of Dreams,* trans. James Strachey (New York: Avon/Discus, 1965), p. 279.

[47] Sigmund Freud, *Introductory Lectures on Psychoanalysis,* trans. James Strachey (New York: Norton/ Liveright, 1977), p. 153.

[48] Freud, *Lectures,* p. 136.

[49] Ibid., p. 217.

[50] All citations are from Ernest Marchand, ed., *Ormond* (New York and London: Hafner, 1962).

[51] Krause, KSU *Ormond.*

[52] Ibid.

[53] Hans Borchers, ed., *Memoirs of Stephen Calvert* (Frankfurt on the Main: Peter Lang, 1978).

[54] Emory Elliott, "Narrative Unity and Moral Resolution in *Arthur Mervyn,*" in Rosenthal, *Critical Essays,*

p. 159. A good discussion of Arthur's own rationalizations is Warner B. Berthoff, "Adventures of the Young Man: An Approach to Charles Brockden Brown," *American Quarterly* 9 (1957):421-34. On the hero's marriage, Berthoff notes, "there remains something distasteful about his love" (p. 432).

55 Norman S. Grabo, "Historical Essay," in *Arthur Mervyn or Memoirs of the Year 1793,* Bicentennial Ed. vol. 3, ed. Sydney J. Krause and S.W. Reid (Kent, Ohio: Kent State University Press, 1980), p. 474.

56 Subsequent citations are from KSU *Arthur Mervyn.*

57 Elliott, "Narrative Unity," p. 152.

58 Ibid.

59 The term is Richard Chase's in *The American Novel and Its Tradition* (Garden City, N.Y.: Doubleday, 1957); it is discussed in Hedges, "Culture of Contradictions," p. 111 ff. I am indebted to Hedges for the term *matronage* (p. 114).

60 Elliott, "Narrative Unity," p. 143.

61 This is the title of an article by James H. Justus, *American Literature* 42 (1970):304-24.

62 *Adoption,* of course, is not used in any legal sense here.

63 The economic and ideological changes affecting women's lives after the revolution were complex and varied by class and region. Women as independent producers of goods and services lost much of their market, whereas the new manufacturers gave employment to a different group of women. Opportunities for them to marry dwindled as a result of the demographic shifts in this period. There is a massive body of literature on the subject, an impressive proof of the impact of women's history. See, for instance, Mari Jo Buhle, Ann G. Gordon, and Nancy Schrom, "Women in American History: An Historical Contribution," *Radical America* 5, no. 1 (July-August 1971):3-66; Mary P. Ryan, *Womanhood in America: From Colonial Times to the Present* (New York: New Viewpoints, 1975), pp. 85-135; Barbara Mayer Wertheimer, *We Were There: The Story of Working Women in America* (New York: Pantheon, 1977), pp. 50-127; Nancy F. Cott, *The Bonds of Womanhood: "Woman's Sphere" in New England, 1780-1835* (New Haven and London: Yale University Press, 1977):19-62 and passim; Carol Hymowitz and Michaele Weissman, *A History of Women in America* (New York: Bantam, 1978), pp. 64-75, 122-37; Linda K. Kerber, *Women of the Republic: Intellect and Ideology in Revolutionary America* (Chapel Hill: University of North Carolina Press, 1980), Ch. 7 and passim.

64 Elliott, "Narrative Unity," p. 148.

65 Barbara Joan Cicardo, "The Mystery of the American Eve: Alienation of the Feminine as a Tragic Theme in American Letters" (Ph.D. diss., St. Louis University, 1971), p. 45.

66 Paul Witherington, "Brockden Brown's Other Novels: *Clara Howard* and *Jane Talbot,*" *Nineteenth Century Fiction* 29 (1974):257.

67 Witherington notes that "Brown came to the epistolary novel when it was being abandoned by other writers" (ibid., p. 267).

68 Krause, "*Clara Howard* and *Jane Talbot,*" p. 186.

69 The young man is named Edward Hartley in the first edition, *Clara Howard; in a Series of Letters* (Philadelphia: Asbury Dickins, 1801). He becomes Philip Stanley in the 1807 British edition, and he is Stanley in the edition that was available to me, *Clara Howard; or the Enthusiasm of Love* (Boston: S. G. Goodrich, 1827). The forthcoming KSU *Clara Howard* will use the original name. To facilitate reference, I give letter numbers (in Roman numerals) as well as page numbers.

70 Printed in Paul Allen, *The Life of Charles Brockden Brown,* ed. Charles E. Bennett (Delmar, N.Y.: Scholars' Facsimiles & Reprints, 1975), pp. 44-46.

71 Wollstonecraft, *Vindication,* p. 356.

72 All references are to *Jane Talbot* (Boston: S. G. Goodrich, 1827).

73 Ibid., p. 37.

74 Krause, "*Clara Howard* and *Jane Talbot,*" p. 196.

75 Charles E. Bennett, "Charles Brockden Brown: Man of Letters," in Rosenthal, *Critical Essays,* pp. 212-23.

76 Krause, "*Clara Howard* and *Jane Talbot,*" p. 185.

Maurice J. Bennett (essay date 1983)

SOURCE: "Charles Brockden Brown's Ambivalence Toward Art and Imagination," in *Essays in Literature,* Vol. X, No. 1, Spring, 1983, pp. 55-69.

[*In the following essay, Bennett contends that Brown's novels reflect his effort to reconcile reason and imagination and concludes that Brown's rejection of fiction was based on the triumph of his "moral distrust" of the form of the romance over his need to create.*]

Recent years have witnessed an increasing tendency to accept Charles Brockden Brown's work on its own terms rather than merely as an awkward provincial imitation of that of Richardson, Godwin, and Radcliffe. There is a greater willingness to regard many of his artistic strengths as conscious achievements and his putative "faults" as equally intentional attempts at innovation.[1] Of course, the haste with which Brown composed is a matter of record, and there are always those critics who regard much of his work in the same manner as James Russell Lowell viewed that of Poe—as so much "fudge."[2] In his recent study of American romance, however, Michael Davitt Bell identifies a fundamental stance toward aesthetic activity that Brown shared with the major writers of pre-Civil War America—a set of attitudes and ambivalences that surfaced directly in the kinds of narrative he composed and that shaped the general contours of his literary career.[3] By examining the miscellaneous magazine sketches in which Brown directly addressed the nature of artistic representation and expressed not only attitudes toward the moral aspects of fiction but also nascent theories concerning fictional characterization and the sociology of literature, the present study seeks a firmer basis than the sensibilities of individual critics for establishing Brown's commitment to the more serious aspects of his art.

The sketches, dialogues, and addresses discussed here certainly do not constitute a formal "art of fiction," but taken as a whole, they reveal Brown consciously wrestling with technical as well as moral issues, the peculiarly aesthetic dimensions of which are not immediately recognizable in his novels. These pieces indicate, however, the degree to which his narratives are themselves densely symbolic structures composed of a consistent and identifiable vocabulary of images and metaphors and requiring other analytical methods than those traditionally directed at the realistic novel. They certainly call into question such observations as Nina Baym's assertion that "there is no real evidence that [Brown's] novelistic aims were very high. His letters, as Dunlap presented them, indicate no concern with any aspect of his fiction other than its salability."[4] The goal of this study, then, is to identify themes, scenarios, intentions that are important for the continuing investigation of Brown's fiction.

In an article devoted to the aesthetics expressed in Brown's critical notices, Ernest Marchand has noted his apparent acceptance of the conventional distinction between "history" and "romance." He remarks Brown's dismissal of the classical epic as the product of ages in which "truth was deformed by tradition and credulity" and "invention supplied defects of memory, and embellished events with causes and circumstances, grotesque, miraculous, and incredible."[5] Brown was particularly outraged by the Aeneid's "embellishment of childish chimera's [sic] and vulgar superstitions."[6] But

such attitudes seem incompatible with a state of mind that could produce works of the quality of his romances. In fact, a letter to William Dunlap, November 28, 1794, indicates that he had not always entertained such uncharitable opinions of epic poetry. "National songs," he writes, "strains which have a peculiar relation to the political or religious transactions of the poet's country, seem to be the most precious morsels, which do not require a dissatisfying brevity, nor preclude the most exalted flights of genius, for in this class I rank the Iliad and Eneid, and Orlando" (D,II,92).[7] Brown's prefaces to his romances announce his interest in becoming the singer of "American" deeds,[8] so that the rejection of Homer and Virgil and the formal denial of his own fiction must be regarded as analogous expressions of a fundamental shift in attitude.[9]

An examination of such sketches as **"The Rhapsodist," "Walstein's School of History,"** or the less well known **"Dialogues"** on music and painting reveals the process by which Brown arrives at the conservative position Marchand notes. Simply stated, Brown's problem was how best to reconcile his need to create with a moral distrust of his medium. His solution was to subordinate literature's purely aesthetic elements to an overriding moral purpose; hence, the preference for Xenophon and Tacitus over Homer and Virgil. He could thus appease the imperatives created by his Enlightenment education and Quaker heritage, while covertly indulging his aesthetic tendencies. But the effort to adjust the expression of an essentially Romantic temperament to Enlightenment canons of taste; to satisfy a poetic sensibility in an intensely pragmatic society that tended to regard art as frivolous; and to indulge a rich imagination within personal and cultural contexts that viewed such indulgence as morally suspect finally ended in Brown's imaginative exhaustion.

Brown's attempt to discover a balance between his creative urge and inherited moral and practical concerns begins with his first extended commentary on aesthetic matters, an address written while he was still in his teens to a group of young Philadelphians calling themselves the Belles Lettres Club.[10] The **"Address"** purports to outline the Club's organizing principles and goals. However, beneath the stated theme, Brown can be observed converting an eighteenth-century vision of unity, balance, and harmony into a personal imperative. The Club is "the noblest species of education" because it seeks to gratify "every propensity to enlarge the circle of . . . faculties, of which the human mind is capable" (D,I,22,23). Brown follows the conventional psychology of the period and divides the mind into the faculties of reason, memory, and imagination. Their simultaneous and harmonious satisfaction becomes the Club's stated goal. Reason and fancy are to be reconciled, and belles lettres itself is presented as a branch of learning in which science and art are united. However, Brown also describes the Club as an intellectualist utopia, proclaiming that "The idea of a perfect commonwealth is not the same extravagant thing in education as in politics" (D,I,24). Such a conception of the Club implies the separation of science and art elsewhere, the fragmentation of reason, memory, and imagination in the world outside its privileged precinct.

There exists at the center of Brown's vision of unity, then, a sense of disharmony, and two important digressions in the **"Address"** indirectly point to his personal inability to maintain the union of reason and imagination. The first occurs in his explanation of the relevance of belles lettres to those unaffected by the "native beauty of the liberal arts." He claims that an enlightened pragmatism itself impels them to study; thus, one might "owe the most valuable of intellectual treasure to motives the most sordid and interested" (D,I,25). However, Brown does not characterize this kind of individual, nor does he offer an account of the manner in which the Philistine is to benefit from belles lettres. But when he turns to the fraternity in which he is himself about to enlist, he becomes eloquent and admits that, "To those who testify a relish for such studies, no argument is necessary to attach them still closer to their favourite object" (D,I,25). He then follows with a description of the poetic sensibility:

> Fondly overcome by the bewitching charms of this their favourite pursuit, they become regardless of the voice of reason, and are totally immersed in the soothing pleasures of the intoxicated fancy. . . . Abhorring equally the noise and clamour of the forum, they fly to solitude and silence, to musing, and to contemplation, frequenters of the shade, and accustomed to indulge the airy flights of a fancy vigorous from use, and bold from the absence of restraint, they are equally governed by imaginary inspiration. They turn their eyes from the insipid scene without, and seek a gayer prospect, and visionary happiness in a world of their own creation. (D,I,25)

This passage introduces an unexpected tension into the reasoned discourse of the **"Address."** In mid-paragraph the subject has suddenly and inexplicably shifted from belles lettres to the "enthusiasm of poetry." There is no equivalent passage on the devotees of science or philosophy, with his peculiar joys and liabilities. Thus, even without the biographical detail that points to Brown's own youthful love of solitude and fantasy, the structural and thematic imbalance created by this exclusive focus on the poet suggests a personal urgency.[11]

The passage is framed by two others that point to the basic tensions underlying Brown's commitment to art. A few sentences before in the paragraph he has written, "various accomplishments are requisite to make any single character complete," and he concludes the paragraph with the admonition: "But those who are superior to the strong attraction of their genius, whose imagination is awed and corrected by their judgement, will still preserve an intimate acquaintance with the liberal sciences in their passage through life" (D,I,25-26). Thus, the poet's "enthusiasm," his predilection for solitude and the intoxication of unrestrained fantasy, is framed by evocations of "balance" and "reason." Particularly in the latter quotation, it is as if Brown were warning himself against the temptations of his poetic "genius."

Poetry and imagination must be brought within the purview of reason; thus, just as he followed the conventional division of the mind into reason, memory, and imagination, Brown accepted Blair's division of belles lettres into the study of rhetoric, grammar, and poetry (D,II,27).[12] In both these series the mind is divided between reason and imagination with the middle term serving as a kind of mediator. Memory, for instance, may be regarded as an aspect of reason in so far as both operate on external phenomena; but it also shares the imagination's capacity to figure objects not sensibly present. Similarly, rhetoric as a discipline functions as a logical system, while poetry is language used imaginatively. For Brown, grammar is essentially the process of metaphor, so that, like memory, it occupies the space between the literal and the fantastic.

Brown's discussion of grammar, then, is the second important digression. Even he recognized that it had little to do with the **"Address's"** ostensible purpose (D,I,31); yet, it forms nearly half the entire text, so that its importance is obvious. Brown defines grammar as the "doctrine of signs" and he concludes by exalting it as an aesthetic and epistemological concern:

> Grammar thus abstractly considered, lies within the bounds of pure metaphysics. The language of man is the intercourse of spirits; it is not the feeble and involuntary respirations of pain and pleasure, but the perfect and pathetic picture of every fixed or transient emotion to which his mind is subject. By one happy faculty is man capable of giving form to spirit, and rendering his soul visible to men. The pictures words exhibit are even more perfect than those produced by the hand of nature. (D,I,30)

Language here is not merely a symbolic system referring to an antecedent and objective reality; rather, it is an instrument through which reality is created. Man's language allows him to compete with nature by creating worlds ("pictures") more perfect than her own. Mimetic and communicative functions are subordinated to language's capacity to contain "the intercourse of spirits" or to express man's subjective preoccupations. Brown's notion of language as grammar approaches Romantic theories on the expressive nature of poetry. As has been noted, however, he is unwilling to commit himself. There are always the alternative ideals of proportion and reason. Brown attempts to solve his conceptual dilemma by perceiving poetry as grammar and thereby drawing on the latter's objective, "rational" associations. As **"Walstein's School of History"** will demonstrate, his formal solution assumes the mode of memory.

"The Rhapsodist" (1789) is perhaps the most widely noted of Brown's sketches. The artist-figure here presents a fuller version of the poetic enthusiast outlined in the **"Address,"** and, as such, he necessarily rejects the intellectual and moral equilibrium to which the **"Address"** is formally dedicated. Brown defines the Rhapsodist as "one who delivers the sentiments suggested by the moment in artless and unpremeditated language" (R,5), but almost as an intellectual and psychological reflex he attempts to keep his artist close to the ideal of rational proportion. Brown claims that even while the Rhapsodist "pours forth the effusions of a sprightly fancy, and describes the devious wanderings of a quick but thoughtful mind," he yet avoids both the "giddy raptures of enthusiasm" and the "didactic strains of dull philosophy" (R,5). But, if this figure foregoes "rapture," then wherefore his designation as a Rhapsodist? Brown is wavering between fidelity to his conception of the artist and the need to justify it to his reason. This momentary qualification is inconsistent with the tone and purport of the sketches that make up this series, and Brown himself ends with the observation that the Rhapsodist is noted for "sudden transitions in his subjects, and hasty discussions" (R,5). In short, he is not given to reasoned, temperate discourse. There is little question of intentional technique with this artist's inspired, ecstatic speech, for he has relinquished all notions of a consciously disciplined utterance.

Like the poet of the **"Address,"** the Rhapsodist rejects the "clamour of the forum" and prefers "solitude and silence." Not only is he an "enemy to conversation," but it is in "his fondness for solitude, that the singularity of his character principally consists" (R,6). And as a final element in this artist-personality, Brown writes that "Love and friendship, and all the social passions, are excluded from his bosom" (R,8). The Rhapsodist is thus an alienated artist. Introverted and emotionally frigid, he actively denies the very ties that would qualify his isolation and bind it to the daily life of some community.

The **"Address"** noted the poet's susceptibility to "imaginary inspiration" and his search for a "visionary happiness in a world of [his] own creation" (D,I,25). Similarly, the Rhapsodist's desire for solitude results from a preference for the realm of his imagination. Brown writes that "He loves to converse with beings of his own creation, and every personage, and every scene, is described with a pencil dipt in the colours of imagination" (R,6). Like

God in the void or the garden of Eden, he strides forth creating worlds and endowing the inanimate with life. "To his strong and vivid fancy, there is scarcely a piece of mere unanimated matter existing in the universe. His presence inspires, being, instinct, and reason into every object, real or imagined, and the air, the water and the woods, whereever he directs his steps, are thronged with unnumerable inhabitants" (R,6).

While the **"Address"** offered only the outline of the poetic temperament, **"The Rhapsodist"** is a portrait of the practicing artist and the art he creates. The passage quoted above presents the poet in his Orphic incarnation. He creates his own world; however, it is a universe that exists solely as an expression of its creator. Art as rhapsody becomes a projection of the idiosyncratic imperatives of the artist; it is the objectification of his subjective reality. Another of Brown's artist-figures, the Scribbler, is quite explicit on this point when he exlaims: "What importance does it give, to have one's *idle reveries* clothed in the typographical vesture, multiplied some thousand fold, and dispersed far and wide among the race of readers!" (D,II,271, emphasis mine).

As a heterocosmic projection of the artist, the work of fiction presents a world in which he is immanent. Thus, The Rhapsodist turns his purely expressive art into an elaborate game in which he attempts to compensate for his alienation from conventional reality. After noting the Rhapsodist's contempt for his peers' desire for ordinary success, and his preference for his favorite grotto or chamber where he can indulge an unrestrained subjectivism, Brown offers this significant description of the artist's activities:

> The clamour of the exulting populace, the shouts of tumultuous joy, murmur hoarsely in the wind. But he is at this moment engaged in improving the grandeur of the scene, . . . He contrives a chariot and a train for his hero, worthy the greatness of his exploits, and gives him the dignity and grace of an immortal.—He then pulls down the pageant from his exalted station, strips him of the purple and the crown, turns him loose among the rabble, and *places himself* in the vacant seat; the sudden shout that invaded his ears, does not interrupt the ceremony of the vision, and it only increases the importance of the imaginary conqueror. (R,11, emphasis mine)

The conception of fictional character expressed in this passage is an important key to reading Brown's romances. Protagonists are drawn from a confluence of objective models with the artist's own complex desires, for which they become surrogates. Art not only expresses the artist's deepest concerns but presents a world in which he is directly participant as hero. In another instance, Brown writes directly of himself as an author whose limitations are the necessary consequence when "the scholar makes his own character the comment" (D,I,50). Brown thus insists that he and his art are reflexive, and the result is an inevitable complication of the reading of the relationships among his major characters and between them and their author. If his aesthetics define fictional character as authorial projection, then many of the important oppositions in his romances—Clara Wieland and Carwin, Constantia Dudley and Ormond, Louisa Calvert, Stephen Calvert, and Clelia Neville—turn upon actual or potential identities that find their source in Brown's own complex personality.[13]

More immediately relevant here, however, is Brown's concern with an expressive art's inescapable duplicity. It does not directly reflect its creator. When the Rhapsodist creates characters that are ultimately fictionalized versions of himself, or when the Scribbler defines art as a "typographical vesture" for his "idle reveries," they distort the subjectivity that is their central concern. The image reflected is fragmented and proliferated, or, as the Scribbler claims, "multiplied some thousand fold." Thus, the artist's constant preoccupation with himself is presented obliquely.

This characteristic doubleness is noted in Letter III of **"The Rhapsodist,"** in which Brown, posing as an "anonymous" reader, complains: "First appearances deceive me, more especially in *an author,* who speaks, as it were from behind a curtain. And while he reveals himself to our view only in the most engaging attitudes, may, by the help of his disguise, render the unfavourable parts of his character perfectly secure from the searching eye of curiosity" (R,16-17).[14] The moral suspicion of aesthetic activity expressed here is anticipated in the **"Address,"** where Brown specifically cites the danger of uninhibited fantasy being carried to a "vicious extreme" when not "corrected by a seasonable mixture of philosophical severity" (D,I,26). In so far as the Rhapsodist is the portrait of a sensibility primarily given to fantasy, he cannot be other than morally suspect.

As a portrait of the artist, then, the Rhapsodist represents tendencies with which Brown never felt quite comfortable. He announced "The Rhapsodist" as a series that would be distinguished by its "sincerity" and "truth," and he went on to write: "Wherever I perceive the least inclination to deceive, I suspect a growing depravity of soul, that will one day be productive of the most dangerous consequences. Falsehood and dissimulation, however embellished with the softest colours, and touched with the most sparing and delicate hand, stamp an infamy upon the character hardly to be equalled by the perpetration of the blackest crimes" (R,2). Yet, in the "Letter" quoted above, Brown complained of the author's *characteristic* duplicity and of his art as a "curtain" behind which he hid personal irregularities. In so far as the Rhapsodist's reveries are fictions, they are also deceptions; and we recall that

Brown's villains are master illusionists: Carwin is a ventriloquist, Ormond loves disguises, and Wellbeck is a forger. Brown can thus be seen questioning the moral legitimacy of art and the artist. Finally, however, he is himself the real embellisher here, the deceiver and dissimulator who, more or less consciously, regarded aesthetic behavior as guilty and himself as criminal.[15]

This sense of guilt becomes another element contributing to Brown's conception of the artist's exile from conventional reality. Society inevitably resents his preference for the world of his imagination, so that he is doubly an "outlaw": his isolation results both from his personal foundness for solitude and social hostility. **"The Man at Home"** (1798) expresses this antagonistic relationship between the artist and society. It offers the portrait of the artist's withdrawal into his subjective world and artistic creation when pursued by a hostile world. The protagonist is threatened with imprisonment for debt and escapes to a rented room where he amuses himself with reveries identical to those recognized as descriptions of the artistic process in "The Rhapsodist." Like many of Brown's protagonists, he writes in order to occupy himself in his isolation and to relieve himself of the anxiety inevitably attendant on his fugitive status. He resembles the Rhapsodist, the Scribbler, and Brown himself when he justifies his resort to literature by claiming, "I must, necessarily, in the wildest of my reveries, exhibit my own character" (R,32). In short, he "makes his own character the comment." All the elements of this sketch suggest that his flight from "debt" is more than a simple denial of financial obligation; rather, it represents a profound apostasy from the dominant commercial ethic of the American community. Brown's rejection of a career in law provides a personal background for the fictional portrait.[16] His refusal to play American life according to its basic rules is echoed in the Man at Home's rejection of the same game.

As a convicted debtor and a fugitive, the Man at Home is a criminal, but hidden in his garret he also becomes a writer. The consequent association of crime, imprisonment, and art expresses both Brown's personal dilemma and a major theme in Romantic literature. The artist and the criminal become synonyms. They are alienated from a bourgeois society committed to social and moral utilitarianism. Both those physically imprisoned and the artist, spiritually imprisoned in conventional reality, console themselves with the imagination.[17] Like the Rhapsodist and Brown himself, the Man at Home is fugitive from the conventional "business" of society. All three project themselves as "enemies" of conversation and as alienated from "love and friendship." Thus, although executed under less favorable circumstances, the Man at Home's flight from society duplicates those of the Rhapsodist and the young Brown, and his criminal status illuminates Brown's attitudes towards his own evasion of conventional roles.

Thus far, all of the artist-figures are committed to an expressive exercise of the imagination during moments of radical isolation, so that art appears essentially as an act of meditation. Brown attributes a capacity for visionary experience to the Rhapsodist when he writes, "Others may wander long on the bare outside of the world of spirits, and meet with nothing but prospects discouraging to the eye. But to thee the impenetrable veil is rent, and thou may'st sit at leisure, and survey the universe within" (R,11). However, the Romantic artist's penetration to realms beyond common perception is a standard feature of our conception of the figure. Most interesting here is the complete breakdown in the communicative aspect of art, the failure of a sense of audience. The man at Home confesses, "I write to myself. The pen is not, in this instance, an instrument of communication," and Brown thus apostrophizes the Rhapsodist: "Vain and Fruitless will be thy endeavours, O thou votary of the wayward must! to disclose the beauty of inchanted scenes, and reveal the splendor of her sceret [sic] habitation. To thee alone is it given to visit 'the bottom of this monstrous world' . . ." (R,11,31). Traditionally, the Romantic artist is not merely an aesthetic sensibility, but also a prophet. He returns from the mystical, aesthetic trance with both the vision of a reality superior to the commonplace and some moral consolation or ethical imperatives for others.[18] But the Rhapsodist remains incommunicative, so that his moral ambiguity finds another source in the solipsism to which his speechlessness confines him.

The **"Dialogues"** on music and painting thus become significant as Brown's first indications of exchanging the Rhapsodist for an artist-figure more responsive to external reality, to moral and social obligations. The artist-figure here is a woman, "L," who, in **"On Music,"** begins by repeating the conception of art as a private meditation advanced in **"The Rhapsodist."** When her companion, "R," asks her to play the harpsichord, she replies, "My music, I told you, is an hymn, played alone, at night, and in my chamber. How then can you expect to be an auditor?" (D,II,126). Music, the most expressive of the arts, is presented as an intensely private act not intended as a mediation between the artist and the world. But "L" eventually allows "R" to stand below her window in order to *overhear* her playing. This attitude is suggestive when one considers that Brown's characteristic narrative, the autobiographical memoir, is more soliloquoy than attempted dialogue with an audience. As with the Man at Home, the act of composition is designed primarily as an expression of the narrative personality. Like "R," the reader is reduced from direct participation to eavesdropping or voyeurism.

"L" has a friend who, on returning to Scotland, leaves behind her books, her pictures, and her harpsichord—the intellectual, visual, and aural aspects of art. She is reluctant to accept these gifts because, as she claims, "My father's frugality, if I may call it by the mildest name, would never allow me to retain, merely for the purpose of luxury, or what he deemed such, what would readily bring upwards of an hundred dollars" (D,II,125). What is merely a suggestion in "The Man at Home" thus becomes explicit in these sketches, for "L" is an American artist and her indictments are directed at the American scene. Art is directly opposed by her father's financial pragmatism and, by extension, the commercial habits of her society. There is more than a little contempt in her claim that she could hardly persuade her father to allow her to keep the harpsichord until her friend returned for it or wrote her concerning its disposal. Further, she claims to be a born painter whose technical development has been inhibited by her environment. The absence of paintings of merit in her own home or those of her friends deprived her of an immediate stimulus, while her father's "parsimony" and narrow prejudices denied her "The materials of the painter, colours, pencils and the like, the instructions of an artist, time and tables . . ." (D,II,129).

As a result of this total aesthetic aridity "L" resorts to "marking and analyzing the forms of nature, or in depicting imaginary scenes in which these forms, without the pencil's aid, were newly combined and arranged" (D,II,129). The artist's alienation also partially results from his aesthetic frustration by his milieu. The inadequacy of the paternal home for aesthetic culture and the absence of the technical means for aesthetic education lead to a retreat to nature or back upon himself in his attempt to create art. The problem of a sensibility struggling with traditions that reject its natural modes of expression is complicated by a specific national idiosyncrasy: the total dominance of commercial and pragmatic values, and a special landscape denuded of art objects. **"On Painting"** responds to this dilemma with the dream that has haunted generations of American artists stranded in their prosaic native land: the flight to Europe and aesthetic fulfillment.[19] "L" escapes the deprivations of her father's house and goes to London where she first becomes a painter, then aspires to authorship.

The most important effect of these companion pieces on the arts, however, is to discredit them as literature's aesthetic rivals. Music is attacked and dismissed by "L," who concludes that "Ignorance of nature or science, sensuality, caprice, and folly, are all consistent with musical skill." She insists that the "time requisite to make a skillfull performer, duty requires us to employ in a better manner." When questioned about her own dabbling in the art, she declares that it is useful for soothing the weak minds of others but that serious intelligence should not mistake it for real achievement.

Similarly, painting is regarded as inferior to literature. "L" not only disclaims her ability to imitate nature's physical wonders but finally asserts: "How many structures of poets and philosophers may be examined in the time mis-devoted to a picture" (D,II,123,137).

"L" resembles the Rhapsodist with her self-admitted incapacity for intellectual discipline and preference for her own imagined worlds. But she rejects music, the artistic form most compatible with her temperament, and is dissatisfied with painting. She arrives at her preference for literature because she specifically desires "intellectual and moral occupation," and she laments the "folly" and "guilt" of her misguided neglect of "poets, historians, and philosophers" (D,II,134). Brown is still warning himself against his "genius" in these sketches. Reason and morality are evoked as a necessary accompaniment of "art," just as these same values were called upon to chasten the poetic enthusiast of the **"Address."** Literature permits the stabilizing intrusion of moral purpose into the aesthetic experience; thus, it balances between music's expressionism and the eighteenth-century conception of painting as mimesis.

"Walstein's School of History" (1799), then, attempts the definition of a fictional form that would satisfy "L's" notion of the nature and function of literature, a form that would mediate between the dangerously fantastic and the confiningly literal. Walstein is the guiding spirit of a group of artists whose works directly address society's fundamental concerns. His pupil, Engel, writes the biography of one Olivo Ronsica, whose story rehearses the plot of **Arthur Mervyn,** Part I. Thus, Engel is Brown's surrogate, and his teacher, Walstein, is Brown's own master spirit.

Walstein writes the histories of Portugal's Marquês de Pombal and of Brown's favorite classical author, Cicero. When compared with conventional histories, these works reveal "a deeper insight into human nature, a more accurate acquaintance with the facts, more concreteness of arrangement, and a deeper concern in the progress and issue of the story" (R,149). This concern with detail, plots, and endings are aesthetic considerations more directly relevant to fiction than to history. When its pronounced psychological interests are also taken into account, the characteristics of the Walstein school accurately describe Brown's romances. This endorsement of history as a specifically "literary" genre rather than as a branch of philosophy is contemporaneous with Brown's preference for Tacitus over Virgil. The review of Southey's *Joan of Arc* in which he dismisses poetry in favor of history was published in the June, 1799, issue of the *Monthly Magazine.* "Walstein" appeared in two parts in the August and Fall issues of the same year. Thus, the sketch may be read as a conscious dramatization of the aesthetic opinions expressed in the review.

The unconventional histories of Walstein and Engel attempt "to illuminate the understanding, to charm curiosity, and sway the passions" (R,148). To this end, "a certain licence of invention" is permitted, so that Walstein's "imaginary history" of Cicero becomes identical with what Brown labels Richardson's "fictitious history," *Clarissa* (R,149,152). Brown's critical vocabulary here depends on eighteenth-century conventions. His notion of the novel as history is but an episode in the traditional conflict between the genre's empirical claims and its fictional content.[20] From its inception, the novel has attempted to present itself as morally significant fact: the preface to *Robinson Crusoe* (1719) announces the tale's "religious Application" and "Instruction," and that "The Editor believes the thing to be a just History of Fact; neither is there any Appearance of Fiction in it"—and although Prévost's famous story is a self-admitted romance, it too pretends to moral significance and is presented as *L'Histoire du chevalier des Grieux et de Manon Lescaut* (1733).[21] Within this general context, however, Brown's use of the term "history" acquires a personal urgency; it is a code word for the kind of biographical (or autobiographical) mode he preferred for his own fiction. Thus, whenever historians appear in his work-and nearly all his major characters play this role at least once—the reader must be aware that "history" is a euphemism for the novelist's art and that the historian-character is, on one level, a portrait of the Brownian artist.

The novel as history focuses on the social context: the real subject of Walstein and Engel is the social welfare, their ultimate goal is the improvement of mankind. Brown writes that "Human society is powerfully modified by individual members," and the Advertisement to **Skywalk** proclaims, "The world is governed, not by the simpleton, but by the man of soaring passions and intellectual energy" (R,147,136). Thus, the question of social good and evil is reduced to the selection of the most effective arena for personal action. "Genius" and "virtue" may work for society, "first, by assailing popular errors and vices, argumentatively and through the medium of books; secondly, by employing legal or ministerial authority to this end" (R,150). Cicero and Pombal were preeminently public men operating in the realm of "legal or ministerial authority," and Brown concludes that "Their fate may evince the insufficiency of the instrument chosen by them, and teach us, that a change of national opinion is the necessary prerequisite of revolutions" (R,150). The case is different, however, with literature, for the author manipulates the subjective sources of all action: "The affections are engaged, the reason is won by incessant attacks," and vague abstractions "exchange the fleeting, misty, and dubious form of inference, for a sensible and present existence" (R,151).

At this point, **"Walstein"** can be seen as an attempt to create a space for the artist in a society preoccupied with business and politics. The scene in which the Rhapsodist replaces his fictional character with himself is a conqueror's triumph, where this profoundly alienated figure imagines himself in a public role. "He swells with transport," Brown writes, "at this new instance of his countrymens [sic] applause, for such, in this monetary paroxism [sic] of his frenzy, he imagines it to be" (R,11). However, as the molders of national consciousness, Walstein and Engel enter directly into the public domain. They escape the solipsistic "frenzy" of their own imaginations to become a part of the social reality.

The works of the Walstein school are the artist's acts of conscious rivalry with, and triumph over, the more obvious agents of history.[22] By questioning the efficacy of Cicero and Pombal, Brown rejected the adequacy of merely public action and indirectly challenged the entire legalistic endeavor of the architects of the American state. Engel is advanced as the real effector of revolutions: he believes that "the narration of public events" is the "most efficacious of moral instruments" (R,150). Brown dramatizes the consciousness-forming role of literature as propaganda in his fictional history of the kingdom of Carsol. The reformer-prince Arthur I first gains control of a papal calendar, which, distributed among the people, is a major source of the Church's power in the kingdom. He then has a book written, *Carsola Restaurata,* directed at those "who possessed the influence resulting from rank, office, riches, and profession" (D,I,184). Through specific literatures directed at the peculiar needs of a mass and an elite audience, Arthur wins public opinion away from the Catholic church and enlists it in his own schemes. Brown seems to have intuited the immense power wielded by the creators of public myth and the manipulators of public communications. Walstein and Engel are prototypes of Whitman's divine literatus and even of the twentieth century's masters of public opinion.[23]

"Walstein," then, responds directly to Brown's conception of the intellectual, moral, and humanistic demands of the period. The devotion of Walstein and Engel to an art in which the purely aesthetic elements are conditioned by obligations to objective fact or the necessities of larger moral considerations is far removed from the Rhapsodist's journey toward the imagination's incommunicable vision. Brown's evocation of "history" is an ultimate attempt to present his creative urge as an endorsable activity. History is the literary equivalent of memory, and just as that faculty partakes of both reason and imagination, history (as described by Brown) occupies the space between philosophy and poetry. It thus becomes another of his terms of mediation; like memory, grammar, or literature itself, it provides a point of balance between the logical and imaginative functions of the mind.

Although Brown's eighteenth-century rhetoric of proportion is sincere, he is also creating a smokescreen for his poetic tendencies. Grammar and history are but his rationalist terms for metaphor, symbol, and the novel. Thus, the sketches discussed in this essay point to a deeper source than the oft-cited haste in composition and failure to revise for the fragmentation and inconsistency that mar even his best work. The characteristic movement of Brown's narratives is toward the control and rejection of imaginative experience: Carwin, Ormond, Wellbeck, and Calvert are each committed to the aesthetic vice of creating illusion, and they are either killed or forced to repent their deceptions. Between the letter to his brother, James, written in 1800, in which he laments the inability of an American writer to earn a living (D,II,100), and the recantation published in 1803, stand his last novels, *Jane Talbot* and *Clara Howard,* both published in 1801. They present protagonists who relinquish lives of imaginative and aesthetic indulgence for marriage and conventional existences. That Brown himself was contemplating marriage at this time and redirecting his career toward the more conventional role of magazine publisher suggests the extent to which the final novels stand as palinodes to his earlier creative effort.

Brown, finally, was fatally ambivalent about his vocation. Committed by culture and education to reason, he was attracted to but distrusted the imagination. The sketches addressed here are often clumsy and inexpert, but even their technical problems bare Brown's struggle to reconcile the various aspects of his personality. These sketches also help us to perceive Brown's rejection of the novelist's trade and repudiation of his fiction as something more than an extreme fit of pique at his failure to achieve popular acclaim and financial success. Fame and money might have forestalled his drastic move, but the seeds of Brown's action were present in his earliest remarks on art. From a youth who dreamed of writing epic poems on the adventure of man in America, he developed into an author who rejected poetry in favor of history on the basis of a supposed moral disparity between the two genres. But those novels written after **"Walstein,"** which dramatize the artist's compromise with convention, possess none of the imaginative power and commitment that raise his major romances above their many technical flaws. For Brown, the movement from his Romantic conception of the artist as Rhapsodist to the more conservatively neo-classic figure of the novelist as historian was the move toward artistic silence.

Notes

[1] Paul Witherington, for instance, regards the "inconsistencies" of character and narrative structure of which Brown's novels are almost universally accused as "aesthetic gambits." And in an essay that reads *Edgar Huntly* as "a surprisingly modern work in its self-conscious attack on the very assumptions and structures

and language that fiction makes possible," he concludes with the refreshing suggestion that "We should now grant Brown the license he claimed as an experimental novelist, and we should slip him some of the linguistic affection we currently lavish on Melville and John Barth." See his "'Not My Tongue Only': Brown's *Edgar Huntly*," in *Critical Essays on Charles Brockden Brown*, ed. Bernard Rosenthal (Boston: G. K. Hall, 1981), pp. 164-83. For further notation of the essentially metafictional concerns of Brown's fiction, see Michael Davitt Bell, "'The Double-Tongued Deceiver': Sincerity and Duplicity in the Novels of Charles Brockden Brown," *Early American Literature*, 9 (Fall, 1974), 150-51. And Mark Seltzer, "Saying Makes It So: Language and Event in Brown's *Wieland*," *Early American Literature*, 13 (Spring, 1979), 81-91.

[2] In "A Minority Reading of *Wieland*," Nina Baym accuses Brown of a fundamental "failure of seriousness" that renders his first published novel hardly more valuable than the work of Rowson, Foster, or William Hill Brown. See *Critical Essays*, pp. 87-107.

[3] See, particularly, his chapter on Brown in his *The Development of American Romance: The Sacrifice of Relation* (Chicago: Univ. of Chicago Press, 1980), pp. 40-61. See also Paul Witherington, "Benevolence and the 'Utmost Sketch': Charles Brockden Brown's Narrative Dilemma," *Criticism*, 14 (1972), 175-91.

[4] *Critical Essays*, p. 87.

[5] Ernest Marchand, "The Literary Opinions of Charles Brockden Brown," *Studies in Philology*, 31 (1934), 541-46. Marchand quotes here from Brown's review of Southey's *Joan of Arc* in his *Monthly Magazine, and American Review*, I (June, 1799), 311-21. Although there are several outstanding studies of Brown's literary technique in specific instances, Marchand's is perhaps the only attempt to describe the particular aesthetics that lead to those techniques.

[6] Brown, loc. cit.

[7] Brown's works cited here will be found either in Dunlap's *The Life of Charles Brockden Brown: together with Selections from the Rarest of His Printed Works, from His Original Letters, and from His Manuscripts Before Unpublished* (Philadelphia: James P. Parke, 1815) designated in the text by "D" followed by volume numeral and page number, or *The Rhapsodist and Other Uncollected Writings by Charles Brockden Brown*, ed. Harry R. Warfel (New York: Scholars' Facsimiles and Reprints, 1943), designated by "R" and page number.

[8] Dunlap recounts Brown's youthful outlines of poems on Columbus's discovery of America and the conquests of Mexico and Peru by the Spanish. In the Advertisement for the unpublished *Skywalk*, Brown claimed that he "who paints, not from books, but from nature, who introduces those lines and hues in which we differ, rather than those in which we resemble our kindred nations beyond the ocean, may lay some claim to the patronage of his countrymen" (R,136). And in the Preface to *Edgar Huntly*, he writes that his purpose is to "exhibit a series of adventures, growing out of the conditions of our country." *Edgar Huntly* (Philadelphia: M. Pollock, 1857), p. 3.

[9] In the Advertisement to the *Literary Magazine and American Register*, reprinted in Dunlap, Brown writes, "I have written much, but take much blame to myself for something which I have written, and take no praise for any thing, I should enjoy a greater share of my own respect, at the present moment, if nothing had ever flowed from my pen, the production of which could be traced to me" (D,II,60).

[10] David Lee Clark lists the members of this club as William Wood Wilkins, Timothy Paxon, Zaccariah Poulson, Jr., Joseph Bringhurst, John Davidson, and a Dr. Minor. See his *Charles Brockden Brown: Pioneer Voice of America* (Durham, NC: Duke Univ. Press, 1952), p. 42.

[11] For Brown's early development of the habit of solitude, see Dunlap, I, pp. 12-14, 40-41. Further, Dunlap writes that for a large portion of his life Brown "loathed the common pursuits and common topics of men, and appeared in society an eccentric, if not an isolated being" (D,I,17).

[12] Brown specifically notes Hugh Blair's *Lectures On Rhetoric and Belles Lettres* (London, 1783). Although Brown's neat divisions do not seem to be a central feature of Blair's work, Brown is probably referring to his broad discussions of the history and nature of language and its uses in speaking and in writing. Blair's Lecture VIII is entitled "Structure of Language" and begins with an exaltation and discussion of grammar.

[13] It is not unusual for an author's psychic conflicts to be projected in his literature as the dramatic conflict of differentiated character. The figure of the *Doppelgänger* is one of the Romantic contributions to fiction resulting from this very process. For an informative study of the process, see Robert Rogers, *A Psychoanalytic Study of the Double in Literature* (Detroit: Wayne State Univ. Press, 1970). For good discussions of the doubling of scene, structure, and character in Brown's work, and the origin of his protagonists in his own personality, see William Hedges, "Charles Brockden Brown and the Culture of Contradictions," *Early American Literature*, 9 (Fall, 1974), 114, and William J. Scheik, "The Problem of Origination in Brown's *Ormond*," *Critical Essays*, 132-33.

[14] Nathaniel Hawthorne, one of Brown's more important admirers and heirs, turns this complex hide-and-seek between author and audience into a major theme. The Rhapsodist's "curtain" becomes the "veil" as a symbol of all forms of artistic duplicity. In "The Old Manse," Hawthorne writes directly of himself, "So far as I am a man of really individual attributes, I veil my face." *The Centenary Edition of the Works of Nathaniel Hawthorne,* ed. William Charvat and others (Columbus: Ohio Univ. Press, 1963), X, p. 33.

[15] Brown's concern with the moral nature of literature finds a source in general eighteenth-century linguistic and aesthetic theories. Edmund Burke's *The Sublime and the Beautiful* located the source of Beauty in those softer, indulgent human qualities that are the very opposite of the stronger virtues on which morality depends. Further, he describes the language of poetry as essentially the falsification of external reality; its primary focus is the subjective reaction of the audience. *The Works of the Right Honorable Edmund Burke* (Boston: Little, Brown, and Company, 1871), I, pp. 188-89, 257-58. For studies of the particularly anti-fictional attitudes in England and America, see W. F. Gallaway, Jr., "The Conservative Attitude toward Fiction, 1770-1830," *PMLA,* 55 (December, 1940), 1041-59, and Harrison G. Orians, "Censure of Fiction in American Romances and Magazines, 1789-1810," *PMLA,* 52 (March, 1937), 195-214.

[16] Dunlap accuses Brown of "indulging in every freak, suggested by his love of literature and fame" and of incarnating his own fictional Rhapsodist while he was ostensibly studying law with Alexander Wilcox. He then recounts Brown's explanations for rejecting the legal profession, which he regarded as committed to a tissue of falsehood and injustice (D,I,16-17; 40-48).

[17] Xavier de Maistre's *Voyage autour de ma chambre* (1795), a work that may have influenced Brown's dialogues on music and painting, explicitly addresses the Romantic themes of physical imprisonment and imaginative liberation, and the anti-imaginative nature of conventional society. On the eve of being freed from his room, the narrator apostrophizes the imagination as a solace for a harsh external reality: "Charmant pays de l'imagination, toi que l'Être bienfaisant par excellence a livré aux hommes pour les consoler de la réalité, il faut que je te quitte" ["Delightful realm of Imagination, which the benevolent being has bestowed upon man to console him for the disappointments he meets in real life, I must quit thee"]. He laments his newly-awarded physical freedom as a rediscovered subjugation to conventional norms ("les affaires," "la bienseance et le devoir" ["office," "politeness and duty"]), and he ends by wishing for "quelque deesse capricieuse" ["some capricious goddess"] to liberate

him from his new captivity. (Paris: Robert Laffont, 1959), p. 73, trans. Henry Attwell (London: Chatto and Windus, 1883), pp. 134, 135.

[18] In the great Romantic apologies for art, the artist invariably appears as a kind of prophet. In Wordsworth's Preface to *Lyrical Ballads* (1800) the poet is a "man speaking to men"; in Shelley's "A Defence of Poetry" he is the "unacknowledged legislator of mankind"; and in Whitman's "Democratic Vistas" he emerges as the "divine literatus" leading men to realms of fulfilled being.

[19] For a brief note on Brown's explicit interest in the fictional possiblities of the international theme later to be exploited by Henry James, see Charles E. Bennett, "Charles Brockden Brown and the International Novel," *Studies in the Novel,* 11 (Spring, 1980), 62-64.

[20] See John Halperin, "Theory of the Novel: A Critical Introduction," in *The Theory of the Novel: New Essays,* ed. John Halperin (New York: Oxford Univ. Press, 1974), pp. 3-18, and the anthology of eighteenth-century prefaces and introductions, *Novel and Romance, 1700-1800: A Documentary Record,* ed. Ioan Williams (New York: Barnes & Noble, 1970).

[21] Daniel Defoe, *Robinson Crusoe,* ed. Michael Shinagel, Norton Critical Editions (New York: W. W. Norton & Company, 1975), p. 3, and Antoine-Francois Prevost d'Exiles, *L'Histoire de Chevalier des Grieux et de Manon Lescaut* (Paris: Garnier-Flammarion, 1967), pp. 29-31.

[22] In "The Symbolism of Literary Alienation," Lewis P. Simpson studies the progressive marginalization of the American writer as the failure of the "republic of letters" that had dominated polity throughout the eighteenth century. It is in such terms that "Walstein" represents a reassertion of the man of letters' claim to social and political preeminence. See Simpson, *The Brazen Face of History: Studies in the Literary Consciousness in America* (Baton Rouge: Louisiana State Univ. Press, 1980), pp. 23-48, *passim.*

[23] In the essay noted above, Simpson observes the American replacement of traditional community structured around Church and state through hierarchy, custom, and ritual with consciousness, public opinion. And in another essay in the collection, "The Printer as American Man of Letters," he notes "an active politics of literacy" which, rather than an attempt to disseminate reading among a large populace, was actually "The quest . . . for a moral government of the world by men of letters." Walstein and Engel are thus Brown's response to the shift of power away from traditional centers of authority to those able to sway and control the public mind. See Simpson, *The Brazen Face of History,* pp. 3-45, *passim.*

Steven Watts (essay date 1994)

SOURCE: "The Writer as Bourgeois Moralist," in *The Romance of Real Life: Charles Brockden Brown and the Origins of American Culture*, The Johns Hopkins University Press, 1994, pp. 131-63.

[*In the following essay, Watts purports that Brown's last two novels,* Clara Howard *and* Jane Talbot, *mark Brown's transition from the radicalism of his earlier novels to the middle-class, moralistic stance of his later essays and journalistic endeavors. Watts argues that in both* Clara Howard *and* Jane Talbot, *Brown uses "sentimental strategies and domestic devices" to present his belief that success and happiness can be achieved through a balance of male ambition and female self-restraint.*]

On or about April 1800 Charles Brockden Brown changed. In a despondent letter to his brother James, the young author confessed that "gloominess and out-of-nature incidents" had tainted his early novels. The time had come, he wearily admitted, "for dropping the doleful tone and assuming a cheerful one, or at least substituting moral causes and daily incidents in place of the prodigious or the singular. I shall not fall hereafter into that strain. Book-making, as you observe, is the dullest of all trades, and the utmost that any American can look for in his native country is to be reimbursed his unavoidable expenses." This rather sullen, forlorn admission seemed to belie the upward trajectory of Brown's literary endeavors. The burst of novel writing over the previous few years had fulfilled his literary agenda, focused his radical social criticism, and relieved his intense adolescent build-up of psychological pressure. The result had been a quartet of brilliant, wild, complex fictions that would elicit much critical commentary over the next few decades. The Philadelphian seemed poised at the threshold of a distinguished literary career, prepared to become, perhaps, America's first entry into the pantheon of great writers in the early modern Atlantic world.[1]

Brown's efforts as a professional writer, however, began to collapse almost as quickly as they had accelerated. His novels sold poorly, and this failure sapped both emotional and financial reserves. The inexorable forces of marketplace individualism in the expanding republic—the very forces Brown had confronted and struggled with in his fiction—seem to have cornered him by the end of the century. Economic success as a writer depended on sales, which in turn demanded popularity. Both of these eluded Brown. Moreover, by 1800 the struggling author's growing desire for a wife, children, and family stability lent even greater urgency to his plight. Genteel poverty, if an acceptable condition for an unmarried and aspiring author, offered no attraction to any respectable young woman.

Thus, by the early nineteenth century, Brown began a significant retrenchment in his life. While earlier pressures of career choice, parental expectations, and emotional upheaval had produced the decision to become a professional writer, a gradual erosion of those hopes now led to a second transformation. Brown began a withdrawal from the literary scene. He took one more half-hearted stab at fiction writing with two domestic novels that seemed deliberately aimed at a popular audience. As this literary endeavor fell flat, he bitterly rejected fiction altogether—at least for the public—and moved in different directions. Brown became involved with his family's mercantile business, married the daughter of a Philadelphia minister, and became a father. In addition, he entered the world of journalism as editor of, successively, three journals of letters and opinion in his native city. In the process, this intense intellectual began to formulate an important new public role: cultural critic and defender of bourgeois values.

Pulling back from radical social criticism, moving away from the breathtaking possibilities of the new novel genre, settling into the routine of family and business life, by 1805 Brown had remade himself once again. He negotiated an uneasy peace with America's expanding market society, and with himself as well, and engaged in a process of cultural and political redefinition. With his customary emotional cycle of fits and starts, deep doubts and utopian enthusiasm, Brown began to reposition himself as a bourgeois moralist in an ascending culture of capitalism. Hints of this dynamic change came in a final, futile attempt at novel writing. Connecting the personal upheaval and creativity of the 1790s with the moral consolidations of the new century, Brown's last two books of fiction built a cultural bridge to the future.

I

Charles Brockden Brown's final pair of published novels offered an obvious contrast to his earlier efforts. Their titles (**Clara Howard** and **Jane Talbot**) indicated a decided shift of gender sensibility away from the male-titled and dominated books of the 1790s. Their content, however, revealed this to be but one part of a broader literary and cultural change. As stories of domestic maneuver in which virtuous, morally willful female characters tamed restless, morally adrift males, these texts fulfilled their author's new determination to abandon "prodigious," "gloomy," and "singular" themes. Yet these works were much more than sentimental, didactic tales cynically aimed at a popular audience, as many critics have long believed. Instead, these domestic novels explored, in fairly complex fashion, the cultural and ideological dimension of Brown's early nineteenth-century adjustment. The author may have utilized the sentimental form in an attempt to sell books, but that form became the vehicle for a more profound reconsideration of American values. These books answered many of the why's and wherefore's of Brown's retreat from radicalism and embrace of bourgeois moralism.[2]

While a certain amount of overlap probably occurred, *Clara Howard* seems to have been written before its counterpart. Likely begun in the late summer of 1800 and finished in the spring of the following year, the novel was published in June 1801.[3] The highly sentimental plot revolved around the romantic and moral entanglements of three primary characters: Edward Hartley, Mary Wilmot, and Clara Howard. Initially, the focus of this epistolary novel fell on Edward, a poor rural boy who had been befriended and tutored by an English gentleman named Mr. Howard. When Howard departed rather suddenly for Europe, his young protégé headed for the city to become a watchmaker's apprentice and begin the climb to social respectability. At this point romance entered the picture. Shortly after his arrival, Edward met Mary Wilmot, a plain young woman almost ten years his elder whose once-wealthy family had fallen into decline. Mary now supported herself and her brother by working as a seamstress, and she fell in love with her new acquaintance. Edward did not reciprocate Mary's love, but considered marriage because of her virtue. He grew more attracted to matrimony, however, when the young woman unexpectedly inherited $5,000. Edward and Mary agreed to wed after a six-month waiting period. In the meantime, Howard surprised everyone by returnign to America with a wife and lovely stepdaughter, Clara. At the same time, a man named Morton suddenly appeared and claimed Mary's inheritance.

Here the novel's narrative became mired in a swamp of complexity. Edward entered Howard's household, was treated as a son, and rapidly became infatuated with the beautiful Clara. Mary, believing that her inheritance was lost and that Edward should not enter a loveless marriage with her, fled the city in the company of friends. When an explanatory letter to her fiancé was misplaced, her disappearance seemed final. At this point, Clara Howard moved to center stage. Although she had fallen in love with Edward, her sense of self-sacrifice proved more powerful. She demanded that her suitor find Mary and wed her, even offering half her fortune to support the match. Edward, forced to marry a woman he did not love by the one he did, dutifully set off in search of Mary. Before finding her, however, he fell ill with a near-fatal fever and the saintly Clara rescinded his banishment. The overjoyed young man revived and departed to make his peace with his former fiancée. The narrative now offered its central, if rather stilted, moral dilemma. After accidentally meeting Mary, Clara insisted once again that Edward marry the older woman. Mary, in the meantime, had fallen in love with a Mr. Sedley, and thus rejected her previous suitor's proposal. Caught in the middle of a tortuous situation in which neither woman seemed to want him, a despairing Edward left the city for life in the wilderness. Again he fell ill, and letters reached him which finally resolved the situation. Mary informed him of her intent to marry Sedley, a move that allowed Clara to drop her opposition and declare her love for Edward. The novel ended with plans in motion for both weddings.

Without doubt, *Clara Howard* was the weakest of all Brown's novels. As critics have observed, the tale liberally borrowed many incidents and situations from the author's earlier works. Its moral situations were contrived, its characters stereotyped and artificial, and its language heavy with overwrought sentimentalism. In terms of literary merit, the book represented a long step backward for Brown. Even with these defects, however, *Clara Howard* contained much of interest for students of early American national culture. Buried beneath the vapid prose and inane plot lay certain ideological and cultural treasures that revealed a great deal about Brown himself and the transforming era in which he wrote. With its self-conscious rendering of gender and morality, and its ongoing juxtaposition of romantic love and utilitarian profit, the novel illuminated certain aspects of the consolidating capitalist culture that its author was coming to embrace. This appeared especially in Brown's central trio of characters.

Edward Hartley, the driving force early in the novel, presented an intriguing portrait of aspiring individualism. His self-description in the book's opening epistle introduced the whole story as a variant on the Franklinian success tale:

> You once knew me as a simple lad, plying the file and tweezers at the bench of a watchmaker, with no prospect before me. . . . I was sprung from obscurity, destitute of property, of parents, of paternal friends; was full of that rustic diffidence, that inveterate humility, which are alone sufficient to divert from us the stream of fortune's favor.

> Such was I three years ago! Now am I rich, happy, crowned with every terrestrial felicity.

Underlining this theme throughout the text, Edward frequently denounced his own rural origins and their quietistic traditions. When his early benefactor, Mr. Howard, urged him to appreciate the dignified integrity of the farmer's life, the young man scoffed. "The rustic life was wholly unsuitable to my temper and taste," he recalled, as the prospect of status and money lured him to the city. Edward admitted that wealth and social position awed him with their "mysterious elevation." Even the friendship of the Howards fired his ambition, as the personal attention "from beings invested with such dazzling superiority, almost intoxicated my senses." In fact, midway through the novel Edward affirmed a dictum—"to retain humility and probity in spite of riches, and to effect the highest good of ourselves and others, by the use of them"—which epitomized his ambitious social creed.[4]

Mary Wilmot provided a study in contrast. In Brown's hands, she became a moral counterweight to the impetuous, aspiring Edward. Nine years older than the young man from the country and full of benevolence, she attracted his intense admiration. Mary fell in love with Edward, but slowly realized that his affection contained no passion. Thus, she refused to accept Edward's dutiful offer of marriage, and sacrificed her contentment to his. As she explained to him, "I sought your happiness. To be the author of it was an object of inexpressible longings. To be happy without you was impossible, but the misery of loneliness, however great, was less than that of being the spectator of your misery, or . . . defrauding you of the felicity attending marriage with a woman whom you could truly love." True to sentimental forms, Mary's nobility took a severe toll on her physical well-being. Emaciated and drained from her moral endeavors, she felt the steady "progress of death" and believed that "every hour accelerates my decay" (p. 16).

Even the virtues of Mary Wilmot, however, paled before those of the novel's namesake, Clara Howard. Combining the older woman's selflessness with a strength of will entirely her own, she was an apostle of self-denial. Denouncing "selfish regards" and "selfish gratification," she insisted that one should derive "more satisfaction from disinterested than selfish conduct." As part of her firm moral code, Clara also rejected mere "sensuality" and placed the material pleasures of wealth and status far back in the rank of values. "Have I not known, from infancy the pleasures of affluence and homage? Cannot I conceive the mortifications to one thus bred up, of poverty and labour?" she exclaimed to Edward. Nonetheless, she made clear her intent to sacrifice such comforts if necessary. Clara's willingness to give up the man she loved seemed to transcend a utilitarian calculus of pleasure and pain, gain and loss. She tried to explain to a puzzled Edward that his despondency reflected

> an heart incapable of perceiving the possibility of sacrificing my own personal gratification to that of another, and of deriving, from that very sacrifice, a purer and more lasting felicity. It shews you unable to comprehend that the welfare of another may demand self-denial from us, and that in bestowing benefits on others, there is a purer delight than in gratifications merely selfish and exclusive. (pp. 71-72, 77-78, 20, 24)

Brown's three primary characters in *Clara Howard* created a fascinating configuration of gender and ide-

ology. Edward suggested that men threatened to become victims of the very social instincts that drove them to success. Lashing out against moral restraints that curbed his passions—"It is the system of nature that deserves my hatred and my curses; that system which makes our very virtues instrumental to our misery"—he acknowledged their validity and his own depravity. Ashamed of his "peasant" background and filled with "self-contempt and humiliation which pertain to that condition," he sought the "confidence and self-respect" that accrued to wealth and social advancement. Such striving produced great ambivalence, however, and Edward frequently chastised himself as a "mere earthworm" and an "obscure clown." In his bitter words, "all my desires are the instigators of guilt, and all my pleasures those of iniquity." Near the end of the novel, he had become so frustrated that he threatened to flee into the wilderness and "make myself akin to savages and tigers, and forget that I was once a man" (pp. 18, 53, 55, 112, 134).

Edward's personal incoherence eventually produced a clear result. He became a moral cripple desperately searching for healing and guidance. Clara Howard happily obliged. Even though in love with the young man, she upbraided Edward for his "cowardly and ignoble designs" in abandoning Mary and warned of the folly attending his greed: "Thou art fiery and impetuous, my friend. Thy spirit is not curbed by reason. There is no outrage or discretion—no crime against thyself—into which thy headlong spirit may not hurry thee." For his part, Edward humbly, even gratefully, submitted to Clara's moral dictations. Calling her "an angel" and his "heavenly monitor," he surrendered with the declaration, "Clara, thou hast conquered me." Even more important, he credited the young woman with healing his inner confusion and putting him on the path to virtue. "I am now master of my actions and thoughts," Edward told her, "and will steadily direct them to a single purpose" (pp. 21, 26, 90, 144, 22).

The force of Clara Howard's benevolence took on another important dimension in Brown's novel. Her task as moral lion-tamer broadened to include women as a group and emerged as a gendered cultural prerogative. By the end of *Clara Howard,* a sisterhood of moral teachers had arisen to dominate the text. For instance, Mary and Clara explicitly joined forces to guide Edward down the correct course of virtue. Only after consulting Mary was Clara prepared to wed Edward and heed "the sweet voice of an approving conscience." For her part, Mary reciprocated by telling her new female friend, "I exult that my feelings are akin to yours, and that it is in my power to vie with you in generosity." As if to underline their sisterhood, Brown disclosed that the two female protagonists were distantly related to one another as second cousins. Most important, perhaps, both women made clear to Edward the goal of this female crusade: moral authority. Near the end of the novel, Mary warned Edward: "Your Clara, the noblest of women, joins me in recalling you . . . to virtue and felicity." Clara put the matter more bluntly. As she told the young man, his "worldly knowledge and acumen may be greater, but in moral discernment much art thou still deficient; here I claim to be more than equal." In the face of this formidable female phalanx, Edward could only retreat while meekly acknowledging that Mary and Clara had rescued him from "disease," "anxiety," and "melancholy," a condition that had made him "half-crazy, shivering and glowing by turns" (pp. 141, 131-32, 96-97, 143, 147, 145).

Thus, *Clara Howard*'s stilted form belied the intriguing cultural content within. Adopting sentimental literary conventions, Brown depicted a male-dominated public ambition harmonizing with female-dominated private self-restraint. Success, wealth, and happiness resulted for everyone: Clara and Edward wed riches and benevolence, while Mary did likewise in agreeing to marry the affluent businessman, Mr. Sedley. So Brown's first fictional foray after his passionate efforts of the 1790s, while doing little for his pocketbook and even less for his literary reputation, represented a critical stage in his ideological development. Distancing himself from the political and cultural radicalism of earlier books like *Alcuin* and *Arthur Mervyn*, the author moved decisively toward the moral consolidations of bourgeois society in early nineteenth-century America.

Jane Talbot, a Novel took an even longer step in the same direction. Although conceived by Brown as a more dramatic moral battleground—here a knot of seduction, religion, and money replaced *Clara Howard*'s rather insipid moral benevolence as the main theme—the story resonated with similar cultural overtones. The Philadelphian's second domestic novel had been started probably in early 1801, set aside while *Clara Howard* was rushed to completion and publication, and then resumed in the late summer of that same year. Finished sometime in the fall, the book finally appeared from a Philadelphia press in December 1801. Even though the novel would see an 1804 publication in England, it received scant critical notice and its sales remained quite low. Once again, however, *Jane Talbot*'s sentimental strategies and domestic devices disguised its important cultural content.[5]

The plot of *Jane Talbot* concerned the frustrated love affair of the novel's heroine, a young widow, and Henry Colden, a Godwinian radical. While deeply in love and determined to marry, these two characters found their plans thwarted by Mrs. Fielder, Jane's strong-willed, adoptive mother, and by Henry's father. The resistance flowed from a combination of political, religious, and moral issues. Mrs. Fielder, Jane's mentor and guardian, grew outraged when informed of Henry's religious skepticism, moral rationalism, and political nonconformity. To make matters even worse, she grew convinced that this profligate had plunged the two into adultery while Jane's husband was still alive. Digging in her heels, Mrs. Fielder used every power at her command to stop the match. The alleged seduction, of course, had never occurred and most of the novel consisted of long epistolary explanations and romantic maneuvers. Jane, caught between love for Henry and respect for her mother, anguished over the correct course of action. Mrs. Fielder refused to budge. Henry, pulled in different directions by his head and his heart, struggled to resolve the situation but ultimately began to crack under the pressure.

Throughout this travail—this is what elevated *Jane Talbot* several notches above the normal run of early sentimental fiction—Brown sustained an ongoing discussion of serious moral, religious, social, and epistemological questions. Arguments over the respective merits of religious faith, worldly wealth, reason and emotion, and male and female sensibility added a strong intellectual element to the book's rather maudlin love story. Such tendencies in the novel were reinforced by its subplots and minor characters. Jane's brother Frank, for instance, occasionally appeared in the text as a spendthrift, embezzler, and insatiable seeker of wealth. Playing on his sister's affection, he successfully overcame her scruples to borrow and waste large sums of money. Jane's late husband, Lewis, also made several ghostly appearances as a paragon of hard-working, self-satisfied bourgeois habits. And Miss Jessup, a flighty young woman carried away by her secret passion for Lewis Talbot, turned out to be a key in the plot: she forged the letter falsely implicating Jane and Henry in adultery. So by the time the story reached its rather predictable conclusion—the two young lovers surmounted all obstacles to finally marry—the novel had ventured beyond mere sentiment to engage some interesting cultural issues.

As in several of his earlier novels, Brown created in *Jane Talbot* a mutable atmosphere of fluctuating financial and moral values. Here, however, the contrast between the stilted, mawkish love story and its fluid social backdrop became striking. In a world increasingly driven by market forces and individualist ambition, the novel's characters slipped and staggered on the shifting cultural ground beneath them. Jane's brother, for instance, with his maneuvering and scheming, prompted from her this reflection: "I know that those who embark on pecuniary schemes are often reduced to temporary straits and difficulties; that ruin and prosperity frequently hang on the decision of the moment; that a gap may be filled up by a small effort seasonably made, which, if neglected, rapidly widens and irrevocably swallows up the ill-fated adventurer." In such a world of contingency and peril, moral fraud seemed even more threatening than financial fraud. As

Jane pointed out, forgery and embezzlement were public crimes that could be punished. A loss of moral character—for example, an accusation that "robs a helpless woman of her reputation"—cut much deeper by producing enmity between the individual and "those whose affection is necessary to render life tolerable." In such a context, it was little wonder that the novel's characters frequently fell into agonizing reappraisals of religion and its correct moral principles. All agreed that "true religion" must consist of more than piety and doctrine, and must somehow include "*rational* activity for others' good." The precise benevolent principles remained elusive, however, and caused Brown's characters to fear a moral "void." Each struggled, in the words of one, "to comprehend myself."[6]

Full of moral flux and social uncertainty, Brown's second domestic novel evinced an additional theme: the nature of correct gender roles. This question centered on the issue of love and morality. Early in the novel, for instance, Jane felt compelled to compare males and females in matters of the heart. Men, she argued, were "sanguine and confident" while inclined to let "their words outstrip their feelings." Those of "ardent temper" could easily, and probably sincerely, love several women in one year. Women, by contrast, were naturally creatures of self-restraint. They "feel deeply but boast not," Jane insisted, and "their words generally fall short of their sentiments." Yet their passion, when aroused, was "hard to be escaped from." As if to illustrate the impulsive nature of men, *Jane Talbot*'s male figures ran the gamut of unacceptable emotional extremes. Lewis Talbot, Jane's first husband, exemplified the sturdy dullness of the bourgeois businessman in the early Republic. His religion was "steadfast and rational" and had produced a highly rationalized conduct that was "regular, sober, and consistent." "He was addicted to industry, was regular and frugal in his manner and economy. He had nothing of that specious and glossy texture which captivates inexperience and youth, and serves a substitute for every other virtue. While others talked about their duty, he was contented with performing it." Lewis's temperament made him an impassive, tedious companion, however, and his marriage to Jane had been a dreary one. At the other extreme, of course, stood Frank. Even as a boy Jane's brother had been "boisterous, ungrateful, imperious," and as an adult appeared "selfish and irascible beyond most other men." He displayed an attraction to "active amusements and sensual pleasures," and had deserted school for the illicit pleasures of gambling and whoring. Frank's embrace of "idleness and dissipation" gradually led him into various speculative schemes that proved financially disastrous. His lack of restraint brought ruin to himself, and near-ruin to his family before he fled the country for France (pp. 170, 223-24, 156-59, 172-200).

Regarding women, *Jane Talbot* offered a contrasting picture of social roles and moral principles. In a liberalizing society in which public activity remained regulated by gender, Brown's female characters sought to solidify their moral dominion in private life and domestic affairs. Their struggles illustrated the complexity of women's cultural plight. As Jane noted early in the narrative, even as a young girl she had become convinced that while males were ambitious, self-seeking, and aggressive, females were "soft, pliant, affectionate." These female qualities could lead to self-destruction, as the example of Miss Jessup showed. With an insatiable hunger for love and emotional connection, the desperate young woman had displayed a "volatile, giddy, thoughtless character." Nearly sick with passion for Lewis Talbot, she was driven to acts of forgery, lying, and character assassination before recanting in a deathbed confession. Mrs. Fielder, however, compensated for the sentimental indulgences of Miss Jessup. As Jane's mother, she emerged in the narrative as a massive, unmovable moral force. When informed of Henry Colden's radical views on social and religious matters, and after learning of Henry and Jane's supposed adultery, she denounced Henry as a sensual "visionary and romantic" who loved "to intoxicate the women with melodious flattery." Bitterly opposed to this dangerous rationalist with his agenda for revolutionary social change, she pictured him as "the grand deceiver." "How nicely does he select, how adroitly manage his tools!" she accused. Both Jane and Henry eventually submitted to this "stern and inflexible spirit" and acknowledged her moral dominion. Significantly, marriage between the two took place after Mrs. Fielder learned the truth about the false adultery charge shortly before her own death, and after Henry had reformed his character to meet her standards. As a counterweight to women like Miss Jessup, this formidable matron became a symbol of female moral influence in the domestic realm (pp. 156, 333-35, 225-29, 303, 376, 326, 394, 431).

This entire mélange of social stresses, religious turmoil, gender definition, and moral struggle settled on the shoulders of the novel's two primary characters, Jane Talbot and Henry Colden. Brown's male protagonist, for instance, stepped forward as a seething mass of emotional insecurities, half-held convictions, and self-loathing. Describing himself as "sensual and volatile," Henry confessed that the "image of myself in my own mind is a sorry compound of hateful or despicable qualities." An alienated Godwinian intellectual struggling in a utilitarian society, his elevated views of science and letters brought spasms of self-doubt: "I cannot labour for bread; I cannot work to live. . . . My very nature unfits me for any profitable business. My dependence must ever be on others or on fortune. . . . I am not indolent, but my activity is vague, profitless, capricious. No lucrative or noble purpose impels me. I aim at nothing but selfish gratification." Henry's inability to find a purposeful career led to fears that a species of "insanity" had destroyed his capacity to act. Desperately seeking to "unfold myself *to* myself," the young man began to believe destiny was slipping ever more out of his control. "Let things take their course," he lamented. "I can do nothing." Following its own emotional logic, this internal fragmentation threatened a dark conclusion. Overwhelmed by "this excruciating, this direful melancholy" and feeling "comfortless and friendless," Henry contemplated suicide as a source of relief: "Nothing is sweet but the prospect of oblivion" (pp. 204, 266, 267, 382, 383, 378).

Henry's death wish never came true. Instead of disintegration completing its fatal course, the faltering young man found his cultural bearings and righted himself emotionally. The way in which he did so—relying upon female morality to restore his shattered persona—proved highly revealing. Despairing over the direction of his life, Henry frantically sought to steady his fluctuating character through "some kind of principle by which to regulate my conduct." When his Godwinian principles—enlightened self-interest, scientific rationalism, utilitarian morality—failed to support him on this count, Jane Talbot stepped into the void. As an advocate of benevolence, self-control, and Christianity she became a source of "steadfastness and virtue" for Henry. His deep respect for "this feminine excellence, this secondary and more valuable self" led him to describe the young woman as "my sweet physician." Her influence was slow-working, however, for only after a long, meditative overseas voyage could Henry truly embrace pious morality as a means to reconnect his fragmented character. Jane's principles of Christian benevolence, he concluded, had shored up his moral framework and "made *my mind whole*" (pp. 390, 228, 309, 382, 311).

As for Jane herself, moral solidity and virtue had not come easily. This heroine had struggled to conquer her own baser instincts as a prerequisite for helping Henry overcome his. "I am very far from being a wise girl," she admitted at the novel's outset, and acknowledged that "there are bounds beyond which passion cannot go without counteracting its own purposes." Fearing that her passions threatened to overwhelm moral barriers, she vowed to "enjoy the rewards of self-denial and forbearance." Through a strong measure of self-control, Jane thus felt able to treat her suitor benevolently. "I want to act with a view to your interests and wishes," she informed Henry in the spirit of self-sacrifice. Jane was so sincere that when Henry's father threatened to disinherit him if he became engaged, she pledged to give him up for his own material well-being. Her explanation summarized the spirit of virtuous self-denial: "What I did was in oblivion of self; [it] was from a duteous regard to his genuine and lasting happiness." Henry became the ultimate object of Jane's moral crusade, as she sought

not only to gain his love but to shape his character. The determined young woman envisioned herself as Henry's wife, happily playing the role of domestic manager, patroness of the cultivated arts, mother, and not least important, moral instructor. His lack of religious belief—"the most deplorable calamity that can befall a human creature"—became the particular target for her endeavors. What Jane called her "unconquerable zeal to rescue him from this calamity" aptly summarized her self-imposed task of moral stewardship (pp. 141-52, 255, 317-20, 399, 284-86, 302-3).

Thus, the conclusion of *Jane Talbot,* with a newly pious Henry set to wed the morally triumphant Jane, reached the same destination as *Clara Howard.* In both cases, sentimental forms and language masked an important cultural realignment at the heart of the stories. Interwined with their author's own personal struggles, Brown's last two published novels suggested the emergence of a profound new pattern in early nineteenth-century America: the old republican tradition of self-sacrificing "virtue" was becoming feminized and privatized, while an emerging liberal imperative of "self-interest" appeared increasingly masculinized and publicized.[7] Most important, these instincts could be, indeed should be, harmonized through the mediation of sentimental love and marriage, with liberty and profit for all. For Charles Brockden Brown, this process rescued him from the ideological and moral upheaval of early manhood in the 1790s, and pulled him into a calming new world of bourgeois stability. It demanded wrenching accommodations on his part, but it was a world that would win both his emotional loyalties and literary talents.

II

Clara Howard and *Jane Talbot,* in terms of sales, failed miserably. Their sentiment and romance did not attract a popular audience, as their despairing author had hoped. Ironically, this collapse of literary hope reinforced the larger cultural accommodations represented in the novels themselves. Brown's psychological state around the dawn of the nineteenth century, for instance, in its evolution from rage to resignation, embodied a process of *embourgeoisment.* So too did his personal life as it became submerged in courtship, marriage, and children. In a marked development from anguished artist to family man, Brown's own life seemed to mirror the social and cultural forces transforming the American republic by the early 1800s.

With the opening of a new century, the Philadelphia author revamped his writing activity, slowly abandoning fiction for other genres. Brown had been involved in several journalistic enterprises throughout the 1790s. In 1798, for example, he had been a primary contributor to the Philadelphia *Weekly Magazine,* a journal of opinion and belles letters. Now Brown's journalistic endeavors quickened as his novelistic ones faded. From April 1799 to the autumn of 1800 he served as editor of the *Monthly Magazine and American Review,* a publication backed by his circle of intellectual friends in New York City. Then, in 1803, the enterprising writer founded another monthly journal in Philadelphia, the *Literary Magazine and American Register,* and edited it until its demise in late 1807. Finally, he was editor of the *American Register, or General Repository of History, Politics, and Science* from 1806 to 1810. Brown also contributed generously throughout the early 1800s to his friend Joseph Dennie's *Port-Folio.*[8]

The abandonment of the novel for journalistic enterprises came at a heavy personal cost. Brown evinced extreme bitterness about his failed literary career and attempted to dismiss it altogether. In a public confession in 1803, he denigrated his earlier writings. "I should enjoy a larger share of my own respect at the present moment," he stated bluntly in the first number of the *Literary Magazine,* "if nothing had ever flowed from my pen, the production of which could be traced to me." This self-hatred also flared outward into a stinging critique of American cultural values. The republic's citizens had become so enamored of the "love of gain" and "the main chance," he angrily wrote, that a genuine appreciation of literature and science was all but impossible. He continued:

> Perhaps there never was such a theatre for *speculation* as the United States have presented for the last twelve or fifteen years. On this theatre thousands have played a part, equally astonishing to the sober calculator and humiliating to the moralist. The influence of this system has extended to the remotest corners of the union; so that perhaps a more mercenary and speculating nation than our own hardly at this day exists.

> The natural and necessary influence of such a state of public taste and public sentiment, must be in various ways highly mischievous. . . . When an idea becomes prevalent, that wealth is everything, and that nothing can atone for the want of property, we may expect to see most men bending their whole attention to this object, and neglecting the cultivation of their minds as an affair of secondary moment.[9]

Brown's reassessment of his writing and its relation to American society also came from deep in his own psyche. Once again, an intense self-absorption boiled to the surface as it had earlier in the 1790s. Now the psychological effects remained more muted, and the lashing out was more controlled. Brown wrestled with a strong sense of social isolation, observing at one point in 1801 that "we know nobody, and can therefore seek employment and amusement only in ourselves." At other times this solitude appeared a mere "wretched possession" far beneath the invigorating "images flowing from society." Such ambiguous reactions eventually settled into a pattern of impassive, morose alienation. Describing "the surface of his life" as "tolerably smooth," he admitted to getting by in terms of mere "food, raiment, and repose." Intellectual vigor seemed to have evaporated. "All the inanimate objects in this city are uniform, monotonous, and dull," Brown wrote a correspondent from Philadelphia in 1800. "I have been surprised at the little power they have over my imagination, at the sameness that everywhere reigns." Literary fame, he decided, was a despicable thing while "obscurity" offered "numberless delights." By 1801 the disgruntled ex-novelist presented a persona that was part self-pity, part sullen resignation.[10]

In this context Brown gradually came to terms with journalism as a career that would allow a modicum of both writing and profit. The task proved difficult, as economic and ideological pressures pulled in several directions. On the one hand, he upheld the journalist's pursuit of gain, albeit a bit defensively. In the 1803 inaugural issue of the *Literary Magazine,* his "Editor's Address" offered self-assurances on this point. "The project is not a mercenary one," he wrote. "At the same time, he [the editor] cannot but be desirous of an ample subscription, not merely because pecuniary profit is acceptable, but because this is the best proof which he can receive that his endeavors to amuse and instruct have not been unsuccessful." On the other hand, however, Brown frequently complained about "the apathy and disregard apparently shown by Americans to literature and science," an attitude that made serious journalistic writing a risky financial proposition. The typical citizen's concern with material interests, the writer noted sourly, did not create a public atmosphere for "estimating the productions of genius, taste, and learning." Overall, Brown was forced to admit that journalistic success depended on the American proclivity for newspapers. This habit was unavoidable in a commercial republic, he granted, where political information and market information were necessary for survival. The journalistic combination of "literature, lucre, and politics," Brown admitted, must be granted its usefulness. In less sanguine moments, however, the editor described popularity as a shallow achievement fleetingly bestowed by "the veneration of the multitude." It usually attended a writing enterprise "with no moral or beneficial purpose whatever."[11]

Such ruminations led Brown to confront head-on a cultural predicament in the expanding liberal republic. The entrepreneurial ambition of the middling orders provided the vitality in American society, he admitted, yet this fact created tremendous difficulties for aspiring writers and artists. The people of the United States, he wrote in 1801, were "more distinguished than those of Europe as a people of business, and by an universal attention to the active and lucrative pursuits of life."

This may have been politically desirable, but the artistic consequences were troubling. Aristocratic wealth, Brown pointed out, traditionally produced a "superfluity" of funds that flowed into the coffers of painters and writers. When wealth was more evenly divided in society, however, people concentrated on "a provision of absolute necessaries, before they think of conveniences; and . . . before they can indulge in the agreeable arts." For the Philadelphian this brought an obvious dilemma. Aristocracy, of course, was ideological anathema to this self-proclaimed radical. He also rejected the romantic opinion that genteel poverty stimulated literary genius, since a struggle for material survival only drained artistic energy. The writer's only alternative was to accept the republic's liberalizing society and work within its confines, attempting to harness its energy. Brown exposed the foundation for his new position in 1805: "Poverty is far from being a spur to genius; wealth is far less unfriendly, though its influence is certainly not propitious to it. It is the middle class that produces every kind of worth in the greatest abundance. We must not look for fertility on the hill top, nor at the bottom of the glen. It is only found in the plains and intermediate slopes."[12]

Brown's reconciliation to America's growing market society in the early nineteenth century appeared clearly in another aspect of his life. After nearly ten years of resistance, he finally caved in to family pressure and became a partner in his brothers' commercial enterprises. In 1801 he began office work in their trans-Atlantic trading company, and particularly focused on problems involved with mercantile and maritime law. In March of that year he ruefully told a correspondent, "I write to you in company, & with all the sounds, tools, & symbols of the gain-pursuing merchant about me." Brown assured friends that his new labors took only part of his time, so that many hours could still be devoted to reading and writing. Equally important, the business provided more financial security than fiction ever had. While mercantile activity certainly had its share of fluctuations and disappointments—particularly when intensification of the Napoleonic Wars brought maritime harassments and blockades—the profits still far outdistanced sales of his books. "This period is eminently prosperous for all with whom I am bound by the dear ties of relationship or friendship," he reported in 1803. "The more so by contrast with ancient difficulties and humiliations."[13]

A brief piece of fiction provided a tantalizing glimpse of the emotional currents that were sweeping Brown from the world of literature to that of business and journalism. Published in the *Monthly Magazine* of July 1800, **"The Trials of Arden"** was a short story about the tribulations of an intellectual wronged by public opinion. The plot involved a young immigrant teacher named Arden who became entangled in a murder mystery. When the eldest daughter in the family whom he tutored, Harriet Finch, was found murdered, suspicion fell immediately upon Arden. Having arrived in this New York town only three months before, the young man had been spotted in the area where the killing took place. His nervous behavior and abrupt resignation from the Finches' service sealed his fate. Smoldering community suspicion flamed into outrage, and Arden was pursued, arrested, and imprisoned. Circumstantial evidence and popular outcry made a guilty verdict at his trial all but inevitable. One juror, however, held out for Arden's innocence. An angry mob then attempted to capture and lynch the prisoner. When he escaped, their wrath turned upon the isolated juror who had insisted on his innocence, and this gentleman also fled the community. Almost a year later, a counterfeiter was arrested in Albany and, under interrogation, confessed to the Finch murder. Arden's vindication prompted embarrassment and apologies from his former accusers, and events reached a happy conclusion. The teacher married a young woman from the community whose support had helped rescue him, and their future prosperity was assured when it was revealed that Harriet Finch had bequeathed to Arden her entire estate.[14]

In the context of Brown's early century retrenchment, **"The Trials of Arden"** had fascinating implications. The protagonist was, as the author considered himself to be, an outsider in American society. The story's plot also involved another issue identified with Brown's own life: the young intellectual struggling to maintain his virtue against unpopularity and mindless persecution. Examining an evil perpetuated upon "the fame, peace, and life of one who merited a better fate," this tale pitted a deluded mob against a dignified, self-contained, even Christ-like individual:

> Nothing confounded observers more, than the sedateness of the man. . . . When called upon to defend himself, he complied with apparent reluctance; but, when he opened his mouth at the bar, averred his purity with astonishing collectiveness and fervency; while, at the same time, he declared his hopelessness of acquittal, his acquiescence in his fate, and his forgiveness of his persecutors.

Brown's sublimation of his own literary fate became even more obvious in his depiction of Mayo, the actual murderer. This criminal not only murdered, but embodied two other "demons" that Brown saw arrayed against him in turn-of-the-century America: the "counterfeiter," who feverishly sought wealth immorally, and the manipulator of false appearances who, "being specious and addressful, insinuated himself into Finch's confidence." In such a society of moral caprice and social distrust, the weary writer could wear his alienation as a badge of honor.[15]

The conclusion of **"The Trials of Arden"** provided a final indicator of Brown's cultural realignment in the early 1800s. Arden's courtship, marriage, and prosperity again paralleled the author's own life. In this period the Philadelphian not only embraced business and journalism, but desperately grasped for the security of marriage and family. As the financial failure of fiction writing had driven him away from the arena of letters, the slow evaporation of his old circle of intellectuals in New York City helped drive him back to the bosom of his family in Philadelphia. The death of Elihu Smith in 1798 had a particularly powerful impact. In January 1799 Brown wrote to his brother: "I have neither wife nor children to look up to me for food; and, in spite of all refinements, conjugal and paternal cares can never be fully transferred to one who has neither offspring nor spouse." Around the same time, he confessed to another correspondent that "my conception of the delights and benefits connected with love and marriage are exquisite." This lonely young man thus began to search for stability in emotional as well as material terms.[16]

In 1801 he began to find it. In that year Brown initiated a serious courtship of Elizabeth Linn, the daughter of a prominent Presbyterian minister from New York City. He had first met the young woman in November 1800 when she visited her brother—the Rev. John Blair Linn, also a minister—at his home in Philadelphia. Taken with her good looks, pleasant manners, and shy demeanor, Brown started to call regularly on Miss Linn and to correspond with her both at her brother's home and at her regular residence back in New York. The courtship would be an extended one—they would not be married until November 1804—and during that time the young writer would become close to the whole Linn clan. He grew quite fond of Elizabeth's three sisters, Susan, Rebecca, and Mary, while a strong friendship evolved with her brother John. The Philadelphia minister was a poet and essayist whose literary interests coincided with Brown's. The two developed a rich personal and professional relationship, with Linn even publishing pieces in Brown's *Literary Magazine*. When the minister died prematurely in August 1804, his brother-in-law wrote a public memorium.[17]

Brown's relationship with Elizabeth Linn proved crucial to his new life. The lonely writer had come to yearn for the security of marriage, as he revealed in 1803. Gaining a wife, he wrote, "may not be the only species of felicity, and of all kinds of terrestrial bliss, it may be . . . [most] precarious in possession, but to *me*, THIS is the highest bliss." With great enthusiasm, and his usual lack of emotional subtlety, Brown plunged headlong into romance and began a barrage of attention and letters. Miss Linn remained cautious. Perhaps bothered by religious reservations—Brown's family had nixed several earlier love affairs because of the young women's non-Quaker status—she also possessed a reserved temperament and was intellectually insecure to. the point of self-deprecation. Hence began a long pro-

cess of maneuver between the impetuous, impassioned Brown and the chary, discreet Miss Linn.[18]

A fascinating record of this romantic minuet has survived in the form of a fat cache of letters from Brown to his future wife. Written from December 1800 up through the spring of 1804—most were posted in 1801—these missives provide much intriguing information about their author's state of mind during this period. They also opened another angle of vision on Brown's social and cultural readjustments in the early nineteenth century. More than just declarations of love for Elizabeth Linn, these didactic letters formulated gender roles and cultural values in the aftermath of the tumultuous, challenging 1790s. Subtly seeking to shape the character of this young woman, and simultaneously realigning his own persona in light of these gendered prerogatives, Brown clarified some of the outlines of an emerging bourgeois culture.

He compulsively stressed the necessity of self-control. Brown's admonitions on this point permeated his letters to "my sweet friend," "my Elisa"—two favorite terms for his correspondent—and most of them focused on his own physical passions and moral character. Not unexpectedly, sexuality emerged as the primary object of repression. The young man wrote frequently of his desire for "that sacred privacy so dear to lovers" and confessed that his "imagination was sometimes in danger of becoming too strong for me." As he told Elisa, the "passion of the sexes is the source of existence and happiness" and it could not be ignored either intellectually or emotionally. "I should not be human," Brown argued, "if I did not muse with rapture on the dear privileges of the wedded life." As soon as sex raised its head, however, he leaped to restrain it on moral grounds. Reflection, he observed in many letters, was the most powerful "antidote to passion" and "the mind of genuine force will need no other expedient to restore its self-possession." Bringing reason to bear on instinct was difficult, he admitted, and "I sometimes have need to struggle with the rising gust of my impatience. But I shall always effectually struggle with it." While reflection and passion tugged in different directions, they were not completely incompatible. As the Philadelphian vowed to his beloved, "My reason, as well as my heart, is thy worshipper."[19]

Brown's search for self-control also transcended the realm of physical lust. His flood of letters to Elizabeth Linn suggested a broader impulse toward character formation defined by sincerity, forthrightness, and moral solidity. This shaping of self involved the regulation of a host of libidinous drives and weaknesses—greed, pride, manipulation, anger. Cumulatively, such restraints would create a coherent, decisive, self-propelled individual. Brown's developing relationship with Elisa, for instance, brought forth an emotional defense of his sincerity. Lengthy assertions of "the purity, the fervency" of his feelings for her tumbled over one another in his letters. An intense struggle to "obtain the victory over my selfishness and vanity" prompted this explanation of his moral character: "My inmost soul is not to be heard or seen. Into that you cannot enter. You must rely for your knowledge on my sentiments, on my words and looks. You have no interest in misapprehending these. If *they* mislead you, who but I am to be blamed . . . for my happiness requires that you know me for what I am." For Brown, this harnessing of emotion and selfishness created a simple imperative: "Self-denial is a wholesome thing." Pronounced with varying degrees of enthusiasm or resignation, this emerged as the motto for many Americans with the cultural *embourgeoisment* of the early nineteenth-century republic.[20]

Brown's "Elisa Letters" also demonstrated, however, that self-control became primarily a gendered directive for males. A stern code of emotional regulation placed somewhat different demands on women. Brown, like other bourgeois moralists in the early nineteenth century, believed that female sexuality was "naturally" less intense and less problematic. Female character formation therefore presented other tasks. Women, as Brown suggested constantly in his missives to Elisa, should strive to become models of genteel sensibility. Less vigorous and willful than men—this was "a sexual distinction, a feminine property: to be addicted to misgivings, reluctances, forebodings"—they were also deficient in the "branches of knowledge." Because of these weaknesses, Brown wrote frankly, "from the multitude of women we may turn away with indifference or contempt." Yet compensation could be found in the female capacity for aesthetic, moral, and cultural refinement. Ensconced in the private realm with "freedom from all brutalizing toils, all ignoble wants, all heart-depressing cares," women could and should read, paint, write, and converse. Wisdom would come to the cultivated female while "truth, by being coupled with delight, shall more easily seduce thee to her side."[21]

An ideologically progressive impulse inspired this idealized vision of feminine culture. In contrast to earlier moralists who downplayed female capabilities, Brown insisted that women did have an important role beyond childbirth and domestic chores. Influenced by revolutionary republicanism and his own earlier concern with women's rights, he roundly condemned John Gregory's *A Father's Legacy to His Daughters* (1774). Having mentioned her reading of this popular American moral primer for young women—a highly conservative work that insisted that vitality and learning were unfeminine and that passive meekness and strict decorum were most appealing in women—Elisa was unprepared for her suitor's outburst.

> Jn. Gregory is an egregious fool, Elisa. Never consign thy conversation and behavior to his government. If I remember rightly, his errors are properly exposed in the "Rights of Women." How remote, indeed, from simplicity and rectitude, are the systems of theorists on the laws of sex. . . . Yet in my narrow and indirect experience, I have met with scarcely anything among women but exceptions to the systems of punctilio.

For Brown, the theorist of gender, Wollstonecraft had distinct advantages over Gregory—but this preference had important limitations.[22]

The writer's litany of instructions to Elisa unveiled a model of active female behavior that was carefully restricted to the realm of genteel culture. Brown urged the young woman to gain confidence, to overcome her tendency to view herself as "homely and unlovely" or "stupid and insipid." He probably contributed to Elisa's self-denigration, as suggested by the comment that "I wish I could cure thee, my love, of thinking thyself a simpleton & me a fastidious hypercritic." Nevertheless, Brown relentlessly urged her to read and write in order to cultivate "reason, reflection, memory" and thus improve herself. He urged her to express emotions frankly, but gracefully, so that "your pen thus faithfully [will] depict your character, your sentiments." Praising Elisa's talents profusely, he pleaded with her to express her inner moral beauty: "your purity, your good sense, your taste, your sensibility, your liberal curiosity, your knowledge, your dignity . . . the unaffected delicacy of your feelings." In a letter of April 1, 1801, the Philadelphian summarized his vision of Elizabeth Linn as idealized woman of genteel learning and discretion: "She will be one whom your reason will as zealously revere, as your heart adore. All that your fondest imagination can conceive of pure, modest, and engaging: with all the benefits of education and society; rectitude of taste; freedom from prejudice & all frivolous propensities."[23]

As part of the cultural bargain, however, the educated and sensitive female of Brown's imagination was expected to perform important emotional tasks. Terming Elisa "my good angel" and "mistress of my destiny," Brown elevated her to a position of moral eminence. She served as a source of religious direction, as an exemplar of "rational piety," and she calmed his libidinous outbursts as a model of "Truth, goodness, virtue, harmony, & love." As Brown confessed rather emotionally to her, she had rescued him from the "ancient difficulties and humiliations" that had plagued him in the 1790s and made his past life a "dreary" one. In the eyes of her suitor, this young woman was such an icon of emotional calm, moral inspiration, and intellectual stability that he must strive to be "not only worthy of you, but in your eyes, worthy."[24]

These gender ideals, however, were but part of a larger project of cultural construction. In Brown's blueprint, willful, self-controlled males and genteel, morally scrupulous females would serve as pillars for a massive edifice of bourgeois respectability. With men striving for success in the competitive marketplace while women served as moral managers in the domestic sphere, the bourgeois vision offered a picture of gender congruity and social harmony. Love, of course, served as the great binder. As Brown explained to Elisa, his love for her was part altruism, part self-interest. "I shall be soothing my own disquiets, beguiling my own pain, in alleviating yours," he observed. Brown elaborated in another letter: "We surely value the happiness of those we love, but then we wish them to owe that happiness to us. We rejoice that they seek their good in our store . . . ; but that they can do without us is our woe." This tug between independence and interdependence suggested how love mediated tensions over individualism in a rapidly growing market society. In the family such fears could be calmed and anxieties overcome. Brown, for instance, wrote of the "vehement longing" and "inebriating rapture" attached to his image of "our home, our fireside." Typically, the writer revealed his longing for domestic happiness by employing a dream motif. Asking Elisa for permission to remain "in quiet possession of my dream," he announced that "my dream will be far exceeded by reality." Thus, home and family, love and marriage promised to provide a great bulwark against the external dangers and internal stresses of a competitive society.[25]

The domestic bliss of Brown's imagination, however, concealed hidden fissures and unrecognized dilemmas. His myriad letters to Elizabeth Linn revealed these clearly. Brown's correspondence, for instance, frequently gave glimpses of the emotional turmoil and power relationships behind the assurances of gender compatibility and social cooperation. His long-standing insecurities often leaped to the fore as he constantly pleaded with Elisa for love and attention. "I will not say you sport with my feelings; but you wound them sorely," he admonished her at one point. "I have *no* security, I tell you, against *you*." Brown accused her of being "full of doubts, mistrusts, misgivings" and of communicating with him only when she had "some request to refuse, some mortification to inflict." Browbeating Elisa into making greater effusions of her love—"do you think I can have patience with your silence? No, I shall insist upon your writing as the only proof admissible that you have not forgotten me"—the young man frequently fell into bouts of whining. His "health of body & peace of mind" depended on the young woman's devotion, one letter insisted, and mortification grew from the fear that he held her "affections by no other tenure than incessant supplication." Falling prostrate at the feet of Elizabeth Linn, Brown appeared as an emotional cripple in desperate need of female succor.[26]

The irony of this situation became clear only in light of Brown's persistent claims of intellectual strength and superiority. While bowing to Elisa's moral and religious eminence, he saw their relationship as a heuristic opportunity. Proclaiming himself her "task setter," "monitor," and "instructor," Brown claimed intellectual authority.

> I would fain now be very wise, be very monitory, very lessonful, I would play the tutor with you; the elder brother with his head a mere storehouse for the harvest of experience; retailing his wisdom with the authoritative air of eldership. . . . Have I any influence over you? Yes, I have. . . . What a sacred duty to employ that influence in cherishing in you the seeds of excellence.

He took this sacred duty to rather extreme lengths. Promising to open new intellectual horizons for Elisa, Brown announced: "I wish to be a sort of visible divinity to my girl, to have all her thoughts, wishes, fears entrusted to my keeping." Such overweaning paternalism involved considerable projection on Brown's part, of course, as became evident in a long letter of March 18, 1801. Contrasting Elisa's pessimism and insecurity with his own supposed emotional confidence, he observed, "Strange, my friend, that thou art not as sanguine as I." To one familiar with Brown's own history of hysteria, self-pity, and outlandish behavior, this claim must appear rather amusing. Clearly concerned with overcoming his own agitated past, the writer seized an opportunity to project those fears onto a "weaker" female and thereby establish a newfound emotional dominion.[27]

These patterns within the developing private relationship of Brown and Miss Linn (at least from his perspective; her letters have not survived) replicated larger archetypes in an emerging culture of capitalism. Maneuvering, accommodating, and defining anew around the onset of the nineteenth century, the young writer's attitudes toward love and life linked a pair of gendered cultural principles. Men, as his many letters to Elisa illustrated, would likely suffer an emotional buffeting from their competitive, assertive roles in the public arena of an acquisitive society. Thus, in the domestic sphere, these weary figures required the security of genteel family life and the serene guidance of females. Women, on the other hand, were to shape themselves as attractive, civilizing public ornaments through modest education in the humanities and fine arts. Yet in the home they were to function as pillars of emotional strength and morality, busily promoting a genteel, religious code of benevolence and self-control. This idealized model of complementary gender behavior unfolded by Brown in the early 1800s was, of course, gradually developed by many other moralists as well. It became the basis of a bourgeois Victorian culture that would slowly become dominant by the 1830s and

1840s, a culture in which the private cult of domesticity reinforced the public world of marketplace endeavor. As the "Elisa Letters" demonstrated with great clarity, Brown's private life at the turn of the century had begun to move in the same cultural channels as his final pair of domestic novels.[28]

III

Brown's wooing of Elizabeth Linn came to a happy, if rather delayed, conclusion. Elisa's caution, in concert with some serious financial setbacks suffered by the Brown family's mercantile business, postponed their marriage until 1804. On November 19 of that year the two were finally married by the Rev. William Linn, the bride's father, in New York City. Predictably, Brown suffered censure and expulsion from the Philadelphia Society of Friends for marrying a non-Quaker. Happier events soon followed. In an interesting twist of fate, given Brown's long-standing fascination with doubled identities, the new couple saw the arrival of twin sons in 1805, Charles Jr. and William. In 1807 there followed another boy, Eugene, and two years later a daughter, Mary.[29]

From all accounts Brown's private life entered a stage of contentment and security, in marked contrast to his personal unhappiness as a young man. Shortly before his marriage, he complained of poor health and the fact that "the world of business has been darkened by unusual vexations, disappointments, and embarrassments." By the end of 1805 the situation had brightened greatly. Reporting to his old companion, William Dunlap, Brown painted a glowing picture of domestic felicity with his "adored wife" and "two healthy and lovely babes." "As to myself, my friend, you judge rightly when you think me situated happily," he wrote. "As to my own personal situation, I have nothing to wish but that it may last." Elizabeth Brown seemed to share her husband's sense of joy at their domestic life. Upon his death several years later, she composed an obituary that stressed her husband's delight in family affairs. "It was in the endearing recesses of domestic life," she wrote, "that the character of the deceased shone with its loveliest lustre."[30]

Brown's series of early nineteenth-century realignments—his immersion in business and journalism, his wholehearted embrace of marriage and family—set the stage for an important new public role: bourgeois cultural critic. During the 1790s this restless young intellectual had challenged cultural, religious, and social traditions as part of his struggles with market-place individualism. Now he moved to occupy a defensive position in protection of bourgeois society. In journals like *The Literary Magazine and American Register* and *The Monthly Magazine,* Brown appeared increasingly in a dual role: articulator of genteel behavior and advocate of cultural stability. A code of self-controlled individualism became his moral map for both private and public endeavor. A young man's intense frustration with a competitive market society, it seemed, developed into a middle-aged man's determination to stabilize that society, clarify its principles, and identify its transgressors.

In 1803 Brown made a dramatic appearance in his new role. The opening issue of the new *Literary Magazine* contained an "Editor's Address to the Public" that was part public confession, part statement of principle. This statement noted somewhat bitterly that the editor took no pride in his earlier writings. Then he announced at some length the cultural maxims that would henceforth guide his work:

> In ages like this, when the foundations of religion and morality have been so boldly attacked, it seems necessary . . . to be particularly explicit as to the path which the editor means to pursue. He therefore avows himself to be, without equivocation or reserve, the ardent friend and willing champion of the Christian religion. . . .

> As, in the conduct of this work, a supreme regard will be paid to the interests of religion and morality, he will scrupulously guard against all that dishonours or impairs that principle. Everything that savours of indelicacy or licentiousness will be rigorously proscribed. His poetical pieces may be dull, but they shall, at least, be free from voluptuousness or sensuality, and his prose . . . shall scrupulously aim at the promotion of public and private virtue.

In the years that followed, the editor attempted to uphold these principles.[31]

Brown vigorously promoted a moral creed of self-control throughout his journalistic essays of the early 1800s. In a startling turnabout from his passionate emotional displays of the 1790s, he now denounced those who acted "according to their impulses without heeding the restraint of rationality." Rampant emotion, he maintained, created a wealth of private and public dangers. It led to widespread mischief and destruction flowing from the consumption of "inebriating liquors." It promoted the perverse blending of honor and violence in the practice of "dueling." It encouraged the pernicious activities of gambling, lotteries, and political partisanship. Finally, it prompted that lust "excited by mere sex, . . . a gross appetite distinguished by no humanity, no delicacy, from that which stimulates the goat and the bull." These activities, Brown insisted, were particularly dangerous in a republic because they enticed "the mechanic and husbandman away from their usual wholesome and virtuous employment, to chimerical and ruinous visions."[32]

The Philadelphia editor leveled some of his sharpest criticism at money making, perhaps the greatest passion in a liberating society of individualism. For too many ambitious Americans, profit had become "the *one thing needful*"in life, and its pursuit had overwhelmed many virtues with "depravity and selfishness." In a *Monthly Magazine* piece entitled "A Miser's Prayer," Brown presented a satirical sketch of the greedy citizen offering his hopes to the Almighty:

> Give humility to the poor and beggarly, and make them contented . . . so they may not pester thy faithful and thrifty servants with their outcries for charity. . . . Save us, we pray thee, from perishing by fire . . . and let a particularly large share of thy regard be bestowed upon the buildings on Third Street, between Vine and Sassafras. . . . Have compassion on all those who are sick and in prison. . . . Have an eye of special regard to Richard Harris, and give him wherewithal to pay thy servant what he oweth him, to wit the sum of three hundred dollars and sixteen cents due, with interests thereon, since the fourth instant.[33]

Such dangerous passions lurking in the shadows of the early nineteenth-century republic led Brown to search for instruments of restraint. He found one in the civilizing influence of women. While tempted by certain cravings—particularly fashion, with its frippery and temptations to physical immodesty—females nonetheless had a unique capacity for self-control. Adopting the model of Lockean psychology, he argued that women were more susceptible to sensory impressions than men because of their worldly inexperience, lack of education, and emotional sensitivity. Yet this was also their greatest source of moral strength. Women, Brown contended, were attuned to the noble sentiments of music and painting and thus were able to promote their "laudable and generous emotions." These activities, however, threatened to degenerate into sensuality or idle amusement, so females needed to engage in serious reading and religious study. Moreover, the editor contended, women should maintain a strict "chastity" in order to control the animal desires of men. While males should seek an "inward conviction of rectitude," women best monitored their conduct through a code of sexual virtue, something that would be "a more effectual preservative against licentiousness, than any penal statute." So while Brown concluded that social equality between the sexes was "quite impossible," he proposed an important public role for women in a bourgeois republic: paragons of self-restraint in a society constantly seduced by self-interest.[34]

In Brown's new cultural ideology, literature emerged as another important means for inspiring sensual repression and social stability. The genre of the novel appeared especially rich with possibilities. While Brown granted that a large number of immoral, insipid, and frivolous stories had come forth under this heading, he insisted that many fictions of "merit and genius" stood out from "the promiscuous crowd." Novels had the capacity to gain an emotional grip over their readers, and then drive home a moral of "virtuous and noble sentiments." Through "the principles they have inculcated, and the sensibilities they have exercised," Brown wrote in 1804, fictional narratives had reached a pinnacle of cultural influence. While the "profligate novel" was a fact of life, Brown focused on the many "novels that may be read with benefit and pleasure by persons of good morals and good taste."[35]

Brown's old hero, Samuel Richardson, stood foremost in the ranks of virtuous novelists. Other fiction writers like Rousseau and Defoe had merit, of course, but in the early 1800s the Philadelphian sang the moral praises of Richardson loudest and longest. Defining the English author as "the father of the modern novel of the serious or pathetic kind," Brown lauded his ability to combine emotional, gripping stories with "salutary maxims" and "dignity of the sentiments." Like no other author, Richardson demonstrated "the beauty and the usefulness of virtue." This figure of "moral grandeur," in Brown's adoring eyes, was like a skillful preacher "in introducing useful maxims and sentiments of virtue . . . and he has besides the power of pressing them upon the heart through the best sensibilities of our nature."[36]

For Brown the bourgeois critic, literature provided only a prelude to his larger movement for cultural stability. From the editor's chair in Philadelphia, he used the *Literary Magazine* in particular to advocate an array of morally uplifting projects. Brown promoted, for instance, a national plan to develop "the fine arts of painting, sculpture, and architecture" in the United States. Urging both a private subscription drive and a congressional grant of public money, he maintained that the construction of art galleries and public monuments would help cohere a "civilized, peaceful, free, industrious, and opulent nation." In addition, by the early 1800s Brown had become a firm advocate of religious instruction. Abandoning his own youthful skepticism, he now insisted that religion must be instilled early in children to "balance the counter-impulse of the passions." If their impressionable minds encountered religion "at a time when the passions are most violent," impulsive behavior could be restrained. Religion, if it was to have social utility, must avoid the extremes of "enthusiasm," on the one side, and "dull conformity" on the other. It "must be taught rationally," drawing upon the individual's reason for comprehension. This cultural critic now saw religion as "the best safeguard against the impulses of the passions."[37]

Given the restless ambition of early nineteenth-century America, education loomed equally large in the Brownian blueprint for stability. He began to address the subject in numerous essays which argued that schooling was critical to the shaping of a virtuous, hard-working citizenry. Education, Brown maintained, worked to "form the mind of youth, . . . to mold the disposition of a new generation." It served as an agent of cultural transmission by handing down "the acquisitions of our forefathers." It helped "produce a virtuous and enlightened race," a necessity in an American society given to licentious temptation. Yet Brown was no simple reactionary on this matter. Granted, he did oppose reformers like Noah Webster who sought to create an American language with its own grammar, spelling, and vocabulary. Instead, he favored an Anglo-American cultural imperialism with a "diffusion of the English lineage and language" throughout the entire New World. Brown also denounced advocates of a "classical education" for American children, arguing that the study of modern languages and science was more appropriate to a utilitarian, market society. As he wrote in the 1805 essay **"On Classical Learning,"** in a voice filled with bittersweet experience,

> If a boy be intended for trade or business, a classical education will be injurious to him. . . . [M]en, who have been educated at the university, seldom make it as active, expert, and successful merchants or tradesmen. . . . Habits of indolence, or of studious industry, are formed at college, which are inimical to the mechanical processes of trade, and to the activity and bustle of a man of business. . . . The dull uniformity and confinement of a shop or accounting room, are irksome to men of genius and studious mind.

Overall, Brown envisioned an educational process that would socially channel and morally restrain the activities of liberated individuals.[38]

As this process of cultural logic unfolded, "taste" emerged as its most intriguing dimension. As a bourgeois critic seeking anchors of stability in a gathering storm of social competition, Brown increasingly formulated principles for correct aesthetic judgment and cultural practice. Such standards, he hoped, would encourage mental stability and moral restraint. In an 1806 essay entitled **"On Standards of Taste,"** Brown made the argument clearly. The laws of taste were partly "natural," in that writing, painting, and music inevitably raised emotional associations and affections in an audience. Yet they were also "partly arbitrary" because of the necessity for "observance of those rules with which critics are conversant." Here Brown minced no words: "As there are rules of taste, which are absolute and universal, and founded only on the common nature of human beings; so the rules of ethics are universal, and obligatory on all intelligent creatures who have received the same constitution as ourselves."[39]

Brown suggested several axioms in elaborating this unbreakable connection between "rules of taste" and morality. First, he demanded a sober-minded sensibil-ity. The habit of witticism was entertaining, but it was also a foolish and "childish practice." Moreover, "the wit" usually proved to be a trite and superficial figure unable "to discuss any subject soberly, to reason or to speculate, or to moralize." Second, the Philadelphian demanded not only seriousness, but realism. The American writer or painter should strive to accurately present "a picture of his age and country, by minutely and faithfully portraying himself." Nature's abundance in the New World provided particular opportunity here. By realistically presenting the "picturesque beauty" of natural landscapes, Brown suggested, the artist could evoke "a gratification the nearest akin and most friendly to the ennobling and domestic virtues."

Turning to his own province of writing, the essayist issued several directives after the turn of the century. In **"The Difference Between History and Romance,"** published in the April 1800 *Monthly Magazine,* Brown set out his mature critical position. The writer should strive to be both a realistic "historian" (one "who carefully watches, and faithfully enumerates the appearances which occur" in life) and an imaginative "romancer" (one "who adorns these appearances with cause and effect, and traces resemblances between the past, and future, with the present"). The narrow scope of history, with its attempts to affirm "what is known by the testimony of our senses," required enrichment from the vast scope of romance, which maintained an "empire absolute and undivided over the motives and tendencies of human action." The result of tasteful artistic endeavor would be an audience of individuals whose "observations are as diligent as their theories are adventurous." The ideal person of "taste"—this included not only producers but consumers of culture, men and women—advanced sober reason against the barriers of mindless custom and tradition. He or she did so calmly and rationally, avoiding wild speculation and unfounded theorizing. Brown envisioned a cultured individual who could fight off "the caprice and instability of human nature" with a wide-ranging curiosity and synthesizing intelligence. Such citizens, he hoped, would bring a forbearing, rational realism to the cause of moral stability in America, and thereby save a volatile market society from its own worst instincts.[40]

One episode, more than any other, illustrated what might happen if human passions were left unrestrained: the French Revolution. Like many American intellectuals and politicians, Brown anguished over the meaning of this upheaval in the life of the Western world. Although he found the course of events in France to be deeply disturbing, he was no reactionary. In fact, by the early nineteenth century Brown developed a reading of the Revolution that was carefully in line with his broader cultural principles. The revolt in France had been initiated by philosophers and moderate republicans, he argued, whose activities were driven by "a love of liberty and a desire of reform." Moreover,

the turbulence of the Revolution was no cause for automatic denunciation. Human nature demanded "the exercise of freedom, and the indulgence of a liberal and beneficent temper" rather than "mere tranquility," Brown insisted. The political disputes, angry meetings, attacks on the monarchy, and general public contention in revolutionary France were to be expected as "the collisions of free society."[41]

However, the Revolution had plunged into disaster, Brown believed, and for specific reasons. Passions had gradually gained the upper hand over reason and sent the French into an abyss of "massacre, confiscation, and exile." Restless popular anger had produced "a reliance on force" and the machinations of demagogues. "Virtuous and enlightened" judgment had been crushed by "acclamations of the mob" and monarchy had given way to "military despotism." Society, Brown believed, was organic in nature with a "natural aristocracy" of leaders who were "the natural organs of a great living body." Such figures, because of their education, status, and wealth, embodied the restrained and rational judgment of the whole. By ignoring this leadership class and indulging themselves in wild political and social experimentation, French revolutionaries had abandoned all hope for reforming the profound "properties and powers" of civil society. For Brown, the triumph of "misguiding passions" in France since 1789 had seriously injured "the cause of rational freedom." This nightmarish scene was one that ambitious Americans ignored only at their peril.[42]

So by the early years of the nineteenth century, Charles Brockden Brown had traveled far on his intellectual and emotional journey. In part, his path reflected a growing conservatism that often typifies the human life cycle. Challenges to the social order had marked his adolescence and early manhood as issues of personal ambition, gender definition, economic pursuit, and cultural performance tormented the young individual. In the same way that American revolutionaries had defied the sovereignty of Great Britain, Brown had worked to undermine traditional paternalism and its restraints. Even in 1800 Brown still emphasized that filial duty was in fact a contractual relationship: "our treatment of parents must be regulated by their characters. When vicious, our duties lie in rejecting their demands," Such freedom, however, could be frightening as well as exciting. The implications of unfettered individualism—its demands and possibilities, pitfalls and liberations—had provided the raw material for his frenzied fiction writing up through the 1790s. After a long struggle, Brown arrived at middle age a different and sobered man. No longer the brash intellectual maverick, he had become a persistent, articulate spokesman for social stability, cultural authority, and self-discipline.[43]

The meaning of this writer's evolution went far beyond personal development. It replicated a broader process of historical change in post-Revolutionary America. First, like many other citizens of the republic, Brown had gradually come to terms with a growing individualism. Fully recognizing the danger of this powerful social and economic force rampaging through the early modern Atlantic world, he grudgingly came to view it as an instrument of progress. This reluctant admission, however, was made possible only by a second crucial proposition. If individual agency was allowed free play in the social arena, the potent forces of "culture" must be mustered out to prevent anarchy and brutality. The passions, in Brown's words, arose from "the deplorable imperfections of human nature, absurd and pernicious." The incredible diversity of the United States—its vast "motliness, the endless variety of habits, ranks, and conditions"—presented additional perils of incoherence and instability. Given these assumptions, Brown the moralist concluded that a culture of self-control provided the strongest barrier to chaos. Genteel standards of conduct, stern moral codes that repressed sexual and violent impulses, and civilizing habits closely tied to the arts stood the best chance of throttling individual licentiousness and its horrors.[44]

Ultimately, the thrust of Brown's social and cultural maneuvers veered in the direction of irony. By elevating "culture" to a level above the tawdry impulses of competitive social and economic life and granting it civilizing powers, Brown in fact helped legitimize a society of marketplace individualism. His promotion of an abstract cultural aesthetic advanced the notion that creativity and imagination had been rationalized out of everyday life and into a specialized realm of human activity. Implicitly, but powerfully, this implied that the social world must be accepted as driven by competition, profit, and productivity. By 1803, for example, Brown had concluded that the typical "poor author" was someone who abandoned steady work for "habits of improvidence and heedlessness, as to all economic matters" and sunk into "the refuge of idleness and poverty." A more admirable kind of writer was one "who devotes to composition the leisure secured to him by hereditary affluence, or by a lucrative profession or office." This artistic role, which clearly disassociated work from creativity, he deemed "the pinnacle of human elevation." Brown's crusade for cultural coherence thus furthered, in unintended fashion, the very social fragmentation that had unsettled him for so many years.[45]

Brown's willingness to don the mantle of cultural "critic" completed this significant historical odyssey. In a public sphere that idealized marketplace social relations—free and equal exchange, debate, and decision making among autonomous individuals—the critic acted as referee. His task of establishing genteel guidelines of rationality and taste was a complex one. The critic sought, in part, to uplift an energetic but provincial mercantile and entrepreneurial class; in part, to

defend the social and property interests of that class; in part, to soothe the pressures and heal the wounds inflicted by expanding market competition. Within this culture, Brown believed, the critic would shape a true "paradigm of reason" inspired yet restrained. As he instructed his countrymen in his 1806 essay **"Standards of Taste,"**

> Criticism is a science, and taste can only be rendered accurate by much study and attention. . . . Nothing is more truly cant, either in morals or in criticism, than the language of those who profess to decide from the impulse of their immediate feelings, without listening to so cold an arbitress as reason. . . . The imagination is the source of all error; and it is hard for taste to keep a rein over so festive a faculty.[46]

In its blending of enlightened reason and genteel repression, this writer's gradual evolution into an arbiter of cultural taste was part of a vast realignment in early modern America. By the early nineteenth century, he was helping validate the hegemony of liberal capitalism by clothing it in the sober, respectable garb of bourgeois civilization. In his final years, Brown would explore his new role, uncovering its capacity both for achievement and self-destruction.

Notes

[1] Brown's letter of April 1800 to his brother James is quoted in David Lee Clark, *Charles Brockden Brown: Pioneer Voice of America* (Durham, N.C., 1952), 195.

[2] My reading of the two novels has been influenced particularly by Sydney J. Krause, "*Clara Howard* and *Jane Talbot:* Godwin on Trial," in Bernard Rosenthal, ed., *Critical Essays on Charles Brockden Brown* (Boston, 1981), 184-211, who suggests that these novels tested and pulled back from an earlier engagement with radicalism. In general, Brown's last two completed books remain far less studied than his four "major" novels of the 1790s. A few exceptions exist. Paul Witherington's "Brockden Brown's Other Novels: *Clara Howard* and *Jane Talbot,*" *Nineteenth-Century Fiction* 29 (1974): 257-72, argues that these two "domestic novels" were linked to his earlier novels in thematic terms of "chastened individualism." Both Clark, *Pioneer Voice,* 181-85, and Charles E. Bennett, "The Brown Canon" (Ph.D. diss., University of North Carolina, 1974), 98-100, 224-25, suggest that Brown knuckled under to sentimental, female, popular literary values in these novels. Norman Grabo, *The Coincidental Art of Charles Brockden Brown* (Chapel Hill, N.C. 1981), 129-57, analyzes the texts as superficial tales that, having abandoned all sense of "complexities and ambiguities," became "trivial and silly." Deborah M. Bingham, "The Identity Crisis of Charles Brockden Brown" (Ph.D. diss., Bowling Green State University, 1977), presents a convincing picture of Brown's re-

treat from "public" literary and intellectual life into a "private" realm of security and family-oriented endeavors during this period, a process that was fed by these two domestic novels. Overall, I have tried to examine these themes and resituate them as parts of a broader process in Brown's life and, indeed, in American culture as a whole: the solidification of a bourgeois sensibility with its moral code based on restraint, gentility, and self-control. This process, I maintain, was part of a response to the dislocations accompanying rapid market growth in the post-Revolutionary decades.

[3] See Donald A. Ringe, "Historical Essay," in Brown, *Clara Howard, in a Series of Letters* and *Jane Talbot, a Novel* (Kent, Ohio, 1986), 441. All subsequent references to these two novels will refer to this bicentennial edition from the Kent State University Press.

[4] Brown, *Clara Howard,* 3, 38, 40, 64, 89.

[5] For a persuasive account of *Jane Talbot*'s publishing history, see Ringe, "Historical Essay," 443-52.

[6] Brown, *Jane Talbot,* 188-89, 314, 305, 307.

[7] For several sophisticated analyses of gendered notions of virtue and self-interest as they developed in the several decades after the American Revolution, see the following works: two articles by Ruth H. Bloch, "American Feminine Ideals in Transition: The Rise of the Moral Mother, 1785-1815," *Feminist Studies* 4 (1978): 101-26, and "The Gendered Meaning of Virtue in Revolutionary America," *Signs* 13 (Autumn 1987): 37-58; Jan Lewis, "The Republican Wife: Virtue and Seduction in the Early Republic," *William and Mary Quarterly* 44 (Oct. 1987): 696-721; and Linda K. Kerber's comments on "republican motherhood" in her *Women of the Republic: Intellect and Ideology in Revolutionary America* (Chapel Hill, N.C. 1980), 269-88.

[8] See Bennett, "Brown Canon," 83-84, 88-92, 98-99, 121-22.

[9] Charles Brockden Brown, "Editor's Address," *Literary Magazine* (Oct. 1803): 4; "On the State of American Literature," by "M," *Monthly Magazine* 1 (Apr. 1799): 16. The latter essay has been identified as Brown's by Sydney Krause in Rosenthal, ed., *Critical Essays,* 209, n. 8.

[10] Brown quoted in Bingham, "Identity Crisis," 173; William Dunlap, *The Life of Brown* (Philadelphia, 1815), 2:49; Brown, quoted in Harry R. Warfel, *Charles Brockden Brown, American Gothic Novelist* (Gainesville, Fla., 1949), 187, 201.

[11] Charles Brockden Brown, "Editor's Address," *Literary Magazine* (1803): 5; "Preface," *Monthly Magazine*

(Oct. 1800): 259-60, 262-63; "Student's Diary," *Literary Magazine* (1803): 327.

12 Charles Brockden Brown, "Preface" to *American Review* (1801), quoted in Robert E. Spiller, *American Literary Revolution, 1783-1837* (Garden City, N.Y., 1967), 32; "Why the Arts Are Discouraged in America," *Literary Magazine* 6 (July 1806): 77; "Alliance between Poverty and Genius," *Literary Magazine* 3 (May 1805): 333.

13 See Bingham, "Identity Crisis," 144-47; Brown's letters to Elizabeth Linn (Humanities Research Center, University of Texas at Austin): Mar. 30, 1801; May 25, 1804; and Dec. 2, 1802.

14 Charles Brockden Brown, "The Trials of Arden," *Monthly Magazine* 3 (July 1800): 19-36.

15 Ibid., 20, 24, 27-28.

16 See the insightful analysis in Bingham, "Identity Crisis," 129, 116-17, 133-34. See also Dunlap, *Life of Brown,* 2:50.

17 See Clark, *Pioneer Voice,* 197-98, 214-15, and Warfel, *Gothic Novelist,* 229.

18 Charles Brockden Brown, "A Student's Diary," *Literary Magazine* 1 (1803): 85; and Clark, *Pioneer Voice,* 197-98.

19 See Brown's letters to Elizabeth Linn (MS, University of Texas): Apr. 4, 1801; Mar. 17, 1801; Apr. 29, 1801; undated letter; Apr. 13, 1801; Mar. 30, 1801.

20 Ibid., "Tuesday afternoon" (n.d.); undated letter; "Tuesday afternoon" (n.d.); Feb. 28, 1801.

21 Ibid., Mar. 27, 1801; Dec. 15, 1800; Apr. 14, 1801. See Carroll Smith-Rosenberg, *Disorderly Conduct: Visions of Gender in Victorian America* (New York, 1985); Ann Douglas, *The Feminization of American Culture* (New York, 1977); and Karen Halttunen, *Confidence Men and Painted Women: A Study of Middle-Class Culture in America, 1830-1870* (New Haven, 1982), for discussions of gender and the development of a bourgeois code of self-control in the nineteenth century.

22 Ibid., Mar. 30, 1801. See Cathy Davidson's discussion of John Gregory in her *Revolution and the Word: The Rise of the Novel in America* (New York, 1986), 126-27. See Mary Beth Norton, *Liberty's Daughters: The Revolutionary Experience of American Women, 1750-1800* (Glenview, Ill., 1980), and Linda K. Kerber, *Women of the Republic: Intellect and Ideology in Revolutionary America* (Chapel Hill, N.C., 1980), for two

superb overviews of transforming gender formulations regarding women in the early American republic.

23 Brown's letters to Elizabeth Linn (MS, University of Texas): Apr. 29, 1801; Apr. 10, 1801; Mar. 31, 1801; Apr. 1, 1801.

24 Ibid., undated (probably Mar. or Apr. 1801); Apr. 1, 1801; Apr. 9, 1801.

25 Ibid., Mar. 6, 1801; Mar. 10, 1801; Apr. 10, 1801; Mar. 27, 1801; Mar. 7, 1801. See Christopher Lasch, *Haven in a Heartless World: The Family Beseiged* (New York, 1977), and Edward Shorter, *The Making of the Modern Family* (New York, 1977), for broad treatments of the development of the bourgeois family.

26 Brown's letters to Elizabeth Linn (MS, University of Texas): Feb. 20, 1801; Mar. 10, 1801; Feb. 17, 1801; Mar. 2, 1801; Apr. 9, 1801.

27 Ibid., Mar. 23, 1801; Apr. 27, 1801; Apr. 9, 1801; Apr. 11, 1801; Apr. 29, 1801; Mar. 18, 1801.

28 On Victorian culture in America, see, in addition to other works cited in nn. for this chapter, Daniel Walker Howe, ed., *Victorian America* (Philadelphia, 1976); Mary Kelly, *Private Women, Public Stage: Literary Domesticity in Nineteenth-Century America* (New York, 1984); and John F. Kasson, *Rudeness and Civility: Manners in Nineteenth-Century America* (New York, 1990).

29 See Warfel, *Gothic Novelist,* 189, 227-29.

30 See Brown's letters in William Dunlap, *Life of Brown,* 2:111-12, 113; and his letter in Clark, *Pioneer Voice,* 213. Elizabeth Brown's obituary can be found in ibid., 292-94.

31 Charles Brockden Brown, "Editor's Address to the Public," *Literary Magazine* 1 (Oct. 1803): 5.

32 Charles Brockden Brown, "On Standards of Taste," *Literary Magazine* 6 (Oct. 1806): 294; "A Student's Diary," *Literary Magazine* 2 (1804): 85 and 1 (1803): 164; "Death of Hamilton," *Literary Magazine,* 2 (Aug. 1804): 337; "Editor's Address," *Literary Magazine* 1 (Oct. 1803): 5; and "Dialogues of the Living," *Monthly Magazine* 1 (Apr. 1799): 19-21.

33 Charles Brockden Brown, "A Miser," *Literary Magazine* 2 (July 1804): 246; "A Miser's Prayer," *Monthly Magazine* 3 (Dec. 1800): 412-13.

34 Charles Brockden Brown, "Female Clothing," *Literary Magazine* 6 (July 1806): 22-23; "On Novel Writing," *Literary Magazine* 2 (Dec. 1804): 697; "On Music as a Female Accomplishment," *Port-Folio* 2 (1802):

292, 307; "On Painting as a Female Accomplishment," *Port-Folio* 2 (1802): 332; "Thoughts on Religion as a Branch of Female Education," *Literary Magazine* 2 (June 1804): 168; Dunlap, *Life of Brown,* 2:119-20.

[35] Brown, "Novels," *Literary Magazine* 3 (Jan. 1805): 16-17; "Novel Writing," *Literary Magazine* (1804): 694, 693; "A Student's Diary," *Literary Magazine* 1 (1803): 404-5.

[36] "Student's Diary," 323-24; "Novel Writing," 696-97, 694; "Original Papers for the Port-Folio: The American Lounger," *Port-Folio* 2 (June 1802): 185-86.

[37] Charles Brockden Brown, "Plan for the Improvement and Diffusion of the Arts, Adapted to the United States," *Literary Magazine* 3 (Mar. 1805): 181-83; "Thoughts on Religion as a Branch of Female Education," *Literary Magazine* 2 (June 1804): 166-167; Brown's final statement, made in 1807, is quoted in Bingham, "Identity Crisis," 169.

[38] Brown, "Religion and Female Education," 166; "On the Scheme of an American Language," *Monthly Magazine* 3 (July 1800): 1-2; "On Classical Learning," *Literary Magazine* 3 (Apr. 1805): 256-57.

[39] Brown, "On Standards of Taste," *Literary Magazine* 6 (Oct. 1806): 294-95.

[40] Brown, "Student's Diary," 6, 81, 408, 328; "On a Scheme for Describing American Manners," *Monthly Magazine* 3 (July 1800): 10; "On a Taste for the Picturesque," *Monthly Magazine* 3 (July 1800): 12; "The Difference between History and Romance," *Monthly Magazine* 2 (Apr. 1800): 251, 253, 252.

[41] Charles Brockden Brown, "On the Merits of the Founders of the French Revolution," *Literary Magazine* 6 (Nov. 1806): 352; "Is a Free or Despotic Government Most Friendly to Human Happiness?" *Literary Magazine* 3 (Mar. 1805): 180.

[42] Brown, "Free and Despotic Governments," 178; "Of the French Revolution," 353-55, 358-59, 356, 354, 351-52.

[43] Brown's comments on paternalism appeared in the 1800 *Monthly Magazine,* and they are quoted in Jay Fliegelman, *Prodigals and Pilgrims: The American Revolution against Patriarchal Authority, 1750-1800* (Cambridge, 1982), 89.

[44] Charles Brockden Brown, "On the Scheme of an American Language," *Monthly Magazine* 3 (July, 1800): 1; "American Manners," 8. See Joseph J. Ellis, *After the Revolution: Profiles of Early American Culture* (New York, 1979); Ronald T. Takaki, *Iron Cages: Race and Culture in 19th-Century America* (Seattle, 1979); and Steven Watts, *Republic Reborn: War and the Making of Liberal America, 1790-1820* (Baltimore, 1987), for various treatments of the cultural campaign to confront individualism and thwart its excesses with an ethic of self-control.

[45] Brown, "Student's Diary," 8. See Raymond Williams, *Culture and Society: 1780-1950* (New York, 1983), xvi-xviii, 47, for a brilliant argument on how the very definition of modern "culture" is rooted in the social relationships of market capitalism.

[46] Brown, "Standards of Taste," 294-95. Terry Eagleton, *The Function of Criticism: From The Spectator to Post-Structuralism* (London, 1984), 10-17, 26, presents a searching theoretical analysis of the role of the "critic" in confirming developing discourses of capitalism.

David Seed (essay date 1996)

SOURCE: "The Mind Set Free: Charles Brockden Brown's *Wieland*" in *Making America/Making American Literature: Franklin to Cooper,* edited by A. Robert Lee and W. M. Verhoeven, Rodopi Amsterdam/Atlanta B.V., 1996, pp. 105-122.

[*In the essay that follows, Seed analyzes the style and structure of* Wieland *and argues that the ambiguity and irresolution in the novel reflect Brown's questioning attitude toward the ability of the mind to "grasp truth and order perceptions." Seed goes on to state that in his presentation of the error of perception and the mind's capacity for self-delusion, Brown anticipates Edgar Allan Poe and Nathaniel Hawthorne*]

When attempting to place Charles Brockden Brown within American literary history Leslie Fiedler locates one central preoccupation in his writings: "the essential human passion to which he hoped to appeal in his examination of society, as well as by his exploration of terror, was curiosity."[1] Curiosity was not only the grounds of Brown's appeal to his readers. It was the very condition of the workings of his imagination. In an address to his Philadelphia literary society he grandiosely declared: "the relations, dependencies, and connections of the several parts of knowledge, have long been a subject of unavailing enquiry with me."[2] Achievement was clearly lagging well behind ambition but in a 1788 sketch, **"The Man at Home"** he figured the scope of the mind as an open expanse ready for exploration: "the world of conjecture is without limits. To speculate on the possible and the future is no ineligible occupation."[3] The latter statement appears to reflect a fairly broad optimism about intellectual enquiry but in his 1798 novel **Wieland,** Brown dramatized the unforeseen consequences of speculation working without social or moral limits. The extraordinary twists and turns of the action and the proliferation of narrative voices has led one critic to conclude that *Wieland* leads to nothing, and in a sense that is true.[4] There is no final resolving certainty which ties all threads together. Rather the novel's ambiguities and very lack of resolution reflect a profound scepticism on Brown's part over the mind's capacity to grasp truth and order perceptions.

The style of *Wieland* both reflects and to a certain extent explains the intricacies of the novel's structure. Take, for example, the following passage describing Wieland senior's state after his first missionary activities with the Indians:

> His previous industry had now enabled him to dispense with personal labour, and direct attention to his own concerns. He enjoyed leisure, and was visited afresh by devotional contemplation. The reading of the scriptures, and other religious books, became once more his favorite employment. His ancient belief relative to the conversion of the savage tribes, was revived with uncommon energy. To the former obstacles were now added the pleadings of parental and conjugal love. The struggle was long and vehement; but his sense of duty would not be stifled or enfeebled, and finally triumphed over every impediment.[5]

It is striking as a general rule how many constatives these lines contain. Characteristically, action becomes reified or nominalized so that Wieland does not emerge as an agent so much as a consciousness to be acted on. This may sound merely like a Lockean expression of the mind as a passive recipient of sense data, but in fact rather more is going on here. The passive verb-forms which recur constantly throughout the whole novel focus the reader's attention on objects and results while leaving origination unspecified. Thus the second sentence of the passage implies that contemplation comes from elsewhere, that the field of consciousness is temporarily occupied by impulses with an unknown provenance. By the end of the paragraph Brown has elaborated this notion into the mental field as the site of conflict between rival impulses: duty against love or pleasure. And it is the "sense of duty" not the self as a whole which wins this struggle. Brown's choice of formulations extends Wieland's conviction of having been addressed by an external spiritual agency into a whole psychological principle whereby the self must endure the conflict between impulses and abide its outcome.

This style, however, is not confined to one character. It runs throughout Clara's narrative, as in the following lines, where she imagines Carwin is returning to her house for no honorable purpose. No sooner has she reflected with satisfaction on a benevolent divinity watching over her than fresh sounds disturb her thoughts:

> Scarcely had I uttered these words, when my attention was startled by the sound of footsteps. They denoted some one stepping into the piazza in front of my house. My new-born confidence was extinguished in a moment. Carwin, I thought, had repented his departure, and was hastily returning. The possibility that his return was prompted by intentions consistent with my safety, found no place in my mind. Images of violation and murder assailed me anew, and the terrors which succeeded almost incapacitated me from taking any measures for my defence. It was an impulse of which I was scarcely conscious, that made me fasten the lock and draw the bolts of my chamber door. (96-97)

Once again all the action is from outside. The one clear action which Clara performs has to be specified as semi-conscious. Otherwise her physical immobility is reflected in her spatialization of her mind as full of threatening possibilities. Rational analysis (sound denoting an arrival) gives way to fears of assault expressed through anticipating "images" which occur within a mental darkness as well as a literal nocturnal setting.

Clara's reactive posture here of tensed anticipation is of course gender specific. Andrew J. Schreiber has argued that Brown's main narrator is in fact a double figure, the product of a contradictory ideology towards women. On the one hand, he states, she is a "child of reason"; on the other as woman she is dependent on the authorization of male power.[6] By the latter Schreiber clearly means her reliance on Pleyel's good opinion and that of her brother. When Pleyel imagines that she has "fallen" from sexual grace his language switches ludicrously from the one extreme of angelic idealization to its opposite melodramatic inference by ruin. Clara's protestations of innocence have a certain legalistic conviction but they do not admit to her consciousness a sexual subtext running through the episodes with Carwin. As soon as they meet a frisson occurs between them and Clara registers how "potent" is the other's eye. Shortly afterwards she composes a decorously romantic meeting between herself and Pleyel in the nearby temple where he would duly declare his love and a cooperative heaven would spare her blushes by sending over clouds just at the appropriate moment. In the event Pleyel does not come and an altogether more sexual fantasy begins to form of a "ravisher" coming to her closet. This closet becomes one within a series of concentric sexual spaces from house to closet, body, and mind. Clara suppresses naming Carwin as the expected visitor but refers to him indirectly through physical synecdoche—a strong hand, a frame which is "all muscle," and so on. Clearly in such episodes, Brown is drawing on the fiction of sensibility, on the works of Richardson, for instance. Carwin's entry into Clara's closet represents an invasion of physical and imaginative intimacy (the latter since he reads her journal), the prelude to a sexual act which never materializes. In her study *Love, Mystery and Misery* (1978) Coral Ann Howells has rightly demonstrated that the heroines of Gothic fiction anticipate threats which thrill them with horror, while the so-called villains might be planning much more mundane purposes like getting their hands on the protagonists' money.[7] Just as Clara does not fit the role of heiress so Carwin makes a poor seducer, claiming as his only success the servant girl Judith. Nothing daunted, Norman S. Grabo sees Carwin as Clara's "own self-generated sexuality—raw, irrational, irresponsible, violent, even criminal."[8] At no point, even in her deepest imaginings, is Clara about to throw decorum to the winds, and Grabo does not recognize the element of anticlimax which attends the nonfulfilment of our anticipations of sexual encounter. And the reason for this is that in *Wieland* we have as many lines of expected plot development as there are narrators.

When approaching the narrative structure of *Wieland,* we should therefore think in terms of multiple accounts rather than of any single entity. Clara's is the primary narrative but this draws on other figures, like her uncle, for information on her father's combustion, and contains other secondary narrators, like Pleyel and her brother. Self-explanation is articulated in narrative terms, a tendency which becomes strikingly evident when Clara is suspected of sexual activity with Carwin. She tells her "tale" (an implied summary of the data she has already given the reader) to Wieland, who, unimpressed, remarks that Pleyel's "proofs . . . are different" (110). Pleyel then prefaces his own account with the warning that the "clearest narrative will add nothing to your present knowledge" (121). In fact this turns out not to be the case because every subsidiary narrative introduces some additional information. Pleyel's statement is best read as an attempt to establish his own credentials in contrast with Carwin, whose "artful tale" he dismisses without even hearing it.

Clearly, then, the novel describes the complex process of its own narrative assembly. Clara functions variously as witness, listener and general narrative conduit more than an agent in her own right, and Harald Kittel has rightly denied that she possesses any retrospective awareness which increases the clarity of the novel. Instead, "the act of narration is contingent upon the physical, mental and overall existential situation of the first- person narrator. Throughout the book, Clara presents herself as intensely self-conscious, but not self-confident, constantly interrupting her narrative to address the reader and confirm the veracity of the tale."[9] Certainly the text is riddled with references to conjecture, inference, and supposition. One biographical reason for this must lie in Brown's legal training. While a member of the Philadelphia Belles Lettre [sic] Society he would recount cases and then scrutinize them for issues of responsiblity and justice. His analysis infers

motivation and comments on the all-important question of probability. For instance, considering a civil action, Brown concludes: "I am of the opinion that the demand and refusal here made, are no sufficient evidence of a conversion."[10] "Evidence" is a key term also in *Wieland,* since what are ingeniously referred to as "tales" turn into testimony either answering the reader's presumption of incredulity, or the moral charges against Clara and the criminal charges against Wieland. The law court functions as a metaphorical context to the former and a literal context to the latter, specifically to Wieland's own account of his actions which refuses the authority of a secular judicial system.

The problem of credibility is written into the novel as a metafictional dimension revealed in three ways. Firstly, there are the many references to reading books, whether on religion, works of tragedy, or Cicero's prose. On her uncle's conclusion to his story of Wieland's mania, Clara reflects: "What a tale had thus been unfolded!" (189). Her intertextual reference to the ghost in *Hamlet* alludes to a passage which simultaneously promises a horrific impact on the listener ("Make thy two eyes like stars start from their spheres," etc.) and contains an embargo on disclosure ("I am forbid / To tell the secrets of my prison0-house").[11] The tension between revelation and disclosure lies at the heart of the novel's action and even finds expression within the style through the device of delayed reference, where a figure is introduced into the action but without immediate identification. The second metafictional strategy Brown follows is to name the central family after the eighteenth-century German writer; indeed, he ensures that the reader will not miss this connection by pointing out that his characters were related. One of the German Wieland's critics has described that novelist's methods in terms virtually identical to those of Brown. Wieland, she declares, follows a pattern set by Richardson and Rousseau where "the events are narrated by various distinctly different personalities whose background, education, experience, moral fibre, and mood colour the presentation of episodes and influence the evaluation of other characters."[12] Transpose this description on to Brown's novel and we find a near paradox in his method, because on the one hand he is applying the discourse of quasi-legal analysis, which sets up an expectation of ultimate coherence; while on the other he is multiplying his narrators so that events are sometimes described for the reader at two removes. The proliferation of narrative sources inevitably muffles the novel's progression towards explanatory closure and prevents it from following Ann Radcliffe's procedure of introducing the supernatural and then explaining it away. No such resolution concludes *Wieland,* which halts prematurely with the collapse of Clara. Discrepancies are left in the explanation of the mysterious voices. Narrative loose-ends remain, hence the tacked on final chapter which tries to swing the focus of narrative interest round to the father of Louisa Conway, a minor figure in the novel proper.[13] And it may be that Brown decided he had not made adequate use of Carwin, commencing the unfinished *Memoirs of Carwin* a few years later.

Indeed, Carwin can be considered as an author in his own right. He is a skilled rhetorician and, for Clara at least, constructs his narratives with so much skill that they demand instant credit. The discussion of his stories in chapter 8, however, does not recount unaminity among Carwin's audience, and the mixed opinions as well as the novel's whole attention to credibility reflect Brown's anxiety on how the "extraordinary and rare" events promised in his Advertisement will be received: hence the novel's opening line as being written in response to an unnamed other. The notion of authoring thus becomes written into the novel as a problem and a search. Clara herself, as we have seen, acts as scribe and assembler of her narrative rather than its originator. The term "author" appears in the latter sense primarily and indicates characters' search for a rational explanation of events. The model which Brown had before him in this respect was Godwin's *Adventures of Caleb Williams,* a work whose "transcendental merits" he valued greatly.[14] This novel starts as an account of the search for explanations ("I was desirous of tracing the variety of effects which might be produced from given causes") whose rationality veers into paranoia as his benefactor-turned-persecutor Falkland comes to possess the knowledge and power Williams has associated with the deity: "Did his power reach through all space, and his eye penetrate every concealment? Was he like that mysterious being, to protect us from whose fierce revenge mountains and hills we are told might fall on us in vain?"[15] Williams' surge of panic at this point occurs as he begins to realize what power wealth might confer.

There is no corresponding moment in *Wieland,* rather a constant suspicion that Carwin might be the "author of this black conspiracy; the intelligence that governed in this storm" (190). Carwin approaches the position occupied by the fantastically powerful schemers of Gothic fiction (he possesses a flashing eye, one of the key attributes of these figures), approaches but never reaches. His name becomes a floating signifier, tantalizingly raising possibilities, but then "Carwin is unknown" even after he tells his story, hence the brilliantly appropriate ambiguity of Brown's coinage "biloquism." In attributing to him a "deep" motive, a "creative" power and a "design," Clara is making him, to use Michael Foucault's terms, a "projection . . . of the operations that we force texts to undergo, the connections that we make, the traits that we establish as pertinent, the continuities that we recognize, or the exclusions that we prac-

tise."[16] Carwin thus personifies a power expressed in textual terms, perhaps as the skills of the author Brown would like to be.

Such skills confer authority and here we must turn to the novel's political dimensions. *Wieland* narrates a series of acts of disobedience against male authority-figures, which is initiated by Grandfather Wieland's refusal to follow his father's wishes and his decision to marry the daughter of a merchant. By so doing he turns his back on Saxon aristocracy and finds an "asylum" in a new home, which satisfies his desire for independence. His son in turn shakes off the restrictions of a mercantile apprenticeship and engages in missionary work among the Pennsylvania Indians. Finally, Theodore Wieland who, we are told, inherits his father's morose religious temperament, develops a "passion" for executing God's will so strong that he can burst free of his fetters in jail (165). This last case is one of submission *and* rebellion, submission to a spiritual father and rebellion against legal authority. Jane Tompkins has shown that the experiences of the grandfather set a trend: "the story of the first Wieland lays down the proposition that it is impossible to rebel against legal authority and not be destroyed."[17] Certainly the acts of rebellion are presented as both necessary and fatal. Even Carwin partly fits the pattern. In the novel he is just a figure at large but in *The Memoirs* he, too, rejects and is rejected by his father for his intellectual precocity, and is taken up by Ludlow as an adopted son.

Already it should be evident that these fictional biographies bear clear resemblances to the ideological portrayal of American history as a struggle for freedom. The first Wieland's new home expresses in miniature Tom Paine's view of America as an "asylum for mankind."[18] His son recapitulates the history of Protestant sects again searching for freedom through emigration and fulfilling a divine mandate through missionary activity. Personal narratives thus take on a historical symbolism just as in his autobiography Franklin describes his struggles for personal autonomy against his father and domineering brother. His achievement of personal independence acts as a prelude to and analogue for the subsequent national maneuverings of the American states. And yet Franklin frames his narrative as advice—advice, not overt instruction—to his son; and he followed the same procedure in his 1758 "Letter from Father Abraham to His Beloved Son," in which he recommended taking on a monitor as personal adviser. Crèvecoeur's *Letters from an American Farmer* made the country-as-parent trope most explicit. The metaphor of adoption naturalizes the process of immigration whereby new arrivals have the following experience: "After a foreigner from any part of Europe is arrived and become a citizen, let him devoutly listen to the voice of our great parent, which says to him, 'Welcome to my shores, distressed European; bless the hour in which thou didst see my verdant fields, my fair navigable rivers, and my green mountains!' . . ."[19] America is given a quasidivine voice, articulating welcome to the new national collectivity as a series of promises of prosperity. Where Crèvecoeur has no misgivings about the steady expansion of the new nation, Brown confuses our sense of purpose and direction by presenting the hopes of his characters as leading to failure. Wieland *père* suffers ridicule by the Indians and is fatally injured by his combustion. His son is led by his convictions to destroy the very group that should be dearest to him—his family. Clara and, as we discover in his **Memoirs,** Carwin can only find peace outside America. As Jane Tompkins points out, the novel evokes an initial state of well-being in the Wielands and their friends in order to maximize the difficulty of explaining their subsequent sufferings: "The question the novel poses . . . is: given the material prosperity of the Wielands, given the ideal nature of their intellectual, moral, and religious education, their location in an innocent rural environment, their freedom from social and political pressures of any kind, given all this, how can one account for the series of catastrophes that ensure?"[20] Neither she nor, she argues, the novel offers any simple answer to this question. The narrative instead raises more questions, implicit and explicit, about the nature of authority and the dramatic consequences of a new culture not possessing any definite social forms.

Brown situates his novel historically and explores a further dimension of authority by his use of voice. Here we should take bearings from the Great Awakening, the wave of religious revivalism which swept through the American colonies in the middle of the eighteenth century. In his *Personal Narrative* Jonathan Edwards records key moments of delight: " . . . an inward sweetness . . . would carry me away in my contemplations . . . by a calm, sweet abstraction of soul from all the concerns of this world, and . . . a kind of vision . . . of being alone in the mountains or some solitary wilderness, far from all mankind, sweetly conversing with Christ. . . ."[21] The experiential pattern of withdrawal into solitude followed by spiritual uplift and privileged communication with the deity is followed by Theodore Wieland, but with a number of crucial differences, as we shall see in a moment. First we need to acknowledge the importance of a news item which ran in the *New York Weekly Magazine* for 1796 and which is now generally acknowledged to have been one of Brown's main sources for **Wieland**. The item concerned a series of murders committed within "one of the most respectable families" of this state in 1781. After an improvised sabbath meeting held at the house in question, as the father subsequently deposed, he had a spiritual experience: "Instantly a new light shone into the room, and upon looking up I beheld two Spirits, one at my right hand and the other at my left; he at the left bade me destroy all my *idols,* and begin

by casting the Bible into the fire; the other spirit dissuaded me, but I obeyed the first, and threw the book into the flames." Understandably his wife protests but her husband embarks on an orgy of destruction, killing one of his horses and two children. By this time the wife has fled but as he catches up with her a brief conflict takes place between "natural feelings" and the voice of a spiritual prompter. The latter convinces him that his wife is also an "idol," whereupon he smashes her face to a pulp with his axe so that he "could not distinguish one feature of her face." After killing the remainder of his children the man is captured and during the hearing repeatedly addresses his spiritual mentor in justification: "my father, thou knowest that it was in obedience to thy commands, and for thy glory that I have done this deed." The case could be placed at the fag end of the Great Awakening and the journalist's conclusion is of particular importance since no sooner has he attributed the events to one cause ("we do not hesitate to pronounce it the act of insanity") than he brings in another possible explanation: "yet upon the other hand . . . we are apt to conclude, that he was under a strong delusion of Satan."[22]

The journalist's hesitation between psychological and religious modes of causality places this article in a period where religious belief was giving way to a new rationalism and a similar ambivalence informs Brown's novel. Theodore Wieland is clearly modeled on the murderer in the article since he, too, acts under the supposed mandate of his father. However, he is referred to as an "enthusiast," a term loaded by the end of the century with negative connotations. Even more pointedly, Brown presents Wieland's experiences as unconscious travesties of biblical prototypes. Let us take as the first instance Wieland senior's combustion in the classical temple in his grounds. The description of this experience stresses light-effects, the gleams and rays which are perceived and in particular a "cloud impregnated with light" (17). Clara's summary both specifies the image and attributes it to the working of his mind: "His fancy immediately pictured to itself, a person bearing a lamp" (18). In fact, the ascription comes too easily because at least one other character has seen this light. Theodore Wieland's equivalent experience occurs in Clara's house at night, again described in terms of a light suddenly shining within the darkness: "I opened my eyes and found all about me luminous and glowing. It was the element of heaven that flowed around. Nothing but a fiery stream was at first visible; but, anon, a shrill voice from behind called upon me to attend" (167). In the Old Testament clouds function as a medium of revelation and the whole nexus of allusions to light revolve around truth, faith, and salvation, the latter sometimes symbolized by the lamp. Theodore Wieland's account draws on the description in Daniel 7. The biblical dream contains its own interpreters whereas Wieland supposedly wakes *from* dream and "sees" only visual flux without the definite figures of the prophet's dream, particularly the Ancient of Days sitting on the throne of judgement.

Up to this point it might seem that Brown was simply drawing on the Bible to compose pastiche moments of revelation, but the novel questions the authenticity of these moments through more diverse means than the overt commentary in Clara's narrative. Wieland senior's withdrawal into his temple, for instance, follows the pattern of abstraction described above in Edwards's *Personal Narrative,* only to render figures of revelation grotesquely physical as a fire which literally scorches the subject. Edwards's 1733 sermon "A Divine and Supernatural light" stresses that the force he is describing has no connection with the senses, nor even with the mind: "This spiritual and divine light does not consist in any impression made upon the imagination. It is no impression upon the mind, as though one saw anything with the bodily eyes."[23] In contrast the novel gives the impression that Wieland's father has been struck by lightning and the restiveness of the critics over this bizarre event grows out of their reluctance to read the event thematically as one of a series of examples where Brown equivocates over the nature of events, over their status as religious, mental or physical happenings. With Theodore Wieland Brown follows a different tactic, one of simple inversion. After Carwin admits that he has fooled him by voice projection, Wieland becomes transformed into a "man of sorrows" (230). The change, signaled in the novel's title, is from faith to despair but the phrase "man of sorrows," which Brown italicizes for special prominence, carries quite different connotations in the Bible. It derives from Isaiah 53, where the prophet describes society's neglect and abuse of a divine messenger who is chastised and imprisoned. It is only when Wieland has *lost* his faith, however, that he is described in these terms, and the same chapter from Isaiah proves to have an ironic relevance to the whole issue of credibility, since it opens with the words, "who hath believed our report? and to whom is the arm of the Lord revealed?"

Wieland, then, does not simply juxtapose a rational "editorial" voice with that of a religious obsessive, as James Hogg was to do in his *Private Memoirs and Confessions of a Justified Sinner* (1824), but assembles a number of contrasting voices which establish radically opposing views on the same events. And he destabilizes the imagery of illumination so that most references to light in the novel indicate the sheer difficulty of visual perception, to say nothing of the relative accessibility of divine truth. Much of the action of *Wieland* takes place in semi-darkness for this reason, not for mere Gothic atmospherics. Finally, despite the airy assertion of an early critic that "Brown delights in solitude of all kinds," this privileged circumstance of mystical revelation is shown instead to be positively dangerous.[24] In *The Rhapsodist* (1798) Brown describes

the luxurious sense of space enjoyed by the "solitary banks of the Ohio" where his persona can "follow the dictates" of his own inclination. Once he goes to the city the contrast unsettles him so severely that he feels to be losing touch with reality itself: " . . . upon my entrance into this city I experienced a temporary paroxism of phrenzy, my fancy was altogether ungovernable, and I frequently mistook the scene which was passing before me for the lively representation of a dream."[25] "Frenzy" is a term which recurs in *Wieland* to suggest the pathological dimension to Theodore's experience. Brown's main source at this point, acknowledged within the text, was Erasmus Darwin's *Zoonomia,* an encyclopedic work of classifying the different forms of organic life. In volume 2, which assembles a taxonomy of diseases, Darwin records the importance of monomania as a symptom: "in every species of madness there is a peculiar idea either of desire or version, which is perpetually excited in the mind with all its connections." He notes that madness can be hereditary (Theodore is explicitly described as possessing his father's melancholy traits) and under "mutable madness" (i.e. mistaking "imagination for realities") Darwin records cases of women imagining that angels tell them not to eat, or to repent for their sins.[26]

Darwin's confident identification of symptoms enters Brown's novel as one of a number of possible explanations of behavior. It is thematically important that self-delusion can occur in terms of voice since the senses of hearing and seeing, which Brown elsewhere describes traditionally as the "inlets to [man's] mind," become in *Wieland* the avenues for perceptual error.[27] The novel clearly positions Carwin as an anti-Wieland because he can project his voice. His function, Alan Axelrod declares, is to "counterfeit knowledge," but it would be better to see him as a counterfeiter of voices since this better explains his role and once again situates the novel historically.[28] The earliest recorded occurrences of the term "ventriloquism" all bear on witchcraft since it was applied to cases of demonic possession whereby evil spirits spoke from their victims' bodies. By 1797, however, the term had become secularized and defined as an "art by which certain persons can so modify their voice, as to make it appear to the audience to proceed from any distance, and in any direction."[29] The *Encyclopedia Britannica* article, which Brown certainly knew, gives examples of deceptions (a whole church congregation is fooled into believing they can hear the voices of those in purgatory, for instance) made possible by our habits of placing sound; in other words it would have given Brown additional material for describing the mind's vulnerability to error.

Ventriloquism features in *Wieland* as a means of trickery and this function helps to explain the peculiarly national significance of Carwin. Gary Lindberg in an important study has argued that the confidence man is the covert culture hero of America, a figure characterized by "plasticity and mimickry." In a more ambiguous way—hence the appropriate ambiguity of Brown's term "biloquism"—Carwin is continuing a pattern recommended by Franklin of easy adaptability to changing experiences. He is an "ideal agent to demonstrate the risks of credulity" because he is himself driven by curiosity (like Caleb Williams and Victor Frankenstein) and a preoccupation with his own skills. Although Lindberg later comments that "in a fluid world of promise, it is easy to regard self-transformation as a matter of *becoming*," he does not apply this point to Carwin.[30] Nevertheless, the latter would fit Lindberg's paradigm exactly. He first appears in the novel as a transient undefined by any specific occupation or even nationality, since he is reported as having been seen in Spain "indistinguishable from a native" (67). He is thus explicitly linked with the theme of transformation and from the very first is perceived by Clara as a figure of secrecy: "Nothing could be discerned through the impenetrable veil of his duplicity" (94). He functions as an enigmatic and elusive signifier around which can cluster fantastic speculations about his power and wickedness, the latter being fed by a handbill naming him as a wanted criminal. Carwin plays the perfect foil to the younger Wieland, the other explicit example of transformation, in that Wieland claims a singular role through biblical discourse whereas Carwin goes from guise to guise, and quotes Lady Macbeth in turn quoting a heavenly voice crying out against murder—"Hold, hold!" Such masking is symptomatic of Carwin who in his confession at once reveals his "gift" to Clara while at the same time scrupulously concealing his past.[31] His fluidity places Carwin in that American tradition of quick-change artists, which produces figures like Ralph Ellison's Rinehart. Ellison himself has confirmed the national symbolism: "Rinehart is my name for the personification of chaos. He is also intended to represent America and change. He has lived so long with chaos that he knows how to manipulate it. It is the old theme of *The Confidence Man*."[32]

The unfinished *Memoirs of Carwin* fill out his dimension as the "living embodiment of a society in which there are no markers that define and fix the self."[33] The *Memoirs* narrate a process of mental growth in Carwin towards an ultimate point of independence. In his childhood his father simply sets limits on his intellectual curiosity. Then, partly as a result of a trick using his talent of ventriloquism, Carwin leaves his family farm and takes up residence with his aunt in Philadelphia. Finally, he comes under the influence of the mysterious Ludlow, who fulfils a quasi-parental role in nurturing his protegé's appetite for knowledge. Their voyage to Ireland is figured as the beginning of an epistemic journey without clear destination or direction. Although the world lies all before him, the description of Carwin's situation carries a certain ambiguity: "Without profession or habits of industry or sources of permanent revenue, the world appeared to me an ocean on which my

bark was set afloat, without compass or sail" (268). His tutor Ludlow specializes in exposing human delusions and in unfettering his pupil's conceptions "from the prejudices which govern the world" (269). While the *Memoirs* privilege the life of the mind over all other activity, Carwin's learning takes a negative direction. Ludlow induces a scepticism towards all presumed knowledge. The influence of *Caleb Williams* on this work emerges in Ludlow's initial role as benefactor and in Brown's modification of the figure of the trunk as a Pandora's box of unpredictable knowledge. Violation of Falkland's privacy in the earlier novel finds a less dramatic but equally important parallel in Ludlow's bookcase. Browsing through its contents, Carwin comes across a cryptic map of some islands which appear to be destined for future colonisation. The result of his discovery is uncertainty: "Could Ludlow have intended that I should see this atlas? . . . Was it an oversight in him to leave it in my way, or could he have intended to lead my curiosity and knowledge a little farther onward by this accidental disclosure?" (300).[34] When the hapless Caleb Williams is caught in the act of rifling Falkland's trunk the novel shifts abruptly from a narrative of patronage to a demonstration of the power which can be exercised by one possessing money and social status. In the *Memoirs,* too, power figures as a central consideration, albeit in a much more ambiguous form. Ludloe invites Carwin to make a complete confession to him and cites his knowledge of the latter's Spanish lover as evidence of the futility of concealment. In other words Ludloe's map becomes a metonym of knowledge itself, tantalizingly left in the atlas and then removed.

Brown constantly reminds us in the *Memoirs* that the process of learning is charged with political implications. Ludloe demonstrates his power over Carwin by pacing this process and by choosing the circumstances of each phase in Carwin's education. The culmination of this process comes with the revelation that Ludloe is a member of a secret society. This disclosure in intself carried a topical significance, since in the same year that *Wieland* was published there also appeared John Robison's sensational *Proofs of a Conspiracy against all the Religions and Governments of Europe.* Robison argued that the Illuminati, founded in Germany in 1775, was a secret society operating through some masonic lodges and behind the facade of reading societies for the "express purpose," he exclaimed, of *rooting out all the religious establishments, and overturning all the existing governments of Europe,* (Robison's emphasis).[35] The founder, Adam Weishaupt, saw his mission as the triumphal assertion of reason and he expressed his purpose through the light-metaphors we have already encountered in Brown: " . . . the means of attaining [universal happiness] is Illumination, enlightening the understanding by the sun of reason, which will dispel the clouds of superstition and prejudice."[36] His declaration of faith in reason anticipates Ludloe's utopian ambition to found a community "where the empire of reason should supplant that of force"; but Ludloe's declaration ("a number of persons are leagued together for an end of some moment") cryptically refuses to specify goals to Carwin (321). One of Robison's strongest criticisms of the Illuminati was that, although they professed a faith in rational progress through understanding, the actual secrecy of their procedures kept the novice in a state of ignorance where blind allegiance is demanded of him: "The pupil can see nothing but this, that there is a set of men, whom he does not know, who may acquire incontroulable power, and may perhaps make use of him, but for what purpose, and in what way, he does not know . . ."[37] This is exactly the position in which Carwin finds himself. Ostensibly Ludloe encourages the free exercise of his intellect; but at the same time he invites a total submission to himself through absolute confession and Carwin is on the verge of making this act of submission just at the points where the **Memoirs** break off. Although they lack the narrative complexity of **Wieland,** nevertheless they continue the same motif of revealing Brown's ambivalence towards the powers of the mind. Carwin's supposed education induces a growing uncertainty in him and a panic-stricken conviction of his tutor's powerful intellectual hold over him despite Ludloe's professions of mental liberation.

Wieland and to a lesser extent the **Memoirs** belong in the line of American fiction which revolves around hermeneutic uncertainty. Brown's depiction of perceptual error and self-delusion clearly looks forward to the tales of Poe and to the monomaniacs of Hawthorne's short stories. While Carwin's activities anticipate the trickery of Melville's *Confidence-Man* the novel's duplicated and reversed perspectives also resemble the contrasted viewpoints of *Moby-Dick.* In Brown's 1799 essay "Walstein's School of History" he writes: "The causes that fashion men into instruments of happiness or misery, are numerous, complex, and operate upon a wide surface. Virtuous activity may, in a thousand ways, be thwarted and diverted by foreign and superior influence."[38] **Wieland** at many points reads like a work of naturalism before the fact in its evocation of the self as the passive plaything of such forces and impulses whose origins lie hidden.

Notes

[1] Leslie A. Fiedler, *Love and Death in the American Novel* (1960; London: Granada, 1970), 139.

[2] Paul Allen, *The Life of Charles Brockden Brown* (Delmar, NY: Scholars' Facsimiles and Reprints, 1975), 18.

[3] Charles Brockden Brown, *The Rhapsodist and Other Uncollected Writings,* ed. Harry R. Warfcl (New York: Scholars' Facsimiles and Reprints, 1943), 46.

[4] Alan Axelrod, *Charles Brockden Brown: An American Tale* (Austin: U of Texas P, 1983), 91.

[5] Charles Brockden Brown, *Wieland: Or, The Transformation: An American Tale* (with *Memoirs of Carwin the Biloquist*), eds Sydney J. Krause and S.W. Reid (1798; Kent, OH: Kent State UP, 1977), 10-11. Hereafter cited parenthetically in the text.

[6] Andrew J. Schreiber, "'The Arm Lifted Against Me': Love, Terror, and the Construction of Gender in *Wieland,*" *Early American Literature* 26 (1991), 174, 186.

[7] Coral Ann Howells, *Love, Mystery, and Misery: Feeling in Gothic Fiction* (London: Athlone P, 1978).

[8] Norman S. Grabo, *The Coincidental Art of Charles Brockden Brown* (Chapel Hill: U of North Carolina P, 1981), 27.

[9] Harald Kittel, "Free Indirect Discourse and the Experiencing Self in Eighteenth-Century American Autobiographical Fiction: The Narration of Consciousness in Charles Brockden Brown's *Wieland,*" *New Comparison* 9 (1990), 77.

[10] Allen, *Life of Charles Brockden Brown,* 33.

[11] *Hamlet,* I.v, 13-16.

[12] Lieselotte E. Kurth-Voigt, *Perspectives and Points of View: The Early Works of Wieland and Their Background* (Baltimore: Johns Hopkins UP, 1974), 44-45. Wieland was, like Brown's character, very interested in the works of Cicero.

[13] Cf. Grabo, *The Coincidental Art of Charles Brockden Brown,* 23.

[14] Allen, *Life of Charles Brockden Brown,* 106.

[15] William Godwin, *Caleb Williams,* ed. David McCracken, (1794; Oxford: Oxford UP, 1970), 4, 240.

[16] Michael Foucault, "What Is An Author?," *Textual Strategies: Perspectives in Post-Structuralist Criticism,* ed. Josué V. Harari (London: Methuen, 1980), 150.

[17] Jane Tompkins, *Sensational Designs: The Cultural Work of American Fiction, 1790-1860* (New York: Oxford UP, 1985), 56.

[18] Thomas Paine, *Common Sense,* ed. Isaac Kramnick (1776; Harmondsworth, UK: Penguin, 1982), 100.

[19] J. Hector St. John de Crèvecoeur, *Letters from an American Farmer* and *Sketches of Eighteenth-Century America,* ed. Albert E. Stone (1782, 1925; Harmondsworth, UK: Penguin, 1981), 89.

[20] Tompkins, *Sensational Designs,* 51.

[21] Jonathan Edwards, *Personal Narrative, Selected Writings of Jonathan Edwards,* ed. Harold P. Simonson (c. 1740; New York: Ungar, 1970), 30.

[22] "An Account of a Murder Committed by Mr. J——Y——, Upon His Family, in December, A.D. 1781," *The New York Weekly Magazine* 2.56 (July 1796), 20, 28.

[23] Edwards, *Selected Writings,* 70.

[24] Unidentified quotation in "On the Writings of Charles Brockden Brown and Washington Irving," *Blackwood's Edinburgh Magazine* 6 (1820), 556.

[25] *The Rhapsodist,* 15,16.

[26] Erasmus Darwin, *Zoonomia; Or, The Laws of Organic Life,* vol. 2 (London: Johnson, 1796), 350, 354, 356-8.

[27] Allen, *Life of Charles Brockden Brown,* 20.

[28] Axelrod, *Charles Brockden Brown,* 76.

[29] "Ventriloquism," *Encyclopedia Britannica,* 3rd ed., vol. 18 (Edinburgh: Bell and Macfarquhar, 1797), 639. Some of the examples given in this article are incorporated into the *Memoirs of Carwin.*

[30] Gary Lindberg, *The Confidence Man in American Literature* (New York: Oxford UP, 1982), 10, 100, 140.

[31] *Macbeth,* I.v, 51-52.

[32] Ralph Ellison, *Shadow and Act* (1964; London: Secker and Warburg, 1967), 181.

[33] Tompkins, *Sensational Designs,* 52.

[34] Brown uses this figure briefly in *Wieland* (Pleyel's trunk), and also in "The Man at Home" where the narrator has a mysterious trunk in his room, apparently left by the previous occupant. Hidden in its false bottom he finds a manuscript which "unfolds the causes, and exhibits the true agents in a transaction of high importance in the American revolution" (*The Rhapsodist,* 69).

[35] John Robison, *Proofs of a Conspiracy against all the Religions and Governments of Europe, Carried on in the Secret meetings of Free Masons, Illuminati, and Reading Societies* (1798; Belmont, MA: Western Islands, 1967), 7. First published in New York, the volume rapidly sold out of its first printing. Although Robison concerned himself with Europe, the publication of his book found a quick and receptive response in American (see Neal Wilgus, *The Illuminoids: Secret Societies and Political Paranoia* [London: New English Library, 1980], 22).

[36] Weishaupt, quoted in Robison, *Proofs of a Conspiracy,* 64. Weishaupt envisaged the transformation of the human race into one big family. In the overthrow of despotism families were to play a special role: "The head of every family will be what Abraham was, the patriarch, the priest, and the unlettered lord of his family, and Reason will be the code of laws to all mankind" (91).

[37] Robison, *Proofs of a Conspiracy,* 131.

[38] *The Rhapsodist,* 152.

FURTHER READING

Axelrod, Alan. *Charles Brockden Brown: An American Tale.* Austin: University of Texas Press, 1983, 203 p.

    Provides a detailed critical analysis of *Wieland, Ormond, Arthur Mervyn,* and *Edgar Huntly.*

Berthoff, W. B. "Adventures of the Young Man: An Approach to Charles Brockden Brown." *American Quarterly* IX, No. 4 (Winter 1957): 421-34.

    Studies Brown's treatment of the theme of initiation in several of his novels.

——."'A Lesson on Concealment': Brockden Brown's Method in Fiction." *Philological Quarterly* XXXVII, No. 1 (January 1958): 45-57.

    Analyzes Brown's short story "A Lesson on Concealment" in order to argue that Brown uses narrative to discover, explore, and test ideas.

Chase, Richard Volney. "Brockden Brown's Melodramas." In *The American Novel and Its Tradition,* pp. 29-41. Garden City, N.Y.: Doubleday, Anchor Books, 1957.

    Examines Brown's use of melodrama in his novels and comments on the influence of Brown's innovations on later American novelists.

Clark, David Lee. *Charles Brockden Brown: Pioneer Voice of America.* Durham, N. C.: Duke University Press, 1952, 363 p.

    Important critical biography emphasizing Brown's radical political and social thought. Clark investigates various aspects of Brown's work and incorporates into his analysis materials from unpublished Brown manuscripts.

Dunlap, William. *Memoirs of Charles Brockden Brown, the American Novelist.* London: Henry Colburn, 1822, 337 p.

Abridged version of Dunlap's 1815 biography of Brown. Considered the most important source of information about Brown's life, however marred by Dunlap's biases.

Ferguson, Robert A. "Literature and Vocation in the Early Republic: The Example of Charles Brockden Brown." *Modern Philology* 78, No. 2 (November 1980): 139-52.

Argues that literature in early America was a by-product of a writer's other efforts in his career, and maintains that Brown dramatizes this relationship between literature and vocation through his use of fiction as "a fantasy world for projecting occupational difficulties."

Hintz, Howard W. "Charles Brockden Brown." In *The Quaker Influence in American Literature,* pp. 34-40. New York: Fleming H. Revell Company, 1940.

Maintains that Brown's Quaker background helped to shape his "romantic social idealism"; it is this quality, Hintz suggests, which most significantly influenced Brown's writings.

Lee, A. Robert. "A Darkness Visible: The Case of Charles Brockden Brown." In *American Horror Fiction: From Brockden Brown to Stephen King,* pp. 13-32. London: Macmillan, 1990.

Examines the characteristics of Brown's novels which contain elements of the genre of horror.

Ringe, Donald A. *Charles Brockden Brown,* revised edition. Boston: Twayne Publishers, 1991, 141 p.

Provides a detailed analysis and evaluation of Brown's life and works.

Snell, George. "Charles Brockden Brown." In *The Shapers of American Fiction, 1798-1947,* pp. 32-87. New York: Cooper Square Publishers, 1961.

Maintains that Brown can be identified as the source of the apocalyptic vision in American fiction—a theme which culminates in the works of William Faulkner.

Stern, Julia A. "A Lady Who Sheds No Tears: Liberty, Contagion, and the Demise of Fraternity in *Ormond.*" In *The Plight of Feeling: Sympathy and Dissent in the Early American Novel,* pp. 153-238. Chicago: University of Chicago Press, 1997.

Argues that in *Ormond,* Brown uncovers as a "national chimera" the "fantasy" of the "vision of sympathy."

Warfel, Harry R. "Charles Brockden Brown's German Sources." *Modern Language Quarterly* 1, No. 3, (1940): 357-65.

Asserts that Brown's interest in German materials reflected similar Biritish interests of the time; that the psychology and rationalism in Brown's novels followed both German and English models; and that the theme of *Wieland* was discovered by Brown in a contemporary German novel.

——. *Charles Brockden Brown: American Gothic Novelist.* Gainesville: University of Florida Press, 1949, 255 p.

A biographical study linking Brown's works to the intellectual atmosphere of his time.

Anna Cora Mowatt

1819-1870

(Also Anna Cora Ogden, Anna Cora Ogden Mowatt Ritchie, Anna Ritchie, Anna Cora Ritchie; wrote under the pseudonyms Helen Berkley, Isabel, Henry C. Browning, and Charles A. Lee, M.D.) American dramatist, novelist, actress, essayist, and poet.

INTRODUCTION

Anna Cora Mowatt, coming from a socially prominent family, was the first upper-middle-class woman to make a public career in the theater, and her successes helped to legitimize acting as an occupation for women. Imaginative and articulate, Mowatt wrote about her stage career in a popular autobiography, and elaborated on the world of the theater in fictional stories. Her best play, *Fashion; or Life in New York* (1845), has been successfully revived in the modern era. Mowatt is generally regarded as a significant contributor to the development of American drama.

Biographical Information

Born on March 5, 1819, in France, Anna Cora Ogden (Mowatt) was one of fourteen children born to Samuel Governeur Ogden and Eliza Lewis, both descendants of old colonial families. When Mowatt was seven, her family moved to the United States and settled in New York. Mowatt did not distinguish herself as a student in the private schools where she was educated. However, her interest in and talent for the theater were manifest early in the writing and performing of creative home theatricals. When Mowatt was fifteen, she eloped with James Mowatt, a well-off New York lawyer. They settled on an estate in Melrose, Long Island. Two years later, in 1836, Mowatt published an historical romance in verse (originally entitled *Pelayo; or The Cavern of Covadonga*) under the name of Isabel. Poor reviews of the work moved Mowatt to reply (also in verse) with *Reviewers Reviewed: A Satire*, printed privately in 1837. Mowatt subsequently became ill with tuberculosis, and went abroad to recover. In London and Paris Mowatt saw performances by the great European actresses of the day and on her return to the United States was inspired to write her first play. This play, entitled *Gulzara; or the Persian Slave*, was published in the well-known *New World* magazine in 1841. Shortly thereafter, Mowatt's husband became ill, lost much of his eyesight, and thus his income. Then, in a financial downturn, he also lost his fortune. Mowatt turned to writing and performing to support herself

and her husband. She began, somewhat cautiously, to give public readings of poems and stories, and was received with great acclaim. She also wrote a variety of non-fiction works under various pseudonyms as well as novels and essays under the pseudonym of Helen Berkley. One of these novels, *The Fortune Hunter; or the Adventures of a Man about Town* (1844), won a prize from *New World*, and prompted one of this magazine's contributors to encourage Mowatt to try play writing. The result, a satirical comedy entitled *Fashion; or Life in New York* (1845), became her best known play. *Fashion* was produced in New York and played for three weeks (a long run for that time). A few months after the production of *Fashion*, Mowatt herself took to the stage, became a well-regarded actress, and remained so for the next eight years. In 1851, Mowatt's husband died. Three years later, Mowatt ended her acting career and married William Ritchie, the editor of the Richmond *Enquirer*. Mowatt continued to write, publishing first an autobiographical account of her years in the theater, entitled *The Autobiography of an Actress* (1854), and then a collection of fictional stories dealing with the same milieu, entitled *Mimic Life; or Before and Behind the Curtain* (1856). Unhappy in her second marriage, Mowatt moved abroad in 1861, and spent the rest of her life in Italy and England. She wrote several more novels and sketches, although they did not achieve the popularity of her earlier works. Mowatt died at the age of fifty-one in Twickingham, England.

Major Works

Mowatt's most important work is her five-act comedy, *Fashion*, written explicitly as an actors-play rather than as a literary endeavor. The first American social comedy, *Fashion* is an engaging satire of nineteenth-century high society in the city of New York. The play pokes good-natured fun at the pretensions, hypocrisy, and shallow materialism of a cast of parvenus as they make their way in society and imitate French fashions. Although *Fashion* has a conventional plot line and stereotyped characters, it is marked by quick action and sharp, witty dialogue. It opened in New York in 1845 to immediate praise and popularity. It subsequently played in Philadelphia and in London (in 1850). The plot turns and humorous characters have proven durable, allowing for successful revivals in 1924 and 1959. Mowatt's most significant work after *Fashion* is her *Autobiography of an Actress*, which offers a lively depiction of life in the theater and the development of her career. It contains humorous and detailed narratives as well as astute social and cultural analysis. Told in a distinctive voice, the autobiography is a valuable portrait of the challenges faced by women in the nineteenth-century and of the conceptions of public and private life. It also serves as an early example of the self-consciousness that characterizes modern autobiography. The collection of tales in *Mimic Life* extends Mowatt's examination of the world of the theater in a fictional context. These tales emphasize the moral tensions and dilemmas that accompanied a theatrical career for a woman in the nineteenth-century, and they portray the minor figures in theatrical productions as dignified and hard-working. Taken with her autobiography, the tales round out a rich historical portrait of a complex social world. Mowatt's other work was well received in her day and was generally successful commercially, but it never achieved a level of recognition or significance equal to that of *Fashion* or the *Autobiography*.

Critical Reception

Mowatt achieved popularity as a writer of both fiction and non-fiction. Her novel *The Fortune Hunter; or the Adventures of a Man about Town* won a prize from *New World* magazine. Her essays written under the pseudonym of Helen Berkley were republished in London and translated into German. Moreover, her autobiography sold extremely well, and was admired by many, including Nathaniel Hawthorne. Mowatt was also a leading figure in the nineteenth-century theater, being well-known in both the United States and England. Furthermore, her dramatic talents and knowledge of the theater helped to make her successful as a playwright. Mowatt's status and esteem in high society helped to change the prevailing notion that the theater was inherently immoral and corrupting, particularly for women. Mowatt's success as a playwright, especially with *Fashion*, challenged those critics who claimed that women could not write plays. Contemporary critics regard Mowatt as the woman with the greatest impact on early American drama, and *Fashion* as the best nineteenth-century comedy. As the most anthologized play of the nineteenth-century, *Fashion* holds a firm place in the canon of nineteenth-century American drama. Historians of the theater have found Mowatt's autobiography and stories about the theater to be valuable sources for details of the daily lives of people who lived and worked behind the curtain. Feminist historians, on the other hand, find Mowatt to be a valuable and articulate example of an unconventional woman, sensitive to the problems of working women and women in the theater.

PRINCIPAL WORKS

Gulzara; or the Persian Slave (drama) 1841
The Fortune Hunter; or the Adventures of a Man about Town (novel) 1844
Fashion; or Life in New York (drama) 1845
Armand; or The Peer and the Peasant (drama) 1847
The Autobiography of an Actress; or Eight Years on the Stage (autobiography) 1854
Mimic Life; or Before and Behind the Curtain (novellas) 1856
Fairy Fingers (novel) 1865

CRITICISM

Mary Howitt

SOURCE: "Memoir of Anna Cora Mowatt," in *Howitt's Journal,* Vol. III, No. 63, March 11, 1848, pp. 167-70.

[*In the following excerpt, Howitt offers an appreciative memoir of the start of Mowatt's writing career and of the public reception of* Fashion.]

Partly in consequence of Mr. Mowatt's residence in Europe, and partly from an affection of the eyes, he gave up his profession of barrister, and was subsequently induced to embark to a large extent in commercial speculations, when unfortunately one of those terrible crises occurring which convulse the whole mercantile world, he, together with thousands of others, found himself on the brink of ruin.

A time of dreadful anxiety succeeded: sleepless nights and days of uncertainty and apprehension. In a few weeks the worst, as they believed, was known, immense loss must be sustained, but still there was a chance of something being saved. Mrs. Mowatt who was extremely attached to their residence, where the brightest and happiest portion of her life had been spent, was willing to make any present sacrifice for the hope of returning in better days to this favourite place.

Misfortunes, however, never come alone; and now, as if to prove the truth of the adage, scarcely had they summoned a cheerful courage to look the future in the face, when a new sorrow, and one more appalling than all the rest, befel them. The affection of the eyes, which had first made its appearance in Germany, again severely attacked Mr. Mowatt. It was impossible for him now to re-commence his professional duties; his sufferings were of the most excruciating character, and for a long period from this time, he was unable to fix his eyes upon a book for above five minutes together.

Here, indeed, was deep cause of anxiety and distress. It was a dark and a melancholy season; yet still out of darkness comes light, and now the young wife, not yet twenty, determined to use some of those splendid gifts which God had given her to retrieve their shipwrecked fortunes, and to lighten, if possible, the load of misfortune which pressed so heavily on her husband. Hitherto her talents had been employed only to embellish life; now they must be used to produce the very means of life; hitherto she had unconsciously been exercising and perfecting her powers amid the joy of youth and the ease of affluence, now their nobler uses must be tried amid the trials of adversity. God truly gives us no powers in vain!

Some time before these domestic events occurred, Mr. Vandenhoff had been giving dramatic readings in various cities of the Union, which had been extremely successful; Mrs. Mowatt had herself attended those which he had given in New York. We know already that she excelled in reading aloud, and in private she had been accustomed to read and recite for the amusement of her friends, and sometimes in large assemblies. Her first idea therefore was to give publicly a course of readings of this class, the taste for them being very great in America.

She had, however, one difficulty to overcome in the very outset, and this was to induce her husband to enter into her plans, for without his full consent she could do nothing. At length this being obtained, she opened her views to a young sister, Mary, who had resided with her since her marriage, but so entirely did this sister, who was of a gentle and shrinking nature, disapprove, so violent was her grief and so earnest her efforts to dissuade, that Mrs. Mowatt determined thenceforth to take counsel of no one, lest thereby her own resolution might be shaken. Silently and sedulously she set about preparing herself for the undertaking, and with the blessing of Heaven she hoped for success. She carefully, therefore, made her selections of poetry from Scott, Byron, Milton, etc, to all of which she wrote appropriate introductions, making at the same time such other preparation as she considered needful. Her resolution and courage never failed her as long as she worked in secret; but so much had she been affected by her much loved sister's grief, that even when all her preparations were finished, and she ready to commence, she thought it best not to consult with her family—her father's disapprobation especially she could not brave.

For reasons which every reader will perfectly appreciate, she felt that she could not commence this new and public life in New York, where she had been known under circumstances so totally different: she, therefore, selected Boston, the most intellectual city of the Union, as the place of her *debût*. We have said already that in part she was induced to make these extraordinary efforts that she might keep the delightful home where she had enjoyed so much happiness. She still resided there—its furniture—its library—its beautiful grounds—its stables with her own and her young sisters' horses—its well-filled green-house—all remained untouched.

Many incidents in the life of this interesting woman are like a page out of a romantic story rather than a passage from real life; this is one of them. From room to room she went gazing fondly on beloved and familiar objects, with a prayer in her heart that God would so bless her as to enable her once more to return to that dear home and to enjoy within its walls something of her former happiness. She walked through garden and grounds; sate in her favourite seats; caressed her animals, and while her sister wept passionately, she herself did not shed one tear. This was the very morning that she set out for Boston.

That same morning she wrote a letter to her father, revealing to him her plans, with all her reasons in favour of them, and earnestly beseeching him not to distress her or to weaken her efforts by his disapproval. She begged of him to write immediately to her in Boston, that she might receive his letter before she made her first appearance in public, and thus, as it were, feel strengthened by his blessing. The dear sister, who was alone the depository of her secret, and who conveyed this letter to her father, parted with her at his very door, which she passed, without taking leave of her family, on her way to the railroad which conveyed her to Boston.

Mrs. Mowatt's name was already favourably known to the press in this city by a number of fugitive poems; and from the first, friends immediately gathered round her, cheering her by the assurance of unquestionable success. According to her earnest wish she received the day before her appearance the much-desired letter from her father; as well as letters from other members of her family; the surprise of all, as might be expected, was great, but as regarded her father, from whom she had inherited her great energy and perseverance, he gave his unqualified consent, approving of her plans and encouraging her to the utmost.

She had to make her *debût* in one of the largest public buildings in Boston; and such was the excitement and interest already created in her behalf, that when she stepped upon the rostrum, she found herself standing before a brilliant assembly, which completely filled the whole building. Her heart almost died within her; all at once she seemed to become aware of the momentous step she had taken; everything was at stake. Had she not over-calculated her powers? She had risked all to save her beloved husband and the remnants of his fortune, and if she had deceived herself, and should now fail, it was a double ruin and disgrace. She had no one to aid her! she stood there a stranger and alone, without even the aid of music to fill up any pause or allow her an interval of rest. These, however, were but the natural doubts of a moment.

The audience, as we have been told, were intensely interested in her appearance, she looked younger, even than she was, and pale as a marble statue—the intensity of her feelings made her cold as death,—she was dressed in plain clear white muslin, with a natural white rose, her favourite flower, in her hair and her bosom. She put up a secret prayer to Heaven for success, and the next moment calmly commenced her reading. How she performed she herself had not the slightest idea, and when the audience applauded she was too much absorbed by her own deep feeling to notice it. It is said that she did not even tremble, and her lips, though colourless as her dress, never quivered. On coming out the people thronged about her; they overwhelmed her with their enthusiastic approval; they congratulated her on her entire success—told her she would go through the whole Union with triumph, and would in the end make a large fortune.

She had not shed a tear through the whole of their misfortunes, nor even on that sad morning when with her sister she took a last farewell of her beautiful home,

now, however, the flood-gates of her feelings seemed opened. She rushed alone into her chamber, and throwing herself on her knees, thanked Heaven from the depths of her soul and wept abundantly!

The sympathy of the whole city was with her. She repeated her readings night after night with increased success. Her heart was cheered and assured, and now she was naturally impatient to return to New York, that she might afford her father an opportunity of hearing her and witnessing her success. Her fame had already gone before her; and on her way thither she gave her readings at the city of Providence. The Americans have a much greater taste for and enjoyment in entertainments of this kind than we have, and the idea of realizing a considerable fortune by means of them appeared anything but chimerical.

Her return to New York afforded the greatest pleasure to her immediate connections and to the public in general: her father, too liberal and high-minded to entertain any petty pride, openly gave her efforts his sanction—her numerous sisters did the same—but she had here to see a new phasis of human nature.

Public applause and sympathy were with her; new friends and admirers gathered around her; she was likely to become an object of universal love and admiration; but many an old and beloved friend, who had flattered her in prosperity, now was ashamed of and coldly deserted her; the dearest friend she had, excepting her sisters, in her own family, one to whom she had looked up as almost to a mother, now totally dissevered herself from her; according to her conventional notions she had lost caste and was degraded. Oh, pride! how cruel and one-sided thou art. She was cut to the heart, she who had bravely faced misfortune, and had shewn a courage through severe trial which surpassed that of a man, was disarmed and enfeebled by the unkindness of those she loved. Her health gave way; she fell dangerously ill, and appeared to all to stand on the brink of the grave. Her medical men gave it as their opinion, that the shock which her feelings had sustained, and not her physical and mental exertions, was killing her. A severe illness succeeded, which confined her to her bed for many months, and which consequently prevented her pursuing her public avocations. For two years she was a confirmed invalid.

A great work, however, was wrought within her soul, which taught her submission and patience, and which shewed her that every trial, however severe, is permitted by the Divine Father as a means of purification and of attracting his creatures still nearer to himself. Under this influence she wrote the following little poem, which we select from a great number of others written at this time, and which all breathe the spirit of the humble and trusting Christian.

THY WILL BE DONE.

Thy will be done! O heavenly King,
   I bow my head to thy decree;
Albeit my soul not yet may wing
   Its upward flight, great God, to thee!

Though I must still on earth abide,
   To toil and groan and suffer here,
To seek for peace on sorrow's tide.
   And meet the world's unfeeling jeer.

When heaven seemed dawning on my view,
   And I rejoiced my race was run,
Thy righteous hand the bliss withdrew;
   And still I say "Thy will be done!"

And though the world can never more
   A world of sunshine be to me,
Though all my fairy dreams are o'er,
   And care pursues where'er I flee.

Though friends I loved—the dearest—best,
   Were scattered by the storm away,
And scarce a hand I warmly pressed
   As fondly presses mine to day.

Yet must I live—must live for those
   Who mourn the shadow on my brow,
Who feel my hand can soothe their woes,
   Whose faithful hearts I gladden now.

Yes, I will live—live to fulfil
   The noble mission scarce begun,
And pressed with grief to murmur still,
   All Wise! All Just! "Thy will be done!"

During this long and severe illness the beautiful home which Mrs. Mowatt had made such extraordinary efforts to save, was sold, and though it had passed away from her for ever, so fondly did her affections still cling to it, that one of the first drives she took during her convalescence was to visit it. The stripped and deserted rooms had a melancholy aspect; the gardens were neglected and overgrown with weeds; it furnished the most complete contrast that could be conceived, to its former state. A pang went to the heart of its young mistress, and yet she returned to her less ostentatious home in the city, though sorrowful, yet submissive to the will of God, let it be whatever it might.

About this time, her husband became the principal partner in a publishing business, and weak as she was, the whole force of her mind was turned to aid him in this undertaking. Wives like this, are truly what wives were meant to be, help-mates in the truest sense of the word. For some time she had written both in her own and under an assumed name in various newspapers and magazines. Under the name of Mrs. Helen Berkley,

she wrote a series of articles which were popular from one end of the Union to the other; which were translated into German, and reprinted in London; the titles of some of these are "Inconvenient Acquaintance," "Practitioners and Patients," "Sketches of Celebrated Persons," and the longest, a one-volume novel, was entitled *The Fortune Hunter.* It may perhaps be as well to remark here that a keen satirical vein runs through most of these works which may be ascribed to the wounds which she had received from her worldly friends and which, while they had tended to open her eyes to the falsehood of the world, had made her *clairvoyant* as it were, to its faults and follies.

The success of these works induced Mrs. Mowatt to write in her own name, and then curious enough, an attack was made upon her by some of the sapient critics for imitating what they called "The witty Helen Berkley." Besides these works we must mention another class which she prepared for her husband's publishing concern, many of them while she was lying upon her bed of sickness, the titles and numbers of which will astonish every one: "On the management of the Sick," "Cookery for the Sick," "Cookery and General House-keeping," "Etiquette for Gentlemen," "Etiquette for Ladies," "Etiquette of Matrimony," "On Knitting, Netting, and Crochet," "On Embroidery," "A Book of the Toilette." This last little book, singular to say, became very popular from its containing some wonderful cosmetics the receipts for which were furnished to her by a relative, to whom they had descended as an heirloom, and which set the ladies, far and wide, to stew and boil the specified roots and ingredients for such cosmetics as had probably belonged to the class which Mrs. Primrose and her daughters prepared. Besides these, she abridged the *Life of Goethe* and Madame D'Arblay's *Life and Letters.* All the above and compilations with the exception of the two last, were extremely successful, edition after edition was sold, and much money was made by them.

We must now relate a little circumstance which appears to us as remarkable as any which have gone before, and which proves that the conscientious discharge of duty, together with a spirit of self-sacrifice and devotion, form the basis of Mrs. Mowatt's character. A singular chance brought her acquainted with a family of British emigrants of the name of Grey, who, after having gone through a series of the most grievous sufferings, were then literally perishing with hunger in that land of plenty. The father was blind, and the mother, in an advanced stage of a mortal malady, was unable to support her family, which consisted of several children, the youngest about two years old. Mrs. Mowatt did not shrink from the picture of abject, hopeless misery before her; on the contrary, all that we have heard of Sisters of Charity doing, was done in this case by this angelic woman; she clothed, she fed, she comforted them; she diffused light amid darkness, hope amid despair. Within a month of each other the parents died, and Mrs. Mowatt found three young orphans upon her hands, but she neither relaxed in her charity nor was dismayed by the weight or the responsibility of the charge.

With the consent of her husband, who had nobly co-operated in her works of Christian love, they adopted the children to whom, having no family of their own, they had become greatly attached. To do all this however much self-sacrifice and self-denial was needed; but they had fortitude enough for this which is the severest trial of the sincerity of charity as well as of any other virtue. For the sake of these otherwise, friendless children, she was willing to bear and to exert herself, often beyond her strength. Among other things, we may mention that she made the clothes even of the boys herself, and gave them all daily instruction. How noble is such a woman! Far more admirable was she making, with her own hands, clothes for her orphans, than if she had remained the brightest ornament merely of wealth and fashion. Three years have passed since these excellent people have become responsible to God and man for these orphan children, and so far, this deed of christianity has brought, and promises yet to bring, abundant blessings. The children are lovely in person and disposition, and devotedly attached to their benefactors.

It was at this time that the works of Miss Bremer, through my translations, made their way into America, and afforded as much pleasure, and created as great a sensation as they have done elsewhere, and must of necessity do, on their first introduction wherever sound moral sentiment forms the foundation of social life. In Mrs. Mowatt's heart they met with the sincerest response; for her mode of action had long been framed instinctively upon the principles advocated and inculcated by Miss Bremer. No wonder therefore, that she seized upon them with the utmost avidity, and hence it is that her longest work, *Evelyn,* written soon after this period, is formed so entirely upon the Bremer model. In this work as well as in *The Fortune Hunter,* the intelligent reader will also become aware of the infusion of another and a nobler spirit, even than that of Miss Bremer—the spirit of Swedenborgian theology which had now been for some time embraced by both Mr. and Mrs. Mowatt.

The history of this conversion, if so it may be called, is not less extraordinary than interesting, but we will hardly venture to communicate all we know, because the world is not yet prepared for the truths of spiritual life. At the important period to which we allude, a period of sickness and deep trial, knowledge was obtained through suffering,—ever one of our divinest teachers, which at once gave a new tone and a new value to this world and the next. The young wife became, as it were, the teacher of the husband, and as in former days, he had guided and tutored her intellect, she now awakened and instructed his nobler spiritual being.

Unfortunately the publishing business in which Mr. Mowatt embarked, was unsuccessful, and new losses and disappointments for the time depressed them. But let no one despair until he have tried every power which is within him. Mrs. Mowatt had many resources yet. It had been told her that nothing which she could write, would be so productive as dramatic literature, for which every one who knew her, believed her eminently qualified. This induced her to make the attempt, and in the spring of 1845, she wrote her first comedy called *Fashion* which was offered to the manager of the Park theatre, New York; no sooner read than accepted, and splendidly brought out.

The design of this piece was to satirise the life of the parvenues of America, and it is undoubtedly indebted for a great deal of its faithful portraiture of life and its keen satire to the author's own experience and sufferings. To the surprise of the young writer, its success was unlimited; no American play was ever so brilliantly successful, and it still keeps its place on the stage.

In Philadelphia it was also brought out and equally well received. The managers of the Walnut-street theatre where it was performed, invited Mr. and Mrs. Mowatt to that city, that they might witness its performance. They accepted the invitation and were entertained three days in the handsomest manner at the expense of these liberal managers. On the night of the performance which Mr. and Mrs Mowatt were to attend, the bills presented to them were printed in letters of gold on white satin. After the play, the audience having discovered that the young authoress was in the house, called for her most enthusiastically. For the first time she that night was compelled to rise from her box and bow to a theatrical audience, little thinking that in less than two months from that time she herself would become familiar with the stage, and make her curtsey before the footlights of that very theatre.

After the play she was requested to go behind the scenes, to be introduced to the principal performers. It was a formidable thing, they were ranged upon the stage in a semicircle to receive her; she made a little acknowledgement to all, as well as her embarrassment would permit, and the following day sent a present to each of the five ladies in the piece. One of these five it will be interesting to our readers to know, was Miss Susan Cushman, now so delightfully familiar to the British public.

The great success of this piece caused the managers of some of the principal theatres to make her very tempting offers to adopt the stage. The acting manager of the Park theatre had two years before, when he witnessed her dramatic readings, offered her the same inducements, but these, at that time, she indignantly refused. Her pride had not yet been wholly conquered, she had, however, since then, suffered a great deal, had gained far greater independence of character, more determination of spirit and greater liberality of views. The shackles which had then, in some degree, bound her to society and its slavish conventionalities were now broken.—She was free and she dared to do whatever was not contrary to her own pure conscience.

The only impediment which stood in her way was the extreme delicacy of her health. However after consultation with physicians she obtained her husband's consent, and after considerable difficulty the consent also of her father, who simply said that if she had but the courage to do in public what he had seen her repeatedly do in private, her success was certain. On the other hand, again came in the opposition of family connections; threats, entreaties, prayers, and tears, were used to deter her. All this caused her so much pain and agitated her mind so fearfully, that to make an end of it, having gained the consent of her husband and father, she determined to expedite the final step that these distressing interferences might be ended. The time for her *debût* was fixed, only allowing about three weeks for the necessary preparatory study and instruction in stage business, and through the whole of that period she was persecuted and annoyed by letters, and warnings; but having advanced thus far, no efforts would turn her back.

She was to make her *debût* at the Park theatre, in the *Lady of Lyons.* The eventful morning of the rehearsal came, and this is a more severe trial to a debutante, than the actual appearing before the public.

The gloomy theatre dimly lighted with gas almost chilled her. All the persons belonging to the theatre were collected round the scenes ready to sneer or laugh, or with malicious pleasure to confuse the novice; but Mrs. Mowatt, summoning all her energies, resolved to do her very best, and regardless of all present, to act her part, exactly as she would do it before the public at night; she took all by surprise, as they afterwards frankly confessed, and when the second act was finished each, in the kindest manner, did his utmost to help her—the very actors themselves applauded, which is the highest species of praise, because it is the most unusual. No one doubted the success which awaited her.

David W. Thompson

SOURCE: "Early Actress-Readers: Mowatt, Kemble, and Cushman," in *Performance of Literature in Historical Perspectives,* edited by David W. Thompson, University Press of America, 1983, pp. 629-50.

[*In the following excerpt, Thompson discusses Mowatt's contributions to the tradition of dramatic reading and characterizes her performing style.*]

Chautauqua marked the climax and not the beginning of the great American interest in public readings of literature. That interest swelled into a passion in the pair of decades just before and after 1900, but that expansion had been prepared for by two earlier developments. One was the patient and wide-spread lecturing on and demonstrating of oral reading by teachers of elocution. The other, complementary to the earnest elocutionists, was the glamorous example of three famous actress-readers touring America between 1841 and 1875. These were Anna Cora Mowatt, Frances Anne Kemble, and Charlotte Cushman.

Prior to the public readings of these three, only a few visiting British actors and actresses had given readings in America, and then only on the fairly rare occasions when they could not find employment with a theatre company. James Fennell and John Vandenhoff, aging British tragedians, occasionally gave readings. A Mrs. Gardner, "actress from Covent Garden," having tried London, Dublin, Jamaica, and Charleston, discovered with some anxiety that she could not find a position in New York. Consequently, she advertised herself giving this reading:

> An Entertainment, rhetorical and oratorical, entitled Fashionable Rallery, or, the Powers of Eloquence Displayed in a spirited and humorous Touch on the Times. Interspersed with Songs and other entertainments, to which will be added a whimsical Mock Heroic after-piece, entitled The Mad Poetess.[1]

In contrast, it would be hard to exaggerate the prestige that Mowatt, Kemble, and Cushman brought to the reading platform. No person of Mowatt's social status and refinement had read or acted publicly in America prior to her. Kemble's own distinction as a professional actress and author before becoming a reader was enlarged by her being the niece of the great Sarah Kemble Siddons, painted by Reynolds as "The Tragic Muse" and sculptured by Chantrey, whose other famous models were George Washington and the Duke of Wellington. Charlotte Cushman brought to the reading platform her outstanding fame as America's first great actress, the only woman to be ranked with Forrest and Booth.

Mowatt, though born after the others, began and ended her readings before those of the other two and, therefore, will be discussed first. Mowatt read at the start of the 1840s, Kemble during the 1850s and 1860s, and Cushman in the 1870s. Their professional careers filled the main body of the nineteenth century and did much to encourage the amount and importance of oral interpretation by the century's end.

I. Anna Cora Mowatt (1819-1870)

Anna Cora Ogden Mowatt Ritchie—to use her full name from childhood through two marriages—is the only one of the three to attempt a career as a professional reader before becoming an actress. Although without professional training, she drew upon her precocious childhood as resources for her success as a reader. She was one of twelve children in a socially prominent family in New York. In her delightful autobiography she tells us she was encouraged to read widely in her father's library, "and at ten years old I had read the whole of Shakespeare's plays many times over."[2] By the age of twelve she was regularly writing, directing, and acting plays with her five sisters for birthdays and other family occasions. This innocent dramatic activity was acceptable then only because it was done in private, but it would have been immodest, or immoral, if performed in public.

Anna Cora Ogden eloped at fifteen to marry a wealthy lawyer. She became Mrs. James Mowatt but went right on with her independent studies:

> From every book which I read I made extracts, and wrote down my impressions of the work. These extracts and critiques I kept in the form of a journal. During several years, this journal testified that I had read and commented upon between ninety and one hundred volumes yearly.[3]

At seventeen she published an epic poem, and when critics condemned it, she challenged them in a verse satire. At eighteen, threatened with consumption, she went to Europe to regain her health. During her fifteen-month convalescence, she wrote magazine articles, visited the theatre, added Italian and German to her knowledge of French, and wrote a five-act play in blank verse which she staged for family and friends in celebration of her return to New York.

When she was twenty-one, her husband lost his considerable fortune in financial speculations, and his health failed. Anna Cora resolved to support the two of them. She had recently attended several evenings of readings by John Vandenhoff; since she had enjoyed her girlhood readings and performances, she promptly decided to earn money in the same way. Only later did she think of the risk of social ostracism for entering what her friends considered the brazen world of public dramatic performance. To have no time for second thoughts, she allowed herself just two weeks to make all programming, rehearsal, scheduling, and travel arrangements "for my new and hazardous career."[4]

She immediately chose selections from her favorite poets and began strengthening her voice by reading aloud for several hours each day in the open air. To delay the likely censure of her friends in New York,

she chose Boston as the place for her first appearances, since it "had been pronounced the most intellectual city of the Union—the American Athens."[5] She and her husband arrived in Boston with letters of introduction to literary and social leaders. As a result, her debut was promptly and easily arranged. Three readings were scheduled at the Masonic Temple on successive nights in late October of 1841. Tickets were put on sale, and newspapers were primed to praise the coming occasion as "one which we have no doubt will be interesting, not chiefly from its novelty, but from its adaptations to gratify a refined taste."[6]

Among the poems she read, Mrs. Mowatt included Byron's "The Dream," Scott's "The Lay of the Last Minstrel," and two American poems, "The Missing Ship" and "The Light of the Lighthouse." The last two were strenuous dramatic narratives written by the poet and playwright Epes Sargent especially for her to read. Her opening anxiety and sense of strain gave way to relief at the warmth and approval of the audiences. They seemed to her "indulgent friends, who were determined to be pleased with my most imperfect efforts." The critics, too, "dealt with me tenderly, as with a spoiled child whom Boston had suddenly adopted and was determined to protect."[7] New York, she knew, would be another matter.

The hostility of her New York friends and relatives for her daring to appear before the public was all she had feared it might be. They excluded her from their social engagements and ignored her when passing on the street, and yet they attended her readings out of curiosity. As a result, in her performances she "could not feel the same easy *abandon*" she had known before. Under this "heavy pressure of mental suffering," added to "the exhaustion produced by unusual exertions" of the performances themselves, her health repeatedly gave way, and scheduled readings had to be postponed. Her inexperience left her at the mercy of any audience, even the unusually friendly one at the Rutger's Institute for Young Ladies. Here the evident pleasure of the lovely young ladies "inspired me to read with more energy and feeling than I had done since my nights in Boston. The effort cost me a relapse of some weeks."[8]

The total of eight New York readings included four nights at Stuyvesant Institute beginning November 18, 1841, one at the Lyceum in Brooklyn on November 27, the Rutger's Institute for Young Ladies on December 8, and two at the Society Library on January 12 and 13, 1842. Those eight readings, preceded by the three in Boston and one in Providence, made up the dozen readings during 1841-42 which constituted Anna Cora Mowatt's entire career as a public reader. For all of them she read poems chosen not only from Byron, Scott, and Sargent, mentioned above, but also from such other poets as Campbell, Holmes, Mrs. Hemans, H. H. Milman, Moore, and Sprague.[9]

Contemporary comments on Mrs. Mowatt's readings suggest something of her methods and effect. A critic in *The Evening Post* held that the poems "gained additional force and brilliancy from her mind and feeling." The close of one poem, "The Brothers," was "a masterpiece of horror" centered on "the expression of intense terror and agony depicted on the face of Mrs. Mowatt." For another poem, "The Fall of Babylon," she "evinced a power and volume of voice which we would have pronounced it impossible for so young and delicate looking a being to possess." Undoubtedly, part of Mrs. Mowatt's dramatic effect was the astonishing contrast between the "very modesty of her appearance" and "her abandonment to her subjects."[10]

One evaluation of the readings was entirely negative. It was an article in the *Ladies' Companion,* Mrs. Mowatt tells us, "by a lady contributor of high literary standing." The article denounced her performances and demanded that "if public readings must be given, I should read before an audience entirely of my own sex!" Apparently, the gentlemen, observes Mrs. Mowatt, "were to be left at the door with the canes and umbrellas."[11]

Anna Cora Mowatt's one season of readings in 1841-42 was a success for her and a new departure in the history of interpretation in America. Before her, only a very few men had occasionally given a professional reading, and almost no women had done so. As she observes with characteristic irony:

> My success gave rise to a host of lady imitators, one of whom announced "Readings and Recitations in the Style of Mrs. Mowatt." I was rather curious to get an idea of my own style, and, had my health permitted, would have gone some distance to have seen it illustrated. At one time there were no less than six advertisements in the papers, of ladies giving readings in different parts of the Union.[12]

Mrs. Mowatt's later great successes as the author of **Fashion** in 1845 and as an actress in America and Britain from 1845 to 1854 make up a separate story. There is no disparagement of that remarkable story— only attempts at aesthetic distinctions—when Joseph Jefferson categorizes Mrs. Mowatt as "always an amateur"[13] and Garff Wilson describes her as the first in an American acting school of "emotionalism."[14] She herself wrote that "I never succeeded in stirring the hearts of others unless I was deeply affected myself," which led her to admit that her reading and acting was not of "the highest school of art . . . in which the actor, Prospero-like, rises or stills tempestuous waves by the magical force of his will."[15] Nevertheless, as Garff Wilson observes, "Mrs. Mowatt's very presence on the stage, whatever her style of performance, did great service to the profession" and weakened the Puritan hostility toward theatre in America. And Wilson concurs with Arthur Hobson Quinn that Anna Cora Mowatt "took into the profession her high heart, her utter refinement, her keen sense of social values, and her infinite capacity for effort, and her effect was a real and a great one."[16]

Notes

[1] George C. D. Odell, *Annals of the New York Stage,* 15 vols. (New York: Columbia Univ. Press, 1927-1949), I, 284.

[2] Anna Cora Mowatt, *Autobiography of an Actress* (Boston: Ticknor, Reed, and Fields, 1854), p. 31.

[3] Mowatt, p. 63.

[4] Mowatt, pp. 137-41.

[5] Mowatt, pp. 141-46.

[6] *The Atlas* (Boston), 18 Oct. 1841, p. 1, quoted in Eric Wollencott Barnes, *The Lady of Fashion: The Life and the Theatre of Anna Cora Mowatt* (New York: Scribners, 1954), p. 71.

[7] Mowatt, p. 151.

[8] Mowatt, pp. 152-53.

[9] The schedule of readings and list of poets are compiled from Mowatt, pp. 152-54; Barnes, pp. 81-83; and Odell, IV, 587.

[10] *The Evening Post* (New York), 13 Jan. 1842, quoted in Odell, IV, 587.

[11] Mowatt, p. 154.

[12] Mowatt, p. 157.

[13] Joseph Jefferson, *Autobiography,* ed. Alan S. Downer (1890; rpt. Cambridge: Harvard Univ. Press, 1964), p. 107.

[14] Garff B. Wilson, *A History of American Acting* (Bloomington: Indiana Univ. Press, 1966), pp. 113-18.

[15] Mowatt, p. 244.

[16] Wilson, pp. 117-18.

Patti P. Gillespie

SOURCE: "Anna Cora Ogden Mowatt Ritchie's *Fairy Fingers:* From Eugène Scribe's?" in *Text and Performance Quarterly,* Vol. 2, April, 1989, 125-34.

[In the following essay, Gillespie analyzes the textual similarities between Mowatt's novel Fairy Fingers *and a contemporary French play of the same name, arguing that Mowatt borrowed her plot from the French play.]*

On March 29, 1858, *Les Doigts de fée* (in English, *Fairy Fingers*) opened at the Comédie française to dismal reviews. Undeterred, French audiences flocked to see this latest play by Eugène Scribe, and publishers immediately offered it to the reading public.[1] Once again Scribe, the father of the well-made play, had a hit on his hands.[2]

In August 1860, Anna Cora Ogden Mowatt Ritchie, author of *Fashion,* arrived in Paris.[3] The recent death of her father, the serious illness of her sister, and—perhaps most important of all—the dallying of her new husband with a slave woman had driven her to leave America for France. In Paris and in need of money, she planned "to eke out an existence with her pen."[4] Almost at once she began work on a novel, a work that she continued after her move to Florence (June 1861) and completed during her visit to New York (1862-1864). By the time ill health forced her return to Florence (1864), the novel, *Fairy Fingers,* had been accepted for publication. It appeared in 1865.[5]

Are the two *Fairy Fingers* mere coincidence? Almost certainly not. As evidence, let us consider this unlikely story:

> Madelaine, an orphan of aristocratic but poor stock, lives in Brittany with a dowager countess and her son (the count), and Bertha, another orphan—who, unlike Madelaine, is rich. The count's son, Maurice, secretly loves Madelaine; a young French businessman, Gaston, secretly loves Bertha. Regrettably, the countess and count intend that Maurice will wed Bertha.

> Madelaine believes that she cannot confess her love or marry Maurice without the count's and the countess's blessing; therefore, Maurice does not know that his love is requited. Likewise, Gaston, thinking that he is not good enough for Bertha, does not declare his love and learn that it is also requited. The count's marriage plans for Maurice and Bertha cause Madelaine, aided by Gaston, to run away. Maurice frantically searches for her, following leads of jewelry, dresses, and handkerchiefs first to London, then Paris, and finally Dresden, where he at last receives a note from Madelaine asking him to abandon his search. He resolves to do so.

> Madelaine, now using the name Mlle. Melanie, flees to America and opens a dress shop that quickly becomes the talk of fashionable Washington society.

> Even while she was living with the count and countess, Madelaine had displayed such magical dexterity with needles and thread that she was called "Fairy Fingers."

> Meanwhile, the count, the countess, Bertha, Gaston, and assorted friends decide to go to America, where Maurice owns land that a railway may buy for a new track. Because the location of the new track will be decided by a committee of nine prominent men, Maurice gives his father power of attorney and sends him to Washington to secure the votes. The count so misuses the power of attorney that soon the railroad track must be secured or the family will be ruined—disgraced and bankrupt.

> Maurice and the count are at the home of a Washington socialite, seeking her husband's vote, when Mlle. Melanie arrives to deliver a breathtakingly beautiful ball gown. All but Gaston are shocked to learn that the famous Mlle. Melanie is in fact their Madelaine. Discovering her new American influence, the count pleads with her to help secure the votes for the railroad so that Maurice can repay the loan. Madelaine agrees, delivers the necessary votes, and repays the loan herself, using money intended for the last installment on her own home.

> The countess is enraged to learn that a poor relative has rescued the family from scandal and ruin. The count falls ill. Madelaine takes him home to nurse, even remodeling her home so the countess can visit unobserved. But the countess grows angrier still, because Madelaine refuses to marry a wealthy nobleman, refuses to close her dress shop, and continues to care for the count in her home. The countess determines to take everyone but Madelaine back to Brittany.

> The impending separation finally causes Madelaine to declare her love for Maurice. The count gives his consent to the marriage—and dies. The countess, overcome with grief, collapses. A huge ornamented curtain crashes down, and Madelaine hurls herself over the countess to protect her. The countess awakens and sees a bleeding Madelaine. She then relents and gives permission for Madelaine and Maurice to marry. Bertha and Gaston, who had refused to wed until Maurice and Madelaine could join them in a double ceremony, embrace.

> The family is reconciled; the complications are resolved; the young lovers are married; and the countess returns happily to Brittany—alone.

This improbable tale encompasses the plot of Anna Cora Ogden Mowatt Ritchie's novel, *Fairy Fingers.* The novel, long even by standards of its day (fifty-seven chapters, made up of four hundred sixty "fine printed pages"),[6] shares both the story and many lengthy verbatim sections with Scribe's play.

The structural relationship between the novel and the play is quite clear. The first seven chapters of Mowatt's novel are the first two acts of Scribe's play, and her chapters twenty-one through thirty-four are his third, fourth, and fifth acts—except that the play's last two scenes are Mowatt's chapters thirty-eight and fifty-two, respectively. A chart can clarify the overall pattern (see Figure 1). Brief sections from the novel and the play can illustrate their verbatim relationship (see Appendix A).

I cannot account for the structural and verbatim similarities with certainty. Three possibilities exist: Mowatt drew from Scribe; Scribe drew from Mowatt; they both drew from a third source. The only compelling argument for either of the last two explanations is that Scribe's play, *Les Doigts de fée,* is quite atypical of his other works. It is more obviously episodic, more rambling, and more sentimental than his typical well-made plays and so might be presumed to draw on some other work, probably a novel.[7]

The weight of evidence, however, clearly favors the first possibility: that is, Mowatt drew from Scribe. The evidence is briefly this:

(1) Scribe's play was first performed at the Comédie française in 1858 and published immediately; Mowatt's novel was not published until 1865.

(2) Mowatt lived in Paris in 1860. Born and raised in France, she spoke and read French fluently. She certainly had access to Scribe's published text, and, because she was both an actor and playwright, her interest in such a text can be safely assumed.[8]

FIGURE 1

Fairy Fingers Compared with *Les doigts de fée*

NOVEL (MOWATT)	PLAY (SCRIBE)
I	1, i, ii, iii, iv, part of v
II	1,vii
III	2,vii; 1,viii in part
IV	1,viii; 2,iv; 2,iii
V	2,i,ii
VI	2,iv, v, vi, vii, viii
VII	2,viii, ix, x
VIII-XIX	
XX	similar to 4,x, xiii; 3,iii
XXI	similar to 3,iv
XXII	3,x, xi, xii, xiii, xiv, xv
XXIII	3,xvi, xvii
XXIV	4,i, ii, iii, iv
XXV	4,v vi
XXVI	4,vii, viii, ix
XXVII	similar to 4,x
XXVIII	4,xi, xii, xiii
XXIX	4,xii, xv
XXX	5,i, iv, x
XXXI	5,xi
XXXII	5,v
XXXIII	5,xi, xii in part
XXXIV	5,ii, vi
XXXV	mostly new, but also 5,vii
XXXVI-XXXVII	
XXXVIII	mostly new, but also 5,xii in part
XXXIX-LI	
LII	5,xii in part
LIII-LVI	

(3) Mowatt was, in the early 1860s, desperately seeking money. She even considered a return to acting, which, with her writing, had supported the family when her first husband, Mr. Mowatt, had lost his money. It seems reasonable to speculate that she felt pressured to write something quickly in order to get paid quickly.

(4) Mowatt had before lifted materials, unattributed, from other sources. When her play ***Armand*** was first in rehearsal, for example, one critic noticed a "strong resemblance to a passage in Byron's *Sardanopolus.*"[9] Mowatt said the resemblance was unintentional and offered to change it. By contrast, Scribe had a reputation for crediting even the most casual contributions to

his plays, citing as co-authors people who contributed only an idea to the finished product.[10]

(5) I have located neither a third source nor references to such a source.

If we can assume that Mowatt used Scribe's play as the basis of her novel, we have a rare opportunity to explore the choices made by an experienced writer. Through her choices, we can glimpse major formal differences between a novel and a play and major social differences between Mowatt's nineteenth-century world and our own. We can, as well, seek insights into Mowatt the writer and Mowatt the woman.

Many of her changes resulted from the formal differences between a novel and a play. For example, Scribe's play (like all plays) could rely on scenery to establish locale (scenery that needed to be only briefly described in stage directions), but Mowatt's novel (like any novel) had to substitute detailed descriptions of each location—various European drawing rooms, an American dress shop, a sick room in a private home, and so on. Whereas Scribe (like any dramatist) could depend on the actors' physical appearance and the details of their costumes for basic characterization, Mowatt (like all novelists) needed to construct portraits of each character with words and, with words, to clothe them. Again in keeping with the formal differences between plays and novels, Scribe as playwright could depend on his actors to embody emotions and relationships that Mowatt as novelist had to describe in detail. It is testament to Mowatt's confidence in writing both plays and novels that she seems to have made the conversion from a play to a novel so surely.

Quite apart from changes occasioned by the shift from the form play to the form novel were others that were more clearly matters of personal choice. Of such changes, four major categories can be adduced.

First, Mowatt lengthened the novel by multiplying the number of complications, introducing many incidents not present in Scribe's work. For example, Scribe closed his second act with Fairy Fingers' running away from home, and he opened his third act with the family's assembling at the fashionable residence to which Fairy Fingers would bring the ball gown and so be recognized. Moving between the same two points, Mowatt introduced fourteen chapters detailing Maurice's frantic searches, false leads, new friendships, serious illness, early career as a lawyer, and trip to America, as well as tracing his family's reasons for joining him there. Again, Scribe moved briskly to the eve of Fairy Fingers' marriage as soon as she delivered the railroad votes and paid off the debt. Mowatt added the illness and death of the count, the illness and rescue of the countess, and the promise of a double wedding before moving to close her novel.

Second, Mowatt sentimentalized both the characters and the action, muting the humor of Scribe's original in favor of "a joy too exquisite for laughter," to borrow Steele's description of the aims of the sentimental.[11] For example, she made the count and countess villainous, while Scribe made them merely foolish. She transformed Scribe's sympathetic heroine into a perfect, flawless heroine, loved by all who encountered her (except, of course, the count and countess). Mowatt had one character describe Madelaine as a woman who "exerts a holy influence upon all with whom she is thrown in contact, and works more good, teaches more truth by the example of a patient, noble, holy life than could be taught by a thousand sermons from the most eloquent lips."[12]

By painting extremes of character and situation, Mowatt heightened the sense of not only the mistreatment of the heroine but also her self-sacrificing response to it. For example, the countess had refused to let Madelaine marry, had rebuked her publicly for repaying the family's debt, had complained about her caring for the count in her home, and had refused her hospitality because the countess did not wish to be seen with a working woman. Still, Mowatt explained how, when the countess was ill, "Madelaine longed to see [the countess], and make some few, needful arrangements for her comfort, but she could not doubt that her presence would do more harm than good. All that she could effect was to instruct Maurice . . . in the requirements of a sick-room, and to have prepared, in her own kitchen, the light food suitable to an invalid. . . . indeed, the only nourishment the invalid tasted was provided [secretly] by the thoughtful Madelaine."[13] Madelaine's was indeed "a nature peculiarly susceptible to the pure delight of serving, aiding, sparing trouble to those whom she loved."[14]

Third, Mowatt set a good part of the action of her novel in America, whose virtues she extolled and whose people she contrasted favorably with the French. Mowatt wrote, for example, that Americans are "in an advantageous position in Paris by the very fact of being an American . . . coming from a land where distinctions of rank are not arbitrarily governed by the accident of birth but where men are assigned their positions in the social scale through a juster, higher, more liberal verdict."[15] American men were characterized as "self-made and self-educated, at an age when young Frenchmen [had] scarcely begun to be aware that they [had] any independent existence."[16] American women were depicted as strong and pragmatic: to the countess's boasts about her ancestry, an American nurse scoffed, "I suppose she don't trace back further than Adam does she? And we all do about that."[17] And of course Madelaine herself had a nature "which responded to the spirit of self-reliance, energy and industry, which are so essentially American characteristics."[18]

Fourth, Mowatt used the play to make a number of social comments—on health, women, and especially work, the dignity of which Mowatt took as her major theme.

On health, Mowatt's views echoed those of Swedenborg, whose spiritual approach to health found important adherents in this country in Dr. Phineas Quimby and his more famous student Mary Baker Eddy.[19] Thus, in *Fairy Fingers* can be found this prescription: "As all *matter* exists from, and is influenced by, spiritual causes, the happy workings of this mental ministry are very comprehensible. Madelaine invariably found medicinal and restorative properties in the pages of an interesting and healthful-toned volume which would draw her out of the contemplation of her own ailments. . . . In this manner she successfully counteracted the depression and unrest that attend bodily disease, and often succeeded in lifting her mind so far above its disordered mortal medium that she was hardly conscious of suffering. . . . Sceptical reader! You smile in doubt, and think that if Madelaine's wisdom and patience could accomplish this feat, she was a rare instance of womanhood. Try her experiment faithfully and then decide!"[20]

Of women, Mowatt wrote most sympathetically, exploring their problems, which were most often caused by men. For example, good women protected men from themselves. Maurice explained to Madelaine: "You do not know the thousand perils [threatening a young man in Paris] . . . the siren lures . . . thrown in his way to ensnare his feet. . . . You do not know that your holy image, rising up before me, shining upon the path I trod, and beckoning me into the right road when I swerved aside, has alone saved me from falling into that vortex of follies and vices by which men are daily swallowed up, and from which they emerge sullied and debased. . . . Would you reign over my soul and keep it stainless? It is under your angel guardianship."[21]

But while protecting men, women had also to protect themselves from men; women in the workplace especially suffered unwanted advances. Mowatt confided in her reader: "We shall not dwell upon the manifold and humiliating trials to which [Madelaine] was subjected."[22] Men often expected sexual favors in return for business favors. When thus propositioned, Madelaine responded angrily: "Under ordinary circumstances, I should have been your debtor. As it is, you and I are quits! The privilege of insulting me will suffice you! And now, my lord, you will excuse me, if, being a woman who earns her livelihood and whose time is valuable, I bring this interview to a close."[23]

Women's lot was made harder still by their capacity for love, a capacity not shared by men. Mowatt repeatedly commented on this vexing difference: "A woman who is gifted with the power of throwing her soul into looks and language and loving ways, runs the risk of producing upon certain men an effect approaching satiety. The woman who has instinctive wisdom will never dash herself against this rock; yet few woman are *wise;* fewer give *too little* of their rich, heart-treasures than *too much.*"[24] And again, "Men are constitutionally, unconsciously ungrateful; give them abundance of what they covet most and they prize the gift less highly than if its measure were stinted. And women have an instinct that warns them not to be too lavish. Those women who love most fervently, most deeply, most internally, seldom frame the full strength of that love into words, or manifest it in looks even; that is, in the waking presence of the one who holds their entire being captive."[25]

Mowatt's most sustained comments, however, were on the importance of work. Indeed, for her, a large part of America's virtue rested on its being a land where honest work was respected above birth. She contrasted the countess's (French) view that Madelaine was disgraced because she worked with an American socialite's view that Madelaine's work should be a source of pride. The American explained, "In this land where *labor* is a *virtue* and the most laborious, . . . become the greatest,—in this land it will be no blot upon her noble name . . . that she has linked that name with *work.* She will rather be held up as an example to the daughters of this young country."[26] Maurice was made sympathetic in part because he adopted the attitudes of America rather than those of his birthplace, France. He congratulated himself: "Thank Heaven, I have lived long enough in this land, where men (and women too) have sufficient courage to use their lives, and senseless idlers are the exceptions; to realize that man's work and woman's work are alike glorious; . . . and that you, Madelaine, the daughter of a duke,—you, the duchess-mantuamaker, have reached a higher altitude through that very labor than your birth could ever command."[27] And, of course, Madelaine—the working woman—taught her colleagues that one "may be very poor and very dependent and yet be the daughter of a duke; and even a duke's daughter may find it less irksome to earn her own bread than to eat the bread of charity."[28]

What can we learn from this brief comparison of the two *Fairy Fingers*?

First, Anna Cora Ogden Mowatt Ritchie's decision, on two separate occasions, to seek money from acting and from writing adds to the growing body of evidence that these two fields offered nineteenth-century women some uncommon chance of financial independence. Occupational data show clearly that female writers and actors were less highly valued than male writers and actors, but the data also confirm that women had better financial opportunities in those fields than in most others of the time.[29]

Second, Anna Cora Ogden Mowatt Ritchie's life—and name—invites our reflection on the social manipulation of a nineteenth-century (and indeed a contemporary) woman's identity. But into a well-known and prestigious family named Ogden, Anna Cora Ogden, when she married, changed her last name to Mowatt, a name with much less social power and panache. After almost twenty years of building an independent international reputation through acting and writing under the name of Mrs. Mowatt, Anna Cora Mowatt became, overnight, Anna Cora Ritchie when she remarried. Thereafter she repeatedly had to explain who she was, as the thirty-third citation in this paper reminds us.

Third, Anna Cora Ogden Mowatt Ritchie was most probably what we would call a plagiarist. But in the absence of an international copyright agreement, her appropriation of Scribe's play was neither illegal nor likely to be viewed as unethical. The history of *Uncle Tom's Cabin,* to cite a single example, testifies to the free-wheeling nature of nineteenth-century borrowing that we now call plagiarism.

Mowatt's decision to plagiarize is probably explained by her acute need for money. Certainly, the structure of the novel—specifically, the nature of Mowatt's additions to the original play—argues for this conclusion: She just added complications. To take over a successful plot and lengthen it merely by adding complications (rather than reworking to make a different point, as with the many versions of Electra, for example) suggests someone who is working quickly.

Fourth, Anna Cora Ogden Mowatt Ritchie understood that writing plays and writing novels were different, and she chose her form knowledgeably. Given the evidence of **Fashion,** we know that Mowatt could have adapted Scribe's work into a play suited for American audiences. She chose, however, to write a novel. Probably the reason was at least in part economic; that is, some income from the publication of a novel was both more certain and more rapid than from the production of a play. But it seems clear as well that Mowatt the writer enjoyed the opportunities granted by the novel's form for commenting on issues that interested her.

For the rest, we can only speculate, for firm evidence is not yet available. Her appropriation of the specific play *Les Doigts de fée* most likely reflects Mowatt's interest in women, especially strong women and working women. Indeed, she seems to have found in Scribe's play, quite serendipitously, a character that had long interested her. We learn from Mowatt's 1853 autobiography that she "could never write mere fiction," that she "needed a groundwork in reality."[31]

We learn as well that she had observed for several years "a young girl, belonging to a ballet company, . . . [who]

supplied the whole wants of the family" by her sewing skills, "only laying down the needles, which her fingers made fly, when she was summoned by the call boy, or required to change her costume by the necessities of the play."[32] This real-life woman worker first found a clear echo as the major secondary character in **Stella,** a vaguely autobiographical story published as a part of Mowatt's book **Mimic Life** in 1856.[33] In Scribe's play, Mowatt found just such a young seamstress cast as the play's central figure, a coincidence perhaps too enticing for Mowatt to resist.

Mowatt's decision to change Scribe's play by moving the action to America and sentimentalizing the characters perhaps reflected her assessment of the market. The middle of the nineteenth century was well into the Victorian age and the age of melodrama, with all that both imply about simple visions of right and wrong, the purity of women, and so on. Moreover, Mowatt may have reasoned that her readers would be American (she had a New York publisher) and that they would be mostly female readers of popular fiction, because she had, early in her career, published regularly in serials like *The Ladies Companion, Graham's Magazine, The Columbia Magazine,* and *Godey's Lady's Book.*[34] She may have adjusted Scribe's comedy in order to cater specifically to this women's readership. If so, her changes provide helpful insights into that readership—its expectations, interests, and tastes.

Her decision to comment on issues of health, women, and work no doubt reflected an assessment of her readership. But the substance of her comments on these issues seems most logically explained by her own life. Married to an older man when she was fifteen, forced to support herself and her sick husband at twenty-five, widowed at twenty-seven, Mowatt early in her life had intense experiences with illness, work, and womanhood. Remarried and retired from the stage at thirty-four, Mowatt soon found herself again forced to be financially independent. Separated from an unfaithful husband and in ill health, Mowatt earned her own way until she died at fifty.

Thus, the novel **Fairy Fingers** is very much the story of a woman who, like Mowatt, had to take control of her own life. On the one hand, Mowatt sought to use this novel as a means to survive. On a different level, she seemingly sought through this novel to teach other women what she had learned about surviving in a man's world: how to avoid the medical establishment and stay healthy, how to ward off seducers and remain virtuous, how to pay men's debts and keep their love.

Notes

[1] Eugène Scribe, *Les Doigts de fee* (Paris: n.p., 1858).

[2] See, for example, Eugene Lataye, "Revue—Chronique," *La Revue de Deux Mondes* 1 June 1858: 716-717.

[3] *Fashion, or Life in New York* was first performed in New York in 1845 and then published in London, by Newberry, in 1850. An American edition (slightly different from the London version) appeared in Anna Cora Mowatt, *Plays* (Boston: Ticknor and Fields, 1855). The play is now widely anthologized and occasionally revived (e.g., Provincetown, 1923-24).

[4] Eric Wollencott Barnes, *The Lady of Fashion; The Life and the Theatre of Anna Cora Mowatt* (New York: Charles Scribner's Sons, 1954), 365. This work, the standard source on Mowatt, is the source for the chronology that follows.

[5] Anna Cora Ritchie, *Fairy Fingers: a Novel* (New York: Carleton, 1865).

[6] The description is by Marius Blesi, "The Life and Times of Anna Cora Mowatt," diss. U of Virginia, 1938, 386.

[7] Patti P. Gillespie, "The Well Made Plays of Eugène Scribe," diss Indiana U, 1970, 130-131.

[8] Mrs. Anna Cora Mowatt, *Autobiography of an Actress: or, Eight Years on the Stage* (Boston: Ticknor, Reed and Fields, 1854); unsigned mss, John Seely Hart Collection, Rare Books Room, Cornell U Library; and Barnes, *The Lady of Fashion,* are the major sources for details of her life and work.

[9] Ritchie, *Autobiography,* 297.

[10] Helene Koon and Richard Switzer, *Eugène Scribe* (Boston: Twayne Publ., 1980), 15-19, 25; and Neil Cole Arvin, *Eugène Scribe and the French Theatre, 1815-1860* (Cambridge: Harvard UP, 1924), 12, 15, 25-26. Ernest Legouvé is listed as coauthor of this play, as several others, but, as is often the case, the nature of the contribution is unclear.

[11] Sir Richard Steele, "Preface to *The Conscious Lovers,*" in Bernard F. Dukore, *Dramatic Theory and Criticism: Greeks to Grotowski* (New York: Holt, Rinehart, and Winston, 1974), 397.

[12] Ritchie, *Fairy Fingers,* 299.

[13] 352.

[14] 371.

[15] 140.

[16] 174.

[17] 398.

[18] 37.

[19] Mowatt was active in the "New Church," one of several holistic health and religion centers in New England at the time. Bliese, 158ff; 170ff. See also Robert Peel, *Mary Baker Eddy* (New York: Holt, Rinehart, and Winston, 1966) and Judith Anderson, *Outspoken Women* (Dubuque, Iowa: Kendall Hunt, 1984), 43-50, on relationships among the various spiritualists, like Swedenborg, and the emergence of Christian Science in this country.

[20] Ritchie, *Fairy Fingers,* 314.

[21] 73-74.

[22] 172.

[23] 288.

[24] 442.

[25] 334.

[26] 220.

[27] 261.

[28] 341.

[29] Claudia Johnson, *American Actresses: Perspective on the Nineteenth Century* (Chicago: Nelson-Hall, 1984); Edna Hammer Cooley, "Women in American Theatre: A Study in Professional Equity," diss. U of Maryland, 1985, esp. chs. two and three.

[30] Mowatt's decision to retain Scribe's title, *Fairy Fingers,* may suggest that she viewed wholesale borrowing as neither illegal nor unethical. On the other hand, its retention may suggest simply that she did not anticipate getting caught: How many Americans were likely to encounter this particular French play, when America was poised for a civil war and American theatre, to the degree that it sought foreign models, sought them in England rather than France? Her reaction to the allegations surrounding *Armand* seem to indicate some sense of guilt about borrowing.

[31] Mowatt, *Autobiography,* 186-187.

[32] Mowatt, *Autobiography,* 314-315.

[33] Anna Cora Ritchie (formerly Mrs. Mowatt), *Mimic Life: or, Before and Behind the Curtain. A Series of Narratives* (Boston: Ticknor and Fields, 1856), esp., 53, 69, 71, 81, 99.

[34] A complete and annotated list of Anna Cora Ogden Mowatt Ritchie's publications can be found in Imogene

J. McCarthy, "Anna Cora Mowatt and Her Audience."
M.A. thesis, U of Maryland, 1953.

Doris Abramson

SOURCE: "'The New Path': Nineteenth-Century
American Women Playwrights," in *Modern American Drama: The Female Canon*, edited by June
Schlueter, Associated University Presses, 1990, pp.
38-51.

[*In the following excerpt, Abramson discusses Mowatt's
Fashion as the foremost woman's play of the nineteenth-century.*]

In 1891, Laurence Hutton had this to say about native
American drama:

> The American drama—such as it is—may be divided
> into several classes, including the Indian Drama,
> and the plays of Frontier Life, which are often
> identical; the Revolutionary and war plays; the
> Yankee, or character plays, like *The Gilded Age*, or
> *The Old Homestead;* the plays of local life and
> character, like *Mose, or Squatter Sovereignty;* and
> the society plays, of which Mrs. Mowatt's *Fashion,*
> and Bronson Howard's *Saratoga Trunk* are fair
> examples.[1]

Writing toward the end of a century noted for a theater
of spectacle, melodrama, and sentiment, a theater continually adapting to an audience of newcomers and an
expanding frontier, he categorized plays written for
that theater, mentioning only a few by title. And a
woman is one of only two playwrights acknowledged
by name. Actually, women wrote plays that fit all these
classes, but it is right that Anna Cora Mowatt should
be named here and elsewhere—*Fashion* is the most
frequently anthologized of all plays by nineteenth-century women playwrights—as the preeminent woman
playwright of the century. Other plays by women of
her time are worth our attention, some even our study,
but only *Fashion* is securely in the canon of American
dramatic literature.

Thanks to her gift for self-advertisement, we know more
about Anna Cora Mowatt than about other women
playwrights of the nineteenth century. Her *Autobiography of An Actress; or Eight Years on the Stage,*
published in 1853, was widely read and extravagantly
admired. Nathaniel Hawthorne put it on a list of a half-
dozen good American books that he was recommending to Richard Monckton Milnes—along with Thoreau's
Walden and *A Week on the Concord and Merrimac
Rivers*.[2] She also wrote two autobiographical novels,
Mimic Life (1855) and *Twin Roses* (1857). These books
are detailed accounts of her personal and professional
life as well as an entertaining record of the American

theater at mid-century. They are self-serving by their
nature—Odell complained that the author was "always
making herself the heroine of a novel, which was her
idea of her own life"[3]—but taken with the usual grains
of salt, they are clearly informative.

Best remembered now as the author of the play *Fashion; or Life in New York* (1845), a lively social
comedy, in her own period she was also noted as an
accomplished actress. Born Anna Cora Ogden, descended from a distinguished American family (her
grandfather on her mother's side, Francis Lewis,
signed the Declaration of Independence), she married James Mowatt, a man twice her age, when she
was fifteen. She had always enjoyed home theatricals, and, when her husband's health failed, she
became first a public reader and then an actress. As
one theater historian put it: "Anna Mowatt . . . was
the first American woman of birth and breeding to
identify herself with the fortunes of the stage."[4]

She became a star in an age of stars, without ever
serving an apprenticeship. She saw her first play at age
fourteen, when she went to the theater reluctantly (like
many ladies of the period she was persuaded by her
minister to view the theater as an abode of the devil)
and saw the bewitching Fanny Kemble. Theater had
been childhood games; later, it became an option when
she was looking for ways to make a living.[5] "I pondered long and seriously upon the consequences of my
entering the profession," she wrote. Her decision was
not made lightly:

> I reviewed my whole past life, and saw, that, from
> earliest childhood, my tastes, studies, pursuits had
> all combined to fit me for this end. I had exhibited
> a passion for dramatic performances when I was
> little more than an infant. I had played plays before
> I had ever entered a theatre. I had written plays
> from the time that I first witnessed a performance.
> My love for the drama was genuine, for it was
> developed at a period when the theatre was an
> unknown place, and actors a species of mythical
> creatures. I determined to fulfill the destiny which
> seemed visibly pointed out by the unerring finger
> of Providence . . . I would become an actress.[6]

She made her debut as an actress in *The Lady of Lyons*
on 13 June 1845, just three months after her debut as
a playwright.

According to her autobiography, her friend Epes Sargent
suggested that she should move from amateur to professional status as a playwright.

> "Why do you not write a play?" said E.S—— to
> me one morning. "You have more decided talent
> for the stage than for anything else. If we can get
> it accepted by the Park Theatre, and if it should
> succeed, you have a new and wide field of exertion

opened to you—one in which success is very rare, but for which your turn of mind has particularly fitted you."

"What shall I attempt, comedy or tragedy?"

"Comedy, decidedly; because you can only write what you feel, and you are 'nothing if not critical'—besides, you will have a fresh channel for the sarcastic ebullitions with which you so constantly indulge us."[7]

The result, of course, was *Fashion,* a satire on American *parvenuism,* intended to be a good-humored and serviceable *"acting comedy."* She claimed she set out to write not a literary but a dramatic play. That it has stood the tests of time, in the theater especially, shows she had studied the strategies used by the best writers of comedy of the past. She wrote a thoroughly American social comedy, following the rules of British comedies of manners of the eighteenth century.

Fashion was accepted as soon as written by the Park Theatre (the manager had been a childhood neighbor), produced "without delay, and in a style of great magnificence," opening on 24 March 1845, and running for three weeks.[8] It had notable success in other American cities and played at London's Olympic Theatre in 1850, the year it was published.[9]

Edgar Allan Poe, then writing criticism for the *Broadway Journal,* did not write about *Fashion* only from the perspective of opening night. He had requested a copy of the play from Mrs. Mowatt and received one before the play's opening. His first review, then, was based on a reading of *Fashion.* Among other things, he wrote: "The general tone is adopted from *The School for Scandal,* to which, indeed, the whole composition bears just such an affinity as the shell of a locust to the locust that tenants it—as the spectrum of a Congreve rocket to the Congreve rocket itself."[10] After seeing the play in production, he became intrigued with it. Although he condemned the ways in which theatrical conventions of the day were being perpetuated—"the coming forward to the footlights when anything of interest was to be told, the reading of private letters in a loud rhetorical tone, the preposterous soliloquizing and even more preposterous asides"—he went on to say that "in many respects (and those of a *telling* character) it is superior to any American play. It has, in especial, the very high merit of simplicity of plot" (29 March 1845). By 5 April 1845, after several viewings of *Fashion,* he wrote:

> In one respect, perhaps, we have done Mrs. Mowatt unintentional injustice. We are not quite sure, upon reflection, that her entire thesis is not an original one. We can call to mind no drama, just now, in which the design can be properly stated as the satirizing of fashion *as* fashion.[11]

It was remarkable that a writer of Poe's stature paid this much attention to Mrs. Mowatt's first play. His opinions of the theater's moribund conventions as well as his judgment of *Fashion* have stood the tests of time.

Fashion's characters are not just caricatures or farcical representations uncomfortably close to those in such plays as Sheridan's *The Rivals* (1775) or Royall Tyler's *The Contrast* (1787). Mrs. Tiffany is a descendant of Mrs. Malaprop, but she is strictly American. The drawing room in which she mangles English and French is an American one. (Tyler's setting could as easily have been London as New York.)

> *Mrs. Tif.* This mode of receiving visitors only upon one specified day of the week is a most convenient custom! It saves the trouble of keeping the house continually in order and of being always dressed. I flatter myself that I was the first to introduce it amongst the New *ee-light.* You are quite sure that it is strictly a Parisian mode, Millinette?
>
> *Mil.* Oh, *oui,* Madame; entirely *mode de Paris.*
>
> *Mrs. Tif.* This girl is worth her weight in gold *(aside).* Millinette, how do you say *arm-chair* in French?
>
> *Mil. Fauteil,* Madame.
>
> *Mrs. Tif.* Fo-tool! That has a foreign—an out-of-the-wayish sound that is perfectly charming—and so genteel! There is something about our American words decidedly vulgar. Fowtool! how refined. (3)[12]

Count Jolimaitre is recognizable as a type of scheming "foreign" fop, but he has an engaging directness in his dealings.

> *Mrs. Tif.* Count, I am so much ashamed,—pray excuse me! Although a lady of large fortune, and one, Count, who can boast of the highest connections, I blush to confess that I have never travelled,—while you, Count, I presume are at home in all the courts of Europe.
>
> *Count. Courts?* Eh? Oh, yes, Madam, very true. I believe I am pretty well known in some of the courts of Europe—*police courts (aside).* In a word, Madam, I had seen enough of civilized life—wanted to refresh myself by a sight of barbarous countries and customs—had my choice between the Sandwich Islands and New York—chose New York! (10)

Zeke (renamed A-dolph by Mrs. Tiffany for its aristocratic sound) is close to a minstrel "darky" in dialect, but he is a fully developed character who shares some of Mrs. Tiffany's pretensions.

Mrs. Tif. Silence! Your business is to obey and not to talk.

Zeke. I'm dumb, Missus!

Mrs. Tif. A-dolph, place that *fow-tool* behind me.

Zeke. (Looking about him.) I hab'nt got dat far in de dictionary yet. No matter, a genus gets his learning by nature. (4)

Later, failing further to understand Mrs. Tiffany's fractured French, he exits saying, "Dem's de defects ob not having a libery education" (4-5).

Gertrude (a role occasionally played by Mrs. Mowatt) is the pure, honest heroine of other plays, but with this difference: she has the sensible intelligence of an all-American girl.

> *Ger.* I have my *mania*—as some wise person declares that all mankind have,—and mine is a love of independence! In Geneva [New York], my wants were supplied by two kind old maiden ladies, upon whom I know not that I have any claim. I had abilities, and desired to use them. I came here at my own request; for here I am no longer *dependent! Voila tout,* as Mrs. Tiffany would say. (20)

Adam Trueman is related in his outspokenness to Mr. Freeman of James K. Paulding's 1831 play, *The Lion of the West,* although he is a farmer instead of a frontiersman. He also is something beyond a stage type. Here is his final speech, just before the epilogue, in answer to the Count's objection to America's lack of *nobility:*

> *True.* Stop there! I object to your use of that word. When justice is found only among lawyers—health among physicians—and patriotism among politicians, *then* may you say that there is no *nobility* where there are no titles! But we *have* kings, princes, and nobles in abundance—of *Nature's stamp,* if not of *Fashion's*—we have honest men, warm hearted and brave, and we have women—gentle, fair, and true, to whom no *title* could add *nobility.* (61)

Anna Cora Mowatt created a play, then, that works on the level of farce comedy but that also attacks folly at every turn.[13]

Fashion is not the first nineteenth-century play by a woman. Louisa H. Medina's melodrama *Nick of the Woods,* based on Robert Montgomery Bird's novel of that title, was first produced in 1838 at the Bowery Theatre in New York.[14] If we were to adopt Frances Wright as she so wholeheartedly adopted America, we could even count her play *Altorf* (1819) as the first play of the century authored by an American woman.[15] It seems easier to speak of foremost than to speak of first. **Fashion** is foremost, and in view of still undiscovered scripts, it is wiser not to try to establish who or what came first.

Notes

[1] Laurence Hutton, *Curiosities of the American Stage* (New York: Harper and Brothers, 1891), p. 8.

[2] Caroline Tichnor, *Hawthorne and His Publisher* (1913; reprint ed., Port Washington, N.Y.: Kennikat Press, 1969), p. 135.

[3] George C. D. Odell, *Annals of the New York Stage,* 15 vol. (New York: Columbia University Press, 1927-49): 5 (1931), p. 99.

[4] Mary Caroline Crawford, *The Romance of the American Theatre* (New York: Halcyon House, 1940), p. 455. Mowatt's career as an actress, novelist, memoirist, and playwright is particularly well documented by Marius Blesi, whose 1938 dissertation has been respectfully plundered by scholars for years.

[5] Between 1842 and 1845, usually under the name of "Helen Berkley," Mowatt wrote pieces for *Godey's Lady's Book, Graham's, The Ladies Companion,* et al. She wrote them to order, for a profit. In the same way, she wrote etiquette books, cook books, and novels. But all this scribbling did not bring in enough money, nor did it put her considerable energies to good enough use. See Anna Cora Mowatt, *Autobiography of an Actress; or Eight Years on the Stage* (Boston: Ticknor, Reed, and Fields, 1854), pp. 184-86.

[6] Mowatt, *Autobiography of an Actress,* p. 216.

[7] Ibid., p. 202.

[8] Ibid., pp. 203-4.

[9] Both of her professionally produced plays were published in one volume in an American edition in 1854. Her second play, *Armand; or, the Peer and the Peasant,* was first produced at the Park Theatre in 1847, subsequently in Boston and London. A historical blank verse play, *Armand* is scarcely known and never revived in our time.

[10] In *Broadway Journal,* 20 March 1845, quoted in *Israfel: The Life and Times of Edgar Allan Poe,* by Hervey Allen (New York: Farrar and Rinehart, 1934), p. 517.

[11] James A. Harrison, ed., *The Complete Works of Edgar Allan Poe,* 17 vol. (1902; reprint ed., New York: AMS Press, 1965), pp. 121, 124.

[12] Anna Cora Mowatt, *Fashion,* in *Plays* (Boston: Ticknor and Fields, 1854), pp. 1-62. Subsequent references are cited parenthetically by page number.

[13] See Daniel F. Havens, *The Columbian Muse of Comedy: The Development of a Native Tradition in Early American Social Comedy: 1787-1845* (Carbondale: Southern Illinois University Press, 1973), 129-48.

[14] L. [Louisa] H. Medina, *Nick of the Woods* (New York: Samuel French, 1838). See illustration in Stanley Appelbaum, ed., *Scenes From the 19th Century Stage in Advertising Woodcuts* (New York: Dover Publications, 1977), p. 4. Shown is "Act II, scene 5: Nick, the Avenger, scares off hostile Indians by shooting the falls in a blazing canoe."

[15] Frances Wright—feminist, radical, reformer—emigrated from Scotland to America at twenty-one, in 1818, and brought with her several play scripts in progress. *Altorf* (a version of the William Tell story) was produced in New York and Philadelphia; although a theatrical failure, it made money as a book. She sent a copy to Thomas Jefferson, then living in retirement, who sent her words of praise and grateful thanks. See Richard Stiller, *Commune on the Frontier: The Story of Frances Wright* (New York: Thomas Y. Crowell, 1972), pp. 43-51.

Lois J. Fowler and David H. Fowler

SOURCE: *Revelations of the Self: American Women in Autobiography,* State University of New York Press, 1990, pp. xvi-xx, 1-2.

[*In the following excerpt, the Fowlers introduce Mowatt's autobiography in the context of nineteenth-century culture.*]

In 1854 there appeared a book entitled ***Autobiography of an Actress, or Eight Years on the Stage,*** by Anna Cora Mowatt, issued by the well-known Boston firm of Ticknor and Fields. The publishers, highly pleased with their record-breaking sales of Harriet Beecher Stowe's recent *Uncle Tom's Cabin,* had good reason to suppose that their new female author, a popular actress, would bring them more profits. In the preceding dozen years Mrs. Mowatt had openly defied conventions governing woman's place in society, winning the public's favor while retaining the respect of much of the upper-middle-class society to which she belonged. Her first appearances in public had been as a dramatic reader of poetry to audiences containing men as well as women. She had next published plays and novels. One of the plays, ***Fashion, or, Life in New York* (1845),** had been staged to great applause in New York and Philadelphia. Turning to acting, Mowatt had gone on to popular successes as a leading lady in both the United States and England. Ticknor and Fields were rewarded: ***Autobiography of an Actress*** sold more that twenty thousand copies in its first year of publication.

These were remarkable achievements. Although prejudice against women speaking before mixed audiences was both traditional and deep, Mrs. Mowatt triumphed in her debut as a reader before an enthusiastic house in Boston. She was very attractive; she performed well— and the time was ripe. As compensation for the defection of some of her friends, who thought such public exposure a disgrace, scores of the liberal-minded, many of them influential in cultural, business, and public life, rallied to her. Their support testified to their acceptance of the idea that talent, when displayed with dignity and moral purpose, ought to be given free play, even in a woman. Some of these supporters applauded her new career even more enthusiastically when they learned that she performed as much for financial gain as for art or fame; with an invalid husband on the verge of bankruptcy, she needed money badly.

For Anna Cora Mowatt to retain her respectability in society through her subsequent career as an actress— an occupation far more suspect than that of literary reader—was even more remarkable. Her previous successes as playwright and novelist were a help. She appeared on the stage as a society matron with literary talent rather than as a girl without money, influence, and reputation, vulnerable to those who ran the theater or patronized it.

If in 1854 one had tried to identify the American woman most likely to offer her life to the public in the form of an autobiography, Anna Cora Mowatt would have seemed a plausible choice. Now a widow, she still needed money. As a well-known person writing about the theater, a familiar source of titillation for the public, she could probably count on financial success. She might also draw inspiration from a memoir by the leading English actress, Frances "Fanny" Kemble Butler, whose *Journal of a Residence in America* (1835) had offered much personal material. And Mowatt had dared so much, so successfully, and had so much to reveal!

Her stated purposes in writing were conventional enough. According to ***Autobiography of an Actress,*** Mowatt wished to fulfill a promise made to her late husband to describe her experiences of life and her profession. But she also hinted at feminist feelings:

> If one struggling sister in the great human family, listening to the history of my life, gain courage to meet and brave severest trials; if she learn to look upon them as blessings in disguise; if she be strengthened in the performance of "daily duties," however "hardly paid;" if she be inspired with faith in the power imparted to a strong will, whose end is good,—then I am amply rewarded for my labor.

She concluded her book with a ringing defense of the theater and the acting profession, adding still another motive for writing.

Mowatt's life, as she presents it in the autobiography, seems to the casual reader an entertainment, its central image a woman of vivid personality playing out a drama influenced by her breach of social convention. Yet the memoirs reveal deeper and more important meanings. Some of them are historical. Her rebellion against conformity symbolizes one of the more striking developments of recent centuries: women in the Western world escaping from their traditional position of legal and social inferiority, which serves as this volume's main historical theme. The memoirs hold further evidence valuable for understanding the broader history of her times, including details of her own importance as a woman who transformed her place in society by becoming a public person, yielding the privacy, protection, and conventional regard given by society to the wife and mother, while risking ridicule, failure, and challenge to reputation in her new role.

Another significance of Mowatt's memoirs is literary. This story of her life became a modest landmark, partly because it displayed the unapologetic consciousness of self that was coming to characterize modern autobiography, but primarily because its author, as a woman, added a distinctive voice to that style of expression. . . .

Women in Nineteenth-Century America

If women's emergence into public life helped to transform their place in American society, how did that emergence come about? What general circumstances in America helped or hindered women intent on change?

The most obvious precondition for change in the status of women was the development of society in directions that would make it possible. During the first century and a half of settlement of the Atlantic coastal colonies, the emigrants from Britain and Europe were largely concerned with survival and security, economic and political. The colonies prospered; but even after the thirteen along the East coast gained independence from Britain, their new nation was still overwhelmingly agricultural and rural. There were only a few American cities of any size, and their cultural opportunities were rudimentary by the standards of London or Paris. Their middle classes were correspondingly small.

By the middle of the nineteenth century, however, the American population had risen from three million to twenty-three million through natural increase and heavy immigration, and it occupied a continental domain. Cities multiplied and grew rapidly. During the early nineteenth century the nation's economy, stimulated by huge production of grain, fiber, and meat for the market, as well as the widespread development of industries, helped to shape a society which was increasingly urban and middle-class in tone, especially in the Northeast, the business center of the country.

By that time Americans had also created a large internal market for ideas. The population boasted more readers, whether in raw numbers or in proportion to the whole, than any other nation. Educational opportunities increased rapidly, and in the 1840s states began to institute the world's first systems of universal public education. A network of rapid transportation in the form of railroads was spreading westward, while the instantaneous communication of the telegraph had begun to match it; both served to carry ideas as well as to aid commerce. More newspapers and magazines circulated in America than anywhere else, aided by liberal subsidies from the federal government through the national postal system, itself a prime carrier of ideas.

While economic opportunism permeated the air, so did democratic politics. The ideas and practices of democracy continually subverted elitist pretensions, championing the right of the masses—with the obvious exclusion of slaves and often free blacks and Native Americans—to literacy, free speech, and political participation as the partners of economic opportunity.

Since all these circumstances favored the ready expression of energy and ideas by individuals, and since women—especially those of the middle and upper classes—enjoyed almost as much literacy and education as men, it might seem inevitable that large numbers of women would assume new roles. But two forces discouraged rapid change of that kind. One was the force of the tradition of female subservience to male authority, still strong and not easily modified. The second was a new feminine ideal which owed much, ironically, to the thrust of economic change.

As breadwinners in an increasingly industrial and commercial society, many men now absented themselves from the home to toil for long hours at factories and offices. Their wives took on heavy—sometimes almost exclusive—responsibility for caring for homes and families much of the time. Many women thus added to their accustomed duties their husbands' traditional roles as primary supervisors of their children's moral and spiritual instruction. While these changing circumstances were real, they helped to generate in nineteenth-century society, in both Britain and America, a new ideal of femininity. Historians have suggested two descriptive terms which together capture the essence of this ideal, "domestic feminism" and "Cult of True Womanhood." In popular thought, expressed in thousands of sermons, speeches, articles, and books, there emerged a glorified image of women as superhuman home managers and spiritual leaders.

Many wives and mothers found attractive the idealizing of femininity generated by this combined tribute and demand. It enhanced the theoretical importance of women to society, and provided recognition for the duties that they had to perform. But the resulting satisfaction in being female could be enjoyed only by women who, more than ever, remained firmly fixed in the home, avoiding outside distractions. Those female deviants who tried to enter the male-run world of affairs felt the force of the ideal in a negative way, as male critics reprimanded them for their departures from domestic duty.

Writing for the Public

Yet if necessity, tradition, and idealized True Womanhood kept most middle-class females in dutiful service at home, it was also true that American society offered venturesome women a respectable mode of courting public attention. This was the occupation (or avocation) of writing for the public. Writing for publication attracted the energies and talents of thousands of American women in the nineteenth century; most of the autobiographers in this anthology first won public attention in that way. The discipline of this work taught a growing number of women to address the public persuasively, and accustomed a rapidly enlarging number of readers of both sexes to listen to what they had to say. Some of the writers were ready to use their pens explicitly for purposes of social reform, and some of these to dramatize their activism through autobiography.

Writing for the public offered a convenient way for a woman to transcend the bounds of home. She could compose poetry, stories, novels, or occasional pieces without leaving home, even submitting work under a pen name to preserve anonymity and privacy, while enjoying vicarious contacts with a wider world. Or she could seek fame, as well as money, by making her identity known to the public, by writing with the authority that came with a literary reputation. There was little male opposition to these women writers; most were thoroughly genteel and celebrated the virtues of True Womanhood, even if they sometimes called attention to large gaps between the pretensions and the practices of the "Lords of Creation," their sarcastic term for the male sex. After all, if a drunken Lord of Creation were endangering home and family, did not the True Woman have the duty of calling him to account?

By the middle of the nineteenth century American women authors were producing sentimental poetry, children's literature, guides to home management, and some literary criticism. They were also publishing novels, tales for magazines and the new cheap story newspapers, and periodical articles so prolifically as to provoke Nathaniel Hawthorne's much-quoted complaint that a "damned army of scribbling women" was giving him unfair competition for the favor of publishers and critics. To illustrate this successful female intrusion into a field earlier dominated by men, Richard B. Morris' *Encyclopedia of American History* notes that ten of the sixteen best-selling books from 1850 to 1860 were written by women (all were novels), and that the only author during those years to publish two best-sellers was the novelist Mrs. E. D. E. N. Southworth.

Such women authors had become deeply involved in an occupation that was both widely visible and influential. They were competing successfully with males and in many cases earning all or part of their livings from it. The five autobiographers here profited from the establishment of writing as an honorable profession for women, for a very large audience of middle-class people, male and female, like themselves.

Who Wrote Autobiographies?

When we look at the identities of our women autobiographers and the contents of their books, however, we realize that the above considerations—literacy, participation in the world of ideas and communication, successful competition with males for the attention of a sizable middle-class audience—do not fully explain why some women were led to reveal their own lives in print. For them to do so, it appears, they needed to involve themselves in important events beyond literature.

That requirement was nearly as true for men as for women; few persons in that day could conceive of placing before the public a wealth of detail about a private life unless they could also claim participation in happenings of special interest to that public. The political leader, the traveler to distant places, the adventurer, and the military hero could make such claims. But on what important matters could women focus their life stories?

Anna Cora Mowatt, as we have seen, was a well-known actress. Mary Antin was a participant in the great migration from the Old World to the New and a notable example of the swift and successful Americanization of many non-English-speaking immigrants. The other women we have chosen were deeply engaged in various movements for social reform, which gave them experience in wrestling with controversial public problems and contending or cooperating with prominent male leaders. Their experiences in dealing with important public questions, coupled with their understandable desire to strengthen the arguments on behalf of their reform interests, furnished them with all the justification they needed to open their lives to the public as examples of work well done.

Unlike the theater and the experience of immigration, these reform causes had flowered only recently. Here the growth in the early nineteenth century of the Evangelical movement within Protestantism, then the overwhelmingly dominant branch of religion in the United States, was important. As historians have shown, this religious movement's powerful emphasis on voluntarism in the saving of souls, as well as the widespread influence of the kind of Perfectionism preached by the Presbyterian revivalist Charles G. Finney, tended to arouse enthusiasm for the reform of many failings, social as well as personal. Those who joined reform movements typically defined them as crusades to attain true morality, as logical outgrowths of personal commitments to religion.

For many women the first stage of participation in reformist activities was in missionary or benevolent organizations sponsored by their own churches. Many then enlisted in women's groups that were more broadly based but aimed at specific goals, such as the reform of prostitutes carried on by the many chapters of the American Society for Moral Reform. Many reform groups contained both male and female members, but often women organized—or were obliged to organize—separate chapters.

The list of pre-War reform groups is a long one. Their aims included the promotion of such things as temperance, better conditions for labor, prisoners, and the insane, free public schools, and socialism through Utopian communities. But it was probably the anti-slavery crusade—in its militant phase beginning in the 1830s—that more than any other movement led women reformers into actions that were politically controversial and often highly unpopular in their own communities, and hence often demanding considerable self-assertion. Agitation for specific legal and other rights for women, which was being organized in the late 1840s, then attracted many of these women, now more accustomed to public activities, into feminist causes. . . .

Anna Cora Mowatt (1819-1870)

Although she was a feminist neither by membership in women's organizations nor through explicit pleas for woman's rights, Anna Cora Mowatt undertook a career that broke dramatically with prescribed roles for nineteenth-century women, especially those of the upper and middle classes. She was born in 1819, ninth of fourteen children of Samuel and Eliza Ogden, both descended from patrician American families. She lived her first six years in southern France, where her father's shipping business had taken him, and went to boarding school on the family's return to New York.

From the first she displayed imagination and talent as amateur actress and playwright, both in her family and at school. When only fifteen she eloped with a young lawyer, James Mowatt, but despite her family's disapproval was soon reconciled with them. She continued to stage amateur productions of her own, and published one play, *Gulzara,* in *The New World,* a magazine suitably genteel for the presentation of a young woman's work. When her husband lost his investments in the business depression of the late 1830s and his sight became impaired through illness, Mowatt turned, with both his and her father's support, to earning an income by giving public readings of poetry. She augmented this income by publishing stories, novels, and plays. Between 1845 and 1854 she won acclaim for the successful staging of her plays and for her appearances as a leading actress in both America and England. Her major work as a playwright, a satire on manners entitled *Fashion,* or, *Life in New York,* was one of the more successful American plays of its time and is virtually the only one of that period still produced today.

For her defiance of convention Mowatt paid a price in the loss of some friends, but compensated for this by acquiring new ones in her own social milieu and in literary and artistic circles. She paid another price in impaired health, suffering severely at times from physical and emotional strain, but found considerable relief in undergoing hypnotism (called mesmerism in that day), and obtained spiritual solace in the Swedenborgian version of Christianity, then growing rapidly in popularity.

James Mowatt died in England in 1851 while she was on tour as an actress there. Without children of their own, the couple had earlier adopted three. By 1854 Mrs. Mowatt was ready to remarry and give up her career in the theater. At this point, at thirty-five, she published her autobiography—fulfilling, she wrote, a promise to her late husband. However, the man she was to marry, William F. Richie, an editor of the *Richmond* (Virginia) *Examiner,* was neither wealthy nor highly paid, and since Mowatt was accustomed to both financial independence and spending money happily, she no doubt viewed her experiences as a potential source of more publishing royalties.

Despite her well-publicized years as an actress, Mowatt threw herself actively and successfully into the highly conservative social life of Richmond, taking a leading part in the efforts of the Mount Vernon Association to purchase and restore the home of George Washington as a national shrine. Her marriage to Ritchie, however, fell into increasing difficulties; she suspected him of dallying with a female slave at a friend's plantation, and in the crisis of the Union she did not wish to support the South. Shortly before the outbreak of the Civil War they separated for good. Mowatt spent the next decade in Europe with brief visits to the United States. She tried to return to the stage, for she had little money left, but failed to attract offers. She died in England in 1870.

James M. Hutchisson

SOURCE: "Poe, Anna Cora Mowatt, and T. Tennyson Twinkle," in *Studies in the American Renaissance,* 1993, pp. 245-54.

[In the following essay, Hutchisson analyzes Mowatt's acquaintanceship with Edgar Allan Poe and argues that one of her characters in Fashion *was a parodic representation of Poe.]*

In Anna Cora Mowatt's drawing-room comedy *Fashion; or, Life in New York,* which premiered at the Park Theatre in New York on 25 March 1845, there appears a minor character named T. Tennyson Twinkle, a diminutive poet who has recently achieved celebrity with a popular poem and who is romantically involved with wealthy older women. Twinkle, who appears only in the first and last scenes of the play, is portrayed as a disputatious literary critic and popular lecturer on poetry in America. Early in the first act, Twinkle arrives at the home of Mrs. Tiffany, the wife of a well-to-do New York merchant, to find her reading a literary periodical which he edits, "The New Monthly Vernal Galaxy," and in reply to Mrs. Tiffany's fulsome remark about the beauty of his poetry, Twinkle says, "Yes, they do read tolerably. And you must take into consideration, ladies, the rapidity with which they were written. Four minutes and a half by the stop watch! The true test of a poet is the *velocity* with which he composes."[1]

I should like to suggest that Mowatt parodistically modeled this character on Edgar Allan Poe. The physical description of Twinkle, his celebrity as a newly-famous poet ("The Raven" had appeared in February 1845), and his reputation as an editor and critic all point to Poe, as does Twinkle's popularity as a lecturer, since at this time Poe was touring the northeast speaking on "Poets and Poetry in America." Another clue to Mowatt's parody might be found in the character's middle name, "Tennyson," which may allude to the much-publicized controversy Poe had started in January 1840 by accusing Henry Wadsworth Longfellow of purloining the central image of "The Death of the Old Year" from Alfred, Lord Tennyson's "Midnight Mass for the New Year." The middle name also recalls Poe's laudatory public statements about Tennyson, whom he much admired.[2] Finally, the brief speech Twinkle makes about "the velocity with which [he] composes" could be a jibe at Poe's extraordinary literary output at this time and at the persona of the workmanlike writer that he projected in various es-

says and reviews. A theory about the "velocity" of composition, in fact, sounds suspiciously like "The Philosophy of Composition," though that is not precisely what Twinkle says, and the debut of *Fashion* predates the publication of "The Philosophy of Composition" in *Graham's Magazine* for January 1846 by nine months. Judging from the contemporary reaction to *Fashion,* however, and from much additional evidence that has never been discussed before, it is very likely that Mowatt had Poe in mind when she created the character of Twinkle.

Poe and Mowatt knew each other by reputation, for they corresponded once, about *Fashion,* and Poe published several articles and reviews of Mowatt and her work. Poe's relationship with Mowatt, a forgotten pioneer of the American theatre, is worth studying in detail, for a good deal of evidence suggests that Poe and Mowatt knew each other better than has previously been supposed. Further, investigating this episode in Poe's career uncovers some hitherto unknown connections between Poe's and Mowatt's circles. It also raises some significant questions about Poe's interest in American drama.

Anna Cora Ogden Mowatt Ritchie (1819-70) was born in Bordeaux, France, and was descended on both sides from colonial American stock. Her paternal grandfather, the Reverend Uzal Ogden, was a distinguished Presbyterian clergyman of New Jersey, and her maternal great-grandfather, Francis Lewis, was a signer of the Declaration of Independence.[3] Except for four years of boarding school in Bordeaux, Mowatt was educated at home in New York City, where the family returned in 1826. At the age of fifteen, she eloped with James Mowatt, a successful New York attorney, and spent her early married life in Flatbush, Long Island, where she and her husband entertained New York society people and many literary figures of the day. In 1841 James Mowatt fell ill, then lost his fortune through speculation. Forced to assume their support, Mowatt decided to give a series of public poetry readings. She was the first American woman to do so, and she became something of a celebrity, inspiring a host of imitators, at least one of whom advertised "Readings and Recitations in the style of Mrs. Mowatt." The strain of making public appearances, however, proved too demanding, so she turned to writing, and between 1842 and 1844 produced, under various pseudonyms, a formidable miscellany of poems, articles, biographies, and cookbooks; manuals on household management, etiquette, and needlework; and two novels, *The Fortune Hunters* and *Evelyn.*

Mowatt then turned to playwriting, and thus *Fashion* was born, the first American comedy of manners and still the best of the early pictures of budding American society. *Fashion* shows the conflict between the homespun ways of nineteenth-century America and the high society manners of the Old World. Its central character, Mrs. Tiffany, is a pretentious *nouveau riche* who tries to lead fashionable New York society by imitating foreign manners. She attempts to thwart her daughter Seraphina's marriage to Adam Trueman, probably the first theatrical portrayal of the diamond-in-the-rough American, and turn Seraphina's attention to Count Jolimaitre, a valet who has fooled Mrs. Tiffany into believing that he is a nobleman. In the end, honest manners triumph and pretension is exposed.

When the play opened at the Park Theatre on 25 March 1845, it was an instant hit and ran for the then-lengthy engagement of twenty-one consecutive performances. Mowatt was seen as a pioneer in the American theatre because the only plays being produced at the time were English plays; she was also seen as a portent of the women's emancipation movement, already well under way, because virtually all of the other American plays of the period were being written by men. *Fashion* later played in Philadelphia and London, and Mowatt began a third successful career as an actress, debuting in June 1845 at the Park Theatre as Pauline, the lead role in Edward Bulwer-Lytton's *The Lady of Lyons*. So began a remarkable career on the American stage, for Mowatt had no theatrical training at all, yet she started at the top of the profession and for eight years held a place as one of the foremost actresses in America and England, where for several seasons she played Juliet, Desdemona, Rosalind, and other Shakespeare heroines. She also performed in many contemporary plays.

James Mowatt died in 1851; three years later his widow decided to leave the stage in order to marry William Foushee Ritchie, the editor of the *Richmond Enquirer*, and move to Virginia. In Richmond she led a successful movement to persuade the Virginia legislature to establish Mount Vernon as a national shrine. But her second marriage proved unhappy, and Mowatt went to live abroad in 1861, spending the last two years of her life in England, where she died of tuberculosis at the age of fifty. By the end of the nineteenth century, Mowatt had been forgotten, but *Fashion* was not. The play was revived on Broadway in 1924 and was staged off Broadway as recently as 1959. It is frequently performed by amateur groups today.

Mowatt began writing *Fashion* in early 1845. On or about 20 March of that year Poe wrote her, asking to see the manuscript of her forthcoming play. Probably that same evening Mowatt wrote her reply, apologizing that she could send only a rough copy of the work, and telling him that his "criticisms [would] be prized."[4] That is the only known record of direct contact between Poe and Mowatt. *Fashion* premiered six nights later. All extant reviews of the play were exuberantly favorable—except for the one by Poe, which appeared in the 29 March 1845 issue of the *Broadway Journal*. In his review, Poe admitted that he had only read the play in manuscript, but he nevertheless lambasted *Fashion* for its lack of verisimilitude and its use of hackneyed conventions of the theatre such as soliloquies, the reading of letters in a "loud, rhetorical tone," "preposterous asides," and other stage tricks.[5] But what Poe found to be distinctly unfunny, everyone else thought hilarious. The reviewer for *The Spirit of the Times*, for example, recorded that the audience laughed uproariously at the long-winded disquisitions by the characters on their claims to being "fashionable."[6] Poe, on the other hand, pointed out the weakness of depending on exaggerated explanations instead of action to bring about the denouement. Poe also objected to the play as a satire of "types of individuals," noting obvious parallels between *Fashion* and Richard Sheridan's *The School for Scandal*, which he said "was comparatively good in its day," but would be "positively bad at the present day," and "imitations" of it "inadmissable at any day" (12:117). In general, Poe complained that the characters were not real human beings but were merely stereotypes, such as "the mad poet reciting his own verses" (12:116). Did Poe see himself in Twinkle? Although he did not single out this role for comment, he was surely sensitive about the attitude of the American public toward poets.

Despite Poe's unfavorable review, *Fashion* continued to attract sizable audiences. Many prominent literary figures saw the play, among them Evert A. Duyckinck, Nathaniel P. Willis, Parke Godwin, William T. Porter, and Park Benjamin.[7] Then, in the 5 April issue of the *Broadway Journal*, twenty days after his review had appeared, Poe offered what amounted to a retraction of his earlier statement, using the occasion of the penultimate performance of the play to comment on the "Prospects of the Drama." In this second article, a recantation that was sometimes characteristic of Poe, he claimed that, having attended every performance of *Fashion* "since its first production," he now judged it to be one of "the clearest indications of a revival of the American drama." He still objected to its being a satire, but he now concluded that its "thesis" was without question "an original one"—a remarkable reversal of opinion.[8] Why the retraction? What seemed significant to Poe was the enthusiastic reception of the play, which indicated to him that there was "an earnest disposition" to see the American drama "revived," an issue that was on Poe's agenda throughout his career. What is jarring about Poe's reason for revising his earlier opinion of *Fashion*, however, is that Poe spent much of his career as a reviewer condemning American critics for shamelessly "puffing" American works simply because they were American. Yet that is largely what Poe was doing here.[9]

In his August 1839 review of Nathaniel P. Willis' *Tortesa; the Usurer* for *Burton's Gentleman's Maga-*

zine, Poe had characteristically demanded high critical standards with which to judge native works and had denounced the growing practice of relaxing those standards for American works in order to encourage people to write and produce them.[10] Poe carried forward these ideas in another essay written for the *American Whig Review* in August 1845, just five months after his laudatory notice of *Fashion,* entitled "The American Drama." Not only did Poe again denounce those who praised American works when they did not deserve praise, but in this essay he listed three specific problems with current American drama that needed to be corrected if a national drama were to flourish in the country. In the two plays he reviewed in this essay, Willis' *Tortesa* (again) and Longfellow's *The Spanish Student,* his criticisms centered on these three deficiencies: "The first thing necessary is to burn or bury the 'old models' and to forget, as quickly as possible, that ever a play has been penned. The second thing is to consider *de novo* what are the *capabilities* of the drama—not merely what hitherto have been its conventional purposes." Poe's "third and last point" had "reference to the composition of a play." In considering Willis' *Tortesa,* he objected to mere complexity passing for plot. Ideally, he said, a plot "is perfect only inasmuch as we shall find ourselves unable to detach from it or *disarrange* any single incident involved, without destruction to the mass."[11] Yet Poe made these same criticisms of *Fashion* in his initial review. He seems to have been willing to suppress his objections to the literary value of the play and to do a little "puffery" himself if in return it would bring about some interest in national drama.

Poe continued to follow Mowatt's career, reviewing her performance that summer in *The Lady of Lyons* on three separate occasions in the *Broadway Journal;* writing a fulsome review of her novel *The Fortune Hunter* in the 2 August 1845 *Broadway Journal;* and a year later including a sketch of her in the second installment of "The Literati of New York City," which appeared in *Godey's Lady's Book* for June 1846.[12] Yet none of these documents supplies clues to the mystery of Twinkle. There is, however, some additional evidence that might help solve the puzzle. Mowatt mentioned Poe several times in her *Autobiography of an Actress,* published in 1854. These remarks are confined to Poe's criticism of *Fashion*—evidently the initial review—which Mowatt found unduly severe: "Edgar A. Poe, one of my sternest critics, wrote of *Fashion,* that it resembled the School for Scandal in the same degree that the *shell* of a locust resembles the living locust. If his severity was but *justice,* it must be that the spirits of the performers infused themselves into the empty shell, and produced a very effective counterfeit of *life.*"[13] Mowatt says nothing about Poe's second review, nor does she say that she modeled the character Twinkle on Poe, but she does defend herself against allegations that she caricatured famous people in the play: "No charge can be more untrue than that with which I have been taxed through the press and in private—the accusation of having held up to ridicule well-known personages."[14] This issue seems to have sparked a controversy in theater circles at the time. Mowatt's friend John William Stanhope Hows, who reviewed *Fashion* in the *Albion,* came to her aid, stating that

> not the least of the merits of [*Fashion*] is that it is only classes that are depicted—*individuals* have not sat for portraits; it would be doing Mrs. Mowatt great injustice to suppose that she would serve up particular persons for public laughter or derision; we believe her incapable of the act—that several persons have been named as models is tolerably conclusive that the application of the satire is a general one.

No one seems to have recorded what characters were thought to have been modeled on which "well-known personages," but Hows praised Mowatt for "the bright idea" of having Twinkle use "the favorite mode of reading verse, very generally in vogue, with poets who prefer to hear the melodious jingle of the rhyme," a description that would fit the character of much of Poe's verse, particularly "The Raven."[15]

Perhaps the most intriguing pieces of the puzzle are the many acquaintances Poe and Mowatt had in common, so many that it is possible that their paths may have crossed on more than the one occasion we know of. Mowatt was good friends with Epes Sargent, Frances Sargent Osgood, John Hill Hewitt, and John R. Thompson. According to Mowatt's *Autobiography,* she wrote *Fashion* at the suggestion of Epes Sargent, a minor poet, critic, and editor of the time. Mowatt later said that Sargent, who was her close friend and literary confidant, had helped her in the composition of the play.[16] Poe's relationship with Sargent is well documented, and recently Gerald E. Gerber has brought to light Poe's possible borrowings in "The Raven" from three of Sargent's poems in *The Light of the Light-House, and Other Poems.*[17] Almost one year before *Fashion* appeared, in June 1844, Poe had unfavorably reviewed Sargent's volume in *Graham's Magazine,* and in July 1848, Sargent, who had just assumed the editorship of the *Boston Evening Transcript,* retaliated by panning Poe's *Eureka* as arrant nonsense. Further, Poe referred to Mowatt in his sketch of Sargent for "The Literati" in August 1846—specifically to the fact that Sargent provided "some assistance" to Mowatt "in the composition of her comedy," and that Mowatt was "guided by his advice in many particulars."[18]

John Hill Hewitt, another of Mowatt's close friends, is remembered in Poe biography for the street brawl he and Poe reportedly engaged in after Hewitt won the

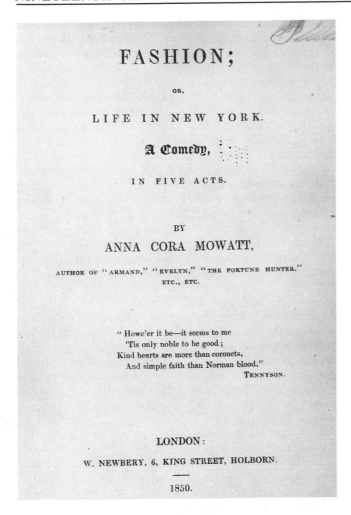

FASHION;

OR,

LIFE IN NEW YORK.

A Comedy,

IN FIVE ACTS.

BY

ANNA CORA MOWATT,

AUTHOR OF "ARMAND," "EVELYN," "THE FORTUNE HUNTER,"
ETC., ETC.

" Howe'er it be—it seems to me
'Tis only noble to be good ;
Kind hearts are more than coronets,
And simple faith than Norman blood."
TENNYSON.

LONDON:

W. NEWBERY, 6, KING STREET, HOLBORN.

——

1850.

poetry prize in the *Baltimore Saturday Visiter* literary contest of June 1833, the contest in which Poe took the fiction prize for "MS. Found in a Bottle." Poe believed that he should have won both prizes because Hewitt was the editor of the *Visiter* and had unfairly entered the contest by submitting his poem under a pseudonym.[19] Mowatt knew Hewitt through her first husband, who had been friendly with the poet, musician, and journalist for some time.[20]

To this point, the facts have unfolded into a scenario that reads more like detective fiction than literary history, with two suspects, each having sufficient motive to lampoon Poe in print. But more interesting is that fact that Hewitt's sister-in-law, Mary Elizabeth Hewitt, was one of Poe's closest associates among the New York bluestockings with whom he associated in the mid- to late 1840s.[21] In fact, Mowatt knew several of Poe's women friends—in particular Frances Sargent Osgood, the most famous member of the circle. The two women met in 1841 after Osgood attended one of Mowatt's poetry readings. Osgood was so moved by the performance that

she wrote a poem in Mowatt's honor, and that began a close friendship which lasted until Osgood's death in 1850.[22]

If Twinkle was modeled on Poe, the character's habit of associating with women who subscribe to the "fashion" of patronizing poets would certainly fit. Mowatt seems to have known something about this phase of Poe's life. She corresponded with Sarah Helen Whitman, and she might have known Elmira Royster Shelton. Certainly she knew *of* her. Among Mrs. Whitman's papers at the John Hay Library of Brown University is an unpublished account of Poe's relationship with Shelton, a two-page manuscript fragment inscribed in Mowatt's hand and titled "J. R. Thompson's account of Poe as given to Mrs. Ritchie and by her related to Mrs. Freeman."[23] Evidently the fragment is a transcription or an oral summary (the account is enclosed in quotation marks) of what John R. Thompson knew of Poe's life. Thompson, the Richmond journalist and poet, became editor of the *Southern Literary Messenger* in November 1847, and, although he did not know Poe especially well, he did correspond with him about writing for the *Messenger* and saw him under various circumstances in 1848 and 1849. "Mrs. Freeman" was Julia Deane Freeman, a poet and friend of both Mowatt and Whitman, who included a discussion of Mowatt's career in an 1860 book entitled *Women of the South Distinguished in Literature*.[24]

The substance of this account appears in a 27 February 1874 letter from Whitman to John H. Ingram, Poe's first English biographer.[25] Evidently Whitman copied from the Mowatt fragment as she wrote the letter to Ingram. The most likely hypothesis for the transmission of the fragment is this: in the spring of 1859, Whitman was corresponding with several of Poe's friends, particularly his women friends, soliciting information for her forthcoming book, *Edgar Poe and His Critics,* published the following year. One of the people Whitman wrote was Anna Mowatt, or so Whitman told Mrs. Maria Clemm, Poe's mother-in-law, in a 4 April 1859 letter: "I answered your letter, I think, by return of mail . . . asking from you some information with regard to Edgar's proposed marriage engagements with a lady of Richmond whose name I did not then know, but which I have since learned through Mrs. Anna Cora Ritchie of that city."[26] The "lady of Richmond" was Elmira Shelton, with whom Poe had first fallen in love as a teenager in 1825, and to whom he eventually became engaged, in July 1849, four months before his death. Whitman's letter to Mrs. Clemm refers to Mowatt a second time: "Can you tell me whether Mr. Allan was twice married?—I ask the question because Mrs. Ritchie (who is intimately acquainted with Mrs. Allan, the widow of Mr. Allan) writes that he was only once married." Sometime before 5 April 1849, then, Whitman wrote Mowatt asking for information about Poe; Mowatt on at least one occasion replied, telling her the information that Whitman related to Mrs. Clemm in the 5 April letter; at some other time, Mowatt wrote Freeman, enclosing the information contained in the fragment (information which Mowatt had been given by Thompson); and Freeman sent the fragment to Whitman, who placed it with her memoranda for *Edgar Poe and His Critics*. Mowatt therefore knew Poe's adoptive family, and the fragment is another link between Mowatt and Whitman, and perhaps between T. Tennyson Twinkle and Edgar Allan Poe. Presumably Mowatt knew of Poe's relationships with Hewitt, Osgood, Shelton, and Whitman, women whom Poe often came to when in need, especially by 1845 and after, when his wife Virginia's health had worsened and she lay ill in Fordham.

Poe surely would have spoken with these literary women about his work (perhaps even about "The Philosophy of Composition," if he was writing it or thinking about it in the spring of 1845 or earlier). With this information, one can safely speculate that Poe was at least partly a parodic model for Twinkle; that Poe and Mowatt knew each other better than has been previously assumed; and some reasons why Poe's reviews of *Fashion* contradict his otherwise stringent standards for native dramatic works may lie in his relationship with Mowatt.

Notes

[1] Anna Cora Mowatt, *Fashion; or, Life in New York* (New York: Samuel French, 1849), pp. 6-7.

[2] The most famous of these statements occurs in "The Poetic Principle," where Poe refers to Tennyson as "the noblest poet that ever lived" (*The Complete Works of Edgar Allan Poe,* ed. James A. Harrison, 17 vols. [New York: Thomas Y. Crowell, 1902], 14:289). See also the September 1842 issue of *Graham's Magazine,* in which Poe welcomes Ticknor's edition of Tennyson's *Poems* by announcing that Tennyson is "a poet, who (in our own humble, but sincere opinion,) is *the greatest* that ever lived" (*Complete Works,* 11:127); and see Poe's observation about the musicality of Tennyson's verse—he "seems to see *with his ear*"—in the December 1844 *Democratic Review* ("Marginalia," *Complete Works,* 16:30). Poe was also compared both favorably and unfavorably to Tennyson many times: see, for example, the essay on "American Poetry" in the London *Foreign Quarterly Review* for January 1844 and the letter to the editor of the *Richmond Compiler* for 9 January 1846, reprinted in Burton R. Pollin, "The Richmond *Compiler* and Poe in 1845: Two Hostile Notices," *Poe Studies,* 18 (June 1985): 6-7.

[3] The earliest biographical account of Mowatt was written by Rufus W. Griswold in the headnote to a selection of Mowatt's poems, which he included in his anthology, *The Female Poets of America* (Philadelphia: Carey and Hart, 1849), pp. 267-69. Brief biographical sketches of Mowatt can be found in *Dictionary of American Biography,* 13:295-97, and in *Notable American Women, 1607-1950,* ed. Edward T. James et al., 3 vols. (Cambridge: Harvard University Press, 1971), 2:596-98. There are two full-length biographies: an unpublished dissertation by Marius Blesi, "Anna Cora Mowatt" (University of Virginia, 1938), and a partly factual, partly reconstructed account of Mowatt's life in the New York theatre world of the nineteenth century by Eric Wollencott Barnes, *The Lady of Fashion: The Life and Theatre of Anna Cora Mowatt* (New York: Scribners, 1954).

[4] Mowatt to Poe, "Thursday Evening / [20 March?] 1845," quoted in John Ward Ostrom, "Fourth Supplement to *The Letters of Poe,*" *American Literature,* 45 (January 1974): 524-25. Poe's letter is not extant.

[5] "The New Comedy by Mrs. Mowatt," *Broadway Journal,* 29 March 1845 (*Complete Works,* 12:112-21); future references to this review will be to the *Complete Works* text and will be cited parenthetically.

[6] *The Spirit of the Times,* 29 March 1845, p. 4. See also "Things Theatrical," *The Spirit of the Times,* 15 March 1845, p. 4.

[7] Barnes, *The Lady of Fashion,* p. 107.

[8] "Prospects of the Drama—Mrs. Mowatt's Comedy," *Broadway Journal,* 5 April 1845 (*Complete Works,* 12:124-29; the passage quoted appears on p. 126).

[9] The most famous of these battles was the one waged against Theodore S. Fay, Nathaniel P. Willis and George P. Morris, editors of the *New York Mirror,* a literary weekly which published fulsome praise of Fay's novel *Norman Leslie*. The *Mirror* and its ally, Lewis Gaylord Clark's *Knickerbocker Magazine,* had printed glowing pre-publication notices of the novel with excerpts from it on several different occasions (see Sidney P. Moss, *Poe's Literary Battles* [Durham: Duke University Press, 1963], esp. chaps. 2 and 3).

[10] "Tortesa The Usurer By Nathaniel P. Willis," *Burton's Gentleman's Magazine,* August 1839 (*Collected Works,* 3:27-30).

[11] "The American Drama," *American Whig Review,* August 1845 (*Collected Works,* 13:33-73; the passage quoted appears on p. 37).

[12] "The Drama," *Broadway Journal,* 19 July, 26 July, 2 August 1845 (*Complete Works,* 12:184-92, 210-12); "The Fortune Hunter; or, The Adventures of a Man About Town. By Mrs. Anna Cora Mowatt," *Broadway Journal,* 2 August 1845 (*Complete Works,* 12:207-10);

"The Literati of New York City—Anna Cora Mowatt," *Godey's Lady's Book,* June 1846 (*Complete Works,* 15:27-32).

[13] Anna Cora Mowatt, *Autobiography of An Actress; or, Eight Years on Stage* (Boston: Ticknor, Reed and Fields, 1854), p. 213.

[14] Mowatt, *Autobiography,* p. 203.

[15] John W. S. Hows, *Albion,* 29 March 1845, p. 178. Hows had already anticipated such objections to the play when one week earlier he had asserted that "Having read the manuscript, we think it but justice to the fair author to state, that the comedy is entirely devoid of personalities—specimens of classes, are presented with bold and graphic skill, but not *individuals* of those classes. . . . it is but just that she should appear, only as censor of general foibles—not the caricaturist of personal foibles" (*Albion,* 22 March 1845, p. 144).

[16] Mowatt, *Autobiography,* p. 202. A review of *Fashion* in the *New York Herald* confirms this: "It is . . . supposed that although attributed to Mrs. Mowatt, that several literary characters have been assisting in [the play's] production, by suggestions, etc; and particular mention is made of the name of Epes Sargent as being connected with its authorship" (24 March 1845, p. 4).

[17] Gerald E. Gerber, "Epes Sargent and 'The Raven,'" *Poe Studies,* 19 (June 1986): 24. The title page of Sargent's volume lists the publisher as "James Mowatt & Co." Blesi states that in early 1843 "James [Mowatt] had launched on a publishing venture with Epes [Sargent]" ("Mowatt," p. 95).

[18] "The Light of the Light-House, and Other Poems," *Graham's Magazine,* June 1844 (reprinted in Thomas Ollive Mabbott, "Newly-Identified Reviews by Edgar Poe," *Notes and Queries,* 163 [17 December 1932]: 441); Sargent, "Eureka," *Boston Evening Transcript,* 20 July 1848, p. 3; "The Literati of New York City—Epes Sargent," *Godey's Lady's Book,* August 1846 (*Complete Works,* 15:91-93; the passage quoted appears on p. 92).

[19] John Hill Hewitt, *Recollections of Poe,* ed. Richard Barksdale Harwell (Atlanta: Emory University Library, 1949), p. 19.

[20] In the Hewitt archives at GAE there are four letters from Mowatt to Hewitt dated in the first months of 1860; these concern church musical activities. Mowatt was then living in Richmond with her second husband William Ritchie. Hewitt, residing in Washington, D.C., arranged musical programs with Mowatt (John Hill Hewitt Collection, Series 1, Box 1, Folder 1, Special Collections, Robert W. Woodruff Library, GAE).

[21] Dwight Thomas and David K. Jackson, *The Poe Log: A Documentary Life of Edgar Allan Poe* (Boston: G. K. Hall, 1987), p. xxviii.

[22] Mowatt speaks admiringly of Osgood throughout her *Autobiography.* Osgood's poem, "To Anna Cora Mowatt (On hearing her read)," appears on pp. 155-56.

[23] Ms. 30.78, Sarah Helen Whitman Papers, John Hay Library, RPB.

[24] Julia Deane Freeman, *Women of the South Distinguished in Literature* (New York: Derby & Jackson, 1861), p. 94.

[25] Whitman to Ingram, 27 February 1874, item 125, in *Poe's Helen Remembers,* ed. John Carl Miller (Charlottesville: University Press of Virginia, 1979), p. 41.

[26] Whitman to Clemm, 4 April 1859, *Complete Works,* 17:423-25.

Jeffrey H. Richards

SOURCE: "Chastity and the Stage in Mowatt's 'Stella,'" in *Studies in American Fiction,* Vol. 24, No. 1, Spring, 1996, pp. 87-100.

[*In the following essay, Richards examines the themes of chastity and the moral dangers of the theater in Mowatt's novella "Stella."*]

At the end of her brief but illustrious theatrical career, the actress and playwright Anna Cora Mowatt returned to a genre she had worked earlier in her life, fiction, in order to convey some ideas she had about stage life. Her collection of three long stories, **Mimic Life; or, Before and Behind the Curtain,** appeared in 1856, approximately a year and a half after she had married William Foushee Ritchie, her second husband. Mowatt, born Anna Cora Ogden, had in younger days dabbled in amateur theater. When her first husband, James Mowatt, began to lose money and through illness grow increasingly incapable of earning a living, Anna Mowatt turned to public reading,[1] then to writing, to make up the loss of income. When her 1845 play **Fashion** proved to be a hit at the Park Theatre in New York, she was encouraged to act as well. Her immediate success as an actress only three months after the opening of **Fashion** led to an astonishing career both in the United States and in England. With the death of her husband, Mowatt continued to act, to considerable acclaim, in order to support herself. Her marriage to Ritchie, subsequently unhappy, gave her the leisure to retire from the stage in 1853. From her experiences in the United States and abroad, Mowatt understood the stage in ways few of her fellow fiction writers could appreciate, and turned to print, rather than public appearance, to share her observations.

Mowatt's choice of medium is itself of interest. As a woman, she understood the prevailing sentiments toward her sex and its relationship to the stage. From a socially prominent New York family, Mowatt had to resist the idea that women of her class could not be seen in public entertainments. Those women who did take up a theatrical career might be praised for their work, but as working women, they had to be on guard always for imputations of sexual impropriety. Despite having an exemplary career on stage, Mowatt seems to have carried with her a lingering concern about the reputation of women on stage. Herself childless, she took her role as a potential model to other young women quite seriously. In reaching those who might follow her, Mowatt understood the demographics of culture. She would have recognized that for all the young women in her audiences—and by midcentury there would be a sizable number of escorted women in the audiences of large urban playhouses—she could touch many more in the reading public. Without much more direct knowledge of stage life than an occasional visit with a parent to a play or perhaps only reading in the press about a performance, this large audience of female fiction readers might still feel the allure of the theater. To them Mowatt aims *Mimic Life.*

Mowatt's publisher Ticknor and Fields no doubt hoped to capitalize on her national notoriety and on the success of her previos volume, *The Autobiography of an Actress; or, Eight Years on the Stage* (1854). In fact, the opening pages to *Mimic Life* include a number of blurbs praising the earlier book. One in particular catches one of Mowatt's own intentions: "The tone is high and unaffectedly religious; and while the author vindicates the profession which she is about to quit, she mingles words of counsel with her farewell, which cannot fail to benefit those for whom they are intended.—*Dollar Newspaper.*" For readers unfamiliar with the particulars of nineteenth-century dramatic production, both books have great value as sources of information on the nitty-gritty details of behind-the-scenes life. At the same time, the "high" tone in *Mimic Life* offers another perspective in recreating theatrical culture in the 1840s and 1850s: by urging upon readers the morality of the stage, Mowatt is able to speak some of the unspoken constraints under which theater people function.

Her purpose in writing these stories would be achieved, she says in her Preface, if the book's "readers will receive a more correct impression of some unlaurelled laborers for the public amusement than is generally entertained."[2] To expose both the trials of those who never achieve anything more than evanescent fame and to raise "the curtain of prejudice" from the lowly are Mowatt's stated themes. Such figures as call boys,

prompters, supernumeraries, ballet girls, and fixed-role bit players people the three narratives in *Mimic Life.* Mowatt's intention—paralleling that of abolitionist writers in presenting slave characters to white audiences—is to establish the humanity and moral goodness of these largely invisible and frequently exploited workers. At the same time, she feels obliged to present a theme connected to her major idea but not precisely named: the maintenance of female sexual virtue in the theater.

This issue seems especially important in the first and longest story, "**Stella**" (*ML,* pp. 7-195). The narrative of a young, virtuous, unmarried woman who tries the stage as a career provides Mowatt with a vehicle through which to test the idea that a woman can act and be chaste at the same time. In many ways, the story follows a familiar sentimental plot. When her father dies, the innocent Stella seeks to support her beloved mother. Rather than follow the usual routes for women in such fictions and engage in domestic labor, Stella decides to go on stage. Despite early setbacks, she succeeds in getting with a company and moves up the ranks into increasingly important roles. Although she could easily use her popularity to justify a star's arrogance, Stella instead takes two impoverished young stage underlings, Floy and Perdita, into her care. Just at the point where we might expect her to fall in love, marry, and leave the stage, she gets sick with "brain fever" after seeing Perdita's father killed during a performance by a falling curtain weight. The disease affects her subsequent performance as Ophelia; sent home to rest, she lingers, then dies. Words from *Romeo and Juliet* provide her eulogy, reinforcing the image of her purity and goodness.

In her *Autobiography,* besides providing the signal events in her life, Mowatt often inserts observations on the relationship of the stage to culture. One of her concerns is the perception that women are degraded by the stage. On the one hand, her *Autobiography* itself is a testament to a woman's retaining the highest moral standards while pursuing a stage career; on the other, that same book gives evidence for the difficulty of that life and warns readers that being an actress requires attributes of character that not all women possess:

> Let me here venture to warn any enthusiastic young aspirant against adopting the stage, unless her qualifications—not to use a much abused word, and say her *mission*—seem particularly to fit her for such a vocation, unless she be strongly impelled by the possession of talents which are unquestionable, unless she be enamoured of Art itself.[3]

To be an actress thus requires a basic dedication to the theater that, if not a "mission," is its artistic equivalent. In a sense, Mowatt seeks to deflect interest in her own story as a model. But she seems in her autobiography not to want to be the cause of other young women—especially those not yet married—embracing the stage with naive and untalented enthusiasm. Not only is this practical advice, it is also a kind of moral imperative.

Indeed, Mowatt seems to be writing to a culture that both supports the stage as its chief medium of public entertainment and condemns its purveyors to a moral second class. Women, she suggests, are particularly vulnerable to the double standard of accolade/condemnation:

> But that the dangers of the profession are such as they are generally accredited to be, I do not believe; for I have known too many women bred upon the stage, whose lives were so blamelessly exemplary, whose manners so refined, whose intellect so cultivated, that they would adorn any sphere of society. The subject is not one into which I can fully enter; but this let me say, that the woman who could be dazzled by the adulation bestowed upon her talents as an actress, would be dazzled and led astray in the blaze of a ball room, in the excitement of social intercourse, in any situation where those talents could be displayed, in any position where she could hear
>
> 'The false glozings of a flattering tongue.'
>
> And from these where will she be shielded, except in utter seclusion? (*Autobiography,* pp. 426-27)

Several things are notable about this passage. The context is Mowatt's final chapter, which she uses largely as a justification of the stage itself. That someone in America in 1854 still felt obliged to defend the theater from the same attacks that had led to the closing of the English theaters in 1642 says a great deal about mass culture moralizing and the public perception of stage life. Despite the proliferation of large theaters in urban areas and the star status given to many actors, Mowatt included, the author writes as if permanent acceptance of the theater as an ennobling art form is far from certain. Of equal importance to the content of her remarks is the tone; her language and subject matter evoke the world of the seduction novels of the previous century.[4]

Mowatt wants to admit no taint of licentiousness in her portrayal of life backstage. In the *Autobiography,* she cannot bring herself more than vaguely to allude to the common prejudice that women who engage in a stage career are doomed to sexual profligacy. In **"Stella,"** Mowatt pursues the same question. When her father dies, Stella Rosenvelt of Boston must confront the limited options for a single woman who suddenly faces economic privation. Her brother is an actor in New York, and to him she writes about the possibility of

her taking up acting as a way of supporting their widowed mother and herself. Ernest's response sets out the thematic space in which Stella will operate. Importantly, Ernest does not object to her acting on moral grounds; like Mowatt in her autobiography, Ernest basically argues that chastity is a product of individual upbringing and choices, not something imposed or removed by an institutional setting:

> You also know that I look upon none of the world's baseless prejudices as more false, more *vulgar,* than that which presupposes that a woman who enters this profession hazards her spotless character, or is even subjected to more than ordinary temptations. (*ML,* p. 32)

If a woman is pure to start with, she will be fine; if she brings in her "infected blood," Ernest continues, there is nothing more in the theater to encourage or prevent her from sexual license than would be found anyplace else in the culture. Of Stella herself, he continues, "whose mind has been precept-strengthened, whose spirit is 'In strong proof of chastity well armed,' I should have no fears of shoals and quicksands" (p. 32). In other words, says Mowatt, a woman whose virtues have already been formed need have no worry that simply by taking up the theater her chastity will be assailed.

Nevertheless, stage life can be hazardous. The rest of Ernest's advice—largely ignored by Stella—deflects worry over loss of virginity to loss of general well-being:

> But to launch you upon this life of turmoil, contention, perpetual struggling!—you, my delicately-nurtured, sensitive, excitable sister!—Heaven forbid! To bid you, who have been environed, from your cradle, with the appliances of ease and opulence, exist upon the capricious breath, the uncertain suffrages, of the public?—never! To throw you, with a nervous system so highly strung that its chords can be played upon by every chance breeze, into this whirlwind of excitement!—never! I implore you to abandon all thoughts of the stage as a profession. Your talents may qualify you for its adoption; your temperament and education do not. (p. 32)

Although this passage surely prepares us for the fact and manner of Stella's demise—the overstimulus caused by the violent death of Perdita's father—the story equivocates. By plot, the narrative fulfills her protective brother's warning; but the bulk of the story largely justifies Stella's bold choice to tackle the entrenched institution of the stage. It is as if Stella's sexual energies are redirected from an orthodox sentimental ending—becoming a wife—into a more platonic desire to embrace the stage itself and reform it, as the angelic Victorian woman was to do the wayward male, husband or lover, into something that more reflects the spirit of chaste womanhood. In other words, the angel of the house becomes the angel of the stage.

The death of Stella's father stimulates her to try her independence; and while her brother takes on the role of older male advice-giver, he does not replace the father in Stella's life. Again, Mowatt shows herself steeped in a kind of thinking rooted in the eighteenth century. As Jay Fliegelman has shown, popular literature and pictures of the Revolutionary period constantly enact the conflict between America and Britain in familial, often parent-daughter terms.[5] Sympathetic cartoonists frequently represent America as a young woman under siege by rapacious British governmental officials; others who draw the symbolic Columbia portray her as a woman alone, in frightening circumstances. In the postwar period, novels like Hannah Webster Foster's *The Coquette* (1798) show a fatherless woman whose bid for independence falters on the rock of the seducing villain. Mowatt—who herself had a largely supportive father at whose house she wrote **Mimic Life**—suggests that for all Stella's courage in braving the theatrical establishment to find a job, her heroine's unprotected status leaves her at risk for a variety of ills. Ironically, the death of Perdita's and Floy's father overstimulates Stella into madness—literally, a loss of mental independence. Freedom from the patriarch leads both to creative brilliance and exposure to terrifying social and economic conditions that threaten to snuff out what independence enables.

In many ways, Stella resembles Mowatt herself.[6] Like her author, Stella enters the profession for reasons of domestic economy, not pursuit of fame. Like Mowatt as well, Stella seeks to alter the style of acting then in vogue. Mowatt practiced a non-melodramatic style; she earned her "points" but not through large gestures and histrionics. In Stella's first role, Virginia in Sheridan Knowles's *Virginius* (1820)—a play that concludes with the murder of Virginia by her father to protect her chastity[7]—she confounds her costumer by preferring a severe, classical style of dress to the heavily brocaded clothes used by earlier generations of actresses. In subsequent roles, she employs techniques similar to those of Method acting:

> Stella never once thought of Mr. Tennent, the supercilious, exacting, self-sufficient tragedian, but of the noble Othello; not of Stella Rosenvelt, the unsophisticated maiden, but of the true-hearted, ingenuous Desdemona, the bride of her Moorish husband. The least undue reserve, the slightest shrinking, would have been an evidence of that painful self-consciousness which is indissolubly allied to mediocrity, but which genius tramples under foot. (*ML*, p. 103)

Dedicated to art, Stella transforms herself into roles which themselves project fierce virginity or "true-

hearted" purity: Virginia, Evadne, Pauline,[8] Juliet, Ophelia. The only ostensible threat to chastity occurs on stage, in public, where all can witness the character's resistance or ingenuousness and admire that. In such acting, the body becomes incidental, the vehicle for portraying the higher passions or the nobility of truth. Reminders of the body as body shatter the picture and threaten shame for being a body at all.

As Mowatt notes frequently here and in her autobiography, sustaining illusion on stage has its own perils and failures. In the performance of *Othello,* for instance, Stella gets too close to the tragedian Tennent, and some black makeup from his face gets on her forehead. After an exchange of lines, Tennent leans over Stella, who is unaware of what has happened, and whispers to her the unsettling news. For the young actress, the illusion is shattered:

> Down fell poor Stella from her poetic heights! the black paint, its begriming touch to her own fair forehead, Mr. Tennent's commonplace tone, dissolved the spell; the loving Venetian quickly melted away. The disenchanted girl shrank from Mr. Tennent's encircling arms; she raised her hand to her forehead to hide the stain, but only smeared the inky hue into her eyes; she was strongly inclined to dart from the stage . . . (*ML*, p. 104)

For Stella, actual contact, body touching body, in any way that transforms stage life into real becomes a "black" thing, a mark of iniquity, covering her with "inky" shame. Stage love turns into filthy sex, the pure Desdemona converted into the dirty Stella. Saved from complete embarrassment by whispers from the older actress playing Emilia (the motherly Mrs. Fairfax), Stella goes offstage and cleans herself up.

Once back, she succeeds in reinserting herself into the role and restoring the illusion; but while serving out her last minutes on stage as a corpse, Stella again finds herself victimized by Tennent's acting. He grabs her in such a way that her head dangles down: "The blood rushed to her head until her brain seemed bursting, crushed by a mountainload. Her senses were leaving her; it was with the greatest difficulty that she could repress a cry. . . . She could endure no more; she tried to groan, to move, but in vain. When the curtain descended, she was found unconscious" (p. 114).[9] Having been marked earlier, but escaping permanent disgrace, Stella again finds that a man's embrace threatens her ability to portray purely. Now, though, the language strongly suggests rape. Stella's cleansing herself earlier is itself an illusion, for it leaves her vulnerable to the more violent and dangerous act at the end. Stained by first contact, Stella nearly succumbs to the symbolic robbery of virtue. Sex and death unite as the corpse of Desdemona becomes the embraced and fainting body of Stella. Only a pitcher of water dumped on her by the intervening mother figure, Mrs. Fairfax, ends her swoon.

Announcing early on that the stage does not in itself rob women of virtue and having her title character play women of unquestionable moral example, Mowatt creates a complex situation in Stella's forced reminders of her physicality. Implicit in Stella's embarrassed circumstances is an aesthetic judgment: the most forceful argument for the morality of the stage occurs when the performance is most artistically rendered. Any form of acting or incompetence that breaks, even for a moment, the belief in actors and audience that the play is the world leads potentially—perhaps inevitably—to interpreting rendered action as sordid and base.

Sometimes, however, acts against the body can, if the actress keeps her poise, be turned into furthering the illusion. In Stella's company is another young woman with whom she sometimes alternates heroine roles. Miss Doran has learned old-school techniques, lots of flash but no fire. Interestingly, her body sends a very different message from that of the more sensitive Stella. Early on, Mowatt explains Stella's beauty as ethereal, like the "soft effulgence of a moonlight lamp," rather than any feature's taking prominence. Most notably, Stella's "figure was slightly above the medium height, with the slender, *spanable* waist, undeveloped proportions, and not very erect bearing, which characterize the American maiden at eighteen" (*ML,* p. 12). Miss Doran, by contrast, has a physique of "the Amazonian order," but—interesting that Mowatt inserts that conjunction here—she has "in a high degree all the physical elements of beauty" (p. 130). When later we learn that Miss Doran chides Stella for her prudishness in not speaking certain indelicate lines in Shakespeare, we recognize that Stella's rival embodies the kind of sexuality that threatens to undo the image of the purified stage that Stella hopes to project.

Miss Doran's jealousy over Stella's playing Evadne[10] leads the first woman to plant nails on a statue that Evadne must clasp during the performance. As she wraps her arms around the statue of her heroic father, Evadne suddenly becomes Stella, uttering and trying to suppress a "half-shriek" not in the script. In the wings, Miss Doran gives a look as if to say, "Her best point is ruined!" (p. 136). Bloodied from the nail punctures she has received, Stella returns quickly to Evadne, whose subsequent speeches are punctuated by references to blood; as her arms are revealed, the "electrifying" effect such a sight produces upon the audience causes the playhouse to shake "with prolonged acclamations" (p. 137).

By turning her "ruin" into triumph, Stella displays the power of the stage—in the hands of a skilled artist—to rewrite the body's literal blood into a figurative display of female virtue and filial loyalty. Yet even this has its dangers, for a new pollution enters the scene. Since in this performance, the offending agent is a woman—albeit one whose erotic potentialities have been hinted at—the matter of surrogate sexual violation is deflected; however, as Stella sweeps past Miss Doran to receive "the enthusiastic summons of the audience," she gives in to an impulse to let "scorn flash from [her] gentle eyes" (p. 138) at her rival. The narrator informs us that Stella has crossed a line she must not traverse by allowing the passions of "bitterness" and "enmity" to "find room within her loving breast":

> Look at them, reckless girl, with self-scanning eyes! Admit all their hideousness; marvel that those wolves and tigers could intrude into the lamb-fold of thy heart's tender affections; then pray the Lord for strength to drive them out! So shall thy untried soul leap with its first impulse towards regeneration. (p. 138)

Representing passion is one thing; feeling it is another. Stella's "fierce passions" threaten to consume her lamb-like purity just as surely as external agency—perhaps even more so. The shedding of blood on stage is nothing to admitting the infection of "hideous" feelings to taint the blood within.

Immediately after the Evadne episode, Stella returns to her dressing room, where she finds a note addressed to her. She sits down, "half disrobed, to break the seal," and finds a poem. Thinking to read it later, she sees it is signed by a young playwright, Edwin Percy, to whose character she has been attracted.[11] Suddenly, she is transformed: "A soft smile, companioned by a blush, threw its radiance over her face as she read" (p. 138). Oblivious to time, she fails to observe that the afterpiece has finished, with the requisite extinguishing of the gas lights soon to follow. Brought back to her senses by the theater manager, Stella gets dressed to leave. "And the poem? Of course it was restored to her dressing-case? No; it found a fairer receptacle where quick pulses beat against the lines which warmer pulses throbbed in penning" (p. 139). Percy's penned poem enters the fair receptacle, not unwanted, but desired. The actress who can rise above the jealousies of rivals and the scorn in her bosom can then open that same bosom to passions that, like those of pure acting, allow the woman to forget her physical circumstances. Only now, offstage, in solitary privacy, out of the public eye and that of the beloved, erotic desire can be indulged without the stigma of personal passions exhibited to the world.

Percy's play, to which Stella has responded with poetic sympathy, proves to be a disaster on stage, largely because of incompetence and perverseness among the other actors. After a restorative of Sabbath service, which Stella has attended with her mother, she meets Percy, whom Mrs. Rosenvelt invites in. They seem to exchange throbbing hearts, but Mowatt observes a difference in male and female apprehensions of love: "the knowledge that flashes upon man penetrates slowly, piercing many a veil and barrier, to woman's recognition" (p. 153). Quick penetration is the male desire; for the female to respond in kind means for her to cede her right to enact her nature. Thus where for some acting seems a type of exposure, for Mowatt's Stella, it has value as a veil, a barrier.

Stricken with disgust at the theater, the dark-eyed romantic Percy does not understand how a woman like Stella can survive in the debased world of the stage. He wants to rescue her, in ways that resemble the stock formula of saving a fallen woman, but ends up comprehending that he would not have her—she not being ruined in fact—had he not essayed the stage with his play.

Mowatt knows most probably that the image of the sexually compromised woman carries with it a variety of meanings in mid-century America. As David S. Reynolds has pointed out, fallen women appear frequently in popular literature during the 1830s-1850s, both the unsuspecting victim of male lust and the sexually aggressive female, who, in her loss of innocence, picks up new and dangerous forms of behavior.[12] From the time of the real-life Helen Jewett, a prostitute whose murder in 1836 led to a war among the penny papers to find new "facts" to feed the public desire,[13] to the heroines and villains of many fictions, including Sylvester Judd's *Margaret* (1845), George Lippard's *The Quaker City* (1845), and Nathaniel Hawthorne's *The Scarlet Letter* (1850), the reading culture had become well-acquainted with the problematic elements of interpreting women who fall—innocently or not—to sexual temptation. Coincident with the reform movement, saving such women became itself an object of moral desire.[14] In addition, prostitutes long inhabited the third tier of large urban playhouses, just above the family tier.[15] Thus the theater presents itself as having all the conditions for corruption, yet simultaneously housing women of undoubted original virtue.[16]

Percy, then, is allied both with the melancholy romantic and the moral reformer, making him, in the context, a sympathetic figure. But Mowatt makes clear that Stella does not need saving from sin—only from stress. Her next role is to be Beatrice in Shakespeare's *Much Ado About Nothing*. On the staging of this in the nineteenth century, Mowatt claims that only expurgated texts were used: "Numerous passages, which were tolerated in the lax days of the Virgin Queen, are suppressed, as a matter of course" (*ML*, p. 155). Still, several "objectionable phrases remain," leaving actors to decide for themselves if they will speak them. Stella's elocution teacher, Mr. Oakland, has already "erased from Stella's volume . . . certain witty but offensive lines," which, when the prompter, unaware of this, urges Stella to

recite in rehearsal, she refuses by saying, "I do not speak those sentences." This opens her further to the ridicule of Miss Doran; Stella once again allows "angry sensations" to enter; and the subsequent performance of the comic Beatrice, played without lightness, is a critical disaster.

For Stella, this is a crucial moment. Unpersuaded by Percy to forget the performance or by Mrs. Fairfax to relax and simply erase the bad night with a subsequent good one, Stella allows herself to be swept up in the tyranny of pleasing the public on stage and fighting her rivals off. Hardly a flattering portrait of any aspect of stage life, "Stella" serves at this point to function as a warning to young women enamored of the stage for its illusions: "'And this—*this is the life*,' exclaimed Stella, bitterly, 'which so many young, light-hearted beings, who watch the brilliant actress through her brief hours of triumph, are panting to adopt!'" (p. 161). Stella, unable to adjust to the conditions as they exist—unable, too, to remove her passions from her life in the theater and transfer them fully to Percy or some other object of desire—becomes increasingly unstable. When in her next role, as Juliet, she witnesses the bloody death of Perdita and Floy's father, she gives way. After all, she has virtually and virtuously adopted the young people as her own. For the virgin mother, the shock of actual violence has the same effect that premarital sex has for the heroines of seduction novels. Stella plays her final role, Ophelia, with a madness that seems too genuine. Taken home, she mutters confused statements of stage speech and memory. Neither Mrs. Fairfax nor Percy can save her. "Brain fever, produced by injudicious mental stimulus" is the diagnosis (p. 191)—death the result.

Throughout, Stella preserves her chastity, but not her rationality. Is this, then, the price of enacted virginity? Her career has been but two weeks: "The meteor, which flashed its resplendent lustre for a moment athwart the dramatic horizon, moved in a heavenlier sphere!" (p. 195). Juliet and Ophelia, her last two roles, like her first, Virginia, are young women for whom purity is death. In creating a fiction of a woman's quick destruction, Mowatt represents far more than an author's wish to give humanity to "unlaurelled laborers" and prove that women in the theater can be virtuous. In speaking Stella's bitterness at her treatment—discounted though it may be by narrative moralizing—Mowatt suggests that desire, converted into art, can be overthrown by the exigencies of stage life. When representation collapses into reality, high passion suddenly turns into inky or bloody physicality.

If not threatened literally by loss of chastity, Stella lives in a world where entrenched attitudes sexualize the world in which she moves. The narrator carefully qualifies Stella's situation—that is, she is unsuited by temperament, if her brother be trusted, to take on an acting career. Nevertheless, Stella's talent and moral integrity show that she is not to be taken as just another fallen woman. Enslaved by public opinion and the ironclad rules that govern theatrical practice, the idealistic actor must forfeit something to survive. For the woman unwilling to give up both virginity and idealism, the wages of purity seem to be madness—and death. This is a far darker message than that with which Mowatt begins.

Notes

1 On this aspect of Mowatt's career, see David W. Thompson, "Early Actress-Readers: Mowatt, Kemble, and Cushman," in *Performance of Literature in Historical Perspectives,* ed. Thompson (Lanham: Univ. Press of America, 1983), pp. 629-34.

2 Anna Cora Ritchie, *Mimic Life; or, Before and Behind the Curtain. A Series of Narratives* (Boston: Ticknor and Fields, 1856), p. 5. Hereafter cited parenthetically in the text.

3 Anna Cora Mowatt, *Autobiography of an Actress; or, Eight Years on the Stage* (Boston: Ticknor, Reed, and Fields, 1854), p. 426. Hereafter cited parenthetically in the text.

4 Mowatt's feeling obligated to confront an archaic moral code seems less remarkable if we consider that the battle to legalize theater in America extended well past the Revolutionary War; only after 1800 was the way clear in most major cities for theater companies to build new playhouses without encountering in law the old moral objections to the theater. Given the sort of culturally determined private/public split encountered by literary women, it is not surprising that Mowatt feels so impelled to argue for a chaste theater. On the division between domesticity and exhibition for women in culture, see Mary Kelley, *Private Woman, Public Stage: Literary Domesticity in Nineteenth-Century America* (New York: Oxford Univ. Press, 1984).

5 Jay Fliegelman, *Prodigals and Pilgrims: The American Revolution Against Patriarchal Authority, 1750-1800* (Cambridge: Cambridge Univ. Press, 1982).

6 Patti P. Gillespie calls "Stella" a "vaguely autobiographical story": "Anna Cora Odgen Mowatt Ritchie's *Fairy Fingers*: From Eugène Scribe's?" in *TPQ [Text and Performance Quarterly]* 2 (1989), 131.

7 For a discussion on the influence of this and other "conservative romance" plays on such American dramas as *Metamora,* see Bruce A. McDonachie, *Melodramatic Formations: American Theatre and Society, 1820-1870* (Iowa City: Univ. of Iowa Press, 1992), pp. 98-100.

8 In Edward Bulwer-Lytton's *The Lady of Lyons* (1838). Pauline Deschappelles—Mowatt's first role as a professional actress—is married by fraud to an idealistic gardener's son who refuses to take her virginity even though their marriage is legal. At first he seeks to shame her pride, but later is himself shamed by her innocence.

9 The smothering of Desdemona ascribed to the fictional tragedian Tennent also happened in real life when Junius Brutus Booth (1796-1852) played *Othello:* Gene Smith, *American Gothic: The Story of America's Legendary Theatrical Family—Junius, Edwin, and John Wilkes Booth* (New York: Simon & Schuster, 1992), pp. 38-39. For a summary of Booth's powerful impact on audiences and actors alike, see David S. Reynolds, *Walt Whitman's America: A Cultural Biography* (New York: Knopf, 1995), pp. 157-61.

10 Although not stated so directly in *Mimic Life,* Stella is probably playing this role as conceived by Irish playwright Richard Lalor Sheil in his play, *Evadne; or, The Statue* (1819).

11 In *Fashion,* Mowatt includes a poet called T. Tennyson Twinkle—suggested by at least one critic to be Poe—whose pathetic lines no one wants to hear: James M. Hutchisson, "Poe, Anna Cora Mowatt, and T. Tennyson Twinkle," *SAR [Studies in the American Renaissance]* (1993), 245-54. Percy, a more sympathetic figure, may have some Poe elements, but he may also be based in part on Mowatt's friend, Epes Sargent, in whose plays she sometimes acted. Mowatt's relationship to Sargent is chronicled by Eric Wollencott Barnes, *The Lady of Fashion: The Life and the Theatre of Anna Cora Mowatt* (New York: Scribner's, 1954).

12 David S. Reynolds, *Beneath the American Renaissance: The Subversive Imagination in the Age of Emerson and Melville* (Cambridge: Harvard Univ. Press, 1989).

13 On the Jewett affair and the penny press, see Andie Tucher, *Froth & Scum: Truth, Beauty, Goodness, and the Ax Murder in America's First Mass Medium* (Chapel Hill: Univ. of North Carolina Press, 1994).

14 Reynolds, *Beneath the American Renaissance,* pp. 360-64.

15 Claudia D. Johnson, "That Guilty Third Tier: Prostitution in Nineteenth-Century American Theater," in *Victorian America,* ed. Daniel Walker Howe (Philadelphia: Univ. of Pennsylvania Press, 1976), pp. 111-20. Complaints about prostitutes were frequent in the first half of the century. Philadelphia manager Francis Wemyss argued that lighting in the seating area should be kept low in order to obscure "the third tier of boxes, where licentiousness prevails in its worst form." Quoted in Francis Hodge, *Yankee Theatre: The Image of America on the Stage, 1825-1850* (Austin: Univ. of Texas Press, 1964), p. 21.

[16] When Mowatt's *Fashion* was first performed at New York's Park Theatre, the owner, John Jacob Astor, expelled the prostitutes and their johns and filled the vacated seats with collegians and other proper young men (Barnes, p. 138). Thus to some extent, Mowatt had already been linked to an impulse to cleanse the theater, even if she can hardly speak about it in her autobiography.

FURTHER READING

Barnes, Eric Wollencott. *The Lady of Fashion: The Life and the Theater of Anna Cora Mowatt*. New York: Charles Scribners Sons, 1954, 402 p.

A full-length study of Mowatt and her theatrical career as both actress and playwright.

Blesi, Marius. *The Life and Letters of Anna Cora Mowatt*. Ph.D. dissertation, University of Virginia, 1938.

A full-length study of Mowatt's life and work.

Matthews, Brander and Laurence Hutton. *Actors and Actresses of Great Britain and the United States*. New York: Cassell and Company, 1886, 319 p.

A comprehensive survey, with a discussion of Mowatt's performing career and excerpts from contemporary reviews.

Odell, George C. D. *Annals of the New York Stage*, 15 vols. New York: Columbia University Press, 1927-49.

An exhaustive theater history, with mentions of Mowatt and performances of *Fashion*.

Sargent, Epes. *The Scientific Basis of Spritualism*. Boston: Colby and Rich, 1882, 396 p.

A study of spiritualism by one of Mowatt's friends, includes an account of Mowatt's therapeutic hypnotism.

Vaughn, Jack A. *Early American Dramatists: From the Beginnings to 1900*. New York: Ungar, 1981, 200 p.

A comprehensive study of the early American theater, with a section on Mowatt as an actress-playwright.

Charles Reade

1814-1884

English novelist and dramatist.

For additional information on Reade's life and works, see *NCLC*, Volume 2.

INTRODUCTION

During his lifetime, Reade was a respected writer whose novels were sometimes compared favorably with those of Charles Dickens and George Eliot. Like Dickens, he often used his fiction as a vehicle for social commentary, and he compiled massive notebooks of material about contemporary abuses for use in his writing. He also wrote several works—notably *Griffith Gaunt* (1866)—in which he portrayed unconventional female characters and explored feminine psychology and sexuality. Reade, however, is best remembered today neither for his novels portraying social problems nor for his fictional studies of women but for his somewhat atypical historical novel, *The Cloister and the Hearth* (1861).

Biographical Information

The youngest son of an Oxfordshire squire, Reade attended Oxford University's Magdalen College, graduating in 1835. His mother wanted him to enter the Catholic Church, but Reade declined. Instead, he studied both medicine and law and was even called to the bar in 1842, but he never practiced either profession. He did, however, go to court more than once in later years as a plaintiff in disputes over his works, and he was fond of satirizing the medical profession. As early as 1835, Reade began collecting information with a view to later producing fiction; he eventually produced a massive accumulation of notebooks containing newspaper clippings, extracts from government reports, and other material that he would later incorporate into his novels and plays. During this period, before he began his literary career, Reade survived in part thanks to a Magdalen College fellowship, which he could hold only as long as he did not marry. Reade abided by this prohibition against marriage, remaining a bachelor all his life, but he wrote very critically about enforced celibacy, notably in *The Cloister and the Hearth*. Reade's first completed literary work, the play *The Ladies' Battle* (adapted from a French work), was performed in London in 1851. Twelve more of his plays were performed over the next five years, including four writ-

ten in collaboration with Tom Taylor. One of these collaborations, *Masks and Faces* (1852), was moderately successful, as was his play *Gold* (1853), about the Australian gold fields, but Reade won greater popularity with his fiction, which he began publishing in 1853, than with his dramas. His first major success came with his novel *It Is Never Too Late to Mend* (1856), although its graphic depiction of abusive practices in prisons also prompted objections from those who believed that Reade was exaggerating. Typically, Reade responded with letters and a pamphlet providing evidence to support his claims. His next major success was in 1861 with *The Cloister and the Hearth*. *Griffith Gaunt* was also popular but provoked an outcry, especially in America, because of its "indecency." Reade responded with a lawsuit and was awarded the derisory sum of six cents. Contentiousness surrounded him throughout his career. He became involved in a dispute with Anthony Trollope after turning Trollope's novel *Ralph the Heir* into the play *Shilly-Shally* (1872) without his permission. This situation was somewhat unusual for Reade because he was more frequently on the other side in cases of unauthorized adaptations and pirated editions; he even published a book, *The Eighth Commandment* (1860), and a series of letters, *The Rights and Wrongs of Authors* (1875), defending authors' rights in these situations. Throughout his career, Reade continually returned to playwriting, and in his final years he insisted on being described first as a dramatist, but it was as a novelist that he gained his greatest fame.

Major Works

Reade's earliest works followed the conventions of Victorian melodrama, but in 1852 the success of Harriet Beecher Stowe's anti-slavery novel *Uncle Tom's Cabin* and the publication of Stowe's "key" explaining the documentary basis of her accomplishment inspired Reade to develop a similar approach to literature. He had already been collecting information on topical matters, but now he began to collect and systematically arrange these materials and to incorporate them in his works. He did this to a certain extent in *Gold*, presenting factual material about Australia, and he practiced this method to a much greater extent in his first socially conscious novel, *It Is Never Too Late to Mend*, in which he included lengthy descriptions of abuses in English prisons. Reade later produced several more novels depicting social issues, including *Hard Cash* (1863), about the evils of lunatic asylums; *Foul Play* (1868), about insurance fraud; and *Put Yourself in His Place* (1870), an attack on labor unions. He did not, however, give up melodrama, combining social commentary with sensational action and resourceful heroes. He is thus often associated with such novelists as Wilkie Collins rather than with the more domestic school of Anthony Trollope and George Eliot. At the same time, however, he was opposed to Carlyle's notions of hero worship, going out of his way in *The Cloister and the Hearth* to celebrate the lives of two ordinary people. That same novel is also notable for its exploration of the choice between a life of spiritual development in isolation from the world (the life of the cloister) and a life spent in the world (at the domestic hearth). Reade's melodramatic inclinations often led him to produce simple conflicts of good and evil, but while his male characters tended to be stock figures, he at times created complex and unconventional female characters, particularly Kate Peyton, whose sexual and emotional conflicts Reade explored in *Griffith Gaunt*.

Critical Reception

Reade referred to several of his novels as "matter-of-fact romances," and his combination of realism and romance led some commentators to fault him for being too realistic, while others found him not realistic enough. Praised in his own day for his didactic purpose and documentary thoroughness, he eventually fell from favor for his excess of factual detail as well as for his unrealistic characterizations and improbable plots. *The Cloister and the Hearth*, with its detailed re-creation of fifteenth-century Europe, came to eclipse all his other works; but Reade stated that only a "lunatic" could call it his best, and it has been written that to judge Reade by this somewhat unrepresentative historical novel is as misleading as judging Dickens by *A Tale of Two Cities*. Reade himself, along with some later commentators, preferred *Griffith Gaunt*. Surprisingly, however, this portrayal of a complex female character has not attracted the attention of modern feminist critics. Indeed, Reade has attracted little attention during the latter half of the twentieth century.

PRINCIPAL WORKS

The Ladies' Battle [adaptor; from the drama *La bataille des dames* by Eugène Scribe and Ernest Legouvé] (drama) 1851

Peregrine Pickle [adaptor; from the novel *Peregrine Pickle* by Tobias Smollett] (drama) 1851

Masks and Faces [with Tom Taylor] (drama) 1852

Gold (drama) 1853

Peg Woffington (novel) 1853

Christie Johnstone (novel) 1853

It Is Never Too Late to Mend (novel) 1856

The Bloomer (short story) 1857

White Lies (novel) 1857

Cream (short stories) 1858

Love Me Little, Love Me Long (novel) 1859

The Eighth Commandment (essay) 1860

The Cloister and the Hearth (novel) 1861

Hard Cash (novel) 1863

It Is Never Too Late to Mend [adaptor; from his own novel] (drama) 1865

Griffith Gaunt (novel) 1866

Foul Play [with Dion Boucicault] (drama) 1868

Put Yourself in His Place (novel) 1870

Free Labour [adaptor; from his own novel *Put Yourself in His Place*] (drama) 1870

A Terrible Temptation (novel) 1871

Shilly-Shally [adaptor; from the novel *Ralph the Heir* by Anthony Trollope] (drama) 1872

Cremona Fiddles (essays) 1872

The Wandering Heir (short story) 1872

A Simpleton (novel) 1873

The Rights and Wrongs of Authors (letters) 1875

A Woman-Hater (novel) 1877

Drink [adaptor; from the novel *L'assomoir* by Emile Zola] (drama) 1879

Love and Money [with Henry Pettitt] (drama) 1882

Singleheart and Double Face (novel) 1884
A Perilous Secret (novel) 1885

*Written circa 1834 and published in 1851.

CRITICISM

Oscar Wilde (essay date 1889)

SOURCE: "The Decay of Lying," in *De Profundis and Other Writings*, edited by Hesketh Pearson, Penguin, 1973, pp. 55-87.

[*In the following excerpt, originally published in 1889 and reprinted in 1973, Wilde laments Reade's decision to abandon his sense of beauty in order to write realistic social-problem novels.*]

I do not know anything in the whole history of literature sadder than the artistic career of Charles Reade. He wrote one beautiful book, *The Cloister and the Hearth,* a book as much above *Romola* as *Romola* is above *Daniel Deronda,* and wasted the rest of his life in a foolish attempt to be modern, to draw public attention to the state of our convict prisons, and the management of our private lunatic asylums. Charles Dickens was depressing enough in all conscience when he tried to arouse our sympathy for the victims of the poor-law administration; but Charles Reade, an artist, a scholar, a man with a true sense of beauty, raging and roaring over the abuses of contemporary life like a common pamphleteer or a sensational journalist, is really a sight for the angels to weep over.

E. W. Hornung (essay date 1921)

SOURCE: "Charles Reade," in *London Mercury*, Vol. 4, June, 1921, pp. 150-63.

[*In the following excerpt, Hornung surveys Reade's novels.*]

Charles Reade was the youngest son of a country gentleman, one of the Reades of Ipsden, in Oxfordshire, where he was born twelve months before Waterloo. His schooling was private and ferocious; but at seventeen, thanks to an English Essay well above the average, he gained a Demyship at Magdalen, and four years later was elected a Fellow of the college. From that moment he considered himself condemned to perpetual celibacy, and observed the letter of an oppressive law inflexibly; yet the other celibates did not altogether approve of him.

In truth there never can have been a Don less donnish, or one less in sympathy with the accepted type. Did he not depict himself, in *A Terrible Temptation,* as "looking like a great fat country farmer" and "walking like a sailor"? Had not his colleagues of the high-table "some of the thickest skulls I have ever encountered"? Not that he saw much of them, unless it was in the year 1851, when Charles Reade was Vice-President of Magdalen. Thereafter his chief use for Oxford was to go down and shut himself up in his rooms to write his book or ransack the Bodleian for the facts on which his books were built. In earlier days he would absent himself altogether on alien enterprises, some of them the reverse of academic. He was called to the Bar, but did not appear in court; he had fought a publisher and lost, though represented by distinguished counsel; then he characteristically conducted a second case himself, won it, but was disallowed his costs. Medicine he tried at Edinburgh, but abandoned upon fainting in the dissecting-room; the Church was considered, though less favourably, under strong domestic pressure. There are traces of all three phases in Reade's novels; most of them contain a lawyer, a doctor, and an ecclesiastic, all drawn with some inside knowledge of their respective jobs.

But it was not only with the learned professions that this fickle Fellow flirted; the six hundred a year his college paid him left a margin for financial ventures as incongruous as they were surreptitious. At one time he was in business partnership with a French fiddle-dealer in the purlieus of Soho, and at another with an Edinburgh fishwife in a fleet of herring-boats. Both ventures were rooted in romance. All his days Reade was a virtuoso in the violin—a fair performer, but a great connoisseur—and his erudite but fascinating articles on Cremona fiddles, his speciality, are worth all the money he can have dropped on the craze. As for the fishwife, she is still deliciously alive as the canny heroine of *Christie Johnstone,* possibly the best Scotch story ever written by an Englishman. Reade's women are too often either shrews or sheep, if not both in turn, but this comely creature trips off his pen as she came into his early life, unencumbered by the knowing generalities bestowed upon so many of her successors.

Not that *Christie Johnstone* was a first novel; it had been preceded by *Peg Woffington,* but only by a matter of months, so that we may look upon the pair as heading the procession of Reade's books in double harness. They had everything in common except a theme: both were one-volume novels, written with extraordinary freshness and dramatic vigour, albeit with certain dubious eccentricities of style. *Peg Woffington* suffers from being the narrative version of a more famous comedy, *Masks and Faces,* in which Reade had the skilled assistance of Tom Taylor. The best scenes depend on stage effects, fall flat without them; but the characters of Triplet and of Peg, Pomander and the Vanes, are lightly and strongly drawn, while as a minor gem Colley Cibber is possibly no loser by the book. Here, at any rate, was a new novelist with whom the world of letters would have to reckon. Yet the two books had no successors for some years, and they were years that might have daunted a less valiant spirit, for it was over these books that Reade took the law of Bentley, with results already given, and on balance a loss to the author of £150. He was now nearly forty, and it seemed still uncertain that he would settle down even to literature. But with all his vagaries he had been for years preparing himself, on a system all his own, for the pursuit he had at last taken up. "I studied the great art of Fiction closely," he declares, "for fifteen years before I wrote a line." But he had written at least fifteen plays, most of which remained, and still remain, unacted. One of them, however, a topical melodrama on the then alluring subject of the Australian diggings, eventually enjoyed a short run at Drury Lane under the auspicious name of *Gold.*

In the first act of *Gold* the leading character, an habitual criminal, is taken up for picking pockets; transported to Australia, he reappears in worthier case, to work out his moral and pecuniary salvation in some thrilling scenes before the finish. As first mentioned in a spasmodic diary, the piece was to be "a great original play" and "make a great hit"; but long before its acceptance, encouraged, no doubt, by the literary success of *Peg Woffington,* Reade was busy turning *Gold* also into a novel. His plan was to split up his melodrama into a mere frame for a terrific picture of prison life in England at that time—the new inspiration sprang from "a noble passage in the *Times* of September 7th or 8th, 1853"—and he went to work with grim gusto on lines long since laid down, but hardly tested hitherto.

> *June* 20. The plan I propose to myself in writing stories will, I see, cost me undeniable labour. I propose never to guess where I can know. For instance, Tom Robinson is in gaol. I have therefore been to Oxford Gaol and visited every inch, and shall do the same at Reading. Having also collected material in Durham Gaol, whatever I write about Tom Robinson's gaol will therefore carry, I hope, a physical exterior of truth. . . .

> My story must cross the water to Australia, and plunge after that into a gold mine. To be consistent with myself I ought to cross-examine at the very least a dozen men that have farmed, dug, or robbed in that land. If I can get hold of two or three that have really been in it, I think I could win the public ear by these means. Failing these I must read books and letters and do the best I can. Such is the mechanism of a novel by Charles Reade. . . .

> Now, I know exactly what I am worth. If I can work the above great system there is enough of me to make one of the writers of the day; without it, NO, NO.

Distrust of a fine imagination was already a perverse yet endearing foible in a man of Reade's outward and combative self-esteem; but concrete fact was not as yet the fetish he was to make of it in after years. Nor was it in *It is Never too Late to Mend* that documentary evidence became his master. He had explored the prisons in person as he describes; and it was the prison part of his book that stirred his countrymen, if it was not the only part to "win the public ear." In York Castle he had been locked up in "the black hole" so long that another five minutes, he felt, would have driven him mad; and none of the prison chapters is more poignant than the one depicting Robinson's agony in the dark cell, unless it be the terrible little chapter devoted to a young suicide's last night on earth; and *that* is nothing if not imaginative. Four years this big book took to write, and after nearly threescore and ten it remains unapproached by any convict story written in English. *For the Term of his Natural Life* is a closer and more accurate study of transportation, written within easy reach of the scenes described; but Marcus Clarke, working on Reade's lines, has nothing like Reade's vivacious sense of character and situation. His superhuman hero is made to endure in his own person the authentic agonies of a number of extreme cases. Reade knew better than to make Tom Robinson even the chief sufferer under the system he laid bare: nor is he by any means the injured innocent of the typical convict yarn, nor yet the villain-hero of the picturesque romance, but just a flashy, bumptious, cunning, altogether realistic scamp. Those two hundred pages, though an ugly hump on the body of the book, are the most powerful that Charles Reade ever wrote. If "a physical exterior of truth" was indeed his modest aim, the furious shame of every decent reader is his achievement.

In prison Robinson is human and himself from first to last. His reformation is a real change of heart, poignant and precarious as in life itself. He is not less excellent in the lively episode of his partial relapse in Sydney. In later phases, as the historic convict who discovered the first gold in Australia and as uncrowned king of the earliest diggings, he will appeal less to the sophisticated reader of to-day; but as moral *nouveau riche* he is still true enough to type. The very full and vigorous account of the great gold-rush must have been a revelation to many who took part in it, for the evidence has been sifted and set out by that rare combination, a judicial yet imaginative mind. It is the work of a great narrator with a genius for assembling diverse facts as the machinery of his tale.

It is interesting to note that the proverbial title, precursor of many with less point in them, was a lively satisfaction to Martin Tupper, who wrote to congratulate the novelist "on having made popular so good and true a *refrain* as *It is Never too Late to Mend.*" It is also said to have been a prophetic *double entendre* on the part of Reade at his own expense, he being forty-two and something of an all-round failure when the one book brought him fame and fortune. Its immediate successors cannot have added much to either. *White Lies,* written as a serial for the *London Journal* and now better known as *The Double Marriage,* was again the narrative version of a hitherto unacted play; and there are sure signs that *Love me Little, Love me Long* was yet such another. The latter story, though a first instalment of *Hard Cash,* is heavy comedy with hardly any sensational relief. This was a dark hour for the author's now innumerable admirers, but Mr. Tupper could have told them what it meant.

In 1859 Messrs. Bradbury & Evans had started *Once a Week* to fill the place of *Household Words,* which had come to an end as the climax of a painful chapter in the life of Dickens. The new journal, making due departure from the old, went in for "names," including Tennyson's in the first number, and for illustrations by Millais and the *Punch* artists. The opening serial was written by Charles Reade and illustrated by Charles Keene, whose work he considered "paltry" and "far below the level of the penny Press." But Reade's eye for a drawing was very much his own, and may have been jaundiced in this instance by a running squabble with the editor on other grounds. That despot was soon being "very annoying, tampering with my text and so on," and, when told "he must distinguish between anonymous contributions and those in which an approved author takes the responsibility by signing his own name," duly refusing to "resign his editorial function." The quarrel is as old as periodical literature and as new as last month's magazines. Reade ended it by ending his story—in an instalment as vindictively abrupt, bald, and unconvincing as the hand of embittered craftsman could make it. You see the editor mop his brow, for the story had arrived on delicate ground, had perhaps elicited the stray anonymous expostulation which carries more weight than the tacit approval of ninety-and-nine just subscribers. But I doubt whether his surviving readers have even now lived long enough to forgive the man; for week after week they had had Charles Reade at something better than Charles Reade's best; week after week they had been making hot love and fighting or flying for their Victorian lives with the young foreign couple of a mediæval romance; and now it was all over until, two years later, *A Great Fight,* as the discontinued story had been called, was fought to a finish in *The Cloister and the Hearth.*

Of a classic that is also a "best seller" to this day, as most publishers of popular reprints can testify, there is very little left to say. Three generations of sober and accredited critics have praised this book in terms of just extravagance; where I venture to think that many have been unjust is in praising it at the expense of Reade's other books. Granted it is his one great book, and the best of the others is but "big," yet the *Cloister and the Hearth* stands as deliberately aloof from the rest of Reade as *A Tale of Two Cities* stands deliber-

ately aloof from the rest of Dickens; if greater heights were reached, higher ground had been chosen; it is a breezy plateau of the past after the dense and tortuous valley of a man's own times. Now a novel ought to be weighed against the same sort of novel by any other hand rather than against an entirely different kind of novel by the same hand. But this is a point which novelists perhaps see clearer, and certainly see redder, than other people. Reade was furious with anybody who suggested that *The Cloister and the Hearth* was his masterpiece. "If that's your opinion," he once retorted, with Johnsonian savagery, "you ought to be in a lunatic asylum"; and his humblest follower, with some stray triumph but many a hard-wrought failure to his name, will enter into Charles Reade's feelings.

Yet I suppose the fact does remain that his historical novel, whether better worth doing or not, was indubitably better done than his modern novels. The truth is that nearly all his novels were written on the system usually reserved and best adapted for the writing of historical novels. He did not use his eyes as other novelists use theirs. He used his eyes to scan the wide world's Press in search of outlandish grist for his mill; he preferred chapter and verse in print to all the raw material that came his way in the shape of ordinary mortals. His imagination did not respond to ordinary flesh and blood (though shortly before his death he was meditating a novel on Zazel, the lady who used to be shot out of a cannon at the Aquarium, and had made her acquaintance as a preliminary step!). "Pen in hand," he confessed, "I am fond of hot passions and pictorial incidents, and, like the historians, care too little for 'the middle of humanity.'" But "like the historians," because he was one, he cared intensely for the extreme case that gets into the papers; had a wondrous faculty for adapting all such to his uses; collected them like stamps, pasted them into large scrapbooks, indexed and cross-indexed these with commercial thoroughness, and so, if he required as much as a common assault in the course of his narrative, knew where to lay his finger on the very thing. Thackeray thumped the desk and cried "That's genius!" with the ink still wet upon a famous touch. Reade was probably as elated when he dived into his home-made tomes and fished up what he called the "warm facts" of a case in point.

It was not an ideal way of writing modern novels; but it must be the only way to give verisimilitude to a story of the past. His "newspapers" were now but crabbed chronicles in monkish Latin; but give him a bone of the decadent language, and Charles Reade, "an artist, a scholar," was the man to reconstruct a living scene. His Dutch interiors were little pictures in print. He throws on a costume in a phrase, betrays a custom as it were by inadvertence, can paint and set his most elaborate scene in a paragraph without a negligible or unwanted word. It is difficult not to describe such art in the terms of sister arts, so pictorial and dramatic is it all; yet to read this book is to have much more than a sense of walking through a picture-gallery or sitting at the play; it is frequently to feel oneself encompassed by the dangers and discomforts of the Middle Ages. The picture ceases to be a picture; it becomes a personal experience of the reader. Thus we tremble with Gerard and Denys at one villainous inn, scratch with them in another, and are no less realistically bored at a third. We feel, indeed, there are too many of these inns, and so there are; but had not Reade picked up in Paris a wonderful Tractate on the Inns of the Middle Ages, and could an artist who was also a virtuoso be expected to leave any of them out? Such are the provocations of research as the handmaid of imagination; and hence those engaging excesses of detail, that unblushing redundancy of adventure, which alone disfigure *The Cloister and the Hearth* artistically. Much as we may love our Gerard, gentle student yet potential demon, and Denys the Burgundian, with his immortal watchword and his innocent immoralities, their tramp across darkest Europe is yet a little long; it even has its *longueurs*. The pair encounter every conceivable kind of peril; just one, you feel, might have been omitted if only to placate the literal mind. The somewhat similar outwitting of two different robber bands reads like alternative adventures, both so splendid that the author could not find it in his heart to forgo either, nor human reader to wish he had. The same may be said of the deplorable entertainment afforded by the heretical Fra Colonna, and even of the fascinating portrait of Pietro Vanucci and other Roman miniatures. These things are off the track of the tale; yet so beautifully are they handled, so deftly introduced, that the true end and aim are never out of sight. And this is only another way of saying that the book throughout is written as Reade never wrote anything else throughout: in a style which, in Stevenson's sentence on Pepys, "condescends to the most fastidious particulars and yet sweeps all away in the forthright current of the narrative." Nor is it ever partly an objective narrative, though the subjectivity is an undercurrent as in life. In the journey of Gerard and Denys, which throws a beam across mediæval Europe, it is not the road alone that is lighted up, nor the dancing motes of obsolete humanity, but always those two wayfaring hearts as well; the one combustible with hot adventure, the other steadily aglow with Margaret's love.

It is not unfair to turn from this acknowledged masterpiece to *Griffith Gaunt,* or *Jealousy,* which Reade himself persisted in proclaiming his masterpiece. It might have been. There were five years between the two, and as big a book as *Hard Cash* was the earlier product of the interval. At the height of his popularity, but only stimulated by success, Charles Reade must have been at his very best when he wrote *Griffith Gaunt;* and signs are not wanting that he was. It opens with as shrewd a "punch" as even he ever delivered:

"Then I say once for all that priest shall never darken my doors again."

"Then I say they are my doors and not yours, and that holy man shall brighten them whenever he will."

After that the "white line" that Reade always used with effect; and after that nearly two hundred pages of pluperfect narrative before we come up to the same two opening sentences in their proper place.

This audacious introductory slab is perhaps the finest example of sustained accomplishment in all Reade's work. The problem has been set in a turn of the hand; it is worked up to a point considerably beyond the one indicated above with the utmost mastery; if the working out were on the same level we should have had the *Othello* of prose fiction. As it is we get, on the whole, our author's best-written book, a book singularly free from the more lurid mannerisms of an innately mannered, though utterly unaffected, style, and richer than any other in that genuine passion which was Reade's noblest quality as a novelist. The pictures of eighteenth-century country-house life never once smell of the reading-lamp; they convince by their masterly incompleteness, the "silence implying sound" that it takes a master to keep. Griffith himself, the rough, riotous, drinking, duelling, hare-brained yet great-hearted young squire, is the creature of his time from top to toe. His Catholic wife is Reade's greatest lady, and her two spiritual directors are notable additions to those studies on the Roman priesthood, begun in *The Cloister and the Hearth,* which by their unbiased breadth and understanding are enough to stamp the Anglican author as a person of essential culture. Father Francis, the "burly ecclesiastic" who was not a gentleman, but a man full of horse-sense and astringent sympathy, is beautifully drawn. Brother Leonard has to play the unlovely part assigned to a sad proportion of the friars of fiction: he is neither a new nor a representative type. The inevitable catastrophe would be more moving had Kate Gaunt been more to blame; but only a tragic expiation could have redeemed Griffith's bigamous reprisal. The "happy" ending wrested from so dire an imbroglio is in fact the most infelicitous feature. It involves a murder mystery and trial which only serve to remind one how admirably Reade dispenses with mysteries in general. Almost alone among "sensation" novelists he achieves suspense entirely by means of the impending event; and this departure from so rare a rule is the more unfortunate inasmuch as the puzzle solves itself at sight. Notwithstanding a fine scene between the wedded and the unwedded wife, the book ends in such bathos that one is almost sorry it was ever finished. Half-written but unspoilt, *Griffith Gaunt* might have ranked with *Weir of Hermiston* as a perfect fragment.

The rest of the novels bear a stronger family likeness. *Hard Cash* deals with private asylums and the sea as faithfully as *It is Never too Late to Mend* dealt with prisons and the gold-diggings. Like its fellows, it has a literary history almost as interesting as the tale itself. Under the less excellent title of **Very Hard Cash** it appeared in *All the Year Round* piecemeal as soon as written, and was none too successful a serial. Indeed, it was said to have lowered the circulation by three thousand copies, and Wills was eventually entrusted by Dickens with the delicate job of requesting Reade to cut the story short. "Peevish nonsense!" wrote the latter, mildly enough for him. "Wills is sure it will be a great success as a book, and Dickens swears by it." Wills was right; but the apparent paradox, in reality one of the commonest experiences in authorship, was especially comprehensible in this case. None of Reade's novels takes so much "getting into" as **Hard Cash.** The first half-dozen chapters—the crucial chapters of any serial—are truly ponderous. Reade, indeed, felt there was "no go" in him at the time; but it is to be doubted whether, with all its wealth of exciting episode, his work ever really lent itself to serial publication. Even when his best was brewing he was not the man to serve it out in thrifty rations; his stuff must simmer for a month or boil over in every column, according to the fire that was in him for the nonce; and facts are kittle fuel. **Hard Cash** is a mass of hard facts. The preparation it required, as recorded in one of his famous notebooks, is not only a concrete instance of Charles Reade's method, but an entertainment to all who take a morbid interest in literary procuration.

HARD CASH

I took notes for this work in various ways. I covered

1. Eight or ten large double folio cards; some of these still survive.

2. I pasted extracts from journals and Dickson's works *on a screen,* where I could see them in one view.

3. I devoted a double sheet each to some of the characters.

4. I took notes on the ordinary system in books.

5. I worked in materials furnished by my brother William, whereof Mathingleyana—the basis of Maxley—and his William's voyage from China survive, I believe. Altogether I bestowed the labour and original research that go to two or three soi-disant learned works.

The pleadings are from Fletcher *v.* Fletcher, which case I had worked from first to last.

I have been accused of inaccuracy in all that relates to asyla, but I offered publicly inspection of my proofs, and my detractors one and all shrank from the test.

My materials are now somewhat scattered, but I shall endeavour to point out where several of my authorities can be found.

Follows a portentous list of technical tomes; on banking, seamanship, Biblical research; lexicons and glossaries of scientific terms; and six or seven medical works! What with the plastered screen it may be imagined there is a good deal of Dr. Dickson, the Sampson of the story, perhaps the most maddening Scotchman in or out of fiction, though some of his phonetic outpourings may be forgiven for the sake of his burlesque prescription for the lovesick heroine herewith appended and construed:

Die Mercur, circa X hor: vespert:
eat in musca ad Aulam oppid:
   Saltet cum xiii canicul: præsertim
meo. Dom: reddita, 6 hora matutin:
dormiat at prand:
   Repetat stultit: pro re nata.

On Wednesday at ten P.M. let her
go in a fly to the Town-Hall,
                      {little dogs
and dance with thirteen   {puppies
                       {whelps
especially with mine: return home
at six A.M. and sleep till dinner, and
repeat the folly as occasion serves.

But this is pure Magdalen. Nor is Sampson the only doctor in the book; the mad-doctors are all excellent, especially the amiable Dr. Wycherley, whose own bonnet had its bee.

Dr. Wycherley, you see, was a collector of mad people, and collectors are always amateurs and very solemn connoisseurs. His turn of mind co-operating with his interests led him to put down any man a lunatic whose intellect was manifestly superior to his own. Alfred Hardie, and one or two more contemporaries, had suffered by this humour of the good doctor's. Nor did the dead escape him entirely. Pascal, according to Wycherley, was a madman with an illusion about a precipice; John Howard a moral lunatic in whom the affections were reversed; Saul a moping maniac with homicidal paroxysms and nocturnal visions; Paul an incoherent lunatic, who in his writings flies off at a tangent, and who admits having once been the victim of a photopsic illusion in broad daylight; Nebuchadnezzar a lycanthropical lunatic; Joan of Arc a theomaniac; Bobby Burton and Oliver Cromwell melancholy maniacs; Napoleon an ambitious maniac in whom the sense of impossibility became gradually extinguished by visceral and cerebral derangement; Porson an oinomaniac; Luther a phrenotic patient of the old demoniac breed, alluded to by Shakespeare:

"One sees more devils than vast Hell can hold. That is the madman."

But without intending any disrespect to any of these gentlemen, he assigned the golden crown of Insanity to Hamlet.

Research cannot build up paragraphs like that or infuse them with so rich an irony. The cracked alienist is a perfect miniature; as for his sane patient, Alfred Hardie, he is as human as Tom Robinson, and his torments in "asyla" as affecting as Robinson's in gaol. As before, all this part is the best; there was something in the mere thought of forcible confinement that put Reade on his mettle. The kidnapping of the bridegroom on his wedding morning, with his running fight for it against cruel odds, is not only one of the most exciting chapters Reade ever wrote, it is one of the most pathetic incidents ever described in terms of action. It takes the reader by the throat, as he feels it must have taken the writer before him. Alfred Hardie does not escape from the asylum; but for once Charles Reade has escaped from his prison-house of prearranged facts and given us one of those scenes which are as coals of fire from the imagination he so strangely distrusted.

Foul Play, again, treats boldly of the sea. In "carpentry" it excels *Hard Cash,* thanks clearly to the collaboration of Boucicault, world's champion at the game; otherwise *Foul Play* is a very much poorer book. It attacks none of those abuses that inspired the novelist with righteous passion; it was just the desert-island story on which every romantic likes to try his hand. Reade, being Reade, assailed his subject scientifically; you would swear to his flora and fauna. But his two castaways leave the male too little, the female too much, to be desired. On learning that her heroic lover is also a convict the lady behaves much as the protagonists of *Etiquette* in a similar quandary; it is a ruinous scene which may well have been the germ of the Bab Ballad in question. *Foul Play* provoked Burnand's *Punch* skit, *Chikkin Hazard,* which Reade (again, being Reade) quite failed to enjoy; and this is sad when one remembers the derelict chair that yielded castor oil, the capers the ready hero cut for the sauce, and other inoffensive joys. Bret Harte's *Handsome Is as Handsome Does* is a more searching parody of a much better book—*Put Yourself in His Place*—the most artistic of the propagandist novels. But the cruellest parodies on Charles Reade were written by himself—or his accomplice—in the later chapters of *Foul Play.*

Though his books are full of the things that betray an author's antecedents, it was many years before he devoted a whole novel to the kind of old-world country-house life that was in his bones; and then he must break new ground for trouble by hitting on his one improper plot! The expression is used with due regard for modern emancipation in these matters. The plain tale of a reformed rake's retributively childless marriage, of his philoprogenitive monomania and his lady wife's desperate remedy for the same, would probably offend in English at any time of day; yet such is the problem plot of *A Terrible Temptation.* Lady Bassett does not indeed resort to infidelity; but, in committing a fraud for which, all things considered, some piety may be claimed, she does that which would be perhaps more difficult to recite to a mixed audience—as written straight from the shoulder by Charles Reade. The motherhood denied to her has been thrust upon her confidential abigail; the two women change figures, as it were, before the reader's eyes, the details being given with as much literary nonchalance as those of the most ordinary masquerade. Nor is the effect on Sir Charles less frankly and casually described. Innocently enchanted with the changeling, he in time becomes own father to a legitimate heir. *Possunt quia posse videntur.*

Such is the plot that Charles Reade treated like any other plot in 1871. In nothing was he more ahead of his time than in the utter simplicity with which he habitually refers to what was invidiously termed "the facts of life"; he to whom life was all facts used no such ignoble euphemisms, but on principle—if he thought twice about it—"the homely expressions of Scripture." As in terminology, so with the veiled language of suggestion and in mere matters of taste. You shall search the works of this old bachelor in vain for the shadow of a joke about childbirth; and adultery in his hands is less offensive than flirtation in the hands of many. None could wish to see such a subject more healthily treated than it is here—in a manner less calculated to debauch an innocent mind. But this is just the trouble with *A Terrible Temptation.* The treatment is too healthy; it is even breezy. With perfect truth Reade claims that there is "more real invention" in the story than in most of his; but this ingenious manipulation of the elemental is one of the very things that jar. The infant impostor is in reality the by-blow of Richard Bassett, heir-presumptive and mortal enemy to the unfortunate baronet; thus there is manifold irony in the situation, which is maintained at a high dramatic level to the end, never sinking to the rank melodrama without which Reade could seldom conclude a novel. As a last aggravation the character-drawing is as much above his average as the general technique of this astounding tale.

One of the characters was, to be sure, the novelist himself, under a transparent *alias* and no disguise at all: a remarkably candid portrait, if not quite so unflattering as Reade rather naïvely protested in answer to those critics who branded it as vile bravado in such a book. Otherwise his defence against a massed attack was in his most slashing vein, and made piquant examples of the Criticaster, the Prurient Prude, the Sham-Sample-Swindler, the Anonymancule, and other "Vermin" at whose expense he enriched the vernacular. Yet these were not the first to condemn the book: it had been declined by many publishers before meeting with acceptance on the worst terms the author had received for years. What is much more astonishing is the fact that it had actually run through *Cassell's Magazine,* of all respected periodicals!

In America, where **Griffith Gaunt** had been a scandalous success on its demerits, **A Terrible Temptation** was held up to nothing less than execration, while in the *Toronto Globe* an old Magdalen score was paid off by one whose anonymity Reade scornfully respected in his passionate rejoinder. He had the temperament, so common among creative artists, which reacts outwardly against criticism as against a blow; but inwardly he took the most preposterous onslaught pathetically to heart. In a notebook of this period is neatly pasted an American notice describing him as "a slimy, snaky, poisonous literary reptile," his book as "this mass of brothel garbage," and himself again as "a gatherer of offal for the hyenas of the human race." Some writers collect that sort of thing to read aloud with roars of merriment. Charles Reade let himself go as follows for our benefit:

> I leave this on record for the instruction of those who complain that authors work for money instead of contenting themselves with the meed of praise they receive.
>
> Was anything of mine ever praised as heartily as here an excellent and innocent story is abused?
>
> Through my whole career it has been so: a little faint reluctant praise—bushels of insolent vituperation.
>
> But with the proceeds of a pen that never wrote a line till I was 35 years of age, I have got me 3 freeholds in the Brompton Road, a leasehold in Albert Terrace, a house full of rich furniture, and pictures—and a few thousands floating, and so I can snap my fingers at a public I despise and a Press I know and loath. To God alone my thanks are due who gave me my good gifts and the sense to see that literature is a trade and that an author is a being secretly despised and who can only raise himself above contempt
>
> by
> *RICHES*

June 8, 1872

A childish outpouring for a famous novelist, on his fifty-eighth birthday too! But a certain childishness is part of the novelist's equipment; and here there is much more of the individual Reade. The distinguished critic who long ago discovered "Reade's essential vulgarity of mind" will find plenty here (besides that unnatural slap at the man's own public) to confirm a youthful judgment. But to me this sad message reveals at least one equally essential, equally demonstrable humility of heart. Only a humble-hearted man, in the position of Charles Reade after Dickens's death, before Mr. Hardy's rise or Meredith's recognition,

could have pointed to the goods and chattels his work had brought him rather than to the work itself.

This is the true clue to a nature more than ordinarily complex and self-contradictory; a truculent and fiery temper, a stubborn though a wayward will, were but the bristling defences of a citadel riven with self-distrust. Hence this inveterate dependence on "warm facts," not only in working up strange cases, but in considering his own. His furniture and his freeholds are the "warm facts," of his success; anything less material might be partly his imagination—that "good gift" which he distrusts the most of all.

You begin to see that he was not altogether wrong; and his books bear him out. They are stronger in episode than in plot, sounder in tactics than in strategy. This is manifest from the last hundred pages of almost any one of them. However fresh the opening, a fatal sameness marks the close of all but two or three. Nothing is harder to finish decently than a sensational story in which all your ends are on the table and no mystery is reserved for solution in the last chapter; but in eschewing this invention Reade had repeated recourse to the same set of devices for reinforcing the intrinsic interest of his tale. The forged, intercepted, or anonymous letter is his favourite instrument of mental torture; it invariably screws the heroine up to a loveless marriage with the villain, as a rule prevented at the altar-rails, though in **Put Yourself in His Place** the actual ceremony is performed by a spurious priest whose handiwork is undone betimes. Such an ending to stories so full of freshness and power would be regret-table enough in a single instance; it is deplorable in book after book. But the pace has been set and must be accelerated at all costs in the straight. "Keep a gallop for the avenue," was Lever's advice to James Payn, who passed it on to the present writer. It was a cardinal rule in the old-fashioned fiction, and is for that matter a plank in the drama of all time. Unfortunately it was just in the avenue that Reade fell off.

An exciting novel ought obviously to become more and more so as the chapters fly, but the excitement must be inherent in the situation and on no account betray the nervous anxiety of an author who is afraid of being dull. This is probably the one form of fear that Charles Reade ever knew; yet it is only another side of a subconscious self-distrust. It shows itself not only in the artificial complications of a natural narrative; it is always showing itself in his style. He distrusts his power of making some specially dramatic point, so has it set up in the largest capitals in the fount; an equally momentous whisper is represented by print that requires a microscope; or the page is broken by a crude wood-cut of clasped hands, as though there were no words for a handshake, or by a miner's knife-blade as large as life, or by a disenchanting diagram of the Southern Cross.

These reflections on the English language, which no English writer has used more pictorially than Charles Reade, are the first faults on which a "criticaster" pounces; they are not, however, the worst. Like all novelists of his day, including his one or two betters, he is continually recalling us from the playground of the story into the august presence of the master whose existence we had forgotten. This bad old habit matters less in Dickens, who is strangely independent of illusion, and hardly at all in Thackeray, whose variations are often as good as the tune. With Reade they are a discord in another key; with Reade, who is always coaxing up steep places, they are the dig in the ribs which is enough to bring one heavily to earth again.

"Forgive my heat, dear reader. I am not an Eden, and these fellows rile me." "Oh, my heroines! When will you learn to be faultless!" "He had not skimmed so many, many books as we have . . . and this, oh men of paper, and oh C. R. in particular, gave him a tremendous advantage over you." Thus he apostrophises his readers, his creatures or himself, with indifferent damage to the context. "Now would you mind closing this book for a minute and making an effort to realise all this? It will save us so much repetition." This in *The Cloister and the Hearth,* of all books; but so are allusions to the crinoline, the Duke of Wellington, and Macready in *Macbeth!* Even in *Griffith Gaunt,* which does on the whole leave the eighteenth century to itself, we are brought back from the duel in the snow to our own fireside by the *bêtise,* "'N.B.—This is rote sarcastical,' as Artemus, the delicious, says." Yet such is the art of the man that all is forgotten in the next sentence every time, and we are back with him on the heights from which his horseplay has dislodged us; for the truth is that his art is author-proof and his style so verily the man that we should suspect his sincerity if he failed to annoy us for many chapters on end.

"I make it a rule," he himself says somewhere, "to put a little good and a little bad into every page I write, so as to suit the average reader." Of course he made it nothing of the sort, but possibly some such consideration did condone some conscious blemishes. "Import some Victor Hugoisms into my Anglo-Saxon" is a darker memorandum, for if ever novelist had a style of his own it was Charles Reade. It was a style quick with colour, vigour, and variety; now economical as stage instructions, now expanding in a fine extravagance; jumpy yet supple, stentorian yet often musical, scholarly yet never academic; in a word, the writing of a gentleman in his shirt-sleeves. And from its very imperfections it was a style which dropped without effort into as good story-telling dialogue as ever was written. Now the relation between narrative and dialogue is an interesting study in any novelist; in the pithiest set-to between his characters will be found a subtle survival of the author's rhythm and imagery. Thus the Wessex peasant takes as kindly to polysyllables as to cider, while the children of Meredith belabour each other with broken epigrams. Thus Charles Reade's characters talk just as naturally and emphatically as Charles Reade wrote.

That they are in themselves a very interesting lot would be a bold contention; but then we never see these people "in themselves." They are shown in collision with circumstances or with each other, and they are not analysed for our benefit either before, during, or after the event; by their behaviour at a pinch we are to judge them; and that, after all, is a test much valued in everyday life. But it is not an everyday test, and on the whole it is more important to know how folks behave at the fireside than at a fire. Time has shown that human nature is better in an emergency than out of one; and we should like to know more of these mettlesome young women in their hours of ease and of their too patient swains when patience has been duly rewarded. The wish is granted in the case of Griffith and Catherine Gaunt, and for a few short pages that tantalising couple are quietly yet tinglingly alive. We know what they are thinking of each other as well as we know what Alfred Hardie, fresh from Oxford, would have thought of *Hard Cash.* The same can hardly be said of the Fieldings or the Littles or the Dodds, though we could swear to David sane or crazy, as we could to Thomas Robinson (unreformed) on a dark night anywhere. On the bulk of their brethren there is more than a dab of prease-paint; the strong men sob oftener and more ladies have downright hysterics than is credible even of early-Victorian times off the stage; in fact, they are *dramatis personæ* rather than characters in novels.

Why, then, was Charles Reade a comparatively unsuccessful, though a most persistent, playwright? All his life he was frankly stage-struck; with the proceeds of a novel he would hasten to put up his own dramatic version, only to lose his money oftener than not; and on his tombstone the words "Dramatist, Novelist, and Journalist" owe their order to his wishes. Yet even in his lifetime no other sane person dreamt of ranking his dramas with his books; and, without going into comparisons, the broad reason is not, I think, very far to seek. Every book Reade ever wrote is replete with the author's personality; this quality goes by the board in all his plays. "In all plays," one might as truly say, were it not for a living dramatist whose worst line would be recognisable as his alone on any moderately articulate gramophone. The run of good plays is none the less as devoid of literary personality as the run of good books is full of it. Reade's books were packed with it from cover to cover; it is the secret of their collective force, their highest common factor. Often enough it is an intensive personality, the jocose or irascible showman with his irritating patter; but from first to last it is a lusty mind that animates the page, a seeing eye that makes it glow before our own, an ardent, uncompromising, and courageous spirit which cannot fail to lift and to enlarge the heart with room in it for a real man and all his foibles. And if he did overdo his doctrine of facts, at least there was something noble in the creed:

> I say before heaven and earth that the man who could grasp the facts of this day and do an immortal writer's duty by them, *i.e.,* so paint them as a later age will be content to engrave them, would be the greatest writer ever lived: such is the force, weight, and number of the grand topics that lie this day on the world's face. I say that he who has eyes to see may now see greater and more poetic things than human eyes have seen since our Lord and His apostles and His miracles left the earth. [*It is Never too Late to Mend.*]

Emerson Grant Sutcliffe (essay date 1931)

SOURCE: "*Fœmina Vera* in Charles Reade's Novels," in *PMLA*, Vol. 46, Autumn, 1931, pp. 1260-79.

[*In the following excerpt, Sutcliffe discusses Reade's often negative portrayal of women and his depiction of women characters who disguise themselves as men or act in traditionally masculine ways.*]

One of the commonest headings in the notebooks on which Charles Reade founded his novels[1] is *fœmina vera*. He considered himself an authority on woman. In a letter to the *Pall Mall Gazette* he calls himself "a patient drudge, who has studied that sex profoundly in various walks of life."[2] Certainly his women are more memorable, and the subject of more comment and criticism, than his men. To them W. D. Howells devoted a long essay in his *Heroines of Fiction*. Though, like his men, they fall into easily recognizable, frequently repeated types, they are more alive, more real, less subordinate to the demands of story structure. The result of more study and more enthusiasm, they are less romanticized, less melodramatized than his heroes and villains.

The idiosyncrasies of his own sex (except under feminine influence) concerned him as little as they concern most men. Or perhaps it would be truer to say that he was as blind to characteristically male fatuity and foible as most men are. Though, as his villains show, he recognized and warmed to indignation at male depravity, minor male weaknesses he does not stigmatize as he does feminine peccadilloes. He drew the egotist willing to murder to have his way; but Meredith's egoist would have been beyond him.

Meredith's name breeds another contrast. He and Reade, contemporaries, drew some sweet young things—the Rose Jocelyn of *Evan Harrington,* the

Lucy of *Richard Feverel;* the Susan Merton of *It is Never too Late to Mend,* the Lucy of *Love Me Little, Love Me Long.* The women of both are high-spirited, yet they differ fundamentally. Meredith's usually have mind, Reade's mother-wit. Reade's women are more like Shaw's. They exploit men to gain their ends, but through instinct rather than reason. They are sly, wily, tricky, but seldom superior to their emotions. Hence they do not develop this or that trait; they have it to begin with. Born petty or noble, they react to experience according to the laws of their nature, spontaneously, for good or evil.

This is why some of Reade's heroines are intolerable. For he occasionally leaves out the liveliness of spirit which enhances most of his feminine personages. The results are disastrous. Susan Merton is so merely amiable that he apologizes for her: "These average women are not the spice of fiction, but they are the salt of real life."[3] This excuse rather opposes his judgment in another novel that "the average woman is under five feet, and rather ugly."[4] But here he is defending himself for not doing justice to a "noble" woman, Ina Klosking. Susan dumbly resists the advances of the villainous suitor, remains passively faithful to the distant hero. More unbearably flabby-minded, incapable indeed of decision, is Grace Carden of *Put Yourself in His Place.* She is afraid of the consequences if she disobeys her father and marries the hero; yet, moved by her nitwit father, and the villain's assiduity, she consents to marry the villain when the hero is thought dead. Her one positive action is to stab the villain after his rascalities are exposed and the hero is found to be alive—when, in other words, she discovers that she has almost reached the condition so often neared or attained by the women in Reade's novels, and the women in the other sensational novels and plays of the period: being "neither maid, wife, nor widow."

Usually Reade treats his women with both more— and less—consideration than he bestows on such jelly-fish heroines. His attitude is that of many persistent bachelors. In fact, all attempts at diagnosis of his feminine point of view must begin with his Magdalen College fellowship, which demanded celibacy, and which he held until his death. Reade, bachelor perforce, is tender, courtly; he admires, he even flutters; but at the same time he scoffs with masculine superiority—and obliquity. The novels frequently, the notebooks always, display an attitude which one, according to his point of view, may call either realistic or cynical.

Instructive comparison is possible between what he selected for the notebooks as truly feminine, and his practical presentation of feminine characteristics in the novels. He conceded something to convention and romance, he condescended somewhat to his readers, he modified for artistic results—and for financial gain. And, as I shall point out, when he reveals his own attitude, he is often strategic.

His undisguised opinion, not trimmed and adjusted to esthetic or popular standards, comes out in the notebooks. There two kinds of data appear, which, with their effects on the novels, I shall take up successively. The first is of a familiar sort, exposing caprice, inconsistency, illogicality, trickiness, softness in the face of maltreatment by beloved men. The second reveals the presence in woman of qualities customarily thought masculine: on the favorable side, physical bravery and activity; on the ugly side, brutality and animalism. He collects material, too, about those abnormal cases where the woman would, if possible, forfeit her sex. This second *fœmina vera* approaches man in heroic strength, in cruel violence, or in dress.

I

Scrutiny of some passages from the notebooks, showing the more conventional aspect of his attitude toward woman, may well precede an inquiry into the means he found in his novels, to evince, to exhibit, or at least to utilize this attitude.

Proof that woman is obedient to instinct, rather than logically consistent, Reade evidently saw in such instances as these:

> A woman jilted by A. gets another and is engaged. Commander in chief will not let B. marry. B. is marched off. Girl hangs herself with a letter in her bosom—to B.? Oh dear no, to A. blowing him up sky high. *Times* Aug. 10 X [18] 56. (*42,* p. 189)

> A lady wrote some verses upon a window, intimating her design of never marrying. A. wrote the following lines underneath:

> The lady whose resolve these words betoken

> Wrote them on glass to show it may be broken.

> A statement of that kind from a woman means this. Marriage is the thing that runs most in my head. How shall I get an offer? I'll put the men on their mettle. I'll say it is not in the power of men to win me. This is a true instinct. (*Journalium,* p. 248.)

Of feminine instability he thought this display worthy of record and comment:

> [A clipping tells of a man long expecting to be a bridegroom who leaves Fife on business. His sweetheart becomes an heiress during his protracted absence and has other suitors. She writes him, but he returns to find her married. Above this there appears in the notebook:]

Fœmina vera.

> Tenacity of purpose under difficulties: broken down or was espiglièrie when it had become easy. It looks as if the woman could hold out a certain time. Circumstances go for nothing or perhaps her letter to her old sweetheart was the last effort of an expiring affection and wounded vanity came in the next moment and caused a reaction. (*Journalium,* p. 248.)

Frequent jottings show a belief in women's mendacity.

> On certain topics the truth is not in them. Madame de la Rochefoucauld the Vendéen heroine marched to the scaffold after lying about her age. She made herself out three years younger than she was. (*42,* p. 253)

> A lie nothing to them. Girl accuses herself falsely of a felony to get a night's lodging rather than knock up the family she is with or be out all night. . . . (*Journalium,* p. 42.)

> Scotch servant lass pretends her mother is dead: gets mistress to lend her black silk, goes to imaginary funeral. (42, p. 178.)

Favorable feminine response to rough treatment, and practical acceptance of a situation, appear in this entry:

> Mary Anne Elton charged Jopling her suitor with attempting her ruin by means of chloroform. But she called out and handed him to a policeman. He was remanded in bail till the 7 May. 7 May the case was proceeded with. Deft. handed in a certificate proving that Mary Anne Elton was Mary Anne Jopling having married him that morning at the church of St. Mary le Strand. Girl's relatives cried out and said she had been entrapped. Mrs. Jopling examined severely said no; it was with her free will. Then looking lovingly on her deft. Oh I am quite sure he will use me well and we shall be happy and comfortable. . . . Then the magistrate instead of saying volenti non fit injuria chose to consider with his male sapience that this marriage was a conspiracy to defeat the ends of justice. The sexes are in all this, & the hard vulgar logic of a woman is at the bottom of it. H.N. [*Household Narrative*] X 50. 109. (*Journalium,* p. 41.)

The natural result of gathering such materials under the head of *fœmina vera* is the tendency to think of women not as individuals, but as a race. This race, as I shall presently demonstrate, is divided in the novels into types; but all these types share the common attributes of true woman. The most comprehensive generalization is this one, used by Vizard, the woman hater (alias Reade):

'Goose!'

'And just now I was a fox.'

'You are both. But so is every woman.'[5]

So Mrs. Bazalgette, elderly flirt, calls Lucy "an innocent fox."[6] The notebooks apply the expression to Mrs. Tilton.

> Fox and Goose. Say the Goose-Fox. Her old business with Parson Beecher and her husband . . . Says she was converted by Griffith Gaunt extract in one of my Giant Folios. (*Antiqua-Wreck:* Fœmina vera.)

Deceit and soft foolishness, which women change to energy and presence of mind when those they love are in need of their help, or when they have marked a man as theirs, these are the principal feminine traits in Reade's estimation. The actions of the women in the novels, then, tend to be essentially feminine rather than personally characteristic. This habit of generalizing appears both when Reade comments as the author, and when, keeping responsibility off himself, he makes use of various devices to animadvert sharply on woman.

Lucy in *Love Me Little, Love Me Long* painstakingly deciphers some old records "with a good-humored patience that belonged partly to her character, partly to her sex. A female who undertakes this sort of work does not skip as we should."[7]

Such generic commentary appears often in *The Cloister and the Hearth.* Margaret and Richt agree that Gerard and Margaret should wed without waiting for parental consent. This gives Reade an excuse for criticizing women:

> Women are creatures brimful of courage. Theirs is not exactly the same quality as manly courage; that would never do, hang it all; we should have to give up trampling on them. No; it is a vicarious courage. They never take part in a bullfight by any chance; but it is remarked that they sit at one, unshaken by those tremors and apprehensions for the combatants to which the male spectator—feeble-minded wretch!—is subject. Nothing can exceed the resolution with which they have been known to send forth men to battle: as some witty dog says, 'Les femmes sont très braves avec le peau d'autrui.'[8]

Not so much her own is the sentiment which Marion, the chambermaid, feels toward Gerard. Rather it is "a triple attraction that has ensnared coquettes in all ages."[9] Similarly, it is because "at her age girls love to be coy and tender, saucy and gentle, by turns," that Margaret delays in offering to tie Gerard's ribbon. And she prolongs the tying unconsciously since "it is not natural to her sex to hurry aught that pertains to the sacred toilet." Here Reade generalizes about feminine physical mannerisms also: "Her mind was not quite easy, till, by a manœuvre peculiar to the female hand, she had made her palm convex, and so applied it . . . to the centre of the knot."[10]

Two more examples from *Griffith Gaunt.* Mrs. Gaunt mothers Father Leonard, shy but eloquent young priest, not because of an especially personal feeling, but because "all true women love to protect".[11] When, in the earlier part of the story, she, then Kate Peyton, folds a letter to keep an address invisible, Reade is provoked to the parenthetic remark: "Small secrecy, verging on deceit, you are bred in woman's bones!"[12]

To prevent the resentment of too many feminine readers, Reade usually puts the more cutting unfavorable generalizations on woman into the mouth of a character who is not to be trusted: a woman hater, as in the novel so called (see especially chap. VIII), or a villain. In this passage from *Put Yourself in His Place,* Coventry, the villain, is the principal speaker:

> 'All women are deceitful.'
>
> 'Oh, come!'
>
> 'Let me explain; all women, worthy of the name, are cowards; and cowardice drives them to deceit, even against their will. . . . '[13]

So the following words from the lips of the rake, Sir Charles Pomander, in *Peg Woffington,* give the author a chance to express without obnoxiousness his own cynical views:

> 'I know that with all women, the present lover is an angel and the past a demon, and so on in turn. And I know that if Satan were to enter the women of the stage, with the wild idea of impairing their veracity, he would come out of their minds a greater liar than he went in, and the innocent darlings would never know their spiritual father had been at them.'[14]

The reader, too, cannot be distressed when the constantly amorous Denys offers sagely experienced advice to Gerard about Marion's probable kindly reception of his affections.[15]

More ingenious is the use of the hero as mouthpiece of Reade's satiric conclusions. In a meditative soliloquy Alfred Hardie of *Hard Cash* incisively remarks about women novelists and their attitude toward their sex:

> 'How many unsuspicious girls have these double-faced mothers deluded so? They do it in half the novels, especially in those written by women: and why? Because these know the perfidy and mendacity of their sex better than we do.'[16]

This slur can be passed over by the sensitive, for Alfred is over-wrought, and, after all, he wishes to make the woman whom he criticizes his mother-in-law. Another situation in which the hero may safely be used is that in which Gerard finds himself. He has met his mate, to whom he is to be faithful throughout the story. Who, then, can with calmer impartiality advise a flirting male companion about feminine untrustworthiness? Gerard brings to bear on Denys in this innocuous fashion some of the by-words of which he—and his creator—were so fond: "Le peu que sont les femmes," and

> Qui hante femmes et dez,
> Il mourra en pauvretez.[17]

It is fair to say that Reade on such occasions puts strongly defensive retorts in the mouths of Denys and others. The maids at the inn snap back: "We say that none run women down but such as are too old, or too ill-favored, or too witless to please them."[18]

A frequent heading in the notebooks is "proclivity toward suicide." From his reading, especially of newspapers, Reade was convinced that young women often committed suicide "for insufficient reasons," as he phrases it. This belief, coupled with the tendency to generalize, has a definite outcome in the novels. It twice affects **The Cloister and the Hearth.** Catherine, Gerard's mother, fears that Margaret may have "made herself away," and tells her daughter of a quarrel in her courting-days that almost caused her to throw herself in the canal.[19] And near the end of the story Margaret is almost wrought up to worse than suicide:

> Margaret, when she ran past Gerard, was almost mad. She was in that state of mind in which affectionate mothers have been known to kill their children, sometimes along with themselves, sometimes alone, which last is certainly maniacal.[20]

In **Put Yourself in His Place** Jael Dence tries to drown herself, self-hypnotized by her own illness, grief over her father's death, the suddenly learned news that her sister has gone to Australia, and the sight of a pool in the moonlight. She is rescued and resuscitated.[21] The heroine of this novel, Grace Carden (about whom I have previously expressed my disgust) has been married, as she thinks, to the villain, and has discovered that the hero, supposed dead, is alive. Under the circumstances the doctor advises Jael Dence to watch Grace closely.

> He had seen a woman start up and throw herself, in one moment, out of a window, for less than this— a woman crushed apparently, and more dead than alive, as Grace Carden was.[22]

Jael accordingly takes away from Grace a stiletto which she is fingering, but is not able to keep her from using it on the supposed bridegroom. Not fatally, of course. Grace is not Tess, and Reade is not Hardy.

II

The inclination to turn any woman into every woman, which was encouraged by the gathering of materials under the head of *fœmina vera,* sometimes has an artificial effect; it is visible in some of the incidents just cited. Often, however, having the nature of the whole sex as background worked out beneficially. Reade thought of his women just as he did his men: he cast them to play certain parts in his story. In **A Woman Hater** Vizard remarks about a new character who has come into the story:

> 'We have got our gusher, likewise our flirt; and it was understood from the first that this was to be a new *dramatis persona,* was not to be a repetition of you or *la* Dover, but—ahem!—the third grace, a virago: solidified vinegar.'[23]

Since the women characters are types, it is fortunate that they are, above all else, feminine. It may be, indeed, that this is one reason why Reade's women are more successful than his men. The more usual procedure is to rely not on sex, but on mutations from type, in creating the impression of individuality. But Reade's women are more individual, paradoxically enough, because the species is always thought of as belonging to the genus. Significantly, the number of feminine character parts in his novels is much smaller than that of male character parts. For the character part is the result of caricature: of varying a type through stress on eccentricities; whereas Reade grounds the type on the genus.

What are the classes into which his women fall? There are flirts, young and old. The young, like Fanny Dover in **A Woman Hater,** and Rose Mayfield in **Clouds and Sunshine,** scheme without scruple to gain their ends. But they are capable of kindness, and unlike the male flirts, who are the villains of the stories in which they appear, they are vouchsafed at the end a respectable partner, though of course not the hero. Fanny may have her prototype in Molière. "Celimène," Reade says, "is a born coquettte, but with a world of good sense and keen wit, and not a bad heart, but an untruthful, a pernicious woman, not a bad one."[24] One of Reade's best feminine characterizations is the decaying Mrs. Bazalgette of **Love Me Little, Love Me Long.** Not especially adroit, she is shameless in her efforts to vamp the young hero, and is not only elderly coy with him, but completely selfish in her relations with Lucy, her ward.

There are the ingenues, who best deserve the description of goose-fox which Reade at times attributed to all women. The vulpine is sometimes lacking; they remain merely geese. Slight individual differences occur, but Mabel Vane of **Peg Woffington,** Susan Merton of **It Is Never too Late to Mend,** Rosa Lusignan of **A Simpleton** (she is the simpleton), Grace Carden of **Put Yourself in His Place,** Zoe Vizard of **A Woman Hater,** born years apart, are, in everything but wig and make-up, more similar than sisters. Indeed, they and Reade's other types, male and female, provide excellent examples of that strange genesis whose products may be called the literary litter.

There are the passionate, who would give all for love. Such are Mrs. Archbold of **Hard Cash,** housekeeper at insane asylums, who threatens the virtuous Alfred Hardie with lunacy if he will not agree to her embraces while sane; Claelia, the Roman princess, who succumbs to Gerard's charms, finds him obdurate, and is afterwards converted by him; Rhoda Somerset, high-class prostitute in **A Terrible Temptation,** who reminds us of Claelia (and Alec D'Urberville) by sublimating amours into evangelism. There are the noble, self-respecting, intelligent heroines whose best example is Margaret in *The Cloister,* and who are also notably, or at least deliberately represented by Ina Klosking, the opera-singer of **A Woman Hater:**

> Remembering how many noble women have shone like stars in every age and every land . . . I have tried to . . . paint La Klosking. But such portraiture is difficult. It is like writing a statue.[25]

There are the self-reliant, strong girls from the country, about whom I shall soon have a great deal to say.

Such a classification is not cleanly complete, and though it shows Reade's favorite methods of composing his women, it perhaps better lists the qualities of which they were composed. What classification quite holds, for instance, Peg Woffington, large-hearted, sparkling woman of passion; Christie Johnstone, child of nature, expert sailor and fisherwoman, vivacious, keen; Phoebe Dale, shrewd, strong, pioneering, beset by a consuming passion for her profligate husband? Nobility and self-respect characterize Mercy Vint, country wife of bigamous Griffith Gaunt; they are softened by traces of physical attraction for a worthless husband in Ina Klosking. Flashing Kate Gaunt is led by her husband's black moods into an almost maternal care of her Roman Catholic chaplain. Here the ingredients are obvious, but so is their mixture. And the binding agent is Reade's conception of *fœmina vera.*

III

So far, it is easy to explain Reade's treatment of his feminine characters as due to his bachelorhood, and to the fictional and dramatic conventions of the mid-century. Not so simple is a sound analysis of the sources of Reade's interest in those women who in one way or another exhibit supposedly masculine characteristics. Surely, partial causes are disappointment and repression. The mother who intervenes in **Christie Johnstone,** to prevent the marriage of fishing girl and painter, had her parallel in Reade's mother. Something, though evidence is lacking to tell just what, must lie behind the many passages in his novels about the evil effects of jealousy, and behind the facts that **Jealousy** is the subtitle of **Griffith Gaunt** and one title Reade gave his adaptation of Sardou's *Andrée.* Perhaps part of the secret lies in the mysterious affair only hinted at in the *Memoir* (chap. xv, which tells of the attraction Reade felt toward some fair woman, herself in love with an ugly, stupid man. There are some odd references in Reade's writings to "beauty and the beast."

Frustration and celibacy, however, cannot be the only explanation. The *Memoir* makes plain that Reade was the occasional victim of deep and prolonged nervous exhaustion and depression of the kind that sometimes seizes his male characters, who have brain-fever and fall into fits, sometimes epileptic. Was Reade's interest in the insane merely part of a large humanitarian benevolence? Is one merely hypnotized by jargon when he finds an inverted, sadistic cruelty in the savage indignation which accompanies Reade's irritation at the spectacle of human suffering? Is his dwelling on the barbarous use of the crank in prisons, which forms so large a part of **It is Never too Late to Mend,** wholly normal? Such thoughts press to the surface, certainly, when one reads the items in the notebooks which record with sardonic, Gilbertian humor instances of feminine cruelty.

A less complicated and perhaps more trustworthy explanation may be offered for the energetic athleticism of his women. He was writing dramatic novels in which swift action was a principal feature. He could not follow altogether the pattern of the medieval romance, which so often took the hero away from the heroine at the beginning of the story, carried him through a series of adventures, and then restored him to the heroine, though there are evidences of this pattern in some of his novels. Some of his women, however, accompany the men through most of the incidents of the story, and under the conditions must act fast and often. If there is an underlying psychological reason for Reade's preference for activity for both sexes—and I think there is—it is to be found in his being primarily, like his brothers, a motor type, and in the fact that, once committed to the writer's life, the easiest way for him to be up and doing was to make his characters active.

As recently as 1911 the *English Review* published in two issues under the title *Androgynism or Woman Playing at Man* an extended account, recovered from Reade's papers, of the life of a woman who persisted in wearing men's clothes and pretending masculinity.

Though his judgment told him such a character was unsuitable for fiction or drama (except farce), he declares that: "Between the years 1858-62, i.e., about the date when I first began to collect from real life materials for the drama . . . I devoted a folio of 250 leaves to tabulating cases of androgynism." This notebook seems to be no longer extant, but the case described in *Androgynism* is like that referred to in the notebooks (*Digest,* p. 51) under the heading of "Living characters." "1859 a woman who has long served as a sailor excuse that she had a sickly husband. Mem! Find this one out photograph her and write her." His interest in the abnormality preceded 1858, for one of his earliest stories is his satire on the bloomer craze, **Propria Quae Maribus,** which, though not printed till 1857, was written, according to his statement in a prefatory note, several years before. The interest is evident, too, in **Peg Woffington** (1852). Peg tells the story of a lover who, she found, intended to marry another:

> 'I found her out; got an introduction to her father; went down to his house three days before the marriage, with a little coal-black mustache, regimentals, and what not. . . .

> 'The first day I flirted and danced with the bride. The second I made love to her, and at night I let her know that her intended was a villain. . . .

> 'So, in a fit of virtuous indignation, the little hypocrite dismissed the little brute; in other words she had fallen in love with me.'[26]

This takes place off-stage. Twenty years later, in another brief novel of the eighteenth century, **The Wandering Heir** (Christmas *Graphic,* 1872), transvestism is an integral part of the plot. It is prepared for by stress, early in the narrative, on Philippa's tomboyish characteristics. At thirteen she wants to be made a boy, thinking that boys' clothes and a hair-cut will bring about the transformation. Her tomboyishness comes for a moment close to the pathological:

> Then, going into a fury, 'Oh! why did not I scratch their eyes out, when they came to christen me a girl? Why cried I not aloud, "No! No! No! A BOY! A BOY!"?'[27]

A few years later, perturbed by the unwelcome suit of Silas, oafish son of a scheming guardian, she runs away to London. There, (at a masquerade shop) she exchanges a new dress for a sailor's costume, and thus attired succeeds in indenting herself as a bookkeeper and overseer to a Delaware planter. She continues to wear her men's clothes, flattering the women and studying the men, in particular the hero, until he and she are on their voyage home.

Even in a historical romance, this epicene feature really does not do. Art and abnormal sexual psychology may have been mated by Proust, but it is reasonably safe to say that transvestism is unacceptable artistically outside farce, Shakespeare, and the pantomime.

Reade seems to have based this part of his plot on the too great strangeness of truth. One of the notebooks (*Bon. fab.,* pp. 181a & b) contains a clipping from the *New Annual Register* of 1781 telling of a girl who becomes a sailor, leaving her uncle in Northumberland in order to see her sweetheart in Bombay.

There is one "new woman" in the Reade novels, Rhoda Gale, the American doctor in **A Woman Hater.** This description of her "clear, silvery voice" is significant of her type of womanliness:

> It was not, like Ina Klosking's, rich, and deep, and tender; yet it had a certain gentle beauty to those who love truth, because it was dispassionate, yet expressive, and cool, yet not cold.[28]

How near this woman comes to the androgynous is suggested by these words which Rhoda speaks when she hears bad news about her mother's health, and lacks money to cross the Atlantic:

> 'My mother . . . forbids me positively to go to her. Oh! but for that, I'd put on boy's clothes, and go as a common sailor to get to her.'[29]

A "generative incident" involving androgynism, which Reade tried to fertilize with his imagination, appears several times in the notebooks of the seventies. In *5g,* p. 21 over, is a clipping telling of an Italian woman who was a corporal in the army until her sex was discovered by a surgeon who was examining a wound. Below the clipping Reade has written:

> Adapt to American Civil War.

> Surgeon girl's unsuccessful lover. She is mad after, follows him to the wars. Surgeon treats them both for wounds: had fought with rival previously.

On p. 56 of the same notebook is an enlargement of the conception:

> American story

> Federal spy female Fol. Mat. Fict. 218. combine with almost a plot Giant Fol. 2. 41. Leave space to mark the combination. The name of the female spy is [space] and she should be interviewed. Some of the adventures are detailed in Fol. Mat. Fict. but not imp[ortant]. Get her interviewed, & get Boucicault's play of Belle Amar.

The other element is a surgeon in love with her; but she loves another and on the grand occasion of the story he tends them both. This is a very generative situation.

IV

A frequent heading in the notebooks is Caliban. This has both masculine and feminine dog-Latin singular and plural forms, and the headings Calibana, Calibanæ, and Calibani are found. Instances of the brutality and bestiality of both sexes are recorded, but there is no doubt that Reade, like D. H. Lawrence, thought feminine brutality noteworthy because not usually admitted. Little of this comes into the novels; Reade's realism is here, as elsewhere, conditioned both by artistic sensitiveness and a regard for sales.

Reade takes a grim, perverted, almost ghoulish delight in setting down under the head of Calibana or Calibanæ such items as these:

> Eliza Smith ætat 17 poisons her master & mistress with arsenic. Admits that they were kind to her, but says that her mistress had come down like a bull-dog that morning. Another excuse that on Sunday she had accused her of killing a fowl. . . .

> Bridget & Julia Conolly kill sheep on large scale & eat; half sheep under petticoats. . . . (*Journalium,* p. 27)

> A woman, Frances Smith, quarreled with her son and his wife: her temper was so bad they turned her out of the house. Then she stole their son, her grandson; and drowned him, to make their hearts ache. She said so. She was hung. (*Antiqua-Wreck,* Calibana)

Such entries, it is important to note, also appear under the head of Fœmina Vera.

> Puella religiosa writes 18 girls, and tries to send them all to heaven with poison. Tantum religio potuit. (51, Fœmina Vera)

> They are child-robbers as well as murderers. Susan Nunn a showily dressed woman of 30 charged with the above. A *swarm* of little girls and boys, nearly 50 ætat. 6-13 brought as witnesses by their friends. Nurse was put in a room with other women and many of the brats identified her at once. (*Journalium,* p. 42)

Numerous in the notebooks as such entries are, the reflection of the interest which prompted them is slight in the novels. Some facts which the notebooks stressed Reade's matter-of-fact romances almost left out. In *A Perilous Secret* he comments: "Men do not ill-treat children. It is only women, who adore them, that kill them and ill-use them accordingly."[30] Attacks on the abuses of baby-farming in the notebooks cast a faint shadow on *Griffith Gaunt:* Caroline Ryder, loose villainess, conceals her child by baby-farming it in a remote county. There is only one incident in the novels in which calibanæ figure. In *Hard Cash* the practice of "tanking" is described. The keeperesses, as Reade calls them, not only taunt the madwomen and feed them vilely, but torture them by putting them naked under cold water again and again: "In the absence of male critics they showed their real selves, and how wise it is to trust that gentle sex in the dark with irresponsible power over females."[31]

V

Reade's interest in androgynism and feminine savagery is akin to his interest in feminine athleticism, the most attractive quality on the sexual border-line. Though the superbly statuesque type of feminine beauty particularly pleased him, he apparently recognized that his age would not allow a novelist to describe a refined Victorian lady as muscularly energetic, at least on her native heath. But when conditions were favorable, he from the beginning of his career gave his women a chance to be as sinewy as his men, and even to use their strength to save the lives of their men associates. He did so when his heroine or other important woman character was of low estate, and particularly when she was a rustic; or when circumstances brought her to an unsettled country; or when she lived at a distant period. With contemporary stay-at-home heroines of the upper middle class the best he could do was negative: he made the heroine of *A Simpleton* a dreadful example of the results of tight-lacing.

There was, however, more safety, and less danger of shocking any one, in taking the feminine characters in a historical novel off the sidelines and putting them into the game of swift action which Reade managed so expertly. Consider the lively part that Margaret plays in *The Cloister,* especially in the earlier chapters. She grasps an arrow that Martin Wittenhaagen is about to shoot at the Duke's leopard. Then:

> She seized his long-pointed knife, almost tore it out of his girdle, and darted from the room. . . . Margaret cut off a huge piece of venison, and ran to the window, and threw it out to the green eyes of fire.[32]

She hides Gerard in a chest.[33] She runs with Gerard and Martin when they are pursued.[34] To put off the bloodhounds, she cuts her arm and smears her hose and shoes.[35] Significantly, too, she anticipates the "new woman" doctor of *A Woman Hater* by playing the physician when her father is stricken by paralysis.[36]

In *Griffith Gaunt,* Kate Peyton, "of ancient family in Cumberland,"

> hunted about twice a week in the season, and was at home in the saddle, for she had ridden from a child; but so ingrained was her character, that this sport, which more or less unsexes most women, had no perceptible effect on her mind, nor even on her manners.[37]

How far Reade reflects his age in this comment on the fox-hunting woman is disputable, but Kate is otherwise active. She interrupts a duel between two of her lovers early in the story, and, falsely accused of murder, at the end of the story pleads her own case. The time of *Griffith Gaunt* is the eighteenth century; here, then, as in *The Cloister,* where Margaret for a time acts the doctor, Reade takes advantage of the historical background to anticipate his time, using an old disguise for a new woman.

In *Foul Play* the heroine is cured of tuberculosis by a life in the open on an uninhabited South Sea island. What more could one ask of the very pattern of a Victorian general's daughter than this lofty resolution, addressed to her fellow castaway: "No," said she, "you are always working for me, and I shall work for you. Cooking and washing are a woman's work, not a man's; and so are plaiting and netting."[38] Nor was this all. For before the story is over, she sailed a boat, in spite of difficulties, and thereby rescued her lover. "She cried like any woman. She persisted like a man."[39]

VI

The most pronounced example of the virile yet feminine woman among Reade's characters is Jael Dence of *Put Yourself in His Place.* Of the earth from which Reade made her there are positive traces in both the novels and the notebooks, worthy of examination by any one who cares to observe closely of what stuff a novelist may shape his characters. Jael is the most highly developed flower of a type: girls rustic, strong, generously built in arm, throat, bosom, and leg, superstitious, full of proverbs, in love usually with the hero, but in one case the villain.

Christie Johnstone, herring-fisher extraordinary, is the first of these. In the second chapter of the novel that bears her name we learn about her physique and that of her friend, and are also told of Reade's physical preferences:

> Their short petticoats revealed a neat ankle, and a leg with a noble swell; for Nature, when she is in earnest, builds beauty on the ideas of ancient sculptors and poets.

We are thus prepared to find Christie making use of her physique. When Sandy Liston is about to solace himself with whiskey for the loss of a dead comrade, she

forgot the wild and savage nature of the man, who had struck his own sister, and seriously hurt her, a month before, . . . and she seized him by the collar, with a grasp from which he in vain attempted to shake himself loose.[40]

And we are not surprised to read of her rescue of Charles Gatty, the hero:

> She flung herself boldly over the gunwale; the man was sinking, her nails touched his hair, her fingers entangled themselves in it, she gave him a powerful wrench, and brought him alongside; the boys pinned him like wild-cats.

> Christie darted away forward to the mast, passed a rope round it, threw it the boys, in a moment it was under his shoulders. Christie hauled on it from the fore thwart, the boys lifted him, and they tumbled him gasping and gurgling like a dying salmon, into the bottom of the boat.[41]

In some subsequent tales there are much fainter foreshadowings of Jael Dence. In *Art,* Susan, Nance Oldfield's cousing and servant, is a thick-headed dairymaid who admires the hero. In *Clouds and Sunshine,* Rose Mayfield, a flirtatious country girl, is described as having a "working arm bare till dinner time," and she and the hero are declared to be "fine specimens of rustic stature and beauty." In *Love Me Little, Love Me Long* Lucy's rustic nurse is an "Amazon."

More distinct is Jacintha, the servant in the novel of the French Revolution, *White Lies.* She is pictured as "a strapping young woman," who "stood in a bold attitude, her massive but well-formed arms folded so that the presence of each against the other made them seem gigantic."[42] Rivière, the hero, jots down some of her "coarse . . . succinct" proverbial comments. Her psychology is also that of the later, more important figure. She was, Reade declares, "a woman, who, though little educated, was full of feeling and shrewdness, and needed but the bare facts: she could add the rest from her own heart and experience."[43]

In *Hard Cash* sinewy femininity is represented unimportantly, but clearly, by a nurse in the asylum in which Alfred Hardie is criminally confined. Hannah, several times called "baby-face biceps," loves Alfred, who bestows her on Brown, an asylum keeper, where her affections had been previously fixed. First, however, he is tender-hearted and complaisant enough to kiss her, to the jealous wrath of Mrs. Archbold, the sensual housekeeper. This buss reminds the reader of the one Gerard grants the chambermaid Marion in *The Cloister.*

Mercy Vint, buxom, blooming, kind, and noble, is the rustic ingenue of *Griffith Gaunt,* but she is not so active as Kate Gaunt.

Next in line is Jael herself, an outgrowth, however, not merely of these figures in the novels, but also of the notebooks of the sixties, which show Reade's interest in feminine physical bravery. Some suggestive items follow:

> Luigina Spazzini, a girl of 15, alone defends the house against a cobbler, whom she wounds so that he is ultimately captured—the Duchess Regent of Parma awarded her a gold medal. (*42*, p. 1)

> Ann Tranter, maid servant to Mr. Swetenham near Congleton, encountering a burglar with her bare arms he armed with a stick. He strikes her. She disarms him. He beats her with his fists. She grapples and throws him. He gets the better again. She rings bell, pushes him out of the house, locks the door—and faints. Ann was [illegible] and stout; but it was partly the power of self-excitement proper to her sex, which enabled her to do this—the penalty, a faint. HC [*Household Chronicle*] 157. Query 1850. Servant at Twickenham near the church, who not only downed and overpowered a burglar but bound him. (*Journalium,* p. 108)

Classified as "Fœm. vera" is a clipping telling of the strength and nerve of Rosa Matthews, a servant. Finding a burglar in her sleeping mistress's bedroom, she took him by his coat-collar down three flights of stairs (*W.B. Reade,* p. 208). In the same notebook (p. 348) are at least two clippings, one headed Heroina, narrating the encounter with another burglar of Elizabeth Storey, another servant girl. Struck by a stick, with two teeth broken, and her face bruised, she caught the miscreant by the hair, called her mistress to get the scissors, and pulled a masking cloth from the man's face.

The parts of Jael Dence's apt name appear in the same notebooks that chronicle these vigorous feminine exertions. It is the result of telescoping the name of a murdered girl, Jael Denny, with that of a woman asylum keeper, Miss Dence.

Like some of the preceding rural characters Jael is superstitious and speaks in proverbs. She tells the hero of her treatment of her drunken brother-in-law, Phil Davis, when he declares that he has married the wrong sister:

> 'I took him by the scruff of the neck and just turned him out of the room and sent him to the bottom of the stairs headforemost.'[44]

When Little requests: "Let us see the arm that flung Phil Davis down stairs,"

> Jael colored a little, but bared her left arm at command.

> 'Good heavens!' cried Little. 'What a limb! Why mine is shrimp compared with it.'

The result of this demonstration is that "Little, with his coat off, and Jael, with her noble arms bare, ground long saws together secretly."[45]

When, in the same chapter, Hill, a union man, is about to shoot an arrow at Little, Jael flings her arm around his neck and deflects the arrow, reminding the reader of Margaret's seizing of an arrow in *The Cloister*.

There follows one of the encounters which Reade does so well.

> Hill twisted violently round, and dropping the bow, struck the woman in the face with his fist; he had not room to use all his force; yet the blow covered her face with blood. She cried out, but gripped him so tight by both shoulders that he could not strike again, but he kicked her savagely. She screamed, but slipped her arms down and got him tight round the waist. Then he was done for: with one mighty whirl she tore him off his feet in a moment, then dashed herself and him under her to the ground with such ponderous violence that his head rang loud on the pavement and he was stunned for a few seconds. Ere he quite recovered she had him turned on his face, and her weighty knee grinding down his shoulders, while her nimble hands whipped off her kerchief and tied his hands behind him in a twinkling.

When Little arrived "she was seated on her prisoner, trembling and crying after her athletic feat, and very little fit to cope with the man if he had not been tied." Then, after one speech, "she became hysterical."[46]

The trembling and loss of control following violent exercise parallel, it will be noticed, the material in the second notebook entry quoted above.

Jael has one more opportunity to show her strength in action. Coventry, the villain, has been successfully intercepting the letters which the hero has been writing from America. His minion, Lally, sees Jael with a letter in Little's writing.

> He seized her hand, and applied his knuckles to the back of it with all his force. That hurt her, and she gave a cry, and twisted away from him and drew back; then, putting her left hand to his breast, she gave a great yaw, and then a forward push with her mighty loins, and a contemporaneous shove with her amazing left arm, that would have pushed down some brick walls, and the weight and strength so suddenly applied sent Lally flying like a feather. His head struck the stone gate-post and he measured his length under it.[47]

If Reade had not obeyed convention and put into his story a stupid, invertebrate heroine, as passive as a Reade character ever can be, he would not have been obliged, as part of the equally conventional final mat-ing process, to marry Jael to Squire Raby, Little's aged uncle. That he dallied with the thought of doing otherwise is shown by his having the hero's mother take Jael in hand and successfully teach her etiquette, according to the best fairy godmother magic method. For a modern instance of an old, old story, see Shaw's *Pygmalion,* and do not laugh too hard at Reade. Restraint of amusement, however, may be difficult for some readers of the following description. Jael has been trained sufficiently to be ready for her début at a formal party.

> [Jael] was blonde, and had a face less perfect in contour, but beautiful in its way, and exquisite in color and peach-like bloom: but the marvel was her form; her comely head, dignified on this occasion with a coronet of pearls, perched on a throat long yet white and massive, and smooth as alabaster; and that majestic throat sat enthroned on a snowy bust and shoulders of magnificent breadth, depth, grandeur, and beauty. Altogether it approached the gigantic; but so lovely was the swell of the broad white bosom, and so exquisite the white and polished skin of the mighty shoulders adorned with two deep dimples, that the awe this grand physique excited was mingled with profound admiration.[48]

At the party Mrs. Little eloquently urges that her son should marry Jael, stressing her face, figure, sense, and heroic devotion; but he asserts that he has only "a great affection and respect for her" and calls her "my sister and my dear friend."[49] There is no doubt where Reade's affections lie: why is he so unkind to his hero?

Jael, though the most impressive, distinct, and alive of her tribe, is not the last. Phoebe Dale, in *A Simpleton,* Reade describes as "the well-fed, erect rustic, with broad, full bust and massive shoulder, and arm as hard as a rock with health and constant use," and he says she belongs "to a small class of women in this island who are not too high to use their arms, not too low to cultivate their minds."[50] She is the victim of a consuming, all-forgiving passion for her philandering husband, and goes pioneering with him to South Africa.

Jael's final presentment is as Deborah Brent in *Singleheart, and Doubleface.* When her sister's drunken husband, James Mansell, wishes to force his way to his wife's room, she "shook him to and fro as a dog does a rat, then . . . with the double power of her loins and her great long arms shot him all across the room into the armchair with such an impetus that the chair went crashing against the wall, and the man in it head down, feet up."[51]

A last word about one way in which the reality of all these characters may be decreased by the demands of the plot and the requirements of Victorian romance. The flirt, the woman of passion, the country damsel are all capable of the self-sacrifice which will bring about if not a happy, at least a conventionally virtuous

ending for the novels. Peg Woffington, the actress, resigns Mr. Vane, whom she has been fondly cosmopolitanizing, to Mrs. Vane, who has come up from the country to London to see her husband. Coquettish Rose Mayfield (in *Clouds and Sunshine*) yields her farmer cousin, whom she might have had on her string, to Rachel, reduced to reaping through a villain's betrayal. Just as Jael Dence resigns Henry Little to Grace Carden, so Mercy Vint, *Griffith Gaunt's* second wife, gives him up to his first wife, Kate. When it is considered that the reconciliation of the two wives was suggested, as the notebooks show, by a newspaper clipping, it may be contended that the point of lack of realism in this instance is not well taken. Dependence on this kind of fact, however, merely indicates the weakness of the documentary system in the hands of a romancer, who, sooner or later, will find in the news an example of the kind that warms his imagination. The essence of news, moreover, is not reality, but the exceptional. Reade's probable private opinion about the embracing cordiality between feminine rivals which sugared so many of his conclusions is expressed in his comment on a French play, *Jeanne.* "Utterly false ad finem. Women are not so generous to women." (*Magd. Coll.,* p. 4.)

[1] The extant notebooks are in the London Library. Passages from them in this article are quoted by permission of the Committee of that library, and its librarian, Dr. C. Hagbert Wright.

[2] *Readiana: The Legal Vocabulary.*

[3] *It is Never too Late to Mend,* chap. LXXXV.

[4] *A Woman Hater,* chap. XXXII.

[5] *A Woman Hater,* chap. XIV.

[6] *Love Me Little, Love Me Long,* chap. XIV.

[7] Chap. VI.

[8] Chap. IX.

[9] Chap. XXXVI.

[10] Chap. II.

[11] Chap. XVI.

[12] Chap. III.

[13] Chap. XXV.

[14] Chap. II.

[15] *The Cloister and the Hearth,* chap. XXXVI.

[16] Chap. V.

[17] *The Cloister and the Hearth,* chap. XXXVI.

[18] *Ibid.*

[19] Chap. XLIX.

[20] Chap. XCIV.

[21] Chap. XXXV. This incident is anticipated in *Griffith Gaunt* (chap. xx) in a speech by Jane, a discharged servant, which indicated Reade's belief that women commit suicide without due cause: "What will father say? He'll give me a hiding. For two pins I'd drown myself in the mere."

[22] Chap. XXXIX.

[23] Chap. XVII or XIX (according to edition).

[24] *Good Stories of Man and Other Animals: Doubles.*

[25] Chap. XXXII or XXXIV (according to edition).

[26] Chap. II.

[27] Chap. III.

[28] Chap. XII.

[29] Chap. XVI.

[30] Chap. III.

[31] Chap. XL.

[32] End chap. VIII. beginning chap. IX.

[33] Chap. XV.

[34] Chap. XIX.

[35] Chap. XX.

[36] Chap. LI.

[37] Chap. I.

[38] Chap. XXXIV.

[39] Chap. XXXVIII.

[40] Chap. XIV.

[41] Chap. XVI.

[42] Chap. II.

[43] Chap. XXXIII.

[44] Chap. XXXI.

[45] *Ibid.*

[46] Chap. XXXIII.

[47] Chap. XXXIX.

[48] Chap. XLI.

[49] Chap. XLII.

[50] Chap. IV.

[51] Chap. II.

Emerson Grant Sutcliffe (essay date 1945)

SOURCE: "Unique and Repeated Situations and Themes in Reade's Fiction," in *PMLA,* Vol. 60, March, 1945, pp. 221-30.

[*In the following excerpt, Sutcliffe discusses plot devices in Reade's novels.*]

Charles Reade had the romancer's fondness for startling and rare, even unparalleled incidents, and heaped up thousands of such incidents in his thoroughly documented notebooks.[1] Yet throughout his fiction he utilized the same formulas and situations over and over again. Here is an anomaly which demands analysis and explanation.

I

The melodrama and the romance (and to some degree the epic) must be made up of swift successions of startling incident. Under the heading of "Striking and Pictorial Incidents" Reade collected in his notebooks the materials which made his novels "sensational," the "matter-of-fact romances" that he desired them to be.[2] Wrecks of vessels,[3] and explosions of a forge,[4] of a grindstone,[5] of a chimney,[6] and in a mine,[7] are matched by such headings as "Accidents," "Disasters," "Wrecks," "Fire," "Burst," in his notebooks. Life-and-death physical encounters are another type of violent incident that forms a necessary part of the plot of any Reade novel. "Pen in hand," he confesses, "I am fond of hot passions and pictorial incidents."[8]

Though he could string together one lively incident after another—as he demonstrates brilliantly, if too lavishly, in *The Cloister and the Hearth,* he was aware that life is never so continuously exciting as his romances. Yet he was never fully at ease in depicting quiet scenes, and always apologized for them when they seemed to him necessary, having a fear that he would thereby lose readers. "I have described in full this day," he says of an eventless twenty-four hours in Gerard's and Denys' march, "because it must stand in this narrative as the representative of many such days. . . . Stirring events come by fits and starts. . . . Life is an intermittent fever. Now all narrators . . . are compelled to slur these barren portions of time,—or else line trunks."[9] He admits that "life has been mainly composed in all ages" of "ordinary personages and incidents,"[10] but he acts on the principle that "Interest flags when trouble ceases."[11]

A long apology to the same effect begins chapter XLVIII of *Hard Cash.* Once more he admits that "No life was ever yet a play: I mean an unbroken sequence of dramatic incidents." But then he takes up and answers a young critic's objection to the sensational writer's falsification of life. "The gospels skip fifteen years of the most interesting life Creation has witnessed. . . . Epics, dramas, novels, histories, chronicles, reports of trials at law . . . all narratives . . . except those which . . . nobody reads, abridge the uninteresting facts . . . and dwell as Nature never did on the interesting." He asks his readers to be patient while he dwells on a quiet year which has succeeded "a year big with strange events."

He gives vent to uneasy distress many times in *Love Me Little, Love Me Long.* This early novel is a quiet love story which pictures county society in Trollope's fashion. It will cause fewer twentieth century readers to laugh at its author's melodramatic violence than any of his other novels. But he wrote it with the same attitude that appears elsewhere: "In the absence of striking incidents, it may be well to notice the progress of character."[12] "Should these characters," he says in the preface, "imbedded in carpet incidents, interest the public at all, they will probably reappear in more potent scenes." Though Mrs. Bazagette says in the first chapter that "great troubles only come in stories," Reade himself refers to "our mild tale";[13] says sympathetically that Arthur, a youngster, "sought out with care such wild romances as give entirely false views of life";[14] and in a footnote defines "domestic" derisively as "Latin for 'tame.' Ex., . . . 'story of domestic interest,' or 'chronicle of small beer'."[15] He asserts, too, that as David Dodd told sea yarns his hearers "were away in thought out of a carpeted temple of wax, small talk, nonentity, and nonentities, away to sea breezes."[16]

When sea-breezes blow through the pages of Reade's novels, out of the ordinary things occur that have little to do with the typical and the universal. In theory Reade preferred the incident that in one way or another seemed to him absolutely new. Early in his writing career, in *Peg Woffington* (1852), the idea of the "matter-of-fact romance" was dawning in his mind, for he speaks approvingly of "one striking incident" in "a piece deficient in facts."[17] In another early work, *Clouds and Sunshine* (before 1854) based on George Sand's *Claudie,* he rejoices in "a strange situation. . . . Marriage offered to a woman

before a man's face who had tried to kill himself for her but yesterday; and offered by a man who had neglected her entirely for five years, and had declined her under more favorable circumstances."[18] In his first long novel, *It is Never too Late to Mend* (1856), he again shows his bent toward the extraordinary. Parson Eden interrogated Gilso, an old soldier, about his life and "fished up all the pearls—the more remarkable passages";[19] and leter in the same novel Reade expresses satisfaction with his selection of another episode by speaking of "the features of this strange incident."[20]

He exults openly in the novelty of three of the incidents in *The Cloister and the Hearth* (1861). He calls the painting of an enemy's corpse with phosphorus an event "unparalleled in the history of mankind";[21] a hired assassin's saving of his intended victim from suicide by drowning "perhaps without a parallel in the history of mankind";[22] the circumstances under which Brother Clement lives with Margaret, "to the best of my belief, unique."[23] He boasts in like manner of incidents in later novels.[24]

He shows in a negative way also that he prizes the unexampled situation; that he does not want to attempt what has too often been done before. To tell how onlookers at a gaming palace gradually become players "would be to write a little comedy that others have already written."[25] "A company of pilgrims" he declares "a subject too well painted by others for me to go and daub."[26] Concerning a babes-in-the-wood episode, he says he does not wish "to dwell too long on what has been so often and so well written by others."[27] "The horrors of entombment in a mine have. . . been described better than any other calamity which befalls living men," he says in connection with such a scene; and he finds his only justification in "the true characteristic feature of *this* sad scene . . . an assassin and his victims were involved in one terrible calamity."[28]

II

Yet when a writer with a melodramatic and romantic mind selects for eventual fictional use materials to put in his notebooks, a curious contradiction results. It appears that the unusual itself falls into patterns and can be classified. The same thing is true of those lurid items which have always shared space with more sober records in respectable newspapers, and from which the tabloids of our day draw their principal sustenance. In the press, at least, history repeats both its dignities and grotesqueries. It is to be expected, then, that Reade's notebooks, largely dependent on newspaper clippings, should show an attraction towards both the startling, and the startling which recurs. It is hard to determine how far life itself, journalists' ideas of what people like to read about, and Reade's own attraction to certain types of abnormal, vivid incident are individually responsible for such recurrence. But the reappearance of some kinds of incident is undeniably conspicuous. Women in men's clothes, premature interment, fires, fights, explosions, accidents, wrecks, disasters are perennial yet extraordinary events which are among the staples of journalism and of Reade's notebooks and novels.

Such an explanation can only partly account for the most peculiar feature of the fiction of a man who stressed the unparalleled and the unique in incident, and who made vast accumulations of such incidents in his notebooks. The fact is that he ever and again employed not only the odd but also the usual situation, the situation that belongs to the common stock of the dramatist and novelist. Furthermore, he incessantly pulled out of his fictional grab-bag the same principal plot, and employed twice, thrice, or oftener a great number of minor incidents.

The main scheme of sending a hero away from home, a romantic staple, is used again and again: in *It is Never too Late to Mend* the hero is in Australia, in *Peg Woffington* in London, in *White Lies* at war, in *The Cloister and the Hearth* on the road to Rome, in *Hard Cash* on shipboard, in *Griffith Gaunt* in a distant English county, in *Hard Cash* and *A Terrible Temptation* in insane asylums, in *Put Yourself in His Place* in America (off stage), in *A Simpleton* in Africa, in *A Wandering Heir* in America.

The reasons why the hero leaves home and the consequences of his departure vary, but they are markedly similar. Sometimes he goes to get enough money to marry on: in *It is Never too Late to Mend, The Cloister and the Hearth, Put Yourself in His Place.* In *A Simpleton* he goes to get enough money to stay married. In *It is Never too Late to Mend* there is a debt on the estate of the hero, in *The Cloister and the Hearth* the heroine's father has long overpaid a debt; and in these two novels, and in *Hard Cash,* the creditor, a designing business man, works against the hero while he is away. The hero's death is falsely reported in *The Cloister and the Hearth,*[29] *White Lies,*[30] and *A Simpleton,*[31] and he is supposed but not really dead in *Hard Cash,*[32] *Griffith Gaunt,* and *Put Yourself in His Place.* The heroine is courted while the hero is away in *The Cloister and the Hearth,*[33] *Hard Cash,*[34] *Griffith Gaunt,*[35] *Foul Play,*[36] and *Put Yourself in His Place.*[37] Attempts are made to seduce the hero while he is away from the heroine in *Hard Cash,*[38] and *The Cloister and the Hearth.*[39]

The hero's being far from home brings about bigamy often, or near bigamy, and especially cases—bigamous or not—in which a woman may truly be said to be "neither maid, wife, nor widow." These situations—and the phrase[40] held, at least in literature, most curious and steady charms for the early and middle Victo-

rians. Reade used the phrase first in *The Lost Husband,*[41] which was one of three adaptations of *La Dame de la Halle* running in London theatres in May, 1852.[42] He used it twice in *The Cloister and the Hearth* to describe Margaret's relationship to Brother Clement.[43] It denotes the bigamous Gaunt's second wife, Mercy Vint,[44] and in *A Perilous Secret* the villain says falsely that Lucy is "neither maid, wife, nor widow."[45] In *Put Yourself in His Place,* when the heroine has just been (apparently) married to the villain, whose perfidy she has just discovered, the comment is made that she might be "maid, wife, and widow all her days."[46] Here, as in the alternative title of *The Cloister and the Hearth*— "Maid, Wife, and Widow"—the heroine, paradoxically, is at the same time "neither." In *Hard Cash,* when Mrs. Dodd does not know whether her husband is alive or not, she is declared to be "wife and no wife."[47] To complete this record of doubtfully marital situations: Bigamy is a vital part of the plot of *Clouds and Sunshine* and *Singleheart, and Doubleface;* and Mr. Vane, who is married, takes Peg Woffington for his mistress as the bigamous Griffith Gaunt takes Mercy Vint as his second wife.

The hero's departure from home on a quest and his love affair with a second woman while on that quest are situations as old as romance. Reade's success with the plot of the travelling hero in his first three-volume novel probably encouraged him to use it in later fiction. His own strong vagrant tendencies are shown in his frequent trips to Paris, and in his maintenance of living quarters at Ipsden, Oxford, and London. Plainly he also satisfied his wanderlust, vicariously, through the journeying heroes of his novels.

Usually not related to this main plot of the hero away from home are further means of creating love interest which are used more than once. For at least three reasons Reade had an interest in clergymen, an interest which affected his plotting: he held a fellowship from Magdalen which demanded celibacy, he fancied himself as lay preacher to the universe, and his mother differed from his father in being an ardent church member. Reade used clergymen thus: A clergyman comes or tries to come between husband and wife in *Griffith Gaunt*[48] and *A Terrible Temptation,*[49] between hero and sweetheart in *Hard Cash.*[50] The comfort of clergymen is looked after by the heroines of *It is Never too Late to Mend* and *Griffith Gaunt:* Susan Merton, of the former novel, straightens Parson Eden's room[51] as Mrs. Gaunt and her maid brighten Father Leonard's.[52] A woman is in church where her lover preaches in *The Cloister and the Hearth*[53] and *Griffith Gaunt.*[54]

The following repeated amatory situations come about without clerical assistance: A passionate woman loves a hero bound to another woman in *Peg Woffington* (Peg), *Hard Cash* (Mrs. Archbold), and *Griffith Gaunt* (Caroline Ryder). The heroine is sooner or later on friendly terms with the wife or woman friend of the hero in *Peg Woffington,*[55] *Griffith Gaunt,*[56] *Put Yourself in His Place*[57] and *A Simpleton.*[58] Reade had no such flattering opinion of what he called "fœmina vera" as these last repetitions might seem to indicate. When he began to write, he had used the situation in *Peg Woffington;* it contributed to a happy ending. Another contribution is made when "bereaved parties console each other." Reade uses this expression when loving women, given up by unfaithful or bigamous husbands, resort to other lovers, who have themselves been unsuccessful elsewhere. It describes the circumstances under which Peg Woffington takes up with Pomander,[59] and Mercy Vint marries Neville.[60]

Some of these situations are obviously as old as fiction, but at the same time especial favorites in the sensational novel. The sensational also characterizes situations in which the love interest is not dominant. A false is substituted for a true heir in *A Terrible Temptation, A Wandering Heir, A Perilous Secret.* A mole is a mark of identification in *The Cloister and the Hearth*[61] and *Griffith Gaunt.* (Cf. the notorious strawberry mark in other sensational novels.)

Death has some connection with the following repetitions, some of which suggest the kinship of the Gothic romance, Victorian melodrama, and the sensational novel. Corpses with dubious identity appear in *Griffith Gaunt,*[62] *Put Yourself in His Place,*[63] and *A Wandering Heir.*[64] There is about to be premature interment (cf. Poe) in *Hard Cash*[65] and in *A Woman Hater;*[66] in both cases the supposed dead man is brought to by water poured from above. A tombstone is set up prematurely in *Love Me Little, Love Me Long*[67] and in *White Lies.*[68] Rings appear on a dangling arm, in *Hard Cash* when the insensible Dodd is under a tarpaulin,[69] in *A Woman Hater* on the finger of a man thought dead,[70] in *Put Yourself in His Place* as a means of identification,[71] and in *Foul Play* on a hand that comes through a wall.[72] In *White Lies* the hero is supposed dead because of the explosion of a bastion,[73] in *Put Yourself in His Place* because of the explosion which wrecks his workshop.[74] Children are killed off by diphtheria (called croup) in *Griffith Gaunt,*[75] *A Terrible Temptation,*[76] and *A Perilous Secret.*[77]

Similar incidents sometimes appear in more than one novel because Reade was expressing a consistent conviction or prejudice. His interest in what he called "medicina laici" often caused a repetition of incidents. In *Clouds and Sunshine* Corporal Patrick would have died if his blood had been let;[78] in *Peg Woffington* Sir Charles Pomander dodges bleeding;[79] in *The Cloister and the Hearth* Gerard refuses to be bled;[80] and in *Griffith Gaunt* a doctor bleeds Gaunt foolishly.[81] Transfusion of blood is an idea in a doctor's mind in *White Lies,*[82] is suggested by Laure for her sister later in the same novel,[83] and is actually resorted to in *Griffith*

Gaunt.[84] As in Molière's *Le Malade Imaginaire* (which Reade adapted under the title of *The Robust Invalid*) and Shaw's *The Doctor's Dilemma,* diagnoses by several doctors differ in *Hard Cash,*[85] *The Cloister and the Hearth,*[86] *Put Yourself in His Place,*[87] and *A Simpleton.*[88] The true cause in all these cases in Reade's fiction—except the last, where tight-lacing is responsible—is that a girl is in love. Reade's own nervous tenseness may be responsible for the fact that his heroes lose their nerve under a strain in *It is Never too Late to Mend,*[89] *The Cloister and the Hearth,*[90] *Griffith Gaunt,*[91] *Put Yourself in His Place.*[92] It may serve to account also for the faints and fits, sometimes followed by brain fever, which especially afflict his heroes, or, sometimes, his villains.[93] His interest in the insane is shown by the fact that a hero is sent to an asylum on a false certificate in *Hard Cash*[94] and *A Terrible Temptation;*[95] and by the fact that a hero is on a ship out of his mind in *Hard Cash*[96] and *A Simpleton.*[97] Prophetic dreams and telepathic divinations especially attracted him: there are sixteen of them in the novels.[98] His amusement at what he called *fœmina vera* caused him to tell of women frightened by a mouse in *Christie Johnstone,*[99] by a rat in *Peg Woffington.*[100]

Though this list of repeated situations is long, and might be extended[101] it is only fair to Reade to say that a catalogue of the incidents which he used only once would be much longer. The keeping of notebooks and the purposive writing of "matter-of-fact romances" made his novels fecund with unfamiliar situations. How did it happen, then, that there are so many repetitions? It seems probable that he followed certain plot formulas for the main outlines of his plot (apparently recognizing his lack of inventiveness here), and that he tied to this chain whatever out-of-the-way incidents he could attach, conveniently or ingeniously. When links in the chain were missing, he again resorted to the minor incidents—whether unusual or usual in drama or romance—which were at the top of his mind because he had used them before. His notebooks show that he was proud of his editorial wisdom in selecting what he called "jewels": incidents buried in some volume of anecdotes, in the newspapers, in the *Annual Register,* or other little read "repertory"; and that he was proud also of his ability to polish them and set them properly. He expected his public to share his enthusiasm for such gems, for the startling incident which he certified as "unparalleled" or "unique." Yet when inspiration flagged, one or more of several things must have happened. He gave his public what, as he knew from previous experience, it liked. Or, having used a plot device or situation before, he saw what appeared a better opportunity for using it; and regardless of any canon demanding that a story-teller should not repeat an incident, with Shakespearian disregard for novelty in plot device he worked it in once more. Or he was impelled to repeat by sheer weariness or forgetfulness or scorn of his readers or a desire to get on with the story. To these explanations must be added, as I have already suggested, the fact that even the sensational features of life repeat themselves, and the fact that his desire to correct social injustice or more positively to improve society's methods caused him to duplicate or reduplicate certain illustrative situations.

III

With regard to the more comprehensive choice of material which gave rise to these incidents, one can hardly quarrel with Reade. As versatile as Bulwer Lytton or Eden Philpotts, he deserves praise indeed for variety and even innovation. He is, most plainly and characteristically, a sensation novelist and a thesis novelist exploiting one or another form of social propaganda. But he also writes colonial novels: *It is Never Too Late to Mend* and *A Simpleton;* novels of the sea: *Christie Johnstone, Love Me Little, Love Me Long, Hard Cash, Foul Play, A Simpleton;* historical novels: *The Cloister and the Hearth, Griffith Gaunt, Peg Woffington, A Wandering Heir;* rural stories: *Clouds and Sunshine* (based on a play by George Sand, but having an Oxfordshire background) and *A Woman Hater.* He brings in the acting or operatic stage in *Art, Peg Woffington,* and *A Woman Hater.* The first believable woman doctor in English fiction is Rhoda Gale in *A Woman Hater.*[102] I know no earlier appearance of the press-agent than Ashmead in that same novel; in him Reade draws a publicity man typical in his disregard for truth in the cause of advertising, but with more heart than many of his species. *Hard Cash* is one of the earliest novels with a pronounced big business element (investment in railroads, banking, the effects of a panic), which appears also in one chapter (XII) of its forerunner, *Love Me Little.* Mention should be made of the mystery and detective ingredients in his fiction, and of his picaresque tale which includes the unique story of the life and murders of a rogue elephant in captivity, *Jack of All Trades,* surely a neglected classic.

One admires Reade's vigor, ingenuity, and versatility; one remembers vividly some of the "unparalleled" situations in his novels. But one deplores the lack of a deep understanding of character and common human relationships, and the lack also of a continuously working artistic conscience, that caused him to seek fame as a novelist too often through the multiplication of startling incidents, many of which other novelists before him and even Reade himself had staled by repetition.

Notes

[1] See my "Charles Reade's Notebooks," *SP,* XXVII.

[2] A footnote to the *Preface* of *Hard Cash* says: "Without sensation there can be no interest." Cf. also *Readiana: The Sham Sample Swindle,* where he commends "striking" and "strong" incidents.

[3] *Hard Cash,* chap. XII-XIII; *Foul Play,* chap. XI.

[4] *Put Yourself in His Place,* chap. V.

[5] *Ibid.,* chap. XII.

[6] *Ibid.,* chap. XXXII.

[7] *A Perilous Secret,* chap. XX.

[8] *Good Stories: Rus.*

[9] *The Cloister and the Hearth,* chap. XXIX.

[10] *Ibid.,* chap. XXXVIII.

[11] *A Perilous Secret,* chap. XXVII.

[12] *Griffith Grant,* Chap. XIV.

[13] Chap. I.

[14] Chap. VIII.

[15] Chap. VI.

[16] Chap. III.

[17] Chap. XIII.

[18] Chap. IX.

[19] Chap. VI.

[20] Chap. XLIX.

[21] Chap. XXXII.

[22] Chap. LXVII.

[23] Chap. XCVI, footnote.

[24] See *Hard Cash,* chap. XXXVII, XL; *Foul Play,* chap. XIX; *Griffith Gaunt,* chap. XIV; *A Perilous Secret,* chap. XXIII; *Singleheart, and Doubleface,* chap. V.

[25] *A Woman Hater,* chap. VII or IX, according to edition.

[26] *The Cloister and the Hearth,* chap. LXXIV.

[27] *A Terrible Temptation,* chap. XXXIX.

[28] *A Perilous Secret,* chap. XXIII.

[29] Chap. LXXXII.

[30] Chap. XXVII.

[31] Chap. XIII, XIV.

[32] Chap. XLIX (David Dodd).

[33] Chap. LXXVI.

[34] Chap. XXXVIII.

[35] Chap. XXX.

[36] Chap. LXIV.

[37] Chap. XXXVIII.

[38] Chap. XL.

[39] Chap. LXI.

[40] Is it proverbial, or improved from *Measure for Measure* (v, 1, 171): "Neither maid' widow, nor wife"? *Jane Eyre* (1847) seems to have ushered in this bigamous era. For Miss Bronte's apparent debt to Le Fanu for the plot, see Edna Kenton: "A Forgotten Creator of Ghosts," *Bookman* (N. Y.), LXIX, 530-531. The Gothic romances are also influential.

[41] Act 1, p. 5, in the Harvard Library copy (Lacy).

[42] *Readiana: The Rights and the Wrongs of Authors,* Fifth Letter.

[43] Chap. XC, XCVI.

[44] *Griffith Gaunt,* chap. XLII.

[45] Chap. XXV.

[46] Chap. XXXIX.

[47] Chap. XLIX.

[48] Chap. XX, XXV, etc.

[49] Chap. XVI.

[50] Chap. XXXVIII.

[51] Chap. XVII.

[52] Chap. XVI.

[53] Chap. LXXXVI.

[54] Chap. XVII.

[55] Chap. XIII.

[56] Chap. XLII.

[57] Jael Dence throughout; Lady Cicely, chap. XIII.

[58] Phoebe Dale.

[59] Chap. XIII.

[60] *Griffith Gaunt,* chap. XLV. Other repeated love situations are these: A leading male character falls off a horse near the door of one who first nurses and later marries him in *Griffith Gaunt* (chap. XXVI) and *A Simpleton* (chap. IV). An aunt or a nurse lives at a distance from the heroine in *Love Me Little, Love Me Long* (chap. XIV), *A Woman Hater* (chap. XXI or XXIII, according to edition), *White Lies* (chap. XXXVI), *A Perilous Secret* (chap. X). At her house the heroine meets the villain in *A Woman Hater,* and the hero in *A Perilous Secret* and *Love Me Little.* In *White Lies* a child is hidden there. There are clandestine marriages or attempts at them in *White Lies* (chap. XXX), *The Cloister and the Hearth* (chap. X), and *A Perilous Secret* (chap. XXV). The heroine's room hides the hero from pursuers in *Hard Cash* (chap. XLV) and *The Cloister and the Hearth* (chap. XIV). A lover is outside the heroine's room in the moonlight in *Hard Cash* (chap. II), *Griffith Gaunt* (chap. X), *Foul Play* (chap. V), *A Woman Hater* (chap. XVII or XIX, according to edition). Duels take place or are imminent in *Griffith Gaunt* (chap. VI) and *Christie Johnstone* (chap. XV). A coach is stuck in the mud in *Art* and *Peg Woffington* (chap. V): in the former story the hero rescues the heroine, in the latter the villain rescues the hero's wife. A father financially embarrassed wishes his daughter to marry a wealthy suitor in *Griffith Gaunt* (chap. VII), and *It is Never too Late to Mend* (chap. LXXX). In *Put Yourself in His Place* (chap. XXVII) and *A Simpleton* (chap. I) a father opposes a poor suitor. A father advises or insists on a son-in-law's taking out insurance in *A Simpleton* (chap. V) and in *Put Yourself in His Place* (chap. VII). A woman's initials are woven in hair into a shirt in *Griffith Gaunt* (chap. XXXII), into a handkerchief in *A Woman Hater* (chap. IX or X, according to edition). A father watches his daughter through binoculars in *A Perilous Secret* (chap. V), and a lover watches his beloved through a telescope in *White Lies* (chap. II).

[61] Chap. XCI. Other plot items in Reade's (and usually in many other novelists') stock-in-trade are these: The heroine of *Put Yourself in His Place* becomes a Protestant nun (chap. XLIII), and in *A Terrible Temptation* a woman disguises herself as a sister of charity (chap. V, VII). The orphan heroine has two guardians in *Love Me Little, Love Me Long* and *A Wandering Heir;* and a male and female protector watch over the heroine and fight with each other in *Love Me Little* and *A Woman Hater* (chap. II). The hero deciphers deeds in *Clouds and Sunshine* (chap. I) and in *Love Me Little;* in *Put Yourself in His Place* he also deciphers brasses (chap. XIX). A locked door, behind which the hero protects himself, is removed

from its hinges in *Hard Cash* (chap. XLV) and *Put Yourself in His Place* (chap. XII). In *Art* and in *A Terrible Temptation* (chap. III) a sister accompanies a woman who comes from the country and leads an immoral life in the city. There are sieges in *White Lies* (chap. XXXIX) and *The Cloister and the Hearth* (chap. XLVII); fox-hunts in *A Terrible Temptation* (chap. XIV) and *Griffith Gaunt* (chap. I); university boat races in *Hard Cash* (chap. I) and *A Terrible Temptation* (chap. XLIV). A bell alarm is set off by an unsuspecting foot in *A Terrible Temptation* (chap. XL) and *It is Never too Late to Mend* (chap. LXV); and one is arranged, but not used, in *White Lies* (chap. VI). Sick witnesses delay a trial in *Hard Cash* (chap. L) and *Foul Play* (chap. LXV); and there is a third delayed trial in *Tit for Tat* (chap. V).

[62] Chap. XXXVIII.

[63] Chap. XXX, XXXIII.

[64] Chap. III.

[65] Chap. XLIX.

[66] Chap. XIII or XIV depending on edition.

[67] Chap. XXI.

[68] Chap. XXXI.

[69] Chap. XIX.

[70] Chap. XIII or XV, according to edition.

[71] Chap. XXXIII.

[72] Chap. LXIII.

[73] Chap. XL.

[74] Chap. XXXII.

[75] Chap. XLV.

[76] Chap. XXXV.

[77] Chap. II.

[78] Chap. III.

[79] Chap. IX.

[80] Chap. XXVI.

[81] Chap. XXVI.

[82] Chap. XV.

[83] Chap. XXXIV.

[84] Chap. XLV.

[85] Chap. III.

[86] Chap. LI.

[87] Chap. XXXVII, XXXVIII.

[88] Chap. II, III.

[89] Chap. XVI, XVII.

[90] Chap. LXI, LXII, LXIII.

[91] Chap. XXV.

[92] Chap. XXXI.

[93] E.g., *The Cloister and the Hearth,* chap. LXI; *Hard Cash,* chap. XVII; *Griffith Gaunt,* chap. XXIV; *Foul Play,* chap. LXIX; *A Simpleton,* chap. XII; *A Terrible Temptation,* chap. V; *A Wandering Heir,* chap. VIII.

[94] Chap. XXIV, etc.

[95] Chap. XX. Cf. also *Put Yourself in His Place,* chap. XLIII.

[96] Chap. LIII.

[97] Chap. XV.

[98] E.g., *The Cloister and the Hearth,* chap. LXVIII; *Hard Cash,* chap. XLIX; *Foul Play,* chap. XV, XX, XXII; *Put Yourself in His Place,* chap. X, XIV, XLIII. Cf. my "Psychological Presentation in Reade's Novels," *SP,* XXXVIII, 533-536.

[99] Chap. XIV.

[100] Chap. III.

[101] For the frequent use of letters as plot links, see my "Plotting in Reade's Novels," *PMLA,* XLVII, 846-848. For frequent adoption in fiction of devices borrowed from the theatre, see my "The Stage in Reade's Novels," *SP,* XXVII, 654-688.

[102] See Louise E. Rorabacker, *Victorian Women in Life and in Fiction* (unpubl. Univ. of Illinois diss.).

Wayne Burns (essay date 1945)

SOURCE: "Pre-Raphaelitism in Charles Reade's Early Fiction" in *PMLA,* Vol. 60, December, 1945, pp. 1149-64.

[*In the following excerpt, Burns considers Reade's theories of art and the influence of those theories on his novel* Christie Johnstone.]

That Charles Reade was interested in art, along with Cremona violins, Scottish herring fisheries, and other such hobbies, has long been known. Coleman listed some of the paintings in Reade's private collection and declared him a connoisseur;[1] Elwin pointed out that he had a genuine taste in art and was the best sort of collector;[2] and Rives added still further information of much the same type.[3] One of Rives' quotations is particularly interesting.

> 1. There is a woman stooping in rather an absurd attitude with her hand touching her foot. Insert at her foot a rose which I could do so that Etty could not tell it from Etty and put a curtain in her left hand, and the absurdity vanishes. We have a woman stealing from behind a curtain, and picking up a gage d'amour which one has thrown at her feet . . .

> 6. Diana waiting for Endymion. Paint out her night cap. Confine her hair by a band glittering in the moonlight, and let this band be surmounted by a crescent as in the picture you sold Mr. Hart . . .[4]

Reade, it would seem, was quite sure of himself when it came to matters of art; and he spoke thus in 1850, at the very time he was writing *Christie Johnstone.*[5]

Yet, despite Reade's pretensions as an art critic, no one (so far as I know)[6] has examined closely what he has to say about art and artists in *Christie Johnstone.* This I propose to do, and by establishing the proper relationship between Reade's theories of painting and those of his contemporaries, I hope to clarify the nature, intent, and originality of the art criticism in *Christie Johnstone,* and thereby give new meaning to the novel itself. Finally, and perhaps most important, I intend to show that Reade's study of Pre-Raphaelite doctrine influenced the development of his "matter-of-fact" theory of fiction.[7]

I

Although Charles Reade dealt with art and artists in other novels, notably *Peg Woffington,*[8] it was only in *Christie Johnstone* that he made full use of his knowledge of painting. The novel is primarily a love idyll,[9] but woven into each of the two parallel romances is a polemic—one dealing with Carlylism, the other with conditions in the art world, more specifically with Pre-Raphaelitism.[10]

Both these are introduced early in the novel. Charles Gatty's first appearance is as a defender of his artistic faith:

With the little band of printers was a young Englishman, the leader of the expedition—Charles Gatty.

His step was elastic, and his manner wonderfully animated, without loudness.

'A bright day,' said he. 'The sun forgot where he was, and shone; everything was in favor of art.'

'Oh dear, no,' replied old Groove, 'not where I was.'

'Why, what was the matter?'

'The flies kept buzzing and biting, and sticking in the work—that's the worst of out o'doors!'

'The flies! is that all? Swear the spiders in special constables next time,' cried Gatty. 'We shall win the day:' and light shot into his hazel eye.

'The world will not always put up with the humbugs of the brush, who, to imitate Nature, turn their back on her. Paint an out-o'-door scene in-doors! I swear by the sun it's a lie! the one stupid, impudent lie, that glitters amongst the lies of vulgar art, like Satan amongst Belial, Mammon, and all those beggars.

'Now look here; the barren outlines of a scene must be looked at, to be done; hence the sketching system slop-sellers of the Academy! but the million delicacies of light, shade, and color, can be trusted to memory, can they?'

'It's a lie big enough to shake the earth out of her course; if any part of the work could be trusted to memory or imagination, it happens to be the bare outlines, and they can't. The million subtleties of light and color; learn them by heart, and say them off on canvas! the highest angel in the sky must have his eye upon them, and look devilish sharp, too, or he shan't paint them: I give him Charles Gatty's word for that . . . '

'Very well,' said Gatty. 'Then I'll say but one word more, and it is this. The artifice of painting is old enough to die; it is time the art was born. Whenever it does come into the world, you will see no more dead corpses of trees, grass, and water, robbed of their life, the sunlight, and flung upon canvas in a studio, by the light of a cigar, and a lie—and'—

'How much do you expect for your picture?' interrupted Jones.

'What has that to do with it? With these little swords (waving his brush), we'll fight for nature-light, truth-light, and sun-light, against a world in arms,—no, worse, in swaddling-clothes.'

'With these little swerrds,' replied poor old Groove, 'we shall cut our own throats if we go against people's prejudices.'

The young artist laughed the old daubster a merry defiance, and then sepaated from the party, for his lodgings were down the street.[11]

The nature of Gatty's allegiance is transparent. It is as though Holman Hunt or the young Millais were speaking;[12] every word fits the Pre-Raphaelite pattern—from the arguments concerning an "out-o'door scene" to the criticism of the Academy and the necessity for reform.[13] To cite further passages and more parallels would be to labor the obvious. One of Ipsden's remarks to Charles Gatty establishes the identification beyond a doubt:

'You, sir,' he went on, 'appear to hang on the skirts of a certain clique, who handle the brush well, but draw ill, and look at nature through the spectacles of certain ignorant painters who spoiled canvas four hundred years ago.'[14]

Reade, it would seem, wanted his readers to know that Gatty was a follower of the P.R.B., just as he wanted them to know that Lady Barbara was a disciple of Carlyle. Both the Pre-Raphaelites and Carlylists were the subject of much controversy in the early fifties, and apparently Reade felt that such topical themes stimulated the interest of readers and helped sell books.[15] Thus, at the very outset of his career Reade began to strive for topicality—one aspect of sensationalism that was to become a staple of his later works.

It would be incorrect, however, to consider Reade's topicality as wholly commercial. He wanted success, to be sure, but he also had other aims:

This story was written three years ago, and one or two topics in it are not treated exactly as they would be if written by the same hand to-day. But if the author had retouched those pages with his colors of 1853, he would (he thinks) have destroyed the only merit they have, viz., that of containing genuine contemporaneous verdicts upon a cant that was flourishing like a peony, and a truth that was struggling for bare life, in the year of truth 1850.

He prefers to deal fairly with the public, and, with this explanation and apology, to lay at its feet a faulty but genuine piece of work.[16]

Since the "truth that was struggling for bare life" was almost certainly the "one great truth" which Reade ascribed to the Pre-Raphaelites,[17] Charles Gatty, as an accredited follower of the P.R.B., assumes a new importance in the novel. To understand Reade's second aim, one must understand his attitude towards Gatty, and the cause he represents.

At first reading, one may be inclined to consider Gatty a weak person, and hence infer that Reade had little sympathy for him or his ideas. But closer scrutiny will reveal that Reade made a distinction between Gatty the lover, and Gatty the struggling young artist—the vacillating lover he treated harshly (Elwin says mercilessly);[18] the artist he treated sympathetically, as in the following passages:

In short, he [Gatty] never left off till he had crushed the non-buyers with eloquence and satire; but he could not crush them into buyers,—they beat him at the passive retort.

Poor Gatty, when the momentary excitement of argument had subsided, drank the bitter cup all must drink awhile, whose bark is alive and strong enough to stem the current down which the dead, weak things of the world are drifting, many of them into safe harbors.[19]

These lines call to mind Reade's own struggles and disappointments. He, too, felt that he was surrounded by stupidity, that he and other original writers and artists had to fight against unfair odds.[20] In 1852, he jotted down the following entry in his *Diary:*

Wait till I get to London, and organize a little society of painters, actors, and writers, all lovers of truth, and sworn to stand or fall together. Why not a Truth Company as well as a Gala Company? *L'un vaut bien l'autre.* Now I think of it, there is, I believe, a company and a steam-engine for everything but truth.[21]

With sentiments like these, he must have felt a keen sympathy for Gatty, and presumably for his Pre-Raphaelite prototypes. At least, it is certain that he later sympathized with Millais, when he was being attacked by what his son called "the rotten criticisms of the period." In 1856 Millais wrote as follows:

I dined at the Garrick with Reade, the author of *It Is Never too Late to Mend.* He is delighted with my pictures, and regards all criticism as worthless. *He has never been reviewed at all in the Times,* although his book has passed through more editions than most of the first-class novels . . . [22]

And in *The Eighth Commandment* Reade explained himself thus:

I can bow to the public when it is right; but I never bow to error and false judgment.

I have purchased Mr. Millais's chef-d'œuvre in the teeth of all the babblers about pictures. . . . [23]

Therefore Elwin was at least partly correct when he said.—

> His [Reade's] own contempt for conventional criticism, his passionate sympathy with the underdog, and his delight in dressing up as a truculent crusader, inspired his espousal of Millais' cause.[24]

But Elwin was unaware of the novelist's intimate acquaintance with Pre-Raphaelite doctrine, and the extent of his sympathy for it. Reade was not more concerned with Gatty's professional battles than with his ideas on art, which are aptly summarized in the following passage:

> 'I have one finished picture, sir,' said the poor boy, 'but the price is high.'
>
> He brought it, in a faint-hearted way, for he had shown it to five picture-dealers, and all five agreed it was hard.
>
> He had painted a lime-tree, distant fifty yards, and so painted it that it looked something like a lime-tree fifty yards off.
>
> 'That was *mesquin,*' said his judges; 'the poetry of painting required abstract trees at metaphysical distance, not the various trees of nature as they appear under positive accidents.'
>
> On this Mr. Gatty had deluged them with words.
>
> 'When it is art, truth, or sense, to fuse a cow, a horse, and a critic, into one undistinguishable quadruped, with six legs, then it will be art to melt an ash, an elm, and a lime, things that differ more than quadrupeds, into what you call abstract trees, that any man who has seen a tree, as well as looked at one, would call drunken stinging-nettles. You, who never look at nature, how can you judge the arts, which are all but copies of nature? At two hundred yards distance, full-grown trees are more distinguishable than the animal tribe. Paint me an abstract human being, neither man nor a woman,' said he, 'and then I will agree to paint a tree that shall be no tree; and if no man will buy it, perhaps the father of lies will take it off my hands, and hang it in the only place it would not disgrace."[25]

Even though the last paragraph is obviously derived from *Modern Painters*,[26] these lines indicate that Reade understood and sanctioned the central aim of the P.R.B.—"to encourage and enforce an entire adherence to the simplicity of nature."[27] Furthermore, when read in context, these lines also indicate that Reade extended his approval to the Pre-Raphaelite method, which, as Gaunt summarized it, was this: " . . . they fitted real people and real backgrounds to imaginary scenes or vice versa, painting these imaginary scenes from nature with the most scrupulous fidelity of detail and pure and vivid colour."[28]

Despite his approval of basic principles and methods, however, Reade was severely critical of Gatty's ancillary doctrines (which were those popularly attributed to the P.R.B.)—as the following quotation illustrates:

> The new-comer [Ipsden] soon showed Mr. Charles Gatty his ignorance of facts.
>
> This man had sat quietly before a multitude of great pictures, new and old, in Europe.
>
> He cooled down Charles Gatty, Esq., monopolist of nature and truth.
>
> He quoted to him thirty painters in Germany, who paint every stroke of a landscape in the open air, and forty in various nations who had done it in times past.
>
> 'You, sir' he went on, 'appear to hang on the skirts of a certain clique, who handle the brush well, but draw ill, and look at nature through the spectacles of certain ignorant painters who spoiled canvas four hundred years ago.'
>
> 'Go no farther in that direction.
>
> 'Those boys, like all quacks, have one great truth which they disfigure with more than one falsehood.
>
> 'Hold fast their truth, which is a truth the world has always possessed, though its practice has been confined to the honest and laborious few.
>
> 'Eschew their want of mind and taste.
>
> 'Shrink with horror from that profane *culte de laideur,* that "love of the lopsided," they have recovered from the foul receptacles of decayed art.'
>
> He reminded him further, that 'Art is not imitation, but illusion; that a plumber and glazier of our day and a mediaeval painter are more alike than any two representatives of general styles that can be found; and for the same reason, namely, that with each of these, art is in its infancy; these two sets of bunglers have not learned how to produce the illusions of art.'[29]

This is Charles Reade speaking, albeit not very originally. The last paragraph probably came from *The Times'* answer to Ruskin's letter in defence of the P.R.B.;[30] but the exact source is not important, since this and all the other arguments represent the conventional staples of newspaper opinion,[31] for the most part written by critics who failed to understand the aims, methods, and accomplishments of the group they condemned. . . .

But if Reade was unoriginal in his adverse criticism, and failed to understand some of the aims and doctrines of the P.R.B.,[36] the fact remains that he was more perceptive and more courageous than most of his contemporaries—for he did understand and defend "the one great truth" which Gatty and "those boys" held so dear. More specifically, he gave unstinted praise to Gatty's picture,[37] and jokingly said that he had always recognized its merits.[38] And later (in real life) he ran counter to prevailing opinion and paid Millais' "Sir Isumbras" an even higher tribute. I quote Millais' son:

> About the sale of this work my mother had a good tale to tell. One evening in 1858, when they were living in London, she was standing outside the house, waiting for the door to be opened, when she was accosted by a grey-haired man in shabby garments, who said he, too, wished to come in. The observation startled her, for she had never seen the man before; and, mistaking him in the darkness for a tramp, she told him to go away. 'But,' pleaded the stranger, with a merry twinkle in his eye, 'I want "The Knight Crossing the Ford," *and I must have it!*' The idea now dawned upon her that he was a harmless lunatic, to be got rid of by a little quiet persuasion. This, therefore, she tried, but in vain. The only reply she got was, 'Oh, beautiful dragon! I am Charles Reade, who wrote *Never Too Late to Mend,* and I simply must have that picture, though I am but a poor man. I would write a whole three-volume novel on it, and then have sentiment enough to spare. I only wish I had someone like you to guard my house!'

And he got the picture! For, though a stranger to my mother, my father knew him well, and was pleased to find on his return home that it had fallen into his hands. Reade was, in fact, an intimate friend of Millais, and when in town they met together almost daily at the Garrick Club.

That he was proud of his purchase the following letter to Millais attests:—

From Charles Reade

'Garrick Club.

'Il Maestro,—The picture is come, and shall be hung in the drawing-room. I cannot pretend to point out exactly what you have done to it, but this I know— it looks admirably well. I hope you will call on me and talk it over. I am very proud to possess it. Either I am an idiot, or it is an immortal work.

Yours sincerely,
Charles Reade.

In another letter he says:—'It is the only picture admitted into the room, and has every justice I can tender it. As I have bought *to keep,* and have no sordid interest in crying it up, you must allow me to write it up a little. It is infamous that a great work of Art should be libelled as this was some time ago.'[39]

In the light of the evidence adduced thus far, one can readily see that those sections of *Christie Johnstone* dealing with art and artists have not always been fully understood. It was not mere chance that caused Reade to make Gatty a painter. Nor was it chance that led the novelist to indulge in whole pages of art criticism. Reade was not an amateur, but a competent art critic— or so he felt at least; and his intention was to write a polemic on art, a polemic of and for his day. In more specific terms his aim was to give a serious criticism of the Pre-Raphaelites: to disabuse them on certain points, to encourage them in their struggle, to aid them in establishing their "one great truth"—in brief, to take upon himself the type of role which Ruskin was later to establish as his own. These aims he fulfilled only indifferently well: his knowledge was incomplete, measured by Ruskin's; his conclusions were often unoriginal and shallow—sometimes nothing more than stale repetition of current fallacies and prejudices; and yet, whether profound or not, his qualified advocacy of Pre-Raphaelite theory and his enthusiastic attempts to defend and encourage Gatty and Millais speak well for his honesty and courage. These facts and conclusions, if sound, clarify the nature and intent of certain passages in the novel, and by so doing give fresh meaning to the novel as a whole.

II

The elucidation of Reade's relationship to the Pre-Raphaelite movement in art also throws new light on still another aspect of his fiction; namely, the development of his theories of documentary realism.

The evidence cited earlier shows that Reade had studied the theories of the P.R.B. as early as 1850—that he had accepted their approach to nature from the very beginning, and continued to embrace this one aspect of their credo throughout the years between 1850 and 1853. Thus, during the very years in which he was formulating his own fictional technique, he was exposed to the influence of Pre-Raphaelite method, which, it may be recalled, was essentially this:

> They [the P.R.B.] fitted real people and real backgrounds to imaginary scenes or vice versa, painting these imaginary scenes from nature with the most scrupulous fidelity of detail and pure and vivid colour. . . . There was no limit to the pains taken to secure accuracy. At Ewell in Surrey, obliging countrymen shot water rats for Millais

and held down sheep for Hunt to copy with the requisite care; and the strawberries in the young aristocrat's hand in Millais' *The Woodman's Daughter* cost five and sixpence at Covent Garden.[40]

In 1853, exactly three days after he had mentioned that he was "busy correcting proofs of ***Christie Johnstone***,"[41] Reade described his own proposed method thus:

> June 20—The plan I propose to myself in writing stories will, I see, cost me undeniable labor. I propose never to guess where I can know. For instance, Tom Robinson is in gaol. I have therefore been to Oxford Gaol and visited every inch, and shall do the same at Reading. Having also collected material in Durham Gaol, whatever I write about Tom Robinson's gaol will therefore carry (I hope) a physical exterior of truth. . . . [42]

The unmistakable similarities in method are made even more striking by one of Gatty's disquisitions:

> 'So I shall go to jail . . . ' [Gatty was faced with imprisonment for debt.]

> Then he took a turn, and began to fall into the artistic, or true view of matters . . .

> 'Look here, Christie,' said he, 'I am sick of conventional assassins, humbugging models, with dirty beards, that knit their brows, and try to look murder; they never murdered so much as a tomcat: I always go in for the real thing, and here I shall find it. . . .

Then I shall find the accessories of a picture I have in my head . . . '[43]

Gatty never painted his picture, but Reade wrote ***It Is Never Too Late To Mend.***

Nor do similarities in method constitute the only points of agreement: other similarities (though not so close) go deeper—to the basic conceptions which underlie both techniques. F. G. Stephens (*alias* John Seward), writing in *The Germ,* explained the "why" of Pre-Raphaelite method in this way:

> That the system of study to which this "entire adherence to the simplicity of nature" would necessarily lead requires a somewhat longer and more devoted course of observation than any other is undoubted; but that it has a reward in a greater effect produced, and more delight in the searching, is, the writer thinks, equally certain. We shall find a greater pleasure in proportion to our closer communion with nature, and by a more exact adherence to all her details, (for nature has no peculiarities or excentricities) in whatsoever direction her study may conduct. . . .

The modern artist does not retire to monasteries, or practice discipline; but he may show his participation in the same high feeling by a firm attachment to truth in every point of representation, which is the most just method. For how can good be sought by evil means, or by falsehood, or by slight in any degree? By a determination to represent the thing and the whole of the thing, by training himself to the deepest observation of its fact and detail, enabling himself to reproduce, as far as is possible, nature herself, the painter will best evince his share of faith.

It is by this attachment to truth in its most severe form that the followers of the Arts have to show that they share in the peculiar character of the present age,—a humility of knowledge, a diffidence of attainment; for, as Emerson has well observed,

> "The time is infected with Hamlet's
>   unhappiness
> Sicklied o'er with the pale cast of thought."

Is this so bad then? Sight is the last thing to be pitied. Would we be blind? Do we fear lest we should outsee Nature and God, and drink truth dry?

. . . Nothing can be more humble than the pretension to the observation of facts alone, and the truthful rendering of them. . . . [44]

Such notions remind one of the art criticism in ***Christie Johnstone;*** and Reade spoke much the same way in his own person, about his own fiction. The following pronouncement is typical:

> Fiction is not lying . . . Let any man look into fiction scientifically, for a change, and he will find all fiction worth a button is founded on fact . . .

> Some things, sir, can never be judged without their alternatives. Suppose I had not used that photograph of an Irish lady's life, what trash should I have written out of the depths of my inner consciousness? It was Swift or lies; for that phase of Irish life he photographs has left no other trace. . . . [Reade had been accused of plagiarizing Swift's *Journal of a Modern Lady.*]

> I tell you this union of fact and imagination is a kind of intellectual copulation, and has procreated the best fiction in every age, by a law of nature.[45]

And again, in "**The Autobiography of a Thief,**" Reade explained:

> You have seen Thomas Robinson, *alias* Hic, *alias* Ille, *alias* Iste, tinted in water-colors by me: now see him painted in oils by himself . . .

Add then this autobiography to his [Thomas Robinson's] character as drawn by me in the novel, and you possess the whole portrait: and now it will be for you to judge whether for once we have taken a character that exists on a large scale in nature, and added it to fiction, or, here too, have printed a shadow, and called it a man.[46]

Reade's criteria were "nature" and "truth"—in essence the same "nature" and "truth" to which Stephens had appealed; in fact the analogy extends to the philosophy underlying both conceptions. Stephens wrote:

It has been said that there is presumption in this movement of the modern school, a want of deference to established authorities, a removing of ancient landmarks. . . . If we are not to depart from established principles, how are we to advance at all? . . .

The sciences have become almost exact within the present century. Geology and chemistry are almost re-instituted. The first has been nearly created; the second expanded so widely that it now searches and measures the creation. And how has this been done but by bringing greater knowledge to bear upon a wider range of experiment; by being precise in the search after truth? If this adherence to fact, to experiment and not theory,—to begin at the beginning and not fly to the end,—has added so much to the knowledge of man in science; why may it not greatly assist the moral purposes of the Arts? It cannot be well to degrade a lesson by falsehood. . . . [47]

Reade was even more explicit: "I will just premise," he said, "that there is, *'me judice,'* but one road to truth in literature, or any human thing; viz., the method of the Naturalist and the Jurist . . ."[48]—a statement he enlarged upon several times, but nowhere more unequivocally than in the following explanatory "note":

There is a little unlicked anonymuncule going scribbling about, whose creed seems to be that a little camel to be known must be examined and compared with other quadrupeds; but that the great arts can be judged out of the depths of a penny-a-liner's inner consciouness, and to be rated and ranked need not be compared *inter se*. Applying the method of the novelist, and diverting the glass from the learned historian's method in history, and the daily chronicler's method in dressing *res gestae* for a journal, this little addle-pate has jumped to a comparative estimate not based on comparison: so that all his blindfold vituperation of a noble art is chimera, not reasoning: it is, in fact, a retrograde step in science and logic. This is to evade the Baconian method, humble and wise, and crawl back to the lazy and self-confident system of the ancients that kept the world dark so many centuries. . . . Avoid this sordid dreamer: and follow in letters as in science the Baconian method. . . . [49]

In revolting against established authority and transcendental thinking, both Reade and the Pre-Raphaelites were espousing an inductive method based on "science." Their indebtedness to empirical philosophy is patent.[50]

Finally, Reade, like the Pre-Raphaelites, used all this paraphernalia to create "romance." His was not the romanticism of the Brotherhood in every respect: for one thing, he could never abide the "Middle Ages"; but on many points there was full agreement, as one can see after reading Gatty's valedictory oration (which is Reade to the core).[51]

"Ay," he burst out again, *"the resources of our art are still unfathomed! Pictures are yet to be painted that shall refresh men's inner souls, and help their hearts against the artificial world, and charm the fiend away, like David's harp! The world, after centuries of lies, will give nature and truth a trial. What a paradise art will be when truths, instead of lies, shall be told on paper, on marble, on canvas, and on the boards!"*[52]

Romantic certainly, and something else besides; for the last line is a more concrete version of earlier dicta—notably " . . . there is, *me judice,* but one road to truth in literature, or any human thing . . ." To Reade apparently there was but one "road," one "nature," and one "truth" for both literature and art—an attitude (Pre-Raphaelite in itself) which helps to account for the nature and closeness of the parallels already established; and which materially strengthens the probability of influence.

At this point I shall rest my case. I could cite still further similarities,[53] but it is not my purpose to suggest that Reade's theories and methods parallel the Pre-Raphaelite credo in every respect. Nor is it my purpose, at the moment, to suggest that Reade borrowed any significant part of his documentary realism directly from the works or writings of the Brotherhood. Since the ideas expressed and practiced by both Reade and the Pre-Raphaelites were in the air, so to speak, some few of the similarities I have listed were undoubtedly fortuitous:[54] other forces, every bit as immediate and powerful as Pre-Raphaelitism, were pushing Reade towards some form of documentary fiction. Consequently, a case for direct and extended influence cannot be established, or even argued, until all the other factors which might have affected the novelist's technique have been given close consideration—a task beyond the scope of the present study.[55]

My aim here is simply to establish the fact of influence, whether great or small, particularly in regard to "method"; and if one accepts the evidence I have mustered, the fact is established. Reade could not have studied the Pre-Rephaelite paintings and writings, at the time he studied them, without absorbing some part of their message—the parallels are too close; the circumstantial evidence too convincing. A method so congenial in every way must, at the very least, have tended to reinforce Reade's own tentative gropings towards the "matter-of-fact romance." And so Pre-Raphaelitism, itself a revolutionary movement in art, played its part in the development of a technique in fiction that, as some critics would have it, "burst the bonds of traditional English realism and 'definitely foreshadowed the modern realistic movement in fiction'."[56]

Notes

[1] John Coleman, *Charles Reade As I Knew Him* (New York, 1903), p. 227.

[2] Malcolm Elwin, *Charles Reade* (London, 1931), pp. 118-120.

[3] Léone Rives, *Charles Reade Sa Vie, Ses Romans* (Toulouse, 1940), pp. 61-62.

[4] Rives identifies her quotation as a "fragment de lettre du 23 mai 1850, addressée à Mr. Gillott . . . communiquée [to Miss Rives] par Mr. Bernard Gillott, Birmingham." Therefore the man to whom Reade gave advice so freely was the famous collector, Mr. Joseph Gillott. See A. G. Temple, *Painting In The Queen's Reign* (London, 1897), p. 16.

[5] Two earlier documents indicate that Reade had long been interested in painting. See Charles L. Reade and Compton Reade, *Charles Reade A Memoir* (New York, 1887), p. 104; and also Malcolm Elwin, *op. cit.*, pp. 63-64.

[6] Mrs. E. V. Smith, in the *North American Review*, criticized *Christie Johnstone* at some length, with due emphasis on the novelist's art criticism, but seemed unaware that Charles Gatty was a follower of the Pre-Raphaelites. Cf. Mrs. E. V. Smith, "Reade's Novels," *North American Review*, LXXXII (1856), 368-388.

[7] Although Professor E. G. Sutcliffe ("The Stage in Reade's Novels," *Studies in Philology*, XXVII [1930], 669-672), has dealt trenchantly with the general influence of paintings, "plates," and "pictures" on Reade's fictional technique, his study is brief, and should be supplemented by a more exhaustive analysis—one similar to Leland Schubert's *Hawthorne, the Artist* (Chapel Hill, 1944). As time permits I hope to make such a study, but in this paper I am concerned only with the early artistic theories of Reade and the Pre-Raphaelites.

[8] Soaper and Snarl, conventional art critics, were made to appear completely ridiculous. See Charles Reade, *Peg Woffington* (Grolier ed.), pp. 147-154. I attach little importance to the novelist's remarks, however, even though they agree with Pre-Raphaelite theory in some respects; for the novel and most of the art criticism that it includes were developed from the play *Masks and Faces,* which is as much Tom Taylor's as Reade's. And Taylor, it will be recalled, was a professional art critic:

"During his [Tom Taylor's] lifetime laymen regarded him as an art critic whose authority was second only to that of Ruskin. . . . Toward the more moderate pre-Raphaelites Taylor displayed tolerance." See Winton Tolles, *Tom Taylor and the Victorian Drama* (New York, 1940), pp. 258-266.

[9] Briefly, the plot of the novel is this: Lord Ipsden, cultured and intelligent, but lackadaisical and bored, is refused by Lady Barbara (a disciple of Carlyle); whereupon he lapses into even greater listlessness than before. At this point an eccentric doctor advises him to acquaint himself with the "lower classes" and see what can be done for them. In following this advice, Ipsden goes to Scotland, does his duty by the lower classes, and even becomes something of a hero when he effects a daring rescue in a storm at sea. In the meantime, Lady Barbara appears in Scotland, becomes disillusioned by the unheroic actions of her Carlylean suitor, and eventually learns the true worth of a modern man—nay, a modern hero! They live happily ever after.

That is one plot. The other concerns Christie Johnstone, a beautiful, intelligent, and talented Scottish fishwife, and Charles Gatty, a weak but well meaning and gifted English painter temporarily living in Scotland. They fall in love, and marriage is in the offing, even though Gatty is penniless and as yet unsuccessful in his work, until Gatty's mother appears on the scene. She dissuades him, and doesn't relent until Christie saves him from drowning. They also live happily ever after.

The two plots are rather mechanically joined. One result is that Ipsden is able to lay down the laws of art to Charles Gatty, and then send him on the way to fame and success.

[10] Here and throughout this paper my intention is to use the expression "Pre-Raphaelite" in the sense originally intended by the Brotherhood. See William Gaunt, *The Pre-Raphaelite Tragedy* (New York, 1942), pp. 15-27; and Percy Bate, *The English Pre-Raphaelite Painters* (London, 1901), pp. 7-9.

[11] Charles Reade, *Christie Johnstone* (Grolier ed.) pp. 43-44.

[12] Millais might have served as one of the originals from whom Gatty was compounded (certain resemblances do appear), but the evidence is too slight to make a convincing case. Thomas Faed, a popular painter

of Reade's acquaintance, is another possibility. See Nathaniel Hawthorne, *The English Notebooks,* ed. Randall Stewart (London, 1941), pp. 316-317.

[13] Any standard work on the Pre-Raphaelites will substantiate my views. See, for example, J. G. Millais, *The Life and Letters of Sir John Everett Millais,* (London 1899), I, 115-120.

[14] *Christie Johnstone,* p. 111. Cf. also *Christie Johnstone,* p. 47.

[15] Cf. *A Memoir,* pp. 194, 196, 201.

[16] *Christie Johnstone,* p. 191. This note is appended to all editions of the novel that I have seen.

[17] See *Christie Johnstone,* p. 111.

[18] *Op. cit.,* pp. 45-46.

[19] *Christie Johnstone,* p. 109.

[20] Cf. Charles Reade, *The Eighth Commandment* (Boston, 1860). This book contains much information about Reade's personal battle for recognition, and incidentally (on pp. 208-212) a comparison of the opportunities open to painters and writers.

[21] *A Memoir,* p. 194.

[22] J. G. Millais, *op. cit.,* p. 305.

[23] *The Eighth Commandment,* p. 124.

[24] *Op. cit.,* p. 119.

[25] *Christie Johnstone,* pp. 108-109.

[26] Cf. John Ruskin, *Modern Painters* (New York, 1866), I, xxxii-xxxiii.

[27] *The Germ,* No. 1, January 1850, prospectus [not paginated]. Cf. also John Seward (F. G. Stephens), "The Purpose and Tendency of Early Italian Art," *The Germ,* No. 2, February, 1850, pp. 58 ff.

[28] *Op. cit.,* p. 26.

[29] *Christie Johnstone,* pp. 111-112.

[30] *The Times,* May 30, 1851. Cf. Henry Ladd, *The Victorian Morality of Art* (New York, 1922), pp. 28-31; 249-254.

[31] Compare, for example, the newspaper and periodical criticisms quoted or summarized by Holman Hunt, *Pre-Raphaelitism and the Pre-Raphaelite Brotherhood* (London, 1905), I, 176-179; 204-206; 218; 244-256. . . .

[36] The note Reade appended to *Christie Johnstone,* in which he stated that he had changed his mind about certain topics in the years between 1850 and 1853, might possibly lead one to believe that he had a fuller understanding of Pre-Raphaelitism in 1853 than when he first wrote the novel, but deliberately suppressed his new information and conclusions, in line with his stated purpose in writing the novel. However, there is no evidence to substantiate such a possibility.

[37] I feel sure that this picture had a real counterpart, but as yet I have been unable to identify it. The words "At present in the collection of Lord Ipsden" may indicate that Reade was describing a painting in his own collection. An article in *The Pall Mall Gazette,* June 20, 1884 (inaccessible to me) discusses Reade's collection of paintings, and might possibly furnish evidence to support my conjecture.

[38] *Christie Johnstone,* p. 112.

[39] *The Life and Letters of Sir John Everett Millais,* I, 313-314. Reade also praised Hunt: "Mr. Holman Hunt has just spent three years on a picture. The result is an immortal work." [*The Eighth Commandment,* p. 209.] And he undoubtedly meant to include the Pre-Raphaelities in the following panegyric:

There are now in this country more independent painters viewing nature for themselves, and interpreting her their way, than in any other nation. All the other schools in Europe are stationary; ours is striding on like a giant. In one branch of art, water colors, we are unrivalled. In the other we very soon shall be. [*The Eighth Commandment,* p. 209.]

[40] Gaunt, *op. cit.,* pp. 26-27. For a fuller and more accurate statement of the Pre-Raphaelite method, see Holman Hunt, *op. cit.,* pp. 25-26; 90-91; 132-152; 202; 262-264; etc.; and J. G. Millais' account of the evolution of his father's paintings in *The Life of Sir John Everett Millais.*

[41] See *A Memoir,* p. 197.

[42] *Ibid.,* p. 198. See also p. 199.

[43] *Christie Johnstone,* p. 55. Reade probably wrote the novel *Christie Johnstone* soon after he had studied thieves at Durham Gaol. See *A Memoir,* pp. 194-197; and Charles Reade, "A Terrible Temptation" (included in *Readiana,* Grolier ed., p. 388).

[44] John Seward (F. G. Stephens), "The Purpose and Tendency of Early Italian Art," *The Germ,* No. 2, February, 1850, pp. 58-59. I quote Stephens because his statement seems to be a fair and yet brief presentation of the views of the Brotherhood—D. G. Rosetti excepted. Cf. Holman Hunt, *op. cit.,* pp. 132-139; 147-

152; 172-179; 220-221. See also Gaunt, *op. cit.,* pp. 22-23, 229-231; and Francis Bickley, *The Pre-Raphaelite Comedy* (New York, n.d.), pp. 164, 251-252

[45] Charles Reade, *The Wandering Heir* (Grolier ed.), pp. 195, 203.

[46] Charles Reade, "The Autobiography of a Thief" (Grolier ed.), XII, 4, 6. Cf. also Rives, *op. cit.,* pp. 189-230.

[47] *The Germ,* No. 2, pp. 59, 61.

[48] *The Eighth Commandment,* p. 9.

[49] Charles Reade, *Love Me Little, Love Me Long* (Grolier ed.), p. 201.

[50] Lewis F. Haines gives a full account of Reade's relationship to English empirical thought. See Lewis F. Haines, "Reade, Mill, and Zola: A Study of the Character and Intention of Charles Reade's Realistic Method," *Studies in Philology,* XL (1943), 466-475.

[51] An excerpt from Henry Ladd's explanation of Ruskin's "Naturalistic principles" can be applied (in a general way) to both Reade and the P.R.B. (Ladd, *op. cit.,* pp. 254-255): Ruskin may thus make extravagant claims for the importance of literal representation—for the Real; but it remains beyond a doubt that the Naturalistic principles arise from an emotional concern for the romance, the poetry, the ideal in the natural world. A faithfulness to the facts of appearance is seldom alien to romantic literature. It was especially common to the literary romantics of the early nineteenth century. . . .

Cf. Holman Hunt, *op. cit.,* p. 150; and E. G. Sutcliffe, "Fact, Realism, and Morality in Reade's Fiction," *Studies in Philology,* XLI (1944), 590-596.

[52] *Christie Johnstone,* p. 180 (Reade's italics). See also T. Earle Welby, *The Victorian Romantics 1850-1870* (London, 1929), pp. 3-33; 48-49; and W. C. Phillips, *Dickens, Reade, and Collins Sensation Novelists* (New York, 1919), pp. 109-151. Speaking *ex cathedra,* Reade later explained (*The Eighth Commandment,* p. 251): [The fine arts] are sisters, and alike in heart though not in the face. Wherefore he who hates any one of them cannot really be in the secrets of her sister.

[53] For example, Reade was almost wholly in agreement with the P.R.B. in defining the "purpose of art and literature; cf. Holman Hunt, *op. cit.,* p. 172 with Charles Reade, *Put Yourself in His Place* (Grolier Ed.), I, 687; and in partial agreement with them in his statements above subject matter; cf. *The Germ,* pp. 17-18 and 120-124, with Léone Rives, *op. cit.,* p. 198. For com-

ment on the articles in *The Germ,* see W. M. Rossetti's *Preface* to "A *Facsimile* Reprint of The Literary Organ Of The Pre-Raphaelite Brotherhood . . ." (London, 1901), pp. 16-17, 21, and *passim.*

[54] The development of realism in French painting and literature furnishes an interesting sidelight on the present problem: L'avènement du réalisme en peinture coïncide avec l'apparition des romans de Champfleury: *L'Enterrement à Ornans* est de 1851, *Les Glaneuses* de 1857. A la même heure, romanciers et peintres se détournent avec le même dédain des exubérances romantiques et des épisodes académiques empruntés à l'histoire et à la légende: Courbet, Millet, Daumier, répondant aux préoccupations de leur époque, peignent le paysan et l'ouvrier, le rustre et le petit bourgeois campagnard. . . . Édouard Maynial, *L'Époque Réaliste* (Paris, 1931), pp. 22-23. See also Bernard Weinberg, *French Realism: The Critical Reaction, 1830-1870,* (New York, 1937), pp. 97-116; and Émile Bouver, *La Bataille Réaliste* (Paris, 1914), pp. 214-256.

It is to be noted, however, that Maynial was speaking of a simultaneous development in a group of writers, whereas Reade alone, among English novelists, adopted a "method" resembling that of the Pre-Raphaelites in painting.

[55] I am now preparing for publication a more comprehensive study that will consider Pre-Raphaelitism in relation to other possible influences.

[56] Haines, *op. cit.,* p. 466.

Wayne Burns and Emerson Grant Sutcliffe (essay date 1946)

SOURCE: "*Uncle Tom* and Charles Reade," in *American Literature,* Vol. 17, January, 1946, pp. 334-47.

[*In the following excerpt, Burns and Sutcliffe suggest that Reade's style of documentary realism was influenced by Harriet Beecher Stowe's* Uncle Tom's Cabin.]

I

Uncle Tom's Cabin (1852) achieved an unparalleled popularity, both in America and Europe. That we all know. What is not so well known is the extent to which the novel, and the accompanying "Key" (*The Key to Uncle Tom's Cabin,* 1853) influenced the thinking and writing of European novelists—among others Charles Reade.

Several scholars have noted a relationship between the work of Mrs. Stowe and that of Reade. Léone Rives, Reade's latest biographer, recognizes similarities in method:

Mrs. Beecher Stowe utilise également une méthode analogue, fondée entièrement sur l'observation. Encore à la manière de Reade, elle fait part au lecteur de son procédé, dans *La case de l'Oncle Tom:*

Les divers incidents que composent ce récit sont en grande partie authentiques; beaucoup d'entre eux ont été observés soit directement par l'auteur, soit par ses amis intimes . . . et la plupart des propos sont retranscrits mot à mot, tels qu'elle les a entendus ou qu'on les lui a rapportés.[1]

This is sound enough, but she summarily dismissed Edmund Ahlers's theory:[2]

Reade wurde zu diesem seinem ersten sozialen Tendenzroman wahrscheinlich durch den 1852 erschienenen Roman *Uncle Tom's Cabin* von Harriet Beecher-Stowe angeregt. *Uncle Tom's Cabin* richtete sich gegen die grausame Behandlung der Negersklaven in einigen Staaten Nordamerikas. Das Thema war also ein ganz ähnliches, wie Reade selbst in **Never too late to Mend** hervorhebt (Vgl. S. 76). Die ungeheure Wirkung, die der Roman der Amerikanerin hatte, muszte in unserem Autor den Wunsch wachrufen, such seiner sozialen Tendenz in Romanform zum Siege zu verhelfen.[3]

There is some truth here, despite Rives; and also in Cross's statement: that "***It is Never Too Late to Mend*** . . . was directly inspired by *Uncle Tom's Cabin*"[4]—just how much truth, however, remains to be determined, for none of these scholars has made a thorough study of the influence. Our aim is to make such a study, and thereby prove that *Uncle Tom* and *The Key* (1) furnished inspiration and ideas for the prison sections of ***It Is Never Too Late To Mend,*** and (2) played a vital role in Reade's development as a novelist of the "Matter-of-Fact."

II

At the time *Uncle Tom's Cabin* was published, Charles Reade was still an obscure writer, known only as an adapter of French plays. He was lonely and despondent, and continued so through-out 1852 and most of 1853.[5] But he kept on writing, almost desperately at times, trying to find a medium, a subject, and a method that would bring him the recognition he so much desired. During the summer and fall of 1852 he completed the drama **Masks and Faces** (in collaboration with Tom Taylor); his first novel, **Peg Woffington;** and his first original drama, **Gold.** All were bids for success, especially **Gold.**[6] His hopes and fears for this play he set down in his "diary":

Sept. 27, Magd. Col., Oxford.—Have nearly finished a great original play, a drama in four acts, containing the matter and characters that go to a five-act piece. I suppose I must go to London to push it.

Mem.—Not to let it go out of my hands. Not to trust it in any theatre, because there are plenty of blackguards about, and any fool could write a play that would go down upon this subject. I am glad in one way of having written this play. I want to show people that, though I adapt French pieces, I can *invent* too, if I choose to take the trouble. And it *is* a trouble to me, I confess.[7]

Reade's fears were soon realized, for on October 23 (or perhaps a day or two earlier) the "Surrey" produced "a new piece entitled 'Off to the Diggins; or, London Schemes in 1852.'"[8] Neither Reade nor any of his biographers refers to this play,[9] but on the very day it was reviewed, Reade vented his feelings thus:

Oct. 23, London.—Charles Reade in account with literature—

	Dr.	£	s.	d.	Cr.
Pens, Paper, Ink, Copying		11	11	0	0
Brains,		4000	0	0	
		4011	11	0	

List of my unacted plays: 1. "The Way Things Turn." 2. "Peregrine Pickle." 3. "Marguerite." 4. "Honor before Title." 5. "Masks and Faces." 6. "Gold." 7. "Nance Oldfield." 8. "The Dangerous Path." 9. "The Hypochondriac." 10. "Fish, Flesh, and Good Red Herring." 11. "Rachel the Reaper." I don't remember the rest. I am a little soured, and no wonder.[10]

The appearance of "Off to the Diggins . . ." may account for some of Reade's bitterness, but not all: for months past he had been "soured"—almost to the point of a complete nervous breakdown. No longer a young man, he apparently felt that he must write a "hit" soon, or resign himself to obscurity and failure.[11]

It was in this mood that he received the impact of *Uncle Tom's Cabin.* Here was a book he admired, and one that was achieving unprecedented popularity. No one, so far as we know, has made a full and detailed study of the novel's reception in England, but the general facts are available. Sampson Low, who later became Mrs. Stowe's English publisher, estimated its success as follows:

From April to December, 1852, twelve different editions (not reissues), at one shilling, were published; and within the twelve months of its first appearance no less than eighteen different houses in London were engaged in supplying the demand that had set in. The total number of editions was forty, varying from the fine illustrated edition of 15 *s.* to the cheap and popular one at *6d.* After carefully analyzing these editions and weighing possibilities with ascertained facts, I am able pretty confidently to say that the aggregate number circulated in Great Britain and her colonies exceeded one million and a half.

It was read everywhere, by all classes of people; talk of it filled the atmosphere. Heated discussions, occasioned by it, resounded in cottage, farmhouse, business offices and palatial residences all over the land. The pity, distress and soulfelt indignation in which it had been written, were by it transferred to the minds and consciences of its readers, and the antagonism it everywhere engendered, threw the social life of this country and England into angry effervescence through all its strata.[12]

Furthermore, the dramatic adaptations were almost as successful as the novel itself. "During 1852 almost every suburban theatre, as well as the Olympic and the Adelphi in the West End, presented a version of the American novel."[13] At least one of these Reade certainly knew intimately, for on November 29, 1852, nine days after the production of **Masks and Faces,** the Adelphi presented *Slave Life,* a dramatization of *Uncle Tom* by Mark Lemon and Tom Taylor.

The popularity of *Uncle Tom's Cabin* must have impressed Reade, the seeker after "hits." It is even conceivable that the novel, or perhaps one of its stage counterparts, influenced the genesis of **Gold,** the play which he later turned into the novel *It Is Never Too Late To Mend.*[14] The dates are right. Reade first mentioned *Gold* on August 10, 1852: "I have sketched the plot of an original drama; I am studying for it a little."[15] The theme, as originally conceived, was concerned with prisons—possibly with prison abuses—[16] a type of subject new to Reade, and a type that might have been suggested by *Uncle Tom's Cabin.* And finally, the method Reade used in writing the play resembled Mrs. Stowe's in certain respects:

> One of my characters is to be a thief. I have the *entrée* of Durham Gaol, and I am studying thieves. I have got lots of their letters, and one or two autobiographies from the chaplain. But the other subject, the gold-diggings makes me very uneasy. I feel my lack of facts at every turn.[17]

However, since the play, as finally produced and printed, did not include the prison section, but was constructed around the other subject, the "gold-diggings," we have no direct evidence to prove that *Uncle Tom* influenced the writing of **Gold.** We are merely suggesting a possibility.

III

But whether or not *Uncle Tom's Cabin* gave Reade any ideas for **Gold,** it is certain that the novel and *The Key* gave him some ideas for *It Is Never Too Late To Mend.*

During the spring and summer of 1853, Reade was still in much the same mood as a year earlier—a bit more sanguine, perhaps, but still striving to become "one of the writers of the day." The modicum of success he had

achieved only increased his desire for a real triumph.[18] In the meantime the popularity of *Uncle Tom's Cabin* continued unabated; and in the early spring of 1853 Mrs. Stowe published *A Key To Uncle Tom's Cabin,* in which she laid bare her creative process, even going so far as to reproduce whole batches of factual material that had gone into the novel. Reade probably read *The Key* soon after it was published in England; or if not, he must have seen the lengthy review of the book in the *Athenæum.*[19] We do not wish to make too much of the point—it may be mere coincidence—but a short time after the appearance of *The Key* and the *Athenæum* review, Reade began to consider the possibility of turning **Gold** into a novel:

> Mem. If I ever write a novel on "Gold," introduce a Jew and a learned Divine (Chaplain of Tom Robinson's gaol), who meet with a holy horror of each other, battle, argue, find they were both in the dark as respects each other, and that all supposed monsters are men—no more, no less.[20]

This was June 14, 1853. By June 20, 1853, he had come to a decision and had begun collecting more data on prison conditions: "For instance, Tom Robinson is in gaol. I have therefore been to Oxford Gaol and visited every inch, and shall do the same at Reading."[21]

Just how or why he came to this decision is not clear. Nor is it clear why he had decided to include the theme of prison reform. On August 22, 1853, Reade described his plans at some length:

> Aug. 22, London.—Tom Taylor has made me over his chambers. They are in a healthier part than Covent Garden, and I feel as if I could set to work. My plans: I will work hard at my tale of "Gold," whether under that title or another. I will hunt up two men who have lived in Australia, and are very communicative; from them I will get real warm facts. I will visit all the London prisons, and get warm facts from them for the Robinson business. I will finish the "Box Tunnel" for Bentley's *Miscellany.* I will write plays with Tom Taylor—his exuberance makes it easy. I will prepare for publication a series of stories under one title. I will play steadily for hits. I will not be worse than the public—or not too much so. I will write better than **"Christie Johnstone."** The story there is dry and husky. I will live moderately. I will take decisive measures for being out of bed at eight.[22]

These last two extracts from Reade's "diary,"[23] while they do not fully explain the genesis of **Never Too Late To Mend,** certainly dispose of the accepted explanation, which, curiously enough, was originally offered by Reade himself. In a letter to the *Times,* August 26, 1871, he wrote as follows: "A noble passage in the *Times* of September 7 or 8, 1853, touched my heart, inflamed my imagination, and was the germ of my first important work. . . . "[24] Yet Reade's own "diary" proves that he had begun work on the novel as early as June 20, 1853. It is a case of Reade *vs.* Reade, and the "diary" entries outweigh the letter, written years later, in a controversial vein.[25] Perhaps, as we shall hypothesize shortly, Reade meant only to imply that the *Times* article was the "germ," not of the whole novel or the prison sections, but of the prison sections in their final form.

In any case, the most likely theory of genesis seems to be this: Reade (perhaps by some adventitious circumstance such as Coleman described)[26] became acquainted with prison conditions about the time *Uncle Tom's Cabin* appeared. Then, whether influenced by *Uncle Tom* or not, he decided to include prison material in his play *Gold;* but for some reason—probably because of the exigencies of dramatic form—he finally decided to eliminate the prison sections when he came to prepare the play for stage production. Therefore, when he chose to make a novel from his play (because of the influence of *Uncle Tom* and/or *The Key,* or for some other reason,[27] he had certain prison materials, such as prisoners' biographies,[28] already at hand. This was in July and August of 1853, and it seems likely that *Never Too Late To Mend,* as he then contemplated it, was to be a double-barreled adventure story (*Gold* plus prisons) of the picaresque type, treating prison conditions incidentally, after the manner of Smollett, Fielding, Goldsmith, Dickens, and a host of others—but with perhaps an added pinch of Mrs. Stowe's melodramatic humanitarianism. At this point in the evolution of the novel, the extent of the Stowe influence is problematical.

Reade had barely begun work on this traditional plan when the article on the Birmingham prison atrocities appeared in the *Times.* Already at work on the prison sections of his novel, he was quick to see in these warm new facts a subject that would enable him to write "a solid fiction" of three full volumes[29]—with something of the aim, scope, and appeal of *Uncle Tom's Cabin.* And he could do all this within the framework of his original story, merely by sending his thief (Tom Robinson of *Gold*) to a "model prison" and exposing him to certain types of maladministration that were being practiced under the name of the "separate system."[30]

In attempting to reconstruct the way Reade evolved the novel in his own mind, we have been careful not to ascribe too much influence to *Uncle Tom* and *The Key,* but in this last stage of the evolvement we are on more certain ground. The chapters on model prisons (presumably added to his original material after the appearance of the *Times* article) clearly reveal traces of both *Uncle Tom* and *The Key,* and suggest strongly that Reade, in

his first attempt to write out-and-out social propaganda, was consciously attempting to emulate Mrs. Stowe.

IV

That *Uncle Tom's Cabin,* or perhaps the novel in conjunction with *The Key,* gave Reade the idea of doing for the prisons what Mrs. Stowe had done for slavery is really not surprising. Many philanthropists had seen the connection between the evils of slavery and those existing in England; among others, Lord Shaftesbury, who had written Mrs. Stowe:

> You are right, too, about Topsy. Our Ragged Schools will afford you many instances of poor children, hardened by kicks, insults, and neglect, moved to tears and to docility by the first word of kindness. It opens new feelings, develops, as it were, a new nature, and brings the wretched outcast into the family of man. I live in hope—God grant it may rise to faith!—that this system is drawing to a close. It seems as though our Lord had sent out this book as the messenger before his face to prepare his way before him. It may be that these unspeakable horrors are now disclosed to drive us to the only "hope of all the ends of the earth," the second advent of our blessed Saviour. Let us continue, as St. Paul says, "fervent and instant in prayer," and may we at the great day of account be found, with millions of this oppressed race, among the sheep at the right hand of our common Lord and Master!

> Believe me, madam, with deep respect,

> Your sincere admirer and servant,

> SHAFTESBURY[31]

Reade himself pointed out certain parallels in an encomiastic reference to *Uncle Tom's Cabin:*

> The book was "Uncle Tom," a story which discusses the largest human topic that ever can arise; for the human race is bisected into black and white. Nowadays a huge subject greatly treated receives justice from the public, and "Uncle Tom" is written in many places with art, in all with red ink and with the biceps muscle.

> Great by theme, and great by skill, and greater by a writer's soul, honestly flung into its pages, "Uncle Tom," to the surprise of many that twaddle traditional phrases in reviews and magazines about the art of fiction, and to the surprise of no man who knows anything about the art of fiction, was all the rage. Not to have read it was like not to have read "The Times" for a week.

> Once or twice during the crucifixion of a prisoner, Mr. Eden had said bitterly to Fry, "Have you read 'Uncle Tom'?"

"No!" would Fry grunt.

But one day that the question was put to him, he asked with some appearance of interest, "Who is Uncle Tom?"

Then Mr. Eden began to reflect. "Who knows?" The cases are in a great measure parallel. Prisoners are a tabooed class in England, as are blacks in some few of the United States. The lady writes better than I can talk. If she once seizes his sympathies by the wonderful power of fiction, she will touch his conscience through his heart. This disciple of Legree is fortified against me; Mrs. Stowe may take him off his guard. He said slyly to Fry, "Not know Uncle Tom! Why, it is a most interesting story—a charming story. There are things in it too, that meet your case."[32]

In another passage, Reade openly called attention to the parallels between Legree and Hawes—and in a manner which suggests that he wished to acknowledge his indebtedness and thereby increase the effectiveness of his own writing. Hawes is talking to his assistant, Fry:

"Well, Fry, thank your stars that you were born in Britain. There are no slaves here, and no buying and selling of human flesh; and one law for high and low, rich and poor, and justice for the weak as well as the strong."

"Yes, sir," said Fry, deferentially—"are you coming into the jail, sir?"—"No," replied Hawes, sturdily, "I won't move till I see what becomes of the negro, and what is done to this eternal ruffian."

"But about the prisoners in my report, sir," remonstrated Fry.

"Oh, you can see to that without my coming," replied Hawes with *nonchalance.* "Put 40 and 45 in the jacket four hours apiece. Mind there's somebody by with the bucket against they sham."—"Yes, sir."

"Put the boy on bread and water, and to-morrow I'll ask the justices to let me flog him. No. 14—humph! stop his supper, and his bed, and gas."

"And Robinson?"—"Oh, give him no supper at all, and no breakfast—not even bread and water; d'ye hear? And at noon I'll put him with his empty belly in the black hole,—that will cow him down to the ground. There, be off!"[33]

From these two quotations one can begin to see the nature of Reade's indebtedness. First, he considered the two themes (slaves and prisoners) to be similar—a fact which may have influenced the genesis of the prison chapters;[34] secondly, he much admired Mrs.

Stowe's zeal;[35] and finally, if our paraphrase is correct, he hoped to receive justice from the public (i.e., financial and artistic recognition) by a judicious imitation of her "theme," "skill," and "soul."

V

The quotations themselves have revealed that the "theme" and "soul" of Reade's novel derived (in part) from *Uncle Tom;* and *The Key* shows that Reade was to some extent indebted to Mrs. Stowe for his "skill," as we interpret the word, his "narrative method."

Mrs. Stowe's *Key,* it will be recalled, appeared in England in the spring of 1853, at a time when Reade was still casting about for a subject and a method. Reade saw *The Key,* or a review of it,[36] and then on June 20, he formulated his new literary credo:

June 20.—The plan I propose to myself in writing stories will, I see, cost me undeniable labor. I propose never to guess where I can know. For instance, Tom Robinson is in gaol. I have therefore been to Oxford Gaol and visited every inch, and shall do the same at Reading. Having also collected material in Durham Gaol, whatever I write about Tom Robinson's gaol will therefore carry (I hope) a physical exterior of truth.

George Fielding is going in a ship to Australia. I know next to nothing about a ship, but my brother Bill is a sailor. I have commissioned him to describe, as he would to an intelligent child, a ship sailing with the wind on her beam—then a lull—a change of wind to dead aft, and the process of making all sail upon a ship under that favorable circumstance.

Simple as this is, it has never been done in human writing so as to be intelligible to *landsmen.*

One of my characters is a Jew—an Oriental Jew. It will be his fate to fall into argument not only with Susan Merton, but with the Chaplain of my gaol. It will be my business to show what is in the head and in the heart of a modern Jew. This entails the reading of at least eight considerable volumes; but those eight volumes read will make my Jew a Truth, please God, instead of a Lie.

My story must cross the water to Australia, and plunge after that into a gold mine. To be consistent with myself, I ought to cross-examine at the very least a dozen men that have farmed, dug, or robbed in that land. If I can get hold of two or three that have really been in it, I think I could win the public ear by these means. Failing these I must read books and letters, and do the best I can. Such is the mechanism of a novel by Charles Reade. I know my system is right; but unfortunately there are few men so little fitted as myself to work this system. A great capacity for labor is the first essential. Now I have a singularly small capacity for acquisitive labor. A patient, indomitable spirit the second. Here I fail miserably. A stout heart the third. My heart is womanish. A vast memory the fourth. My memory is not worth a dump.

Now, I know exactly what I am worth. If I can work the above great system, there is enough of me to make one of the writers of the day; without it, NO, NO.[37]

This "system," which constitutes a formulation, in brief, of Reade's theory of the "Matter-of-Fact Romance," is in all essentials strikingly similar to what Mrs. Stowe outlines in *The Key*—from Reade's emphasis on various types and methods of documentation to his implied belief that factual and literary truth are one and the same. Reade does seem to depart from *The Key* in frankly avowing that his aim is to become "one of the writers of the day," but this is only a seeming difference. He, too, has his share of evangelical piety (*It Is Never Too Late To Mend* is full of it) and wrote by his own admission, as a reformer, not merely as a novelist.[38] He even went so far as to write a "key" in reply to charges against *It Is Never Too Late To Mend*.[39]

Reade's technique also reveals borrowings of a more specific nature. In many instances he used Mrs. Stowe's very terms: he labeled certain of the materials in his famous notebooks, "nigri loci"; he used the term "dark places" in the novels and in *Readiana;*[40] and in his notebooks he called his proofs of the material in *Never Too Late To Mend* "Key to Sera Nunquam."[41]

Finally, the novel itself reveals that his application of the documentary technique is quite similar to Mrs. Stowe's. His social criticism is fundamentally different in that he blames the men, not the system; but after all, he is not dealing with the same subject. In other respects, his treatment of documentary materials bears a close resemblance to that of his American prototype. His handling of the Birmingham prison atrocities, as presented in the *Times* articles, is a case in point. He culls all the sensational facts available, borrowing freely, even literally at times; and he uses these facts to fit his own melodramatic and humanitarian aims—much as Mrs. Stowe used the personal histories and newspaper articles presented in *The Key*.[42]

VI

Now that the case for the influence of Mrs. Stowe's method has been made, it is necessary to consider the counterevidence. Many forces other than *The Key* and *Uncle Tom* were pushing Reade toward documentary realism. Apart from his personal, intellectual, and sociological background, which certainly had an effect, but which cannot be discussed here, other and more specific influences were at work. Painting, especially Pre-Raphaelitism;[43] the drama, both French and English;[44] empirical philosophy;[45] the traditions of the English novel;[46] and more specifically the realistic and sensational literature of the thirties and forties—all these exerted a demonstrable influence on Reade's art, and all contributed to his theory and practice of sensational realism. In fact, Reade had already used social materials and research techniques in writing *Peg Woffington* and *Christie Johnstone;* and also in writing *Gold*,[47] which may or may not have been influenced by *Uncle Tom*. Hence, we must admit that Reade was on the way to becoming a writer of the "Matter-of-Fact" before the American novel appeared.[48]

And yet the Stowe influence is uniquely important. *Uncle Tom* served as an inspiration and guide to Reade in his first attempt to write fiction of unmixed social purpose; and *The Key* (together with *Uncle Tom*) was one of the proximate influences that led him to modify his creative method, and to espouse the type of thorough-going documentary realism now associated with his name.

Notes

[1] Léone Rives, *Charles Reade: sa vie ses romans* (Toulouse, 1940), p. 197.

[2] *Ibid.,* p. 258: Edmond [*sic*] Ahlers, affirme que Reade fut poussé à écrire ce roman, après la lecture de *La Case de L'Oncle Tom*. Or, ces deux oeuvres n'offrent aucune similitude de sujects, à proprement parler. Ils n'ont de commun, à part le réalisme de la technique, que la peinture de la souffrance humaine. Si l'on veut, Reade a autant fait pour les prisonniers du Royaume-Uni, que Mrs. Beecher Stowe pour les esclaves noirs d'Amérique.

[3] Edmund Ahlers, *Charles Reades Romane und ihr Verhältnis zu ihren literarischen Vorbildern* (Münster, 1914), p. 85.

[4] Wilbur L. Cross, *The Development of the English Novel* (New York, 1899), p. 213. Cf. also E. G. Sutcliffe, "Plotting in Reade's Novels," *PMLA,* XLVII, 835, 843 (Sept., 1932).

[5] Charles L. Reade and Compton Reade, *Charles Reade: A Memoir* (New York, 1887), pp. 177-201. Hereinafter referred to as *Memoir*.

[6] Not one of the three was received at first with general and unqualified approval: *Masks and Faces* eventually became "pretty successful," to quote Reade's own words, and something much less might be said for *Gold;* but the novel *Peg Woffington* (Dec. 17, 1852) and later the novel *Christie Johnstone* (Aug. 25, 1853) achieved in the fifties only a *succès d'estime.* Malcolm Elwin

interprets the evidence differently—in contradiction, it seems, to Reade's own statements. See Malcolm Elwin, *Charles Reade A Biography* (London, 1931), pp. 84-86.

[7] *Memoir,* p. 196.

[8] The *Illustrated London News* (Oct. 23, 1852) described the play thus:

Surrey

> A new piece entitled "Off to the Diggins; or, London Schemes in 1852," has been produced here. The scene is laid both in London and California; and, in the second act, the diggers are shown at work, with all the picturesque accompaniments of dingy linen, spades, pick-axes, cradles and lynch-law weaponry. The bustle, excitement, and fun of the piece are extreme, and promise much success.

[9] Coleman mentioned a French play, *Les Chercheurs d'or.* See John Coleman, *Charles Reade As I Knew Him* (London, 1903), p. 121; and *Memoir,* p. 223. A version of *Gold* in the Harvard Library substitutes California for Australia and turns Robinson into an adventurer. The adapter was Edward L. Davenport.

[10] *Memoir,* pp. 196-197.

[11] Cf. *ibid.,* p. 225.

[12] Quoted by Grace Edith Maclean, *Uncle Tom's Cabin in Germany* (New York, 1910), p. 19. For a more complete analysis of *Uncle Tom's* reception in England, see Clarence Gohdes, *American Literature in Nineteenth-Century England* (New York, 1944), pp. 29-33.

[13] Winton Tolles, *Tom Taylor and the Victorian Drama* (New York, 1940), p. 95.

[14] The origin of *Gold* is not known, unless one is willing to accept Coleman's account. See Coleman, *op. cit.,* pp. 118-119.

[15] *Memoir,* p. 195. The *Illustrated London News* listed *Uncle Tom's Cabin* in "Publications of the Month" on July 31, 1852.

[16] A passage in the essay "A Terrible Temptation" (included in *Readiana,* Grolier ed., p. 388) seems to refer to his investigations of Durham Gaol in August, 1852: "I had also personally inspected many gaols, and discovered terrible things; a cap of torture and infection in one northern gaol . . ."; and the next few lines on the same page may also refer in part to his prison investigations preparatory to writing *Gold:* " . . . in a southern gaol the prisoners were wakened several times at night, and their reason shaken thereby. In another

gaol I found an old man sinking visibly to his grave under the system; nobody doubted it, nobody cared. In another, the chaplain, though a great enthusiast, let out that a woman had been put into the 'black hole' by the gaoler against his advice, and taken out a lunatic, and was still a lunatic, and the visiting justices had treated the case with levity. . . . "

[17] *Memoir,* p. 195. One or both of the autobiographies mentioned might possibly have furnished the basis for "The Autobiography of a Thief," originally intended for use in *Never Too Late To Mend.*

[18] *Memoir,* p. 201.

[19] The review was continued through the following issues: March 26, 1853; April 2, 1853; and April 9, 1853. That Reade was well acquainted with the *Athenæum* at this time seems fairly certain: his first two novels were reviewed at some length and rather favorably (*Athenæum,* Jan. 1, 1852; and Oct. 1, 1853); moreover, in reference to the review of *Peg Woffington,* he wrote a letter that was published in the issue of Jan. 15, 1853.

We cite only the *Athenæum,* but of course many other reviews of *The Key* were also available to Reade.

[20] *Memoir,* p. 197.

[21] *Ibid.,* p. 198.

[22] *Ibid.,* p. 201.

[23] We have quoted only two extracts, in part. See *Memoir,* pp. 197-201.

[24] "Facts Must Be Faced," *Readiana* (Grolier ed.), p. 437. In a "Terrible Temptation" (*ibid.,* pp. 388-389) Reade explained further: the *Times* article was followed by "an onslaught on the gaols" from "a hundred anonymous writers." Then, "I studied the two extraordinary Bluebooks, viz., the Royal Commissioners' Report on Birmingham Gaol, and also on Leicester Gaol. . . . Then I conversed with one of the Royal Commissioners, and he told me the horrors of Leicester Gaol had so affected one of the Commissioners that it had made him seriously ill for more than a month. Enlightened by all these studies . . . I did what the anonymous Press had done on a vast scale . . . : I struck a blow in defense of outraged law and outraged humanity. But unlike the Press, to whom the prison rules are unknown, I did *not* confound the system with all its abuses; on the contrary, I conducted the case thus: I placed before the reader not one government official, but two—the gaoler eternally breaking *the prison rules,* and the chaplain eternally appealing to the prison rules."

[25] Since many of our conclusions are wholly dependent on the chronology of the "diary" entries presented in

the *Memoir,* we find it necessary to acknowledge one seeming discrepancy, previously overlooked: under the date June 14, 1853, appears this statement, "Still, I ought to make a great hit with my drama 'Gold.'" Yet *Gold* was produced on Monday, Jan. 10, 1853, and ran only six weeks. Perhaps Reade wrote "drama" when he meant "novel," or perhaps the authors of the *Memoir* did not transcribe correctly? In any case, since this is the only inconsistency we have found, it is probably more curious than important. Cf. *Memoir,* p. 197.

[26] Cf. above, footnote 14. However, one need not accept Coleman. Since prisons and prison abuses were very live topics in the years between 1849 and 1852, Reade might have derived his interest from newspapers or books. See, for example, Hepworth Dixon, *The London Prisons* (London, 1850), Preface, *passim.* Furthermore, one must not forget that "prisons" had furnished themes for Fielding, Smollett, Goldsmith, and Dickens, to name only four of Reade's favorite novelists. See Rives, *op. cit.,* pp. 236-241.

The preceding suggestions presume that the prison element came first in the genesis of *Gold.* If (contrary to Coleman) the Australian element came first, then it might have brought up the idea of prisons, since Australia was settled partly by British convicts.

[27] Cf. above, p. 340.

[28] Cf. above, p. 338. Some prison chapters in *It Is Never Too Late To Mend* are written in play form, but there is no proof that any of the stagelike dialogue may first have been written for *Gold* and then rejected.

[29] See E. G. Sutcliffe, "Plotting in Reade's Novels," *PMLA,* XLVII, 834-835 (Sept., 1932). Reade had originally planned to write a "two-volume" novel. See Elwin, *op. cit.,* p. 98.

[30] See Wayne Burns, "More Reade Notebooks," *Studies in Philology,* XLII, 829-830 (Oct., 1945).

[31] The last paragraph of a letter from Lord Shaftesbury to Mrs. Stowe, dated Dec. 14, 1852, quoted in the "Introduction" to *Uncle Tom's Cabin* (The Riverside Press, 1881), p. xxviii. Comparisons of a similar nature were commonplace: see, for example, Frances Trollope, *Life and Adventures of Michael Armstrong, the Factory Boy* (London, 1840), II, 67-68, 164-165, 202, 254-256.

[32] Charles Reade, *It Is Never Too Late To Mend* (Grolier ed.), I, 283-284. Mr. Eden speaks for Reade in the prison scenes.

[33] *Ibid.,* pp. 357-358.

[34] Cf. above, pp. 338, 341, 342.

[35] As is well known, Reade himself was a congenitally quarrelsome reformer.

[36] Cf. above, p. 339. *The Key,* we realize, was not absolutely necessary to an understanding of Mrs. Stowe's "method." The anonymous author of *Uncle Tom in England,* for example, borrowed his "method" from Mrs. Stowe before the appearance of *The Key.* See *Uncle Tom in England; or a Proof that Black's White* (London, 1852), pp. iii-iv, 206.

[37] *Memoir,* pp. 198-199.

[38] Many of Reade's tracts and "keys" can be found in *Readiana,* which is a collection of his shorter nonfictional works.

[39] Unfortunately, no copy of this pamphlet is known to exist. See Michael Sadleir, *Excursions in Victorian Bibliography* (London, 1922), p. 161.

[40] Malcolm Elwin (p. 327) apparently did not fully understand what Reade meant by "Nigri Loci." Reade, in his "list of subjects entered as headings" in his notebooks (see *Charles Reade's Notebooks,* p. 108), defined the term thus: "NIGRI LOCI, or the dark places of the land. This is a heading of vast extent, comprising cruelties and iniquities in Prisons, Police cells, Asyla, Ships, Emigrant Ships especially, Mines, Secret or demi-secret tribunals, like the Committee of Privileges, House of Lords, Public Schools, Workhouses, Convents, Factories, violent exclusion of females, China Painters, female robbed of the maul stick, milliners' work rooms, etc."

Compare the terms "Nigri Loci" and "dark places" with *Uncle Tom's Cabin,* p. 404.

[41] See E. G. Sutcliffe, "Charles Reade's Notebooks," *Studies in Philology,* XXVII, 94 (Jan., 1930).

[42] Forrest Wilson has pointed out that *The Key* was not made up of the materials Mrs. Stowe had before her when she wrote *Uncle Tom's Cabin;* that *The Key* has consequently given many critics a false notion of Mrs. Stowe's creative method in writing *Uncle Tom.* We cannot accept this conclusion without qualification; but the nature and extent of our disagreement are of no immediate concern: Reade undoubtedly understood the essential elements of *The Key* as Mrs. Stowe intended them to be understood. See above, n. 19; and Charles E. Stowe, *The Life of Harriet Beecher Stowe* (Boston and New York, 1891), pp. 173-174, 188-189. See also Forrest Wilson, *Crusader in Crinoline* (New York, 1941), pp. 332-333; Catherine Gilbertson, *Harriet Beecher Stowe* (New York, 1937), pp. 172-180; and *The Life and Letters of Harriet Beecher Stowe,* edited by Annie Fields (Boston and New York, 1898), pp. 171, 177, 209.

[43] Wayne Burns, "Pre-Raphaelitism in Charles Reade's Early Fiction," *PMLA*, LX, 1149-1164 (Dec., 1945).

[44] E. G. Sutcliffe, "The Stage in Reade's Novels," *Studies in Philology*, XXVII, 654-688 (Oct., 1930).

[45] Lewis F. Haines, "Reade, Mill, and Zola: A Study of the Character and Intention of Charles Reade's Realistic Method," *Studies in Philology*, XL, 463-480 (July, 1943).

[46] Edmund Ahlers, *op. cit., passim.*

[47] See above, p. 338.

[48] Elwin, *op. cit.*, pp. 40, 67.

Sheila M. Smith (essay date 1960)

SOURCE: "Propaganda and Hard Facts in Charles Reade's Didactic Novels: A Study of *It Is Never Too Late to Mend* and *Hard Cash*," in *Renaissance and Modern Studies*, Vol. 4, 1960, pp. 135-49.

[*In the following excerpt, Smith contends that although Reade drew on factual sources for his didactic novels, he exaggerated and introduced melodramatic elements in the tradition of the sensation novel.*]

'Eccentric fact makes improbable fiction, and improbable fiction is not impressive.'

The Times, 2 Jan. 1864, reviewing *Hard Cash.*

'All fiction, worth a button, is founded on facts,' wrote Charles Reade in the preface to his novel *A Simpleton* (1873). To help him write his novels he evolved a 'system', which can be summed up as the use of a great deal of fact and of a little imagination. The novel was not his favourite medium, so it was convenient for him to have a rule-of-thumb to work by. For him a good plot was essential in a novel. He found invention difficult, and his imagination needed a ground plan of facts to work upon, so he made a virtue of necessity and insisted that good fiction is founded on fact.

In Reade's fourteen novels the proportion and kind of 'hard fact' vary considerably. Sometimes he used factual evidence to substantiate social criticism which is only subsidiary to the main theme, for example the description of a lunatic asylum in *A Terrible Temptation* (1871); the story of the prostitute, Rhoda Somerset, in the same novel; Rhoda Gale's struggles to be recognised as a doctor in *A Woman Hater* (1877); or a businessman's evil practices to cheat the underwriters of insurance money in *Foul Play* (written with Dion Boucicault 1868). But the three 'novels with a purpose'—*It is Never Too Late to Mend* (1856), *Hard Cash* (1863) and *Put Yourself in His Place* (1870)—had as their shaping impulse indignation at contemporary abuses and were meant to silence criticism by their factual accuracy. In *Hard Cash* Reade assumes an air of authority as he writes of Alfred's letter to the Commissioners of Lunacy:

To the best of my belief no madman, however slightly touched, or however cunning, ever wrote a letter so gentle yet strong, so earnest yet calm, so short yet full, and withal so lucid and cleanly jointed as this was: and I am no contemptible judge; for I have accumulated during the last few years a large collection of letters from persons deranged in various degrees, and studied them minutely, more minutely than most Psychologicals study anything but Pounds, Shillings and Verbiage (*Hard Cash,* Chapter 34, pp. 382, 383).[1]

Criticism, however, obstinately refused to be silenced. While the book was appearing as *Very Hard Cash* in *All the Year Round* (28 March-26 Dec., 1863) a Dr. Bushnan protested to the *Daily News* against 'the terrible slander cast upon a body of professional men to which I am proud to belong', and challenged Reade to quote evidence to prove that a sane man could be unlawfully imprisoned in a private lunatic asylum. He replied spiritedly, marshalling an impressive array of cases. (See letter dated 5 Dec., 1868, quoted at the beginning of *Hard Cash,* Chatto and Windus 1895; and letters at beginning of undated Chatto and Windus edition marked 'new edition'.)

When a novelist protests so vehemently that the basis of his social novels is factual, the strength of his social criticism may be tested by comparing the source of the facts with the facts as they appear in the novel. This kind of comparison also indicates how the novelist's imagination works on the 'hard facts' and what he makes of them in the novel as a whole. It is outside the scope of this essay to examine in detail the sources of *It is Never Too Late to Mend, Hard Cash* and *Put Yourself in His Place,* but as an example of Reade's use of factual evidence in novels purporting to criticise abuses in contemporary society, I intend to examine the facts on which were based the prison scenes in *It is Never Too Late to Mend* and the lunacy scenes in *Hard Cash,* as these are more interesting and more successful novels than *Put Yourself in His Place.*

The main source for the scenes in . . . Gaol is the Royal Commissioners' Report on Birmingham Borough Prison after Edward Andrews, aged fifteen, had hanged himself on 28 April, 1853. At the time the prison was governed by William Austin, who had established there the system of confining the prisoners separately. The chaplain was the Rev. Ambrose Sherwin who, after Andrews's suicide, had made a statement about the 'illegal and excessive punishments inflicted on the deceased and on other prisoners'.[2] Whereupon Mr. Perry, the district inspector of prisons, instituted an enquiry.

Among the facts of the Report are these. Andrews was imprisoned for stealing four pounds of beef. It was his third offence. The chaplain described him as 'a very ignorant poor boy' and 'a very neglected desolate child' but 'a mild, quiet, docile boy'. The governor thought him 'sullen' and 'dogged'.

In the prison there were cranks which the prisoners had to turn—10,000 revolutions for a day's work:

> . . . we were assured that, in order to accomplish such a task, a boy would necessarily exert a force equal to one fourth of the ordinary work of a draught horse; . . . that no human being, whether adult or juvenile, could continue to perform such an amount of labour of this kind for several consecutive days, especially on prison diet, without wasting much and suffering greatly (Report of the Commissioners on Birmingham Borough Prison, *op. cit.*, p. vi).

A prisoner who failed to achieve his task at the crank was illegally put on a bread and water diet. Also in the prison was the 'punishment jacket', originally meant to restrain violent and dangerous prisoners but illegally used by Austin as a punishment:

> . . . it must be an engine of positive torture . . . This mode of punishment, —which was of ordinary and indeed almost daily occurrence in the prison during the greater part of the year 1852 and the early part of 1853, which was unquestionably altogether illegal, and was of a very cruel, painful, and irritating nature . . . (*ibid.*, p. viii).

The visiting magistrates were lax. Mr. Howard Luckcock, seeing a boy strapped into a jacket and being told that he had damaged a crank and been violent to the warders, made no inquiry as to the authority for the infliction of the punishment, nor reported it to the board of visiting justices, but

> . . . in the prisoner's presence, expressed his opinion that 'It was very proper; that he hoped he (the prisoner) would soon be sorry for his conduct, and then the governor, he had no doubt, would release him' (*ibid.*, p. viii).

A prisoner who fainted in a punishment jacket was drenched with water. The Prisoners' Misconduct Book was not a faithful record of punishments inflicted. For example, all cases of the use of the punishment jacket were not noted in the book.

After passing several days at the crank, and continually being deprived of his food and punished in the jacket,

On the 26th of April, Andrews broke the bar of his cell window, and again damaged his crank, and his cell was found to be dirty. On that occasion the governor intimated to him that he should not punish him again, but should report him to the justices, and ordered that he should be without his bed till 10 o'clock P.M.; that is, from 5.30 P.M., the ordinary time of locking up. On the 27th, the prisoner broke the glass of his crank machine, and was also detected talking through the window to another boy, and expressing his determination, in coarse language, not to do the work. The governor in consequence visited him, and repeated the intimation that he should not punish him, but report him to the justices. On the same night, about 10 o'clock, the night watchman, coming into his cell to give him his bed (of which he had on that evening been again deprived), found him hanging by his hammock strap to his handkerchief from one of the bars of the window, dead. The chaplain expressed a decided opinion that the sufferings this boy endured, from the punishments he underwent and from the pangs of hunger, drove him to the commission of suicide (*ibid.*, p. x).

The description of the sufferings in . . . Gaol, then, is based on fact. The Report proves the existence of illegal punishments and lax magistrates like the Mr. Woodcock (obviously a play on Luckcock) of Reade's novel. Young Josephs's history and the opinions the chaplain, Mr. Eden, and the governor, Mr. Hawes, had of him are also based on fact.

In the prison scenes of *It is Never Too Late to Mend* Reade used the novelist's appeal to publicise two specific abuses, illegal cruelty practised in prisons, especially in Birmingham Prison by Lieutenant Austin, and the lack of imagination evident in the legalised 'separate' system. He needed ineluctable facts. But he was writing a novel, not a pamphlet, and 'in order to give the glow of life to brute fact it must be transmuted by passion' (Somerset Maugham, *A Writer's Notebook*, 1952, Preface, p.vi). Reade's passion was a burning indignation against inhuman cruelty and senseless waste of human energy, but a contemporary critic considered that it distorted rather than transmuted the facts:

> . . . the general conclusion which we have drawn from a careful examination of Mr. Reade's book, with the authorities on which it professes to be founded, is, that it hardly contains a single statement of a matter of fact which can be entirely depended upon, though every statement respecting . . . Gaol, which it contains, is founded upon something mentioned in the Report of the Commissioners who inquired into Birmingham Prison ('The Licence of Modern Novelists', *Edinburgh Review*, July 1857).

The critic carefully marshals the facts of Josephs's life in *It is Never Too Late to Mend* and compares them with the Report's description of Andrews's life. At first the differences seem trivial enough. There is no mention in the Report that the jacket's leather collar was jagged and so more painful, as Reade described it:

> This collar, by a refinement of cruelty, was made with unbound edges, so that when the victim, exhausted with the cruel cramp that racked his aching bones in the fierce grip of Hawes' infernal machine, sank his heavy head and drooped his chin, the jagged collar saved him directly, and, lacerating the flesh, drove him away from even this miserable approach to ease (Chapter 11, p. 104).

Andrews, unlike Josephs, was not confined in the jacket the afternoon before he committed suicide. He was never deprived of his bed for a whole night, as Josephs is, and the proximate cause of suicide was the threat to report him to the magistrates, not Austin's punishment. (Here, however, it can be argued that Austin had threatened to report him before, but the threat had not induced suicide. Also it is ironical that Austin should threaten the report, declaring that he himself would punish Andrews no more, when that very night Andrews's bed was removed. Reade was justified in making the suicide the cumulative result of ill-treatment.)

The writer points out that there is no evidence that Austin abused Andrews, as Reade made Hawes abuse Josephs the afternoon before the suicide:

> 'I'll make your life hell to you, you young vagabond. You are hardly used, are you? all you have ever known isn't a stroke with a feather to what I'll make you know by and by. Wait till tomorrow comes, you shall see what I can do when I am put to it' (Chapter 18, p. 218).

The writer omits several other divergences between the fact and the fiction. Josephs has served no previous sentences, and he is not rebuked for bad language. Also in the novel there is the sentimental addition of the starving mother for whom the boy stole. Again, all the cranks in . . . Gaol are non-productive, wasting man's energy:

> This clergyman (Eden) had a secret horror and hatred of the crank. He called it a monster got by folly upon science to degrade labour below theft; for 'theft is immoral, but crank labour is immoral and idiotic too', said he. The crank is a diabolical engine to keep thieves from ever being anything but thieves . . . This antipathy to the crank quite overpowered him . . . It cut his understanding like a knife to see a man turn a handle for hours and nothing come of it (Chapter 14, p. 131).

But, according to the Report, the cranks in Birmingham Prison were productive:

> Not long after the opening of the prison, two crank machines were put up, which were used to turn corn mills; subsequently, while Lieutenant Austin was deputy governor, twelve others, and after he became governor fourteen more . . . (*op. cit.,* p. vii).

In *It is Never Too Late to Mend,* the prison chaplain's nondescript character is transformed into Mr. Eden, a kind of Archangel Michael with superhuman persistence and a taste for melodramatic gestures, who insists that the Home Office make an inquiry into the den of cruelty which the prison becomes under Reade's pen:

> The victims of the Inquisition would have gained but little by becoming the victims of the separate and silent system in . . . Gaol (Chapter 11, p. 104).

> A thick dark pall of silence and woe hung over its huge walls. If a voice was heard above a whisper, it was sure to be either a cry of anguish or a fierce command to inflict anguish. Two or three were crucified (N.B. the emotional effect of this exaggerated use of the word) every day; the rest expected crucifixion from morning till night. No man felt safe an hour; no man had the means of averting punishment; all were at the mercy of a tyrant. Threats, frightful, fierce, and mysterious, hung like weights over every soul and body. Whenever a prisoner met an officer, he cowered and hurried, crouching by like a dog passing a man with a whip in his hand; and as he passed he trembled at the thunder of his own footsteps, and wished to Heaven they would not draw so much attention to him by ringing so clear through that huge silent tomb. When an officer met the governor, he tried to slip by with a hurried salute, lest he should be stopped, abused and sworn at (Chapter 18, pp. 211, 212).

It appears from the Report that Austin was a stern disciplinarian, attempting to maintain what he thought to be the ideal prison system, not a sadistic brute, as Hawes is. Mr. Justice Coleridge's words to Austin at his trial may seem a little complacent in view of the cruelties revealed in the Report, but they appear nearer the truth than Reade's emotional denunciation:

> The Court are satisfied, from the character you have borne for a number of years, and from statements in your affidavits, that deliberate cruelty and inhumanity were never conceived by you.

The cumulative effect of Reade's slight but persistent exaggeration of the cruelties inflicted by Hawes and his officers, the suppression of any taint in Josephs's character or behaviour, and the creation of Mr. Eden, are not a convincing and impressive protest against cruelty, but a sensational picture of a melodramatic struggle between devilish brutality and angelic mercy, created, moreover, not from a lurid source[3] but from a sober, unemotional Commissioners' Report.

The lurid quality of the imagination which worked upon the hard facts of Reade's research is amply illustrated by the description of Eden ejecting Hawes from the prison. The first paragraph might be a badly-rendered account of Michael expelling Lucifer from Heaven:

> 'Away! Away! Wash those red hands and that black soul in years and years of charity, in tears and tears of penitence, and in our Redeemer's blood. Begone, and darken and trouble us here no more.'

> The cowed jailer shrank and cowered before the thunder and lightning of the priest, who, mild by nature, was awful when he rebuked an impenitent sinner out of Holy Writ. He slunk away, his knees trembling under him, and the first fiery seeds of remorse sown in his dry heart. He met the printing-press coming in, and the loom following it (naturally); he scowled at them and groaned. Evans held the door open for him with a look of joy that stirred all his bile again. He turned on the very threshold, and spat a volley of oaths upon Evans. Evans at this put down his head like a bull, and running fiercely with the huge door, slammed it close on his heel with such ferocity, that the report rang like a thunderclap through the entire building, and the ex-gaoler was in the street (Chapter 26, p. 286).

These words, written about a living and recently disgraced man, are in questionable taste. Also, Reade's attempt to arouse hatred against Austin by presenting the facts is defeated, for the modern reader, by the over-emphasis of the language and the melodramatic gestures used. The reader's mind, though perhaps responding to Reade's indignation, questions the facts, suspecting that they may be distorted by the violence of the author's feelings.[4]

It is Never Too Late to Mend can be described as a propaganda novel. In it Reade attempts to inculcate an emotion in the reader, hatred against Hawes and his system, rather than soberly to explore a problem affecting society. The situation is therefore distorted to make this propaganda plausible. Contrast Mrs. Gaskell's masterly attempt to see both sides of the employment problem in *North and South,* notwithstanding her intense sympathy with the workers' sufferings.

She, too, possessed the facts of the case. She had read intelligently on the subject and she lived in Manchester where she knew something of the people and their problems; she attended discussions at workmen's clubs and attempted, like her friend Susanna Winkworth, personally to alleviate the sufferings of the poor. But she used her facts, transmuted by sympathy and human understanding, to present a social conflict which makes

its appeal long after the particular situation has lost its significance. To a lesser degree, Disraeli's *Sybil* is still good reading, in spite of the sentimental treatment of Sybil herself, because although it advocates the Young England movement, dead long since, this solution to England's problem gradually evolves after an exploration of English society in which flaws are evident in both aristocracy and Chartists. Reade's novel is not one of patient exploration, but of dogmatic statement.

The novel can be successfully used to explore the human implications of a social problem. It is not such a happy medium for propaganda, because the necessary distortion makes too sharp a divorce between the events in the novel and normal living.

When we turn to **Hard Cash** we find that the lunatic asylum scenes here also have a factual basis. In spite of Dr. Bushnan's protests, a glance at the *Minutes of Evidence Taken Before the Select Committee on Lunatics* (Ordered by the House of Commons to be printed, 11 April, 1859) confirms that there were grave cases of ill-treatment and illegal confinement in private lunatic asylums.[5] Fifteen years after the publication of **Hard Cash** the Reverend Charles Garrett Jones wrote a pathetic comment on an article in the *Pall Mall Budget* which had criticised certain practices in private lunatic asylums and had suggested that closer inspection was necessary:

> I wish it to be understood that I was cast into a ward, and there kept for 15 months with some of the worst cases, whose habits and manners were most disgusting . . . My life in Peckham Private Asylum I consider was much worse than it would have been, had I been imprisoned in Newgate Gaol.[6]

He maintains that, however poorly the inmates are clad and fed, relatives have to pay heavy bills. He describes the kind of trickery exposed in **Hard Cash**:

> Relations are quite helpless against this form of extortion. If they pay a visit to the Asylum the patient is quickly dressed up in decent clothes taken from his own, or some other patient's wardrobe; he is conducted to a handsome suit of rooms, where perhaps the farce is played of sticking a cigar into his mouth, and making him cosy near a fire with a picture book on his knees, meanwhile a couple of attendants told off for special duty on the occasion are ready, with glib patter as to how kindly the patient is treated, so that the relatives go away quite comfortable . . . A fearful sense of abandonment and hopelessness falls upon the partially sane patient, who finds himself confined with human beings who are treated *like brutes* (ibid., p. 3).

And, after the novel, as **Very Hard Cash,** had appeared in *All the Year Round* a contributor wrote:

We all recollect the assaults made upon Mr. Charles Reade for his exposure of the abuses of the madhouse institutions, and many readers are yet disposed to suspect exaggeration, when the probability is that worse horrors have been actually committed; but which, for their unfitness for a work of art, have never yet found their way into a novel of real life ('The Spirit of Fiction', *AYR,* [27 July, 1867,] XVIII, p. 120).

The germ of *Hard Cash* was the case of Fletcher v. Fletcher, in which Reade had helped to free a sane, wealthy man from a private lunatic asylum. Alfred Hardie's confinement, at the will of his hard father who wants his money and his absence, is founded on fact.

At first sight it seems that Reade explores this case more impartially than the cruelties at Birmingham Prison. Alfred is subjected to unpleasant physical restraint at Silverton Grove House until he gives up all attempt to get free, but some of his keepers feel pity for him and even try to effect his escape. Reade indicates that all private lunatic asylums are not the same. At Dr. Wycherley's asylum, whither he is later moved, Alfred is treated like a gentleman and allowed books to continue his studies. Finally, at Drayton House, he himself wins respect although some of the other prisoners are cruelly treated.

These attempts to give a complete picture of private lunatic asylums may have been made by Reade out of deference to Dickens and Forster. At the conclusion of *Very Hard Cash* in *All the Year Round* 26 Dec., 1863, Dickens commented:

> The statements and opinions of this Journal generally, are, of course, to be received as the statements and opinions of its Conductor. But this is not so, in the case of a work of fiction first published in these pages as a serial story, with the name of an eminent writer attached to it. When one of my literary brothers does me the honour to undertake such a task, I hold that he executes it on his own personal responsibility, and for the sustainment of his own reputation; and I do not consider myself at liberty to exercise that control over his text which I claim as to other contributions.

He was clearly disturbed by some of the ideas in the novel, and it has been suggested that the episode of the kindly Commissioner in Lunacy (Chapter 46, cf. *AYR,* Sat. 14 Nov., 1863) was introduced to appease Forster, who was himself a Commissioner and had been offended at some of the earlier episodes in the novel (cf. W. C. Phillips, *Dickens, Reade and Collins: Sensation Novelists,* N.Y. 1919, Chapter 3, p. 115).[7]

So the personal relationships involved in the serial publication of *Very Hard Cash* may have forced Reade to consider his facts concerning abuses in private lunatic asylums in a light less hysterical than that in which he viewed Lieutenant Austin's misdemeanours in *It is Never Too Late to Mend.* However, the central situation in *Hard Cash* is, none the less, given a startling explanation. Alfred's father is a banker, outwardly respectable and fabulously wealthy, but in secret he speculates with his children's money and takes the opportunity of David Dodd's apoplexy to rob him of £14,000. There are many exaggerated incidents which tax the reader's credulity. Alfred is lured to an asylum on his wedding morning, and the reader is spared none of the agonies of the shamed bride, Julia Dodd. Mrs. Archbold, an asylum keeper, is a vampire who pursues Alfred passionately until he impatiently rejects her love, whereupon she threatens him with vengeance. David Dodd is confined at Drayton House. Mrs. Dodd visits him, but Mrs. Archbold takes care that Alfred shall never see her. However, he manages to get a message into her parasol:

> If you are a Christian, if you are human, pity a sane man here confined by fraud, and take this to the Board of Lunacy at Whitehall. Torn by treachery from her I love, my letters all intercepted, pens and paper kept from me, I write this with a toothpick and my blood on a rim of 'The Times'. O God, direct it to someone who has suffered, and can feel for another's agony (Chapter 42, p. 476).

The combination of blood, toothpick and a rim of *The Times* makes it impossible for the reader at this point to take Alfred's plight seriously! Finally Alfred, in a melodramatic scene, escapes with David Dodd while the asylum is burning. Their lives are saved by Edward Dodd, Julia's brother, who has become, in a short space of time, remarkably proficient as a fireman. Alfred is proved sane in a court of law, gets his First Class and is married to Julia.

In *Hard Cash* Reade's hatred for cruelty bred by greed, and his admiration for generous feeling, for affection, for beauty and for the impulsiveness of youth, betrayed him into ludicrous exaggeration.

In *The Quarterly Review,* April 1863, appeared an article denouncing 'sensation novels', the literature which 'preaches to the nerves'. The writer explains the growth of this ephemeral kind of reading matter by the fashion of running serials in periodicals, the development of circulating libraries and the existence of railway bookstalls which offered exciting tales to relieve a tedious journey.

'A sensation novel, as a matter of course', continues the article, 'abounds in incident. Indeed, as a general rule, it consists of nothing else.'

Often it has a superficially didactic purpose:

> Let a writer have a prejudice against the religion of
> his neighbour, against the government of his country,
> against the administration of the law . . . against the
> social position of women who have lapsed from
> virtue . . . against any institution, custom, or fact of
> the day—forthwith comes out a tale to exhibit in
> glowing colours the evil which might be produced
> by the obnoxious object in an imaginary case . . .
> heightened by every kind of exaggeration.

This is a fair comment on the prison scenes in *It is Never Too Late to Mend,* or on *Hard Cash.*

One sentence in the article is particularly interesting to a student of Reade's work:

> The sensation novel, be it mere trash or something
> worse, is usually a tale of our own times. Proximity
> is, indeed, one great element of sensation.

So also, remarks the writer, is 'personality' and many a 'sensation novel' is written from contemporary incidents, the well-known characters faintly disguised. This kind of novel appeals to the reader's love of scandal and challenges his ingenuity to solve the puzzle of identity. In this way Reade used the Austin trial and the case of Fletcher v. Fletcher in *It is Never Too Late to Mend* and *Hard Cash.*

So two of Reade's most important didactic novels accord with a contemporary definition of a 'sensation novel', and from an examination of Reade's use of research in *It is Never Too Late to Mend* and *Hard Cash* it is obvious that even in the novels which had an overtly social purpose, he used his facts as a 'sensation' rather than a social novelist.[8] The 'sensation novel' was the novelistic counterpart of the popular stage-melodrama and appealed to the same desire for crude excitement, and to this end Reade used his facts which were in themselves startling.[9] And although it may be argued that an exaggerated treatment of them was justified to shock the reading public into thought, the evident distortion of fact proves that the novelist was, in part at least, satisfying the contemporary craving for 'sensation' rather than soberly exploring a social problem.

In the Preface to *Hard Cash* Reade protests against the 'little easy cant about Sensation Novelists' with which the madhouse scenes have been met.

'In reality', he continues, 'those passages have been written on the same system as the nautical, legal, and other scenes: the best evidence has been ransacked . . . '

This indicates a danger of his belief in facts as a novel's foundation. If they were facts, no matter of what kind, they were good and ensured artistic reality.[10] When his mind, delighted by the unusual, led him to surprising and startling facts, the result would not be lurid 'sensation' but artistic truth. The 'sensation novelist' of the mid nineteenth century often used facts in this way, but without attempting to justify his practice by evolving a wrong-headed artistic theory, as did Reade.

To discover romance, wonder and horror in the facts of 'real life' was a profitable way of writing a novel in the mid decades of the nineteenth century. There was a large market for this kind of romanticism, possibly a debasement of the romanticism preached by Wordsworth in the early years of the nineteenth century—the wonder and delight in common things (cf. Mario Praz *The Hero in Eclipse in Victorian Fiction,* O.U.P. 1956). Collins, Dickens and Reade all produced the 'sensation novels' which found eager readers and some bitter critics. The writer in the *Edinburgh Review*[11] attacked Dickens as well as Reade for his distortion of facts to produce 'sensation'—particularly in *Little Dorrit.* Each of the three writers, while favouring 'sensation', produced very individual 'sensation novels'. Dickens, in novels like *Oliver Twist* and *Bleak House,* took a broad, general problem, the working of the Poor Law or the transactions of the Chancery Court, conceived the problem in terms of imaginary human beings, set them against a powerfully-evoked background and relied for his effect on comedy and well-timed climaxes. Collins, in his best 'sensation novels', *The Woman in White* and *The Moonstone,* carefully worked out a plot which should tantalise the reader until the dramatic revelation at the end of the book. The subsidiary dramatic climaxes led to the last grand climax. Reade chose specific incidents which aroused his indignation because of their injustice or inhumanity, transferred them thinly disguised into his novel, and relied upon melodramatic climaxes and occasional direct harangues to the reader to get his indignation across. In these books he did not attempt to depict the upper classes or nobility.

There was a great variety of standard in the 'sensation novel' when Reade was writing. The 'sensation novelists' ranged from Dickens and Wilkie Collins to Mrs. Henry Wood and Miss Braddon.[12] *It is Never Too Late to Mend* and *Hard Cash,* in spite of their crudities, have their moments of sympathetic insight into the plights of the characters concerned and are inspired by a genuine zeal for reform, though they are not such good novels as *Oliver Twist,* with its powerful images of menacing evil and of isolated torment, or *The Woman in White,* a classic in suspense and plot-manipulation. Unfortunately, some of Reade's later novels, written for a fashionable public, such as *A Woman Hater* (1877) and *A Perilous Secret* (1884) come close to the empty excitement of *Lady Audley's Secret.*

The particular danger of the 'sensation novel' in its lowest form was its encouragement of 'crooked thinking'.

The novelist pandered to his reader's love of the 'sensational' and the melodramatic while persuading him that he was assisting in the discussion of a 'serious moral problem' of the day. For example, the novelist revelled in the sordid story of an undergraduate's introduction to sensuality and vice, persuading himself and his readers that he was showing, by a high-minded moral story, the dangers of youthful liberty, as in Winwood Reade's *Liberty Hall, Oxon.* This muddled thinking, far from presenting the reader with moral truths, often produced statements of dubious accuracy and moral effect:

> . . . when the soul is good at bottom, vice may be led back to virtue by a tender hand. The courtezan makes often the most faithful wife, the criminal the best Christian, the poacher the most upright gamekeeper and the rake the most sincere adviser. Real vice sickens in its own looking-glass, and regrets; the sinner mediocre is in most danger, for he smiles with his eyes blind-folded (*Liberty Hall, Oxon.* I, Chapter 2, p. 21. Charles J. Skeet, London, 1860).

The writer takes a small fragment of truth and twists it into a lie. It is true that a sincere conversion may take place after an evil life and that the courtezan *may* become a model wife, but the writer is inaccurate and makes sweeping statements unsupported by evidence—'makes *often* the most faithful wife'—and weights the scales sentimentally in favour of the intrinsic goodness of most courtezans. A vicious man *may* eventually realise the enormity of his crimes and turn to better things, but all vice does not 'sicken in its own looking-glass' as Winwood Reade would have us believe. His paragraph can be interpreted: better be a criminal, with 'sensational' adventures and an equally 'sensational' conversion, than a hum-drum sinner whose deeds are not interesting to the 'sensationalist'. Vice is so interesting (from the moral point of view, of course,) that the writer comes to feel a certain affection for it.

Reade's novels are not of this morbid kind. Even in the crudest of them, there is something virile about his writing, and there is no doubt that he was sincere in his desire for certain social reforms. But, for Reade, to emphasise was to caricature and, remembering the ogre Hawes in a novel purporting to expose the cruelties of the 'separate' system and the laxities of Governmental supervision in prisons, and the melodramatic Richard Hardie and arch-vampire Mrs. Archbold in the novel meant to explore the abuses of private lunatic asylums, 'we are bound to protest' with the writer in the *Quarterly Review* 'against the levity which mixes up the solemn reflections which belong to these' (moral) 'aspects of the question with the claptrap devices and theatrical artifices of a fourth-rate sensation story.'

Notes

[1] The edition of Reade's novels used for reference throughout this essay is the Library Edition, Chatto and Windus, London 1895-6.

[2] *The Report of the Commissioners appointed to inquire into the Condition and Treatment of the Prisoners confined in Birmingham Borough Prison, and the conduct, management, and discipline of the said prison; together with the Minutes of Evidence,* p.v. London, Eyre and Spottiswoode, for Her Majesty's Stationery Office, 1854.

[3] There are many instances, in Reade's fiction, of his use of lurid facts in such a way as to make them even more lurid. For example, the scenes described after the bursting of the reservoir in *Put Yourself in His Place* (see Wayne Burns, 'The Sheffield Flood: A Critical Study of Charles Reade's Fiction', *PMLA*, LXIII, 1948, pp. 686-695). But in these scenes Reade is wholly concerned with producing exciting fiction, not with propaganda for the purpose of social reform, which is the subject of my essay. A sensational source was not necessary to 'inflame his most dangerous sensibilities' (as Wayne Burns considers that Samuel Harrison's *History of the Great Flood at Sheffield* [London, 1864] inflamed them in *Put Yourself in His Place*), and a sober source was no guarantee of sober fiction when Reade worked. The Commissioners' Report on Birmingham Prison, which deals with startling facts, has nothing in common with 'the crudities and sentimentalities of Harrison's yellow journalism' (Wayne Burns, *op. cit.,* p. 694); Reade's imagination was such that even soberly-stated facts became lurid.

[4] On Reade's exaggeration of social abuses for which there was factual evidence see Emerson Grant Sutcliffe's comment in 'Fact, Realism, and Morality in Reade's Fiction', *Studies in Philology,* XLI, 1944, pp. 593, 594.

[5] See particularly the Earl of Shaftesbury's comments pp. 14 and 39; Sir Erskine Perry's remarks p. 218. Also cf. Report from the Select Committee on Lunatics, printed 5 Aug., 1859, p. 35—evidence of cruelty in private asylums, and Report printed 30 July, 1877, p. 209—the case of Mrs. Petschler who was illegally confined in Macclesfield Asylum by her sister.

[6] 'Extracts taken from the "Pall Mall Budget" of November 9th, 1878, by the Reverend Charles Garrett Jones, (Rector of Magdalen Laver, Essex), upon the Treatment of Lunatics in "Private Madhouses,"' British Museum copy, dated 1 June, 1885, p. 2.

[7] At this point in my discussion I am indebted to a conversation with Mr. P. A., W. Collins, of Leicester University.

⁸ For a discussion of Reade's failure to produce a serious social drama partly because of his 'sensational' use of realistic effects see my essay in *English,* XII, 1958, No. 69, pp. 94-100.

⁹ 'He chose facts which were as violently colored as his own temperament,' Emerson Grant Sutcliffe, *op. cit.,* p. 583. Nevertheless, it must be remembered that Reade found some of these facts in sober, unemotional documents, as I have tried to show above.

¹⁰ Wayne Burns makes a similar comment, *op. cit.,* p. 694.

¹¹ July 1857. Quoted above.

¹² Reade much admired Miss Braddon and to her he dedicated his long short-story *The Wandering Heir* (appeared in the Christmas number of the *Graphic,* 1872).

Wayne Burns (essay date 1961)

SOURCE: "*It Is Never Too Late to Mend*: The Immortal Part of the Work," in *Charles Reade: A Study in Victorian Authorship*, Bookman Associates, 1961, pp. 155-71.

[*In the following excerpt, Burns discusses the epic qualities of the novel version of* It Is Never Too Late to Mend.]

In a letter to *The Times* (August 26, 1871) Reade wrote: "A noble passage in *The Times* of September 7 or 8, 1853, touched my heart, inflamed my imagination, and was the germ of my first important work."² Taken literally—the way it has so often been taken—this statement implies that Reade had never thought of prisons or prison reform as a subject for a novel before September 7 or 8 (actually September 12) when he encountered the noble passage in *The Times* detailing the atrocities in Birmingham Gaol. But this is not the way Reade intended the statement, or at least it is not the way, in all honesty, he should have intended it, for the *Diary* shows that he had begun his prison researches in 1852, in connection with his play *Gold,* "August 10,—I have sketched the plot of an original drama; I am studying for it a little. One of my characters is to be a thief. I have the *entrée* of Durham Gaol, and I am studying thieves. I have got lots of their letters, and one or two autobiographies from the chaplain. But the other subject, the gold-diggings, makes me very uneasy. I feel my lack of facts at every turn. . . . "

At this juncture Reade was seemingly on the point of dropping "the other subject, the gold-diggings," in favor of his first subject, prisons. Why he followed the opposite procedure is not clear. Perhaps he felt that his

Australian facts, though meager, were more immediately topical and better suited to Keanian methods of staging. In any case he did not abandon his prison investigations until he had "personally inspected many gaols, and discovered terrible things; a cap of torture and infection in one northern gaol . . . in a southern gaol the prisoners were wakened several times at night, and their reason shaken thereby. In another gaol I found an old man sinking visibly to his grave under the system; nobody doubted it, nobody cared. In another, the chaplain, though a great enthusiast, let out that a woman had been put into the 'black hole' by the gaoler against his advice, and taken out a lunatic, and was still a lunatic, and the visiting justices had treated the case with levity. . . . "³

These "terrible things" seemed all the more terrible to Reade because of *Uncle Tom's Cabin.* The conditions of slaves had been likened to that of prisoners by philanthropists and novelists from Shaftesbury to Mrs. Trollope,⁴ and Reade, with the example of *Uncle Tom* before him, was quick to see how readily he could exploit that likeness in a novel based on *Gold*—by sending the thief of the play to prison, and thus reintroducing the prison theme he had originally intended to include in the play: "June 14 . . . Mem. If ever I write a novel on 'Gold,' introduce . . . a learned Divine (Chaplain of Tom Robinson's gaol). . . . "

Reade's plans for documenting the new prison section indicate that at this time he envisaged it as a realistic protest against the cruelties of prisons, cast in the traditional picaresque mode of Smollett and Fielding, but enlivened and made more sensationally realistic through the application of the great system, after the manner of Mrs. Stowe (as revealed in "The Key to Uncle Tom's Cabin"). By June 20, the *Diary* reveals, he had already "been to Oxford Gaol and visited every inch . . ." and was planning to "do the same at Reading"—a plan which he carried out with due thoroughness (July 10-17), even extending his researches to the prison chapel, where, in his own words, he "heard and saw a parson drone the liturgy, and hum a common-place dry-as-dust discourse to two hundred great culprits and beginners. Most of those men's lives have been full of stirring and thrilling adventures. They are now by the mighty force of a system arrested in their course, and for two whole hours to-day were chained under a pump, which ought to pump words of fire into their souls; but this pump of a parson could not do his small share . . . he droned away as if he had been in a country parish church. He attacked the difficult souls with a buzz of conventional commonplaces, that have come down from book of sermons to book of sermons for the last century; but never in that century knocked at the door of a man in passing—nor ever will. . . . "

Though characteristically Readian in tone the substance of this indictment suggests that Reade, following his new system, had been consulting books as well as men, and was viewing "'the Reading system"—with its unique emphasis on religious instruction—from the perspective provided by Hepworth Dixon, in the chapter he devoted to Reading Gaol in his *The London Prisons* (1850). Certainly Reade studied Dixon's chapter later, if not at this time, for in describing his fictional prison, modelled after Reading, he borrowed Dixon's phrases as well as his observations, and in his fictional indictment of "the silent and solitary system as practised at Reading and other County Gaols," he reiterated every single one of Dixon's charges, along with a number of his specific examples.[5]

Of the other books Reade apparently consulted at this time, J. Field's *Field on Prison Discipline* (1848) and Joseph Kingsmill's *Chapters on Prisons and Prisoners* (Second Edition, 1852) are among the most significant. Indeed it would seem that these books, along with Dixon's, provided Reade with dramatic and stylistic as well as factual and philosophic models. *The London Standard,* in reviewing Kingsmill's book pointed out that "from Gay and Fielding to Dickens, various writers of fiction have given us glimpses of the race of thieves, but the creations of these writers are imaginary, and therefore subject to exaggerations; Mr. Kingsmill, however, gives us reality, which far exceeds anything that has ever yet been presented in fictious narrative."[6] In other words Kingsmill's was just the reality that Reade was striving to reproduce in fiction, and he did not scruple to incorporate its effects, as well as its facts, in everything from the treatment of scenic details to the characterization of Parson Eden, the Resourceful Hero of this section.

II

In the light of these borrowings it would appear that Reade had worked out his titular thesis and completed a draft of the prison section long before the appearance of the articles on the Birmingham atrocities. At least it is certain that he had worked out two of his three main characters. Robinson, the thief of *Gold* who exemplifies the titular thesis of the novel, he derived from the "one or two autobiographies" he secured in August, 1852, from the chaplain of Durham Prison. In his Preface to "**The Autobiography of a Thief**" (published separately in 1857 but originally intended for inclusion in the novel) he dedicated "this strange but true story of Robinson . . . to such as will deign to accept this clew to my method in writing. . . . I feign probabilities; I record improbabilities: the former are conjectures, the latter truths: mixed they make a thing not so true as gospel nor so false as history; viz. fiction. . . . Add then this autobiography to his character as drawn by me in the novel, and you possess the whole portrait: and now it will be for you to judge whether for once we have taken a character that exists

on a large scale in nature, and added it to fiction, or here too, have printed a shadow, and called it a man."[7]

While the fallacy inherent in this theory of imitation is no doubt obvious enough, it should be noted, in Reade's defense, that he was consciously abjuring the techniques of Trollope and the domestic novelists (whose works he dismissed as "chronicles of small beer") in an effort to create epic characters equal to what he conceived to be his epic theme. "A 3 vol. novel," he wrote his publisher, "is a great prose epic," and in the novel itself he time and again invoked the epic tradition to justify his methods and techniques, as in his anti-Carlylean paean to the Nineteenth Century, in which, after announcing that he cannot sing the song of gold because he is "neither Lamartine nor Hugo nor Walter Scott," he goes on to proclaim that the present age "is a giant compared with the past, and full of mighty materials for any great pen in prose or verse":

> God has been bountiful to the human race in this age. Most bountiful to poets; most bountiful to all of us who have a spark of nobleness in ourselves, and so can see and revere at sight the truly grand and noble. . . .
>
> I say before heaven and earth that the man who could grasp the facts of this day and do an immortal writer's duty by them, i.e., so paint them as a later age will be content to engrave them, would be the greatest writer ever lived: such is the force, weight, and number of the grand topics that lie this day on the world's face. I say that he who has eyes to see may now see greater and far more poetic things than human eyes have seen since our Lord and His apostles and His miracles left the earth. . . .
>
> When we write a story or sing a poem of the great nineteenth century, there is but one fear—not that our theme will be beneath us, but we miles below it; that we shall lack the comprehensive vision a man must have from heaven to catch the historical, the poetic, the lasting features, of the Titan events that stride so swiftly past IN THIS GIGANTIC AGE.[8]

With such poetic stories to write—and despite his rhetorical modesty, Reade believed he was writing them—there was no time for George Eliot's type of character analysis, which in any case "microscoped poodles into lions." The best if not the only way to create a fictional lion, or thief, was to copy an actual one, employing the techniques of "character painting used by the old epic and dramatic writers" to transfer the thief of the factual autobiography first to *Gold,* then to the novel.

But in fashioning Robinson in this way Reade was not really copying an actual thief; he was copying the actual thief's self-portrait, in which the actual thief presents himself, not as an individual man, but as a type of outlaw common to Newgate and Dickensian fiction. Like Bulwer Lytton's Paul Clifford he is so brave, sensitive, and talented that he could, and presumably would, have succeeded in any type of honest endeavor—had he not been led into a life of crime as a result of personal misfortunes and adverse circumstances. And like Mrs. Gaskell's John Barton and Kingsley's Alton Locke, he is finally led back to the path of bourgeois righteousness, after much suffering and many struggles, by virtuous friends and Christian eloquence. In short the factual thief of the autobiography is himself a literary type, and in transferring him to the novel Reade merely reproduced, from fact, a character he could just as easily have copied directly from any one of a dozen novels.

As for the touches that Reade himself added, in fitting the thief of the autobiography into the novel, they are of no positive consequence, except in so far as he endows Robinson with his own sensitivity to the tortures of the solitary and silent system. Robinson's climactic hours in "the black hole," for example, represent a convincing account of the terrors a sensitive man might experience in his efforts to cope with utter darkness and isolation.[9] Even here, however, Robinson's reactions are more typical than individual; and in many instances they are not merely typical, but crudely theatrical, as in the scene in which he is deterred from reverting to a life of crime by accidentally discovering, at just the right moment, one of Parson Eden's tracts, "The Wages of Sin Are Death." As the scene opens, it is night, and Robinson, who is about to take part in a "house-breaking," has decided to have a look at one of a series of supposedly pornographic pamphlets he has just purchased:

> . . . He knelt down and took off his hat, and put his dark lantern inside it before he ventured to move the slide; then undid the paper, and, putting it into the hat, threw the concentrated rays on the contents, and peered in to examine them. Now the various little pamphlets had been displaced by mephisto, and the first words that met the thief's eye, in large letters on the back of a tract, were these: 'THE WAGES OF SIN ARE DEATH.'

> Thomas Robinson looked at these words with a stupid gaze. At first he did not realize all that lay in them. He did not open the tract: he gazed benumbed at the words, and they glared at him like the eyes of green fire when we come in the dark on some tiger-cat crouching in his lair.

> Oh, that I were a painter, and could make you see what cannot be described! the features of this strange incident that sounds so small and was so great. The black night, the hat, the renegade peering under it in the wall's deep shadows to read something trashy,

and the half-open lantern shooting its little strip of intense fire, and the grim words springing out in a moment from the dark face of night and dazzling the renegade's eyes and chilling his heart: 'THE WAGES OF SIN ARE DEATH.'[10]

That Reade could declare Robinson's reactions to be those of a "man," the scene itself (along with those that follow) "true to nature . . . the immortal part of the work,"[11] shows how naïvely and completely he identified nature and truth with his Dickensian preconceptions.

III

Along with his epic thief, Reade created an epic hero in Parson Eden (first referred to as "the chaplain of Tom Robinson's gaol") who is in all but name an idealized self-portrait and therefore the ultimate Resourceful Hero of the novel. Parson Eden's goodness is difficult to describe; to find anyone to compare with him one must turn to such paragons as Squire Allworthy, John Jarndyce, or Tom Newcome, and even these characters are inferior in that they are *merely* good. In addition to his perfect goodness, which is completely selfless and of course sexless, Eden is blessed with the intelligence of a Newton, the eloquence of a Whitefield . . . and when the occasion demands he is also an expert wrestler, a pupil of Bendigo. His one seeming weakness—a tendency to sicken at the sight of blood and torture—is not really a weakness at all, it turns out, but a necessary concomitant of his sensitivity. Indeed he is so much the perfect hero that Swinburne, ordinarily so indulgent to Reade's heroes, was obliged to dismiss him as "that athletico-seraphic chaplain . . . Prince Rodolphe (of the *Mystères de Paris*) in Anglican order."[12]

As in the case of Robinson, however, there is the matter of Reade's intention. He was not trying to create a commonplace parson, like George Eliot's Mr. Irwine; he was trying to create a modern hero who was also a modern saint. **Christie Johnstone** he had intended as, in part, a votive offering to his mother, and it would appear that in Eden, he was endeavoring to present her with the ideal parson she had intended him to be—a Christian clergyman who would represent God and Bacon and Progress, in contrast and opposition to the "infernal little disciples of Carlyle."

IV

As yet, however, Reade's sources had not provided him with a Carlylean hero whom he could cast in the role of villain. Nor was he content with the documentary evidence he had thus far collected. To duplicate the art and purpose of *Uncle Tom* he knew that he had to have more sensational facts, and as late as August 22, 1853, he was still resolving to find them: "I will visit all the London prisons, and get warm facts for the prison business. . . . ”[13] A few weeks later, however, the articles on the Birmingham atrocities appeared (*Times*, September 6-16) to provide the ultimate answer to his Baconian prayers. For the articles were more than warm, they laid bare the workings of a nineteenth century Buchenwald, and in doing so provided leads towards the exposure of still further atrocities—leads that he immediately followed up. In his own words: “I studied the two extra-ordinary Bluebooks, viz., the Royal Commissioners’ Report on Birmingham Gaol, and also on Leicester Gaol. . . . Then I conversed with one of the Royal Commissioners, and he told me the horrors of Leicester Gaol had so affected one of the Commissioners that it had made him seriously ill for more than a month. Enlightened by all these studies . . . I did what the anonymous Press had done on a vast scale . . . I struck a blow in defense of outraged law and outraged humanity. But unlike the Press, to whom the prison rules are unknown, I did *not* confound the system with all its abuses; on the contrary, I conducted the case thus: I placed before the reader not one government official, but two—the gaoler eternally breaking *the prison rules,* and the chaplain eternally appealing to the prison rules. At last, after inflicting many miseries by repeated breaches of the prison rules, the gaoler does a poor boy to death; and then I bring in a third government official, who dismisses the gaoler.”[14]

Reade’s statement shows how neatly he fitted his new facts to his old thesis through a slight extension of his old epic framework. He did not, like his master Dickens, challenge the prevailing theories of penology which in America were presented under the aegis of the “Pennsylvania System,” and in England, with slight modifications, were known as “the silent and solitary system.”[15] Later, in his notebooks and in two of his novels, he condemned “the system” roundly, but at this time, following Dixon, he accepted it with minor reservations, basing his entire case on Dixon’s key distinction between the system and its abuses. In one of his Notebooks he pasted in a printed copy of the “Rules relating to the conduct and treatment of prisoners in the County Gaol and House of Correction at Reading,” and beneath these rules he wrote: “These are the Prison rules I used in writing ‘It is never too late to mend.’ They were repeatedly broken in the gaols whose abuses I explored. . . . I attacked the abuses but not the theory of those gaols. . . . ”[16]

By thus taking his stand behind the system, Reade gained a number of advantages—not the least of which was a ready-made factual villain in the person of Lieutenant Austin, the warden responsible for the Birmingham atrocities. The one difficulty, from a reformist point of view, was that Austin had already been tried, dismissed, and held up to public scorn. But that did not deter Reade. He was looking for an excuse to harrow his readers—after the manner of *Uncle Tom*—and in Austin he had found his Simon Legree.

He therefore transferred the factual Austin directly to the novel, then proceeded to vilify him as that Carlylean demon of cruelty, that “lurid specimen of barbarism,” that “black ray of the narrow, self-deceiving bloody past . . . earnest Hawes.”[17] At times—the few times he tried to probe the whys and wherefores of Hawes’s cruelties—Reade showed considerable insight. He recognized that “this unhappy dolt Hawes . . . must still, like his prisoners and the rest of us, have some excitement to keep him from going dead. What more natural than that such a nature should find its excitement in tormenting, and that by degrees this excitement should become first a habit, then a need? Growth is the nature of habit, not of one sort or another but of all—even of unnatural habit. Gin grows on a man—tobacco grows on a man—blood grows on a man.”[18] But Reade the philanthropist was too close to Hawes the sadist to recognize the implications of his own analysis—either as it applied to Hawes or to himself. In any case his aim was not to understand Hawes, but to expose him as a nineteenth century Himmler—a monster so monstrous that he, Charles Reade (alias Charles Eden), could hound and beat and destroy him in the name of “outraged law and humanity.” And in pursuing this aim he believed that he was writing in the epic tradition, that he was emulating Milton as well as Dickens and Mrs. Stowe. Hence his efforts to liken Hawes to Nero, Pharaoh, the inquisitors, and Carlyle’s Great Men, and thus establish him as a modern Satan at war with a modern Christ for the souls of modern Christians as represented by Robinson, the human Adam.

V

The discrepancy between Reade’s epic design and melodramatic treatment is evident as early as the first few pages of the prison section in which Reade presents a picture of the entire gaol—a factual reproduction based in part on Dixon’s elaborate description of Reading Gaol, but with added rhetorical touches intended to show the evil lurking beneath the order and cleanliness.[19] Into this gaol—seemingly a model of its kind—Reade introduces Robinson and through him unveils the rigors of “the silent and separate system” as enforced by Hawes—rigors that soon reduce the intelligent and sensitive but misguided Robinson to a vicious animal, ready to strike back against and, if possible, kill his tormentor.

Then, just at the moment that Robinson is about to commit murder, and the other prisoners are for various reasons also at the breaking point, Parson Eden enters upon the scene. In contrast to his predecessor, Chaplain Jones, a well-meaning but in Reade’s own terminology a “commonplace man,”[20] Eden sets about his new duties with all the zeal and acumen of Charles Reade himself. In one of his sermons to the prisoners "he suddenly opens his arms, wth wonderful grace and warmth and energy," and speaks to them as only he can: "My poor wandering sheep, come—come back to the heavenly fold! Let me gather you as a hen gathers her chickens under her wing. You are my anxiety, my terror—be my joy, my consolation here, and hereafter the brightest jewel in my crown." In this strain, according to Reade, Eden soared higher than earth-clogged wings can follow: "Gracious words of entreaty and encouragement gushed from him in a crystal stream with looks and tones of more than mortal charity. Men might well doubt was this a man, or was it Christianity speaking? Christianity, born in a stable, was she there, illuminating a gaol?"[21]

At this point the reader may be tempted to interrupt Reade's Christ metaphor—which he carries on through another half page—with the type of witticism visited upon Dickens' Wopsle. Yet there is a certain amount of Readian logic in this seeming rhetorical madness, for Eden's Christlike love gives him the Godlike right to hate—and he hates cruelty, which is the subject of his next sermon:

> "No crime is so thoroughly without excuse as this. Other crimes have sometimes an adequate temptation, this never. The path to other crimes is down-hill; to cruelty is up-hill. In the very act, Nature, who is on the side of some crimes, cries out within us against this monstrous sin. The blood of our victim flowing from our blows, its groans and sighs and pallor, stay the uplifted arm and appeal to the furious heart. Wonderful they should ever appeal in vain . . . God has written his abhorrence of this monstrous sin in letters of fire and blood on every page of history."

Here he ransacked history, and gave them some thirty remarkable instances of human cruelty, and of its being punished in kind so strangely, and with such an exactness of retribution, that the finger of God seemed visible writing on the world—"God hates cruelty."

At the end of his examples he instanced two that happened under his own eye—a favorite custom of this preacher.

"A man was tried in London for cruelty to animals; he was acquitted by a legal flaw, though the evidence was clear against him. This man returned homeward triumphant. The train in which he sat was drawn up by the side of a station. An express-train passed on the up-line at full speed. At the moment of passing, the fly-wheel of the engine broke; a large fragment was driven into the air, and fell upon the stationary train: it burst through one of the carriages, and killed a man upon the spot. That man was seated between two other men, neither of whom received the slightest

injury. The man so singled out was the cruel man who had evaded man's justice, but could not escape His hand who created the beasts as well as man, and who abhors all men who are cruel to any creature He has formed."[22]

Nor does Eden stop here. He continues on for some four more pages, and when it seems that even he has exhausted his powers of Biblical rhetoric, he works himself up into a hell-fire and damnation finale: "Tremble, ye cruel, God hates ye!" And so, by making God a humanitarian with sadistic propensities, in support of his cruelty-hating Christ, Reade secured every possible sanction for expressing his own "abhorrence of cruelty" in "letters of fire and blood."

VI

The struggle between Eden and Hawes is therefore grotesquely unequal from the start. Eden finds a copy of the prison rules, mentioned earlier, and then proceeds to prove, point by point, that practically every single punishment employed by Hawes is illegal and must be stopped. Any prison official who so much as tampers with a prisoner's diet is, he declares, "a felon," and he, Charles Francis Eden, will proceed against any such official "by the dog-whip of the criminal law, by the gibbet of the public press, and by every weapon that wit and honesty have ever found to scourge cruelty . . . since civilization dawned upon the earth."[23] And Eden carries out this threat to the letter. In fact he works himself into such a frenzy—just by recounting Hawes's cruelties—that he steps forth in his own person to revoke Justice Coleridge's decision in the Austin Case:

> I revoke that sentence [of Justice Coleridge] with all the blunders on which it was founded. Instead of becoming, as other judicial proceedings do, a precedent for future judges, I condemn it to be a beacon they shall avoid. It shall lie among the decisions of lawyers, but it shall never mix with them. It shall stand alone in all its oblique pity, its straightforward cruelty, and absurdity; and no judge shall dare copy it while I am alive; for if he does, I swear to him by the God that made me, that all I have yet said is to what I will print of *him,* as a lady's riding whip to a thresher's flail. I promise him, on my honour as a writer and no hireling, that I will buy a sheet of paper as big as a barn-door, and nail him to it by his name as we nail a pole-cat by the throat. I will take him by one ear to Calcutta, and from Calcutta to Sydney; and by the other from London via Liverpool to New York and Boston. The sun shall never set upon his gibbet, and when his bones are rotten his shame shall live—Ay! though he was thirty years upon the bench. Posterity shall know little about his name, and *feel* nothing about it but this—that it is the name of a muddle-head who gained and merited my loathing, my horror and my scorn.

The civilized races, and I their temporary representative revoke that sentence from the rising to the setting sun in every land where the English tongue is spoken.[24]

The indignation expressed in this passage borders so closely on the psychopathic that it not only fails of its intended effect but reflects back upon Reade himself.[25] And other passages in which Eden anathematizes Hawes have a similar effect. Eden's humanitarianism is but Hawes's sadism, plus moral sanctions, and the moral sanctions are in themselves rationalizations.

VII

Although, for strategic reasons, Reade does not challenge the system directly in the novel, he can and does criticize the system and its workings indirectly—by making Eden ill, and then permitting him to air his notions in the form of a dream: "But one day it so happened that he was light-headed and greatly excited, holding a conversation [with an imaginary companion] . . . The enthusiast was building a prison in the air. A prison with a farm, a school, and a manufactory attached. Here were combined the good points of every system, and others of his own . . . there shall be both separation and silence for those whose moral case it suits—for all, perhaps, at first—but not for all always. Away with your Morrisons's pill-system, your childish monotony of moral treatment in cases varying and sometimes opposed." Continuing in this vein Eden outlines a theory of prison reform quite advanced for the time—although he is careful to point out that "systems avail less than supposed . . . all depends on your men, not your machinery." For this reason, he argues, old-fashioned gaolers and turnkeys and visiting justices must go. "As they were in the days of Fielding so they are in the days of light, and as they are now so will they remain until they are swept away from the face of the soil. . . . " Then, after these "men of the past" have been swept away, they must be replaced by men of light—as in Eden's Utopian dream: "Now we have really a governor and warders instead of jailers and turnkeys. The nation has discovered these are high offices, not mean ones. . . . Our officers are men picked out of all England for intelligence and humanity. . . . Our jail is one of the nation's eyes; it is a school, thank Heaven, it is not a dungeon."[26]

Yet even in such a Utopian prison, manned by such model officials, there was still the need for outside surveillance. For no matter how intelligent or humane the officials might be there was always the possibility of their becoming enmeshed in red tape. As a final safeguard he therefore insisted that all prisons be kept open for public inspection—to enable the people, under the guidance of zealots like himself, to keep the prison under constant surveillance. "Justice," Reade constantly reiterated, "is the daughter of publicity."[27]

In designating the people, in the guise of "public opinion," the final arbiter in matters relating to prisons (as well as in all matters social, political, and literary) Reade doubtless thought that he was being republican if not democratic—in line with his own Benthamitic beliefs and in opposition to the authoritarian doctrines of his *bête noir,* Carlyle. Yet it should be obvious that he too subscribed to a form of hero-worship. His final appeal is not to the people as such (elsewhere, in a statement reminiscent of Bumble's remarks on the law, he says flatly: "the public is an ass") but only to the people as informed and guided by "modern" heroes. And while it can of course be argued that Reade's heroes are liberal, intelligent leaders, not medieval despots, and therefore not authoritarian in the Carlylean sense at all, this is to overlook the spirit of their words and actions. For if Eden ordinarily speaks the language of Bacon, the Mills and the Evangelical pulpit (rather than that of Fichte, Cromwell, and Carlyle's captains of industry) he speaks this language with a peculiarly Readian accent that is much closer to Carlyle than to, say, Mill, or even Arnold. Eden seldom if ever speaks as Eden; it is always as the representative of God, humanity, law and order, the government, the Home Office . . . and he invariably invokes the power of these concepts and institutions in an effort to crush anyone who opposes him—from Hawes, to the gaolers, to the Visiting Justices, to Justice Coleridge.

VIII

Reade, it need hardly be added, saw nothing ludicrous in presenting his Christ as an authoritarian representative of the Home Office. Nor did he see anything reprehensible about using his Christ to gibbet an actual prison official (Lieutenant Austin) who had already been tried and punished. Reade's argument, which anticipates the morality now exemplified in the work of Mickey Spillane, was that Lieutenant Austin had not suffered enough, that, consequently, he had to be tried and sentenced again—this time by the public, with the Christlike Eden as prosecuting attorney and Reade himself as judge.

Having thus reduced his epic structure to a sadistic formula Reade could exploit to the full the blackness of his black facts—as he did in the scene in which Hawes and the gaolers amuse themselves by stuffing salt down the throat of a half-witted prisoner who has been confined in the punishment jacket for hours and is already crazed with fear, pain, and thirst. *The Times's* comment on the factual counterpart of this scene—that it "eclipses any scene in *Uncle Tom's Cabin,* those in which Legree figures not excluded"—applies with equal force to Reade's fictional treatment, which in this and similar instances eclipses Dickens (as well as Stowe) in its sheer sadistic intensity, and can hardly be matched outside the pages that Marcus Clarke (in his *For the Term of His Natural Life*) modelled after Reade. Indeed it was one of the factual scenes taken directly from the novel—in which a boy named Josephs faints after being confined in the punishment jacket—that very nearly precipitated a riot when Reade later produced the play *It's Never Too Late to Mend.*[29]

Dramatically, however, these scenes are open to the same criticism that Samuel Warren levels against the "frightful scenes" in *Uncle Tom's Cabin* when he declares that "one might as well describe, in detail, the slaughter of an ox by the slaughterer and his two assistants."[30] Warren's implication, of course, is that the slaughterer cannot be held morally responsible for his slaughter. And neither can Hawes. The facts reveal that Lieutenant Austin was more sick than satanic, more of a Bumble than a Pharaoh, and Reade's Baconian dramatization of the facts conveys the same impression—an impression that his rhetoric and invective fail to alter. Hawes remains Hawes, and in gibbeting him as he does Eden tends to negate the very humanitarianism Reade is trying to enforce; just as, to cite a comparable but inferior modern example, Laura Hobson's treatment of the anti-semites tends to negate the avowed purpose of *Gentleman's Agreement,* by showing the anti-anti-semites to be as authoritarian and as bloodthirsty as the anti-semites.

The most telling prison scenes—in terms of Reade's avowed intentions—are therefore those scenes (previously described) in which Eden plays little if any part, in which Reade draws directly upon his black facts to show the prisoners alone and helpless, the victims of a dolt who is himself the victim of a system. Yet even these scenes, which, in themselves, are at least as compelling as the comparable scenes in *For the Term of his Natural Life,* or those in James Jones's *From Here to Eternity,* actually come to very little in the context of the novel. For when Reade (in the person of Christ-like Eden) assumes the role of father to the prisoners, he immediately reduces the prisoners, along with Hawes, to the pattern of his own sadistic phantasy—a pattern in which he anticipates Freud's "A Child is being Beaten" with his own "A Prisoner is being Beaten."

But of course Reade did not know that he had negated his humanitarian as well as his epic intentions, that in his efforts to emulate Milton and Mrs. Stowe he had anticipated Mickey Spillane and Laura Hobson—as well as Freud's case histories. To him Eden's feelings of obsessive tenderness for the prisoners—the sadistic feelings that compel him to torment their tormentor—were neither obsessive nor sadistic. They were the feelings of humane men and women everywhere, and in giving them fictional expression, in harrowing his readers as he himself had been harrowed by his factual investigations, he believed that he had, at long last, done justice to the teachings of his master—that he had, in fact, vindicated both himself and his great system.

Notes

[2] Quoted in "Facts Must Be Faced," *Readiana,* p. 437.

[3] "A Terrible Temptation," in *Readiana,* p. 388.

[4] For a more complete and more fully documented study of prisons and prisoners in relation to the genesis of Reade's chapters see my unpublished thesis, *Charles Reade: The Making of a Social Novelist* (Cornell, 1946) pp. 216-255.

[5] See Hepworth Dixon, *The London Prisons* (London, 1850), pp. 391-412.

[6] See "Extracts from various Notices of the Work," quoted on the last page of Kingsmill. Joseph Kingsmill, *Chapters on Prisons and Prisoners* (London, 1852).

[7] "The Autobiography of a Thief," p. 4, Reade's opening statement seems to derive from the following passage in Kingsley's *Yeast* (New York, 1885), pp. 20-21:

> "Then let the reader believe, that whatsoever is commonplace in my story is my own invention. Whatsoever may seem extravagant or startling is most likely to be historic fact . . ."

[8] *It Is Never Too Late To Mend,* II, pp. 75-78.

[9] *It Is Never Too Late To Mend,* I, pp. 216-219.

[10] *It Is Never Too Late To Mend,* I, pp. 537-538.

[11] See the epigraph to the present chapter. This is one of the letters reproduced in Annie Fields, "Charles Reade," *The Century Magazine* (November, 1884), p. 70.

[12] Algernon Charles Swinburne, *Miscellanies* (London, 1886), p. 273.

[13] Charles L. Reade and Compton Reade, *Charles Reade . . . A Memoir* (London, 1887), p. 201.

[14] "A Terrible Temptation," *Readiana,* pp. 388-389.

[15] For a full and accurate description of the "Pennsylvania system" see William Parker Foulke, *Remarks on Cellular Separation* (Philadelphia, 1861). Foulke (pp. 108-112) reprints a letter in which William Peter endeavors to refute Dickens' charges against "the system."

[16] Emerson Grant Sutcliffe, "Charles Reade's Notebooks," *Studies in Philology* 28(1930), p. 82.

[17] *It Is Never Too Late To Mend,* I, p. 307.

[18] *Ibid,* I, p. 286.

[19] Cf. Dixon, *op. cit.,* pp. 391-394 with *It Is Never Too Late To Mend,* I, pp. 128-131.

[20] *It Is Never Too Late To Mend,* I, pp. 182-183.

[21] *Ibid,* I, p. 240.

[22] *Ibid,* I, pp. 242-243.

[23] *Ibid,* I, p. 253.

[24] This passage appears in *It Is Never Too Late To Mend* (Boston, Ticknor And Fields, 1856) II, pp. 421-422. Reade later deleted this passage, along with others in a similar vein (II, pp. 415-423). See *Memoir,* pp. 244 and 365.

[25] Cf. Fitzjames Stephen, "The License of Modern Novelists" (*The Edinburgh Review,* CVI, 1857), pp. 136-143.

[26] *It Is Never Too Late To Mend,* I, pp. 298-299.

[27] In "Our Dark Places," for instance, Reade opened his second letter with the statement: "In England Justice is the daughter of Publicity." See *Readiana,* p. 155. Reade also repeated the statement in *Hard Cash,* III, p. 217, and on the Notecards, under the heading *Arundiniana.* See Douglas Bankson, "Charles Reade's Manuscript Notecards for **Hard Cash**" (unpublished doctoral thesis, University of Washington, 1954), p. 54.

[28] *The Times,* September, 12, 1853.

[29] See John Hollingshead, *My Lifetime* (London, 1895), I, p. 167; also Henry Morley, *The Journal of a London Playgoer* (London, 1866), pp. 380-381. For an informed and thorough analysis of "the connexion between spectacular realism and serious social purpose in Reade's work," see Sheila M. Smith, "Realism in the Drama of Charles Reade," *English* (XII), pp. 94-100. In this article Sheila M. Smith discusses *It's Never Too Late To Mend* at some length, comparing its realism with that of Reade's later plays, including *Free Labour, Foul Play,* and *Love and Money.*

[30] Samuel Warren, *Miscellanies, Critical, Imaginative, and Juridical* (Edinburgh and London, 1855), I, p. 413.

Wayne Burns (essay date 1961)

SOURCE: "*Griffith Gaunt*: 'The Great Passions that Poets Have Sung,'" in *Charles Reade: A Study in Victorian Authorship,* Bookman Associates, 1961, pp. 231-67.

[*In the following excerpt, Burns discusses Reade's portrayal of feminine psychology and sexuality in* Griffith Gaunt.]

III

In the midst of this turmoil [over the stage version of *It Is Never Too Late to Mend*] Reade still managed to keep up his Notebooks, and to start work on a new novel, although, duplicating the practice he had followed after completing his prison epic, he did not immediately attempt another matter-of-fact romance. After **Hard Cash** and **The Cloister** that would have been too strenuous. Instead he essayed another and to his way of thinking less demanding type of novel. "It is a tale of the heart," he wrote Fields (Oct. 13, 1865), "and does not straggle into any eccentric topics. Need I say I shall make it as exciting and interesting as I can."

The outlines of this tale Reade seems to have drawn primarily from the two sources first identified in *The Round Table* (Dec. 1, 1867): 1) a fifty page story in Wilkie Collins' *Queen of Hearts* (1859) entitled "Brother Griffith's Story of a Plot in Private Life," and 2) "The Frenchman of Two Wives," an article in *Household Words* (Dec. 6, 1856) that was seemingly Collins' own immediate source for "Brother Griffith's Story. . . . " And behind this source was still another, a story called "Le Mort-vivant" which C. L. Connelly (*The Overland Monthly,* October, 1873) declared the source of both **Griffith Gaunt** and "Brother Griffith's Story"—although it would seem, on the basis of the evidence adduced by Edmund Morrison (in his *Charles Reade and his Novels,* 1940), that "Le Mort-vivant" was the source, not of Reade's novel or Collins' story, but of the "Frenchman of Two Wives."[7]

But there is no need to rehearse Morrison's arguments. Intelligent and restrained as they are they still tend to equate "source" with "conception," and in doing so necessarily oversimplify the creative process. Reade did not write **Griffith Gaunt** because he quite by chance stumbled onto a source or sources for its plot; he searched out these sources because he wanted to write such a "tale of the heart." The Notebooks are filled with "Plots" and "Plagianda" having to do with jealousy, priests, celibacy, bigamy, and the like. And these entries in turn reflect his autobiographical interests and experiences from the time of his first meeting with his Scotch wife, to his unhappy love affairs with Mrs. Stirling, to his more settled life (dating from 1853) with Mrs. Seymour. In all these love relationships Reade saw himself as the victim, not of his mother and his own Oedipal feelings, but of the rule of celibacy imposed by his Magdalen Fellowship. As late as 1876 he wrote in one of his Notebooks: "In my medieval romance **The Cloister and the Hearth** I use this expression celibacy of the clergy, an invention truly devilish. . . . The opinion I uttered in 1860 was even then twenty years old in me; it is now thirty-six."[8]

Cherishing these feelings, which he had been able to express only in *The Cloister and the Hearth,* and then not fully, owing to the limits of its historical framework, Reade was, the Notebooks indicate, constantly on the lookout for "Plagianda" that might enable him to write a modern variation on his medieval theme. And in Collins' story, and its even more lurid original, he found just the sources he needed. For "The Frenchman of Two Wives" is a circumstantial account of a late seventeenth century Frenchman who first becomes convinced that his wife is having an adulterous relationship with a priest, then commits bigamy himself—the whole affair ending in a confusion of wives and husbands and violence and murder trials. Given Reade's aims and interests these materials were invaluable in themselves, and to have them combined within a Sensation plot ideally suited to his needs and techniques (as in Collins' version) was, for Reade, to discover the basic form and substance of another masterpiece.

IV

The prime virtue of Collins' plot, considered as "Plagianda" or "Bon. Fab.," was that it lent itself to his time tried techniques of adaptation. To expand Collins' fifty page story of crime and detection into a five hundred page tale of the heart he needed, on the structural level, only a sufficient number of "generative incidents," and these he apparently found ready to hand in the Notebooks.[9] In any event he completely disregards plot in his notes for the novel (on the reverse side of the Notecard labelled "Notes for Griffith Gaunt"), taking the structure of his action for granted and concentrating on aspects of theme and character not to be found in his sources. . . .

In form as well as substance these notes, loosely strung out on one side of one Notecard, appear incomplete and tentative—as if Reade had in mind further additions and developments that for some reason he failed to carry through. As the notes appear on the Notecard, those having to do with Father Leonard and the Church are by far the most fully developed—not only because they involve Reade's deepest personal interests but also, it would seem, because they mark a radical departure from his sources. In Collins' story, for instance, the parson's character is summarized, Dickensian fashion, in his name (Mr. Meek), and in any but a Victorian story he would be a comic figure. Nor is there the slightest hint, either in Collins' story or "The Frenchman of Two Wives," that the priest's actions have any serious moral or religious implications. The thematic development Reade suggests is entirely his own, and seems designed to present the conflict between the young priest and the young wife as another conflict between the novel centering around Kate and Father Leonard; the rest he considered a matter of extending and filling out his sources, and for this he apparently felt very little special preparation was required.

The remaining Notecards devoted wholly or in part to the novel are singularly bare, and the few entries they do contain are of no great significance, except as they indicate how cursory were his preparations, even in matters relating to the historical setting of the novel. Indeed there is but one entry on one Notecard to indicate that he was at all concerned with historical accuracy—an entry (on the otherwise blank Notecard headed "Notes for Griffith Gaunt") which seems to be a collection of eighteenth century words, idioms, and turns of speech:

> Has been the ruin of one woman
> already who was wife to his bosom friend.
> I am out of countenance. P. for ashamed
> Pray present my humble duty to my Mama
> Made me some amends for what I had suff.
> I stick close to my spinnet. daughter for God
>   daughter
> [One word illegible] excuse to me was bad
>   tenants and a cheeky steward
> Run mad for gone mad. He designs to enter
>   himself.
> Eternally yours, Lansdowne We had pure
>   sport. [Thin?] of company to what it used to
>   be. We were twelve in company; and it was
>   proposed we should sit a man and a
>   woman.
> The loss you have made. The company—were
>   free [libertine?] people
> Old harridan mother in law
> French ladies their faces and persons are so
>   hid he does not know what to make of
>   them.
> Foemina Vera That morning I was entertained
>   with [Cuzzoni?]
> Oh how charming! How did I wish for all I
>   love and like to be with me at that instant
>   of time
> The Babe is to be made a Ztian next Sunday
> Mrs. Badge nor I could not rightly understand
>   about the Bohea tea. [pondering?] gown
>   Sweetheart applied to children frighted
>   hackneys for h. coaches Harpsichord
>
> Upon my permission up comes the gentleman
>   so spruce and finical.

Except for these rather desultory notes Reade showed less concern for historical accuracy than in his very first novel, *Peg Woffington,* written before he had developed his elaborate Baconian theories and techniques. The reason for this apparent inconsistency it seems clear, is that for all his emphasis on "the very period Henry Fielding has described" he did not really intend *Griffith Gaunt* to be an historical novel. His first interest was not "history" but "the heart," and he chose to set his tale in the period of Fielding, not because, like Thackeray, he understood the period, and found it spiritually congenial, but because its manners and morals and speech "were somewhat blunter than now-a-days" and in consequence lent themselves more readily to the expression of "the great passions that poets have sung."

V

The heart of Reade's tale, as set forth in these Notes, is also the heart of the novel. And if he had not felt obliged to be tri-voluminous he might conceivably have been content to write a one-volume novel entitled *Kate Gaunt* or *Father Leonard*. As it was, having committed himself to three volumes, he had no choice but to lengthen his tale with an introduction and a long drawn-out bigamous conclusion. In consequence **Griffith Gaunt** falls into three parts or dramatic sequences (corresponding roughly to the acts of a three-act play) which may be designated 1) courtship (Chs. 1-13, pp. 3-151); 2) temptation (Chs. 14-25, pp. 152-251); 3) bigamy (Chs. 26-46, pp. 252-489).

In the first or courtship sequence Reade (following Collins) sets his scene, introduces his leading characters, and establishes his theme, introducing Griffith's foible as early as page thirteen, and developing it through such commentaries as the following: "The mind as well as the body has its self-protecting instincts. This of Griffith's was after all an instinct of that class, and under certain circumstances, is true wisdom. But Griffith, I think, carried the instinct to excess; and that is why I call it his foible."[11] Here and elsewhere Reade's psychological analyses and commentaries are remarkably acute—though in his efforts to dramatize Griffith's excess he invariably falls back upon the language and techniques of *The Actors' Hand-Book:* "Hitherto she had but beheld the feeling of jealousy, but now she witnessed the livid passion of jealousy writhing in every lineament of a human face. That terrible passion had transfigured its victim in a moment: the ruddy, genial, kindly Griffith, with his soft brown eye, was gone; and in his place lowered a face older and discolored and convulsed, and almost demoniacal."[12]

But if Griffith's melodramatic duality is not convincing in itself it does provide a means of exploring Kate's responses, more especially her sexual responses, and Reade makes the most of it to introduce her as "a dreamy virgin" who for all her girlish enthusiasm and Catholic piety is yet a woman. The opening scene of the novel, in which Kate rides to the hounds, calls to mind the early scenes of *Daniel Deronda*. And the succeeding scenes, though more theatrical than Eliot's, are at times equally revealing, particularly those in which Reade shows Kate responding to both her suitors (Griffith and his rival, George Neville) not merely by turns but at the same time, on one occasion with both lovers in full view. While she watched Griffith ride away, "the inflammable George made hot love to her again"—and not without effect, despite her conscious efforts to repulse him:

> Fire and water were in his eyes, passion in every tone; his manly hand grasped hers and trembled, and drew her gently towards him.

> Her bosom heaved; his passionate male voice and manner electrified her, and made her flutter. "Spare me this pain," she faltered; and she looked through the window and thought, "Poor Griffith was right after all, and I was wrong. He had cause for jealousy, and CAUSE FOR FEAR."

> And then she pitied him who panted at her side, and then was sorry for him who rode away disconsolate, still lessening to her eye; and what with this conflict, and the emotion her quarrel with Griffith had already caused her, she leaned her head back against the shutter, and began to sob low, but almost hysterically.

Although the language is tritely theatrical, Kate's thoughts and actions are certainly not those of the stock Victorian heroine. For even as she sobs, "almost hysterically," she is aware of her duplicity, and when she seeks to justify it falls into still further confusion:

> Catherine turned her dreamy eyes on him [Neville].

> "You have had a good master. Why did you not come to me sooner?"

> She was thinking more of him than of herself, and in fact paying too little heed to her words. But she had no sooner uttered this inadvertent speech than she felt she had said too much.

Thus Reade, by the technically simple device of playing off Kate's words against her thoughts and impulses, probes the depths of her confusion. She does not know her own mind because what she feels for Neville she wants to feel for Griffith—not only because his inferior position and prospects render him more worthy, in terms of her ideals, but because for all his physical prowess, his more tentative maleness, as expressed in his slavish devotion, poses less of a threat to her own personality. Married to Neville she would have to be merely his wife; married to Griffith she could continue to be herself, submitting physically but retaining her emotional and intellectual independence, and in fact treating Griffith as she had treated her father.

What Kate finally wanted, it seems clear, was marriage and sexual fulfillment without emotional submission to a husband. Yet her feelings for Neville were so strong that she could not choose Griffith until she had inadvertently caused him to be wounded in a duel and robbed of his inheritance. Then she could no longer resist him. On the very night he was disinherited in her favor, she called him to her bedroom window, knowing that he was drunk, to say that she would be his wife:

> Griffith burst into raptures; Kate listened to them with a complacent smile; then delivered herself after this fashion: "You have very little to thank me for, dear Griffith. I don't exactly downright love you; but I could not rob you of those unlucky farms, and you refuse to take them back any way but this; so what can I do? And then, for all I don't love you, I find I am always unhappy if you are unhappy, and happy when you are happy; so it comes pretty much to the same thing. I declare I am sick of giving you pain, and a little sick of crying in consequence. There, I have cried more in the last fortnight than in all my life before, and you know nothing spoils one's beauty like crying; and then you are so good, and kind, and true, and brave; and everybody is so unjust, and so unkind to you; papa and all. You were quite in the right about the duel, dear; he *is* an impudent puppy; and I threw dust in your eyes, and made you own you were in the wrong; and it was a great shame of me; but it was because I liked you best. I could take liberties with *you,* dear. And you are wounded for me; and now I have disinherited you; oh, I can't bear it, and I won't. My heart yearns for you; bleeds for you. I would rather die than you should be unhappy; I would rather follow you in rags round the world than marry a prince and make you wretched. Yes, dear, I am yours. Make me your wife; and then some day I dare say I shall love you as I ought."

In these lines Kate reveals the full implications of her choice. She is consciously rejecting love, the love she had begun to feel for Neville, in favor of self-sacrifice and devotion. And if she is rather wistful, despite the bantering tone of her remarks on beauty, she is also pleased and proud. For in giving herself to Griffith she feels she is expressing a higher kind of love, the love that she feels for the Church, and that she on one occasion expresses in almost exactly the same words: "My heart bleeds for the Church . . . and when I see her present condition I long to be of service."

In the light of this and similar statements it seems clear that, to Kate, marriage to Griffith is the next best alternative to becoming a nun—her ultimate ideal. But before she can marry Griffith, she must overcome the opposition of her father, as well as the still more formidable opposition of Father Francis, who has already squelched her romantic notions about entering a nunnery and is urging her, for practical reasons, to marry Neville. To ensure her own steadfastness she therefore offers Griffith "a friend's advice": "Then," she said, "I'll do a downright brazen thing, now my hand is in. I declare I'll tell you how to secure me. You make me plight my troth with you this minute, and exchange rings with you, *whether I like or not;* engage my honor in this foolish business, and if you do that, I really do think you will have me in spite of them all." Having so bound herself she then uses her wit and charm to disarm her father and Father Francis, and when, in Father Francis' case, her stratagems prove ineffectual, she resorts to tears and supplications:

> "Spare me!" muttered Kate, faintly.

> "Then do you drop deceit and the silly cunning of your sex, and speak to me from your heart, or not at all." (Diapason.)

> At this Kate began to whimper. "Father," she said, "show me some mercy," Then, suddenly clasping her hands: "HAVE PITY ON HIM, AND ON ME."

> This time Nature herself seemed to speak, and the eloquent cry went clean through the priest's heart. "Ah!" said he; and his own voice trembled a little, "now you are as strong as your cunning was weak. Come, I see how it is with you; and I am human, and have been young, and a lover into the bargain, before I was a priest. There, dry thy eyes, child, and go to thy room; he thou couldst not trust shall bear the brunt for thee; this once."

> Then Kate bowed her fair head and kissed the horrid paw of him that had administered so severe but salutary a pat. She huried away up-stairs, right joyful at the unexpected turn things had taken.

While this scene is patently of the usual Reade construction—with Father Francis, the priestly embodiment of the elderly Readian adviser, evincing the manly emotions demanded by the plot—Kate's theatricality is in part redeemed by the dramatic context. If she speaks and acts like an actress it is because she is acting. She has learned the feminine appeals that touch the hearts of men, whether they be elderly priests or young suitors, and has no scruples about using them to serve her own ends, since, as she sees these ends, they are wholly unselfish and noble. It is only after she has completed her conquest of the male opposition by securing her father's consent to the marriage that she feels any compunction, and then her primary concern is to justify herself to Neville, whose forgiveness she entreats in a note so disarming in its seeming honesty that it leaves him no choice but to suffer nobly.

In these latter phases of the courtship Kate may be compared with the young Dorothea of *Middlemarch.* And while Reade's characterization lacks the Tolstoyan depth and finish of Eliot's, it is almost equally perceptive in its grasp of feminine psychology, and more daring, if not more perceptive, in its treatment of disguised sexual motivation. It shows that Kate, "the dreamy young virgin," is not so dreamy after all, that in sacrificing herself to Griffith she is seeking to fulfill her personal as well as her religious ideals. For Griffith, in contrast to Neville, does not demand emotional submission; he is rather the object of her charity and compassion—a man for whom she can bleed without staining the pristine purity of her virginal self-image.

VI

The second or temptation sequence of the novel Reade opens with a summary and a challenge:

> Mr. and Mrs. Gaunt lived happily together—as times went. A fine girl and boy were born to them; and need I say how their hearts expanded and exulted; and seemed to grow twice as large?

> The little boy was taken from them at three years old: and how can I convey to any but a parent the anguish of that first bereavement?

> Well, they suffered it together, and that poignant grief was one tie more between them.

> For many years they did not furnish any exciting or even interesting matter to this narrator. . . . In the absence of striking incidents, it may be well to notice the progress of character, and note the tiny seeds of events to come.

This is rather bold, even for Reade, since in thus reiterating his Sensation theories and relegating character analysis to the secondary position he feels it deserves, he is, in effect, challenging the Eliotians on their own ground. He is promising to delineate, within the space of a few pages, psychological developments that, in a George Eliot novel, might be analyzed through an entire volume.

Yet if the challenge itself is quixotic, and based on a misconception of Eliot's aims and techniques, there is no denying the validity of his own performance. The incisiveness of his commentary shows how inevitable was Kate's frustration, as Griffith, following the accepted pattern of the time, developed into a boozy country squire. Finding it impossible to bleed for such a husband, she again decided to bleed for the Church, only to be once again held in check by her spiritual director, Father Francis, whose common sense had by this time become so irksome to her that she felt relieved when he was ordered to another part of the country: "His mind," said she, "is set on earthly things. Instead of helping the angels to raise my thought to heaven and heavenly things, he drags me down to earth. Oh, that man's soul was born without wings. . . . There are plenty of honest men in the world," said she; "but in one's spiritual director, one needs something more than that, and I have pined for it like a thirsty soul in the desert all these years."

The something more Kate pined for remained undefined until she met Father Francis' successor: "His skin was dark and his eyes coal black; yet his ample but symmetrical forehead was singularly white and delicate. Very tall and spare, and both face and figure were of that exalted kind which make ordinary beauty seem dross. . . . This Brother Leonard looked and moved like a being who had come down from some higher sphere to pay the world a very little visit, and be very kind and patient with it all the time." None of these features were lost upon Kate, who "almost started at first sight . . . of a man so remarkable." He seemed to her "Religion embodied," and in her innocence she set about winning his approval in the same way she had won that of every other man she had encountered—with flutters, and blushes, and displays of feminine charm. But to no avail. Only when she began talking about "the prospects of the Church" did Leonard show the slightest interest, and then he dismissed her remarks with a "cold, lofty look of polite but grave disapproval."

The "look" is no more convincing than Leonard himself, who throughout this scene remains, in his stately aloofness, a clerical counterpart of Jane Austen's Darcy. But Kate's reactions to his rebuffs are convincing enough, particularly as they reveal her almost masochistic delight in having at long last discovered a man who could make her feel inferior. Even while she continued to resist his domination, out of wounded pride, she secretly hoped in "her woman's nature" that he would overcome her resistance—as he eventually did, to her entire satisfaction, through the overwhelming strength of his eloquence: "His first sermon was an era in her life. After twenty years of pulpit prosers, there suddenly rose before her a sacred orator . . . in the exercise of this great gift the whole man seemed transfigured; abroad, he was a languid, rather slouching priest, who crept about, a picture of delicate humility, but with a shade of meanness; for, religious prejudice apart, it is ignoble to sweep the wall in passing as he did, and eye the ground; but, once in the pulpit, his figure rose and swelled majestically, and seemed to fly over them all like a guardian angel's; his sallow cheek burned, his great Italian eye shot black lightning at the impenitent, and melted ineffably when he soothed the sorrowful."

In so far as this rhetorical portrait represents Kate's view of Leonard's preaching—and that is how it is primarily intended—its theatricalities are to some extent justified. In her state of mind she was prepared to see his figure rise and swell majestically and to respond accordingly:

> Mrs. Gaunt sat thrilled, enraptured, melted. She hung upon his words; and, when they ceased, she still sat motionless, spell-bound; loath to believe that accents so divine could really come to an end.

Even whilst all the rest were dispersing, she sat quite still, and closed her eyes. For her soul was too high-strung now to endure the chit-chat she knew would attack her on the road home—chit-chat that had been welcome enough, coming home from other preachers.

And by this means she came hot and undiluted to her husband; she laid her white hand on his shoulder, and said, "Oh, Griffith, I have heard the voice of God."

The sexual connotations of "hot and undiluted," clear enough in themselves and substantiated by Reade's entries on the Notecards, serve to emphasize the sexual implications of Kate's words and actions, as she, in her "enthusiastic admiration," identified Leonard first with St. Paul, then with Christ. Nor was she much sobered by Griffith's disapproval, or his impatience at having to delay Sunday dinner because of Leonard's eloquence. That Griffith could even mention dinner at such a time seemed to her incredibly gross, an impression that was deepened on the following Sunday by his refusal to accompany her to chapel, on the ground that it would look as if he were tied "to his wife's apron" and in any case would offend his own Anglican parson. To Kate these arguments seemed at best "stupid," and when, on the following Sunday, he once again fell to complaining about her being late for dinner, pointing out that the delay might upset the servants and spoil their Sunday, she expressed her sense of outrage in a speech that is all the more dramatically effective for being a direct answer to his bumbling attempts to equate Sunday dinner with the sanctity of the home: "Dinner! dinner! What! shall I starve my soul, by hurrying away from the oracles of God to a sirloin? Oh, these gross appetites! how they deaden the immortal half, and wall out heaven's music! For my part, I wish there was no such thing as eating and drinking; 'tis like falling from heaven down into the mud, to come back from such divine discourse and be greeted with 'dinner! dinner! dinner!'" These sentiments Kate presumably derived from the Sermon on the Mount (Matthew 6, 25), but the words, and more particularly the images, were of her own devising. And their crudity, not to say cruelty, reveals that her rejection of Sunday dinner was also a symbolic rejection of her husband and his animal appetites.

Having thus freed herself Kate became ever more devoted to her heavenly oracle, who had finally begun to succumb to her presence: "She was always there whenever he preached, and her rapt attention never flagged. Her gray eyes never left his face, and, being upturned, the full orbs came out in all their grandeur, and seemed an angel's come down from heaven to hear him. . . . " After leaving the pulpit, "and cooling," Leonard invariably remembered that Kate "was no angel but a woman of the world." The illusion, however, had be-come so necessary to him that, to avoid dispelling it through personal contact, he commissioned his assistant to visit her and receive her confessions. While this explanation of Leonard's motives may seem rather arbitrary, and certainly involves Reade in some rather arbitrary plotting, it provides just about the only possible circumstances in which such an ethereal love could take root and grow. So long as Leonard saw Kate only from the pulpit he felt no obligation to censor his feelings; after all, she was his inspiring angel. And so he made love to her, never realizing that he had in effect substituted the pulpit for the divan, holy words and looks for more conventional forms of endearment. And she, equally innocent in her idealism, met his words and looks with adoring looks of her own.

In consequence Leonard found it increasingly difficult to maintain the purity of his angelic image. More and more he tended to transform the ideal image into the real woman. And she, in her womanliness, hastened the transformation, when, stopping to chat with Mrs. Gough, the housekeeper of the parsonage and an old servant of hers, she discovered that Leonard's saintliness, as manifested in his obliviousness to food and comfort, caused him to experience periods of melancholy. Deeply moved by this information, she not only bribed Mrs. Gough to adulterate Leonard's food with meat but also arranged, again with Mrs. Gough's connivance, to have his study "filled with geraniums and jessamine. . . . " Then, having permitted Mrs. Gough to sweep aside her one doubt—that it might "be a sin, and a sacrilege to boot . . . for us to play the woman so, and delude a saint for his mere bodily weal"—she departed "with feelings strangely but sweetly composed of veneration and pity. In that Leonard was a great orator and a high-minded priest, she revered him; in that he was solitary and sad, she pitied him; in that he wanted common sense, she felt like a mother, and must take him under her wing. All true women love to protect; perhaps it is a part of the great maternal element; but to protect a man, and yet look up to him, this is delicious."

"Delicious," applied to a woman's feelings, nearly always carries sexual overtones in Reade's usage, and the present instance is no exception—though Reade, looking forward to the climactic action and the need for maintaining Kate's purity, stresses her maternal and reverential feelings (rather than the impulses that underlie them), and in manipulating the plot goes out of his way to absolve her of any real complicity in the matter of the flowers: "Now Mrs. Gaunt, after eight years of married life, was too sensible and dignified a woman to make a romantic mystery out of nothing. She concealed the gravy, because there secrecy was necessary; but she never dreamed of hiding that she had sent her spiritual adviser a load of flowers. She did not tell her neighbors, for she was not ostentatious; but she told her husband, who grunted, but did not object."

Although this bit of editorializing is not, in itself, wholly convincing, Kate's own words and actions substantiate the essential innocence of her naïve high-mindedness. She could not know that Leonard, already in love with his angelic image of her, would cherish the flowers because they were "from her hand," or that he would be even more delighted with two watering pots with gold crosses on them because they not only were "from her hand" but intended "for his hands." Nor could she know that "watering the flowers that she had given him . . . with his own hands" would become for Leonard a physical if ritualized act of love: "He had a Madonna that cared for him in secret. She was human, but good, beautiful, and wise. . . . And she knows me better than myself. . . . Since I had these flowers from her hand, I am another man."

Yet if these were not the reactions that Kate intended or expected the fact remains that she was quick to recognize and accept them:

> One evening Mrs. Gaunt rode by with Griffith, and saw him watering them. His tall figure, graceful, though inclined to stoop, bent over them with feminine delicacy, and the simple act, which would have been nothing in vulgar hands, seemed to Mrs. Gaunt so earnest, tender, and delicate in him, that her eyes filled, and she murmured, "Poor Brother Leonard!"

> "Why, what's wrong with him now?" asked Griffith, a little peevishly.

> "That was him watering his flowers."

> "Oh, is that all?" said Griffith carelessly.

These last few lines of dialogue are quite masterful, revealing as they do the full extent of the psychic distance that separates the naïve wife from the even more naïve husband. Griffith, having taken refuge in peevish male jealousy could not possibly comprehend Kate's response, much less the more subtle evasiveness of her reply, which suggests that she sensed more than she knew, or at least more than she was willing to admit, even to herself.

In any event she was pleased and not at all surprised when, a few days later, she heard that Brother Leonard had called on her in person while she was out. What she did not know, however, was that he had been directed to the grove (known as the "Dames Haunt" because she so much frequented it) and that while there, walking "to and fro, in religious meditation," his meditative eye had "happened to fall on a terrestrial object that startled and thrilled him . . . a lady's glove. . . . He stooped and picked it up. He opened the little fingers, and called up in fancy the white and tapering hand that glove could fit. He laid the glove softly on his own palm, and eyed it with dreamy tenderness. 'So this is the hand that hath solaced my loneliness,' said he: 'a hand fair as that angelical face, and sweet as the kind heart that doeth good by stealth. . . . ' He put the little glove in his bosom, and paced thoughtfully home through the woods. . . . "

VII

This episode of the glove marks the end of Leonard's innocence—though not, of course, his self-deception. In Reade's words: "Love stole on him, masked with religious zeal, and robed in a garment of light that seemed celestial. When the mask fell, it was too late: the power to resist . . . was gone. The solitary man was too deep in love." And so he cherished the glove, and when he felt frustrated in his efforts "to sketch the inspired face he had learned to preach to," actually desecrated the pulpit by using it as an easel: "On his return home, he threw himself on his knees, and prayed forgiveness of God with many sighs and tears, and hid the sacrilegious drawing out of his own sight. Two days after, he was at work coloring it; and the hours flew by like minutes, as he laid the mellow, melting tints on with infinite care and delicacy. *Labor ipse voluptas.*"

Kate, on the other hand, remained innocent in her responsiveness until, quite by chance, she discovered her glove and portrait in Leonard's room. Then she too experienced feelings that brought her close to self-awareness—feelings that Reade describes imagistically in a passage that at once looks back to Bacon and anticipates Freud: "Her meditations were no longer so calm and speculative as heretofore. She found her mind constantly recurring to one person, and, above all, to the discovery she had made of her portrait in his possession. She had turned it off to Betty Gough; but here, in her calm solitude and umbrageous twilight, her mind crept out of its cave, like wild and timid things at dusk, and whispered to her heart that Leonard perhaps admired her more than was safe or prudent. Then this alarmed her, yet caused her a secret complacency: and that, her furtive satisfaction, alarmed her still more."

It was to such passages as this that Henry James was referring when he spoke of "those great sympathetic guesses with which a real master attacks the truth."[13] And in the dramatic passage that follows—the first personal meeting between Kate and Leonard—Reade does full justice to his insight by having Kate draw upon her suppressed awareness of Leonard's love to break down his reserves and to bring him to the point of sharing with her his hopes and ambitions for the Church.

After this meeting Kate departed from Leonard "like one in a dream . . . the world seemed dead to her forever." And in the weeks and months that followed, as she devoted herself wholly to Leonard and his religious activities, the world, including her husband, actually did come to mean less and less to her. She lived only for her meetings with Leonard—meetings that, for her as for Leonard, soon developed into disguised love trysts:

> Every syllable that passed between these two might have been published without scandal. But the heart does not speak by words alone: there are looks, and there are tones of voice that belong to Love, and are his signs, his weapons; and it was in these very tones the priest murmured to his gentle listener about "the angelic life" between spirits still lingering on earth, but purged from earthly dross; and even about other topics less captivating to the religious imagination. He had persuaded her to found a school in this dark parish, and in it he taught the poor with exemplary and touching patience. Well, when he spoke to her about this school, it was in words of practical good sense, but in tones of love; and she, being one of those feminine women who catch the tone they are addressed in, and instinctively answer in tune, and, moreover, seeing no ill but good in the *subject* of their conversation, replied sometimes, unguardedly enough, in accents almost as tender.

> In truth, if Love was really a personage, as the heathens feigned, he must have often perched on a tree, in that quiet grove, and chuckled and mocked when this man and woman sat and murmured together in the soft seducing twilight about the love of God.

This final paragraph underlines the fact that Kate was almost as deeply in love with Leonard as he with her, that, for all her innocence, she was well on the way to replacing her husband with her priest. But this, given his plot, theories, and techniques, Reade could not permit. To justify Kate's actions and to add sensational interest, he introduced Mrs. Ryder, a "female-rake" (patterned after Mrs. Archbold) who is also a "she-Machiavel," and therefore a fit instrument for working out the complications of the plot outlined on the Notecards. It is Mrs. Ryder who goads Griffith into a jealous fury; it is she who foils as well as foments his scheme to have Leonard dragged through the horse-pond; and it is she, in her role of "she-Machiavel," who reveals to both Leonard and Kate Griffith's part in the scheme—with a view to bringing the wife and priest together and thereby securing the husband for her rakish self.

Hopelessly melodramatic as they are in themselves these nefarious machinations and threats of violence do enable Reade to bring his pure heroine to the point of seduction without sacrificing her innocence: "It was an evil hour when Griffith attacked her saint with violence. The woman was too high-spirited, and too sure of her own rectitude, to endure that; so, instead of crushing her, it drove her to retaliation, and to imprudence." Since Leonard could no longer come to her she would go to him:

> One day, as he sat drooping and listless, there came a light foot along the passage, a light tap at the door, and the next moment she stood before him, a little paler than usual, but lovelier than ever, for celestial pity softened her noble features.

> The priest started up with a cry of joy that ought to have warned her; but it only brought a faint blush of pleasure to her cheek, and the brimming tears to her eyes.

> 'Dear father and friend,' said she. 'What! have you missed me? Think, then, how I have missed *you*. But 'twas best for us both to let their vile passions cool first.'

> Leonard could not immediately reply. The emotion of seeing her again so suddenly almost choked him.

> He needed all the self-possession he had been years acquiring, not to throw himself at her knees and declare his passion to her.

> Mrs. Gaunt saw his agitation, but did not interpret it aright.

> She came eagerly and sat on a stool beside him. 'Dear father,' she said, 'do not let their insolence grieve you. They have smarted for it, and *shall* smart till they make their submission to you, and beg and entreat you to come to us again. Meantime, since you cannot visit me, I visit you. Confess me, father, and then direct me with your counsels.'

> . . . . .

> By this time Leonard had recovered his self-possession, and he spent an hour of strange intoxication, confessing his idol, sentencing his idol to light penances, directing and advising his idol, and all in the soft murmurs of a lover. . . .

> Two days only elapsed, and she came again. Visit succeeded to visit; and her affection seemed boundless.

Kate's "confess me, father" is so tantalizing, in context, as to be very nearly pornographic, and presumably she intensified her "tenderness" on her succeeding visits—though Reade dared not say as much. He had reached the end of his Victorian tether—as demonstrated by his frantic efforts to maintain Kate's innocence and purity, first by shifting the burden of moral responsibility wholly onto Leonard, then by interpolating moral platitudes to account for her seductive acts.

So that, if one accepts Reade's commentary, rather than the full text, she is guilty of nothing more than indiscretion.

But Kate's actions and words speak for themselves, and they, together with Reade's hints and incidental revelations (e.g., that Kate had not been sleeping with Griffith since his threatened violence to Leonard) do much to redeem the otherwise stock melodramatic features of Leonard's attempted seduction and its aftermath. In fact Reade's treatment of Kate's reaction to the attempted seduction is in all essentials sound, and in certain of its touches remarkably perceptive:

> She went home straight to her husband . . . 'Griffith,' she said, 'will you grant your wife a favor? You once promised to take me abroad: I desire to go now: I long to see foreign countries: I am tired of this place. I want a change. Prithee, prithee, take me hence this very day.' . . .

> 'Well, but what a fancy to take all of a sudden!'

> 'Oh, Griffith, don't deny me what I ask you, with my arm around your neck, dearest. It is no fancy. I want to be alone with *you,* far from this place where coolness has come between us.' And with this she fell to crying and sobbing, and straining him tight to her bosom, as if she feared to lose him, or be taken from him.

> Griffith kissed her, and told her to cheer up, he was not the man to deny her anything. 'Just let me get my hay in,' said he, 'and I'll take you to Rome, if you like.' . . .

> Mrs. Gaunt had gradually sunk almost to her knees. She now started up with nostrils expanding and her blue eyes glittering. 'Your hay!' she cried, with bitter contempt; 'your hay before your wife? That is how *you* love me.'

The final "you," contrasting Griffith with Leonard, accounts for Kate's slipping on the stairs (just after the hay was in); also for her having an invalid's bed sent "by the doctor at her own request, and placed on a small bedstead," thus leaving Griffith once again "as good as a widower." And to spell out the full implications of Kate's illness, which would now be labelled psychosomatic, Reade arranged for his "she-Machiavel" (now become a "female Iago") to disillusion the sorrowful Griffith:

> 'It is nothing,' said she; then she paused and added, 'but my folly. I can't bear to see you waste your feelings. She is not so ill as you fancy.'

> 'Do you mean to say that my wife is pretending?'

> 'How can I say that? I wasn't there: *nobody saw her fall;* nor *heard her either;* and the house full of people. No doubt there is something the matter with her; but I do believe her heart is in more trouble than her back.'

> 'And what troubles her heart? Tell me, and she shall not fret long.'

> 'Well, sir: then just you send for Father Leonard: and she will get up and walk as she used. . . . That man is the main of her sickness, you take my word.'

Here as elsewhere Reade used his "female Iago" quite skillfully, not only to further his plot but also to reveal aspects of his heroine's feelings that he, as Victorian author, could not treat directly. For whatever Ryder's motives her words are true—as Griffith discovers when he returns home unexpectedly to find his invalid wife in the grove with Leonard, "springing along, elastic as a young greyhound, and full of fire and animation."

Further than this, however, Reade dared not go. Indeed he apparently felt that he had gone too far already, for in the climactic scene that follows Kate has no sympathy whatsoever for Leonard, even after he has been trampled by the maniacal Griffith. Her sole concern is for her own dignity and honor, so cruelly besmirched by Griffith's curses, and she consequently dismisses Leonard on the spot—in a manner appropriate to an Adelphi heroine: "Mrs. Gaunt turned and flung her arm around so that the palm of her hand, high raised, confronted Leonard. I am thus particular, because it was a gesture grand and terrible as the occasion that called it forth: a gesture that *spoke,* and said, 'Put the whole earth and sea between us forever after this.'"

VIII

That Leonard should quail before Kate's meaninglessly theatrical gesture was as necessary to Reade's moral purpose as to his melodramatic plot, and helps to explain why, following the episode of the glove, he presented Leonard as he did, drawing upon the Notecards to demonstrate that not Leonard but the Church itself must be held responsible for his actions: "Father Leonard was a pious, pure, and noble-minded man who had undertaken to defy nature with religious aid; and, after years of successful warfare, now sustained one of those defeats to which such warriors have always been liable." Moreover the Church provided the means as well as the justification for Leonard's attempted seduction. It was through the confessional that he gained the knowledge which finally brought him to the point of openly declaring his passion; and to gain this knowledge "Leonard . . . had only to follow precedents and ask questions his Church has printed for the use of confessors. . . . "

While these passages serve to enforce Reade's moral argument, their dramatic effect, most evident in the seduction scene, is to reduce Leonard to a weak-willed exemplar of the evils of celibacy. In consequence his cries of "jealous agony" and his torrents of "burning, melting words" have no personal or moral meaning whatever. At best they raise the question: "Will he or won't he manage to seduce our Kate?" And that soap-opera question lacks even the elementary quality of suspense, since the reader knows Kate will never give in, no matter how passionate his priestly importunings.

But Reade's failure with Leonard, serious as it is, does not weaken the later scenes of temptation nearly so much as might be expected, primarily because these scenes are so much Kate's. It is her temptation, not Leonard's, that is central and significant; and her temptation has little to do with Leonard. In fact she does not require or even want a lover: she wants only an embodiment of her romantic ideal and the more passive that embodiment the better. For she is still the same Kate who rejected Neville and married Griffith, and her feelings are still, in D. H. Lawrence's sense of the word, "masturbatory." She insists upon having the intimacy, the thrills, of a man-woman relationship without permitting the man in the case to be a man. He must remain her image of a man, i.e., a man who is not a man, but a priest (a man in skirts) who is besides effeminate in looks and manner. And when this, her ideal, violates itself by speaking hot words of physical love, she is both shocked and indignant.

IX

The third or final section of the novel, which presents the manifold consequences of Jealousy (" . . . of which Bigamy is one . . ."), follows directly from the climactic scene in which Griffith confronts Kate and Leonard in the grove. After trampling "upon the poor priest with both feet" and damning the pair of them, he gallops away from Hearnshaw in a maniacal rage, never stopping until he reaches an obscure inn, some ninety miles away, where he experiences an attack of brain fever that might have proved fatal but for the efforts of the innkeeper's daughter, a dove-eyed milkmaid and Puritan named Mercy Vint. She nurses Griffith back to health, and innocently encourages his advances; whereupon he, in his bitterness and despair, courts and finally marries her—to settle down to a bigamous and happy life.

But not for long. Circumstances force him to return to Hearnshaw, where Kate completely vindicates herself, and he, too late, sees the crime he has committed. For he is now the husband of two wives (one with child, and the other, Kate, soon to be) and finds himself unable to desert either one or the other. So he temporizes until Kate, discovering his crime, threatens to stab him; then he leaves Hearnshaw, quite mysteriously, in circum-

stances that lead to Kate's being tried and very nearly convicted on charges of murder—despite her gallant and brilliant defense. At the last moment, however, Mercy Vint appears on the scene, having walked all the way from Lancashire with her child on her arm, to win Kate's love and to save her life—at the sacrifice of her own good name. For in proving that Griffith is still alive Mercy is forced to expose her own bigamous marriage. Nevertheless it all works out nicely in the end: with Henry Neville, Kate's old suitor, married to Mercy, and the Gaunts united as never before through the effects of a remarkable blood transfusion in which Griffith's "bright red blood" is sent "smoking hot into Kate Gaunt's veins." Henceforth the Gaunts are as happy as the Nevilles, and while the two families cannot appear in public together, because of the gossip, they remain close friends. In Reade's words:

> The wives . . . corresponded, and Lady Neville easily induced Mrs. Gaunt to co-operate with her in her benevolent acts, especially in saving young women who had been betrayed, from sinking deeper.

> Living a good many miles apart, Lady Neville could send her stray sheep to service near Mrs. Gaunt, and *vice versa;* and so, merciful, but discriminating, they saved many a poor girl who had been weak, not wicked.

> So, then, though they could not eat nor dance together in earthly mansions, they could do good together; and, methinks, in the eternal world, where years of social intercourse will prove less than cobwebs, these their joint acts of mercy will be links of a bright, strong chain, to bind their souls in everlasting amity.

In thus uniting the two wives in good sexual works that serve to remind them of their own inadvertent sexual transgressions Reade provides a fitting conclusion to this final section. The banality of his treatment derives in the first place from his efforts to combine so many wild and disparate actions within the confines of his borrowed plot—efforts so strained that he has little chance to develop or motivate even his leading characters, but must endow them with the stock responses necessitated by the action. On Griffith and the lesser melodramatic types carried over from the first two sections the effects of this treatment are hardly discernible. But on Kate they are disastrous. She degenerates from the complex woman of the first two sections to a female embodiment of conventional Victorian virtues, including many virtues ordinarily reserved for men: she bears her wrongs and sufferings "like a man"; she pleads her case in court with Portia-like charm and masculine logic; and in speaking to Neville of Mercy's plight she declares: "I wish I was a man: I'd cure her of Griffith before we reached the 'Packhorse.' And, now I think of it, you are a very happy man to travel eighty miles with an angel, a dove-eyed angel." Yet as Reade presents these traits they do not enhance or develop the androgynous side of Kate's make-up; they merely add piquancy to her bigamous predicament.

Nor is Reade's portrait of Mercy, who shares the feminine lead with Kate in this section, any more convincing or meaningful. Her piety is too patent, her mercy too strained, her womanliness too pure. Seemingly intended to combine the salient qualities of Dinah Morris and Hetty Sorrel she actually combines the stock features of these two characters—most obviously in the early scenes of pastoral courtship, in which she continually nurses and churns and sings and simpers, but also in the more crucial scenes of bigamous married life, in which she allegedly brings "our hero, now malefactor," a "sweet content" he had never enjoyed in his legitimate married life with Kate. Although the point of this intended contrast ("to clear away some vague conventional notions" about crime in general and bigamy in particular) may be legitimate enough, Reade's efforts to give it dramatic substance come to very little. Mercy is so theatrically obsequious in her wifely affection—what with tending the fire and tuning his viol da gambo—that the only significant effect of contrasting her love with Kate's is, once again, to heighten the piquancy of Griffith's bigamous situation.

And the scenes in which Mercy and Kate meet, glare, weep, embrace, examine Mercy's child, and then, quite literally, sleep together, have much the same effect, despite the purity of Reade's avowed intentions. Dickens, in politely refusing Wilkie Collins' invitation to defend the novel in court, discussed these scenes (along with others he found objectionable) in a letter that by implication defines the moral code to which all serious novelists were expected to adhere:

MY DEAR WILKIE,

I have read Charles Reade's book, and here follows my state of mind—*as a witness*—respecting it.

I have read it with the strongest interest and admiration. I regard it as the work of a highly accomplished writer and a good man; a writer with a brilliant fancy and a graceful and tender imagination. I could name no other living writer who could, in my opinion, write such a story nearly so well. As regards a so-called critic who should decry such a book as Holywell Street literature, and the like, I should have merely to say of him that I could desire no stronger proof of his incapacity in, and his unfitness for, the post to which he has elected himself.

Cross-examined, I should feel myself in danger of being put on unsafe ground, and should try to set my wits against the cross-examiner, to keep well off it. But if I were reminded (as I probably should be, supposing the evidence to be allowed at all) that I was the editor of a periodical of large circulation in which the Plaintiff himself had written, and if I had read to me in court those passages about Gaunt's going up to his wife's bed drunk and that last child's being conceived, and was asked whether, as Editor, I would have passed those passages, whether written by the Plaintiff or anybody else, I should be obliged to reply No. Asked why? I should say that what was pure to an artist might be impurely suggestive to inferior minds (of which there must necessarily be many among a large mass of readers) and that I should have called the writer's attention to the likelihood of those passages being perverted in such quarters. Asked if I should have passed the passage where Kate and Mercy have the illegitimate child upon their laps and look over its little points together? I should again be obliged to reply No, for the same reason. Asked whether, as author or Editor, I should have passed Neville's marriage to Mercy, and should have placed those four people, Gaunt, his wife, Mercy, and Neville, in those relative situations towards one another, I should again be obliged to reply No. Hard pressed upon this point, I must infallibly say that I consider those relative situations extremely coarse and disagreeable.[14]

The prime difficulty with this criticism, considered from a modern point of view, is that it denies Reade his subject as well as his treatment, and would apply with even greater force to such a modern novel as Nabokov's *Lolita*. Nor is Dickens' attempt to distinguish between the "artist" and "inferior minds" much more helpful, confusing as it does moral with artistic values. The passages in question are not "impurely suggestive to inferior minds," they are purely (or merely) "suggestive" (or pornographic) to all perceptive minds, and for this reason tend to oversimplify or invalidate the sexual responses of the characters involved. No doubt Kate was curious about "every feature" of Mercy's little boy, but in having the two women immediately set about examining and kissing the boy's "limbs and extremities after the manner of their sex" Reade endowed his heroine with "female traits" that, in context, appear less characteristic than titillating.

To such a charge Reade would doubtless have replied by citing various items in the Notebooks, among others the following (included in the Notebook entitled "Foemina Vera" under the heading "Traits"):

Fonder of their own children than men,
and kiss them ten times oftener
fonder of children generally and [pillage
   them?]
of their clothes in the
street, which no male
malefactor does.

A few pages further on, in the same Notebook, Reade includes a clipping (Telegraph, April 7 X 64) illustrating the above observation, then on the next page repeats the observation itself—with slight variations and additions:

> Women in connection
> with children
> Love children ten times more than
> men do; and kiss them thirty
> times more
> women are the child strippers
> See Theta 2
> woman throws a babe out of window
> Epsilon 12

But these factual traits do not in any sense justify those of Kate and Mercy—even if one accepts Reade's Baconian premises. For in adapting the facts to his characters he has oversimplified the facts (as well as the characters) by choosing to overlook or evade the sexual implications of the violence and child-stripping that render the facts meaningful. In other words the pornography is the result not of frankness but of evasiveness—an evasiveness that leads, first to the suppression of the full sexual responses of the two heroines, then to the presentation of their partial responses as conventionally pure manifestations of womanly curiosity.

And Reade bowdlerized· nearly all the other sexual passages in much the same way to much the same effect—although the passages that most upset Dickens ("those . . . about Gaunts going up to his wife's bed drunk and that last child's being conceived") are perhaps more ludicrous than pornographic, since Reade's efforts to purify Griffith's actions (by attributing them to "habit") so closely parallel *Tristram Shandy's* explanation of his father's sex habits as to suggest the possibility that Reade was consciously drawing upon the well known fourth chapter of *Tristram Shandy.* Needless to say he was not, in fact could not, without compromising his work as well as his own moral position. If he was borrowing from anyone, the Notecards reveal, it was Michelet, whose observations on "habit" were entirely staid. Yet the Sternean parallels are still there—whether intended or not—and their effect is to render farcical Reade's strained efforts to purify Griffith's habit.

X

Also farcical are many of the passages Reade consciously intended to be Shakespearean—notably those in which Kate emulates Portia and Mrs. Ryder plays female Iago to Griffith's Othello. For by stressing these parallels and seeking to reinforce them with Shakespearean language Reade but calls attention to the discrepancy between his conventionally melodramatic characters and Shakespeare's—a discrepancy so great that it renders foolish passages that might otherwise be acceptable, such as those in which Kate pleads her own case. So long as she confines herself to reporting the bare facts or cross-examining witnesses her performance is genuinely moving, but when she resorts to the Shakespearean manner of Charles Kean in declaring her wrongs there is little to choose between her eloquence and that of her melodramatic predecessors.

The remaining passages in this section—in which Reade presents the scenes of blood, violence, and mistaken identity necessary to the resolution of his plot—are likewise conventionally melodramatic. Only in treating the blood transfusion, based directly on the Notebooks (*Red Digest,* p. 25),[15] does Reade manage to integrate his Sensation with his theme, and even then his efforts to develop the metaphoric and symbolic aspects of the transfusion hardly fulfill his intention—to render credible Kate's final submission to Griffith: "She wanted a good excuse for loving him as frankly as before, and now he had given her one. She used to throw it in his teeth in the prettiest way. Whenever she confessed a fault, she was sure to turn slyly round and say, 'But what could one expect of me? I have his blood in my veins.' . . . Once she told Father Francis, quite seriously, that she had never been quite the same woman since she lived by Griffith's blood; she was turned jealous; and, moreover, it had given him a fascinating power over her, and she could tell blindfold when he was in the room."

Reade's object in bringing Kate to such a point of abject love and submission is of course to qualify her for the concluding marital quadrille, in which, all passion presumably purified, the two heroines join hands with one another (as well as with their former husbands and lovers) to prove that Love and Charity can triumph over Jealousy and Bigamy. And while there is no doubting the sincerity of Reade's intention, the effect of this finalé (as might be expected) is to prove just the opposite, and in the process to carry the pornography and Sensation of the preceding scenes right down to the penultimate paragraph—in which Reade, in a final attempt at pietistic justification, actually stresses the carnal knowledge that the two heroines still share on earth and will presumably still share in heaven.

XI

In itself Reade's ending is perhaps no more banal than, say, the insipidly happy ending that Dickens, in deference to his readers and Bulwer-Lytton, tacked onto *Great Expectations.* But whereas the ending of *Great Expectations* merely provides a means for closing off the action, that of **Griffith Gaunt** represents the necessary fulfillment of the entire final section of the novel, which in turn represents the necessary fulfillment of the plot and ostensible theme that Reade formally announces as early as page thirteen in speaking of Griffith's foible.

Yet—and this is what saves the novel—Jealousy does not, accurately speaking, constitute the theme or even the subject of the novel; at most it provides the titular hero with a "humour" convenient for organizing the disparate elements of the action into a loose melodramatic plot. The subject of the novel, in Percy Lubbock's sense of "subject," is not Griffith but Kate; and the theme, in so far as it can be defined in a word, is not Jealousy but Adultery—the theme that Reade himself adumbrates on the Notecards and in the opening lines of the novel:

CHAPTER I

"THEN I say once for all, that priest shall never darken my doors again."

"Then I say they are my doors and not yours, and that holy man shall brighten them whenever he will."

The gentleman and lady, who faced each other, pale and furious, and interchanged this bitter defiance, were man and wife. And had loved each other well.

In this dialogue, repeated verbatim half-way through the novel (p. 210), Kate makes her choice: "The matrimonial throne for him till he resisted her priest; and then a stool at her feet and his." And in the following scenes Reade develops the implications of this choice, using Griffith's Jealousy and Mrs. Ryder's melodramatic machinations as a subordinate means of furthering and justifying his treatment of Kate. It is not until he has brought Kate to the point of seeming adultery, in the climactic grove scene, that he permits Griffith's *foible* to become dominant, and at this point he is obviously preparing to substitute Jealousy and its Bigamous consequences for the theme of Adultery.

Had Reade ended the novel here it might now be an acknowledged Victorian masterpiece; certainly if he had carried the theme of adultery to the ultimate conclusions prefigured in both his text and the Notecards its claims would be beyond dispute. But given Reade's theories and techniques and the moral demands of his readers he could neither conclude nor develop his adulterous theme. In fact he could not even abandon it: he had to replace it, then purify it. Hence the introduction (into this final bigamous section) of Kate's letters to Leonard proving that she had never really felt what, according to the dramatic text, she certainly had felt. Hence too the resourceful explanations of Father Francis, proving that her temptation had not been a temptation at all, but a series of misunderstandings brought about by her "imprudence"—

not ordinary imprudence but imprudence derived from "Christian Charity . . . true and rare and exalted piety."

Taken at face value, these attempts at purification cancel out nearly the whole of the temptation sequence. But of course they cannot be taken at face value: their function—an accepted one in Sensation fiction—is akin to that of the last act in a "well-made" stage comedy, which consists, according to Shaw, "of clearing up the misunderstanding, and generally getting the audience out of the theatre as best you can."[16] One essential difference, however, is that Reade did not apply this conventional stratagem cynically: to him as to his readers it represented a moral necessity as well as a literary convention, and he saw no conflict between the two. The purification simply justified him in presenting aspects of his heroine's character that would otherwise have been morally reprehensible. And while the modern reader, acquainted with Zola, Hardy, Lawrence, *et al,* may consider this conception of morality in fiction to be naïve and contradictory, if not downright hypocritical, the fact remains that it was shared by nearly all the Victorian novelists, Dickens included, and therefore constitutes a necessary if limiting condition of their art.

Indeed it can be argued that the entire final section of the novel is of a piece with Reade's attempts at purification, and should be dismissed on similar grounds— as a conventional appendage corresponding in function to the closing chapters of so many other Sensational novels. But this argument, appealing as it may be to the modern reader, verges on the arbitrary when applied to a section that constitutes, in bulk, nearly half the novel, and that represents, on the plot level, the fulfillment of the announced theme of the novel. After all, the novel is entitled **Griffith Gaunt,** not *Kate Peyton,* and the melodramatic and pornographic aspects of the action that become dominant in the final bigamous section cannot be dismissed or rationalized away simply because they tend to mar and distort what is artistically valid in the first two sections.

The best if not the only critical alternative is to acknowledge that the novel, considered as a whole, is radically flawed—much as *Vanity Fair,* for instance, is radically flawed, with Mercy's bigamous purity corresponding to Amelia's widowed purity, Gaunt's insane Jealousy to Dobbins' insane devotion. As for pornography there is nothing more flagrant in **Griffith Gaunt** than the scene in *Vanity Fair* (already discussed) in which Thackeray descants on the charms of his sleeping heroine. And like parallels can be drawn from nearly all the other great Victorian novels—the point being, of course, that in Victorian fiction such blemishes are the necessary concomitants of creative expression, particularly in matters sexual. Thackeray could never have created Becky Sharp if he had not, in the very beginning of the novel, paired her off against Amelia; nor could he have developed her as he did, if he had not, towards the end of the novel, reduced her to a tawdry whore.

To apply the currently modish standards of Jamesian criticism to such fiction is therefore, as Percy Lubbock himself acknowledges, a bit ridiculous. Unless some of the greatest Victorian novels (including all of Dickens' novels, with the possible exception of *Great Expectations*) are to be rejected out of hand, the critic must recognize that the final test of a novel is not its perfection of Jamesian form but the intensity of expression it achieves in spite of or apart from its imperfections. By this test, which is James's own positive test, Thackeray's inanities are more than redeemed by what Lubbock has defined as its "richness of life."[17] And by the same token Reade's inanities are more than redeemed by the intensity he achieves in his dramatic portrait of Kate—an intensity, paraphrasing Reade's own words, that penetrates beneath the calm solitude and umbrageous twilight of Kate's idealism to reveal, with rare perceptiveness, the warped and twisted feelings that underlie it. And if James, in his encomiastic reference to "those great sympathetic guesses," overpraises Reade at George Eliot's expense, the fact remains that Reade's portrait (as it is developed in relation to the theme of adultery) will bear comparison, not only with the corresponding portraits of Eliot, but with those of the later Hardy— and that, in itself, should be sufficient to restore the novel to the first rank of Victorian fiction.

Notes

[7] See Edmund Morrison, unpublished dissertation, University of California pp. 197-199.

[8] Quoted in Emerson Grant Sutcliffe, "Charles Reade's Notebooks," *Studies in Philology* 28 (1930), p. 103.

[9] See "Charles Reade's Notebooks," *passim*. . . .

[11] *Griffith Gaunt,* p. 13.

[12] *Ibid.,* p. 17. Since I shall be quoting from *Griffith Gaunt* often and at length (throughout the rest of this chapter) there seems to be little point in footnoting individual passages. Ordinarily my commentary will provide an identifiable context for these passages.

[13] *Notes and Reviews By Henry James* with a preface by Pierre De Chaignon La Rose (Cambridge, Mass., 1921), p. 207.

[14] Quoted by Malcolm Elwin, *Charles Reade* (London, 1931), pp. 188-189.

[15] See "Charles Reade's Notebooks," p. 86.

[16] George Bernard Shaw, "Preface" to *Three Plays By Brieux* (New York, 1911), p. xxiii.

[17] See Percy Lubbock, *The Craft of Fiction* (New York, Charles Scribner's Sons, n.d.) p. 117.

C. H. Muller (essay date 1971)

SOURCE: "Charles Reade and *The Cloister and the Hearth*: A Survey of the Novel's Literary Reception and Its Historic Fidelity," in *Unisa English Studies*, Vol. IX, No. 1, March, 1971, pp. 18-26.

[*In the following excerpt, Muller explores the reasons for the popularity of* The Cloister and the Hearth.]

I

Numerous reasons can be put forward to explain why nineteenth-century critics declined to place Charles Reade in the foremost rank of novelists; but there are three main and obvious reasons: his polemical purpose was frequently injurious to, and incompatible with, his artistic purpose, his reliance on documentary sources like law reports and prison blue-books persuaded critics that he lacked true imagination, or genius, and his invective spirit, apart from damaging his art, made enemies of numerous critics. *Never too late to Mend*—the most characteristic of Reade's didactic works—was one of the most popular novels of the Victorian era, and the novel by which the author first secured his reputation in the eyes of a vast reading public; but to a large number of critics the novel was not welcome, and on its publication (in 1856) a great outcry arose. The author was accused of having indulged in wilful exaggeration of facts concerning the penal system; notwithstanding the heated defence of the author, who showed by Government reports and by the evidence of prison officials that everything he had represented concerning the cruel treatment of prisoners in Birmingham Gaol was true, the prevailing critical attitude that he had written the didactic scenes with much less light than heat shortened the life of the book. Another unfortunate result of Reade's reliance on documentary material occurred when he extended his research to the works of other authors, by which means he exposed himself to charges of plagiarism. Reade denied that he was a plagiarist, yet virtually admitted the truth of the accusation by saying he borrowed from other writers in as much as Shakespeare, Byron and Scott had borrowed from, and improved upon, the works of their predecessors. The matter rests on the question whether Reade was great enough to do what Shakespeare and Byron and Scott could do. In the *Cloister and the Hearth* (1861) he certainly succeeded, and utilized the literature of the middle ages in a historic novel to better effect than any of his contemporaries. Whether

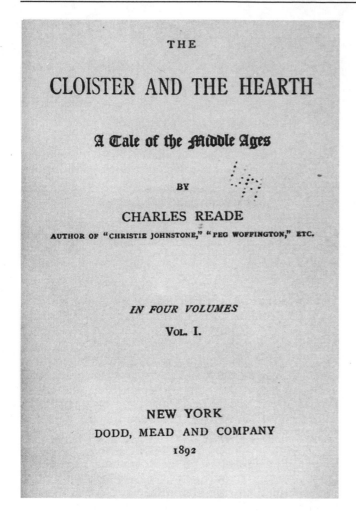

THE

CLOISTER AND THE HEARTH

A Tale of the Middle Ages

BY

CHARLES READE

AUTHOR OF "CHRISTIE JOHNSTONE," "PEG WOFFINGTON," ETC.

IN FOUR VOLUMES

VOL. I.

NEW YORK
DODD, MEAD AND COMPANY
1892

It was as a result of his critics' animosity that Reade became inspired with the indomitable spirit that drove him to the self-denying task of writing the *Cloister and the Hearth;* their criticism lashed him into an almost vindictive fury of determination, as is clear from a letter to Mrs Seymour, an actress who became the life-long friend of the author:

> A man who steps out of the beaten track in every way, as I do, must expect greater difficulties than other people. The question whether I can overcome them or not, is not settled. When I produce another **'Never too Late'**, and the Cabal succeed in burking it, then I will give in.

Not before!

Reade nevertheless considered the 'Cabal' of the English press an insurmountable barrier, and so he consoled himself with the prospect of a higher reputation in France; he was on good terms with Maquet, thanks to his gentlemanly dealings with him concerning international copyright, and this, he hoped, would pave the way for a literary reputation in the Parisian press; hence he wrote to Mrs Seymour: 'Brisebarre writes from Paris and promises to back me in the Parisian press Maquet ditto. Of the English press I have no hope, as you are well aware'. In case the Cabal did succeed in burking his novel. Reade gained a further consolation by persuading himself of a secure future reputation—'I need try and keep my temper, and remember that my lines will outlive theirs by many years'.

In spite of these preliminary doubts and fears, the *Cloister and the Hearth,* after the preceding low ebb of Reade's reputation, struck the reading public as well as the American and English press like a tidal wave. It was particularly in America that the novel swept the continent, the pressure of orders being so great that, according to a short notice in the *New York Herald,* the publishers had to delay publication on account of orders requiring to be filled at once. Later an advertisement stated that the seventh thousand copy was being printed although the book had been out less than a week. The *Saturday Evening Courier* noted that the book had rapidly passed through eight editions within a few weeks after it was published. As a historical novel, the work was a masterpiece, according to the American reviewers. The *New York Herald* noted that the *Cloister and the Hearth* 'has eclipsed all [Reade's] previous efforts, and presented us with a masterpiece of historic fiction', and the *Saturday Evening Courier* readily pronounced Reade's novel 'the best historical romance' the world possessed, acclaiming Reade 'an honest artist and a great author'. Even Nathaniel Hawthorne considered the book 'one of the finest of historical novels'. This success across the Atlantic actually received its impetus from the huge success that had already greeted

he was as successful in his other works is less certain. His novel *White Lies* (1857), it must be admitted, is, in dialogue and incident, largely a translation of Auguste Maquet's *Château de Grantier.* For many of his works he took his plots wherever he happened to find them, and for this purpose his favourite hunting-ground was the French theatre. Reade furthermore invoked the disfavour of critics by means of his wild explosions of printed rage against them, when they dared to question the artistic merit of his work, the truth of his factual data, or the originality of his ideas. His private notebooks, now in the *London Library,* testify that the author entered whole-heartedly into his guerilla warfare with critics; his heartfelt contempt for 'criticasters' and 'pseudonymuncules' (anonymous and pseudonymous critics—most nineteenth-century reviews were anonymous) is expressed, for example, in his notebook *Index Variorum et Manuscriptorum* where, under the heading of 'criticaster', he wrote, 'One does not expect an everlasting reason for tenpence; and under the heading, 'Pseudonymuncule', he observed, 'Impudence and conceit of . . . shown in the names he assumes'.

the novel in Reade's own country. Reade had complained that his success was always greater in the United States. Ironically, it was in American newspapers that his success in England was now reflected. Thus his American publisher advertised the novel by referring to its successful reception by the English press.

Years later, in 1898, W. J. Johnston[1] observed that the *Cloister* was accepted by the critics and the public as a great work, but had created no burst of enthusiasm, since 1861, the year when the novel appeared, was prolific in great works: novels like *Silas Marner, Great Expectations* and the *Woman in White* had fully engaged critical appreciation, so that little attention could be devoted to a comparatively new author like Reade. This conclusion is erroneous, since a survey of reviews in the English press clearly reveals the burst of enthusiasm with which Reade's masterpiece was received. Many reviews paid tribute to Reade's reputation by placing him in the foremost rank of literature. *The Westminster Review,* for example, reviewed the *Cloister and the Hearth* together with and at the expense of Dickens's *Great Expectations* and Thackeray's *Lovel the Widower;* the reviewer followed George Eliot's custom of beginning with a long discussion of the book selected to receive the most prominent notice for the quarter, passing on to notice a handful of lesser novels which were given considerably less space. In this case the most prominent place was given to Reade's novel, the reviewer placing it amongst those novels 'of which the general excellence is so conspicuous, that judges need not hesitate about stamping them with the seal of their approbation'. Whereas the reviewer considered no creation of 'modern fiction' truer to nature and more lovable than Reade's heroine, he predicted that not a character or passage in *Great Expectations* would afford enjoyment to anyone 'twenty years hence'! Indeed, the reviewer felt critics were beginning to tire of Dickens's style 'which grates on the ears of those who were once his warmest admirers'. No doubt Reade's terse and epigrammatic style struck the reviewer as refreshing after Dickens. Thackeray received even less critical attention—'Had not Mr Thackeray been the author of the . . . book, we should have passed it over without notice, and the reading public would have done the same'.

The *Westminster Review* was not alone in ranking Reade on a par, if not above, some of his great contemporaries. The *London Review,* while pronouncing that the 'excellence of Mr Thackeray seems unapproachable', remarked that with the exception of Thackeray 'Reade need hardly fear a comparison with any of his contemporaries'.

The impact of Reade's historical novel on the nineteenth-century literary scene was such that George Eliot, in addition to Dickens and Thackeray, was later to suffer by comparison with Reade. Thus in 1872 a highly flattering article appeared in *Once a Week* in which the *Cloister and the Hearth* was vindicated in exuberant language at the expense of George Eliot's historical novel, *Romola;* it was averred by the anonymous critic that in the historical novel the two writers met in an arena that tested the highest quality they both pretended to—imagination. The result was that in Reade's novel a true and living picture of the Middle Ages was portrayed, whereas the 'narrow canvas' of *Romola* portrayed characters who were 'little more than voluble shadows'. Thus the *Cloister and the Hearth* emerged triumphant:

> **The Cloister and the Hearth** is one of the most scholarlike and learned, as well as one of the most artistic and beautiful, works of fiction in any language. This splendid production can only be compared with the best books of one author Walter Scott. And in all things it is as good as *Kenilworth* and *Ivanhoe:* In some points it is better.

Later, in 1887, the writers of the *Memoir* (Reade's godson and nephew) referred to this article, observing that *Once a Week* may possibly have designed it as an *amende,* since the editor had previously quarrelled with Reade on account of the serialized form of a novel which had since proven its merit; thus the *Memoir* concluded, 'We take it to be in intention an apologetic criticism, as genuine as it is honourable'.[2] Unfortunately the article's high praise cannot be taken seriously, since, according to a writer[3] in the *Bookman,* it was later discovered that its anonymous author was none other than Charles Reade himself. The truth of the matter was that George Eliot's *Romola* had won the plaudits of the press as readily as the *Cloister and the Hearth,* and this, for Reade, was galling, since he firmly believed that the authoress's success was achieved through judicious wire-pulling. Furthermore, he was certain that his own historical romance was George Eliot's chief source of inspiration; thus he asked Mrs Seymour, 'Is it egotism, or am I right in thinking that this story of the fifteenth century [*Romola*] has been called into existence by my success with the same epoch?'

No doubt it was egotism which led Reade to write his own eulogy in *Once a Week;* but his more important motive was to give his reputation a boost at a time when many critics were angrily raising their voices against moral improprieties in his later novels; and since he knew the *Cloister and the Hearth* was his trump card, he gave it his most lavish praise, indicating that no one had previously had the courage to compare George Eliot's novel with a novel critics had compared with the works of Scott. It seems that the bait was taken, that the article had its desired effect, and that it became the fashion to compare Reade with George Eliot at the expense of the latter. Thus some years later Swinburne spoke of the 'now fashionable comparison or contrast of Charles Reade with George Eliot' which to him seemed less profitable and less reasonable than a contrast or comparison of Reade's work with that of 'the two most copious and spontaneous masters of romance', Scott and Dumas.[4] Walter Besant, in 1882, was the first of the more notable writers to follow the trend:

> Comparison between **'The Cloister and the Hearth'** and 'Romola' is forced upon one. Both books treat of the same period; similar pictures should be presented in the pages of both. Yet—what a difference! In the man's work we find action, life, movement, surprise, reality. In the woman's work we find languor, tedium, and the talk of nineteenth-century puppets dressed in fifteenth-century clothes.[5]

Although he thought a comparison between Reade and George Eliot idle, since both writers could achieve equally great heights in their own spheres, Swinburne was himself inclined to rank Reade's historical novel higher than that of George Eliot:

> A story better conceived or better composed, better constructed or better related, than *The Cloister and the Hearth,* it would be difficult to find anywhere; while the most enthusiastic devotees of Romola must surely admit the wellnigh puerile insufficiency of some of the resources by which the story has to be pushed forward or warped round before it can be got into harbour.[6]

A year later the writers of the *Memoir* willingly endorsed this opinion, referring to Swinburne's praise as a 'magnificent exordium', concluding rather extravagantly, 'His noble words tell in an excess of majestic language his enthusiasm, and that . . . is the highest form of intelligent criticism'. Thus, in exaggerated language, Reade's nephew and godson attempted to give the author's reputation a second boost: but no boost could have been more effective than that given to the *Cloister and the Hearth* by Reade himself; under its impetus the book was easily propelled into the twentieth century.

Just before the turn of the century W. J. Johnston noted in the *Gentleman's Magazine* that time had stamped the *Cloister and the Hearth* with the seal of immortality, saying that 'the sweetest, saddest, and most tender love story ever devised by wit of man' could never die. Walter Besant's verdict that the novel was 'the greatest historical novel in the language' was reiterated by Johnston, who went on to observe that it was then almost as well known and appreciated as *David Copperfield, Ivanhoe* or the *Newcomes*. And so, after being repeatedly acclaimed a masterpiece since the day of its publication, the *Cloister and the Hearth* secured more than an ephemeral reputation, and by the beginning of the twentieth century passed

into the region of classical fiction. Thus in 1906 Lewis Melville confidently predicted that the book would rank among the masterpieces 'so long as English novels are read',[7] and E. W. Hornung, in 1921, observed that it was a classic, and still a best seller: 'Three generations of sober and accredited critics have praised this book in terms of just extravagance'.[8]

It was, indeed, this very extravagance of praise given to the *Cloister and the Hearth* which after 1900 caused it to eclipse all of Reade's other works, as the sun extinguishes the lesser lights of the stars. Already in 1906, Lewis Melville considered that the *Cloister and the Hearth,* compared with Reade's other works, was 'as gold to dross', and noted that Reade was 'one of the few great authors whose reputation is founded upon a single book'. By the nineteen-twenties the process was almost complete, and it seemed clear to Hornung that the success of Reade's best book had almost completely suppressed his others; hence Hornung felt that critics had been unjust in praising Reade's one book at the expense of the others:

> Granted it is his one great book, and the best of the others is but 'big', yet the *Cloister and the Hearth* stands as deliberately aloof from the rest of Reade as *A Tale of Two Cities* stands deliberately aloof from the rest of Dickens.[9]

Ironically, a study of Reade's notebooks reveals that he may well have anticipated this trend in his literary reputation; it was a trend he recognised as the typical outcome of the determination of 'criticasters' to pervert the truth by praising past authors at the expense of living ones; thus in the notebook *Digest* which belongs largely to 1858-9, the years immediately preceding the *Cloister and the Hearth,* he wrote under the heading, 'Recipes. Criticaster's cookery book', the following:

> How to write Truth down and Falsehood up without lying . . . State the facts of the past in the language of Epic Poetry, and of the present in the language of Satire. If well done, there will be scarcely any sediment of truth left. This is the test.

> Another method.

> Define a dead author by his best work, and a living author by his worst. Let the [true?] Defoe stand all through your work as the author of Robinson Crusoe & nothing else . . . Understand by Dickens the author of Little Dorrit and nothing else, by Fielding the author of Tom Jones and no feeble stories & bad plays . . . This at first sight seems impossible but there is evidence to prove it has been done, and by human beings.

This was written when Reade was still smarting from the wounds inflicted by Fitzjames Stephen who, in the

Edinburgh Review, had come close to condemning both Reade and Dickens almost entirely on the basis of a single novel—*Never too Late to Mend* in Reade's case, and *Little Dorrit* in Dickens's case—whereas he praised the wholesome works of the past. When the twentieth century dawned, it was Reade's turn to be considered as an author of a past era; and so, as a dead author, his controversial ***Never too Late to Mend*** was forgotten since the trend of criticism was to define him solely on the basis of his best work. A similar trend, as Hornung indicated, affected Dickens, who was in the early part of the century remembered more for *A Tale of Two Cities* than for *Little Dorrit.* Although it could be concluded that Reade might have been gratified had he known that he would be remembered for what was adjudged his best work, that conclusion is doubtful, since he himself did not consider the ***Cloister and the Hearth*** his masterpiece; this may be concluded from the *Memoir,* which records that when a stranger once complimented him on the ***Cloister and the Hearth*** as his best novel, the author indignantly informed his eulogist that if that was his opinion, he was only fit for a lunatic asylum. It is quite possible, then, that Reade would have looked upon his twentieth-century eulogists as either mentally deficient, or as latter-day criticasters.

II

It is specifically by means of the painful application of the 'Baconian principle' that Reade believed good novels were written. The painful acquisition of knowledge was the first step; thus he wrote in the ***Eighth Commandment,*** a work on international copyright published in the year preceding the appearance of the ***Cloister and the Hearth:***

> Nothing in man is an inch deep, but knowledge painfully acquired, partly by personal observation, partly from the testimony of other eye-witnesses. Nothing in man is a foot deep, but knowledge acquired by the science of sciences, statistic. That science, sneered at by buzzards, is 'the soi-disant *Baconian principle*' worked by a vast machinery . . . of eyes and hands.

Reade felt that the Baconian principle was the only means whereby an author could attain a respectable position in the world of letters, and preserve his dignity; and so, at about the same time (1858-9) he copied the following Baconian quotation under the heading, 'An Author's dignity', into his notebook *Digest:*

> For there is no power on Earth which setteth up a throne in the spirits and souls of men and in their cogitations, imagination, opinions and beliefs, save only Knowledge and Learning.

Undoubtedly one of the main reasons for the vast success of the novel and its lasting fame was that Reade's

Baconian methods and Keanian notions of realism were best suited to the sort of antiquarian research necessary in the resuscitation of a past era. Writing in 1856 on nineteenth-century drama, E. S. Dallas alluded to Charles Kean who laid great stress on the 'virtues of antiquarian research and historical fidelity'; Kean, according to Dallas, believed that scenic illustration adorned and gave dignity 'to works of genius' provided it had the 'weight of authority'. Kean asserted that 'in decoration of every kind, whether scenic or otherwise', he had aimed at truth with the 'grand object of conveying to the stage an accurate portraiture and a living picture of a bygone age'.[10] Like Kean, Reade aimed at historical truth and accurate scenic illustration to add the weight of authority to his living picture of the past; hence he consulted innumerable volumes, many with plates from which he drew his descriptions of typical mediaeval costumes and customs, ranging from works on the fine arts like Alexandre du Sommerard's *Les Arts au Moyen Age,* to literary works that included Walter Scott's *Monastery* and *Quentin Durward.* Ironically, while writing the novel, Reade expressed his doubts as to whether this was the right method for a historical novel; he resolved that henceforth he would remember the advice, *soyez de votre siècle*—'I am convinced that learning and research should be applied to passing, not past, events. In the same sense alone is Dickens a learned man, and mark the result!'[11] Nevertheless, it was only when he applied his learning and research to past events that Reade achieved a success in any way comparable to that of Dickens. In applying his documentary method to 'passing events', he was obliged to scan the wide world's press in search of what Hornung has called the outlandish grist for his mill; but the historical novelist must of necessity work from documents, and so by means of the documentary method Reade succeeded in deepening his understanding of the fifteenth-century milieu.

George Orwell[12] selected 'the charm of useless knowledge' as the chief attraction of Reade's novels. Indeed, Reade's notebooks abound with scraps of 'useless knowledge' collected from innumerable newspapers; in his notebook *Bon. Fab.—Mat. Fict.* is a clipping from the *Newcastle Chronicle* on Yew trees; and in his notebook *Red Digest,* under the heading 'Memorabilia', is a page from a periodical, crammed with advertisements explaining the use of various items such as skates, seven-shooters, sewing-machines, pianos, etc. It is understandable that this sort of information, when incorporated into a 'novel of the day', would be little more than tedious. But when meticulous research of this kind is applied to a past age, it is equally understandable that the 'useless knowledge' thus uncovered would be flavoured with considerable historical interest. This, in conjunction with his readable style, was responsible for the peculiar charm that invested the driest details of the author's picture of the

Middle Ages. Hence an unidentified review in Reade's scrapbook praised at length various items of interest such as the narration of how soldiers of the Middle Ages drove the poor from overpopulated areas, and the account of a curious custom of preserving fresh rosebuds through the winter. It concluded that novels like Reade's would do more to instruct one in the history of ancient times 'than all the dry, political volumes that ever were published'.

Pure historical interest and Reade's readable style were not the only factors that revivified the dry information of old chronicles. Reade was particularly successful in adding human interest to the past, since the human actors are constantly before the reader's eyes. Thus when Margaret van Eyck describes in detail how her brother Jan van Eyck ground his colours and prepared his oil, we sense her own enthusiasm as well as Gerard's enchantment; he listens to her with rapt attention while she speaks with sparkling eyes. She does not relate her facts dispassionately, since they take the form of advice to the young Gerard who accordingly drinks in every word; this advice, Reade appropriately concludes, Gerard 'received . . . like a legacy from Heaven, so interesting are some things that read uninteresting'. And when Margaret Brandt's aging father, a mediaeval quack, rambles about the origin and medicinal virtues of *soupe au vin,* his tale becomes a part of his character. He speaks amidst his daughter's protestations which elicit our patience, and at the same time make us more acutely aware of Peter Brandt's fanatic enthusiasm in the field of medicine; and so we swallow all the background information as easily as the old man swallows Gerard's supply of *soupe au vin.* Similarly, information concerning a mediaeval crossbow is put into the mouth of Denys, the Burgundian crossbowman, who airs mediaeval prejudices in favour of the crossbow's chances of outliving such newfangled inventions as gunpowder:

> 'Pooh! pooh!' said Denys warmly; 'petrone nor harquebuss shall ever put down Sir Arbalest. Why, we can shoot ten times while they are putting their charcoal and their lead into their leathern smoke belchers . . . All that is too fumbling for the field of battle; there a soldier's weapon needs be aye ready, like his heart'. (Ch. XXIV.)

Since the facts of erudition are thus couched in the soldier's picturesque and quaint speech, they are by no means presented in a scholarly fashion. It is through Denys's own distinct personality, his warm and impetuous nature, that an impression of the Renaissance age is conveyed—an age of progress jostling with ignorance.

In this way the reader is conducted through Germany and France to Italy, and introduced to many figures who have not just emerged from the Dark Ages, but stand on the brink of a more enlightened age to come. It is through a venerable monk, Father Anselm, that Mediaeval superstitions are expressed in pious terms relating to the virtues of relics—'We steep the hair or the bones of some dead saint in the medicine, and thus work marvellous cures' (Ch. XXX). Reade portrays the mediaeval mind with its unenlightened reasoning, with true veneration and without scoffing at mediaeval prejudices. Indeed, Anselm's character is given verisimilitude because his notions are put forward as sincere beliefs; at the same time the verisimilitude is enhanced since the monk is portrayed as being on the brink of realising that relics may well not be efficacious on account of their intrinsic merit, but on account of the faith and powers of auto-suggestion they engender in the patient. In this way the characters become the spokesmen of their age; and so Reade never crams our minds with the details he has unearthed so that we forget the human actors; the characters themselves win our sympathy to understand the times in which they lived.

The same can be said of Fra Colonna, the Dominican friar of whom the reviewers had very different opinions. One journal, the *Critic,* spoke of Fra Colonna's 'tiresome twaddle' in the long dissertation the friar gives on the ceremonies borrowed from Paganism by Christianity, and the *Morning Herald* objected to having its mind improved by 'musty erudition' when it sought amusement. The majority of critics, however, were more appreciative of Reade's treatment of pedantry. the *Era* considered Colonna's dissertation 'one of the most remarkable bits of controversial scholarship' that it had met 'for many a long day'. Similarly the *Daily News* thought it 'a marvellous collection of curious learning and admirable reasoning', and the *Illustrated London News* went so far as to call it the most remarkable passage in the book. There is certainly little of 'musty erudition' in Colonna's long dissertation in which he endeavours to show with a rush of learning and eloquence how every doctrine, ceremony and observance of the Romish church is derived, directly and immediately, from pagan sources, since it is coloured with his own naive scepticism, enthusiasm and respect for antiquity. Furthermore, still supremely a dramatist, Reade does not simply narrate Colonna's arguments, but literally has them enacted; just as Plato would have dramatised a learned matter between teacher and pupil, so Reade portrays Colonna as instructing Gerard while the figures watch, first the processions of Holy Thursday, and later, amidst the crowds in the church, the religious ceremonies. As each ceremony is enacted before them, Colonna explains its pagan origin amidst Gerard's wonder and astonishment. In this way the reader becomes a spectator as well as a listener, and is again made to feel that he is living in a bygone age in company with the very figures that peopled it. In this Reade was more successful than Bulwer Lytton who, in the *Last Days of Pompeii,* traced the origin and cultivation of magic while speaking in his own person, thereby breaking the illusion of reality by appearing to the reader as a learned and pedantic historian who tediously strings together ancient names like Ostanes, Xerxes, and Hellas.

Reade's superiority to Lytton in portraying factual detail intended for historical colouring may be seen in their different descriptions of the festive board. Lytton portrays the abundant and luxurious wealth of a Roman feast, evoking a sense of sumptuous richness by indicating, instead of the repast, the costly ornamentation of the setting; thus the splendour and profusion of wealth is conveyed by the candelabras and vases, the various images of gods wrought from numerous precious metals, all grouped about the spacious hall, and bathed in myrrh and frankincense. The description, however, has an artificial stamp to it; the ostentatious finery detracts the reader's attention from the characters, who thereby become little more than dim shadows, and recalls the profuse and perfumed luxury of Ouida's fashionable novels. Lytton, furthermore, unwittingly destroys the illusion he creates by repeatedly drawing attention to the reader ('The reader understands that the festive board was composed of three tables' . . .) and to the present time (' . . . ornaments . . . were ranged . . . with the same ostentation . . . that we find displayed at a modern feast'). Reade's description is more to the point, relating the sumptuous wealth of a duke's feast to the repast itself, elaborately portrayed with its extravaganza of cathedrals of sugar, all 'gilt and painted in the interstices of the bas-reliefs'—works of art 'made to be destroyed'. (Ch. II.) The characters themselves are not forgotten, since Margaret, her father, and Gerard are humble guests who through simple but vivid human touches are portrayed as visibly impressed and gratified at the sight of so much extravagance; we share with them their surprise and delight, and at the same time find amusement in their reactions: when Peter, faint with hunger after his long journey, is confronted with the repast, he clasps his hands in pious admiration, his face 'expanding and shining'; and when the wild boar is served up with a winning smile and eyes of coloured sugar glowing in its head, Margaret has occasion to wheel round, squeaking and pinching Gerard, with horror-stricken eyes.

In this way Reade explores the world of the fifteenth century through his characters and narrative: his story is a fast-flowing river that envelops the paintings of the Renaissance artists of the Netherlands, the frescoes of Perugino, the illuminated missals of the convents, the religious observances of the Romish church, the customs and superstitions of the people, throwing a beam of light across mediaeval Europe by creating for us the men and women who lived in the midst of those wonders and peculiarities. Lytton, on the other hand, creates a sense of unreality, since he describes

the art and customs of Pompeii in isolation from the narrative that concerns his characters; with one eye on his story, the other on museum-pieces, he constantly forgets his characters in order to tell his reader in which museum the various articles he describes may still be seen. This is not the way to animate the past, but to fossilize it. But Reade, in delving into the complicated facts of history, incidentally produces a medley of living portraits, including that of a Burgundian soldier, a zealous monk, a cultured and fanatic scholar, and various other humble folk who were shaped and influenced by those facts. Consequently, although there are, as in Bulwer Lytton's work, numerous direct addresses to the reader, they rarely become obtrusive, and barely take the reader out of the fifteenth-century milieu. In writing a historical novel, Reade was more successful in forgetting the nineteenth century;[13] indeed, the inability to do so was a fault he knew many writers of historical novels were prone to make, as is evident from a comment in one of his notebooks: 'Falsehood of antiquarian novels— Characters look forward instead of back and are before their age'. Reade so fully enters into the age he describes, that the *Press* unintentionally complimented him by raising the objection that he told his tale as if he were a prejudiced partisan of the fifteenth century. The *New York Times* was less fastidious and openly recognised his success, saying that by a masterly movement of mental retrogression' he seemed to have moved his soul out of the present, forgotten the future, and wrapped himself in the past.

Notes

[1] W. J. Johnston, 'Charles Reade and His Books', *Gentleman's Magazine,* CCLXXV (July-Dec., 1898). p. 369.

[2] Charles L. Reade and Rev. Compton Reade, *Charles Reade: A Memoir* (Chapman and Hall, 1887), II, p. 116.

[3] 'M', 'Charles Reade's Opinion of Himself and His Opinion of George Eliot', *The Bookman,* XVIII (Nov., 1903), p. 260. According to this writer, who was himself anonymous, the article in *Once a Week* was written by Reade himself in his own hand—'It is a chapter of autobiography; it is an essay in self-criticism'.

[4] A. C. Swinburne, 'Charles Reade', *Miscellanies* (Chatto and Windus, 1886), p. 279.

[5] Besant, 'Charles Reade's Novels', *Gentleman's Magazine,* CCLIII (Aug., 1882), p. 214.

[6] Swinburne, *op. cit.,* p. 281.

[7] Melville, *Victorian Novelists* (Constable and Co., 1906), p. 167.

[8] Hornung, 'Charles Reade', *London Mercury,* IV (June, 1921), p. 153.

[9] *Ibid.*

[10] 'The Drama', *Blackwood's Magazine,* LXXIX (Feb., 1856), p. 218.

[11] *Memoir, ed. cit.,* II, p. 109.

[12] Orwell, *New Statesman,* XX (17 Aug., 1940), p. 162.

[13] However Reade was not always able to forget his own century. When Gerard is imprisoned by the Burgomaster, for example, he cannot refrain from criticizing the 'solitary system' of nineteenth-century gaols which caused 'a great many persons [to] commit suicide during the first twenty-four hours of the solitary cell'. (Ch. X.)

Elton E. Smith (essay date 1976)

SOURCE: "Novels: On Social Issues," in *Charles Reade*, Twayne, 1976, pp. 104-34.

[*In the following excerpt, Smith discusses Reade's general approach to writing novels about social issues and discusses specific aspects of* It Is Never Too Late to Mend.]

The last sentence of ***Put Yourself in His Place*** reveals Charles Reade's intention for his novels about current social issues: " . . . I have taken a few undeniable truths out of many, and have laboured to make my readers realize those appalling facts of the day which most men know, but not one in a thousand comprehends, and not one in a hundred thousand realizes, until fiction—which, whatever you may have been told to the contrary, is the highest, widest, noblest, and greatest of all the arts—comes to his aid, studies, penetrates, digests the hard facts of chronicles and blue-books, and makes their dry bones live." Reade's friend Wilkie Collins collected all the remarkable police cases and judicial narratives he could find; and, out of the vast accumulation of bizarre criminal facts, he chose the bricks to go into the solid fabric of his mystery stories. As the author of *Woman in White* and *The Moonstone,* Collins was ever on the alert for perplexing criminal oddities; but the author of ***It Is Never Too Late to Mend, Hard Cash,*** and ***Put Yourself in His Place*** cast himself in the pleasing romantic role of knight-errant who went striding across a kingdom to find those legal or social wrongs that he believed only the writer of fiction could redress.

Reade was by no means alone in such an attempt. Charles Dickens struck at the dark places of society with lavish outpourings of comedy, eccentricities galore, involved and coincidental plots, pathos and bathos; he buried his social criticisms in so rich a tissue of humanity that they tended to become particular peccadilloes rather than a general indictment.[1] Harriet Martineau made up her characteristically dry little stories about the application of morality to social economy, and Benjamin Disraeli bound together scurrilous gossip of high society with excerpts from his own parliamentary speeches and called them "social novels." For Reade, all the facts had to be there on the printed page; but he so fused them with plot and character that to tell the story or to describe the character's predicament was automatically to expose social abuse. He was not always successful, however, in producing exactly the proper fusion of fact and fiction.

Unfortunately the social novel, in the hands of whatever practitioner, tends to become the story of colorless people set in elaborately accurate staging. Although Reade was unquestionably, in this department of literary activity, a forerunner of Emile Zola and of the realistic and naturalistic movements, he nevertheless often assured that the "facts" of his blue books and newspaper accounts necessarily became the "truth" of literature. Indeed, it is interesting to note that Zola was doing editorial and translator's work for the French firm of Hachette et Frères at the very time that the company was publishing pirated translations of Reade's novels for the French reading public. Reade's information was always valuable, delightfully available, and necessary to his forensic purpose; but he often permitted it to degenerate into the clutter that jumbled Victorian architecture, crowded Victorian parlors, and finally became so eccentrically eclectic that it ruined Victorian taste. Nonetheless, his factual novels suited an age suspicious of poetic fancy, enamored with the ideal of scientific observation, and busy collecting every kind of monstrosity and knickknack as if it were all authentic treasure.

In 1940, George Orwell addressed himself to the factuality of Reade's novels and at the same time estimated that three of his works (***Foul Play, Hard Cash,*** and ***It Is Never Too Late to Mend***) would outlive the entire works of Meredith and George Eliot:

> What is the attraction of Reade? . . . it is the charm of useless knowledge. Reade was a man of what one might call penny-encyclopaedic learning. He possessed vast stocks of disconnected information which a lively narrative gift allowed him to cram into books. . . . If you have . . . the sort of mind that likes knowing exactly how a medieval catapult worked or just what objects a prison cell of the eighteen-forties contained, then you can hardly help enjoying Reade. He himself, of course, did not see his work in quite this light. He prided himself on his accuracy and compiled his books largely from

newspaper cuttings, but the strange facts which he collected were subsidiary to what he would have regarded as his "purpose." For he was a social reformer in a fragmentary way, and made vigorous attacks on such diverse evils as blood-letting, the treadmill, private lunatic asylums, clerical celibacy and tight-lacing.[2]

Years before the Goncourts coined the expression "the human document," Reade was busily compiling large volumes and cards of newspaper clippings and personal testimony of persons who had worked or lived in highly specialized surroundings. Before writing novels about sheep raisers, gold miners, and fishermen, he read the standard travel books and collected special accounts from individuals who could speak from experience. Members of his own family could brief him on nautical matters,[3] he kept hack writers busy at the Bodleian Library and in the British Museum culling facts and writing up cases for his files.[4] As he so bluntly put it, he milked about two hundred cows into the pail of each story and thus created a highly mixed but not very homogenized product.

As for what his elaborate system of cards, notes, clippings, research writers, travel diaries, and much, much more did for Reade, the answer has never been better and more fully stated than by Walter Frewen Lord in 1906:

> "In the course of that career he wrote very well indeed about Australia without having been there; he wrote in great detail about banking without having been in business; he wrote of strikes and "rattening" as if he had been a picketed operative; he described accidents and incidents in coal-mines much better than most men who pass their lives in that kind of work. . . . His knowledge of prison life makes one marvel how it could have been acquired except as a warder or an amateur convict. Lunatic asylums had a special attraction for him; they were fruitful . . . of blood-curdling melodrama where almost every page contains not only a judicious thrill, but a valuable piece of information (laboriously acquired by the author) and a handsome moral. It is inconceivable that any man could write the sea-fight in *Hard Cash* without having himself commanded, and fought, a merchant vessel. . . . He is equally at home with respectability and with crime; and when he tells us of a forgery it is our own fault if we cannot go away and do likewise . . . he laboured over detail to an extent that far out-distances any other writer of his time.[5]

I It Is Never Too Late to Mend: A Matter of Fact Romance *(1856)*

On June 10, 1852, Charles Reade had finished the novel *Peg Woffington,* which was based on his play *Masks and Faces.* Almost immediately, he sketched, in a great burst of energy, the plot outline of *Gold,* the genesis of his novel *It Is Never Too Late to Mend.* By December, 1852, Reade had begun, between the demanding productions of *Masks and Faces* and *Gold,* to write *Christie Johnstone.* He finished this work in the early summer and at once began the familiar task of making a novel out of *Gold.* This novel, first called "Susan Merton," was later given the proverbial title Swinburne so deplored—*It Is Never Too Late to Mend.* When the two-volume work was published on August 1, 1856, it was reviewed in *Bentley's Miscellany* as "incomparably the best novel of the season";[6] other major critics (with the exception of the writers for the *Saturday Review*) were unanimous in its praise, but each had some minor criticisms to make.

Much comment was made by these critics about the seeming independence of the two halves of the book: Berkshire is the beginning and the end, but English prisons and Australian goldfields are sandwiched in between. The explanation for this cleavage is that Reade meant to use his melodrama as the mere frame for a terrifying picture of prison life in England of the time. Reade's source for the inserted material came from "a noble passage in the *Times* of September 7th or 8th, 1853"; and with it, Reade set out, somewhat grimly, to test the lines of procedure he had for long accepted intellectually but had as yet hardly used. On June 20, he wrote: "I propose never to guess where I can know." Since his story crossed the sea to Australia and plunged the reader into gold mines there, Reade began to make lists of the necessary preparations for the author. "To be consistent with myself I ought to cross-examine at the very least a dozen men that have farmed, dug, or robbed in that land. . . . Failing these I must read books and letters and do the best I can. Such is the mechanism of a novel by Charles Reade." After this complacent boast, he faces the potentialities of success and failure: "Now, I know exactly what I am worth. If I can work the above great system there is enough of me to make one of the writers of the day; without it, NO, NO."[7]

Other than the usual objections to the use of unwieldy and proverbial titles, not enough attention has been given to the title of this novel as a clue to its central meaning. It may, in addition, have been a prophetic double entendre that Reade aimed at himself, for he was forty-two at the time and may have felt very much a failure so far as both drama and the novel were concerned. But an analysis of the patterns of characterization indicates that this novel is clearly an Evangelical study of the conversion experience. If a person sees the error of his ways, no matter how old nor how hardened in them he may be, if he truly repents, can he really begin afresh on a new path and can he maintain it? The central character was probably meant to be Tom Robinson, who, in the first section of the book, is a free man but is despaired of by the decent people who know his past. The second section depicts him in prison among other criminals, where he meets a saintly chaplain who does not despair of Tom's possibilities for reform. The third section, which portrays the new life of the redeemed man, is honestly enough presented to admit a temporary fall from grace in Sydney, which is followed by a humbled and fearful return to the path the chaplain had laid out for him. Reade treats this solemn theme with enough lightness to show how indignant a reformed thief can become when someone has stolen a hard-earned fortune from him!

But what is true of Robinson is also true to a lesser degree of the other characters. When Robinson is being taken to the Black Hole, he screams at the new chaplain (Mr. Francis Eden): "Do you see this, you in the black coat? You that told us the other day you loved us, and now stand coolly there and see me taken to the black hole to be got ready for the mad-house? D'ye hear?" The chaplain replies, gravely and gently, "I hear you" (Chapter XIII). Thus, all Mr. Eden's inspired preaching will do no good until he "gravely and gently" accepts the responsibility of making his idealism work in the lives of the prisoners and in the conduct of a British prison.

Even the resolutely good *émigré* George Fielding, in Australia to earn enough to marry Susan, has to learn the odd lesson that mere goodness is not enough. Robinson ponders about the case of Fielding with amazement, for here is an honest man who never prospers. Is this the unrewarded honesty to which he has been converted? Reade permits the former felon to come to an astonishing but nevertheless honest conclusion: success in the world does not come from goodness alone, but from the combination of virtue with that cluster of circumstances which is generally called "luck." George, who left England cursing his fate and feeling like a British Job suffering unmerited punishment, must come to a humbler definition of self. When George is at last glad just to be alive, the tide turns, and he begins to receive his due reward.

The novel has been criticized not only for the two somewhat separate halves but also because it seems to have no single hero. If it is only a romance, this lack is a real difficulty; but, if it is a book written to illustrate the title, enrichment results from three very different heroes—thief, good man, and saint—since for each of them "it is never too late to mend." Reade's stubborn extension of this thesis to the bitter end is illustrated by the departure abroad of the thwarted villain Meadows, his mother, and her servant. Not satisfied to send him away with all his schemes awry and his life in ruins around him, Reade tells his readers that Meadow's mother has plans to make him repent his evil past and to lead him to conversion.

Dedicated, oddly enough, to the president, fellows, and demies of Magdalen College, Reade's "attempt at a solid fiction" is an almost complete denial of academic posture. The story claims that knowledge comes from experience, not from books; that self-knowledge is not everything; and that human personality can undergo remarkable transformations through the power of the Gospel. The thesis rejects idea, ideal, and theory until each has proved its adequacy by operating successfully in the real world. Of course, the nature of the book cannot help but suggest the author's great admiration for Charles Dickens. Like his master, Reade seizes upon some glaring public and social evil, footlights it with the dramatic techniques he had learned from the stage, and holds the illuminated and magnified evil up to public indignation. Just as *Bleak House* exposes the glacial cruelty of the Court of Chancery, *Hard Times* shows human life strangled by the red tape of officialdom, and *Little Dorrit* reveals the hopelessness of imprisonment for debt, **It Is Never Too Late to Mend** presents a powerful and unforgettable picture of the bestial inhumanity with which prisoners were treated in some nineteenth-century British jails.

Beyond mere choice of topics, many Dickensian touches are noticeable in character, dialogue, and incident. In Chapter XI, Reade echoes Dickens's insistence on the influence of environment on character by claiming that prison treatment harmed Robinson's "soul more than had years of burglary and petty larceny." It is a highly Dickensian feast, both as to irony and menu, to which Mr. Williams, the prison overseer, sits down after deciding that the prison gruel was too thick and rich: soup with tapioca, salmon, lobster patties, rissoles, turkey, tongue, mutton, pigeon, greengage tart, yellow custard, iced pudding, Stilton cheese, salad, muscadel grapes, guava jelly, and wines. Dickensian also is the death of prisoner Edward Josephs, aged fifteen, who hangs himself in his cell by his own pocket handkerchief; Dickensian are the sentimental references to mother and friends; Dickensian is the quiet malice of the public indictment. While a fifteen-year-old lad is hanging himself, the author appends the soothing refrain "ILS EST DEUX HEURES: TOUT EST TRANQUILLE: DORMEZ, MAITRES, DORMEZ!"[8]

Reade, with his legal training, often slips into the highly effective rhetoric of legal indictment:

> Thus in the nineteenth century, in a kind-hearted nation, under the most humane sovereign the world has ever witnessed on an earthly throne . . . Edward Josephs has been done to death in the queen's name, in the name of England, and in the name of the law. . . . For the present, the account between Josephs and the law stands thus:—Josephs has committed the smallest theft imaginable. He has stolen food. For this the law, professing to punish him with certain months imprisonment, has inflicted capital punishment; has overtasked, crucified, starved—

overtasked, starved, crucified—robbed him of light, of sleep, of hope, of life; has destroyed his body, and perhaps his soul. (Chapter XXVII)

The versatile author then turns to the technique of the financial accountant: "Sum total—1st page of account—

Josephs	The Law
a larcenist and	a liar and
a corpse.	a felon."

Never Too Late (or as even Reade, oppressed by the excessive length of its title, called it in his notebooks, "Sera Nunquam") is, like many of Dickens's works, a study in contrasts. Isaac Levi, the righteous but unforgiving Jewish usurer, balances John Meadows, the Christian but unrighteous Gentile usurer. Contrasted are the two unfavored lovers: William Fielding fights temptation by staying away from Susan Merton, but John Meadows feeds his desire by hovering closer and closer to the flame. Two prison systems are contrasted: The old higgledy-piggledy massing of all levels of criminals in large dormitory accommodations provided not only dangerous exposure of all to the worst but also comforting warmth of contact with others suffering the same penalties. Solitary confinement, the new system, which sounds sensible because of its careful classification of prisoners, is actually inhuman because of the intolerable loneliness it inflicts.

A contrast also exists between the visiting prison chaplain from the north of England, the Reverend James Lepel, who gets along splendidly with the sadistic governor, Mr. Hawes, and Mr. Francis Eden, who sets himself resolutely to break Hawes's illegal discipline and to reform the prison administration. The small cells and the tiny fields of tight little England, contrast with the vastness of space in the subcontinent of Australia. In England, propertied vallainy, in the form of Mr. Meadows, is victorious; in Australia, with its extreme flexibility of economic status, the virtuous triumph and are able to return to triumph in England. Of course, the most striking contrast is between the two Robinsons: the thief who in England helped to destroy George's standing in his home community, and the partner who in Australia was a tower of resourcefulness and the molder of his fortune.

As usual, elements of melodramatic excess hurt the emotional motivation of the characters. Mr. Eden is one of Reade's fainting heroes: he writes a "stiff memorial" to the secretary for the Home Department demanding an inquiry into the conduct of the jail; sends a copy to the prison governor Hawes, directs and seals his own copy, and then falls onto a sofa in a dead faint. This melodramatic swoon gives the author an opportunity for a melodramatic rescue, for Susan arrives with her Aunt Davies and posts the letter (Chapter XVII).

When Robinson has been committed to the dark hole and is about to lose his mind after six hours of incarceration, he hears the voice of the new chaplain comforting him with the word "brother." This scene is quite believable and even acceptable to modern readers, but it becomes incredibly effusive when Robinson, in an access of emotion, cries to his comforter: "I am kissing your dear hand. There! There! There! I bless you! I love you! I adore you! I am kissing your hand, and I am on my knees blessing you and kissing. Oh, my heart! my heart! my heart!" (Chapter XV).

Once again, this Reade novel is rich in irony. It is comic irony that the villainous Mr. Hawes hates Simon Legree (villain of Harriet Beecher Stowe's *Uncle Tom's Cabin*) and fervently hopes that his cruelty will be punished. It is heroic irony that Robinson should discover large "sheets of gold" in the roof and walls of the very tunnel the villains laboriously dug to rob the hero of his little hoard. Rhetorical irony echoes from Isaac Levi's revelation that he had fitted Meadow's house with piping that carries the sounds of every word spoken to Levi's house: "You had no mercy on the old Jew. You took his house from him, not for your need but for hate. So he made that house a trap and caught you in your villainy!" (Chapter L).

Reade also found it pleasant to indulge in some of his old sensational tricks. He enjoys substituting little pictures for words—a bit like rotogravure pages for children—and so he draws for the reader a picture of a little nugget of gold balanced for scale on the end of a prospector's knife. As enamored as ever with the disguise technique, he dresses his villain in donkey skins and has him wear a donkey head, but that villain is quite capable, even in this ponderous costume, of crawling on his hands and knees with a dagger held between his teeth. The French technique of the false *dénouement* is dragged out again when Susan is given false news of George's marriage abroad, thus setting her free to marry Meadows as an expression of her appreciation for his kindness and because of family pressure. One of the incredible moments of melodrama occurs when Tom Robinson is able to identify all his stolen money—seven thousand pounds—because he had memorized the serial numbers on the bills.

The Victorian earnestness responsible for Reade's inception of the work also marked it completion. In the twenty-second chapter of volume two, Reade extols the Victorian doctrine of progress and its consummation in the nineteenth century: "When we write a story or sing a poem of the great nineteenth century I give you my sacred word of honour there is but one fear—not that our theme will be beneath us, but we shall lack the comprehensive vision a man must have from heaven to catch the historical the poetic the lasting features of the Titan events that stride so swiftly past IN THIS GIGANTIC AGE!!!"

One of the things about "Sera Nunquam" that struck contemporaries was the marvelous factuality of the Australian settings, the cattle-raising country and the gold-mining areas. In an essay about Henry Kingsley, written when Henry James was only twenty-two, the critic cited Reade to make his point:

> It is one of those rudimentary truths which cannot be too often repeated, that to write a novel it is not necessary to have been a traveller, an adventurer, a sightseer; it is simply necessary to be an artist. Mr. Kingsley's descriptions of Australia are very pretty; but they are not half so good as those of Mr. Charles Reade, who, as far as we know, has never visited the country. . . . Mr. Reade went to Australia—that is, his imagination went—on purpose to compose certain chapters in **Never Too Late to Mend.** Mr. Kingsley went in the flesh; but Mr. Kingsley in the flesh is not equal to Mr. Reade in the spirit.[9]

Australian writers have questioned James's judgment; but most agree that, whether on the stage or in a novel, whether through the eyes of experience or the reading glasses of the study, Reade's descriptions were always "vivid."

Notes

[1] Professor William H. Scheuerle considers that "particular peccadillo" may describe the earlier Dickens novels but that his later works, especially *Our Mutual Friend,* often make a strong "general indictment."

[2] George Orwell, *New Statesman and Nation* (August 17, 1940) and *The Collected Essays, Journalism and Letters of George Orwell,* eds. Sonia Orwell and Ian Angus (London: Secker & Warburg, 1968), II, pp. 34, 35.

[3] In Reade's notebooks, an untitled folio dated 1867-70 is mostly in the handwriting of William Barrington Reade, Charles's nautical brother. London Library, St. James' Square.

[4] Reade's notebooks, "Digest"—*"memoranda agenda":* "13. Having wasted too many years to be learned I must use cunning. Think of some way to make young active fellows run and collect materials for me. Think of a Machinery. Government though not very brainful produces books Briareus like; why might not I, and lick the rough cub into shape. Thus start the conception. Learn the sources by Watts Bibliotheca, Mr. Donne, Bandinel etc. Then put my hacks on, *leaving gaps;* so that they may not see the whole design, and steal the capital idea. German hacks good for this. University hacks ditto. Pay them well and keep them dark."

[5] Walter Frewen Lord, *The Mirror of the Century;* pp. 252-54.

[6] Malcolm Elwin, *Charles Reade,* p. 114.

[7] E. W. Hornung, "Charles Reade," pp. 151-52.

[8] "It is two o'clock: All is well: sleep, masters, sleep!"

[9] Professor Scheuerle, in defense of Henry Kingsley, points out that although the youthful Henry James was ostensibly reviewing Henry Kingsley's *The Hillyars and the Burtons,* he was actually launching an attack on Charles Kingsley and the whole "Noble School of Fiction." Thus James was almost committed to find things wrong with the Kingsleys, and by contrast, things right with writers who were not part of the "Noble" circle.

Dianna Vitanza (essay date 1986)

SOURCE: "*The Cloister and the Hearth*: A Popular Response to the Oxford Movement," in *Religion and Literature*, Vol. 18, No. 3, Fall, 1986, pp. 71-88.

[*In the following excerpt, Vitanza observes that* The Cloister and the Hearth *not only faults the enforced celibacy but also the isolation from worldly concerns associated with the Oxford Movement.*]

Charles Reade, the nineteenth-century novelist whom the young Henry James called "to our mind the most readable of living English novelists and . . . a distant kinsman of Shakespeare" (207) and who, in the estimation of many of his contemporaries, "after the death of Thackeray and of Dickens . . . divided with George Eliot the reputation of being the greatest living novelist" (Phillips 20), is all but ignored in literary criticism today. Except for passing comment in literary histories, Reade is the subject of only an occasional article or dissertation. This current neglect leads one to forget the strength of Reade's reputation at the height of his career. William Dean Howells, who observed first hand the rise and decline of Reade's reputation, testifies to Reade's popularity with his contemporary audience. Recalling in *My Literary Passions* the writers who had most influenced him, Howells writes,

> I ought not to omit from the list of the favorites an author who was then beginning to have his greatest vogue, and who somehow just missed of being a very great one. We were all reading his jaunty, nervy, knowing books, and some of us were questioning whether we ought not to set him above Thackeray and Dickens and George Eliot, *tulli quanti,* so great was the effect that Charles Reade had with our generation. (144)

Though Reade's novels have not sustained the writer's reputation, they are, nevertheless, of interest to scholars today because they treat issues and themes which reflect the popular concerns of the Victorians, from women's rights and women's dress to abuses in mental hospitals and prisons and because, as Howells attests, they had a significant impact on the readers of the time.

The only one of Reade's novels to achieve any lasting popularity is his historical novel, *The Cloister and the Hearth,* which presents a fictionalized version of the life of Gerard Eliason, the father of Erasmus. The theme of this novel has usually been interpreted to be the preferability of marital sexual union, represented as the "Hearth," over celibacy, represented by the "Cloister." Malcolm Elwin in his biography of Reade states that the "epic theme" of the novel is "the misery caused by the vow of celibacy demanded by the Roman Church. The situation of Margaret, who loves and is beloved by Gerard, is the mother of his child, and yet is denied the privilege of being his wife because he is a priest, is described with excruciating pathos" (44). Similarly, Wayne Burns argues that Gerard's "'good fight' (the title of Reade's first version of the novel) is his fight against his sexual love for Margaret—a fight so all consuming that even after her death, when he thinks he has won, his actions belie his professions" (319).

This theme of the conflict between celibacy and marriage is usually interpreted as a reflection of Reade's own personal experiences. John Coleman first makes the suggestion, and Elwin and Burns agree, that Reade probably at one time had a Scottish mistress whom he could not marry because of the vow of celibacy which he had to take in order to maintain a university fellowship at Oxford.[1] Elwin and Burns cite a comment made by Reade on the problem of celibacy in *The Cloister and the Hearth* as evidence that Reade's central concern in the novel is indeed the issue of celibacy. In 1876 Reade wrote in his notebooks,

> In my mediaeval romance The Cloister and the Hearth I use this expression celibacy of the clergy, an invention truly devilish. A French critic is surprised at this violence in me since the rest of my work in general deals benevolently and benignly with Pope, Priests, Convents, and the unreformed Church in general. . . . The opinion I uttered in 1860 was even then twenty years old in me: it is now thirty-six. (quoted in Elwin 44)

Elwin, commenting on this statement, says, "Apparently something occurred in or about the year 1840 which incited Reade to vehement resentment of the celibate condition imposed by the statutes upon him as a fellow of his college" (44).

But the relationship between Gerard and Margaret takes up only a small part of the action of the novel.

The larger part of the action concerns Gerard's journey through medieval Europe from Holland through Germany and France to Italy, his rise to success in copying and illuminating manuscripts in Rome, his decision to enter the priesthood when he believes Margaret to be dead, and his journey back to his platonic reunion with Margaret. This larger portion of the novel is usually simply dismissed as a series of colorful incidents and picaresque adventures played out against the background of the Middle Ages.[2] However, a closer examination of Reade's comment and its context and of the work itself reveals that the novel is unified by a consistent concern with a social-political-religious issue that also occupied the attention of many of his better-known contemporaries: the Oxford Movement. *The Cloister and the Hearth* is Reade's response to the Oxford Movement and to the religious attitude toward mankind which Reade and many others, particularly the Broad Church Anglicans such as Charles Kingsley and F. D. Maurice, felt that the leaders of the Oxford Movement advocated.

Though Reade's own mandatory vow of celibacy may have influenced his choice of subject and may have enabled him to treat Gerard with greater understanding, Reade's statement about Gerard's plight concerns the religious doctrine of celibacy of the clergy, not the sort of personal restrictions of celibacy imposed upon him by the conditions of his fellowship. Moreover, in Reade's statement the doctrine of "celibacy of the clergy" is clearly linked to the other religious questions of "Pope, Priests, Convents, and the unreformed Church in general." In the early 1840s, the date at which Reade's opposition to the doctrine began, all of these questions, including celibacy, were in the air, subjects of religious debate aroused by the Oxford Movement.

The Oxford Movement, which also came to be known as Tractarianism after a series of doctrinal tracts published from 1833 to 1841 by John Henry Newman, John Keble, E. B. Pusey and others in which they explained their doctrinal position, emphasized re-establishing "a religion of holiness" (DeLaura 8) by purging the Church of England of what they considered to be the contamination of secularization which had been growing since the Reformation. They insisted upon the separation of the Church from the world and generally advocated a movement back toward the practices of the Catholic Church before the Reformation. More specifically, the Oxford Movement, according to Joseph Ellis Baker in *The Novel and the Oxford Movement,* "insisted on the doctrine of Apostolical Succession, on the importance of the Sacraments (with Mass as the central act of worship), on confession and absolution. It led to the establishment of monastic institutions, to some practice of celibacy among the clergy, and to hope for reconciliation with Rome" (4).

When Reade went up to Oxford in 1831, John Henry Newman had been the pastor at the university church of St. Mary's for three years. In 1833, while Reade was still an undergraduate, John Keble preached the Assize sermon on "National Apostasy" that initiated the Oxford Movement, and the *Tracts for the Times* series began. In 1835 Reade graduated from Oxford and the same year become a fellow at Magdalen. He received his M.A. in 1838, and though he left Oxford to study law in London from 1838 to 1842, he was, nevertheless, elected Junior Dean of Arts at Magdalen in 1841, the year Newman published his famous *Tract 90,* which caused widespread reaction and which led to Newman's retreat to Littlemore, to his consequent resignation from St. Mary's in 1843, and to his entering the Roman Catholic Church in 1845. During these years of Newman's struggle, Reade's connection with Oxford was still strong. In 1842 Reade was elected Vinerian Fellow at Magdalen and 1844 was made Bursar. Though Newman entered the Roman Catholic Church in 1845, leaving the Oxford Movement to the leadership of Pusey, fifteen years later when Reade was writing *The Cloister and the Hearth* in his rooms at Magdalen, the controversy aroused by the Oxford Movement was still raging. In fact, as late as 1864, Newman, in a letter to a fellow priest, quotes a resident of Oxford who said, "We are all becoming High Church again as fast as we can, a fact which it is difficult for the country to understand. It is so nevertheless. England will awake one morning, astonished to find itself Tractarian" (Ward I 593). And it was not until later that same year, 1864, that Charles Kingsley's comment questioning the veracity of the Roman Catholic clergy appeared in *MacMillan's* and led Newman to write his *Apologia Pro Vita Sua.*

Clearly then, Reade as a student and later as a fellow at Magdalen was thoroughly aware of the turmoil caused by the Tractarian Movement. To be sure, Elwin is correct when he declares that the Tractarians "could scarcely have influenced Reade, since his mother's religious views were diametrically opposed to what she termed Newman's 'disloyalty'" (Elwin 29). Having come from an Evangelical, Anti-Puseyite background, Reade might be expected to oppose the Tractarians, but his opposition was probably personal as well as doctrinal. One of his closest friends, Bernard Smith, a theological student at Oxford, had been persuaded by the Tractarian arguments and had become a Catholic even before Newman left the Anglican Church.[3] According to Charles L. and Compton Reade in their biography of the novelist, Reade "cherished a sincere affection for Bernard Smith and . . . was positivity chagrined when his friend elected to merge himself in the Church of Rome, and not only so, but to embrace Roman orders. He always spoke of that gentleman as a brother whom he had lost by the sort of misadventure which he could neither comprehend nor quite tolerate" (85). . . .

In *The Cloister and the Hearth* Reade argues against [the] basic tenets of the Tractarians, but he does not do so systematically or analytically. Instead, he often adopts a satiric tone with which he ridicules the claim of apostolic succession and the Tractarian view of Church tradition and authority, and attacks specific doctrines held by the Tractarians, such as transubstantiation, the primacy and infallibility of the Pope as the voice of the Apostolic Church, and monasticism and clerical celibacy. *The Cloister and the Hearth* is set in the medieval period when everyone belonged to one religious body. Thus, Reade presents both the Tractarian and anti-Tractarian positions as opposing attitudes within the Catholic Church. The method which Reade often uses to undercut the Tractarian doctrines is to present a scene in which a naïve Gerard espouses a belief which corresponds to a Tractarian tenet and then to allow someone more knowledgeable and sophisticated, usually a cleric, to illuminate his error.

In Rome, the innocent and believing Gerard goes with Fra Colonna to see the heads of St. Paul and of St. Peter, the traditional founder of the Church. With the people gathered to watch, a curtain is drawn three times to reveal "at a height of about thirty feet . . . two human heads with bearded faces, that seemed alive" (435). Believing that the heads are indeed the actual heads of the apostles reverently preserved by the Church, Gerard is astounded when Fra Colonna calls them "waxen images." A confused Gerard asks,

> "Waxen images? What, are they not the apostles themselves, embalmed, or the like?"
>
> The friar moaned.
>
> "They did not exist in the year 800. The great old Roman families always produced at their funerals a series of these 'imagines,' thereby tying past and present history together, and showing the populace the features of far-famed worthies. I can conceive nothing more thrilling or instructive. But then the effigies were portraits made during life or at the hour of death. These of St. Paul and St. Peter are moulded out of pure fancy." (436)

Reade's reference to the heads of St. Paul and St. Peter is surely an allusion to Newman's treatment of the same question in his novel *Loss and Gain* (1848). Charles Reding, the largely autobiographical central character in the novel, is in conversation with his Oxford friend Willis, who has already left the Anglican Church and become a Catholic. Willis argues that it might be true that the human heads preserved in Rome might not be the heads of the apostles; nevertheless, he says, "it is very well for secular historians to give up a tradition or testimony at once, and for a generation to oh-oh it; but the Church cannot do so; she has a religious responsibility, and must move slowly.

Take the chance of its turning out that the heads at St. John Lateran were, after all, those of the two Apostles, and that she had cast them aside" (221). He continues,

> There is no doubt in the world that at least they are the heads of martyrs: the only question is this, and no more, whether they are the very heads of the two Apostles. From time immemorial they have been preserved upon or under the altar as the heads of saints or martyrs; and it requires to know very little of Christian antiquities to be perfectly certain that they really are saintly relics, even though unknown. Hence the sole mistake is, that Catholics have venerated, what ought to be venerated anyhow, under a wrong name; perhaps have expected miracles (which they had a right to expect), and have experienced them (as they might well experience them), because they were the relics of saints, although they were in error as to what saints. This surely is no great matter. (223)

For Newman clearly the question of the veneration of relics was linked to the crucial issue of Church authority and tradition. Newman, in attempting to reconcile the Thirty Nine Articles to Catholic doctrine, argues in *Tract 90* that Article xxii, which describes "the Romish doctrine concerning purgatory, pardons (de indulgentiis), worshipping (de veneratione) and adoration, as well of images as of relics, and also invocation of saints" as "repugnant (contradicit) to the Word of God," is not really a condemnation of these practices themselves but only of certain excesses. He contends that "None of these doctrines does the Article condemn; any of them may be held by the Anglo-Catholic as a matter of private belief" (297).

But by describing the effigies at St. John Lateran as "waxen images" "moulded out of pure fancy," Reade denies that the heads are authentic martyrs' heads at all, much less those of the founders of the Church which have been carefully preserved and passed on by the clergy, and he thus implies that the doctrine of apostolic succession, too, is a fiction created by the Church to support the claim of authority. Moreover, because the heads are false relics, Reade argues that to venerate them is simply to perpetuate superstition and pretence.

Reade also includes numerous other incidents which argue against the veneration of relics, against the worshipping of images, and against the invocation of the saints. For example, when the naïve Gerard meets a seller of relics, the tradesman confesses to him.

> I tell thee, Bon Bec, . . . there is not one true relic on earth's face. The Saints died a thousand years agone, and their bones mixed with the dust; but the trade in relics, it is of yesterday; and there are forty thousand tramps in Europe live by it; selling relics of forty or fifty bodies. (365)

And when Gerard includes in a letter to Margaret the list of a wealth of religious relics he has viewed with awe in Venice, his comment must be a satiric reflection of Reade's feeling about such objects. Gerard writes that he saw "also a stone Christ sat on, preaching at Tyre; but some say it is one the patriarch Jacob laid his head on, and I hold with them, by reason our Lord never preached at Tyre" (394).

Similarly, Reade clarifies his position on the worshipping of images and the invocation of the saints, which Newman had condoned, when Gerard on his journey to Rome finds himself aboard a sinking ship. All about him the other passengers begin frantically praying: "An English merchant vowed a heap of gold to Our Lady of Walsingham; but a Genoese merchant vowed a silver collar of four pounds to Our Lady of Loretto, and a Tuscan noble promised ten pounds of wax lights to Our Lady of Ravena; and with a similar rage for diversity they pledged themselves, not on the true Cross, but on the true Cross in this, that, or the other modern city" (399). Because Gerard does not do the same, the other travelers blame him for their distress: "'Here is the cause of all,' they cried. 'He has never invoked a single saint. He is a heathen; here is a pagan aboard.'" But Gerard replies,

> Friends, I do honor the saints—but I dare not pray to them now—there is no time—(oh!) what avail me Dominic, and Thomas, and Catherine? Nearer God's throne than these St. Peter sitteth; and if I pray to him, it's odds but I shall be drowned ere he has time to plead my cause with God. . . . I must need go straight to Him that made the sea, and the saints, and me. Our Father, which are in heaven, save these poor souls and me that cry for the bare life! Oh, sweet Jesus, pitiful Jesus, that didst walk Gennesaret when Peter sank, and wept for Lazarus dead when the apostles' eyes were dry, oh, save poor Gerard—for dear Margaret's sake! (401)

After the sailors abandon the ship and passengers, Gerard acts quickly to aid a mother and her child. When he sees "one on his knees praying over the wooden statue of the Virgin Mary, as large as life, which the sailors had reverently detached from the mast," he snatches up the image "and, heedless of a wail that issued from its worshiper, like a child robbed of its toy," lashes the mother and child to it and sets them afloat to save them (402). Gerard's practical use of the wooden image of the Virgin to rescue the woman and child achieves more, Reade seems to say, than one's prayers to it would accomplish.

The origin of traditions and the apostolic ordination of church practices are also questioned by Reade's work. Reade points out that many Church traditions come from pagan, not Christian, sources and that the Church simply appropriated and adapted them for Christian observance. Fra Colonna, a student of antiquity, informs both Gerard and the devout Brother Jerome that the

> kissing of images, and the Pope's toe, is Eastern Paganism. . . . Our infant baptism is Persian, with the font and the signing of the child's brow. Our throwing three handfuls of earth on the coffin, and saying dust to dust, is Egyptian.
>
> Our incense is Oriental, Roman, Pagan; and the early Fathers of the Church regarded it with superstitious horror, and died for refusing to handle it. Our holy water is Pagan, and all its uses. . . .
>
> We celebrate the miraculous Conception of the Virgin on the 2nd of February. The old Romans celebrated the miraculous Conception of Juno on the 2nd of February. Our feast of All Saints is on the 2nd of November. The Festum Die Mortis was on the feast; neither the date nor the ceremony altered one tittle. (494)

By indicating the pagan origin of Church rites and the attitude of the Church Fathers toward them, Reade questions both the idea of inherent separation of the Church from the world and the idea that Church practices are derived from apostolically ordained tradition.

In addition to questioning the fundamental Tractarian position on apostolic succession and the primacy of Church authority and tradition, Reade also argues against the Tractarians on more specific doctrinal issues. Many of the Tractarians subscribed to the doctrine of transubstantiation, that in the mass the bread and wine are miraculously transformed into the very substance of Christ. . . .

The anti-Tractarians rejected transubstantiation and argued that the Tractarian position on the issue was "undistinguishable from Roman doctrine" (Cornish 285) "which the declaration made by our Reformers and inserted in our Prayer Books was meant to deny" ("Transubstantiation" 600). Indeed they argued that "the framers of the Articles went to the fire for denying it" (Cornish 278). Gerard's experience at a papal mass at Rome implies Reade's agreement with this anti-Tractarian position. When Gerard sees someone taste the bread and wine before the Pope officiates, he asks who it could be. Fra Colonna replies:

> "Oh, that is the Preguste, and he tastes the eucharist by way of precaution. This is the country for poison;
>
> and none fall oftener by it than the poor Popes."
>
> "Alas! so I have heard; but after the miraculous change of the bread and wine to Christ His body and blood, poison cannot remain; gone is the bread with all its properties and accidents; gone is the wine."

> "So says Faith; but experience tells another tale. Scores have died in Italy poisoned in the host." (435)

Another specific Tractarian doctrine with which Reade disagrees is that of papal supremacy and infallibility. Though the leaders of the Oxford Movement obviously did not accept the idea of papal supremacy as long as they remained within the Anglican Church, they saw it as a crucial issue in the decision to remain in the Anglican Church or to enter the Catholic communion. As a Roman Catholic, Newman defended the primacy of the Pope in *Loss and Gain* and the infallibility of the Pope in the *Apologia*. In *Loss and Gain*, after his conversion to Catholicism Charles Reding declares, "The Popedom is the true Apostolate, the Pope is the successor of the Apostles, particularly of St. Peter. . . . And hence Catholics call him Vicar of Christ, Bishop of Bishops, and the like; and I believe, consider that he, in a pre-eminent sense, is the one pastor or ruler of the Church, the source of jurisdiction, the judge of controversies, and the centre of unity, as having the powers of the Apostles, and specially of St. Peter (270-71).

Reade attempts to undermine this special view of the Pope by having the Pope himself appear as a character in the novel. Everything the character says or does argues not only for his ordinariness, but also for his own recognition that he is as fallible as other men. Far from being a man of spiritual depth, the Pope is "*Le gentilhomme blasé.* A high-bred, and highly cultivated gentleman, who had done, and said, and seen, and known everything, and whose body was nearly worn out" (438). When the Pope is asked "to give us your infallible judgment" on a novel he had written before becoming Pope, he refuses since "pope's novels are not matters of faith." He is persuaded, however, to make a pronouncement on a religious question even though he does it reluctantly since, he says, "I have had a life of controversy, and am sick on't, sick as death." Moreover, even after he makes his judgment, he encourages Gerard not to accept his words "as delivered *ex cathedra,* but uttered carelessly, in a free hour, by an aged clergyman" (440). And Reade insures that the reader does not miss his meaning by adding that the Pope "seemed to be gently probing the matter in concert with his hearers, not playing Sir Oracle" (440-41).

Clearly Reade's treatment of specific doctrines and practices near to the heart of the Tractarian movement reveals his bias against the teachings of the Oxford group. And the number and variety of examples indicate that their presence in the novel is more than coincidental. But as a popular response to the Oxford Movement, *The Cloister and the Hearth* does more than attack specific doctrines; it also more generally opposes what was popularly perceived to be the Tractarian view of the relationship between the Church and the secular world. In stressing Church authority and discipline the Tractarians argued for the separation of the Church from wordly concerns and many Tractarians acted on this belief by supporting clerical celibacy and monasticism. When Newman and his circle retreated to Littlemore before his decision to enter the Catholic Church, they lived an ascetic, monastic life of fasting, morning silence, and prayer. And for many Tractarians, Newman foremost among them, the highest religious life included celibacy. In *Loss and Gain* when Charles's Anglican friend Carlton argues that "celibacy is unnatural," Charles replies, "smiling," that celibacy is "supernatural," "the pefection of nature" (137).

But the Broad Churchmen and the Evangelicals would have agreed with Carlton's view that "Celibacy has no place in our idea or our system of religion," that "it is not a question about formal enactments, but whether the genius of Anglicanism is not utterly at variance with it" (136). For the anti-Tractarians, the primary function of the church was to work within and to be a part of the world and for the clergy to participate fully in the human experience. F. D. Maurice, for example, "condemned as Manichaeism the idea that the world was an alien society from which the Church of religious people was radically separated" (Bowen 368). Maurice rejected the idea of the Church as he believed the Tractarians formulated it, for he saw the purpose of such a church as being "not to love the world, not to save the world, not to convince the world, but to set itself up as a rival competitor to the world, to plot against the world, to undermine the world" (I 249). Bowen says that Maurice "believed that Newman and all those who promoted religion instead of showing God to the world were guilty of heresy and that the clergy should 'seek for the evidence of the compassion of God at work in the world in the ordinary life of man, not in the abstract speculations of academic churchmen'" (369).

Indeed many opponents of Tractarianism such as Charles Kingsley saw the Oxford Movement not as a religious but as a political movement which would undermine the freedom and well-being of the common man. In the revised 1862 edition of his novel *Alton Locke,* Kingsley has Alton describe the Tractarian movement in political terms. Responding to his cousin's arguments in support of Tractarianism, Alton says that his cousin

> tried to assure me—and did so with a great deal of cleverness—that this Tractarian movement was not really an aristocratic, but a democratic one; that the Catholic Church had been in all ages the Church of the poor; that the clergy were commissioned by Heaven to vindicate the rights of the people, and to stand between them and the tyranny of Mammon. I did not care to answer him that the 'Catholic Church'

> had always been a Church of slaves, and not of free men; that the clergy had in every age been the enemies of light, of liberty; the oppressors of their flocks; and that to exalt a sacerdotal caste over other aristocracies, whether of birth or wealth, was merely to change our tyrants. (106-7)

Though Reade is much less vehement than Kingsley, he nevertheless also rejects what was popularly perceived to be the Tractarian view of the Church. In *The Cloister and the Hearth* he embraces the socially-oriented, more humanistic religion of the Broad Churchmen and Evangelicals and argues against a religion of dogma. Thus, the meanings of "cloister" and "hearth" go beyond "celibacy" and "marriage." A "cloister" connotes the isolation and separation from the secular community endorsed by the Oxford Movement and acted out by Newman's decision to withdraw to Littlemore and ultimately to leave the Anglican communion. The "hearth" of the novel connotes not only marriage and family life, but also the larger meanings of participation in common human experience, of the affirmation of the value of the secular or earthly community, and of the recognition of the joy of human relationships whether they be those of marriage, of the family or of friendship. In short, the "hearth" represents humanitarianism in all its forms.

Only when one takes into account these larger meanings of the conflict between the "cloister" and the "hearth" can one see that there does exist in the novel a consistent theme which unifies the Gerard-Margaret sequences and the journey sequences. The keynote of the novel is embodied in the words of Gerard's mother, Catherine, when she says: "A heart to share joy and grief with is a great comfort to man or woman" (45). The journey from Holland to Rome is unmistakably to be taken as the traditional symbolic representation of life's journey. And the argument of the novel that one ought to overcome isolation and to establish connections with other human beings by reaching out to them is developed through a series of relationships which Gerard establishes through his journey, the most important of which are those with Margaret and Denys, and through brief encounters with other human beings who reveal compassion, a recognition of human kinship, and a willingness to act in another's behalf. Margaret represents a life's companion in marriage; Denys, the Burgundian soldier whom Gerard meets in Germany, acts as Gerard's companion through a journey which presents the joys and obstacles of the human experience; and those individuals who aid Gerard in some way argue for the importance of humanitarian acts of kindness and fellowship. This humanitarian attitude is epitomized by the woman in a German inn who gives Gerard food when she sees he is hungry. He tries to pay her for it, but she refuses the money, saying, "For what do you take me? . . . we are travellers and strangers the same as you, and bound to feel for those in like plight." Then, Reade says, after this act of compassion, "they parted, and never met again in this world" (112). Again and again throughout the novel, Reade expresses the view that "There is nothing but meeting and parting in this world" (509), and that it is not cold religion or the performance of religious duties but rather acts of benevolence and human fellowship that give meaning to life.

In effect, Gerard's entrance into the monastery when he believes Margaret to be dead ends all human relationships that have developed through the novel. His new commitment to the Church and to the spiritual world forces him to forsake all earthly concerns: "The Church would not share with earth. Nor could even the Church cure the great love without annihilating the smaller ones" (504). Throughout Gerard's experience as a friar, Reade shows him being torn between the demands of his monastic vows and his feelings of compassion for humanity. This conflict intensifies when Gerard reaches Holland to discover that Margaret is not dead as he had believed. Now all his longing to be a part of human life, to marry, to have a family, to participate in the earthly community, is given new impetus. But because he takes his vows seriously, he decides that the only way he can survive as a priest is to cease all intercourse with other people and become a hermit. In his hermit's cell he struggles to extinguish every earthly desire, particularly his love for Margaret.

In the arguments which Margaret presents to Gerard to convince him to leave the "foul place," the hermit's cave with its solitude and isolation, for the position of Vicar of Gouda with its "pretty vicarage" and the social intercourse of family and friends, Reade makes his attitude toward Tractarianism and the role of religion in the world inescapably clear. It is, as Margaret argues, "only a higher kind of selfishness, spiritual egotism" (627) to cloister oneself away from society by devotion to the Church. As long as there is evil and suffering in the world, Reade seems to say, the priest's first obligation is to help others. In language that might have come straight from a Broad Churchman or Evangelical of the nineteenth century, Margaret argues for something which sounds much like Kingsley's "muscular Christianity" and against a doctrinal religion which leads the individual to concentrate foremost on his own spiritual development through the observation of sacraments, confession, and absolution. She contends that

> a priest had no more right to care only for his own soul than only for his own body. That was not *his* path to heaven. "But," said she, "whoever yet lost his soul by saving the souls of others! the Almighty loves him who thinks of others. . . . So long as Satan walks the whole earth, tempting men, and so long as the sons of Belial do never lock themselves in caves, but run like ants to and fro corrupting others, the good man that

> skulks apart plays the devil's game, or at least gives him the odds; thou a soldier of Christ? ask thy comrade Denys, who is but a soldier of the Duke, ask him if ever he skulked in a hole and shunned the battle because forsooth in battle is danger as well as glory and duty. (627)

But it is not Margaret's argument alone which convinces Gerard to leave his hermit's cell. He comes to his own recognition of the joy and goodness of earthly affections. It is through his and Margaret's child, a child he did not know existed, that Gerard's isolation is broken. The child, though the product of sexual love, represents all human affection and earthly ties. He is, as Gerard calls him, a "little human flower" (615). When he finds the child asleep in his cell, not knowing he is his own son, Gerard still experiences love for him. He blesses the child and vows, "I would not change thee for e'en a cherub in heaven" (616). The child becomes the human link which will "anchor his father forever to humanity" (632).

When Margaret returns finally to convince Gerard to go to Gouda to accept the roles of son to his parents, brother to his siblings, father to his young son, companion to Margaret, and vicar to the community, he leaves his hermit's cell because, he says, "the affections of earth curl softly round my heart! I cannot help it: God made them after all" (626). After he is reintegrated into human society, he learns that "the cave which had been his hermit's cell has verily fallen in" and concludes that if he had not left it to take his proper place in the world "it had assuredly buried me dead there where I had buried myself alive" (635).

It is not accidental that the child who brings about this transformation in Gerald is one who would later come to be known as Erasmus, one of the leaders of the Reformation. An 1850 article in the *Christian Examiner* points out that "Erasmus, it has been said, picked the lock of the door, which Luther pushed open and entered. The common saying was, in the days of the Reformation, that 'Erasmus laid the egg, and Luther hatched it'" (86). The nineteenth-century reader would surely not have missed the significance of Erasmus's role in Reade's novel as a response to Tractarianism. Erasmus's work "The Praise of Folly" was, according to an 1854 article in the *Eclectic Magazine,* "a favorite class-book with our teachers" (320), and in this work and others, Erasmus puts forth a humanist position which corresponds to that of the anti-Tractarians. H. Hyma states that to Erasmus "it mattered little whether the miracles recorded in the Bible actually happened or not. As for the doctrine of transubstantiation, of purgatory, and of justification by faith and words, he believed that they might be interpreted in various ways. . . . He said on many occasions that to imitate the life of Jesus was far more important than to argue about dogma" (quoted in Erasmus 10). Like the anti-Tractarians after him,

Erasmus also rejected the position that the final source of authority was the Church. Erasmus sought the final source of authority in Scripture.

Reade, in re-telling the life of the father of Erasmus, was clearly putting forth his position on a debate which had occupied many of his contemporaries for almost thirty years. Though his understanding of the Oxford Movement was perhaps overly simplistic and his response to the Tractarians was satiric and unsystematic, Reade nevertheless represents a popular reaction to a religious position which to many Victorians seemed to counter to the general movement of their time. The unsettling events surrounding the Oxford Movement forced Reade and many other Victorians to re-examine their beliefs on religious and doctrinal matters and to re-evaluate the relationship between the Church and the secular world. By saying that Gerard's proper place was in the secular world and not in the isolation of a monastery or a hermit's cell and by arguing that the Church and the clergy ought to devote itself not to reaffirming its religious authority and engaging in doctrinal disputes but, rather, to alleviating the suffering of those human beings who are a part of the secular world, Reade was reflecting the dominant Victorian attitude toward religion. ***The Cloister and the Hearth,*** which was among the most widely read novels of the nineteenth century, is a reflection of a popular attitude among many Victorians who saw the Oxford Movement as an abdication of social and religious obligation.

[1] See Coleman. Though they do not mention a mistress, Charles L. and Compton Reade say that "Celibacy also with its cruel claws held Charles Reade prisoner" (281).

[2] For example, Burns goes so far as to argue that the novel is "little more than a long sequence of excellent melodramatic scenes (complete with historical settings), very neatly worked into the form of a 'good story' (79). Butterfield concurs that the novel concerns "loyalties that cut across each other and pull different ways: but that Reade simply uses this theme as an excuse for sending his hero on a journey, so that his story becomes very largely a story of travel." The only unity that Butterfield finds in the incidents is that "they all happen to the same person" (43-44).

[3] Ward relates that during Newman's period of retreat in Littlemore the interest in whether he would enter the Catholic Church was intense and that "Dr. Wiseman's eagerness to know more of the prospect was especially keen. He had with him at Oscott, as a theological student, Bernard Smith, a recent convert, formerly rector of Leadenham, an old friend and quondam curate of Newman. Mr. Smith consented to pay Newman a visit at Littlemore to ascertain how matters really stood. His visit was on June 26. Newman received him coldly at first, and left him to the care of the rest of the Littlemore community. Later on he reappeared and asked Mr. Smith to remain for dinner. The guest from Oscott was on the look-out for the smallest sign of his intentions from one who was apt, as Dean Stanley has said, 'like the slave of Midas to whisper his secret to the reeds.' And a sign came—slight but unmistakable. At dinner Newman was attired in grey trousers—which to Bernard Smith, who knew his punctiliousness in matters of dress, was conclusive evidence that he no longer regarded himself as a clergyman. Mr. Smith returned to Oscott and reported that the end was near" (83).

Works Cited

Baker, Joseph Ellis. *The Novel and The Oxford Movement.* Princeton Studies in English, No. 8. Princeton: Princeton UP, 1932.

Bowen, Desmond. *The Idea of the Victorian Church: A Study of the Church of England, 1883-1889.* Montreal: McGill UP, 1968.

Burns, Wayne. *Charles Reade: A Study in Victorian Authorship.* New York: Bookman Associates, 1961.

Butterfield, Herbert. *The Historical Novel: An Essay.* Cambridge: Cambridge UP, 1924.

Chapman, Raymond. *Faith and Revolt.* London: Weidenfeld and Nicolson, 1970.

Coleman, John. *Charles Reade As I Knew Him.* London: Treherne and Co., 1903.

Cornish, Francis Warre. *The English Church in the Nineteenth Century, Part 1.* A History of the English Church, vol. 8. Ed. W. R. W. Stephens and William Hunt. London: Macmillan, 1933.

DeLaura, David J. *Hebrew and Hellene in Victorian England: Newman, Arnold, and Pater.* Austin: U of Texas P, 1969.

Elwin, Malcolm. *Charles Reade.* London: Jonathan Cape, 1931.

"Erasmus." *The Christian Examiner,* 49 (1850): 80-100.

"Erasmus." *Eclectic Magazine,* 33 (1854): 310-326.

Erasmus, Desiderius, *In Praise of Folly.* In *The Essential Erasmus,* ed. and trans. John Dolan. New York: New American Library, 1964.

Howells, William Dean. *My Literary Passions.* New York: Harper Brothers, 1895.

James, Henry. "Felix Holt the Radical." *Notes and Reviews.* 1921; rpt. Freeport, N.Y.: Books for Libraries Press, 1968.

Kingsley, Charles. *Alton Locke.* Rev. ed., 1862; rpt. London: Macmillan and Co., 1900.

Maurice, F. D. *Sermons Preached in Lincoln's Inn Chapel.* Vol. 1. New York: Macmillan, 1891.

Newman, John Henry. "Remarks on Certain Passages of the Thirty-Nine Articles (Being No. 90 of the Tracts for the Times) 1841." In *The Via Media of the Anglican Church.* 2 vols. Ed. John Henry Newman. London: Longmans, Green and Co., 1891.

Phillips, Walter Clarke. *Dickens, Reade and Collins: Sensation Novelists.* 1919; rpt. New York: Russell and Russell, 1962.

Reade, Charles. *The Works of Charles Reade.* Vol. XI. 1895; rpt. New York: AMS Press, Inc., 1978.

Reade, Charles L. and Compton. *Charles Reade . . . A Memoir.* New York: Harper, 1884.

"Tractarian View of the Doctrine of Transubstantiation." *Christian Observer,* 47 (1847): 599-603.

Ward, Wilfrid. *The Life of John Henry Cardinal Newman.* 2 vols. London: Longmans, Green and Co., 1912.

Daniel Barrett (essay date 1993)

SOURCE: "*It is Never Too Late to Mend* and Prison Conditions in Nineteenth-Century England," in *Theatre Research International,* Vol. 18, No. 1, 1993, pp. 4-15.

[*In the following excerpt, Barrett discusses the controversial premiere of Reade's play* It is Never Too Late to Mend.]

The première of *It Is Never Too Late to Mend* at the Princess's Theatre on 4 October 1865 marked the appropriately tumultuous return of Charles Reade to the London stage after an absence of nine years. That night, one of the most memorable disturbances in the nineteenth-century theatre occurred when the drama critics in attendance, led by Frederick Guest Tomlins of the *Morning Advertiser,* demanded that the play be halted because of its offensive subject matter and one particularly shocking scene. The dispute became a *cause célèbre* among critics, dramatists, and the general public and was recalled (with varying degrees of accuracy) years later by its participants, witnesses, and other interested parties.

Today the incident raises several questions. Why did Reade decide to return to stage writing after his self-imposed hiatus, since he had long criticized the inability of playwrights to receive proper compensation for their work and to protect it through inadequate copyright laws? Why was Reade's dramatization of his novel so much more provocative than the novel itself, published in 1856, and how did it gain a licence from the Examiner of Plays? What actually happened on opening night, since the fracas was remembered so differently by many people, most of whom had strong motives for their recollections? What effect did the uproar have on the play itself and its reception, both during the first run and in revivals? Reade's drama deserves at least a footnote in history, for it establishes a point in the nineteenth century when an angry audience could no longer condemn a controversial play to extinction, but could be defied by a manager and playwright who defended their production and eventually made it a success. The play also informs us about penal practices in Victorian England, an unpleasant subject to middle-class playgoers but one that Reade either courageously thrust before their eyes or exploited for his own profit, depending on one's interpretation of the events.

It Is Never Too Late to Mend had already accumulated a contentious and litigious history before it ever appeared on stage, beginning on 10 January 1853 when Reade's drama, *Gold,*[1] was first performed at Drury Lane. Wishing to depict the recent discovery of gold in Australia through a stage realization, Reade composed a 'Surrey piece' in which three Englishmen, drawn by their misfortunes to the gold fields, eventually find wealth and vindication. Although better written than most dramas of this genre, *Gold* won acclaim for its pictorial rather than its literary merits:

> The scene of the 'diggins' in Australia, with all the mechanism of 'cradles', the chymistry of testing, and instances of the rude administration of justice in a lawless state of society, furnishes a living picture of a region which now engrosses the attention of every class of the community, and those who care little for the piece may go to see this particular scene, as they would go to one of the numerous dioramas of the day.[2]

Because one of the characters, Tom Robinson, is a thief, Reade made it his business to educate himself in the ways of convicts and prisons. He recorded in his diary, 'I have the *entree* of Durham Gaol, and I am studying thieves.'[3] Reade did not display all the fruits of his research in *Gold,* but his enquiries later contributed to the prison scene in *It Is Never Too Late to Mend,* both the novel and play. During a respectable run of six weeks at Drury Lane, *Gold* 'crowded the theatre, and saved the manager [E. T. Smith]', at least by Reade's reckoning, with Reade earning £20 a week.[4]

The play also served Reade well as both a rough draft for the plot of *It Is Never Too Late to Mend* and as an unlikely repository of his performance rights, as determined by a notable court case in 1862.

By that year, Reade had made his reputation as one of London's leading dramatists and author of two perennial favorites, *The Ladies' Battle* (1851) and *Masks and Faces* (1852), the latter written with Tom Taylor. He was also a famous and wealthy novelist, thanks in large part to the publication of *It Is Never Too Late to Mend* in 1856. But the novel's gain had been the drama's loss, for Reade had abandoned stage writing after his final collaboration with Taylor, *The First Printer,* produced by Charles Kean in 1856. In later years, Reade complained that he had been 'driven off the stage against my will, and compelled to go into a sister art, for which I think I have not the same ability'. When asked to elaborate, he launched into a well-rehearsed polemic:

> It was in consequence of the extreme narrowness of the market, and above all, the competition in those days of the stolen goods from the French, under circumstances particularly unfavourable to dramatic inventors. . . . The case was this: the play-wrights, who steal pieces from the French, are journalists, most of them (at least at that time they were so), and that gave them the power to shut the manager's doors to the inventor; it operated like this: the inventor asked the manager to read a piece, and at the same time a man who had taken a French piece without paying for it, and could get it praised in the newspapers by his colleagues, brought those two temptations to the manager, and he could undersell me, because you cannot invent a piece as cheaply as you can steal one.[5]

Although these are legitimate complaints, Reade is being wilfully deceitful. For one thing, he had profited from the same practice he criticizes: at least five of his performed plays had been adapted from the French. More important, he never mentions his primary motive for embracing novel-writing: money. He had earned far more from *It Is Never Too Late to Mend* than from all his previous stage writing, especially in America, where literary copyright was protected while performance right was legally ignored.

However much Reade exaggerates his grievances, he is most sincere when he regrets his isolation from the theatre. 'During my period of enforced exile from the stage I suffered intellectual hell', he wrote. 'I used to go to the theatres and see that one piece of unnatural trash after another could get a hearing, yet the market was hermetically sealed to me.'[6] With the popular reception of *It Is Never Too Late to Mend,* Reade set about writing a stage adaptation, one that incorporated scenes from *Gold* as well as the novel, but to no avail: managers uniformly rejected the play. Mean-

while he witnessed the indignity of seeing his novel adapted by others 'with a success unparalleled in those days. . . . Managers made at least seventy thousand pounds out of my brains, stolen.'[7]

Finally he struck back. When Thomas Hailes Lacy published an adaptation of *It Is Never Too Late to Mend* by Colin Hazlewood, Reade sued Lacy in 1861 for infringement of copyright—not of the novel, but of its dramatic precursor, *Gold.* Lacy knew he could adapt any novel he chose without recompense to the author. But he had not anticipated Reade's argument that since the novel included scenes from the play, and the play had been published, Lacy had violated Reade's copyright once removed. Lacy pleaded that he knew nothing of *Gold* (conveniently forgetting he had published the play himself), but the court was not persuaded, concluding, '[Reade] did not, by transferring these passages into his novel, lose any part of the copyright which he had in his drama; nor can ignorance of the existence of the drama on the part of the Defendant be urged as a valid defence.'[8]

Thus an unauthorized adaptation could not be published; but could it be performed? During 1861 Reade brought two lawsuits against Benjamin Conquest, manager of the Grecian Theatre, where an adaptation of *It Is Never Too Late to Mend* written by Conquest's brother, George, had been presented for eighty nights. To the extent that the adaptation was taken from the *novel,* Conquest could safely produce the play without obligation to Reade.[9] But by proving that the adaptation was partially (and unintentionally) derived from *Gold,* Reade was protected and won his case, receiving damages of £160.[10] In other words, in 1861 an author could protect his novel from being freely adapted only by first writing a play on the same subject and having it published.

These successes did little to mitigate Reade's frustration at seeing his own adaptation lie unperformed for seven years. Then early in 1865, John Coleman, manager of the Theatres Royal in Leeds, York, Lincoln, and Cambridge, applied personally to Reade for permission to stage an adaptation of *It Is Never Too Late to Mend.* Coleman later recalled his first encounter with Reade:

> When I said that I wanted to dramatize his book, he told me he had dramatized it already; that he had sent printed copies to every manager in London, and they had not had the decency even to acknowledge his letters on the subject. He had lost all hope and heart about it, he said, but if I liked I might take the play and read it, and form my own opinion as to its chances of success. I read it that night, and breakfasted with him the next morning, when we arranged to produce it forthwith at my theatre in Leeds.[11]

Although advised by Dion Boucicault to sell the play for no less than one-sixth of the box-office receipts,

Reade was so favorably impressed by Coleman's initiative and personality that, as he later admitted, 'I made great concessions. I agreed to let him work it in certain first-class theatres, not his own, for 1/10 the nightly receipts, and I actually let him play it at his own four theatres for 1 gu[ine]a per representation, which was a mere peppercorn rent.'[12] For his part, Coleman received performance rights for one year, with the stipulations that 'the said drama to be thoroughly well rehearsed, and the words perfect before performance. Three new scenes at least to be painted[.] First, a . . . Farmhouse scene[;] a prison scene, built, and with real gas-light[;] and an Australian scene with gold-digging business.'[13] Believing that 'A play of mine loses so enormously when not rehearsed by me',[14] Reade came down to Leeds to attend rehearsals and make life miserable for at least one member of the company before opening night of 28 February 1865.[15]

In most respects, Reade's adaptation of *It Is Never Too Late to Mend* is a conventional melodrama. George Fielding, an 'upright, downright honest man', is too poor to marry his fiancée of three years, Susan Merton, and decides to leave his Berkshire farm and seek his fortune in Australia. His departure is hastened by a villainous moneylender, John Meadows, who secretly wishes to marry Susan and has entrapped Fielding and his brother, William, in debt. (The first act ends with Fielding's tearful departure from family and friends, whereupon Meadows immediately advances toward Susan, saying, 'Mine! mine!') Meanwhile Tom Robinson, an acquaintance of Fielding's, is accused of larceny and sent to prison, accompanied by a boy, Josephs, who has been caught stealing potatoes. There they suffer the brutalities inflicted by the fiendish governor of the prison, Hawes, with Josephs dying from mistreatment and Robinson escaping only by being transported. Eventually Fielding and Robinson are reunited in Australia, where Robinson persuades Fielding to give up sheep-farming and take up prospecting. The results are predictable: with the help of Fielding's aborigine companion, Jacky, the two friends find a huge gold nugget and return to England £7,000 richer. They arrive just in time to prevent the marriage of Meadows and Susan, who has been deceived into thinking that Fielding had taken a wife in Australia. All ends happily as Fielding and Susan are to be married, Meadows meets the fate of most melodramatic villains by being dispatched to jail, and Robinson offers himself as living proof of the moralistic title of the play.[16]

Reade and Coleman agreed that the prison scene would be '*the* act of the play',[17] as it had been *the* scene of the novel. In fact, Reade had written the novel primarily to publicize the abuses of the 'silent system' as practised at Birmingham Borough Gaol in 1851-3. In the most sensational of the many cases reported by the *Times*,[18] a 15-year-old boy, Edward Andrews, had

hanged himself in his cell as a final refuge from the tortures meted out by the governor of the prison, Lieutenant Austin. A government inquiry into these abuses led to the publication in 1854 of a 'Blue Book' on the subject,[19] the name given to official government reports (usually bound in blue covers) on a variety of social problems. In his thorough way of exhaustively researching a subject before writing about it, Reade studied this Blue Book carefully and invented Josephs and Hawes as counterparts to Andrews and Austin. His outrage at the barbarous treatment of those prisoners never abated, and years later he still fumed that Austin should have been drawn and quartered rather than simply dismissed from his position.[20]

For the opening production at Leeds, Reade wished to present as grimly realistic a prison scene as possible, complete with a treadmill on which prisoners could be seen labouring. Here Coleman balked, repulsed by 'the revolting realism of the incident', and since the treadmill was not written into the contract, he prevailed over Reade.[21] Coleman's discretion helped to ensure a triumphant first night, the reviewer from the *Era* commenting that 'a success more brilliant and complete has seldom been achieved anywhere'.[22] The play was performed twelve nights at Leeds, but despite enthusiastic audiences, Coleman recalled that 'it was never played a single week to its current expenses'.[23] He then arranged a provincial tour of the production, beginning in Lincoln on 17 April 1865, and although Coleman wrote that 'from that moment the success of the piece was assured, and wherever we went the theatre was crowded nightly',[24] a transcript of his box-office ledger tells a different tale. *It Is Never Too Late to Mend* lost £56.11.6 at Lincoln in the first six of nine performances; Coleman noted, 'Never Too Late ought to have been withdrawn after the first night.' The play then averaged receipts of £8.5.2 for eight nights at York, and after a promising first two nights at Cambridge (receipts of £40.3.6, which Coleman nevertheless called 'The worst opening I ever had here'), lost £27.17.9 over the next six nights.[25] In the midst of this dismal tour, George Vining of the Princess's Theatre in London, having read the script, came down to York on 7 June to see a performance. Despite low attendance that night, Vining saw potential in the play and arranged for a London production, with Reade earning one-quarter of the profits through a sharing agreement.[26]

Reade thereupon submitted a printed copy of the play to the Lord Chamberlain's office for licencing. The soon-to-be-controversial prison scenes aroused no suspicions in William Bodham Donne, the Examiner of Plays, and the licence was duly issued on 24 July. Reade, an experienced dramatist, had anticipated Donne's blue pencil, and although there are many excised passages in the licence copy, all the deletions were made by Reade himself, sometimes with the initials 'C.R.' appearing in the margin next to a certain cut. For example, in a monologue at the start of Act Two, scene three, Robinson, sitting alone in his cell, says, 'And when they let us run in the yard for a mouthful of air, do we get it? Not we! A great filthy cap is put on our faces, to keep the light from our eyes, and health from our lungs. Sometimes the last victim that wore that cap was diseased; then you catch his disease, that is all. It is only a prisoner settled; 'tisn't as if it was a dog.' Reade correctly surmised that these lines would be disgusting to audiences and to their official protector, Donne. Later in the same speech, referring to the prison officers, Robinson adds, 'and, but for good Mr. Eden, I should hate Him who made them the heartless miscreants I find them here'. Again Reade cut the line, aware of Donne's distaste for all references to the Almighty.

Through these and similar alterations, Reade gave the appearance of improving the play for public consumption but left its provocative substance intact. Perhaps his self-censorship lulled Donne into a false sense of security. In his study of Victorian stage censorship, John Russell Stephens writes that Donne was 'perfectly content' with *It Is Never Too Late to Mend* 'mainly because [Reade's] social points were generally obscured in the dramatist's love of sensational effect'.[27] Actually, many of the play's powerful effects were concealed in the cursory descriptions of stage settings, properties, and acting in the script. Even so perceptive a reader as Donne could not anticipate how graphically the prison scenes would come to life on the Princess's stage.

In 1865, the Princess's was the home of sensation drama in the West End, largely because of its talented scene designer, Frederick Lloyds, a holdover from the Princess's glory days during Charles Kean's tenure in the 1850s. Since May 1862, when Vining began his management, the Princess's had recorded two triumphs by the master of sensation drama, Dion Boucicault: *The Streets of London* (1864), which ran 209 nights, followed by *Arrah-na-Pogue* (1865) and another long run of 164 performances. Both plays featured a thrilling sensation scene—a burning tenement and horse-drawn fire engine coming to the rescue in *The Streets of London,* and the famous escape by Shaun-the-Post up the walls of the prison tower in *Arrah-na-Pogue*—scenes wondrous to behold as well as technical masterpieces of the stage designer's art. As *Arrah-na-Pogue* reached the end of its run and preparations began for *It Is Never Too Late to Mend,* Vining and Lloyds were determined to fulfil Reade's intentions and meet or exceed the standards they had set.

When the curtain rose on opening night of 4 October, spectators immediately broke into applause as they feasted their eyes on Lloyds's rendering of the Grove Farm. The reviewer for the *Era* admired its rustic realism: 'The farm labourers are employed thrashing the wheat, real horses are brought on and taken into real stables, piles of hay and straw are scattered about the barn in most natural disorder, pigeons are resting on the dove-cote above, and real water is drawn from the pump below, whilst moving figures animate the background, and windmills are seen breezily and busily at work.[28] The cheery, wholesome atmosphere set the tone for Act One, which was well received by the audience, but made the transition to the shadowy, forbidding scenes which followed in Act Two all the more abrupt and disturbing. Reade's stage directions specify only, *'A corridor in the borough gaol, a line of cell doors represented on flats or on a drop scene'*. What confronted spectators was nothing less than a modern prison yard, rendered with a fidelity never before achieved on a London stage. To my knowledge, no artist's drawing of the scene survives. However, an illustration from Henry Mayhew and John Binny's *The Criminal Prisons of London and Scenes of Prison Life* contains some of the elements of Lloyds's prison and provides at least an approximation of the set. To realize the full impact of this scene, we need first to understand its different components—a virtual catalogue of nineteenth-century prison practices.

1. The treadmill. Although the treadmill is not mentioned in the script, it was by far the most scandalous of Lloyds's creations and dominated people's impressions of Act Two. . . . the treadmill (or treadwheel) must have figured . . . prominently on the Princess's stage; the playbill description of this scene says simply 'TREADMILL'. The treadmill was basically a long paddle wheel sixteen feet in circumference on which a dozen prisoners at a time would slowly step for fifteen minutes, rest for the same amount of time, work again for fifteen minutes, and so on for as many as fifteen periods in a day. As Mayhew and Binny explain, the prisoners would support themselves by leaning on a handrail,

> and they move their legs as if they were mounting a flight of stairs; but with this difference, that instead of their *ascending,* the steps pass from under them, and, as one of the officers remarked, it is this peculiarity which causes the labour to be so tiri[n]g, owing to the want of a firm tread. The sight of the prisoners on the wheel suggested to us the idea of a number of squirrels working outside rather than inside the barrels of their cages.[29]

The labour was so exhausting that prisoners would take desperate measures, such as self-inflicted indigestion or wounds, to avoid the hated 'shin-scraper'. Not only could it reduce grown men to tears, but sometimes a prisoner would slip on the treadmill and be crushed under its tremendous weight. Nor did it serve any purpose besides supplying a form of hard labour. Although originally conceived in 1818 as a means of grinding corn or pumping water, most treadmills were designed only to 'grind the air'—an unintentional lesson to the prisoners on the futility of hard work. One justice described the treadmill *approvingly* as 'the most tiresome, distressing, exemplary punishment that has ever been contrived by human ingenuity'.[30]

2. The crank. The critic for the *Sunday Times* noticed a crank in the prison yard,[31] a bit of artistic licence on Lloyds's part since the crank was always relegated to a 'crank cell' where a prisoner toiled alone, usually as a punishment. Next to the treadmill, the crank was the most dreaded form of hard labour. With the machine placed next to the cell wall and a long handle protruding to the side, a prisoner would use his entire weight to turn the handle in a circular motion, the resistance being imperfectly adjusted according to the age and size of the prisoner. (During Act Two, young Josephs responds to Hawes's charge that he refused to turn the crank by crying, 'You know I never said I *wouldn't;* I said I *couldn't:* that crank is a man's crank; it is too heavy for a lad like me.') The crank had figured prominently in the 1854 Blue Book, and the commissioners found that 'although in pressing the handle downwards the prisoner has only the five pounds [for a juvenile] or the ten pounds [for an adult] to bear down, yet in lifting it up, when nearest his body, he has to exert a force equal to at least three times those weights respectively'.[32] Prisoners were forced to spend hours at this debilitating, monotonous labour. At one point Hawes says to Tom Robinson, 'So, No. 12, you have been REFRACTORY at the crank again: only done 3,350 revolutions out of your 3,500.' Reade actually understates the punishment: the standard task was 10,000 revolutions which, at a rate of 20 per minute, required over eight hours.[33] At the Birmingham Borough Gaol (and in Reade's play), prisoners were punished for not completing the required number of revolutions, at times being put on a diet of bread and water which sapped their strength and made them even less able to finish their quota. Needless to say, the crank served no more utilitarian purpose than the treadmill. Both existed only to punish, to humiliate, and to intimidate.

3. Picking oakum. Although now forgotten, picking oakum was as closely associated in the public mind with convicts as breaking rocks—reason enough for Lloyds to include some oakum pickers in his prison yard. Oakum picking consisted of shredding thickly tarred rope obtained from ships until the strands were reduced to the texture of floss, later to be used for caulking. This mind-numbing task was not as simple as it seems: many prisoners could not pick their required amount of oakum even over a 14-hour period, and the effort left their hands bleeding, blistered, and covered with tar. The work had little to recommend it

as either a punishment or a worthwhile enterprise, since the financial return on a prisoner's three-pound ball of oakum amounted to about three pence a day. Yet oakum picking continued for years, according to Philip Priestley, 'because of its simplicity and its tediousness and because no one could think of any better way of keeping so many unskilled hands from idleness'.[34]

4. Silence. Even with all the visual semblances of prison life, one of the features that most unsettled the Princess's audience was the intense silence on stage. The rule of silence was imposed on prisoners to keep them from communicating, and infractions thus accounted for 70-80% of all prison offences.[35] On the stage as in real life, the sight of prisoners silently picking oakum or walking in file was 'assuredly the most appalling and depressing sight we can look upon', the whole scene having a '*goblin* character' to it.[36] In the play, one of the prison turnkeys extols the silent system with unintentional irony: 'The SYSTEM is a grand SYSTEM, a beautiful SYSTEM, dissolves the varmints into tears, and grinds 'em into bible texts and bone dust; but somehow they do hang themselves SYSTEMATIC, to get out of the SYSTEM.' Again Reade is referring to the Birmingham Borough Gaol, where twelve prisoners had attempted suicide and three of them (including Edward Andrews) had succeeded. In the theatre where spoken language was the lifeblood of performance, the ominous silence, relieved only by 'mournful music', added considerably to the 'dismal and revolting horror' of the scene.[37]

During this bleak parade of Victorian prison customs, a few protests from the audience were heard, but they were only the prelude to the storm. For in the next scene, Lloyds introduced the even more appalling spectacle of a prison interior, apparently based on the model prison at Pentonville. Near the centre of the stage were the cells of Josephs and Tom Robinson, separated by a corridor and with the fourth wall removed in each so the audience could view what was happening both inside and outside the cells. From this central point, gas-lit corridors radiated in a multi-tiered maze of cells disappearing into the gloomy depths, with the galleries connected by circular iron staircases. Only the critics paused to marvel at Lloyds's artistry and wonder how he had arranged such an intricate set during the relatively short interval. The rest of the audience felt a premonition of horror at this moment, especially when Josephs was revealed strapped to the corridor wall with a 'punishment jacket'. Another of Reade's borrowings from the Blue Book, the punishment jacket was simply a straitjacket with a leather collar strapped around the prisoner's neck. With their arms pinned to the wall by straps, prisoners were forced to stand for hours in excruciating pain, often unable to breathe freely because of the collar. Josephs does not exaggerate the torture of the punishment as applied at Birmingham Borough Gaol when he pleads to Hawes,

Oh no! no no! anything but that; it chokes me, it cuts me, it robs my breath, it crushes my heart, it makes me faint away, it kills me by inches: I cannot go on like this—first the jacket, till I faint away; then buckets of water thrown over me, and to lie all night in my wet clothes; then starved, and then the jacket again, because you have starved me down too weak to work. Oh, pray, pray have mercy on me and hang me! You mean to kill me; why not have a little, little, little pity, and kill me quicker!

Although Hawes and his minions do not grant Josephs's wish, the boy soon decides his own fate. Deprived of both bed and gaslight in his cell, Josephs (played in heart-rending fashion by Louisa Moore) hurriedly ties a handkerchief around one of the iron staircases and, in full view of the audience, prepares to hang himself.

At this point the playhouse erupted into shouts of 'Revolting!' 'Shame!' and 'Stop the piece!' and indeed the play did stop. A confrontation ensued between Vining, who approached the front of the stage dressed as the convict Robinson, and the drama critics represented by their unofficial spokesman, Tomlins. Vining then made a short speech which the *Era* recorded:

> Ladies and Gentlemen,—With all due submission to public opinion, permit me to call your attention to one fact, which appears to have been overlooked. It has been acknowledged that the work from which this piece is taken has done a great deal of good. We are not here representing a system as it is, but the abuses of a system, and I may refer to the Blue Book—here a voice from the pit shouted out 'We want no Blue Books on the stage'—for the truthfulness of these things. This question can be discussed elsewhere, and I believe that I am not wrong in supposing that most of the dissentient persons have not[sic]—Here the Manager paused significantly—Come in Free.[38]

This last reference to the 'dissentient persons' of the press, whom Vining and Reade loathed in equal measure, touched off immediate shouts of 'Apologize!'[39] Instead, Vining asked the audience for permission to continue the performance and, remarkably, they agreed. The sombre mood of the play was quickly dissipated by Lloyds's dioramic re-creation in Act Three of a ravine in Australia, seen first by moonlight, then by the light of dawn, and described as 'one of the most magnificent sets ever witnessed'.[40] By the time the play ended at midnight, the audience applauded so enthusiastically that they called for Reade (who made his bows from a private box) as Vining reappeared on stage to assure the press that he had been honored by their presence and had intended no slight to them.

The critics wasted no time in responding to the performance, and their comments fall into three categories.

First, they complained that the mistreatment of criminals and the depiction of prison life were totally unsuitable subjects for the theatre. In his column the next morning, Tomlins justified his protest the night before:

> If the theatre is to be made a one-sided and exaggerated advocate for every political opinion, it certainly will be avoided by all persons who frequent it in hopes of finding relaxation and amusement. There are ample opportunities for persons riding their particular hobbies, without making the stage a polemical and political arena. If Mr. Vining were judicious he would cut out the second act, which would have the double advantage of shortening the piece (now five hours long), and also of getting rid of the most painful and disgusting scenes we ever witnessed in a theatre.[41]

Reade's novel had successfully exposed prison abuses and helped to curtail them, but what could be described in a book could not necessarily be brought to life in a theatre. 'The exigencies of dramatic presentation forbid argument, qualification, moderation', wrote the *Pall Mall Gazette*. 'No time is left for reflection; everything must carry conviction as it appears.' Besides, what purpose could Reade and Vining have intended? 'Is it to call attention to that question which increasingly presses itself on the notice of all of us—the existence of a criminal population and the best methods by which the evil may be mitigated? A more ludicrous effort of benevolence than that of enlightening public opinion through a sensation drama was never suggested by a philanthropist.'[42]

While questioning the theatre's role as a forum for ideas rather than a place for diversion, reviewers also criticized the sensations themselves. T. W. Robertson, who would inaugurate a very different type of realistic comedy at the Prince of Wales's Theatre with *Society* the following month, reflected the majority opinion when he wrote

> if any person should dare to place upon the stage, for the mere greed of gain, a 'sensation' scene in the likeness of the ward of a hospital, and simulate the operation of amputating the leg of the hero, or the arm of the heroine[,] with real bandages, real tourniquets, real unguents, real saws, real needles, real arteries, and real blood, and the rest of the sickening apparatus, then the newspaper critic would be *dans son droit* to rise and hiss loudly, and it is to be hoped that he would be aided by audiences whose length of suffering is as extraordinary as is their patience.[43]

If the proper role of art was to inspire, enlighten, and entertain, then such scenes had no place in the theatre. Over thirty years later, Clement Scott recalled being at the Princess's on opening night, and the experience reinforced his dramatic credo: 'all that happened on the stage was doubtless true; the author had authority for everything he wrote in his play; but the stage insists that realism shall have a stopping point. Art does not countenance such horror as this.'[44]

The most serious accusation, however, was that Reade and Vining were portraying horrors that were no longer possible, given the reforms arising from the 1854 Blue Book and, indirectly, Reade's novel. The *Era* pointed out, 'The atrocities perpetrated in the Birmingham Borough Gaol . . . have long since ceased to exist, and it seemed therefore felt by the audience . . . that an unnecessary shock was given to their feelings by forcing upon their notice the sight of brutalities which made the heart sicken and the mind shudder to contemplate.' One could only conjecture whether 'these thrilling examples of bygone cruelty were simply brought forward to no more profitable purpose than that of creating a "stage sensation"'.[45] Reade had not brought his prison scenes up to date in the nine years since the novel's publication, and a monster like Hawes or an instrument of torture like the punishment jacket would not be found in a modern prison.[46] The melodramatic excesses of the characters seemed even more unreal when placed against the lifelike appearance of Lloyds's set. In his defence, Reade might have argued (though he chose not to) that the treatment of criminals was as inhumane and ineffective as ever, however much conditions had changed since 1856. The practises of the British penal system were still based on punishment rather than reform, a condition that would continue until the 1898 Prison Act finally banned such measures as the treadmill and crank.

Reade responded to the clamour in typical fashion: having cultivated his own animosity toward critics for years, he attributed their complaints to the same motive. On 24 November he wrote to his American publisher, 'I have just atchieved [sic] a great dramatic success. The whole London Press caballed to crush it; and the public put its foot on them with a decision they will not forget in a hurry. d—n them.'[47] He later embellished this interpretation in his bitter memoir, 'Reade's Luck', in which he charged that Tomlins was drunk during the performance and was incited by his fellow critics to make his protest, only to be put down by galleryites who shouted, 'Turn the blackguards out.'[48] Vining was equally unrepentant—and deficient in memory. After his first-night challenge to the critics, he taunted them in newspaper advertisements that trumpeted the success of the production.[49] Ten years later, he attributed the entire controversy to Louisa Moore's being accidentally thrown to the stage too roughly, with 'a smack similar to a cod's tail slapped on the marble slab of a fishmonger's shop—the effect was horrible'.[50]

Despite the bravado shown by Reade and Vining, the audience response had an immediate effect on the production. By the second night, both the treadmill and Josephs's attempted suicide were gone. The *Era* reported only 'a slight outburst of sibilation' at the diminished prison horrors, and no protests since then.[51] Boucicault later testified that the crank had gone the way of the treadmill 'after two or three nights'.[52] Beyond these concessions to decorum, Vining and Reade apparently made no other alterations—nor did they need to. The production amply fulfilled one reviewer's prediction that 'in the [public's] anxiety to learn what has created such a sensation, the Manager will doubtless find a remunerative source of profit'.[53] Besides the attraction of Lloyds's splendid scenery, the production featured fine performances by Vining and Dominick Murray (as Peter Crawley, a grovelling agent of Meadows's) and an astonishing piece of character acting by Stanislaus Calhaem, who portrayed Jacky with supposed fidelity to the customs and temperament of the Australian aborigine. The initial run of 140 performances gratified both Reade's ego and his bank account, earning him £2,000 from total profits of £8,000.[54]

It Is Never Too Late to Mend went on to become a repertory staple, particularly in the provinces, where it proved a durable source of income for Reade. The play was also revived in London, first at Astley's in 1874 (with Reade directing the production and Ellen Terry starring as Susan), later at the Adelphi in 1881. But as the memories of its sensational première faded, the play stood revealed as only the 'commonplace transpontine drama'[55] that survives on the page today. In a whimsical passage from his *English Dramatists of To-Day,* William Archer dismissed Reade as a 'dramatist of yesterday' as he recalled the recent Adelphi production. The play had always seemed too long to Archer—he thought the title should be changed to *It's Never Too Late to End*—and despite his determination to see a performance through, he finally succumbed in Act Three: 'When the irrepressible Jacky took the centre of the stage and set himself to solve the mysteries of a cotton umbrella, I reflected that art is long and life is fleeting, and went.' As for the notorious second act, Archer admits he did not see the original staging, but 'If the scene was more horrible and more absurd than it is at present, it must have been a wonderful production'.[56]

In retrospect, the play that Reade always considered his masterpiece served two important functions. First, the original production signalled the end of democracy in the Victorian theatre, a time when a first-night audience could force the removal of a play with the manager powerless to resist. The playwright Shirley Brooks, testifying before the 1866 Parliamentary committee, recognized the end of an era when he said of the outburst on opening night, 'I suppose that in other days that would have been accepted as what is called damnation; but the manager did not recognise the right of the audience to pronounce any such opinion; he pushed the piece on, and gradually the public came, and at last you could not get into the theatre at all.'[57] The age of the autocratic actor-manager had begun.

Second, Reade's success in introducing a controversial subject like prison conditions into his play opened new possibilities for the theatre as an intellectual medium suitable for the portrayal and discussion of serious social issues. One can certainly fault Reade for not adhering strictly to the facts in his rendering of prison life. But in both his play and novel, he wanted to shock his audience, to force them to confront the harsh realities of a well-hidden penal system. When he received a letter in 1857 objecting to the details of *It Is Never Too Late to Mend,* he defended the novel with gusto:

> Those black facts have been before the public, before ever I handled them; they have been told, and tolerably well told, by many chroniclers. But it is my business, and my art, and my duty, to make you Ladies and Gentlemen *realize* things, which the chronicler presents to you in his dim, and cold, and shadowy way; and so they pass over your mind like idle wind.

> This you sometimes call 'being harrowed', but ask yourselves two questions:

> (1) Do you think you are harrowed one tenth part as much as I have been; as I could harrow you?

> (2) I, one tenth part as much as Josephs, who died under the harrow?[58]

By persevering in bringing his play to the stage, Reade 'realized' his vision once more, to the benefit of both the theatre and the social principles he supported.[59]

Notes

[1] Charles Reade, *Gold* (London; Thomas Hailes Lacy, c. 1853). Lacy's Acting Edition of Plays, vol. 11.

[2] *Times,* 11 January 1853, p. 8.

[3] Wayne Burns, *Charles Reade: A Study in Victorian Authorship* (New York: Bookman, 1961), p. 103.

[4] Charles L. Reade and the Rev. Compton Reade, *Charles Reade: A Memoir,* 2 vols. (London: Chapman and Hall, 1887), II, 164; John Coleman, *Charles Reade as I Knew Him* (London: Treherne, 1903), pp. 143-44.

[5] *Report from the Select Committee on Theatrical Licences and Regulations* (1866; rpt. Shannon: Irish Univ. Press, 1970), p. 235, questions 6724-26.

[6] Reade and Reade, II, 162-63.

[7] Ibid., II, 164-65.

[8] Reade *v.* Lacy, 1861, 1 J. & H. 528.

[9] Reade *v.* Conquest, 1861, 9 C. B. (N. S.) 755.

[10] Reade *v.* Conquest, 1862, 11 C. B. (N. S.) 479. For discussion of these cases and their influence on adaptations by Dickens, see K. J. Fielding, 'Charles Reade and Dickens—A Fight Against Piracy', *Theatre Notebook,* 10 (1956), 106-11.

[11] John Coleman, *Players and Playwrights I have Known,* 2 vols. (London: Chatto and Windus, 1888), II, 26.

[12] ALS, Reade to Laurie and Keen (his solicitors), 2 February 1867, Parrish Collection, Princeton University Library. All quotations from the Parrish Collection are printed with the permission of the Princeton University Library.

[13] Contract between Coleman and Reade, 7 February 1865, Parrish Collection, Princeton University Library.

[14] Reade and Reade, I, 311.

[15] As recounted in Coleman, *Charles Reade,* pp. 173-74.

[16] All references to *It Is Never Too Late to Mend* are from the printed licence copy, British Library Add. MS. 53044 D. This copy is the privately printed edition that Reade showed to Coleman, with some additions, excisions, and transpositions made by Reade. The text is similar to that in the most recent edition of the play, *Plays by Charles Reade,* ed. Michael Hammet (Cambridge: Cambridge Univ. Press, 1986). Hammet, who does not disclose his copy-text or editorial principles, includes one scene (Act Four, scene two) that Reade himself cut, and excludes short scenes at the start of Acts Three and Four which, Reade specified, were intended to be read but not performed. I have also consulted Reade's manuscript of *It Is Never Too Late to Mend,* contained in three notebooks and preserved in the Parrish Collection, Princeton University Library.

[17] Coleman, *Charles Reade,* p. 11.

[18] *Times,* 12 September 1853, pp. 9-10.

[19] *Report of the Commissioners Appointed to Inquire into the Condition and Treatment of the Prisoners Confined in Birmingham Borough Prison* (London: Eyre and Spottiswoode, 1854).

[20] Coleman, *Charles Reade,* p. 11.

[21] Ibid., p. 171.

[22] Ibid., p. 176.

[23] Coleman, *Players and Playwrights,* II, 31.

[24] Ibid., II, 32.

[25] ALS, M. H. Davies (Coleman's treasurer) to Charles Reade, 19 December 1866, Parrish Collection, Princeton University Library. Davies prepared a transcript of the ledger because Reade questioned the payments he had received from Coleman. Other documents in the Parrish Collection show that Reade and Coleman continued to wrangle over Coleman's managerial practices and accounts. In particular, Reade objected to Coleman's unauthorized leasing of the play to J. P. Weston of the Theatre Royal Bolton for 20% of the receipts while paying Reade 10%, with Coleman reserving the balance 'for my humble expence in providing prompt book, music, sketches[,] models of scenery [,] posters, wood cuts, &c.' Reade also believed he was owed forty guineas for performances in Cambridge and York. On the whole, however, Reade thought that 'Coleman and I have done business together very fairly and agreeably'. Not only did he like Coleman, but as he confided to his solicitors, '[Coleman] may be useful to me by starting another play and so forcing it on those idiots the London managers.'

[26] Reade and Reade, II, 168.

[27] John Russell Stephens, *The Censorship of English Drama 1824-1901* (Cambridge: Cambridge Univ. Press, 1980), pp. 124-25.

[28] *Era,* 8 October 1865, p. 11.

[29] Henry Mayhew and John Binny, *The Criminal Prisons of London and Scenes of Prison Life* (London: Charles Griffin, [1862]), p. 304.

[30] Michael Ignatieff, *A Just Measure of Pain: The Penitentiary in the Industrial Revolution, 1750-1850* (London: Macmillan, 1978), p. 177.

[31] *Sunday Times,* 8 October 1865, p. 3.

[32] *Report of the Commissioners,* pp. vi-vii.

[33] Ibid., p. vii; Mayhew and Binny, p. 308.

[34] Philip Priestley, *Victorian Prison Lives: English Prison Biography 1830-1914* (London: Methuen, 1985), p. 123.

[35] Ibid., p. 197.

[36] Mayhew and Binny, p. 311.

[37] *Morning Advertiser,* 5 October 1865, p. 6.

[38] *Era,* 8 October 1865, p. 11. Given the ensuing outcry, Vining must indeed have said, ' . . . that most of the dissentient persons *have* Come in Free', although the article in the *Era* reads ' . . . the dissentient persons have *not* . . . '

[39] Clement Scott, *The Drama of Yesterday and To-day,* 2 vols. (London: Macmillan, 1899), II, 274.

[40] *Illustrated London News,* 7 October 1865, p. 334.

[41] *Morning Advertiser,* 5 October 1865, p. 6.

[42] *Pall Mall Gazette,* 6 October 1865, pp. 10-11.

[43] *Fun,* 21 October 1865, p. 53. Robertson's unsigned contribution is identified through the Proprietor's Copy of *Fun* at the Huntington Library.

[44] Scott, II, 274.

[45] *Era,* 8 October 1865, p. 11.

[46] *Pall Mall Gazette,* 6 October 1865, pp. 10-11; *Daily News,* 5 October 1865, p. 2.

[47] Burns, p. 236.

[48] Reade and Reade, II, 167-68.

[49] See *Fun,* 25 November 1865, p. 103.

[50] Malcolm Elwin, *Charles Reade* (London: Jonathan Cape, 1931), p. 183.

[51] *Era,* 15 October 1865, p. 11. The *Era* (8 October 1865, p. 11) noted that the suicide attempt and other 'more prominent causes of disapprobation' had been removed by the second night. According to Coleman, Reade himself decided that the treadmill must be banished before the second performance (Coleman, *Charles Reade,* p. 210). I have not found any mention of the treadmill being used after the première.

[52] *Report from the Select Committee,* p. 143, question 4064.

[53] *Era,* 8 October 1865, p. 11.

[54] Reade and Reade, II, 168.

[55] Henry Morley, *The Journal of a London Playgoer* (1866; rpt. Leicester: Leicester Univ. Press, 1974), p. 313.

[56] William Archer, *English Dramatists of To-Day* (London: Sampson Low, 1882), pp. 27, 32, 34.

[57] *Report from the Select Committee,* p. 160, question 4511.

[58] Reade and Reade, II, 37-8.

[59] Research for this article was supported by a Travel to Collections grant from the National Endowment for the Humanities.

Michael Hays (essay date 1995)

SOURCE: "Representing Empire: Class, Culture, and the Popular Theatre in the Nineteenth Century," in *Imperialism and Theatre: Essays on World Theatre, Drama, and Performance,* edited by J. Ellen Gainor, Routledge, 1995, pp. 132-47.

[*In the following excerpt, Hays discusses the way Reade's play* It is Never Too Late to Mend *reflects the newly developing ideology of harmony between the social classes in England based on exploitation of the colonies.*]

[If] we turn to the melodrama of the early 1860s, we can do so with the sense that the discursive unity [Edward] Said discovers in the age of Conrad had not only not (yet) prevailed earlier in the century, but that it was held in abeyance by an active struggle for cultural dominance, both in the public realm (forcefully manifest in the Chartist and Corn Law conflicts) *and* in the "aesthetic" realm. Indeed it is only with the plays of Robertson, Pinero and Jones, and the "modernist" preoccupations of Shaw, that what might be called "aestheticized" dramatic culture and imperialism are functionally integrated as fully as in Conrad's novels.[5] Prior to this, the project of political enclosure and cultural submersion suggested in [Jane Austen's] *Mansfield Park* had yet to be completed. To get to that point, both the popular drama and its audience had to be reconfigured, included fully within the cultural politics legitimated by Austen's narrative. The drama (and its audience) had to, as it were, learn to speak differently, to accept the binding closure of the discourse and practice of imperialism instead of producing a cultural rhetoric of its own. Likewise, the "better" classes had to reconfigure their perceptions of certain segments of the lower-class public—find ways to merge them positively in the political and economic spaces of their wordly practice and in the cultural spaces open to representation in the theatre.

An interesting marker of this process, and of the resistances still to be overcome, can be found in Charles Reade's *It's Never Too Late to Mend* (1865).[6] It seems to me that this play participates in a socio-political reinscription that was also being advanced at the time in a number of other fields of cultural production: the fabulation of a new set of social models of the "nation" and its inhabitants, a picture of social integration, control, and stability which historians (Michelet, for example, in France) and early sociologists (e.g. Spencer) sought to theorize as a means of defining proper,

inclusive positions for all classes (even the criminal)—a social recodification that made possible the psychological and anthropological representations of the individual and the nation that were crucial to the development of the culture of high imperialism, and to a description (and concomitant marginalization) of colonial peoples outside the national "center." Reade's play contributes to this project by enacting an idealized transformation of representative figures from these groups. Thus, it can document for us a liminal moment, a moment at which the impoverishment and abuse actually experienced by unemployed and displaced (potentially rebellious) artisans, laborers, and smallholders in England are staged as the occasion for the production of willing participants in middle-class political economy at home and the imperialist adventure abroad.

Initially, it seems that the play is merely organized around a classic "melodramatic" situation. A young man, George Fielding, is deeply in love with his neighbor, Susan Merton, but finds himself rejected as a suitor because Susan's father will not allow her to marry a man marked as he is by his failure to pay the rent on his farm. This seems especially cruel because George's mother had, years before, helped Susan's father out of serious difficulties. Of course, behind all of this lurks the villain, Meadows, a moneylender and land speculator whose name is ironically evocative of one of his primary interests. He has bought up the debt on a number of houses in the village and is anxious to foreclose whenever possible. At the very beginning of the play Meadows states his position quite clearly. "I have always put my foot on whatever has stood in my path" (20). Needless to say, he, too, is desperately in love with the beautiful Susan, and, therefore, also anxious to get George out of the way.

Meadows conspires to force George to leave his village and voyage to Australia in search of the money he needs to wed Susan, and then tricks Susan into believing that George has married someone else. Because of this Susan, after putting up great resistance, agrees to marry Meadows; but on the very eve of their wedding Fielding returns, and after some further moments of tension the play ends happily with George and Susan together and Meadows on his way to prison. In other words, the play fits our modern understanding of a rigorously formulaic melodrama. But what is of interest here is not the possibility of proving that there might have been such a formula. What matters is the way in which the formula is *used* to both figure and occult social and economic issues that, if confronted directly would no doubt have produced a far more threatening picture of the political situation in England at the time. The formulaic aspect of the play, precisely because of its familiarity, allows the audience to easily identify with the young lovers and, at the same time, understand concrete formulations of social, political, and economic inequity as parts of a *momentary* dilemma.

What then is the "historical" ground that is engaged by the generic practice of the play? If we turn to the opening scene we note that it begins with Meadows trying to foreclose on the home of Isaac Levi, an aging Jew who, like Meadows, was also a moneylender, but who now simply wants to live out his final days in the peace of his own home. This, and his treatment of Fielding, provide examples of speculation and exploitation that are not merely "melodramatic" tropes. They correspond to economic practices which, at the time the play was written, were in fact driving numbers of people off their land. Laws that allowed absentee landlords to amass extensive holdings and extract impoverishing rents from tenants had already been denounced a decade and more earlier, but with the growth of suburbs around the major manufacturing towns, the problem had gotten much worse. Indeed, at the time the play was written, land-reform agitation had been further spurred by the attempts of London landlords to appropriate common lands for building development.[7] But here the topical issue of land speculation and economic exploitation on the part of large landholders as a group is displaced by a portrayal of the isolated evil caused by one individual in particular. Meadows' "melodramatic" cruelty places him outside the "normal" socio-economic order, in a position defined as much by literary tradition as by his specific actions: the echo of Shylock faintly preserved in the figure of the Jewish moneylender reduces Meadows' status to that of social pariah, since Levi is, in comparison, a worthy member of the world figured by the play.

This shift of focus also helps blunt the force of the complaints voiced by another character in the opening act: Tom Robinson, an old friend of George's who has been visiting from the city, gives voice to some very serious though not very well elaborated political and economic charges. England is not livable, he says:

> This very morning I heard one of your clodhoppers say, "The Squire be a good gentleman; he often gives me a day's work!" I should think it was the clodhopper *gave* the gentleman a day's work, and the gentleman gave him a shilling and made five by it. . . . Come George, England is the spot if you happen to be married to a duke's daughter: and got fifty thousand a year—and two houses and a coach. . . . But this island is the Dead Sea to a poor man. (27)

Such sentiments, when expressed in the context of Chartist and labor agitation of the recent past, had been sufficient cause for the speaker to be transported as a fomenter of criminal activity, but here they have a different effect.[8] While the mere fact that Robinson is allowed to give voice to these ideas implies their operative existence in the real world of the audience, the ultimate role they play in this drama is in fact to under-

mine the historical ground on which they stand. Rather than marking a confrontational situation, one which would delineate the class, economic, and political inequities in England that had been further exacerbated by the economic downturn of the late 1850s, they open the way to a transformation of the real social and economic tensions in England into a discursive unity made possible by the Empire.[9] Even before this happens, however, the truth value of Robinson's comments is diminished by our discovery that he is really a thief who has fled the city in order to avoid arrest. The fact that the play shows such malcontents are "criminal" and also under surveillance no doubt served to reduce the anxiety of the "better" parts of an audience that would surely object to the politics implicit in his lines. Nonetheless, they have been introduced into the play, just as Meadows' land speculation has; class divisions, political and economic conflict upset the small world on stage, and by the end of the first act the original social nexus of the village has been thoroughly upset.

If the play implicitly asks whether England could be the politically and economically fragmented and oppressive place suggested by these characters, the answer to this question is also already available in the situation and the characters present at the close of the act. "England" is not just the space occupied by these individuals or this village. Australia is proposed to George and to the audience as an extension of the English domain, a territory of promise for energetic workers in search of a better future—not as penal colony where lower-class troublemakers such as Robinson had habitually been sent.[10] Likewise, his discourse of resistance to social and economic exploitation will be transformed in the rest of the play, emerging finally as a positive evocation of participation in an imperial project that allows free movement between the colonies and England for all native Englishmen.

The difference between this treatment of the Australian colonies and that found in Dickens is worth noting here, since it provides some sense of the rapid transformation of their status as the need to recast the relationship between the lower classes and the colonies grew. As Hughes points out, Dickens' treatment of Magwitch in *Great Expectations* (1861) shows that he retains a far more restrained view of the Australian convict (586). Since the novel is set in an earlier period, Dickens is historically justified in barring Magwitch's return to England, but at the same time the novel clearly retains the idea that although transported convicts may redeem themselves through hard work, both they and the colonies remain segregated from the metropolitan center. Of course, in *David Copperfield,* Micawber willingly emigrates to Australia, but his choice and his situation are exemplary of a literary function assigned to the colonies in the industrial novel of the 1840s and early 1850s where, as Raymond Williams has pointed out, they served as a means of resolving conflict through a physical displacement of the characters to a space outside England.

Said presents Magwitch in particular as yet another demonstration of the way in which the novelists he invokes make use of the colonies without ever really allowing these places formal space or presence. In contrast, Reade, in both the novel and the play, boasts of the authenticity of his representations of both the place and the practices that are available for lower-class self-transformation, a transformation that does not evict them from the metropolis, but provides them with the wherewithal to return and re-establish themselves in England as model burghers. The Empire holds out its hand here to the poor Englishman in need—George Fielding will attempt to found a new and better life by farming and prospecting for gold in the Australian colonies, and Robinson will join him later, after he spends some time in one of the new prisons where he will be disciplined by the silent and solitary system of which Foucault has written so much—and which Dickens so distrusted.

The next two acts of the play offer us further insights into both locales, but only to legitimate the roles these places play in making good fellow citizens of what would have earlier been regarded by the upper classes as potentially dangerous individuals. From the contemporary audience's point of view, the most startling of these acts was surely the second, which takes us into the new "borough gaol" in which Robinson has been confined along with Josephs, a young lad who, in the first act, had been caught stealing potatoes from Meadows. Here again it is Meadows who is the source of an injustice over which the audience will be free to weep—without ever calling the political and legal systems into question. Indeed, this is probably the most important function of the act as a whole: to allow for a compassionate reconciliation between the audience and its counterparts on stage. We enter the prison milieu along with dear, good Susan, who has brought gifts to Robinson, and so, with her and through her eyes, experience the legitimation of the judicial order and the reintegration of Robinson into society.

In the second scene of this act Robinson describes his condition as follows:

> When I first came here I hadn't a bad heart, though my conduct was bad. I was a felon, but I was a man. And I had a secret respect for the law; who hasn't? unless he is a fool as well as a rogue. But here I find the law as great a felon as any of my pals. Here the law breaks the law; steals a prisoner's food contrary to the law and claps a prisoner in a black hole contrary to the law, and forces him to self-murder contrary to the law. So now . . . I despise the law because it is a liar and a thief. I loathe the law because it is a murderer. (45)

This is strong stuff. But we must keep in mind that Robinson's remarks are also representative of the liberal penal doctrine of the time insofar as he presents himself as someone who has been bad but is not bad of heart. In other words, he is potentially open to self-discipline and reform—if given the opportunity—which is precisely what the new prison system (as opposed to the old jail regime) was supposed to offer. In effect, the play tests this notion by pitting two figures seemingly representative of the state against each other: Eden, the prison chaplain, and Hawes, the prison governor. Eden confronts Hawes, saying "you have no right to reduce a prisoner's food, nor to torment him in a punishment jacket." When Hawes insists that he, not Eden, is master of the prison, Eden responds: "the law is your master and mine." Hawes persists, and Eden vows he will appeal to the Home Secretary, and if that doesn't work, to the Crown, and beyond that to the people (in other words, to the audience of this play) in order to see whether "the law can penetrate a prison" (44). Nevertheless, Hawes sends Robinson to the "black hole" and causes Josephs to suffer so horribly that he finally commits suicide. But these are solely the acts of a governor who has failed to follow the rules set down by the state. As with Meadows, it is the individual who is delinquent, not the order that had made their activities possible.

This exculpation of the regime seems to me to be exactly parallel to the public response precipitated by an event in the colonies which actually took place somewhat later in the year that Reade's play was staged: when E. J. Eyre, the Governor of Jamaica ordered a retaliatory massacre after some black islanders had killed some whites during an uprising, the response in England focused primarily on Eyre, not on the institutions that made his regime possible. The important difference, of course, lies in the fact that for Robinson, a white Englishman, the final result is integrative: he is ultimately to be reunited with the social body in England, while the blacks living in Jamaica are either included in the imperium as its servants, or as "subjects" that had a theoretical right to protection from arbitrary murder, but not to socio-political equity. As Edward Said points out when he briefly discusses this incident, Ruskin, Carlyle, and Arnold *supported* Eyre's actions (as did Charles Kingsley, Tennyson, and Dickens, who for some reason Said fails to mention) while Mill, Huxley, Darwin, Herbert Spencer, and Goldwin Smith denounced Eyre as a tyrant and murderer who violated the "natural rights" of English subjects. These rights, however, did not include the "native" right to resist imperial authority.[11]

It is precisely this difference that helps explain the functional importance of the prison scenes in Reade's play. Robinson, who would have earlier been regarded as a potentially dangerous subject and, like his Irish counterparts, would have been cast away in one of the white colonies in Australia, is, here, first "reformed" and then recast as a legitimate participant in a new national order that, as we shall see, promises a new harmony of interests in England, a harmony based on a new understanding of interpersonal relations at home and a common mastery of subject people abroad. Henry Fawcett, a contemporary of Reade's, best sums up this wished-for new order in his *Economic Position of the British Labourer* (1865). He looks forward to a society of well-fed, well-educated citizens, with skilled artisans and peasant proprietors at the base—"scavenged for and waited upon by Negroes and Chinese."[12]

This idea seems to be the imperial, economic equivalent of the "coherent heterogeneity" that Spencer had theorized in his *First Principles* (1862) as the necessary upshot of biological evolution and as the founding principle in the progress of human societies as they move toward "the greatest perfection and the most complete happiness" (340-71, 407, 530). Even if the "nature" of this process emerges somewhat differently in the play, the goal appears to be the same. And to the degree that Robinson is successfully coerced into participation, the audience too may be convinced to set aside certain historical animosities. Artisan and lower middle class spectators can unite with their betters in appreciation of the colonial adventure that unfolds in the next act. Indeed, this seems to be one of the functional values of the play as a whole. Its unifying discourse and representation of an internally coherent England allow the members of the audience to surmount their own class differences, just as their peers were later expected to unite in "common interest" when limited franchise was extended to certain artisans and members of the lower middle class in 1867.[13]

This new cultural paradigm begins to take shape when Robinson is freed on parole as part of the "ticket of leave" program that had in fact recently been introduced in England. He is enjoined to "repent, and . . . labour with [his] hands, and steal no more" (50). After receiving a letter from Susan to George, he sets off for Australia to build a new life. Thus, the tension produced by the violence of the prison scenes and by Josephs' death finds release both in a confirmation of the justness of the order behind the penal system and, once again, in the idea of the colonies as a place to work out one's authentic relation to the metropolitan center. Thanks to the Empire, George and Robinson will be united in their quest to become true, fulfilled Englishmen. This then becomes the core of the third act and central moment of the play: the ultimate transformation of Australia from penal colony into a land of opportunity, and the legitimation of colonial exploitation as a necessary adjunct of such opportunity, exploitation defined as a "profitable" interaction between colonials of every class and the colonized natives whom they supervise.

Reade claims to have done extensive research for the scenes in Australia and for his presentation of Jacky, the token Aborigine of the play. Nonetheless, it is obvious that he (like Isaac Levi, whom I mentioned earlier) is actually a literary artifact, a revised example of the stage Black,[14] put into play here to confirm a larger fiction of the general relation between the colonist and the colonized subject. It is Reade's *claim* that what he offers here is historically accurate that makes Jacky different from other, earlier stage figures of this type. Reade himself had, for example, included several other "Australian Blacks" along with Jacky in the play **Gold,** but none of them were focused upon as instances of the racial distinctions that found and justify colonial exploitation. They were merely useful (comic) "background," as was the stereotypical stage Irishwoman, Mary McDoggherty, who appeared with them. In the novel and in the later play, however, a new element is introduced. Jacky's presence, especially in the more tightly focused context of the second play, serves to delineate what Reade claimed was the "reality" of Australian life. He proudly announced that he had read "some thirty books" on Australia while preparing the novel, just as he had done preparatory research for the prison scenes. This new "realism" helps create a visual/spatial context that transforms characters such as Jacky from mere stock figures in the genre into authoritative ("anthropological") representations of cultural groups and their relations.[15]

Thus it is that when George reappears in the play he is accompanied by Jacky, who, needless to say, is his servant. Together they configure and justify the fundamental structures of imperial cultural relations. We see "Massa George" take on what can only be understood as 'the white man's burden' of educating Jacky—in "comic" scenes about such things as Jacky's inability to negotiate the change in temperature from the heat of midday to the chill of evening, a change that George's "friend" is apparently not able to predict: "When Jacky a good deal hot here . . . he can't feel a berry little cold a long way off . . . Jacky not white fellow" (59). From here, the play moves to a portrayal of Jacky as the stereotypical happy savage—willing to serve, but lacking mental and moral sufficiency: George comments on his "poor shallow brain" (62). But Jacky is above all *loyal*. When George gets sick, Jacky stays with him and tends him as best he can, but, of course, he doesn't do too well. Fortunately, Robinson appears on the scene just in time; it is he, not Jacky that knows how to get George back on his feet. Robinson's arrival also makes possible the introduction of more comic business demonstrating both Jacky's ignorance and an Englishman's "pluck": when Jacky threatens Robinson, he is easily put in his place by a few strong words (67).

After this series of patronizing and emphatically racist representations, the play moves on to the crucial moment when Jacky enacts the ideal role of the colonized subject. Learning that George and Robinson are in search of gold, he leads them to a nugget large enough to secure both their futures. This moment not only sets up the "happy end" the audience expects, it also gives George and Robinson an opportunity to comment further on Jacky's character. He is presented both as a savage and as "natural" man: "these poor savages have got an eye like a hawk for everything in nature" (76). Jacky is the "noble savage" who gladly reveals the existence of a great nugget, which he refers to as a "yellow stone," to his white masters, and Robinson says to George: "Here is a true philosopher. Here's Ebony despises Gold" (77). Idealism combines nicely with capital at this point to prove that the "philosophical" Aborigine *desires* to help his white master to empire and economic well-being. This is no doubt the Englishman's compensation for being cut off from nature.

What is interesting about this section of the play is that it is in fact based in real events. But those events, which had been widely publicized in England in the early 1850s, are *not* reproduced in the play. Instead of the story of an educated, native Australian who worked for a Dr W. J. Kerr, and who, after reporting the existence of a huge gold nugget, was rewarded (albeit insufficiently) with "two flocks of sheep, two saddle horses, . . . a quantity of rations, and . . . a team of bullocks to plow some land in which [he and his brother] are about to sow maize and potatoes," and instead of factual reportage on the waning of the gold boom in Australia, or the political unrest among the (white) workers there, or the anti-Chinese sentiment that had grown up around 1860 (there were about 15,000 Chinese in Australia at the time) when there was less land to prospect, we are offered Jacky.[16]

Of course, the play does not move quite so simply or directly as I have presented it. Events in the last act unfold, as did those of the first and second, in a context of "melodramatic" tension that leaves the audience no time to reflect on the possible discrepancies between known facts and the situation, the play's characters, and their actions. Jacky is quickly left behind in the final scenes of the play so that we can have a joyous reunion between George and Susan—a reunion that also brings together the various figures of the first act in such a way as to re-establish (on a new socioeconomic plane) the community that had initially been disrupted by Meadow's corrupt and anti-social activities. It seems love, hard work, and moral righteousness conquer all, but their (melo)drama also functions superbly as a means of uniting all classes in the audience in their desire to further experience representations— if not the practice—of the unifying and sustaining project of empire.

Fictions of English superiority over the colonized other invert and dispel the real conditions of lower-class existence, while the image of the imperial domain provides the idea of distant land and wealth as compensation for the otherwise painful need to submit to the actual constraints—spatial, economic, and political—that define life in metropolitan England. It is not surprising therefore that the discourse of empire enters the vocabulary of the working-class movement more fully at this time, and that a (false) consciousness of national superiority impedes the development of an alternative critical analysis, while not preventing the later re-emergence of class confrontation in England. Minds as well as bodies are being mobilized for the struggles that lie ahead, and to replace those that have already fallen in England's name.[17] Indeed, it is only if we make the effort to see how this came about, only if we can seek out the cultural moments that mark the difference between individual experience and the universalizing discourse that masks, trivializes, or distorts it that we can avoid the tendency to produce equally reductive counter-discourses in our criticism, discourses that, in the name of resistance and identity formation may overlook the internal differences that are always the initial targets of cultural subjugation—and that also can provide the initial instance in the process of building new modes of (inter)cultural understanding.

Notes

5 As J. Ellen Gainor has shown, Shaw, like Conrad, is aware of the complex and destructive relationship that exists between England and its colonies. But he also enacts imperial culture in ways that are fully in accord with its projects.

6 The play is Reade's dramatized version of his novel of the same name, which carried the subtitle "A Matter of Fact Romance" (1856) and which was itself developed form his early play, *Gold* (1852, first staged January 1853). With each new version of the tale there are shifts in character and emphasis that mark the evolving context in which it appeared.

7 Perkin (106-10) indicates several such efforts. See as well Golby and Purdue, (145). The year after Reade's play appeared, the Metropolitan Commons Act (1866) was passed to prevent this kind of encroachment.

8 For some examples of the transportation of these "criminals," see Thompson (222, 226-27, 249, 513).

9 The degree to which this discursive shift succeeded in changing the story of lower-class emigraton is evident if one compares the events limned by the play with the explanation offered by a later historian of the empire. G. M. Trevelyan's confidence in the imperial discourse with which he was raised allows him to assert that:

until the end of the Victorian era there were still large numbers of persons born and bred as agriculturalists, and desiring no better than to obtain land of their own beyond the ocean. It is only of recent years that a fear has arisen lest the English race, at home and in the Dominions, may by choice eschew the rural life and crowd too exclusively in the cities.

(Trevelyan 207)

As Eric Hobsbawm later demonstrates, it was enforced poverty, the result of economic undermining of the agrarian life, rather than free choice, that was the primary cause of such emigration (Hobsbawm 181ff, 200).

[10] Transportation to Australia officially ended in 1868, but had been under criticism for some years, particularly after the discovery of gold that figures so importantly in this play. On this subject see Hughes, especially chs. 15-16. A clear picture of the effort undertaken to encourage working-class emigration to Australia is provided by Clacy: "Much is done now-a-days to assist emigration, but far greater exertions are needed before either the demand for labour in the colonies or the oversupply of it in England can be exhausted" (158). At the time Reade wrote his play only the latter condition still obtained.

[11] For further information on the Eyre controversy see Semmel and Workman.

[12] Fawcett's comments are cited in Young (111).

[13] On the Reform Act and political value of this overcoming of difference through a limited franchise as well as the resultant split between artisans and the "masses," see Hobsbawm (224), but cf. Trevelyan (203-6).

[14] In addition to other sources, Reade's portrait of Jacky certainly owes something to Stowe's *Uncle Tom's Cabin*. That book's proclaimed factual basis had, in part, inspired Reade's own "realism." See Burns (131-33).

[15] The historical role and the significance of this development of "realism" in the drama in the 1860s has not yet been explored in any detail and certainly merits further inquiry. The question that imposes itself here is the degree to which this shift marks the absorption of the theatre—particularly the melodrama and the audience for whom it might have embodied vestiges of resistance and difference—into the imperialist cultural project as a whole.

[16] The earliest report of the discovery of the Kerr nugget, which is obviously the source of the incident in *It's Never Too Late to Mend,* appeared in the *Bathurst Free Press,* July 16, 1851. Several of the original reports have been reprinted in *Gold Fever* (39-44).

[17] Foster provides further, quite interesting documentation of the development of this nationalist and racist "English" consciousness in his discussion of the impact of the Crimean War and the emergence of the anti-Irish movement in 1861 (329-46).

Works Cited

Burns, Wayne. *Charles Reade: A Study in Victorian Authorship.* New York: Bookman Associates, 1961.

Clacy, Ellen. *A Lady's Visit to the Gold Diggings of Australia.* Ed. Patricia Thompson. London: Angus and Richardson, 1963.

Foster, John. *Class Struggle and the Industrial Revolution: Early Industrial Capitalism in Three English Towns.* New York: St. Martins Press, 1974.

Gainor, J. Ellen. "Bernard Shaw: The Drama of Imperialism." *The Performance of Power. Theatrical Discourse and Politics.* Ed. Sue-Ellen Case and Janelle Reinelt. Iowa City: University of Iowa Press, 1991, 56-74.

Golby, J. M. and A. W. Purdue. *The Civilization of the Crowd: Popular Culture in England 1750-1900.* New York: Schocken Books, 1985.

Hobsbawm, E. J. *The Age of Capital.* New York: Scribner, 1975.

Hughes, Robert. *The Fatal Shore: The Epic of Australia's Founding.* New York: Knopf, 1987.

Gold Fever: The Australian Goldfields 1851 to the 1890's. Ed. Nancy Keesing. Sydney and London: Angus and Richardson, 1967.

Perkin, Harold. *The Structured Crowd: Essays in English Social History.* Brighton, Sussex: Harvester Press, 1981.

Reade, Charles. *It's Never Too Late to Mend.* An edition of Charles Reade's unpublished drama with an introduction and notes by Léone Rives. Toulouse: Impr. Toulousaine, 1940.

Said, Edward W. *Culture and Imperialism.* New York: Knopf, 1993.

Semmel, Bernard. *Jamaican Blood and Victorian Conscience: The Governor Eyre Controversy.* Boston: Houghton Mifflin, 1963.

Spencer, Herbert. *First Principles.* New York: D. Appleton and Company, 4th edn, 1904.

Thompson, E. P. *The Making of the English Working Class.* New York: Random House, 1977.

Trevelyan, G. M. *History of England,* Vol. 3 (1926). Garden City, NY: Doubleday and Company, 1956.

Workman, Gillian. "Thomas Carlyle and the Governor Eyre Controversy: An Account with Some New Material." *Victorian Studies* 18 (1974), 77-102.

Young, G. M. *Victorian England: Portrait of an Age.* London, New York: Oxford University Press, 2nd edn, 1953.

FURTHER READING

Bibliographies

Parrish, M. L. *Wilkie Collins and Charles Reade.* London: Constable, 1940.

> Descriptive bibliography of the first editions of Reade's works.

Sadleir, Michael. "Charles Reade: Note and Bibliography." In *Excursions in Victorian Bibliography*, pp. 159-79. London: Chaundy & Cox, 1922.

> Lists first editions of Reade's novels and plays.

Biographies

Booth, Bradford A. "Trollope, Reade, and 'Shilly-Shally'." *Trollopian* 1, No. 4 (1947): 43-54; 2, No. 1 (1947): 43-51.

> Examines the dispute between Trollope and Reade over Reade's dramatization of Trollope's novel *Ralph the Heir.*

Coleman, John. *Charles Reade as I Knew Him.* London: Traherne, 1903.

> Based on the memoir by Reade's relatives (see below).

Elwin, Malcolm. *Charles Reade.* London: Cape, 1931.

> Focuses on details of Reade's career and includes bibliographies of Reade's novels and plays.

Reade, Charles L., and Compton Reade. *Charles Reade ... A Memoir.* London: Chapman and Hall, 1887.

> A discreet and not always trustworthy account written by members of Reade's family.

Rives, Léone. *Charles Reade, sa vie, ses romans.* Toulouse: Toulousaine, 1940.

> Draws on previously unavailable family papers and includes a complete bibliography of primary and secondary sources.

Criticism

Burns, Wayne. "*The Cloister and the Hearth*: A Classic Reconsidered." *Trollopian* 2 (1947): 71-81.

> Contends that *The Cloister and the Hearth* is not a great novel and is no better than Reade's other works.

Haines, Lewis. "Reade, Mill and Zola: A Study of the Character and Intention of Charles Reade's Realistic Method." *Studies in Philology* 40 (1943): 466-75.

> Examines the influence on Reade of John Stuart Mill and empirical thought.

Phillips, Walter C. *Dickens, Reade, and Collins: Sensation Novelists.* New York: Russell, 1962 (reprint of 1919 edition).

> Studies the relationship between the works of Charles Dickens, Wilkie Collins, and Reade as well as the nature of their fiction.

Sutcliffe, Emerson Grant. "Charles Reade's Notebooks." *Studies in Philology* 27 (1930): 64-109.

> Describes the massive collection of notes, articles, and reports which Reade compiled to assist him in composing his novels.

——. "Psychological Presentation in Reade's Novels." *Studies in Philology* 38 (1941): 521-42.

> Examines Reade's handling of character in his fiction.

Turner, Albert Morton. *The Making of "The Cloister and the Hearth."* Chicago: University of Chicago Press, 1938.

> A study of Reade's sources and his methods of composition.

Additional coverage of Reade's life and career is contained in the following source published by The Gale Group: *Dictionary of Literary Biography*, Vol. 21.

Frances Wright

1795-1852

Scottish-born social reformer.

INTRODUCTION

One of the first advocates of emancipation and equal rights, Frances Wright deeply influenced the social reform movements of the nineteenth century, particularly in the United States. Her eloquence and dedication in these matters earned her both support and outrage from the American and British public. Wright's intellectual legacy reflects the founding impulses of democracy, and it combines a belief in individual liberty with a strong sense of community ethics and the importance of education. Wright's contribution to the earliest beginnings of the feminist movement remains her best known work, but her concern in general was to liberate humanity from all forms of oppression— including ignorance, poverty, and prejudice.

Biographical Information

Wright was born into a wealthy merchant family in 1795 in Dundee, Scotland. She was related to the Scottish aristocracy through her mother, and to the intellectuals and political liberals of Glasgow through her father. Both of Wright's parents died in 1798, and she and her younger sister Camilla went to live with her maternal aunt, Frances Campbell. Soon afterward Wright's aunt moved the family south to Devonshire. At the age of eight Wright became heiress to family properties in India. At this time Wright was occupied with the study of languages, literature, history, and philosophy, and her well-known scorn for propriety and social convention evidently dates from this period. Wright began to notice the social inequities that pervaded British rural life, and she was particularly interested in the newly-independent nation of the United States. In 1813, Wright and Camilla moved to Glasgow to live with their uncle, James Mylne, who held liberal political beliefs and taught moral philosophy at the University of Glasgow. In Glasgow, Wright cultivated her intellectual and political interests, and began to write seriously—primarily poetry. In 1818, she visited the United States with Camilla in order to observe the social and political experiment in democracy and individual freedom. Her family wealth gave her an immediate entrance into New York society, and her play *Altorf* was produced there in 1819. Wright trav-

elled extensively in the United States, and wrote about her perceptions in *Views of Society and Manners in America—In a Series of Letters from That Country to a Friend in England, During the Years 1818, 1819, 1820* (1821). Wright became convinced of the need to establish a "colony" where slaves might both work for their freedom (in a plan of gradual emancipation) and become educated. She bought land in Tennessee in 1825, and named her new community Nashoba. In her attempts to support and draw attention to her endeavors, she lectured widely and edited the *New Harmony Gazette*, a periodical that grew out of Robert Owen's experimental utopian community in New Harmony, Indiana. Nashoba never became economically self-sufficient, and was dissolved in 1829. The ex-slaves from the Nashoba community were transported to the new republic of Haiti. After the dissolution of the community of Nashoba, Wright wrote an essay entitled "Explanatory Notes, Respecting the Nature and Objects of the Institution of Nashoba, and of the Principles upon which it is Founded: Addressed to the Friends of Human Improvement, in All Countries and of All Nations" (1830). In 1831, the year following the publication of the essay on Nashoba, Camilla died and Wright returned to England. In the same year, Wright married William Phiquepal D'Arusmont. D'Arusmont had been a former member of Owen's experimental utopian community, and had followed Wright to England. With D'Arusmont, Wright had two children, but only the second, Frances Sylva D'Arusmont, survived infancy. At this time Wright limited her public activities, but managed to publish her lectures on educational reform in England as *A Course of Popular Lectures* (1834). In 1835 Wright returned to her political activities in the United States, particularly to her advocacy of the gradual emancipation of slaves. But after 1839 she began to spend more time writing at her home in Cincinnati than speaking in public, and the public furor that had accompanied her attempts at social reform dissipated. During this period Wright wrote *England the Civilizer: Her History Developed in Its Principles* (1848) and an autobiography entitled *Biography, Notes, and Political Letters of Frances Wright D'Arusmont* (1849). In 1852, shortly after divorcing D'Arusmont, Frances Wright died after a prolonged illness caused by a fall at her home.

Major Works

Wright's first major literary production was her play, *Altorf*. This play, produced in the United States in 1819, takes its setting and plot from the fourteenth-century Swiss independence movement. In 1822, she wrote a dialogue on Epicurean philosophy entitled *A Few Days in Athens—Being the Translation of a Greek Manuscript Discovered in Herculeaneum* (1822). This treatise reflects Wright's interest in tolerance and self-reliance. However, unlike the original Epicurus, Wright was not an advocate of the spiritual renunciation of worldly pleasures. In Celia Eckhardt's words, Wright "dares to honor happiness" in this work. Furthermore, Wright's Epicurus is noted for his lack of discrimination against women students. Wright's works grew increasingly political in emphasis. Her "Explanatory Notes, Respecting the Nature and Objects of the Institution of Nashoba, and of the Principles upon which it is Founded: Addressed to the Friends of Human Improvement, in All Countries and of All Nations," her many editorials in the *New Harmony Gazette* (later renamed the *Free Enquirer*) and in the *Boston Investigator*, and her *A Course of Popular Lectures* reflect her abiding concern with slavery, economic disparities, inequities between genders, lack of public education, and the problematic authority of religious institutions. Among her intellectual influences were Thomas Jefferson, Jeremy Bentham, Robert Owen, and Mary Wollstonecraft. Her work, particularly in her

later years, focused upon rewriting and developing earlier lectures given in major cities around the United States and England. Some of these lectures were revised and collected in *England the Civilizer: Her History Developed in Its Principles*, her last published work.

Critical Reception

While Wright provoked some of the most scathing denunciations of the women's movement of the nineteenth century, she also earned the praise and respect of prominent liberal thinkers of that century. According to George Holyoake, John Stuart Mill (who shared with Wright the ideals of equality and individual liberty) considered her to be "one of the most important women of her day." Walt Whitman attended many of her lectures and sympathized with her passionate struggle for the fulfillment of the democratic promise latent in the new nation. According to critic Celia Eckhardt, Frances Wright's reception by the American and European public shows "how much people love the rhetoric of equality and how little they are inclined to make equality possible." The fact that ten thousand people attended one of Wright's lectures in New York City in 1837 provides evidence for the popularity of Wright's writings and lectures. However, Wright's attempts to put into practice her beliefs regarding gradual emancipation, sexual freedom, racial equality, economic justice, and public education were consistently condemned as radical, blasphemous, and unfeminine. This public outrage, led by the established press and religious authorities, must be counted as one of the principal reasons for the failure of the community of Nashoba. Wright is recognized by more recent critics for the power of her rhetoric and for the profound influence that she exerted over the feminist movements of the nineteenth century. Lucretia Mott, Susan B. Anthony and Elizabeth Cady Stanton all refer to Frances Wright as a pioneer in women's rights. Current feminist scholarship acknowledges her impact on the struggle for social justice, but also notes the extent to which her own philosophical inheritances influence her views. Elizabeth Bartlett claims that Wright was more interested in supporting the rights of humanity in general than of women in particular. Bartlett also claims that Wright "sought the liberty of women to be like men" rather than criticized that ideal itself. Yet Wright's fervent attempts to argue for the independence and equality of all human beings formed a strong foundation for later feminist and liberal activists.

PRINCIPAL WORKS

Altorf (drama) 1819
Views of Society and Manners in America—In a Series

of Letters from that Country to a Friend in England, During the Years 1818, 1819, 1820 (letters) 1821
"Explanatory Notes, Respecting the Nature and Object of the Institution at Nashoba, and of the Principles upon which it is Founded: Addressed to the Friends of Human Improvement, in All Countries and of All Nations" (essay) 1830
Course of Popular Lectures (lectures) 1834
England the Civilizer: Her History Developed in Its Principles (history) 1848
Biography, Notes, and Political Letters of Frances Wright D'Arusmont (autobiography) 1849

*Reprinted in *Life, Letters and Lectures, 1834-44* (1972)

CRITICISM

William Randall Waterman (essay date 1924)

SOURCE: "Nashoba Concluded," in *Frances Wright*, Columbia University Press, 1924, pp. 111-33.

[*In the following excerpt, Waterman reviews Frances Wright's published plan for her cooperative community of Nashoba and argues that Wright's advocacy of equal rights and sexual freedom contributed to her reputation as a radical.*]

Shortly after her return [from England in 1827] Frances [Wright] carried out the suggestion in her letter to James Richardson, and made public her famous **"Explanatory Notes, respecting the Nature and Object of the Institution at Nashoba, and of the principles upon which it is founded: Addressed to the Friends of Human Improvement, in all Countries and all Nations."**[1] In this remarkable document she plainly stated that it was now the purpose of Nashoba to carry into practice certain principles which had been long advocated by liberal thinkers, but which the world would never receive unsupported by experiment. At Nashoba it was hoped to convince mankind of their moral beauty and their utility, and within herself Miss Wright felt there existed the qualifications necessary for successfully carrying on such an experiment—mental courage and a passion for the improvement of the human race.

Observation had taught her that "men are virtuous in proportion as they are happy; and happy in proportion as they are free!" In the present state of society, however, they were not free, but bound by a thousand unhappy conventions and conditions, which prevented the attainment of true happiness and virtue. An unequal division of labor separated them into artificial classes, condemning the greater half to a life of physical toil, and the lesser to one of pernicious idleness, or to mental exertion only, so that

nowhere could one find "even a single individual, male or female, whose mental and physical powers have been fairly cultivated and developed." A false economy conceived of men as but so much machinery for the creation of wealth, and held a nation rich, "not in proportion to the number of its individuals who enjoy, but to the mass of ideal wealth, thrown into commercial circulation." The most necessary occupations were considered degrading, while those which throve upon the quarrels and credulity of men were exalted. The repressive force of public opinion too often failed to influence those classes most needing it, and crushed those "whose feelings and intellects have been most cultivated, and who consequently, are best fitted to a healthy and intellectual race." And finally there was the unfortunate effect of present institutions upon women, for

> in what class do we find the largest proportion of childless females, and devoted victims to unnatural restraints? Certainly among the cultivated, talented and independent women, who . . . shrink equally from the servitude of matrimony, and from the opprobrium stamped upon unlegalized connexions.

Something, indeed, men had done to throw off the bonds which fettered their progress to freedom. In one country, at least, political liberty had been achieved; but political liberty, "the liberty of speech and of action, without incurring the violence of authority, or the penalties of law," was only half the victory. True freedom—"universal in all the objects it embraces and equal for all classes of men"—could come only with the attainment of moral liberty—"the free exercise of the liberty of speech and of action, without incurring the intolerance of popular prejudice, and ignorant public opinion." With political liberty attained, a people had but "to will it," to secure moral liberty, and with moral liberty men might rationally enquire into their institutions, without fear of popular prejudice, and free society from the ills which burdened it.

> It is much to have declared men free and equal, but it shall be more, when they are rendered so—when the means shall be sought, and found, and employed to develope all the intellectual and physical powers of all human beings, without regard to sex or condition—class, race, or color.

It would be even more when men learned

> to view each other as members of one great family, with equal claims to enjoyment and equal capacities for labor and instruction—admitting always the sole differences arising out of the varieties exhibited in the individual organization.

To show that moral freedom could produce so happy a result was the duty of Nashoba.

For the times these were radical views, but they were not very dissimilar to those avowed by Owen at New Harmony, and it seems probable that had it not been for an effort to apply them to the racial problem but little attention would have been paid to them. However, in establishing at Nashoba a cooperative community, based upon principles of moral freedom, Frances Wright had to consider the original object of her experiment. To raise the slave to the level of the European intellect, and an appreciation of the theory and practice of voluntary cooperation, seemed impossible. The benumbing mental effects of slavery were too great a handicap. It was, therefore, decided that the best interests of the negro race would be consulted by limiting the number of slaves at Nashoba to the original purchase, and by admitting to membership, upon terms of absolute equality, respectable free negroes, whose children would receive a rational education in the school of the institution, thus raising the intellectual and moral character of the race. In self-emancipation, as a solution of the slave problem, Miss Wright had apparently lost faith. Slavery, she now believed, was destined to disappear in a comparatively few years, due to economic causes, leaving behind it a serious race problem. Then,

> the principles avowed at Nashoba may . . . attract the national attention, and the olive peace of brotherhood be embraced by the white man & the black, and their children approached in feeling and education gradually blend into one, their blood and their hue.

Indeed, it was in the amalgamation of the races alone that she could now see a solution of the problem which she had so vigorously attacked two years before:

> It [emancipation] can only be progressive thro' the feelings; and, thro' that medium, be finally complete and entire, involving at once, political equality, and the amalgamation of the races. . . . The only question is, whether it shall take place in good taste and good feeling, & be made at once the means of sealing the tranquility, & perpetuating the liberty of the country, and of peopling it with a race more suited to its southern climate, than the pure European,—or whether it shall proceed, as it now does, viciously and degradingly, mingling hatred and fear with ties of blood—denied, indeed, but stamped by nature on the skin.

In view of her frank advocacy of the amalgamation of the races in a country where race feeling ran high, it is no wonder that Miss Wright's name became anathema in the South, and that gentlemen should intimate that they would "not be surprised if Miss Wright should, one of these mornings, find her throat cut!"[2] Madison wrote to Lafayette that with all her rare talents, and still rarer disinterestedness,

she has I fear created insuperable obstacles to the good fruits of which they might be productive by her disregard or rather open defiance of the most established opinion & vivid feelings. Besides her views of amalgamating the white & black population so universally obnoxious, she gives an eclât to her notions on the subject of Religion & of marriage, the effect of which your knowledge of this Country can readily estimate.[3]

By the few papers of liberal tendencies the **"Notes"** were well received, although they commented upon the daring of the author, and the New York *Correspondent* felt that it might be wise, at first, to confine the practice of the views set forth to a community.[4]

Notes

[1] This was written on board the "Edward" on her return from Europe, and is dated December 4, 1827. It was published in the *New Harmony Gazette,* January 30, 1828.

[2] Wright MSS. Mary Carroll to Frances Wright, New Orleans, February 4, 1828. Miss Carroll was a young lady of New Orleans who had given up her millinery business to start a "philosophical bookshop." She was a friend of Owen and Maclure, and was much interested in Miss Wright.

[3] Madison, James, *Writings,* edited by Gaillard Hunt, 9 vols., New York, 1900-1910, vol. ix, pp. 310-313.

[4] *New Harmony Gazette,* January 30, 1828; The New York *Correspondent,* February 29, 1828.

Helen Heineman (essay date 1983)

SOURCE: "Frances Wright and the Second Utopia," in *Restless Angels: The Friendship of Six Victorian Women.* Ohio University Press, 1983, pp. 23-62

[*In the following excerpt, Heineman discusses Frances Wright's correspondence concerning the establishment of Nashoba, a colony intended to serve as a model of emancipation and equality.*]

We have seen that among early peoples the quite normal man is warrior and hunter, and the quite normal woman house-wife and worker-round-the-house; and it is quite conceivable that if no intermediate types had arisen, human society might have remained stationary in these simple occupations. But when types of men began to appear who had no taste for war and slaughter—men, perhaps, of a more gentle or feminine disposition; or when types of women arose who chafed at the slavery of the house, and longed for the open field of adventure and activity—women, in fact, of a more masculine tendency—then necessarily and quite naturally these new-comers had to find, and found, for themselves, new occupations and new activities. The intermediate types of human beings created intermediate spheres of social life and work.

Edward Carpenter, *Intermediate Types among Primitive Folk: A Study in Social Evolution* (1919)

Take up some one pursuit or occupation with persevering determination. I can truly declare that I have never enjoyed tranquility but when my time has been steadily employed.

Frances Wright to Julia Garnett, 1 December 1825

Fanny Wright's revulsion against slavery, always intense, now combined with her passion for reform and found a favorable growing climate in the atmosphere of radical hopes that were then sweeping across certain areas of the United States. Change, conversion, awakening—these were the watchwords of the time and the place. It seemed time for every human institution to be questioned. As Ralph Waldo Emerson subsequently noted, "In the history of the world the doctrine of Reform had never such scope as at the present hour." And so, after Lafayette's return to the old world, Fanny turned to find inspiration in transforming ideas of reform. Once again, she was attracted to a powerful man and his vision.

On New Year's Day 1825, when Robert Owen,[1] the English industrial magnate and utopian reformer completed the purchase of the large Harmony community of George Rapp in western Indiana, it seemed as though anyone who had ever dreamed a dream or hankered after an ideal was ready to make concrete what had hitherto been only a subject for conversation or debate. Owen believed things were in the best possible state for beneficial change. People were talking about the perfectibility of man and taking the subject seriously. Owen's intellectual friends argued that Chinese children could be made Indian, and vice versa, were they simply removed early enough from one situation to another. For centuries, man had wondered about limits and potentialities. "Know then thyself," Pope had cautioned, and now people like Robert Owen, George Rapp, and William MacClure were convinced that they did. They were ready to test their theories on the virgin soil of America, hoping to raise up a society such as the world had never seen—free, open, peaceful, intelligent, and harmonious. People were ready to leave comfortable homes and dear relatives and journey to New Harmony, which shone with the aura of a bright new planet. Into this quest for earthly perfection, like moths to a destructive flame, Frances and Camilla

Wright were drawn. For Cam, the attraction had ever been Fanny herself. But Frances Wright was fascinated by utopian experiments because she saw in them a hope for ridding the world of a ruinous system of exploitation. She also saw the chance to shape her own life anew, to make her own story, to escape the impediments of social class and gender. In saving others, she would also save herself and her friends.

Increasingly, Fanny's thoughts revolved around the subject of slavery. She wrote the Garnetts:

> Alas, Alas! The more I consider this subject the more I shudder, the more I tremble. This plague spot so soils the beauty of the robe of American liberty that I often turn in disgust from the freest country in the world. . . . American industry—morals—enterprise—all is benumbed. The heart is hardened—the character depraved. Our course is still to lie through the benighted & guilty regions [i.e., the South]. I could hardly execute the project did I not propose to turn my observations to account.[2]

As she had traveled, she had been struck by the awesome vastness of America. But she could take no pleasure in its beauty, when she thought of the blight of slavery. Emotionally, she wrote:

> I could have wept when gazing on the lovely face of nature in the state of Mississippi—such woods, such lawns, such gently swelling hills, such glorious trees, such exquisite flowers, & the giant river wafting the rich produce of this unrivalled land to the ocean. I could have wept as I thought that such a garden was wrought by the hands of slaves! But when following the course of these mighty streams you traverse varying latitudes and climates marking an extent greater than the continent of Europe, and reflect that this plague is gradually spreading under the cover of the forests & along the track of the rivers over this huge territory, the heart truly sickens and curses the progress of cultivation.[3]

But writing letters about the problem was not enough. For Fanny, thoughts and words must be translated into action. A specific plan took root as she prepared an article for the *Westminster Review* on the subject of American Negro slavery. Though the essay never appeared, the research permitted Fanny to gather her emotions into thought on the problem which continued to engross her. On a visit to New Orleans, she found slavery "in all its horrors," from the clank of chains to the "dark-eyed rich-complexioned damsels" of mulatto blood whose offspring could never be acknowledged by their white fathers. In the seven months she had spent in slave states, she had mulled over various modes of curing this great evil. But not until she had made her second visit to Harmony did specific ideas take shape. Curiously enough, the communities of New Harmony had made no provision for slaves, freed or otherwise. Blacks were absolutely excluded from Owen's experiment. Fanny Wright decided to try Owen's principles on a project of slave emancipation. Her first idea was "that the slaves on a plantation should be led to work from the incentive of working out their liberty with a view to their being afterwards employed as waged laborers." Then, at Harmony, "a vague idea" crossed her mind, "that there was something in the system of united labor as there was in operation which might be rendered subservient to the emancipation of the South." United labor would undersell the slave labor of the South, even as slaves worked out their freedom and became educated at the same time. Thus engrossed, Fanny rode about the country seeking advice and support of her plan for the amelioration and, eventually, the abolition of slavery in the United States of America. By April 1826 she had purchased the necessary tract of land, along with eight Negroes who would be the first laborers there. In all, to set up her colony, she would spend over $10,000 in expenses, more than a third of her total property. She was ready to start creating her world.[4] . . .

Fanny's dreams had more clarity. They were two-fold, the parts separate but hinged, like contrasting but connected pictures in a locket. Ever since she had watched Father Rapp leading his people out of the Promised Land and Mr. Owen establishing a harmonious new order there, Frances had longed to be part of some great work. For her, the first purpose of Nashoba was the abolishing of slavery, a problem her fellow reformers had thus far largely ignored.

But at the same time, she had hopes for those who would dedicate their lives to this purpose. They would find not the peaceful haven of Camilla's thinking, but useful, if strenuous occupation, for women who were proud and strong enough to grasp the opportunity. Fanny had watched the women of her acquaintance—the Garnett sisters, her dear friend Mrs. Millar, the Lafayette daughters, her own sister—and she had come to some painful conclusions about the lives of women in general.

> Without some fixed and steady occupation of labor—of business, of study, something which keeps in habitual exercise our physical or mental energies—and the better when it is both—it is impossible to make our existence glide smoothly. We must know moments, nay hours of vexation and lassitude. It is this which makes the pretty universally marked difference between men & women, that gives to the former good health and good nerves, and fits them more or less to taste the enjoyments of life without being dependent upon any and to bear or brave its ills with a resisting spirit.[5]

She recalled one of the observations of John Garnett, who had educated his daughters so well in the old days in America:

> Geometry had been his best friend and most consoling companion. Rousseau said the same of botany—Gibbon of his historical research and composition and every poet has said or sung the same of his muse.[6]

Frances resolved that her physical and mental energy would be directed away from the conventional, life-consuming activities of women, and toward some more satisfying and independent work of her own. She admitted that such activity was for her an absolute necessity. "I can truly declare that I have never enjoyed tranquility but when my time has been steadily employed."[7] While those interests with which most women filled their lives—"amusements, social intercourse, friendship, love"—were "the precious diamond sparks in the hourglass of human existence," she was sure that "the mass of the sand is composed of homelier materials." Unless she found whereof this latter material was made, she would become like her other women friends, distracted, her blood "fevered," and full of vague "disquietude." She had, after all, tried with painful consequences being the faithful daughter to Lafayette. Her sermons to her friends, lengthy and perhaps tedious, and surely perplexing, she could not forswear. She continued to sound the theme of occupation across the measures of her whole life.

Depositing the still weak Cam at New Harmony and Albion (George Flower's colony across the river), Fanny at once set out to find land that would provide the arena where she would shape her fate and, she hoped, that of America itself. She had already seen much of good and evil in the West. She had ridden through the forests of Indiana, en route to Tennessee, where the good land lay, and witnessed the cruel kidnapping of a poor hunted black boy. She had tried to rescue the boy, recovering him for a brief moment, only to lose him again. But such failures only increased her determination, despite the surrounding dangers, to start the work of abolishing the evil of slavery. The secret of her plans for an educational colony aimed at slave emancipation must be kept for at least a year, for in the southern states, news of her scheme would be a devouring flame, running from Virginia to Georgia, from Kentucky to Louisiana. Her ultimate goal was nothing less than a holy conversion of the entire country. Her friend Robert Dale Owen, son of Harmony's founder, was her fellow warrior. She saw him and herself as partners in a dramatic transformation of American society. "He is working miracles and promises fair to revolutionize a second time the North as I pray we may do in the South."

She was ready to work hard and pay much for the accomplishment of her own prospective miracle. After much negotiation and discussion, she purchased two hundred acres of land in Tennessee, on the Chickasaw bluffs near the Wolf River, about five miles from the Indian line. Hoping to avoid the American "fever," she chose a spot "dry and rolling and second rate only as to richness of soil." Tennessee was "one of the most favored" states, "abundantly watered by navigable streams flowing in all directions and affording all varieties of wood and many of climate." Its prevailing summer sun, she had heard, was "genial." Now Frances sent for Camilla and her new friends George and Eliza Flower. The great experiment was imminent. . . .

Aware as she must have been of the recent troubles at New Harmony, Fanny Wright was still convinced that her colony would work. Part of her optimism stemmed from her faith in the people who now surrounded her. George Flower, who had helped found the English settlement at Albion, Illinois, was to be a resident trustee of Nashoba. Some had accused him of bigamy, saying that he had married two wives and divorced none. In England, the stories went, he and his first wife had separated by mutual consent. Then, "wounded in spirit and almost heartbroken," he had passed to America, where he found "the beautiful, the gay, the attractive Eliza Andrews," whom he had married, winning her away from her fatherly protector, Morris Birkbeck, who had also proposed to her. The resultant breach between the two men had damaged their hopes of colonizing land in Edwards County for English settlers, and also produced the luxuriant crop of gossip which Fanny Wright ignored in inviting the Flowers to become part of her colony. Cam, of course, supported her sister in this defense of the outcasts, calling Eliza Flower "one of the most noble, generous, and candid minds I have ever known in life," whose "affections are entirely centered in her husband and children." Still, Cam was not completely comfortable with Mrs. Flower, and told the Garnetts what she kept from Fanny: "While I admire and esteem her as my friend, I do not & shall never feel for her that species of affection which constitutes real friendship."[8] Cam's rendition of the complicated relationship between the Flowers and Mr. Birkbeck reveals her loyal support of her sister's choices in the face of "all that the ill-nature and malice of a misjudging world can suggest. . . . " The fact that Flower was being called an "immoral man," and that he and his wife could find no place in "polite society," made them ripe to share the perils of the Nashoba experiment, although, as Cam admitted, Mrs. Flower had "not the least faith" in this new colony, having seen their own settlement collapse and the New Harmony venture almost in ruins. As she told Cam, "she feels, herself, that she will never again be equal to the unheard of exertions she has undergone since her first arrival in this country, and well may she dread entering a second time the difficulties and hardships of a new settlement." Mrs. Flower's disenchantment with utopian ventures, like that of Sarah Pears before her, was another example of the sharp conflict between personal hopes and the communal regimen which seemed starkest in women.

Still, recruits were quickly made among the ranks of other "promising" outsiders. Fanny picked up James Richardson, a Scotchman who had studied medicine at Edinburgh, in Memphis where he was "recovering slowly from a long and painful illness." Once again, Fanny's eloquence about finding a sense of purpose had produced a worker for Nashoba. "Our conversation and friendship," she wrote, "first cheered his spirits and the prospect of assisting in our undertaking seems to have supplied him with what he wanted—an object in life suited to his feelings and opinions."[9] She told the Garnetts that he "unites to the invaluable qualities of trust, prudence & accurate attention to business, a finely cultivated mind with every liberal and generous opinion and sentiment." Money to outfit the store ($550 worth of goods) came from a wealthy Quaker merchant in New York. And so, with eight purchased Negroes, five men and three women, who had arrived by steamboat from Nashville, a family of a mother and six daughters from South Carolina, a carpenter, a blacksmith, and, she hoped, a shoemaker, Fanny, Cam, Richardson, and the Flowers were ready to begin. Another recent addition, also a trustee, should be mentioned. Richeson Whitby, a Shaker, formerly resident of New Harmony and director of the commissary there, had early become disenchanted with Owen's experiment, leaving Harmony in December 1826 for Nashoba. Ironically, his position had been filled by Thomas Pears. Whether his intention was solely to make another try at living by utopian principles, or whether he felt already that attraction for the Wright sisters which would ultimately end with his marriage to Camilla Wright, is unknown. Nevertheless, he became part of the new world at Nashoba. It had not been difficult to attract male workers to Fanny's colony.

The only ingredient missing was the community of female friends, in particular, the Garnetts, who still lagged behind in Europe. Fanny chafed with resentment to think that her dearest friends still lived the old, outworn conventional life. When Julia and Harriet begged her for news and descriptions of Nashoba, Fanny's answer was a pointed reminder of what they were missing:

> Remember dear loves that we are not ladies of leisure with nothing to do but to follow up the correspondence of friendship. I wish I knew you engaged in some pursuit that could call forth your energies and prevent your indulging in melancholy and vain regrets.[10]

When Fanny Wright spoke of calling forth the energies of her female friends, she had in mind that kind of imagination which can envision a self and a society as yet unformed in the given world. She herself had found both energy and will enough to abandon home, family, and religion to brave the social taboos which sought to confine her within a limited female sphere. She was ready to do yet more in her slave emancipation colony, testing the world's resistance to the society she envisioned for others and the self she was fashioning for herself. The Garnetts, too, had energies, and clearly, Miss Wright feared they would ultimately turn them inward by "indulging in melancholy and vain regrets," and be finally destroyed. . . .

As Fanny viewed the world to which she had temporarily returned, she recognized the decreasing probability that any of the women she knew would join her at Nashoba. Like the sensible woman she was, she began looking elsewhere for recruits. While there was always Cam, she was not the commanding equal Fanny could respect and admire. Mrs. Trollope had called Fanny Wright "the most interesting woman in Europe"; Fanny wanted a female companion at least equally fascinating. Her search began on August 22 with a letter to a total stranger. With all the exalted eloquence of which she was ever the master, Fanny Wright addressed the widow of Percy Bysshe Shelley.

> As the daughter of your father and mother (known to me only by their works and opinions), as the friend and companion of a man distinguished during life, and preserved in the remembrance of the public as one distinguished not by genius merely, but, as I imagine, by the strength of his opinions and his fearlessness in their expression;—viewed only in these relations you would be to me an object of interest and . . . of curiosity.[11]

But Fanny had heard that Mary Shelley shared her father's opinions and her mother's generous feelings; thus, she was ready to travel far, just to see her. "It is rare in this world, especially in our sex, to meet with those opinions united with those feelings, and with the manners and disposition calculated to command respect and conciliate affection."

Excusing her bold intrusion, Fanny pleaded the rare opportunity of finding someone with whom she could share her dedication to "moral truth and moral liberty." Should she "neglect any means for discovering a real friend of that cause," she wrote, "I were almost failing to a duty." Briefly, she explained her determination to undermine a variety of slaveries: of color, of mind, of rank, of wealth, of instruction, and last, but not least, of sex. Her determination was to create an entirely new world order.

> Our circle already comprises a few united cooperators, whose choice of associates will be guided by their moral fitness only; saving that, for the protection and support of all, each must be fitted to exercise some useful employment, or to supply 200 dollars as an equivalent for their support. The present generation will in all probability supply but a limited number of individuals suited in opinion and disposition to such a state of society; but that, that number, however limited, may best find their happiness and best exercise their utility by uniting their interests, their society, and their talents, I feel a conviction. In this conviction, I have devoted my time and fortune to laying the foundations of an establishment where affection shall form the only marriage, kind feeling and kind action the only religion, respect for the feelings and liberties of others the only restraint, and union of interest the bond of peace and security.[12]

Such were her extensive goals, and fifteen months had placed her establishment in what she called "a fair way of progress." Come to Europe only for reasons of health, she was now ready to return to her "forest home." Whatever happened, Fanny concluded, "I wish to convey to Mary Wollstonecraft Godwin Shelley my respect and admiration of those from whom she holds those names, and my fond desire to connect her with them in my esteem, and in the knowledge of mutual sympathy to sign myself her friend."

Mary Shelley answered at once. She was, as Robert Dale Owen subsequently noted, "genial, gentle, sympathetic, thoughtful, and matured in opinion beyond her years." Fanny had touched upon "the right chord" to win her attention.

> The memory of my mother [she wrote] has always been the pride and delight of my life and the admiration of others for her, has been the cause of most of the happiness I have enjoyed. Her greatness of soul and my father's high talents have perpetually reminded me that I ought to degenerate as little as I could from those from whom I derived my being. For several years with Mr. Shelley I was blessed with the companionship of one, who fostered this ambition & inspired that of being worthy of him. He who was single among men for Philanthropy—devoted generosity—talent—goodness— yet you must not fancy that I am what I wish I were, and my chief merit must always be derived, first from the glory these wonderful beings have shed around me; and then for the enthusiasms I have for excellence & the ardent admiration I feel for those who sacrifice themselves for the public good.

> If you feel curiosity concerning me—how much more in the refined sense of the word, must I not feel for yourself—a woman, young, rich & independent, quits the civilization of England for a life of hardship in the forests of America, that by so doing she may contribute to the happiness of her species. Her health fails in the attempt, yet scarcely restored to that, she is eager to return again to the scene of her labours, & again to spend the flower of her life in arduous struggles and beneficent, self-sacrificing devotion to others. Such a tale cannot fail to inspire the deepest interest and

the most ardent admiration. You do honour to our species and what perhaps is dearer to me, to the feminine part of it.—and that thought, while it makes me doubly interested in you, makes me tremble for you. Women are so particularly the victims of their generosity and their purer, & more sensitive feelings render them so much less than men, capable of battling the selfishness, hardness, and ingratitude which is so often the return made, for the noblest efforts to benefit others. But you seem satisfied with your success, so I hope the ill-fortune which too usually frustrates our best view, will spare to harm the family of love, which you represent to have assembled at Nashoba.[13]

Having only Fanny's letter to tell her about Nashoba, she wondered about the settlement's real success.

Is it all you wish? Do you find the motives you mention sufficient to tame that strange human nature, which is perpetually the source of wonder to me? It takes a simpler form probably in a forest abode— yet can enthusiasm for public good rein in passion, motive benevolence, & unite families? It were a divine right to behold the reality of such a picture. Yet do not be angry with me that I am so much of a woman that I am far more interested in you than in (except as it is yours) your settlement.

She invited Fanny to England, and asked to hear from her again. "At least, I pray you, write again—write about yourself—tell me whether happiness & content repay your exertions. I have fancied that the first of these blessings can only be found in the exercise of the affections—yet I have not found mine there.—for where moral evil does not interfere, dreadful Death has come to deprive me of all I enjoyed. My life has not been like yours publicly active, but it has been one of tempestuous suffering."

Mrs. Shelley was here asking a crucial question, one which Fanny had already begun to answer. Could women find happiness in work or were they required to find their deepest satisfactions in the realm of the affections? Living in seclusion with her only surviving son and with a beloved female friend, Mary Shelley drew back before the risk of a call to work at Nashoba, even while she entreated Fanny to maintain their correspondence. "I fully trust that I shall hear from you again. Do not, public spirited as you are, turn from me, because private interests too much engross me. At least, tho' mine be a narrow circle, yet I am willing at all times to sacrifice my being to it, & derive my only pleasures from contributing to the happiness and welfare of others." Was ever the century's ideal for women better expressed?

But Fanny Wright had already differentiated between the kind of love demanded by men and that possible among women who were truly equals. In an enig-

matic letter of October 1827, Fanny referred to one of her relationships with men, a dashing young adventurer named Dutrone, who had gone to fight in the war of Greek independence and with whom she had been briefly and passionately involved. He had offered to follow her to Nashoba. She told Julia: "Always to support others has cost me too much. To hold in check the passions of others, if it has aided me in mastering my own, has too much used up my strength and my life. In the annihilation of self, one enjoys calm and an inner peace, but it is not happiness. There are moments when it takes effort not to give way, when one's self feels the need of sympathy and the support of a strong and understanding spirit. Am I able to make myself understood?"[14] And while Mary Shelley probably did understand, since she had herself devoted her whole being to the needs of a powerful man, she was unable to rouse herself to the active life Fanny was now describing.

But since the gates of friendship and feeling had opened, Fanny freely articulated her more selfish motive in wanting Mary to come. Relationships with men had been demanding and debilitating. She was ready to restate the idea of sisterhood, inextricably associating it with the work ahead.

I do want one of my own sex to commune with and sometimes to lean upon in all the confidence and equality of friendship. You see, I am not so disinterested as you suppose. Delightful it is indeed to aid the progress of human improvement and sweet is the peace we derive from aiding the happiness of others, but still the heart craves something more ere it can say, I am satisfied.[15]

In Fanny's mind, sisterhood was connected with the goal of useful occupation. For her, they were the companion parts of a complete life, both necessary in her Faustian quest for satisfaction. She offered to come to Brighton, to Arundel, "anywhere you may name," to convince Mrs. Shelley that she, too, could achieve this dual goal.

The last section of her letter contained Fanny's compelling self-portrait, a heroic picture, somewhat masculine and even Arthurian, with its suggestion of a dangerous and vigorous search for moral improvement. The passage gives insight into the created self of Frances Wright—strenuous, spartan, alienated from the masses—above all, a leader. She had transformed Cam's quiet haven of kindred spirits into an amazonian circle of strong souls ready to change the world at any cost.

A delicate nursling of European luxury and aristocracy, I thought and felt for myself, and for martyrised humankind, and have preferred all hazards, all privations in the forests of the New World to the dear-bought comforts of miscalled civilization. I have made the hard earth my bed, the saddle of my horse my pillow, and have staked my life and fortune on an experiment having in view moral liberty and human improvement. Many of course think me mad, and if to be mad means to be one of a minority, I am so, and very mad indeed, for our minority is very small. Should that few succeed in mastering the first difficulties, weaker spirits, though often not less amiable, may carry forward the good work. But the fewer we are who now think alike, the more we are of value to each other. To know you, therefore, is a strong desire of my heart, and all things consistent with my engagements, which I may call duties, since they are connected with the work I have in hand, will I do to facilitate our meeting.[16]

But Mary's daring days were clearly over. And for Fanny Wright, the eligible women were vanishing fast. . . .

Sismondi called Fanny "insanely religious," seeing her, in anticipation of George Eliot's description of Dorothea in *Middlemarch,* as "a new St. Theresa in whom the love of principle and usefulness moves, but not that of the soul or the love of God." He hoped she would stay quiet, discussing Owen's system with other philosophers so that she might in the end see the truth. "Let her return quickly," he wrote, "to an equilibrium which has been upset because the only man of spirit who has approached her for some time was a fool."

And so, despite Fanny's continued importunings, her friends, amid such powerful tutelage and rumors of scandal, were reluctant to join Fanny on her return to America. At the last, she tried once more to convince Harriet Garnett.

> I cannot bear to think of your solitude [with Julia's impending marriage] and yet I cannot but think of it, day and night. A whole year, my Harry! It is too long—too long. Why should you not go with me? You did not convince me by any of your reasons at the time and now when I look back to them I am still less convinced.[17]

The hoped-for female companionship was proving increasingly elusive. These early Victorian women were finding it still difficult to translate individual goals into anything as specific as, say, an infamous slave emancipation colony thousands of miles away.

All the talk of eternal pacts and friendship forever was over. From now on, sisterhood would prove to be mainly an intellectual and emotional mainstay, based on the connections forged by language, not actions. Whenever the demands made by one or another of the women approached an area requiring tangible support—a move to Nashoba, or Hanover, the braving of convention to take someone in—the sisterhood faltered. Never con-

crete, it remained a compelling idea which provided a continuing, if often fragile bond among members of the circle, a force which the women could draw upon only in personal, inward ways.

Notes

[1] In 1814, George Rapp (1757-1847), leader of a religious group called Harmonists, founded the village of Harmonie in Indiana. In 1825 he sold the town to a social reformer and pioneer in cooperative movements, Robert Owen (1771-1858) who renamed the settlement "New Harmony." William Maclure, a wealthy scientist and "Father of American Geology," taught at New Harmony.

[2] "Alas, Alas! . . ." FW/HG & JGP [Frances Wright/ Harriet Garnett & Julia Garnett Pertz], January or February 1825, GPC [Garnett-Pertz Collection, Houghton Library of Harvard University].

[3] "I could have wept . . ." FW/HG & JGP, 12 April 1825, GPC.

[4] "start creating her world. . . . " For published selections from the Nashoba letters, see Cecilia Helena Payne-Gaposchkin, ed., "The Nashoba Plan for Removing the Evil of Slavery: Letters of Frances and Camilla Wright, 1820-1829," *Harvard Library Bulletin* 23 (1975).

[5] "Without some fixed . . ." FW/HG & JGP, 4 December 1825, GPC.

[6] "Geometry had been . . ." FW/HG & JGP, 4 December 1825, GPC.

[7] "I can truly declare . . ." FW/HG & JGP, 4 December 1825, GPC.

[8] "While I admire . . ." [Camilla Wright]/HG & JGP, 10 January 1826, GPC. For George and Eliza Flower, see *Dictionary of National Biography.*

[9] "Our conversation and friendship . . ." FW/HG & JGP, 11 April 1826, GPC.

[10] "Remember dear loves . . ." FW/HG & JGP, 11 April 1826, GPC.

[11] "As the daughter . . ." FW to Mary Shelley, 22 August 1827, in Florence A. Marshall, *The Life and Letters of Mary Shelley,* pp. 168-71.

[12] "Our circle already . . ." FW to Mary Shelley, 22 August 1827, in Marshall, *Shelley.*

[13] "The memory of my mother . . ." Mary Shelley to FW, 12 September 1827, copy in JGP's hand, GPC.

[14] "Always to support . . ." FW/HG & JGP, October 1827, GPC.

[15] "I do want one . . ." FW to Mary Shelley, 15 September 1827, in Marshall, *Shelley,* pp. 172-4.

[16] "A delicate nursling . . ." FW to Mary Shelley, 15 September 1827, in Marshall, *Shelley.*

[17] "I cannot bear to think . . ." FW/HG, Autumn 1827, GPC.

Celia Morris Eckhardt (essay date 1984)

SOURCE: "Jane Austen and the Rebel," in *Fanny Wright: Rebel in America,* Harvard University Press, 1984, pp. 1-24.

[*In the following excerpt, Eckhardt contrasts Frances Wright, who even in her youth expressed outrage at oppression and willfully entered into political activism, with the more iconic and conventional figure of femininity drawn by Jane Austen.*]

On the sixth of September, 1795, a child was born on the southeast coast of Scotland whose life proved as vital as any could be in the nineteenth century, and almost as full of pain. Her name was Frances Wright, and John Stuart Mill would call her one of the most important women of her day.[1]

She was important because she dared to take Thomas Jefferson seriously when he wrote, "All men are created equal," and to assume that "men" meant "women" as well. She was important because she made of her life a determined search for a place where she could help forge the institutions that would allow that principle to govern society. She was important because she had the integrity and courage to renounce the upper middle-class world to which she was born—a world whose prizes and comforts were hers for the taking—and to risk her health, her fortune, and her good name to realize, in the United States of America, the ideals on which it was founded.

In 1825 she became the first woman in America to act publicly to oppose slavery. Twenty miles outside the little trading post so presumptuously named Memphis, in Tennessee, she established a commune whose purpose was to discover and then to demonstrate how slaves might be educated and responsibly freed. In 1828 she became the first woman in America to speak in public to a large secular audience of men and women, and the first to argue that women were men's equals and must be granted an equal role in all the business of public life. Along with Robert Owen's eldest son, Robert Dale Owen, she edited a liberal weekly newspaper, the *Free Enquirer,* and from 1828 to 1830 she

used its pages, as she used lecture halls throughout the country, to fight for all the victims of the social and political hierarchies of her time.

The pampered daughter of a favored class, Fanny cast her lot with working people and, as speaker and journalist, involved herself in the beginnings of the labor movement in New York. She attacked an economic system that allowed not only slavery in the South but what she called wage slavery in the North, a system that made black women the sexual prey of white men and drove poor women everywhere to the workhouse, to crime, and to prostitution. She came to see what Alexis de Tocqueville did not: that America was by no means a society in which people lived as equals, but one marked by extremes of wealth and poverty which were growing rather than diminishing. She understood that such disparities of wealth made an authentic republic impossible.

Nor did the churches escape her wrath. She showed her skepticism of the religious and sexual pieties of her time when she wrote Mary Wollstonecraft Shelley that men, "like their old progenitor, Father Adam . . . walk about boasting of their wisdom, strength, and sovereignty, while they have not sense so much as to swallow an apple without the aid of an Eve to put it down their throats." She attacked a morality that taught people to spend their money building churches and sending missionaries abroad but that closed their eyes to the destitution and injustice around them. She took on the churches in part because she thought men used religion to keep women foolish, dependent, and at home.[2]

At a time when women's virtue was said to depend on their chastity, she spoke of sexual passion as "the strongest and . . . the noblest of the human passions" and the source of "the best joys of our existence." With the possible exception of Walt Whitman, she wrote more powerfully of sexual experience than any other American in the nineteenth century. In 1827, when propriety forbade women even to mention sexuality, she publicly endorsed miscegenation as a way to solve the race problem in America. She looked to the day when "the olive of peace" would be "embraced by the white man and the black, and their children, approached in feeling and education, [would] gradually blend into one their blood and hue."[3]

In the 1840s she came to believe that governments men had made inclined to war, and was convinced that they did so because they elevated the selfish principle over the generous, in part by restricting women to "the narrowest precincts of the individual family circle . . . by forcibly closing [their] eyes upon the claims of the great human family without that circle." Justice, she argued, could come only when "the two persons in human kind—man and woman—shall exert equal influences in a state of equal independence."[4]

A woman so at odds with the conventions of her time was bound to divide her contemporaries, and Frances Wright was loved and hated with equal extravagance. By the time she was thirty, she had met and dazzled the famous on both sides of the Atlantic. Jeremy Bentham observed that she had "the sweetest and strongest mind that ever was lodged in a female body." The Marquis de Lafayette called her his daughter, his adored Fanny, and paid his attentions so openly that he scandalized not only his social circle but his own family. In old age Walt Whitman remembered that "we all loved her: fell down before her: her very appearance seemed to enthrall us." She was "sweeter, nobler, grander—multiplied by twenty—than all who traduced her."[5]

Because she attacked the churches, however, endorsed miscegenation, and most of all, because she shunned the pedestal prescribed for women, she was labeled "The Red Harlot of Infidelity." In 1829 a New York editor called her "a bold blasphemer, and a voluptuous preacher of licentiousness . . . impervious to the voice of virtue, and case-hardened against shame!" In 1836 Catharine Beecher, exemplar of respectable women, charged that Fanny "stands, with brazen front and brawny arms, attacking the safeguards of all that is venerable and sacred in religion, all that is safe and wise in law, all that is pure and lovely in domestic virtue . . . I cannot conceive any thing in the shape of a woman, more intolerably offensive and disgusting." In 1837, while the press manipulated the opposition to her for partisan political ends, ten thousand people thronged the streets of New York to hear her speak, and the entire police force had to be called out to protect her and her followers.[6]

Some seventy-five years after Fanny Wright was born, a great English novelist mused on the problems of women like her. George Eliot, remembering Saint Theresa of Avila, an ascetic and mystic who founded sixteen convents and fourteen monasteries in Spain, remarked that her "passionate, ideal nature demanded an epic life" rather than the "many-volumed romances of chivalry and the social conquests of a brilliant girl." The latter-day Theresas, Eliot knew, seldom found an "epic life wherein there was a constant unfolding of far-resonant action." Their spiritual grandeur ill-matched with mean opportunities, their lives slipped obscurely by.[7]

Fanny Wright's resemblance to the pragmatic Catholic saint did not escape at least one of her contemporaries. In 1827 the Swiss economist J. C. L. de Sismondi wrote, "She is a new St. Theresa, in whom the love of principle and usefulness operates as the love of God did in the other." The problem for Fanny was to discover how she might be useful—for any woman in the first half of the nineteenth century who aspired to a spacious, dedicated life faced a formidable set of bar-riers. She could not matriculate in a university, much less teach in one. Neither in America nor in Great Britain could she vote. The laws that governed her and the creeds by which she lived were all written, interpreted, and enforced by men. A married woman could neither sign a contract, own money she earned, nor hold title to property originally hers by dowry or inheritance. Her children belonged legally to her husband. Her job lay in raising those children, though she was forbidden to know the world for which she shaped them. Modesty and self-sacrifice were the goals held up to her. No one expected her to excel; no one demanded that she be great. No matter how intelligent, ambitious, and dedicated, she was ineligible for a profession and had no natural role to play in any established institution that battled publicly to make the good prevail.[8]

Defying the conventions that would contain her, Fanny Wright chose to live tempestuously and to try for greatness. She traveled farther than perhaps any other woman of her time, and as she ranged, she broke one barrier after another.

For all this, the story of Fanny Wright is hard and disquieting. It tells more about the losses than the gains of America in the nineteenth century. It tells how much people love the rhetoric of equality and how little they are inclined to make equality possible. It tells how self-righteously men fight to hold their power over half the human race. It tells how women crucify the would-be saviors of their sex and how men mock them with that fact. It tells how fragile reason is, and how deadly isolation. It tells of a woman whose strength was tightly bound to her frailty. It is a story of courage, boldness, and waste. Most of all, it is a story not merely of the past: to learn it is to recover a part of our democratic heritage, and to discover that the time for Fanny Wright has not yet come.

The most terrifying thing that ever happened to Fanny Wright happened when she was two and a half: her mother died in February 1798, and her father three months later. Fanny was then torn from her five-year-old brother and baby sister and their home in Dundee, on the coast of Scotland, and taken to be raised in London by her grandfather and her eighteen-year-old aunt. In neither her public nor her private writings would there be a sense of childhood.[9]

A letter from Fanny's mother, Camilla, suggests what might have been. While visiting her sister in the north of England, Camilla wrote her husband on their anniversary: "I need not say how much more rejoiced I should be to have your dear self here, but when I think how tenderly you are employed in caring for our beloved children I less regret your absence, tho it is on the day I regard as the most valued of my life." Camilla's family was among the British lettered aristocracy. She named her son for her uncle, Richard Robinson, who had become Baron Rokeby in 1777. For a quarter of a century he was vice chancellor of the University of Dublin, and he served as Archbishop of Armagh from 1765 until his death in 1794. Camilla's great-aunt and devoted godmother was the gifted bluestocking Elizabeth Robinson Montagu, whom Dr. Samuel Johnson fondly called "Queen of the Blues." Mrs. Montagu defended Shakespeare against Voltaire's attack, and established a salon that attracted people as different as the painter Sir Joshua Reynolds and the author and reformer Hannah More. So brilliantly did she entertain "all the leaders of thought and fashion in the London of the day" that she caught the attention of royalty. Not long before Fanny was born, the papers wrote that the Queen and her six daughters had breakfasted with Mrs. Montagu. And like her aunt, Camilla Wright drew people who admired her and found her charming.[10]

Fanny's father, James Wright, Jr., was a Dundee merchant, related through his mother to Glasgow intellectuals who helped to give the Scottish Enlightenment its name. For more than forty years his uncle, James Mylne, was professor of moral philosophy at the University of Glasgow. James Wright too was a serious student: his special interest was in coins, and his collection was rare and valuable. In his mid-twenties he challenged the authority on the subject on some points of accuracy and insisted that he underrated the excellence of Scottish coinage. James despised aristocracy and those who used "the silly morsels of heraldry" in designing coins, and he argued for representations of "emblems of industry and commerce," such as weavers at their work, mail-coaches, and "whale-fishing."[11]

Like James Mylne, Wright admired Thomas Paine and the principles of the French Revolution, and he was politically suspect for his enthusiasm. According to Fanny, he was the object of government espionage in 1794 for promoting a cheap edition of *The Rights of Man,* and Dundee legend had it that to escape prosecution, he rowed out alone at midnight and dumped his radical coins and literature into the river Tay. When Fanny later discovered some of his papers, she marveled at "a somewhat singular coincidence in views between a father and daughter, separated by death when the first had not reached the age of twenty-nine, and when the latter was in infancy."[12]

James was a poor businessman. He begrudged the time work took away from his family, his coins, and his politics, and the times were hard for trade. But the Wrights lived comfortably in Miln's Buildings at the Nethergate in a new apartment busy with children and the servants on which their class depended. The life there augured well for raising responsible, good-natured young people who would take their places in the community among their peers. Had death not intervened, the world would never have heard of Fanny Wright.[13]

Her brother and sister seemed less deeply scarred than Fanny by the tragedy of their childhood. Richard was raised in James Mylne's home in Glasgow along with his own five children. Camilla, a year and a half younger than Fanny, was left with foster parents in Dundee, of whom she later wrote with the love a child might feel for parents who were especially kind. For the next eight years, however, Fanny had to learn the hard lessons of childhood solitude. In a time and place where children were treated as small adults, she learned to be her own shaping spirit.[14]

She lived in London with her maternal grandfather, Major General Duncan Campbell of the Royal Marines, and his daughter Frances, and it was in rebellion against her Tory guardians that Fanny began to understand the life around her. She later wrote of her "absence of all sympathy with the views and characters of those among whom her childhood was thrown." Her brother's sketch of their grandfather suggests the nature of her rebellion, for Campbell was indolent and convivial, a man who loved the good life as it paraded itself in a great metropolis. In 1809, when Richard passed through London on his way to serve with the East India Company, he wrote home that his grandfather knew nobody but "Lords and Generals" and never dined at home alone. "He is going out today, and we were out yesterday at Mr. Kerr's M.P., who to be sure had a grand dinner, and ten or twelve different sorts of wine . . . we are going to the Opera tonight." By her own account, Fanny came early to distrust the self-indulgence that made that life so sweet.[15]

The beggars of London first inspired Fanny to compassion for the poor. As she walked about the city with Duncan Campbell, she saw thousands begging pennies to buy bread. When she asked her grandfather why these tattered mothers and their children were so poor, he said it was because they were too lazy to work. But once, when he answered a knock at the door to find a gaunt man dressed in rags who said he had eaten nothing for three days and begged to work just for food and clothing, Duncan Campbell turned him away. When Fanny wished aloud that she had money to give the man to keep him from starving, her grandfather called her "a foolish simple girl" who knew "but little of the world." When she asked him why rich people who did not work did not become beggars, he answered that work was shameful: "I could not associate with rich people if I worked . . . God intended there should be poor, and there should be rich." And when Fanny wondered if the rich robbed the poor, he replied indignantly that if she indulged such thoughts, she would not be admitted into good society.[16]

Late in 1803, Fanny's uncle Major William Campbell, who was Frances' brother, was killed in action against the Mahrattas at Saswarree in India. Of his property in the provinces of Bengal, Behar, and Orissa, and in the Zemindary of Benares, he willed half to his sister and the other half to his nieces, Frances and Camilla Wright. And William had clearly been a very wealthy man.[17]

The legacy that made the girls heiresses no doubt also made possible Frances Campbell's move, in 1806, to the coastal village of Dawlish, in Devonshire. The nine-year-old Camilla apparently joined her and Fanny then, and soon became the foil for her sister's dazzling presence. The pattern soon was set: Fanny confronted the world while Camilla kept the house. By all accounts gentle and bright, Camilla was also intensely loyal. She looked to Fanny "for guidance, and leaned upon her for support," and life for her became unthinkable apart from her sister.[18]

Death had separated them once before; in 1809 it came again to strengthen their dependence on each other. Late in the spring, en route to India, their brother Richard was killed in a skirmish with the French, and in November of the same year their grandfather died. By the time she was fourteen, Fanny had seen her mother, her father, her brother, and her grandfather die. This was radical deprivation. And she seems to have transformed the turbulent emotions of fear and anger that such deprivation would provoke into lifelong outrage at human suffering.[19]

The two girls probably lived with their aunt in the twenty-room mansion that she called The Cottage, for Richard wrote that Miss Campbell lived in great style, and Fanny remarked that she was "surrounded at all times by rare and extensive libraries, and commanding whatever masters she desired." The Cottage topped a hill and looked down on Lyme Bay, just where the English Channel flows into the Atlantic Ocean. A visitor called it an earthly paradise, with its grand view and terraced walks, its fine magnolia and banks of rhododendron, its kitchen garden with peach trees and apricots.[20]

And for the next seven years, until 1813, Fanny and Camilla Wright lived with Miss Campbell in Dawlish in the gracious style of the British upper middle class. Servants waited on them: they never had to dress themselves or pack a trunk. Governesses and tutors came to their call, and what intellectual nourishment they did not find at home they could get from the group of worldly and experienced men settled nearby. On Sundays they worshiped with their aunt at Dawlish Church in the decorous fashion of the Anglican communion. The seasons came gently as the rolling hills, and the abundant fruits and flowers of Devonshire graced their table. Fanny lived there from the time she was eleven until she was eighteen, as she and Camilla mastered their lessons, learned to swim and ride their horses, paid their calls and took their tea.

For an insight into Fanny's and Camilla's adolescence, we are in debt to another great English novelist. In 1811 Jane Austen published *Sense and Sensibility,* in which a man seems surprised that anybody could live in Devonshire without living near Dawlish. Sharp and conservative, Frances Campbell was a lady from one of Jane Austen's novels, and she brought up her nieces to triumph in the world the author so zestfully describes—a world dominated by manor and parsonage, regulated for those of consequence by the London social season, enlivened by visits for tea. People entertained themselves with hunting, whist, picnics, and balls. Ladies did needlework and on occasion sang for their friends.

In such a world, propriety was a great dictator. It decreed, among other things, that well-bred men like Duncan Campbell should not work. One of Jane Austen's characters, for example, describes himself as having nothing to do: "idleness was pronounced on the whole to be the most advantageous and honourable, and a young man of eighteen is not in general so earnestly bent on being busy as to resist the solicitations of his friends to do nothing. I was therefore entered at Oxford, and have been properly idle ever since."[21]

For women, the possibilities of vocation were a good deal more meager. Jane Austen's heroines concentrate on sorting the worthy suitor from the unworthy—"worthy" invariably having a close, if complicated, relationship to "rich." The first line of *Pride and Prejudice* announces the game played in all her novels: "It is a truth universally acknowledged, that a single man in possession of a good fortune must be in want of a wife." In *Emma* the possibility that a spirited woman will have to become a governess is looked upon as a disaster of sorts—even by those who do not wish her well. It was a world with which Fanny Wright was almost ludicrously at odds.[22]

Had Jane Austen tried to portray the adolescent Fanny, she would have drawn a tall, thin, conspicuous woman, for Fanny was very tall at fourteen and, when full-grown, was at least five feet ten inches. She might have shown Fanny jumping her horse while others trotted, talking of higher mathematics to a suitor who knew nothing but hounds, insisting on the virtues of Byron to people who read only Cowper. In fact, when "a deep and shrewd mathematician and physician" observed that a question of hers was "dangerous," Fanny asked if truth could be dangerous. From his reply, "It is thought so," she concluded "that Truth had still to be found . . . [and] men were afraid of it." Jane Austen obviously could not have put Frances Wright in her frame, for while Fanny learned exquisite manners, she also asked unsettling, radical questions. She asked,

"What is justice?" and "Why are so many poor?" She was too hungry to content herself with Jane Austen's high tea.[23]

More important, Fanny did not develop the psychic protection of a sense of humor. She wrote later that "experience taught her, in very childhood, how little was to be learned in drawing-rooms, and inspired her with a disgust for frivolous reading, conversation, and occupation." Jane Austen could have said, with one of her heroines, "Follies and nonsense, whims and inconsistencies, *do* divert me, I own, and I laugh at them whenever I can." Fanny was not amused.[24]

She never learned to be as tough as the comic novelist. She could not use irony or humor to help her live with those for whom she felt contempt. She could not manipulate people, as the novelist did, for her own amusement. She was not subtle enough, or cruel enough, for her own good—if one imagined her good to consist of an accommodation to the small world around her. Fanny, of course, did not so imagine it.

If these were unhappy years, Fanny emerged from them with a strength that people invariably found startling. Her disdain for drawing rooms prompted her to pour her energies into becoming a scholar, and from the small but distinguished group of educated men around Dawlish, she caught the excitement of the life of the mind. She undoubtedly knew John Schank, a gifted naval engineer. She probably knew Sir William Watson, whose many visitors included Sir William Herschel, the astronomer who discovered the planet Uranus. Joseph Drury, who retired to Dawlish after his tenure as headmaster of Harrow, entertained scientists and scholars from all over England; and the naturalist Thomas Comyns had one of the best private museums in the country there. These men set high standards that governed those of her class, and even by such standards Fanny was well educated. She learned French and Italian. She read classical literature. She spent years confronting the disciplines of history, philosophy, and mathematics.[25]

Her scholarship led her to classical drama as well as to European and English poetry, which she studied in the most fruitful way, by imitation. She found relief through writing: to name her feelings was to understand and to control them. In a poem apparently from this period she wrote of losing a beloved friend:

Fair star! may every joy be thine!
May thou ne'er prove the bitter anguish
Of love so true, so fond as mine,
Doomed without hope untold to languish.

Oh had I but the Lesbyan's lyre,
Blue-eyed Sappho's fervid strain;
Then might I hope thy blood to fire;
Then should I make thee share my pain.

She learned when she was young that language gives power: if she could be eloquent, she would not suffer alone. She began to perfect that command of language so crucial to the legend she would become.[26]

Dawlish itself deeply influenced her. The Cottage looked down on a coastline that was sinuously beautiful, and at a time when Wordsworth was teaching the English-speaking world to feel the power of nature and the virtue of simple people, Fanny was looking to rural Devonshire for solace. A small village, and remote, Dawlish depended primarily on its own artisans and tradesmen. The most memorable event in its history occurred in Fanny's time: the 1810 flood, which washed away a number of houses. And if Fanny learned in Dawlish the respect for plain people that marked her always, she also learned that life was not the idyll it might seem.

Thomas Hardy began a lifetime of indignant questioning when he saw a boy die of starvation in the fruitful field he had helped to cultivate. By the time she was fifteen Fanny too had discovered that a good deal of human suffering had human causes. She saw how painfully old English peasants labored and how, nevertheless, they were "ejected, under various pretexts, from the estates of the wealthy proprietors of the soil among whom she moved." She saw that wealth had power in the world which age and infirmity did not.[27]

At least three men were building empires for themselves in that part of Devonshire, and Fanny watched these local enclosures as they drove peasants from their ancestral homes and took away the traditional rights to gather food and firewood that had made their lives tolerable. In the 1790s, Drury of Harrow had taken over eight small holdings, consolidated them, and built himself a mansion. What had been a patchwork of small cultivated plots and common lands, he transformed into gardens and parkland, surrounded with a few cultivated fields. A few years later Charles Hoare, who was richer than Drury, bought a number of adjoining farms and made them into the Luscombe Estate. He built a castle and laid out parks, and for years he continued to accumulate the farms nearby. At about the same time, John Inglet Fortescue bought the manor of Dawlish from the dean and chapter of Exeter Cathedral, who had held it since before the Norman Conquest, and sold it piecemeal to the highest bidders.

As Fanny watched these rich men drive the poor from land on which their ancestors had lived as far back as memory and legend could trace, she "pronounced to herself a solemn oath, to wear ever in her heart the cause of the poor and the helpless; and to aid in all that she could in redressing the grievous wrongs which seemed to prevail in society." It was an oath that became the motive force in her life.[28]

Her anger at the cruelty her aunt's gracious world inflicted on the poor led readily into what became her life's obsession: the United States of America. When she was seventeen, she chanced upon Carlo Bocca's *Storia della Guerra dell' Independenza degli Stati Uniti d'America,* a history of the thirteen colonies' struggle to become a young republic. At that moment of discovery, she later recalled, she glimpsed a new life: "There existed a country consecrated to freedom, and in which man might awake to the full knowledge and full exercise of his powers." While those around her were absorbed in the war against Napoleon, Fanny determined secretly to see the nation across the Atlantic against which, in that Tory corner of England, there seemed to be a conspiracy of silence.[29]

Not long after her discovery of America, the anger that had simmered for years between niece and aunt boiled to the surface. Frances Campbell was a woman who reveled in her life of modest grandeur. She was respectable enough, and good enough company, that in later years the Hoares invited her to live with them in nearby Luscombe Castle. It seems unlikely that she was malicious to her nieces, but she was at least inept. Only eighteen when death forced the two-year-old Fanny upon her, she assumed a premature responsibility that may well have made her rigid. Richard Wright described her as a fussy woman who told him to eat just so much and to wear his gloves constantly. He wished someone would teach her how to give advice: "I would not give one of Mr. Mylne's advices for 10,000 of hers . . . It would make a horse laugh."[30]

But Fanny despised her. She believed her aunt deceitful and cruel, and saw in her "the image of an enemy." Scarred by a bitterness she knew she would carry till death, Fanny felt that she had been victimized since infancy by the "crying wrongs" her aunt had heaped upon her, and whatever the rights and wrongs of each side in their quarrel, it had a profound emotional impact on Frances Wright. The pattern of her relationship with her aunt repeated itself throughout her life: she would feel someone wrong her and turn harshly against him, as though the child whom death had torn from those she loved could never let herself be vulnerable again. She left Dawlish marked with a psychic inflexibility that would never soften. As though freed from a trap and wary of being caught again, she looked suspiciously on permanent commitment and inclined to move restlessly through the world. Rather than put her trust in people who would die or betray, Fanny Wright came to put her trust in ideas.[31]

Fanny's formidable will had its first major triumph in 1813, when she whisked herself and Camilla away from Frances Campbell's home before they were legally of an age to go. They went to Glasgow, to their uncle James Mylne and his wife Agnes, who had nurtured Richard and now welcomed them. They joined the five Mylne children in a college house said to be very cramped, but one that opened onto a university court romantically like the close of an English cathedral. Glasgow, a port on the river Clyde, was a mercantile city where citizens took public affairs and their own responsibilities seriously. The currents of social reform swirled past the sisters' door, and they began to feel the insurgent pulls of modern life.[32]

Glasgow was also the home of one of Scotland's oldest and most distinguished universities, and Fanny and Camilla now lived with a man who had taken the chair of moral philosophy less than thirty-five years after Adam Smith had left it. Oxford and Cambridge for the most part confined their teaching to the learned languages and the transmission of what Edward Gibbon called "the prejudices and infirmities of the age," but Glasgow's intellectual life was both utilitarian and democratic. Although the university excluded women, it took pride in furthering the country's economic and industrial development and even concerned itself with educational reforms: most classes were taught in English rather than Latin, and dedicated and inspiring teachers like James Mylne were objects of respect. Little had changed since Adam Smith had called the Scottish universities "without exception the best seminaries of learning that are to be found anywhere in Europe."[33]

The extended family that Fanny and Camilla joined in Glasgow had been powerfully shaped by its patriarch, John Millar, a friend and disciple of both Smith and David Hume, and professor of civil law and jurisprudence at the university until his death in 1801. Nine of Millar's children survived him, and they and their families offered models of human possibility far more congenial to Fanny than Frances Campbell or her Tory friends had been. Her Aunt Agnes was Millar's daughter. Robina Craig Millar, who would try to replace the mother Fanny had lost so young, had married his eldest son. Another son, James, was professor of mathematics and, with Mylne, showed the family instinct for dissent by regularly voting in the minority on issues of university policy.

The women in the Millar circle cultivated literature and the arts as eagerly as the men did. Frederick Lamb remarked that all the ladies around Millar were "contaminated with an itch for philosophy and learning" and seemed to enjoy themselves wonderfully. "After cheese they hand around the table a bottle of whisky and another of brandy, and the whole company, males and females . . . indulge in a dram. It is very comfortable and exhilarating, and affords an opportunity for many jokes." It seems unlikely that Millar's children would have turned, intellectually or socially, to a frugal table after he died, and Fanny and Camilla boarded richly among them.[34]

The coincidence between Fanny's ideas and those of John Millar can hardly be accidental. A Whig when Scotland was run for the most part by Tories, Millar enthusiastically endorsed the fight against the slave trade. He supported the American Revolution in the interests of "that love of liberty, so congenial to the mind of man, which nothing but imperious necessity is able to subdue." He vigorously upheld the principles on which the French Revolution was fought, and his dismay at the course it took did not lead him, as it did so many others, to support Edmund Burke's crusade and the war against France. A believer in gradual progress and the good effects of manufacture and commerce, he nonetheless wrote that "the pursuit of riches becomes a scramble, in which the hand of every man is against every other." His work is a model of the cool, dispassionate inquiry Fanny later tried to emulate, and his pages explore many of the ideas she later preached to a startled America.[35]

As for James Mylne, he was said to be "probably the most independent thinker of the Scottish philosophical professoriate" of his day. His students called him "Old Sensation," an allusion to the philosophical position which Fanny soon took, that we can know nothing beyond the evidence provided by our senses. A Church of Scotland minister, Mylne exalted reason, self-control, and duty. Like his father-in-law, he opposed the slave trade and endorsed the principle of utility, which looks to the greater happiness of the greater number. And he delighted in Fanny and Camilla: "girls of whom I may be justly vain—well-principled, well-informed, elegantly accomplished, fit to take their places among society of any rank and to be received in it with esteem and respect."[36]

In Scotland, Fanny and Camilla found two sets of sisters, the Millars and the Cullens, who heightened their sense of how accomplished women can become. They often stayed at Milheugh, the Millar family's estate not far from Glasgow, where the Millar sisters so fired one visitor's love of knowledge that she called the days she spent there "the acme of her intellectual existence." The Cullen sisters were equally distinguished, their father, Dr. William Cullen, having been one of the outstanding professors and scientists at the University of Edinburgh. Robina Craig Millar, the youngest of the Cullens, was the bridge between these remarkable people, and she became the most important older woman in Fanny's life. She had married John Millar, Jr., and emigrated with him to the United States, but after he died suddenly in Pennsylvania in 1796, she returned to live with her sister Margaret, whom the Wright sisters called the "Good Spirit." Fanny turned to Robina as to a mother. Talented, charming, and radical in her sympathies, Mrs. Millar lavished her affections on Fanny and Camilla. And one of her letters shows the kind of adulation the elder Miss Wright inspired in those around her: "what an existence you gave and what a world you have carried away! . . . you . . . will soon have all the world at your feet."[37]

At least once, when she was twenty, Fanny flirted briefly with marriage. The man's name was Watson. He formally proposed, and James Mylne thought him "a man of honor and integrity, of generous and affectionate dispositions, of correct habits, of rational and moderate views." Mylne told Watson that if he could accumulate enough money to support a family "of education and habits such as yours and Fanny's," Mylne could approve their eventual marriage. Their engagement, however, enjoyed no very long duration. After Fanny broke it off, Robina Millar observed that she had never thought them suited to each other. Although Watson was amiable and steady and might have saved Fanny "from many rocks on which in your voyage thro' life you might be in danger of being driven . . . a character of his caliber could never have rendered you happy," and she congratulated Fanny on her escape.[38]

About the same time Fanny was doing what was expected of young women—getting engaged—she was doing something altogether presumptuous: she was taking herself seriously as a writer. Mrs. Millar, who became the voice of propriety in relation to her work, assured her that she was a born poet: "You have the imagination, the temperament, the just confidence of genius." Fanny began a long poem, *Thoughts of a Recluse,* and her interest in it lasted a good deal longer than her interest in Watson. She continued for years to write additional passages and tried more than once to have it published. The poem, of which only fragments remain, was apparently Byronic in tone, world-weary and contemptuous when not simply angry. And though Mrs. Millar admired it, she discouraged Fanny's attempts to publish it on the grounds that "no Bookseller would venture upon it because they as well as the author are compelled to suffer for libels." She thought it contained opinions that would seem arrogant in one so young and was afraid it might prejudice readers against Fanny's other work.[39]

Only a few short poems from this period have survived. In some of them Fanny echoed the romanticism of her time and embraced nature, the first of many panaceas she would try and find wanting. More important, she had the stunning self-assurance to talk to Genius as to a familiar, if difficult, friend, and to write of her "fond desire / Of fame immortal." She introduced an idea that, althoug fashionable, also seems genuine and recurs in her work—the idea that her experience had destroyed some quality vital to life:

> And now, the worst—a heart whose pulse is killed,
> And hath no more to give or to receive,
> Shrunk in itself, all passive, mute and chilled,
> That hopes not, cares not, joys not, nor can grieve.

Fanny thought of this paralysis as a response to the cruelty she had watched and suffered herself, though the sexual suppression that propriety demanded of women of her class might well have been equally to blame. But she also gave a glimpse of the pleasant side of her life, among people who cared for her and for one another:

> Good night! Good night! if we, this day,
>   Have spoke in wrath, be it forgiven
> And may we, on our pillows lay,
>   At peace with Man, at peace with Heaven!
>
> Good night! Good night! Oh, may we greet,
>   In health and joy, tomorrow's light!
> And, as we part, so may we meet
>   In peace and love! Good night! Good night![40]

By Fanny's own account she "passed three years in Scotland, during which period she employed her summers in visiting its Highlands and Lowlands; and her winters in closet study." They were fruitful years for her, and people helped when they could. The university librarian Lockhart Muirhead allowed her free access to everything about the United States, and, no doubt for Fanny's sake, James Mylne took out various books on America. She made one of an informal group that gathered to talk of literature and philosophy, and it was for them she wrote several plays, only one of which, *Altorf,* survives in its published form. It was also for them she wrote a treatise on Epicurean philosophy, later published under the title *A Few Days in Athens.*[41]

Its fable is simple. Theon, a young Greek who has come to Athens to study philosophy, believes a fellow student who slanders Epicurus. On a walk outside town, Theon then tells a stranger how shocked he is that Epicurus has been allowed to corrupt young people, and the stranger turns out to be Epicurus. Ashamed of himself, Theon goes back with him to the garden where he teaches, and there he sheds his biases, learns to weigh evidence, and grows in compassion. The life Fanny imagines as the locus of morality is the life of a school, a self-contained world of talk, and the message it preaches is a generous, high-minded self-sufficiency. Epicurus teaches that a sage must become independent of all he cannot command within himself: "What is poverty, if we have temperance, and can be satisfied with a crust, and a draught from the spring?"[42]

Remarkable for its intellectual vigor, the book is a highly competent representation of certain Greek philosophical schools. Its flaws reflect Fanny's characteristic impatience: the writing is often inflated, and the plot flimsy. But *A Few Days* stands as a moving plea for tolerance, self-restraint, and loyalty. It is also iconoclastic—and not merely as the work of an eighteen-year-old. Implicitly attacking Christianity as an ethical guide, Fanny describes a moral life in which neither guilt, sacrifice, nor suffering plays a leading role. Her hero dares to honor happiness: a garden is a place of beauty, and in Epicurean philosophy refined pleasure is the supreme guide. Epicurus teaches his students to discipline themselves to avoid both evil passions and uncontrolled appetites: "I think virtue only the highest pleasure, and vice, or ungoverned passions and appetites, the worst misery."[43]

As Fanny sees him, Epicurus, the first Greek philosopher to accept women as students, is a worthy teacher who can "instantly give security to the timid, and draw love from the feeling heart," and he shows life's purpose as the struggle toward wisdom. The book juxtaposes Epicurus and the Stoic Zeno, the former generous and tolerant, the latter autocratic and unbending, and Fanny weights Epicurus' side of the scale. Though he knows the power he has over his students, "he exerts it in no other way," according to one, "than to mend our lives, or to keep them innocent."[44]

Leontium, alleged to be Epicurus' first female disciple, is modeled on Fanny herself, who clearly enjoyed the role of reverent student to a wise, elderly man whom she could then explain to others. Fanny describes Leontium as having "the self-possessed dignity of ripened womanhood, and the noble majesty of mind, that asked respect and promised delight and instruction. The features were not those of Venus, but Minerva. The eye looked deep and steady from beneath two even brows, that sense, not years, had slightly knit in the centre of the forehead, which else was uniformly smooth and polished as marble. The nose was rather Roman than Grecian, yet perfectly regular, and though not masculine, would have been severe in expression, but for a mouth where all that was lovely and graceful habited . . . Her stature was much above the female standard, but every limb and every motion was symmetry and harmony." More learned than the other students, Leontium has "the most acute, elegant, and subtle pen of Athens." Accustomed to receiving adulation as her due, she is called on to silence disputes and give definitive answers, which she does with graceful precision. The attention Fanny attracted suggests that the portrait is not inaccurate, but its self-confidence verges on self-congratulation, a trait that would unnerve and on occasion offend people she met—and one that would in part betray her.[45]

Fanny then, spent this time in Scotland with good people alive to ideas—to literature, to politics, and to art—and yet she was not satisfied. Making a distinction in her journal between the misanthrope and the cynic, she implicitly identified herself with the former, who "will generally be found to have entered life with a warm heart, a lively imagination, and a sanguine temperament; the latter with a cold heart, a shrewd understanding, and a phlegmatic temper. The misanthrope is made by disappointment, the cynic I take to be fashioned by nature." Like the misanthrope, Fanny had a grand conception of what men and women might be and was disgusted when she discovered what they were. The wounds she had suffered so young were the source of her restless anger: they never let her look benignly on the world or rest content with quiet happiness and the fond respect of her peers.[46]

While those long winter months of study, writing, and talk nourished Fanny intellectually, the summers, when she and Camilla traveled in the Highlands, fed her contempt for the social ethics of her time. The year 1814, just after she and Camilla came to Scotland, has gone down in Gaelic history as the Year of the Burnings, when landlords set fire to cottages to force their tenants off the land. In the name of "progress," they cleared people from the Highlands and replaced them with sheep. The Marquess of Stafford, later the Duke of Sutherland, drove five thousand people from their ancestral homes: "He was the product of a class to whom Property was becoming a sacred trust and its improvement an obligation that must take precedence over all others. This class, owning the land, controlling the legislature, officering the Army, dividing mankind into Gentility and Commons, and transporting a child for the stealing of a handkerchief (because it was Property), sincerely believed that its own enrichment must bring a greater good to a greater number." In boats as far south as the river Clyde, Fanny saw uprooted peasants bound for the United States. And in the Highlands, from which her father's people had come in the fifteenth century, she heard grim tales from those who remained.[47]

The Highlanders were an amalgam of Norse and Gael who "raised goats and black cattle, potatoes and inferior oats, brewed a rough beer and distilled a raw whisky for their dreams." The Lowlanders, who for the most part were the agents of the northerners' eviction, looked contemptuously on what seemed their indifference to progress, their satisfaction with poor food and meager huts, their fondness for illicit stills and belief in the Evil Eye. James Loch, a Lowlander who spent forty years helping to move them out, considered himself "at war with indolence, superstition, inefficiency, the obstinacy of a primitive people and the intransigence of the earth itself." One of his critics would say Loch's object was "to drive out that master-piece of sloth and uselessness—man and all his retinue."[48]

The spectacle of the Highland clearances, in addition to the enclosures that Fanny had seen in Dawlish, gave her a suspicion of "progress" that would run as a counterpoint through all her writing. She listened to people assuage their consciences by considering their victims not quite human. She saw the church collaborating with the rich to defraud the poor. With few exceptions, "the churchmen gave God's authority to Improvement, and threatened the more truculent of the evicted with damnation." Or as one spectator described it, the clergy "maintained in their sermons that the whole was a merciful interposition of Providence to bring them to repentance." If Fanny had not doubted the church before, she doubted it now, and her skepticism was unremitting.[49]

Some years later Fanny wrote that Robert Owen would transform the world, and she no doubt first learned about this utopian reformer in Glasgow. He was a friend of James Mylne's, and his industrial experiments at New Lanark, no more than thirty miles from the city, caught the attention of people as far away as Russia. While the government was hanging Luddites for trying to destroy the machines that were taking away their jobs, and while ambitious "improvers" were driving people from the Highlands to make room for sheep, Robert Owen was demonstrating that the successful operation of cotton mills was not incompatible with human welfare.[50]

Owen's was one of the dazzling success stories of early industrialism. Before he was twenty, he ran a factory with five hundred workers; well before he was thirty, he was part owner and manager of the largest mills in Scotland. But fifteen years before Fanny and Camilla came to Glasgow, he had decided he wanted to do something more than make money. He wanted benevolently to interfere with workers' lives. He wanted to practice the theory that the purpose of society was to make people happy, as well as to show that such a purpose was economically feasible. He captured Fanny's imagination in part because he was eager to spend his life for ordinary people, and he seemed to know how to translate idealism into practical terms.

Owen was an odd sort in an age when most mill owners were willing to keep children as young as six breathing cotton fluff and standing fourteen to sixteen hours in temperatures well over 75 degrees. By 1806, he had stopped importing the pauper children who were a standard source of labor for mills in remote places. He had prohibited the hiring of children under ten, shortened the hours of work, and abolished all punishments except fines, or dismissal for the hopelessly intractable. He had added a story to his workers' houses and developed clever inducements to cleanliness in the village and efficiency in the factory. He had replaced the profiteering shopkeepers and brought in good coal and clothes, pure food, and even pure whiskey, which he sold at minimal prices. He succeeded in making his factory and its town a decent, humane place, and he wanted to persuade others to follow his example.

Between 1815 and 1817, while Fanny and Camilla were in Glasgow, Owen published a series of essays about the effect of the manufacturing system on the working class, and especially on children. His arguments altered the thrust of the received wisdom of political economy. It was one thing for John Millar to comment on the demoralizing and dehumanizing tendencies of mechanization. It was quite another for an eminently successful manufacturer to say that though Britain's wealth and power had indeed increased remarkably because of the development of machinery, the accompanying social evils were so great that the loss from them might well be greater than the gain from mechanization. Owen found the laboring classes "infinitely more degraded and miserable than they were before the introduction of these manufactories, upon the success of which their bare subsistence now depends." He inveighed against the profit motive as "destructive of that open, honest sincerity, without which man cannot make others happy, nor enjoy happiness himself." Long before Carlyle, Ruskin, and Marx thundered against the modern system that pitted one person against another and class against class, Owen spoke out against industrialism's legacy of social devastation and argued that it was unnecessary and could be reversed.[51]

Owen insisted to his peers, the British master manufacturers, that the talk about the freedom of the working classes was cant, since the only alternatives they had to working nine to fifteen hours a day were the workhouse, crime, or starvation. His fellow manufacturers tried to discredit him. When he testified before a committee of the House of Commons on a bill to regulate the conditions of work in textile mills, a cotton lord questioned him with such hostility about his religious beliefs that the cross-examination was later expunged from the records. More important, the manufacturers had decisive power in Parliament, and the bill that finally passed in 1819 had been so amended to meet their demands that Owen, disclaiming any responsibility for it, turned to communitarian experiments to find his lever to move the world.

The essence of Owen's philosophy was that people's characters are formed for them, not by them; that all religions and all earlier philosophies had falsely held people responsible for their condition; that society brought them up in circumstances that inevitably made them vicious and criminal, and then punished them for being so; and that it was demonstrably possible to alter society radically, with no violence or loss to anyone, so that people would grow up to cooperate rather than to distrust or despise one another. The state to which he looked forward was governed, quite simply, by the precepts of primitive Christianity.

A man of action, Owen believed that the millennium was just around the corner, and he dedicated his life to bringing it into existence. He created a model that Fanny Wright was to find profoundly congenial. Ultimately he influenced her more, perhaps, than any other person she met in adult life, although it was an influence she came to rue.

In 1816, when she was twenty-one, Fanny began casting about for something to do. She had grown restless; her pleasant, self-contained world of good talk and good feelings had begun to pall. She had read some of the new romantic poets—certainly Byron, Shelley, and Schiller—and had caught their tone. She thrilled, as they did, to the cry of liberty, and with them she despised the tyrants of their time. She envied their moody heroes stalking the world, contemptuous of mediocrity and ready to die for a cause. More pertinent, she felt trapped by the decorum that narrowly bound the women of her class and denied them meaningful work. Among the poor, such decorum was irrelevant, because people worked to survive and women typically drudged longer hours than men did. The same was true in places like the American frontier, where hands were scarce and therefore dear, and where women worked alongside men and at many of the same jobs. Among the aristocracy, girls were often educated with their brothers, and queens and duchesses had proved how capable a gifted woman could be. But for women of the great middle class, from which Fanny came, productive work began to disappear in the last half of the eighteenth century, when the tide of industrialism began to carry work into the factories. The many jobs necessary to maintain a household—spinning, weaving, candle- and soap-making—were now done outside the home, leaving many women with idle hands. Those idle hands became a mark of distinction, a coveted badge that proclaimed the economic security and well-being of a class.

Idleness, however, offended Fanny Wright and made her uneasy, so after three years in Scotland, she and Camilla left the Mylnes and went to London. Fanny said they needed to arrange their financial affairs, perhaps by settling a lawsuit with Frances Campbell over the money held for them in trust. But their finances were also a convenient excuse. Fanny hoped to find something worthy to do, and what she saw and heard in London made her even more skeptical that she could find it in her native land. Looking with a critical eye on the men who governed England, she saw how thoroughly they were the beneficiaries of a society based on class. She began to despair of their ever voluntarily giving up their power and became more convinced that they would use it always against the poor.

The past twenty years had in fact been bad for the poor and politically tempestuous for everyone. The Industrial Revolution had developed machinery that permanently altered the nature of work, bringing a rapidly growing population from the countryside into un-planned cities and destroying ancient structures of community life, but the chances for dealing constructively with these changes had been frustrated by a political counter-revolution in response to the Terror in France. The British manufacturers had joined the aristocracy in making common cause against reforms from below. The landowners worked to repress any Jacobin "conspiracies" to gain political power; the manufacturers worked to defeat "conspiracies" to increase wages and improve working conditions. Even play and laughter, especially on Sunday, became politically suspect.[52]

By 1815, the men who ran England seemed to be turning the thumbscrews on the poor. A landowners' Parliament passed the protectionist Corn Laws, which, by prohibiting the importation of cheap grain, raised the price of bread and devastated people who depended on it. In 1816, when Fanny reached London, she might well have wondered if the binding strings of British society would hold, as it seemed that the country was on the verge of a class war.

She was introduced to new strains in radical thought and tactics. The period from 1815 to 1820, the years of Fanny's early adulthood, has been called the heroic age of popular radicalism in Great Britain. William Cobbett, its most unrelenting journalist, and Henry Hunt, its most powerful orator, attacked abuses they saw coming from a venal, self-interested group of landowners and politicians. Dissidents pushed to extend the franchise and reform the House of Commons—the radicals arguing for universal manhood suffrage, the moderates for reduced property restrictions on those allowed to vote. They taught Fanny that others shared her disbelief in a Providence that decreed human suffering. With Robert Owen, they taught her to hope that society could be changed.

But by 1816 it was clear that the men who ruled England thought modest change revolutionary. For four years Major John Cartwright had been touring England and Scotland trying to "divert insurrectionary discontent into constitutional forms, and to lay the basis of a nation-wide movement continually petitioning Parliament." But the authorities were frightened and quartered soldiers all over the country. In the fall of 1816 three reform meetings held just outside London were disrupted. In January 1817 a convention Cartwright himself had called in London ended in rioting. The political crisis coincided with extreme economic distress, unemployment in the textile and iron districts, and soaring prices. The Prince Regent was mobbed in the London streets and his carriage window broken. The government suspended habeas corpus and reenacted an arsenal of repressive laws. Later in the year, thirty-five men who had been part of an abortive insurrection were arraigned for high treason, and four were

condemned to die. A man executed for high treason was hanged, cut down before he was dead, and his entrails were cut out and burned in front of him. He was then beheaded and his head was brandished on a spike for the crowd's benefit. These outrages were enough for Fanny. In the summer of 1818 she and Camilla decided to go to America.[53]

Fanny wanted to see if life in a republic was as promising as it seemed, but she made her decision for other reasons as well. It was one step further in her rejection of the comfortable role that women of her class were expected to play. She decided apparently at the same time to write Robina Millar a series of letters from America that would serve as the basis for a book. When she and Camilla spent ten weeks that summer with the two Cullen sisters in the north of England, no doubt the four women talked of how Fanny should approach her task.

The act of writing would not itself violate the decorum expected of ladies: Fanny's poems and plays had been her apprentice work and won her a measure of the attention she craved. It was her choice of America that stretched the bounds of propriety. But America offered a subject on which she could try her powers, and a chance to catch the public ear by using a tone quite different from the carping and contempt she found in most British writing on the topic.

Notes

[1] George Jacob Holyoake, *The History of Co-operation* (London: T. F. Unwin, 1908), I, 240-241.

[2] [Frances Wright (FW)] to Mary Wollstonecraft Shelley, 20 March 1828, *The Life and Letters of Mary Wollstonecraft Shelley,* ed. Mrs. Julian Marshall (1889; reprint New York: Haskell House, 1970), II, 180.

[3] FW, "Explanatory Notes on Nashoba," *New Harmony Gazette,* 30 Jan., 6 and 13 Feb. 1828.

[4] FW, *England the Civilizer: Her History Developed in Its Principles* (London, 1848), pp. 13, 22.

[5] Lafayette to Jeremy Bentham, 10 Nov. 1828, *Works of Jeremy Bentham,* ed. John Bowring (Edinburgh, 1843), XI, 4-5; Horace Traubel, *With Walt Whitman in Camden* (New York: Appleton, 1908), II, 205, 499.

[6] *New York Commercial Advertiser,* 12 Jan. 1829; Catharine E. Beecher, *Letters on the Difficulties of Religion* (Hartford, 1836), p. 23.

[7] George Eliot, *Middlemarch* (London: J. M. Dent, 1959), I, xiii.

[8] J. C. L. de Sismondi to [Julia Garnett (JG)], 9 Sept. 1827, [Garnett Letters, Houghton Library, Harvard University (G Letters)].

[9] *Gentleman's Magazine* 68 (March 1798): 259; *Scots Magazine* 60 (May 1798): 364. See also *Biography, Notes, and Political Letters of Frances Wright D'Arusmont* (1844), reprinted in FW, *Life, Letters and Lectures, 1834-1844* (New York: Arno Press, 1972).

[10] Camilla Campbell Wright to James Wright, Jr., 11 April 1796, Theresa Wolfson Papers, Martin P. Catherwood Library, Cornell University; George Edward Cokayne, *The Complete Peerage* (London: St. Catherine Press, 1949), XI, 70-71; John Busse, *Mrs. Montagu: Queen of the Blues* (1928; reprint Folcroft, Pa.: Folcroft Library Editions, 1977), p. 4; Elizabeth Montagu, "An Essay on the Writings and Genius of Shakespear, Compared with the Greek and French Dramatic Poets" (New York: Augustus M. Kelley, 1970); Elizabeth Robinson Montagu to unknown addressee, 1791 (#11 MS. 392S), National Library of Scotland. The Theresa Wolfson Papers at Cornell include voluminous notes made by Alice Perkins early in the twentieth century from diaries, letters, and manuscripts in a trunk then owned by Fanny's grandson, the Reverend William Norman Guthrie. The trunk has since disappeared. Letters cited here in the Theresa Wolfson Papers rarely refer to original manuscript material, but rather to Perkins' notes.

[11] James Wright, Jr., to John Pinkerton, 14 Aug. 1795, Pinkerton Papers, National Library of Scotland.

[12] *The Reasoner* 7 (Nov. 1849): 325; FW, *Biography*, p. 6.

[13] The property James Wright, Jr., inherited from his father, Alexander Wright, was eventually transferred to his uncle, James Wright, Sr., to satisfy his creditors. General Register of Sasines, #RS 3/2286/12-23, Scottish Record Office.

[14] In her autobiography Fanny wrote: "Her brother passed his boyhood under the charge of his grand-uncle, Professor Mylne," adding that her "infant sister remained some years at nurse in the neighborhood of her native town." FW, *Biography*, pp. 8-9; Alice Perkins and Theresa Wolfson, however, wrote: "The boy Richard . . . was placed with the family of Watson cousins, children of Duncan Campbell's elder sister . . . The two little girls, however, were taken at once to England." *Frances Wright Free Enquirer: The Study of a Temperament* (New York: Harper Bros., 1939), p. 7. Because of discrepancies or mistakes such as these, I have depended on Perkins and Wolfson only when I have been unable to find other sources. Because Alice Perkins was the last to have access to Fanny Wright's trunk, however, her notes are a crucial source of information. I do not always follow her spelling, her abbreviations, or her punctuation, and in other quotations I sometimes substitute "and" for "&." Translations are not indicated.

[15] FW, *Biography*, p. 9; Richard Wright to Miss Watson, 3 June 1809, W Papers.

[16] Joel Brown, unpub. memoir of FW, Public Library of Cincinnati and Hamilton County, pp. 19-21. The memoir is written on the backs of stationery with a letterhead dated September 1893. According to a note signed, "Alexis Brown, son of Joel Brown," the memoir was written about 1889. It therefore represents the memory of a very old man, as Joel Brown had first worked for Fanny in 1843, and he is often mistaken.

[17] See Sir Duncan Campbell, *Records of Clan Campbell in the Honourable East India Company, 1600-1858* (London: Longmans and Green, 1925), pp. 268-269; William Campbell's will, dated 30 Aug. 1803 and probated 27 May 1805, Public Record Office (PROB 11/1425), London.

[18] FW, *Biography*, p. 9.

[19] Ibid., p. 8; *Gentleman's Magazine* 79 (Nov. 1809): 1176.

[20] Richard Wright to Betsy Watson, 12 June 1809, W Papers; FW, *Biography*, p. 9; Beatrix F. Cresswell, *Dawlish—The Estuary of the Exe and Notes on Chudleigh* (Dawlish and London, 1902), p. 18.

[21] Jane Austen, *Sense and Sensibility* (London: Macmillan, 1951), p. 90.

[22] Jane Austen, *Pride and Prejudice* (London: J. M. Dent, 1954), p. 1.

[23] FW, *Biography*, p. 10.

[24] Ibid., p. 15; Austen, *Pride and Prejudice*, p. 49.

[25] Henry G. Morgan to the author, 5 Aug. 1977. I am indebted to the late Mr. Morgan, chairman of the Dawlish Museum Society, for information about Miss Campbell and her neighbors and about Dawlish during this period.

[26] W Papers.

[27] FW, *Biography*, p. 11.

[28] Ibid.

[29] Ibid.

[30] Richard Wright to Betsy Watson, 25 July 1809, W Papers.

[31] FW to Frances Campbell, 1820(?), W Papers.

[32] See James Coutts, *A History of the University of Glasgow, 1451-1909* (Glasgow: J. Maclehose, 1909); David Murray, *Memories of the Old College of Glasgow* (Glasgow: Jackson and Wylie, 1927); Douglas Sloan, *The Scottish Enlightenment and the American College Ideal* (New York: Teachers College Press, 1971).

[33] Adam Smith to Dr. William Cullen, 20 Sept. 1774, quoted in Sloan, *The Scottish Enlightenment,* p. 32.

[34] Frederick Lamb to Lady Melbourne, n.d., quoted in William C. Lehmann, *John Millar of Glasgow, 1735-1801* (Cambridge: Cambridge University Press, 1960), p. 82.

[35] Ibid., pp. 376, 387.

[36] Quoted in Murray, *Memories of Glasgow,* p. 103; James Mylne to Mr. Watson, 15 July 1815, W Papers.

[37] Elizabeth Dawson Fletcher, *The Autobiography of Mrs. Fletcher* (Boston, 1876), p. 344; [Robina Craig Millar (RCM)] to FW and [Camilla Wright (CW)] 26 July 1818, W Papers.

[38] James Mylne to Mr. Watson, 15 July 1815, RCM to FW, 4 Sept. 1816, W Papers.

[39] RCM to FW, 28 July 1817, 9 Oct. 1818, W Papers.

[40] W Papers.

[41] FW, *Biography,* p. 13

[42] FW, *A Few Days in Athens* (Boston, 1850), p. 122.

[43] Ibid., p. 40.

[44] Ibid., pp. 12, 112.

[45] Ibid., pp. 24-25.

[46] FW, 23 July 1818, "Commonplace Book," W Papers.

[47] John Prebble, *The Highland Clearances* (London: Secker and Warburg, 1963), p. 58.

[48] Ibid., pp. 63, 78, 117.

[49] Ibid., pp. 71, 109.

[50] See *The Life of Robert Owen Written by Himself* (1857; reprint London: Frank Cass, 1967); Frank Podmore, *Robert Owen: A Biography* (London: Hutchinson, 1906); G. D. H. Cole, *The Life of Robert Owen* (London: Ernest Benn, 1925); Margaret Cole, *Robert Owen of New Lanark* (London: Batchworth Press, 1953); J. F. C. Harrison, *Quest for the New Moral World: Robert Owen and the Owenites in Britain and America* (London: Routledge and Kegan Paul, 1969). For the influence of Owen on women and the feminist movement, see Barbara Taylor, *Eve and the New Jerusalem: Socialism and Feminism in the Nineteenth Century* (New York: Pantheon, 1983).

[51] Robert Owen, "Observations on the Effect of the Manufacturing System," in his *A New View of Society* (London: Everyman's Library, 1963), pp. 121-122.

[52] See Asa Briggs, *The Age of Improvement* (London: Longmans and Green, 1959); Elie Halévy, *The Liberal Awakening, 1815-1830* (London: Ernest Benn, 1949); E. P. Thompson, *The Making of the English Working Class* (London: Penguin Books, 1976).

[53] Thompson, *The Making of the English Working Class,* p. 666.

Susan S. Kissel (essay date 1993)

SOURCE: "Wright, the American Suffragists, Mill, and Whitman," in *In Common Cause: The "Conservative" Frances Trollope and the "Radical" Frances Wright,* Bowling Green State University Popular Press, 1993, pp. 94-114.

[*In the following essay, Kissel contends that Frances Wright, by generating both public opprobrium and sympathy, significantly advanced the cause of women's rights in the United States and Britain.*]

Rejected by the majority, Frances Wright's ideas nevertheless came to affect every level of American society. Those who have focused attention on her career have agreed on the paradox of her life, its electricity and color reduced to seeming paralysis and invisibility before her death. Yet her ideas would have impact on the mainstream of American culture. In 1924 William Randall Waterman concluded his study of Frances Wright with these words:

> Just how deeply she influenced American thought it is difficult to say. . . . Probably it would be safe to say that through her lectures and editorials she did much to popularize and stimulate the demand for a more liberal religion, more liberal marriage laws, the protection of the property rights of married women, a more generous system of education, and the abolition of capital punishment and of imprisonment for debt. Slavery she opposed as irrational, and an obstacle to the progress of America. . . . Perhaps Miss Wright's greatest

contribution was to the intellectual emancipation of women. A pioneer, she was scoffed at, hooted and reviled, but she showed what the feminine mind was capable of, and having blazed the way, other courageous women were not wanting to follow in her footsteps. (255-56)

While stressing that Wright's contributions were "'broader' than the single issue of equal rights for women," Waterman could attest to Wright's continuing importance in one of the most significant movements of his own period: "At a moment when the women of the United States are rapidly bringing to a successful conclusion their long struggle for equal rights a study of the life of Frances Wright seems most fitting, for Frances Wright was one of the foremost pioneers in the cause, although never a participant in the organized movement" (9).

Twenty years later, Merle Curti in *The Growth of American Thought* similarly stresses that the feminist movement in the United States "owed much to the clear logic and forceful argument by which this courageous crusader denounced the subjection of women by law and custom and pleaded for their emancipation on every level—economic, social, and cultural" (385). More recently, Eleanor Flexner in *Century of Struggle* comments on America's mistreatment of Frances Wright, asserting,

> Yet her influence was enduring. No woman in the first half of the nineteenth century who challenged tradition escaped the effect of Frances Wright's leavening thought; nor was its impact limited to women alone. The lectures which she delivered in New York, Philadelphia, Baltimore, Boston, Cincinnati, Louisville, St. Louis, and elsewhere were largely before audiences of workingmen, who also read accounts of her addresses in the active labor press of the day; they helped to feed the rising popular demand for free education. (28)

Frances Wright's ideas appeared everywhere in American society—as did unrelenting attacks against her.

Naming Frances Wright as especially offensive, the Reverend Parsons Cooke justified the prohibition against woman's speaking, explaining, "Even if it were true, that some woman in an assembly had more talents than all the men present, the excess of her talents so far from making a reason why she should display them, would make it a still stronger case of usurping authority over the man" (9-10). Despite attacks from the pulpit, Frances Wright's brilliance was attracting a growing, loyal following among all classes of women as well as of men. Margaret Fuller was one of those who took advantage of the new paths Frances Wright was opening for women, even though she wished to do so at as much distance from the embattled Frances Wright as safety seemed to require.

Already carefully educated by her father and encouraged by him to believe "girls were the intellectual equals of boys" (Rosenthal v), Margaret Fuller must have been gratified to find women such as Frances Wright embarking on public careers to proclaim the rights of women and society's other oppressed groups. Marie Urbanski—agreeing with Fuller's earlier biographer, Madeline Stern—concludes that Margaret Fuller "undoubtedly had heard of Fanny Wright . . . since [Wright] lectured in Boston in August 1829, when Fuller was living in Cambridge and the Reverend Lyman Beecher in one of his sermons on political atheism complained that females of education and refinement were among her votaries . . ." (Urbanski 63).[1] Since Wright's views were being debated everywhere she had spoken, Margaret Fuller most certainly would have been aware of the controversy surrounding the Scottish reformer's appearances and editorials.

Nevertheless, Margaret Fuller's debt to Frances Wright must be inferred from the similarity of the views she expressed in *Woman in the Nineteenth Century* (1845) when compared to the public statements of Frances Wright more than a decade earlier. As Bernard Rosenthal has suggested, *Woman in the Nineteenth Century* "did not come from a political or social vacuum" (vi). Clearly Margaret Fuller is echoing Frances Wright's views when she asserts, "improvement in the daughters will best aid in the reformation of the sons of this age" (24); the American wife or mother "misses the education which should enlighten [her] influence [on her husband or children]" (72); "women are, indeed, the easy victims both of priestcraft and self-delusion; but this would not be, if the intellect was developed in proportion to the other powers" (105); and, finally, in effecting female "self-dependence, and a greater . . . fulness of being" society must "look to the young; . . . [for] action and conservation, not of old habits, but of a better nature, enlightened by hopes that daily grow brighter" (96). These words can barely be distinguished from those earlier pronouncements of Frances Wright on the same topics.

Had she lived longer, Fuller might have acknowledged the incendiary Wright's influence as she matured and became herself more and more actively involved in politics. Urbanski concludes, "Frances Wright's type of revolutionary fervor came to Margaret Fuller later in Europe as her ideas developed under the tutelage of Adam Mickiewicz and Guiseppe Mazzini" (65). Fuller's tragic death, in 1850 at the age of only 40, cut short her intellectual development and her influential career even before the elder Frances Wright's own death. We will never know if Margaret Fuller might have returned to the United States as politically committed and outspoken as she had been in Italy (immediately prior to her death) during the ferment of the Italian revolution.

In contrast, other leading women reformers of nineteenth century America went out of their way to recognize and praise Frances Wright's pioneering efforts for human rights. The first of these followers would be Ernestine Rose, the Polish-born reformer, "whose path often crossed" Frances Wright's as she petitioned and spoke for women's causes in the United States during the 1830s and 1840s (Neidle 40). Although Cecyle Neidle contends that Rose worked with Frances Wright (37), I can find no existing record of personal meetings or interchanges between them. However, Ernestine Rose openly and often expressed the bond of sympathy and respect she felt for Frances Wright.

Coming to the United States in 1836 after rejecting a marriage arranged by her father, suing him in the Polish courts for control of her inheritance (then returning it to her father after she had won her suit against him), supporting herself in Europe and in England before her marriage to the British Owenite, William Rose, Ernestine Rose already had proven her own political acumen and her commitment to women's independence at a young age. Nevertheless, she expressed gratitude for the work Frances Wright had begun in America as she followed in her footsteps to address the same issues: the injustices of slavery and child labor; the mistreatment of working people; the inadequacies of existing public education; as well as the need for married women's property rights, woman's suffrage, and more liberal divorce laws. Ernestine Rose insisted, as had Wright, that American rhetoric must parallel American legal practices. She demanded, "Carry out the republican principle of universal suffrage, or strike it from your banners and substitute 'Freedom and Power to one half of society, and Submission and Slavery to the other.' Give women the elective franchise. Let married women have the same right to property that their husbands have. . . . " (Stanton *et al.* 1: 258).

Rose often directly expressed her admiration for Frances Wright. In Waverly, New York, at a Friends of Progress social-reform convention, a woman paid tribute to Ernestine Rose by asking Rose to name her newborn baby. According to Rose's biographer, Yuri Suhl, Rose responded by publicly and permanently linking herself to her Scottish-born predecessor, declaring "'Then I name her Ernestine Frances Lyons' . . . The Frances was for Frances Wright" (121).

In 1860, at the Tenth National Woman's Rights Convention at the Cooper Institute in New York, Ernestine Rose once more commemorated Frances Wright's heroic life struggle for justice in the United States, saying

> Frances Wright was the first woman in this country who spoke on the equality of the sexes. She had indeed a hard task before her. The elements were entirely unprepared. She had to break up the time-

hardened soil of conservatism; and her reward was sure—the same reward that is always bestowed upon those who are in the vanguard of any great movement. She was subjected to public odium, slander, and persecution. But these were not the only things that she received. Oh, she had her reward!— . . . the eternal reward of knowing that she had done her duty; the reward springing from the consciousness of rights, of endeavoring to benefit unborn generations. How delightful to see the molding of the minds around you, the infusing of your thoughts and aspirations into others, until one by one they stand by your side, without knowing how they came there! That reward she had. It has been her glory, it is the glory of her memory; and the time will come when society will have outgrown its old prejudices, and stepped with one foot, at least, upon the elevated platform on which she took her position. (Stanton *et al.* 1: 692)

It was Frances Wright's example, Rose explained, which had given her strength when she campaigned for married women's property rights in New York, obtaining five signatures in five months, working on for 12 long years for final passage of the Married Women's Property Bill in the New York State legislature in 1848.[2]

Rose knew well how it felt to be ridiculed and slandered for expressing her convictions both as a contributer to the *Boston Investigator* and as a tireless public speaker whose "addresses were regarded as revolutionary. At times she came close to being tarred and feathered" (Neidle 40). But Ernestine Rose wrote and spoke as passionately as had Frances Wright on behalf of the "general reconstruction of American society" (Seller 256). For both women, Yuri Suhl concludes, "woman's rights [were] part of a larger struggle for human rights" (40), part of a "new form of society, based on the social philosophy of Owenism, [which they believed] would be the ultimate solution to mankind's ills" (42).

Rose's fellow suffragist, the Quaker reformer and abolitionist, Lucretia Mott, also paid on-going tribute to Frances Wright. Whether Mott actually had a personal relationship with Wright, as Perkins and Wolfson contended in their 1939 study, *Frances Wright Free Enquirer* (363), and Judith Nies more recently suggests, as well (*Seven Women* 121), she and her husband were both familiar with Wright's work and her philosophy from the beginning of Wright's public appearances. Both husband and wife had taken a courageous stand after Wright gave early lectures in Wilmington, Delaware, on knowledge and education. When Quakers who had attended Wright's lectures were disowned, and subsequently appealed their cases at the Philadelphia Yearly Meeting, the Motts, as Lucretia wrote friends, "came close to 'losing our place' by uttering our indignant protest against their intolerance" (Bacon 38).

Lucretia Mott not only defended Frances Wright's right to speak in public (and the rights of others to listen to Wright's ideas), Mott agreed with her and helped to disseminate Wright's views both within and beyond the Quaker community—most importantly to younger women such as Elizabeth Cady Stanton and Susan B. Anthony. Kathleen Barry recounts how Susan Anthony, while a student at Deborah Moulson's seminary, "listened to [Mott] with rapt attention" while Ellen DuBois relates Mott's critical role in Elizabeth Cady Stanton's intellectual development:

> Meeting Lucretia Mott greatly accelerated Elizabeth Stanton's development as a feminist. . . . Despite [Mott's] Quakerism and her piety, Mott was familiar with and sympathetic to the traditions of secular radicalism. . . . Mott had read Wollstonecraft and Paine, knew Robert Owen the elder and, perhaps most important for Stanton's development, was acquainted with and sympathetic to the feminist ideas of Frances Wright. Mott cultivated Stanton's intellect and encouraged her feminism. She urged her to read Wollstonecraft, Wright, and the Grimkes' writings, which Stanton herself circulated in the early 1840s. (Barry 29; DuBois, *Elizabeth Cady Stanton* 11)

Mott spread Wright's views further as she spoke throughout the country.

In 1847, Mott addressed the yearly meeting of Hicksite Friends in Ohio, arguing for women's political equality and the need for comparable education for women (Melder 126). In 1848, she and Stanton organized the Seneca Falls Women's Rights Convention to put forth a series of resolutions, including woman's right to speak in public, her right to vote, her right to participate equally with men in the world, and her right to enter into occupations of all varieties (Melder 145-47). At the Rochester Women's Rights Convention in 1848, having elaborated on the plight of seamstresses and working women, Lucretia Mott noted that the oppressed, black or white, must demand their freedom. She advised her female audience no longer to be duped by "the flattery typically used to deceive women."[3] The following year, 1849, Mott defended the expansion of woman's role in a major speech in Philadelphia. After Frances Wright's death, Lucretia Mott lamented America's neglect of Wright's ideas, as of those of Robert Owen and Mary Wollstonecraft. Mott looked to the day when all three, Wright, Wollstonecraft, and Owen, would "have justice done them, and the denunciations of bigoted sectarianism [would] fall into merited contempt" (Hallowell 357).

With the elder suffragists, Lucretia Mott and Ernestine Rose, so insistent on Wright's importance to American society's political development, and so respectful of her personal courage and wisdom, it is little wonder,

then, to find Susan B. Anthony and Elizabeth Cady Stanton commemorating Frances Wright throughout their careers. Along with Matilda Joslyn Gage, editors Stanton and Anthony made Wright's picture the frontispiece for their massive *History of Woman Suffrage* (1881) and wrote this dedication:

> These volumes are Affectionately Inscribed to The Memory of Mary Wollstonecraft, Frances Wright, Lucretia Mott, Harriet Martineau, Lydia Maria Child, Margaret Fuller, Sarah and Angela Grimke, Josephine S. Griffing, Martha C. Wright, Harriot K. Hunt, M.D., Marianna W. Johnson, Alice and Phebe Carey, Ann Preston, M.D., Paulina Wright Davis, Whose Earnest Lives and Fearless Words, in Demanding Political Rights for Women, have been in the Preparation of these Pages, a Constant Inspiration to the Editors.

In the *History of Woman Suffrage,* the editors "identified three precipitating factors [for the Seneca Falls Convention of 1848]: the radical ideas of Wright and Rose on religion and democracy; the initial reforms in women's property law in the 1830s and 1840s; and . . . women's experiences in the antislavery movement" (DuBois, *Elizabeth Cady Stanton* 8-9). They honored Frances Wright's contributions to women's causes, and to the advancement of American women in the field of journalism through her editorship of the *Free Enquirer,* "the first periodical established in the United States for the purpose of fearless and unbiased inquiry on all subjects" (Stanton *et al.* 1: 44-45). Wright's "able lectures . . . on political, religious, and social questions" they deemed vital to the growth of American thought—with Ernestine Rose following "to deepen and perpetuate the impression Frances Wright had made on the minds of unprejudiced hearers" (Stanton *et al.* 1: 51).

The editors of the *History of Woman Suffrage* further decried the way Wright's reputation had been degraded and her character attacked throughout her lifetime. They tried to reinterpret Frances Wright for the American public, concluding that Wright was

> a person of extraordinary powers of mind, . . . the first woman who gave lectures on political subjects in America. . . . . Her ideas on theology, slavery and the social degradation of woman, now generally accepted by the best minds of the age, were then denounced by both press and pulpit, and maintained by her at the risk of her life. Although the Government of the United States was framed on the basis of entire separation of Church and State, yet from an early day the theological spirit had striven to unite the two, in order to strengthen the Church by its union with the civil power. . . . The clergy at once became her most bitter opponents . . . though her work was of vital importance to the country and under-taken from the purest philanthropy. (1: 35-36)

Stanton and Anthony shared concern with Frances Wright's causes and an empathy created by their own experiences for the way Wright had been publicly degraded.

In their *History,* Stanton, Anthony, and Gage also included a long, commemorative speech on Frances Wright given by Chair Paulina W. Davis at the twentieth anniversary Woman's Rights Convention in Apollo Hall, New York. Recounting Wright's political career, Davis celebrated "this heroic woman," reminding her audience that "[Wright] pitied and endured the scoffs and jeers of the multitude and fearlessly continued to utter her rebukes against oppression, ignorance and bigotry. Women joined in the hue and cry against her, little thinking that men were building the gallows and making them the executioners. Women have crucified in all ages the redeemers of their own sex, and men mocked them with the fact" (Stanton *et al., History* 1: 430). Similarly, Elizabeth Cady Stanton had recalled Frances Wright's career when writing Lucretia Mott about the debate over Victoria Woodhull's morality,

> We have had women enough sacrificed to this sentimental, hypocritical prating about purity. This is one of man's most effective engines for our division and subjugation. He creates the public sentiment, builds the gallows, and then makes us hangmen for our own sex. Women have crucified the Mary Wollstonecrafts, the Fanny Wrights, the George Sands, the Fanny Kembles, the Lucretia Motts of all ages, and now men mock us with the fact, and say we are ever cruel to each other. Let us end this ignoble record and henceforth stand by womanhood. (Lutz 218)

Again Susan B. Anthony defended Wright in May 1860, at the New York City Women's Rights meeting at the Cooper Institute, demanding to know, "who of our literary women . . . has yet ventured one word of praise or recognition of the heroic enunciators of the great idea of woman's equality—of Mary Wollstonecraft, Frances Wright, Ernestine L. Rose, Lucretia Mott, Elizabeth Cady Stanton?" (Suhl 138). Attempting to remove the stains from Frances Wright's reputation, Stanton and Anthony revived both her memory and her ideas in American political thought.

Keeping Frances Wright's picture on the wall of her study, Susan B. Anthony read Wright's *A Few Days in Athens* in 1855 and published articles on Wright and Wright's writings in *The Revolution.*[4] Continuing in the tradition of Frances Wright's *Free Enquirer,* Stanton and Anthony—along with fellow editor of *The Revolution,* Parker Pillsbury—addressed numerous ills of American society. They "wrote and reprinted articles on prostitution, infanticide, the need for sex education, cooperative housekeeping, and the monogamous practices of Oneida communitarians and Utah Mormons. They published the writings of Frances

Wright and Mary Wollstonecraft and discovered a feminist heritage that was many centuries old" (DuBois, *Feminism* 104). In 1868 in *The Revolution* they argued for "educated suffrage, irrespective of sex or color, equal pay for equal work, eight hours labor, abolition of standing armies and party despotisms." They cried, "Down with the Politicians—Up with the People" (Burnett 170).

In addition to Stanton's editorials on women's rights topics, *The Revolution* "pioneered fearlessly . . . as it pointed out labor's valuable contribution to the development of the country. It also called attention to the vicious contrasts in large cities, where many lived in tumble-down tenements in abject poverty while the few, with more wealth than they knew what to do with, spent lavishly and built themselves palaces . . . The Chicago *Workingman's Advocate* observed, 'We have no doubt [*The Revolution*] will prove an able ally of the labor reform movement'" (Lutz, *Susan B. Anthony* 142-43). The progressive causes espoused by *The Revolution* from 1868 to 1870 were, for the most part, ones that Frances Wright had spearheaded several decades earlier on behalf of working men and women, blacks, the impoverished, the disenfranchised, uneducated, and mistreated throughout the United States.

As Susan B. Anthony and Elizabeth Cady Stanton grew older, they became as politically and philosophically at odds with American culture as Frances Wright had been. This was particularly true of Stanton. When Dr. W. W. Patton of Howard University in 1885 preached in Washington's Congregational Church on the topic of "Woman and Skepticism," warning that "freedom for woman led to skepticism and immorality, he illustrated his position by pointing to Hypatia, Mary Wollstonecraft, Frances Wright, George Eliot" and others; it was said that

> at the close of the sermon [Anthony and Stanton] went directly up to Dr. Patton to remonstrate with him. "Doctor," ejaculated Susan with cutting bluntness, "Your mother, if you have one, should lay you across her knee and give you a good spanking for that sermon." (Stanton, *Eighty Years* 382)

> "Oh no," interposed Elizabeth . . . "allow me to congratulate you. I have been trying for years to make women understand that the worst enemy they have is in the pulpit, and you have illustrated the truth of it." (Lutz, *Created Equal* 274)

Stanton followed Frances Wright in battling the American clergy throughout her life.

Stanton's *Woman's Bible,* published in 1898 when she was 80, no doubt was an inevitable outgrowth of her disagreement with institutionalized Christianity in the

United States and her early sympathy with the anti-clerical humanism of Frances Wright. With the publication of the *Woman's Bible,* Stanton

> was repudiated by the very organization she had helped to found. In her efforts to challenge religious teachings, which relentlessly preached women's inferiority, she stirred up the clergy, caused libraries to refuse to circulate the book, and fostered a storm of criticism in various newspapers. (Nies 91)

Stanton came to know the same kinds of attacks from clergy as those made against Frances Wright, yet, unlike Wright, Stanton had the comfort of Wright's pioneering efforts in America to help strengthen her resolve, as well as a long life in which, as she comments in her autobiography, she witnessed one "mistake" after another become recognized as "a step in progress." At 80 and "still considered a dangerous radical," Stanton felt she had gained

> confidence in my judgment and patience with the opposition of my coadjutors, with whom on so many points I disagree. It requires no courage now to demand the right of suffrage, temperance legislation, liberal divorce laws, or for women to fill church offices—these battles have been fought and won. But it still requires courage to question the divine inspiration of the Hebrew Writings as to the position of woman. Why should the myths, fables, and allegories of the Hebrews be held more sacred than those of the Assyrians and Egyptians from whose literature most of them were derived? Seeing that the religious superstitions of women perpetuate their bondage more than all other adverse influences, I feel impelled to reiterate my demands for justice, liberty and equality in the Church as well as in the State. (*Eighty Years and More* 467-68)

Stanton's adamant stance against institutionalized Christianity in the United States became as unacceptable as had Frances Wright's.

In fact, in her last decade of life, Elizabeth Cady Stanton would advance her attacks on many American institutions. She "began to study socialism" to redress the labor issues which had arisen in America in the latter part of the nineteenth century. She warned, "although we forget and neglect [the masses'] interests and our duties, we do it at the peril of all . . . there must be a radical change in the relations of capital and labor" (Nies 91). In 1894, writing about the railroad strikes in Chicago, she announced, "My sympathies are with [Debs and his strikers]" (Nies 91) and, three years before her death, she wrote in 1898 in the *New York Journal,*

> We have a higher duty than the demand for suffrage. . . . We see that the right of suffrage avails nothing for the masses in competition with the wealthy classes, and, worse still, with each other. . . . Agitation of the broader question of philosophical socialism is now in order. (Nies 62)

For Elizabeth Cady Stanton, as for Susan B. Anthony, Lucretia Mott, Ernestine Rose, and Frances Wright, women's rights were seen as part of a larger social picture. All envisioned a more compassionate, feminized, and "generous" society—and had lectured throughout the United States and written in numerous publications to achieve that end.

Frances Wright's ideas were viewed with equal sympathy in England by one of the leading social theorists of the nineteenth century. It was not so much that John Stuart Mill had been influenced by Frances Wright as that both had, in their youth, been influenced by the same individuals. Mill first had become acquainted with Wright when she was entertained in his home, along with his parents' fellow guests, Jeremy Bentham and Joseph Hume (Eckhardt, *Fanny Wright* 63). Mill at the time was studying with his father under an intensive curriculum designed by Jeremy Bentham—while Wright, then in her early twenties, had become Bentham's disciple for several years following the publication of her *Views of Society and Manners in America.* In addition, both Frances Wright and John Stuart Mill would come to know well the person and philosophy of the elder Robert Owen.

From Bentham and Owen, Frances Wright and John Stuart Mill would learn a philosophy of social reform—that society's ills could, and should, be addressed through political and institutional change. As with Wright, Mill too would develop an early, messianic ambition—as Mill expressed it, "to be a reformer of the world" (Stillinger 112). To this end, Wright and Mill both dedicated their lives, attempting to improve human society and human life through their efforts, the former in America and the latter in Britain, primarily. As F. W. Garforth writes of Mill,

> His dominant purpose was clearly "the improvement of mankind," and if Mill may be said to have had *an* educational aim inclusive of all others, this was it. In one phrasing or another the idea of human improvement, of human well-being in its widest possible extension, occurs repeatedly in his writings. (*Educative Democracy* 2)

As we have seen, the same was true of Frances Wright. Buoyed up by a shared faith in human progress, by the promise of science, and by the seeming mutability (and improveability) both of individuals and of governments, Wright and Mill continued throughout their lives to believe in the principles learned in their youths. As we have already seen with Wright, and as F. W. Garforth says of Mill, "Later in life, after the disappointment of his early enthusiasms, he came to accept that the improvement must be gradual; but that it is possible he never doubted" (*Theory of Education* 36; *Educative Democracy* 97).

It is little wonder, then, as George Jacob Holyoake reported, that John Stuart Mill "held [Frances Wright] in regard as one of the most important women of her day, and pointed this out to the present writer on her last visit to England" (380). The similarity of their writings and their views reflects a common philosophy and common influences. Mill, however, would never know the humiliation and degradation experienced by Frances Wright in America. He could argue, as had she, for a socialist society and, in "The Utility of Religion," for a "religion of humanity" to replace Christianity, without inviting assaults on his person or on his character (Garforth, *Educative Democracy* 2). Mill had been born into his father's challenging circle of prestigious philosophers and associates—and would continue to be recognized as a leading figure in Britain's intellectual history, one of the

> few Englishmen who have given themselves so un-reservedly . . . to the task of improving the intellectual, moral, political, economic, and cultural life of his own country, especially among the "labouring classes." (Garforth, *Educative Democracy* 3)

Wright would not enjoy such continuing veneration and historical prominence in either the Britain she had fled or the America she embraced.

In addition to sharing with Frances Wright continuous efforts to improve the lives of the working classes, Mill agreed with her in opposing slavery and capital punishment, promoting birth control, advancing the rights of women, and repudiating the social and legal inequities of traditional marriage (although Mill favored reforming marriage, not—as with Wright—abandoning it—agreeing with her, however, on the need for more liberal divorce laws). In each case a dedication to education acted as a common thread binding together many of their social reform efforts.

Mill and Wright both believed that, as Garforth says of Mill, "people must be educated into democracy . . . as an on-going process which continually expands and enriches the possibilities of their communal experience" (*Educative Democracy* 52). While more concerned from the outset about the effects of democracy than Wright, the need "to protect against [democracy's] dangers—mediocrity, the commercial spirit, and the diminution of individuality"—Mill nevertheless argued in *On Liberty* (as had Wright in speeches given in the United States) for institutionalizing

> the peculiar training of a citizen, the practical part of the political education of a free people, taking them out of the narrow circle of personal

and family selfishness and accustoming them to the comprehension of joint interests, the management of joint concerns . . . which unite instead of isolating them from one another. (Garforth, *Educative Democracy* 52; Mill, *On Liberty* 134)

This was, of course, as both Mill and Wright understood, particularly necessary for women.

In a speech on female suffrage given in 1867, more than a decade after Frances Wright's death, Mill echoes the earlier reformer's American speeches, arguing.

> We continually hear that the most important part of national education is that of mothers, because they educate the future men. Is this importance really attached to it? Are there many fathers who care as much, or are willing to expend as much for the education of their daughters as of their sons? Where are the Universities, where the high schools, or the schools of any description, for them? If it be said that girls are better educated at home, where are the training-schools for governesses? (Garforth, *Educative Democracy* 130).

In "The Enfranchisement of Women" (1851) and *The Subjection of Women* (1869) Mill would also urge improved education for women.

> pointing to the injustice of socially approved male domination; to the moral influence of women both in the family—wives on husbands, mothers on children—and in society at large; to the competitive stimulus educated women would exercise on men; to the need for a greater national reserve of intellectual power; to the degradation of the marriage relationship by the existing inequality between man and wife; to the enormous gain in personal happiness and liberation of potential that would come from offering women equality of opportunity with men. (Garforth, *Educative Democrary* 132)

Wright had made these same arguments on behalf of education for women in speeches throughout the United States in the 1820s and 1830s. While Harriet Taylor has taken the blame for many of her husband's advanced views on women's rights, it is clear that many of these ideas had already been implanted in Mill, as in Wright, early on through the influence of Robert Owen and of Jeremy Bentham.

Mill's personal courage in his relationship with Harriet Taylor would prove his one area of public vulnerability during a long and much-respected career. Drawing up an agreement with Harriet Taylor prior to their marriage in 1851, he "put on record a formal protest against the existing law of marriage . . . and [gave] a solemn promise never in any case or under any circumstances to use [the legal powers marriage conferred upon the male over the female]." Further, he made clear his views that his future wife should have "the same absolute freedom of action and freedom of disposal of herself and of all that does or may at any time belong to her, as if no such marriage had taken place" (*Letters of John Stuart Mill* 58). (Frances Wright, of course, had not been granted such freedom in her own marriage.)

While Phyllis Rose in *Parallel Lives: Five Victorian Marriages* perpetuates the myth of Mill's subjugation to his wife (positing Mill's need to subordinate himself to a stronger personality, found first in his father and then in Harriet Taylor), Rose explains well the difficulty Mill was confronting:

> The Mills were embarked upon a great experiment, something new in the history of relations between men and women—a true marriage of equals. But so unusual was the situation that for Harriet to be anywhere near equal she had to be "more than equal." . . .

> Mill intended both the fact and the written portrait of their friendship—and later of their marriage— to be an *acte provocateur*. However, in attempting to perform a revolutionary act, setting up woman as ruler, he was tracing an ancient pattern more accessible to ordinary minds, the man besotted by love into yielding his rule to a woman, Hercules with a distaff, a figure of fun for centuries. What Mill saw as a daring political gesture seemed to others no more than a grievous case of uxoriousness. (136)

Mill's integrity demanded that he do more than pay lip-service to equality for women; at some cost to himself, he practiced his philosophy through his marriage to Harriet Taylor and the respect he paid her life and memory.

The Subjection of Women (1869) is Mill's lasting tribute to the philosophical and relational harmony he experienced with his wife—and his contribution to the nineteenth century's political struggle for women's rights.[5] Again, the work recalls Wright's earlier speeches and writings on similar subjects, as well as points made in her last work, **England, the Civilizer.** For instance, Mill concludes, as did Wright, that historically, "The moral education of mankind has hitherto emanated chiefly from the law of force, and is adapted almost solely to the relations which force creates" (*Subjection* 79). He rues, as did Wright, the way in which, " . . . by the mere fact of being born a male [man] is by right the superior of all and every one of an entire half of the human race. . . . What must be the effect on his character, of this lesson?" (*Subjection* 149). He asserts, "But so long as the right of the strong to power over the weak rules in the very heart of society, the attempt to make the equal rights of the weak the principle of its outward actions will always be an uphill struggle. . . . " (*Subjection*

153). Thus Mill followed Wright in calling for an end to "the legal subordination of one sex to the other— . . . wrong in itself, and now one of the chief hindrances to human improvement," advising that it "be replaced by a principle of perfect equality, admitting no power or privilege on the one side, no disability on the other" (*Subjection* 1).

Acknowledging the consequences of having divided human qualities up by gender, Mill agrees with Wright that men have become too abstract in their thinking, able to "lose sight of the legitimate purpose of speculation altogether," while "a woman seldom runs wild after an abstracton . . . her more lively interest in the present feelings of persons . . . makes her consider, first of all . . . in what manner persons will be affected by [ideas]" (*Subjection* 108-09). Therefore, Mill concludes that, "Women's thoughts are thus as useful in giving reality to those of thinking men, as men's thoughts [are] in giving width and largeness to those of women" (*Subjection* 109). Mill and Wright both believed that men and women must come together, through equal education and equal relationships, to join their strengths and work together for the betterment of society. He knew, from the personal experience of his own marriage, that "when the two persons both care for great objects, and are a help and encouragement to each other in whatever regards these . . . each can enjoy the luxury of looking up to the other, and can have alternately the pleasure of leading and of being led in the path of development" (*Subjection* 174; 177). The result of such sexual equality, Mill agreed with Wright, would be the personal betterment of individuals and the advancement of civilization.

After reading Mill's *The Subjection of Women* in 1869, Elizabeth Cady Stanton reflected:

> I lay the book down with a peace and joy I never felt before, for it is the first response from any man to show he is capable of seeing and feeling all the nice shades and degrees of woman's wrongs and the central points of her weakness and degradation. (Lutz, *Created Equal* 171-72)

She was not quite so enthusiastic about Wright's most important male sympathizer—and Mill's contemporary—Walt Whitman. Betsy Erkkila reports that, after reading in Whitman's *Leaves of Grass* (1856),

> I am stern, acrid, large, undissuadable—but I
> love you,
> I do not hurt you any more than is necessary
> for you,
> I pour the stuff to start sons and daughters fit
> for These States—I press with slow rude
> muscle,

I brace myself effectually—I listen to no
   entreaties,
I dare not withdraw till I deposit what has so
   long accumulated in me,

(241-42)

Stanton wrote in her diary in 1883, "He speaks as if
the female must be forced to the creative act apparently ignorant of the great natural fact that a healthy
woman has as much passion as a man, that she needs
nothing stronger than the law of attraction to draw her
to the male" (Erkkila 137-138).

Whitman, in fact, while ambivalent about female sexuality, never deviated from his belief in the need for a
powerful female influence on American society. So
strong were Whitman's portraits of Americans women,
so open was he in depicting their bodies (including,
at times, their erotic desires), in addition to venerat-
ing their spirits, that "by 1882 the female body of
Whitman's poems was deemed dangerous to the public morality. Not only was *Leaves of Grass* banned in
Boston, but those who attempted to publish his offending poems were persecuted" (Erkkila 310).[6] In
spite of these attacks on Whitman's portraits of women
(his love poems to men ironically passed unnoticed),
"women readers loved him and defended him passionately in letters and reviews . . . [he had beck-
oned] women readers out of domestic confinement
toward an open road of equality and comradeship with
men. To Eliza Farnham in her study *Woman and Her
Era* (1864), Whitman was one of the pioneering feminists of his age. . . . " (Erkkila 311, 315).

Frances Wright's influence on Whitman's view of
women, as well as on his understanding of religion,
history, and society, cannot be overestimated. She
was, as he told Horace Traubel, one of the three
individuals (Elias Hicks and Thomas Paine being
the other two) who were "the superber characters
of my day or America's early days" (Traubel 2:
206), individuals he desired to remember and com-
memorate in his writing. While there are those who
contend that Frances Wright was less formative than
Whitman himself believed,[7] the evidence seems very
much to the contrary. Whitman, of course, would
tell Horace Traubel that *A Few Days in Athens,*
Frances Wright's "book about Epicurus was daily food
to me" as he was growing up—reading, as well, her
editorials in the *Free Enquirer* to which his father subscribed (Traubel 2: 445). Still later, as a young journalist in New York attending Wright's lectures in
Tammany Hall, he "read over and over again [Wright's]
little Socratic dialogue"; once more, as late as " . . . the
spring of 1851, [when his] friends invited him to lecture at the newly formed Brooklyn Art Union, on
Fuller Street . . . [he spoke about] the reading [he]
was doing at the time: Emerson's *Nature* and 'Divinity School Address,' Carlyle's *Sartor Resartus,*

Epictetus, Frances Wright's *A Few Days in Athens*"
(Asselineau, 45-46; Zewig 128). From his youth on
into his thirties, Whitman tells us that he had continued to read and reread *A Few Days in Athens.* It is
not surprising, then, that, as David Goodale revealed
in 1938, Whitman had been so influenced by Wright's
A Few Days in Athens that he echoed many of its
words and phrases, especially in his poem "Pictures."[8]

More important than Whitman's direct quotes and
paraphrasings of *A Few Days in Athens,* however,
are Whitman's other borrowings from Wright's work.
Gay Wilson Allen explains that Metrodorus's lesson
about the eternity of all things in *A Few Days in
Athens* became central to Whitman's concept of
Leaves of Grass. Other teachings in *A Few Days in
Athens*—about the need for harmony between the
body and the soul, as about the naturalness of death—
also had a formative influence on Whitman's thinking (Allen, *The Solitary Singer* 139-40).[9] Whitman
incorporates into "Song of Myself" the respect for
all forms of life Frances Wright had expressed in *A
Few Days in Athens,* the sense "that everything that
exists is equally wonderful." Similarly, he follows
Wright in expressing his loathing for theologies which
inculcate fear and guilt instead of self-love and love
of humanity in their followers (Allen, *Reader's Guide*
22; 21).[10] In addition, as Henry Seidel Canby speculates, Whitman absorbed from *A Few Days in Athens* a desire "to appear an Epicurus of his own times,
since, like Epicurus, he believed virtue could be
learned through pleasure, and that life was to be lived,
not shrunk from" (Canby 160). Certainly, Whitman
would succeed in embodying for and advocating to
the nineteenth century American public Epicurus's
message of sensuality and pleasure in living.

In the person of Frances Wright herself, as well as
that of her character Epicurus in *A Few Days in
Athens,* Walt Whitman found much to emulate. As
Newton Arvin explains, in the 1830s Whitman "had
gone repeatedly to her public lectures and received
from them a profoundly personal and intellectual
impression which nothing was ever to efface . . ."
(Arvin 163). David Goodale theorized in 1938 that
"it may well have been that Whitman's admiration
for Frances Wright as a lecturer motivated his own
early ambition to become a public speaker" (Goodale
207), a desire he continued to hold as late as 1879,
when, "after his lecture on Lincoln in New York
City . . . he wrote in his diary: 'I intend to go up and
down the land (in moderation,) seeking whom I may
devour with lectures'" (Goodale 207). As a young
man, he had been "devoured" by Frances Wright's
rhetoric, gaining from her a sense of the power of
words, the power of ideas, the power of one individual to move audiences. He no doubt drew on his
memories of Frances Wright when he pictured "the
orator advancing . . . ascend[ing] the platform, silent,

rapid, stern, almost fierce—and deliver[ing] an oration of liberty—up-braiding, full of invective—with enthusiasm" (Furness 74).

David Goodale compares Frances Wright's picture of the orator in *Views of Society and Manners in America* with Whitman's poem about oratory, showing the similarities of word choice and concepts between the two works (207). Whitman evokes "the orator's joys":

> To inflate the chest, to roll the thunder of the
>   voice out from the ribs and throat,
> To make the people rage, weep, hate, desire,
>   with yourself, . . .
> To speak with a full and sonorous voice out
>   of a broad chest . . .

>   (Holloway, *Leaves* 152-53)

while Frances Wright recommended that successful orators evince:

> animation, energy, high moral feeling, ardent patriotism, a sublime love of liberty, a rapid flow of ideas and of language, a happy vein of irony, an action at once vehement and dignified, and a voice full, sonorous, distinct, and flexible; exquisitely adapted to all the varieties of passion or argument. (*Views of Society* 374)

Frances Wright's words about public speaking, as well her example as a lecturer, had moved Whitman to imitate her very phrases as well as many of her ideas and goals.

In the persona of his poems, as Betsy Erkkila points out, Whitman would continue to emulate the orator, seeking "to project the sense of personal presence and magnetism he admired in such orators as Elias Hicks and George Fox . . . the egalitarian and millennial language . . . the rhetorical tinges of the proletarian, anticapitalist appeals of Frances Wright and William Leggett" (4; 48). His sense of mission, to move his readers to action, was that of the orator. Whitman insisted

> on the reader's creative role . . . [as] part of his revolutionary strategy, his attempt to collapse the traditionally authoritarian relation between poet and audience, text and reader by transferring the ultimate power of creation to the reader. "A great poem is no finish to a man or woman but rather a beginning," he said in the 1855 preface [of *Leaves of Grass*]. . . . "The touch of [the great poet] tells in action." (Erkkila 91)

To move his audience to action, Whitman created a sense of personal self for the reader, not only through placing pictures of himself as the democratic poet at the beginning of successive editions of *Leaves of Grass,* but also, as David Simpson argues, by

turn[ing] writing into speech, the absent into the present . . . [through] the vocatic markers and incantory rhythms of the text, which thus seeks constantly to express itself as voice. . . . Everything possible is done to create . . . a sense of the incarnate presence of the poet's voice and body. (179)

Whitman's rhetorical rhythms, David Goodale argues, bear witness to Frances Wright as a source of "his characteristic poetic idiom" (213).

Most importantly, it can be shown that Frances Wright profoundly influenced Whitman's ideas, from his earliest writings to his last. If, as David Goodale contends, "clues to the secret of Whitman's prose style and his early ideas of reform, especially in such of his writings as 'The Eighteenth Presidency' may be found in Frances Wright's political writings" (207), these same signifiers remain in evidence throughout Whitman's life works. His "vision of a harmonious society of artisans, farmers, and laborers owning homesteads in fee simple, his association of virtue with the laboring classes, and his emphasis on the interactive values of independence and cooperation, freedom and community," had been Frances Wright's before him, conveyed to Whitman in his youth through her *Free Enquirer* editorials, her speeches to New York workers in the 1830s, and her prose writings (from *Views of Society and Manners in America* and *A Few Days in Athens,* to her final *England, the Civilizer*) (Erkkila 27).

As editor of the *Aurora* (a New York penny paper for workers) in the early 1840s, as editor of the *Brooklyn Daily Eagle* (1846-48), and as author of his early "proletarian" tales, as well as of later works of prose and poetry, Whitman continued to emphasize recurring themes inculcated in him by Frances Wright:

> reform in the relation of labor and capital, urging improvements in the factory system, wages, working conditions, and the treatment of women laborers. He agitated against the slave trade and the extension of slavery. He urged reforms in education and the prison system, and he spoke out against corporal punishment and capital punishment. (Erkkila 27-32; 34)

In the final passages of "Song of Myself," Whitman voiced once more his ongoing sympathy with working-class people, with those on "a plain public road" (Cowley, *Leaves* 80), battling injustices, expressing his democratic feeling for the

> Many sweating and ploughing and thrashing,
>   and then the chaff for payment receiving,
> A few idly owning, and they the wheat
>   continually claiming.

>   (Cowley, *Leaves* 73)

While as disillusioned by the events of his lifetime as Frances Wright came to be in her final years, Walt Whitman would continue to share Wright's persistent, republican dream, expressing in *Democratic Vistas* his hope for a post-Civil War America which would learn to balance "self-interest with social love, matter with spirit, science with religion, money with soul" (Erkkila 254). Betsy Erkkila argues that Whitman divorced himself from the individualism Emerson and Thoreau advocated, offering instead "a form of freedom that exists not in an isolated self or a romanticized state of nature but in relation to others . . . he was moving closer to the socialist concept of the individual finding her or his greatest freedom within a political community" (255). In other words, Whitman had kept alive in himself, and alive in his readers, Frances Wright's belief in the union of the individual with the community, the selfish with the generous human principle, the male with the female, a dream of a cooperative community, through his "grammar of reconciliation and union [in response] to a world of rupture and dislocation" (Erkkila 11). He maintained this dream to the last, as had Frances Wright in *England, the Civilizer.*

In expressing his vision, Whitman felt that he must transcend the restrictions of gender. As Justin Kaplan explains, "The 'I' of *Leaves of Grass* is almost as often a woman as a man, and the book is a supremely passionate argument for the androgynous union of strength and tenderness, sagicity and impulse" (63). Whitman had always "accept[ed] . . . genuine intellectuality in women"—in Frances Wright, George Sand, and Margaret Fuller, among others (Killingsworth 246-47). And Whitman had always celebrated women's strengths, as Frances Wright had done before him. David Goodale shows that Frances Wright, in *Views of Society and Manners in America,* advocated the teaching of American women (in words that Whitman would later echo), saying that they needed "in early youth to excel in the race, to hit a mark, to swim, and, in short, to use every exercise which would impart vigour to their frames and independence to their minds" (317). Whitman would turn Wright's hopes for American women into their accomplishments, praising them because, he said,

> They know how to swim, row, ride, wrestle,
>   shoot, run,
> strike, retreat, advance, resist, defend
> themselves.
>
>   (Holloway, *Leaves* 87)

Whitman did more, however, than simply sing the praises of American women, advocate their causes, and promote both a public and a political role for them. He insisted, more and more, on the need for

what his culture had defined as "female" values to predominate in society and in individuals.

Having insisted always on the equality of women, Whitman would come in the last part of his career to desire the supremacy of their traditional virtues over those of men. Betsy Erkkila explains that, "As America during the [Civil] war moved toward the traditionally masculine polarity of militarism, violence, and aggression, Whitman in his person and his writing moved toward the traditionally feminine polarity of nurturance, compassion, and love" (199). Having nursed the dying and wounded of both the North and the South, the black and white races, during the Civil War, Whitman subsequently, in *Democratic Vistas* and in his late poetry, "sought to remove motherhood from the private sphere and release the values of nurturance, love, generativity, and community into the culture at large" (Erkkila 259). Whitman's "democratic mother . . . came to symbolize the creative and democratizing force of history itself," Erkkila contends, a cultural pattern he sought to strengthen in order to counteract the "corporate, centralized, male-identified model of power" he saw threatening not only the future of America but humanity's future—the future of the world (262). Throughout his career, as a lecturer, editor, prose writer, and poet, Whitman heeded the early lessons he learned from reading and listening to Frances Wright. As his fear for the future increased, he became even more adamant in "challeng[ing] a political economy based on the separation of female and male, private and public, home and world, by placing the values of community, equality, creation, and love at the center rather than at the margins of democratic culture" (Erkkila 316).

Whitman never found any vision of society more moving or more just than the one Frances Wright had inspired in him as a young man. She had moved him to passion, called forth his idealism, and, most certainly, strengthened in him an individual sense of self-worth and personal creativity. In his seventies, he would continue to speak of the "majesty" of her character with awe and respect (Traubel 2: 499), for she had helped to give him passion, hope, a sense of career, and personal resolve to inspire in others the wonder and vision he had come to know through her. For Whitman, as for the American suffragists—Ernestine Rose, Lucretia Mott, Susan B. Anthony, and Elizabeth Cady Stanton—Frances Wright would be remembered always as a model and an inspiration. They agreed with John Stuart Mill's assessment of her. For each of these historic individuals, Frances Wright would remain one of the most important women of her era—a personal guide as well as a shaper of Anglo-American culture.

Notes

[1] See also Madeline B. Stern, *The Life of Margaret Fuller* (New York: E. P. Dutton and Co., Inc., 1942).

[2] See Cecyle S. Neidle, *America's Immigrant Women* (Boston: Twayne Publ., 1975) 37-9; Yuri Suhl, *Eloquent Crusader: Ernestine Rose* (New York: Julian Messner, 1970) 139.

[3] See Lucretia Mott, *Discourse on Woman, Delivered at the Assembly Building,* Dec. 17, 1849 (Philadelphia, 1850), 21, qtd. in Keith E. Melder, *Beginnings of Sisterhood: The American Women's Rights Movement, 1800-1850* (New York: Schoken Books, 1977) 126; qtd. in Melder, 148.

[4] See Ida Husted Harper, *Life and Work of Susan B. Anthony,* Vol. 2, 1898 (Salem, New Hampshire: Ayer Co. Publ., Inc., 1983) 935; Alma Lutz, *Susan B. Anthony: Rebel, Crusader, Humanitarian* (Boston: Beacon, 1959) 52, 142; Ellen Carol DuBois, *Feminism and Suffrage: The Emergence of an Independent Women's Movement in America: 1848-1869* (Ithaca: Cornell P, 1978) 104.

[5] See Alice Rossi's study of the respective contributions of each partner to *The Subjection of Women* in *Essays on Sex and Equality: John Stuart Mill and Harriet Taylor Mill* (Chicago: U of Chicago P, 1970).

[6] For differing perspectives on Whitman's attitude toward female sexuality and women's roles see Harold Aspiz, *Walt Whitman and the Body Beautiful* (Urbana: U of Illinois P, 1980) 218-48; Roger Asselineau, *The Evolution of Walt Whitman: The Creation of a Book* (Cambridge, MA: The Belknap P of Harvard UP, 1962) 159-61; Myrth Jimmie Killingsworth, "Whitman and Motherhood: A Historical View" (1982), in Edwin H. Cady and Louis J. Budd, *On Whitman: The Best From American Literature* (Durham, NC: Duke UP, 1987) 245-61; Merle Curti, *Human Nature in American Thought: A History* (Madison: U of Wisconsin P, 1980) 161; and Floyd Stovall, *The Foreground of Leaves of Grass* (Charlottesville: U of Virginia P, 1974) 22.

[7] See T. R. Rajasekharaiah, *The Roots of Whitman's Grass* (Rutherford: Farleigh Dickinson UP, 1970) 31.

[8] See David Goodale, "Some of Walt Whitman's Borrowings," *American Literature,* 10 (May 1938) 202-13.

[9] See also [Betsy] Erkkila, [*Whitman the Political Poet* (New York: Oxford UP, 1989)] 18, for other of Whitman's thematic borrowings from Frances Wright.

[10] See also Asselineau, *The Evolution of Walt Whitman: The Creation of a Book* (Cambridge: The Belknap P

of Harvard UP, 1962) 45-48, for a discussion of Whitman's anticlerical views, so similar to those he heard and read in Frances Wright.

Works Cited

Allen, Gay Wilson. *A Reader's Guide to Walt Whitman.* New York: Octagon Books of Farrar, Straus and Giroux, 1981.

_____. *The Solitary Singer: A Critical Biography of Walt Whitman.* New York: The MacMillan Co., 1955.

Arvin, Newton. *Whitman.* 1938. New York: Russell and Russell, 1969.

Asselineau, Roger. *The Evolution of Walt Whitman: The Creation of a Book.* Cambridge: The Belknap P of Harvard UP, 1962.

Bacon, Margaret Hope. *Valiant Friend: The Life of Lucretia Mott.* New York: Walker and Co., 1980.

Barry, Kathleen. *Susan B. Anthony: A Biography of a Singular Feminist.* New York: New York UP, 1988.

Beecher, Lyman. *Lectures on Political Atheism.* Boston: Jewett, 1852.

Burnett, Constance Buel. *Five for Freedom.* 1953. Westport CN: Greenwood, 1976.

Canby, Henry Seidel. *Walt Whitman: An American.* Boston: Houghton Mifflin Co., 1943.

Cooke, Parsons. "Female Preaching Unlawful and Inexpedient." Lynn, MA: 1837. In *Beginnings of Sisterhood: The American Woman's Rights Movement, 1800-1850.* Keith E. Melder. New York: Schocken Books, 1977.

Curti, Merle. *The Growth of American Thought.* New York: Harper and Brothers, Publ., 1943.

DuBois, Ellen Carol, ed. *Elizabeth Cady Stanton and Susan B. Anthony: Correspondence, Writings, Speeches.* New York: Schocken Books, 1981.

Eckhardt, Celia. *Fanny Wright: Rebel in America.* Cambridge: Harvard UP, 1984.

Erkkila, Betsy. *Whitman the Political Poet.* New York and Oxford: Oxford UP, 1989.

Flexner, Eleanor. *Century of Struggle: The Women's Rights Movement in the United States,* rev. ed. Cambridge, MA: Belknap P of Harvard U, 1975.

Fuller, Margaret. *Woman in the Nineteenth Century.* (1855). New York: W.W. Norton and Co., Inc., 1971.

Furness, Clifton Joseph, ed. *Walt Whitman's Workshop.* New York: Russell and Russell, 1964.

Garforth, F. W. *Educative Democracy: John Stuart Mill on Education in Society.* Oxford UP, 1980.

_____. *John Stuart Mill's Theory of Education.* New York: Barnes and Noble, 1979.

Goodale, David. "Some of Walt Whitman's Borrowings." *American Literature.* 10 May 1938.

Hallowell, A. D., ed. *James and Lucretia Mott: Life and Letters.* Boston and New York: Houghton Mifflin and Co., 1884.

Holyoake, George Jacob. *The History of Co-operation in England: Its Literature and Its Advocates.* Vol. I. London: T. F. Unwin, 1908.

Killingsworth, Myrth J. "Whitman and Motherhood: A Historical View (1982)." In *On Whitman: The Best From American Literature.* Eds. Edwin H. Cady and Louis J. Budd. Durham, NC: Duke UP, 1987.

Lutz, Alma. *Created Equal: A Biography of Elizabeth Cady Stanton, 1815-1902.* 1940. New York: Farrar, Straus and Girouz, 1974.

_____. *Susan B. Anthony: Rebel, Crusader, Humanitarian.* Boston: Beacon, 1959.

Melder, Keith E. *Beginnings of Sisterhood: The American Women's Rights Movement, 1800-1850.* New York: Schoken Books, 1977.

Mill, John Stuart. *On Liberty.* Ed. M. G. Fawcett. Oxford: Oxford UP, 1912.

_____. *The Letters of John Stuart Mill.* Vol. I. Ed. Hugh S. Elliot, 6 March 1851. London: Longmans, Green and Co., 1910. In ed. Alice S. Rossi. *Essays on Sex and Equality: John Stuart Mill and Harriet Taylor Mill.* Chicago: U of Chicago P, 1970.

_____. *The Subjection of Women.* 1869. New York: Source, 1970.

Neidle, Cecyle S. *America's Immigrant Women.* Boston: Twayne Publ., 1975.

Nies, Judith. *Seven Women: Portraits from the American Radical Tradition.* New York: Viking, 1977.

Patten, Robert. *Charles Dickens and His Publishers.* Oxford: Clarendon P, 1978.

Perkins, H. J. G. and Theresa Wolfson. *Frances Wright Free Enquirer: The Study of a Temperament.* New York and London: Harper Brothers, Publ., 1939.

Rose, Phyllis. *Parallel Lives: Five Victorian Marriages.* New York: Vintage, 1983.

Rosenthal, Bernard, ed. Introduction. *Woman in the Nineteenth Century.* 1855. New York: W. W. Norton and Co., Inc., 1971.

Seller, Maxine Schwartz, ed. *Immigrant Women.* Philadelphia: Temple UP, 1981.

Simpson, David. "Destiny Made Manifest: The Styles of Whitman's Poetry." *Nation and Narration.* Ed. Homi K. Bhabha. London: Routledge, 1990.

Stanton, Elizabeth Cady. *Eighty Years and More (1815-1897); Reminiscences of Elizabeth Cady Stanton.* 1898. New York: Source, 1970.

Stanton, Elizabeth Cady, Susan B. Anthony and Matilda Joslyn Gage, eds. *History of Woman Suffrage 1848-1861.* Vol. I. 1881. New York: Arno P and *The New York Times,* 1969.

Stern, Madeline B. *The Life of Margaret Fuller.* New York: E. P. Dutton and Co., Inc., 1942.

Stillinger, J. ed. *The Early Draft of John Stuart Mill's Autobiography.* Champaign: U of Illinois P, 1961.

Suhl, Yuri. *Eloquent Crusader: Ernestine Rose.* New York: Julian Messner, 1970.

Traubel, Horace. *With Walt Whitman in Camden.* 2 vols. New York: Appleton, 1908.

Urbanski, Marie Mitchell Olesen. *Margaret Fuller's Woman in the Nineteenth Century: A Literary Study.* Westport and London: Greenwood P, 1980.

Waterman, William Randall. *Frances Wright.* New York: Columbia UP, 1924.

Whitman, Walt. *Leaves of Grass: Facsimile of 1856 Edition.* Norwood, PA: Norwood, PA: Norwood Editions, 1976.

_____. *Leaves of Grass: Inclusive Edition.* Ed. Emory Holloway. New York: Doubleday, 1926.

_____. *Leaves of Grass: The First (1855) Edition.* Ed. Malcolm Cowley. New York: Viking, 1959.

Wright, Frances [Mme. D'Arusmont]. *Views of Society and Manners in America.* Ed. Paul R. Baker. Cambridge: Belknap P of Harvard UP, 1963.

Elizabeth Ann Bartlett (essay date 1994)

SOURCE: "Frances Wright," in *Liberty, Equality, Sorority: The Origins and Interpretation of American Feminist Thought: Frances Wright, Sarah Grimke, and Margaret Fuller,* Carlson Publishing, 1994, pp. 25-55.

[*In the following excerpt, Bartlett considers Wright's moral and political convictions, which grew out of her intellectual commitments to liberal democracy and utopian socialism.*]

Wright's Feminist Thought

The juxtaposition of all of the contrasting philosophical backgrounds and assumptions of moral sense, utilitarianism, and utopian socialism creates a complexity and richness in Wright's feminism. From the Enlightenment Wright drew the importance of education in shaping character and thus in defining the equality or inequality of the sexes. From utilitarian liberalism she gained her appreciation of the liberty of individual thought and action. She drew her passion for justice and equality from moral sense and utopian socialist thought. As a moral sense theorist, she justified her feminism with moral righteousness; as a utilitarian, she justified it as a useful solution to a practical problem.

Wright was a liberal feminist, a minimalist who saw no significant differences between men and women with regard to their physical, mental, moral, and sexual capacities. Along utilitarian liberal lines, Wright argued that the emancipation of women was called for by the right of self-determination and just treatment, and would result in the happiness and improvement of the individual and society. She was also a feminist socialist, believing that the freedom and the equality of both sexes would best be established and enhanced through equal and communal education and living and working conditions. Along utopian socialist lines, Wright argued that women claim equality as members of the common humanity and that liberty, happiness, and all other benefits of society were contingent on first achieving equality. She sought the moral autonomy of all as guaranteed through free inquiry, which is in turn guaranteed through equality. In essence, in her feminism Wright sought the full inclusion of women into every aspect of society, to the point that little or no distinctions would be drawn between the sexes. She sought the liberty of women primarily through their equality to men, not through their sorority to one another.

Liberty

Frances Wright was a champion of free inquiry, the unfettered pursuit of knowledge and truth. All other aspects of freedom followed from this. She believed that most people led lives of submission and domination out of fear, fear grounded in lack of knowledge.

Educate people, give them the knowledge of facts and the principles of reason and understanding, and they would be able to rule their own lives.

While valuable in and of itself, the freedom to search and to question and to discover one's truths is essential to the development of moral autonomy. Through knowledge, individuals could understand the consequences of their actions, giving themselves a basis on which to make moral decisions. Further, a portion of the populace so enlightened would mitigate the oppressive intolerance and ignorance of popular prejudices and public opinion. As an entire society became educated, individuals would be free to think and to act without restraint of public law or popular opinion.

Thus it is that Wright's concept of freedom is strongly associated with autonomy and independence. To be free is to depend only on one's own senses and reason. Dependence on anything or anyone else was the worst evil, and the dependence of women was especially deplorable.

> Alas for the morals of a country when female dignity is confounded with helplessness and the guardianship of a woman's virtue transfigured from herself to others! . . . Of the two extremes it is better to see a woman, as in Scotland, bent over the glebe, mingling the sweat of her brow with that of her husband or more churlish son, than to see her gradually sinking into the childish dependence of a Spanish donna.[56]

The dependence of women was fostered primarily by three causes: the neglected state of the female mind, lack of sufficient economic reward, and marriage. Women were deprived of education, and thereby deprived of the resources on which to base rational decisions. They were left dependent on those who dispensed formulas of belief and actions, and they were particularly vulnerable to the quackery practiced in the name of religion.[57]

Wright felt that the main stumbling block to knowledge, especially to free inquiry, was religion. She objected to religion as taught and practiced not only because it was not true knowledge (empirically based) and was therefore useless,[58] but also because it was the cause of much suffering. Misery and evil, she claimed, are always conjoined with ignorance, and religion is willful ignorance. Its indifference to the visible causes of tangible evil and the visible sources of tangible happiness were the primary causes of suffering. "[The problem] is not that religion is merely useless; it is mischievous. It is mischievous by its idle terrors; it is mischievous by its false morality; it is mischievous by its hypocrisy; by its fanaticism; by its dogmatism; by its threats; by its hopes; by its promises."[59] Wright was especially concerned about the subjection of women by religion.[60] Women were particularly vulnerable to the sway of religion because they had not developed their reason. The liberation of women from the domination of religion is a recurrent theme in her feminism.

Wright found two reasons for women's lack of education. First, women were viewed by fathers, who made those decisions, as nothing. Even if women could learn, fathers would argue, they could not apply it in a trade or profession. Whatever earnings they might have would become their husbands'. In the eyes of the law, married women did not exist. In the eyes of educators, they had no value. Second, men thought women were more useful ignorant. Ignorant women would be more likely to accept complacently their subservient position. Deprived of reason and thereby of autonomy, women would be dependent on men, who desired women's dependence to flatter their own egos. Wright countered this view by arguing that this principle, to hold up, must hold for *all* cases, not just for women, and since no one would argue that a man is more useful when ignorant, it must not be true of women. More likely, men simply do not want the competition of women.[61]

Deprived of a proper education, most occupations were closed to women. Those that were available did not pay a living wage. Then as now, men were paid higher wages "because they had a family to support," and the only viable option for women was to depend on that support for survival.

Driven into marriage by economic and social pressure, the dependence of women was assured. By law they were deprived of all rights to property and person; by sheer drudgery they were deprived of any means of improvement. In marriage women became economically, physically, legally, and morally dependent on their male partners.

Wright attacked the legal institution of marriage on three fronts: it is unnecessary, unjust, and the cause of much suffering of women.

Wright felt that the affections between a man and a woman are personal in nature. They can't be regulated like traffic or contracted like any other business relation, and it is unwarranted that the state should try to do so. It was ludicrous that men and women had to be given permission to live together, or apart, and that relations formed without this sanction, no matter how loving and caring, were regarded as morally evil; just as relations given this sanction, no matter how miserable and mean, were thought to be morally blessed. Even louder did she decry the travesty of the state declaring illegitimate the children of such unsanctioned unions.

Wright found the whole notion of state permission and regulation of adult relations paternalistic. She argued that men and women should be treated as autonomous beings and that their affections should be their private concern only. Love should be sufficient reason to bring men and women together, and lack of love sufficient reason for them to part. Legal and public sanctions of marriage and divorce were unnecessary and undesirable. Their only purpose was to fill the coffers of the priest with a fee of union and those of the lawyer with a fee of parting.[62]

In her condemnation of the role of the state in regulating relations between adults, Wright made explicit the political nature of the marriage institution. She recognized it as just one more tool to suppress women. She viewed the marriage contract as a means for the law and the government "to deprive the female of *all defense,* by abrogating all her natural rights as a human being, and all her artificial rights as a citizen."[63]

Wright criticized the absurdity and injustice of the common law of England, adopted by the United States, whereby a married woman was deprived of her very personhood. Under these laws of coverture, a woman at marriage literally ceased to exist in the eyes of the law. All her property and earnings belonged to her husband; all contracts and other legal associations had to be made through him. Her husband was even responsible for any criminal actions on her part (and often for whatever punishment ensued as well). Wright condemned a system of laws that so completely abrogated the rights of women as to make every woman a slave.[64]

She argued that women were by marriage deprived not only of their rights, but also of any possibility of peace and happiness.[65] Further, their mental bondage was secured. Entering into marriage ignorant and naive, women were soon submerged in the never-ending drudgery of domestic chores and child producing. Marriage left women at the disposal of their partners. Deprived of their rights, of economic self-sufficiency, and of opportunity for improvement, they were dependent on and defenseless against the whims of their husbands and were often the victims of neglect, misery, and brutality.[66]

> The unfortunate dependence of women too often makes them . . . victims to all evils which the error of their partner entails.[67]

> See her, moreover, compelled to endure the company of her destroyer, experience its vitiating example, and entail its evils on a yearly multiplying progeny![68]

Wright advocated better divorce laws, primarily so that a woman could get out of a bad situation. She argued that all states should adopt the divorce laws of Rhode Island, which permitted an annulment of the marriage contract on the grounds of a simple declaration of incompatibility and two years' separation.[69]

In her discussion of marital relations, Wright indicated that the problems originate in the legal stipulations of the marriage contract, rather than in the more fundamental association of women with men. She clearly felt that men and women were capable of tender and loving relations outside of the bonds of a legal contract. The marriage laws had no force in her own community of Nashoba, and yet she encouraged love relations between men and women. Thus it would appear that Wright believed that the marriage laws, by ensuring the dependence of women, fostered a situation in which men would take advantage of the powerlessness of their partners.

Men, Wright argued, finding women's dependence flattering to their egos, fostered that dependence. After all, it was men who determined the laws, men who determined wages, and men who determined the scope of the educational system. It was well within the power of men to grant women independence, but they had consistently refused. Given the political liberties available to the men in the United States, Wright felt reforms were possible. American men had the right of popular sovereignty. They needed only to exercise that right to bring about changes in the laws that would assure liberty, equality, prosperity, and happiness to all.

Paradoxically, in calling on the enfranchised citizenry—men—to exercise their liberty of popular sovereignty to invoke liberty and equality for all, Wright was suggesting that men relinquish the very dependence of women that they found so flattering. It is not clear how men would be persuaded to do so.

The freedom Wright claimed for women is their intellectual and moral independence and autonomy. This required above all the free pursuit of knowledge. And in order for this liberty to be secured, it must be shared equally. In that knowledge is power, as long as it is distributed unequally, some will be more powerful and others will be dependent and submissive. In particular, men, who monopolized knowledge, would ensure the submission and dependence of women. Thus we come to the subject of equality.

Equality

Equality of all humankind is the central tenet of Wright's thought. All are born with equal mental, moral, and physical capabilities. We bring with us no inherent female or male traits. Each comes into the world equally blank. Any distinctions that occur are the result of education and circumstances.

Also, relying on moral sense principles, Wright argued that regardless of whatever privileges or distinctions, intelligence or talents, circumstances may have brought our way, they have no relevance to our capacity to act morally. The moral faculty is inherent in all. Separate from our physical powers, it is not circumscribed by merely physical differences of sex; separate from our intellectual powers, it is not affected by differences in intelligence or education. With respect at least to moral truth, Wright argued that "the mind of the savage, *equally* with that of the sage, acknowledges the self-evidence."[70] All are equal in the moral sense notion that all are capable of being useful and happy, of being guided by reason and senses in a course of practice consistent with their own and the common good.[71]

Finally, Wright's assumption of equality stemmed as a necessary corollary from the utopian socialist assertion of our common species. We are first and foremost human beings—not citizens, not sects, not lawyers or merchants, and particularly not men and women. Our humanity is fundamental. It overrides and mitigates any distinctions between the sexes.

However, Wright was acutely aware that differences in education and environment create inequalities of privilege and condition. She felt keenly the wretchedness and squalor of the masses of humanity. She knew well the oppression of the working classes and of women. Believing strongly in the right of every human being to equal chances for development, reward, and happiness in this life, she dedicated her life to promoting educational and economic reforms. She sought

> the equal claim of all the members of the human family to equal chances; to equal care in infancy, equal protection and equal opportunities for mental and physical development in childhood and youth; equal credit according to the powers of his or her individual industry and genius in manhood or womanhood; equal certainty of reward in precise accordance with his or her services thro' life; equal security in the present and for the future of enjoying what his or her services may have fairly earned.[72]

An equal chance depends primarily on two conditions: equal educational opportunities and fair reward for labor. In pursuing the first condition, Wright developed a plan of national republican education that she promoted on every speaking tour. Her plan called for a government-supported and government-run system that would take responsibility for the care and education of *all* children, from the age of two years on up. The pattern of equality was to be set in the nurseries, in which all would be fed at a common board, wear common clothes, and be given similar duties, habits, and training, and would continue from infancy to adulthood.[73]

Wright was particularly concerned with equalizing the benefits, powers, and privileges of the sexes, and she saw a system of equal education as the key. Wright was severely critical of the lack of education for women. The facilities and the subjects of study for men were far superior to those for women. What education some women did receive was of little value. Women were usually educated in the European tradition, obtaining knowledge of only those things necessary for polite amusement—French, Italian, dancing, and drawing.

Since women had been educated only in the moral aspects of their nature, Wright was especially concerned that the two other aspects—the intellectual and the physical—be given equal cultivation. Whereas many did not regard women as rational beings, and were skeptical that women's intellect could be developed at all, Wright asserted that the mind has no innate characteristics of sex—or any other distinction—but only those characteristics that habit and education give it.[74] Women's intellects had been stifled. Even "in the happiest country, their condition is sufficiently hard. Have they talents? It is difficult to turn them to account. Ambition? The road to honorable distinction is shut against them. A vigorous intellect? It is broken down by sufferings, bodily and mental."[75]

However, that women did indeed have intellects, which were equal of any man's, Wright herself was proof, an argument she frequently advanced in speeches to challenge her male taunters.[76] Given that women's intellectual capabilities were equal to that of men, Wright argued that they should be equally developed, with equal education in philosophy, history, political economy, and sciences.

Even those who advocated the equal intellectual education of women often did not believe women should receive the same physical training. Though she occasionally referred to women as "the weaker sex," Wright felt that any physical differences between the sexes could be minimized by women being taught to race, swim, and shoot. The physical aspect of human character was just as important as the moral and intellectual, and Wright emphasized the need to exercise it equally with them. "I often lament that in rearing of women so little attention should be commonly paid to the exercise of the bodily organs; to invigorate the body is to invigorate the mind, and Heaven knows that the weaker sex have much cause to be rendered strong in both."[77]

Unlike many of her contemporaries, who sought the education of women so that they might be better mothers and teachers of men, Wright felt that the education of women as complete human beings was of the utmost importance for themselves, as individuals.[78] Education would enable women to reason, to fulfill their capabilities, to become autonomous.

It is important to remember that for Wright knowledge was the one key to all other societal goods. Without knowledge a woman could not be free or equal; she could not progress; she had no power. Moreover, Wright adopted the Epicurean belief that knowledge is the foundation of all other virtues. Thus, without education a woman could attain neither virtue nor happiness. Deprived of knowledge, women were deprived of all that is worthwhile in life. One cannot say of Wright that she *merely* sought education for women. In seeking education she sought all.

Wright also presented a very utilitarian argument (presumably addressed to men, to whom all of her utilitarian arguments seem to be addressed) for the education of women. Not only would education equalize benefits to women, it would extend these benefits to the nation as a whole. "The wonderful advance which this nation has made, . . . may yet be doubly accelerated when the education of women shall be equally a national concern with that of the other sex."[79]

In its equalization of knowledge, equal education would serve the Epicurean/utilitarian purposes of the extension of other equal benefits to all individuals and society as a whole. Wright also thought that equal education would serve the utopian socialist purposes of establishing a sense of community and equality of condition by providing similar habits, views, and interests. She argued "that a nation to be strong, must be united, to be united, must be equal in condition, to be equal in condition, must be similar in habits and in feeling, to be similar in habits and feelings, must be raised in national institutions as the children of a common family, and citizens of a common country."[80] By providing similar habits, pursuits, views, feelings, and interests, education would serve to bind individuals together in the common interests and the equality of a family.[81] This is an important notion for her feminism, for as all would come to recognize their common interests and bonds, the degradation of women by men would cease.

We do, however, encounter here the tension in Wright's thought between individual liberty and the collective good. Wright seems to be suggesting that equality and unity can be achieved by educating everyone to think alike. She tries to argue that given the proper education, each would independently recognize his or her responsibility to the community.

> Practical equality, or, the universal and *equal improvement of the condition* of all, until, by the gradual change in the views and habits of men, and the change consequent upon the same, in the whole social arrangement of the body politic, the American people shall present, in another generation, but in one class, as it were, but *one family—each independent* in his and her own thoughts, actions, rights, person, and possessions, and all *co-operating,* according to their *individual* tastes and ability, to the promotion of the common weal.[82]

The predominant question this raises for her feminism is how the nature of this similar education is to be determined. Perhaps constrained by the male bias in utopian socialism, Wright implied that this sense of community is ultimately male-defined. She had no concept of female awareness or self-definition. Rather, we get the impression that women should be able to become equal to the best of men.

Wright was equally concerned with achieving equality for all, but especially for women, through a fair reward for one's labor. Again, following in the utopian socialist tradition, Wright felt that the monetary system of rewarding the rich for idleness while the hard labors of the masses went unrewarded was immoral and unjust and was at the basis of the evils of society. Only by securing to all equal opportunity and affording them useful occupations and full and fair fruits of their labors would happiness and abundance be attainable by the whole of humanity.[83]

Wealth, as Wright defined it, is the fruit of industry and, in justice, should be owned by those who create it—the laboring classes. The estimate of value should be based on the average time employed in the production of an article, and workers should be rewarded according to the labor they invest. The substitution of just for unjust money and the fair reward of labor would lead to reform in all of society, equalizing the condition of humankind, bringing plenty to each, as well as honesty, ease, independence, and "brotherly" love.

Wright was particularly concerned with ensuring a just reward for women's labor. Women were deprived of economic equality in several ways. To begin with, they were not given sufficient training or skills to pursue a career. Their rights to property were denied by laws of marriage and primogeniture. Most significant, their labor was not rewarded equally to that of men. This economic discrimination rendered women incapable of supporting themselves, leaving them the choice between living independently in poverty or trading their independence for survival. Wright stated her case eloquently.

> We might ask if the brightest half of our race whose wisdom best might guard and guide the interests and happiness of the whole, could ever be found selling their persons for a subsistence, weighing in useless idleness on their relatives or male help-mates, or struggling in want and wretchedness under unrequited toil, if the fruits of industry, and not metal from the bowels of a mine were accounted wealth, if all were trained to create those fruits, and if, by whomsoever created, they bore ever their own value, and could neither be depreciated nor exalted below nor beyond the same.[84]

Wright believed that the labor of women is not inferior to that of men, and in any case, sex is not a legitimate basis of distinction. The labor of women should be rewarded equally to that of men,[85] and the labor of all should be rewarded according to the amount of service rendered. As a practical course to the achievement of equality of condition, Wright sought to institute what she called the "self-evident axiom: *To every man, woman, and child, according to his and to her works.*"[86]

In sum, Wright sought to put the principles of equality and justice into effect through equal educational opportunity and a fair reward for labor. Both were particularly important to women, who had consistently been denied them. She believed that women and men were equal in their mental, moral, and physical capacities and that women needed only be given equal opportunities in order for that equality to be realized. For Wright, the standard of excellence, privilege, and power was male. Equality of the sexes meant the extension of male opportunities, privileges, responsibilities, and rewards to women. Her goal was that women be equal to men—and this brings us to sorority.

Sorority

The concept of sorority is not as central to Wright's feminist thought as are the concepts of liberty and equality. Her utopian socialist collectivism was strong, and she sought not so much the identity and unity of women as the identity of humanity.

Wright believed any differences between the sexes to be minimal. She made little mention of sex-related behavior or sex roles. She discussed the educational and economic distinctions that society imposed on the sexes, but had no further discussion of the effects of such distinctions on behavior or attitudes. Unlike most of her contemporaries, including Fuller and Grimké, Wright made no mention of masculine/feminine character traits, or sexually separate "spheres."

One important reason for this lack of emphasis on sex roles and sexual distinctions is that Wright did not develop a concept of womanhood. Her concern was humankind. The equality and liberty she sought for woman was that of humanity in general.

I believe that Wright's inattention to sex roles stemmed in part from her allegiance with and concern for working-class women. It was one thing for middle-class women to address the issue of sex roles because their lives of domesticity were so far removed from their husbands' and brothers' professional lives. It was quite another to expect working-class women to regard their roles as unique, when they went to work in the factories just as their husbands and brothers did. Neither did working-class women need solitude for reflecting on their nature as women so much as they needed a decent wage. Better for them to aspire to the lives of middle-class men than to those of middle-class women.

Another reason Wright did not focus on sex role differences is that she did not regard women as first and foremost wives and mothers. She questioned the institution of marriage and family by her very acceptance of divorce, by her advice that women not marry, by her suggestion that men and women could sustain loving and committed relations outside of marriage, and by her advocacy of taking children out of the home and placing them in common nurseries. Thus Wright made a new perception of the role of women possible. No longer viewed solely in terms of domestic functions, women would be regarded as human beings, with all their potential and possibilities. Because Wright went beyond the restrictive assumption of the family unit, she viewed women as something other than wives and mothers. Able to break through this most basic of women's roles, she did not view any roles whatsoever as significant.

Another reason for Wright's lack of emphasis on culturally defined sex differences may be her belief that there were no significant differences between the sexes in their sexuality. Unlike her contemporaries, Wright did not condemn or deny sexuality. Wright was irritated by the dictums of propriety that rendered the mere mention of an arm or leg indecent. She condemned the fact that women were afraid of their own bodies, and were, in fact, often viewed as having no bodies at all.[87] Wright advocated that rather than shrouding their bodies, desires, and faculties, women address them openly.[88]

That men had healthy appetites and passions was readily acknowledged. Wright, however, was among the first to acknowledge that women have any sex drive whatsoever, let alone one that is as "healthy" as a man's. Wright viewed both men and women as sexual beings, and felt the temperate expression of their passions was a natural outgrowth of their nature as human beings.[89] It was the denial of these feelings that was undesirable. "Let us not teach that virtue consists in the crucifying of affections and appetites, but in their judicious government," Wright admonished. "Let us not attack ideas of purity to monastic chastity, impossible to man *or woman* without consequences fraught with evil, nor ideas of vice to connections formed under the auspices of kind feelings."[90]

Wright believed that men and women were each other's equals, even in their most sex-defined relationships. This underscored artificial distinctions between the sexes. The one exception to this is that, like her contemporaries, she sometimes argued that women are morally superior to men. At times she made the distinction between "brute males" and "the brightest half" of the species.[91] Wright felt that women were more noble and generous than men, and exerted a special

moral influence over all of society.[92] In fact, the moral character of a whole society is determined by the influence that women have in that society. The position of women is a gauge for the morals of a country.[93]

Wright made a passionate argument that the current depravity of the human condition was a direct result of the degradation of the nobler instincts of women.

> The first master of measure employed for the more certain enslavement of the species was the subjugation of woman in her body and her soul. She—the intellect, the soul, the providence of society—being made a tool of that sex which looks to individual conservation and selfish gratification—the nobler instinct enshrined in her—that which looks to the conservation and happiness of the species—was necessarily made subservient to the baser. The consequence has been what we witness at this hour: brute force quelling the inspirations of the mind; noise drowning reason; disputation knowledge; fraud subtracting from weakness what violence may have failed to rob; law usurping the place of justice; selfish interest that of generous friendship; prostitution, contraband or legal, that of love; theology of religion, and rapacious government that of benign administration.[94]

Wright went so far as to argue that all of human improvement is contingent on the position of women. Her belief that men will ever rise or fall to the level of women is put forth in her most famous statement.

> However novel it may appear, I shall venture the assertion, that, until women assume the place in society which good sense and good feeling alike assign to them, human improvement must advance but feebly. It is in vain that we would circumscribe the power of one half of our race, and that half by far the most important and influential. If they exert it not for good, they will for evil, if they advance not knowledge, they will perpetrate ignorance. Let women stand where they may in the scale of improvement, their position decides that of the race. Are they cultivated?—so is society polished and enlightened. Are they ignorant?—so is it gross and insipid. Are they wise?—so is the human condition prosperous. Are they foolish?—so is it unstable and unpromising. Are they free?—so is the human character elevated. Are they enslaved?—so is the whole race degraded.[95]

If one is looking for consistency in Wright's thought, the question must be asked, Why, if women are in all respects equal to men, do they exert such a unique influence over the morals of society? This may be answered in part by her own statement that "the fate of the sexes is so entwined that the dignity of the one must rise or fall with that of the other."[96] So, as women were then denied their full dignity, so were men; and as women came into their own, so would men and thus society.

This may also be answered in part by her observations that women, though receiving no physical or intellectual training, did receive moral training whereas men did not. Thus women may be more moral than men simply because their moral faculties have been enlightened and developed.

However, it may also be true that Wright is inconsistent. It may be that she was presenting the cultural stereotype of her day. Or perhaps in these affirmations of women's moral nature are the seeds of a bolder affirmation of womanhood in general and an incipient notion of sorority.

Wright occasionally hinted at a sisterhood among women. Certainly she affirmed her sisterhood with working-class women in a way that most middle-class feminists did not. She also recognized the common suffering that all women endured as a class. Wright separated the afflictions of humanity into those of men and those of women, the latter always being more burdensome. "It is difficult, in walking through the world, not to laugh at the consequences which, sooner or later, overtake men's follies, but when these are visited upon women I feel more disposed to sigh. Born to endure the worst afflictions of fortune, they are enervated in soul and body lest the storm should not visit them sufficiently rudely."[97]

Wright made occasional reference to women's oppression by men. In general, however, she did not regard the relations between women and men to be that of the solidarity of the oppressed versus the oppressors. Wright did not view the relations between the sexes as antagonistic. She felt that women were oppressed by clergy and bankers and lawyers and husbands; not by men *as men,* but by men as representatives of institutions—the church, the bank, the state, marriage. In the utopian socialist tradition, it was institutions, not people, that were responsible for the character of society, and in her evaluation of male/female relations, Wright viewed the problem as one of institutions, not sexes, and not persons.

Far from urging an independent struggle for women, Wright urged men and women to cooperate to achieve the goals of collective humanity.[98] Wright viewed our humanity as fundamental, and she denied the significance of subdivision by sex, race, or any other category. Humanity, with its inherent equality, takes precedence over sorority.

For Wright to believe in and affirm a unique nature of womanhood would be to go against her Enlightenment assumptions that human character is shaped by education and environment, rather than by such physical characteristics as sex. For Wright to affirm a sisterhood of women separate and apart from men would be at odds with her utopian socialist beliefs in the essential commonality and solidarity of all humanity.

But beyond the issue of Wright's beliefs, her own life story gave her little experience of sorority on which to draw as a feminist. Wright's life and work were not within the common world of women, but among the world of men. Unlike most women, she was highly educated and her intellectual companions were men; unlike most women, she traveled extensively; she chose and pursued what was typically a "man's" occupation and her working relationships were with men. Indeed, all of Wright's closest and best relationships were with men—her uncle, General Lafayette, Jeremy Bentham, Robert Owen, Robert Dale Owen.[99] Men were her peers, and they treated her as such.

Wright had relatively few correspondingly close relationships with women. Except for her brief association with Mrs. Millar, who was more like a mother, and her reliance on her sister, who was more like a wife, there were no women with whom Wright related as a sister.

Wright felt much more at home with men than with women. Men and their lives and works were more familiar to her. So estranged from the lives and the world of most women, it is no wonder that Wright did not develop a stronger notion of sorority.

Rather than being an appeal to women to recognize and affirm their autonomy and identity as women and their sisterhood with other women, the whole tenor of Wright's feminism is an appeal to men. She wrote and spoke as though by far the more important and certainly the more influential members of her audience were male. Her arguments for improving the condition of women so as to improve that of men were addressed to the interests and concerns of men. Her appeals for equal education, fair wages, and just marriage laws were addressed to fathers and husbands, not to those she hoped would benefit. The general argument put forth by Wright is for men to take the yoke of servitude off of women, rather than encouraging women to do so themselves. Unlike Fuller and Grimké, Wright trusted and relied on men to help women, who she felt were not in a position to help themselves. This position is consistent with the rest of Wright's philosophy. She felt that unless a person were educated, he or she was powerless. To address her argument to women would have been futile, for women were incapable of doing anything to improve their situation. Wright had to appeal to those who were capable of changing society, and at that time, this meant addressing her arguments to men.

Once freed from their yoke, women would enter equally into the lives and knowledge and power and work of men, as Wright had, rather than affirm their own particular identity and vision.

Only in her later life, after years of bitter marriage, divorce, and being cheated and lied to by her husband

and her attorney, did Wright change her sentiments. She openly admitted that she was afraid of men, that she would not trust them, and with what she believed to be good reason.[100] I suggest that had Wright written after this point in her life, she might have been hesitant to address her feminism to men, and the approach of her feminism might have been based more on the concept of sorority.

Conclusion

Wright's feminism is a balanced tension between liberty and equality. As she wrote, "equality is the soul of liberty, there is, in fact, no liberty without it."[101] She sought free inquiry only in conjunction with equal education for all; she sought equality of economic condition only in conjunction with political and legal liberties. For Wright, the liberty of free inquiry was guaranteed only by the equal distribution of that inquiry. If knowledge was held as a monopoly of a few, then the masses would lead lives of submission and domination to the knowledge keepers—priests, doctors, lawyers, governors. The lives of all would be restricted by the ignorance and prejudices of all. The purpose of providing everyone with an equal education is so that each can discover his or her own truths, not to enforce conformity. It is the equality of the education that guarantees its liberty. Liberty unaccompanied by equality is nonexistent. Similarly, women's independence could be guaranteed only through a fair and equal wage for their labor. Without this, women would continue to depend on men for economic support, usually through marriage.

Whereas liberty and equality are well balanced in Wright's thought, there is no corresponding tension with the concept of sorority. The value of this for Wright's feminism is that it helped to break down the stereotypes of female behavior and roles prevalent in the 1830s. She broke from the view of women as wives and mothers—and, ironically, as asexual or antisexual beings. Her feminism is liberating, stressing the liberty of women to exercise fully their physical, moral, intellectual, and sexual capacities.

However, Wright's feminism also suffers from this lack of balance with sorority. Her standard of virtue becomes maleness. She wanted women to be able to think, work, run, shoot, act like men. She sought the liberty of women to be like men; she sought the equality of women to men. Wright failed to see the paradox in her thought. She recognized the oppressiveness of certain institutions and sought to eliminate them. However, she did not make the connection that these oppressive institutions were shaped by the very men to whom she thought women should aspire. She did not recognize that these institutions were outgrowths of a patriarchal culture and male-defined reality. She did not see that in encouraging

women to be like men, she was encouraging the perpetuation of male-defined institutions.

Nor did Wright recognize how the knowledge she sought to convey had been defined, recorded, and interpreted by men. Or if she did, she did not regard this as a problem. Neither did she recognize the limitations in a male-defined "truth," a truth discernible only through reason. She did not see that her rejection of "women's ways of knowing," that is, intuition and personal knowledge,[102] was perpetuation of a male-defined reality that denied the equality of women's experiences and perceptions.

Contemporary feminist critiques of the academy show the male bias in the existing knowledge base. They show as well how the questions and concepts and even facts of academic disciplines have necessarily, though often reluctantly, changed in response to challenges raised by a feminist perspective.[103] For example, feminists have challenged the validity of traditional theories of moral development such as those of Freud and Kohlberg, because women have been excluded from these studies.[104] Similarly, in political theory, the liberal theory of justice has been challenged by the feminist ethic of care.[105]

To Wright's credit, this feminist challenge of the canon of knowledge could not have begun without the inclusion of women in the academy, which Wright demanded. However, generations of women have passed through the academy simply following in the male tradition. It took more than the inclusion of women in the academy to change it. It took the challenges of those who valued women's experience and women's perspectives.

Thus, Wright's notions of liberty and equality are limited. Without the inclusion of women's experiences and unique knowledge base, without the acknowledgment of a "woman's reality,"[106] women's true liberty is denied. They are free to be like men. They have equal pay, but are they free to pursue those aspects of their nature that are regarded as traditionally feminine? Will women who choose to be homemakers or mothers be considered of less worth than those who pursue an education and a career? Will women's truths, based on intuition and personal experience, be regarded as of little or no value? How can women be free or equal with their experiences and perspectives denied? I argue that in a society that regards maleness as the standard for the liberty and equality of women, women—and men—continue to be oppressed by male-defined institutions and a male-defined reality.

Wright made necessary and important strides for women. She helped break the path for women escaping the traditional molds that had been in part designed by men to serve their purposes. However, the alternative molds she proposed are male-defined as well. Wright herself was a victim of this. Her feminism is more deeply rooted in male traditions than the more gynocentric feminism of Grimké and Fuller.

The whole notion of sorority was at odds with her deep sense of the collectivity of humanity. For Wright, women could not be *just sisters,* because they have *brothers,* who are as important. The importance of the equality of humanity for Wright could not be superseded by the division inherent in sorority. Wright's feminism is first and foremost an eloquent appeal for independence as individuals and equality as human beings.

Notes

[56] Wright, *Views of Society,* pp. 219-20.

[57] Berg, *Remembered Gate,* p. 9.

[58] Wright, "Religion," in D'Arusmont, *Life, Letters, and Lectures,* p. 192.

[59] Wright, *Athens,* p. 150.

[60] Wright, *Popular Lectures,* p. 9.

[61] Wright, "Lectures," in Rossi, *Feminist Papers,* pp. 115-16.

[62] *The Free Enquirer,* May 13, 1829, p. 230.

[63] Ibid., October 1, 1828, p. 391.

[64] Ibid., April 29, 1829, p. 213.

[65] Ibid.

[66] Wright, *Views of Society,* p. 22.

[67] *The Free Enquirer,* July 22, 1829, p. 309.

[68] Ibid., April 29, 1829, p. 213.

[69] Wright, *Views of Society,* p. 220.

[70] Wright, "Six Epochs" (emphasis added).

[71] *The Free Enquirer,* April 30, 1831, p. 219.

[72] Wright, "Six Epochs."

[73] Wright preferred the Pestalozzi method of instruction, which first addresses the senses and through them awakens the faculties by commanding the attention of reason. (D'Arusmont, *Life, Letters, and Lectures,* p. 58.) Wright's husband, Phequepal D'Arusmont, was a Pestalozzi instructor.

[74] Apparently even Wright's good friend Lafayette was skeptical of the intellectual potential of women. She stated her thesis in a letter to him: "Trust me, my beloved friend, the mind has no sex but what habit and education give it, and I, who was thrown in infancy upon the world like a wreck upon the waters, have learned as well to struggle with the elements as any child of Adam's." (Frances Wright to Lafayette, February 9, 1823, quoted in Perkins and Wolfson, *Frances Wright,* p. 74.)

[75] Wright, *Views of Society,* p. 220.

[76] *The Free Enquirer,* January 7, 1829, p. 83. Waterman has argued that Wright's own demonstration of the intellectual capabilities of a woman was her greatest contribution because "she showed what the feminine mind was capable of." (William Randall Waterman, *Frances Wright* [New York: AMS Press, 1967], p. 256.)

[77] Wright, *Views of Society,* p. 220.

[78] Schramm, *Plow Women,* p. 87.

[79] Wright, *Views of Society,* p. 22. Notice the similarity to Mill's argument for the equality of women. For reasons mentioned above, it is possible that Mill got his arguments from Wright.

[80] Wright, *Existing Evils,* p. 10.

[81] Assuming this is true of a family. *The Free Enquirer,* March 3, 1831, p. 176.

[82] Wright, *Parting Address,* p. 16 (emphasis added).

[83] The basic outline of Wright's economic theories is found in *The Free Enquirer,* September 25, 1830, pp. 382-83; October 2, 1830, pp. 390-91; October 9, 1830, pp. 397-98; October 16, 1830, pp. 402-6; October 23, 1830, pp. 410-12.

[84] Ibid., November 9, 1830, p. 398.

[85] Ibid., July 3, 1830, p. 286.

[86] D'Arusmont, *Biography,* part 2, p. 26.

[87] This masculine vision of female sexuality, that women were passionless, was tied to the rise of evangelical religion between the 1790s and the 1830s. See Nancy F. Cott, "Passionless," *Signs: Journal of Women in Culture and Society* 4 (Winter 1978): 227-28.

[88] *The Free Enquirer,* February 6, 1828, p. 132.

[89] In so defining female sexuality, Wright broke out of the more typical male-defined visions of female sexuality as either passionless (Mary) or evilly se-

ductive (Eve). See Elizabeth Janeway, "Who is Sylvia? On the Loss of Sexual Paradigms," *Signs: Journal of Women in Culture and Society* 5 (Summer 1980): 573-89.

[90] *The Free Enquirer,* February 6, 1828, p. 132.

[91] See, for example, *The Free Enquirer,* October 9, 1830, p. 398.

[92] Ibid., February 6, 1828, p. 133.

[93] Wright, *Views of Society,* p. 219.

[94] D'Arusmont, *Biography,* part 2, p. 16.

[95] Wright, "Lectures," in Rossi, *Feminist Papers,* p. 109.

[96] Wright, *Views of Society,* p. 221.

[97] Ibid.

[98] Wright, "Lectures," in Rossi, *Feminist Papers,* p. 109.

[99] Wright, *Views of Society,* p. 221.

[100] Frances Wright to W. G. Gholson, Letters and Documents, Cincinnati Historical Society.

[101] Wright, "Lectures," in Rossi, *Feminist Papers,* p. 110.

[102] Belerky, *Women's Ways of Knowing.*

[103] See, for example, Florence Howe, *Myths of Co-education* (Bloomington: Indiana University Press, 1984); Sandra Harding, *Feminism and Methodology* (Bloomington: Indiana University Press, 1987); and Christie Farnham, ed., *The Impact of Feminist Research in the Academy* (Bloomington: Indiana University Press, 1987).

[104] Gilligan, *Different Voice.*

[105] See for example, Nel Noddings, *Caring: A Feminine Approach to Ethics and Moral Education* (Berkeley: University of California Press, 1984); and Eva Feder Kittay and Diana T. Meyers, *Women and Moral Theory* (Totowa, N.J.: Rowman and Littlefield, 1987).

[106] Anne Wilson Schaef, *Women's Reality* (Minneapolis: Winston Press, 1981).

Works Cited

Unpublished Sources

Frances Wright Letters. Houghton Library, Cambridge, Massachusetts.

Wright MSS. Cincinnati Historical Society, Cincinnati, Ohio.

Wright Lectures. Cornell University Library, Ithaca, New York.

Published Sources

Belerky, Mary Field, et al. *Women's Ways of Knowing: The Development of Self, Voice, and Mind.* New York: Basic Books, 1986.

Berg, Barbara J. *The Remembered Gate: Origins of American Feminism: The Woman and the City, 1800-1860.* New York: Oxford University Press, 1978.

Cott, Nancy F. "Passionlessness: An Interpretation of Victorian Sexual Ideology, 1790-1850," *Signs: Journal of Women in Culture and Society* 4 (Winter 1978): 219-316.

D'Arusmont, Frances Wright. *Biography, Notes, and Political Letters of Frances Wright D'Arusmont, Parts 1 and 2.* New York: John Windt, 1844.

Farnham, Christie, ed. *The Impact of Feminist Research in the Academy.* Bloomington: Indiana University Press, 1987.

Free Enquirer. 1825-33.

Gilligan, Carol. *In a Different Voice: Psychological Theory and Women's Development.* Cambridge: Harvard University Press, 1982.

Harding, Sandra. *Feminism and Methodology.* Bloomington: Indiana University Press, 1987.

Howe, Florence. *Myths of Coeducation.* Bloomington: Indiana University Press, 1984.

Janeway, Elizabeth. "Who is Sylvia? On the Loss of Sexual Paradigms," *Signs: Journal of Women in Culture and Society* 5 (Summer 1980): 573-89.

Kittay, Eva Feder, and Diana T. Meyers. *Women and Moral Theory.* Totowa, N.J.: Rowman and Littlefield, 1987.

Noddings, Nel. *Caring: A Feminine Approach to Ethics and Moral Education.* Berkeley: University of California Press, 1984.

Perkins, A. J. G., and Theresa Wolfson. *Frances Wright: Free Enquirer: The Study of a Temperament.* New York: Harper, 1939.

Rossi, Alice S., ed. *The Feminist Papers: From Adams to de Beauvoir.* New York: Columbia University Press, 1973.

Schaef, Anne Wilson. *Women's Reality*. Minneapolis: Winston Press, 1981.

Schramm, Sarah Slavin. *Plow Women Rather Than Reapers: An Intellectual History of Feminism in the United States*. Metuchen, N.J.: Scarecrow Press, 1979.

Waterman, William Randall. *Frances Wright*. New York: AMS Press, 1967.

Wright, Frances. *Course of Popular Lectures; with Three Addresses, on Various Public Occasions, and a Reply to the Charges against the French Reformers of 1789 and Supplement Course of Lectures*. London: James Watson, 1834; reprint ed. Frances Wright D'Arusmont. *Life, Letters, and Lectures 1834-1844*. New York: Arno Press, 1972.

_____. *A Few Days in Athens; Being the Translation of a Greek Manuscript Discovered in Herculaneum*. London: Longmans, 1822.

_____. *A Lecture on Existing Evils and Their Remedy, as delivered in the Arch Street Theater, Philadelphia, June 2, 1829*. New York: George Evans, 1829.

_____. *Parting Address: as delivered in Bowery Theatre to People in New York, June, 1830*. New York: Free Enquirer, 1830.

_____. *Views of Society and Manners in America*. Edited by Paul R. Baker. Cambridge: Belknap Press, 1963.

FURTHER READING

Eckhardt, Celia. "Of Fanny and Camilla Wright: Their Sisterly Love." In *The Sister Bond: A Feminist View of a Timeless Connection*, edited by Toni A. H. McNaron, pp. 37-50. New York: Pergamon Press, 1985.

> Describes the relationship between Frances and Camilla Wright, which was instrumental in supporting Frances Wright's political ideals and activism.

Lane, Margaret. *Frances Wright and the "Great Experiment."* Totowa, New Jersey: Rowman & Littlefield, 1972. 50 p.

> Provides biographical information, particularly for the period in which Frances Wright began the experimental community of Nashoba.

Nineteenth-Century Literature Criticism

Cumulative Indexes
Volumes 1-74

How to Use This Index

The main references

> **Calvino, Italo**
> 1923-1985.....CLC 5, 8, 11, 22, 33, 39,
>   73; SSC 3

list all author entries in the following Gale Literary Criticism series:

BLC = Black Literature Criticism
CLC = Contemporary Literary Criticism
CLR = Children's Literature Review
CMLC = Classical and Medieval Literature Criticism
DA = DISCovering Authors
DC = Drama Criticism
HLC = Hispanic Literature Criticism
LC = Literature Criticism from 1400 to 1800
NCLC = Nineteenth-Century Literature Criticism
PC = Poetry Criticism
SSC = Short Story Criticism
TCLC = Twentieth-Century Literary Criticism
WLC = World Literature Criticism, 1500 to the Present

The cross-references

> See also CANR 23; CA 85-88;
>   obituary CA 116

list all author entries in the following Gale biographical and literary sources:

AAYA = Authors & Artists for Young Adults
AITN = Authors in the News
BEST = Bestsellers
BW = Black Writers
CA = Contemporary Authors
CAAS = Contemporary Authors Autobiography Series
CABS = Contemporary Authors Bibliographical Series
CANR = Contemporary Authors New Revision Series
CAP = Contemporary Authors Permanent Series
CDALB = Concise Dictionary of American Literary Biography
CDBLB = Concise Dictionary of British Literary Biography
DLB = Dictionary of Literary Biography
DLBD = Dictionary of Literary Biography Documentary Series
DLBY = Dictionary of Literary Biography Yearbook
HW = Hispanic Writers
JRDA = Junior DISCovering Authors
MAICYA = Major Authors and Illustrators for Children and Young Adults
MTCW = Major 20th-Century Writers
NNAL = Native North American Literature
SAAS = Something about the Author Autobiography Series
SATA = Something about the Author
YABC = Yesterday's Authors of Books for Children

Literary Criticism Series
Cumulative Author Index

20/1631
See Upward, Allen

A/C Cross
See Lawrence, T(homas) E(dward)

Abasiyanik, Sait Faik 1906-1954
See Sait Faik
See also CA 123

Abbey, Edward 1927-1989 **CLC 36, 59**
See also CA 45-48; 128; CANR 2, 41

Abbott, Lee K(ittredge) 1947- **CLC 48**
See also CA 124; CANR 51; DLB 130

Abe, Kobo 1924-1993 **CLC 8, 22, 53, 81; DAM NOV**
See also CA 65-68; 140; CANR 24, 60; DLB 182; MTCW 1

Abelard, Peter c. 1079-c. 1142 **CMLC 11**
See also DLB 115

Abell, Kjeld 1901-1961 **CLC 15**
See also CA 111

Abish, Walter 1931- **CLC 22**
See also CA 101; CANR 37; DLB 130

Abrahams, Peter (Henry) 1919- **CLC 4**
See also BW 1; CA 57-60; CANR 26; DLB 117; MTCW 1

Abrams, M(eyer) H(oward) 1912- **CLC 24**
See also CA 57-60; CANR 13, 33; DLB 67

Abse, Dannie 1923- **CLC 7, 29; DAB; DAM POET**
See also CA 53-56; CAAS 1; CANR 4, 46, 74; DLB 27

Achebe, (Albert) Chinua(lumogu) 1930- **CLC 1, 3, 5, 7, 11, 26, 51, 75; BLC 1; DA; DAB; DAC; DAM MST, MULT, NOV; WLC**
See also AAYA 15; BW 2; CA 1-4R; CANR 6, 26, 47, 73; CLR 20; DLB 117; MAICYA; MTCW 1; SATA 40; SATA-Brief 38

Acker, Kathy 1948-1997 **CLC 45, 111**
See also CA 117; 122; 162; CANR 55

Ackroyd, Peter 1949- **CLC 34, 52**
See also CA 123; 127; CANR 51, 74; DLB 155; INT 127

Acorn, Milton 1923- **CLC 15; DAC**
See also CA 103; DLB 53; INT 103

Adamov, Arthur 1908-1970 **CLC 4, 25; DAM DRAM**
See also CA 17-18; 25-28R; CAP 2; MTCW 1

Adams, Alice (Boyd) 1926- **CLC 6, 13, 46; SSC 24**
See also CA 81-84; CANR 26, 53; DLBY 86; INT CANR-26; MTCW 1

Adams, Andy 1859-1935 **TCLC 56**
See also YABC 1

Adams, Brooks 1848-1927 **TCLC 80**
See also CA 123; DLB 47

Adams, Douglas (Noel) 1952- **CLC 27, 60; DAM POP**
See also AAYA 4; BEST 89:3; CA 106; CANR 34, 64; DLBY 83; JRDA

Adams, Francis 1862-1893 **NCLC 33**

Adams, Henry (Brooks) 1838-1918 **TCLC 4, 52; DA; DAB; DAC; DAM MST**
See also CA 104; 133; DLB 12, 47, 189

Adams, Richard (George) 1920- **CLC 4, 5, 18; DAM NOV**
See also AAYA 16; AITN 1, 2; CA 49-52; CANR 3, 35; CLR 20; JRDA; MAICYA; MTCW 1; SATA 7, 69

Adamson, Joy(-Friederike Victoria) 1910-1980 **CLC 17**
See also CA 69-72; 93-96; CANR 22; MTCW 1; SATA 11; SATA-Obit 22

Adcock, Fleur 1934- **CLC 41**
See also CA 25-28R; CAAS 23; CANR 11, 34, 69; DLB 40

Addams, Charles (Samuel) 1912-1988 **CLC 30**
See also CA 61-64; 126; CANR 12

Addams, Jane 1860-1945 **TCLC 76**

Addison, Joseph 1672-1719 **LC 18**
See also CDBLB 1660-1789; DLB 101

Adler, Alfred (F.) 1870-1937 **TCLC 61**
See also CA 119; 159

Adler, C(arole) S(chwerdtfeger) 1932- **CLC 35**
See also AAYA 4; CA 89-92; CANR 19, 40; JRDA; MAICYA; SAAS 15; SATA 26, 63, 102

Adler, Renata 1938- **CLC 8, 31**
See also CA 49-52; CANR 5, 22, 52; MTCW 1

Ady, Endre 1877-1919 **TCLC 11**
See also CA 107

A.E. 1867-1935 **TCLC 3, 10**
See Russell, George William

Aeschylus 525B.C.-456B.C. **CMLC 11; DA; DAB; DAC; DAM DRAM, MST; DC 8; WLCS**
See also DLB 176

Aesop 620(?)B.C.-564(?)B.C. **CMLC 24**
See also CLR 14; MAICYA; SATA 64

Affable Hawk
See MacCarthy, Sir(Charles Otto) Desmond

Africa, Ben
See Bosman, Herman Charles

Afton, Effie
See Harper, Frances Ellen Watkins

Agapida, Fray Antonio
See Irving, Washington

Agee, James (Rufus) 1909-1955 **TCLC 1, 19; DAM NOV**
See also AITN 1; CA 108; 148; CDALB 1941-1968; DLB 2, 26, 152

Aghill, Gordon
See Silverberg, Robert

Agnon, S(hmuel) Y(osef Halevi) 1888-1970 **CLC 4, 8, 14; SSC 30**
See also CA 17-18; 25-28R; CANR 60; CAP 2; MTCW 1

Agrippa von Nettesheim, Henry Cornelius 1486-1535 **LC 27**

Aherne, Owen
See Cassill, R(onald) V(erlin)

Ai 1947- **CLC 4, 14, 69**
See also CA 85-88; CAAS 13; CANR 70; DLB 120

Aickman, Robert (Fordyce) 1914-1981 **CLC 57**

See also CA 5-8R; CANR 3, 72

Aiken, Conrad (Potter) 1889-1973 **CLC 1, 3, 5, 10, 52; DAM NOV, POET; SSC 9**
See also CA 5-8R; 45-48; CANR 4, 60; CDALB 1929-1941; DLB 9, 45, 102; MTCW 1; SATA 3, 30

Aiken, Joan (Delano) 1924- **CLC 35**
See also AAYA 1, 25; CA 9-12R; CANR 4, 23, 34, 64; CLR 1, 19; DLB 161; JRDA; MAICYA; MTCW 1; SAAS 1; SATA 2, 30, 73

Ainsworth, William Harrison 1805-1882 **NCLC 13**
See also DLB 21; SATA 24

Aitmatov, Chingiz (Torekulovich) 1928- **CLC 71**
See also CA 103; CANR 38; MTCW 1; SATA 56

Akers, Floyd
See Baum, L(yman) Frank

Akhmadulina, Bella Akhatovna 1937- **CLC 53; DAM POET**
See also CA 65-68

Akhmatova, Anna 1888-1966 **CLC 11, 25, 64; DAM POET; PC 2**
See also CA 19-20; 25-28R; CANR 35; CAP 1; MTCW 1

Aksakov, Sergei Timofeyvich 1791-1859 **NCLC 2**
See also DLB 198

Aksenov, Vassily
See Aksyonov, Vassily (Pavlovich)

Akst, Daniel 1956- **CLC 109**
See also CA 161

Aksyonov, Vassily (Pavlovich) 1932- **CLC 22, 37, 101**
See also CA 53-56; CANR 12, 48

Akutagawa, Ryunosuke 1892-1927 **TCLC 16**
See also CA 117; 154

Alain 1868-1951 **TCLC 41**
See also CA 163

Alain-Fournier **TCLC 6**
See also Fournier, Henri Alban
See also DLB 65

Alarcon, Pedro Antonio de 1833-1891 **NCLC 1**

Alas (y Urena), Leopoldo (Enrique Garcia) 1852-1901 **TCLC 29**
See also CA 113; 131; HW

Albee, Edward (Franklin III) 1928- **CLC 1, 2, 3, 5, 9, 11, 13, 25, 53, 86, 113; DA; DAB; DAC; DAM DRAM, MST; WLC**
See also AITN 1; CA 5-8R; CABS 3; CANR 8, 54, 74; CDALB 1941-1968; DLB 7; INT CANR-8; MTCW 1

Alberti, Rafael 1902- **CLC 7**
See also CA 85-88; DLB 108

Albert the Great 1200(?)-1280 **CMLC 16**
See also DLB 115

Alcala-Galiano, Juan Valera y
See Valera y Alcala-Galiano, Juan

Alcott, Amos Bronson 1799-1888 **NCLC 1**
See also DLB 1

See also DLB 151, 172

Andrews, Cicily Fairfield
See West, Rebecca

Andrews, Elton V.
See Pohl, Frederik

Andreyev, Leonid (Nikolaevich) 1871-1919
TCLC 3
See also CA 104

Andric, Ivo 1892-1975   **CLC 8**
See also CA 81-84; 57-60; CANR 43, 60; DLB
147; MTCW 1

Androvar
See Prado (Calvo), Pedro

Angelique, Pierre
See Bataille, Georges

Angell, Roger 1920-   **CLC 26**
See also CA 57-60; CANR 13, 44, 70; DLB 171,
185

Angelou, Maya 1928-CLC 12, 35, 64, 77; BLC
1; DA; DAB; DAC; DAM MST, MULT,
POET, POP; WLCS
See also Johnson, Marguerite (Annie)
See also AAYA 7, 20; BW 2; CA 65-68; CANR
19, 42, 65; CLR 53; DLB 38; MTCW 1;
SATA 49

Anna Comnena 1083-1153   **CMLC 25**

Annensky, Innokenty (Fyodorovich) 1856-1909
TCLC 14
See also CA 110; 155

Annunzio, Gabriele d'
See D'Annunzio, Gabriele

Anodos
See Coleridge, Mary E(lizabeth)

Anon, Charles Robert
See Pessoa, Fernando (Antonio Nogueira)

Anouilh, Jean (Marie Lucien Pierre) 1910-1987
**CLC 1, 3, 8, 13, 40, 50; DAM DRAM; DC
8**
See also CA 17-20R; 123; CANR 32; MTCW 1

Anthony, Florence
See Ai

Anthony, John
See Ciardi, John (Anthony)

Anthony, Peter
See Shaffer, Anthony (Joshua); Shaffer, Peter
(Levin)

Anthony, Piers 1934-   **CLC 35; DAM POP**
See also AAYA 11; CA 21-24R; CANR 28, 56,
73; DLB 8; MTCW 1; SAAS 22; SATA 84

Anthony, Susan B(rownell) 1916-1991 **T C L C
84**
See also CA 89-92; 134

Antoine, Marc
See Proust, (Valentin-Louis-George-Eugene-)
Marcel

Antoninus, Brother
See Everson, William (Oliver)

Antonioni, Michelangelo 1912-   **CLC 20**
See also CA 73-76; CANR 45

Antschel, Paul 1920-1970
See Celan, Paul
See also CA 85-88; CANR 33, 61; MTCW 1

Anwar, Chairil 1922-1949   **TCLC 22**
See also CA 121

Apess, William 1798-1839(?)NCLC 73; DAM
MULT
See also DLB 175; NNAL

Apollinaire, Guillaume 1880-1918TCLC 3, 8,
51; DAM POET; PC 7
See also Kostrowitzki, Wilhelm Apollinaris de
See also CA 152

Appelfeld, Aharon 1932-   **CLC 23, 47**
See also CA 112; 133

Apple, Max (Isaac) 1941-   **CLC 9, 33**
See also CA 81-84; CANR 19, 54; DLB 130

Appleman, Philip (Dean) 1926-   **CLC 51**
See also CA 13-16R; CAAS 18; CANR 6, 29,
56

Appleton, Lawrence
See Lovecraft, H(oward) P(hillips)

Apteryx
See Eliot, T(homas) S(tearns)

Apuleius, (Lucius Madaurensis) 125(?)-175(?)
CMLC 1

Aquin, Hubert 1929-1977   **CLC 15**
See also CA 105; DLB 53

Aragon, Louis 1897-1982   **CLC 3, 22; DAM
NOV, POET**
See also CA 69-72; 108; CANR 28, 71; DLB
72; MTCW 1

Arany, Janos 1817-1882   **NCLC 34**

Arbuthnot, John 1667-1735   **LC 1**
See also DLB 101

Archer, Herbert Winslow
See Mencken, H(enry) L(ouis)

Archer, Jeffrey (Howard) 1940-   **CLC 28;
DAM POP**
See also AAYA 16; BEST 89:3; CA 77-80;
CANR 22, 52; INT CANR-22

Archer, Jules 1915-   **CLC 12**
See also CA 9-12R; CANR 6, 69; SAAS 5;
SATA 4, 85

Archer, Lee
See Ellison, Harlan (Jay)

Arden, John 1930-CLC 6, 13, 15; DAM DRAM
See also CA 13-16R; CAAS 4; CANR 31, 65,
67; DLB 13; MTCW 1

Arenas, Reinaldo 1943-1990   **CLC 41; DAM
MULT; HLC**
See also CA 124; 128; 133; CANR 73; DLB
145; HW

Arendt, Hannah 1906-1975   **CLC 66, 98**
See also CA 17-20R; 61-64; CANR 26, 60;
MTCW 1

Aretino, Pietro 1492-1556   **LC 12**

Arghezi, Tudor 1880-1967   **CLC 80**
See also Theodorescu, Ion N.
See also CA 167

Arguedas, Jose Maria 1911-1969 CLC 10, 18
See also CA 89-92; CANR 73; DLB 113; HW

Argueta, Manlio 1936-   **CLC 31**
See also CA 131; CANR 73; DLB 145; HW

Ariosto, Ludovico 1474-1533   **LC 6**

Aristides
See Epstein, Joseph

Aristophanes 450B.C.-385B.C.CMLC 4; DA;
DAB; DAC; DAM DRAM, MST; DC 2;
WLCS
See also DLB 176

Aristotle 384B.C.-322B.C.   **CMLC 31; DA;
DAB; DAC; DAM MST; WLCS**
See also DLB 176

Arlt, Roberto (Godofredo Christophersen)
1900-1942TCLC 29; DAM MULT; HLC
See also CA 123; 131; CANR 67; HW

Armah, Ayi Kwei 1939-   **CLC 5, 33; BLC 1;
DAM MULT, POET**
See also BW 1; CA 61-64; CANR 21, 64; DLB
117; MTCW 1

Armatrading, Joan 1950-   **CLC 17**
See also CA 114

Arnette, Robert
See Silverberg, Robert

**Arnim, Achim von (Ludwig Joachim von
Arnim)** 1781-1831   **NCLC 5; SSC 29**
See also DLB 90

Arnim, Bettina von 1785-1859   **NCLC 38**
See also DLB 90

Arnold, Matthew 1822-1888NCLC 6, 29; DA;
DAB; DAC; DAM MST, POET; PC 5;
WLC
See also CDBLB 1832-1890; DLB 32, 57

Arnold, Thomas 1795-1842   **NCLC 18**
See also DLB 55

Arnow, Harriette (Louisa) Simpson 1908-1986
CLC 2, 7, 18
See also CA 9-12R; 118; CANR 14; DLB 6;
MTCW 1; SATA 42; SATA-Obit 47

Arouet, Francois-Marie
See Voltaire

Arp, Hans
See Arp, Jean

Arp, Jean 1887-1966   **CLC 5**
See also CA 81-84; 25-28R; CANR 42

Arrabal
See Arrabal, Fernando

Arrabal, Fernando 1932-   **CLC 2, 9, 18, 58**
See also CA 9-12R; CANR 15

Arrick, Fran   **CLC 30**
See also Gaberman, Judie Angell

Artaud, Antonin (Marie Joseph) 1896-1948
TCLC 3, 36; DAM DRAM
See also CA 104; 149

Arthur, Ruth M(abel) 1905-1979   **CLC 12**
See also CA 9-12R; 85-88; CANR 4; SATA 7,
26

Artsybashev, Mikhail (Petrovich) 1878-1927
TCLC 31
See also CA 170

Arundel, Honor (Morfydd) 1919-1973CLC 17
See also CA 21-22; 41-44R; CAP 2; CLR 35;
SATA 4; SATA-Obit 24

Arzner, Dorothy 1897-1979   **CLC 98**

Asch, Sholem 1880-1957   **TCLC 3**
See also CA 105

Ash, Shalom
See Asch, Sholem

Ashbery, John (Lawrence) 1927-CLC 2, 3, 4,
6, 9, 13, 15, 25, 41, 77; DAM POET
See also CA 5-8R; CANR 9, 37, 66; DLB 5,
165; DLBY 81; INT CANR-9; MTCW 1

Ashdown, Clifford
See Freeman, R(ichard) Austin

Ashe, Gordon
See Creasey, John

Ashton-Warner, Sylvia (Constance) 1908-1984
CLC 19
See also CA 69-72; 112; CANR 29; MTCW 1

Asimov, Isaac 1920-1992 CLC 1, 3, 9, 19, 26,
76, 92; DAM POP
See also AAYA 13; BEST 90:2; CA 1-4R; 137;
CANR 2, 19, 36, 60; CLR 12; DLB 8; DLBY
92; INT CANR-19; JRDA; MAICYA;
MTCW 1; SATA 1, 26, 74

Assis, Joaquim Maria Machado de
See Machado de Assis, Joaquim Maria

Astley, Thea (Beatrice May) 1925-   **CLC 41**
See also CA 65-68; CANR 11, 43

Aston, James
See White, T(erence) H(anbury)

Asturias, Miguel Angel 1899-1974 CLC 3, 8,
13; DAM MULT, NOV; HLC
See also CA 25-28, 49-52; CANR 32; CAP 2;
DLB 113; HW; MTCW 1

Atares, Carlos Saura
See Saura (Atares), Carlos

Atheling, William
See Pound, Ezra (Weston Loomis)

Atheling, William, Jr.

See Blish, James (Benjamin)

Atherton, Gertrude (Franklin Horn) 1857-1948
TCLC 2
See also CA 104; 155; DLB 9, 78, 186

Atherton, Lucius
See Masters, Edgar Lee

Atkins, Jack
See Harris, Mark

Atkinson, Kate   **CLC 99**
See also CA 166

Attaway, William (Alexander) 1911-1986**CLC
92; BLC 1; DAM MULT**
See also BW 2; CA 143; DLB 76

Atticus
See Fleming, Ian (Lancaster); Wilson, (Thomas)
Woodrow

Atwood, Margaret (Eleanor) 1939-**CLC 2, 3,
4, 8, 13, 15, 25, 44, 84; DA; DAB; DAC;
DAM MST, NOV, POET; PC 8; SSC 2;
WLC**
See also AAYA 12; BEST 89:2; CA 49-52;
CANR 3, 24, 33, 59; DLB 53; INT CANR-
24; MTCW 1; SATA 50

Aubigny, Pierre d'
See Mencken, H(enry) L(ouis)

Aubin, Penelope 1685-1731(?)   **LC 9**
See also DLB 39

Auchincloss, Louis (Stanton) 1917-**CLC 4, 6,
9, 18, 45; DAM NOV; SSC 22**
See also CA 1-4R; CANR 6, 29, 55; DLB 2;
DLBY 80; INT CANR-29; MTCW 1

Auden, W(ystan) H(ugh) 1907-1973**CLC 1, 2,
3, 4, 6, 9, 11, 14, 43; DA; DAB; DAC; DAM
DRAM, MST, POET; PC 1; WLC**
See also AAYA 18; CA 9-12R; 45-48; CANR
5, 61; CDBLB 1914-1945; DLB 10, 20;
MTCW 1

Audiberti, Jacques 1900-1965 **CLC 38; DAM
DRAM**
See also CA 25-28R

Audubon, John James 1785-1851 **NCLC 47**

Auel, Jean M(arie) 1936- **CLC 31, 107; DAM
POP**
See also AAYA 7; BEST 90:4; CA 103; CANR
21, 64; INT CANR-21; SATA 91

Auerbach, Erich 1892-1957   **TCLC 43**
See also CA 118; 155

Augier, Emile 1820-1889   **NCLC 31**
See also DLB 192

August, John
See De Voto, Bernard (Augustine)

Augustine, St. 354-430   **CMLC 6; DAB**

Aurelius
See Bourne, Randolph S(illiman)

Aurobindo, Sri
See Ghose, Aurabinda

Austen, Jane 1775-1817 **NCLC 1, 13, 19, 33,
51; DA; DAB; DAC; DAM MST, NOV;
WLC**
See also AAYA 19; CDBLB 1789-1832; DLB
116

Auster, Paul 1947-   **CLC 47**
See also CA 69-72; CANR 23, 52

Austin, Frank
See Faust, Frederick (Schiller)

Austin, Mary (Hunter) 1868-1934 **TCLC 25**
See also CA 109; DLB 9, 78

Autran Dourado, Waldomiro
See Dourado, (Waldomiro Freitas) Autran

Averroes 1126-1198   **CMLC 7**
See also DLB 115

Avicenna 980-1037   **CMLC 16**
See also DLB 115

Avison, Margaret 1918- **CLC 2, 4, 97; DAC;
DAM POET**
See also CA 17-20R; DLB 53; MTCW 1

Axton, David
See Koontz, Dean R(ay)

Ayckbourn, Alan 1939- **CLC 5, 8, 18, 33, 74;
DAB; DAM DRAM**
See also CA 21-24R; CANR 31, 59; DLB 13;
MTCW 1

Aydy, Catherine
See Tennant, Emma (Christina)

Ayme, Marcel (Andre) 1902-1967   **CLC 11**
See also CA 89-92; CANR 67; CLR 25; DLB
72; SATA 91

Ayrton, Michael 1921-1975   **CLC 7**
See also CA 5-8R; 61-64; CANR 9, 21

Azorin   **CLC 11**
See also Martinez Ruiz, Jose

Azuela, Mariano 1873-1952 **TCLC 3; DAM
MULT; HLC**
See also CA 104; 131; HW; MTCW 1

Baastad, Babbis Friis
See Friis-Baastad, Babbis Ellinor

Bab
See Gilbert, W(illiam) S(chwenck)

Babbis, Eleanor
See Friis-Baastad, Babbis Ellinor

Babel, Isaac
See Babel, Isaak (Emmanuilovich)

Babel, Isaak (Emmanuilovich) 1894-1941(?)
TCLC 2, 13; SSC 16
See also CA 104; 155

Babits, Mihaly 1883-1941   **TCLC 14**
See also CA 114

Babur 1483-1530   **LC 18**

Bacchelli, Riccardo 1891-1985   **CLC 19**
See also CA 29-32R; 117

Bach, Richard (David) 1936- **CLC 14; DAM
NOV, POP**
See also AITN 1; BEST 89:2; CA 9-12R; CANR
18; MTCW 1; SATA 13

Bachman, Richard
See King, Stephen (Edwin)

Bachmann, Ingeborg 1926-1973   **CLC 69**
See also CA 93-96; 45-48; CANR 69; DLB 85

Bacon, Francis 1561-1626   **LC 18, 32**
See also CDBLB Before 1660; DLB 151

Bacon, Roger 1214(?)-1292   **CMLC 14**
See also DLB 115

Bacovia, George   **TCLC 24**
See also Vasiliu, Gheorghe

Badanes, Jerome 1937-   **CLC 59**

Bagehot, Walter 1826-1877   **NCLC 10**
See also DLB 55

Bagnold, Enid 1889-1981 **CLC 25; DAM
DRAM**
See also CA 5-8R; 103; CANR 5, 40; DLB 13,
160, 191; MAICYA; SATA 1, 25

Bagritsky, Eduard 1895-1934   **TCLC 60**

Bagrjana, Elisaveta
See Belcheva, Elisaveta

Bagryana, Elisaveta   **CLC 10**
See also Belcheva, Elisaveta
See also DLB 147

Bailey, Paul 1937-   **CLC 45**
See also CA 21-24R; CANR 16, 62; DLB 14

Baillie, Joanna 1762-1851   **NCLC 71**
See also DLB 93

Bainbridge, Beryl (Margaret) 1933-**CLC 4, 5,
8, 10, 14, 18, 22, 62; DAM NOV**
See also CA 21-24R; CANR 24, 55; DLB 14;
MTCW 1

Baker, Elliott 1922-   **CLC 8**

See also CA 45-48; CANR 2, 63

Baker, Jean H.   **TCLC 3, 10**
See also Russell, George William

Baker, Nicholson 1957- **CLC 61; DAM POP**
See also CA 135; CANR 63

Baker, Ray Stannard 1870-1946   **TCLC 47**
See also CA 118

Baker, Russell (Wayne) 1925-   **CLC 31**
See also BEST 89:4; CA 57-60; CANR 11, 41,
59; MTCW 1

Bakhtin, M.
See Bakhtin, Mikhail Mikhailovich

Bakhtin, M. M.
See Bakhtin, Mikhail Mikhailovich

Bakhtin, Mikhail
See Bakhtin, Mikhail Mikhailovich

Bakhtin, Mikhail Mikhailovich 1895-1975
CLC 83
See also CA 128; 113

Bakshi, Ralph 1938(?)-   **CLC 26**
See also CA 112; 138

Bakunin, Mikhail (Alexandrovich) 1814-1876
NCLC 25, 58

Baldwin, James (Arthur) 1924-1987**CLC 1, 2,
3, 4, 5, 8, 13, 15, 17, 42, 50, 67, 90; BLC 1;
DA; DAB; DAC; DAM MST, MULT, NOV,
POP; DC 1; SSC 10; WLC**
See also AAYA 4; BW 1; CA 1-4R; 124; CABS
1; CANR 3, 24; CDALB 1941-1968; DLB
2, 7, 33; DLBY 87; MTCW 1; SATA 9;
SATA-Obit 54

Ballard, J(ames) G(raham) 1930-**CLC 3, 6, 14,
36; DAM NOV, POP; SSC 1**
See also AAYA 3; CA 5-8R; CANR 15, 39, 65;
DLB 14; MTCW 1; SATA 93

Balmont, Konstantin (Dmitriyevich) 1867-1943
TCLC 11
See also CA 109; 155

Balzac, Honore de 1799-1850**NCLC 5, 35, 53;
DA; DAB; DAC; DAM MST, NOV; SSC
5; WLC**
See also DLB 119

Bambara, Toni Cade 1939-1995 **CLC 19, 88;
BLC 1; DA; DAC; DAM MST, MULT;
WLCS**
See also AAYA 5; BW 2; CA 29-32R; 150;
CANR 24, 49; DLB 38; MTCW 1

Bamdad, A.
See Shamlu, Ahmad

Banat, D. R.
See Bradbury, Ray (Douglas)

Bancroft, Laura
See Baum, L(yman) Frank

Banim, John 1798-1842   **NCLC 13**
See also DLB 116, 158, 159

Banim, Michael 1796-1874   **NCLC 13**
See also DLB 158, 159

Banjo, The
See Paterson, A(ndrew) B(arton)

Banks, Iain
See Banks, Iain M(enzies)

Banks, Iain M(enzies) 1954-   **CLC 34**
See also CA 123; 128; CANR 61; DLB 194;
INT 128

Banks, Lynne Reid   **CLC 23**
See also Reid Banks, Lynne
See also AAYA 6

Banks, Russell 1940-   **CLC 37, 72**
See also CA 65-68; CAAS 15; CANR 19, 52,
73; DLB 130

Banville, John 1945-   **CLC 46**
See also CA 117; 128; DLB 14; INT 128

Banville, Theodore (Faullain) de 1832-1891

Beecher, Catharine Esther 1800-1878 **N C L C 30**
See also DLB 1
Beecher, John 1904-1980 **CLC 6**
See also AITN 1; CA 5-8R; 105; CANR 8
Beer, Johann 1655-1700 **LC 5**
See also DLB 168
Beer, Patricia 1924- **CLC 58**
See also CA 61-64; CANR 13, 46; DLB 40
Beerbohm, Max
See Beerbohm, (Henry) Max(imilian)
Beerbohm, (Henry) Max(imilian) 1872-1956
TCLC 1, 24
See also CA 104; 154; DLB 34, 100
Beer-Hofmann, Richard 1866-1945 **TCLC 60**
See also CA 160; DLB 81
Begiebing, Robert J(ohn) 1946- **CLC 70**
See also CA 122; CANR 40
Behan, Brendan 1923-1964 **CLC 1, 8, 11, 15, 79; DAM DRAM**
See also CA 73-76; CANR 33; CDBLB 1945-1960; DLB 13; MTCW 1
Behn, Aphra 1640(?)-1689 **LC 1, 30, 42; DA; DAB; DAC; DAM DRAM, MST, NOV, POET; DC 4; PC 13; WLC**
See also DLB 39, 80, 131
Behrman, S(amuel) N(athaniel) 1893-1973
CLC 40
See also CA 13-16; 45-48; CAP 1; DLB 7, 44
Belasco, David 1853-1931 **TCLC 3**
See also CA 104; 168; DLB 7
Belcheva, Elisaveta 1893- **CLC 10**
See also Bagryana, Elisaveta
Beldone, Phil "Cheech"
See Ellison, Harlan (Jay)
Beleno
See Azuela, Mariano
Belinski, Vissarion Grigoryevich 1811-1848
NCLC 5
See also DLB 198
Belitt, Ben 1911- **CLC 22**
See also CA 13-16R; CAAS 4; CANR 7; DLB 5
Bell, Gertrude (Margaret Lowthian) 1868-1926
TCLC 67
See also CA 167; DLB 174
Bell, J. Freeman
See Zangwill, Israel
Bell, James Madison 1826-1902 **TCLC 43; BLC 1; DAM MULT**
See also BW 1; CA 122; 124; DLB 50
Bell, Madison Smartt 1957- **CLC 41, 102**
See also CA 111; CANR 28, 54, 73
Bell, Marvin (Hartley) 1937- **CLC 8, 31; DAM POET**
See also CA 21-24R; CAAS 14; CANR 59; DLB 5; MTCW 1
Bell, W. L. D.
See Mencken, H(enry) L(ouis)
Bellamy, Atwood C.
See Mencken, H(enry) L(ouis)
Bellamy, Edward 1850-1898 **NCLC 4**
See also DLB 12
Bellin, Edward J.
See Kuttner, Henry
Belloc, (Joseph) Hilaire (Pierre Sebastien Rene Swanton) 1870-1953 **TCLC 7, 18; DAM POET; PC 24**
See also CA 106; 152; DLB 19, 100, 141, 174; YABC 1
Belloc, Joseph Peter Rene Hilaire
See Belloc, (Joseph) Hilaire (Pierre Sebastien Rene Swanton)

Belloc, Joseph Pierre Hilaire
See Belloc, (Joseph) Hilaire (Pierre Sebastien Rene Swanton)
Belloc, M. A.
See Lowndes, Marie Adelaide (Belloc)
Bellow, Saul 1915-**CLC 1, 2, 3, 6, 8, 10, 13, 15, 25, 33, 34, 63, 79; DA; DAB; DAC; DAM MST, NOV, POP; SSC 14; WLC**
See also AITN 2; BEST 89:3; CA 5-8R; CABS 1; CANR 29, 53; CDALB 1941-1968; DLB 2, 28; DLBD 3; DLBY 82; MTCW 1
Belser, Reimond Karel Maria de 1929-
See Ruyslinck, Ward
See also CA 152
Bely, Andrey **TCLC 7; PC 11**
See also Bugayev, Boris Nikolayevich
Belyi, Andrei
See Bugayev, Boris Nikolayevich
Benary, Margot
See Benary-Isbert, Margot
Benary-Isbert, Margot 1889-1979 **CLC 12**
See also CA 5-8R; 89-92; CANR 4, 72; CLR 12; MAICYA; SATA 2; SATA-Obit 21
Benavente (y Martinez), Jacinto 1866-1954
TCLC 3; DAM DRAM, MULT
See also CA 106; 131; HW; MTCW 1
Benchley, Peter (Bradford) 1940- **CLC 4, 8; DAM NOV, POP**
See also AAYA 14; AITN 2; CA 17-20R; CANR 12, 35, 66; MTCW 1; SATA 3, 89
Benchley, Robert (Charles) 1889-1945 **T C L C 1, 55**
See also CA 105; 153; DLB 11
Benda, Julien 1867-1956 **TCLC 60**
See also CA 120; 154
Benedict, Ruth (Fulton) 1887-1948 **TCLC 60**
See also CA 158
Benedict, Saint c. 480-c. 547 **CMLC 29**
Benedikt, Michael 1935- **CLC 4, 14**
See also CA 13-16R; CANR 7; DLB 5
Benet, Juan 1927- **CLC 28**
See also CA 143
Benet, Stephen Vincent 1898-1943 **TCLC 7; DAM POET; SSC 10**
See also CA 104; 152; DLB 4, 48, 102; DLBY 97; YABC 1
Benet, William Rose 1886-1950 **TCLC 28; DAM POET**
See also CA 118; 152; DLB 45
Benford, Gregory (Albert) 1941- **CLC 52**
See also CA 69-72; CAAS 27; CANR 12, 24, 49; DLBY 82
Bengtsson, Frans (Gunnar) 1894-1954**T C L C 48**
See also CA 170
Benjamin, David
See Slavitt, David R(ytman)
Benjamin, Lois
See Gould, Lois
Benjamin, Walter 1892-1940 **TCLC 39**
See also CA 164
Benn, Gottfried 1886-1956 **TCLC 3**
See also CA 106; 153; DLB 56
Bennett, Alan 1934-**CLC 45, 77; DAB; DAM MST**
See also CA 103; CANR 35, 55; MTCW 1
Bennett, (Enoch) Arnold 1867-1931 **TCLC 5, 20**
See also CA 106; 155; CDBLB 1890-1914; DLB 10, 34, 98, 135
Bennett, Elizabeth
See Mitchell, Margaret (Munnerlyn)
Bennett, George Harold 1930-

See Bennett, Hal
See also BW 1; CA 97-100
Bennett, Hal **CLC 5**
See also Bennett, George Harold
See also DLB 33
Bennett, Jay 1912- **CLC 35**
See also AAYA 10; CA 69-72; CANR 11, 42; JRDA; SAAS 4; SATA 41, 87; SATA-Brief 27
Bennett, Louise (Simone) 1919-**CLC 28; BLC 1; DAM MULT**
See also BW 2; CA 151; DLB 117
Benson, E(dward) F(rederic) 1867-1940
TCLC 27
See also CA 114; 157; DLB 135, 153
Benson, Jackson J. 1930- **CLC 34**
See also CA 25-28R; DLB 111
Benson, Sally 1900-1972 **CLC 17**
See also CA 19-20; 37-40R; CAP 1; SATA 1, 35; SATA-Obit 27
Benson, Stella 1892-1933 **TCLC 17**
See also CA 117; 155; DLB 36, 162
Bentham, Jeremy 1748-1832 **NCLC 38**
See also DLB 107, 158
Bentley, E(dmund) C(lerihew) 1875-1956
TCLC 12
See also CA 108; DLB 70
Bentley, Eric (Russell) 1916- **CLC 24**
See also CA 5-8R; CANR 6, 67; INT CANR-6
Beranger, Pierre Jean de 1780-1857**NCLC 34**
Berdyaev, Nicolas
See Berdyaev, Nikolai (Aleksandrovich)
Berdyaev, Nikolai (Aleksandrovich) 1874-1948
TCLC 67
See also CA 120; 157
Berdyayev, Nikolai (Aleksandrovich)
See Berdyaev, Nikolai (Aleksandrovich)
Berendt, John (Lawrence) 1939- **CLC 86**
See also CA 146
Beresford, J(ohn) D(avys) 1873-1947 **T C L C 81**
See also CA 112; 155; DLB 162, 178, 197
Bergelson, David 1884-1952 **TCLC 81**
Berger, Colonel
See Malraux, (Georges-)Andre
Berger, John (Peter) 1926- **CLC 2, 19**
See also CA 81-84; CANR 51; DLB 14
Berger, Melvin H. 1927- **CLC 12**
See also CA 5-8R; CANR 4; CLR 32; SAAS 2; SATA 5, 88
Berger, Thomas (Louis) 1924-**CLC 3, 5, 8, 11, 18, 38; DAM NOV**
See also CA 1-4R; CANR 5, 28, 51; DLB 2; DLBY 80; INT CANR-28; MTCW 1
Bergman, (Ernst) Ingmar 1918- **CLC 16, 72**
See also CA 81-84; CANR 33, 70
Bergson, Henri(-Louis) 1859-1941 **TCLC 32**
See also CA 164
Bergstein, Eleanor 1938- **CLC 4**
See also CA 53-56; CANR 5
Berkoff, Steven 1937- **CLC 56**
See also CA 104; CANR 72
Bermant, Chaim (Icyk) 1929- **CLC 40**
See also CA 57-60; CANR 6, 31, 57
Bern, Victoria
See Fisher, M(ary) F(rances) K(ennedy)
Bernanos, (Paul Louis) Georges 1888-1948
TCLC 3
See also CA 104; 130; DLB 72
Bernard, April 1956- **CLC 59**
See also CA 131
Berne, Victoria
See Fisher, M(ary) F(rances) K(ennedy)

Bernhard, Thomas 1931-1989 **CLC 3, 32, 61**
See also CA 85-88; 127; CANR 32, 57; DLB 85, 124; MTCW 1

Bernhardt, Sarah (Henriette Rosine) 1844-1923 **TCLC 75**
See also CA 157

Berriault, Gina 1926- **CLC 54, 109; SSC 30**
See also CA 116; 129; CANR 66; DLB 130

Berrigan, Daniel 1921- **CLC 4**
See also CA 33-36R; CAAS 1; CANR 11, 43; DLB 5

Berrigan, Edmund Joseph Michael, Jr. 1934-1983
See Berrigan, Ted
See also CA 61-64; 110; CANR 14

Berrigan, Ted **CLC 37**
See also Berrigan, Edmund Joseph Michael, Jr.
See also DLB 5, 169

Berry, Charles Edward Anderson 1931-
See Berry, Chuck
See also CA 115

Berry, Chuck **CLC 17**
See also Berry, Charles Edward Anderson

Berry, Jonas
See Ashbery, John (Lawrence)

Berry, Wendell (Erdman) 1934- **CLC 4, 6, 8, 27, 46; DAM POET**
See also AITN 1; CA 73-76; CANR 50, 73; DLB 5, 6

Berryman, John 1914-1972 **CLC 1, 2, 3, 4, 6, 8, 10, 13, 25, 62; DAM POET**
See also CA 13-16; 33-36R; CABS 2; CANR 35; CAP 1; CDALB 1941-1968; DLB 48; MTCW 1

Bertolucci, Bernardo 1940- **CLC 16**
See also CA 106

Berton, Pierre (Francis Demarigny) 1920- **CLC 104**
See also CA 1-4R; CANR 2, 56; DLB 68; SATA 99

Bertrand, Aloysius 1807-1841 **NCLC 31**
Bertran de Born c. 1140-1215 **CMLC 5**
Beruni, al 973-1048(?) **CMLC 28**
Besant, Annie (Wood) 1847-1933 **TCLC 9**
See also CA 105

Bessie, Alvah 1904-1985 **CLC 23**
See also CA 5-8R; 116; CANR 2; DLB 26

Bethlen, T. D.
See Silverberg, Robert

Beti, Mongo **CLC 27; BLC 1; DAM MULT**
See also Biyidi, Alexandre

Betjeman, John 1906-1984 **CLC 2, 6, 10, 34, 43; DAB; DAM MST, POET**
See also CA 9-12R; 112; CANR 33, 56; CDBLB 1945-1960; DLB 20; DLBY 84; MTCW 1

Bettelheim, Bruno 1903-1990 **CLC 79**
See also CA 81-84; 131; CANR 23, 61; MTCW 1

Betti, Ugo 1892-1953 **TCLC 5**
See also CA 104; 155

Betts, Doris (Waugh) 1932- **CLC 3, 6, 28**
See also CA 13-16R; CANR 9, 66; DLBY 82; INT CANR-9

Bevan, Alistair
See Roberts, Keith (John Kingston)

Bey, Pilaff
See Douglas, (George) Norman

Bialik, Chaim Nachman 1873-1934 **TCLC 25**
See also CA 170

Bickerstaff, Isaac
See Swift, Jonathan

Bidart, Frank 1939- **CLC 33**
See also CA 140

Bienek, Horst 1930- **CLC 7, 11**
See also CA 73-76; DLB 75

Bierce, Ambrose (Gwinett) 1842-1914(?) **TCLC 1, 7, 44; DA; DAC; DAM MST; SSC 9; WLC**
See also CA 104; 139; CDALB 1865-1917; DLB 11, 12, 23, 71, 74, 186

Biggers, Earl Derr 1884-1933 **TCLC 65**
See also CA 108; 153

Billings, Josh
See Shaw, Henry Wheeler

Billington, (Lady) Rachel (Mary) 1942- **C L C 43**
See also AITN 2; CA 33-36R; CANR 44

Binyon, T(imothy) J(ohn) 1936- **CLC 34**
See also CA 111; CANR 28

Bioy Casares, Adolfo 1914-1984 **CLC 4, 8, 13, 88; DAM MULT; HLC; SSC 17**
See also CA 29-32R; CANR 19, 43, 66; DLB 113; HW; MTCW 1

Bird, Cordwainer
See Ellison, Harlan (Jay)

Bird, Robert Montgomery 1806-1854 **NCLC 1**
See also DLB 202

Birkerts, Sven 1951- **CLC 116**
See also CA 128; 133; CAAS 29; INT 133

Birney, (Alfred) Earle 1904-1995 **CLC 1, 4, 6, 11; DAC; DAM MST, POET**
See also CA 1-4R; CANR 5, 20; DLB 88; MTCW 1

Bishop, Elizabeth 1911-1979 **CLC 1, 4, 9, 13, 15, 32; DA; DAC; DAM MST, POET; PC 3**
See also CA 5-8R; 89-92; CABS 2; CANR 26, 61; CDALB 1968-1988; DLB 5, 169; MTCW 1; SATA-Obit 24

Bishop, John 1935- **CLC 10**
See also CA 105

Bissett, Bill 1939- **CLC 18; PC 14**
See also CA 69-72; CAAS 19; CANR 15; DLB 53; MTCW 1

Bitov, Andrei (Georgievich) 1937- **CLC 57**
See also CA 142

Biyidi, Alexandre 1932-
See Beti, Mongo
See also BW 1; CA 114; 124; MTCW 1

Bjarme, Brynjolf
See Ibsen, Henrik (Johan)

Bjoernson, Bjoernstjerne (Martinius) 1832-1910 **TCLC 7, 37**
See also CA 104

Black, Robert
See Holdstock, Robert P.

Blackburn, Paul 1926-1971 **CLC 9, 43**
See also CA 81-84; 33-36R; CANR 34; DLB 16; DLBY 81

Black Elk 1863-1950 **TCLC 33; DAM MULT**
See also CA 144; NNAL

Black Hobart
See Sanders, (James) Ed(ward)

Blacklin, Malcolm
See Chambers, Aidan

Blackmore, R(ichard) D(oddridge) 1825-1900 **TCLC 27**
See also CA 120; DLB 18

Blackmur, R(ichard) P(almer) 1904-1965 **CLC 2, 24**
See also CA 11-12; 25-28R; CANR 71; CAP 1; DLB 63

Black Tarantula
See Acker, Kathy

Blackwood, Algernon (Henry) 1869-1951 **TCLC 5**

See also CA 105; 150; DLB 153, 156, 178

Blackwood, Caroline 1931-1996 **CLC 6, 9, 100**
See also CA 85-88; 151; CANR 32, 61, 65; DLB 14; MTCW 1

Blade, Alexander
See Hamilton, Edmond; Silverberg, Robert

Blaga, Lucian 1895-1961 **CLC 75**
See also CA 157

Blair, Eric (Arthur) 1903-1950
See Orwell, George
See also CA 104; 132; DA; DAB; DAC; DAM MST, NOV; MTCW 1; SATA 29

Blais, Marie-Claire 1939- **CLC 2, 4, 6, 13, 22; DAC; DAM MST**
See also CA 21-24R; CAAS 4; CANR 38; DLB 53; MTCW 1

Blaise, Clark 1940- **CLC 29**
See also AITN 2; CA 53-56; CAAS 3; CANR 5, 66; DLB 53

Blake, Fairley
See De Voto, Bernard (Augustine)

Blake, Nicholas
See Day Lewis, C(ecil)
See also DLB 77

Blake, William 1757-1827 **NCLC 13, 37, 57; DA; DAB; DAC; DAM MST, POET; PC 12; WLC**
See also CDBLB 1789-1832; CLR 52; DLB 93, 163; MAICYA; SATA 30

Blasco Ibanez, Vicente 1867-1928 **TCLC 12; DAM NOV**
See also CA 110; 131; HW; MTCW 1

Blatty, William Peter 1928- **CLC 2; DAM POP**
See also CA 5-8R; CANR 9

Bleeck, Oliver
See Thomas, Ross (Elmore)

Blessing, Lee 1949- **CLC 54**

Blish, James (Benjamin) 1921-1975 **CLC 14**
See also CA 1-4R; 57-60; CANR 3; DLB 8; MTCW 1; SATA 66

Bliss, Reginald
See Wells, H(erbert) G(eorge)

Blixen, Karen (Christentze Dinesen) 1885-1962
See Dinesen, Isak
See also CA 25-28; CANR 22, 50; CAP 2; MTCW 1; SATA 44

Bloch, Robert (Albert) 1917-1994 **CLC 33**
See also CA 5-8R; 146; CAAS 20; CANR 5; DLB 44; INT CANR-5; SATA 12; SATA-Obit 82

Blok, Alexander (Alexandrovich) 1880-1921 **TCLC 5; PC 21**
See also CA 104

Blom, Jan
See Breytenbach, Breyten

Bloom, Harold 1930- **CLC 24, 103**
See also CA 13-16R; CANR 39; DLB 67

Bloomfield, Aurelius
See Bourne, Randolph S(illiman)

Blount, Roy (Alton), Jr. 1941- **CLC 38**
See also CA 53-56; CANR 10, 28, 61; INT CANR-28; MTCW 1

Bloy, Leon 1846-1917 **TCLC 22**
See also CA 121; DLB 123

Blume, Judy (Sussman) 1938- **CLC 12, 30; DAM NOV, POP**
See also AAYA 3, 26; CA 29-32R; CANR 13, 37, 66; CLR 2, 15; DLB 52; JRDA; MAICYA; MTCW 1; SATA 2, 31, 79

Blunden, Edmund (Charles) 1896-1974 **C L C 2, 56**
See also CA 17-18; 45-48; CANR 54; CAP 2; DLB 20, 100, 155; MTCW 1

BLC 1; DAM MULT; DC 1
See also DLB 3, 50

Browne, (Clyde) Jackson 1948(?)-   CLC 21
See also CA 120

Browning, Elizabeth Barrett 1806-1861
NCLC 1, 16, 61, 66; DA; DAB; DAC; DAM
MST, POET; PC 6; WLC
See also CDBLB 1832-1890; DLB 32, 199

Browning, Robert 1812-1889 NCLC 19; DA;
DAB; DAC; DAM MST, POET; PC 2;
WLCS
See also CDBLB 1832-1890; DLB 32, 163;
YABC 1

Browning, Tod 1882-1962   CLC 16
See also CA 141; 117

Brownson, Orestes Augustus 1803-1876
NCLC 50
See also DLB 1, 59, 73

Bruccoli, Matthew J(oseph) 1931-   CLC 34
See also CA 9-12R; CANR 7; DLB 103

Bruce, Lenny   CLC 21
See also Schneider, Leonard Alfred

Bruin, John
See Brutus, Dennis

Brulard, Henri
See Stendhal

Brulls, Christian
See Simenon, Georges (Jacques Christian)

Brunner, John (Kilian Houston) 1934-1995
CLC 8, 10; DAM POP
See also CA 1-4R; 149; CAAS 8; CANR 2, 37;
MTCW 1

Bruno, Giordano 1548-1600   LC 27

Brutus, Dennis 1924- CLC 43; BLC 1; DAM
MULT, POET; PC 24
See also BW 2; CA 49-52; CAAS 14; CANR 2,
27, 42; DLB 117

Bryan, C(ourtlandt) D(ixon) B(arnes) 1936-
CLC 29
See also CA 73-76; CANR 13, 68; DLB 185;
INT CANR-13

Bryan, Michael
See Moore, Brian

Bryant, William Cullen 1794-1878 NCLC 6,
46; DA; DAB; DAC; DAM MST, POET;
PC 20
See also CDALB 1640-1865; DLB 3, 43, 59,
189

Bryusov, Valery Yakovlevich 1873-1924
TCLC 10
See also CA 107; 155

Buchan, John 1875-1940   TCLC 41; DAB;
DAM POP
See also CA 108; 145; DLB 34, 70, 156; YABC
2

Buchanan, George 1506-1582   LC 4
See also DLB 152

Buchheim, Lothar-Guenther 1918-   CLC 6
See also CA 85-88

Buchner, (Karl) Georg 1813-1837 NCLC 26

Buchwald, Art(hur) 1925-   CLC 33
See also AITN 1; CA 5-8R; CANR 21, 67;
MTCW 1; SATA 10

Buck, Pearl S(ydenstricker) 1892-1973CLC 7,
11, 18; DA; DAB; DAC; DAM MST, NOV
See also AITN 1; CA 1-4R; 41-44R; CANR 1,
34; DLB 9, 102; MTCW 1; SATA 1, 25

Buckler, Ernest 1908-1984   CLC 13; DAC;
DAM MST
See also CA 11-12; 114; CAP 1; DLB 68; SATA
47

Buckley, Vincent (Thomas) 1925-1988CLC 57
See also CA 101

Buckley, William F(rank), Jr. 1925-CLC 7, 18,
37; DAM POP
See also AITN 1; CA 1-4R; CANR 1, 24, 53;
DLB 137; DLBY 80; INT CANR-24; MTCW
1

Buechner, (Carl) Frederick 1926-CLC 2, 4, 6,
9; DAM NOV
See also CA 13-16R; CANR 11, 39, 64; DLBY
80; INT CANR-11; MTCW 1

Buell, John (Edward) 1927-   CLC 10
See also CA 1-4R; CANR 71; DLB 53

Buero Vallejo, Antonio 1916-   CLC 15, 46
See also CA 106; CANR 24, 49; HW; MTCW
1

Bufalino, Gesualdo 1920(?)-   CLC 74
See also DLB 196

Bugayev, Boris Nikolayevich 1880-1934
TCLC 7; PC 11
See also Bely, Andrey
See also CA 104; 165

Bukowski, Charles 1920-1994CLC 2, 5, 9, 41,
82, 108; DAM NOV, POET; PC 18
See also CA 17-20R; 144; CANR 40, 62; DLB
5, 130, 169; MTCW 1

Bulgakov, Mikhail (Afanas'evich) 1891-1940
TCLC 2, 16; DAM DRAM, NOV; SSC 18
See also CA 105; 152

Bulgya, Alexander Alexandrovich 1901-1956
TCLC 53
See also Fadeyev, Alexander
See also CA 117

Bullins, Ed 1935- CLC 1, 5, 7; BLC 1; DAM
DRAM, MULT; DC 6
See also BW 2; CA 49-52; CAAS 16; CANR
24, 46, 73; DLB 7, 38; MTCW 1

Bulwer-Lytton, Edward (George Earle Lytton)
1803-1873   NCLC 1, 45
See also DLB 21

Bunin, Ivan Alexeyevich 1870-1953 TCLC 6;
SSC 5
See also CA 104

Bunting, Basil 1900-1985   CLC 10, 39, 47;
DAM POET
See also CA 53-56; 115; CANR 7; DLB 20

Bunuel, Luis 1900-1983   CLC 16, 80; DAM
MULT; HLC
See also CA 101; 110; CANR 32; HW

Bunyan, John 1628-1688   LC 4; DA; DAB;
DAC; DAM MST; WLC
See also CDBLB 1660-1789; DLB 39

Burckhardt, Jacob (Christoph) 1818-1897
NCLC 49

Burford, Eleanor
See Hibbert, Eleanor Alice Burford

Burgess, AnthonyCLC 1, 2, 4, 5, 8, 10, 13, 15,
22, 40, 62, 81, 94; DAB
See also Wilson, John (Anthony) Burgess
See also AAYA 25; AITN 1; CDBLB 1960 to
Present; DLB 14, 194

Burke, Edmund 1729(?)-1797 LC 7, 36; DA;
DAB; DAC; DAM MST; WLC
See also DLB 104

Burke, Kenneth (Duva) 1897-1993 CLC 2, 24
See also CA 5-8R; 143; CANR 39, 74; DLB
45, 63; MTCW 1

Burke, Leda
See Garnett, David

Burke, Ralph
See Silverberg, Robert

Burke, Thomas 1886-1945   TCLC 63
See also CA 113; 155; DLB 197

Burney, Fanny 1752-1840   NCLC 12, 54
See also DLB 39

Burns, Robert 1759-1796   PC 6
See also CDBLB 1789-1832; DA; DAB; DAC;
DAM MST, POET; DLB 109; WLC

Burns, Tex
See L'Amour, Louis (Dearborn)

Burnshaw, Stanley 1906-   CLC 3, 13, 44
See also CA 9-12R; DLB 48; DLBY 97

Burr, Anne 1937-   CLC 6
See also CA 25-28R

Burroughs, Edgar Rice 1875-1950 TCLC 2,
32; DAM NOV
See also AAYA 11; CA 104; 132; DLB 8;
MTCW 1; SATA 41

Burroughs, William S(eward) 1914-1997CLC
1, 2, 5, 15, 22, 42, 75, 109; DA; DAB; DAC;
DAM MST, NOV, POP; WLC
See also AITN 2; CA 9-12R; 160; CANR 20,
52; DLB 2, 8, 16, 152; DLBY 81, 97; MTCW
1

Burton, Richard F. 1821-1890   NCLC 42
See also DLB 55, 184

Busch, Frederick 1941-   CLC 7, 10, 18, 47
See also CA 33-36R; CAAS 1; CANR 45, 73;
DLB 6

Bush, Ronald 1946-   CLC 34
See also CA 136

Bustos, F(rancisco)
See Borges, Jorge Luis

Bustos Domecq, H(onorio)
See Bioy Casares, Adolfo; Borges, Jorge Luis

Butler, Octavia E(stelle) 1947-CLC 38; BLCS;
DAM MULT, POP
See also AAYA 18; BW 2; CA 73-76; CANR
12, 24, 38, 73; DLB 33; MTCW 1; SATA 84

Butler, Robert Olen (Jr.) 1945-CLC 81; DAM
POP
See also CA 112; CANR 66; DLB 173; INT 112

Butler, Samuel 1612-1680   LC 16, 43
See also DLB 101, 126

Butler, Samuel 1835-1902   TCLC 1, 33; DA;
DAB; DAC; DAM MST, NOV; WLC
See also CA 143; CDBLB 1890-1914; DLB 18,
57, 174

Butler, Walter C.
See Faust, Frederick (Schiller)

Butor, Michel (Marie Francois) 1926-CLC 1,
3, 8, 11, 15
See also CA 9-12R; CANR 33, 66; DLB 83;
MTCW 1

Butts, Mary 1892(?)-1937   TCLC 77
See also CA 148

Buzo, Alexander (John) 1944-   CLC 61
See also CA 97-100; CANR 17, 39, 69

Buzzati, Dino 1906-1972   CLC 36
See also CA 160; 33-36R; DLB 177

Byars, Betsy (Cromer) 1928-   CLC 35
See also AAYA 19; CA 33-36R; CANR 18, 36,
57; CLR 1, 16; DLB 52; INT CANR-18;
JRDA; MAICYA; MTCW 1; SAAS 1; SATA
4, 46, 80

Byatt, A(ntonia) S(usan Drabble) 1936- C L C
19, 65; DAM NOV, POP
See also CA 13-16R; CANR 13, 33, 50; DLB
14, 194; MTCW 1

Byrne, David 1952-   CLC 26
See also CA 127

Byrne, John Keyes 1926-
See Leonard, Hugh
See also CA 102; INT 102

Byron, George Gordon (Noel) 1788-1824
NCLC 2, 12; DA; DAB; DAC; DAM MST,
POET; PC 16; WLC
See also CDBLB 1789-1832; DLB 96, 110

Byron, Robert 1905-1941   **TCLC 67**
See also CA 160; DLB 195

C. 3. 3.
See Wilde, Oscar (Fingal O'Flahertie Wills)

Caballero, Fernan 1796-1877   **NCLC 10**

Cabell, Branch
See Cabell, James Branch

Cabell, James Branch 1879-1958   **TCLC 6**
See also CA 105; 152; DLB 9, 78

Cable, George Washington 1844-1925 **TCLC 4; SSC 4**
See also CA 104; 155; DLB 12, 74; DLBD 13

Cabral de Melo Neto, Joao 1920-   **CLC 76; DAM MULT**
See also CA 151

Cabrera Infante, G(uillermo) 1929-**CLC 5, 25, 45; DAM MULT; HLC**
See also CA 85-88; CANR 29, 65; DLB 113; HW; MTCW 1

Cade, Toni
See Bambara, Toni Cade

Cadmus and Harmonia
See Buchan, John

Caedmon fl. 658-680   **CMLC 7**
See also DLB 146

Caeiro, Alberto
See Pessoa, Fernando (Antonio Nogueira)

Cage, John (Milton, Jr.) 1912-1992   **CLC 41**
See also CA 13-16R; 169; CANR 9; DLB 193; INT CANR-9

Cahan, Abraham 1860-1951   **TCLC 71**
See also CA 108; 154; DLB 9, 25, 28

Cain, G.
See Cabrera Infante, G(uillermo)

Cain, Guillermo
See Cabrera Infante, G(uillermo)

Cain, James M(allahan) 1892-1977**CLC 3, 11, 28**
See also AITN 1; CA 17-20R; 73-76; CANR 8, 34, 61; MTCW 1

Caine, Mark
See Raphael, Frederic (Michael)

Calasso, Roberto 1941-   **CLC 81**
See also CA 143

Calderon de la Barca, Pedro 1600-1681   **L C 23; DC 3**

Caldwell, Erskine (Preston) 1903-1987**CLC 1, 8, 14, 50, 60; DAM NOV; SSC 19**
See also AITN 1; CA 1-4R; 121; CAAS 1; CANR 2, 33; DLB 9, 86; MTCW 1

Caldwell, (Janet Miriam) Taylor (Holland) 1900-1985**CLC 2, 28, 39; DAM NOV, POP**
See also CA 5-8R; 116; CANR 5; DLBD 17

Calhoun, John Caldwell 1782-1850**NCLC 15**
See also DLB 3

Calisher, Hortense 1911-**CLC 2, 4, 8, 38; DAM NOV; SSC 15**
See also CA 1-4R; CANR 1, 22, 67; DLB 2; INT CANR-22; MTCW 1

Callaghan, Morley Edward 1903-1990**CLC 3, 14, 41, 65; DAC; DAM MST**
See also CA 9-12R; 132; CANR 33, 73; DLB 68; MTCW 1

Callimachus c. 305B.C.-c. 240B.C. **CMLC 18**
See also DLB 176

Calvin, John 1509-1564   **LC 37**

Calvino, Italo 1923-1985**CLC 5, 8, 11, 22, 33, 39, 73; DAM NOV; SSC 3**
See also CA 85-88; 116; CANR 23, 61; DLB 196; MTCW 1

Cameron, Carey 1952-   **CLC 59**
See also CA 135

Cameron, Peter 1959-   **CLC 44**

See also CA 125; CANR 50

Campana, Dino 1885-1932   **TCLC 20**
See also CA 117; DLB 114

Campanella, Tommaso 1568-1639   **LC 32**

Campbell, John W(ood, Jr.) 1910-1971 **C L C 32**
See also CA 21-22; 29-32R; CANR 34; CAP 2; DLB 8; MTCW 1

Campbell, Joseph 1904-1987   **CLC 69**
See also AAYA 3; BEST 89:2; CA 1-4R; 124; CANR 3, 28, 61; MTCW 1

Campbell, Maria 1940-   **CLC 85; DAC**
See also CA 102; CANR 54; NNAL

Campbell, (John) Ramsey 1946-**CLC 42; SSC 19**
See also CA 57-60; CANR 7; INT CANR-7

Campbell, (Ignatius) Roy (Dunnachie) 1901-1957   **TCLC 5**
See also CA 104; 155; DLB 20

Campbell, Thomas 1777-1844   **NCLC 19**
See also DLB 93; 144

Campbell, Wilfred   **TCLC 9**
See also Campbell, William

Campbell, William 1858(?)-1918
See Campbell, Wilfred
See also CA 106; DLB 92

Campion, Jane   **CLC 95**
See also CA 138

Campos, Alvaro de
See Pessoa, Fernando (Antonio Nogueira)

Camus, Albert 1913-1960**CLC 1, 2, 4, 9, 11, 14, 32, 63, 69; DA; DAB; DAC; DAM DRAM, MST, NOV; DC 2; SSC 9; WLC**
See also CA 89-92; DLB 72; MTCW 1

Canby, Vincent 1924-   **CLC 13**
See also CA 81-84

Cancale
See Desnos, Robert

Canetti, Elias 1905-1994**CLC 3, 14, 25, 75, 86**
See also CA 21-24R; 146; CANR 23, 61; DLB 85, 124; MTCW 1

Canfield, Dorothea F.
See Fisher, Dorothy (Frances) Canfield

Canfield, Dorothea Frances
See Fisher, Dorothy (Frances) Canfield

Canfield, Dorothy
See Fisher, Dorothy (Frances) Canfield

Canin, Ethan 1960-   **CLC 55**
See also CA 131; 135

Cannon, Curt
See Hunter, Evan

Cao, Lan 1961-   **CLC 109**
See also CA 165

Cape, Judith
See Page, P(atricia) K(athleen)

Capek, Karel 1890-1938   **TCLC 6, 37; DA; DAB; DAC; DAM DRAM, MST, NOV; DC 1; WLC**
See also CA 104; 140

Capote, Truman 1924-1984**CLC 1, 3, 8, 13, 19, 34, 38, 58; DA; DAB; DAC; DAM MST, NOV, POP; SSC 2; WLC**
See also CA 5-8R; 113; CANR 18, 62; CDALB 1941-1968; DLB 2, 185; DLBY 80, 84; MTCW 1; SATA 91

Capra, Frank 1897-1991   **CLC 16**
See also CA 61-64; 135

Caputo, Philip 1941-   **CLC 32**
See also CA 73-76; CANR 40

Caragiale, Ion Luca 1852-1912   **TCLC 76**
See also CA 157

Card, Orson Scott 1951-**CLC 44, 47, 50; DAM POP**

See also AAYA 11; CA 102; CANR 27, 47, 73; INT CANR-27; MTCW 1; SATA 83

Cardenal, Ernesto 1925-   **CLC 31; DAM MULT, POET; HLC; PC 22**
See also CA 49-52; CANR 2, 32, 66; HW; MTCW 1

Cardozo, Benjamin N(athan) 1870-1938   **TCLC 65**
See also CA 117; 164

Carducci, Giosue (Alessandro Giuseppe) 1835-1907   **TCLC 32**
See also CA 163

Carew, Thomas 1595(?)-1640   **LC 13**
See also DLB 126

Carey, Ernestine Gilbreth 1908-   **CLC 17**
See also CA 5-8R; CANR 71; SATA 2

Carey, Peter 1943-   **CLC 40, 55, 96**
See also CA 123; 127; CANR 53; INT 127; MTCW 1; SATA 94

Carleton, William 1794-1869   **NCLC 3**
See also DLB 159

Carlisle, Henry (Coffin) 1926-   **CLC 33**
See also CA 13-16R; CANR 15

Carlsen, Chris
See Holdstock, Robert P.

Carlson, Ron(ald F.) 1947-   **CLC 54**
See also CA 105; CANR 27

Carlyle, Thomas 1795-1881   **NCLC 70; DA; DAB; DAC; DAM MST**
See also CDBLB 1789-1832; DLB 55; 144

Carman, (William) Bliss 1861-1929 **TCLC 7; DAC**
See also CA 104; 152; DLB 92

Carnegie, Dale 1888-1955   **TCLC 53**

Carossa, Hans 1878-1956   **TCLC 48**
See also CA 170; DLB 66

Carpenter, Don(ald Richard) 1931-1995**C L C 41**
See also CA 45-48; 149; CANR 1, 71

Carpenter, Edward 1844-1929   **TCLC 88**
See also CA 163

Carpentier (y Valmont), Alejo 1904-1980**CLC 8, 11, 38, 110; DAM MULT; HLC**
See also CA 65-68; 97-100; CANR 11, 70; DLB 113; HW

Carr, Caleb 1955(?)-   **CLC 86**
See also CA 147; CANR 73

Carr, Emily 1871-1945   **TCLC 32**
See also CA 159; DLB 68

Carr, John Dickson 1906-1977   **CLC 3**
See also Fairbairn, Roger
See also CA 49-52; 69-72; CANR 3, 33, 60; MTCW 1

Carr, Philippa
See Hibbert, Eleanor Alice Burford

Carr, Virginia Spencer 1929-   **CLC 34**
See also CA 61-64; DLB 111

Carrere, Emmanuel 1957-   **CLC 89**

Carrier, Roch 1937-**CLC 13, 78; DAC; DAM MST**
See also CA 130; CANR 61; DLB 53

Carroll, James P. 1943(?)-   **CLC 38**
See also CA 81-84; CANR 73

Carroll, Jim 1951-   **CLC 35**
See also AAYA 17; CA 45-48; CANR 42

Carroll, Lewis   NCLC 2, 53; PC 18; WLC
See also Dodgson, Charles Lutwidge
See also CDBLB 1832-1890; CLR 2, 18; DLB 18, 163, 178; JRDA

Carroll, Paul Vincent 1900-1968   **CLC 10**
See also CA 9-12R; 25-28R; DLB 10

Carruth, Hayden 1921- **CLC 4, 7, 10, 18, 84; PC 10**

See also CA 9-12R; CANR 4, 38, 59; DLB 5, 165; INT CANR-4; MTCW 1; SATA 47

Carson, Rachel Louise 1907-1964 **CLC 71; DAM POP**
See also CA 77-80; CANR 35; MTCW 1; SATA 23

Carter, Angela (Olive) 1940-1992 **CLC 5, 41, 76; SSC 13**
See also CA 53-56; 136; CANR 12, 36, 61; DLB 14; MTCW 1; SATA 66; SATA-Obit 70

Carter, Nick
See Smith, Martin Cruz

Carver, Raymond 1938-1988 **CLC 22, 36, 53, 55; DAM NOV; SSC 8**
See also CA 33-36R; 126; CANR 17, 34, 61; DLB 130; DLBY 84, 88; MTCW 1

Cary, Elizabeth, Lady Falkland 1585-1639 **LC 30**

Cary, (Arthur) Joyce (Lunel) 1888-1957 **TCLC 1, 29**
See also CA 104; 164; CDBLB 1914-1945; DLB 15, 100

Casanova de Seingalt, Giovanni Jacopo 1725-1798 **LC 13**

Casares, Adolfo Bioy
See Bioy Casares, Adolfo

Casely-Hayford, J(oseph) E(phraim) 1866-1930 **TCLC 24; BLC 1; DAM MULT**
See also BW 2; CA 123; 152

Casey, John (Dudley) 1939- **CLC 59**
See also BEST 90:2; CA 69-72; CANR 23

Casey, Michael 1947- **CLC 2**
See also CA 65-68; DLB 5

Casey, Patrick
See Thurman, Wallace (Henry)

Casey, Warren (Peter) 1935-1988 **CLC 12**
See also CA 101; 127; INT 101

Casona, Alejandro **CLC 49**
See also Alvarez, Alejandro Rodriguez

Cassavetes, John 1929-1989 **CLC 20**
See also CA 85-88; 127

Cassian, Nina 1924- **PC 17**

Cassill, R(onald) V(erlin) 1919- **CLC 4, 23**
See also CA 9-12R; CAAS 1; CANR 7, 45; DLB 6

Cassirer, Ernst 1874-1945 **TCLC 61**
See also CA 157

Cassity, (Allen) Turner 1929- **CLC 6, 42**
See also CA 17-20R; CAAS 8; CANR 11; DLB 105

Castaneda, Carlos 1931(?)- **CLC 12**
See also CA 25-28R; CANR 32, 66; HW; MTCW 1

Castedo, Elena 1937- **CLC 65**
See also CA 132

Castedo-Ellerman, Elena
See Castedo, Elena

Castellanos, Rosario 1925-1974 **CLC 66; DAM MULT; HLC**
See also CA 131; 53-56; CANR 58; DLB 113; HW

Castelvetro, Lodovico 1505-1571 **LC 12**

Castiglione, Baldassare 1478-1529 **LC 12**

Castle, Robert
See Hamilton, Edmond

Castro, Guillen de 1569-1631 **LC 19**

Castro, Rosalia de 1837-1885 **NCLC 3; DAM MULT**

Cather, Willa
See Cather, Willa Sibert

Cather, Willa Sibert 1873-1947 **TCLC 1, 11, 31; DA; DAB; DAC; DAM MST, NOV; SSC 2; WLC**

See also AAYA 24; CA 104; 128; CDALB 1865-1917; DLB 9, 54, 78; DLBD 1; MTCW 1; SATA 30

Catherine, Saint 1347-1380 **CMLC 27**

Cato, Marcus Porcius 234B.C.-149B.C. **CMLC 21**

Catton, (Charles) Bruce 1899-1978 **CLC 35**
See also AITN 1; CA 5-8R; 81-84; CANR 7, 74; DLB 17; SATA 2; SATA-Obit 24

Catullus c. 84B.C.-c. 54B.C. **CMLC 18**

Cauldwell, Frank
See King, Francis (Henry)

Caunitz, William J. 1933-1996 **CLC 34**
See also BEST 89:3; CA 125; 130; 152; CANR 73; INT 130

Causley, Charles (Stanley) 1917- **CLC 7**
See also CA 9-12R; CANR 5, 35; CLR 30; DLB 27; MTCW 1; SATA 3, 66

Caute, (John) David 1936- **CLC 29; DAM NOV**
See also CA 1-4R; CAAS 4; CANR 1, 33, 64; DLB 14

Cavafy, C(onstantine) P(eter) 1863-1933 **TCLC 2, 7; DAM POET**
See also Kavafis, Konstantinos Petrou
See also CA 148

Cavallo, Evelyn
See Spark, Muriel (Sarah)

Cavanna, Betty **CLC 12**
See also Harrison, Elizabeth Cavanna
See also JRDA; MAICYA; SAAS 4; SATA 1, 30

Cavendish, Margaret Lucas 1623-1673 **LC 30**
See also DLB 131

Caxton, William 1421(?)-1491(?) **LC 17**
See also DLB 170

Cayer, D. M.
See Duffy, Maureen

Cayrol, Jean 1911- **CLC 11**
See also CA 89-92; DLB 83

Cela, Camilo Jose 1916- **CLC 4, 13, 59; DAM MULT; HLC**
See also BEST 90:2; CA 21-24R; CAAS 10; CANR 21, 32; DLBY 89; HW; MTCW 1

Celan, Paul **CLC 10, 19, 53, 82; PC 10**
See also Antschel, Paul
See also DLB 69

Celine, Louis-Ferdinand **CLC 1, 3, 4, 7, 9, 15, 47**
See also Destouches, Louis-Ferdinand
See also DLB 72

Cellini, Benvenuto 1500-1571 **LC 7**

Cendrars, Blaise 1887-1961 **CLC 18, 106**
See also Sauser-Hall, Frederic

Cernuda (y Bidon), Luis 1902-1963 **CLC 54; DAM POET**
See also CA 131; 89-92; DLB 134; HW

Cervantes (Saavedra), Miguel de 1547-1616 **LC 6, 23; DA; DAB; DAC; DAM MST, NOV; SSC 12; WLC**

Cesaire, Aime (Fernand) 1913- **CLC 19, 32, 112; BLC 1; DAM MULT, POET**
See also BW 2; CA 65-68; CANR 24, 43; MTCW 1

Chabon, Michael 1963- **CLC 55**
See also CA 139; CANR 57

Chabrol, Claude 1930- **CLC 16**
See also CA 110

Challans, Mary 1905-1983
See Renault, Mary
See also CA 81-84; 111; CANR 74; SATA 23; SATA-Obit 36

Challis, George

See Faust, Frederick (Schiller)

Chambers, Aidan 1934- **CLC 35**
See also AAYA 27; CA 25-28R; CANR 12, 31, 58; JRDA; MAICYA; SAAS 12; SATA 1, 69

Chambers, James 1948-
See Cliff, Jimmy
See also CA 124

Chambers, Jessie
See Lawrence, D(avid) H(erbert Richards)

Chambers, Robert W(illiam) 1865-1933 **TCLC 41**
See also CA 165; DLB 202

Chandler, Raymond (Thornton) 1888-1959 **TCLC 1, 7; SSC 23**
See also AAYA 25; CA 104; 129; CANR 60; CDALB 1929-1941; DLBD 6; MTCW 1

Chang, Eileen 1920-1995 **SSC 28**
See also CA 166

Chang, Jung 1952- **CLC 71**
See also CA 142

Chang Ai-Ling
See Chang, Eileen

Channing, William Ellery 1780-1842 **NCLC 17**
See also DLB 1, 59

Chaplin, Charles Spencer 1889-1977 **CLC 16**
See also Chaplin, Charlie
See also CA 81-84; 73-76

Chaplin, Charlie
See Chaplin, Charles Spencer
See also DLB 44

Chapman, George 1559(?)-1634 **LC 22; DAM DRAM**
See also DLB 62, 121

Chapman, Graham 1941-1989 **CLC 21**
See also Monty Python
See also CA 116; 129; CANR 35

Chapman, John Jay 1862-1933 **TCLC 7**
See also CA 104

Chapman, Lee
See Bradley, Marion Zimmer

Chapman, Walker
See Silverberg, Robert

Chappell, Fred (Davis) 1936- **CLC 40, 78**
See also CA 5-8R; CAAS 4; CANR 8, 33, 67; DLB 6, 105

Char, Rene(-Emile) 1907-1988 **CLC 9, 11, 14, 55; DAM POET**
See also CA 13-16R; 124; CANR 32; MTCW 1

Charby, Jay
See Ellison, Harlan (Jay)

Chardin, Pierre Teilhard de
See Teilhard de Chardin, (Marie Joseph) Pierre

Charles I 1600-1649 **LC 13**

Charriere, Isabelle de 1740-1805 **NCLC 66**

Charyn, Jerome 1937- **CLC 5, 8, 18**
See also CA 5-8R; CAAS 1; CANR 7, 61; DLBY 83; MTCW 1

Chase, Mary (Coyle) 1907-1981 **DC 1**
See also CA 77-80; 105; SATA 17; SATA-Obit 29

Chase, Mary Ellen 1887-1973 **CLC 2**
See also CA 13-16; 41-44R; CAP 1; SATA 10

Chase, Nicholas
See Hyde, Anthony

Chateaubriand, Francois Rene de 1768-1848 **NCLC 3**
See also DLB 119

Chatterje, Sarat Chandra 1876-1936(?)
See Chatterji, Saratchandra
See also CA 109

Chatterji, Bankim Chandra 1838-1894 **NCLC 19**

Chatterji, Saratchandra   **TCLC 13**
See also Chatterje, Sarat Chandra
Chatterton, Thomas 1752-1770 **LC 3; DAM POET**
See also DLB 109
Chatwin, (Charles) Bruce 1940-1989 **CLC 28, 57, 59; DAM POP**
See also AAYA 4; BEST 90:1; CA 85-88; 127; DLB 194
Chaucer, Daniel
See Ford, Ford Madox
Chaucer, Geoffrey 1340(?)-1400 **LC 17; DA; DAB; DAC; DAM MST, POET; PC 19; WLCS**
See also CDBLB Before 1660; DLB 146
Chaviaras, Strates 1935-
See Haviaras, Stratis
See also CA 105
Chayefsky, Paddy   **CLC 23**
See also Chayefsky, Sidney
See also DLB 7, 44; DLBY 81
Chayefsky, Sidney 1923-1981
See Chayefsky, Paddy
See also CA 9-12R; 104; CANR 18; DAM DRAM
Chedid, Andree 1920-   **CLC 47**
See also CA 145
Cheever, John 1912-1982 **CLC 3, 7, 8, 11, 15, 25, 64; DA; DAB; DAC; DAM MST, NOV, POP; SSC 1; WLC**
See also CA 5-8R; 106; CABS 1; CANR 5, 27; CDALB 1941-1968; DLB 2, 102; DLBY 80, 82; INT CANR-5; MTCW 1
Cheever, Susan 1943-   **CLC 18, 48**
See also CA 103; CANR 27, 51; DLBY 82; INT CANR-27
Chekhonte, Antosha
See Chekhov, Anton (Pavlovich)
Chekhov, Anton (Pavlovich) 1860-1904 **TCLC 3, 10, 31, 55; DA; DAB; DAC; DAM DRAM, MST; DC 9; SSC 2, 28; WLC**
See also CA 104; 124; SATA 90
Chernyshevsky, Nikolay Gavrilovich 1828-1889 **NCLC 1**
Cherry, Carolyn Janice 1942-
See Cherryh, C. J.
See also CA 65-68; CANR 10
Cherryh, C. J.   **CLC 35**
See also Cherry, Carolyn Janice
See also AAYA 24; DLBY 80; SATA 93
Chesnutt, Charles W(addell) 1858-1932 **TCLC 5, 39; BLC 1; DAM MULT; SSC 7**
See also BW 1; CA 106; 125; DLB 12, 50, 78; MTCW 1
Chester, Alfred 1929(?)-1971   **CLC 49**
See also CA 33-36R; DLB 130
Chesterton, G(ilbert) K(eith) 1874-1936 **TCLC 1, 6, 64; DAM NOV, POET; SSC 1**
See also CA 104; 132; CANR 73; CDBLB 1914-1945; DLB 10, 19, 34, 70, 98, 149, 178; MTCW 1; SATA 27
Chiang, Pin-chin 1904-1986
See Ding Ling
See also CA 118
Ch'ien Chung-shu 1910-   **CLC 22**
See also CA 130; CANR 73; MTCW 1
Child, L. Maria
See Child, Lydia Maria
Child, Lydia Maria 1802-1880   **NCLC 6, 73**
See also DLB 1, 74; SATA 67
Child, Mrs.
See Child, Lydia Maria
Child, Philip 1898-1978   **CLC 19, 68**

See also CA 13-14; CAP 1; SATA 47
Childers, (Robert) Erskine 1870-1922 **TCLC 65**
See also CA 113; 153; DLB 70
Childress, Alice 1920-1994 **CLC 12, 15, 86, 96; BLC 1; DAM DRAM, MULT, NOV; DC 4**
See also AAYA 8; BW 2; CA 45-48; 146; CANR 3, 27, 50, 74; CLR 14; DLB 7, 38; JRDA; MAICYA; MTCW 1; SATA 7, 48, 81
Chin, Frank (Chew, Jr.) 1940-   **DC 7**
See also CA 33-36R; CANR 71; DAM MULT
Chislett, (Margaret) Anne 1943-   **CLC 34**
See also CA 151
Chitty, Thomas Willes 1926-   **CLC 11**
See also Hinde, Thomas
See also CA 5-8R
Chivers, Thomas Holley 1809-1858 **NCLC 49**
See also DLB 3
Chomette, Rene Lucien 1898-1981
See Clair, Rene
See also CA 103
Chopin, Kate TCLC 5, 14; DA; DAB; SSC 8; WLCS
See also Chopin, Katherine
See also CDALB 1865-1917; DLB 12, 78
Chopin, Katherine 1851-1904
See Chopin, Kate
See also CA 104; 122; DAC; DAM MST, NOV
Chretien de Troyes c. 12th cent. - **CMLC 10**
Christie
See Ichikawa, Kon
Christie, Agatha (Mary Clarissa) 1890-1976 **CLC 1, 6, 8, 12, 39, 48, 110; DAB; DAC; DAM NOV**
See also AAYA 9; AITN 1, 2; CA 17-20R; 61-64; CANR 10, 37; CDBLB 1914-1945; DLB 13, 77; MTCW 1; SATA 36
Christie, (Ann) Philippa
See Pearce, Philippa
See also CA 5-8R; CANR 4
Christine de Pizan 1365(?)-1431(?)   **LC 9**
Chubb, Elmer
See Masters, Edgar Lee
Chulkov, Mikhail Dmitrievich 1743-1792 **LC 2**
See also DLB 150
Churchill, Caryl 1938-   **CLC 31, 55; DC 5**
See also CA 102; CANR 22, 46; DLB 13; MTCW 1
Churchill, Charles 1731-1764   **LC 3**
See also DLB 109
Chute, Carolyn 1947-   **CLC 39**
See also CA 123
Ciardi, John (Anthony) 1916-1986 **CLC 10, 40, 44; DAM POET**
See also CA 5-8R; 118; CAAS 2; CANR 5, 33; CLR 19; DLB 5; DLBY 86; INT CANR-5; MAICYA; MTCW 1; SAAS 26; SATA 1, 65; SATA-Obit 46
Cicero, Marcus Tullius 106B.C.-43B.C. **CMLC 3**
Cimino, Michael 1943-   **CLC 16**
See also CA 105
Cioran, E(mil) M. 1911-1995   **CLC 64**
See also CA 25-28R; 149
Cisneros, Sandra 1954- **CLC 69; DAM MULT; HLC; SSC 32**
See also AAYA 9; CA 131; CANR 64; DLB 122, 152; HW
Cixous, Helene 1937-   **CLC 92**
See also CA 126; CANR 55; DLB 83; MTCW 1
Clair, Rene   **CLC 20**
See also Chomette, Rene Lucien

Clampitt, Amy 1920-1994   **CLC 32; PC 19**
See also CA 110; 146; CANR 29; DLB 105
Clancy, Thomas L., Jr. 1947-
See Clancy, Tom
See also CA 125; 131; CANR 62; INT 131; MTCW 1
Clancy, Tom   **CLC 45, 112; DAM NOV, POP**
See also Clancy, Thomas L., Jr.
See also AAYA 9; BEST 89:1, 90:1
Clare, John 1793-1864 **NCLC 9; DAB; DAM POET; PC 23**
See also DLB 55, 96
Clarin
See Alas (y Urena), Leopoldo (Enrique Garcia)
Clark, Al C.
See Goines, Donald
Clark, (Robert) Brian 1932-   **CLC 29**
See also CA 41-44R; CANR 67
Clark, Curt
See Westlake, Donald E(dwin)
Clark, Eleanor 1913-1996   **CLC 5, 19**
See also CA 9-12R; 151; CANR 41; DLB 6
Clark, J. P.
See Clark, John Pepper
See also DLB 117
Clark, John Pepper 1935- **CLC 38; BLC 1; DAM DRAM, MULT; DC 5**
See also Clark, J. P.
See also BW 1; CA 65-68; CANR 16, 72
Clark, M. R.
See Clark, Mavis Thorpe
Clark, Mavis Thorpe 1909-   **CLC 12**
See also CA 57-60; CANR 8, 37; CLR 30; MAICYA; SAAS 5; SATA 8, 74
Clark, Walter Van Tilburg 1909-1971 **CLC 28**
See also CA 9-12R; 33-36R; CANR 63; DLB 9; SATA 8
Clark Bekederemo, J(ohnson) P(epper)
See Clark, John Pepper
Clarke, Arthur C(harles) 1917- **CLC 1, 4, 13, 18, 35; DAM POP; SSC 3**
See also AAYA 4; CA 1-4R; CANR 2, 28, 55, 74; JRDA; MAICYA; MTCW 1; SATA 13, 70
Clarke, Austin 1896-1974   **CLC 6, 9; DAM POET**
See also CA 29-32; 49-52; CAP 2; DLB 10, 20
Clarke, Austin C(hesterfield) 1934- **CLC 8, 53; BLC 1; DAC; DAM MULT**
See also BW 1; CA 25-28R; CAAS 16; CANR 14, 32, 68; DLB 53, 125
Clarke, Gillian 1937-   **CLC 61**
See also CA 106; DLB 40
Clarke, Marcus (Andrew Hislop) 1846-1881 **NCLC 19**
Clarke, Shirley 1925-   **CLC 16**
Clash, The
See Headon, (Nicky) Topper; Jones, Mick; Simonon, Paul; Strummer, Joe
Claudel, Paul (Louis Charles Marie) 1868-1955 **TCLC 2, 10**
See also CA 104; 165; DLB 192
Clavell, James (duMaresq) 1925-1994 **CLC 6, 25, 87; DAM NOV, POP**
See also CA 25-28R; 146; CANR 26, 48; MTCW 1
Cleaver, (Leroy) Eldridge 1935-1998 **CLC 30; BLC 1; DAM MULT**
See also BW 1; CA 21-24R; 167; CANR 16
Cleese, John (Marwood) 1939-   **CLC 21**
See also Monty Python
See also CA 112; 116; CANR 35; MTCW 1
Cleishbotham, Jebediah

Cooke, M. E.
See Creasey, John

Cooke, Margaret
See Creasey, John

Cook-Lynn, Elizabeth 1930-   CLC 93; DAM
    MULT
See also CA 133; DLB 175; NNAL

Cooney, Ray   CLC 62

Cooper, Douglas 1960-   CLC 86

Cooper, Henry St. John
See Creasey, John

Cooper, J(oan) California   CLC 56; DAM
    MULT
See also AAYA 12; BW 1; CA 125; CANR 55

Cooper, James Fenimore 1789-1851 NCLC 1,
    27, 54
See also AAYA 22; CDALB 1640-1865; DLB
    3; SATA 19

Coover, Robert (Lowell) 1932- CLC 3, 7, 15,
    32, 46, 87; DAM NOV; SSC 15
See also CA 45-48; CANR 3, 37, 58; DLB 2;
    DLBY 81; MTCW 1

Copeland, Stewart (Armstrong) 1952-CLC 26

Copernicus, Nicolaus 1473-1543   LC 45

Coppard, A(lfred) E(dgar) 1878-1957 T C L C
    5; SSC 21
See also CA 114; 167; DLB 162; YABC 1

Coppee, Francois 1842-1908   TCLC 25
See also CA 170

Coppola, Francis Ford 1939-   CLC 16
See also CA 77-80; CANR 40; DLB 44

Corbiere, Tristan 1845-1875   NCLC 43

Corcoran, Barbara 1911-   CLC 17
See also AAYA 14; CA 21-24R; CAAS 2;
    CANR 11, 28, 48; CLR 50; DLB 52; JRDA;
    SAAS 20; SATA 3, 77

Cordelier, Maurice
See Giraudoux, (Hippolyte) Jean

Corelli, Marie 1855-1924   TCLC 51
See also Mackay, Mary
See also DLB 34, 156

Corman, Cid 1924-   CLC 9
See also Corman, Sidney
See also CAAS 2; DLB 5, 193

Corman, Sidney 1924-
See Corman, Cid
See also CA 85-88; CANR 44; DAM POET

Cormier, Robert (Edmund) 1925-CLC 12, 30;
    DA; DAB; DAC; DAM MST, NOV
See also AAYA 3, 19; CA 1-4R; CANR 5, 23;
    CDALB 1968-1988; CLR 12; DLB 52; INT
    CANR-23; JRDA; MAICYA; MTCW 1;
    SATA 10, 45, 83

Corn, Alfred (DeWitt III) 1943-   CLC 33
See also CA 104; CAAS 25; CANR 44; DLB
    120; DLBY 80

Corneille, Pierre 1606-1684   LC 28; DAB;
    DAM MST

Cornwell, David (John Moore) 1931- CLC 9,
    15; DAM POP
See also le Carre, John
See also CA 5-8R; CANR 13, 33, 59; MTCW 1

Corso, (Nunzio) Gregory 1930-   CLC 1, 11
See also CA 5-8R; CANR 41; DLB 5, 16;
    MTCW 1

Cortazar, Julio 1914-1984CLC 2, 3, 5, 10, 13,
    15, 33, 34, 92; DAM MULT, NOV; HLC;
    SSC 7
See also CA 21-24R; CANR 12, 32; DLB 113;
    HW; MTCW 1

CORTES, HERNAN 1484-1547   LC 31

Corvinus, Jakob
See Raabe, Wilhelm (Karl)

Corwin, Cecil
See Kornbluth, C(yril) M.

Cosic, Dobrica 1921-   CLC 14
See also CA 122; 138; DLB 181

Costain, Thomas B(ertram) 1885-1965 C L C
    30
See also CA 5-8R; 25-28R; DLB 9

Costantini, Humberto 1924(?)-1987 CLC 49
See also CA 131; 122; HW

Costello, Elvis 1955-   CLC 21

Cotes, Cecil V.
See Duncan, Sara Jeannette

Cotter, Joseph Seamon Sr. 1861-1949 T C L C
    28; BLC 1; DAM MULT
See also BW 1; CA 124; DLB 50

Couch, Arthur Thomas Quiller
See Quiller-Couch, SirArthur (Thomas)

Coulton, James
See Hansen, Joseph

Couperus, Louis (Marie Anne) 1863-1923
    TCLC 15
See also CA 115

Coupland, Douglas 1961-CLC 85; DAC; DAM
    POP
See also CA 142; CANR 57

Court, Wesli
See Turco, Lewis (Putnam)

Courtenay, Bryce 1933-   CLC 59
See also CA 138

Courtney, Robert
See Ellison, Harlan (Jay)

Cousteau, Jacques-Yves 1910-1997 CLC 30
See also CA 65-68; 159; CANR 15, 67; MTCW
    1; SATA 38, 98

Coventry, Francis 1725-1754   LC 46

Cowan, Peter (Walkinshaw) 1914-   SSC 28
See also CA 21-24R; CANR 9, 25, 50

Coward, Noel (Peirce) 1899-1973CLC 1, 9, 29,
    51; DAM DRAM
See also AITN 1; CA 17-18; 41-44R; CANR
    35; CAP 2; CDBLB 1914-1945; DLB 10;
    MTCW 1

Cowley, Abraham 1618-1667   LC 43
See also DLB 131, 151

Cowley, Malcolm 1898-1989   CLC 39
See also CA 5-8R; 128; CANR 3, 55; DLB 4,
    48; DLBY 81, 89; MTCW 1

Cowper, William 1731-1800   NCLC 8; DAM
    POET
See also DLB 104, 109

Cox, William Trevor 1928-   CLC 9, 14, 71;
    DAM NOV
See also Trevor, William
See also CA 9-12R; CANR 4, 37, 55; DLB 14;
    INT CANR-37; MTCW 1

Coyne, P. J.
See Masters, Hilary

Cozzens, James Gould 1903-1978CLC 1, 4, 11,
    92
See also CA 9-12R; 81-84; CANR 19; CDALB
    1941-1968; DLB 9; DLBD 2; DLBY 84, 97;
    MTCW 1

Crabbe, George 1754-1832   NCLC 26
See also DLB 93

Craddock, Charles Egbert
See Murfree, Mary Noailles

Craig, A. A.
See Anderson, Poul (William)

Craik, Dinah Maria (Mulock) 1826-1887
    NCLC 38
See also DLB 35, 163; MAICYA; SATA 34

Cram, Ralph Adams 1863-1942   TCLC 45
See also CA 160

Crane, (Harold) Hart 1899-1932 TCLC 2, 5,
    80; DA; DAB; DAC; DAM MST, POET;
    PC 3; WLC
See also CA 104; 127; CDALB 1917-1929;
    DLB 4, 48; MTCW 1

Crane, R(onald) S(almon) 1886-1967CLC 27
See also CA 85-88; DLB 63

Crane, Stephen (Townley) 1871-1900 T C L C
    11, 17, 32; DA; DAB; DAC; DAM MST,
    NOV, POET; SSC 7; WLC
See also AAYA 21; CA 109; 140; CDALB 1865-
    1917; DLB 12, 54, 78; YABC 2

Cranshaw, Stanley
See Fisher, Dorothy (Frances) Canfield

Crase, Douglas 1944-   CLC 58
See also CA 106

Crashaw, Richard 1612(?)-1649   LC 24
See also DLB 126

Craven, Margaret 1901-1980 CLC 17; DAC
See also CA 103

Crawford, F(rancis) Marion 1854-1909TCLC
    10
See also CA 107; 168; DLB 71

Crawford, Isabella Valancy 1850-1887N C L C
    12
See also DLB 92

Crayon, Geoffrey
See Irving, Washington

Creasey, John 1908-1973   CLC 11
See also CA 5-8R; 41-44R; CANR 8, 59; DLB
    77; MTCW 1

Crebillon, Claude Prosper Jolyot de (fils) 1707-
    1777   LC 1, 28

Credo
See Creasey, John

Credo, Alvaro J. de
See Prado (Calvo), Pedro

Creeley, Robert (White) 1926- CLC 1, 2, 4, 8,
    11, 15, 36, 78; DAM POET
See also CA 1-4R; CAAS 10; CANR 23, 43;
    DLB 5, 16, 169; DLBD 17; MTCW 1

Crews, Harry (Eugene) 1935- CLC 6, 23, 49
See also AITN 1; CA 25-28R; CANR 20, 57;
    DLB 6, 143, 185; MTCW 1

Crichton, (John) Michael 1942-CLC 2, 6, 54,
    90; DAM NOV, POP
See also AAYA 10; AITN 2; CA 25-28R; CANR
    13, 40, 54; DLBY 81; INT CANR-13; JRDA;
    MTCW 1; SATA 9, 88

Crispin, Edmund   CLC 22
See also Montgomery, (Robert) Bruce
See also DLB 87

Cristofer, Michael 1945(?)-   CLC 28; DAM
    DRAM
See also CA 110; 152; DLB 7

Croce, Benedetto 1866-1952   TCLC 37
See also CA 120; 155

Crockett, David 1786-1836   NCLC 8
See also DLB 3, 11

Crockett, Davy
See Crockett, David

Crofts, Freeman Wills 1879-1957 TCLC 55
See also CA 115; DLB 77

Croker, John Wilson 1780-1857   NCLC 10
See also DLB 110

Crommelynck, Fernand 1885-1970 CLC 75
See also CA 89-92

Cromwell, Oliver 1599-1658   LC 43

Cronin, A(rchibald) J(oseph) 1896-1981C L C
    32
See also CA 1-4R; 102; CANR 5; DLB 191;
    SATA 47; SATA-Obit 25

Cross, Amanda

See Heilbrun, Carolyn G(old)
Crothers, Rachel 1878(?)-1958 **TCLC 19**
See also CA 113; DLB 7
Croves, Hal
See Traven, B.
Crow Dog, Mary (Ellen) (?)- **CLC 93**
See also Brave Bird, Mary
See also CA 154
Crowfield, Christopher
See Stowe, Harriet (Elizabeth) Beecher
Crowley, Aleister **TCLC 7**
See also Crowley, Edward Alexander
Crowley, Edward Alexander 1875-1947
See Crowley, Aleister
See also CA 104
Crowley, John 1942- **CLC 57**
See also CA 61-64; CANR 43; DLBY 82; SATA 65
Crud
See Crumb, R(obert)
Crumarums
See Crumb, R(obert)
Crumb, R(obert) 1943- **CLC 17**
See also CA 106
Crumbum
See Crumb, R(obert)
Crumski
See Crumb, R(obert)
Crum the Bum
See Crumb, R(obert)
Crunk
See Crumb, R(obert)
Crustt
See Crumb, R(obert)
Cryer, Gretchen (Kiger) 1935- **CLC 21**
See also CA 114; 123
Csath, Geza 1887-1919 **TCLC 13**
See also CA 111
Cudlip, David 1933- **CLC 34**
Cullen, Countee 1903-1946**TCLC 4, 37; BLC 1; DA; DAC; DAM MST, MULT, POET; PC 20; WLCS**
See also BW 1; CA 108; 124; CDALB 1917-1929; DLB 4, 48, 51; MTCW 1; SATA 18
Cum, R.
See Crumb, R(obert)
Cummings, Bruce F(rederick) 1889-1919
See Barbellion, W. N. P.
See also CA 123
Cummings, E(dward) E(stlin) 1894-1962**CLC 1, 3, 8, 12, 15, 68; DA; DAB; DAC; DAM MST, POET; PC 5; WLC 2**
See also CA 73-76; CANR 31; CDALB 1929-1941; DLB 4, 48; MTCW 1
Cunha, Euclides (Rodrigues Pimenta) da 1866-1909 **TCLC 24**
See also CA 123
Cunningham, E. V.
See Fast, Howard (Melvin)
Cunningham, J(ames) V(incent) 1911-1985 **CLC 3, 31**
See also CA 1-4R; 115; CANR 1, 72; DLB 5
Cunningham, Julia (Woolfolk) 1916- **CLC 12**
See also CA 9-12R; CANR 4, 19, 36; JRDA; MAICYA; SAAS 2; SATA 1, 26
Cunningham, Michael 1952- **CLC 34**
See also CA 136
Cunninghame Graham, R(obert) B(ontine) 1852-1936 **TCLC 19**
See also Graham, R(obert) B(ontine) Cunninghame
See also CA 119; DLB 98
Currie, Ellen 19(?)- **CLC 44**

Curtin, Philip
See Lowndes, Marie Adelaide (Belloc)
Curtis, Price
See Ellison, Harlan (Jay)
Cutrate, Joe
See Spiegelman, Art
Cynewulf c. 770-c. 840 **CMLC 23**
Czaczkes, Shmuel Yosef
See Agnon, S(hmuel) Y(osef Halevi)
Dabrowska, Maria (Szumska) 1889-1965**CLC 15**
See also CA 106
Dabydeen, David 1955- **CLC 34**
See also BW 1; CA 125; CANR 56
Dacey, Philip 1939- **CLC 51**
See also CA 37-40R; CAAS 17; CANR 14, 32, 64; DLB 105
Dagerman, Stig (Halvard) 1923-1954 **TCLC 17**
See also CA 117; 155
Dahl, Roald 1916-1990**CLC 1, 6, 18, 79; DAB; DAC; DAM MST, NOV, POP**
See also AAYA 15; CA 1-4R; 133; CANR 6, 32, 37, 62; CLR 1, 7, 41; DLB 139; JRDA; MAICYA; MTCW 1; SATA 1, 26, 73; SATA-Obit 65
Dahlberg, Edward 1900-1977 **CLC 1, 7, 14**
See also CA 9-12R; 69-72; CANR 31, 62; DLB 48; MTCW 1
Daitch, Susan 1954- **CLC 103**
See also CA 161
Dale, Colin **TCLC 18**
See also Lawrence, T(homas) E(dward)
Dale, George E.
See Asimov, Isaac
Daly, Elizabeth 1878-1967 **CLC 52**
See also CA 23-24; 25-28R; CANR 60; CAP 2
Daly, Maureen 1921- **CLC 17**
See also AAYA 5; CANR 37; JRDA; MAICYA; SAAS 1; SATA 2
Damas, Leon-Gontran 1912-1978 **CLC 84**
See also BW 1; CA 125; 73-76
Dana, Richard Henry Sr. 1787-1879**NCLC 53**
Daniel, Samuel 1562(?)-1619 **LC 24**
See also DLB 62
Daniels, Brett
See Adler, Renata
Dannay, Frederic 1905-1982 **CLC 11; DAM POP**
See also Queen, Ellery
See also CA 1-4R; 107; CANR 1, 39; DLB 137; MTCW 1
D'Annunzio, Gabriele 1863-1938**TCLC 6, 40**
See also CA 104; 155
Danois, N. le
See Gourmont, Remy (-Marie-Charles) de
Dante 1265-1321 **CMLC 3, 18; DA; DAB; DAC; DAM MST, POET; PC 21; WLCS**
d'Antibes, Germain
See Simenon, Georges (Jacques Christian)
Danticat, Edwidge 1969- **CLC 94**
See also CA 152; CANR 73
Danvers, Dennis 1947- **CLC 70**
Danziger, Paula 1944- **CLC 21**
See also AAYA 4; CA 112; 115; CANR 37; CLR 20; JRDA; MAICYA; SATA 36, 63, 102; SATA-Brief 30
Da Ponte, Lorenzo 1749-1838 **NCLC 50**
Dario, Ruben 1867-1916 **TCLC 4; DAM MULT; HLC; PC 15**
See also CA 131; HW; MTCW 1
Darley, George 1795-1846 **NCLC 2**
See also DLB 96

Darrow, Clarence (Seward) 1857-1938**TCLC 81**
See also CA 164
Darwin, Charles 1809-1882 **NCLC 57**
See also DLB 57, 166
Daryush, Elizabeth 1887-1977 **CLC 6, 19**
See also CA 49-52; CANR 3; DLB 20
Dasgupta, Surendranath 1887-1952**TCLC 81**
See also CA 157
Dashwood, Edmee Elizabeth Monica de la Pasture 1890-1943
See Delafield, E. M.
See also CA 119; 154
Daudet, (Louis Marie) Alphonse 1840-1897 **NCLC 1**
See also DLB 123
Daumal, Rene 1908-1944 **TCLC 14**
See also CA 114
Davenant, William 1606-1668 **LC 13**
See also DLB 58, 126
Davenport, Guy (Mattison, Jr.) 1927-**CLC 6, 14, 38; SSC 16**
See also CA 33-36R; CANR 23, 73; DLB 130
Davidson, Avram 1923-
See Queen, Ellery
See also CA 101; CANR 26; DLB 8
Davidson, Donald (Grady) 1893-1968**CLC 2, 13, 19**
See also CA 5-8R; 25-28R; CANR 4; DLB 45
Davidson, Hugh
See Hamilton, Edmond
Davidson, John 1857-1909 **TCLC 24**
See also CA 118; DLB 19
Davidson, Sara 1943- **CLC 9**
See also CA 81-84; CANR 44, 68; DLB 185
Davie, Donald (Alfred) 1922-1995 **CLC 5, 8, 10, 31**
See also CA 1-4R; 149; CAAS 3; CANR 1, 44; DLB 27; MTCW 1
Davies, Ray(mond Douglas) 1944- **CLC 21**
See also CA 116; 146
Davies, Rhys 1901-1978 **CLC 23**
See also CA 9-12R; 81-84; CANR 4; DLB 139, 191
Davies, (William) Robertson 1913-1995 **CLC 2, 7, 13, 25, 42, 75, 91; DA; DAB; DAC; DAM MST, NOV, POP; WLC**
See also BEST 89:2; CA 33-36R; 150; CANR 17, 42; DLB 68; INT CANR-17; MTCW 1
Davies, W(illiam) H(enry) 1871-1940**TCLC 5**
See also CA 104; DLB 19, 174
Davies, Walter C.
See Kornbluth, C(yril) M.
Davis, Angela (Yvonne) 1944- **CLC 77; DAM MULT**
See also BW 2; CA 57-60; CANR 10
Davis, B. Lynch
See Bioy Casares, Adolfo; Borges, Jorge Luis
Davis, Harold Lenoir 1896-1960 **CLC 49**
See also CA 89-92; DLB 9
Davis, Rebecca (Blaine) Harding 1831-1910 **TCLC 6**
See also CA 104; DLB 74
Davis, Richard Harding 1864-1916 **TCLC 24**
See also CA 114; DLB 12, 23, 78, 79, 189; DLBD 13
Davison, Frank Dalby 1893-1970 **CLC 15**
See also CA 116
Davison, Lawrence H.
See Lawrence, D(avid) H(erbert Richards)
Davison, Peter (Hubert) 1928- **CLC 28**
See also CA 9-12R; CAAS 4; CANR 3, 43; DLB 5

Davys, Mary 1674-1732   **LC 1, 46**
   See also DLB 39

Dawson, Fielding 1930-   **CLC 6**
   See also CA 85-88; DLB 130

Dawson, Peter
   See Faust, Frederick (Schiller)

Day, Clarence (Shepard, Jr.) 1874-1935
   TCLC 25
   See also CA 108; DLB 11

Day, Thomas 1748-1789   **LC 1**
   See also DLB 39; YABC 1

Day Lewis, C(ecil) 1904-1972   **CLC 1, 6, 10;**
   DAM POET; PC 11
   See also Blake, Nicholas
   See also CA 13-16; 33-36R; CANR 34; CAP 1;
   DLB 15, 20; MTCW 1

Dazai Osamu 1909-1948   **TCLC 11**
   See also Tsushima, Shuji
   See also CA 164; DLB 182

de Andrade, Carlos Drummond
   See Drummond de Andrade, Carlos

Deane, Norman
   See Creasey, John

de Beauvoir, Simone (Lucie Ernestine Marie Bertrand)
   See Beauvoir, Simone (Lucie Ernestine Marie Bertrand) de

de Beer, P.
   See Bosman, Herman Charles

de Brissac, Malcolm
   See Dickinson, Peter (Malcolm)

de Chardin, Pierre Teilhard
   See Teilhard de Chardin, (Marie Joseph) Pierre

Dee, John 1527-1608   **LC 20**

Deer, Sandra 1940-   **CLC 45**

De Ferrari, Gabriella 1941-   **CLC 65**
   See also CA 146

Defoe, Daniel 1660(?)-1731   **LC 1, 42; DA;**
   DAB; DAC; DAM MST, NOV; WLC
   See also AAYA 27; CDBLB 1660-1789; DLB
   39, 95, 101; JRDA; MAICYA; SATA 22

de Gourmont, Remy(-Marie-Charles)
   See Gourmont, Remy (-Marie-Charles) de

de Hartog, Jan 1914-   **CLC 19**
   See also CA 1-4R; CANR 1

de Hostos, E. M.
   See Hostos (y Bonilla), Eugenio Maria de

de Hostos, Eugenio M.
   See Hostos (y Bonilla), Eugenio Maria de

Deighton, Len   **CLC 4, 7, 22, 46**
   See also Deighton, Leonard Cyril
   See also AAYA 6; BEST 89:2; CDBLB 1960 to
   Present; DLB 87

Deighton, Leonard Cyril 1929-
   See Deighton, Len
   See also CA 9-12R; CANR 19, 33, 68; DAM
   NOV, POP; MTCW 1

Dekker, Thomas 1572(?)-1632   **LC 22; DAM DRAM**
   See also CDBLB Before 1660; DLB 62, 172

Delafield, E. M. 1890-1943   **TCLC 61**
   See also Dashwood, Edmee Elizabeth Monica
   de la Pasture
   See also DLB 34

de la Mare, Walter (John) 1873-1956 **TCLC 4, 53; DAB; DAC; DAM MST, POET; SSC 14; WLC**
   See also CA 163; CDBLB 1914-1945; CLR 23;
   DLB 162; SATA 16

Delaney, Franey
   See O'Hara, John (Henry)

Delaney, Shelagh 1939- **CLC 29; DAM DRAM**
   See also CA 17-20R; CANR 30, 67; CDBLB

1960 to Present; DLB 13; MTCW 1

Delany, Mary (Granville Pendarves) 1700-1788
   LC 12

Delany, Samuel R(ay, Jr.) 1942- **CLC 8, 14, 38;**
   BLC 1; DAM MULT
   See also AAYA 24; BW 2; CA 81-84; CANR
   27, 43; DLB 8, 33; MTCW 1

De La Ramee, (Marie) Louise 1839-1908
   See Ouida
   See also SATA 20

de la Roche, Mazo 1879-1961   **CLC 14**
   See also CA 85-88; CANR 30; DLB 68; SATA
   64

De La Salle, Innocent
   See Hartmann, Sadakichi

Delbanco, Nicholas (Franklin) 1942- **CLC 6, 13**
   See also CA 17-20R; CAAS 2; CANR 29, 55;
   DLB 6

del Castillo, Michel 1933-   **CLC 38**
   See also CA 109

Deledda, Grazia (Cosima) 1875(?)-1936
   TCLC 23
   See also CA 123

Delibes, Miguel   **CLC 8, 18**
   See also Delibes Setien, Miguel

Delibes Setien, Miguel 1920-
   See Delibes, Miguel
   See also CA 45-48; CANR 1, 32; HW; MTCW
   1

DeLillo, Don 1936- **CLC 8, 10, 13, 27, 39, 54, 76; DAM NOV, POP**
   See also BEST 89:1; CA 81-84; CANR 21; DLB
   6, 173; MTCW 1

de Lisser, H. G.
   See De Lisser, H(erbert) G(eorge)
   See also DLB 117

De Lisser, H(erbert) G(eorge) 1878-1944
   TCLC 12
   See also de Lisser, H. G.
   See also BW 2; CA 109; 152

Deloney, Thomas 1560(?)-1600   **LC 41**
   See also DLB 167

Deloria, Vine (Victor), Jr. 1933-   **CLC 21; DAM MULT**
   See also CA 53-56; CANR 5, 20, 48; DLB 175;
   MTCW 1; NNAL; SATA 21

Del Vecchio, John M(ichael) 1947-   **CLC 29**
   See also CA 110; DLBD 9

de Man, Paul (Adolph Michel) 1919-1983
   CLC 55
   See also CA 128; 111; CANR 61; DLB 67;
   MTCW 1

De Marinis, Rick 1934-   **CLC 54**
   See also CA 57-60; CAAS 24; CANR 9, 25, 50

Dembry, R. Emmet
   See Murfree, Mary Noailles

Demby, William 1922- **CLC 53; BLC 1; DAM MULT**
   See also BW 1; CA 81-84; DLB 33

de Menton, Francisco
   See Chin, Frank (Chew, Jr.)

Demijohn, Thom
   See Disch, Thomas M(ichael)

de Montherlant, Henry (Milon)
   See Montherlant, Henry (Milon) de

Demosthenes 384B.C.-322B.C.   **CMLC 13**
   See also DLB 176

de Natale, Francine
   See Malzberg, Barry N(athaniel)

Denby, Edwin (Orr) 1903-1983   **CLC 48**
   See also CA 138; 110

Denis, Julio

See Cortazar, Julio

Denmark, Harrison
   See Zelazny, Roger (Joseph)

Dennis, John 1658-1734   **LC 11**
   See also DLB 101

Dennis, Nigel (Forbes) 1912-1989   **CLC 8**
   See also CA 25-28R; 129; DLB 13, 15; MTCW
   1

Dent, Lester 1904(?)-1959   **TCLC 72**
   See also CA 112; 161

De Palma, Brian (Russell) 1940-   **CLC 20**
   See also CA 109

De Quincey, Thomas 1785-1859   **NCLC 4**
   See also CDBLB 1789-1832; DLB 110; 144

Deren, Eleanora 1908(?)-1961
   See Deren, Maya
   See also CA 111

Deren, Maya 1917-1961   **CLC 16, 102**
   See also Deren, Eleanora

Derleth, August (William) 1909-1971 **CLC 31**
   See also CA 1-4R; 29-32R; CANR 4; DLB 9;
   DLBD 17; SATA 5

Der Nister 1884-1950   **TCLC 56**

de Routisie, Albert
   See Aragon, Louis

Derrida, Jacques 1930-   **CLC 24, 87**
   See also CA 124; 127

Derry Down Derry
   See Lear, Edward

Dersonnes, Jacques
   See Simenon, Georges (Jacques Christian)

Desai, Anita 1937- **CLC 19, 37, 97; DAB; DAM NOV**
   See also CA 81-84; CANR 33, 53; MTCW 1;
   SATA 63

de Saint-Luc, Jean
   See Glassco, John

de Saint Roman, Arnaud
   See Aragon, Louis

Descartes, Rene 1596-1650   **LC 20, 35**

De Sica, Vittorio 1901(?)-1974   **CLC 20**
   See also CA 117

Desnos, Robert 1900-1945   **TCLC 22**
   See also CA 121; 151

Destouches, Louis-Ferdinand 1894-1961 **CLC 9, 15**
   See also Celine, Louis-Ferdinand
   See also CA 85-88; CANR 28; MTCW 1

de Tolignac, Gaston
   See Griffith, D(avid Lewelyn) W(ark)

Deutsch, Babette 1895-1982   **CLC 18**
   See also CA 1-4R; 108; CANR 4; DLB 45;
   SATA 1; SATA-Obit 33

Devenant, William 1606-1649   **LC 13**

Devkota, Laxmiprasad 1909-1959 **TCLC 23**
   See also CA 123

De Voto, Bernard (Augustine) 1897-1955
   TCLC 29
   See also CA 113; 160; DLB 9

De Vries, Peter 1910-1993 **CLC 1, 2, 3, 7, 10, 28, 46; DAM NOV**
   See also CA 17-20R; 142; CANR 41; DLB 6;
   DLBY 82; MTCW 1

Dexter, John
   See Bradley, Marion Zimmer

Dexter, Martin
   See Faust, Frederick (Schiller)

Dexter, Pete 1943-   **CLC 34, 55; DAM POP**
   See also BEST 89:2; CA 127; 131; INT 131;
   MTCW 1

Diamano, Silmang
   See Senghor, Leopold Sedar

Diamond, Neil 1941-   **CLC 30**

See also CA 108

Diaz del Castillo, Bernal 1496-1584   **LC 31**

di Bassetto, Corno
See Shaw, George Bernard

Dick, Philip K(indred) 1928-1982**CLC 10, 30, 72; DAM NOV, POP**
See also AAYA 24; CA 49-52; 106; CANR 2, 16; DLB 8; MTCW 1

Dickens, Charles (John Huffam) 1812-1870
NCLC 3, 8, 18, 26, 37, 50; DA; DAB; DAC; DAM MST, NOV; SSC 17; WLC
See also AAYA 23; CDBLB 1832-1890; DLB 21, 55, 70, 159, 166; JRDA; MAICYA; SATA 15

Dickey, James (Lafayette) 1923-1997 **CLC 1, 2, 4, 7, 10, 15, 47, 109; DAM NOV, POET, POP**
See also AITN 1, 2; CA 9-12R; 156; CABS 2; CANR 10, 48, 61; CDALB 1968-1988; DLB 5, 193; DLBD 7; DLBY 82, 93, 96, 97; INT CANR-10; MTCW 1

Dickey, William 1928-1994   **CLC 3, 28**
See also CA 9-12R; 145; CANR 24; DLB 5

Dickinson, Charles 1951-   **CLC 49**
See also CA 128

Dickinson, Emily (Elizabeth) 1830-1886
NCLC 21; DA; DAB; DAC; DAM MST, POET; PC 1; WLC
See also AAYA 22; CDALB 1865-1917; DLB 1; SATA 29

Dickinson, Peter (Malcolm) 1927-**CLC 12, 35**
See also AAYA 9; CA 41-44R; CANR 31, 58; CLR 29; DLB 87, 161; JRDA; MAICYA; SATA 5, 62, 95

Dickson, Carr
See Carr, John Dickson

Dickson, Carter
See Carr, John Dickson

Diderot, Denis 1713-1784   **LC 26**

Didion, Joan 1934-**CLC 1, 3, 8, 14, 32; DAM NOV**
See also AITN 1; CA 5-8R; CANR 14, 52; CDALB 1968-1988; DLB 2, 173, 185; DLBY 81, 86; MTCW 1

Dietrich, Robert
See Hunt, E(verette) Howard, (Jr.)

Difusa, Pati
See Almodovar, Pedro

Dillard, Annie 1945-   **CLC 9, 60, 115; DAM NOV**
See also AAYA 6; CA 49-52; CANR 3, 43, 62; DLBY 80; MTCW 1; SATA 10

Dillard, R(ichard) H(enry) W(ilde) 1937-
CLC 5
See also CA 21-24R; CAAS 7; CANR 10; DLB 5

Dillon, Eilis 1920-1994   **CLC 17**
See also CA 9-12R; 147; CAAS 3; CANR 4, 38; CLR 26; MAICYA; SATA 2, 74; SATA-Obit 83

Dimont, Penelope
See Mortimer, Penelope (Ruth)

Dinesen, Isak   **CLC 10, 29, 95; SSC 7**
See also Blixen, Karen (Christentze Dinesen)

Ding Ling   **CLC 68**
See also Chiang, Pin-chin

Diphusa, Patty
See Almodovar, Pedro

Disch, Thomas M(ichael) 1940-   **CLC 7, 36**
See also AAYA 17; CA 21-24R; CAAS 4; CANR 17, 36, 54; CLR 18; DLB 8; MAICYA; MTCW 1; SAAS 15; SATA 92

Disch, Tom

See Disch, Thomas M(ichael)

d'Isly, Georges
See Simenon, Georges (Jacques Christian)

Disraeli, Benjamin 1804-1881   **NCLC 2, 39**
See also DLB 21, 55

Ditcum, Steve
See Crumb, R(obert)

Dixon, Paige
See Corcoran, Barbara

Dixon, Stephen 1936-   **CLC 52; SSC 16**
See also CA 89-92; CANR 17, 40, 54; DLB 130

Doak, Annie
See Dillard, Annie

Dobell, Sydney Thompson 1824-1874 **NCLC 43**
See also DLB 32

Doblin, Alfred   **TCLC 13**
See also Doeblin, Alfred

Dobrolyubov, Nikolai Alexandrovich 1836-1861
NCLC 5

Dobson, Austin 1840-1921   **TCLC 79**
See also DLB 35; 144

Dobyns, Stephen 1941-   **CLC 37**
See also CA 45-48; CANR 2, 18

Doctorow, E(dgar) L(aurence) 1931- **CLC 6, 11, 15, 18, 37, 44, 65, 113; DAM NOV, POP**
See also AAYA 22; AITN 2; BEST 89:3; CA 45-48; CANR 2, 33, 51; CDALB 1968-1988; DLB 2, 28, 173; DLBY 80; MTCW 1

Dodgson, Charles Lutwidge 1832-1898
See Carroll, Lewis
See also CLR 2; DA; DAB; DAC; DAM MST, NOV, POET; MAICYA; SATA 100; YABC 2

Dodson, Owen (Vincent) 1914-1983 **CLC 79; BLC 1; DAM MULT**
See also BW 1; CA 65-68; 110; CANR 24; DLB 76

Doeblin, Alfred 1878-1957   **TCLC 13**
See also Doblin, Alfred
See also CA 110; 141; DLB 66

Doerr, Harriet 1910-   **CLC 34**
See also CA 117; 122; CANR 47; INT 122

Domecq, H(onorio) Bustos
See Bioy Casares, Adolfo; Borges, Jorge Luis

Domini, Rey
See Lorde, Audre (Geraldine)

Dominique
See Proust, (Valentin-Louis-George-Eugene-) Marcel

Don, A
See Stephen, SirLeslie

Donaldson, Stephen R. 1947- **CLC 46; DAM POP**
See also CA 89-92; CANR 13, 55; INT CANR-13

Donleavy, J(ames) P(atrick) 1926-**CLC 1, 4, 6, 10, 45**
See also AITN 2; CA 9-12R; CANR 24, 49, 62; DLB 6, 173; INT CANR-24; MTCW 1

Donne, John 1572-1631**LC 10, 24; DA; DAB; DAC; DAM MST, POET; PC 1**
See also CDBLB Before 1660; DLB 121, 151

Donnell, David 1939(?)-   **CLC 34**

Donoghue, P. S.
See Hunt, E(verette) Howard, (Jr.)

Donoso (Yanez), Jose 1924-1996**CLC 4, 8, 11, 32, 99; DAM MULT; HLC**
See also CA 81-84; 155; CANR 32, 73; DLB 113; HW; MTCW 1

Donovan, John 1928-1992   **CLC 35**
See also AAYA 20; CA 97-100; 137; CLR 3; MAICYA; SATA 72; SATA-Brief 29

Don Roberto

See Cunninghame Graham, R(obert) B(ontine)

Doolittle, Hilda 1886-1961**CLC 3, 8, 14, 31, 34, 73; DA; DAC; DAM MST, POET; PC 5; WLC**
See also H. D.
See also CA 97-100; CANR 35; DLB 4, 45; MTCW 1

Dorfman, Ariel 1942-   **CLC 48, 77; DAM MULT; HLC**
See also CA 124; 130; CANR 67, 70; HW; INT 130

Dorn, Edward (Merton) 1929-   **CLC 10, 18**
See also CA 93-96; CANR 42; DLB 5; INT 93-96

Dorris, Michael (Anthony) 1945-1997   **CLC 109; DAM MULT, NOV**
See also AAYA 20; BEST 90:1; CA 102; 157; CANR 19, 46; DLB 175; NNAL; SATA 75; SATA-Obit 94

Dorris, Michael A.
See Dorris, Michael (Anthony)

Dorsan, Luc
See Simenon, Georges (Jacques Christian)

Dorsange, Jean
See Simenon, Georges (Jacques Christian)

Dos Passos, John (Roderigo) 1896-1970 **CLC 1, 4, 8, 11, 15, 25, 34, 82; DA; DAB; DAC; DAM MST, NOV; WLC**
See also CA 1-4R; 29-32R; CANR 3; CDALB 1929-1941; DLB 4, 9; DLBD 1, 15; DLBY 96; MTCW 1

Dossage, Jean
See Simenon, Georges (Jacques Christian)

Dostoevsky, Fedor Mikhailovich 1821-1881
NCLC 2, 7, 21, 33, 43; DA; DAB; DAC; DAM MST, NOV; SSC 2; WLC

Doughty, Charles M(ontagu) 1843-1926
TCLC 27
See also CA 115; DLB 19, 57, 174

Douglas, Ellen   **CLC 73**
See also Haxton, Josephine Ayres; Williamson, Ellen Douglas

Douglas, Gavin 1475(?)-1522   **LC 20**
See also DLB 132

Douglas, George
See Brown, George Douglas

Douglas, Keith (Castellain) 1920-1944 **TCLC 40**
See also CA 160; DLB 27

Douglas, Leonard
See Bradbury, Ray (Douglas)

Douglas, Michael
See Crichton, (John) Michael

Douglas, (George) Norman 1868-1952 **TCLC 68**
See also CA 119; 157; DLB 34, 195

Douglas, William
See Brown, George Douglas

Douglass, Frederick 1817(?)-1895**NCLC 7, 55; BLC 1; DA; DAC; DAM MST, MULT; WLC**
See also CDALB 1640-1865; DLB 1, 43, 50, 79; SATA 29

Dourado, (Waldomiro Freitas) Autran 1926-
CLC 23, 60
See also CA 25-28R; CANR 34

Dourado, Waldomiro Autran
See Dourado, (Waldomiro Freitas) Autran

Dove, Rita (Frances) 1952-**CLC 50, 81; BLCS; DAM MULT, POET; PC 6**
See also BW 2; CA 109; CAAS 19; CANR 27, 42, 68; DLB 120

Doveglion

See Villa, Jose Garcia

Dowell, Coleman 1925-1985   **CLC 60**
See also CA 25-28R; 117; CANR 10; DLB 130

Dowson, Ernest (Christopher) 1867-1900
  TCLC 4
See also CA 105; 150; DLB 19, 135

Doyle, A. Conan
See Doyle, Arthur Conan

Doyle, Arthur Conan 1859-1930 **TCLC 7; DA;
  DAB; DAC; DAM MST, NOV; SSC 12;
  WLC**
See also AAYA 14; CA 104; 122; CDBLB 1890-
  1914; DLB 18, 70, 156, 178; MTCW 1;
  SATA 24

Doyle, Conan
See Doyle, Arthur Conan

Doyle, John
See Graves, Robert (von Ranke)

Doyle, Roddy 1958(?)-   **CLC 81**
See also AAYA 14; CA 143; CANR 73; DLB
  194

Doyle, Sir A. Conan
See Doyle, Arthur Conan

Doyle, Sir Arthur Conan
See Doyle, Arthur Conan

Dr. A
See Asimov, Isaac; Silverstein, Alvin

Drabble, Margaret 1939- **CLC 2, 3, 5, 8, 10, 22,
  53; DAB; DAC; DAM MST, NOV, POP**
See also CA 13-16R; CANR 18, 35, 63; CDBLB
  1960 to Present; DLB 14, 155; MTCW 1;
  SATA 48

Drapier, M. B.
See Swift, Jonathan

Drayham, James
See Mencken, H(enry) L(ouis)

Drayton, Michael 1563-1631   **LC 8; DAM
  POET**
See also DLB 121

Dreadstone, Carl
See Campbell, (John) Ramsey

Dreiser, Theodore (Herman Albert) 1871-1945
  **TCLC 10, 18, 35, 83; DA; DAC; DAM
  MST, NOV; SSC 30; WLC**
See also CA 106; 132; CDALB 1865-1917;
  DLB 9, 12, 102, 137; DLBD 1; MTCW 1

Drexler, Rosalyn 1926-   **CLC 2, 6**
See also CA 81-84; CANR 68

Dreyer, Carl Theodor 1889-1968   **CLC 16**
See also CA 116

Drieu la Rochelle, Pierre(-Eugene) 1893-1945
  TCLC 21
See also CA 117; DLB 72

Drinkwater, John 1882-1937   **TCLC 57**
See also CA 109; 149; DLB 10, 19, 149

Drop Shot
See Cable, George Washington

Droste-Hulshoff, Annette Freiin von 1797-1848
  NCLC 3
See also DLB 133

Drummond, Walter
See Silverberg, Robert

Drummond, William Henry 1854-1907 **TCLC
  25**
See also CA 160; DLB 92

Drummond de Andrade, Carlos 1902-1987
  CLC 18
See also Andrade, Carlos Drummond de
See also CA 132; 123

Drury, Allen (Stuart) 1918-1998   **CLC 37**
See also CA 57-60; 170; CANR 18, 52; INT
  CANR-18

Dryden, John 1631-1700 **LC 3, 21; DA; DAB;**

**DAC; DAM DRAM, MST, POET; DC 3;
  WLC**
See also CDBLB 1660-1789; DLB 80, 101, 131

Duberman, Martin (Bauml) 1930-   **CLC 8**
See also CA 1-4R; CANR 2, 63

Dubie, Norman (Evans) 1945-   **CLC 36**
See also CA 69-72; CANR 12; DLB 120

Du Bois, W(illiam) E(dward) B(urghardt) 1868-
  1963   **CLC 1, 2, 13, 64, 96; BLC 1; DA;
  DAC; DAM MST, MULT, NOV; WLC**
See also BW 1; CA 85-88; CANR 34; CDALB
  1865-1917; DLB 47, 50, 91; MTCW 1; SATA
  42

Dubus, Andre 1936- **CLC 13, 36, 97; SSC 15**
See also CA 21-24R; CANR 17; DLB 130; INT
  CANR-17

Duca Minimo
See D'Annunzio, Gabriele

Ducharme, Rejean 1941-   **CLC 74**
See also CA 165; DLB 60

Duclos, Charles Pinot 1704-1772   **LC 1**

Dudek, Louis 1918-   **CLC 11, 19**
See also CA 45-48; CAAS 14; CANR 1; DLB
  88

Duerrenmatt, Friedrich 1921-1990 **CLC 1, 4,
  8, 11, 15, 43, 102; DAM DRAM**
See also CA 17-20R; CANR 33; DLB 69, 124;
  MTCW 1

Duffy, Bruce (?)-   **CLC 50**

Duffy, Maureen 1933-   **CLC 37**
See also CA 25-28R; CANR 33, 68; DLB 14;
  MTCW 1

Dugan, Alan 1923-   **CLC 2, 6**
See also CA 81-84; DLB 5

du Gard, Roger Martin
See Martin du Gard, Roger

Duhamel, Georges 1884-1966   **CLC 8**
See also CA 81-84; 25-28R; CANR 35; DLB
  65; MTCW 1

Dujardin, Edouard (Emile Louis) 1861-1949
  TCLC 13
See also CA 109; DLB 123

Dulles, John Foster 1888-1959   **TCLC 72**
See also CA 115; 149

Dumas, Alexandre (pere)
See Dumas, Alexandre (Davy de la Pailleterie)

Dumas, Alexandre (Davy de la Pailleterie)
  1802-1870   **NCLC 11; DA; DAB; DAC;
  DAM MST, NOV; WLC**
See also DLB 119, 192; SATA 18

Dumas, Alexandre (fils) 1824-1895 **NCLC 71;
  DC 1**
See also AAYA 22; DLB 192

Dumas, Claudine
See Malzberg, Barry N(athaniel)

Dumas, Henry L. 1934-1968   **CLC 6, 62**
See also BW 1; CA 85-88; DLB 41

du Maurier, Daphne 1907-1989 **CLC 6, 11, 59;
  DAB; DAC; DAM MST, POP; SSC 18**
See also CA 5-8R; 128; CANR 6, 55; DLB 191;
  MTCW 1; SATA 27; SATA-Obit 60

Dunbar, Paul Laurence 1872-1906 **TCLC 2,
  12; BLC 1; DA; DAC; DAM MST, MULT,
  POET; PC 5; SSC 8; WLC**
See also BW 1; CA 104; 124; CDALB 1865-
  1917; DLB 50, 54, 78; SATA 34

Dunbar, William 1460(?)-1530(?)   **LC 20**
See also DLB 132, 146

Duncan, Dora Angela
See Duncan, Isadora

Duncan, Isadora 1877(?)-1927   **TCLC 68**
See also CA 118; 149

Duncan, Lois 1934-   **CLC 26**

See also AAYA 4; CA 1-4R; CANR 2, 23, 36;
  CLR 29; JRDA; MAICYA; SAAS 2; SATA
  1, 36, 75

Duncan, Robert (Edward) 1919-1988 **CLC 1,
  2, 4, 7, 15, 41, 55; DAM POET; PC 2**
See also CA 9-12R; 124; CANR 28, 62; DLB
  5, 16, 193; MTCW 1

Duncan, Sara Jeannette 1861-1922 **TCLC 60**
See also CA 157; DLB 92

Dunlap, William 1766-1839   **NCLC 2**
See also DLB 30, 37, 59

Dunn, Douglas (Eaglesham) 1942- **CLC 6, 40**
See also CA 45-48; CANR 2, 33; DLB 40;
  MTCW 1

Dunn, Katherine (Karen) 1945-   **CLC 71**
See also CA 33-36R; CANR 72

Dunn, Stephen 1939-   **CLC 36**
See also CA 33-36R; CANR 12, 48, 53; DLB
  105

Dunne, Finley Peter 1867-1936   **TCLC 28**
See also CA 108; DLB 11, 23

Dunne, John Gregory 1932-   **CLC 28**
See also CA 25-28R; CANR 14, 50; DLBY 80

Dunsany, Edward John Moreton Drax Plunkett
  1878-1957
See Dunsany, Lord
See also CA 104; 148; DLB 10

Dunsany, Lord   **TCLC 2, 59**
See also Dunsany, Edward John Moreton Drax
  Plunkett
See also DLB 77, 153, 156

du Perry, Jean
See Simenon, Georges (Jacques Christian)

Durang, Christopher (Ferdinand) 1949- **CLC
  27, 38**
See also CA 105; CANR 50

Duras, Marguerite 1914-1996 **CLC 3, 6, 11, 20,
  34, 40, 68, 100**
See also CA 25-28R; 151; CANR 50; DLB 83;
  MTCW 1

Durban, (Rosa) Pam 1947-   **CLC 39**
See also CA 123

Durcan, Paul 1944- **CLC 43, 70; DAM POET**
See also CA 134

Durkheim, Emile 1858-1917   **TCLC 55**

Durrell, Lawrence (George) 1912-1990 **CLC
  1, 4, 6, 8, 13, 27, 41; DAM NOV**
See also CA 9-12R; 132; CANR 40; CDBLB
  1945-1960; DLB 15, 27; DLBY 90; MTCW
  1

Durrenmatt, Friedrich
See Duerrenmatt, Friedrich

Dutt, Toru 1856-1877   **NCLC 29**

Dwight, Timothy 1752-1817   **NCLC 13**
See also DLB 37

Dworkin, Andrea 1946-   **CLC 43**
See also CA 77-80; CAAS 21; CANR 16, 39;
  INT CANR-16; MTCW 1

Dwyer, Deanna
See Koontz, Dean R(ay)

Dwyer, K. R.
See Koontz, Dean R(ay)

Dwyer, Thomas A. 1923-   **CLC 114**
See also CA 115

Dye, Richard
See De Voto, Bernard (Augustine)

Dylan, Bob 1941-   **CLC 3, 4, 6, 12, 77**
See also CA 41-44R; DLB 16

Eagleton, Terence (Francis) 1943-
See Eagleton, Terry
See also CA 57-60; CANR 7, 23, 68; MTCW 1

Eagleton, Terry   **CLC 63**
See also Eagleton, Terence (Francis)

PC 18; WLC
See also CDALB 1640-1865; DLB 1, 59, 73

Eminescu, Mihail 1850-1889   **NCLC 33**

Empson, William 1906-1984**CLC 3, 8, 19, 33, 34**
See also CA 17-20R; 112; CANR 31, 61; DLB 20; MTCW 1

Enchi, Fumiko (Ueda) 1905-1986   **CLC 31**
See also CA 129; 121

Ende, Michael (Andreas Helmuth) 1929-1995 **CLC 31**
See also CA 118; 124; 149; CANR 36; CLR 14; DLB 75; MAICYA; SATA 61; SATA-Brief 42; SATA-Obit 86

Endo, Shusaku 1923-1996 **CLC 7, 14, 19, 54, 99; DAM NOV**
See also CA 29-32R; 153; CANR 21, 54; DLB 182; MTCW 1

Engel, Marian 1933-1985   **CLC 36**
See also CA 25-28R; CANR 12; DLB 53; INT CANR-12

Engelhardt, Frederick
See Hubbard, L(afayette) Ron(ald)

Enright, D(ennis) J(oseph) 1920-**CLC 4, 8, 31**
See also CA 1-4R; CANR 1, 42; DLB 27; SATA 25

Enzensberger, Hans Magnus 1929-   **CLC 43**
See also CA 116; 119

Ephron, Nora 1941-   **CLC 17, 31**
See also AITN 2; CA 65-68; CANR 12, 39

Epicurus 341B.C.-270B.C.   **CMLC 21**
See also DLB 176

Epsilon
See Betjeman, John

Epstein, Daniel Mark 1948-   **CLC 7**
See also CA 49-52; CANR 2, 53

Epstein, Jacob 1956-   **CLC 19**
See also CA 114

Epstein, Joseph 1937-   **CLC 39**
See also CA 112; 119; CANR 50, 65

Epstein, Leslie 1938-   **CLC 27**
See also CA 73-76; CAAS 12; CANR 23, 69

Equiano, Olaudah 1745(?)-1797 **LC 16; BLC 2; DAM MULT**
See also DLB 37, 50

ER   **TCLC 33**
See also CA 160; DLB 85

Erasmus, Desiderius 1469(?)-1536   **LC 16**

Erdman, Paul E(mil) 1932-   **CLC 25**
See also AITN 1; CA 61-64; CANR 13, 43

Erdrich, Louise 1954-   **CLC 39, 54; DAM MULT, NOV, POP**
See also AAYA 10; BEST 89:1; CA 114; CANR 41, 62; DLB 152, 175; MTCW 1; NNAL; SATA 94

Erenburg, Ilya (Grigoryevich)
See Ehrenburg, Ilya (Grigoryevich)

Erickson, Stephen Michael 1950-
See Erickson, Steve
See also CA 129

Erickson, Steve 1950-   **CLC 64**
See also Erickson, Stephen Michael
See also CANR 60, 68

Ericson, Walter
See Fast, Howard (Melvin)

Eriksson, Buntel
See Bergman, (Ernst) Ingmar

Ernaux, Annie 1940-   **CLC 88**
See also CA 147

Erskine, John 1879-1951   **TCLC 84**
See also CA 112; 159; DLB 9, 102

Eschenbach, Wolfram von
See Wolfram von Eschenbach

Eseki, Bruno
See Mphahlele, Ezekiel

Esenin, Sergei (Alexandrovich) 1895-1925 **TCLC 4**
See also CA 104

Eshleman, Clayton 1935-   **CLC 7**
See also CA 33-36R; CAAS 6; DLB 5

Espriella, Don Manuel Alvarez
See Southey, Robert

Espriu, Salvador 1913-1985   **CLC 9**
See also CA 154; 115; DLB 134

Espronceda, Jose de 1808-1842   **NCLC 39**

Esse, James
See Stephens, James

Esterbrook, Tom
See Hubbard, L(afayette) Ron(ald)

Estleman, Loren D. 1952-**CLC 48; DAM NOV, POP**
See also AAYA 27; CA 85-88; CANR 27, 74; INT CANR-27; MTCW 1

Euclid 306B.C.-283B.C.   **CMLC 25**

Eugenides, Jeffrey 1960(?)-   **CLC 81**
See also CA 144

Euripides c. 485B.C.-406B.C.**CMLC 23; DA; DAB; DAC; DAM DRAM, MST; DC 4; WLCS**
See also DLB 176

Evan, Evin
See Faust, Frederick (Schiller)

Evans, Caradoc 1878-1945   **TCLC 85**

Evans, Evan
See Faust, Frederick (Schiller)

Evans, Marian
See Eliot, George

Evans, Mary Ann
See Eliot, George

Evarts, Esther
See Benson, Sally

Everett, Percival L. 1956-   **CLC 57**
See also BW 2; CA 129

Everson, R(onald) G(ilmour) 1903-   **CLC 27**
See also CA 17-20R; DLB 88

Everson, William (Oliver) 1912-1994 **CLC 1, 5, 14**
See also CA 9-12R; 145; CANR 20; DLB 5, 16; MTCW 1

Evtushenko, Evgenii Aleksandrovich
See Yevtushenko, Yevgeny (Alexandrovich)

Ewart, Gavin (Buchanan) 1916-1995**CLC 13, 46**
See also CA 89-92; 150; CANR 17, 46; DLB 40; MTCW 1

Ewers, Hanns Heinz 1871-1943   **TCLC 12**
See also CA 109; 149

Ewing, Frederick R.
See Sturgeon, Theodore (Hamilton)

Exley, Frederick (Earl) 1929-1992 **CLC 6, 11**
See also AITN 2; CA 81-84; 138; DLB 143; DLBY 81

Eynhardt, Guillermo
See Quiroga, Horacio (Sylvestre)

Ezekiel, Nissim 1924-   **CLC 61**
See also CA 61-64

Ezekiel, Tish O'Dowd 1943-   **CLC 34**
See also CA 129

Fadeyev, A.
See Bulgya, Alexander Alexandrovich

Fadeyev, Alexander   **TCLC 53**
See also Bulgya, Alexander Alexandrovich

Fagen, Donald 1948-   **CLC 26**

Fainzilberg, Ilya Arnoldovich 1897-1937
See Ilf, Ilya
See also CA 120; 165

Fair, Ronald L. 1932-   **CLC 18**
See also BW 1; CA 69-72; CANR 25; DLB 33

Fairbairn, Roger
See Carr, John Dickson

Fairbairns, Zoe (Ann) 1948-   **CLC 32**
See also CA 103; CANR 21

Falco, Gian
See Papini, Giovanni

Falconer, James
See Kirkup, James

Falconer, Kenneth
See Kornbluth, C(yril) M.

Falkland, Samuel
See Heijermans, Herman

Fallaci, Oriana 1930-   **CLC 11, 110**
See also CA 77-80; CANR 15, 58; MTCW 1

Faludy, George 1913-   **CLC 42**
See also CA 21-24R

Faludy, Gyoergy
See Faludy, George

Fanon, Frantz 1925-1961   **CLC 74; BLC 2; DAM MULT**
See also BW 1; CA 116; 89-92

Fanshawe, Ann 1625-1680   **LC 11**

Fante, John (Thomas) 1911-1983   **CLC 60**
See also CA 69-72; 109; CANR 23; DLB 130; DLBY 83

Farah, Nuruddin 1945-**CLC 53; BLC 2; DAM MULT**
See also BW 2; CA 106; DLB 125

Fargue, Leon-Paul 1876(?)-1947   **TCLC 11**
See also CA 109

Farigoule, Louis
See Romains, Jules

Farina, Richard 1936(?)-1966   **CLC 9**
See also CA 81-84; 25-28R

Farley, Walter (Lorimer) 1915-1989 **CLC 17**
See also CA 17-20R; CANR 8, 29; DLB 22; JRDA; MAICYA; SATA 2, 43

Farmer, Philip Jose 1918-   **CLC 1, 19**
See also CA 1-4R; CANR 4, 35; DLB 8; MTCW 1; SATA 93

Farquhar, George 1677-1707   **LC 21; DAM DRAM**
See also DLB 84

Farrell, J(ames) G(ordon) 1935-1979 **CLC 6**
See also CA 73-76; 89-92; CANR 36; DLB 14; MTCW 1

Farrell, James T(homas) 1904-1979**CLC 1, 4, 8, 11, 66; SSC 28**
See also CA 5-8R; 89-92; CANR 9, 61; DLB 4, 9, 86; DLBD 2; MTCW 1

Farren, Richard J.
See Betjeman, John

Farren, Richard M.
See Betjeman, John

Fassbinder, Rainer Werner 1946-1982**CLC 20**
See also CA 93-96; 106; CANR 31

Fast, Howard (Melvin) 1914-   **CLC 23; DAM NOV**
See also AAYA 16; CA 1-4R; CAAS 18; CANR 1, 33, 54; DLB 9; INT CANR-33; SATA 7

Faulcon, Robert
See Holdstock, Robert P.

Faulkner, William (Cuthbert) 1897-1962**CLC 1, 3, 6, 8, 9, 11, 14, 18, 28, 52, 68; DA; DAB; DAC; DAM MST, NOV; SSC 1; WLC**
See also AAYA 7; CA 81-84; CANR 33; CDALB 1929-1941; DLB 9, 11, 44, 102; DLBD 2; DLBY 86, 97; MTCW 1

Fauset, Jessie Redmon 1884(?)-1961 **CLC 19, 54; BLC 2; DAM MULT**
See also BW 1; CA 109; DLB 51

See also CA 109; 117; CANR 50, 74; DLB 5, 193; INT 117

Ford, Elbur
See Hibbert, Eleanor Alice Burford

Ford, Ford Madox 1873-1939 **TCLC 1, 15, 39, 57; DAM NOV**
See also CA 104; 132; CANR 74; CDBLB 1914-1945; DLB 162; MTCW 1

Ford, Henry 1863-1947　　　**TCLC 73**
See also CA 115; 148

Ford, John 1586-(?)　　　　　　**DC 8**
See also CDBLB Before 1660; DAM DRAM; DLB 58

Ford, John 1895-1973　　　　**CLC 16**
See also CA 45-48

Ford, Richard 1944-　　　　**CLC 46, 99**
See also CA 69-72; CANR 11, 47

Ford, Webster
See Masters, Edgar Lee

Foreman, Richard 1937-　　　**CLC 50**
See also CA 65-68; CANR 32, 63

Forester, C(ecil) S(cott) 1899-1966　**CLC 35**
See also CA 73-76; 25-28R; DLB 191; SATA 13

Forez
See Mauriac, Francois (Charles)

Forman, James Douglas 1932-　**CLC 21**
See also AAYA 17; CA 9-12R; CANR 4, 19, 42; JRDA; MAICYA; SATA 8, 70

Fornes, Maria Irene 1930-　　**CLC 39, 61**
See also CA 25-28R; CANR 28; DLB 7; HW; INT CANR-28; MTCW 1

Forrest, Leon (Richard) 1937-1997　**CLC 4; BLCS**
See also BW 2; CA 89-92; 162; CAAS 7; CANR 25, 52; DLB 33

Forster, E(dward) M(organ) 1879-1970 **C L C 1, 2, 3, 4, 9, 10, 13, 15, 22, 45, 77; DA; DAB; DAC; DAM MST, NOV; SSC 27; WLC**
See also AAYA 2; CA 13-14; 25-28R; CANR 45; CAP 1; CDBLB 1914-1945; DLB 34, 98, 162, 178, 195; DLBD 10; MTCW 1; SATA 57

Forster, John 1812-1876　　　**NCLC 11**
See also DLB 144, 184

Forsyth, Frederick 1938- **CLC 2, 5, 36; DAM NOV, POP**
See also BEST 89:4; CA 85-88; CANR 38, 62; DLB 87; MTCW 1

Forten, Charlotte L.　　　**TCLC 16; BLC 2**
See also Grimke, Charlotte L(ottie) Forten
See also DLB 50

Foscolo, Ugo 1778-1827　　　**NCLC 8**

Fosse, Bob　　　　　　　　**CLC 20**
See also Fosse, Robert Louis

Fosse, Robert Louis 1927-1987
See Fosse, Bob
See also CA 110; 123

Foster, Stephen Collins 1826-1864 **NCLC 26**

Foucault, Michel 1926-1984　**CLC 31, 34, 69**
See also CA 105; 113; CANR 34; MTCW 1

Fouque, Friedrich (Heinrich Karl) de la Motte 1777-1843　　　**NCLC 2**
See also DLB 90

Fourier, Charles 1772-1837　　**NCLC 51**

Fournier, Henri Alban 1886-1914
See Alain-Fournier
See also CA 104

Fournier, Pierre 1916-　　　**CLC 11**
See also Gascar, Pierre
See also CA 89-92; CANR 16, 40

Fowles, John (Philip) 1926- **CLC 1, 2, 3, 4, 6, 9, 10, 15, 33, 87; DAB; DAC; DAM MST**

See also CA 5-8R; CANR 25, 71; CDBLB 1960 to Present; DLB 14, 139; MTCW 1; SATA 22

Fox, Paula 1923-　　　　　　**CLC 2, 8**
See also AAYA 3; CA 73-76; CANR 20, 36, 62; CLR 1, 44; DLB 52; JRDA; MAICYA; MTCW 1; SATA 17, 60

Fox, William Price (Jr.) 1926-　**CLC 22**
See also CA 17-20R; CAAS 19; CANR 11; DLB 2; DLBY 81

Foxe, John 1516(?)-1587　　　**LC 14**
See also DLB 132

Frame, Janet 1924- **CLC 2, 3, 6, 22, 66, 96; SSC 29**
See also Clutha, Janet Paterson Frame

France, Anatole　　　　　　**TCLC 9**
See also Thibault, Jacques Anatole Francois
See also DLB 123

Francis, Claude 19(?)-　　　　**CLC 50**

Francis, Dick 1920- **CLC 2, 22, 42, 102; DAM POP**
See also AAYA 5, 21; BEST 89:3; CA 5-8R; CANR 9, 42, 68; CDBLB 1960 to Present; DLB 87; INT CANR-9; MTCW 1

Francis, Robert (Churchill) 1901-1987　**C L C 15**
See also CA 1-4R; 123; CANR 1

Frank, Anne(lies Marie) 1929-1945 **TCLC 17; DA; DAB; DAC; DAM MST; WLC**
See also AAYA 12; CA 113; 133; CANR 68; MTCW 1; SATA 87; SATA-Brief 42

Frank, Bruno 1887-1945　　　**TCLC 81**
See also DLB 118

Frank, Elizabeth 1945-　　　**CLC 39**
See also CA 121; 126; INT 126

Frankl, Viktor E(mil) 1905-1997　**CLC 93**
See also CA 65-68; 161

Franklin, Benjamin
See Hasek, Jaroslav (Matej Frantisek)

Franklin, Benjamin 1706-1790　**LC 25; DA; DAB; DAC; DAM MST; WLCS**
See also CDALB 1640-1865; DLB 24, 43, 73

Franklin, (Stella Maria Sarah) Miles (Lampe) 1879-1954　　　　**TCLC 7**
See also CA 104; 164

Fraser, (Lady) Antonia (Pakenham) 1932- **CLC 32, 107**
See also CA 85-88; CANR 44, 65; MTCW 1; SATA-Brief 32

Fraser, George MacDonald 1925-　**CLC 7**
See also CA 45-48; CANR 2, 48, 74

Fraser, Sylvia 1935-　　　　**CLC 64**
See also CA 45-48; CANR 1, 16, 60

Frayn, Michael 1933- **CLC 3, 7, 31, 47; DAM DRAM, NOV**
See also CA 5-8R; CANR 30, 69; DLB 13, 14, 194; MTCW 1

Fraze, Candida (Merrill) 1945-　**CLC 50**
See also CA 126

Frazer, J(ames) G(eorge) 1854-1941 **TCLC 32**
See also CA 118

Frazer, Robert Caine
See Creasey, John

Frazer, Sir James George
See Frazer, J(ames) G(eorge)

Frazier, Charles 1950-　　　**CLC 109**
See also CA 161

Frazier, Ian 1951-　　　　　**CLC 46**
See also CA 130; CANR 54

Frederic, Harold 1856-1898　　**NCLC 10**
See also DLB 12, 23; DLBD 13

Frederick, John
See Faust, Frederick (Schiller)

Frederick the Great 1712-1786　　**LC 14**

Fredro, Aleksander 1793-1876　　**NCLC 8**

Freeling, Nicolas 1927-　　　**CLC 38**
See also CA 49-52; CAAS 12; CANR 1, 17, 50; DLB 87

Freeman, Douglas Southall 1886-1953 **T C L C 11**
See also CA 109; DLB 17; DLBD 17

Freeman, Judith 1946-　　　**CLC 55**
See also CA 148

Freeman, Mary Eleanor Wilkins 1852-1930 **TCLC 9; SSC 1**
See also CA 106; DLB 12, 78

Freeman, R(ichard) Austin 1862-1943 **T C L C 21**
See also CA 113; DLB 70

French, Albert 1943-　　　　**CLC 86**
See also CA 167

French, Marilyn 1929- **CLC 10, 18, 60; DAM DRAM, NOV, POP**
See also CA 69-72; CANR 3, 31; INT CANR-31; MTCW 1

French, Paul
See Asimov, Isaac

Freneau, Philip Morin 1752-1832　**NCLC 1**
See also DLB 37, 43

Freud, Sigmund 1856-1939　　　**TCLC 52**
See also CA 115; 133; CANR 69; MTCW 1

Friedan, Betty (Naomi) 1921-　**CLC 74**
See also CA 65-68; CANR 18, 45, 74; MTCW 1

Friedlander, Saul 1932-　　　**CLC 90**
See also CA 117; 130; CANR 72

Friedman, B(ernard) H(arper) 1926- **CLC 7**
See also CA 1-4R; CANR 3, 48

Friedman, Bruce Jay 1930-　**CLC 3, 5, 56**
See also CA 9-12R; CANR 25, 52; DLB 2, 28; INT CANR-25

Friel, Brian 1929- **CLC 5, 42, 59, 115; DC 8**
See also CA 21-24R; CANR 33, 69; DLB 13; MTCW 1

Friis-Baastad, Babbis Ellinor 1921-1970 **C L C 12**
See also CA 17-20R; 134; SATA 7

Frisch, Max (Rudolf) 1911-1991 **CLC 3, 9, 14, 18, 32, 44; DAM DRAM, NOV**
See also CA 85-88; 134; CANR 32, 74; DLB 69, 124; MTCW 1

Fromentin, Eugene (Samuel Auguste) 1820-1876　　　**NCLC 10**
See also DLB 123

Frost, Frederick
See Faust, Frederick (Schiller)

Frost, Robert (Lee) 1874-1963 **CLC 1, 3, 4, 9, 10, 13, 15, 26, 34, 44; DA; DAB; DAC; DAM MST, POET; PC 1; WLC**
See also AAYA 21; CA 89-92; CANR 33; CDALB 1917-1929; DLB 54; DLBD 7; MTCW 1; SATA 14

Froude, James Anthony 1818-1894 **NCLC 43**
See also DLB 18, 57, 144

Froy, Herald
See Waterhouse, Keith (Spencer)

Fry, Christopher 1907- **CLC 2, 10, 14; DAM DRAM**
See also CA 17-20R; CAAS 23; CANR 9, 30, 74; DLB 13; MTCW 1; SATA 66

Frye, (Herman) Northrop 1912-1991 **CLC 24, 70**
See also CA 5-8R; 133; CANR 8, 37; DLB 67, 68; MTCW 1

Fuchs, Daniel 1909-1993　　　**CLC 8, 22**
See also CA 81-84; 142; CAAS 5; CANR 40;

See also Green, Julian (Hartridge)

Green, Paul (Eliot) 1894-1981 **CLC 25; DAM DRAM**
See also AITN 1; CA 5-8R; 103; CANR 3; DLB 7, 9; DLBY 81

Greenberg, Ivan 1908-1973
See Rahv, Philip
See also CA 85-88

Greenberg, Joanne (Goldenberg) 1932- **CLC 7, 30**
See also AAYA 12; CA 5-8R; CANR 14, 32, 69; SATA 25

Greenberg, Richard 1959(?)-   **CLC 57**
See also CA 138

Greene, Bette 1934-   **CLC 30**
See also AAYA 7; CA 53-56; CANR 4; CLR 2; JRDA; MAICYA; SAAS 16; SATA 8, 102

Greene, Gael   **CLC 8**
See also CA 13-16R; CANR 10

Greene, Graham (Henry) 1904-1991**CLC 1, 3, 6, 9, 14, 18, 27, 37, 70, 72; DA; DAB; DAC; DAM MST, NOV; SSC 29; WLC**
See also AITN 2; CA 13-16R; 133; CANR 35, 61; CDBLB 1945-1960; DLB 13, 15, 77, 100, 162, 201; DLBY 91; MTCW 1; SATA 20

Greene, Robert 1558-1592   **LC 41**
See also DLB 62, 167

Greer, Richard
See Silverberg, Robert

Gregor, Arthur 1923-   **CLC 9**
See also CA 25-28R; CAAS 10; CANR 11; SATA 36

Gregor, Lee
See Pohl, Frederik

Gregory, Isabella Augusta (Persse) 1852-1932 **TCLC 1**
See also CA 104; DLB 10

Gregory, J. Dennis
See Williams, John A(lfred)

Grendon, Stephen
See Derleth, August (William)

Grenville, Kate 1950-   **CLC 61**
See also CA 118; CANR 53

Grenville, Pelham
See Wodehouse, P(elham) G(renville)

Greve, Felix Paul (Berthold Friedrich) 1879-1948
See Grove, Frederick Philip
See also CA 104; 141; DAC; DAM MST

Grey, Zane 1872-1939 **TCLC 6; DAM POP**
See also CA 104; 132; DLB 9; MTCW 1

Grieg, (Johan) Nordahl (Brun) 1902-1943 **TCLC 10**
See also CA 107

Grieve, C(hristopher) M(urray) 1892-1978 **CLC 11, 19; DAM POET**
See also MacDiarmid, Hugh; Pteleon
See also CA 5-8R; 85-88; CANR 33; MTCW 1

Griffin, Gerald 1803-1840   **NCLC 7**
See also DLB 159

Griffin, John Howard 1920-1980   **CLC 68**
See also AITN 1; CA 1-4R; 101; CANR 2

Griffin, Peter 1942-   **CLC 39**
See also CA 136

Griffith, D(avid Lewelyn) W(ark) 1875(?)-1948 **TCLC 68**
See also CA 119; 150

Griffith, Lawrence
See Griffith, D(avid Lewelyn) W(ark)

Griffiths, Trevor 1935-   **CLC 13, 52**
See also CA 97-100; CANR 45; DLB 13

Griggs, Sutton Elbert 1872-1930(?) **TCLC 77**

See also CA 123; DLB 50

Grigson, Geoffrey (Edward Harvey) 1905-1985 **CLC 7, 39**
See also CA 25-28R; 118; CANR 20, 33; DLB 27; MTCW 1

Grillparzer, Franz 1791-1872   **NCLC 1**
See also DLB 133

Grimble, Reverend Charles James
See Eliot, T(homas) S(tearns)

Grimke, Charlotte L(ottie) Forten 1837(?)-1914
See Forten, Charlotte L.
See also BW 1; CA 117; 124; DAM MULT, POET

Grimm, Jacob Ludwig Karl 1785-1863**NCLC 3**
See also DLB 90; MAICYA; SATA 22

Grimm, Wilhelm Karl 1786-1859   **NCLC 3**
See also DLB 90; MAICYA; SATA 22

Grimmelshausen, Johann Jakob Christoffel von 1621-1676 **LC 6**
See also DLB 168

Grindel, Eugene 1895-1952
See Eluard, Paul
See also CA 104

Grisham, John 1955-   **CLC 84; DAM POP**
See also AAYA 14; CA 138; CANR 47, 69

Grossman, David 1954-   **CLC 67**
See also CA 138

Grossman, Vasily (Semenovich) 1905-1964 **CLC 41**
See also CA 124; 130; MTCW 1

Grove, Frederick Philip   **TCLC 4**
See also Greve, Felix Paul (Berthold Friedrich)
See also DLB 92

Grubb
See Crumb, R(obert)

Grumbach, Doris (Isaac) 1918-**CLC 13, 22, 64**
See also CA 5-8R; CAAS 2; CANR 9, 42, 70; INT CANR-9

Grundtvig, Nicolai Frederik Severin 1783-1872 **NCLC 1**

Grunge
See Crumb, R(obert)

Grunwald, Lisa 1959-   **CLC 44**
See also CA 120

Guare, John 1938- **CLC 8, 14, 29, 67; DAM DRAM**
See also CA 73-76; CANR 21, 69; DLB 7; MTCW 1

Gudjonsson, Halldor Kiljan 1902-1998
See Laxness, Halldor
See also CA 103; 164

Guenter, Erich
See Eich, Guenter

Guest, Barbara 1920-   **CLC 34**
See also CA 25-28R; CANR 11, 44; DLB 5, 193

Guest, Judith (Ann) 1936- **CLC 8, 30; DAM NOV, POP**
See also AAYA 7; CA 77-80; CANR 15; INT CANR-15; MTCW 1

Guevara, Che   **CLC 87; HLC**
See also Guevara (Serna), Ernesto

Guevara (Serna), Ernesto 1928-1967
See Guevara, Che
See also CA 127; 111; CANR 56; DAM MULT; HW

Guild, Nicholas M. 1944-   **CLC 33**
See also CA 93-96

Guillemin, Jacques
See Sartre, Jean-Paul

Guillen, Jorge 1893-1984   **CLC 11; DAM MULT, POET**

See also CA 89-92; 112; DLB 108; HW

Guillen, Nicolas (Cristobal) 1902-1989 **CLC 48, 79; BLC 2; DAM MST, MULT, POET; HLC; PC 23**
See also BW 2; CA 116; 125; 129; HW

Guillevic, (Eugene) 1907-   **CLC 33**
See also CA 93-96

Guillois
See Desnos, Robert

Guillois, Valentin
See Desnos, Robert

Guiney, Louise Imogen 1861-1920 **TCLC 41**
See also CA 160; DLB 54

Guiraldes, Ricardo (Guillermo) 1886-1927 **TCLC 39**
See also CA 131; HW; MTCW 1

Gumilev, Nikolai (Stepanovich) 1886-1921 **TCLC 60**
See also CA 165

Gunesekera, Romesh 1954-   **CLC 91**
See also CA 159

Gunn, Bill   **CLC 5**
See also Gunn, William Harrison
See also DLB 38

Gunn, Thom(son William) 1929-**CLC 3, 6, 18, 32, 81; DAM POET**
See also CA 17-20R; CANR 9, 33; CDBLB 1960 to Present; DLB 27; INT CANR-33; MTCW 1

Gunn, William Harrison 1934(?)-1989
See Gunn, Bill
See also AITN 1; BW 1; CA 13-16R; 128; CANR 12, 25

Gunnars, Kristjana 1948-   **CLC 69**
See also CA 113; DLB 60

Gurdjieff, G(eorgei) I(vanovich) 1877(?)-1949 **TCLC 71**
See also CA 157

Gurganus, Allan 1947- **CLC 70; DAM POP**
See also BEST 90:1; CA 135

Gurney, A(lbert) R(amsdell), Jr. 1930- **CLC 32, 50, 54; DAM DRAM**
See also CA 77-80; CANR 32, 64

Gurney, Ivor (Bertie) 1890-1937   **TCLC 33**
See also CA 167

Gurney, Peter
See Gurney, A(lbert) R(amsdell), Jr.

Guro, Elena 1877-1913   **TCLC 56**

Gustafson, James M(oody) 1925-   **CLC 100**
See also CA 25-28R; CANR 37

Gustafson, Ralph (Barker) 1909-.   **CLC 36**
See also CA 21-24R; CANR 8, 45; DLB 88

Gut, Gom
See Simenon, Georges (Jacques Christian)

Guterson, David 1956-   **CLC 91**
See also CA 132; CANR 73

Guthrie, A(lfred) B(ertram), Jr. 1901-1991 **CLC 23**
See also CA 57-60; 134; CANR 24; DLB 6; SATA 62; SATA-Obit 67

Guthrie, Isobel
See Grieve, C(hristopher) M(urray)

Guthrie, Woodrow Wilson 1912-1967
See Guthrie, Woody
See also CA 113; 93-96

Guthrie, Woody   **CLC 35**
See also Guthrie, Woodrow Wilson

Guy, Rosa (Cuthbert) 1928-   **CLC 26**
See also AAYA 4; BW 2; CA 17-20R; CANR 14, 34; CLR 13; DLB 33; JRDA; MAICYA; SATA 14, 62

Gwendolyn
See Bennett, (Enoch) Arnold

H. D.   CLC 3, 8, 14, 31, 34, 73; PC 5
See also Doolittle, Hilda

H. de V.
See Buchan, John

Haavikko, Paavo Juhani 1931-   CLC 18, 34
See also CA 106

Habbema, Koos
See Heijermans, Herman

Habermas, Juergen 1929-   CLC 104
See also CA 109

Habermas, Jurgen
See Habermas, Juergen

Hacker, Marilyn 1942- CLC 5, 9, 23, 72, 91;
DAM POET
See also CA 77-80; CANR 68; DLB 120

Haeckel, Ernst Heinrich (Philipp August) 1834-
1919   TCLC 83
See also CA 157

Haggard, H(enry) Rider 1856-1925 TCLC 11
See also CA 108; 148; DLB 70, 156, 174, 178;
SATA 16

Hagiosy, L.
See Larbaud, Valery (Nicolas)

Hagiwara Sakutaro 1886-1942 TCLC 60; PC
18

Haig, Fenil
See Ford, Ford Madox

Haig-Brown, Roderick (Langmere) 1908-1976
CLC 21
See also CA 5-8R; 69-72; CANR 4, 38; CLR
31; DLB 88; MAICYA; SATA 12

Hailey, Arthur 1920- CLC 5; DAM NOV, POP
See also AITN 2; BEST 90:3; CA 1-4R; CANR
2, 36; DLB 88; DLBY 82; MTCW 1

Hailey, Elizabeth Forsythe 1938-   CLC 40
See also CA 93-96; CAAS 1; CANR 15, 48;
INT CANR-15

Haines, John (Meade) 1924-   CLC 58
See also CA 17-20R; CANR 13, 34; DLB 5

Hakluyt, Richard 1552-1616   LC 31

Haldeman, Joe (William) 1943-   CLC 61
See also CA 53-56; CAAS 25; CANR 6, 70,
72; DLB 8; INT CANR-6

Haley, Alex(ander Murray Palmer) 1921-1992
CLC 8, 12, 76; BLC 2; DA; DAB; DAC;
DAM MST, MULT, POP
See also AAYA 26; BW 2; CA 77-80; 136;
CANR 61; DLB 38; MTCW 1

Haliburton, Thomas Chandler 1796-1865
NCLC 15
See also DLB 11, 99

Hall, Donald (Andrew, Jr.) 1928- CLC 1, 13,
37, 59; DAM POET
See also CA 5-8R; CAAS 7; CANR 2, 44, 64;
DLB 5; SATA 23, 97

Hall, Frederic Sauser
See Sauser-Hall, Frederic

Hall, James
See Kuttner, Henry

Hall, James Norman 1887-1951   TCLC 23
See also CA 123; SATA 21

Hall, Radclyffe
See Hall, (Marguerite) Radclyffe

Hall, (Marguerite) Radclyffe 1886-1943
TCLC 12
See also CA 110; 150; DLB 191

Hall, Rodney 1935-   CLC 51
See also CA 109; CANR 69

Halleck, Fitz-Greene 1790-1867   NCLC 47
See also DLB 3

Halliday, Michael
See Creasey, John

Halpern, Daniel 1945-   CLC 14

See also CA 33-36R

Hamburger, Michael (Peter Leopold) 1924-
CLC 5, 14
See also CA 5-8R; CAAS 4; CANR 2, 47; DLB
27

Hamill, Pete 1935-   CLC 10
See also CA 25-28R; CANR 18, 71

Hamilton, Alexander 1755(?)-1804 NCLC 49
See also DLB 37

Hamilton, Clive
See Lewis, C(live) S(taples)

Hamilton, Edmond 1904-1977   CLC 1
See also CA 1-4R; CANR 3; DLB 8

Hamilton, Eugene (Jacob) Lee
See Lee-Hamilton, Eugene (Jacob)

Hamilton, Franklin
See Silverberg, Robert

Hamilton, Gail
See Corcoran, Barbara

Hamilton, Mollie
See Kaye, M(ary) M(argaret)

Hamilton, (Anthony Walter) Patrick 1904-1962
CLC 51
See also CA 113; DLB 10

Hamilton, Virginia 1936-   CLC 26; DAM
MULT
See also AAYA 2, 21; BW 2; CA 25-28R;
CANR 20, 37, 73; CLR 1, 11, 40; DLB 33,
52; INT CANR-20; JRDA; MAICYA;
MTCW 1; SATA 4, 56, 79

Hammett, (Samuel) Dashiell 1894-1961 C L C
3, 5, 10, 19, 47; SSC 17
See also AITN 1; CA 81-84; CANR 42; CDALB
1929-1941; DLBD 6; DLBY 96; MTCW 1

Hammon, Jupiter 1711(?)-1800(?)   NCLC 5;
BLC 2; DAM MULT, POET; PC 16
See also DLB 31, 50

Hammond, Keith
See Kuttner, Henry

Hamner, Earl (Henry), Jr. 1923-   CLC 12
See also AITN 2; CA 73-76; DLB 6

Hampton, Christopher (James) 1946- CLC 4
See also CA 25-28R; DLB 13; MTCW 1

Hamsun, Knut   TCLC 2, 14, 49
See also Pedersen, Knut

Handke, Peter 1942- CLC 5, 8, 10, 15, 38; DAM
DRAM, NOV
See also CA 77-80; CANR 33; DLB 85, 124;
MTCW 1

Hanley, James 1901-1985   CLC 3, 5, 8, 13
See also CA 73-76; 117; CANR 36; DLB 191;
MTCW 1

Hannah, Barry 1942-   CLC 23, 38, 90
See also CA 108; 110; CANR 43, 68; DLB 6;
INT 110; MTCW 1

Hannon, Ezra
See Hunter, Evan

Hansberry, Lorraine (Vivian) 1930-1965 CLC
17, 62; BLC 2; DA; DAB; DAC; DAM
DRAM, MST, MULT; DC 2
See also AAYA 25; BW 1; CA 109; 25-28R;
CABS 3; CANR 58; CDALB 1941-1968;
DLB 7, 38; MTCW 1

Hansen, Joseph 1923-   CLC 38
See also CA 29-32R; CAAS 17; CANR 16, 44,
66; INT CANR-16

Hansen, Martin A(lfred) 1909-1955 TCLC 32
See also CA 167

Hanson, Kenneth O(stlin) 1922-   CLC 13
See also CA 53-56; CANR 7

Hardwick, Elizabeth (Bruce) 1916- CLC 13;
DAM NOV
See also CA 5-8R; CANR 3, 32, 70; DLB 6;

MTCW 1

Hardy, Thomas 1840-1928 TCLC 4, 10, 18, 32,
48, 53, 72; DA; DAB; DAC; DAM MST,
NOV, POET; PC 8; SSC 2; WLC
See also CA 104; 123; CDBLB 1890-1914;
DLB 18, 19, 135; MTCW 1

Hare, David 1947-   CLC 29, 58
See also CA 97-100; CANR 39; DLB 13;
MTCW 1

Harewood, John
See Van Druten, John (William)

Harford, Henry
See Hudson, W(illiam) H(enry)

Hargrave, Leonie
See Disch, Thomas M(ichael)

Harjo, Joy 1951-   CLC 83; DAM MULT
See also CA 114; CANR 35, 67; DLB 120, 175;
NNAL

Harlan, Louis R(udolph) 1922-   CLC 34
See also CA 21-24R; CANR 25, 55

Harling, Robert 1951(?)-   CLC 53
See also CA 147

Harmon, William (Ruth) 1938-   CLC 38
See also CA 33-36R; CANR 14, 32, 35; SATA
65

Harper, F. E. W.
See Harper, Frances Ellen Watkins

Harper, Frances E. W.
See Harper, Frances Ellen Watkins

Harper, Frances E. Watkins
See Harper, Frances Ellen Watkins

Harper, Frances Ellen
See Harper, Frances Ellen Watkins

Harper, Frances Ellen Watkins 1825-1911
TCLC 14; BLC 2; DAM MULT, POET;
PC 21
See also BW 1; CA 111; 125; DLB 50

Harper, Michael S(teven) 1938- CLC 7, 22
See also BW 1; CA 33-36R; CANR 24; DLB
41

Harper, Mrs. F. E. W.
See Harper, Frances Ellen Watkins

Harris, Christie (Lucy) Irwin 1907- CLC 12
See also CA 5-8R; CANR 6; CLR 47; DLB 88;
JRDA; MAICYA; SAAS 10; SATA 6, 74

Harris, Frank 1856-1931   TCLC 24
See also CA 109; 150; DLB 156, 197

Harris, George Washington 1814-1869 N C L C
23
See also DLB 3, 11

Harris, Joel Chandler 1848-1908   TCLC 2;
SSC 19
See also CA 104; 137; CLR 49; DLB 11, 23,
42, 78, 91; MAICYA; SATA 100; YABC 1

Harris, John (Wyndham Parkes Lucas) Beynon
1903-1969
See Wyndham, John
See also CA 102; 89-92

Harris, MacDonald   CLC 9
See also Heiney, Donald (William)

Harris, Mark 1922-   CLC 19
See also CA 5-8R; CAAS 3; CANR 2, 55; DLB
2; DLBY 80

Harris, (Theodore) Wilson 1921-   CLC 25
See also BW 2; CA 65-68; CAAS 16; CANR
11, 27, 69; DLB 117; MTCW 1

Harrison, Elizabeth Cavanna 1909-
See Cavanna, Betty
See also CA 9-12R; CANR 6, 27

Harrison, Harry (Max) 1925-   CLC 42
See also CA 1-4R; CANR 5, 21; DLB 8; SATA
4

Harrison, James (Thomas) 1937- CLC 6, 14,

33, 66; SSC 19
See also CA 13-16R; CANR 8, 51; DLBY 82;
INT CANR-8
Harrison, Jim
See Harrison, James (Thomas)
Harrison, Kathryn 1961-   CLC 70
See also CA 144; CANR 68
Harrison, Tony 1937-   CLC 43
See also CA 65-68; CANR 44; DLB 40; MTCW
1
Harriss, Will(ard Irvin) 1922-   CLC 34
See also CA 111
Harson, Sley
See Ellison, Harlan (Jay)
Hart, Ellis
See Ellison, Harlan (Jay)
Hart, Josephine 1942(?)- CLC 70; DAM POP
See also CA 138; CANR 70
Hart, Moss 1904-1961 CLC 66; DAM DRAM
See also CA 109; 89-92; DLB 7
Harte, (Francis) Bret(t) 1836(?)-1902 TCLC 1,
25; DA; DAC; DAM MST; SSC 8; WLC
See also CA 104; 140; CDALB 1865-1917;
DLB 12, 64, 74, 79, 186; SATA 26
Hartley, L(eslie) P(oles) 1895-1972 CLC 2, 22
See also CA 45-48; 37-40R; CANR 33; DLB
15, 139; MTCW 1
Hartman, Geoffrey H. 1929-   CLC 27
See also CA 117; 125; DLB 67
Hartmann, Sadakichi 1867-1944   TCLC 73
See also CA 157; DLB 54
Hartmann von Aue c. 1160-c. 1205 CMLC 15
See also DLB 138
Hartmann von Aue 1170-1210   CMLC 15
Haruf, Kent 1943-   CLC 34
See also CA 149
Harwood, Ronald 1934-   CLC 32; DAM
DRAM, MST
See also CA 1-4R; CANR 4, 55; DLB 13
Hasegawa Tatsunosuke
See Futabatei, Shimei
Hasek, Jaroslav (Matej Frantisek) 1883-1923
TCLC 4
See also CA 104; 129; MTCW 1
Hass, Robert 1941-   CLC 18, 39, 99; PC 16
See also CA 111; CANR 30, 50, 71; DLB 105;
SATA 94
Hastings, Hudson
See Kuttner, Henry
Hastings, Selina   CLC 44
Hathorne, John 1641-1717   LC 38
Hatteras, Amelia
See Mencken, H(enry) L(ouis)
Hatteras, Owen   TCLC 18
See also Mencken, H(enry) L(ouis); Nathan,
George Jean
Hauptmann, Gerhart (Johann Robert) 1862-
1946   TCLC 4; DAM DRAM
See also CA 104; 153; DLB 66, 118
Havel, Vaclav 1936-   CLC 25, 58, 65; DAM
DRAM; DC 6
See also CA 104; CANR 36, 63; MTCW 1
Haviaras, Stratis   CLC 33
See also Chaviaras, Strates
Hawes, Stephen 1475(?)-1523(?)   LC 17
See also DLB 132
Hawkes, John (Clendennin Burne, Jr.) 1925-
1998   CLC 1, 2, 3, 4, 7, 9, 14, 15, 27, 49
See also CA 1-4R; 167; CANR 2, 47, 64; DLB
2, 7; DLBY 80; MTCW 1
Hawking, S. W.
See Hawking, Stephen W(illiam)
Hawking, Stephen W(illiam) 1942-   CLC 63,

105
See also AAYA 13; BEST 89:1; CA 126; 129;
CANR 48
Hawkins, Anthony Hope
See Hope, Anthony
Hawthorne, Julian 1846-1934   TCLC 25
See also CA 165
Hawthorne, Nathaniel 1804-1864 NCLC 39;
DA; DAB; DAC; DAM MST, NOV; SSC
3, 29; WLC
See also AAYA 18; CDALB 1640-1865; DLB
1, 74; YABC 2
Haxton, Josephine Ayres 1921-
See Douglas, Ellen
See also CA 115; CANR 41
Hayaseca y Eizaguirre, Jorge
See Echegaray (y Eizaguirre), Jose (Maria
Waldo)
Hayashi, Fumiko 1904-1951   TCLC 27
See also CA 161; DLB 180
Haycraft, Anna
See Ellis, Alice Thomas
See also CA 122
Hayden, Robert E(arl) 1913-1980 CLC 5, 9,
14, 37; BLC 2; DA; DAC; DAM MST,
MULT, POET; PC 6
See also BW 1; CA 69-72; 97-100; CABS 2;
CANR 24; CDALB 1941-1968; DLB 5, 76;
MTCW 1; SATA 19; SATA-Obit 26
Hayford, J(oseph) E(phraim) Casely
See Casely-Hayford, J(oseph) E(phraim)
Hayman, Ronald 1932-   CLC 44
See also CA 25-28R; CANR 18, 50; DLB 155
Haywood, Eliza 1693(?)-1756   LC 44
See also DLB 39
Haywood, Eliza (Fowler) 1693(?)-1756 LC 1,
44
Hazlitt, William 1778-1830   NCLC 29
See also DLB 110, 158
Hazzard, Shirley 1931-   CLC 18
See also CA 9-12R; CANR 4, 70; DLBY 82;
MTCW 1
Head, Bessie 1937-1986 CLC 25, 67; BLC 2;
DAM MULT
See also BW 2; CA 29-32R; 119; CANR 25;
DLB 117; MTCW 1
Headon, (Nicky) Topper 1956(?)-   CLC 30
Heaney, Seamus (Justin) 1939- CLC 5, 7, 14,
25, 37, 74, 91; DAB; DAM POET; PC 18;
WLCS
See also CA 85-88; CANR 25, 48; CDBLB
1960 to Present; DLB 40; DLBY 95; MTCW
1
Hearn, (Patricio) Lafcadio (Tessima Carlos)
1850-1904   TCLC 9
See also CA 105; 166; DLB 12, 78, 189
Hearne, Vicki 1946-   CLC 56
See also CA 139
Hearon, Shelby 1931-   CLC 63
See also AITN 2; CA 25-28R; CANR 18, 48
Heat-Moon, William Least   CLC 29
See also Trogdon, William (Lewis)
See also AAYA 9
Hebbel, Friedrich 1813-1863 NCLC 43; DAM
DRAM
See also DLB 129
Hebert, Anne 1916- CLC 4, 13, 29; DAC; DAM
MST, POET
See also CA 85-88; CANR 69; DLB 68; MTCW
1
Hecht, Anthony (Evan) 1923- CLC 8, 13, 19;
DAM POET
See also CA 9-12R; CANR 6; DLB 5, 169

Hecht, Ben 1894-1964   CLC 8
See also CA 85-88; DLB 7, 9, 25, 26, 28, 86
Hedayat, Sadeq 1903-1951   TCLC 21
See also CA 120
Hegel, Georg Wilhelm Friedrich 1770-1831
NCLC 46
See also DLB 90
Heidegger, Martin 1889-1976   CLC 24
See also CA 81-84; 65-68; CANR 34; MTCW
1
Heidenstam, (Carl Gustaf) Verner von 1859-
1940   TCLC 5
See also CA 104
Heifner, Jack 1946-   CLC 11
See also CA 105; CANR 47
Heijermans, Herman 1864-1924   TCLC 24
See also CA 123
Heilbrun, Carolyn G(old) 1926-   CLC 25
See also CA 45-48; CANR 1, 28, 58
Heine, Heinrich 1797-1856   NCLC 4, 54
See also DLB 90
Heinemann, Larry (Curtiss) 1944-   CLC 50
See also CA 110; CAAS 21; CANR 31; DLBD
9; INT CANR-31
Heiney, Donald (William) 1921-1993
See Harris, MacDonald
See also CA 1-4R; 142; CANR 3, 58
Heinlein, Robert A(nson) 1907-1988 CLC 1, 3,
8, 14, 26, 55; DAM POP
See also AAYA 17; CA 1-4R; 125; CANR 1,
20, 53; DLB 8; JRDA; MAICYA; MTCW 1;
SATA 9, 69; SATA-Obit 56
Helforth, John
See Doolittle, Hilda
Hellenhofferu, Vojtech Kapristian z
See Hasek, Jaroslav (Matej Frantisek)
Heller, Joseph 1923- CLC 1, 3, 5, 8, 11, 36, 63;
DA; DAB; DAC; DAM MST, NOV, POP;
WLC
See also AAYA 24; AITN 1; CA 5-8R; CABS
1; CANR 8, 42, 66; DLB 2, 28; DLBY 80;
INT CANR-8; MTCW 1
Hellman, Lillian (Florence) 1906-1984 CLC 2,
4, 8, 14, 18, 34, 44, 52; DAM DRAM; DC 1
See also AITN 1, 2; CA 13-16R; 112; CANR
33; DLB 7; DLBY 84; MTCW 1
Helprin, Mark 1947- CLC 7, 10, 22, 32; DAM
NOV, POP
See also CA 81-84; CANR 47, 64; DLBY 85;
MTCW 1
Helvetius, Claude-Adrien 1715-1771   LC 26
Helyar, Jane Penelope Josephine 1933-
See Poole, Josephine
See also CA 21-24R; CANR 10, 26; SATA 82
Hemans, Felicia 1793-1835   NCLC 71
See also DLB 96
Hemingway, Ernest (Miller) 1899-1961 C L C
1, 3, 6, 8, 10, 13, 19, 30, 34, 39, 41, 44, 50,
61, 80; DA; DAB; DAC; DAM MST, NOV;
SSC 1, 25; WLC
See also AAYA 19; CA 77-80; CANR 34;
CDALB 1917-1929; DLB 4, 9, 102; DLBD
1, 15, 16; DLBY 81, 87, 96; MTCW 1
Hempel, Amy 1951-   CLC 39
See also CA 118; 137; CANR 70
Henderson, F. C.
See Mencken, H(enry) L(ouis)
Henderson, Sylvia
See Ashton-Warner, Sylvia (Constance)
Henderson, Zenna (Chlarson) 1917-1983 S S C
29
See also CA 1-4R; 133; CANR 1; DLB 8; SATA
5

DRAM
See also CA 29-32R; 120; CANR 42; MTCW 1

Hochwalder, Fritz
See Hochwaelder, Fritz

Hocking, Mary (Eunice) 1921-   **CLC 13**
See also CA 101; CANR 18, 40

Hodgins, Jack 1938-   **CLC 23**
See also CA 93-96; DLB 60

Hodgson, William Hope 1877(?)-1918 **T C L C 13**
See also CA 111; 164; DLB 70, 153, 156, 178

Hoeg, Peter 1957-   **CLC 95**
See also CA 151

Hoffman, Alice 1952-   **CLC 51; DAM NOV**
See also CA 77-80; CANR 34, 66; MTCW 1

Hoffman, Daniel (Gerard) 1923-**CLC 6, 13, 23**
See also CA 1-4R; CANR 4; DLB 5

Hoffman, Stanley 1944-   **CLC 5**
See also CA 77-80

Hoffman, William M(oses) 1939-   **CLC 40**
See also CA 57-60; CANR 11, 71

Hoffmann, E(rnst) T(heodor) A(madeus) 1776-1822   **NCLC 2; SSC 13**
See also DLB 90; SATA 27

Hofmann, Gert 1931-   **CLC 54**
See also CA 128

Hofmannsthal, Hugo von 1874-1929**TCLC 11; DAM DRAM; DC 4**
See also CA 106; 153; DLB 81, 118

Hogan, Linda 1947-   **CLC 73; DAM MULT**
See also CA 120; CANR 45, 73; DLB 175; NNAL

Hogarth, Charles
See Creasey, John

Hogarth, Emmett
See Polonsky, Abraham (Lincoln)

Hogg, James 1770-1835   **NCLC 4**
See also DLB 93, 116, 159

Holbach, Paul Henri Thiry Baron 1723-1789   **LC 14**

Holberg, Ludvig 1684-1754   **LC 6**

Holden, Ursula 1921-   **CLC 18**
See also CA 101; CAAS 8; CANR 22

Holderlin, (Johann Christian) Friedrich 1770-1843   **NCLC 16; PC 4**

Holdstock, Robert
See Holdstock, Robert P.

Holdstock, Robert P. 1948-   **CLC 39**
See also CA 131

Holland, Isabelle 1920-   **CLC 21**
See also AAYA 11; CA 21-24R; CANR 10, 25, 47; JRDA; MAICYA; SATA 8, 70

Holland, Marcus
See Caldwell, (Janet Miriam) Taylor (Holland)

Hollander, John 1929-   **CLC 2, 5, 8, 14**
See also CA 1-4R; CANR 1, 52; DLB 5; SATA 13

Hollander, Paul
See Silverberg, Robert

Holleran, Andrew 1943(?)-   **CLC 38**
See also CA 144

Hollinghurst, Alan 1954-   **CLC 55, 91**
See also CA 114

Hollis, Jim
See Summers, Hollis (Spurgeon, Jr.)

Holly, Buddy 1936-1959   **TCLC 65**

Holmes, Gordon
See Shiel, M(atthew) P(hipps)

Holmes, John
See Souster, (Holmes) Raymond

Holmes, John Clellon 1926-1988   **CLC 56**
See also CA 9-12R; 125; CANR 4; DLB 16

Holmes, Oliver Wendell, Jr. 1841-1935**T C L C**

77
See also CA 114

Holmes, Oliver Wendell 1809-1894 **NCLC 14**
See also CDALB 1640-1865; DLB 1, 189; SATA 34

Holmes, Raymond
See Souster, (Holmes) Raymond

Holt, Victoria
See Hibbert, Eleanor Alice Burford

Holub, Miroslav 1923-1998   **CLC 4**
See also CA 21-24R; 169; CANR 10

Homer c. 8th cent. B.C.-   **CMLC 1, 16; DA; DAB; DAC; DAM MST, POET; PC 23; WLCS**
See also DLB 176

Hongo, Garrett Kaoru 1951-   **PC 23**
See also CA 133; CAAS 22; DLB 120

Honig, Edwin 1919-   **CLC 33**
See also CA 5-8R; CAAS 8; CANR 4, 45; DLB 5

Hood, Hugh (John Blagdon) 1928-**CLC 15, 28**
See also CA 49-52; CAAS 17; CANR 1, 33; DLB 53

Hood, Thomas 1799-1845   **NCLC 16**
See also DLB 96

Hooker, (Peter) Jeremy 1941-   **CLC 43**
See also CA 77-80; CANR 22; DLB 40

hooks, bell   **CLC 94; BLCS**
See also Watkins, Gloria

Hope, A(lec) D(erwent) 1907-   **CLC 3, 51**
See also CA 21-24R; CANR 33, 74; MTCW 1

Hope, Anthony 1863-1933   **TCLC 83**
See also CA 157; DLB 153, 156

Hope, Brian
See Creasey, John

Hope, Christopher (David Tully) 1944-   **C L C 52**
See also CA 106; CANR 47; SATA 62

Hopkins, Gerard Manley 1844-1889   **NCLC 17; DA; DAB; DAC; DAM MST, POET; PC 15; WLC**
See also CDBLB 1890-1914; DLB 35, 57

Hopkins, John (Richard) 1931-1998   **CLC 4**
See also CA 85-88; 169

Hopkins, Pauline Elizabeth 1859-1930**T C L C 28; BLC 2; DAM MULT**
See also BW 2; CA 141; DLB 50

Hopkinson, Francis 1737-1791   **LC 25**
See also DLB 31

Hopley-Woolrich, Cornell George 1903-1968
See Woolrich, Cornell
See also CA 13-14; CANR 58; CAP 1

Horatio
See Proust, (Valentin-Louis-George-Eugene-) Marcel

Horgan, Paul (George Vincent O'Shaughnessy) 1903-1995   **CLC 9, 53; DAM NOV**
See also CA 13-16R; 147; CANR 9, 35; DLB 102; DLBY 85; INT CANR-9; MTCW 1; SATA 13; SATA-Obit 84

Horn, Peter
See Kuttner, Henry

Hornem, Horace Esq.
See Byron, George Gordon (Noel)

Horney, Karen (Clementine Theodore Danielsen) 1885-1952   **TCLC 71**
See also CA 114; 165

Hornung, E(rnest) W(illiam) 1866-1921   **TCLC 59**
See also CA 108; 160; DLB 70

Horovitz, Israel (Arthur) 1939-**CLC 56; DAM DRAM**
See also CA 33-36R; CANR 46, 59; DLB 7

Horvath, Odon von
See Horvath, Oedoen von
See also DLB 85, 124

Horvath, Oedoen von 1901-1938   **TCLC 45**
See also Horvath, Odon von
See also CA 118

Horwitz, Julius 1920-1986   **CLC 14**
See also CA 9-12R; 119; CANR 12

Hospital, Janette Turner 1942-   **CLC 42**
See also CA 108; CANR 48

Hostos, E. M. de
See Hostos (y Bonilla), Eugenio Maria de

Hostos, Eugenio M. de
See Hostos (y Bonilla), Eugenio Maria de

Hostos, Eugenio Maria
See Hostos (y Bonilla), Eugenio Maria de

Hostos (y Bonilla), Eugenio Maria de 1839-1903   **TCLC 24**
See also CA 123; 131; HW

Houdini
See Lovecraft, H(oward) P(hillips)

Hougan, Carolyn 1943-   **CLC 34**
See also CA 139

Household, Geoffrey (Edward West) 1900-1988   **CLC 11**
See also CA 77-80; 126; CANR 58; DLB 87; SATA 14; SATA-Obit 59

Housman, A(lfred) E(dward) 1859-1936   **TCLC 1, 10; DA; DAB; DAC; DAM MST, POET; PC 2; WLCS**
See also CA 104; 125; DLB 19; MTCW 1

Housman, Laurence 1865-1959   **TCLC 7**
See also CA 106; 155; DLB 10; SATA 25

Howard, Elizabeth Jane 1923-   **CLC 7, 29**
See also CA 5-8R; CANR 8, 62

Howard, Maureen 1930-   **CLC 5, 14, 46**
See also CA 53-56; CANR 31; DLBY 83; INT CANR-31; MTCW 1

Howard, Richard 1929-   **CLC 7, 10, 47**
See also AITN 1; CA 85-88; CANR 25; DLB 5; INT CANR-25

Howard, Robert E(rvin) 1906-1936 **TCLC 8**
See also CA 105; 157

Howard, Warren F.
See Pohl, Frederik

Howe, Fanny (Quincy) 1940-   **CLC 47**
See also CA 117; CAAS 27; CANR 70; SATA-Brief 52

Howe, Irving 1920-1993   **CLC 85**
See also CA 9-12R; 141; CANR 21, 50; DLB 67; MTCW 1

Howe, Julia Ward 1819-1910   **TCLC 21**
See also CA 117; DLB 1, 189

Howe, Susan 1937-   **CLC 72**
See also CA 160; DLB 120

Howe, Tina 1937-   **CLC 48**
See also CA 109

Howell, James 1594(?)-1666   **LC 13**
See also DLB 151

Howells, W. D.
See Howells, William Dean

Howells, William D.
See Howells, William Dean

Howells, William Dean 1837-1920**TCLC 7, 17, 41**
See also CA 104; 134; CDALB 1865-1917; DLB 12, 64, 74, 79, 189

Howes, Barbara 1914-1996   **CLC 15**
See also CA 9-12R; 151; CAAS 3; CANR 53; SATA 5

Hrabal, Bohumil 1914-1997   **CLC 13, 67**
See also CA 106; 156; CAAS 12; CANR 57

Hroswitha of Gandersheim c. 935-c. 1002

Ishikawa, Hakuhin
See Ishikawa, Takuboku
Ishikawa, Takuboku 1886(?)-1912 **TCLC 15;**
  DAM POET; PC 10
  See also CA 113; 153
Iskander, Fazil 1929-   **CLC 47**
  See also CA 102
Isler, Alan (David) 1934-   **CLC 91**
  See also CA 156
Ivan IV 1530-1584   **LC 17**
Ivanov, Vyacheslav Ivanovich 1866-1949
  TCLC 33
  See also CA 122
Ivask, Ivar Vidrik 1927-1992   **CLC 14**
  See also CA 37-40R; 139; CANR 24
Ives, Morgan
  See Bradley, Marion Zimmer
J. R. S.
  See Gogarty, Oliver St. John
Jabran, Kahlil
  See Gibran, Kahlil
Jabran, Khalil
  See Gibran, Kahlil
Jackson, Daniel
  See Wingrove, David (John)
Jackson, Jesse 1908-1983   **CLC 12**
  See also BW 1; CA 25-28R; 109; CANR 27;
  CLR 28; MAICYA; SATA 2, 29; SATA-Obit
  48
Jackson, Laura (Riding) 1901-1991
  See Riding, Laura
  See also CA 65-68; 135; CANR 28; DLB 48
Jackson, Sam
  See Trumbo, Dalton
Jackson, Sara
  See Wingrove, David (John)
Jackson, Shirley 1919-1965 **CLC 11, 60, 87;**
  DA; DAC; DAM MST; SSC 9; WLC
  See also AAYA 9; CA 1-4R; 25-28R; CANR 4,
  52; CDALB 1941-1968; DLB 6; SATA 2
Jacob, (Cyprien-)Max 1876-1944   **TCLC 6**
  See also CA 104
Jacobs, Harriet A(nn) 1813(?)-1897**NCLC 67**
Jacobs, Jim 1942-   **CLC 12**
  See also CA 97-100; INT 97-100
Jacobs, W(illiam) W(ymark) 1863-1943
  TCLC 22
  See also CA 121; 167; DLB 135
Jacobsen, Jens Peter 1847-1885   **NCLC 34**
Jacobsen, Josephine 1908-   **CLC 48, 102**
  See also CA 33-36R; CAAS 18; CANR 23, 48
Jacobson, Dan 1929-   **CLC 4, 14**
  See also CA 1-4R; CANR 2, 25, 66; DLB 14;
  MTCW 1
Jacqueline
  See Carpentier (y Valmont), Alejo
Jagger, Mick 1944-   **CLC 17**
Jahiz, Al- c. 776-869   **CMLC 25**
Jahiz, al- c. 780-c. 869   **CMLC 25**
Jakes, John (William) 1932- **CLC 29; DAM**
  NOV, POP
  See also BEST 89:4; CA 57-60; CANR 10, 43,
  66; DLBY 83; INT CANR-10; MTCW 1;
  SATA 62
James, Andrew
  See Kirkup, James
James, C(yril) L(ionel) R(obert) 1901-1989
  CLC 33; BLCS
  See also BW 2; CA 117; 125; 128; CANR 62;
  DLB 125; MTCW 1
James, Daniel (Lewis) 1911-1988
  See Santiago, Danny
  See also CA 125

James, Dynely
  See Mayne, William (James Carter)
James, Henry Sr. 1811-1882   **NCLC 53**
James, Henry 1843-1916 **TCLC 2, 11, 24, 40,**
  47, 64; DA; DAB; DAC; DAM MST, NOV;
  SSC 8, 32; WLC
  See also CA 104; 132; CDALB 1865-1917;
  DLB 12, 71, 74, 189; DLBD 13; MTCW 1
James, M. R.
  See James, Montague (Rhodes)
  See also DLB 156
James, Montague (Rhodes) 1862-1936 **T C L C**
  6; SSC 16
  See also CA 104; DLB 201
James, P. D. 1920-   **CLC 18, 46**
  See also White, Phyllis Dorothy James
  See also BEST 90:2; CDBLB 1960 to Present;
  DLB 87; DLBD 17
James, Philip
  See Moorcock, Michael (John)
James, William 1842-1910   **TCLC 15, 32**
  See also CA 109
James I 1394-1437   **LC 20**
Jameson, Anna 1794-1860   **NCLC 43**
  See also DLB 99, 166
Jami, Nur al-Din 'Abd al-Rahman 1414-1492
  LC 9
Jammes, Francis 1868-1938   **TCLC 75**
Jandl, Ernst 1925-   **CLC 34**
Janowitz, Tama 1957-   **CLC 43; DAM POP**
  See also CA 106; CANR 52
Japrisot, Sebastien 1931-   **CLC 90**
Jarrell, Randall 1914-1965**CLC 1, 2, 6, 9, 13,**
  49; DAM POET
  See also CA 5-8R; 25-28R; CABS 2; CANR 6,
  34; CDALB 1941-1968; CLR 6; DLB 48, 52;
  MAICYA; MTCW 1; SATA 7
Jarry, Alfred 1873-1907   **TCLC 2, 14; DAM**
  DRAM; SSC 20
  See also CA 104; 153; DLB 192
Jarvis, E. K.
  See Bloch, Robert (Albert); Ellison, Harlan
  (Jay); Silverberg, Robert
Jeake, Samuel, Jr.
  See Aiken, Conrad (Potter)
Jean Paul 1763-1825   **NCLC 7**
Jefferies, (John) Richard 1848-1887**NCLC 47**
  See also DLB 98, 141; SATA 16
Jeffers, (John) Robinson 1887-1962**CLC 2, 3,**
  11, 15, 54; DA; DAC; DAM MST, POET;
  PC 17; WLC
  See also CA 85-88; CANR 35; CDALB 1917-
  1929; DLB 45; MTCW 1
Jefferson, Janet
  See Mencken, H(enry) L(ouis)
Jefferson, Thomas 1743-1826   **NCLC 11**
  See also CDALB 1640-1865; DLB 31
Jeffrey, Francis 1773-1850   **NCLC 33**
  See also DLB 107
Jelakowitch, Ivan
  See Heijermans, Herman
Jellicoe, (Patricia) Ann 1927-   **CLC 27**
  See also CA 85-88; DLB 13
Jen, Gish   **CLC 70**
  See also Jen, Lillian
Jen, Lillian 1956(?)-
  See Jen, Gish
  See also CA 135
Jenkins, (John) Robin 1912-   **CLC 52**
  See also CA 1-4R; CANR 1; DLB 14
Jennings, Elizabeth (Joan) 1926- **CLC 5, 14**
  See also CA 61-64; CAAS 5; CANR 8, 39, 66;
  DLB 27; MTCW 1; SATA 66

Jennings, Waylon 1937-   **CLC 21**
Jensen, Johannes V. 1873-1950   **TCLC 41**
  See also CA 170
Jensen, Laura (Linnea) 1948-   **CLC 37**
  See also CA 103
Jerome, Jerome K(lapka) 1859-1927**TCLC 23**
  See also CA 119; DLB 10, 34, 135
Jerrold, Douglas William 1803-1857 **NCLC 2**
  See also DLB 158, 159
Jewett, (Theodora) Sarah Orne 1849-1909
  TCLC 1, 22; SSC 6
  See also CA 108; 127; CANR 71; DLB 12, 74;
  SATA 15
Jewsbury, Geraldine (Endsor) 1812-1880
  NCLC 22
  See also DLB 21
Jhabvala, Ruth Prawer 1927-**CLC 4, 8, 29, 94;**
  DAB; DAM NOV
  See also CA 1-4R; CANR 2, 29, 51, 74; DLB
  139, 194; INT CANR-29; MTCW 1
Jibran, Kahlil
  See Gibran, Kahlil
Jibran, Khalil
  See Gibran, Kahlil
Jiles, Paulette 1943-   **CLC 13, 58**
  See also CA 101; CANR 70
Jimenez (Mantecon), Juan Ramon 1881-1958
  TCLC 4; DAM MULT, POET; HLC; PC
  7
  See also CA 104; 131; CANR 74; DLB 134;
  HW; MTCW 1
Jimenez, Ramon
  See Jimenez (Mantecon), Juan Ramon
Jimenez Mantecon, Juan
  See Jimenez (Mantecon), Juan Ramon
Jin, Ha 1956-   **CLC 109**
  See also CA 152
Joel, Billy   **CLC 26**
  See also Joel, William Martin
Joel, William Martin 1949-
  See Joel, Billy
  See also CA 108
John, Saint 7th cent. -   **CMLC 27**
John of the Cross, St. 1542-1591   **LC 18**
Johnson, B(ryan) S(tanley William) 1933-1973
  CLC 6, 9
  See also CA 9-12R; 53-56; CANR 9; DLB 14,
  40
Johnson, Benj. F. of Boo
  See Riley, James Whitcomb
Johnson, Benjamin F. of Boo
  See Riley, James Whitcomb
Johnson, Charles (Richard) 1948-**CLC 7, 51,**
  65; BLC 2; DAM MULT
  See also BW 2; CA 116; CAAS 18; CANR 42,
  66; DLB 33
Johnson, Denis 1949-   **CLC 52**
  See also CA 117; 121; CANR 71; DLB 120
Johnson, Diane 1934-   **CLC 5, 13, 48**
  See also CA 41-44R; CANR 17, 40, 62; DLBY
  80; INT CANR-17; MTCW 1
Johnson, Eyvind (Olof Verner) 1900-1976
  CLC 14
  See also CA 73-76; 69-72; CANR 34
Johnson, J. R.
  See James, C(yril) L(ionel) R(obert)
Johnson, James Weldon 1871-1938 **TCLC 3,**
  19; BLC 2; DAM MULT, POET; PC 24
  See also BW 1; CA 104; 125; CDALB 1917-
  1929; CLR 32; DLB 51; MTCW 1; SATA 31
Johnson, Joyce 1935-   **CLC 58**
  See also CA 125; 129
Johnson, Lionel (Pigot) 1867-1902 **TCLC 19**

See also CA 117; DLB 19

Johnson, Marguerite (Annie)
See Angelou, Maya

Johnson, Mel
See Malzberg, Barry N(athaniel)

Johnson, Pamela Hansford 1912-1981 **CLC 1, 7, 27**
See also CA 1-4R; 104; CANR 2, 28; DLB 15; MTCW 1

Johnson, Robert 1911(?)-1938   **TCLC 69**

Johnson, Samuel 1709-1784 **LC 15; DA; DAB; DAC; DAM MST; WLC**
See also CDBLB 1660-1789; DLB 39, 95, 104, 142

Johnson, Uwe 1934-1984   **CLC 5, 10, 15, 40**
See also CA 1-4R; 112; CANR 1, 39; DLB 75; MTCW 1

Johnston, George (Benson) 1913-   **CLC 51**
See also CA 1-4R; CANR 5, 20; DLB 88

Johnston, Jennifer 1930-   **CLC 7**
See also CA 85-88; DLB 14

Jolley, (Monica) Elizabeth 1923- **CLC 46; SSC 19**
See also CA 127; CAAS 13; CANR 59

Jones, Arthur Llewellyn 1863-1947
See Machen, Arthur
See also CA 104

Jones, D(ouglas) G(ordon) 1929-   **CLC 10**
See also CA 29-32R; CANR 13; DLB 53

Jones, David (Michael) 1895-1974 **CLC 2, 4, 7, 13, 42**
See also CA 9-12R; 53-56; CANR 28; CDBLB 1945-1960; DLB 20, 100; MTCW 1

Jones, David Robert 1947-
See Bowie, David
See also CA 103

Jones, Diana Wynne 1934-   **CLC 26**
See also AAYA 12; CA 49-52; CANR 4, 26, 56; CLR 23; DLB 161; JRDA; MAICYA; SAAS 7; SATA 9, 70

Jones, Edward P. 1950-   **CLC 76**
See also BW 2; CA 142

Jones, Gayl 1949-   **CLC 6, 9; BLC 2; DAM MULT**
See also BW 2; CA 77-80; CANR 27, 66; DLB 33; MTCW 1

Jones, James 1921-1977   **CLC 1, 3, 10, 39**
See also AITN 1, 2; CA 1-4R; 69-72; CANR 6; DLB 2, 143; DLBD 17; MTCW 1

Jones, John J.
See Lovecraft, H(oward) P(hillips)

Jones, LeRoi   **CLC 1, 2, 3, 5, 10, 14**
See also Baraka, Amiri

Jones, Louis B. 1953-   **CLC 65**
See also CA 141; CANR 73

Jones, Madison (Percy, Jr.) 1925-   **CLC 4**
See also CA 13-16R; CAAS 11; CANR 7, 54; DLB 152

Jones, Mervyn 1922-   **CLC 10, 52**
See also CA 45-48; CAAS 5; CANR 1; MTCW 1

Jones, Mick 1956(?)-   **CLC 30**

Jones, Nettie (Pearl) 1941-   **CLC 34**
See also BW 2; CA 137; CAAS 20

Jones, Preston 1936-1979   **CLC 10**
See also CA 73-76; 89-92; DLB 7

Jones, Robert F(rancis) 1934-   **CLC 7**
See also CA 49-52; CANR 2, 61

Jones, Rod 1953-   **CLC 50**
See also CA 128

Jones, Terence Graham Parry 1942- **CLC 21**
See also Jones, Terry; Monty Python
See also CA 112; 116; CANR 35; INT 116

Jones, Terry
See Jones, Terence Graham Parry
See also SATA 67; SATA-Brief 51

Jones, Thom 1945(?)-   **CLC 81**
See also CA 157

Jong, Erica 1942- **CLC 4, 6, 8, 18, 83; DAM NOV, POP**
See also AITN 1; BEST 90:2; CA 73-76; CANR 26, 52; DLB 2, 5, 28, 152; INT CANR-26; MTCW 1

Jonson, Ben(jamin) 1572(?)-1637   **LC 6, 33; DA; DAB; DAC; DAM DRAM, MST, POET; DC 4; PC 17; WLC**
See also CDBLB Before 1660; DLB 62, 121

Jordan, June 1936- **CLC 5, 11, 23, 114; BLCS; DAM MULT, POET**
See also AAYA 2; BW 2; CA 33-36R; CANR 25, 70; CLR 10; DLB 38; MAICYA; MTCW 1; SATA 4

Jordan, Neil (Patrick) 1950-   **CLC 110**
See also CA 124; 130; CANR 54; INT 130

Jordan, Pat(rick M.) 1941-   **CLC 37**
See also CA 33-36R

Jorgensen, Ivar
See Ellison, Harlan (Jay)

Jorgenson, Ivar
See Silverberg, Robert

Josephus, Flavius c. 37-100   **CMLC 13**

Josipovici, Gabriel 1940-   **CLC 6, 43**
See also CA 37-40R; CAAS 8; CANR 47; DLB 14

Joubert, Joseph 1754-1824   **NCLC 9**

Jouve, Pierre Jean 1887-1976   **CLC 47**
See also CA 65-68

Jovine, Francesco 1902-1950   **TCLC 79**

Joyce, James (Augustine Aloysius) 1882-1941 **TCLC 3, 8, 16, 35, 52; DA; DAB; DAC; DAM MST, NOV, POET; PC 22; SSC 3, 26; WLC**
See also CA 104; 126; CDBLB 1914-1945; DLB 10, 19, 36, 162; MTCW 1

Jozsef, Attila 1905-1937   **TCLC 22**
See also CA 116

Juana Ines de la Cruz 1651(?)-1695 **LC 5; PC 24**

Judd, Cyril
See Kornbluth, C(yril) M.; Pohl, Frederik

Julian of Norwich 1342(?)-1416(?)   **LC 6**
See also DLB 146

Junger, Sebastian 1962-   **CLC 109**
See also CA 165

Juniper, Alex
See Hospital, Janette Turner

Junius
See Luxemburg, Rosa

Just, Ward (Swift) 1935-   **CLC 4, 27**
See also CA 25-28R; CANR 32; INT CANR-32

Justice, Donald (Rodney) 1925- **CLC 6, 19, 102; DAM POET**
See also CA 5-8R; CANR 26, 54, 74; DLBY 83; INT CANR-26

Juvenal c. 55-c. 127   **CMLC 8**
See also Juvenalis, Decimus Junius

Juvenalis, Decimus Junius 55(?)-c. 127(?)
See Juvenal

Juvenis
See Bourne, Randolph S(illiman)

Kacew, Romain 1914-1980
See Gary, Romain
See also CA 108; 102

Kadare, Ismail 1936-   **CLC 52**
See also CA 161

Kadohata, Cynthia   **CLC 59**
See also CA 140

Kafka, Franz 1883-1924 **TCLC 2, 6, 13, 29, 47, 53; DA; DAB; DAC; DAM MST, NOV; SSC 5, 29; WLC**
See also CA 105; 126; DLB 81; MTCW 1

Kahanovitsch, Pinkhes
See Der Nister

Kahn, Roger 1927-   **CLC 30**
See also CA 25-28R; CANR 44, 69; DLB 171; SATA 37

Kain, Saul
See Sassoon, Siegfried (Lorraine)

Kaiser, Georg 1878-1945   **TCLC 9**
See also CA 106; DLB 124

Kaletski, Alexander 1946-   **CLC 39**
See also CA 118; 143

Kalidasa fl. c. 400-   **CMLC 9; PC 22**

Kallman, Chester (Simon) 1921-1975 **CLC 2**
See also CA 45-48; 53-56; CANR 3

Kaminsky, Melvin 1926-
See Brooks, Mel
See also CA 65-68; CANR 16

Kaminsky, Stuart M(elvin) 1934-   **CLC 59**
See also CA 73-76; CANR 29, 53

Kane, Francis
See Robbins, Harold

Kane, Paul
See Simon, Paul (Frederick)

Kane, Wilson
See Bloch, Robert (Albert)

Kanin, Garson 1912-   **CLC 22**
See also AITN 1; CA 5-8R; CANR 7; DLB 7

Kaniuk, Yoram 1930-   **CLC 19**
See also CA 134

Kant, Immanuel 1724-1804   **NCLC 27, 67**
See also DLB 94

Kantor, MacKinlay 1904-1977   **CLC 7**
See also CA 61-64; 73-76; CANR 60, 63; DLB 9, 102

Kaplan, David Michael 1946-   **CLC 50**

Kaplan, James 1951-   **CLC 59**
See also CA 135

Karageorge, Michael
See Anderson, Poul (William)

Karamzin, Nikolai Mikhailovich 1766-1826 **NCLC 3**
See also DLB 150

Karapanou, Margarita 1946-   **CLC 13**
See also CA 101

Karinthy, Frigyes 1887-1938   **TCLC 47**
See also CA 170

Karl, Frederick R(obert) 1927-   **CLC 34**
See also CA 5-8R; CANR 3, 44

Kastel, Warren
See Silverberg, Robert

Kataev, Evgeny Petrovich 1903-1942
See Petrov, Evgeny
See also CA 120

Kataphusin
See Ruskin, John

Katz, Steve 1935-   **CLC 47**
See also CA 25-28R; CAAS 14, 64; CANR 12; DLBY 83

Kauffman, Janet 1945-   **CLC 42**
See also CA 117; CANR 43; DLBY 86

Kaufman, Bob (Garnell) 1925-1986 **CLC 49**
See also BW 1; CA 41-44R; 118; CANR 22; DLB 16, 41

Kaufman, George S. 1889-1961 **CLC 38; DAM DRAM**
See also CA 108; 93-96; DLB 7; INT 108

Kaufman, Sue   **CLC 3, 8**

See also DLB 21, 32, 163, 190; YABC 2

Kingsley, Sidney 1906-1995   **CLC 44**
See also CA 85-88; 147; DLB 7

Kingsolver, Barbara 1955-**CLC 55, 81; DAM POP**
See also AAYA 15; CA 129; 134; CANR 60; INT 134

Kingston, Maxine (Ting Ting) Hong 1940-
CLC 12, 19, 58; DAM MULT, NOV; WLCS
See also AAYA 8; CA 69-72; CANR 13, 38, 74; DLB 173; DLBY 80; INT CANR-13; MTCW 1; SATA 53

Kinnell, Galway 1927- **CLC 1, 2, 3, 5, 13, 29**
See also CA 9-12R; CANR 10, 34, 66; DLB 5; DLBY 87; INT CANR-34; MTCW 1

Kinsella, Thomas 1928-   **CLC 4, 19**
See also CA 17-20R; CANR 15; DLB 27; MTCW 1

Kinsella, W(illiam) P(atrick) 1935- **CLC 27, 43; DAC; DAM NOV, POP**
See also AAYA 7; CA 97-100; CAAS 7; CANR 21, 35, 66; INT CANR-21; MTCW 1

Kipling, (Joseph) Rudyard 1865-1936 **TCLC 8, 17; DA; DAB; DAC; DAM MST, POET; PC 3; SSC 5; WLC**
See also CA 105; 120; CANR 33; CDBLB 1890-1914; CLR 39; DLB 19, 34, 141, 156; MAICYA; MTCW 1; SATA 100; YABC 2

Kirkup, James 1918-   **CLC 1**
See also CA 1-4R; CAAS 4; CANR 2; DLB 27; SATA 12

Kirkwood, James 1930(?)-1989   **CLC 9**
See also AITN 2; CA 1-4R; 128; CANR 6, 40

Kirshner, Sidney
See Kingsley, Sidney

Kis, Danilo 1935-1989   **CLC 57**
See also CA 109; 118; 129; CANR 61; DLB 181; MTCW 1

Kivi, Aleksis 1834-1872   **NCLC 30**

Kizer, Carolyn (Ashley) 1925-**CLC 15, 39, 80; DAM POET**
See also CA 65-68; CAAS 5; CANR 24, 70; DLB 5, 169

Klabund 1890-1928   **TCLC 44**
See also CA 162; DLB 66

Klappert, Peter 1942-   **CLC 57**
See also CA 33-36R; DLB 5

Klein, A(braham) M(oses) 1909-1972**CLC 19; DAB; DAC; DAM MST**
See also CA 101; 37-40R; DLB 68

Klein, Norma 1938-1989   **CLC 30**
See also AAYA 2; CA 41-44R; 128; CANR 15, 37; CLR 2, 19; INT CANR-15; JRDA; MAICYA; SAAS 1; SATA 7, 57

Klein, T(heodore) E(ibon) D(onald) 1947-
CLC 34
See also CA 119; CANR 44

Kleist, Heinrich von 1777-1811 **NCLC 2, 37; DAM DRAM; SSC 22**
See also DLB 90

Klima, Ivan 1931-   **CLC 56; DAM NOV**
See also CA 25-28R; CANR 17, 50

Klimentov, Andrei Platonovich 1899-1951
See Platonov, Andrei
See also CA 108

Klinger, Friedrich Maximilian von 1752-1831
NCLC 1
See also DLB 94

Klingsor the Magician
See Hartmann, Sadakichi

Klopstock, Friedrich Gottlieb 1724-1803
NCLC 11

See also DLB 97

Knapp, Caroline 1959-   **CLC 99**
See also CA 154

Knebel, Fletcher 1911-1993   **CLC 14**
See also AITN 1; CA 1-4R; 140; CAAS 3; CANR 1, 36; SATA 36; SATA-Obit 75

Knickerbocker, Diedrich
See Irving, Washington

Knight, Etheridge 1931-1991**CLC 40; BLC 2; DAM POET; PC 14**
See also BW 1; CA 21-24R; 133; CANR 23; DLB 41

Knight, Sarah Kemble 1666-1727   **LC 7**
See also DLB 24, 200

Knister, Raymond 1899-1932   **TCLC 56**
See also DLB 68

Knowles, John 1926- **CLC 1, 4, 10, 26; DA; DAC; DAM MST, NOV**
See also AAYA 10; CA 17-20R; CANR 40, 74; CDALB 1968-1988; DLB 6; MTCW 1; SATA 8, 89

Knox, Calvin M.
See Silverberg, Robert

Knox, John c. 1505-1572   **LC 37**
See also DLB 132

Knye, Cassandra
See Disch, Thomas M(ichael)

Koch, C(hristopher) J(ohn) 1932-   **CLC 42**
See also CA 127

Koch, Christopher
See Koch, C(hristopher) J(ohn)

Koch, Kenneth 1925-   **CLC 5, 8, 44; DAM POET**
See also CA 1-4R; CANR 6, 36, 57; DLB 5; INT CANR-36; SATA 65

Kochanowski, Jan 1530-1584   **LC 10**

Kock, Charles Paul de 1794-1871 **NCLC 16**

Koda Shigeyuki 1867-1947
See Rohan, Koda
See also CA 121

Koestler, Arthur 1905-1983**CLC 1, 3, 6, 8, 15, 33**
See also CA 1-4R; 109; CANR 1, 33; CDBLB 1945-1960; DLBY 83; MTCW 1

Kogawa, Joy Nozomi 1935- **CLC 78; DAC; DAM MST, MULT**
See also CA 101; CANR 19, 62; SATA 99

Kohout, Pavel 1928-   **CLC 13**
See also CA 45-48; CANR 3

Koizumi, Yakumo
See Hearn, (Patricio) Lafcadio (Tessima Carlos)

Kolmar, Gertrud 1894-1943   **TCLC 40**
See also CA 167

Komunyakaa, Yusef 1947-**CLC 86, 94; BLCS**
See also CA 147; DLB 120

Konrad, George
See Konrad, Gyoergy

Konrad, Gyoergy 1933-   **CLC 4, 10, 73**
See also CA 85-88

Konwicki, Tadeusz 1926- **CLC 8, 28, 54, 117**
See also CA 101; CAAS 9; CANR 39, 59; MTCW 1

Koontz, Dean R(ay) 1945-   **CLC 78; DAM NOV, POP**
See also AAYA 9; BEST 89:3, 90:2; CA 108; CANR 19, 36, 52; MTCW 1; SATA 92

Kopernik, Mikolaj
See Copernicus, Nicolaus

Kopit, Arthur (Lee) 1937-**CLC 1, 18, 33; DAM DRAM**
See also AITN 1; CA 81-84; CABS 3; DLB 7; MTCW 1

Kops, Bernard 1926-   **CLC 4**

See also CA 5-8R; DLB 13

Kornbluth, C(yril) M. 1923-1958 **TCLC 8**
See also CA 105; 160; DLB 8

Korolenko, V. G.
See Korolenko, Vladimir Galaktionovich

Korolenko, Vladimir
See Korolenko, Vladimir Galaktionovich

Korolenko, Vladimir G.
See Korolenko, Vladimir Galaktionovich

Korolenko, Vladimir Galaktionovich 1853-
1921   **TCLC 22**
See also CA 121

Korzybski, Alfred (Habdank Skarbek) 1879-
1950   **TCLC 61**
See also CA 123; 160

Kosinski, Jerzy (Nikodem) 1933-1991**CLC 1, 2, 3, 6, 10, 15, 53, 70; DAM NOV**
See also CA 17-20R; 134; CANR 9, 46; DLB 2; DLBY 82; MTCW 1

Kostelanetz, Richard (Cory) 1940- **CLC 28**
See also CA 13-16R; CAAS 8; CANR 38

Kostrowitzki, Wilhelm Apollinaris de 1880-
1918
See Apollinaire, Guillaume
See also CA 104

Kotlowitz, Robert 1924-   **CLC 4**
See also CA 33-36R; CANR 36

Kotzebue, August (Friedrich Ferdinand) von
1761-1819   **NCLC 25**
See also DLB 94

Kotzwinkle, William 1938-   **CLC 5, 14, 35**
See also CA 45-48; CANR 3, 44; CLR 6; DLB 173; MAICYA; SATA 24, 70

Kowna, Stancy
See Szymborska, Wislawa

Kozol, Jonathan 1936-   **CLC 17**
See also CA 61-64; CANR 16, 45

Kozoll, Michael 1940(?)-   **CLC 35**

Kramer, Kathryn 19(?)-   **CLC 34**

Kramer, Larry 1935-**CLC 42; DAM POP; DC 8**
See also CA 124; 126; CANR 60

Krasicki, Ignacy 1735-1801   **NCLC 8**

Krasinski, Zygmunt 1812-1859   **NCLC 4**

Kraus, Karl 1874-1936   **TCLC 5**
See also CA 104; DLB 118

Kreve (Mickevicius), Vincas 1882-1954**TCLC 27**
See also CA 170

Kristeva, Julia 1941-   **CLC 77**
See also CA 154

Kristofferson, Kris 1936-   **CLC 26**
See also CA 104

Krizanc, John 1956-   **CLC 57**

Krleza, Miroslav 1893-1981   **CLC 8, 114**
See also CA 97-100; 105; CANR 50; DLB 147

Kroetsch, Robert 1927-**CLC 5, 23, 57; DAC; DAM POET**
See also CA 17-20R; CANR 8, 38; DLB 53; MTCW 1

Kroetz, Franz
See Kroetz, Franz Xaver

Kroetz, Franz Xaver 1946-   **CLC 41**
See also CA 130

Kroker, Arthur (W.) 1945-   **CLC 77**
See also CA 161

Kropotkin, Peter (Aleksieevich) 1842-1921
TCLC 36
See also CA 119

Krotkov, Yuri 1917-   **CLC 19**
See also CA 102

Krumb
See Crumb, R(obert)

Krumgold, Joseph (Quincy) 1908-1980 **C L C 12**
See also CA 9-12R; 101; CANR 7; MAICYA; SATA 1, 48; SATA-Obit 23

Krumwitz
See Crumb, R(obert)

Krutch, Joseph Wood 1893-1970 **CLC 24**
See also CA 1-4R; 25-28R; CANR 4; DLB 63

Krutzch, Gus
See Eliot, T(homas) S(tearns)

Krylov, Ivan Andreevich 1768(?)-1844 **N C L C 1**
See also DLB 150

Kubin, Alfred (Leopold Isidor) 1877-1959 **TCLC 23**
See also CA 112; 149; DLB 81

Kubrick, Stanley 1928- **CLC 16**
See also CA 81-84; CANR 33; DLB 26

Kumin, Maxine (Winokur) 1925- **CLC 5, 13, 28; DAM POET; PC 15**
See also AITN 2; CA 1-4R; CAAS 8; CANR 1, 21, 69; DLB 5; MTCW 1; SATA 12

Kundera, Milan 1929- **CLC 4, 9, 19, 32, 68, 115; DAM NOV; SSC 24**
See also AAYA 2; CA 85-88; CANR 19, 52, 74; MTCW 1

Kunene, Mazisi (Raymond) 1930- **CLC 85**
See also BW 1; CA 125; DLB 117

Kunitz, Stanley (Jasspon) 1905-**CLC 6, 11, 14; PC 19**
See also CA 41-44R; CANR 26, 57; DLB 48; INT CANR-26; MTCW 1

Kunze, Reiner 1933- **CLC 10**
See also CA 93-96; DLB 75

Kuprin, Aleksandr Ivanovich 1870-1938 **TCLC 5**
See also CA 104

Kureishi, Hanif 1954(?)- **CLC 64**
See also CA 139; DLB 194

Kurosawa, Akira 1910-1998 **CLC 16; DAM MULT**
See also AAYA 11; CA 101; 170; CANR 46

Kushner, Tony 1957(?)-**CLC 81; DAM DRAM**
See also CA 144; CANR 74

Kuttner, Henry 1915-1958 **TCLC 10**
See also Vance, Jack
See also CA 107; 157; DLB 8

Kuzma, Greg 1944- **CLC 7**
See also CA 33-36R; CANR 70

Kuzmin, Mikhail 1872(?)-1936 **TCLC 40**
See also CA 170

Kyd, Thomas 1558-1594**LC 22; DAM DRAM; DC 3**
See also DLB 62

Kyprianos, Iossif
See Samarakis, Antonis

La Bruyere, Jean de 1645-1696 **LC 17**

Lacan, Jacques (Marie Emile) 1901-1981 **CLC 75**
See also CA 121; 104

Laclos, Pierre Ambroise Francois Choderlos de 1741-1803 **NCLC 4**

Lacolere, Francois
See Aragon, Louis

La Colere, Francois
See Aragon, Louis

La Deshabilleuse
See Simenon, Georges (Jacques Christian)

Lady Gregory
See Gregory, Isabella Augusta (Persse)

Lady of Quality, A
See Bagnold, Enid

La Fayette, Marie (Madelaine Pioche de la

Vergne Comtes 1634-1693 **LC 2**

Lafayette, Rene
See Hubbard, L(afayette) Ron(ald)

Laforgue, Jules 1860-1887**NCLC 5, 53; PC 14; SSC 20**

Lagerkvist, Paer (Fabian) 1891-1974 **CLC 7, 10, 13, 54; DAM DRAM, NOV**
See also Lagerkvist, Par
See also CA 85-88; 49-52; MTCW 1

Lagerkvist, Par **SSC 12**
See also Lagerkvist, Paer (Fabian)

Lagerloef, Selma (Ottiliana Lovisa) 1858-1940 **TCLC 4, 36**
See also Lagerlof, Selma (Ottiliana Lovisa)
See also CA 108; SATA 15

Lagerlof, Selma (Ottiliana Lovisa)
See Lagerloef, Selma (Ottiliana Lovisa)
See also CLR 7; SATA 15

La Guma, (Justin) Alex(ander) 1925-1985 **CLC 19; BLCS; DAM NOV**
See also BW 1; CA 49-52; 118; CANR 25; DLB 117; MTCW 1

Laidlaw, A. K.
See Grieve, C(hristopher) M(urray)

Lainez, Manuel Mujica
See Mujica Lainez, Manuel
See also HW

Laing, R(onald) D(avid) 1927-1989 **CLC 95**
See also CA 107; 129; CANR 34; MTCW 1

Lamartine, Alphonse (Marie Louis Prat) de 1790-1869**NCLC 11; DAM POET; PC 16**

Lamb, Charles 1775-1834 **NCLC 10; DA; DAB; DAC; DAM MST; WLC**
See also CDBLB 1789-1832; DLB 93, 107, 163; SATA 17

Lamb, Lady Caroline 1785-1828 **NCLC 38**
See also DLB 116

Lamming, George (William) 1927- **CLC 2, 4, 66; BLC 2; DAM MULT**
See also BW 2; CA 85-88; CANR 26; DLB 125; MTCW 1

L'Amour, Louis (Dearborn) 1908-1988 **C L C 25, 55; DAM NOV, POP**
See also AAYA 16; AITN 2; BEST 89:2; CA 1-4R; 125; CANR 3, 25, 40; DLBY 80; MTCW 1

Lampedusa, Giuseppe (Tomasi) di 1896-1957 **TCLC 13**
See also Tomasi di Lampedusa, Giuseppe
See also CA 164; DLB 177

Lampman, Archibald 1861-1899 **NCLC 25**
See also DLB 92

Lancaster, Bruce 1896-1963 **CLC 36**
See also CA 9-10; CANR 70; CAP 1; SATA 9

Lanchester, John **CLC 99**

Landau, Mark Alexandrovich
See Aldanov, Mark (Alexandrovich)

Landau-Aldanov, Mark Alexandrovich
See Aldanov, Mark (Alexandrovich)

Landis, Jerry
See Simon, Paul (Frederick)

Landis, John 1950- **CLC 26**
See also CA 112; 122

Landolfi, Tommaso 1908-1979 **CLC 11, 49**
See also CA 127; 117; DLB 177

Landon, Letitia Elizabeth 1802-1838 **N C L C 15**
See also DLB 96

Landor, Walter Savage 1775-1864 **NCLC 14**
See also DLB 93, 107

Landwirth, Heinz 1927-
See Lind, Jakov
See also CA 9-12R; CANR 7

Lane, Patrick 1939- **CLC 25; DAM POET**
See also CA 97-100; CANR 54; DLB 53; INT 97-100

Lang, Andrew 1844-1912 **TCLC 16**
See also CA 114; 137; DLB 98, 141, 184; MAICYA; SATA 16

Lang, Fritz 1890-1976 **CLC 20, 103**
See also CA 77-80; 69-72; CANR 30

Lange, John
See Crichton, (John) Michael

Langer, Elinor 1939- **CLC 34**
See also CA 121

Langland, William 1330(?)-1400(?) **LC 19; DA; DAB; DAC; DAM MST, POET**
See also DLB 146

Langstaff, Launcelot
See Irving, Washington

Lanier, Sidney 1842-1881 **NCLC 6; DAM POET**
See also DLB 64; DLBD 13; MAICYA; SATA 18

Lanyer, Aemilia 1569-1645 **LC 10, 30**
See also DLB 121

Lao-Tzu
See Lao Tzu

Lao Tzu fl. 6th cent. B.C.- **CMLC 7**

Lapine, James (Elliot) 1949- **CLC 39**
See also CA 123; 130; CANR 54; INT 130

Larbaud, Valery (Nicolas) 1881-1957**TCLC 9**
See also CA 106; 152

Lardner, Ring
See Lardner, Ring(gold) W(ilmer)

Lardner, Ring W., Jr.
See Lardner, Ring(gold) W(ilmer)

Lardner, Ring(gold) W(ilmer) 1885-1933 **TCLC 2, 14; SSC 32**
See also CA 104; 131; CDALB 1917-1929; DLB 11, 25, 86; DLBD 16; MTCW 1

Laredo, Betty
See Codrescu, Andrei

Larkin, Maia
See Wojciechowska, Maia (Teresa)

Larkin, Philip (Arthur) 1922-1985**CLC 3, 5, 8, 9, 13, 18, 33, 39, 64; DAB; DAM MST, POET; PC 21**
See also CA 5-8R; 117; CANR 24, 62; CDBLB 1960 to Present; DLB 27; MTCW 1

Larra (y Sanchez de Castro), Mariano Jose de 1809-1837 **NCLC 17**

Larsen, Eric 1941- **CLC 55**
See also CA 132

Larsen, Nella 1891-1964 **CLC 37; BLC 2; DAM MULT**
See also BW 1; CA 125; DLB 51

Larson, Charles R(aymond) 1938- **CLC 31**
See also CA 53-56; CANR 4

Larson, Jonathan 1961-1996 **CLC 99**
See also CA 156

Las Casas, Bartolome de 1474-1566 **LC 31**

Lasch, Christopher 1932-1994 **CLC 102**
See also CA 73-76; 144; CANR 25; MTCW 1

Lasker-Schueler, Else 1869-1945 **TCLC 57**
See also DLB 66, 124

Laski, Harold 1893-1950 **TCLC 79**

Latham, Jean Lee 1902-1995 **CLC 12**
See also AITN 1; CA 5-8R; CANR 7; CLR 50; MAICYA, SATA 2, 68

Latham, Mavis
See Clark, Mavis Thorpe

Lathen, Emma **CLC 2**
See also Hennissart, Martha; Latsis, Mary J(ane)

Lathrop, Francis
See Leiber, Fritz (Reuter, Jr.)

75
Lengyel, Jozsef 1896-1975   **CLC 7**
  See also CA 85-88; 57-60; CANR 71
Lenin 1870-1924
  See Lenin, V. I.
  See also CA 121; 168
Lenin, V. I.   **TCLC 67**
  See also Lenin
Lennon, John (Ono) 1940-1980   **CLC 12, 35**
  See also CA 102
Lennox, Charlotte Ramsay 1729(?)-1804
  NCLC 23
  See also DLB 39
Lentricchia, Frank (Jr.) 1940-   **CLC 34**
  See also CA 25-28R; CANR 19
Lenz, Siegfried 1926-   **CLC 27**
  See also CA 89-92; DLB 75
Leonard, Elmore (John, Jr.) 1925-**CLC 28, 34,**
  71; DAM POP
  See also AAYA 22; AITN 1; BEST 89:1, 90:4;
    CA 81-84; CANR 12, 28, 53; DLB 173; INT
    CANR-28; MTCW 1
Leonard, Hugh   **CLC 19**
  See also Byrne, John Keyes
  See also DLB 13
Leonov, Leonid (Maximovich) 1899-1994
  CLC 92; DAM NOV
  See also CA 129; CANR 74; MTCW 1
Leopardi, (Conte) Giacomo 1798-1837**NCLC**
  22
Le Reveler
  See Artaud, Antonin (Marie Joseph)
Lerman, Eleanor 1952-   **CLC 9**
  See also CA 85-88; CANR 69
Lerman, Rhoda 1936-   **CLC 56**
  See also CA 49-52; CANR 70
Lermontov, Mikhail Yuryevich 1814-1841
  NCLC 47; PC 18
Leroux, Gaston 1868-1927   **TCLC 25**
  See also CA 108; 136; CANR 69; SATA 65
Lesage, Alain-Rene 1668-1747   **LC 2, 28**
Leskov, Nikolai (Semyonovich) 1831-1895
  NCLC 25
Lessing, Doris (May) 1919-**CLC 1, 2, 3, 6, 10,**
  15, 22, 40, 94; DA; DAB; DAC; DAM MST,
  NOV; SSC 6; WLCS
  See also CA 9-12R; CAAS 14; CANR 33, 54;
    CDBLB 1960 to Present; DLB 15, 139;
    DLBY 85; MTCW 1
Lessing, Gotthold Ephraim 1729-1781   **LC 8**
  See also DLB 97
Lester, Richard 1932-   **CLC 20**
Lever, Charles (James) 1806-1872 **NCLC 23**
  See also DLB 21
Leverson, Ada 1865(?)-1936(?)   **TCLC 18**
  See also Elaine
  See also CA 117; DLB 153
Levertov, Denise 1923-1997 **CLC 1, 2, 3, 5, 8,**
  15, 28, 66; DAM POET; PC 11
  See also CA 1-4R; 163; CAAS 19; CANR 3,
    29, 50; DLB 5, 165; INT CANR-29; MTCW
    1
Levi, Jonathan   **CLC 76**
Levi, Peter (Chad Tigar) 1931-   **CLC 41**
  See also CA 5-8R; CANR 34; DLB 40
Levi, Primo 1919 1987   **CLC 37, 50; SSC 12**
  See also CA 13-16R; 122; CANR 12, 33, 61,
    70; DLB 177; MTCW 1
Levin, Ira 1929-   **CLC 3, 6; DAM POP**
  See also CA 21-24R; CANR 17, 44, 74; MTCW
    1; SATA 66
Levin, Meyer 1905-1981   **CLC 7; DAM POP**
  See also AITN 1; CA 9-12R; 104; CANR 15;

DLB 9, 28; DLBY 81; SATA 21; SATA-Obit
27
Levine, Norman 1924-   **CLC 54**
  See also CA 73-76; CAAS 23; CANR 14, 70;
    DLB 88
Levine, Philip 1928-   **CLC 2, 4, 5, 9, 14, 33;**
  DAM POET; PC 22
  See also CA 9-12R; CANR 9, 37, 52; DLB 5
Levinson, Deirdre 1931-   **CLC 49**
  See also CA 73-76; CANR 70
Levi-Strauss, Claude 1908-   **CLC 38**
  See also CA 1-4R; CANR 6, 32, 57; MTCW 1
Levitin, Sonia (Wolff) 1934-   **CLC 17**
  See also AAYA 13; CA 29-32R; CANR 14, 32;
    CLR 53; JRDA; MAICYA; SAAS 2; SATA
    4, 68
Levon, O. U.
  See Kesey, Ken (Elton)
Levy, Amy 1861-1889   **NCLC 59**
  See also DLB 156
Lewes, George Henry 1817-1878   **NCLC 25**
  See also DLB 55, 144
Lewis, Alun 1915-1944   **TCLC 3**
  See also CA 104; DLB 20, 162
Lewis, C. Day
  See Day Lewis, C(ecil)
Lewis, C(live) S(taples) 1898-1963**CLC 1, 3, 6,**
  14, 27; DA; DAB; DAC; DAM MST, NOV,
  POP; WLC
  See also AAYA 3; CA 81-84; CANR 33, 71;
    CDBLB 1945-1960; CLR 3, 27; DLB 15,
    100, 160; JRDA; MAICYA; MTCW 1; SATA
    13, 100
Lewis, Janet 1899-   **CLC 41**
  See also Winters, Janet Lewis
  See also CA 9-12R; CANR 29, 63; CAP 1;
    DLBY 87
Lewis, Matthew Gregory 1775-1818**NCLC 11,**
  62
  See also DLB 39, 158, 178
Lewis, (Harry) Sinclair 1885-1951 **TCLC 4,**
  13, 23, 39; DA; DAB; DAC; DAM MST,
  NOV; WLC
  See also CA 104; 133; CDALB 1917-1929;
    DLB 9, 102; DLBD 1; MTCW 1
Lewis, (Percy) Wyndham 1882(?)-1957**TCLC**
  2, 9
  See also CA 104; 157; DLB 15
Lewisohn, Ludwig 1883-1955   **TCLC 19**
  See also CA 107; DLB 4, 9, 28, 102
Lewton, Val 1904-1951   **TCLC 76**
Leyner, Mark 1956-   **CLC 92**
  See also CA 110; CANR 28, 53
Lezama Lima, Jose 1910-1976**CLC 4, 10, 101;**
  DAM MULT
  See also CA 77-80; CANR 71; DLB 113; HW
L'Heureux, John (Clarke) 1934-   **CLC 52**
  See also CA 13-16R; CANR 23, 45
Liddell, C. H.
  See Kuttner, Henry
Lie, Jonas (Lauritz Idemil) 1833-1908(?)
  TCLC 5
  See also CA 115
Lieber, Joel 1937-1971   **CLC 6**
  See also CA 73-76; 29-32R
Lieber, Stanley Martin
  See Lee, Stan
Lieberman, Laurence (James) 1935- **CLC 4,**
  36
  See also CA 17-20R; CANR 8, 36
Lieh Tzu fl. 7th cent. B.C.-5th cent. B.C.
  CMLC 27
Lieksman, Anders

See Haavikko, Paavo Juhani
Li Fei-kan 1904-
  See Pa Chin
  See also CA 105
Lifton, Robert Jay 1926-   **CLC 67**
  See also CA 17-20R; CANR 27; INT CANR-
    27; SATA 66
Lightfoot, Gordon 1938-   **CLC 26**
  See also CA 109
Lightman, Alan P(aige) 1948-   **CLC 81**
  See also CA 141; CANR 63
Ligotti, Thomas (Robert) 1953-**CLC 44; SSC**
  16
  See also CA 123; CANR 49
Li Ho 791-817   **PC 13**
Liliencron, (Friedrich Adolf Axel) Detlev von
  1844-1909   **TCLC 18**
  See also CA 117
Lilly, William 1602-1681   **LC 27**
Lima, Jose Lezama
  See Lezama Lima, Jose
Lima Barreto, Afonso Henrique de 1881-1922
  TCLC 23
  See also CA 117
Limonov, Edward 1944-   **CLC 67**
  See also CA 137
Lin, Frank
  See Atherton, Gertrude (Franklin Horn)
Lincoln, Abraham 1809-1865   **NCLC 18**
Lind, Jakov   **CLC 1, 2, 4, 27, 82**
  See also Landwirth, Heinz
  See also CAAS 4
Lindbergh, Anne (Spencer) Morrow 1906-
  CLC 82; DAM NOV
  See also CA 17-20R; CANR 16, 73; MTCW 1;
    SATA 33
Lindsay, David 1878-1945   **TCLC 15**
  See also CA 113
Lindsay, (Nicholas) Vachel 1879-1931 **TCLC**
  17; DA; DAC; DAM MST, POET; PC 23;
  WLC
  See also CA 114; 135; CDALB 1865-1917;
    DLB 54; SATA 40
Linke-Poot
  See Doeblin, Alfred
Linney, Romulus 1930-   **CLC 51**
  See also CA 1-4R; CANR 40, 44
Linton, Eliza Lynn 1822-1898   **NCLC 41**
  See also DLB 18
Li Po 701-763   **CMLC 2**
Lipsius, Justus 1547-1606   **LC 16**
Lipsyte, Robert (Michael) 1938-**CLC 21; DA;**
  DAC; DAM MST, NOV
  See also AAYA 7; CA 17-20R; CANR 8, 57;
    CLR 23; JRDA; MAICYA; SATA 5, 68
Lish, Gordon (Jay) 1934-   **CLC 45; SSC 18**
  See also CA 113; 117; DLB 130; INT 117
Lispector, Clarice 1925(?)-1977   **CLC 43**
  See also CA 139; 116; CANR 71; DLB 113
Littell, Robert 1935(?)-   **CLC 42**
  See also CA 109; 112; CANR 64
Little, Malcolm 1925-1965
  See Malcolm X
  See also BW 1; CA 125; 111; DA; DAB; DAC;
    DAM MST, MULT; MTCW 1
Littlewit, Humphrey Gent.
  See Lovecraft, H(oward) P(hillips)
Litwos
  See Sienkiewicz, Henryk (Adam Alexander
    Pius)
Liu, E 1857-1909   **TCLC 15**
  See also CA 115
Lively, Penelope (Margaret) 1933- **CLC 32,**

50; DAM NOV
See also CA 41-44R; CANR 29, 67; CLR 7; DLB 14, 161; JRDA; MAICYA; MTCW 1; SATA 7, 60, 101

Livesay, Dorothy (Kathleen) 1909-**CLC 4, 15, 79; DAC; DAM MST, POET**
See also AITN 2; CA 25-28R; CAAS 8; CANR 36, 67; DLB 68; MTCW 1

Livy c. 59B.C.-c. 17 **CMLC 11**

Lizardi, Jose Joaquin Fernandez de 1776-1827 **NCLC 30**

Llewellyn, Richard
See Llewellyn Lloyd, Richard Dafydd Vivian
See also DLB 15

Llewellyn Lloyd, Richard Dafydd Vivian 1906-1983 **CLC 7, 80**
See also Llewellyn, Richard
See also CA 53-56; 111; CANR 7, 71; SATA 11; SATA-Obit 37

Llosa, (Jorge) Mario (Pedro) Vargas
See Vargas Llosa, (Jorge) Mario (Pedro)

Lloyd, Manda
See Mander, (Mary) Jane

Lloyd Webber, Andrew 1948-
See Webber, Andrew Lloyd
See also AAYA 1; CA 116; 149; DAM DRAM; SATA 56

Llull, Ramon c. 1235-c. 1316 **CMLC 12**

Lobb, Ebenezer
See Upward, Allen

Locke, Alain (Le Roy) 1886-1954 **TCLC 43; BLCS**
See also BW 1; CA 106; 124; DLB 51

Locke, John 1632-1704 **LC 7, 35**
See also DLB 101

Locke-Elliott, Sumner
See Elliott, Sumner Locke

Lockhart, John Gibson 1794-1854 **NCLC 6**
See also DLB 110, 116, 144

Lodge, David (John) 1935-**CLC 36; DAM POP**
See also BEST 90:1; CA 17-20R; CANR 19, 53; DLB 14, 194; INT CANR-19; MTCW 1

Lodge, Thomas 1558-1625 **LC 41**
See also DLB 172

Lodge, Thomas 1558-1625 **LC 41**

Loennbohm, Armas Eino Leopold 1878-1926
See Leino, Eino
See also CA 123

Loewinsohn, Ron(ald William) 1937-**CLC 52**
See also CA 25-28R; CANR 71

Logan, Jake
See Smith, Martin Cruz

Logan, John (Burton) 1923-1987 **CLC 5**
See also CA 77-80; 124; CANR 45; DLB 5

Lo Kuan-chung 1330(?)-1400(?) **LC 12**

Lombard, Nap
See Johnson, Pamela Hansford

London, Jack **TCLC 9, 15, 39; SSC 4; WLC**
See also London, John Griffith
See also AAYA 13; AITN 2; CDALB 1865-1917; DLB 8, 12, 78; SATA 18

London, John Griffith 1876-1916
See London, Jack
See also CA 110; 119; CANR 73; DA; DAB; DAC; DAM MST, NOV; JRDA; MAICYA; MTCW 1

Long, Emmett
See Leonard, Elmore (John, Jr.)

Longbaugh, Harry
See Goldman, William (W.)

Longfellow, Henry Wadsworth 1807-1882 **NCLC 2, 45; DA; DAB; DAC; DAM MST, POET; WLCS**

See also CDALB 1640-1865; DLB·1, 59; SATA 19

Longinus c. 1st cent. - **CMLC 27**
See also DLB 176

Longley, Michael 1939- **CLC 29**
See also CA 102; DLB 40

Longus fl. c. 2nd cent. - **CMLC 7**

Longway, A. Hugh
See Lang, Andrew

Lonnrot, Elias 1802-1884 **NCLC 53**

Lopate, Phillip 1943- **CLC 29**
See also CA 97-100; DLBY 80; INT 97-100

Lopez Portillo (y Pacheco), Jose 1920-**CLC 46**
See also CA 129; HW

Lopez y Fuentes, Gregorio 1897(?)-1966**CLC 32**
See also CA 131; HW

Lorca, Federico Garcia
See Garcia Lorca, Federico

Lord, Bette Bao 1938- **CLC 23**
See also BEST 90:3; CA 107; CANR 41; INT 107; SATA 58

Lord Auch
See Bataille, Georges

Lord Byron
See Byron, George Gordon (Noel)

Lorde, Audre (Geraldine) 1934-1992**CLC 18, 71; BLC 2; DAM MULT, POET; PC 12**
See also BW 1; CA 25-28R; 142; CANR 16, 26, 46; DLB 41; MTCW 1

Lord Houghton
See Milnes, Richard Monckton

Lord Jeffrey
See Jeffrey, Francis

Lorenzini, Carlo 1826-1890
See Collodi, Carlo
See also MAICYA; SATA 29, 100

Lorenzo, Heberto Padilla
See Padilla (Lorenzo), Heberto

Loris
See Hofmannsthal, Hugo von

Loti, Pierre **TCLC 11**
See also Viaud, (Louis Marie) Julien
See also DLB 123

Louie, David Wong 1954- **CLC 70**
See also CA 139

Louis, Father M.
See Merton, Thomas

Lovecraft, H(oward) P(hillips) 1890-1937 **TCLC 4, 22; DAM POP; SSC 3**
See also AAYA 14; CA 104; 133; MTCW 1

Lovelace, Earl 1935- **CLC 51**
See also BW 2; CA 77-80; CANR 41, 72; DLB 125; MTCW 1

Lovelace, Richard 1618-1657 **LC 24**
See also DLB 131

Lowell, Amy 1874-1925 **TCLC 1, 8; DAM POET; PC 13**
See also CA 104; 151; DLB 54, 140

Lowell, James Russell 1819-1891 **NCLC 2**
See also CDALB 1640-1865; DLB 1, 11, 64, 79, 189

Lowell, Robert (Traill Spence, Jr.) 1917-1977 **CLC 1, 2, 3, 4, 5, 8, 9, 11, 15, 37; DA; DAB; DAC; DAM MST, NOV; PC 3; WLC**
See also CA 9-12R; 73-76; CABS 2; CANR 26, 60; DLB 5, 169; MTCW 1

Lowndes, Marie Adelaide (Belloc) 1868-1947 **TCLC 12**
See also CA 107; DLB 70

Lowry, (Clarence) Malcolm 1909-1957**TCLC 6, 40; SSC 31**
See also CA 105; 131; CANR 62; CDBLB

1945-1960; DLB 15; MTCW 1

Lowry, Mina Gertrude 1882-1966
See Loy, Mina
See also CA 113

Loxsmith, John
See Brunner, John (Kilian Houston)

Loy, Mina **CLC 28; DAM POET; PC 16**
See also Lowry, Mina Gertrude
See also DLB 4, 54

Loyson-Bridet
See Schwob, Marcel (Mayer Andre)

Lucas, Craig 1951- **CLC 64**
See also CA 137; CANR 71

Lucas, E(dward) V(errall) 1868-1938 **TCLC 73**
See also DLB 98, 149, 153; SATA 20

Lucas, George 1944- **CLC 16**
See also AAYA 1, 23; CA 77-80; CANR 30; SATA 56

Lucas, Hans
See Godard, Jean-Luc

Lucas, Victoria
See Plath, Sylvia

Ludlam, Charles 1943-1987 **CLC 46, 50**
See also CA 85-88; 122; CANR 72

Ludlum, Robert 1927-**CLC 22, 43; DAM NOV, POP**
See also AAYA 10; BEST 89:1, 90:3; CA 33-36R; CANR 25, 41, 68; DLBY 82; MTCW 1

Ludwig, Ken **CLC 60**

Ludwig, Otto 1813-1865 **NCLC 4**
See also DLB 129

Lugones, Leopoldo 1874-1938 **TCLC 15**
See also CA 116; 131; HW

Lu Hsun 1881-1936 **TCLC 3; SSC 20**
See also Shu-Jen, Chou

Lukacs, George **CLC 24**
See also Lukacs, Gyorgy (Szegeny von)

Lukacs, Gyorgy (Szegeny von) 1885-1971
See Lukacs, George
See also CA 101; 29-32R; CANR 62

Luke, Peter (Ambrose Cyprian) 1919-1995 **CLC 38**
See also CA 81-84; 147; CANR 72; DLB 13

Lunar, Dennis
See Mungo, Raymond

Lurie, Alison 1926- **CLC 4, 5, 18, 39**
See also CA 1-4R; CANR 2, 17, 50; DLB 2; MTCW 1; SATA 46

Lustig, Arnost 1926- **CLC 56**
See also AAYA 3; CA 69-72; CANR 47; SATA 56

Luther, Martin 1483-1546 **LC 9, 37**
See also DLB 179

Luxemburg, Rosa 1870(?)-1919 **TCLC 63**
See also CA 118

Luzi, Mario 1914- **CLC 13**
See also CA 61-64; CANR 9, 70; DLB 128

Lyly, John 1554(?)-1606**LC 41; DAM DRAM; DC 7**
See also DLB 62, 167

L'Ymagier
See Gourmont, Remy (-Marie-Charles) de

Lynch, B. Suarez
See Bioy Casares, Adolfo; Borges, Jorge Luis

Lynch, David (K.) 1946- **CLC 66**
See also CA 124; 129

Lynch, James
See Andreyev, Leonid (Nikolaevich)

Lynch Davis, B.
See Bioy Casares, Adolfo; Borges, Jorge Luis

Lyndsay, Sir David 1490-1555 **LC 20**

Lynn, Kenneth S(chuyler) 1923-   **CLC 50**
See also CA 1-4R; CANR 3, 27, 65

Lynx
See West, Rebecca

Lyons, Marcus
See Blish, James (Benjamin)

Lyre, Pinchbeck
See Sassoon, Siegfried (Lorraine)

Lytle, Andrew (Nelson) 1902-1995   **CLC 22**
See also CA 9-12R; 150; CANR 70; DLB 6;
DLBY 95

Lyttelton, George 1709-1773   **LC 10**

Maas, Peter 1929-   **CLC 29**
See also CA 93-96; INT 93-96

Macaulay, Rose 1881-1958   **TCLC 7, 44**
See also CA 104; DLB 36

Macaulay, Thomas Babington 1800-1859
NCLC 42
See also CDBLB 1832-1890; DLB 32, 55

MacBeth, George (Mann) 1932-1992 **CLC 2, 5, 9**
See also CA 25-28R; 136; CANR 61, 66; DLB
40; MTCW 1; SATA 4; SATA-Obit 70

MacCaig, Norman (Alexander) 1910- **CLC 36;
DAB; DAM POET**
See also CA 9-12R; CANR 3, 34; DLB 27

MacCarthy, Sir (Charles Otto) Desmond 1877-
1952   **TCLC 36**
See also CA 167

MacDiarmid, Hugh **CLC 2, 4, 11, 19, 63; PC 9**
See also Grieve, C(hristopher) M(urray)
See also CDBLB 1945-1960; DLB 20

MacDonald, Anson
See Heinlein, Robert A(nson)

Macdonald, Cynthia 1928-   **CLC 13, 19**
See also CA 49-52; CANR 4, 44; DLB 105

MacDonald, George 1824-1905   **TCLC 9**
See also CA 106; 137; DLB 18, 163, 178;
MAICYA; SATA 33, 100

Macdonald, John
See Millar, Kenneth

MacDonald, John D(ann) 1916-1986 **CLC 3,
27, 44; DAM NOV, POP**
See also CA 1-4R; 121; CANR 1, 19, 60; DLB
8; DLBY 86; MTCW 1

Macdonald, John Ross
See Millar, Kenneth

Macdonald, Ross   **CLC 1, 2, 3, 14, 34, 41**
See also Millar, Kenneth
See also DLBD 6

MacDougal, John
See Blish, James (Benjamin)

MacEwen, Gwendolyn (Margaret) 1941-1987
CLC 13, 55
See also CA 9-12R; 124; CANR 7, 22; DLB
53; SATA 50; SATA-Obit 55

Macha, Karel Hynek 1810-1846   **NCLC 46**

Machado (y Ruiz), Antonio 1875-1939 **TCLC 3**
See also CA 104; DLB 108

Machado de Assis, Joaquim Maria 1839-1908
TCLC 10; BLC 2; SSC 24
See also CA 107; 153

Machen, Arthur   **TCLC 4; SSC 20**
See also Jones, Arthur Llewellyn
See also DLB 36, 156, 178

Machiavelli, Niccolo 1469-1527 **LC 8, 36; DA;
DAB; DAC; DAM MST; WLCS**

MacInnes, Colin 1914-1976   **CLC 4, 23**
See also CA 69-72; 65-68; CANR 21; DLB 14;
MTCW 1

MacInnes, Helen (Clark) 1907-1985 **CLC 27,
39; DAM POP**

See also CA 1-4R; 117; CANR 1, 28, 58; DLB
87; MTCW 1; SATA 22; SATA-Obit 44

Mackay, Mary 1855-1924
See Corelli, Marie
See also CA 118

Mackenzie, Compton (Edward Montague)
1883-1972   **CLC 18**
See also CA 21-22; 37-40R; CAP 2; DLB 34,
100

Mackenzie, Henry 1745-1831   **NCLC 41**
See also DLB 39

Mackintosh, Elizabeth 1896(?)-1952
See Tey, Josephine
See also CA 110

MacLaren, James
See Grieve, C(hristopher) M(urray)

Mac Laverty, Bernard 1942-   **CLC 31**
See also CA 116; 118; CANR 43; INT 118

MacLean, Alistair (Stuart) 1922(?)-1987 **CLC
3, 13, 50, 63; DAM POP**
See also CA 57-60; 121; CANR 28, 61; MTCW
1; SATA 23; SATA-Obit 50

Maclean, Norman (Fitzroy) 1902-1990 **CLC
78; DAM POP; SSC 13**
See also CA 102; 132; CANR 49

MacLeish, Archibald 1892-1982 **CLC 3, 8, 14,
68; DAM POET**
See also CA 9-12R; 106; CANR 33, 63; DLB
4, 7, 45; DLBY 82; MTCW 1

MacLennan, (John) Hugh 1907-1990 **CLC 2,
14, 92; DAC; DAM MST**
See also CA 5-8R; 142; CANR 33; DLB 68;
MTCW 1

MacLeod, Alistair 1936- **CLC 56; DAC; DAM
MST**
See also CA 123; DLB 60

Macleod, Fiona
See Sharp, William

MacNeice, (Frederick) Louis 1907-1963 **CLC
1, 4, 10, 53; DAB; DAM POET**
See also CA 85-88; CANR 61; DLB 10, 20;
MTCW 1

MacNeill, Dand
See Fraser, George MacDonald

Macpherson, James 1736-1796   **LC 29**
See also Ossian
See also DLB 109

Macpherson, (Jean) Jay 1931-   **CLC 14**
See also CA 5-8R; DLB 53

MacShane, Frank 1927-   **CLC 39**
See also CA 9-12R; CANR 3, 33; DLB 111

Macumber, Mari
See Sandoz, Mari(e Susette)

Madach, Imre 1823-1864   **NCLC 19**

Madden, (Jerry) David 1933-   **CLC 5, 15**
See also CA 1-4R; CAAS 3; CANR 4, 45; DLB
6; MTCW 1

Maddern, Al(an)
See Ellison, Harlan (Jay)

Madhubuti, Haki R. 1942- **CLC 6, 73; BLC 2;
DAM MULT, POET; PC 5**
See also Lee, Don L.
See also BW 2; CA 73-76; CANR 24, 51, 73;
DLB 5, 41; DLBD 8

Maepenn, Hugh
See Kuttner, Henry

Maepenn, K. H.
See Kuttner, Henry

Maeterlinck, Maurice 1862-1949   **TCLC 3;
DAM DRAM**
See also CA 104; 136; DLB 192; SATA 66

Maginn, William 1794-1842   **NCLC 8**
See also DLB 110, 159

Mahapatra, Jayanta 1928-   **CLC 33; DAM
MULT**
See also CA 73-76; CAAS 9; CANR 15, 33, 66

Mahfouz, Naguib (Abdel Aziz Al-Sabilgi)
1911(?)-
See Mahfuz, Najib
See also BEST 89:2; CA 128; CANR 55; DAM
NOV; MTCW 1

Mahfuz, Najib   **CLC 52, 55**
See also Mahfouz, Naguib (Abdel Aziz Al-
Sabilgi)
See also DLBY 88

Mahon, Derek 1941-   **CLC 27**
See also CA 113; 128; DLB 40

Mailer, Norman 1923- **CLC 1, 2, 3, 4, 5, 8, 11,
14, 28, 39, 74, 111; DA; DAB; DAC; DAM
MST, NOV, POP**
See also AITN 2; CA 9-12R; CABS 1; CANR
28, 74; CDALB 1968-1988; DLB 2, 16, 28,
185; DLBD 3; DLBY 80, 83; MTCW 1

Maillet, Antonine 1929-   **CLC 54; DAC**
See also CA 115; 120; CANR 46, 74; DLB 60;
INT 120

Mais, Roger 1905-1955   **TCLC 8**
See also BW 1; CA 105; 124; DLB 125; MTCW
1

Maistre, Joseph de 1753-1821   **NCLC 37**

Maitland, Frederic 1850-1906   **TCLC 65**

Maitland, Sara (Louise) 1950-   **CLC 49**
See also CA 69-72; CANR 13, 59

Major, Clarence 1936- **CLC 3, 19, 48; BLC 2;
DAM MULT**
See also BW 2; CA 21-24R; CAAS 6; CANR
13, 25, 53; DLB 33

Major, Kevin (Gerald) 1949-   **CLC 26; DAC**
See also AAYA 16; CA 97-100; CANR 21, 38;
CLR 11; DLB 60; INT CANR-21; JRDA;
MAICYA; SATA 32, 82

Maki, James
See Ozu, Yasujiro

Malabaila, Damiano
See Levi, Primo

Malamud, Bernard 1914-1986 **CLC 1, 2, 3, 5,
8, 9, 11, 18, 27, 44, 78, 85; DA; DAB; DAC;
DAM MST, NOV, POP; SSC 15; WLC**
See also AAYA 16; CA 5-8R; 118; CABS 1;
CANR 28, 62; CDALB 1941-1968; DLB 2,
28, 152; DLBY 80, 86; MTCW 1

Malan, Herman
See Bosman, Herman Charles; Bosman, Herman
Charles

Malaparte, Curzio 1898-1957   **TCLC 52**

Malcolm, Dan
See Silverberg, Robert

Malcolm X   **CLC 82, 117; BLC 2; WLCS**
See also Little, Malcolm

Malherbe, Francois de 1555-1628   **LC 5**

Mallarme, Stephane 1842-1898 **NCLC 4, 41;
DAM POET; PC 4**

Mallet-Joris, Francoise 1930-   **CLC 11**
See also CA 65-68; CANR 17; DLB 83

Malley, Ern
See McAuley, James Phillip

Mallowan, Agatha Christie
See Christie, Agatha (Mary Clarissa)

Maloff, Saul 1922-   **CLC 5**
See also CA 33-36R

Malone, Louis
See MacNeice, (Frederick) Louis

Malone, Michael (Christopher) 1942- **CLC 43**
See also CA 77-80; CANR 14, 32, 57

Malory, (Sir) Thomas 1410(?)-1471(?) **LC 11;
DA; DAB; DAC; DAM MST; WLCS**

See Chekhov, Anton (Pavlovich)
Myers, L(eopold) H(amilton) 1881-1944
  TCLC 59
  See also CA 157; DLB 15
Myers, Walter Dean 1937- **CLC 35; BLC 3;**
  DAM MULT, NOV
  See also AAYA 4, 23; BW 2; CA 33-36R;
  CANR 20, 42, 67; CLR 4, 16, 35; DLB 33;
  INT CANR-20; JRDA; MAICYA; SAAS 2;
  SATA 41, 71; SATA-Brief 27
Myers, Walter M.
  See Myers, Walter Dean
Myles, Symon
  See Follett, Ken(neth Martin)
Nabokov, Vladimir (Vladimirovich) 1899-1977
  CLC 1, 2, 3, 6, 8, 11, 15, 23, 44, 46, 64;
  DA; DAB; DAC; DAM MST, NOV; SSC
  11; WLC
  See also CA 5-8R; 69-72; CANR 20; CDALB
  1941-1968; DLB 2; DLBD 3; DLBY 80, 91;
  MTCW 1
Nagai Kafu 1879-1959   **TCLC 51**
  See also Nagai Sokichi
  See also DLB 180
Nagai Sokichi 1879-1959
  See Nagai Kafu
  See also CA 117
Nagy, Laszlo 1925-1978   **CLC 7**
  See also CA 129; 112
Naidu, Sarojini 1879-1943   **TCLC 80**
Naipaul, Shiva(dhar Srinivasa) 1945-1985
  CLC 32, 39; DAM NOV
  See also CA 110; 112; 116; CANR 33; DLB
  157; DLBY 85; MTCW 1
Naipaul, V(idiadhar) S(urajprasad) 1932-
  CLC 4, 7, 9, 13, 18, 37, 105; DAB; DAC;
  DAM MST, NOV
  See also CA 1-4R; CANR 1, 33, 51; CDBLB
  1960 to Present; DLB 125; DLBY 85;
  MTCW 1
Nakos, Lilika 1899(?)-   **CLC 29**
Narayan, R(asipuram) K(rishnaswami) 1906-
  CLC 7, 28, 47; DAM NOV; SSC 25
  See also CA 81-84; CANR 33, 61; MTCW 1;
  SATA 62
Nash, (Frediric) Ogden 1902-1971 **CLC 23;**
  DAM POET; PC 21
  See also CA 13-14; 29-32R; CANR 34, 61; CAP
  1; DLB 11; MAICYA; MTCW 1; SATA 2,
  46
Nashe, Thomas 1567-1601(?)   **LC 41**
  See also DLB 167
Nashe, Thomas 1567-1601   **LC 41**
Nathan, Daniel
  See Dannay, Frederic
Nathan, George Jean 1882-1958   **TCLC 18**
  See also Hatteras, Owen
  See also CA 114; 169; DLB 137
Natsume, Kinnosuke 1867-1916
  See Natsume, Soseki
  See also CA 104
Natsume, Soseki 1867-1916   **TCLC 2, 10**
  See also Natsume, Kinnosuke
  See also DLB 180
Natti, (Mary) Lee 1919-
  See Kingman, Lee
  Scc also CA 5-8R; CANR 2
Naylor, Gloria 1950-**CLC 28, 52; BLC 3; DA;**
  DAC; DAM MST, MULT, NOV, POP;
  WLCS
  See also AAYA 6; BW 2; CA 107; CANR 27,
  51, 74; DLB 173; MTCW 1
Neihardt, John Gneisenau 1881-1973**CLC 32**

See also CA 13-14; CANR 65; CAP 1; DLB 9,
  54
Nekrasov, Nikolai Alekseevich 1821-1878
  NCLC 11
Nelligan, Emile 1879-1941   **TCLC 14**
  See also CA 114; DLB 92
Nelson, Willie 1933-   **CLC 17**
  See also CA 107
Nemerov, Howard (Stanley) 1920-1991**CLC 2,**
  6, 9, 36; DAM POET; PC 24
  See also CA 1-4R; 134; CABS 2; CANR 1, 27,
  53; DLB 5, 6; DLBY 83; INT CANR-27;
  MTCW 1
Neruda, Pablo 1904-1973**CLC 1, 2, 5, 7, 9, 28,**
  62; DA; DAB; DAC; DAM MST, MULT,
  POET; HLC; PC 4; WLC
  See also CA 19-20; 45-48; CAP 2; HW; MTCW
  1
Nerval, Gerard de 1808-1855**NCLC 1, 67; PC**
  13; SSC 18
Nervo, (Jose) Amado (Ruiz de) 1870-1919
  TCLC 11
  See also CA 109; 131; HW
Nessi, Pio Baroja y
  See Baroja (y Nessi), Pio
Nestroy, Johann 1801-1862   **NCLC 42**
  See also DLB 133
Netterville, Luke
  See O'Grady, Standish (James)
Neufeld, John (Arthur) 1938-   **CLC 17**
  See also AAYA 11; CA 25-28R; CANR 11, 37,
  56; CLR 52; MAICYA; SAAS 3; SATA 6,
  81
Neville, Emily Cheney 1919-   **CLC 12**
  See also CA 5-8R; CANR 3, 37; JRDA;
  MAICYA; SAAS 2; SATA 1
Newbound, Bernard Slade 1930-
  See Slade, Bernard
  See also CA 81-84; CANR 49; DAM DRAM
Newby, P(ercy) H(oward) 1918-1997 **CLC 2,**
  13; DAM NOV
  See also CA 5-8R; 161; CANR 32, 67; DLB
  15; MTCW 1
Newlove, Donald 1928-   **CLC 6**
  See also CA 29-32R; CANR 25
Newlove, John (Herbert) 1938-   **CLC 14**
  See also CA 21-24R; CANR 9, 25
Newman, Charles 1938-   **CLC 2, 8**
  See also CA 21-24R
Newman, Edwin (Harold) 1919-   **CLC 14**
  See also AITN 1; CA 69-72; CANR 5
Newman, John Henry 1801-1890   **NCLC 38**
  See also DLB 18, 32, 55
Newton, (Sir)Isaac 1642-1727   **LC 35**
Newton, Suzanne 1936-   **CLC 35**
  See also CA 41-44R; CANR 14; JRDA; SATA
  5, 77
Nexo, Martin Andersen 1869-1954 **TCLC 43**
Nezval, Vitezslav 1900-1958   **TCLC 44**
  See also CA 123
Ng, Fae Myenne 1957(?)-   **CLC 81**
  See also CA 146
Ngema, Mbongeni 1955-   **CLC 57**
  See also BW 2; CA 143
Ngugi, James T(hiong'o)   **CLC 3, 7, 13**
  See also Ngugi wa Thiong'o
Ngugi wa Thiong'o 1938- **CLC 36; BLC 3;**
  DAM MULT, NOV
  See also Ngugi, James T(hiong'o)
  See also BW 2; CA 81-84; CANR 27, 58; DLB
  125; MTCW 1
Nichol, B(arrie) P(hillip) 1944-1988 **CLC 18**
  See also CA 53-56; DLB 53; SATA 66

Nichols, John (Treadwell) 1940-   **CLC 38**
  See also CA 9-12R; CAAS 2; CANR 6, 70;
  DLBY 82
Nichols, Leigh
  See Koontz, Dean R(ay)
Nichols, Peter (Richard) 1927- **CLC 5, 36, 65**
  See also CA 104; CANR 33; DLB 13; MTCW
  1
Nicolas, F. R. E.
  See Freeling, Nicolas
Niedecker, Lorine 1903-1970   **CLC 10, 42;**
  DAM POET
  See also CA 25-28; CAP 2; DLB 48
Nietzsche, Friedrich (Wilhelm) 1844-1900
  TCLC 10, 18, 55
  See also CA 107; 121; DLB 129
Nievo, Ippolito 1831-1861   **NCLC 22**
Nightingale, Anne Redmon 1943-
  See Redmon, Anne
  See also CA 103
Nightingale, Florence 1820-1910   **TCLC 85**
  See also DLB 166
Nik. T. O.
  See Annensky, Innokenty (Fyodorovich)
Nin, Anais 1903-1977 **CLC 1, 4, 8, 11, 14, 60;**
  DAM NOV, POP; SSC 10
  See also AITN 2; CA 13-16R; 69-72; CANR
  22, 53; DLB 2, 4, 152; MTCW 1
Nishida, Kitaro 1870-1945   **TCLC 83**
Nishiwaki, Junzaburo 1894-1982   **PC 15**
  See also CA 107
Nissenson, Hugh 1933-   **CLC 4, 9**
  See also CA 17-20R; CANR 27; DLB 28
Niven, Larry   **CLC 8**
  See also Niven, Laurence Van Cott
  See also AAYA 27; DLB 8
Niven, Laurence Van Cott 1938-
  See Niven, Larry
  See also CA 21-24R; CAAS 12; CANR 14, 44,
  66; DAM POP; MTCW 1; SATA 95
Nixon, Agnes Eckhardt 1927-   **CLC 21**
  See also CA 110
Nizan, Paul 1905-1940   **TCLC 40**
  See also CA 161; DLB 72
Nkosi, Lewis 1936-   **CLC 45; BLC 3; DAM**
  MULT
  See also BW 1; CA 65-68; CANR 27; DLB 157
Nodier, (Jean) Charles (Emmanuel) 1780-1844
  NCLC 19
  See also DLB 119
Noguchi, Yone 1875-1947   **TCLC 80**
Nolan, Christopher 1965-   **CLC 58**
  See also CA 111
Noon, Jeff 1957-   **CLC 91**
  See also CA 148
Norden, Charles
  See Durrell, Lawrence (George)
Nordhoff, Charles (Bernard) 1887-1947
  TCLC 23
  See also CA 108; DLB 9; SATA 23
Norfolk, Lawrence 1963-   **CLC 76**
  See also CA 144
Norman, Marsha 1947-**CLC 28; DAM DRAM;**
  DC 8
  See also CA 105; CABS 3; CANR 41; DLBY
  84
Normyx
  See Douglas, (George) Norman
Norris, Frank 1870-1902   **SSC 28**
  See also Norris, (Benjamin) Frank(lin, Jr.)
  See also CDALB 1865-1917; DLB 12, 71, 186
Norris, (Benjamin) Frank(lin, Jr.) 1870-1902
  TCLC 24

See also Norris, Frank
See also CA 110; 160
Norris, Leslie 1921-   **CLC 14**
  See also CA 11-12; CANR 14; CAP 1; DLB 27
North, Andrew
  See Norton, Andre
North, Anthony
  See Koontz, Dean R(ay)
North, Captain George
  See Stevenson, Robert Louis (Balfour)
North, Milou
  See Erdrich, Louise
Northrup, B. A.
  See Hubbard, L(afayette) Ron(ald)
North Staffs
  See Hulme, T(homas) E(rnest)
Norton, Alice Mary
  See Norton, Andre
  See also MAICYA; SATA 1, 43
Norton, Andre 1912-   **CLC 12**
  See also Norton, Alice Mary
  See also AAYA 14; CA 1-4R; CANR 68; CLR
    50; DLB 8, 52; JRDA; MTCW 1; SATA 91
Norton, Caroline 1808-1877   **NCLC 47**
  See also DLB 21, 159, 199
Norway, Nevil Shute 1899-1960
  See Shute, Nevil
  See also CA 102; 93-96
Norwid, Cyprian Kamil 1821-1883 **NCLC 17**
Nosille, Nabrah
  See Ellison, Harlan (Jay)
Nossack, Hans Erich 1901-1978   **CLC 6**
  See also CA 93-96; 85-88; DLB 69
Nostradamus 1503-1566   **LC 27**
Nosu, Chuji
  See Ozu, Yasujiro
Notenburg, Eleanora (Genrikhovna) von
  See Guro, Elena
Nova, Craig 1945-   **CLC 7, 31**
  See also CA 45-48; CANR 2, 53
Novak, Joseph
  See Kosinski, Jerzy (Nikodem)
Novalis 1772-1801   **NCLC 13**
  See also DLB 90
Novis, Emile
  See Weil, Simone (Adolphine)
Nowlan, Alden (Albert) 1933-1983   **CLC 15;**
  DAC; DAM MST
  See also CA 9-12R; CANR 5; DLB 53
Noyes, Alfred 1880-1958   **TCLC 7**
  See also CA 104; DLB 20
Nunn, Kem   **CLC 34**
  See also CA 159
Nye, Robert 1939- **CLC 13, 42; DAM NOV**
  See also CA 33-36R; CANR 29, 67; DLB 14;
    MTCW 1; SATA 6
Nyro, Laura 1947-   **CLC 17**
Oates, Joyce Carol 1938-**CLC 1, 2, 3, 6, 9, 11,**
  15, 19, 33, 52, 108; DA; DAB; DAC; DAM
  MST, NOV, POP; SSC 6; WLC
  See also AAYA 15; AITN 1; BEST 89:2; CA 5-
    8R; CANR 25, 45, 74; CDALB 1968-1988;
    DLB 2, 5, 130; DLBY 81; INT CANR-25;
    MTCW 1
O'Brien, Darcy 1939-1998   **CLC 11**
  See also CA 21-24R; 167; CANR 8, 59
O'Brien, E. G.
  See Clarke, Arthur C(harles)
O'Brien, Edna 1936- **CLC 3, 5, 8, 13, 36, 65,**
  116; DAM NOV; SSC 10
  See also CA 1-4R; CANR 6, 41, 65; CDBLB
    1960 to Present; DLB 14; MTCW 1
O'Brien, Fitz-James 1828-1862   **NCLC 21**

See also DLB 74
O'Brien, Flann   **CLC 1, 4, 5, 7, 10, 47**
  See also O Nuallain, Brian
O'Brien, Richard 1942-   **CLC 17**
  See also CA 124
O'Brien, (William) Tim(othy) 1946- **CLC 7,**
  19, 40, 103; DAM POP
  See also AAYA 16; CA 85-88; CANR 40, 58;
    DLB 152; DLBD 9; DLBY 80
Obstfelder, Sigbjoern 1866-1900   **TCLC 23**
  See also CA 123
O'Casey, Sean 1880-1964 **CLC 1, 5, 9, 11, 15,**
  88; DAB; DAC; DAM DRAM, MST;
  WLCS
  See also CA 89-92; CANR 62; CDBLB 1914-
    1945; DLB 10; MTCW 1
O'Cathasaigh, Sean
  See O'Casey, Sean
Ochs, Phil 1940-1976   **CLC 17**
  See also CA 65-68
O'Connor, Edwin (Greene) 1918-1968 **CLC 14**
  See also CA 93-96; 25-28R
O'Connor, (Mary) Flannery 1925-1964 **C L C**
  1, 2, 3, 6, 10, 13, 15, 21, 66, 104; DA; DAB;
  DAC; DAM MST, NOV; SSC 1, 23; WLC
  See also AAYA 7; CA 1-4R; CANR 3, 41;
    CDALB 1941-1968; DLB 2, 152; DLBD 12;
    DLBY 80; MTCW 1
O'Connor, Frank   **CLC 23; SSC 5**
  See also O'Donovan, Michael John
  See also DLB 162
O'Dell, Scott 1898-1989   **CLC 30**
  See also AAYA 3; CA 61-64; 129; CANR 12,
    30; CLR 1, 16; DLB 52; JRDA; MAICYA;
    SATA 12, 60
Odets, Clifford 1906-1963 **CLC 2, 28, 98; DAM**
  DRAM; DC 6
  See also CA 85-88; CANR 62; DLB 7, 26;
    MTCW 1
O'Doherty, Brian 1934-   **CLC 76**
  See also CA 105
O'Donnell, K. M.
  See Malzberg, Barry N(athaniel)
O'Donnell, Lawrence
  See Kuttner, Henry
O'Donovan, Michael John 1903-1966 **CLC 14**
  See also O'Connor, Frank
  See also CA 93-96
Oe, Kenzaburo 1935- **CLC 10, 36, 86; DAM**
  NOV; SSC 20
  See also CA 97-100; CANR 36, 50, 74; DLB
    182; DLBY 94; MTCW 1
O'Faolain, Julia 1932-   **CLC 6, 19, 47, 108**
  See also CA 81-84; CAAS 2; CANR 12, 61;
    DLB 14; MTCW 1
O'Faolain, Sean 1900-1991 **CLC 1, 7, 14, 32,**
  70; SSC 13
  See also CA 61-64; 134; CANR 12, 66; DLB
    15, 162; MTCW 1
O'Flaherty, Liam 1896-1984 **CLC 5, 34; SSC 6**
  See also CA 101; 113; CANR 35; DLB 36, 162;
    DLBY 84; MTCW 1
Ogilvy, Gavin
  See Barrie, J(ames) M(atthew)
O'Grady, Standish (James) 1846-1928 **T C L C**
  5
  See also CA 104; 157
O'Grady, Timothy 1951-   **CLC 59**
  See also CA 138
O'Hara, Frank 1926-1966 **CLC 2, 5, 13, 78;**
  DAM POET
  See also CA 9-12R; 25-28R; CANR 33; DLB
    5, 16, 193; MTCW 1

O'Hara, John (Henry) 1905-1970 **CLC 1, 2, 3,**
  6, 11, 42; DAM NOV; SSC 15
  See also CA 5-8R; 25-28R; CANR 31, 60;
    CDALB 1929-1941; DLB 9, 86; DLBD 2;
    MTCW 1
O Hehir, Diana 1922-   **CLC 41**
  See also CA 93-96
Okigbo, Christopher (Ifenayichukwu) 1932-
  1967 **CLC 25, 84; BLC 3; DAM MULT,**
  POET; PC 7
  See also BW 1; CA 77-80; CANR 74; DLB 125;
    MTCW 1
Okri, Ben 1959-   **CLC 87**
  See also BW 2; CA 130; 138; CANR 65; DLB
    157; INT 138
Olds, Sharon 1942-   **CLC 32, 39, 85; DAM**
  POET; PC 22
  See also CA 101; CANR 18, 41, 66; DLB 120
Oldstyle, Jonathan
  See Irving, Washington
Olesha, Yuri (Karlovich) 1899-1960   **CLC 8**
  See also CA 85-88
Oliphant, Laurence 1829(?)-1888   **NCLC 47**
  See also DLB 18, 166
Oliphant, Margaret (Oliphant Wilson) 1828-
  1897   **NCLC 11, 61; SSC 25**
  See also DLB 18, 159, 190
Oliver, Mary 1935-   **CLC 19, 34, 98**
  See also CA 21-24R; CANR 9, 43; DLB 5, 193
Olivier, Laurence (Kerr) 1907-1989 **CLC 20**
  See also CA 111; 150; 129
Olsen, Tillie 1912- **CLC 4, 13, 114; DA; DAB;**
  DAC; DAM MST; SSC 11
  See also CA 1-4R; CANR 1, 43, 74; DLB 28;
    DLBY 80; MTCW 1
Olson, Charles (John) 1910-1970 **CLC 1, 2, 5,**
  6, 9, 11, 29; DAM POET; PC 19
  See also CA 13-16; 25-28R; CABS 2; CANR
    35, 61; CAP 1; DLB 5, 16, 193; MTCW 1
Olson, Toby 1937-   **CLC 28**
  See also CA 65-68; CANR 9, 31
Olyesha, Yuri
  See Olesha, Yuri (Karlovich)
Ondaatje, (Philip) Michael 1943- **CLC 14, 29,**
  51, 76; DAB; DAC; DAM MST
  See also CA 77-80; CANR 42, 74; DLB 60
Oneal, Elizabeth 1934-
  See Oneal, Zibby
  See also CA 106; CANR 28; MAICYA; SATA
    30, 82
Oneal, Zibby   **CLC 30**
  See also Oneal, Elizabeth
  See also AAYA 5; CLR 13; JRDA
O'Neill, Eugene (Gladstone) 1888-1953 **TCLC**
  1, 6, 27, 49; DA; DAB; DAC; DAM DRAM,
  MST; WLC
  See also AITN 1; CA 110; 132; CDALB 1929-
    1941; DLB 7; MTCW 1
Onetti, Juan Carlos 1909-1994   **CLC 7, 10;**
  DAM MULT, NOV; SSC 23
  See also CA 85-88; 145; CANR 32, 63; DLB
    113; HW; MTCW 1
O Nuallain, Brian 1911-1966
  See O'Brien, Flann
  See also CA 21-22; 25-28R; CAP 2
Ophuls, Max 1902-1957   **TCLC 79**
  See also CA 113
Opie, Amelia 1769-1853   **NCLC 65**
  See also DLB 116, 159
Oppen, George 1908-1984   **CLC 7, 13, 34**
  See also CA 13-16R; 113; CANR 8; DLB 5,
    165
Oppenheim, E(dward) Phillips 1866-1946

TCLC 45
See also CA 111; DLB 70
Opuls, Max
See Ophuls, Max
Origen c. 185-c. 254   **CMLC 19**
Orlovitz, Gil 1918-1973   **CLC 22**
See also CA 77-80; 45-48; DLB 2, 5
Orris
See Ingelow, Jean
Ortega y Gasset, Jose 1883-1955   **TCLC 9;**
  DAM MULT; HLC
See also CA 106; 130; HW; MTCW 1
Ortese, Anna Maria 1914-   **CLC 89**
See also DLB 177
Ortiz, Simon J(oseph) 1941- **CLC 45; DAM**
  MULT, POET; PC 17
See also CA 134; CANR 69; DLB 120, 175;
  NNAL
Orton, Joe   **CLC 4, 13, 43; DC 3**
See also Orton, John Kingsley
See also CDBLB 1960 to Present; DLB 13
Orton, John Kingsley 1933-1967
See Orton, Joe
  See also CA 85-88; CANR 35, 66; DAM
  DRAM; MTCW 1
Orwell, George **TCLC 2, 6, 15, 31, 51; DAB;**
  WLC
See also Blair, Eric (Arthur)
See also CDBLB 1945-1960; DLB 15, 98, 195
Osborne, David
See Silverberg, Robert
Osborne, George
See Silverberg, Robert
Osborne, John (James) 1929-1994**CLC 1, 2, 5,**
  11, 45; DA; DAB; DAC; DAM DRAM,
  MST; WLC
  See also CA 13-16R; 147; CANR 21, 56;
  CDBLB 1945-1960; DLB 13; MTCW 1
Osborne, Lawrence 1958-   **CLC 50**
Oshima, Nagisa 1932-   **CLC 20**
See also CA 116; 121
Oskison, John Milton 1874-1947 **TCLC 35;**
  DAM MULT
See also CA 144; DLB 175; NNAL
Ossian c. 3rd cent. -   **CMLC 28**
See also Macpherson, James
Ossoli, Sarah Margaret (Fuller marchesa d')
  1810-1850
See Fuller, Margaret
See also SATA 25
Ostrovsky, Alexander 1823-1886**NCLC 30, 57**
Otero, Blas de 1916-1979   **CLC 11**
See also CA 89-92; DLB 134
Otto, Rudolf 1869-1937   **TCLC 85**
Otto, Whitney 1955-   **CLC 70**
See also CA 140
Ouida   **TCLC 43**
See also De La Ramee, (Marie) Louise
See also DLB 18, 156
Ousmane, Sembene 1923-   **CLC 66; BLC 3**
See also BW 1; CA 117; 125; MTCW 1
Ovid 43B.C.-18(?)**CMLC 7; DAM POET; PC**
  2
Owen, Hugh
See Faust, Frederick (Schiller)
Owen, Wilfred (Edward Salter) 1893-1918
  TCLC 5, 27; DA; DAB; DAC; DAM MST,
  POET; PC 19; WLC
  See also CA 104; 141; CDBLB 1914-1945;
  DLB 20
Owens, Rochelle 1936-   **CLC 8**
See also CA 17-20R; CAAS 2; CANR 39
Oz, Amos 1939-**CLC 5, 8, 11, 27, 33, 54; DAM**

NOV
See also CA 53-56; CANR 27, 47, 65; MTCW
  1
Ozick, Cynthia 1928- **CLC 3, 7, 28, 62; DAM**
  NOV, POP; SSC 15
See also BEST 90:1; CA 17-20R; CANR 23,
  58; DLB 28, 152; DLBY 82; INT CANR-
  23; MTCW 1
Ozu, Yasujiro 1903-1963   **CLC 16**
See also CA 112
Pacheco, C.
See Pessoa, Fernando (Antonio Nogueira)
Pa Chin   **CLC 18**
See also Li Fei-kan
Pack, Robert 1929-   **CLC 13**
See also CA 1-4R; CANR 3, 44; DLB 5
Padgett, Lewis
See Kuttner, Henry
Padilla (Lorenzo), Heberto 1932- **CLC 38**
See also AITN 1; CA 123; 131; HW
Page, Jimmy 1944-   **CLC 12**
Page, Louise 1955-   **CLC 40**
See also CA 140
Page, P(atricia) K(athleen) 1916- **CLC 7, 18;**
  DAC; DAM MST; PC 12
See also CA 53-56; CANR 4, 22, 65; DLB 68;
  MTCW 1
Page, Thomas Nelson 1853-1922   **SSC 23**
See also CA 118; DLB 12, 78; DLBD 13
Pagels, Elaine Hiesey 1943-   **CLC 104**
See also CA 45-48; CANR 2, 24, 51
Paget, Violet 1856-1935
See Lee, Vernon
See also CA 104; 166
Paget-Lowe, Henry
See Lovecraft, H(oward) P(hillips)
Paglia, Camille (Anna) 1947-   **CLC 68**
See also CA 140; CANR 72
Paige, Richard
See Koontz, Dean R(ay)
Paine, Thomas 1737-1809   **NCLC 62**
See also CDALB 1640-1865; DLB 31, 43, 73,
  158
Pakenham, Antonia
See Fraser, (Lady) Antonia (Pakenham)
Palamas, Kostes 1859-1943   **TCLC 5**
See also CA 105
Palazzeschi, Aldo 1885-1974   **CLC 11**
See also CA 89-92; 53-56; DLB 114
Paley, Grace 1922- **CLC 4, 6, 37; DAM POP;**
  SSC 8
See also CA 25-28R; CANR 13, 46, 74; DLB
  28; INT CANR-13; MTCW 1
Palin, Michael (Edward) 1943-   **CLC 21**
See also Monty Python
See also CA 107; CANR 35; SATA 67
Palliser, Charles 1947-   **CLC 65**
See also CA 136
Palma, Ricardo 1833-1919   **TCLC 29**
See also CA 168
Pancake, Breece Dexter 1952-1979
See Pancake, Breece D'J
See also CA 123; 109
Pancake, Breece D'J   **CLC 29**
See also Pancake, Breece Dexter
See also DLB 130
Panko, Rudy
See Gogol, Nikolai (Vasilyevich)
Papadiamantis, Alexandros 1851-1911**TCLC**
  29
See also CA 168
Papadiamantopoulos, Johannes 1856-1910
See Moreas, Jean

See also CA 117
Papini, Giovanni 1881-1956   **TCLC 22**
See also CA 121
Paracelsus 1493-1541   **LC 14**
See also DLB 179
Parasol, Peter
See Stevens, Wallace
Pardo Bazan, Emilia 1851-1921   **SSC 30**
Pareto, Vilfredo 1848-1923   **TCLC 69**
Parfenie, Maria
See Codrescu, Andrei
Parini, Jay (Lee) 1948-   **CLC 54**
See also CA 97-100; CAAS 16; CANR 32
Park, Jordan
See Kornbluth, C(yril) M.; Pohl, Frederik
Park, Robert E(zra) 1864-1944   **TCLC 73**
See also CA 122; 165
Parker, Bert
See Ellison, Harlan (Jay)
Parker, Dorothy (Rothschild) 1893-1967**CLC**
  15, 68; DAM POET; SSC 2
See also CA 19-20; 25-28R; CAP 2; DLB 11,
  45, 86; MTCW 1
Parker, Robert B(rown) 1932-**CLC 27; DAM**
  NOV, POP
See also BEST 89:4; CA 49-52; CANR 1, 26,
  52; INT CANR-26; MTCW 1
Parkin, Frank 1940-   **CLC 43**
See also CA 147
Parkman, Francis, Jr. 1823-1893 **NCLC 12**
See also DLB 1, 30, 186
Parks, Gordon (Alexander Buchanan) 1912-
  CLC 1, 16; BLC 3; DAM MULT
  See also AITN 2; BW 2; CA 41-44R; CANR
  26, 66; DLB 33; SATA 8
Parmenides c. 515B.C.-c. 450B.C. **CMLC 22**
See also DLB 176
Parnell, Thomas 1679-1718   **LC 3**
See also DLB 94
Parra, Nicanor 1914-   **CLC 2, 102; DAM**
  MULT; HLC
See also CA 85-88; CANR 32; HW; MTCW 1
Parrish, Mary Frances
See Fisher, M(ary) F(rances) K(ennedy)
Parson
See Coleridge, Samuel Taylor
Parson Lot
See Kingsley, Charles
Partridge, Anthony
See Oppenheim, E(dward) Phillips
Pascal, Blaise 1623-1662   **LC 35**
Pascoli, Giovanni 1855-1912   **TCLC 45**
See also CA 170
Pasolini, Pier Paolo 1922-1975 **CLC 20, 37,**
  106; PC 17
See also CA 93-96; 61-64; CANR 63; DLB 128,
  177; MTCW 1
Pasquini
See Silone, Ignazio
Pastan, Linda (Olenik) 1932- **CLC 27; DAM**
  POET
See also CA 61-64; CANR 18, 40, 61; DLB 5
Pasternak, Boris (Leonidovich) 1890-1960
  CLC 7, 10, 18, 63; DA; DAB; DAC; DAM
  MST, NOV, POET; PC 6; SSC 31; WLC
  See also CA 127; 116; MTCW 1
Patchen, Kenneth 1911-1972   **CLC 1, 2, 18;**
  DAM POET
See also CA 1-4R; 33-36R; CANR 3, 35; DLB
  16, 48; MTCW 1
Pater, Walter (Horatio) 1839-1894 **NCLC 7**
See also CDBLB 1832-1890; DLB 57, 156
Paterson, A(ndrew) B(arton) 1864-1941

TCLC 32
See also CA 155; SATA 97

Paterson, Katherine (Womeldorf) 1932- **C L C 12, 30**
See also AAYA 1; CA 21-24R; CANR 28, 59; CLR 7, 50; DLB 52; JRDA; MAICYA; MTCW 1; SATA 13, 53, 92

Patmore, Coventry Kersey Dighton 1823-1896 **NCLC 9**
See also DLB 35, 98

Paton, Alan (Stewart) 1903-1988 **CLC 4, 10, 25, 55, 106; DA; DAB; DAC; DAM MST, NOV; WLC**
See also AAYA 26; CA 13-16; 125; CANR 22; CAP 1; DLBD 17; MTCW 1; SATA 11; SATA-Obit 56

Paton Walsh, Gillian 1937-
See Walsh, Jill Paton
See also CANR 38; JRDA; MAICYA; SAAS 3; SATA 4, 72

Patton, George S. 1885-1945 **TCLC 79**

Paulding, James Kirke 1778-1860 **NCLC 2**
See also DLB 3, 59, 74

Paulin, Thomas Neilson 1949-
See Paulin, Tom
See also CA 123; 128

Paulin, Tom **CLC 37**
See also Paulin, Thomas Neilson
See also DLB 40

Paustovsky, Konstantin (Georgievich) 1892-1968 **CLC 40**
See also CA 93-96; 25-28R

Pavese, Cesare 1908-1950 **TCLC 3; PC 13; SSC 19**
See also CA 104; 169; DLB 128, 177

Pavic, Milorad 1929- **CLC 60**
See also CA 136; DLB 181

Payne, Alan
See Jakes, John (William)

Paz, Gil
See Lugones, Leopoldo

Paz, Octavio 1914-1998 **CLC 3, 4, 6, 10, 19, 51, 65; DA; DAB; DAC; DAM MST, MULT, POET; HLC; PC 1; WLC**
See also CA 73-76; 165; CANR 32, 65; DLBY 90; HW; MTCW 1

p'Bitek, Okot 1931-1982 **CLC 96; BLC 3; DAM MULT**
See also BW 2; CA 124; 107; DLB 125; MTCW 1

Peacock, Molly 1947- **CLC 60**
See also CA 103; CAAS 21; CANR 52; DLB 120

Peacock, Thomas Love 1785-1866 **NCLC 22**
See also DLB 96, 116

Peake, Mervyn 1911-1968 **CLC 7, 54**
See also CA 5-8R; 25-28R; CANR 3; DLB 15, 160; MTCW 1; SATA 23

Pearce, Philippa **CLC 21**
See also Christie, (Ann) Philippa
See also CLR 9; DLB 161; MAICYA; SATA 1, 67

Pearl, Eric
See Elman, Richard (Martin)

Pearson, T(homas) R(eid) 1956- **CLC 39**
See also CA 120; 130; INT 130

Peck, Dale 1967- **CLC 81**
See also CA 146; CANR 72

Peck, John 1941- **CLC 3**
See also CA 49-52; CANR 3

Peck, Richard (Wayne) 1934- **CLC 21**
See also AAYA 1, 24; CA 85-88; CANR 19, 38; CLR 15; INT CANR-19; JRDA;

MAICYA; SAAS 2; SATA 18, 55, 97

Peck, Robert Newton 1928- **CLC 17; DA; DAC; DAM MST**
See also AAYA 3; CA 81-84; CANR 31, 63; CLR 45; JRDA; MAICYA; SAAS 1; SATA 21, 62

Peckinpah, (David) Sam(uel) 1925-1984 **C L C 20**
See also CA 109; 114

Pedersen, Knut 1859-1952
See Hamsun, Knut
See also CA 104; 119; CANR 63; MTCW 1

Peeslake, Gaffer
See Durrell, Lawrence (George)

Peguy, Charles Pierre 1873-1914 **TCLC 10**
See also CA 107

Peirce, Charles Sanders 1839-1914 **TCLC 81**

Pena, Ramon del Valle y
See Valle-Inclan, Ramon (Maria) del

Pendennis, Arthur Esquir
See Thackeray, William Makepeace

Penn, William 1644-1718 **LC 25**
See also DLB 24

PEPECE
See Prado (Calvo), Pedro

Pepys, Samuel 1633-1703 **LC 11; DA; DAB; DAC; DAM MST; WLC**
See also CDBLB 1660-1789; DLB 101

Percy, Walker 1916-1990 **CLC 2, 3, 6, 8, 14, 18, 47, 65; DAM NOV, POP**
See also CA 1-4R; 131; CANR 1, 23, 64; DLB 2; DLBY 80, 90; MTCW 1

Percy, William Alexander 1885-1942 **TCLC 84**
See also CA 163

Perec, Georges 1936-1982 **CLC 56, 116**
See also CA 141; DLB 83

Pereda (y Sanchez de Porrua), Jose Maria de 1833-1906 **TCLC 16**
See also CA 117

Pereda y Porrua, Jose Maria de
See Pereda (y Sanchez de Porrua), Jose Maria de

Peregoy, George Weems
See Mencken, H(enry) L(ouis)

Perelman, S(idney) J(oseph) 1904-1979 **C L C 3, 5, 9, 15, 23, 44, 49; DAM DRAM; SSC 32**
See also AITN 1, 2; CA 73-76; 89-92; CANR 18; DLB 11, 44; MTCW 1

Peret, Benjamin 1899-1959 **TCLC 20**
See also CA 117

Peretz, Isaac Loeb 1851(?)-1915 **TCLC 16; SSC 26**
See also CA 109

Peretz, Yitzkhok Leibush
See Peretz, Isaac Loeb

Perez Galdos, Benito 1843-1920 **TCLC 27**
See also CA 125; 153; HW

Perrault, Charles 1628-1703 **LC 2**
See also MAICYA; SATA 25

Perry, Brighton
See Sherwood, Robert E(mmet)

Perse, St.-John
See Leger, (Marie-Rene Auguste) Alexis Saint-Leger

Perutz, Leo 1882-1957 **TCLC 60**
See also DLB 81

Peseenz, Tulio F.
See Lopez y Fuentes, Gregorio

Pesetsky, Bette 1932- **CLC 28**
See also CA 133; DLB 130

Peshkov, Alexei Maximovich 1868-1936
See Gorky, Maxim

See also CA 105; 141; DA; DAC; DAM DRAM, MST, NOV

Pessoa, Fernando (Antonio Nogueira) 1898-1935 **TCLC 27; HLC; PC 20**
See also CA 125

Peterkin, Julia Mood 1880-1961 **CLC 31**
See also CA 102; DLB 9

Peters, Joan K(aren) 1945- **CLC 39**
See also CA 158

Peters, Robert L(ouis) 1924- **CLC 7**
See also CA 13-16R; CAAS 8; DLB 105

Petofi, Sandor 1823-1849 **NCLC 21**

Petrakis, Harry Mark 1923- **CLC 3**
See also CA 9-12R; CANR 4, 30

Petrarch 1304-1374 **CMLC 20; DAM POET; PC 8**

Petrov, Evgeny **TCLC 21**
See also Kataev, Evgeny Petrovich

Petry, Ann (Lane) 1908-1997 **CLC 1, 7, 18**
See also BW 1; CA 5-8R; 157; CAAS 6; CANR 4, 46; CLR 12; DLB 76; JRDA; MAICYA; MTCW 1; SATA 5; SATA-Obit 94

Petursson, Halligrimur 1614-1674 **LC 8**

Peychinovich
See Vazov, Ivan (Minchov)

Phaedrus 18(?)B.C.-55(?) **CMLC 25**

Philips, Katherine 1632-1664 **LC 30**
See also DLB 131

Philipson, Morris H. 1926- **CLC 53**
See also CA 1-4R; CANR 4

Phillips, Caryl 1958- **CLC 96; BLCS; DAM MULT**
See also BW 2; CA 141; CANR 63; DLB 157

Phillips, David Graham 1867-1911 **TCLC 44**
See also CA 108; DLB 9, 12

Phillips, Jack
See Sandburg, Carl (August)

Phillips, Jayne Anne 1952- **CLC 15, 33; SSC 16**
See also CA 101; CANR 24, 50; DLBY 80; INT CANR-24; MTCW 1

Phillips, Richard
See Dick, Philip K(indred)

Phillips, Robert (Schaeffer) 1938- **CLC 28**
See also CA 17-20R; CAAS 13; CANR 8; DLB 105

Phillips, Ward
See Lovecraft, H(oward) P(hillips)

Piccolo, Lucio 1901-1969 **CLC 13**
See also CA 97-100; DLB 114

Pickthall, Marjorie L(owry) C(hristie) 1883-1922 **TCLC 21**
See also CA 107; DLB 92

Pico della Mirandola, Giovanni 1463-1494 **LC 15**

Piercy, Marge 1936- **CLC 3, 6, 14, 18, 27, 62**
See also CA 21-24R; CAAS 1; CANR 13, 43, 66; DLB 120; MTCW 1

Piers, Robert
See Anthony, Piers

Pieyre de Mandiargues, Andre 1909-1991
See Mandiargues, Andre Pieyre de
See also CA 103; 136; CANR 22

Pilnyak, Boris **TCLC 23**
See also Vogau, Boris Andreyevich

Pincherle, Alberto 1907-1990 **CLC 11, 18; DAM NOV**
See also Moravia, Alberto
See also CA 25-28R; 132; CANR 33, 63; MTCW 1

Pinckney, Darryl 1953- **CLC 76**
See also BW 2; CA 143

Pindar 518B.C.-446B.C. **CMLC 12; PC 19**
See also DLB 176

Pineda, Cecile 1942- **CLC 39**
See also CA 118
Pinero, Arthur Wing 1855-1934 **TCLC 32;
DAM DRAM**
See also CA 110; 153; DLB 10
Pinero, Miguel (Antonio Gomez) 1946-1988
CLC 4, 55
See also CA 61-64; 125; CANR 29; HW
Pinget, Robert 1919-1997 **CLC 7, 13, 37**
See also CA 85-88; 160; DLB 83
Pink Floyd
See Barrett, (Roger) Syd; Gilmour, David; Mason, Nick; Waters, Roger; Wright, Rick
Pinkney, Edward 1802-1828 **NCLC 31**
Pinkwater, Daniel Manus 1941- **CLC 35**
See also Pinkwater, Manus
See also AAYA 1; CA 29-32R; CANR 12, 38;
CLR 4; JRDA; MAICYA; SAAS 3; SATA 46,
76
Pinkwater, Manus
See Pinkwater, Daniel Manus
See also SATA 8
Pinsky, Robert 1940-**CLC 9, 19, 38, 94; DAM
POET**
See also CA 29-32R; CAAS 4; CANR 58;
DLBY 82
Pinta, Harold
See Pinter, Harold
Pinter, Harold 1930-**CLC 1, 3, 6, 9, 11, 15, 27,
58, 73; DA; DAB; DAC; DAM DRAM,
MST; WLC**
See also CA 5-8R; CANR 33, 65; CDBLB 1960
to Present; DLB 13; MTCW 1
Piozzi, Hester Lynch (Thrale) 1741-1821
NCLC 57
See also DLB 104, 142
Pirandello, Luigi 1867-1936**TCLC 4, 29; DA;
DAB; DAC; DAM DRAM, MST; DC 5;
SSC 22; WLC**
See also CA 104; 153
Pirsig, Robert M(aynard) 1928-**CLC 4, 6, 73;
DAM POP**
See also CA 53-56; CANR 42, 74; MTCW 1;
SATA 39
Pisarev, Dmitry Ivanovich 1840-1868 **NCLC
25**
Pix, Mary (Griffith) 1666-1709 **LC 8**
See also DLB 80
Pixerecourt, (Rene Charles) Guilbert de 1773-
1844 **NCLC 39**
See also DLB 192
Plaatje, Sol(omon) T(shekisho) 1876-1932
TCLC 73; BLCS
See also BW 2; CA 141
Plaidy, Jean
See Hibbert, Eleanor Alice Burford
Planche, James Robinson 1796-1880**NCLC 42**
Plant, Robert 1948- **CLC 12**
Plante, David (Robert) 1940- **CLC 7, 23, 38;
DAM NOV**
See also CA 37-40R; CANR 12, 36, 58; DLBY
83; INT CANR-12; MTCW 1
Plath, Sylvia 1932-1963 **CLC 1, 2, 3, 5, 9, 11,
14, 17, 50, 51, 62, 111; DA; DAB; DAC;
DAM MST, POET; PC 1; WLC**
See also AAYA 13; CA 19-20; CANR 34; CAP
2; CDALB 1941-1968; DLB 5, 6, 152;
MTCW 1; SATA 96
Plato 428(?)B.C.-348(?)B.C. **CMLC 8; DA;
DAB; DAC; DAM MST; WLCS**
See also DLB 176
Platonov, Andrei **TCLC 14**
See also Klimentov, Andrei Platonovich

Platt, Kin 1911- **CLC 26**
See also AAYA 11; CA 17-20R; CANR 11;
JRDA; SAAS 17; SATA 21, 86
Plautus c. 251B.C.-184B.C. **CMLC 24; DC 6**
Plick et Plock
See Simenon, Georges (Jacques Christian)
Plimpton, George (Ames) 1927- **CLC 36**
See also AITN 1; CA 21-24R; CANR 32, 70;
DLB 185; MTCW 1; SATA 10
Pliny the Elder c. 23-79 **CMLC 23**
Plomer, William Charles Franklin 1903-1973
CLC 4, 8
See also CA 21-22; CANR 34; CAP 2; DLB
20, 162, 191; MTCW 1; SATA 24
Plowman, Piers
See Kavanagh, Patrick (Joseph)
Plum, J.
See Wodehouse, P(elham) G(renville)
Plumly, Stanley (Ross) 1939- **CLC 33**
See also CA 108; 110; DLB 5, 193; INT 110
Plumpe, Friedrich Wilhelm 1888-1931**T C L C
53**
See also CA 112
Po Chu-i 772-846 **CMLC 24**
Poe, Edgar Allan 1809-1849 **NCLC 1, 16, 55;
DA; DAB; DAC; DAM MST, POET; PC
1; SSC 1, 22; WLC**
See also AAYA 14; CDALB 1640-1865; DLB
3, 59, 73, 74; SATA 23
Poet of Titchfield Street, The
See Pound, Ezra (Weston Loomis)
Pohl, Frederik 1919- **CLC 18; SSC 25**
See also AAYA 24; CA 61-64; CAAS 1; CANR
11, 37; DLB 8; INT CANR-11; MTCW 1;
SATA 24
Poirier, Louis 1910-
See Gracq, Julien
See also CA 122; 126
Poitier, Sidney 1927- **CLC 26**
See also BW 1; CA 117
Polanski, Roman 1933- **CLC 16**
See also CA 77-80
Poliakoff, Stephen 1952- **CLC 38**
See also CA 106; DLB 13
Police, The
See Copeland, Stewart (Armstrong); Summers,
Andrew James; Sumner, Gordon Matthew
Polidori, John William 1795-1821 **NCLC 51**
See also DLB 116
Pollitt, Katha 1949- **CLC 28**
See also CA 120; 122; CANR 66; MTCW 1
Pollock, (Mary) Sharon 1936-**CLC 50; DAC;
DAM DRAM, MST**
See also CA 141; DLB 60
Polo, Marco 1254-1324 **CMLC 15**
Polonsky, Abraham (Lincoln) 1910- **CLC 92**
See also CA 104; DLB 26; INT 104
Polybius c. 200B.C.-c. 118B.C. **CMLC 17**
See also DLB 176
Pomerance, Bernard 1940- **CLC 13; DAM
DRAM**
See also CA 101; CANR 49
Ponge, Francis (Jean Gaston Alfred) 1899-1988
CLC 6, 18; DAM POET
See also CA 85-88; 126; CANR 40
Pontoppidan, Henrik 1857-1943 **TCLC 29**
See also CA 170
Poole, Josephine **CLC 17**
See also Helyar, Jane Penelope Josephine
See also SAAS 2; SATA 5
Popa, Vasko 1922-1991 **CLC 19**
See also CA 112; 148; DLB 181
Pope, Alexander 1688-1744 **LC 3; DA; DAB;**

DAC; DAM MST, POET; WLC
See also CDBLB 1660-1789; DLB 95, 101
Porter, Connie (Rose) 1959(?)- **CLC 70**
See also BW 2; CA 142; SATA 81
Porter, Gene(va Grace) Stratton 1863(?)-1924
TCLC 21
See also CA 112
Porter, Katherine Anne 1890-1980**CLC 1, 3, 7,
10, 13, 15, 27, 101; DA; DAB; DAC; DAM
MST, NOV; SSC 4, 31**
See also AITN 2; CA 1-4R; 101; CANR 1, 65;
DLB 4, 9, 102; DLBD 12; DLBY 80; MTCW
1; SATA 39; SATA-Obit 23
Porter, Peter (Neville Frederick) 1929-**CLC 5,
13, 33**
See also CA 85-88; DLB 40
Porter, William Sydney 1862-1910
See Henry, O.
See also CA 104; 131; CDALB 1865-1917; DA;
DAB; DAC; DAM MST; DLB 12, 78, 79;
MTCW 1; YABC 2
Portillo (y Pacheco), Jose Lopez
See Lopez Portillo (y Pacheco), Jose
Post, Melville Davisson 1869-1930 **TCLC 39**
See also CA 110
Potok, Chaim 1929- **CLC 2, 7, 14, 26, 112;
DAM NOV**
See also AAYA 15; AITN 1, 2; CA 17-20R;
CANR 19, 35, 64; DLB 28, 152; INT CANR-
19; MTCW 1; SATA 33
Potter, (Helen) Beatrix 1866-1943
See Webb, (Martha) Beatrice (Potter)
See also MAICYA
Potter, Dennis (Christopher George) 1935-1994
CLC 58, 86
See also CA 107; 145; CANR 33, 61; MTCW 1
Pound, Ezra (Weston Loomis) 1885-1972**CLC
1, 2, 3, 4, 5, 7, 10, 13, 18, 34, 48, 50, 112;
DA; DAB; DAC; DAM MST, POET; PC
4; WLC**
See also CA 5-8R; 37-40R; CANR 40; CDALB
1917-1929; DLB 4, 45, 63; DLBD 15;
MTCW 1
Povod, Reinaldo 1959-1994 **CLC 44**
See also CA 136; 146
Powell, Adam Clayton, Jr. 1908-1972**CLC 89;
BLC 3; DAM MULT**
See also BW 1; CA 102; 33-36R
Powell, Anthony (Dymoke) 1905-**CLC 1, 3, 7,
9, 10, 31**
See also CA 1-4R; CANR 1, 32, 62; CDBLB
1945-1960; DLB 15; MTCW 1
Powell, Dawn 1897-1965 **CLC 66**
See also CA 5-8R; DLBY 97
Powell, Padgett 1952- **CLC 34**
See also CA 126; CANR 63
Power, Susan 1961- **CLC 91**
Powers, J(ames) F(arl) 1917-**CLC 1, 4, 8, 57;
SSC 4**
See also CA 1-4R; CANR 2, 61; DLB 130;
MTCW 1
Powers, John J(ames) 1945-
See Powers, John R.
See also CA 69-72
Powers, John R. **CLC 66**
See also Powers, John J(ames)
Powers, Richard (S.) 1957- **CLC 93**
See also CA 148
Pownall, David 1938- **CLC 10**
See also CA 89-92; CAAS 18; CANR 49; DLB
14
Powys, John Cowper 1872-1963**CLC 7, 9, 15,
46**

Rakosi, Carl 1903-   **CLC 47**
  See also Rawley, Callman
  See also CAAS 5; DLB 193
Raleigh, Richard
  See Lovecraft, H(oward) P(hillips)
Raleigh, Sir Walter 1554(?)-1618 **LC 31, 39**
  See also CDBLB Before 1660; DLB 172
Rallentando, H. P.
  See Sayers, Dorothy L(eigh)
Ramal, Walter
  See de la Mare, Walter (John)
Ramana Maharshi 1879-1950   **TCLC 84**
Ramon, Juan
  See Jimenez (Mantecon), Juan Ramon
Ramos, Graciliano 1892-1953   **TCLC 32**
  See also CA 167
Rampersad, Arnold 1941-   **CLC 44**
  See also BW 2; CA 127; 133; DLB 111; INT
  133
Rampling, Anne
  See Rice, Anne
Ramsay, Allan 1684(?)-1758   **LC 29**
  See also DLB 95
Ramuz, Charles-Ferdinand 1878-1947**TCLC 33**
  See also CA 165
Rand, Ayn 1905-1982 **CLC 3, 30, 44, 79; DA;
  DAC; DAM MST, NOV, POP; WLC**
  See also AAYA 10; CA 13-16R; 105; CANR
  27, 73; MTCW 1
Randall, Dudley (Felker) 1914-**CLC 1; BLC 3;
  DAM MULT**
  See also BW 1; CA 25-28R; CANR 23; DLB
  41
Randall, Robert
  See Silverberg, Robert
Ranger, Ken
  See Creasey, John
Ransom, John Crowe 1888-1974 **CLC 2, 4, 5,
  11, 24; DAM POET**
  See also CA 5-8R; 49-52; CANR 6, 34; DLB
  45, 63; MTCW 1
Rao, Raja 1909-   **CLC 25, 56; DAM NOV**
  See also CA 73-76; CANR 51; MTCW 1
Raphael, Frederic (Michael) 1931-**CLC 2, 14**
  See also CA 1-4R; CANR 1; DLB 14
Ratcliffe, James P.
  See Mencken, H(enry) L(ouis)
Rathbone, Julian 1935-   **CLC 41**
  See also CA 101; CANR 34, 73
Rattigan, Terence (Mervyn) 1911-1977**CLC 7;
  DAM DRAM**
  See also CA 85-88; 73-76; CDBLB 1945-1960;
  DLB 13; MTCW 1
Ratushinskaya, Irina 1954-   **CLC 54**
  See also CA 129; CANR 68
Raven, Simon (Arthur Noel) 1927- **CLC 14**
  See also CA 81-84
Ravenna, Michael
  See Welty, Eudora
Rawley, Callman 1903-
  See Rakosi, Carl
  See also CA 21-24R; CANR 12, 32
Rawlings, Marjorie Kinnan 1896-1953**TCLC
  4**
  See also AAYA 20; CA 104; 137; DLB 9, 22,
  102; DLBD 17; JRDA; MAICYA; SATA 100;
  YABC 1
Ray, Satyajit 1921-1992   **CLC 16, 76; DAM
  MULT**
  See also CA 114; 137
Read, Herbert Edward 1893-1968   **CLC 4**
  See also CA 85-88; 25-28R; DLB 20, 149

Read, Piers Paul 1941-   **CLC 4, 10, 25**
  See also CA 21-24R; CANR 38; DLB 14; SATA
  21
Reade, Charles 1814-1884   **NCLC 2, 74**
  See also DLB 21
Reade, Hamish
  See Gray, Simon (James Holliday)
Reading, Peter 1946-   **CLC 47**
  See also CA 103; CANR 46; DLB 40
Reaney, James 1926-   **CLC 13; DAC; DAM
  MST**
  See also CA 41-44R; CAAS 15; CANR 42; DLB
  68; SATA 43
Rebreanu, Liviu 1885-1944   **TCLC 28**
  See also CA 165
Rechy, John (Francisco) 1934- **CLC 1, 7, 14,
  18, 107; DAM MULT; HLC**
  See also CA 5-8R; CAAS 4; CANR 6, 32, 64;
  DLB 122; DLBY 82; HW; INT CANR-6
Redcam, Tom 1870-1933   **TCLC 25**
Reddin, Keith   **CLC 67**
Redgrove, Peter (William) 1932- **CLC 6, 41**
  See also CA 1-4R; CANR 3, 39; DLB 40
Redmon, Anne   **CLC 22**
  See Nightingale, Anne Redmon
  See also DLBY 86
Reed, Eliot
  See Ambler, Eric
Reed, Ishmael 1938-**CLC 2, 3, 5, 6, 13, 32, 60;
  BLC 3; DAM MULT**
  See also BW 2; CA 21-24R; CANR 25, 48, 74;
  DLB 2, 5, 33, 169; DLBD 8; MTCW 1
Reed, John (Silas) 1887-1920   **TCLC 9**
  See also CA 106
Reed, Lou   **CLC 21**
  See also Firbank, Louis
Reeve, Clara 1729-1807   **NCLC 19**
  See also DLB 39
Reich, Wilhelm 1897-1957   **TCLC 57**
Reid, Christopher (John) 1949-   **CLC 33**
  See also CA 140; DLB 40
Reid, Desmond
  See Moorcock, Michael (John)
Reid Banks, Lynne 1929-
  See Banks, Lynne Reid
  See also CA 1-4R; CANR 6, 22, 38; CLR 24;
  JRDA; MAICYA; SATA 22, 75
Reilly, William K.
  See Creasey, John
Reiner, Max
  See Caldwell, (Janet Miriam) Taylor (Holland)
Reis, Ricardo
  See Pessoa, Fernando (Antonio Nogueira)
Remarque, Erich Maria 1898-1970 **CLC 21;
  DA; DAB; DAC; DAM MST, NOV**
  See also AAYA 27; CA 77-80; 29-32R; DLB
  56; MTCW 1
Remizov, A.
  See Remizov, Aleksei (Mikhailovich)
Remizov, A. M.
  See Remizov, Aleksei (Mikhailovich)
Remizov, Aleksei (Mikhailovich) 1877-1957
  TCLC 27
  See also CA 125; 133
Renan, Joseph Ernest 1823-1892   **NCLC 26**
Renard, Jules 1864-1910   **TCLC 17**
  See also CA 117
Renault, Mary   **CLC 3, 11, 17**
  See also Challans, Mary
  See also DLBY 83
Rendell, Ruth (Barbara) 1930- **CLC 28, 48;
  DAM POP**
  See also Vine, Barbara

  See also CA 109; CANR 32, 52, 74; DLB 87;
  INT CANR-32; MTCW 1
Renoir, Jean 1894-1979   **CLC 20**
  See also CA 129; 85-88
Resnais, Alain 1922-   **CLC 16**
Reverdy, Pierre 1889-1960   **CLC 53**
  See also CA 97-100; 89-92
Rexroth, Kenneth 1905-1982 **CLC 1, 2, 6, 11,
  22, 49, 112; DAM POET; PC 20**
  See also CA 5-8R; 107; CANR 14, 34, 63;
  CDALB 1941-1968; DLB 16, 48, 165;
  DLBY 82; INT CANR-14; MTCW 1
Reyes, Alfonso 1889-1959   **TCLC 33**
  See also CA 131; HW
Reyes y Basoalto, Ricardo Eliecer Neftali
  See Neruda, Pablo
Reymont, Wladyslaw (Stanislaw) 1868(?)-1925
  TCLC 5
  See also CA 104
Reynolds, Jonathan 1942-   **CLC 6, 38**
  See also CA 65-68; CANR 28
Reynolds, Joshua 1723-1792   **LC 15**
  See also DLB 104
Reynolds, Michael Shane 1937-   **CLC 44**
  See also CA 65-68; CANR 9
Reznikoff, Charles 1894-1976   **CLC 9**
  See also CA 33-36; 61-64; CAP 2; DLB 28, 45
Rezzori (d'Arezzo), Gregor von 1914-1998
  CLC 25
  See also CA 122; 136; 167
Rhine, Richard
  See Silverstein, Alvin
Rhodes, Eugene Manlove 1869-1934**TCLC 53**
Rhodius, Apollonius c. 3rd cent. B.C.- **CMLC
  28**
  See also DLB 176
R'hoone
  See Balzac, Honore de
Rhys, Jean 1890(?)-1979 **CLC 2, 4, 6, 14, 19,
  51; DAM NOV; SSC 21**
  See also CA 25-28R; 85-88; CANR 35, 62;
  CDBLB 1945-1960; DLB 36, 117, 162;
  MTCW 1
Ribeiro, Darcy 1922-1997   **CLC 34**
  See also CA 33-36R; 156
Ribeiro, Joao Ubaldo (Osorio Pimentel) 1941-
  CLC 10, 67
  See also CA 81-84
Ribman, Ronald (Burt) 1932-   **CLC 7**
  See also CA 21-24R; CANR 46
Ricci, Nino 1959-   **CLC 70**
  See also CA 137
Rice, Anne 1941-   **CLC 41; DAM POP**
  See also AAYA 9; BEST 89:2; CA 65-68; CANR
  12, 36, 53, 74
Rice, Elmer (Leopold) 1892-1967 **CLC 7, 49;
  DAM DRAM**
  See also CA 21-22; 25-28R; CAP 2; DLB 4, 7;
  MTCW 1
Rice, Tim(othy Miles Bindon) 1944- **CLC 21**
  See also CA 103; CANR 46
Rich, Adrienne (Cecile) 1929-**CLC 3, 6, 7, 11,
  18, 36, 73, 76; DAM POET; PC 5**
  See also CA 9-12R; CANR 20, 53, 74; DLB 5,
  67; MTCW 1
Rich, Barbara
  See Graves, Robert (von Ranke)
Rich, Robert
  See Trumbo, Dalton
Richard, Keith   **CLC 17**
  See also Richards, Keith
Richards, David Adams 1950- **CLC 59; DAC**
  See also CA 93-96; CANR 60; DLB 53

Richards, I(vor) A(rmstrong) 1893-1979 **C L C 14, 24**
    See also CA 41-44R; 89-92; CANR 34, 74; DLB 27
Richards, Keith 1943-
    See Richard, Keith
    See also CA 107
Richardson, Anne
    See Roiphe, Anne (Richardson)
Richardson, Dorothy Miller 1873-1957 **TCLC 3**
    See also CA 104; DLB 36
Richardson, Ethel Florence (Lindesay) 1870-1946
    See Richardson, Henry Handel
    See also CA 105
Richardson, Henry Handel   **TCLC 4**
    See also Richardson, Ethel Florence (Lindesay)
    See also DLB 197
Richardson, John 1796-1852 **NCLC 55; DAC**
    See also DLB 99
Richardson, Samuel 1689-1761 **LC 1, 44; DA; DAB; DAC; DAM MST, NOV; WLC**
    See also CDBLB 1660-1789; DLB 39
Richler, Mordecai 1931- **CLC 3, 5, 9, 13, 18, 46, 70; DAC; DAM MST, NOV**
    See also AITN 1; CA 65-68; CANR 31, 62; CLR 17; DLB 53; MAICYA; MTCW 1; SATA 44, 98; SATA-Brief 27
Richter, Conrad (Michael) 1890-1968 **CLC 30**
    See also AAYA 21; CA 5-8R; 25-28R; CANR 23; DLB 9; MTCW 1; SATA 3
Ricostranza, Tom
    See Ellis, Trey
Riddell, Charlotte 1832-1906   **TCLC 40**
    See also CA 165; DLB 156
Riding, Laura   **CLC 3, 7**
    See also Jackson, Laura (Riding)
Riefenstahl, Berta Helene Amalia 1902-
    See Riefenstahl, Leni
    See also CA 108
Riefenstahl, Leni   **CLC 16**
    See also Riefenstahl, Berta Helene Amalia
Riffe, Ernest
    See Bergman, (Ernst) Ingmar
Riggs, (Rolla) Lynn 1899-1954   **TCLC 56; DAM MULT**
    See also CA 144; DLB 175; NNAL
Riis, Jacob A(ugust) 1849-1914   **TCLC 80**
    See also CA 113; 168; DLB 23
Riley, James Whitcomb 1849-1916 **TCLC 51; DAM POET**
    See also CA 118; 137; MAICYA; SATA 17
Riley, Tex
    See Creasey, John
Rilke, Rainer Maria 1875-1926 **TCLC 1, 6, 19; DAM POET; PC 2**
    See also CA 104; 132; CANR 62; DLB 81; MTCW 1
Rimbaud, (Jean Nicolas) Arthur 1854-1891 **NCLC 4, 35; DA; DAB; DAC; DAM MST, POET; PC 3; WLC**
Rinehart, Mary Roberts 1876-1958 **TCLC 52**
    See also CA 108; 166
Ringmaster, The
    See Mencken, H(enry) L(ouis)
Ringwood, Gwen(dolyn Margaret) Pharis 1910-1984   **CLC 48**
    See also CA 148; 112; DLB 88
Rio, Michel 19(?)-   **CLC 43**
Ritsos, Giannes
    See Ritsos, Yannis
Ritsos, Yannis 1909-1990   **CLC 6, 13, 31**

    See also CA 77-80; 133; CANR 39, 61; MTCW 1
Ritter, Erika 1948(?)-   **CLC 52**
Rivera, Jose Eustasio 1889-1928   **TCLC 35**
    See also CA 162; HW
Rivers, Conrad Kent 1933-1968   **CLC 1**
    See also BW 1; CA 85-88; DLB 41
Rivers, Elfrida
    See Bradley, Marion Zimmer
Riverside, John
    See Heinlein, Robert A(nson)
Rizal, Jose 1861-1896   **NCLC 27**
Roa Bastos, Augusto (Antonio) 1917- **CLC 45; DAM MULT; HLC**
    See also CA 131; DLB 113; HW
Robbe-Grillet, Alain 1922- **CLC 1, 2, 4, 6, 8, 10, 14, 43**
    See also CA 9-12R; CANR 33, 65; DLB 83; MTCW 1
Robbins, Harold 1916-1997   **CLC 5; DAM NOV**
    See also CA 73-76; 162; CANR 26, 54; MTCW 1
Robbins, Thomas Eugene 1936-
    See Robbins, Tom
    See also CA 81-84; CANR 29, 59; DAM NOV, POP; MTCW 1
Robbins, Tom   **CLC 9, 32, 64**
    See also Robbins, Thomas Eugene
    See also BEST 90:3; DLBY 80
Robbins, Trina 1938-   **CLC 21**
    See also CA 128
Roberts, Charles G(eorge) D(ouglas) 1860-1943 **TCLC 8**
    See also CA 105; CLR 33; DLB 92; SATA 88; SATA-Brief 29
Roberts, Elizabeth Madox 1886-1941 **TCLC 68**
    See also CA 111; 166; DLB 9, 54, 102; SATA 33; SATA-Brief 27
Roberts, Kate 1891-1985   **CLC 15**
    See also CA 107; 116
Roberts, Keith (John Kingston) 1935- **CLC 14**
    See also CA 25-28R; CANR 46
Roberts, Kenneth (Lewis) 1885-1957 **TCLC 23**
    See also CA 109; DLB 9
Roberts, Michele (B.) 1949-   **CLC 48**
    See also CA 115; CANR 58
Robertson, Ellis
    See Ellison, Harlan (Jay); Silverberg, Robert
Robertson, Thomas William 1829-1871 **NCLC 35; DAM DRAM**
Robeson, Kenneth
    See Dent, Lester
Robinson, Edwin Arlington 1869-1935 **TCLC 5; DA; DAC; DAM MST, POET; PC 1**
    See also CA 104; 133; CDALB 1865-1917; DLB 54; MTCW 1
Robinson, Henry Crabb 1775-1867 **NCLC 15**
    See also DLB 107
Robinson, Jill 1936-   **CLC 10**
    See also CA 102; INT 102
Robinson, Kim Stanley 1952-   **CLC 34**
    See also AAYA 26; CA 126
Robinson, Lloyd
    See Silverberg, Robert
Robinson, Marilynne 1944-   **CLC 25**
    See also CA 116
Robinson, Smokey   **CLC 21**
    See also Robinson, William, Jr.
Robinson, William, Jr. 1940-
    See Robinson, Smokey
    See also CA 116

Robison, Mary 1949-   **CLC 42, 98**
    See also CA 113; 116; DLB 130; INT 116
Rod, Edouard 1857-1910   **TCLC 52**
Roddenberry, Eugene Wesley 1921-1991
    See Roddenberry, Gene
    See also CA 110; 135; CANR 37; SATA 45; SATA-Obit 69
Roddenberry, Gene   **CLC 17**
    See also Roddenberry, Eugene Wesley
    See also AAYA 5; SATA-Obit 69
Rodgers, Mary 1931-   **CLC 12**
    See also CA 49-52; CANR 8, 55; CLR 20; INT CANR-8; JRDA; MAICYA; SATA 8
Rodgers, W(illiam) R(obert) 1909-1969 **CLC 7**
    See also CA 85-88; DLB 20
Rodman, Eric
    See Silverberg, Robert
Rodman, Howard 1920(?)-1985   **CLC 65**
    See also CA 118
Rodman, Maia
    See Wojciechowska, Maia (Teresa)
Rodriguez, Claudio 1934-   **CLC 10**
    See also DLB 134
Roelvaag, O(le) E(dvart) 1876-1931 **TCLC 17**
    See also CA 117; DLB 9
Roethke, Theodore (Huebner) 1908-1963 **CLC 1, 3, 8, 11, 19, 46, 101; DAM POET; PC 15**
    See also CA 81-84; CABS 2; CDALB 1941-1968; DLB 5; MTCW 1
Rogers, Samuel 1763-1855   **NCLC 69**
    See also DLB 93
Rogers, Thomas Hunton 1927-   **CLC 57**
    See also CA 89-92; INT 89-92
Rogers, Will(iam Penn Adair) 1879-1935 **TCLC 8, 71; DAM MULT**
    See also CA 105; 144; DLB 11; NNAL
Rogin, Gilbert 1929-   **CLC 18**
    See also CA 65-68; CANR 15
Rohan, Koda   **TCLC 22**
    See also Koda Shigeyuki
Rohlfs, Anna Katharine Green
    See Green, Anna Katharine
Rohmer, Eric   **CLC 16**
    See also Scherer, Jean-Marie Maurice
Rohmer, Sax   **TCLC 28**
    See also Ward, Arthur Henry Sarsfield
    See also DLB 70
Roiphe, Anne (Richardson) 1935-   **CLC 3, 9**
    See also CA 89-92; CANR 45, 73; DLBY 80; INT 89-92
Rojas, Fernando de 1465-1541   **LC 23**
Rolfe, Frederick (William Serafino Austin Lewis Mary) 1860-1913   **TCLC 12**
    See also CA 107; DLB 34, 156
Rolland, Romain 1866-1944   **TCLC 23**
    See also CA 118; DLB 65
Rolle, Richard c. 1300-c. 1349   **CMLC 21**
    See also DLB 146
Rolvaag, O(le) E(dvart)
    See Roelvaag, O(le) E(dvart)
Romain Arnaud, Saint
    See Aragon, Louis
Romains, Jules 1885-1972   **CLC 7**
    See also CA 85-88; CANR 34; DLB 65; MTCW 1
Romero, Jose Ruben 1890-1952   **TCLC 14**
    See also CA 114; 131; HW
Ronsard, Pierre de 1524-1585   **LC 6; PC 11**
Rooke, Leon 1934- **CLC 25, 34; DAM POP**
    See also CA 25-28R; CANR 23, 53
Roosevelt, Theodore 1858-1919   **TCLC 69**
    See also CA 115; 170; DLB 47, 186
Roper, William 1498-1578   **LC 10**

Roquelaure, A. N.
See Rice, Anne
Rosa, Joao Guimaraes 1908-1967   **CLC 23**
See also CA 89-92; DLB 113
Rose, Wendy 1948-**CLC 85; DAM MULT; PC 13**
See also CA 53-56; CANR 5, 51; DLB 175; NNAL; SATA 12
Rosen, R. D.
See Rosen, Richard (Dean)
Rosen, Richard (Dean) 1949-   **CLC 39**
See also CA 77-80; CANR 62; INT CANR-30
Rosenberg, Isaac 1890-1918   **TCLC 12**
See also CA 107; DLB 20
Rosenblatt, Joe   **CLC 15**
See also Rosenblatt, Joseph
Rosenblatt, Joseph 1933-
See Rosenblatt, Joe
See also CA 89-92; INT 89-92
Rosenfeld, Samuel
See Tzara, Tristan
Rosenstock, Sami
See Tzara, Tristan
Rosenstock, Samuel
See Tzara, Tristan
Rosenthal, M(acha) L(ouis) 1917-1996 **C L C 28**
See also CA 1-4R; 152; CAAS 6; CANR 4, 51; DLB 5; SATA 59
Ross, Barnaby
See Dannay, Frederic
Ross, Bernard L.
See Follett, Ken(neth Martin)
Ross, J. H.
See Lawrence, T(homas) E(dward)
Ross, John Hume
See Lawrence, T(homas) E(dward)
Ross, Martin
See Martin, Violet Florence
See also DLB 135
Ross, (James) Sinclair 1908- **CLC 13; DAC; DAM MST; SSC 24**
See also CA 73-76; DLB 88
Rossetti, Christina (Georgina) 1830-1894
NCLC 2, 50, 66; DA; DAB; DAC; DAM MST, POET; PC 7; WLC
See also DLB 35, 163; MAICYA; SATA 20
Rossetti, Dante Gabriel 1828-1882 **NCLC 4; DA; DAB; DAC; DAM MST, POET; WLC**
See also CDBLB 1832-1890; DLB 35
Rossner, Judith (Perelman) 1935-**CLC 6, 9, 29**
See also AITN 2; BEST 90:3; CA 17-20R; CANR 18, 51, 73; DLB 6; INT CANR-18; MTCW 1
Rostand, Edmond (Eugene Alexis) 1868-1918
TCLC 6, 37; DA; DAB; DAC; DAM DRAM, MST
See also CA 104; 126; DLB 192; MTCW 1
Roth, Henry 1906-1995   **CLC 2, 6, 11, 104**
See also CA 11-12; 149; CANR 38, 63; CAP 1; DLB 28; MTCW 1
Roth, Philip (Milton) 1933-**CLC 1, 2, 3, 4, 6, 9, 15, 22, 31, 47, 66, 86; DA; DAB; DAC; DAM MST, NOV, POP; SSC 26; WLC**
See also BEST 90:3; CA 1-4R; CANR 1, 22, 36, 55; CDALB 1968-1988; DLB 2, 28, 173; DLBY 82; MTCW 1
Rothenberg, Jerome 1931-   **CLC 6, 57**
See also CA 45-48; CANR 1; DLB 5, 193
Roumain, Jacques (Jean Baptiste) 1907-1944
TCLC 19; BLC 3; DAM MULT
See also BW 1; CA 117; 125
Rourke, Constance (Mayfield) 1885-1941

TCLC 12
See also CA 107; YABC 1
Rousseau, Jean-Baptiste 1671-1741   **LC 9**
Rousseau, Jean-Jacques 1712-1778**LC 14, 36; DA; DAB; DAC; DAM MST; WLC**
Roussel, Raymond 1877-1933   **TCLC 20**
See also CA 117
Rovit, Earl (Herbert) 1927-   **CLC 7**
See also CA 5-8R; CANR 12
Rowe, Elizabeth Singer 1674-1737   **LC 44**
See also DLB 39, 95
Rowe, Nicholas 1674-1718   **LC 8**
See also DLB 84
Rowley, Ames Dorrance
See Lovecraft, H(oward) P(hillips)
Rowson, Susanna Haswell 1762(?)-1824
NCLC 5, 69
See also DLB 37, 200
Roy, Arundhati 1960(?)-   **CLC 109**
See also CA 163; DLBY 97
Roy, Gabrielle 1909-1983 **CLC 10, 14; DAB; DAC; DAM MST**
See also CA 53-56; 110; CANR 5, 61; DLB 68; MTCW 1
Royko, Mike 1932-1997   **CLC 109**
See also CA 89-92; 157; CANR 26
Rozewicz, Tadeusz 1921-   **CLC 9, 23; DAM POET**
See also CA 108; CANR 36, 66; MTCW 1
Ruark, Gibbons 1941-   **CLC 3**
See also CA 33-36R; CAAS 23; CANR 14, 31, 57; DLB 120
Rubens, Bernice (Ruth) 1923-   **CLC 19, 31**
See also CA 25-28R; CANR 33, 65; DLB 14; MTCW 1
Rubin, Harold
See Robbins, Harold
Rudkin, (James) David 1936-   **CLC 14**
See also CA 89-92; DLB 13
Rudnik, Raphael 1933-   **CLC 7**
See also CA 29-32R
Ruffian, M.
See Hasek, Jaroslav (Matej Frantisek)
Ruiz, Jose Martinez   **CLC 11**
See also Martinez Ruiz, Jose
Rukeyser, Muriel 1913-1980**CLC 6, 10, 15, 27; DAM POET; PC 12**
See also CA 5-8R; 93-96; CANR 26, 60; DLB 48; MTCW 1; SATA-Obit 22
Rule, Jane (Vance) 1931-   **CLC 27**
See also CA 25-28R; CAAS 18; CANR 12; DLB 60
Rulfo, Juan 1918-1986   **CLC 8, 80; DAM MULT; HLC; SSC 25**
See also CA 85-88; 118; CANR 26; DLB 113; HW; MTCW 1
Rumi, Jalal al-Din 1297-1373   **CMLC 20**
Runeberg, Johan 1804-1877   **NCLC 41**
Runyon, (Alfred) Damon 1884(?)-1946**T C L C 10**
See also CA 107; 165; DLB 11, 86, 171
Rush, Norman 1933-   **CLC 44**
See also CA 121; 126; INT 126
Rushdie, (Ahmed) Salman 1947- **CLC 23, 31, 55, 100; DAB; DAC; DAM MST, NOV, POP; WLCS**
See also BEST 89:3; CA 108; 111; CANR 33, 56; DLB 194; INT 111; MTCW 1
Rushforth, Peter (Scott) 1945-   **CLC 19**
See also CA 101
Ruskin, John 1819-1900   **TCLC 63**
See also CA 114; 129; CDBLB 1832-1890; DLB 55, 163, 190; SATA 24

Russ, Joanna 1937-   **CLC 15**
See also CANR 11, 31, 65; DLB 8; MTCW 1
Russell, George William 1867-1935
See Baker, Jean H.
See also CA 104; 153; CDBLB 1890-1914; DAM POET
Russell, (Henry) Ken(neth Alfred) 1927-**C L C 16**
See also CA 105
Russell, William Martin 1947-   **CLC 60**
See also CA 164
Rutherford, Mark   **TCLC 25**
See also White, William Hale
See also DLB 18
Ruyslinck, Ward 1929-   **CLC 14**
See also Belser, Reimond Karel Maria de
Ryan, Cornelius (John) 1920-1974   **CLC 7**
See also CA 69-72; 53-56; CANR 38
Ryan, Michael 1946-   **CLC 65**
See also CA 49-52; DLBY 82
Ryan, Tim
See Dent, Lester
Rybakov, Anatoli (Naumovich) 1911-**CLC 23, 53**
See also CA 126; 135; SATA 79
Ryder, Jonathan
See Ludlum, Robert
Ryga, George 1932-1987**CLC 14; DAC; DAM MST**
See also CA 101; 124; CANR 43; DLB 60
S. H.
See Hartmann, Sadakichi
S. S.
See Sassoon, Siegfried (Lorraine)
Saba, Umberto 1883-1957   **TCLC 33**
See also CA 144; DLB 114
Sabatini, Rafael 1875-1950   **TCLC 47**
See also CA 162
Sabato, Ernesto (R.) 1911-**CLC 10, 23; DAM MULT; HLC**
See also CA 97-100; CANR 32, 65; DLB 145; HW; MTCW 1
Sa-Carniero, Mario de 1890-1916 **TCLC 83**
Sacastru, Martin
See Bioy Casares, Adolfo
Sacher-Masoch, Leopold von 1836(?)-1895
NCLC 31
Sachs, Marilyn (Stickle) 1927-   **CLC 35**
See also AAYA 2; CA 17-20R; CANR 13, 47; CLR 2; JRDA; MAICYA; SAAS 2; SATA 3, 68
Sachs, Nelly 1891-1970   **CLC 14, 98**
See also CA 17-18; 25-28R; CAP 2
Sackler, Howard (Oliver) 1929-1982 **CLC 14**
See also CA 61-64; 108; CANR 30; DLB 7
Sacks, Oliver (Wolf) 1933-   **CLC 67**
See also CA 53-56; CANR 28, 50; INT CANR-28; MTCW 1
Sadakichi
See Hartmann, Sadakichi
Sade, Donatien Alphonse Francois, Comte de 1740-1814   **NCLC 47**
Sadoff, Ira 1945-   **CLC 9**
See also CA 53-56; CANR 5, 21; DLB 120
Saetone
See Camus, Albert
Safire, William 1929-   **CLC 10**
See also CA 17-20R; CANR 31, 54
Sagan, Carl (Edward) 1934-1996**CLC 30, 112**
See also AAYA 2; CA 25-28R; 155; CANR 11, 36, 74; MTCW 1; SATA 58; SATA-Obit 94
Sagan, Francoise   **CLC 3, 6, 9, 17, 36**
See also Quoirez, Francoise

See also DLB 83

Sahgal, Nayantara (Pandit) 1927-   **CLC 41**
See also CA 9-12R; CANR 11

Saint, H(arry) F. 1941-   **CLC 50**
See also CA 127

St. Aubin de Teran, Lisa 1953-
See Teran, Lisa St. Aubin de
See also CA 118; 126; INT 126

Saint Birgitta of Sweden c. 1303-1373 **C M L C 24**

Sainte-Beuve, Charles Augustin 1804-1869
NCLC 5

Saint-Exupery, Antoine (Jean Baptiste Marie Roger) de 1900-1944 **TCLC 2, 56; DAM NOV; WLC**
See also CA 108; 132; CLR 10; DLB 72; MAICYA; MTCW 1; SATA 20

St. John, David
See Hunt, E(verette) Howard, (Jr.)

Saint-John Perse
See Leger, (Marie-Rene Auguste) Alexis Saint-Leger

Saintsbury, George (Edward Bateman) 1845-1933   **TCLC 31**
See also CA 160; DLB 57, 149

Sait Faik   **TCLC 23**
See also Abasiyanik, Sait Faik

Saki   **TCLC 3; SSC 12**
See also Munro, H(ector) H(ugh)

Sala, George Augustus   **NCLC 46**

Salama, Hannu 1936-   **CLC 18**

Salamanca, J(ack) R(ichard) 1922- **CLC 4, 15**
See also CA 25-28R

Sale, J. Kirkpatrick
See Sale, Kirkpatrick

Sale, Kirkpatrick 1937-   **CLC 68**
See also CA 13-16R; CANR 10

Salinas, Luis Omar 1937-   **CLC 90; DAM MULT; HLC**
See also CA 131; DLB 82; HW

Salinas (y Serrano), Pedro 1891(?)-1951
TCLC 17
See also CA 117; DLB 134

Salinger, J(erome) D(avid) 1919- **CLC 1, 3, 8, 12, 55, 56; DA; DAB; DAC; DAM MST, NOV, POP; SSC 2, 28; WLC**
See also AAYA 2; CA 5-8R; CANR 39; CDALB 1941-1968; CLR 18; DLB 2, 102, 173; MAICYA; MTCW 1; SATA 67

Salisbury, John
See Caute, (John) David

Salter, James 1925-   **CLC 7, 52, 59**
See also CA 73-76; DLB 130

Saltus, Edgar (Everton) 1855-1921 **TCLC 8**
See also CA 105; DLB 202

Saltykov, Mikhail Evgrafovich 1826-1889
NCLC 16

Samarakis, Antonis 1919-   **CLC 5**
See also CA 25-28R; CAAS 16; CANR 36

Sanchez, Florencio 1875-1910   **TCLC 37**
See also CA 153; HW

Sanchez, Luis Rafael 1936-   **CLC 23**
See also CA 128; DLB 145; HW

Sanchez, Sonia 1934-   **CLC 5, 116; BLC 3; DAM MULT; PC 9**
See also BW 2; CA 33-36R; CANR 24, 49, 74; CLR 18; DLB 41; DLBD 8; MAICYA; MTCW 1; SATA 22

Sand, George 1804-1876 NCLC **2, 42, 57; DA; DAB; DAC; DAM MST, NOV; WLC**
See also DLB 119, 192

Sandburg, Carl (August) 1878-1967 CLC **1, 4, 10, 15, 35; DA; DAB; DAC; DAM MST,**

POET; **PC 2; WLC**
See also AAYA 24; CA 5-8R; 25-28R; CANR 35; CDALB 1865-1917; DLB 17, 54; MAICYA; MTCW 1; SATA 8

Sandburg, Charles
See Sandburg, Carl (August)

Sandburg, Charles A.
See Sandburg, Carl (August)

Sanders, (James) Ed(ward) 1939-   **CLC 53**
See also CA 13-16R; CAAS 21; CANR 13, 44; DLB 16

Sanders, Lawrence 1920-1998 CLC **41; DAM POP**
See also BEST 89:4; CA 81-84; 165; CANR 33, 62; MTCW 1

Sanders, Noah
See Blount, Roy (Alton), Jr.

Sanders, Winston P.
See Anderson, Poul (William)

Sandoz, Mari(e Susette) 1896-1966   **CLC 28**
See also CA 1-4R; 25-28R; CANR 17, 64; DLB 9; MTCW 1; SATA 5

Saner, Reg(inald Anthony) 1931-   **CLC 9**
See also CA 65-68

Sannazaro, Jacopo 1456(?)-1530   **LC 8**

Sansom, William 1912-1976 **CLC 2, 6; DAM NOV; SSC 21**
See also CA 5-8R; 65-68; CANR 42; DLB 139; MTCW 1

Santayana, George 1863-1952   **TCLC 40**
See also CA 115; DLB 54, 71; DLBD 13

Santiago, Danny   **CLC 33**
See also James, Daniel (Lewis)
See also DLB 122

Santmyer, Helen Hoover 1895-1986   **CLC 33**
See also CA 1-4R; 118; CANR 15, 33; DLBY 84; MTCW 1

Santoka, Taneda 1882-1940   **TCLC 72**

Santos, Bienvenido N(uqui) 1911-1996 **C L C 22; DAM MULT**
See also CA 101; 151; CANR 19, 46

Sapper   **TCLC 44**
See also McNeile, Herman Cyril

Sapphire
See Sapphire, Brenda

Sapphire, Brenda 1950-   **CLC 99**

Sappho fl. 6th cent. B.C.-   **CMLC 3; DAM POET; PC 5**
See also DLB 176

Sarduy, Severo 1937-1993   **CLC 6, 97**
See also CA 89-92; 142; CANR 58; DLB 113; HW

Sargeson, Frank 1903-1982   **CLC 31**
See also CA 25-28R; 106; CANR 38

Sarmiento, Felix Ruben Garcia
See Dario, Ruben

Saro-Wiwa, Ken(ule Beeson) 1941-1995 **C L C 114**
See also BW 2; CA 142; 150; CANR 60; DLB 157

Saroyan, William 1908-1981 CLC **1, 8, 10, 29, 34, 56; DA; DAB; DAC; DAM DRAM, MST, NOV; SSC 21; WLC**
See also CA 5-8R; 103; CANR 30; DLB 7, 9, 86; DLBY 81; MTCW 1; SATA 23; SATA-Obit 24

Sarraute, Nathalie 1900- CLC **1, 2, 4, 8, 10, 31, 80**
See also CA 9-12R; CANR 23, 66; DLB 83; MTCW 1

Sarton, (Eleanor) May 1912-1995 CLC **4, 14, 49, 91; DAM POET**
See also CA 1-4R; 149; CANR 1, 34, 55; DLB

48; DLBY 81; INT CANR-34; MTCW 1; SATA 36; SATA-Obit 86

Sartre, Jean-Paul 1905-1980 CLC **1, 4, 7, 9, 13, 18, 24, 44, 50, 52; DA; DAB; DAC; DAM DRAM, MST, NOV; DC 3; SSC 32; WLC**
See also CA 9-12R; 97-100; CANR 21; DLB 72; MTCW 1

Sassoon, Siegfried (Lorraine) 1886-1967 C L C 36; DAB; DAM MST, NOV, POET; PC 12
See also CA 104; 25-28R; CANR 36; DLB 20, 191; DLBD 18; MTCW 1

Satterfield, Charles
See Pohl, Frederik

Saul, John (W. III) 1942- CLC **46; DAM NOV, POP**
See also AAYA 10; BEST 90:4; CA 81-84; CANR 16, 40; SATA 98

Saunders, Caleb
See Heinlein, Robert A(nson)

Saura (Atares), Carlos 1932-   **CLC 20**
See also CA 114; 131; HW

Sauser-Hall, Frederic 1887-1961   **CLC 18**
See also Cendrars, Blaise
See also CA 102; 93-96; CANR 36, 62; MTCW 1

Saussure, Ferdinand de 1857-1913 **TCLC 49**

Savage, Catharine
See Brosman, Catharine Savage

Savage, Thomas 1915-   **CLC 40**
See also CA 126; 132; CAAS 15; INT 132

Savan, Glenn 19(?)-   **CLC 50**

Sayers, Dorothy L(eigh) 1893-1957 **TCLC 2, 15; DAM POP**
See also CA 104; 119; CANR 60; CDBLB 1914-1945; DLB 10, 36, 77, 100; MTCW 1

Sayers, Valerie 1952-   **CLC 50**
See also CA 134; CANR 61

Sayles, John (Thomas) 1950-   **CLC 7, 10, 14**
See also CA 57-60; CANR 41; DLB 44

Scammell, Michael 1935-   **CLC 34**
See also CA 156

Scannell, Vernon 1922-   **CLC 49**
See also CA 5-8R; CANR 8, 24, 57; DLB 27; SATA 59

Scarlett, Susan
See Streatfeild, (Mary) Noel

Schaeffer, Susan Fromberg 1941- CLC **6, 11, 22**
See also CA 49-52; CANR 18, 65; DLB 28; MTCW 1; SATA 22

Schary, Jill
See Robinson, Jill

Schell, Jonathan 1943-   **CLC 35**
See also CA 73-76; CANR 12

Schelling, Friedrich Wilhelm Joseph von 1775-1854   **NCLC 30**
See also DLB 90

Schendel, Arthur van 1874-1946   **TCLC 56**

Scherer, Jean-Marie Maurice 1920-
See Rohmer, Eric
See also CA 110

Schevill, James (Erwin) 1920-   **CLC 7**
See also CA 5-8R; CAAS 12

Schiller, Friedrich 1759-1805 **NCLC 39, 69; DAM DRAM**
See also DLB 94

Schisgal, Murray (Joseph) 1926-   **CLC 6**
See also CA 21-24R; CANR 48

Schlee, Ann 1934-   **CLC 35**
See also CA 101; CANR 29; SATA 44; SATA-Brief 36

Schlegel, August Wilhelm von 1767-1845
NCLC 15

See also DLB 94

Schlegel, Friedrich 1772-1829 **NCLC 45**
See also DLB 90

Schlegel, Johann Elias (von) 1719(?)-1749**L C 5**

Schlesinger, Arthur M(eier), Jr. 1917-**CLC 84**
See also AITN 1; CA 1-4R; CANR 1, 28, 58;
DLB 17; INT CANR-28; MTCW 1; SATA
61

Schmidt, Arno (Otto) 1914-1979 **CLC 56**
See also CA 128; 109; DLB 69

Schmitz, Aron Hector 1861-1928
See Svevo, Italo
See also CA 104; 122; MTCW 1

Schnackenberg, Gjertrud 1953- **CLC 40**
See also CA 116; DLB 120

Schneider, Leonard Alfred 1925-1966
See Bruce, Lenny
See also CA 89-92

Schnitzler, Arthur 1862-1931**TCLC 4; SSC 15**
See also CA 104; DLB 81, 118

Schoenberg, Arnold 1874-1951 **TCLC 75**
See also CA 109

Schonberg, Arnold
See Schoenberg, Arnold

Schopenhauer, Arthur 1788-1860 **NCLC 51**
See also DLB 90

Schor, Sandra (M.) 1932(?)-1990 **CLC 65**
See also CA 132

Schorer, Mark 1908-1977 **CLC 9**
See also CA 5-8R; 73-76; CANR 7; DLB 103

Schrader, Paul (Joseph) 1946- **CLC 26**
See also CA 37-40R; CANR 41; DLB 44

Schreiner, Olive (Emilie Albertina) 1855-1920
TCLC 9
See also CA 105; 154; DLB 18, 156, 190

Schulberg, Budd (Wilson) 1914- **CLC 7, 48**
See also CA 25-28R; CANR 19; DLB 6, 26,
28; DLBY 81

Schulz, Bruno 1892-1942**TCLC 5, 51; SSC 13**
See also CA 115; 123

Schulz, Charles M(onroe) 1922- **CLC 12**
See also CA 9-12R; CANR 6; INT CANR-6;
SATA 10

Schumacher, E(rnst) F(riedrich) 1911-1977
CLC 80
See also CA 81-84; 73-76; CANR 34

Schuyler, James Marcus 1923-1991**CLC 5, 23;
DAM POET**
See also CA 101; 134; DLB 5, 169; INT 101

Schwartz, Delmore (David) 1913-1966**CLC 2,
4, 10, 45, 87; PC 8**
See also CA 17-18; 25-28R; CANR 35; CAP 2;
DLB 28, 48; MTCW 1

Schwartz, Ernst
See Ozu, Yasujiro

Schwartz, John Burnham 1965- **CLC 59**
See also CA 132

Schwartz, Lynne Sharon 1939- **CLC 31**
See also CA 103; CANR 44

Schwartz, Muriel A.
See Eliot, T(homas) S(tearns)

Schwarz-Bart, Andre 1928- **CLC 2, 4**
See also CA 89-92

Schwarz-Bart, Simone 1938- **CLC 7; BLCS**
See also BW 2; CA 97-100

Schwob, Marcel (Mayer Andre) 1867-1905
TCLC 20
See also CA 117; 168; DLB 123

Sciascia, Leonardo 1921-1989 **CLC 8, 9, 41**
See also CA 85-88; 130; CANR 35; DLB 177;
MTCW 1

Scoppettone, Sandra 1936- **CLC 26**

See also AAYA 11; CA 5-8R; CANR 41, 73;
SATA 9, 92

Scorsese, Martin 1942- **CLC 20, 89**
See also CA 110; 114; CANR 46

Scotland, Jay
See Jakes, John (William)

Scott, Duncan Campbell 1862-1947 **TCLC 6;
DAC**
See also CA 104; 153; DLB 92

Scott, Evelyn 1893-1963 **CLC 43**
See also CA 104; 112; CANR 64; DLB 9, 48

Scott, F(rancis) R(eginald) 1899-1985**CLC 22**
See also CA 101; 114; DLB 88; INT 101

Scott, Frank
See Scott, F(rancis) R(eginald)

Scott, Joanna 1960- **CLC 50**
See also CA 126; CANR 53

Scott, Paul (Mark) 1920-1978 **CLC 9, 60**
See also CA 81-84; 77-80; CANR 33; DLB 14;
MTCW 1

Scott, Sarah 1723-1795 **LC 44**
See also DLB 39

Scott, Walter 1771-1832 **NCLC 15, 69; DA;
DAB; DAC; DAM MST, NOV, POET; PC
13; SSC 32; WLC**
See also AAYA 22; CDBLB 1789-1832; DLB
93, 107, 116, 144, 159; YABC 2

Scribe, (Augustin) Eugene 1791-1861 **N C L C
16; DAM DRAM; DC 5**
See also DLB 192

Scrum, R.
See Crumb, R(obert)

Scudery, Madeleine de 1607-1701 **LC 2**

Scum
See Crumb, R(obert)

Scumbag, Little Bobby
See Crumb, R(obert)

Seabrook, John
See Hubbard, L(afayette) Ron(ald)

Sealy, I. Allan 1951- **CLC 55**

Search, Alexander
See Pessoa, Fernando (Antonio Nogueira)

Sebastian, Lee
See Silverberg, Robert

Sebastian Owl
See Thompson, Hunter S(tockton)

Sebestyen, Ouida 1924- **CLC 30**
See also AAYA 8; CA 107; CANR 40; CLR 17;
JRDA; MAICYA; SAAS 10; SATA 39

Secundus, H. Scriblerus
See Fielding, Henry

Sedges, John
See Buck, Pearl S(ydenstricker)

Sedgwick, Catharine Maria 1789-1867**N C L C
19**
See also DLB 1, 74

Seelye, John (Douglas) 1931- **CLC 7**
See also CA 97-100; CANR 70; INT 97-100

Seferiades, Giorgos Stylianou 1900-1971
See Seferis, George
See also CA 5-8R; 33-36R; CANR 5, 36;
MTCW 1

Seferis, George **CLC 5, 11**
See also Seferiades, Giorgos Stylianou

Segal, Erich (Wolf) 1937- **CLC 3, 10; DAM
POP**
See also BEST 89:1; CA 25-28R; CANR 20,
36, 65; DLBY 86; INT CANR-20; MTCW 1

Seger, Bob 1945- **CLC 35**

Seghers, Anna **CLC 7**
See also Radvanyi, Netty
See also DLB 69

Seidel, Frederick (Lewis) 1936- **CLC 18**

See also CA 13-16R; CANR 8; DLBY 84

Seifert, Jaroslav 1901-1986 **CLC 34, 44, 93**
See also CA 127; MTCW 1

Sei Shonagon c. 966-1017(?) **CMLC 6**

Selby, Hubert, Jr. 1928-**CLC 1, 2, 4, 8; SSC 20**
See also CA 13-16R; CANR 33; DLB 2

Selzer, Richard 1928- **CLC 74**
See also CA 65-68; CANR 14

Sembene, Ousmane
See Ousmane, Sembene

Senancour, Etienne Pivert de 1770-1846
NCLC 16
See also DLB 119

Sender, Ramon (Jose) 1902-1982**CLC 8; DAM
MULT; HLC**
See also CA 5-8R; 105; CANR 8; HW; MTCW
1

Seneca, Lucius Annaeus 4B.C.-65 **CMLC 6;
DAM DRAM; DC 5**

Senghor, Leopold Sedar 1906- **CLC 54; BLC
3; DAM MULT, POET**
See also BW 2; CA 116; 125; CANR 47, 74;
MTCW 1

Serling, (Edward) Rod(man) 1924-1975 **C L C
30**
See also AAYA 14; AITN 1; CA 162; 57-60;
DLB 26

Serna, Ramon Gomez de la
See Gomez de la Serna, Ramon

Serpieres
See Guillevic, (Eugene)

Service, Robert
See Service, Robert W(illiam)
See also DAB; DLB 92

Service, Robert W(illiam) 1874(?)-1958**TCLC
15; DA; DAC; DAM MST, POET; WLC**
See also Service, Robert
See also CA 115; 140; SATA 20

Seth, Vikram 1952-**CLC 43, 90; DAM MULT**
See also CA 121; 127; CANR 50, 74; DLB 120;
INT 127

Seton, Cynthia Propper 1926-1982 **CLC 27**
See also CA 5-8R; 108; CANR 7

Seton, Ernest (Evan) Thompson 1860-1946
TCLC 31
See also CA 109; DLB 92; DLBD 13; JRDA;
SATA 18

Seton-Thompson, Ernest
See Seton, Ernest (Evan) Thompson

Settle, Mary Lee 1918- **CLC 19, 61**
See also CA 89-92; CAAS 1; CANR 44; DLB
6; INT 89-92

Seuphor, Michel
See Arp, Jean

**Sevigne, Marie (de Rabutin-Chantal) Marquise
de** 1626-1696 **LC 11**

Sewall, Samuel 1652-1730 **LC 38**
See also DLB 24

Sexton, Anne (Harvey) 1928-1974**CLC 2, 4, 6,
8, 10, 15, 53; DA; DAB; DAC; DAM MST,
POET; PC 2; WLC**
See also CA 1-4R; 53-56; CABS 2; CANR 3,
36; CDALB 1941-1968; DLB 5, 169;
MTCW 1; SATA 10

Shaara, Michael (Joseph, Jr.) 1929-1988**C L C
15; DAM POP**
See also AITN 1; CA 102; 125; CANR 52;
DLBY 83

Shackleton, C. C.
See Aldiss, Brian W(ilson)

Shacochis, Bob **CLC 39**
See also Shacochis, Robert G.

Shacochis, Robert G. 1951-

See Shacochis, Bob
See also CA 119; 124; INT 124
Shaffer, Anthony (Joshua) 1926-   **CLC 19;**
  DAM DRAM
  See also CA 110; 116; DLB 13
Shaffer, Peter (Levin) 1926-**CLC 5, 14, 18, 37,**
  60; DAB; DAM DRAM, MST; DC 7
  See also CA 25-28R; CANR 25, 47, 74; CDBLB
  1960 to Present; DLB 13; MTCW 1
Shakey, Bernard
  See Young, Neil
Shalamov, Varlam (Tikhonovich) 1907(?)-1982
  CLC 18
  See also CA 129; 105
Shamlu, Ahmad 1925-   **CLC 10**
Shammas, Anton 1951-   **CLC 55**
Shange, Ntozake 1948-**CLC 8, 25, 38, 74; BLC**
  3; DAM DRAM, MULT; DC 3
  See also AAYA 9; BW 2; CA 85-88; CABS 3;
  CANR 27, 48, 74; DLB 38; MTCW 1
Shanley, John Patrick 1950-   **CLC 75**
  See also CA 128; 133
Shapcott, Thomas W(illiam) 1935-   **CLC 38**
  See also CA 69-72; CANR 49
Shapiro, Jane   **CLC 76**
Shapiro, Karl (Jay) 1913-   **CLC 4, 8, 15, 53**
  See also CA 1-4R; CAAS 6; CANR 1, 36, 66;
  DLB 48; MTCW 1
Sharp, William 1855-1905   **TCLC 39**
  See also CA 160; DLB 156
Sharpe, Thomas Ridley 1928-
  See Sharpe, Tom
  See also CA 114; 122; INT 122
Sharpe, Tom   **CLC 36**
  See also Sharpe, Thomas Ridley
  See also DLB 14
Shaw, Bernard   **TCLC 45**
  See also Shaw, George Bernard
  See also BW 1
Shaw, G. Bernard
  See Shaw, George Bernard
Shaw, George Bernard 1856-1950**TCLC 3, 9,**
  21; DA; DAB; DAC; DAM DRAM, MST;
  WLC
  See also Shaw, Bernard
  See also CA 104; 128; CDBLB 1914-1945;
  DLB 10, 57, 190; MTCW 1
Shaw, Henry Wheeler 1818-1885   **NCLC 15**
  See also DLB 11
Shaw, Irwin 1913-1984 **CLC 7, 23, 34; DAM**
  DRAM, POP
  See also AITN 1; CA 13-16R; 112; CANR 21;
  CDALB 1941-1968; DLB 6, 102; DLBY 84;
  MTCW 1
Shaw, Robert 1927-1978   **CLC 5**
  See also AITN 1; CA 1-4R; 81-84; CANR 4;
  DLB 13, 14
Shaw, T. E.
  See Lawrence, T(homas) E(dward)
Shawn, Wallace 1943-   **CLC 41**
  See also CA 112
Shea, Lisa 1953-   **CLC 86**
  See also CA 147
Sheed, Wilfrid (John Joseph) 1930-**CLC 2, 4,**
  10, 53
  See also CA 65-68; CANR 30, 66; DLB 6;
  MTCW 1
Sheldon, Alice Hastings Bradley 1915(?)-1987
  See Tiptree, James, Jr.
  See also CA 108; 122; CANR 34; INT 108;
  MTCW 1
Sheldon, John
  See Bloch, Robert (Albert)

Shelley, Mary Wollstonecraft (Godwin) 1797-
  1851**NCLC 14, 59; DA; DAB; DAC; DAM**
  MST, NOV; WLC
  See also AAYA 20; CDBLB 1789-1832; DLB
  110, 116, 159, 178; SATA 29
Shelley, Percy Bysshe 1792-1822   **NCLC 18;**
  DA; DAB; DAC; DAM MST, POET; PC
  14; WLC
  See also CDBLB 1789-1832; DLB 96, 110, 158
Shepard, Jim 1956-   **CLC 36**
  See also CA 137; CANR 59; SATA 90
Shepard, Lucius 1947-   **CLC 34**
  See also CA 128; 141
Shepard, Sam 1943- **CLC 4, 6, 17, 34, 41, 44;**
  DAM DRAM; DC 5
  See also AAYA 1; CA 69-72; CABS 3; CANR
  22; DLB 7; MTCW 1
Shepherd, Michael
  See Ludlum, Robert
Sherburne, Zoa (Morin) 1912-   **CLC 30**
  See also AAYA 13; CA 1-4R; CANR 3, 37;
  MAICYA; SAAS 18; SATA 3
Sheridan, Frances 1724-1766   **LC 7**
  See also DLB 39, 84
Sheridan, Richard Brinsley 1751-1816**NCLC**
  5; DA; DAB; DAC; DAM DRAM, MST;
  DC 1; WLC
  See also CDBLB 1660-1789; DLB 89
Sherman, Jonathan Marc   **CLC 55**
Sherman, Martin 1941(?)-   **CLC 19**
  See also CA 116; 123
Sherwin, Judith Johnson 1936-   **CLC 7, 15**
  See also CA 25-28R; CANR 34
Sherwood, Frances 1940-   **CLC 81**
  See also CA 146
Sherwood, Robert E(mmet) 1896-1955**TCLC**
  3; DAM DRAM
  See also CA 104; 153; DLB 7, 26
Shestov, Lev 1866-1938   **TCLC 56**
Shevchenko, Taras 1814-1861   **NCLC 54**
Shiel, M(atthew) P(hipps) 1865-1947**TCLC 8**
  See also Holmes, Gordon
  See also CA 106; 160; DLB 153
Shields, Carol 1935-   **CLC 91, 113; DAC**
  See also CA 81-84; CANR 51, 74
Shields, David 1956-   **CLC 97**
  See also CA 124; CANR 48
Shiga, Naoya 1883-1971   **CLC 33; SSC 23**
  See also CA 101; 33-36R; DLB 180
Shilts, Randy 1951-1994   **CLC 85**
  See also CA 115; 127; 144; CANR
  45; INT 127
Shimazaki, Haruki 1872-1943
  See Shimazaki Toson
  See also CA 105; 134
Shimazaki Toson 1872-1943   **TCLC 5**
  See also Shimazaki, Haruki
  See also DLB 180
Sholokhov, Mikhail (Aleksandrovich) 1905-
  1984   **CLC 7, 15**
  See also CA 101; 112; MTCW 1; SATA-Obit
  36
Shone, Patric
  See Hanley, James
Shreve, Susan Richards 1939-   **CLC 23**
  See also CA 49-52; CAAS 5; CANR 5, 38, 69;
  MAICYA; SATA 46, 95; SATA-Brief 41
Shue, Larry 1946-1985**CLC 52; DAM DRAM**
  See also CA 145; 117
Shu-Jen, Chou 1881-1936
  See Lu Hsun
  See also CA 104
Shulman, Alix Kates 1932-   **CLC 2, 10**

See also CA 29-32R; CANR 43; SATA 7
Shuster, Joe 1914-   **CLC 21**
Shute, Nevil   **CLC 30**
  See also Norway, Nevil Shute
Shuttle, Penelope (Diane) 1947-   **CLC 7**
  See also CA 93-96; CANR 39; DLB 14, 40
Sidney, Mary 1561-1621   **LC 19, 39**
Sidney, Sir Philip 1554-1586 **LC 19, 39; DA;**
  DAB; DAC; DAM MST, POET
  See also CDBLB Before 1660; DLB 167
Siegel, Jerome 1914-1996   **CLC 21**
  See also CA 116; 169; 151
Siegel, Jerry
  See Siegel, Jerome
Sienkiewicz, Henryk (Adam Alexander Pius)
  1846-1916   **TCLC 3**
  See also CA 104; 134
Sierra, Gregorio Martinez
  See Martinez Sierra, Gregorio
Sierra, Maria (de la O'LeJarraga) Martinez
  See Martinez Sierra, Maria (de la O'LeJarraga)
Sigal, Clancy 1926-   **CLC 7**
  See also CA 1-4R
Sigourney, Lydia Howard (Huntley) 1791-1865
  NCLC 21
  See also DLB 1, 42, 73
Siguenza y Gongora, Carlos de 1645-1700**LC**
  8
Sigurjonsson, Johann 1880-1919   **TCLC 27**
  See also CA 170
Sikelianos, Angelos 1884-1951   **TCLC 39**
Silkin, Jon 1930-   **CLC 2, 6, 43**
  See also CA 5-8R; CAAS 5; DLB 27
Silko, Leslie (Marmon) 1948-**CLC 23, 74, 114;**
  DA; DAC; DAM MST, MULT, POP;
  WLCS
  See also AAYA 14; CA 115; 122; CANR 45,
  65; DLB 143, 175; NNAL
Sillanpaa, Frans Eemil 1888-1964   **CLC 19**
  See also CA 129; 93-96; MTCW 1
Sillitoe, Alan 1928-   **CLC 1, 3, 6, 10, 19, 57**
  See also AITN 1; CA 9-12R; CAAS 2; CANR
  8, 26, 55; CDBLB 1960 to Present; DLB 14,
  139; MTCW 1; SATA 61
Silone, Ignazio 1900-1978   **CLC 4**
  See also CA 25-28; 81-84; CANR 34; CAP 2;
  MTCW 1
Silver, Joan Micklin 1935-   **CLC 20**
  See also CA 114; 121; INT 121
Silver, Nicholas
  See Faust, Frederick (Schiller)
Silverberg, Robert 1935- **CLC 7; DAM POP**
  See also AAYA 24; CA 1-4R; CAAS 3; CANR
  1, 20, 36; DLB 8; INT CANR-20; MAICYA;
  MTCW 1; SATA 13, 91
Silverstein, Alvin 1933-   **CLC 17**
  See also CA 49-52; CANR 2; CLR 25; JRDA;
  MAICYA; SATA 8, 69
Silverstein, Virginia B(arbara Opshelor) 1937-
  CLC 17
  See also CA 49-52; CANR 2; CLR 25; JRDA;
  MAICYA; SATA 8, 69
Sim, Georges
  See Simenon, Georges (Jacques Christian)
Simak, Clifford D(onald) 1904-1988**CLC 1, 55**
  See also CA 1-4R; 125; CANR 1, 35; DLB 8;
  MTCW 1; SATA-Obit 56
Simenon, Georges (Jacques Christian) 1903-
  1989   **CLC 1, 2, 3, 8, 18, 47; DAM POP**
  See also CA 85-88; 129; CANR 35; DLB 72;
  DLBY 89; MTCW 1
Simic, Charles 1938-   **CLC 6, 9, 22, 49, 68;**
  DAM POET

See also CA 29-32R; CAAS 4; CANR 12, 33, 52, 61; DLB 105

Simmel, Georg 1858-1918   **TCLC 64**
See also CA 157

Simmons, Charles (Paul) 1924-   **CLC 57**
See also CA 89-92; INT 89-92

Simmons, Dan 1948-   **CLC 44; DAM POP**
See also AAYA 16; CA 138; CANR 53

Simmons, James (Stewart Alexander) 1933-
CLC 43
See also CA 105; CAAS 21; DLB 40

Simms, William Gilmore 1806-1870 **NCLC 3**
See also DLB 3, 30, 59, 73

Simon, Carly 1945-   **CLC 26**
See also CA 105

Simon, Claude 1913-1984   **CLC 4, 9, 15, 39;**
DAM NOV
See also CA 89-92; CANR 33; DLB 83; MTCW 1

Simon, (Marvin) Neil 1927-**CLC 6, 11, 31, 39,**
70; DAM DRAM
See also AITN 1; CA 21-24R; CANR 26, 54; DLB 7; MTCW 1

Simon, Paul (Frederick) 1941(?)-   **CLC 17**
See also CA 116; 153

Simonon, Paul 1956(?)-   **CLC 30**

Simpson, Harriette
See Arnow, Harriette (Louisa) Simpson

Simpson, Louis (Aston Marantz) 1923-**CLC 4,**
7, 9, 32; DAM POET
See also CA 1-4R; CAAS 4; CANR 1, 61; DLB 5; MTCW 1

Simpson, Mona (Elizabeth) 1957-   **CLC 44**
See also CA 122; 135; CANR 68

Simpson, N(orman) F(rederick) 1919-**CLC 29**
See also CA 13-16R; DLB 13

Sinclair, Andrew (Annandale) 1935-   **CLC 2,**
14
See also CA 9-12R; CAAS 5; CANR 14, 38; DLB 14; MTCW 1

Sinclair, Emil
See Hesse, Hermann

Sinclair, Iain 1943-   **CLC 76**
See also CA 132

Sinclair, Iain MacGregor
See Sinclair, Iain

Sinclair, Irene
See Griffith, D(avid Lewelyn) W(ark)

Sinclair, Mary Amelia St. Clair 1865(?)-1946
See Sinclair, May
See also CA 104

Sinclair, May 1863-1946   **TCLC 3, 11**
See also Sinclair, Mary Amelia St. Clair
See also CA 166; DLB 36, 135

Sinclair, Roy
See Griffith, D(avid Lewelyn) W(ark)

Sinclair, Upton (Beall) 1878-1968 **CLC 1, 11,**
15, 63; DA; DAB; DAC; DAM MST, NOV;
WLC
See also CA 5-8R; 25-28R; CANR 7; CDALB 1929-1941; DLB 9; INT CANR-7; MTCW 1; SATA 9

Singer, Isaac
See Singer, Isaac Bashevis

Singer, Isaac Bashevis 1904-1991**CLC 1, 3, 6,**
9, 11, 15, 23, 38, 69, 111; DA; DAB; DAC;
DAM MST, NOV; SSC 3; WLC
See also AITN 1, 2; CA 1-4R; 134; CANR 1, 39; CDALB 1941-1968; CLR 1; DLB 6, 28, 52; DLBY 91; JRDA; MAICYA; MTCW 1; SATA 3, 27; SATA-Obit 68

Singer, Israel Joshua 1893-1944   **TCLC 33**
See also CA 169

Singh, Khushwant 1915-   **CLC 11**
See also CA 9-12R; CAAS 9; CANR 6

Singleton, Ann
See Benedict, Ruth (Fulton)

Sinjohn, John
See Galsworthy, John

Sinyavsky, Andrei (Donatevich) 1925-1997
CLC 8
See also CA 85-88; 159

Sirin, V.
See Nabokov, Vladimir (Vladimirovich)

Sissman, L(ouis) E(dward) 1928-1976**CLC 9,**
18
See also CA 21-24R; 65-68; CANR 13; DLB 5

Sisson, C(harles) H(ubert) 1914-   **CLC 8**
See also CA 1-4R; CAAS 3; CANR 3, 48; DLB 27

Sitwell, Dame Edith 1887-1964 **CLC 2, 9, 67;**
DAM POET; PC 3
See also CA 9-12R; CANR 35; CDBLB 1945-1960; DLB 20; MTCW 1

Siwaarmill, H. P.
See Sharp, William

Sjoewall, Maj 1935-   **CLC 7**
See also CA 65-68; CANR 73

Sjowall, Maj
See Sjoewall, Maj

Skelton, Robin 1925-1997   **CLC 13**
See also AITN 2; CA 5-8R; 160; CAAS 5; CANR 28; DLB 27, 53

Skolimowski, Jerzy 1938-   **CLC 20**
See also CA 128

Skram, Amalie (Bertha) 1847-1905 **TCLC 25**
See also CA 165

Skvorecky, Josef (Vaclav) 1924- **CLC 15, 39,**
69; DAC; DAM NOV
See also CA 61-64; CAAS 1; CANR 10, 34, 63; MTCW 1

Slade, Bernard   **CLC 11, 46**
See also Newbound, Bernard Slade
See also CAAS 9; DLB 53

Slaughter, Carolyn 1946-   **CLC 56**
See also CA 85-88

Slaughter, Frank G(ill) 1908-   **CLC 29**
See also AITN 2; CA 5-8R; CANR 5; INT CANR-5

Slavitt, David R(ytman) 1935-   **CLC 5, 14**
See also CA 21-24R; CAAS 3; CANR 41; DLB 5, 6

Slesinger, Tess 1905-1945   **TCLC 10**
See also CA 107; DLB 102

Slessor, Kenneth 1901-1971   **CLC 14**
See also CA 102; 89-92

Slowacki, Juliusz 1809-1849   **NCLC 15**

Smart, Christopher 1722-1771   **LC 3; DAM**
POET; PC 13
See also DLB 109

Smart, Elizabeth 1913-1986   **CLC 54**
See also CA 81-84; 118; DLB 88

Smiley, Jane (Graves) 1949-**CLC 53, 76; DAM**
POP
See also CA 104; CANR 30, 50, 74; INT CANR-30

Smith, A(rthur) J(ames) M(arshall) 1902-1980
CLC 15; DAC
See also CA 1-4R; 102; CANR 4; DLB 88

Smith, Adam 1723-1790   **LC 36**
See also DLB 104

Smith, Alexander 1829-1867   **NCLC 59**
See also DLB 32, 55

Smith, Anna Deavere 1950-   **CLC 86**
See also CA 133

Smith, Betty (Wehner) 1896-1972   **CLC 19**

See also CA 5-8R; 33-36R; DLBY 82; SATA 6

Smith, Charlotte (Turner) 1749-1806 **N C L C**
23
See also DLB 39, 109

Smith, Clark Ashton 1893-1961   **CLC 43**
See also CA 143

Smith, Dave   **CLC 22, 42**
See also Smith, David (Jeddie)
See also CAAS 7; DLB 5

Smith, David (Jeddie) 1942-
See Smith, Dave
See also CA 49-52; CANR 1, 59; DAM POET

Smith, Florence Margaret 1902-1971
See Smith, Stevie
See also CA 17-18; 29-32R; CANR 35; CAP 2; DAM POET; MTCW 1

Smith, Iain Crichton 1928-   **CLC 64**
See also CA 21-24R; DLB 40, 139

Smith, John 1580(?)-1631   **LC 9**
See also DLB 24, 30

Smith, Johnston
See Crane, Stephen (Townley)

Smith, Joseph, Jr. 1805-1844   **NCLC 53**

Smith, Lee 1944-   **CLC 25, 73**
See also CA 114; 119; CANR 46; DLB 143; DLBY 83; INT 119

Smith, Martin
See Smith, Martin Cruz

Smith, Martin Cruz 1942-   **CLC 25; DAM**
MULT, POP
See also BEST 89:4; CA 85-88; CANR 6, 23, 43, 65; INT CANR-23; NNAL

Smith, Mary-Ann Tirone 1944-   **CLC 39**
See also CA 118; 136

Smith, Patti 1946-   **CLC 12**
See also CA 93-96; CANR 63

Smith, Pauline (Urmson) 1882-1959**TCLC 25**

Smith, Rosamond
See Oates, Joyce Carol

Smith, Sheila Kaye
See Kaye-Smith, Sheila

Smith, Stevie   **CLC 3, 8, 25, 44; PC 12**
See also Smith, Florence Margaret
See also DLB 20

Smith, Wilbur (Addison) 1933-   **CLC 33**
See also CA 13-16R; CANR 7, 46, 66; MTCW 1

Smith, William Jay 1918-   **CLC 6**
See also CA 5-8R; CANR 44; DLB 5; MAICYA; SAAS 22; SATA 2, 68

Smith, Woodrow Wilson
See Kuttner, Henry

Smolenskin, Peretz 1842-1885   **NCLC 30**

Smollett, Tobias (George) 1721-1771**LC 2, 46**
See also CDBLB 1660-1789; DLB 39, 104

Snodgrass, W(illiam) D(e Witt) 1926-**CLC 2,**
6, 10, 18, 68; DAM POET
See also CA 1-4R; CANR 6, 36, 65; DLB 5; MTCW 1

Snow, C(harles) P(ercy) 1905-1980 **CLC 1, 4,**
6, 9, 13, 19; DAM NOV
See also CA 5-8R; 101; CANR 28; CDBLB 1945-1960; DLB 15, 77; DLBD 17; MTCW 1

Snow, Frances Compton
See Adams, Henry (Brooks)

Snyder, Gary (Sherman) 1930-**CLC 1, 2, 5, 9,**
32; DAM POET; PC 21
See also CA 17-20R; CANR 30, 60; DLB 5, 16, 165

Snyder, Zilpha Keatley 1927-   **CLC 17**
See also AAYA 15; CA 9-12R; CANR 38; CLR 31; JRDA; MAICYA; SAAS 2; SATA 1, 28,

See also CA 113; DLB 9, 102

Sudermann, Hermann 1857-1928   **TCLC 15**
See also CA 107; DLB 118

Sue, Eugene 1804-1857   **NCLC 1**
See also DLB 119

Sueskind, Patrick 1949-   **CLC 44**
See also Suskind, Patrick

Sukenick, Ronald 1932-   **CLC 3, 4, 6, 48**
See also CA 25-28R; CAAS 8; CANR 32; DLB 173; DLBY 81

Suknaski, Andrew 1942-   **CLC 19**
See also CA 101; DLB 53

Sullivan, Vernon
See Vian, Boris

Sully Prudhomme 1839-1907   **TCLC 31**

Su Man-shu   **TCLC 24**
See also Su, Chien

Summerforest, Ivy B.
See Kirkup, James

Summers, Andrew James 1942-   **CLC 26**

Summers, Andy
See Summers, Andrew James

Summers, Hollis (Spurgeon, Jr.) 1916-**CLC 10**
See also CA 5-8R; CANR 3; DLB 6

Summers, (Alphonsus Joseph-Mary Augustus)
   Montague 1880-1948   **TCLC 16**
See also CA 118; 163

Sumner, Gordon Matthew   **CLC 26**
See also Sting

Surtees, Robert Smith 1803-1864   **NCLC 14**
See also DLB 21

Susann, Jacqueline 1921-1974   **CLC 3**
See also AITN 1; CA 65-68; 53-56; MTCW 1

Su Shih 1036-1101   **CMLC 15**

Suskind, Patrick
See Sueskind, Patrick
See also CA 145

Sutcliff, Rosemary 1920-1992 **CLC 26; DAB;**
   DAC; DAM MST, POP
See also AAYA 10; CA 5-8R; 139; CANR 37;
   CLR 1, 37; JRDA; MAICYA; SATA 6, 44,
   78; SATA-Obit 73

Sutro, Alfred 1863-1933   **TCLC 6**
See also CA 105; DLB 10

Sutton, Henry
See Slavitt, David R(ytman)

Svevo, Italo 1861-1928 **TCLC 2, 35; SSC 25**
See also Schmitz, Aron Hector

Swados, Elizabeth (A.) 1951-   **CLC 12**
See also CA 97-100; CANR 49; INT 97-100

Swados, Harvey 1920-1972   **CLC 5**
See also CA 5-8R; 37-40R; CANR 6; DLB 2

Swan, Gladys 1934-   **CLC 69**
See also CA 101; CANR 17, 39

Swarthout, Glendon (Fred) 1918-1992**CLC 35**
See also CA 1-4R; 139; CANR 1, 47; SATA 26

Sweet, Sarah C.
See Jewett, (Theodora) Sarah Orne

Swenson, May 1919-1989**CLC 4, 14, 61, 106;**
   **DA; DAB; DAC; DAM MST, POET; PC
   14**
See also CA 5-8R; 130; CANR 36, 61; DLB 5;
   MTCW 1; SATA 15

Swift, Augustus
See Lovecraft, H(oward) P(hillips)

Swift, Graham (Colin) 1949-   **CLC 41, 88**
See also CA 117; 122; CANR 46, 71; DLB 194

Swift, Jonathan 1667-1745   **LC 1, 42; DA;**
   **DAB; DAC; DAM MST, NOV, POET; PC
   9; WLC**
See also CDBLB 1660-1789; CLR 53; DLB 39,
   95, 101; SATA 19

Swinburne, Algernon Charles 1837-1909

**TCLC 8, 36; DA; DAB; DAC; DAM MST,
POET; PC 24; WLC**
See also CA 105; 140; CDBLB 1832-1890;
   DLB 35, 57

Swinfen, Ann   **CLC 34**

Swinnerton, Frank Arthur 1884-1982**CLC 31**
See also CA 108; DLB 34

Swithen, John
See King, Stephen (Edwin)

Sylvia
See Ashton-Warner, Sylvia (Constance)

Symmes, Robert Edward
See Duncan, Robert (Edward)

Symonds, John Addington 1840-1893 **NCLC
34**
See also DLB 57, 144

Symons, Arthur 1865-1945   **TCLC 11**
See also CA 107; DLB 19, 57, 149

Symons, Julian (Gustave) 1912-1994 **CLC 2,
14, 32**
See also CA 49-52; 147; CAAS 3; CANR 3,
   33, 59; DLB 87, 155; DLBY 92; MTCW 1

Synge, (Edmund) J(ohn) M(illington) 1871-
   1909   **TCLC 6, 37; DAM DRAM; DC 2**
See also CA 104; 141; CDBLB 1890-1914;
   DLB 10, 19

Syruc, J.
See Milosz, Czeslaw

Szirtes, George 1948-   **CLC 46**
See also CA 109; CANR 27, 61

Szymborska, Wislawa 1923-   **CLC 99**
See also CA 154; DLBY 96

T. O., Nik
See Annensky, Innokenty (Fyodorovich)

Tabori, George 1914-   **CLC 19**
See also CA 49-52; CANR 4, 69

Tagore, Rabindranath 1861-1941**TCLC 3, 53;**
   DAM DRAM, POET; PC 8
See also CA 104; 120; MTCW 1

Taine, Hippolyte Adolphe 1828-1893 **NCLC
15**

Talese, Gay 1932-   **CLC 37**
See also AITN 1; CA 1-4R; CANR 9, 58; DLB
   185; INT CANR-9; MTCW 1

Tallent, Elizabeth (Ann) 1954-   **CLC 45**
See also CA 117; CANR 72; DLB 130

Tally, Ted 1952-   **CLC 42**
See also CA 120; 124; INT 124

Talvik, Heiti 1904-1947   **TCLC 87**

Tamayo y Baus, Manuel 1829-1898 **NCLC 1**

Tammsaare, A(nton) H(ansen) 1878-1940
   TCLC 27
See also CA 164

Tam'si, Tchicaya U
See Tchicaya, Gerald Felix

Tan, Amy (Ruth) 1952-**CLC 59; DAM MULT,
   NOV, POP**
See also AAYA 9; BEST 89:3; CA 136; CANR
   54; DLB 173; SATA 75

Tandem, Felix
See Spitteler, Carl (Friedrich Georg)

Tanizaki, Jun'ichiro 1886-1965**CLC 8, 14, 28;
   SSC 21**
See also CA 93-96; 25-28R; DLB 180

Tanner, William
See Amis, Kingsley (William)

Tao Lao
See Storni, Alfonsina

Tarassoff, Lev
See Troyat, Henri

Tarbell, Ida M(inerva) 1857-1944   **TCLC 40**
See also CA 122; DLB 47

Tarkington, (Newton) Booth 1869-1946**TCLC**

9
See also CA 110; 143; DLB 9, 102; SATA 17

Tarkovsky, Andrei (Arsenyevich) 1932-1986
   CLC 75
See also CA 127

Tartt, Donna 1964(?)-   **CLC 76**
See also CA 142

Tasso, Torquato 1544-1595   **LC 5**

Tate, (John Orley) Allen 1899-1979**CLC 2, 4,
   6, 9, 11, 14, 24**
See also CA 5-8R; 85-88; CANR 32; DLB 4,
   45, 63; DLBD 17; MTCW 1

Tate, Ellalice
See Hibbert, Eleanor Alice Burford

Tate, James (Vincent) 1943-   **CLC 2, 6, 25**
See also CA 21-24R; CANR 29, 57; DLB 5,
   169

Tavel, Ronald 1940-   **CLC 6**
See also CA 21-24R; CANR 33

Taylor, C(ecil) P(hilip) 1929-1981   **CLC 27**
See also CA 25-28R; 105; CANR 47

Taylor, Edward 1642(?)-1729   **LC 11; DA;
   DAB; DAC; DAM MST, POET**
See also DLB 24

Taylor, Eleanor Ross 1920-   **CLC 5**
See also CA 81-84; CANR 70

Taylor, Elizabeth 1912-1975   **CLC 2, 4, 29**
See also CA 13-16R; CANR 9, 70; DLB 139;
   MTCW 1; SATA 13

Taylor, Frederick Winslow 1856-1915 **TCLC
76**

Taylor, Henry (Splawn) 1942-   **CLC 44**
See also CA 33-36R; CAAS 7; CANR 31; DLB
   5

Taylor, Kamala (Purnaiya) 1924-
See Markandaya, Kamala
See also CA 77-80

Taylor, Mildred D.   **CLC 21**
See also AAYA 10; BW 1; CA 85-88; CANR
   25; CLR 9; DLB 52; JRDA; MAICYA; SAAS
   5; SATA 15, 70

Taylor, Peter (Hillsman) 1917-1994**CLC 1, 4,
   18, 37, 44, 50, 71; SSC 10**
See also CA 13-16R; 147; CANR 9, 50; DLBY
   81, 94; INT CANR-9; MTCW 1

Taylor, Robert Lewis 1912-1998   **CLC 14**
See also CA 1-4R; 170; CANR 3, 64; SATA 10

Tchekhov, Anton
See Chekhov, Anton (Pavlovich)

Tchicaya, Gerald Felix 1931-1988   **CLC 101**
See also CA 129; 125

Tchicaya U Tam'si
See Tchicaya, Gerald Felix

Teasdale, Sara 1884-1933   **TCLC 4**
See also CA 104; 163; DLB 45; SATA 32

Tegner, Esaias 1782-1846   **NCLC 2**

Teilhard de Chardin, (Marie Joseph) Pierre
   1881-1955   **TCLC 9**
See also CA 105

Temple, Ann
See Mortimer, Penelope (Ruth)

Tennant, Emma (Christina) 1937-**CLC 13, 52**
See also CA 65-68; CAAS 9; CANR 10, 38,
   59; DLB 14

Tenneshaw, S. M.
See Silverberg, Robert

Tennyson, Alfred 1809-1892   **NCLC 30, 65;
   DA; DAB; DAC; DAM MST, POET; PC
   6; WLC**
See also CDBLB 1832-1890; DLB 32

Teran, Lisa St. Aubin de   **CLC 36**
See also St. Aubin de Teran, Lisa

Terence 195(?)B.C.-159B.C. **CMLC 14; DC 7**

Teresa de Jesus, St. 1515-1582 **LC 18**

Terkel, Louis 1912-
See Terkel, Studs
See also CA 57-60; CANR 18, 45, 67; MTCW
1

Terkel, Studs **CLC 38**
See also Terkel, Louis
See also AITN 1

Terry, C. V.
See Slaughter, Frank G(ill)

Terry, Megan 1932- **CLC 19**
See also CA 77-80; CABS 3; CANR 43; DLB 7

Tertullian c. 155-c. 245 **CMLC 29**

Tertz, Abram
See Sinyavsky, Andrei (Donatevich)

Tesich, Steve 1943(?)-1996 **CLC 40, 69**
See also CA 105; 152; DLBY 83

Tesla, Nikola 1856-1943 **TCLC 88**

Teternikov, Fyodor Kuzmich 1863-1927
See Sologub, Fyodor
See also CA 104

Tevis, Walter 1928-1984 **CLC 42**
See also CA 113

Tey, Josephine **TCLC 14**
See also Mackintosh, Elizabeth
See also DLB 77

Thackeray, William Makepeace 1811-1863
**NCLC 5, 14, 22, 43; DA; DAB; DAC; DAM
MST, NOV; WLC**
See also CDBLB 1832-1890; DLB 21, 55, 159,
163; SATA 23

Thakura, Ravindranatha
See Tagore, Rabindranath

Tharoor, Shashi 1956- **CLC 70**
See also CA 141

Thelwell, Michael Miles 1939- **CLC 22**
See also BW 2; CA 101

Theobald, Lewis, Jr.
See Lovecraft, H(oward) P(hillips)

Theodorescu, Ion N. 1880-1967
See Arghezi, Tudor
See also CA 116

Theriault, Yves 1915-1983 **CLC 79; DAC;
DAM MST**
See also CA 102; DLB 88

Theroux, Alexander (Louis) 1939- **CLC 2, 25**
See also CA 85-88; CANR 20, 63

Theroux, Paul (Edward) 1941- **CLC 5, 8, 11,
15, 28, 46; DAM POP**
See also BEST 89:4; CA 33-36R; CANR 20,
45, 74; DLB 2; MTCW 1; SATA 44

Thesen, Sharon 1946- **CLC 56**
See also CA 163

Thevenin, Denis
See Duhamel, Georges

Thibault, Jacques Anatole Francois 1844-1924
See France, Anatole
See also CA 106; 127; DAM NOV; MTCW 1

Thiele, Colin (Milton) 1920- **CLC 17**
See also CA 29-32R; CANR 12, 28, 53; CLR
27; MAICYA; SAAS 2; SATA 14, 72

Thomas, Audrey (Callahan) 1935-**CLC 7, 13,
37, 107; SSC 20**
See also AITN 2; CA 21-24R; CAAS 19; CANR
36, 58; DLB 60; MTCW 1

Thomas, D(onald) M(ichael) 1935- **CLC 13,
22, 31**
See also CA 61-64; CAAS 11; CANR 17, 45,
74; CDBLB 1960 to Present; DLB 40; INT
CANR-17; MTCW 1

Thomas, Dylan (Marlais) 1914-1953**TCLC 1,
8, 45; DA; DAB; DAC; DAM DRAM,
MST, POET; PC 2; SSC 3; WLC**

See also CA 104; 120; CANR 65; CDBLB
1945-1960; DLB 13, 20, 139; MTCW 1;
SATA 60

Thomas, (Philip) Edward 1878-1917 **T C L C
10; DAM POET**
See also CA 106; 153; DLB 19

Thomas, Joyce Carol 1938- **CLC 35**
See also AAYA 12; BW 2; CA 113; 116; CANR
48; CLR 19; DLB 33; INT 116; JRDA;
MAICYA; MTCW 1; SAAS 7; SATA 40, 78

Thomas, Lewis 1913-1993 **CLC 35**
See also CA 85-88; 143; CANR 38, 60; MTCW
1

Thomas, Paul
See Mann, (Paul) Thomas

Thomas, Piri 1928- **CLC 17**
See also CA 73-76; HW

Thomas, R(onald) S(tuart) 1913- CLC 6, 13,
48; DAB; DAM POET
See also CA 89-92; CAAS 4; CANR 30;
CDBLB 1960 to Present; DLB 27; MTCW 1

Thomas, Ross (Elmore) 1926-1995 **CLC 39**
See also CA 33-36R; 150; CANR 22, 63

Thompson, Francis Clegg
See Mencken, H(enry) L(ouis)

Thompson, Francis Joseph 1859-1907**TCLC 4**
See also CA 104; CDBLB 1890-1914; DLB 19

Thompson, Hunter S(tockton) 1939- **CLC 9,
17, 40, 104; DAM POP**
See also BEST 89:1; CA 17-20R; CANR 23,
46, 74; DLB 185; MTCW 1

Thompson, James Myers
See Thompson, Jim (Myers)

Thompson, Jim (Myers) 1906-1977(?)**CLC 69**
See also CA 140

Thompson, Judith **CLC 39**

Thomson, James 1700-1748 **LC 16, 29, 40;
DAM POET**
See also DLB 95

Thomson, James 1834-1882 **NCLC 18; DAM
POET**
See also DLB 35

Thoreau, Henry David 1817-1862**NCLC 7, 21,
61; DA; DAB; DAC; DAM MST; WLC**
See also CDALB 1640-1865; DLB 1

Thornton, Hall
See Silverberg, Robert

Thucydides c. 455B.C.-399B.C. **CMLC 17**
See also DLB 176

Thurber, James (Grover) 1894-1961 **CLC 5,
11, 25; DA; DAB; DAC; DAM DRAM,
MST, NOV; SSC 1**
See also CA 73-76; CANR 17, 39; CDALB
1929-1941; DLB 4, 11, 22, 102; MAICYA;
MTCW 1; SATA 13

Thurman, Wallace (Henry) 1902-1934 **T C L C
6; BLC 3; DAM MULT**
See also BW 1; CA 104; 124; DLB 51

Ticheburn, Cheviot
See Ainsworth, William Harrison

Tieck, (Johann) Ludwig 1773-1853 **NCLC 5,
46; SSC 31**
See also DLB 90

Tiger, Derry
See Ellison, Harlan (Jay)

Tilghman, Christopher 1948(?)- **CLC 65**
See also CA 159

Tillinghast, Richard (Williford) 1940-**CLC 29**
See also CA 29-32R; CAAS 23; CANR 26, 51

Timrod, Henry 1828-1867 **NCLC 25**
See also DLB 3

Tindall, Gillian (Elizabeth) 1938- **CLC 7**
See also CA 21-24R; CANR 11, 65

Tiptree, James, Jr. **CLC 48, 50**
See also Sheldon, Alice Hastings Bradley
See also DLB 8

Titmarsh, Michael Angelo
See Thackeray, William Makepeace

Tocqueville, Alexis (Charles Henri Maurice
Clerel, Comte) de 1805-1859**NCLC 7, 63**

Tolkien, J(ohn) R(onald) R(euel) 1892-1973
**CLC 1, 2, 3, 8, 12, 38; DA; DAB; DAC;
DAM MST, NOV, POP; WLC**
See also AAYA 10; AITN 1; CA 17-18; 45-48;
CANR 36; CAP 2; CDBLB 1914-1945; DLB
15, 160; JRDA; MAICYA; MTCW 1; SATA
2, 32, 100; SATA-Obit 24

Toller, Ernst 1893-1939 **TCLC 10**
See also CA 107; DLB 124

Tolson, M. B.
See Tolson, Melvin B(eaunorus)

Tolson, Melvin B(eaunorus) 1898(?)-1966
CLC 36, 105; BLC 3; DAM MULT, POET
See also BW 1; CA 124; 89-92; DLB 48, 76

Tolstoi, Aleksei Nikolaevich
See Tolstoy, Alexey Nikolaevich

Tolstoy, Alexey Nikolaevich 1882-1945**T C L C
18**
See also CA 107; 158

Tolstoy, Count Leo
See Tolstoy, Leo (Nikolaevich)

Tolstoy, Leo (Nikolaevich) 1828-1910**TCLC 4,
11, 17, 28, 44, 79; DA; DAB; DAC; DAM
MST, NOV; SSC 9, 30; WLC**
See also CA 104; 123; SATA 26

Tomasi di Lampedusa, Giuseppe 1896-1957
See Lampedusa, Giuseppe (Tomasi) di
See also CA 111

Tomlin, Lily **CLC 17**
See also Tomlin, Mary Jean

Tomlin, Mary Jean 1939(?)-
See Tomlin, Lily
See also CA 117

Tomlinson, (Alfred) Charles 1927-**CLC 2, 4, 6,
13, 45; DAM POET; PC 17**
See also CA 5-8R; CANR 33; DLB 40

Tomlinson, H(enry) M(ajor) 1873-1958**TCLC
71**
See also CA 118; 161; DLB 36, 100, 195

Tonson, Jacob
See Bennett, (Enoch) Arnold

Toole, John Kennedy 1937-1969 **CLC 19, 64**
See also CA 104; DLBY 81

Toomer, Jean 1894-1967**CLC 1, 4, 13, 22; BLC
3; DAM MULT; PC 7; SSC 1; WLCS**
See also BW 1; CA 85-88; CDALB 1917-1929;
DLB 45, 51; MTCW 1

Torley, Luke
See Blish, James (Benjamin)

Tornimparte, Alessandra
See Ginzburg, Natalia

Torre, Raoul della
See Mencken, H(enry) L(ouis)

Torrey, E(dwin) Fuller 1937- **CLC 34**
See also CA 119; CANR 71

Torsvan, Ben Traven
See Traven, B.

Torsvan, Benno Traven
See Traven, B.

Torsvan, Berick Traven
See Traven, B.

Torsvan, Berwick Traven
See Traven, B.

Torsvan, Bruno Traven
See Traven, B.

Torsvan, Traven

See Traven, B.

Tournier, Michel (Edouard) 1924-CLC **6, 23, 36, 95**
  See also CA 49-52; CANR 3, 36, 74; DLB 83; MTCW 1; SATA 23

Tournimparte, Alessandra
  See Ginzburg, Natalia

Towers, Ivar
  See Kornbluth, C(yril) M.

Towne, Robert (Burton) 1936(?)-   **CLC 87**
  See also CA 108; DLB 44

Townsend, Sue   **CLC 61**
  See also Townsend, Susan Elaine
  See also SATA 55, 93; SATA-Brief 48

Townsend, Súsan Elaine 1946-
  See Townsend, Sue
  See also CA 119; 127; CANR 65; DAB; DAC; DAM MST

Townshend, Peter (Dennis Blandford) 1945-
  CLC 17, 42
  See also CA 107

Tozzi, Federigo 1883-1920   **TCLC 31**
  See also CA 160

Traill, Catharine Parr 1802-1899 **NCLC 31**
  See also DLB 99

Trakl, Georg 1887-1914   **TCLC 5; PC 20**
  See also CA 104; 165

Transtroemer, Tomas (Goesta) 1931-CLC **52, 65; DAM POET**
  See also CA 117; 129; CAAS 17

Transtromer, Tomas Gosta
  See Transtroemer, Tomas (Goesta)

Traven, B. (?)-1969   **CLC 8, 11**
  See also CA 19-20; 25-28R; CAP 2; DLB 9, 56; MTCW 1

Treitel, Jonathan 1959-   **CLC 70**

Tremain, Rose 1943-   **CLC 42**
  See also CA 97-100; CANR 44; DLB 14

Tremblay, Michel 1942- **CLC 29, 102; DAC; DAM MST**
  See also CA 116; 128; DLB 60; MTCW 1

Trevanian   **CLC 29**
  See also Whitaker, Rod(ney)

Trevor, Glen
  See Hilton, James

Trevor, William 1928-CLC **7, 9, 14, 25, 71, 116; SSC 21**
  See also Cox, William Trevor
  See also DLB 14, 139

Trifonov, Yuri (Valentinovich) 1925-1981
  CLC 45
  See also CA 126; 103; MTCW 1

Trilling, Lionel 1905-1975   **CLC 9, 11, 24**
  See also CA 9-12R; 61-64; CANR 10; DLB 28, 63; INT CANR-10; MTCW 1

Trimball, W. H.
  See Mencken, H(enry) L(ouis)

Tristan
  See Gomez de la Serna, Ramon

Tristram
  See Housman, A(lfred) E(dward)

Trogdon, William (Lewis) 1939-
  See Heat-Moon, William Least
  See also CA 115; 119; CANR 47; INT 119

Trollope, Anthony 1815-1882NCLC **6, 33; DA; DAB; DAC; DAM MST, NOV; SSC 28; WLC**
  See also CDBLB 1832-1890; DLB 21, 57, 159; SATA 22

Trollope, Frances 1779-1863   **NCLC 30**
  See also DLB 21, 166

Trotsky, Leon 1879-1940   **TCLC 22**
  See also CA 118; 167

Trotter (Cockburn), Catharine 1679-1749L C 8
  See also DLB 84

Trout, Kilgore
  See Farmer, Philip Jose

Trow, George W. S. 1943-   **CLC 52**
  See also CA 126

Troyat, Henri 1911-   **CLC 23**
  See also CA 45-48; CANR 2, 33, 67; MTCW 1

Trudeau, G(arretson) B(eekman) 1948-
  See Trudeau, Garry B.
  See also CA 81-84; CANR 31; SATA 35

Trudeau, Garry B.   **CLC 12**
  See also Trudeau, G(arretson) B(eekman)
  See also AAYA 10; AITN 2

Truffaut, Francois 1932-1984   **CLC 20, 101**
  See also CA 81-84; 113; CANR 34

Trumbo, Dalton 1905-1976   **CLC 19**
  See also CA 21-24R; 69-72; CANR 10; DLB 26

Trumbull, John 1750-1831   **NCLC 30**
  See also DLB 31

Trundlett, Helen B.
  See Eliot, T(homas) S(tearns)

Tryon, Thomas 1926-1991 **CLC 3, 11; DAM POP**
  See also AITN 1; CA 29-32R; 135; CANR 32; MTCW 1

Tryon, Tom
  See Tryon, Thomas

Ts'ao Hsueh-ch'in 1715(?)-1763   **LC 1**

Tsushima, Shuji 1909-1948
  See Dazai Osamu
  See also CA 107

Tsvetaeva (Efron), Marina (Ivanovna) 1892-1941   **TCLC 7, 35; PC 14**
  See also CA 104; 128; CANR 73; MTCW 1

Tuck, Lily 1938-   **CLC 70**
  See also CA 139

Tu Fu 712-770   **PC 9**
  See also DAM MULT

Tunis, John R(oberts) 1889-1975   **CLC 12**
  See also CA 61-64; CANR 62; DLB 22, 171; JRDA; MAICYA; SATA 37; SATA-Brief 30

Tuohy, Frank   **CLC 37**
  See also Tuohy, John Francis
  See also DLB 14, 139

Tuohy, John Francis 1925-
  See Tuohy, Frank
  See also CA 5-8R; CANR 3, 47

Turco, Lewis (Putnam) 1934-   **CLC 11, 63**
  See also CA 13-16R; CAAS 22; CANR 24, 51; DLBY 84

Turgenev, Ivan 1818-1883   **NCLC 21; DA; DAB; DAC; DAM MST, NOV; DC 7; SSC 7; WLC**

Turgot, Anne-Robert-Jacques 1727-1781 **L C 26**

Turner, Frederick 1943-   **CLC 48**
  See also CA 73-76; CAAS 10; CANR 12, 30, 56; DLB 40

Tutu, Desmond M(pilo) 1931-CLC **80; BLC 3; DAM MULT**
  See also BW 1; CA 125; CANR 67

Tutuola, Amos 1920-1997CLC **5, 14, 29; BLC 3; DAM MULT**
  See also BW 2; CA 9-12R; 159; CANR 27, 66; DLB 125; MTCW 1

Twain, MarkTCLC 6, 12, 19, 36, 48, 59; SSC 6, 26; WLC
  See also Clemens, Samuel Langhorne
  See also AAYA 20; DLB 11, 12, 23, 64, 74

Tyler, Anne 1941- **CLC 7, 11, 18, 28, 44, 59, 103; DAM NOV, POP**
  See also AAYA 18; BEST 89:1; CA 9-12R; CANR 11, 33, 53; DLB 6, 143; DLBY 82; MTCW 1; SATA 7, 90

Tyler, Royall 1757-1826   **NCLC 3**
  See also DLB 37

Tynan, Katharine 1861-1931   **TCLC 3**
  See also CA 104; 167; DLB 153

Tyutchev, Fyodor 1803-1873   **NCLC 34**

Tzara, Tristan 1896-1963   **CLC 47; DAM POET**
  See also CA 153; 89-92

Uhry, Alfred 1936- **CLC 55; DAM DRAM, POP**
  See also CA 127; 133; INT 133

Ulf, Haerved
  See Strindberg, (Johan) August

Ulf, Harved
  See Strindberg, (Johan) August

Ulibarri, Sabine R(eyes) 1919-CLC **83; DAM MULT**
  See also CA 131; DLB 82; HW

Unamuno (y Jugo), Miguel de 1864-1936
  TCLC 2, 9; DAM MULT, NOV; HLC; SSC 11
  See also CA 104; 131; DLB 108; HW; MTCW 1

Undercliffe, Errol
  See Campbell, (John) Ramsey

Underwood, Miles
  See Glassco, John

Undset, Sigrid 1882-1949TCLC **3; DA; DAB; DAC; DAM MST, NOV; WLC**
  See also CA 104; 129; MTCW 1

Ungaretti, Giuseppe 1888-1970CLC **7, 11, 15**
  See also CA 19-20; 25-28R; CAP 2; DLB 114

Unger, Douglas 1952-   **CLC 34**
  See also CA 130

Unsworth, Barry (Forster) 1930-   **CLC 76**
  See also CA 25-28R; CANR 30, 54; DLB 194

Updike, John (Hoyer) 1932-CLC **1, 2, 3, 5, 7, 9, 13, 15, 23, 34, 43, 70; DA; DAB; DAC; DAM MST, NOV, POET, POP; SSC 13, 27; WLC**
  See also CA 1-4R; CABS 1; CANR 4, 33, 51; CDALB 1968-1988; DLB 2, 5, 143; DLBD 3; DLBY 80, 82, 97; MTCW 1

Upshaw, Margaret Mitchell
  See Mitchell, Margaret (Munnerlyn)

Upton, Mark
  See Sanders, Lawrence

Upward, Allen 1863-1926   **TCLC 85**
  See also CA 117; DLB 36

Urdang, Constance (Henriette) 1922-CLC **47**
  See also CA 21-24R; CANR 9, 24

Uriel, Henry
  See Faust, Frederick (Schiller)

Uris, Leon (Marcus) 1924- **CLC 7, 32; DAM NOV, POP**
  See also AITN 1, 2; BEST 89:2; CA 1-4R; CANR 1, 40, 65; MTCW 1; SATA 49

Urmuz
  See Codrescu, Andrei

Urquhart, Jane 1949-   **CLC 90; DAC**
  See also CA 113; CANR 32, 68

Ustinov, Peter (Alexander) 1921-   **CLC 1**
  See also AITN 1; CA 13-16R; CANR 25, 51; DLB 13

U Tam'si, Gerald Felix Tchicaya
  See Tchicaya, Gerald Felix

U Tam'si, Tchicaya
  See Tchicaya, Gerald Felix

Vachss, Andrew (Henry) 1942-   **CLC 106**

See also CA 118; CANR 44

Vachss, Andrew H.
See Vachss, Andrew (Henry)

Vaculik, Ludvik 1926-   **CLC 7**
See also CA 53-56; CANR 72

Vaihinger, Hans 1852-1933   **TCLC 71**
See also CA 116; 166

Valdez, Luis (Miguel) 1940-   **CLC 84; DAM
    MULT; HLC**
See also CA 101; CANR 32; DLB 122; HW

Valenzuela, Luisa 1938- **CLC 31, 104; DAM
    MULT; SSC 14**
See also CA 101; CANR 32, 65; DLB 113; HW

Valera y Alcala-Galiano, Juan 1824-1905
    TCLC 10
See also CA 106

Valery, (Ambroise) Paul (Toussaint Jules) 1871-
    1945   **TCLC 4, 15; DAM POET; PC 9**
See also CA 104; 122; MTCW 1

Valle-Inclan, Ramon (Maria) del 1866-1936
    TCLC 5; DAM MULT; HLC
See also CA 106; 153; DLB 134

Vallejo, Antonio Buero
See Buero Vallejo, Antonio

Vallejo, Cesar (Abraham) 1892-1938**TCLC 3,
    56; DAM MULT; HLC**
See also CA 105; 153; HW

Vallette, Marguerite Eymery
See Rachilde

Valle Y Pena, Ramon del
See Valle-Inclan, Ramon (Maria) del

Van Ash, Cay 1918-   **CLC 34**

Vanbrugh, Sir John 1664-1726 **LC 21; DAM
    DRAM**
See also DLB 80

Van Campen, Karl
See Campbell, John W(ood, Jr.)

Vance, Gerald
See Silverberg, Robert

Vance, Jack   **CLC 35**
See also Kuttner, Henry; Vance, John Holbrook
See also DLB 8

Vance, John Holbrook 1916-
See Queen, Ellery; Vance, Jack
See also CA 29-32R; CANR 17, 65; MTCW 1

**Van Den Bogarde, Derek Jules Gaspard Ulric
    Niven** 1921-
See Bogarde, Dirk
See also CA 77-80

Vandenburgh, Jane   **CLC 59**
See also CA 168

Vanderhaeghe, Guy 1951-   **CLC 41**
See also CA 113; CANR 72

van der Post, Laurens (Jan) 1906-1996**CLC 5**
See also CA 5-8R; 155; CANR 35

van de Wetering, Janwillem 1931-   **CLC 47**
See also CA 49-52; CANR 4, 62

Van Dine, S. S.   **TCLC 23**
See also Wright, Willard Huntington

Van Doren, Carl (Clinton) 1885-1950 **TCLC
    18**
See also CA 111; 168

Van Doren, Mark 1894-1972   **CLC 6, 10**
See also CA 1-4R; 37-40R; CANR 3; DLB 45;
    MTCW 1

Van Druten, John (William) 1901-1957**TCLC
    2**
See also CA 104; 161; DLB 10

Van Duyn, Mona (Jane) 1921- **CLC 3, 7, 63,
    116; DAM POET**
See also CA 9-12R; CANR 7, 38, 60; DLB 5

Van Dyne, Edith
See Baum, L(yman) Frank

van Itallie, Jean-Claude 1936-   **CLC 3**
See also CA 45-48; CAAS 2; CANR 1, 48; DLB
    7

van Ostaijen, Paul 1896-1928   **TCLC 33**
See also CA 163

Van Peebles, Melvin 1932- **CLC 2, 20; DAM
    MULT**
See also BW 2; CA 85-88; CANR 27, 67

Vansittart, Peter 1920-   **CLC 42**
See also CA 1-4R; CANR 3, 49

Van Vechten, Carl 1880-1964   **CLC 33**
See also CA 89-92; DLB 4, 9, 51

Van Vogt, A(lfred) E(lton) 1912-   **CLC 1**
See also CA 21-24R; CANR 28; DLB 8; SATA
    14

Varda, Agnes 1928-   **CLC 16**
See also CA 116; 122

Vargas Llosa, (Jorge) Mario (Pedro) 1936-
    **CLC 3, 6, 9, 10, 15, 31, 42, 85; DA; DAB;
    DAC; DAM MST, MULT, NOV; HLC**
See also CA 73-76; CANR 18, 32, 42, 67; DLB
    145; HW; MTCW 1

Vasiliu, Gheorghe 1881-1957
See Bacovia, George
See also CA 123

Vassa, Gustavus
See Equiano, Olaudah

Vassilikos, Vassilis 1933-   **CLC 4, 8**
See also CA 81-84

Vaughan, Henry 1621-1695   **LC 27**
See also DLB 131

Vaughn, Stephanie   **CLC 62**

Vazov, Ivan (Minchov) 1850-1921   **TCLC 25**
See also CA 121; 167; DLB 147

Veblen, Thorstein B(unde) 1857-1929 **T C L C
    31**
See also CA 115; 165

Vega, Lope de 1562-1635   **LC 23**

Venison, Alfred
See Pound, Ezra (Weston Loomis)

Verdi, Marie de
See Mencken, H(enry) L(ouis)

Verdu, Matilde
See Cela, Camilo Jose

Verga, Giovanni (Carmelo) 1840-1922 **T C L C
    3; SSC 21**
See also CA 104; 123

Vergil 70B.C.-19B.C.   **CMLC 9; DA; DAB;
    DAC; DAM MST, POET; PC 12; WLCS**

Verhaeren, Emile (Adolphe Gustave) 1855-1916
    TCLC 12
See also CA 109

Verlaine, Paul (Marie) 1844-1896**NCLC 2, 51;
    DAM POET; PC 2**

Verne, Jules (Gabriel) 1828-1905**TCLC 6, 52**
See also AAYA 16; CA 110; 131; DLB 123;
    JRDA; MAICYA; SATA 21

Very, Jones 1813-1880   **NCLC 9**
See also DLB 1

Vesaas, Tarjei 1897-1970   **CLC 48**
See also CA 29-32R

Vialis, Gaston
See Simenon, Georges (Jacques Christian)

Vian, Boris 1920-1959   **TCLC 9**
See also CA 106; 164; DLB 72

Viaud, (Louis Marie) Julien 1850-1923
See Loti, Pierre
See also CA 107

Vicar, Henry
See Felsen, Henry Gregor

Vicker, Angus
See Felsen, Henry Gregor

Vidal, Gore 1925-**CLC 2, 4, 6, 8, 10, 22, 33, 72;**

DAM NOV, POP
See also AITN 1; BEST 90:2; CA 5-8R; CANR
    13, 45, 65; DLB 6, 152; INT CANR-13;
    MTCW 1

Viereck, Peter (Robert Edwin) 1916- **CLC 4**
See also CA 1-4R; CANR 1, 47; DLB 5

Vigny, Alfred (Victor) de 1797-1863**NCLC 7;
    DAM POET**
See also DLB 119, 192

Vilakazi, Benedict Wallet 1906-1947**TCLC 37**
See also CA 168

Villa, Jose Garcia 1904-1997   **PC 22**
See also CA 25-28R; CANR 12

Villaurrutia, Xavier 1903-1950   **TCLC 80**
See also HW

**Villiers de l'Isle Adam, Jean Marie Mathias
    Philippe Auguste, Comte de** 1838-1889
    NCLC 3; SSC 14
See also DLB 123

Villon, Francois 1431-1463(?)   **PC 13**

Vinci, Leonardo da 1452-1519   **LC 12**

Vine, Barbara   **CLC 50**
See also Rendell, Ruth (Barbara)
See also BEST 90:4

Vinge, Joan (Carol) D(ennison) 1948-**CLC 30;
    SSC 24**
See also CA 93-96; CANR 72; SATA 36

Violis, G.
See Simenon, Georges (Jacques Christian)

Virgil
See Vergil

Visconti, Luchino 1906-1976   **CLC 16**
See also CA 81-84; 65-68; CANR 39

Vittorini, Elio 1908-1966   **CLC 6, 9, 14**
See also CA 133; 25-28R

Vivekananda, Swami 1863-1902   **TCLC 88**

Vizenor, Gerald Robert 1934-**CLC 103; DAM
    MULT**
See also CA 13-16R; CAAS 22; CANR 5, 21,
    44, 67; DLB 175; NNAL

Vizinczey, Stephen 1933-   **CLC 40**
See also CA 128; INT 128

Vliet, R(ussell) G(ordon) 1929-1984 **CLC 22**
See also CA 37-40R; 112; CANR 18

Vogau, Boris Andreyevich 1894-1937(?)
See Pilnyak, Boris
See also CA 123

Vogel, Paula A(nne) 1951-   **CLC 76**
See also CA 108

Voigt, Cynthia 1942-   **CLC 30**
See also AAYA 3; CA 106; CANR 18, 37, 40;
    CLR 13, 48; INT CANR-18; JRDA;
    MAICYA; SATA 48, 79; SATA-Brief 33

Voigt, Ellen Bryant 1943-   **CLC 54**
See also CA 69-72; CANR 11, 29, 55; DLB 120

Voinovich, Vladimir (Nikolaevich) 1932-**C L C
    10, 49**
See also CA 81-84; CAAS 12; CANR 33, 67;
    MTCW 1

Vollmann, William T. 1959-   **CLC 89; DAM
    NOV, POP**
See also CA 134; CANR 67

Voloshinov, V. N.
See Bakhtin, Mikhail Mikhailovich

Voltaire 1694-1778   **LC 14; DA; DAB; DAC;
    DAM DRAM, MST; SSC 12; WLC**

von Daeniken, Erich 1935-   **CLC 30**
See also AITN 1; CA 37-40R; CANR 17, 44

von Daniken, Erich
See von Daeniken, Erich

von Heidenstam, (Carl Gustaf) Verner
See Heidenstam, (Carl Gustaf) Verner von

von Heyse, Paul (Johann Ludwig)

See Heyse, Paul (Johann Ludwig von)
von Hofmannsthal, Hugo
See Hofmannsthal, Hugo von
von Horvath, Odon
See Horvath, Oedoen von
von Horvath, Oedoen
See Horvath, Oedoen von
von Liliencron, (Friedrich Adolf Axel) Detlev
See Liliencron, (Friedrich Adolf Axel) Detlev von
Vonnegut, Kurt, Jr. 1922- CLC 1, 2, 3, 4, 5, 8, 12, 22, 40, 60, 111; DA; DAB; DAC; DAM MST, NOV, POP; SSC 8; WLC
See also AAYA 6; AITN 1; BEST 90:4; CA 1-4R; CANR 1, 25, 49; CDALB 1968-1988; DLB 2, 8, 152; DLBD 3; DLBY 80; MTCW 1
Von Rachen, Kurt
See Hubbard, L(afayette) Ron(ald)
von Rezzori (d'Arezzo), Gregor
See Rezzori (d'Arezzo), Gregor von
von Sternberg, Josef
See Sternberg, Josef von
Vorster, Gordon 1924- CLC 34
See also CA 133
Vosce, Trudie
See Ozick, Cynthia
Voznesensky, Andrei (Andreievich) 1933- CLC 1, 15, 57; DAM POET
See also CA 89-92; CANR 37; MTCW 1
Waddington, Miriam 1917- CLC 28
See also CA 21-24R; CANR 12, 30; DLB 68
Wagman, Fredrica 1937- CLC 7
See also CA 97-100; INT 97-100
Wagner, Linda W.
See Wagner-Martin, Linda (C.)
Wagner, Linda Welshimer
See Wagner-Martin, Linda (C.)
Wagner, Richard 1813-1883 NCLC 9
See also DLB 129
Wagner-Martin, Linda (C.) 1936- CLC 50
See also CA 159
Wagoner, David (Russell) 1926- CLC 3, 5, 15
See also CA 1-4R; CAAS 3; CANR 2, 71; DLB 5; SATA 14
Wah, Fred(erick James) 1939- CLC 44
See also CA 107; 141; DLB 60
Wahloo, Per 1926-1975 CLC 7
See also CA 61-64; CANR 73
Wahloo, Peter
See Wahloo, Per
Wain, John (Barrington) 1925-1994 CLC 2, 11, 15, 46
See also CA 5-8R; 145; CAAS 4; CANR 23, 54; CDBLB 1960 to Present; DLB 15, 27, 139, 155; MTCW 1
Wajda, Andrzej 1926- CLC 16
See also CA 102
Wakefield, Dan 1932- CLC 7
See also CA 21-24R; CAAS 7
Wakoski, Diane 1937- CLC 2, 4, 7, 9, 11, 40; DAM POET; PC 15
See also CA 13-16R; CAAS 1; CANR 9, 60; DLB 5; INT CANR-9
Wakoski-Sherbell, Diane
See Wakoski, Diane
Walcott, Derek (Alton) 1930- CLC 2, 4, 9, 14, 25, 42, 67, 76; BLC 3; DAB; DAC; DAM MST, MULT, POET; DC 7
See also BW 2; CA 89-92; CANR 26, 47; DLB 117; DLBY 81; MTCW 1
Waldman, Anne (Lesley) 1945- CLC 7
See also CA 37-40R; CAAS 17; CANR 34, 69;

DLB 16
Waldo, E. Hunter
See Sturgeon, Theodore (Hamilton)
Waldo, Edward Hamilton
See Sturgeon, Theodore (Hamilton)
Walker, Alice (Malsenior) 1944- CLC 5, 6, 9, 19, 27, 46, 58, 103; BLC 3; DA; DAB; DAC; DAM MST, MULT, NOV, POET, POP; SSC 5; WLCS
See also AAYA 3; BEST 89:4; BW 2; CA 37-40R; CANR 9, 27, 49, 66; CDALB 1968-1988; DLB 6, 33, 143; INT CANR-27; MTCW 1; SATA 31
Walker, David Harry 1911-1992 CLC 14
See also CA 1-4R; 137; CANR 1; SATA 8; SATA-Obit 71
Walker, Edward Joseph 1934-
See Walker, Ted
See also CA 21-24R; CANR 12, 28, 53
Walker, George F. 1947- CLC 44, 61; DAB; DAC; DAM MST
See also CA 103; CANR 21, 43, 59; DLB 60
Walker, Joseph A. 1935- CLC 19; DAM DRAM, MST
See also BW 1; CA 89-92; CANR 26; DLB 38
Walker, Margaret (Abigail) 1915- CLC 1, 6; BLC; DAM MULT; PC 20
See also BW 2; CA 73-76; CANR 26, 54; DLB 76, 152; MTCW 1
Walker, Ted CLC 13
See also Walker, Edward Joseph
See also DLB 40
Wallace, David Foster 1962- CLC 50, 114
See also CA 132; CANR 59
Wallace, Dexter
See Masters, Edgar Lee
Wallace, (Richard Horatio) Edgar 1875-1932 TCLC 57
See also CA 115; DLB 70
Wallace, Irving 1916-1990 CLC 7, 13; DAM NOV, POP
See also AITN 1; CA 1-4R; 132; CAAS 1; CANR 1, 27; INT CANR-27; MTCW 1
Wallant, Edward Lewis 1926-1962 CLC 5, 10
See also CA 1-4R; CANR 22; DLB 2, 28, 143; MTCW 1
Walley, Byron
See Card, Orson Scott
Walpole, Horace 1717-1797 LC 2
See also DLB 39, 104
Walpole, Hugh (Seymour) 1884-1941 TCLC 5
See also CA 104; 165; DLB 34
Walser, Martin 1927- CLC 27
See also CA 57-60; CANR 8, 46; DLB 75, 124
Walser, Robert 1878-1956 TCLC 18; SSC 20
See also CA 118; 165; DLB 66
Walsh, Jill Paton CLC 35
See also Paton Walsh, Gillian
See also AAYA 11; CLR 2; DLB 161; SAAS 3
Walter, Villiam Christian
See Andersen, Hans Christian
Wambaugh, Joseph (Aloysius, Jr.) 1937- CLC 3, 18; DAM NOV, POP
See also AITN 1; BEST 89:3; CA 33-36R; CANR 42, 65; DLB 6; DLBY 83; MTCW 1
Wang Wei 699(?)-761(?) PC 18
Ward, Arthur Henry Sarsfield 1883-1959
See Rohmer, Sax
See also CA 108
Ward, Douglas Turner 1930- CLC 19
See also BW 1; CA 81-84; CANR 27; DLB 7, 38
Ward, Mary Augusta

See Ward, Mrs. Humphry
Ward, Mrs. Humphry 1851-1920 TCLC 55
See also DLB 18
Ward, Peter
See Faust, Frederick (Schiller)
Warhol, Andy 1928(?)-1987 CLC 20
See also AAYA 12; BEST 89:4; CA 89-92; 121; CANR 34
Warner, Francis (Robert le Plastrier) 1937- CLC 14
See also CA 53-56; CANR 11
Warner, Marina 1946- CLC 59
See also CA 65-68; CANR 21, 55; DLB 194
Warner, Rex (Ernest) 1905-1986 CLC 45
See also CA 89-92; 119; DLB 15
Warner, Susan (Bogert) 1819-1885 NCLC 31
See also DLB 3, 42
Warner, Sylvia (Constance) Ashton
See Ashton-Warner, Sylvia (Constance)
Warner, Sylvia Townsend 1893-1978 CLC 7, 19; SSC 23
See also CA 61-64; 77-80; CANR 16, 60; DLB 34, 139; MTCW 1
Warren, Mercy Otis 1728-1814 NCLC 13
See also DLB 31, 200
Warren, Robert Penn 1905-1989 CLC 1, 4, 6, 8, 10, 13, 18, 39, 53, 59; DA; DAB; DAC; DAM MST, NOV, POET; SSC 4; WLC
See also AITN 1; CA 13-16R; 129; CANR 10, 47; CDALB 1968-1988; DLB 2, 48, 152; DLBY 80, 89; INT CANR-10; MTCW 1; SATA 46; SATA-Obit 63
Warshofsky, Isaac
See Singer, Isaac Bashevis
Warton, Thomas 1728-1790 LC 15; DAM POET
See also DLB 104, 109
Waruk, Kona
See Harris, (Theodore) Wilson
Warung, Price 1855-1911 TCLC 45
Warwick, Jarvis
See Garner, Hugh
Washington, Alex
See Harris, Mark
Washington, Booker T(aliaferro) 1856-1915 TCLC 10; BLC 3; DAM MULT
See also BW 1; CA 114; 125; SATA 28
Washington, George 1732-1799 LC 25
See also DLB 31
Wassermann, (Karl) Jakob 1873-1934 TCLC 6
See also CA 104; DLB 66
Wasserstein, Wendy 1950- CLC 32, 59, 90; DAM DRAM; DC 4
See also CA 121; 129; CABS 3; CANR 53; INT 129; SATA 94
Waterhouse, Keith (Spencer) 1929- CLC 47
See also CA 5-8R; CANR 38, 67; DLB 13, 15; MTCW 1
Waters, Frank (Joseph) 1902-1995 CLC 88
See also CA 5-8R; 149; CAAS 13; CANR 3, 18, 63; DLBY 86
Waters, Roger 1944- CLC 35
Watkins, Frances Ellen
See Harper, Frances Ellen Watkins
Watkins, Gerrold
See Malzberg, Barry N(athaniel)
Watkins, Gloria 1955(?)-
See hooks, bell
See also BW 2; CA 143
Watkins, Paul 1964- CLC 55
See also CA 132; CANR 62
Watkins, Vernon Phillips 1906-1967 CLC 43

See also CA 9-10; 25-28R; CAP 1; DLB 20

Watson, Irving S.
See Mencken, H(enry) L(ouis)

Watson, John H.
See Farmer, Philip Jose

Watson, Richard F.
See Silverberg, Robert

Waugh, Auberon (Alexander) 1939-   **CLC 7**
See also CA 45-48; CANR 6, 22; DLB 14, 194

Waugh, Evelyn (Arthur St. John) 1903-1966
  **CLC 1, 3, 8, 13, 19, 27, 44, 107; DA; DAB;
  DAC; DAM MST, NOV, POP; WLC**
See also CA 85-88; 25-28R; CANR 22; CDBLB
  1914-1945; DLB 15, 162, 195; MTCW 1

Waugh, Harriet 1944-   **CLC 6**
See also CA 85-88; CANR 22

Ways, C. R.
See Blount, Roy (Alton), Jr.

Waystaff, Simon
See Swift, Jonathan

Webb, (Martha) Beatrice (Potter) 1858-1943
  TCLC 22
See also Potter, (Helen) Beatrix
See also CA 117; DLB 190

Webb, Charles (Richard) 1939-   **CLC 7**
See also CA 25-28R

Webb, James H(enry), Jr. 1946-   **CLC 22**
See also CA 81-84

Webb, Mary (Gladys Meredith) 1881-1927
  TCLC 24
See also CA 123; DLB 34

Webb, Mrs. Sidney
See Webb, (Martha) Beatrice (Potter)

Webb, Phyllis 1927-   **CLC 18**
See also CA 104; CANR 23; DLB 53

Webb, Sidney (James) 1859-1947   **TCLC 22**
See also CA 117; 163; DLB 190

Webber, Andrew Lloyd   **CLC 21**
See also Lloyd Webber, Andrew

Weber, Lenora Mattingly 1895-1971 **CLC 12**
See also CA 19-20; 29-32R; CAP 1; SATA 2;
  SATA-Obit 26

Weber, Max 1864-1920   **TCLC 69**
See also CA 109

Webster, John 1579(?)-1634(?)   **LC 33; DA;
  DAB; DAC; DAM DRAM, MST; DC 2;
  WLC**
See also CDBLB Before 1660; DLB 58

Webster, Noah 1758-1843   **NCLC 30**

Wedekind, (Benjamin) Frank(lin) 1864-1918
  TCLC 7; DAM DRAM
See also CA 104; 153; DLB 118

Weidman, Jerome 1913-   **CLC 7**
See also AITN 2; CA 1-4R; CANR 1; DLB 28

Weil, Simone (Adolphine) 1909-1943 **TCLC 23**
See also CA 117; 159

Weininger, Otto 1880-1903   **TCLC 84**

Weinstein, Nathan
See West, Nathanael

Weinstein, Nathan von Wallenstein
See West, Nathanael

Weir, Peter (Lindsay) 1944-   **CLC 20**
See also CA 113; 123

Weiss, Peter (Ulrich) 1916-1982 **CLC 3, 15, 51;
  DAM DRAM**
See also CA 45-48; 106; CANR 3; DLB 69, 124

Weiss, Theodore (Russell) 1916- **CLC 3, 8, 14**
See also CA 9-12R; CAAS 2; CANR 46; DLB
  5

Welch, (Maurice) Denton 1915-1948 **TCLC 22**
See also CA 121; 148

Welch, James 1940-   **CLC 6, 14, 52; DAM
  MULT, POP**

See also CA 85-88; CANR 42, 66; DLB 175;
  NNAL

Weldon, Fay 1931- **CLC 6, 9, 11, 19, 36, 59;
  DAM POP**
See also CA 21-24R; CANR 16, 46, 63; CDBLB
  1960 to Present; DLB 14, 194; INT CANR-
  16; MTCW 1

Wellek, Rene 1903-1995   **CLC 28**
See also CA 5-8R; 150; CAAS 7; CANR 8; DLB
  63; INT CANR-8

Weller, Michael 1942-   **CLC 10, 53**
See also CA 85-88

Weller, Paul 1958-   **CLC 26**

Wellershoff, Dieter 1925-   **CLC 46**
See also CA 89-92; CANR 16, 37

Welles, (George) Orson 1915-1985 **CLC 20, 80**
See also CA 93-96; 117

Wellman, John McDowell 1945-
See Wellman, Mac
See also CA 166

Wellman, Mac 1945-   **CLC 65**
See also Wellman, John McDowell; Wellman,
  John McDowell

Wellman, Manly Wade 1903-1986   **CLC 49**
See also CA 1-4R; 118; CANR 6, 16, 44; SATA
  6; SATA-Obit 47

Wells, Carolyn 1869(?)-1942   **TCLC 35**
See also CA 113; DLB 11

Wells, H(erbert) G(eorge) 1866-1946 **TCLC 6,
  12, 19; DA; DAB; DAC; DAM MST, NOV;
  SSC 6; WLC**
See also AAYA 18; CA 110; 121; CDBLB 1914-
  1945; DLB 34, 70, 156, 178; MTCW 1;
  SATA 20

Wells, Rosemary 1943-   **CLC 12**
See also AAYA 13; CA 85-88; CANR 48; CLR
  16; MAICYA; SAAS 1; SATA 18, 69

Welty, Eudora 1909- **CLC 1, 2, 5, 14, 22, 33,
  105; DA; DAB; DAC; DAM MST, NOV;
  SSC 1, 27; WLC**
See also CA 9-12R; CABS 1; CANR 32, 65;
  CDALB 1941-1968; DLB 2, 102, 143;
  DLBD 12; DLBY 87; MTCW 1

Wen I-to 1899-1946   **TCLC 28**

Wentworth, Robert
See Hamilton, Edmond

Werfel, Franz (Viktor) 1890-1945   **TCLC 8**
See also CA 104; 161; DLB 81, 124

Wergeland, Henrik Arnold 1808-1845 **N C L C
  5**

Wersba, Barbara 1932-   **CLC 30**
See also AAYA 2; CA 29-32R; CANR 16, 38;
  CLR 3; DLB 52; JRDA; MAICYA; SAAS 2;
  SATA 1, 58

Wertmueller, Lina 1928-   **CLC 16**
See also CA 97-100; CANR 39

Wescott, Glenway 1901-1987   **CLC 13**
See also CA 13-16R; 121; CANR 23, 70; DLB
  4, 9, 102

Wesker, Arnold 1932-   **CLC 3, 5, 42; DAB;
  DAM DRAM**
See also CA 1-4R; CAAS 7; CANR 1, 33;
  CDBLB 1960 to Present; DLB 13; MTCW 1

Wesley, Richard (Errol) 1945-   **CLC 7**
See also BW 1; CA 57-60; CANR 27; DLB 38

Wessel, Johan Herman 1742-1785   **LC 7**

West, Anthony (Panther) 1914-1987   **CLC 50**
See also CA 45-48; 124; CANR 3, 19; DLB 15

West, C. P.
See Wodehouse, P(elham) G(renville)

West, (Mary) Jessamyn 1902-1984 **CLC 7, 17**
See also CA 9-12R; 112; CANR 27; DLB 6;
  DLBY 84; MTCW 1; SATA-Obit 37

West, Morris L(anglo) 1916-   **CLC 6, 33**
See also CA 5-8R; CANR 24, 49, 64; MTCW 1

West, Nathanael 1903-1940 **TCLC 1, 14, 44;
  SSC 16**
See also CA 104; 125; CDALB 1929-1941;
  DLB 4, 9, 28; MTCW 1

West, Owen
See Koontz, Dean R(ay)

West, Paul 1930-   **CLC 7, 14, 96**
See also CA 13-16R; CAAS 7; CANR 22, 53;
  DLB 14; INT CANR-22

West, Rebecca 1892-1983   **CLC 7, 9, 31, 50**
See also CA 5-8R; 109; CANR 19; DLB 36;
  DLBY 83; MTCW 1

Westall, Robert (Atkinson) 1929-1993 **CLC 17**
See also AAYA 12; CA 69-72; 141; CANR 18,
  68; CLR 13; JRDA; MAICYA; SAAS 2;
  SATA 23, 69; SATA-Obit 75

Westermarck, Edward 1862-1939   **TCLC 87**

Westlake, Donald E(dwin) 1933-   **CLC 7, 33;
  DAM POP**
See also CA 17-20R; CAAS 13; CANR 16, 44,
  65; INT CANR-16

Westmacott, Mary
See Christie, Agatha (Mary Clarissa)

Weston, Allen
See Norton, Andre

Wetcheek, J. L.
See Feuchtwanger, Lion

Wetering, Janwillem van de
See van de Wetering, Janwillem

Wetherald, Agnes Ethelwyn 1857-1940 **T C L C
  81**
See also DLB 99

Wetherell, Elizabeth
See Warner, Susan (Bogert)

Whale, James 1889-1957   **TCLC 63**

Whalen, Philip 1923-   **CLC 6, 29**
See also CA 9-12R; CANR 5, 39; DLB 16

Wharton, Edith (Newbold Jones) 1862-1937
  **TCLC 3, 9, 27, 53; DA; DAB; DAC; DAM
  MST, NOV; SSC 6; WLC**
See also AAYA 25; CA 104; 132; CDALB 1865-
  1917; DLB 4, 9, 12, 78, 189; DLBD 13;
  MTCW 1

Wharton, James
See Mencken, H(enry) L(ouis)

Wharton, William (a pseudonym) CLC 18, 37
See also CA 93-96; DLBY 80; INT 93-96

Wheatley (Peters), Phillis 1754(?)-1784 **LC 3;
  BLC 3; DA; DAC; DAM MST, MULT,
  POET; PC 3; WLC**
See also CDALB 1640-1865; DLB 31, 50

Wheelock, John Hall 1886-1978   **CLC 14**
See also CA 13-16R; 77-80; CANR 14; DLB
  45

White, E(lwyn) B(rooks) 1899-1985 **CLC 10,
  34, 39; DAM POP**
See also AITN 2; CA 13-16R; 116; CANR 16,
  37; CLR 1, 21; DLB 11, 22; MAICYA;
  MTCW 1; SATA 2, 29, 100; SATA-Obit 44

White, Edmund (Valentine III) 1940- **CLC 27,
  110; DAM POP**
See also AAYA 7; CA 45-48; CANR 3, 19, 36,
  62; MTCW 1

White, Patrick (Victor Martindale) 1912-1990
  CLC 3, 4, 5, 7, 9, 18, 65, 69
See also CA 81-84; 132; CANR 43; MTCW 1

White, Phyllis Dorothy James 1920-
See James, P. D.
See also CA 21-24R; CANR 17, 43, 65; DAM
  POP; MTCW 1

White, T(erence) H(anbury) 1906-1964 **C L C**

Literary Criticism Series
Cumulative Topic Index

This index lists all topic entries in Gale's *Classical and Medieval Literature Criticism, Contemporary Literary Criticism, Literature Criticism from 1400 to 1800, Nineteenth-Century Literature Criticism,* and *Twentieth-Century Literary Criticism.*

NCLC Cumulative Nationality Index

Kotzebue, August (Friedrich Ferdinand) von **25**
Ludwig, Otto **4**
Marx, Karl (Heinrich) **17**
Morike, Eduard (Friedrich) **10**
Müller, Wilhelm **73**
Novalis **13**
Schelling, Friedrich Wilhelm Joseph von **30**
Schiller, Friedrich **39, 69**
Schlegel, August Wilhelm von **15**
Schlegel, Friedrich **45**
Schopenhauer, Arthur **51**
Storm, (Hans) Theodor (Woldsen) **1**
Tieck, (Johann) Ludwig **5, 46**
Wagner, Richard **9**
Wieland, Christoph Martin **17**

GREEK
Solomos, Dionysios **15**

HUNGARIAN
Arany, Janos **34**
Madach, Imre **19**
Petofi, Sandor **21**

INDIAN
Chatterji, Bankim Chandra **19**
Dutt, Toru **29**
Ghalib **39**

IRISH
Allingham, William **25**
Banim, John **13**
Banim, Michael **13**
Boucicault, Dion **41**
Carleton, William **3**
Croker, John Wilson **10**
Darley, George **2**
Edgeworth, Maria **1, 51**
Ferguson, Samuel **33**
Griffin, Gerald **7**
Jameson, Anna **43**
Le Fanu, Joseph Sheridan **9, 58**
Lever, Charles (James) **23**
Maginn, William **8**
Mangan, James Clarence **27**
Maturin, Charles Robert **6**
Merriman, Brian **70**
Moore, Thomas **6**
Morgan, Lady **29**
O'Brien, Fitz-James **21**

ITALIAN
Collodi, Carlo (Carlo Lorenzini) **54**
Da Ponte, Lorenzo **50**
Foscolo, Ugo **8**
Gozzi, (Conte) Carlo **23**
Leopardi, (Conte) Giacomo **22**
Manzoni, Alessandro **29**
Mazzini, Guiseppe **34**
Nievo, Ippolito **22**

JAPANESE
Higuchi Ichiyo **49**
Motoori, Norinaga **45**

LITHUANIAN
Mapu, Abraham (ben Jekutiel) **18**

MEXICAN
Lizardi, Jose Joaquin Fernandez de **30**

NORWEGIAN
Collett, (Jacobine) Camilla (Wergeland) **22**
Wergeland, Henrik Arnold **5**

POLISH
Fredro, Aleksander **8**
Krasicki, Ignacy **8**
Krasinski, Zygmunt **4**
Mickiewicz, Adam **3**
Norwid, Cyprian Kamil **17**
Slowacki, Juliusz **15**

ROMANIAN
Eminescu, Mihail **33**

RUSSIAN
Aksakov, Sergei Timofeyvich **2**
Bakunin, Mikhail (Alexandrovich) **25, 58**
Bashkirtseff, Marie **27**
Belinski, Vissarion Grigoryevich **5**
Chernyshevsky, Nikolay Gavrilovich **1**
Dobrolyubov, Nikolai Alexandrovich **5**
Dostoevsky, Fedor Mikhailovich **2, 7, 21, 33, 43**
Gogol, Nikolai (Vasilyevich) **5, 15, 31**
Goncharov, Ivan Alexandrovich **1, 63**
Herzen, Aleksandr Ivanovich **10**
Karamzin, Nikolai Mikhailovich **3**
Krylov, Ivan Andreevich **1**
Lermontov, Mikhail Yuryevich **5**
Leskov, Nikolai (Semyonovich) **25**

Nekrasov, Nikolai Alekseevich **11**
Ostrovsky, Alexander **30. 57**
Pisarev, Dmitry Ivanovich **25**
Pushkin, Alexander (Sergeyevich) **3, 27**
Saltykov, Mikhail Evgrafovich **16**
Smolenskin, Peretz **30**
Turgenev, Ivan **21**
Tyutchev, Fyodor **34**
Zhukovsky, Vasily **35**

SCOTTISH
Baillie, Joanna **2, 71**
Beattie, James **25**
Campbell, Thomas **19**
Carlyle, Thomas **22, 70**
Ferrier, Susan (Edmonstone) **8**
Galt, John **1**
Hogg, James **4**
Jeffrey, Francis **33**
Lockhart, John Gibson **6**
Mackenzie, Henry **41**
Oliphant, Margaret (Oliphant Wilson) **11**
Scott, Walter **15, 69**
Stevenson, Robert Louis (Balfour) **5, 14, 63**
Thomson, James **18**
Wilson, John **5**
Wright, Frances **74**

SPANISH
Alarcon, Pedro Antonio de **1**
Caballero, Fernan **10**
Castro, Rosalia de **3**
Espronceda, Jose de **39**
Larra (y Sanchez de Castro), Mariano Jose de **17**
Tamayo y Baus, Manuel **1**
Zorrilla y Moral, Jose **6**

SWEDISH
Almqvist, Carl Jonas Love **42**
Bremer, Fredrika **11**
Tegner, Esaias **2**

SWISS
Amiel, Henri Frederic **4**
Burckhardt, Jacob **49**
Charriere, Isabelle de **66**
Keller, Gottfried **2**
Wyss, Johann David Von **10**

UKRAINIAN
Taras Shevchenko **54**

Nationality Index

NCLC-74 Title Index